1972-1979
WHA MEDIA GUIDES

edited by
TIMOTHY GASSEN

PCMP PRESS
P.O. Box 121
Tucson, Arizona
85702 USA

www.purple-cactus.tv

Copyright ©2018 by PCMP LLC & Timothy Gassen

The logo of the WHA Hall of Fame is a registered trademark, used with permission.

www.WHAhof.com

All rights reserved. No part of this publication may be reproduced, stored in a retrieval system, or transmitted in any form or by any means electronic, mechanical, photocopy, recording, or otherwise without the prior written permission of the publisher.

ISBN 978-0-9797337-5-8

Manufactured in the United States of America

First Reprint Edition published June 2018

Front Cover: adapted from the 1978-1979 WHA media guide cover

Back Cover: the 1972-1979 WHA media guide front covers

Trademarks remain the property of their owners and are shown for historical purposes.

Thank you to the talented writers, editors, and media staff for WHA teams, and the WHA league offices, who made these materials possible.

Table of Contents

Introduction 4

1972-73 5

1973-74 55

1974-75 139

1975-76 255

1976-77 369

1977-78 483

1978-79 565

About the WHA HOF & Author 799

Introduction

Paper media guides were once the norm for all professional hockey teams. They were small in physical dimensions, usually around 6 inches wide and 8 inches long – perfect to fit into a pocket or briefcase. Their main purpose was to give newspaper, radio, and TV media professionals a quick reference guide for their reporting, but they were also used widely by team and league personnel.

Like paper game programs, the paper team media guides were phased out by the early 2000s, and today they are sadly replaced by electronic download files and periodically updated web site pages.

Back in the 1970s, though, each World Hockey Association team would publish their own media guide, and the league would also print a tome that covered the entire circuit. It is those WHA league guides, from 1972-1979, that we have restored as an archive and are reproducing here. They are fascinating artifacts of a major league's birth, expansion, contraction, and then concerted stab at cementing a merger with the rival NHL.

It is that last-season 1978-1979 WHA league media guide that indirectly makes the merger pitch. While the league's yearly media guide fluctuated between 50 to 116 pages, the '78-'79 publication topped out at a whopping 236 pages. The two leagues had toyed with merger talks previously, and the negotiations were at a critical point before that 1978-1979 season. That thick, final WHA media guide seems to trumpet the point: "We have a real history and we will not go away. Merge with us now!"

And so they did – the NHL took four teams from the WHA for the 1979-1980 season, and the rebel league was no more.

But evidence of the league's incredible hockey journey still exists. Enjoy the following 800 pages of league information, painstakingly restored and re-printed by the WHA Hall of Fame.

All that hard work – for the league and for this archival project – was certainly worth it.

> – Timothy Gassen
> President, WHA Hall of Fame
> Summer 2018

EDITOR'S NOTE: Each media guide page is reproduced at actual size within an outline box. The original page numbers for the interior of each season's media guide are inside that box. The running page numbers for the entire book are placed outside that box, and referenced in the Table of Contents. Each original media guide contained several advertisements and these ads have been omitted here. Several naming errors in the original printings are corrected in this edition, though no statistics or other data have been altered.

CONTENTS

GARY L. DAVIDSON 5
WHA DIRECTORY 7
CHRONOLOGY OF THE WHA 8
WHA RULES 10
ALBERTA OILERS 12
CHICAGO COUGARS 14
CLEVELAND CRUSADERS 16
HOUSTON AEROS 18
LOS ANGELES SHARKS 20
MINNESOTA FIGHTING SAINTS 22
NEW ENGLAND WHALERS 24
NEW YORK RAIDERS 26
OTTAWA NATIONALS 28
PHILADELPHIA BLAZERS 30
QUEBEC NORDIQUES 32
WINNIPEG JETS 34
1972-73 SCHEDULE 37
WHA REFEREES 46
1972-73 STARTING TIMES 47
WHA TRAVELOG 48
WHA ON CBS AND CBC 49

Litho in U.S.A.

GARY L. DAVIDSON
President
World Hockey Association

There have been only two successful expansion major leagues in modern professional sports—the American Football League and the American Basketball Association.

From all appearances, the World Hockey Association will be a third.

Somewhere down the road in sports history, Gary L. Davidson will be remembered as the man who put together two of the three.

The 38-year-old Santa Ana, Calif., attorney is one-of-a-kind.

He and his close friend, Dennis Murphy, now president and general manager of the Los Angeles Sharks, are the men who created both the ABA and the WHA.

They had the ideas. They found the owners. And, with those owners, nurtured both leagues to reality.

A graduate of UCLA Law School, Davision does not approach professional sports like the former athlete he is. Rather, he calls himself a professional financial manager who puts together financial packages for professional sports and other business ventures.

"I don't practice law anymore," Davidson says. "I'm basically oriented to do financing."

A partner in the law firm of Nagel, Regan and Davidson, Gary is the originator of the WHA's unique position on player contracts. The WHA has neither a reserve clause or option clause.

"I believe if a major league is to be truly successful," he says, "it has to be a league that holds the interests of the owners in the same esteem."

Born in Missoula, Mont., on August 13, 1934, Davidson and his mother moved to California when Gary was in first grade, following his parents' separation.

Athletics became an important part of his life. He was a four-sport letterman in football, basketball, baseball and track at Garden Grove High School. He also was a straight-A student.

Davidson owns a minority interest in the Dallas Chaparrals of the ABA and the Los Angeles Sharks. He also is Chairman of the Board of General Residential Corporation, a firm that builds residential care homes; President of Mammoth Sports, Inc., a leisure development company, and Chairman of the Board of FIS, Inc., a temporary employment services company.

5

James W. Browitt
Executive Vice-President/Administrator

Donald J. Regan
General Counsel

Ed Fitkin
Assistant to the President

Lee L. Meade
Public Relations Director

Max Muhleman
WHA Properties

Steve Arnold
Director of Player Personnel

Vern Buffey
Referee-in-Chief

WHA DIRECTORY

LEAGUE OFFICE

1010 North Main Street, Suite 623
Santa Ana, Calif. 92701
(714) 558-3044

STAFF

President . . . . Gary L. Davidson

Exec. Vice President / Administrator . . James W. Browitt

General Counsel . . . . Donald J. Regan

Asst. to the President . . . . Ed Fitkin

Public Relations Director . . . . Lee L. Meade
   P.O. Box 657   Home: (612) 938-5729
   Hopkins, Minn. 55343   Office: (612) 938-6792

Director of Player Personnel . . . . Steve Arnold
   10 Manzanita Court
   Corte Madera, Calif. 94925

Referee-in-Chief . . . . Vern Buffey
   111 Timberbank Blvd.
   Agincourt, Ontario, Canada

WHA PROPERTIES COMPANY

3371 Via Lido, Suite 204
Newport Beach, Calif. 92660
(714) 675-4640

Executive Director . . . . Max Muhleman

Assistant Director . . . . Jack Long

7

CHRONOLOGY
OF THE
WHA

 FROM... ...TO

JANUARY 1971
Dennis Murphy, then general manager of the Floridians in the American Basketball Association, telephoned his close friend, Gary Davidson in Santa Ana, Calif., to tell him of an idea to start a new professional hockey major league.

MARCH 1971
The ABA season over, Murphy and Davidson agree to investigate the feasibility of a second hockey league.

APRIL 1971
Murphy returns to California and the plan is launched.

JUNE 1971
Articles of Incorporation are filed in Delaware on June 10 for the World Hockey Association.

JULY 1971
By-Laws for the WHA are approved by the first Board of Trustees. Signatures on the document are Gary L. Davidson, Donald J. Regan and Dennis A. Murphy . . . Murphy meets with Edmonton hockey promoter W. D. (Bill) Hunter and interests him in the project.

AUGUST 1971
Murphy and Davidson travel around North America, explaining their plan and meeting prospective franchise holders.

SEPTEMBER 1971
The first meeting of the new league is in Los Angeles (Sept. 23-24) where representatives of interested ownership groups discuss the organization program.

OCTOBER 1971
Davidson announces in Chicago on Oct. 20 the WHA will operate without a reserve clause or "any substitute therefore, such as an option clause," in all player contracts.

NOVEMBER 1971
Following two days of meetings at the American Hotel in New York, the World Hockey Association is formally organized on Nov. 1 with 10 franchises: Calgary, Chicago, Dayton, Edmonton, Los Angeles, Miami, New York, St. Paul, San Francisco and Winnipeg . . . Two additional franchises are granted in Tampa, Fla., on Nov. 21 to groups from Ontario and New England, bringing membership in the WHA to 12 . . . Steve Arnold is named Director of Player Personnel on Nov. 22.

DECEMBER 1971
Lee Meade, who has been helping in the organization of the new league for several months, becomes Director of Public Relations and Statistician.

JANUARY 1972
Richard I. (Dick) Wood and Seymour E. (Sy) Siegel, partners in a Trenton, N.J., law firm, purchase the franchise rights for New York . . . Vern Buffey is named Referee-in-Chief . . . Two outstanding college coaches—Boston University's Jack Kelley and Minnesota's Glen Sonmor—join the New England Whalers and Minnesota Fighting Saints in dual capacities as General Manager and Coach.

FEBRUARY 1972
A group of Quebec City businessmen purchase the San Francisco franchise on Feb. 11 . . . WHA holds its first player draft Feb. 12-13 at the Royal

8

Coach Inn in Anaheim, Calif. . . . New England locates in Boston . . . Ontario settles in Ottawa . . . Goaltender Bernie Parent signs an agreement on Feb. 27 with the Miami Screaming Eagles to join the WHA team.

MARCH 1972

U.S. Olympic goaltender Mike Curran becomes the first player to sign a WHA standard player's contract, joining Minnesota . . . WHA Properties Company is formed with Max Muhleman as Executive Director . . . Ed Fitkin joins the WHA as Assistant to the President . . . A group of businessmen from the Chicago suburban area of Oak Brook acquires ownership of the Chicago Cougars . . . Owners of the Dayton Aeros transfer the franchise to Houston.

APRIL 1972

Right wing Wayne Connelly and goaltender George Gardner join Minnesota and the Los Angeles Sharks, respectively, becoming the first two NHL players to sign with the WHA . . . Ten teams post $100,000 performance bonds at Continental Plaza Hotel in Chicago on April 14 . . . Two teams—Calgary and Miami—are notified their franchises are in default and given two weeks to get back in good standing . . . On April 28, Davidson cancels the franchises held by groups in Calgary and Miami.

MAY 1972

New York Raiders sign a lease to play all regular season games in Madison Square Garden . . . James W. Browitt, who had been working for the WHA as a consultant, is appointed League Administrator and Executive Vice-President, succeeding Murphy, who left the league office to become President and General Manager of the Los Angeles franchise.

JUNE 1972

James L. Cooper and Bernard A. Brown, a pair of New Jersey businessmen, obtain the 11th WHA franchise, name it the Philadelphia Blazers and sign Parent . . . Nick J. Mileti, who already owns major league teams in baseball and basketball, obtains 12th WHA franchise for Cleveland . . . Chicago real estate developers Jordon and Walter Kaiser take over controlling interest in the Chicago franchise . . . John McKenzie signs as player-coach of the Blazers . . . Bobby Hull signs a $2.75 million, 10-year contract with the Winnipeg Jets and the WHA . . . Davidson presents Hull with a $1 million certified check from WHA Properties, Ltd., in St. Paul, and Hull is flown to Winnipeg to sign a playing and coaching contract with Jets as more than 10,000 gather at corner of Portage and Main.

JULY 1972

J. C. Tremblay signs with Quebec Nordiques . . . WHA has one of its most active weeks as 28 players sign . . . Among them are goaltender Gerry Cheevers with Cleveland, defenseman Teddy Green with New England and center Bobby Sheehan with New York . . . Hall of Famer Maurice (Rocket) Richard joins the Nordiques as coach.

AUGUST 1972

Derek Sanderson signs with the Philadelphia Blazers for $2.325 million over 10 years . . . With more than 300 players under contract, WHA announces a 78-game schedule for its first season.

SEPTEMBER 1972

WHA teams begin training camps, with Philadelphia leading the way, on Sept. 10 . . . Rookie teams play first WHA games ever on Sept. 23 . . . New England defeats Philadelphia 5-3 at Roanoke, Va., and Minnesota beats Chicago 10-7 at Hibbing, Minn.

OCTOBER 1972

Veteran players report to training camps on Oct. 1 . . . Davidson announces WHA will use a colored puck—blue—and hopes to develop a bright red puck for future use . . . He also signs league's first television contract with Canadian Broadcasting Corporation . . . League's first regular season games are set Wednesday, Oct. 11, with Quebec meeting Cleveland at Cleveland and Alberta playing Ottawa at Ottawa.

WHA RULES

*Something Old,
Something New,
Something Borrowed,
Something Blue (the puck)*

A new league has one big advantage over an existing league. The new league cannot say, "But we've always done it that way."

The World Hockey Association is taking full advantage of its position by making some changes in the already exciting game of hockey that will offer fans even more thrills.

The areas of change are:

OVERTIME PLAY

From the beginning, WHA organizers have been adamant about tie games. If regulation time fails to produce a winner, a 10-minute sudden-death or sudden-victory, if you prefer, overtime session will be played.

Bill Hunter, President of the Alberta Oilers and chairman of the WHA Rules Committee, was asked about the possibility of disappointing fans if sudden-death doesn't break the deadlock.

"After 10 minutes of sudden-death," responded Hunter, "I'll show you an arena full of people so tired from cheering, they won't be able to complain."

SHOOT-OUTS?

With an eye toward the future and the possible elimination of tie games completely, the WHA experimented with a shoot-out during its preseason games.

Under the plan, if the score remains tied after three regulation periods and a 10-minute sudden-death overtime, each coach designates a shooting order. The players then skate in on the opposing goaltender one-on-one, ala a penalty shot.

The visiting team goes first, followed by the first shooter for the home team. And so on, until one team scores and the other doesn't. The home team always has a chance to tie, much like extra innings in baseball.

Coaches and players were strongly opposed to such goings-on, but the WHA is taking the shoot-out under advisement because of its great popularity with the fans.

There was one shoot-out during the exhibition season. Houston's Aeros edged the Minnesota Fighting Saints 7-6 in Duluth, Minn., October 6. Regulation play ended 4-4 and the overtime period was, of course, scoreless. Eighteen players, nine from each team, had a chance to win it in the shoot-out before the Aeros prevailed on a goal by Don Grierson. Two Aeros—Larry Lund and Murray Hall—had scored on Saint goaltender Jack McCartan, but two Saints—Jimmy Johnson and Ted Hampson—got the goals back for Minnesota in their turns.

The WHA Board of Trustees voted 9-2 against using the shoot-out in regular season play this year, but they'll more than likely take another look at it for 1973-74. Philadelphia, which sponsored the rule, and Minnesota, the only WHA shoot-out victim, were the two teams voting in favor of using it this season. Quebec abstained.

PASSES ACROSS TWO LINES

In the WHA, a team may begin a breakaway by headmanning the puck virtually to the other team's blue line. But the maneuver will require excellent timing.

The puck may be passed from a team's defensive end to the other team's blue line, provided the puck precedes the receiving player across the red line and he takes it ahead of his body. The puck, of course, also must precede his body across the opponent's blue line.

NEW LOOK AT ICING

A new version of the icing rule will provide some added difficulties for short-handed teams. Simply, a short-handed team in the WHA cannot clear the puck by dumping it to the other end of the ice. That will be ruled icing.

Instead, short-handed teams must carry or pass the puck, at least past its own blue line. From there, the puck may be shot down the ice without resulting in an icing call.

THIRD MAN RULE

Like the National Hockey League, the WHA has a "third man" rule, but the new league's guidelines are designed to keep players on the ice.

In the NHL, the third man in a fight, whether it's as a peacemaker or added combatant, is given a game misconduct penalty. In the WHA, the third man receives a 10-minute misconduct penalty and a $100 fine. If the same player is the third man a second time in the same game, he gets an early shower.

Vern Buffey, Referee-in-Chief for the WHA, explained the reasoning behind the interpretation.

"We want to keep our stars on the ice," said Buffey. "For instance, if Bobby Hull pulled one of his Winnipeg teammates away from a fight, he would be the third man. In the NHL in that situation, Hull would be out of the game."

"We're not promoting fighting," Buffey added. "We just want our fans to see the stars."

CURVED STICKS

The WHA's position on curved sticks should please Hull, too.

NHL goaltenders remember Hull's blazing-fast shot that dipped and broke off his curved blade. Then, the NHL limited the curvature of a player's stick to one-half inch.

This year, Hull and the rest of the WHA players will be able to use a stick with up to an inch and a quarter of curvature.

COLORED PUCK

Why is the puck black? Because it's always been black.

Not in the WHA. With no restricting precedence to follow, the WHA boldly decided on a colored puck.

Early experiments with a blazing red puck were not satisfactory, so the league settled on a deep blue coloring.

"We haven't given up on red, though," WHA President Gary L. Davidson points out. "We're still working on it."

Most of the changes adopted give indication the WHA will be a higher-scoring league than the NHL. If it is, don't blame the goalkeepers.

The rules have been written so that power plays should be more effective, there will be more breakaways and, of course, fewer and fewer tie games.

Which was the idea all along. © 2018 WHA HOF / PCMP LLC

ALBERTA OILERS 1972-73 ROSTER

No.	Player	Pos	S	Ht	Wt	Birth Date	1971-72 Club (League)	GP	G	A	Pts	PIM
10	Ron Anderson	RW	R	6-0	190	July 29, 1945	Buffalo (NHL)	37	0	4	4	19
19	Ken Baird	D	L	6-0	190	February 1, 1951	Oklahoma City (CHL)	59	5	11	16	196
							California (NHL)	10	0	2	2	15
5	Doug Barrie	D	R	5-9	175	October 2, 1946	Los Angeles (NHL)	75	5	18	23	92
21	Jim Benzelock	RW	R	5-10	187	June 21, 1947	Dayton (IHL)	69	44	32	76	125
14	Brian Carlin	LW	L	5-10	175	June 13, 1950	Springfield (AHL)	67	35	31	66	6
20	Steve Cartyle	D	L	5-10	180	March 10, 1950	Alberta (College)	20	14	20	34	—
2	Roger Cote	D	L	5-9	184	December 22, 1939	Cleveland (AHL)	73	4	21	25	141
6	Bob Falkenberg	D	L	6-0	195	January 1, 1946	Tidewater (AHL)	74	4	21	25	57
8	Val Fonteyne	LW	L	5-9	160	December 2, 1933	Pittsburgh (NHL)	68	6	13	19	0
3	Al Hamilton	D	R	6-2	195	August 20, 1946	Buffalo (NHL)	76	4	30	34	105
27	Derek Harker	D	R	6-0	185	January 7, 1951	Flint (IHL)	33	0	9	9	49
7	Jim Harrison	C	R	5-11	180	July 9, 1947	Toronto (NHL)	66	19	17	36	104
12	Bill Hicke	RW	L	5-8	176	March 31, 1938	Pittsburgh (NHL)	12	2	0	2	6
							Tidewater (AHL)	16	4	2	6	6
							Fort Worth (CHL)	34	9	10	19	51
16	Ed Joyal	C	L	6-0	180	May 8, 1940	Philadelphia (NHL)	70	14	7	21	25
15	Dennis Kassian	LW	L	5-11	170	July 14, 1941	Salt Lake City (WHL)	72	22	20	42	39
18	Bob McAneeley	LW	L	5-8	175		British Columbia (College)	—	29	32	61	—
17	Rusty Patenaude	RW	R	5-9	175	October 17, 1949	Fort Wayne (IHL)	70	32	41	73	111
9	Ross Perkins	C	R	5-10	176	November 4, 1946	Fort Worth (CHL)	68	41	56	97	47
4	Bob Wall	LW	L	5-10	180	December 1, 1942	Detroit (NHL)	46	2	4	6	9
11	Ron Walters	C	R	6-0	175	March 9, 1948	Tidewater (AHL)	17	2	4	6	12
							Tidewater (AHL)	75	14	27	41	21

No.	Player	Pos	S	Ht	Wt	Birth Date	1971-72 Club (League)	GP	GA	SO	AVG
1	Ken Brown	G	L	5-11	175	December 19, 1948	Dallas (CHL)	31	90	2	3.20
30	Jack Norris	G	L	5-10	175	August 5, 1942	Springfield (AHL)	10	36	0	3.60

Allard   Feldman   Hunter   Kinasewich

ALBERTA OILERS

Operated by Edmonton World Hockey Enterprises Ltd.
MacDonald Hotel
Edmonton, Alberta T5J ON6, Canada
Telephone: (403) 422-4049
Telex: 037-3595 HOCKEY EDM

Chairman of the Board .... Charles A. Allard
Alternate Trustee and President .... Zane Feldman
Trustee, Vice-President and General Manager .. W.D. (Bill) Hunter
Comptroller .... Ray Barth
Coach .... Ray Kinasewich
Assistant Coach .... Glenn Hall
Director of Player Personnel .... Bob Freeman
Trainer .... Ron Walters Sr.
Public Relations Director .... Don LeRose
Home Phone: (403) 466-9995

Colors: Royal Blue, Orange and White.
Arena: Edmonton Gardens, Edmonton Exhibition Grounds, Edmonton, Alberta, Canada (Capacity 5,200).
Radio: CJCA (930 kc), all games, play-by-play Bryan Hall.
Television: None.

EDMONTON:
Fort Edmonton, built in 1795, was related to the fur trade, but today's Edmonton is a rapidly-expanding industrial and refining center. Petrochemical-based secondary industries such as plastics and fertilizers, as well as steel tube mills, are making increasingly important contributions to the economic growth of the largest refining center in Western Canada. The city also has the nation's second-largest meat packing industry. The prosperous mixed-farming economy of the region was transformed by the discovery of oil at Leduc (20 miles south) in 1947, which touched off Alberta's oil boom. Edmonton is the originating terminus of five pipelines transporting oil and natural gas to eastern Canada and the U.S. The city's population doubled in the 15 years from 1955 to 1970. Now, with a metropolitan area population in excess of 437,000, is one of the fastest growing metro areas in Canada. Edmonton also is the home of the Eskimos of the Canadian Football League and the Oil Kings junior team of the Western Canada Hockey League.

13

CHICAGO COUGARS 1972-73 ROSTER

No.	Player	Pos	S	Ht	Wt	Birth Date	1971-72 Club (League)	GP	G	A	Pts	PIM
18	Ron Anderson	D	L	6-0	190	November 15, 1948	Greensboro (EHL)	71	13	45	58	98
2	Butch Barber	D	L	5-10	180	August 31, 1943	Hershey (AHL)	71	2	19	21	87
22	Bernie Blanchette	RW	R	6-0	185	July 11, 1947	Kansas City (CHL)	43	24	21	45	40
5	Larry Cahan	D	R	6-1	215	December 25, 1933	Seattle (WHL)	50	4	12	16	44
6	Reggie Fleming	LW-D	L	5-10	190	April 21, 1936	Salt Lake City (WHL)	56	20	28	48	134
27	Brian Glenwright	LW	L	6-3	210	October 8, 1949	Denver (WHL)	65	21	20	41	28
12	Ed Hatoum	RW	R	5-10	185	December 7, 1947	Rochester (AHL)	67	9	23	32	29
11	Darrel Knibbs	C-RW	R	6-1	185	September 21, 1949	Muskegon (IHL)	71	42	33	75	12
7	Bob Liddington	LW	L	5-11	180	September 14, 1948	Phoenix (WHL)	72	22	19	41	58
14	Dan Lodboa	LW-RW		5-9	178	September 25, 1946	Dallas (CHL)	64	20	23	43	24
4	Dick McGlynn	D	R	6-2	184	July 19, 1948	U.S. Olympic (Amateur)	51	7	27	34	87
10	Rick Morris	LW	L	5-11	176	July 5, 1946	Laurentian U. (College)	17	20	26	46	61
9	Rosie Paiement	RW	R	5-11	183	August 12, 1945	Vancouver (NHL)	69	10	19	29	117
19	Jan Popiel	LW	L	5-9	184	October 9, 1947	Tulsa (CHL)	63	24	37	61	109
3	Dick Proceviat	D	L	6-0	187	June 25, 1946	Kansas City (CHL)	67	7	47	54	137
17	Bob Sicinski	C	L	5-11	181	November 13, 1946	Dallas (CHL)	67	23	61	84	14
20	Pierre Viau	D	L	6-2	187	January 29, 1952	Cornwall (QJHL)	31	1	7	8	27
15	Bobby Whitlock	C	L	5-10	187	July 16, 1949	Phoenix (WHL)	65	33	46	79	69
8	Rod Zaine	C	L	5-10	179	May 18, 1946	Buffalo (NHL)	24	2	1	3	4
							Cincinnati (AHL)	32	8	15	23	6

No.	Player	Pos	S	Ht	Wt	Birth Date	1971-72 Club (League)	GP	GA	SO	AVG
30	Andre Gill	G	L	5-7	175	September 19, 1941	Hershey (AHL)	40	114	2	2.96
31	Keith Le Lievre	G	R	5-7	162	November 19, 1949	U. of New Brunswick (College)	13	66	0	4.92
1	Jimmy McLeod	G	L	5-9	174	April 7, 1937	St. Louis (NHL)	16	44	0	3.00
							Portland (WHL)	13	34	0	2.79

J. Kaiser   W. Kaiser   Ladner   Short   Pronovost

CHICAGO COUGARS

Operated by Chicago Cougars Hockey Club, Inc.
222 North Michigan Ave.
Chicago, Ill. 60601
Telephone: (312) 346-4344
Telex: 25-3357 COUGARS CGO

Trustee and Chairman of the Board . . . . Jordon H. Kaiser
President . . . . Walter Kaiser
Alternate Trustee and Executive
    Vice-President . . . . John J. Ladner, Jr.
General Manager . . . . Edwin G. Short
Coach . . . . Marcel Pronovost
Trainer . . . . Eddie Swiss
Public Relations Director . . . . Michael Haggerty
                         Home Phone: (312) 771-5082

    Colors: Jungle Green and Cougar Gold.
    Arena: International Amphitheatre, 4300 South Halstead St., Chicago, Ill. 60609 (Capacity 9,000).
    Radio: WJJB-FM (104.3 mc), all home games, play-by-play Duane Dow.
    Television: WSNS-TV (Channel 44), minimum 12 away games, play-by-play Bud Palmer.

CHICAGO:

Geography has helped make Chicago the nation's center of industrial distribution and transportation. Indians named the area Checagou for its strong-smelling wild onions. Wagon trains set up camp south of Fort Dearborn in the 1830s on what was to become Michigan Avenue. In 1837, Chicago was incorporated by 4,170 pioneers. At the time of the Chicago fire in 1871, it had 300,000 residents. Now as the nation's second largest city, Chicago proper has 3,369,359 people. Metropolitan Chicago, defined as the Illinois counties of Cook, Lake, McHenry, DuPage, Kane and Will and Lake and Porter counties in Indiana, has 7,612,314 people. Chicago's biggest industry is primary metals. Next is food and kindred products, then electrical equipment and supplies. In professional sports, Chicago also has the baseball White Sox and Cubs of the American and National Leagues, respectively; the Bulls of the National Basketball Association; the Bears of the National Football League, and the Black Hawks of the National Hockey League.

15

CLEVELAND CRUSADERS 1972-73 ROSTER

No.	Player	Pos	S	Ht	Wt	Birth Date	1971-72 Club (League)	GP	G	A	Pts	PIM
21	Paul Andrea	RW	L	5-10	170	July 31, 1941	Cincinnati (AHL)	69	14	58	72	18
9	Doug Brindley	C	L	5-11	175	June 8, 1949	Rochester (AHL)	74	20	27	47	12
10	Ron Buchanan	C	L	6-3	170	November 15, 1944	Denver (WHL)	69	38	42	80	10
6	Ray Clearwater	D	L	5-11	175	November 10, 1942	Providence (AHL)	76	12	36	48	69
24	Bob Dillabough	C	L	5-11	170	April 24, 1941	Tidewater (AHL)	15	0	0	0	4
16	Grant Erickson	LW	L	5-9	165	April 28, 1947	Cleveland (AHL)	76	26	24	50	45
2	John Hanna	RW	L	5-9	170	May 2, 1952	Medicine Hat (WCHL Jr.)	68	59	57	116	99
25	Joe Hardy	C	L	6-0	185	December 5, 1944	Nova Scotia (AHL)	69	18	42	60	105
11	Ted Hodgson	RW	R	5-11	175	June 30, 1945	Salt Lake City (WHL)	72	22	17	39	86
4	Ralph Hopiavuori	D	L	6-1	185	July 15, 1951	Port Huron (IHL)	45	3	12	15	134
26	Bill Horton	D	L	6-0	180	September 5, 1946	Flint (IHL)	69	4	25	29	116
12	Gary Jarrett	D	L	5-8	180	September 3, 1942	California (NHL)	55	5	10	15	18
17	Skip Krake	C	R	5-11	170	October 14, 1943	Salt Lake City (WHL)	53	15	36	51	59
22	Jim McMasters	D	R	5-10	180	September 20, 1952	Calgary (WCHL Jr.)	65	12	48	60	94
5	Wayne Muloin	D	L	5-8	175	December 24, 1941	Cleveland (AHL)	71	1	14	15	82
7	Gerry Pinder	LW	R	5-8	165	September 15, 1948	California (NHL)	74	23	31	54	59
23	Dick Pumple	C	L	6-3	200	November 2, 1948	Muskegon (IHL)	71	25	19	44	60
19	Al Rycroft	RW	R	5-9	170	January 10, 1950	Fort Wayne (IHL)	38	19	26	45	4
							Seattle (WHL)	24	3	4	7	8
3	Paul Shmyr	D	L	5-10	170	January 28, 1946	California (NHL)	69	6	21	27	156
							Rochester (AHL)	13	4	8	12	2
14	Jim Wiste	C	L	5-10	185	February 18, 1946	Seattle (WHL)	4	0	0	0	0
							Providence (AHL)	53	12	26	38	35

No.	Player	Pos	S	Ht	Wt	Birth Date	1971-72 Club (League)	GP	GA	SO	AVG
30	Gerry Cheevers	G	L	5-11	185	December 7, 1940	Boston (NHL)	41	101	2	2.50
1	Bob Whidden	G	R	5-10	165	July 27, 1946	Baltimore (AHL)	44	143	2	3.33

Mileti Zayac Needham

CLEVELAND CRUSADERS

Operated by Cleveland Crusaders Limited
3717 Euclid Avenue
Cleveland, Ohio 44115
Telephone: (216) 361-3700
Telex: 985-376 CAVALIERS CLV

Trustee and President ....Nick J. Mileti
Alternate Trustee and Operations Manager ....Stephen Zayac Jr.
Director of Player Personnel ....Chuck Catto
Coach ....Bill Needham
Trainer ....Steve Thomas
Public Relations Director ....Bob Brown
                            Home Phone: (216) 671-4089
Publicity Director ....Barry Swinehart
                            Home Phone: (216) 234-1191

Colors: Crusader Purple, Black and White.
Arena: Cleveland Arena, 3717 Euclid Ave., Cleveland, Ohio 44115. (Capacity 9,500).
Radio: WKYC (1100 kc), 59 games, play-by-play Steve Albert.
Television: WUAB-TV (Channel 43), 10 away games, play-by-play Frank Sweeney. Also, all home games will be televised to Akron by Akron Cablevision.

CLEVELAND:

Visitors to "The Best Location in the Nation," as Cleveland calls itself, are greeted by a large sign as they leave the city's Hopkins International Airport. Within 500 miles, it says, are 53 per cent of the U.S. population, 55 per cent of the nation's retail sales, 60 per cent of the nation's industries and 67 per cent of the billion-dollar markets. It was here—where the twisting Cuyahoga River flows into Lake Erie—that General Moses Cleveland established the first settlement in 1796. Now the 10th largest city in the U.S. with 750,879 population, Cleveland has a metro area of more than 2 million. No single industry dominates its economy, but the making of steel and the manufacturing of metal products are mainstays. In professional sports, Cleveland also is the home of the baseball Indians of the American League, the Browns of the National Football League, the Cavaliers of the National Basketball Association and the Barons of the American Hockey League.

17

HOUSTON AEROS 1972-73 ROSTER

No.	Player	Pos	S	Ht	Wt	Birth Date	1971-72 Club (League)	GP	G	A	Pts	PIM
21	Don Grierson	RW	R	6-0	180	June 18, 1947	Port Huron (Int.)	72	45	32	77	234
17	Larry Hale	D	L	6-1	187	October 9, 1941	Richmond (AHL)	68	11	33	44	68
							Philadelphia (NHL)	6	0	1	1	0
11	Murray Hall	RW-C	R	5-11	174	November 24, 1940	Rochester (AHL)	37	10	32	42	70
							Vancouver (NHL)	32	6	6	12	6
15	Duke Harris	RW	R	6-0	190	February 25, 1942	Rochester (AHL)	74	27	34	61	24
16	Andre Hinse	LW	L	5-9	175	April 19, 1945	Phoenix (WHL)	66	33	43	76	61
12	Ed Hoekstra	RW-C	L	5-11	175	November 4, 1937	Springfield (AHL)	74	16	69	85	32
7	Frank Hughes	RW	L	5-10	180	October 1, 1949	Phoenix (WHL)	53	34	28	62	41
5	Gordon Kannegiesser	D	L	6-0	190	December 21, 1945	Denver (WHL)	70	8	25	33	57
10	Gordon Labossiere	RW-C	L	6-1	185	January 2, 1940	Cleveland (AHL)	66	40	45	85	71
3	Ray Larose	D	L	6-0	190	November 20, 1941	Denver (WHL)	65	12	23	35	63
13	Larry Lund	C	R	6-0	190	September 9, 1940	Phoenix (WHL)	66	30	66	96	149
4	Dunc McCallum	D	R	6-1	193	March 29, 1940	San Diego (NHL)	61	10	30	40	99
8	Brian McDonald	RW-C	L	5-11	190	March 23, 1945	San Diego (WHL)	63	24	22	46	88
9	Keke Mortson	RW	R	5-9	170	March 29, 1934	Cincinnati (AHL)	76	17	50	67	133
6	Paul Popiel	D	L	5-10	176	February 28, 1943	Rochester (AHL)	12	7	4	11	10
							Vancouver (NHL)	38	1	1	2	36
2	John Schella	D	R	6-0	180	May 9, 1947	Vancouver (NHL)	77	2	13	15	166
18	Jack Stanfield	LW	L	5-11	176	May 30, 1942	Rochester (AHL)	62	11	16	27	74
14	Ted Taylor	RW	L	6-0	175	February 25, 1942	Vancouver (NHL)	69	9	13	22	88

No.	Player	Pos	S	Ht	Wt	Birth Date	1971-72 Club (League)	GP	GA	SO	AVG
29	Bill Hughes	Out of Hockey – 1971-72									
1	Don McLeod	G	L	6-1	190	August 24, 1946	Providence (AHL)	19	66	0	2.73
							Philadelphia (NHL)	4	14	0	4.64
							Richmond (AHL)	5	14	0	2.80
30	Wayne Rutledge	G	L	6-2	205	January 5, 1942	Salt Lake City (WHL)	60	206	1	3.51

Deneau — Smith — Dineen

HOUSTON AEROS

Operated by Houston Hockey Club, Inc.
810 Bagby
Houston, Texas 77002
Telephone: (713) 228-6437
Telex: 775-520 AEROS HOU

Trustee and Chairman of the Board .... Paul H. Deneau
Alternate Trustee, President and
   General Manager .... James S. Smith
Coach .... Bill Dineen
Trainer .... Dick Bielus
Public Relations Director and
   Business Manager .... Sonny Tate
                               Home Phone: (713) 626-8178

    Colors: Powder Blue, Navy Blue and White.
    Arena: Sam Houston Coliseum, 810 Bagby, Houston, Texas 77002. (Capacity 9,300).
    Radio: KLYX-FM (102.5 mc), all games, play-by-play Jerry Trupiano.
    Television: Arrangements pending.

HOUSTON:
Houston is the nation's sixth largest and fastest growing major city. Located on the Golf Coast prairies, connected to Galveston Bay by a 50-mile ship canal, its average temperature is 68.6 degrees and the climate is devoid of extremes. The Manned Spacecraft Center, which gives Houston its nickname, "Space City, U.S.A.", is 22 miles south from downtown. A $250,000,000 complex of 1,620 acres, the installation is the center of astronaut training, equipment testing and Mission Control for the space program. The population of the metropolitan Houston area is 1,957,688, up 38 percent from the 1960 census. The Astrodome, America's largest enclosed sports stadium, is the home of the baseball Houston Aeros of the National League and the Houston Oilers of the National Football League. The city also is the home of the Houston Rockets of the National Basketball Association.

LOS ANGELES SHARKS 1972-73 ROSTER

No.	Player	Pos	S	Ht	Wt	Birth Date	1971-72 Club (League)	GP	G	A	Pts	PIM
9	Mike Byers	RW	R	5-10	185	September 11, 1946	Buffalo (NHL)	74	13	12	25	23
7	Bart Crashley	D	R	6-0	178	June 15, 1946	Dallas (CHL)	56	20	38	58	24
12	Tom Gilmore	LW	L	5-11	190	May 14, 1948	Tidewater (AHL)	76	30	31	61	141
22	Howie Heggedal	C	L	6-0	185	September 15, 1949	Toldeo (IHL)	72	23	32	55	198
16	Earl Heiskala	RW	L	6-0	185	November 30, 1942	San Diego (WHL)	72	15	22	37	169
8	Bob Jones	LW	L	6-2	195	November 27, 1945	Portland (WHL)	45	13	11	24	19
23	Pat Kropicka	RW		5-9	160		Zurich (Europe)	–	–	–	–	–
10	J. P. LeBlanc	C	L	5-10	170	October 20, 1946	Dallas (CHL)	70	22	68	90	117
20	Bernie MacNeil	LW	L	5-11	180	March 7, 1950	Fort Wayne (IHL)	67	19	13	32	140
4	Ralph MacSweyn	D	R	5-11	195	September 8, 1942	Philadelphia (NHL)	2	0	0	0	0
							Richmond (AHL)	60	0	15	15	52
5	Larry Mavety	D	R	5-11	185	May 29, 1942	Salt Lake City (WHL)	62	15	38	53	114
11	Ted McCaskill	C	L	6-1	190	October 29, 1936	Phoenix (WHL)	71	18	37	55	237
3	Jim Niekamp	D	R	6-1	185	March 11, 1946	Detroit (NHL)	5	0	0	0	10
							Tidewater (AHL)	65	6	11	17	216
6	Gerry Odrowski	D	L	5-10	190	October 4, 1938	St. Louis (NHL)	55	1	2	3	8
14	Peter Slater	C	L	5-11	170	January 31, 1948	Des Moines (IHL)	67	27	27	54	151
19	Steve Sutherland	LW	L	5-11	172	September 1, 1946	Port Huron (IHL)	52	21	23	44	219
15	Joe Szura	C	L	6-3	198	December 18, 1938	Baltimore (AHL)	72	38	38	76	20
18	Gary Veneruzzo	RW	L	5-8	165	June 28, 1943	Denver (WHL)	72	41	45	96	41
2	Jim Watson	D	L	6-2	195	June 28, 1943	Buffalo (HNL)	66	2	6	8	101
17	Bill Young	LW	L	6-2	195	July 5, 1947	Dallas (CHL)	49	11	14	25	41

No.	Player	Pos	S	Ht	Wt	Birth Date	1971-72 Club (League)	GP	GA	SO	AVG
30	George Gardner	G	L	5-10	165	October 8, 1942	Vancouver (NHL)	24	86	1	4.17
1	Russ Gillow	G	L	5-10	165	September 2, 1940	Spokane (WIHL)	–	–	–	–

Murphy   Davidson   Slater

LOS ANGELES SHARKS

Operated by Los Angeles Sharks, Inc.
3939 S. Figueroa Ave.
Los Angeles, Calif. 90037
Telephone: (213) 741-2111
Telex: 677-337 SHARKS LSA

Trustee, President and General Manager .... Dennis Murphy
Executive Vice-President .... Gary L. Davidson
Assistant to the General Manager .... John Kanel
Coach .... Terry Slater
Trainer .... Al Olsen
Public Relations Director .... Hank Ives
                                     Home Phone: (714) 534-6802

Colors: Red, Black and White.
Arena: L.A. Sports Arena, 3939 S. Figueroa St., Los Angeles, Calif. 90053 (Capacity 14,700), 35 games; Long Beach Arena, 300 Ocean Blvd., Long Beach, Calif. 90802 (Capacity 11,325), 4 games.
Radio: KUTE-FM (102.0 mc), all games, play-by-play Gary Morrell.
Television: Arrangements pending.

LOS ANGELES:

Until 1817, Los Angeles alternated with Monterey as the capital of the Mexican territory of Alta California. In 1842, the first gold discovery in California was made at Placerita Canyon, in the northern part of Los Angeles County, six years before the famous strike was made at Sutter's mill. Today, the City of Los Angeles has a population of 2,816,061, and covers 458.2 square miles. Los Angeles County has a total population of 7,032,075. Including Orange County (where WHA offices are located in Santa Ana) the total reaches nearly 8.5 million. Since the first movie was made in Los Angeles in 1908, the city has become the film capital of the world. Hollywood was annexed to the city in 1910 and a recent report showed 617 firms engaged, somehow, in the motion picture industry. Among its professional sports teams, Los Angeles has the Rams of the National Football League, the baseball Dodgers of the National League, the Lakers of the National Basketball Association and the Kings of the National Hockey League. The baseball California Angels of the American League play in Anaheim in Orange County.

21

MINNESOTA FIGHTING SAINTS 1972-73 ROSTER

No.	Player	Pos	S	Ht	Wt	Birth Date	1971-72 Club (League)	GP	G	A	Pts	PIM
12	Mike Antonovich	C	L	5-8	160	October 18, 1951	Minnesota College	–	8	4	12	–
17	John Arbour	D	L	5-11	194	September 28, 1945	St. Louis (NHL)	17	0	0	0	10
21	Terry Ball	D	R	5-9	165	November 29, 1944	Denver (WHL)	20	4	12	16	73
6	Keith Christiansen	C	R	5-5	155	July 14, 1944	Cincinnati (AHL)	68	17	39	56	62
7	Wayne Connelly	RW	R	5-10	175	December 16, 1939	U.S. Olympics	–	25	50	75	–
16	Craig Falkman	RW	R	5-11	190	August 1, 1943	Vancouver (NHL)	68	19	25	44	14
10	Ted Hampson	C	L	5-8	170	December 11, 1936	Did not play	–	–	–	–	–
20	Jimmy Johnson	LW	L	5-9	185	November 7, 1942	Minnesota (NHL)	78	5	14	19	6
8	Billy Klatt	RW	R	5-10	180	October 16, 1947	Los Angeles (NHL)	74	21	24	45	18
19	George Konik	D	L	5-10	195	May 4, 1934	Oklahoma City (CHA)	66	34	41	75	26
15	Len Lilyholm	LW	L	5-8	163	April 1, 1941	Did not play	–	–	–	–	–
14	Bob MacMillan	C	L	5-10	175	December 3, 1952	Kitzbuehel, Aus.	–	33	58	91	–
23	Mike McMahon	D	L	5-11	182	August 30, 1941	St. Catherines (OHA JRA)	39	12	41	53	41
9	George Morrison	LW	L	6-1	175	December 24, 1948	Rochester (AHL)	48	3	29	32	78
2	Dick Paradise	D	L	5-11	194	April 21, 1945	St. Louis (NHL)	42	2	11	13	7
26	Mel Pearson	LW	L	5-10	175	April 29, 1938	Tidewater (AHL)	51	3	1	4	80
18	Terry Ryan	C	L	5-10	178	September 10, 1952	Portland (WHL)	72	21	38	59	45
4	Frank Sanders	D	R	6-3	230	March 8, 1949	Hamilton (OHA JRA)	61	47	45	92	59
11	Fred Speck	C	L	5-9	165	July 22, 1947	U.S. Olympics	–	–	–	–	–
							Vancouver (NHL)	18	1	2	3	0
							Cleveland (AHL)	27	6	8	14	21
							Seattle (WHL)	6	3	3	6	0

No.	Player	Pos	S	Ht	Wt	Birth Date	1971-72 Club (League)	GP	GA	SO	AVG
1	Mike Curran	G	L	5-9	175	April 14, 1944	U.S. Olympics	–	–	–	–
30	Jack McCartan	G	L	6-1	195	August 5, 1935	San Diego (WHL)	36	112	0	3.44
35	Carl Wetzel	G	L	6-2	190	December 12, 1938	Kitzbuhel, Aus.	–	–	2	3.00

Marzitelli   Grothe   Kaplan   Sonmor

MINNESOTA FIGHTING SAINTS

Operated by Midwest Saints, Inc.
Metro Square, Suite 240
St. Paul, Minn. 55101
Telephone: (612) 222-3040
Telex: 29-7499 SAINTS STP

Chairman of the Board .... Frank Marzitelli
*Alternate Trustee, President and
    Executive Director* .... Fred Grothe
Trustee and Chairman Emeritus .... Lou Kaplan
General Manager and Coach .... Glen Sonmor
Assistant General Manager .... Harry Neale
Trainer .... Glenn Gostick
Public Relations Director .... Bob Halverson
                            Home Phone: (715) 386-5302

    Colors: Royal Blue, New Gold and White.
    Arena: St. Paul Auditorium, 143 West 4th St., St. Paul, Minn. 55102. (Capacity 8,000), until December 1972; St. Paul Civic Center, 143 West 4th St., St. Paul, Minn. 55102. (Capacity 16,180), after January 1973.
    Radio: WLOL (1330 kc), all games, play-by-play Frank Buetel.
    Television: Arrangements pending.

ST. PAUL:
St. Paul, capital city of Minnesota, has a population of 309,828, second only in the state to its neighbor, Minneapolis. The Twin Cities and their suburbs have a metropolitan area population of 1,874,380. Located on the hilly banks of the Mississippi River in eastern Minnesota, St. Paul is close to Minnesota and Wisconsin vacationlands and is noted for manufacturing, transportation, shopping and education. The first settler (1838) was a trader, Piere "Pig's Eye" Parrant, who was removed from Fort Snelling in 1840 and settled in what is now the heart of the city. In 1841, Father Lucien Galtier built a chapel to serve the community, dedicating it to St. Paul, which supplanted Pig's Eye as the community name. The Twin Cities is the fourth largest electronics center in the nation. St. Paul is fourth largest in printing and publishing, fifth in cosmetics production in the nation and the largest refiner of petroleum products in the northern Midwest. The Twin Cities are also the home of the Minnesota Vikings of the National Football League, the baseball Minnesota Twins of the American League and the Minnesota North Stars of the National Hockey League.

23

NEW ENGLAND WHALERS 1972-73 ROSTER

No.	Player	Pos	S	Ht	Wt	Birth Date	1971-72 Club (League)	GP	G	A	Pts	PIM
14	Kevin Ahearn	LW	L	5-10	170	June 20, 1948	U.S. Olympics	7	—	1	2	—
							Nova Scotia (AHL)	31	1	1	2	0
18	Bob Brown	D	R	6-1	195	December 18, 1950	Boston U. (College)	31	14	36	50	36
7	Terry Caffery	C	R	5-9	165	April 1, 1949	Cleveland (AHL)	65	29	59	88	18
22	Don Cahoon	LW	L	5-9	175	April 13, 1949	Boston U. (College)	31	13	17	30	14
17	John Cunniff	LW	L	5-9	175	July 9, 1944	Rochester (AHL)	66	16	29	45	57
12	John Danby	C	R	5-10	165	July 20, 1948	Boston U. (College)	26	26	24	50	14
10	Jim Dorey	D	L	6-1	190	August 17, 1947	Toronto (NHL)	50	4	19	23	56
							New York (NHL)	1	0	0	0	0
27	Tom Earl	RW	R	5-11	180	January 27, 1947	Kansas City (CHL)	64	15	18	33	23
11	John French	C	L	5-11	175	August 25, 1950	Baltimore (AHL)	69	17	29	46	14
6	Ted Green	D	R	5-10	209	March 22, 1940	Boston (NHL)	54	1	16	17	21
5	Paul Hurley	D	R	5-11	195	July 12, 1946	Boston (AHL)	74	7	28	35	65
21	Mike Hyndman	RW	R	6-1	195	December 8, 1945	Boston U. (College)	75	20	14	34	38
20	Ric Jordan	D	L	6-3	195	March 31, 1950	Boston U. (College)	31	13	27	40	34
2	Rick Ley	D	L	5-9	185	November 2, 1948	Toronto (NHL)	67	1	14	15	124
4	Larry Pleau	C	L	6-1	185	June 29, 1947	Nova Scotia (AHL)	11	7	6	13	19
							Montreal (NHL)	55	7	10	17	14
16	Dick Sarrazin	RW	R	6-0	187	January 22, 1946	Richmond (AHL)	42	11	11	22	4
							Philadelphia (NHL)	28	3	4	7	4
3	Brad Selwood	D	L	6-1	188	March 18, 1948	Toronto (NHL)	72	4	17	21	60
15	Tim Sheehy	C	R	6-1	185	September 3, 1948	U.S. Olympics	—	—	—	—	—
1	Guy Smith	RW	R	6-1	180	January 2, 1950	New Hampshire (College)	29	21	41	62	—
8	Tom Webster	RW	R	5-10	185	October 4, 1948	California (NHL)	12	3	2	5	10
9	Tommy Williams	C	R	5-11	177	April 17, 1940	California (NHL)	32	3	9	12	2
							Boston (AHL)	31	8	15	23	8

No.	Player	Pos	S	Ht	Wt	Birth Date	1971-72 Club (League)	GP	GA	SO	AVG
30	Bruce Landon	G	R	5-9	180	October 5, 1949	Springfield (AHL)	32	118	2	3.69
29	Geoff McMullen	G	R	5-9	158	April 23, 1949	Colgate (College)	19	80	0	5.13
1	Al Smith	G	L	6-1	200	November 10, 1945	Detroit (NHL)	43	135	4	3.24

Schmertz   Baldwin   Coburn   Barnes   Kelley

NEW ENGLAND WHALERS

Operated by New England Whalers Hockey Club
705 Statler Office Building
Boston, Mass. 02116
Telephone: (617) 357-9012
Telex: 357-9012 WHALERS BSN

Chairman of the Board ....Robert J. Schmertz
Trustee and President ....Howard L. Baldwin
Alternate Trustee and Executive
  Vice-President ....John Coburn Jr.
Executive Vice-President of Marketing ....William E. Barnes
General Manager and Coach ....John H. (Jack) Kelley
Assistant General Manager and
  Director of Player Personnel ....Ronald K. Ryan
Trainer .... Joseph R. Altott
Public Relations Director .... Arthur L. Dunphy
                              Home Phone: (617) 545-6907

Colors: Forest Green and White with Black.
Arena: Boston Garden, 150 Causeway St., Boston, Mass. 02114. (Capacity 14,994), 19 games; Boston Arena, St. Botolph St. and Massachusetts Ave., Boston, Mass. 02116. (Capacity 6,000), 20 games.
Radio: WHDH (850 kc), all games, play-by-play Dave Martin.
Television: WKBG-TV (Channel 56), minimum of 25 games home and away.

BOSTON:

Boston, founded in 1630 by a company of Puritans under the leadership of John Winthrop and incorporated as a city in 1822, has been known variously as The Hub, the Athens of America and, more recently, as a result of broad programs of urban renewal and a quickening of civic interest, as The New Boston. The city's population in the 1970 census was 641,071 while in the standard metropolitan area, including 78 cities and towns, the population was 2,753,700. The New England area is steeped in tradition, especially dating to the days prior to and during the American Revolution. Boston is the world's leading wholesale wool market and a major medical center. In professional sports, the area also claims the baseball Boston Red Sox of the American League, the Boston Celtics of the National Basketball Association and the Boston Bruins of the National Hockey League. The New England Patriots of the National Football League play in Foxboro, 25 miles south of Boston.

25

NEW YORK RAIDERS 1972-73 ROSTER

No.	Player	Pos	S	Ht	Wt	Birth Date	1971-72 Club (League)	GP	G	A	Pts	PIM
17	Ken Block	D	L	5-10	184	March 18, 1944	Rochester (AHL)	71	4	29	33	69
14	Brian Bradley	LW	L	5-10	174	December 14, 1944	Oklahoma City (CHL)	69	18	21	39	30
22	Claude Chartre	C	L	6-0	176	December 21, 1949	Jersey (EHL)	75	40	32	72	44
21	Kent Douglas	D	L	5-10	195	February 6, 1936*	Baltimore (AHL)	75	6	31	37	130
9	Norm Ferguson	RW	R	5-8	165	October 16, 1945	California (NHL)	77	14	20	34	13
3	Jean Gauthier	D	R	6-1	196	April 29, 1937	Baltimore (AHL)	64	3	37	40	104
16	James Kennedy	RW	L	5-8	175	September 7, 1946	Jersey (EHL)	75	50	42	92	119
18	Mike Laughton	C	L	6-2	185	February 21, 1944	Nova Scotia (AHL)	73	23	28	51	6
15	Brian Morenz	RW	L	5-10	185	May 11, 1949	Denver (College)	–	–	35	45	74
4	Wally Olds	D		6-2	200		U.S. Olympics	–	–	–	–	–
25	Gene Peacosh	C	L	5-11	175	September 28, 1948	Johnstown (EHL)	75	43	64	107	28
19	Brian Perry	LW	L	5-10	176	April 6, 1944	Providence (AHL)	76	24	25	49	52
11	Craig Reichmuth	LW	L	5-11	185	September 22, 1947	Tidewater (AHL)	10	0	0	0	10
							Fort Worth (CHL)	58	9	17	26	143
11	Wayne Rivers	RW	R	5-9	179	February 1, 1942	Springfield (AHL)	68	48	33	81	67
20	Ted Scharf	RW	R	5-11	185	October 3, 1951	Jersey (EHL)	75	24	33	57	221
7	Bobby Sheehan	C	L	5-8	160	January 11, 1949	California (NHL)	78	20	26	46	12
24	Bill Speer	D	L	5-11	205	March 20, 1942	Boston (AHL)	–	0	0	0	2
							Providence (AHL)	59	5	27	32	38
6	Ron Ward	D	R	5-11	175	September 12, 1944	Vancouver (NHL)	71	2	4	6	4
10	Alton White	RW	R	5-8	175	May 31, 1945	Providence (AHL)	76	30	34	64	18
5	Hal Willis	D	L	6-2	215	June 8, 1946	Seattle (WHL)	66	3	8	11	155
							Denver (WHL)	–	0	6	6	79

No.	Player	Pos	S	Ht	Wt	Birth Date	1971-72 Club (League)	GP	GA	SO	AVG
23	Peter Donnelly	G		5-8	155		Jersey (EHL)	73	276	2	3.78
36	Joe Junkin	G		5-11	175	September 8, 1946	Fenlon Falls (IOHA)	–	–	–	–
30	Gary Kurt	G	R	6-2	181	March 9, 1947	California (NHL)	16	60	0	4.29
1	Ian Wilkie	G		5-9	160	July 20, 1949	Brit. Columbia (College)	21	73	1	3.59

26

Wood   Siegel   Milkes   Henry

NEW YORK RAIDERS

Operated by Metropolitan Hockey Club, Inc.
Statler-Hilton Hotel, Suite 62
401 Seventh Avenue
New York, N.Y. 10001
Telephone: (212) 239-4875
Telex: 12-6059 RAIDERS NYK

Trustee and President .... Richard I. (Dick) Wood
Alternate Trustee and Chairman
  of the Board .... Seymour E. (Sy) Siegel
General Manager .... Marvin Milkes
Coach .... Camille Henry
Trainer .... Fraser Gleeson
Public Relations Director and
  Assistant General Manager .... Herb Elk
                    Home Phone: (212) 736-5000

Colors: Orange and Blue.
Arena: Madison Square Garden, Pennsylvania Plaza, New York, N.Y. 10001 (Capacity 17,250.)
Radio: WCMA Radio (570 kc), 34 home games and 15 road games, play-by-play John Sterling.
Television: Arrangements pending.

NEW YORK:
New York is the nation's largest city, its richest port and its leader in business, manufacturing, service industries, communications, fashion, art, music and literature, as well as the world's chief financial center and, as host to the headquarters of the United Nations, the "capital" of the world. The population is 7,895,563. The city credits Giovanni de Verrazano with discovering its magnificent harbor in 1524. During the American Revolution, New York was a focal point for both the Continentals and the British. New York has more professional sports teams than any city in the world. Also on the sports rolls are baseball's Yankees (American League) and Mets (National League), the Jets and Giants of the National Football League, the Knicks of the National Basketball Association, the Nets of the American Basketball Association, the Rangers and Islanders of the National Hockey League and the Cosmos of the North American Soccer League.

27

OTTAWA NATIONALS 1972-73 ROSTER

No.	Player	Pos	S	Ht	Wt	Birth Date	1971-72 Club (League)	GP	G	A	Pts	PIM
5	Mike Amodeo	D	L	5-10	195	June 22, 1952	Oshawa (OHA Jr.)	63	6	34	40	130
10	Mike Boland	RW	R	5-10	183	December 16, 1949	Springfield (AHL)	48	4	20	24	47
9	Wayne Carleton	LW	L	6-3	217	August 4, 1946	California (NHL)	76	17	14	31	45
16	Bob Charlebois	LW	L	5-11	170	May 27, 1944	Tulsa (CHL)	6	0	0	0	04
23	Ron Climie	LW	L	5-11	180	March 5, 1950	Kansas City (CHL)	71	31	30	61	13
20	Brian Conacher	C	L	6-3	195	August 31, 1941	Detroit (NHL)	25	3	1	4	4
							Fort Worth (CHL)	40	13	13	26	4
3	Rich Cunningham	D		5-10	190	March 3, 1951	Trent (College)	–	–	–	–	–
24	John Donnelly	D		6-0	190	September 28, 1948	Loyola (College)	–	–	–	–	–
6	Brian Gibbons	D	L	6-3	190	July 7, 1947	Springfield (AHL)	65	2	12	14	111
21	Jack Gibson	LW		6-0	185	August 18, 1948	Alberta (College)	–	–	–	–	–
12	Steve King	C	R	5-9	160	September 8, 1948	Tulsa (CHL)	59	20	16	36	12
11	Gavin Kirk	C	L	5-10	165	December 6, 1951	Loyola (College)	–	–	–	–	–
							Phoenix (WHL)	3	1	2	3	2
19	Bob Leduc	C	L	5-10	185	May 24, 1944	Providence (AHL)	76	13	30	43	46
17	Tom Martin	RW	R	5-9	167	October 16, 1947	Fort Worth (CHL)	31	14	21	35	17
22	Chris Meloff	D	L	5-11	185	May 7, 1952	Kitchener (OHA Jr.)	59	4	37	41	83
15	Ron Riley	LW	L	6-0	189	July 20, 1948	Loyola (College)	–	–	–	–	–
8	Rich Sentes	LW	L	5-11	180	January 10, 1947	Tidewater (AHL)	74	32	21	53	104
14	Tom Simpson	RW	R	5-10	200	August 15, 1952	Oshawa (OHA Jr.)	44	29	18	47	53
4	Ken Stephanson	D		5-11	193	November 13, 1941	Did not play					
7	Guy Trottier	RW	R	5-8	165	April 1, 1941	Toronto (NHL)	52	9	12	21	16
2	Steve Warr	D		5-11	185	January 5, 1951	Clarkson (College)	–	–	–	–	–

No.	Player	Pos	S	Ht	Wt	Birth Date	1971-72 Club (League)	GP	GA	SO	AVG
30	Les Binkley	G	R	6-0	170	June 6, 1934	Pittsburgh (NHL)	31	98	4	3.51
33	Gilles Gratton	G		5-11	155	July 28, 1952	Oshawa (OHA Jr.)	50	178	3	3.55

Michel   Trbovich   Houle   Harris

OTTAWA NATIONALS

Operated by Ontario Nationals Hockey Teams, Inc.
Ottawa Civic Centre
Lansdowne Park
Ottawa 1, Ontario, Canada
Telephone: (613) 237-5356
Telex: 053-4339 NATIONALS OTT

Trustee and President .... Douglas P. Michel
Alternate Trustee .... Nick Trbovich
General Manager .... A. J. (Buck) Houle
Coach .... Billy Harris
Trainer .... Peter Unwin
Public Relations Director .... Mike Mulhall

                               Office Phone: (613) 238-1101
                               Home Phone: (613) 236-2013

    Colors: Red and White with Blue.
    Arena: Ottawa Civic Centre, Lansdowne Park, Ottawa, Ontario, Canada (Capacity 9,300).
    Radio: CKOY Radio (1310 kc), all games, play-by-play Jack Dailey. CJRC Radio (1150 kc), 15 to 20 games to be announced, French language play-by-play Rene Le Cavalier.
    Television: Arrangements pending.

OTTAWA:

Ottawa is Canada's national capital and fifth largest city with a population just under 300,000. Founded in 1827 as Bytown, it was renamed Ottawa in 1855. The name is the Anglicized form of Outaouac or Outaouais, a tribe of Indians from Lake Huron who were prominent in trade with the French in the 17th Century. Now spread over 30,481 acres of land, of which 3,256 acres are covered with water, Ottawa is located on the provincial border of Ontario and Quebec at a point where the Ottawa River tumbles over Chaudiere Falls. It is just across the river from Hull, Quebec, a city of 130,000. Among Ottawa's sports teams are the Ottawa Rough Riders, members of the Canadian Football League, and the Ottawa 67s, members of the Ontario Junior Hockey Association.

29

PHILADELPHIA BLAZERS 1972-73 ROSTER

No.	Player	Pos	S	Ht	Wt	Birth Date	1971-72 Club (League)	GP	G	A	Pts	PIM
20	John Bennett	LW	R	6-1	175	January 19, 1950	Brown (College)	22	6	13	19	30
8	Don Burgess	LW	L	6-0	170	June 8, 1946	Greensboro (EHL)	73	39	58	97	29
14	Bryan Campbell	C	L	6-0	175	March 27, 1944	Chicago (NHL)	75	5	13	18	22
6	Rychard Campeau	D	R	6-0	200	April 9, 1952	Sorel (QJHL)	75	26	47	73	102
5	Jim Cardiff	D	L	5-9	165	August 29, 1944	San Diego (WHL)	71	7	18	25	197
10	Frank Golembrosky	RW	R	6-0	190	May 3, 1945	Charlotte (EHL)	73	39	67	106	174
17	Don Herriman	LW	L	5-10	165	January 2, 1946	Clinton (EHL)	65	30	30	60	170
3	Dave Hutchison	D	L	6-3	205	May 2, 1952	London (OHA)	46	3	11	14	151
7	Andre Lacroix	D	L	5-8	175	June 5, 1945	Chicago (NHL)	51	4	7	11	6
11	Danny Lawson	RW	R	5-11	185	October 30, 1947	Buffalo (NHL)	78	10	6	16	15
19	John McKenzie	RW	R	5-9	178	December 12, 1937	Boston (NHL)	77	22	47	69	126
18	John Migneault	D	L	5-11	180	February 4, 1949	Muskegon (IHL)	72	12	22	34	70
21	Wayne Mosdell	D	R	6-3	185	December 4, 1944	Roanoke (EHL)	73	13	31	44	82
12	Don O'Donoghue	RW	R	5-10	180	August 27, 1949	Boston (AHL)	16	0	3	3	0
24	Michel Plante	C	L	6-0	170	January 19, 1952	Drummondville (QJHL)	62	35	55	90	70
4	Ron Plumb	D	L	5-10	175	July 17, 1950	Oklahoma City (CHL)	72	10	42	52	90
2	Nick Polano	D	L	6-0	187	March 25, 1941	Providence (AHL)	59	4	9	13	92
9	Mike Rouleau	C	L	5-10	170	September 28, 1944	Charlotte (EHL)	70	35	70	105	224
16	Derek Sanderson	C	L	6-0	170	June 16, 1946	Boston (NHL)	28	25	33	58	108

No.	Player	Pos	S	Ht	Wt	Birth Date	1971-72 Club (League)	GP	GA	SO	AVG
1	Marcel Paille	G	L	5-8	185	December 8, 1932	Providence (AHL)	34	110	3	3.33
00	Bernie Parent	G	L	5-10	170	April 3, 1945	Toronto (NHL)	47	116	3	2.56

Cooper   Brown   Freeman   Iannarelli   McKenzie

PHILADELPHIA BLAZERS

Operated by Philadelphia World Hockey Club, Inc.
P. O. Box 8494
Philadelphia, Pa. 19101
Telephone: (215) 382-5220
Telex: 831-521 BLAZERS PHA

Trustee and President .... James L. Cooper
*Alternate Trustee and Chairman of
  the Board* .... Bernard A. Brown
Executive Vice-President .... Hal Freeman
Administrative Vice-President .... Donald D. Iannarelli
Assistant General Manager .... Jerry Rafter
Coach .... John McKenzie
Director of Player Personnel .... Phil Watson
Trainer .... Warren Elliott
Public Relations Director .... Kevin Johnson
                         Home Phone: (215) 849-6865

    Colors: Orange and Gold.
    Arena: Philadelphia Civic Center, Civic Center Boulevard, Philadelphia, Pa. 19101 (Capacity 9,000).
    Radio: Arrangements pending.
    Television: WHYY (Channel 12), 10 away games, play-by-play Bob McLean and Dan Baker.

PHILADELPHIA:

Philadelphia, birthplace of the U.S., is a major center of commerce, finance and culture with a population of nearly 5,000,000 in its eight-county metropolitan area. William Penn founded the city in 1682 and gave it a name that means "City of Brotherly Love." His grid pattern of streets and public squares dictated the modern shape of the center city area from the Delaware to the Schuykill River. Philadelphia has the largest fresh water port in the world with 50 miles of waterfront and is the second largest petroleum refining center in the nation. Its other sports teams include the Philadelphia Phillies of the National Baseball League, the Philadelphia Eagles of the National Football League, the Philadelphia 76ers of the National Basketball Association and the Philadelphia Flyers of the National Hockey League.

31

QUEBEC NORDIQUES 1972-73 ROSTER

No.	Player	Pos	S	Ht	Wt	Birth Date	1971-72 Club (League)	GP	G	A	Pts	PIM
9	Michel Archambault	LW	L	5-8	175	September 27, 1950	Dallas (CHL)	65	31	26	57	115
17	Yves Bergeron	RW	R	5-9	165	January 11, 1952	Shawinigan (QJHL)	57	31	60	91	54
5	Jacques Blain	D	L	6-0	200	July 19, 1947	Long Island (EHL)	75	10	41	51	58
22	Ken Desjardine	D	L	6-0	184	August 23, 1947	Tulsa (CHL)	60	2	17	19	100
20	Guy Dufour	RW	R	5-11	180	February 9, 1946	Roanoke (EHL)	54	17	30	47	14
16	Andre Gaudette	C	L	5-7	165	December 16, 1947	Richmond (AHL)	74	17	31	48	30
7	Jean Guy Gendron	LW	L	5-8	163	August 30, 1934	Philadelphia (NHL)	56	6	13	19	36
25	Robert Guindon	LW	L	5-9	170	November 19, 1950	Fort Worth (CHL)	72	22	26	48	36
6	Pierre Guite	LW	L	6-1	192	April 17, 1952	Pennsylvania (College)	–	7	5	12	4
18	Rejean Giroux	RW	R	5-11	160	September 13, 1952	Quebec (QJHL)	57	58	51	109	99
10	Mike Harvey	C	L	5-11	180	January 31, 1938	Did not play	–	–	–	–	–
4	Francois Lacombe	D	L	5-10	188	February 24, 1948	Cincinnati (AHL)	35	4	10	14	26
14	Paul Larose	RW	L	5-9	170	November 1, 1950	Syracuse (EHL)	75	67	62	129	61
15	Renald Leclerc	C	R	5-11	165	November 12, 1947	San Diego (WHL)	28	6	7	13	39
							Fort Worth (CHL)	2	0	0	0	0
24	Mike McNamara	LW	L	5-9	175	March 28, 1949	Tidewater (AHL)	31	6	6	12	51
							William (College)	36	15	34	49	50
12	Michel Parizeau	LW	L	5-9	165	April 9, 1948	Philadelphia (NHL)	40	2	12	14	10
							St. Louis (NHL)	18	1	2	3	8
8	Jean Payette	C	L	6-0	180	March 29, 1946	Tulsa (CHL)	72	33	64	97	44
2	Pierre Roy	D	L	6-0	175	March 12, 1952	Quebec (QJHL)	50	3	22	25	137
11	Brit Selby	LW	L	5-10	178	March 27, 1945	St. Louis (NHL)	6	0	0	0	8
							Kansas City (CHL)	63	11	24	35	82
3	J.C. Tremblay	D	L	5-10	178	January 22, 1939	Montreal (NHL)	76	6	51	57	24

								GP	GA	SO		AVG
1	Serge Aubry	G		5-8	170	January 2, 1942	Rochester (AHL)	37	137	0		4.53
30	Richard Brodeur	G	R	5-7	160	September 15, 1952	Cornwall (QJHL)	58	170	5		2.93
30	Jacques Lemelin	G	R	5-8	155	November 11, 1949	Laval (College)	–	–	–		–

Racine   Lesage   Fortier   Filion

QUEBEC NORDIQUES

Operated by Le Club de Hockey les Nordiques Inc.
Quebec Coliseum
Quebec 3, P.Q., Canada
Telephone: (418) 529-4161
Telex: 0-113-068 NORDIQUES QBC

Trustee and President . . . . Paul Racine
Chairman of the Board . . . . Jean Lesage
Alternate Trustee and General Manager . . . . Marius Fortier
Coach . . . . Maurice Filion
Trainer . . . . Rene Lacasse
Public Relations Director . . . . Serge Lamarre
                                                                   Home Phone: (418) 626-1790

    Colors: Nordique Blue, Red and White.
    Arena: Quebec Coliseum, Exhibition Grounds, Quebec 3, P.Q.,
            Canada (Capacity 10,000).
    Radio: CJRP (1060 kc), away games, play-by-play Claude
            Bedard.
    Television: TVA (French Network), 9 games, play-by-play.

QUEBEC:

Quebec is the seventh largest city in Canada with a metropolitan area population of 424,000. The province is one of the original provinces, along with Ontario, Nova Scotia and New Brunswick, and is the largest in size (594,860 square miles) and second largest in population (6,030,000). It is a province of vivid contrast in everything from geography to its economy and history. The great Canadian Shield occupies much of the area north of the St. Lawrence River. Quebec, capital of the province, is North America's only fortified city, part of the upper town still being encircled by walls that are a magnet to tourists. The cliffs of Quebec are famous in the history of both Canada and the U.S. and give the name to the Quebec Remparts of the Quebec Junior Hockey League.

33

WINNIPEG JETS 1972-73 ROSTER

No.	Player	Pos	S	Ht	Wt	Birth Date	1971-72 Club (League)	GP	G	A	Pts	PIM
3	Bob Ash	D	L	5-9	170	September 29, 1943	Omaha (CHL)	64	5	26	31	66
22	Duke Asmundson	RW	R	6-2	195	August 17, 1943	Des Moines (IHL)	72	35	47	82	48
11	Norm Beaudin	RW	R	5-9	170	November 28, 1941	Cleveland (AHL)	75	33	33	66	16
19	Milt Black	RW	R	6-0	190	June 20, 1949	Dallas (CHL)	32	9	9	18	39
7	Chirs Bordeleau	LW	L	5-8	152	September 23, 1947	Chicago (NHL)	66	14	17	31	12
8	Wally Boyer	C	L	5-8	170	August 27, 1937	Hershey (AHL)	64	18	30	48	43
27	Brian Cadle	LW	L	6-1	165	September 13, 1948	Columbus (IHL)	34	4	11	15	105
6	Steve Cuddie	D	R	5-11	203	June 18, 1950	Cincinnati (AHL)	57	2	1	3	64
16	Jean-Guy Gratton	RW	R	5-9	173	March 8, 1949	Hershey (AHL)	74	30	34	64	42
5	Larry Hornung	D	L	5-11	185	October 10, 1945	St. Louis (NHL)	47	2	9	11	10
							Kansas City (CHL)	26	2	20	22	23
9	Bobby Hull	LW	L	5-10	170	January 3, 1939	Chicago (NHL)	78	50	43	93	24
17	Danny Johnson	C	L	5-11	178	October 1, 1944	Detroit (NHL)	54	3	8	11	8
14	Ab McDonald	LW	L	6-2	194	February 18, 1936	Tidewater (AHL)	41	5	7	12	4
							Detroit (NHL)	19	2	3	5	0
15	Garth Rizzuto	C	L	5-10	180	September 11, 1947	Rochester (AHL)	36	6	8	14	11
							Seattle (WHL)	23	4	15	19	36
12	Dunc Rousseau	LW	L	6-0	195	February 10, 1945	Baltimore (AHL)	66	12	9	21	96
18	Cal Swenson	C	L	5-11	182	April 16, 1948	Tulsa (CHL)	66	35	46	81	80
10	Bill Sutherland	LW	L	5-10	175	November 10, 1934	Detroit (NHL)	16	2	4	6	4
							Tidewater (AHL)	40	6	10	16	26
2	Bob Woytowich	D	R	5-11	195	August 18, 1941	Los Angeles (NHL)	67	1	8	9	14
4	Joe Zanussi	D	R	5-10	180	September 25, 1947	Fort Worth (CHL)	48	4	24	28	69

No.	Player	Pos	S	Ht	Wt	Birth Date	1971-72 Club (League)	GP	GA	SO	PIM
1	Joe Daley	G	L	5-10	160	February 20, 1943	Detroit (NHL)	29	85	0	3.14
30	Ernie Wakely	G	L	5-11	170	November 27, 1940	St. Louis (NHL)	30	92	1	3.42

34

    Hatskin   Hind   Stukus   Hull

WINNIPEG JETS

Operated by Winnipeg Jets Hockey Club Ltd.
15 - 1430 Maroons Road
Winnipeg, Manitoba R3G OL5, Canada
Telephone: (204) 772-9491
Telex: 07-587-810 HOCKEY WPG

Trustee and President .... Ben Hatskin
Executive Manager .... Terry Hind
General Manager .... Annis Stukus
Coach .... Bobby Hull
Assistant Coach .... Nick Mickoski
Director of Player Personnel .... Bill Robinson
Trainer .... Diarmid McVicar
Public Relations Director .... Ron Lyon
                                  Home Phone: (204) 889-3888

    Colors: Blue with Red and White.
    Arena: Winnipeg Arena, 15 - 1430 Maroons Road, Winnipeg,
        Manitoba R3G OL5, Canada (Capacity 11,000).
    Radio: CJOB (680 kc), all games, play-by-play Ken Nicolson.
    Television: Arrangements pending.

WINNIPEG:

Winnipeg, Canada's fourth largest metropolitan area with an estimated population of 529,000 is at the junction of the historic Red and Assiniboine Rivers near the geographical center of North America. The city covers an area of 166.6 square miles and is the capital of the province of Manitoba. The city area attracted its first settlers, the Lord Selkirk colonists, in 1812. A fur-trading post, Winnipeg was incorporated as a city in 1873. It had a population of 1,869. Manufacturing, emerging as a major economic factor in the Western grain capital, is the largest source of employment and income. Winnipeg's other professional sports teams are the Winnipeg Blue Bombers of the Canadian Football League and the baseball Winnipeg Whips of the International League. The junior Jets, members of the Western Canada Hockey League, also play in the Winnipeg Arena.

35

1972-73 SCHEDULE

#	Day	Mo	Date	Visitor		Home
1	Wed	Oct	11	Alberta	at	Ottawa
2				Quebec	at	Cleveland
3	Thurs	"	12	Winnipeg	at	New York
4				Chicago	at	Houston
5				Philadelphia	at	New England (BG)
6	Fri	"	13	Houston	at	Los Angeles
7				Winnipeg	at	Minnesota
8				Alberta	at	Quebec
9				New England	at	Philadelphia
10	Sat	"	14	Ottawa	at	New York
11				Alberta	at	Cleveland
12	Sun	"	15	Philadelphia	at	New York
13				Cleveland	at	Ottawa
14				Chicago	at	Minnesota
15				Los Angeles	at	Houston
16				Alberta	at	Winnipeg
17	Mon	"	16	Chicago	at	New England (BG)
18	Tues	"	17	Quebec	at	Philadelphia
19				New York	at	Cleveland
20				Los Angeles	at	Minnesota
21				Winnipeg	at	Alberta
22	Wed	"	18	New England	at	Houston
23	Thurs	"	19	Cleveland	at	New York
24				Minnesota	at	Houston
25				Chicago	at	Ottawa
26				Philadelphia	at	Los Angeles
27				Quebec	at	New England (BG)
28	Fri	"	20	Minnesota	at	Winnipeg
29				Philadelphia	at	Alberta
30	Sat	"	21	Houston	at	New York
31				Ottawa	at	Cleveland
32				New England	at	Quebec
33	Sun	"	22	Minnesota	at	New York
34				Ottawa	at	Quebec
35				Philadelphia	at	Winnipeg
36				Chicago	at	Los Angeles
37	Mon	"	23	Minnesota	at	New England (BG)
38	Tues	"	24	New England	at	Cleveland
39				Chicago	at	Alberta
40				Philadelphia	at	Winnipeg
41				Houston	at	Quebec
42	Wed	"	25	Ottawa	at	Los Angeles
43				Cleveland	at	Philadelphia
44	Thurs	"	26	New England	at	New York
45				Ottawa	at	Houston
46				Minnesota	at	Quebec

37

47	Fri	Oct	27	Alberta	at	Cleveland
48				Chicago	at	Winnipeg
49				Los Angeles	at	Philadelphia
50	Sat	"	28	Los Angeles	at	New York
51				Ottawa	at	Philadelphia
52				Alberta	at	New England (BA)
53	Sun	"	29	Alberta	at	New York
54				Cleveland	at	Quebec
55				Houston	at	Winnipeg
56	Tues	"	31	Winnipeg	at	Chicago
57				Los Angeles	at	Quebec
58				Houston	at	Alberta
59	Wed	Nov	1	Winnipeg	at	Minnesota
60				Philadelphia	at	Cleveland
61				Chicago	at	New England (BA)
62	Thurs	"	2	Los Angeles	at	Ottawa
63				New York	at	Minnesota
64				Philadelphia	at	Quebec
65	Fri	"	3	Houston	at	Alberta
66				New York	at	Winnipeg
67	Sat	"	4	Los Angeles	at	Chicago
68				Philadelphia	at	New England (BG)
69				Quebec	at	Cleveland
70	Sun	"	5	New York	at	Winnipeg
71				Houston	at	Los Angeles
72				Philadelphia	at	Minnesota
73				Ottawa	at	Alberta
74				Chicago	at	Quebec
75	Mon	"	6	Winnipeg	at	New England (BG)
76	Tues	"	7	Houston	at	Chicago
77				New York	at	Alberta
78	Wed	"	8	New York	at	Los Angeles
79				Winnipeg	at	Quebec
80	Thurs	"	9	Los Angeles	at	Alberta
81				Winnipeg	at	Ottawa
82	Fri	"	10	Minnesota	at	Winnipeg
83	Sat	"	11	New York	at	New England (BG)
84				Los Angeles	at	Alberta
85				Houston	at	Quebec
86				Cleveland	at	Chicago
87	Sun	"	12	Los Angeles	at	Winnipeg
88				Philadelphia	at	Ottawa
89				Cleveland	at	Alberta
90	Mon	"	13	Houston	at	New England (BG)
91	Tues	"	14	Cleveland	at	Minnesota
92				Los Angeles	at	Winnipeg
93				Philadelphia	at	Chicago

94	Wed	Nov	15	New York	at Quebec
95				Los Angeles	at Houston
96				Winnipeg	at Alberta
97	Thurs	"	16	Ottawa	at Cleveland
98				Quebec	at Minnesota
99	Fri	"	17	Winnipeg	at Los Angeles (LB)
100				New England	at Cleveland
101				Chicago	at Alberta
102	Sat	"	18	Quebec	at New York
103				Ottawa	at New England (BA)
104				Minnesota	at Philadelphia
105	Sun	"	19	Winnipeg	at Los Angeles
106				Cleveland	at Houston
107				Philadelphia	at New York
108				Chicago	at Minnesota
109	Mon	"	20	Ottawa	at New England (BG)
110	Tues	"	21	Winnipeg	at Houston
111				Cleveland	at Los Angeles
112				Quebec	at Ottawa
113				Alberta	at Minnesota
114	Wed	"	22	New England	at New York
115				Alberta	at Philadelphia
116	Thurs	"	23	Winnipeg	at Houston
117				Los Angeles	at Minnesota
118				Chicago	at Ottawa
119	Fri	"	24	Quebec	at Winnipeg
120				Los Angeles	at Cleveland
121				Alberta	at New England (BA)
122				Minnesota	at Philadelphia
123	Sat	"	25	Houston	at Cleveland
124				Alberta	at New York
125				Chicago	at Philadelphia
126	Sun	"	26	Quebec	at Winnipeg
127				Los Angeles	at New York
128				Alberta	at Ottawa
129				New England	at Minnesota
130	Mon	"	27	Cleveland	at New England (BG)
131	Tues	"	28	Alberta	at Winnipeg
132				Houston	at Cleveland
133				Minnesota	at Ottawa
134				Los Angeles	at Philadelphia
135				Chicago	at Quebec
136	Wed	"	29	New England	at New York
137	Thurs	"	30	Winnipeg	at Alberta
138				Minnesota	at New York
139				Cleveland	at Ottawa
140				Houston	at Los Angeles
141	Fri	Dec	1	Minnesota	at Alberta
142				Ottawa	at Winnipeg

39

143	Fri	Dec	1	New England	at	Philadelphia
144				Los Angeles	at	Chicago
145	Sat	"	2	Houston	at	New York
146				Quebec	at	New England (BG)
147				Philadelphia	at	Cleveland
148				Los Angeles	at	Chicago
149	Sun	"	3	Minnesota	at	Winnipeg
150				Houston	at	Ottawa
151				Cleveland	at	New York
152				Quebec	at	Alberta
153	Mon	"	4	Ottawa	at	New England (BG)
154	Tues	"	5	New York	at	Houston
155				Quebec	at	Winnipeg
156				Chicago	at	Minnesota
157				Cleveland	at	Philadelphia
158	Wed	"	6	New York	at	New England (BG)
159				Chicago	at	Winnipeg
160	Thurs	"	7	New England	at	Ottawa
161				Houston	at	Minnesota
162				Cleveland	at	Quebec
163	Fri	"	8	Minnesota	at	Chicago
164				Houston	at	Winnipeg
165				Alberta	at	Los Angeles
166				New York	at	Philadelphia
167	Sat	"	9	Quebec	at	Chicago
168				Winnipeg	at	Cleveland
169				Ottawa	at	Philadelphia
170				New York	at	New England (BG)
171	Sun	"	10	Quebec	at	Ottawa
172				Cleveland	at	Minnesota
173				Alberta	at	Los Angeles
174	Mon	"	11	Winnipeg	at	New England (BG)
175				Chicago	at	New York
176	Tues	"	12	Minnesota	at	Los Angeles
177				Philadelphia	at	Quebec
178				Alberta	at	Houston
179	Wed	"	13	New England	at	Chicago
180				Quebec	at	New York
181				Alberta	at	Houston
182				Winnipeg	at	Philadelphia
183	Thurs	"	14	New York	at	Ottawa
184				New England	at	Los Angeles
185				Minnesota	at	Chicago
186	Fri	"	15	Houston	at	Minnesota
187				Winnipeg	at	Philadelphia
188				Ottawa	at	Alberta
189	Sat	"	16	Quebec	at	Cleveland
190				New England	at	Philadelphia
191	Sun	"	17	Chicago	at	Minnesota

40

192	Fri	Dec	17	Los Angeles	at	Houston
193				Philadelphia	at	New England (BG)
194				Winnipeg	at	New York
195				Cleveland	at	Quebec
196				Ottawa	at	Alberta
197	Tues	"	19	Cleveland	at	Chicago
198				New England	at	Minnesota
199				New York	at	Philadelphia
200				Ottawa	at	Quebec
201				Los Angeles	at	Houston
202	Wed	"	20	Chicago	at	Philadelphia
203	Thurs	"	21	Los Angeles	at	Ottawa
204				New York	at	Cleveland
205				Winnipeg	at	Minnesota
206				New England	at	Alberta
207	Fri	"	22	Ottawa	at	New York
208				Winnipeg	at	Chicago
209	Sat	"	23	Los Angeles	at	Quebec
210				Minnesota	at	Cleveland
211				Alberta	at	Chicago
212				Philadelphia	at	Houston
213	Sun	"	24	Quebec	at	Ottawa
214				Los Angeles	at	New England (BG)
215	Mon	"	25	New England	at	New York
216				Philadelphia	at	Cleveland
217				Alberta	at	Chicago
218	Tues	"	26	Houston	at	Ottawa
219				Philadelphia	at	Minnesota
220				New York	at	Quebec
221				Chicago	at	Winnipeg
222	Thurs	"	28	Philadelphia	at	Chicago
223				Minnesota	at	Los Angeles (LB)
224				New England	at	Quebec
225	Fri	"	29	Quebec	at	Cleveland
226				Houston	at	New England (BA)
227				Minnesota	at	Los Angeles
228	Sat	"	30	Houston	at	Cleveland
229				Ottawa	at	Chicago
230	Sun	"	31	Philadelphia	at	Los Angeles
231				Ottawa	at	Quebec
232				New England	at	New York
233	Mon	Jan	1	Houston	at	Minnesota
234				Philadelphia	at	New York
235				Winnipeg	at	Alberta
***	Wed	"	3	WHA ALL-STARS VS CZECHS AT QUEBEC		
236	Thurs	"	4	Ottawa	at	New York
***	Fri	"	5	WHA ALL-STARS VS CZECHS AT WINNIPEG		
***	Sun	"	7	WHA ALL-STARS VS CZECHS AT ST. PAUL		

41

237	Mon	Jan	8	Quebec	at	New York
238	Tues	"	9	Quebec	at	Ottawa
239				Los Angeles	at	Minnesota
240				New England	at	Houston
241	Wed	"	10	Alberta	at	Winnipeg
242				Los Angeles	at	Chicago
243				New York	at	Philadelphia
244	Thurs	"	11	Houston	at	Chicago
245				New York	at	Ottawa
246				Cleveland	at	Minnesota
247	Fri	"	12	Quebec	at	Minnesota
248				Alberta	at	Los Angeles
249				Cleveland	at	Winnipeg
250				Ottawa	at	Philadelphia
251	Sat	"	13	Quebec	at	Philadelphia
252				Chicago	at	Houston
253				New York	at	New England (BA)
254				Alberta	at	Los Angeles
255	Sun	"	14	Cleveland	at	Winnipeg
256				Ottawa	at	Minnesota
257	Mon	"	15	Los Angeles	at	Alberta
258				Chicago	at	Houston
259	Tues	"	16	Los Angeles	at	Alberta
260				Minnesota	at	Winnipeg
261				Cleveland	at	Philadelphia
262				Ottawa	at	Quebec
263	Wed	"	17	Cleveland	at	Houston
264				New England	at	Chicago
265	Thurs	"	18	Houston	at	Chicago
266				Minnesota	at	Ottawa
267				New York	at	Quebec
268	Fri	"	19	New England	at	Winnipeg
269				Cleveland	at	Los Angeles
270				Ottawa	at	Philadelphia
271	Sat	"	20	Minnesota	at	Quebec
272				Chicago	at	Alberta
273				Houston	at	Philadelphia
274	Sun	"	21	New England	at	Winnipeg
275				Cleveland	at	Los Angeles
276				Ottawa	at	Houston
277	Mon	"	22	Chicago	at	Alberta
278				Minnesota	at	New York
279	Tues	"	23	Quebec	at	Chicago
280				Winnipeg	at	Cleveland
281				Ottawa	at	Houston
282	Wed	"	24	Winnipeg	at	New England (BG)
283				Philadelphia	at	Quebec
284	Thurs	"	25	New England	at	Ottawa

285	Thurs	Jan	25	Philadelphia	at	Cleveland
286				New York	at	Chicago
287				Houston	at	Minnesota
288	Fri	"	26	Ottawa	at	Minnesota
289				Winnipeg	at	Quebec
290				New York	at	Los Angeles
291	Sat	"	27	Philadelphia	at	Alberta
292				Quebec	at	New England (BA)
293				Cleveland	at	Chicago
294	Sun	"	28	Philadelphia	at	Alberta
295				Winnipeg	at	Ottawa
296				New York	at	Los Angeles
297				Chicago	at	Houston
298	Mon	"	29	New England	at	Cleveland
299	Tues	"	30	New York	at	Alberta
300				Cleveland	at	New England (BG)
301				Philadelphia	at	Ottawa
302				Minnesota	at	Chicago
303				Los Angeles	at	Houston
304	Thurs	Feb	1	Minnesota	at	Quebec
305				New York	at	Alberta
306				New England	at	Houston
307				Ottawa	at	Cleveland
308	Fri	"	2	Alberta	at	Winnipeg
309				Ottawa	at	Chicago
310				New England	at	Los Angeles
311				Philadelphia	at	Cleveland
312	Sat	"	3	New York	at	Chicago
313				Minnesota	at	Houston
314	Sun	"	4	Cleveland	at	Ottawa
315				Winnipeg	at	Alberta
316				New England	at	Los Angeles
317				Quebec	at	New York
318	Mon	"	5	Chicago	at	Cleveland
319				Minnesota	at	Houston
320	Tues	"	6	New York	at	Minnesota
321				Philadelphia	at	Ottawa
322				New England	at	Alberta
323	Wed	"	7	Winnipeg	at	Houston
324				New England	at	Alberta
325				Philadelphia	at	Quebec
326	Thurs	"	8	Winnipeg	at	Houston
327				New York	at	Ottawa
328				Quebec	at	Chicago
329				Minnesota	at	Los Angeles
330	Fri	"	9	Minnesota	at	Alberta
331	Sat	"	10	Winnipeg	at	Los Angeles
332				Ottawa	at	New England (BA)
333				New York	at	Cleveland

43

334	Sat	Feb	10	Houston	at	Chicago
335				Quebec	at	Philadelphia
336	Sun	"	11	Winnipeg	at	Los Angeles
337				Ottawa	at	New York
338				Cleveland	at	Philadelphia
339				Minnesota	at	Alberta
340				New England	at	Quebec
341	Mon	"	12	New York	at	Cleveland
342	Tues	"	13	Chicago	at	Los Angeles
343				Winnipeg	at	Minnesota
344				Houston	at	Alberta
345				New England	at	Philadelphia
346	Wed	"	14	Ottawa	at	Quebec
347				Cleveland	at	Philadelphia
348	Thurs	"	15	Houston	at	Alberta
349				Los Angeles	at	New England (BA)
350				Winnipeg	at	Chicago
351				Ottawa	at	Minnesota
352	Fri	"	16	New York	at	Philadelphia
353				Houston	at	Winnipeg
354				Los Angeles	at	Quebec
355	Sat	"	17	New England	at	Quebec
356				Minnesota	at	Cleveland
357				Ottawa	at	Chicago
358	Sun	"	18	Houston	at	Winnipeg
359				Chicago	at	Minnesota
360				Los Angeles	at	Philadelphia
361	Tues	"	20	Los Angeles	at	Ottawa
362				Alberta	at	Cleveland
363				Chicago	at	Quebec
364	Wed	"	21	Alberta	at	New York
365	Thurs	"	22	Philadelphia	at	Ottawa
366				Quebec	at	Houston
367	Fri	"	23	Alberta	at	New England (BA)
368	Sat	"	24	Quebec	at	Los Angeles
369				Chicago	at	Cleveland
370	Sun	"	25	Philadelphia	at	Winnipeg
371				Cleveland	at	New York
372				Alberta	at	Ottawa
373				Quebec	at	Los Angeles
374				Minnesota	at	Houston
375	Tues	"	27	Chicago	at	Winnipeg
376				Philadelphia	at	Minnesota
377				Alberta	at	Houston
378				Cleveland	at	Ottawa
379	Wed	"	28	Alberta	at	Houston
380	Thurs	Mar	1	New York	at	Ottawa
381				Los Angeles	at	Minnesota

44

382	Fri	Mar	2	Los Angeles	at Winnipeg
383	Sat	"	3	Quebec	at Houston
384				Cleveland	at New York
385	Sun	"	4	Los Angeles	at Winnipeg
386				Philadelphia	at New York
387				Chicago	at Ottawa
388				Quebec	at Houston
389				New England	at Minnesota
390	Mon	"	5	Chicago	at New York
391	Tues	"	6	Quebec	at Los Angeles
392				Winnipeg	at Ottawa
393				Philadelphia	at Chicago
394				Alberta	at Minnesota
395	Wed	"	7	Cleveland	at New England (BA)
396				Houston	at Los Angeles
397	Thurs	"	8	Winnipeg	at Quebec
398				Alberta	at Chicago
399				Minnesota	at Philadelphia
400	Fri	"	9	Houston	at Los Angeles (LB)
401				Cleveland	at New England (BA)
402				Quebec	at Philadelphia
403	Sat	"	10	Minnesota	at New England (BA)
404				Winnipeg	at New York
405				Alberta	at Chicago
406	Sun	"	11	Ottawa	at Los Angeles
407				New York	at Quebec
408				Alberta	at Minnesota
409				Houston	at Philadelphia
410				Cleveland	at Winnipeg
411	Mon	"	12	Chicago	at New York
412	Tues	"	13	Cleveland	at Alberta
413				New England	at Chicago
414				Ottawa	at Los Angeles
415				Houston	at Philadelphia
416	Wed	"	14	Cleveland	at Alberta
417				New England	at Winnipeg
418				Houston	at New York
419	Thurs	"	15	Minnesota	at Chicago
420				Los Angeles	at New York
421	Fri	"	16	Ottawa	at Winnipeg
422				Minnesota	at New England (BA)
423				Quebec	at Alberta
424	Sat	"	17	Los Angeles	at Cleveland
425				Philadelphia	at New England (BA)
426				Quebec	at Alberta
427				New York	at Chicago
428	Sun	"	18	Ottawa	at Winnipeg
429				New York	at Houston

45

430	Mon	Mar	19	Los Angeles	at	Cleveland
431				Philadelphia	at	Houston
432	Tues	"	20	Minnesota	at	Alberta
433				Los Angeles	at	New England (BA)
434				Cleveland	at	Quebec
435	Wed	"	21	Philadelphia	at	Houston
436	Thurs	"	22	Alberta	at	Winnipeg
437				Minnesota	at	Chicago
438				New England	at	Ottawa
439	Fri	"	23	Chicago	at	New England (BA)
440				Philadelphia	at	Los Angeles
441	Sat	"	24	Minnesota	at	Cleveland
442				Alberta	at	Quebec
443	Sun	"	25	Minnesota	at	Ottawa
444				Alberta	at	Quebec
445				Chicago	at	Los Angeles
446				New York	at	Winnipeg
447				Cleveland	at	Houston
448	Mon	"	26	New England	at	Cleveland
449	Tues	"	27	New York	at	Minnesota
450				Quebec	at	Ottawa
451				Houston	at	New England (BA)
452				Chicago	at	Los Angeles (LB)
453	Wed	"	28	Winnipeg	at	Chicago
454				Alberta	at	Philadelphia
455	Thurs	"	29	Quebec	at	Minnesota
456				Alberta	at	Philadelphia
457				New England	at	Ottawa
458				New York	at	Houston
459	Fri	"	30	Alberta	at	Minnesota
460				Winnipeg	at	Cleveland
461	Sat	"	31	New York	at	New England (BA)
462				Houston	at	Quebec
463				Ottawa	at	Cleveland
464				Chicago	at	Philadelphia
465	Sun	Apr	1	Houston	at	Ottawa
466				Chicago	at	Cleveland
467				Quebec	at	New England (BA)
468				Winnipeg	at	Philadelphia

WHA REFEREES
Vern Buffey, Referee-in-Chief

Referees:
1. Bill Friday
2. Bob Sloan
3. Ron Ego
4. Brent Casselman
7. Willie Papp
8. Ray Thomas
9. Ron Asselstine
10. Pierre Belanger

Linesmen:
18. Ron Asselstine
19. Wayne Mundey
20. Bobby Frampton
21. Pierre Belanger
22. Gene Kusy
23. Mike Entwistle
24. Ross Keenan

46

1972-73 STARTING TIMES

ALL TIMES LOCAL
ALBERTA
Week nights .... 8:00 p.m.
Sundays .... 7:30 p.m.

CHICAGO
All games .... 7:30 p.m.

CLEVELAND
Week nights .... 8:00 p.m.
Dec. 25 and April 1 .... 2:00 p.m.

HOUSTON
All games .... 7:30 p.m.

LOS ANGELES
Week nights .... 8:00 p.m.
Sundays .... 7:00 p.m.
Jan. 28; Feb. 10, 24, 25 and March 11 .... 2:30 p.m.

MINNESOTA
All games .... 7:30 p.m.

NEW ENGLAND
Mondays .... 7:00 p.m.
Other week nights .... 7:30 p.m.
Nov. 4, 11; Dec. 2, 9, 17, 24 .... 1:30 p.m.

NEW YORK
Week nights .... 7:30 p.m.
Saturdays and Sundays .... 1:30 p.m.
Feb. 11 .... 7:00 p.m.

OTTAWA
Week nights .... 8:00 p.m.
Sundays .... 7:30 p.m.
Nov. 12 .... 2:00 p.m.

PHILADELPHIA
Week nights .... 7:35 p.m.
Sundays .... 7:00 p.m.
Dec. 9; Jan. 20; March 11, 31 .... 1:35 p.m.

QUEBEC
All games .... 8:05 p.m.

WINNIPEG
Week nights .... 8:00 p.m.
Sundays .... 7:30 p.m.

47

WHA TRAVELOG

Approximate Air Mileage

	Alberta	Chicago	Cleveland	Houston	Los Angeles	Minnesota	New England	New York	Ottawa	Philadelphia	Quebec	Winnipeg
Alberta	W	1646	1754	1864	1752	1252	2600	2457	1963	2018	2016	835
Chicago	1646	O	312	932	1746	334	865	719	656	675	893	834
Cleveland	1754	312	R	1104	2046	624	558	410	413	365	656	1017
Houston	1864	932	1104	L	1372	1046	1603	1416	1596	1336	1746	1469
Los Angeles	1752	1746	2046	1372	D	1940	2610	2454	2401	2396	2628	1990
Minnesota	1252	334	624	1046	1940		1385	1253	1006	985	1227	440
New England	2600	865	558	1603	2610	1385	H	186	320	274	403	1765
New York	2457	719	410	1416	2454	1253	186	O	329	84	477	1645
Ottawa	1963	656	413	1596	2401	1006	320	329	C	384	230	1160
Philadelphia	2018	675	365	1336	2396	985	274	84	384	K	540	1375
Quebec	2016	893	656	1746	2628	1227	403	477	230	540	E	1277
Winnipeg	835	834	1017	1469	1990	440	1765	1645	1160	1375	1277	Y

WHA on CBS and CBC

Two networks in two nations will carry World Hockey Association games during the 1972-73 season.

The Canadian Broadcasting Corporation will broadcast a minimum of six WHA games, beginning with the WHA opener featuring the Ottawa Nationals and the Alberta Oilers in Ottawa.

Global Sports Enterprises Ltd. actually holds the Canadian TV rights to WHA games and will work in conjunction with the CBC. Global Sports is an offshoot of the Global Television Network, which will be Canada's third such chain, licensed to commence broadcasting Jan. 1, 1974. The network will have 10 stations ready to go on that day and the WHA will be the cornerstone of its sports programming schedule.

Gary L. Davidson, WHA President, described the package as a "multi-year deal that could be worth in excess of $3 million."

Exactly which games the CBC will telecast has not yet been determined.

In the United States, the Columbia Broadcasting System has purchased U.S. network television rights for WHA games in a five-year, multi-million dollar agreement.

CBS will broadcast a minimum of five games this season. There will be regular season game broadcasts on Sunday, Jan. 7 and Sunday, Feb. 25. Telecasts of postseason playoff games are scheduled April 22, April 29 and May 6. All three dates are Sundays.

In the event the playoffs are still in progress, a fourth playoff game will be carried Sunday, May 13. There is also a possibility that additional regular season games will be added to the schedule.

In future years, CBS plans to expand its coverage of the WHA.

In making the announcement, Robert D. Wood, President of CBS, said, "We are looking forward to expanding our coverage to a Game of the Week in three years."

49

1973-74 MEDIA GUIDE

EDITOR
WALT MARLOW

STATISTICIAN
FRANK POLNASZEK

THE COVER

Two of Hockey's greatest — Bobby Hull (top) and Gordie Howe caught in action by Bob Rush.

CONTENTS

Gary L. Davidson	3
WHA Directory	5
Chicago Cougars	6
Cleveland Crusaders	8
Edmonton Oilers	10
Houston Aeros	12
Los Angeles Sharks	14
Minnesota Saints	16
New England Whalers	18
New York Golden Blades	20
Quebec Nordiques	22
Toronto Toros	24
Vancouver Blazers	26
Winnipeg Jets	28
Final 1972-73 League Standings	30
Scoring Leaders	32
Goaltending	34
Multiple Goal Nights	36
Attendance	39
All-Star Teams	40
All-Star Game	42
Overtime Facts	44
Team Totals	46-48
Team Records	48
Individual Records	54
Playoffs	55
Playoff Statistics	57
WHA Officials	61
1973-74 Schedule	62
Travelog	72
Chronology of WHA	73
WHA Rules	77
Minor Officials	79

THE BACK COVER

The champion New England Whalers, winners of the first World Trophy.

FRONT — Al Smith, Tom Williams, Asst. Coach Ron Ryan, Coach-GM Jack Kelley, Ted Green (Capt.), Pres. Howard Baldwin, Jim Dorey, Larry Pleau, Bruce Landon.

MIDDLE — Guy Smith, Mike Byers, Brad Selwood, Tim Sheehy, Ric Jordan, Paul Hurley, Brit Selby, Skip Cunningham (Equipment Mgr.), Howie Hewitt (stick boy), trainer Joe Altott.

BACK ROW — Tom Earl, John Danby, John French, Rick Ley, Terry Caffery, Tom Webster, John Cuniff, Kevin Ahearn.

PRINTED IN U.S.A—All rights reserved, World Hockey Association.

Gary L. Davidson

President
World Hockey Association

As a sports executive, Gary L. Davidson is dedicated to the proposition that nothing is impossible. He resides in a positive world. He regards negativism as an instrument of failure.

It was on such structured thinking that the World Hockey Association was founded. Anything less and the incredible birth of hockey's second major league never would have materialized.

What the bystanders and critics first labeled a study in futility, the WHA — as it embarks on its' second season — is now solidly entrenched.

"It has been conclusively proven by the players themselves that there is room in hockey for a second major league," said Davidson, whose administrative genius also launched the American Basketball Association and has been a vital force in numerous other sports endeavors.

"That those players had the courage to follow the leadership of the WHA's equally courageous owners is ample testimony to our credibility," Davidson added.

As the architect of the unique non-reserve clause in standard player contracts, Davidson — a Montana native who moved to Southern California when he was in the first grade — forecasts a historic future for the WHA.

"You measure an enterprise by its' growth," advised the charismatic Davidson, who, at 39, is still young enough to exercise his high school and college basketball skills in an industrial Orange County winter league. "WHA franchises have risen in value from $25,000 to $2 million within a mere 18 months.

"That growth will be further reflected next season when expansion takes the WHA into three new cities — Cincinnati, Indianapolis and Phoenix. There are other cities that want in. The future of this league is infinite."

While playing facilities are a perennial problem for any new league, the WHA — as Davidson points up — has and is making giant strides in that direction.

"In most instances, we had adequate existing facilities," reflected Davidson. "But our status will be greatly enhanced with the completion of new arenas in Cleveland, Chicago, Toronto, Edmonton, Boston, and Cincinnati."

A graduate of the UCLA law school, Davidson — by his own admission — practices little law since he and Dennis Murphy elected to launch the WHA.

As a professional financial manager, Davidson assembles the financial packages that put a league in business. Legal matters are the domain of Nagel, Regan and Davidson, the Orange County law firm of which he is a partner.

James W. Browitt
Executive Vice-President / Administrator

Ed Fitkin
Assistant to the President

Donald J. Regan
General Counsel

Walt Marlow
Director of Press Relations

Max Muhleman
WHA Properties

Vern Buffey
Referee-In-Chief

Steve Arnold
Director of Player Personnel

4

WHA DIRECTORY

LEAGUE OFFICES
4299 MacArthur Blvd.
Newport Beach, California 92660
(714) 833-9461

PRESIDENT
Gary L. Davidson

EXEC. VICE-PRESIDENT
AND ADMINISTRATOR
James W. Browitt

ASSISTANT TO
THE PRESIDENT
J. Edward Fitkin

GENERAL COUNSEL
SECRETARY
Donald J. Regan

DIRECTOR OF
PRESS RELATIONS
Walt Marlow
Home (714) 549-4163

DIRECTOR OF
PLAYER PERSONNEL
R. Steven Arnold
10 Manzanita Court
Corte Madera, Calif. 94925

REFEREE-IN-CHIEF
Vern Buffey
111 Timberbank Blvd.
Agincourt, Ontario, Canada

WHA PROPERTIES
4299 MacArthur Blvd.
Newport Beach, Calif. 92660

EXECUTIVE DIRECTOR
Max Muhleman

TRUSTEES

W. D. (Bill) Hunter
Edmonton

Jordon H. Kaiser
Chicago

Nick J. Mileti
Cleveland

Paul H. Deneau
Houston

Dennis A. Murphy
Los Angeles

Lou Kaplan
Minnesota

Howard L. Baldwin
New England

Ralf Brent
New York

John F. Bassett, Jr.
Toronto

Paul Racine, Sr.
Quebec

Ben Hatskin
Winnipeg

Tiff Trimble
Vancouver

CHICAGO COUGARS 1973-74 ROSTER

No.	Player	Pos.	S	Ht.	Wt.	Birth Date	1972-73 Club	GP	G	A	Pts.	PIM
3	Dick Proceviat	RD	L	6-0	187	6/25/46	Chicago Cougars (WHA)	56	4	14	18	33
4	Darryl Maggs	RD	R	6-3	202	4/6/49	Chi. Black Hawks (NHL)	17	0	0	0	4
							Calif. Golden Seals (NHL)	54	7	15	22	50
5	Hank Cahan	RD	R	6-1	215	12/25/33	Chicago Cougars (WHA)	76	1	10	11	44
6	Reg Fleming	RW	L	5-10	190	4/21/36	Chicago Cougars (WHA)	74	23	45	68	91
7	Bob Liddington	LW	L	5-11	180	9/14/48	Chicago Cougars (WHA)	78	20	11	31	24
8	Rod Zaine	C	L	5-11	179	5/18/46	Chicago Cougars (WHA)	72	3	14	17	25
9	Rosaire Paiement	RW	R	5-11	183	8/12/45	Chicago Cougars (WHA)	78	33	36	69	135
10	Rick Morris	LW	L	5-11	176	7/5/46	Chicago Cougars (WHA)	76	31	17	48	84
11	Brian Coates	C	L	6-0	195	9/22/52	Cape Cod (EHL)	76	36	46	82	97
							Boston Braves (AHL)	8	0	0	0	0
12	Pat Stapleton	LD	L	5-8	185	7/4/40	Chi. Black Hawks (NHL)	75	10	21	31	14
14	Ralph Backstrom	C	L	5-10	180	9/18/37	Los Angeles Kings (NHL)	63	19	25	44	6
							Chi. Black Hawks (NHL)	16	7	7	14	2
							(Coached in Lausanne, Switzerland last season)					
15	Eric Nesterenko	RW	R	6-2	199	10/31/33	Chicago Cougars (WHA)	75	23	28	51	53
16	Bobby Whitlock	RW	L	5-11	187	7/16/49	Chicago Cougars (WHA)	77	25	63	88	18
17	Bobby Sicinski	C	L	5-11	181	11/13/46	Chicago Cougars (WHA)	73	3	26	29	34
18	Ron Anderson	LD	L	6-0	190	11/15/48	Chicago Cougars (WHA)	76	31	34	65	77
19	Jan Popiel	LW	L	5-9	184	10/9/47	Houston Aeros (WHA)	75	30	12	42	14
20	Duke Harris	RW	R	6-0	191	2/25/42	L.A. Sharks (WHA)	2	1	0	1	2
21	Larry Mavety	RD	R	5-11	185	5/29/42	Phila. Blazers (WHA)	4	0	0	0	14
							Chicago Cougars (WHA)	67	9	40	49	73
							Alberta Oilers (WHA)	26	1	1	2	10
22	Jim Benzelock	RW	R	5-10	195	6/21/47	Chicago Cougars (WHA)	43	9	12	21	23
23	Frankie Rochon	LW	L	5-11	181	4/18/53	Sherb. Beavers (QJHL)	63	52	57	109	52
24	Brian Glenwright	LW	L	6-3	210	10/8/49	Chicago Cougars (WHA)	48	2	5	7	0
25	Joe Hardy	C	L	6-0	185	12/5/44	Cleve. Crusaders (WHA)	72	17	33	50	80

No.	Player	Pos.	S	Ht.	Wt.	Birth Date	1972-73 Club	GP	GA	SO	AVG.
1	Andre Gill	G	L	5-7	175	9/19/41	Chicago Cougars (WHA)	28	118	0	4.21
30	Cam Newton	G	R	5-10	165	2/25/50	Hershey Bears (AHL)	19	53	2	2.84
							Pittsburgh (NHL)	10	35	0	3.94

Coach—Pat Stapleton   Head Trainer—Eddie Swiss   Asst. Trainer—Mike Cairns

CHICAGO COUGARS HOCKEY CLUB, INC.
Illinois Center
111 East Wacker Drive
Chicago, Illinois 60601   (312) 565-1900

Trustee and Chairman of the Board:
JORDON H. KAISER

President:
WALTER KAISER

Director of Player Personnel:
JACQUES DEMERS

Coach:
PAT STAPLETON

Public Relations Director:
MICHAEL HAGGERTY

Trainer:
EDDIE SWISS

KAISER

KAISER

STAPLETON

DEMERS

ARENA—International Amphitheatre, 4300 South Halstead, Chicago, Illinois. Capacity: 9,000.
TEAM COLORS — Jungle Green and Cougar Gold.
TELEVISION — 25 away games. Play-by-play Red Rush.
RADIO — All home games, 3-station network — WWMM-FM, WLNR-FM, WGSB-AM. Play-by-play Howard Balson and Bud Kelly.

CLEVELAND CRUSADERS 1973-74 ROSTER

No.	Player	Pos.	S	Ht.	Wt.	Birth Date	1972-73 Club	GP	G	A	Pts.	PIM
2	Larry Hillman	D	—	6-0	181	2/5/37	Buffalo (NHL)	73	5	44	49	169
3	Paul Shmyr	D	L	5-10	170	1/28/46	Cleveland (WHA)	67	2	13	15	64
5	Wayne Muloin	D	L	5-8	175	12/24/41	Cleveland (WHA)	78	30	36	66	121
7	Gerry Pinder	RW	R	5-8	165	9/15/48	Cleveland (WHA)					
8	Wayne Hillman	D		6-0	205	11/13/38	Philadelphia (NHL)			10	10	20
10	Ron Buchanan	C	L	6-3	170	11/15/44	Cleveland (WHA)	75	37	44	81	79
12	Gary Jarrett	LW	L	5-8	180	9/3/42	Cleveland (WHA)	77	40	38	78	24
14	Jim Wiste	C	L	5-10	185	2/18/46	Cleveland (WHA)	70	28	43	71	
15	Bill Heindl	LW	—	5-10	175	5/13/46	Providence (AHL)	4	1	1	2	0
16	Grant Erickson	LW	L	5-9	165	4/28/47	New York (NHL)	77	15	29	44	23
17	Skip Krake	RW	R	5-11	170	2/18/46	Cleveland (WHA)	28	9	10	19	61
18	Tom Edur	D	—	6-0	180	11/18/54	Toronto (OHA)	—	14	48	62	32
20	Bill Young	LW	—	6-2	195	7/5/47	Los Angeles (WHA)	50	14	12	26	46
							Minnesota (WHA)	23	5	6	11	20
21	Paul Andrea	LW	L	5-10	170	7/31/41	Cleveland (WHA)	67	21	30	51	12
23	Rich Pumple	RW	L	6-3	200	11/2/48	Cleveland (WHA)	78	21	20	41	45
28	Russ Walker	RW	—	6-1	185	5/24/53	Saskatoon (WCHL)	—	42	38	80	193
29	Robbie Neale	C	—	6-0	190	4/17/53	Brandon (WCHL)	—	41	57	98	94

Goalies							1972-73 Club	GP	GA	SO	AVG.	
30	Gerry Cheevers	G	L	5-11	185	12/7/40	Cleveland (WHA)	52	149		2.83	
1	Bob Whidden	G	R	5-10	165	7/27/46	Cleveland (WHA)	26	88		3.28	

General Manager—Jack Vivian; Coach—Bill Needham

CLEVELAND CRUSADERS LIMITED
3717 Euclid Avenue
Cleveland, Ohio 44115 (216) 361-3700

President and Trustee:
NICK J. MILETI

Alternate Trustee and Operations Manager:
STEPHEN ZAYAC, JR.

General Manager:
JACK VIVIAN

Administrative Assistant:
HANK KELLY

Coach:
BILL NEEDHAM

Public Relations Director:
BARRY SWINEHART

Trainer:
STEVE THOMAS

MILETI

NEEDHAM

VIVIAN

ARENA — Cleveland Arena, 3717 Euclid Avenue, Cleveland, Ohio 44115. Capacity: 9,500.
TEAM COLORS — Crusader Purple, Black and White.
TELEVISION — 12 away games (WUAB). Play-by-play Steve Albert, color Joe Tait, Gib Shanley, Sue Needham.
RADIO — 62 home and away games (WWWE, 1100). Play-by-play Steve Albert.

9

EDMONTON OILERS 1973-74 ROSTER

No.	Player	Pos.	S	Ht.	Wt.	Birth Date	1972-73 Club	GP	G	A	Pts.	PIM
1	Doug Barrie	D	R	5-9	175	10/2/46	Edmonton (WHA)	54	9	22	31	109
4	Bob Wall	D	L	5-10	180	12/1/42	Edmonton (WHA)	78	16	29	45	20
3	Al Hamilton	D	R	6-2	195	8/20/46	Edmonton (WHA)	78	11	49	60	126
6	Bob Falkenberg	D	L	6-0	195	1/1/46	Edmonton (WHA)	77	6	23	29	44
2	Roger Cote	D	L	5-9	184	12/22/39	Edmonton (WHA)	60	3	5	8	44
20	Steve Carlyle	D	L	5-10	180	3/10/50	Edmonton (WHA)	67	7	10	17	35
19	Ken Baird	D	L	6-0	190	2/1/51	Edmonton (WHA)	75	14	15	29	112
22	Jim McCrimmon	D	R	6-1	210	(age 20)	Medicine Hat (WCHL)					
21	Eddie Joyal	C	L	6-0	180	5/8/40	Edmonton (WHA)	71	22	16	38	16
22	Bob Fitchner	C	L	6-1	190	12/22/50	Ft. Wayne (EHL)	73	26	37	63	157
16	Jim Harrison	C	R	5-11	180	7/9/47	Edmonton (WHA)	65	39	48	87	93
7	Ross Perkins	C	R	5-10	176	11/4/46	Edmonton (WHA)	71	21	37	58	19
9	Brian McKenzie	LW	L	5-10	180	3/16/51						
11	Ron Climie	LW	L	5-11	180	3/5/50	Ottawa (WHA)	31	12	19	31	2
8	Val Fonteyne	LW	L	5-9	160	12/2/33	Edmonton (WHA)	77	7	32	39	6
18	Bob McAneeley	LW	L	5-8	175	11/7/50	Edmonton (WHA)	51	5	7	12	24
27	Len Lunde	LW	L	6-0	194	11/13/36	Finnish National Team					
14	Blair McDonald	RW	R	5-11	180	(age 19)	Cornwall (OHA)	64	63	39	102	44
17	Rusty Patenaude	RW	R	5-9	175	10/17/49	Edmonton (WHA)	78	29	27	56	59
15	Tom Gilmore	RW	R	5-11	190	5/14/48	Los Angeles (WHA)	70	17	18	35	191

No.	Goalies	Pos.	S	Ht.	Wt.	Birth Date	1972-73 Club	GP	GA	SO	AVG.
30	Jack Norris	G	L	5-10	175	8/5/42	Edmonton (WHA)	64	189		3.06
1	Chris Worthy	G	L	6-0	186	10/23/47	Denver	38	98		4.43

General Manager—Bill Hunter; Coach—Brian Shaw

EDMONTON WORLD HOCKEY ENTERPRISES LTD.
MacDonald Hotel
Edmonton, Alberta T5J 0N6, Canada
(403) 429-2802   429-2803   429-2804

Chairman of the Board:
DR. CHARLES A. ALLARD

President and Alternate Trustee:
ZANE FELDMAN

Vice-President, General Manager and Trustee:
W. D. (BILL) HUNTER

Comptroller:
RAY BARTH

Coach:
BRIAN SHAW

Director of Player Personnel:
RAY KINASEWICH

Public Relations Director:
DON LEROSE

Trainer:
DICK BIELOUS

ALLARD

FELDMAN

HUNTER

SHAW

ARENA — Edmonton Gardens, Edmonton Exhibition Grounds, Edmonton, Alberta, Canada. Capacity: 5,200.
TEAM COLORS — Royal Blue, Orange and White.
TELEVISION — none.
RADIO — All home and away (CFRN). Play-by-play Al McGann and Rod Phillips. Pre-game and post game shows — Norm Williams and Cecil (Tiger) Goldstick.

HOUSTON AEROS 1973-74 ROSTER

No.	Player	Pos.	S	Ht.	Wt.	Birth Date	1972-73 Club	GP	G	A	Pts.	PIM
3	Marty Howe	D	L	6-1	185	2/18/54	Toronto (OHA)	38	11	17	28	81
17	Larry Hale	D	L	6-1	187	10/9/41	Houston (WHA)	68	4	26	30	65
5	G. Kannegeisser	D	R	6-0	190	12/2/45	Houston (WHA)	45	0	10	10	37
2	John Schella	D	R	6-0	190	12/2/45	Houston (WHA)	77	2	24	26	239
20	Dunc McCallum	D	R	6-1	193	3/29/40	Houston (WHA)	69	9	20	29	112
6	Poul Popiel	D	L	5-10	176	2/28/43	Houston (WHA)	73	16	48	64	153
22	Bill Prentice	D	R	6-1	190	6/10/50	Mich. Tech	21	3	7	10	50
11	Murray Hall	C	R	5-11	174	11/24/40	Houston (WHA)	76	28	42	70	84
10	Gord Labossiere	C	R	6-1	185	1/2/40	Houston (WHA)	77	36	60	96	56
12	Ed Hoekstra	C	R	5-11	175	11/4/37	Houston (WHA)	71	11	28	39	12
13	Larry Lund	C	R	6-0	190	9/9/40	Houston (WHA)	77	21	45	66	120
8	Joe Szura	C	L	6-3	198	12/18/38	Los Angeles (WHA)	73	13	32	45	25
23	Jim Sherrit	C	R	5-7	170	9/29/48	Cape Cod (EHL)	76	42	81	123	49
4	Mark Howe	LW	L	5-11	180	5/28/55	Toronto (OHA)	60	38	66	104	27
16	Andre Hinse	LW	L	5-9	175	4/19/45	Phoenix (WHL)	72	34	42	76	25
18	Jack Stanfield	LW	L	5-11	176	5/30/42	Houston (WHA)	71	8	12	12	8
9	Gordon Howe	RW	R	6-0	205	3/31/28	Retired					
21	Don Grierson	RW	R	6-0	180	6/18/47	Houston (WHA)	78	22	22	44	33
7	Frank Hughes	RW	L	5-10	180	10/1/49	Houston (WHA)	77	22	19	41	41
14	Ted Taylor	RW	L	6-0	175	2/25/42	Houston (WHA)	72	34	42	76	101

No.	Player	Pos.	S	Ht.	Wt.	Birth Date	1972-73 Club	GP	GA	SO	AVG.
30	Wayne Rutledge	G	L	6-2	205	1/5/42	Houston	37	110		2.96
1	Don McLeod	G	L	6-1	190	8/24/46	Houston	40	143		3.65

General Manager—Jim Smith; Coach—Bill Dineen

HOUSTON HOCKEY CLUB, INC.
810 Bagby
Houston, Texas 77002   (713) 228-6437

Trustee and Chairman of the Board:
PAUL H. DENEAU

President, General Manager
and Alternate Trustee:
JAMES S. SMITH

Coach:
BILL DINEEN

Assistant Coach and Chief Scout:
DOUG HARVEY

Public Relations Director
and Business Manager:
SONNY TATE

Trainer:
BOBBY BROWN

DENEAU

SMITH

DINEEN

ARENA — Sam Houston Coliseum, 810 Bagby, Houston, Texas 77002. Capacity: 9,300.
TEAM COLORS — Powder Blue, Navy Blue and White.
TELEVISION — 10 road games, channel 26. Play-by-play Jerry Trupiano.
RADIO — All home and away (KULF). Play-by-play Jerry Trupiano.

13

LOS ANGELES SHARKS 1973-74 ROSTER

No.	Player	Pos.	S	Ht.	Wt.	Birth Date	1972-73 Club	GP	G	A	Pts.	PIM
9	Marc Tardif	LW	L	6-1	180	6/12/49	Montreal (NHL)	76	25	25	50	48
16	Earl Heiskala	LW	L	6-0	185	11/30/42	Los Angeles (WHA)	70	12	17	29	148
18	Gary Veneruzzo	LW	L	5-8	165	6/28/43	Los Angeles (WHA)	78	43	30	73	34
19	Steve Sutherland	LW	L	5-11	175	9/1/46	Los Angeles (WHA)	43	11	6	17	96
13	Peter Slater	RW	R	5-11	170	1/31/48	Los Angeles (WHA)	72	12	12	12	87
23	Alton White	RW	R	5-9	175	5/31/45	New York (WHA)	13	1	4	5	2
							Los Angeles (WHA)	57	20	17	37	22
20	Don Gordon	RW	R	5-11	180	4/17/48	Dallas (CHL)		28	35	63	70
17	Brian McDonald	RW	R	5-11	190	3/23/45	Houston (WHA)	71	20	20	40	81
24	Tommy Serviss	C	R	5-10	185	5/25/48	Los Angeles (WHA)	73	11	26	37	32
8	Fred Speck	C	L	5-9	165	7/22/27	Minnesota (WHA)	47	13	16	29	53
							Los Angeles (WHA)	28	3	13	16	23
10	J. P. LeBlanc	C	L	5-10	170	10/20/46	Los Angeles (WHA)	77	19	50	69	49
11	Ted McCaskill	C	L	6-1	190	10/29/36	Los Angeles (WHA)	73	11	11	22	150
21	Reg Thomas	C	L	5-10	180	5/21/53	London (OHL)		52	83	135	41
2	Jim Watson	D	L	6-2	195	6/28/43	Los Angeles (WHA)	75	5	15	20	123
3	Jim Niekamp	D	R	6-1	185	3/11/47	Los Angeles (WHA)	78	7	22	29	151
4	Ralph MacSweyn	D	L	5-11	195	9/8/42	Los Angeles (WHA)	78	0	23	23	39
6	Gerry Odrowski	D	L	5-10	190	10/4/38	Los Angeles (WHA)	78	6	31	37	89
7	Bart Crashley	D	R	6-0	195	6/15/46	Los Angeles (WHA)	70	18	27	45	10
5	Bill Horton	D	L	6-0	180	9/5/46	Cleveland (WHA)		2	17	19	55
12	Ron Garwasiuk	D	L	5-8	160	2/17/49	Providence (AHL)	74	19			

No.	Player			Ht.	Wt.	Birth Date	1972-73 Club	GP	GA	SO	AVG.
1	Russ Gillow			5-10	165	9/2/40	Los Angeles (WHA)	38	96		2.88
30	George Gardner			5-10	180	10/8/42	Los Angeles (WHA)	49	149		3.29
—	Paul Hoganson			6-0	180	11/12/49	Hershey (AHL)		111		2.95

General Manager—Dennis Murphy; Coach—Terry Slater

PROFESSIONAL HOCKEY CORP.
3939 S. Figueroa Street
Los Angeles, California 90037
(213) 741-2111

Trustee and General Manager:
DENNIS A. MURPHY

Coach:
TERRY SLATER

Assistant General Manager:
GARY MORRELL

Director of Public Relations:
HANK IVES

Promotion Director:
BRUCE BLAIR

MURPHY

SLATER

ARENA — L.A. Sports Arena, 3939 S. Figueroa St., Los Angeles, CA. Capacity: 14,700.
TEAM COLORS — Red, Black and White.
TELEVISION — Check local listing.
RADIO — All home and away games (KGBS-FM, 91.7). Play-by-play Gary Morrell, color Bud Tucker.

15

MINNESOTA FIGHTING SAINTS 1973-74 ROSTER

No.	Player	Pos.	S	Ht.	Wt.	Birth Date	1972-73 Club	GP	G	A	Pts.	PIM
2	Dick Paradise	D	L	5-11	194	4/21/45	Minnesota (WHA)	77	3	15	18	189
3	Rick Smith	D	L	5-11	200	5/29/48	California (NHL)	64	9	24	33	77
4	Mike Walton	LW	L	5-9	185	1/3/45	Boston (NHL)	52	25	22	47	32
5	Rob Walton	C	L	5-9	165	9/3/49	Seattle Totems (WHL)	72	40	61	101	43
6	Keith Christiansen	C	R	5-5	155	7/14/44	Minnesota (WHA)	64	12	30	42	24
7	Wayne Connelly	RW	R	5-10	175	12/16/39	Minnesota (WHA)	78	40	30	70	16
8	Billy Klatt	RW	R	5-10	180	10/16/47	Minnesota (WHA)	78	36	22	58	22
9	George Morrison	LW	L	6-1	175	12/24/48	Minnesota (WHA)	70	16	24	40	20
10	Ted Hampson	C	L	5-8	170	12/11/36	Minnesota (WHA)	76	17	45	62	20
11	Murray Heatley	LW	L	5-8	185	11/7/48	Phoenix (WHL)	72	43	55	98	62
12	Mike Antonovich	C	L	5-8	160	10/18/51	Minnesota (WHA)	75	20	19	39	44
14	Bob MacMillan	C	L	5-10	175	12/3/52	Minnesota (WHA)	75	13	27	40	48
16	Gordon Gallant	LW	L	5-11	178	10/27/50	Syracuse (EHL)	53	17	34	51	232
17	John Arbour	D	L	5-11	194	9/28/45	Minnesota (WHA)	76	6	27	33	188
20	Jimmy Johnson	LW	L	5-9	185	11/7/42	Minnesota (WHA)	33	9	14	23	12
21	Terry Ball	LW	R	5-9	165	11/29/44	Minnesota (WHA)	76	6	34	40	66
22	Blaine Rydman	D	L	6-2	195	12/16/49	Minnesota (WHA)	31	0	1	1	69
23	Mike McMahon	D	L	5-11	182	8/30/41	Minnesota (WHA)	75	12	39	51	87
24	Bob Boyd	D	R	6-0	190	11/27/51	Mich. State (WCHA)	35	7	41	48	124
33	Steve Cardwell	LW	L	5-11	190	8/18/49	Pittsburgh (NHL)	20	2	2	4	2
							Hershey (AHL)	30	16	23	39	18

No.	Player	Pos.	S	Ht.	Wt.	Birth Date	1972-73 Club	GP	GA	SO	AVG.
1	Mike Curran	G	L	5-9	175	4/14/44	Minnesota (WHA)	43	131	4	3.09
30	Jack McCartan	G	L	6-1	195	8/5/35	Minnesota (WHA)	38	129	1	3.59
35	John Garrett	G	L	5-8	170	5/17/51	Richmond (AHL)	37	117	0	3.26

General Manager—Glen Sonmor; Coach—Harry Neale

MIDWEST SAINTS, INC.
Metro Square, Suite 240
St. Paul, Minnesota 55101   (612) 222-3040

President and Executive Director:
JOHN T. FINLEY

Chairman of the Board and Alternate Trustee:
FRED GROTHE

Trustee:
LOU KAPLAN

General Manager:
GLEN SONMOR

Coach:
HARRY NEALE

Public Relations Director:
MIKE LAMEY

Trainer:
GLENN GOSTICK

FINLEY

GROTHE

KAPLAN

SONMOR

ARENA — St. Paul Civic Center, 143 West 4th Street, St. Paul, Minnesota 55102. Capacity: 16,180.
TEAM COLORS — Royal Blue, New Gold and White.
TELEVISION — Check local listing.
RADIO — All home and away games (WLOL). Play-by-play Frank Buetel.

17

NEW ENGLAND WHALERS 1973-74 ROSTER

No.	Player	Pos.	S	Ht.	Wt.	Birth Date	1972-73 Club	GP	G	A	Pts.	PIM
2	Rick Ley	D	L	5-9	185	10/2/48	New England (WHA)	77	3	27	30	108
3	Brad Selwood	D	L	6-1	190	3/18/49	New England (WHA)	77	13	21	34	110
4	Larry Pleau	C	L	6-1	185	6/29/47	New England (WHA)	76	39	48	87	44
5	Paul Hurley	D	R	5-11	195	7/12/46	New England (WHA)	77	3	15	18	60
6	Ted Green (C)	D	R	5-10	210	3/23/40	New England (WHA)	78	16	30	46	47
7	Terry Caffery	C	R	5-9	165	4/1/49	New England (WHA)	74	39	61	100	14
8	Tom Webster	RW	R	5-10	185	10/4/48	New England (WHA)	77	53	50	103	83
9	Tom Williams	C	R	5-11	175	4/17/40	New England (WHA)	69	10	21	31	16
10	Jim Dorey	D	L	6-1	190	8/17/47	New England (WHA)	74	7	56	63	95
11	John French	LW	R	5-11	175	8/25/50	New England (WHA)	76	24	35	59	43
12	John Danby	C	R	5-10	175	7/20/48	New England (WHA)	76	14	23	37	10
14	Al Karlander	C	L	5-8	174	11/5/46	Detroit (NHL)	77	15	22	37	25
15	Tim Sheehy	RW	R	6-1	185	9/3/48	New England (WHA)	78	33	38	71	30
16	Hugh Harris	LW	L	6-0	190	6/7/48	Buffalo (NHL)	60	12	26	38	17
17	John Cunniff	LW	L	5-9	175	7/9/44	Ottawa (WHA)	32	3	5	8	16
18	Bob Charlebois	LW	L	5-11	170	5/27/44	New England (WHA)	78	24	39	63	28
21	Mike Byers	RW	R	5-10	185	9/11/46	Los Angeles (WHA)	19	6	4	10	4
22	Don Blackburn	LW	L	6-0	175	5/14/38	New York Is. (NHL)	56	19	17	36	20
							Minnesota (NHL)	56	7	10	17	24
								4	0	0	0	0
27	Tom Earl	RW	R	5-11	180	1/27/47	New England (WHA)	77	10	13	23	4

No.	Player	Pos.	S	Ht.	Wt.	Birth Date	1972-73 Club	GP	GA	SO	AVG.
1	Al Smith	G	R	6-1	200	11/10/45	New England (WHA)	50.5	162	3	3.18
30	Bruce Landon	G	R	5-9	180	10/5/49	New England (WHA)	27.5	100	1	3.58

General Manager—Jack Kelley Assistant Coach—Jack Ferreira
Coach—Ron Ryan Trainer—Joe Altott

NEW ENGLAND PROFESSIONAL HOCKEY CLUB, INC.
705 Statler Office Building
Boston, Massachusetts 02116
(617) 357-9012

Chairman of the Board:
ROBERT J. SCHMERTZ

President and Trustee:
HOWARD L. BALDWIN

Vice-President and Secretary:
W. GODFREY WOOD

Executive Vice-President of Marketing:
WILLIAM E. BARNES

General Manager:
JOHN H. (JACK) KELLEY

Coach and Assistant General Manager:
RONALD K. RYAN

Director of Player Personnel
and Assistant Coach:
JACK FERREIRA

Public Relations Director:
KEVIN WALSH

Trainer:
JOSEPH R. ALTOTT

SCHMERTZ

BALDWIN

BARNES

KELLEY

ARENA — Boston Garden, 150 Causeway Street, Boston, Massachusetts 02114. Capacity: 14,994.
TEAM COLORS: Forest Green and White with Black.
TELEVISION — 25 home and away games (WKBG, 56). Play-by-play John Carlson. Color Shirley and Stan Fischler.
RADIO — All home and away games (WHDH). Play-by-play John Moynoihan.

NEW YORK GOLDEN BLADES 1973-74 ROSTER

No.	Player	Pos.	S	Ht.	Wt.	Birth Date	1972-73 Club	GP	G	A	Pts.	PIM
3	Harry Howell	D		6-1	200	12/28/32	Los Angeles Kings	73	4	11	15	28
4	Kevin Morrison	D		5-11	210	10/28/49	New Haven Nighthawks	74	7	28	33	154
5	Dean Boylan	D		5-11	180	(Age 20)	Yale University	22	4	14	18	36
6	Bobby Sheehan	C		5-9	170	1/11/49	N.Y. Raiders	75	35	53	88	17
7	Andre Lacroix	C		5-8	175	6/5/45	Philadelphia Blazers	78	50	74	124	83
8	Garry Peters	C		5-10	180	10/9/42	N.Y. Raiders	23	2	7	9	25
9	Norm Ferguson	RW		5-8	165	10/16/45	N.Y. Raiders	56	28	40	68	8
10	Bob Jones	C		6-2	195	11/27/45	Los Angeles Sharks	20	2	7	9	8
12	Wayne Rivers	RW		5-9	179	2/1/42	N.Y. Raiders	56	11	12	23	24
14	Brian Bradley	LW		5-10	174	12/14/44	N.Y. Raiders	75	37	40	77	47
15	Brian Morenz	RW		5-10	185	5/11/49	N.Y. Raiders	78	22	33	55	20
17	Ken Block	D		5-10	184	3/18/44	N.Y. Raiders	30	7	1	8	23
18	Mike Laughton	C		6-2	185	2/21/44	N.Y. Raiders	78	5	53	58	43
19	Brian Perry	RW		5-10	176	4/6/44	N.Y. Raiders	67	16	20	36	44
21	Lee Inglis	LW		6-0	190		Played in Holland—record not available	74	13	20	33	30
22	Claude Chartre	C		6-0	176	12/21/49	N.Y. Raiders	12	2	3	5	0
23	Ray Larose	D		6-0	190	11/20/41	Long Island Ducks	52	34	40	74	23
24	Bill Speer	D		5-10	210	3/20/42	Houston Aeros	68	1	10	11	25
25	Gene Peacosh	LW		6-0	175	9/28/48	N.Y. Raiders	69	3	23	26	40
26	Bob Brown	D		6-1	195	12/18/50	Rhode Island Eagles	67	37	34	71	25
							N.Y. Raiders	47	9	25	34	33
								17	0	4	4	6

Goalies

No.	Player	Pos.	S	Ht.	Wt.	Birth Date	1972-73 Club	GP	GA	SO	AVG.
1	Jimmy McLeod	G		5-9	174	4/7/37	Chicago Cougars	54	166	1	3.32
36	Joe Junkin	G		5-11	175	9/8/46	Syracuse Blazers	35	90	5	2.60

Managing Director of Hockey—Jerry DeLise
Coach—Camille Henry
Head Trainer—Peter Unwin
Assistant Trainer—Bob Sarnas

GOLDEN BLADES HOCKEY, INC.
Two Pennsylvania Plaza, Suite 2844
New York, N.Y. 10001   (212) 239-4875

President and Trustee:
RALF BRENT

Executive Vice-President
and Alternate Trustee:
LEE MATISON

Managing Director of Hockey Personnel:
JERRY DE LISE

Director of Player Personnel:
BILL MCDERMOTT

Coach:
CAMILLE HENRY

Public Relations Director:
ROBERT BOYLES

ARENA: Madison Square Garden, Pennsylvania Plaza, New York, N.Y. 10001. Capacity: 17,250.
TEAM COLORS: Purple, Gold and White.
TELEVISION — Selected games on cable.
RADIO — WRVR-FM. Play-by-play Barry Landers.

21

QUEBEC NORDIQUES 1973-74 ROSTER

No.	Player	Pos.	S	Ht.	Wt.	Birth Date	1972-73 Club	GP	G	A	Pts.	PIM
2	Alain Beaule	D	L	6-0	195	4/7/46	Springfield (AHL)	57	7	23	30	72
3	J.-C. Tremblay	D	L	5-10	185	1/22/39	Quebec (WHA)	75	14	76	90	26
4	Francois Lacombe	D	L	5-10	188	2/24/48	Quebec (WHA)	61	10	17	27	123
5	Rejean Houle	LW	L	5-11	165	10/25/49	Montreal (NHL)	72	13	35	48	36
6	Pierre Guite	LW	L	6-1	192	4/17/52	Quebec (WHA)	68	10	8	18	136
8	Jean Payette	C	L	6-0	180	3/29/46	Quebec (WHA)	73	15	29	44	46
12	Michel Parizeau	C	L	5-9	165	4/9/48	Quebec (WHA)	75	25	48	73	50
15	Renald Leclerc	RW	R	5-11	165	11/12/47	Quebec (WHA)	62	25	28	53	104
16	Andre Gaudette	C	L	5-7	165	12/16/47	Quebec (WHA)	78	28	43	71	12
17	Jeannot Gilbert	C	L	5-9	170	9/28/44	Hershey (AHL)	68	31	58	89	—
19	Alain Caron	RW	R	5-9	180	4/27/38	Quebec (WHA)	70	36	28	64	27
20	Guy Dufour	RW	R	5-11	180	9/2/46	Quebec (WHA)	11	3	2	5	2
21	Serge Bernier	RW	R	6-1	190	4/29/47	Los Angeles (NHL)	75	22	46	68	43
22	Ken Desjardine	D	L	6-0	184	8/23/47	Quebec (WHA)	38	2	6	8	36
24	N. Descoteaux	D	L	5-9	175	1/3/48	Europe	40	40	40	80	60
25	Robert Guindon	LW	L	5-9	170	11/19/50	Quebec (WHA)	70	28	28	56	31
33	Dale Hoganson	D	L	5-10	190	7/8/49	Montreal (NHL)	26	0	2	2	2

Goalies								GP	GA	SO		AVG.
1	Serge Aubry	G	L	5-9	160	1/2/42	Quebec (WHA)	52	177	2		3.59
30	Michel Deguise	G	L	5-8	150	11/6/51	Nova Scotia (AHL)	—	68			2.65
—	Richard Brodeur	G	R	5-7	160	9/15/52	Quebec (WHA)	24	95			4.75

Coach and General Manager—Jacques Plante

**LE CLUB DE HOCKEY
LES NORDIQUES INC.**
Quebec Coliseum   2025 Ave. Du Colisee
Quebec P.Q., Quebec, Canada G1L 4W7
(418) 529-4161

President and Trustee:
PAUL RACINE

Chairman of the Board:
HON. JEAN LESAGE

Vice-President and Alternate Trustee:
MARIUS FORTIER

General Manager and Head Coach:
JACQUES PLANTE

Assistant Coach:
CLAUDE STE.-MARIE

Trainer:
GUY GIRARDREAU

Chief Scout:
MAURICE FILION

Public Relations Director:
DONALD D'AMOURS

RACINE

LESAGE

FORTIER

PLANTE

ARENA — Quebec Coliseum, Exhibition Grounds, Quebec 3, P.Q., Canada. Capacity: 10,000.
TEAM COLORS: Blue, Red and White.
TELEVISION — 14 games, Channel 10 Montreal French Network.
RADIO — All home (CKCV) and away (CGRP). Play-by-play Guy Turbide and Claude Bedard.

23

TORONTO TOROS 1973-74 ROSTER

No.	Player	Pos.	S	Ht.	Wt.	Birth Date	1972-73 Club	GP	G	A	Pts.	PIM
5	Mike Amodeo	D	L	5-10	195	6/22/52	Ottawa (WHA)	60	1	14	15	77
2	Carl Brewer	D	L	5-10	185	10/21/38	St. Louis (NHL)	(Out of Hockey)				42
9	Wayne Carleton	LW	L	6-3	215	8/4/46	Ottawa (WHA)	75	42	49	91	121
4	Steve Cuddie	D	R	5-11	198	6/18/50	Winnipeg (WHA)	77	7	15	22	141
3	Rick Cunningham	D	R	5-10	190	3/3/51	Ottawa (WHA)	78	9	31	40	25
18	Wayne Dillon	C	L	6-0	180	5/25/55	Toronto (OHA)	59	47	60	107	60
6	Brian Gibbons	D	L	6-3	190	7/7/47	Ottawa (WHA)	73	7	35	42	40
23	Gerard Gibbons	D	L	6-3	185	1/7/53	St. Mary's Univ.	22	8	20	28	50
21	Jack Gibson	LW	L	6-0	185	8/18/48	Ottawa (WHA)	59	22	12	34	80
16	Pat Hickey	C-RW	L	6-1	185	5/14/53	Hamilton (OHA)	63	32	47	79	28
12	Steve King	RW	R	5-9	175	9/8/48	Ottawa (WHA)	68	18	34	52	54
11	Gavin Kirk	C	L	5-11	185	12/6/51	Ottawa (WHA)	78	28	40	68	71
19	Bob Leduc	C	L	5-10	178	5/24/44	Ottawa (WHA)	77	22	33	55	22
17	Tom Martin	RW	R	5-9	175	10/16/47	Ottawa (WHA)	75	19	27	46	40
20	Peter Marrin	C-RW	R	5-10	180	7/8/53	Toronto (OHA)	58	42	64	106	52
15	Brit Selby	LW	L	5-10	175	3/27/45	New England (WHA)	72	13	30	43	75
8	Rick Sentes	LW	L	6-0	184	1/10/47	Ottawa (WHA)	73	22	19	41	45
14	Tom Simpson	RW	R	5-11	192	8/15/52	Ottawa (WHA)	58	10	7	17	25
7	Guy Trottier	RW	R	5-8	165	4/1/41	Ottawa (WHA)	71	26	32	58	

No.	Goalies	Pos.	S	Ht.	Wt.	Birth Date	1972-73 Club	GP	GA	SO	AVG.
30	Les Binkley	G	L	6-0	170	6/6/34	Ottawa (WHA)	30	106		3.72
33	Gilles Gratton	G	L	5-11	155	7/28/52	Ottawa (WHA)	51	187		3.71
—	Frank Blum	G	R	6-0	180	6/29/52	Clinton (EHL)	17	71		4.35

General Manager—Buck Houle; Coach—Billy Harris

CAN SPORTS INC.
238 Bloor Street West, Suite 107
Toronto, Ontario, Canada   (416) 961-7441

President and Trustee:
JOHN F. BASSETT, JR.

Alternate Trustee:
NICK TRBOVICH

General Manager:
A. J. (BUCK) HOULE

Coach:
BILLY HARRIS

Public Relations Director:
MIKE MCCLURE

Trainer:
PETER UNWIN

BASSETT

HOULE

ARENA — Varsity Arena, Toronto (30 Games). Capacity: 5,000. Civic Center, Ottawa (9 Games). Capacity: 9,300.
TEAM COLORS: Blue, Red and White.
TELEVISION — 15 home games. Play-by-play Joe Spence.
RADIO — none.

VANCOUVER BLAZERS 1973-74 ROSTER

No.	Player	Pos.	S	Ht.	Wt.	Birth Date	1972-73 Club	GP	G	A	Pts.	PIM
7	Jim Adair	C	L	6-0	185	9/29/48	Fort Worth (GHL)	20	5	20	25	24
8	Don Burgess	LW	L	6-0	175	6/8/46	Philadelphia (WHA)	74	20	22	42	15
14	Bryan Campbell	C	L	6-0	180	3/27/44	Philadelphia (WHA)	75	25	48	73	85
2	Colin Campbell	D	L	5-11	190	1/28/53	Peterboro (OHA)	77	9	48	57	322
6	Rychard Campeau	D	R	6-0	200	4/9/52	Roanoke (EHL)					
5	Jim Cardiff	D	L	5-9	165	8/29/44	Philadelphia (WHA)	78	3	24	27	185
16	Mike Chernoff	LW	L	5-10	175	6/13/46	Jacksonville (EHL)	76	35	33	68	37
21	Sam Gellard	LW	L	6-0	195	3/15/50	Rhode Island (EHL)	36	21	20	41	43
3	Dave Hutchison	D	L	6-3	205	5/2/52	Roanoke (EHL)	32	7	18	25	158
11	Danny Lawson	RW	R	5-11	185	10/30/47	Philadelphia (WHA)	28	0	2	2	34
19	McKenzie John	RW	R	5-6	175	12/12/37	Philadelphia (WHA)	60	28	50	78	157
15	Dennis Meloche	C	L	5-9	160	6/16/52	Roanoke (EHL)	58	30	49	79	60
18	John Migneault	LW	L	5-10	185	2/4/49	Roanoke (EHL)	18	4	13	17	15
12	Don O'Donoghue	RW	L	6-0	190	9/27/49	Philadelphia (WHA)	74	16	23	39	43
4	Ron Plumb	D	R	5-10	175	7/17/50	Philadelphia (WHA)	78	10	41	51	66
23	Irvin Spencer	D	L	5-10	180	12/4/37	Rhode Island (EHL)	11	3	3	6	4
22	Claude St. Sauveur	C	L	6-1	175	8/15/52	Roanoke (EHL)	62	55	52	107	99
10	Ron Ward	C	R	5-10	180	9/12/44	New York (WHA)	77	51	67	118	28

Goalies							1972-73 Club	GP	GA	SO	AVG.	
30	Yves Archambault	G	L	6-0	170	6/22/52	Roanoke	29	0		3.51	
1	Peter Donnelly	G	L	5-8	160	6/14/48	New York	47	2		3.56	

General Manager—Phil Watson; Coach—John McKenzie

**VANCOUVER BLAZERS
HOCKEY TEAM LTD.**
Pacific Coliseum, Exhibition Park
Vancouver 6, B.C., Canada   (604) 253-4181

Owner:
JIM PATTISON

President and Trustee:
TIFF TRIMBLE

Administrative Assistant:
IRV MULDOWAN

General Manager:
PHIL WATSON

Playing Coach:
JOHN MCKENZIE

Trainer:
WARREN ELLIOTT

Public Relations Director:
RON LYON

PATTISON

TRIMBLE

WATSON

McKENZIE

ARENA — Pacific Coliseum, Exhibition Park, Vancouver 6, B.C., Canada. Capacity: 15,569.
TEAM COLORS — Orange and Gold.
TELEVISION — Check local listing.
RADIO — All games home and away (CJJC, 800). Play-by-play Ron Oakes; Color — Ed Clarke and Gary Raible.

27

WINNIPEG JETS 1973-74 ROSTER

No.	Player	Pos.	S	Ht.	Wt.	Birth Date	1972-73 Club	GP	G	A	Pts.	PIM
	Bob Ash	D	L	5-9	173	9/29/43	Winnipeg Jets (WHA)	74	3	14	17	39
	Duke Asmundson	RW	R	6-2	194	8/17/43	Winnipeg Jets (WHA)	78	2	15	17	56
	Norm Beaudin	RW	R	5-8	172	11/28/41	Winnipeg Jets (WHA)	78	38	65	103	15
	Milt Black	RW	R	5-10	179	6/20/49	Winnipeg Jets (WHA)	77	18	16	34	31
	Chris Bordeleau	C	R	5-9	172	9/23/47	Winnipeg Jets (WHA)	77	47	54	101	12
	Wally Boyer	C	L	5-8	171	8/27/37	Winnipeg Jets (WHA)	70	6	28	34	27
	Jean Guy Gratton	RW	R	5-9	181	3/8/47	Winnipeg Jets (WHA)	73	15	12	27	37
	Jim Hargreaves	D	R	5-11	200	5/2/50	Vancouver Canucks (NHL)	67	1	10	11	85
							Seattle (WHL)	12			13	30
	Ted Hargreaves	C	L	5-11	180	11/4/43	Nels. Maple Leafs (WIHL)	48	20	37	57	70
	Larry Hornung	D	L	5-11	184	10/10/45	Winnipeg Jets (WHA)	77	13	45	58	28
	Bobby Hull	LW	L	5-11	191	1/3/39	Winnipeg Jets (WHA)	63	51	52	103	37
	Danny Johnson	LW	L	5-11	178	10/1/44	Winnipeg Jets (WHA)	76	19	23	42	17
	Ab McDonald	LW	L	6-2	194	2/18/36	Winnipeg Jets (WHA)	77	17	24	41	16
	Kelly Pratt	RW	R	5-8	175	2/8/53	S. C. Broncos (WCHL)	64	55	37	82	99
	Garth Rizzuto	LW	L	5-10	182	9/11/47	Winnipeg Jets (WHA)	61	10	10	20	32
	Dunc Rousseau	LW	L	6-0	197	2/10/45	Winnipeg Jets (WHA)	74	16	17	33	75
	John Shmyr	D	L	6-0	170	1/2/45	Winnipeg Jets (WHA)	7	0	0	0	2
	Ron Snell	RW	R	5-10	171	8/11/48	Hershey (AHL)	76	33	38	71	90
	Dan Spring	C	R	6-0	180	10/13/51	Dallas (CHL)	47	13	19	32	—
	Ken Stephenson	D	L	5-11	195	11/13/41	Ottawa Nationals (WHA)	78	3	16	19	91
	Cal Swenson	D	L	5-11	182	4/16/48	Winnipeg Jets (WHA)	78	7	22	29	19
	Bob Woytowich	D	R	5-11	196	8/18/41	Winnipeg Jets (WHA)	62	2	4	6	47
	Joe Zanussi	D	R	5-10	181	9/25/47	Winnipeg Jets (WHA)	73	4	21	25	53

No.	Goalies	Pos.	S	Ht.	Wt.	Birth Date	1972-73 Club	GP	GA	SO		AVG.
	Joe Daley	G	L	5-10	171	2/20/43	Winnipeg Jets (WHA)	29	83	2		2.90
	Ernie Wakely	G		5-11	171	11/27/40	Winnipeg Jets (WHA)	48	152	2		3.16

Playing Coach—Bobby Hull; General Manager—Annis Stukus; Assistant Coach—Nick Mickoski.

SPORTS CENTREPOINT ENTERPRISES INC.
15-1430 Maroons Road
Winnipeg, Manitoba, Canada R3G 0L5
(204) 772-9491

President and Trustee:
BEN HATSKIN

General Manager:
ANNIS STUKUS

Playing Coach:
BOBBY HULL

Assistant Coach:
NICK MICKOSKI

Director of Player Personnel:
BILL ROBINSON

Trainer:
DIARMID MCVICAR

Public Relations Director:
J. A. BOYD

HATSKIN

HULL

STUKUS

ARENA — Winnipeg Arena, 15-1430 Maroons Road, Winnipeg, Manitoba, Canada R3G 0L5. Capacity: 11,000.
TEAM COLORS — Blue with Red and White.
TELEVISION — none.
RADIO — All home and away games (CJOB). Play-by-play Ken Nicolson. Color Stu MacPherson.

29

YEAR ONE OF THE WHA

1972-73 Final Standings

EASTERN	GP	W	L	T	Pts	GF	GA	Pct.	HOME W-L-T	AWAY W-L-T
New England	78	46	30	2	94	318	263	.602	30- 8-1	16-22-1
Cleveland	78	43	32	3	89	287	239	.570	26-11-2	17-21-1
Philadelphia	78	38	40	0	76	288	305	.487	24-15-0	14-25-0
Ottawa	78	35	39	4	74	279	301	.474	21-15-3	14-24-1
Quebec	78	33	40	5	71	276	313	.455	22-12-5	11-28-0
New York	78	33	43	2	68	303	334	.435	23-15-1	10-28-1

WESTERN	GP	W	L	T	Pts	GF	GA	Pct.	HOME W-L-T	AWAY W-L-T
Winnipeg	78	43	31	4	90	285	249	.576	26-11-2	17-20-2
Houston	78	39	35	4	82	284	269	.525	22-16-1	17-19-3
Los Angeles	78	37	35	6	80	259	250	.512	18-20-1	19-15-5
Alberta	78	38	37	3	79	269	256	.506	25-12-2	13-25-1
Minnesota	78	38	37	3	79	250	269	.506	24-14-1	14-23-2
Chicago	78	26	50	2	54	245	295	.346	17-22-0	9-28-2

STANDINGS DIVISION-BY-DIVISION

EASTERN		Against Own Division							Against Other Division				
	W	L	T	Pts	GF	GA	Pct.	W	L	T	Pts	GF	GA	Pct.
New England Whalers	25	16	1	51	177	145	.607	21	14	1	43	141	118	.597
Cleveland Crusaders	24	16	2	50	166	134	.595	19	16	1	39	121	108	.541
Philadelphia Blazers	21	21	0	42	167	178	.500	17	19	0	34	121	127	.472
Ottawa Nationals	18	23	1	37	158	172	.440	17	16	3	37	121	126	.513
Quebec Nordiques	15	24	3	33	154	192	.392	18	16	2	38	122	121	.527
New York Raiders	19	22	1	39	167	168	.464	14	21	1	29	136	166	.402

	W	L	T	Pts	GF	GA	Pct.
EASTERN							
New England	27	12	3	57	153	100	.678
Cleveland	22	18	2	46	145	146	.547
Philadelphia	20	20	2	42	138	137	.500
Ottawa	21	18	3	45	152	135	.535
Quebec	17	22	3	37	124	146	.440
New York	12	29	1	25	114	162	.297
WESTERN							
Winnipeg Jets	16	19	1	33	132	149	.458
Houston Aeros	17	17	2	36	139	123	.500
Los Angeles Sharks	17	15	4	38	121	113	.527
Alberta Oilers	17	19	0	34	117	121	.472
Minnesota Saints	21	15	1	42	126	123	.583
Chicago Cougars	14	21	1	29	131	133	.402

WON-LOST-TIED RECORDS CLUB BY CLUB

	N.E.	Cle.	Phil.	Ott.	Que.	N.Y.	Win.	Hou.	L.A.	Alb.	Minn.	Chi.
EASTERN												
New England	—	5-3-0	4-4-0	5-3-0	4-3-1	7-3-0	5-1-0	2-3-1	3-3-0	3-3-0	3-3-0	5-1-0
Cleveland	3-5-0	—	6-4-0	4-3-1	5-2-1	6-2-0	3-3-0	3-3-0	3-2-1	4-2-0	2-4-0	4-2-0
Philadelphia	4-4-0	4-6-0	—	5-3-0	4-4-0	4-4-0	3-3-0	2-4-0	4-2-0	3-3-0	2-4-0	3-3-0
Ottawa	3-5-0	3-4-1	3-5-0	—	7-3-0	2-6-0	4-2-0	1-4-1	2-2-2	3-3-0	3-3-0	4-2-0
Quebec	3-4-1	2-5-1	4-4-0	3-7-0	—	3-4-1	2-3-1	5-1-0	2-3-1	3-3-0	3-3-0	3-3-0
New York	3-7-0	2-6-0	4-4-0	6-2-0	4-3-1	—	2-4-0	4-2-0	1-5-0	3-3-0	2-4-0	2-3-1
WESTERN												
Winnipeg	1-5-0	3-3-0	3-3-0	2-4-0	3-2-1	4-2-0	—	6-2-0	8-0-0	3-5-2	4-3-1	6-2-0
Houston	3-2-1	3-3-0	4-2-0	4-1-0	1-5-0	2-4-0	2-6-0	—	3-6-1	5-3-0	5-2-1	7-1-0
Los Angeles	3-3-0	2-3-1	2-4-0	2-2-2	3-2-1	5-1-0	0-8-0	6-3-1	—	3-5-0	5-2-1	6-2-0
Alberta	3-3-0	2-4-0	3-3-0	3-3-0	3-3-0	3-3-0	5-3-2	3-5-0	5-3-0	—	4-4-0	4-3-1
Minnesota	3-3-0	4-2-0	4-2-0	3-3-0	4-2-0	4-2-0	3-4-1	2-5-1	2-5-1	4-4-0	—	6-4-0
Chicago	1-5-0	2-4-0	3-3-0	2-4-0	3-3-0	3-2-1	2-6-0	1-7-0	2-6-0	3-4-1	4-6-0	—

INDIVIDUAL SCORING
(The Top 50)

Player, Team	GP	G	A	Pts	PIM	WG	PP	SH
Andre Lacroix, Philadelphia	78	50	74	124	83	11	16	0
Ron Ward, New York	77	51	67	118	28	5	12	1
Danny Lawson, Philadelphia	78	61	45	106	35	6	20	3
Tom Webster, New England	77	53	50	103	89	6	12	0
Bobby Hull, Winnipeg	63	51	52	103	37	7	15	2
Norm Beaudin, Winnipeg	78	38	65	103	15	5	5	0
Chris Bordeleau, Winnipeg	78	47	54	101	12	7	6	3
Terry Caffery, New England	74	39	61	100	14	7	9	1
Gordon Labossiere, Houston	77	36	60	96	56	1	10	0
Wayne Carleton, Ottawa	75	42	49	91	42	4	6	1
J. C. Tremblay, Quebec	76	14	75	89	32	3	5	0
Bobby Sheehan, New York	75	35	53	88	17	5	18	0
Bobby Sicinski, Chicago	77	25	63	88	18	2	7	1
Jim Harrison, Alberta	66	39	47	86	93	6	8	6
Larry Pleau, New England	78	39	48	87	42	4	10	0
Ron Buchanan, Cleveland	75	37	44	81	20	5	6	0
Gary Jarrett, Cleveland	77	40	39	79	79	7	8	0
John McKenzie, Philadelphia	60	28	50	78	157	7	8	1
Wayne Rivers, New York	75	37	40	77	47	4	4	0
Ted Taylor, Houston	72	34	42	76	103	4	5	1
Gary Veneruzzo, Los Angeles	78	43	30	73	34	5	12	0
Bryan Campbell, Philadelphia	75	25	48	73	85	1	6	0
Michel Parizeau, Quebec	75	25	48	73	50	4	10	1
Don Herriman, Philadelphia	78	24	48	72	63	4	9	0
Gene Peacosh, New York	67	37	34	71	25	3	10	1
Tim Sheehy, New England	78	33	38	71	25	4	4	0
Jim Wiste, Cleveland	70	28	43	71	24	3	4	0
Andre Gaudette, Quebec	78	27	44	71	12	3	0	5
Wayne Connelly, Minnesota	78	40	30	70	16	6	10	0
Murray Hall, Houston	76	28	42	70	84	7	7	2
Rosaire Paiement, Chicago	78	33	36	69	135	4	5	0
J. P. LeBlanc, Los Angeles	77	19	50	69	49	3	2	1
Norm Ferguson, New York	56	28	40	68	8	5	8	1
Gavin Kirk, Ottawa	78	28	40	68	54	2	5	0
Reggie Fleming, Chicago	75	23	45	68	93	2	7	1
Gerry Pinder, Cleveland	78	30	36	66	121	3	7	3
Larry Lund, Houston	77	21	45	66	120	2	4	0
Jan Popiel, Chicago	76	31	34	65	77	4	6	0
Poul Popiel, Houston	73	16	48	64	158	2	5	0
Alain Caron, Quebec	68	36	27	63	14	5	15	0
Bob Charlebois, Ottawa	78	24	40	64	28	5	5	1
Jim Dorey, New England	75	7	56	63	95	1	0	1
Ted Hampson, Minnesota	77	17	45	62	20	2	4	0
Al Hamilton, Alberta	78	11	50	61	124	1	3	1
John French, New England	74	24	35	59	43	3	2	0
Billy Klatt, Minnesota	78	36	22	58	22	5	12	0
Guy Trottier, Ottawa	72	26	32	58	25	1	10	0
Ross Perkins, Alberta	71	21	37	58	19	2	5	0
Larry Hornung, Winnipeg	77	13	45	58	28	2	5	2
Ken Block, New York	78	5	53	58	43	1	0	1

THOSE WITH THE MOST

MOST GOALS

Danny Lawson, Philadelphia	61
Tom Webster, New England	53
Bobby Hull, Winnipeg	51
Ron Ward, New York	51
Andre Lacroix, Philadelphia	50
Chris Bordeleau, Winnipeg	47
Gary Veneruzzo, Los Angeles	43
Wayne Carleton, Ottawa	42
Wayne Connelly, Minnesota	40
Gary Jarrett, Cleveland	40

MOST ASSISTS

J. C. Tremblay, Quebec	75
Andre Lacroix, Philadelphia	74
Ron Ward, New York	67
Norm Beaudin, Winnipeg	65
Bobby Sicinski, Chicago	63
Terry Caffery, New England	61
Gordon Labossiere, Houston	60
Jim Dorey, New England	56
Chris Bordeleau, Winnipeg	54
Ken Block, New York	53
Bobby Sheehan, New York	53

MOST PENALTY MINUTES

John Schella, Houston	239
Tom Gilmore, Los Angeles	191
Dick Paradise, Minnesota	189
John Arbour, Minnesota	188
Jim Cardiff, Philadelphia	185
Paul Shmyr, Cleveland	169
Pierre Roy, Quebec	167
Hal Willis, New York	159
Poul Popiel, Houston	158
John McKenzie, Philadelphia	157
Mike Rouleau, Quebec	157

MOST GAME-WINNING GOALS: 1—Andre Lacroix, Philadelphia 11; 2. Bobby Hull, Winnipeg; Chris Bordeleau, Winnipeg; Terry Caffery, New England; Gary Jarrett, Cleveland, and John McKenzie, Philadelphia, Murray Hall, Houston all tied with 7.   © 2018 WHA HOF / PCMP LLC

MOST POWER GOALS: 1—Danny Lawson, Philadelphia, 20; 2. Bobby Sheehan, New York, 18; 3. Andre Lacroix, Philadelphia, 16.

MOST SHORTHANDED GOALS: 1—Jim Harrison, Alberta, Bob Dillabough, Cleveland, and Terry Ryan, Minnesota, all tied with 6.

GOALTENDING STATISTICS
(Final Official)

	GPI	MIN.	W	L	T	Pct.	SOG	GA	SVS	GAA	EN	SA%	GAF	SG	SP
CLEVELAND															
Gerry Cheevers	78	4753	43	32	3	.570	2581	237	2344	2.98	2	.908	10.89	5	90
Bob Whidden	52	3144	32	20	0	.615	1695	149	1546	2.83	2	.912	11.37	5	64
	26	1609	11	12	3	.480	886	88	798	3.28	0	.900	10.06	0	26
WINNIPEG															
Joe Daley	78	4750	43	31	4	.576	2252	245	2007	3.09	4	.891	9.19	4	96
Ernie Wakely	29	1718	17	10	1	.625	776	83	693	2.89	2	.893	9.34	2	35
Gordon Tumilson	49	2894	26	19	3	.572	1411	152	1259	3.15	2	.892	9.28	2	60
	3	138	0	2	0	.000	65	10	55	4.34	0	.846	6.50	0	1
LOS ANGELES															
Bob Perreault	78	4765	37	35	6	.512	2106	247	1859	3.11	3	.882	8.52	3	88
Russ Gillow	1	60	1	0	0	1.000	17	2	15	2.00	0	.882	8.50	0	1
George Gardner	38	1982	17	13	2	.562	851	96	755	2.88	3	.887	8.86	2	36
	49	2713	19	22	4	.466	1238	149	1089	3.29	3	.879	8.30	1	51
ALBERTA															
Jack Norris	78	4739	38	37	3	.506	2487	252	2235	3.19	4	.898	9.86	2	89
Ken Brown	64	3705	28	29	3	.491	1947	189	1758	3.06	3	.902	10.30	1	71
	20	1034	10	8	0	.555	540	63	477	3.65	1	.883	8.57	1	18
MINNESOTA															
Carl Wetzel	78	4760	38	37	3	.506	2653	263	2390	3.31	6	.900	10.08	5	96
Mike Curran	1	60	0	1	0	.000	35	3	32	3.00	0	.914	11.66	—	1
Jack McCartan	44	2540	23	17	2	.571	1437	131	1306	3.09	3	.908	10.69	4	53
	38	2160	15	19	1	.442	1181	129	1052	3.58	3	.890	9.15	1	42
NEW ENGLAND															
Al Smith	78	4730	46	30	2	.602	2423	262	2161	3.32	1	.891	9.24	4	80
Bruce Landon	51	3059	31	19	1	.617	1535	162	1373	3.17	1	.894	9.47	3	54
	30	1671	15	11	1	.574	888	100	788	3.59	0	.887	8.88	1	26
HOUSTON															
Wayne Rutledge	78	4743	39	35	4	.525	2510	264	2246	3.33	5	.894	9.50	1	77
Don McLeod	37	2223	21	14	2	.594	1192	110	1082	2.96	3	.907	10.83	0	41
Bill Hughes	40	2350	18	20	1	.474	1230	143	1087	3.65	1	.883	8.60	1	33
	3	170	0	1	1	.250	88	11	77	3.88	1	.875	8.00	0	3

GOALTENDING STATISTICS
(Final Official)

	GPI	MIN.	W	L	T	Pct.	SOG	GA	SVS	GAA	EN	SA%	GAF	SG	SP
CHICAGO															
Jim McLeod	78	4750	26	50	2	.346	2747	289	2458	3.65	6	.894	9.50	1	77
Andre Gill	54	2996	22	25	2	.469	1742	166	1576	3.32	4	.904	10.49	1	55
Paul Menard	33	1709	4	24	0	.142	982	118	864	4.14	2	.879	8.32	0	22
	1	45	0	1	0	.000	23	5	18	6.66	0	.782	4.60	0	0
OTTAWA															
Gilles Gratton	78	4758	35	39	4	.474	2508	296	2212	3.74	5	.881	8.47	0	71
Les Binkley	51	3021	25	22	3	.530	1591	187	1404	3.71	4	.882	8.50	0	45
Frank Blum	30	1709	10	17	1	.375	930	106	794	3.72	1	.882	8.49	0	26
	2	28	0	0	0	.000	17	3	14	6.42	0	.823	5.66	0	0
PHILADELPHIA															
Danny Sullivan	78	4706	38	40	0	.487	2534	297	2237	3.78	8	.882	8.53	2	72
Bernie Parent	1	60	1	0	0	1.000	34	3	31	3.00	0	.912	11.33	0	0
Yves Archambault	63	3653	33	28	0	.540	1936	220	1716	3.61	2	.886	8.80	2	61
Tom Cottringer	6	260	1	3	0	.250	122	17	105	3.92	5	.861	7.18	0	2
Marcel Paille	2	122	1	1	0	.500	65	8	57	3.93	0	.877	8.13	0	2
	15	611	2	8	0	.200	377	49	328	4.81	3	.865	7.69	0	7
QUEBEC															
Serge Aubry	78	4758	33	40	5	.455	2713	313	2400	3.94	0	.884	8.66	2	67
Jacques Lemelin	52	3036	25	22	3	.530	1781	182	1599	3.59	0	.897	9.78	2	47
Richard Brodeur	9	434	3	4	0	.429	99	29	170	4.00	0	.854	6.86	0	6
	24	1288	5	14	2	.285	733	102	631	4.75	0	.860	7.18	0	14
NEW YORK															
Peter Donnelly	78	4740	33	43	2	.435	2534	332	2202	4.20	2	.868	7.63	2	66
Gary Kurt	47	2606	22	19	2	.534	1328	155	1173	3.56	0	.883	8.56	2	44
Ian Wilkie	36	1881	10	21	0	.322	1034	150	884	4.78	1	.854	6.89	0	21
	5	253	1	3	0	.250	172	27	145	6.40	0	.843	6.35	0	1

KEY TO GOALTENDING ABBREVIATIONS: GPI—Games Played In. MIN.—Minutes Played. W—Games Won. L—Games Lost. T—Games Tied. PCT.—Percentage. SOG—Shots on Goal. GA—Goals Against. SVS—Saves. GAA—Goals Against Average for 60 Minutes. EN—Empty Net Goals. SA%—Save Percentage. GAF—Goals Allowed Frequency (Number of Shots for Each Goal Allowed). SG—Shutout Games. SP—Shutout Periods.

THREE-GOAL NIGHTS

Date	Player	Team	Opp.	Final Score	Elapsed Time	Opp. Goalie	Shots Taken	WHA Game #	Three Goal Game #	H or R
10/15/72	Hardy	Clev.	Otwa.	Clev.-7 Otwa.-5	32:20	Gratton	5	14	1	
10/18/72	Webster	N.E.	Hstn.	N.E.-4 Hstn.-1	42:46	Rutledye	5	22	1	R
10/19/72	Labossiere	Hstn.	Minn.	Hstn.-5 Minn.-1	30:34	McCarten	4	23	1	R
10/20/72	Walters	Alb.	Phil.	Alb.-4 Phil.-1	54:10	Parent	6	28	1	H
10/25/72	Hodgson	Clev.	Phil.	Clev.-8 Phil.-2	46:14	Parent	6	43	1	R
10/26/72	Rivers	N.Y.	N.E.	N.Y.-7 N.E.-6	39:50	Smith	8	44	1	
10/28/72	Martin	Otwa.	Phil.	Otwa.-5 Phil.-3	29:06	Archambault	5	50	1	H
11/6/72	Webster	N.E.	Wpg.	N.E.-8 Wpg.-2	45:19	Wakely	5	75	2	
11/11/72	Pinder	Clev.	Chi.	Clev.-4 Chi.-1	36:31	Gill	12	86	1	H
11/15/72	Caron	Que.	N.Y.	Que.-7 N.Y.-4	40:37	Donnelly	8	94	1	H
11/29/72	Ward	N.Y.	N.E.	N.Y.-7 N.E.-6	6:44	Smith	9	136	1	
12/2/72	Veneruzzo	L.A.	Chi.	L.A.-4 Chi.-2	56:45	McLeod & Gill	3	148	1	H
12/3/72	Carleton	Otwa.	Hstn.	Otwa.-5 Hstn.-4	41:44	McLeod	10	150	1	R
12/5/72	Peacosh	N.Y.	Hstn.	N.Y.-6 Hstn.-4	36:34	McLeod	4	154	1	
12/6/72	Gratton	Wpg.	Chi.	Wpg.-7 Chi.-1	27:12	Gill	3	159	1	H
12/10/72	Byers	L.A.	Alb.	L.A.-5 Alb.-3	16:09	Norriss	5	173	1	H
12/12/72	Gaudette	Que.	Phil.	Que.-5 Phil.-2	55:00	Parent	5	177	1	H
12/13/72	Popiel	Chi.	N.E.	Chi.-6 N.E.-3	33:23	Landon	5	179	1	
12/13/72	Sheehan	N.Y.	Que.	N.Y.-9 Que.-1	37:20	Lemelin & Brodner	4	180	1	
12/17/72	Herriman	Phil.	N.E.	Phil.-6 N.E.-3	19:44	Smith	6	193	1	H
12/23/72	Grierson	Hstn.	Phil.	Hstn.-7 Phil.-3	32:09	McLeod	3	212	1	R
12/24/72	Pleau	N.E.	L.A.	N.E.-5 L.A.-3	51:19	Gardner	8	214	1	
12/26/72	Lawson	Phil.	Minn.	Phil.-6 Minn.-2	49:58	McCarten	11	219	1	
1/1/73	Perkins	Alb.	Wpg.	Alb.-7 Wpg.-3	17:07	Wakely	6	235	1	R
1/9/73	Labossiere	Hstn.	N.E.	Hstn.-7 N.E.-5	47:45	Smith	5	240	2	
1/10/73	White	L.A.	Chi.	L.A.-8 Chi.-5	6:58	McLeod	4	242	1	R

THREE-GOAL NIGHTS

Date	Player	Team	Opp.	Final Score	Elapsed Time	Opp. Goalie	Shots Taken	WHA Game #	Three Goal Game #	H or R
1/10/73	Morris	Chi.	L.A.	L.A.-8 Chi.-5	27:02	Gillow	4	242	1	H
1/13/73	Lawson	Phil.	Que.	Phil.-9 Que.-4	44:29	Brodeur	7	251	2	H
1/20/73	Antonovich	Minn.	Que.	Minn.-10 Que.-5	57:48	Aubry	4	271	1	
1/23/73	Paiement	Chi.	Que.	Chi.-7 Que.-1	37:18	Brodeur-2 Lemelin-1				R
1/24/73	McKenzie	Phil.	Que.	Phil.-6 Que.-4	33:21	Aubry	8	279	1	H
1/25/73	Lodboa	Chi.	N.Y.	Chi.-9 N.Y.-2	52:45	Kurt-1 & Donnelly-2	8	283	1	R
1/30/73	Harrison	Alb.	N.Y.	Alb.-11 N.Y.-3	47:45	Wilkie	6	286	1	H
2/1/73	Selby	N.E.	Hstn.	N.E.-5 Hstn.-4	59:01	Rutledge	10	299	1	H
2/4/73	Hull	Wpg.	Alb.	Wpg.-5 Alb.-3	9:00	Norris	3	306	1	R
2/16/73	McKenzie	Phil.	N.Y.	Phil.-9 N.Y.-2	15:53	Donnelly	4	315	2	R
2/25/73	Beaudin	Wpg.	Phil.	Wpg.-5 Phil.-3	15:59	Parent	3	352	1	
2/25/73	Rivers	N.Y.	Clev.	N.Y.-9 Clev.-5	29:23	Cheevers	5	370	2	H
2/25/73	Peacosh	N.Y.	Clev.	N.Y.-9 Clev.-5	35:57	Cheevers	9	371	2	H
3/9/73	White	L.A.	Minn.	L.A.-4 Minn.-1	30:09	McCarten	7	371	2	H
3/9/73	Gilmore	L.A.	Hstn.	L.A.-5 Hstn.-1	50:37	Rutledge	2*	381	1	R
3/9/73	Lacroix	Phil.	Que.	Phil.-11 Que.-3	54:03	Aubry-2 Brodeur-1	6	400	1	H
3/11/73	Buchanen	Clev.	Wpg.	Clev.-11 Wpg.-2	37:05	Wakely	9	402	1	H
3/12/73	Fleming	Chi.	N.Y.	N.Y.-8 Chi.-7	29:39	Kurt	4	410	1	R
3/14/73	Hull	Wpg.	N.E.	N.E.-7 Wpg.-5	33:49	Landon	5	411	2	R
3/21/73	Lacroix	Phil.	Hstn.	Hstn.-7 Phil.-3	35:23	McLeod	7	417	2	H
3/29/73	Kirk	Otwa.	N.E.	Otwa.-5 N.E.-2	32:16	Smith	5	435	1	R
3/29/73	Hull	Hstn.	N.Y.	Hstn.-5 N.Y.-3	44:03	Kurt	6	457	2	
3/30/73	Caffery	N.E.	N.Y.	N.E.-5 N.Y.-4	54:34	Kurt	8	458	1	H
3/31/73	Lawson	Phil.	Chi.	Phil.-5 Chi.-1	13:26	Gill	3	461	3	H
4/1/73	Taylor	Hstn.	Otwa.	Hstn.-6 Otwa.-3	26:36	Gratton	5	464	1	
4/1/73	Webster	N.E.	Que.	N.E.-8 Que.-3	29:14	Brodeur	3	465	3	H
							8	467	3	

*Third goal awarded when stick was thrown from Minnesota Bench. White had a breakaway on an open net.

FOUR-GOAL NIGHTS

Date	Player	Team	Opp.	Final Score	Opp. Goalie	Elapsed Time	Shots Taken	WHA Game #	Four Goal Number	H or R
10/12/72	Bordeleau	Wpg.	N.Y.	Wpg.-6 N.Y.-4	Kurt	46:39	7	3	1	R
11/1/72	Lawson	Phil.	Clev.	Phil.-7 Clev.-5	Cheevers	41:22	6	60	1	R
11/16/72	Buchanan	Clev.	Otwa.	Clev.-6 Otwa.-3	Binkley	33:43	6	97	1	H
12/19/72	McDonald	Hstn.	L.A.	Hstn.-7 L.A.-5	Gillow	19:22	6	201	1	H
12/20/72	Lawson	Phil.	Chi.	Phil.-8 Chi.-5	Gill (Last Goal Eng)	54:28	7	202	(2)	H
1/13/73	Lacroix	Phil.	Que.	Phil.-9 Que.-4	Brodeur	31:05	8	251	1	H
2/13/73	Lawson	Phil.	N.E.	Phil.-5 N.E.-4	Smith	24:29	5	345	(3)	H
2/15/73	Hull	Wpg.	Chi.	Wpg.-7 Chi.-2	McLeod	47:29	12	350	1	R
3/16/73	Martin	Otwa.	Wpg.	Otwa.-6 Wpg.-1	Wakely	50:38	8	421	1	R

FIVE-GOAL NIGHT

Date	Player	Team	Opp.	Final Score	Opp. Goalie	Elapsed Time	Shots Taken	WHA Game #
1/4/73	Ward	N.Y.	Otwa.	N.Y.-9 Otwa.-4	Gratton	25:55	12	236

ATTENDANCE BREAKDOWN
1972-1973

CLUB	ATTENDANCE	(39 Games) AVERAGE
NEW ENGLAND	272,255	6,981
QUEBEC	269,979	6,923
WINNIPEG	237,982	6,102
LOS ANGELES	233,285	5,982
NEW YORK	228,857	5,868
MINNESOTA	228,360	5,855
CLEVELAND	206,202	5,287
HOUSTON	180,037	4,616
CHICAGO	178,960	4,589
PHILADELPHIA	168,680	4,325
ALBERTA	150,089	3,848
OTTAWA	125,802	3,226
GAMES: 468	2,479,679	5,298

PLAYOFF GAMES

GAMES: 31	215,092	6,938
TOTAL LEAGUE & PLAYOFF: 499	2,694,771	5,400

DECISION RATIO

1—Goal Decisions	— 139	29.7%	
2—Goal Decisions	— 137	29.2%	
2—Goal that had ENG	— 38	8.1%	
Readjusted 1 Goal	— (177	37.8%)	—If there had been no ENG
3—Goal Decisions	— 78	16.6%	
3—Goal with ENG	— 8	1.7%	
Readjusted 2 Goal	— (99	21.1%)	—If there had been no ENG
4—Goal Decisions	— 42	8.9%	
5—Goal Decisions	— 28	5.9%	
6—Goal Decisions	— 13	2.7%	
7—Goal Decisions	— 5	1.0%	
8—Goal Decisions	— 6	1.2%	
9—Goal Decisions	— 1	.2%	
TIES	— 38	8.1%	

39

Bobby Hull   Andre Lacroix   Danny Lawson

First Team

Pos.	Player, Team	Ht.	Wt.	Hometown
G	Gerry Cheevers, Cleveland	5-11	185	St. Catherines, Ont.
D	J. C. Tremblay, Quebec	5-10	178	Bagotville, Que.
D	Paul Shmyr, Cleveland	5-10	170	Cudworth, Sask. *
LW	Bobby Hull, Winnipeg	5-10	170	Point Anne, Ont.
C	Andre Lacroix, Philadelphia	5-8	175	Lauzon, Que.
RW	Danny Lawson, Philadelphia	5-11	185	Toronto, Ont.

Individual Awards

GARY L. DAVIDSON TROPHY
   (Most Valuable Player) ....BOBBY HULL

W. D. (BILL) HUNTER TROPHY
   (Scoring Champion) ....ANDRE LACROIX

LOU KAPLAN AWARD
   (Rookie of the Year) ....TERRY CAFFERY

BEN HATSKIN TROPHY
   (Best Goaltender) ....GERRY CHEEVERS

DENNIS A. MURPHY AWARD
   (Best Defenseman) ....J. C. TREMBLAY

PAUL DENEAU AWARD
   (Most Sportsmanlike Player) ....Unselected

HOWARD BALDWIN AWARD
   (Coach of the Year) ....JACK KELLEY

Gerry Cheevers   Paul Shmyr   J. C. Tremblay

Second Team

Pos.	Player, Team	Ht.	Wt.	Hometown
G	Bernie Parent, Philadelphia	5-10	170	Montreal, Que.
D	Jim Dorey, New England	6-1	192	Kingston, Ont.
D	Larry Hornung, Winnipeg	6-0	190	Weyburn, Sask.
LW	Gary Jarrett, Cleveland	5-8	180	Toronto, Ont.
C	Ron Ward, New York	5-11	175	Cornwall, Ont.
RW	Tom Webster, New England	5-9	169	Kirkland Lake, Ont.

Third Team

G — **AL SMITH**
New England
D — **RICK LEY**
New England
TED GREEN
New England
LW — **WAYNE CARLETON**
Ottawa
C — **CHRIS BORDELEAU**
Winnipeg
RW — **NORM BEAUDIN**
Winnipeg

Gary Jarrett   Ron Ward   Tom Webster

Larry Hornung   Jim Dorey   Bernie Parent

41

WHA FIRST ANNUAL ALL-STAR GAME
JAN. 6/72 QUEBEC CITY, QUEBEC

(Players selected by vote of league coaches)

EAST LINEUP

GOALTENDERS
 Al Smith, New England; Gerry Cheevers, Cleveland; Serge Aubry, Quebec;

DEFENSEMEN
 Rick Ley, New England; J. C. Tremblay, Quebec; Paul Shymr, Cleveland; Jim Dorey, New England; Gary Jarrett, Cleveland; Ken Block, New York;

FORWARDS
 Larry Pleau, New England; Ron Ward, New York; Bobby Sheehan, New York; Wayne Carleton, Ottawa; Gerry Pinder, Cleveland; Michel Parizeau, Quebec; Tom Webster, New England; Danny Lawson, Philadelphia; Norm Ferguson, New York; John McKenzie, Philadelphia. *Ron Climie, Ottawa; John Hanna, Cleveland. **Guy Trottier, Ottawa.

COACH
 Jack Kelley, New England. *—Did not appear due to injury. **—Replaced Ron Climie.

WEST LINEUP

GOALTENDERS
 Mike Curran, Minnesota; Ernie Wakely, Winnipeg; Jack Norris, Alberta;

DEFENSEMEN
 Al Hamilton, Alberta; Larry Hornung, Winnipeg; Gerry Odrowski, Los Angeles; Terry Ball, Minnesota;

FORWARDS
 Bobby Hull, Winnipeg; Chris Bordeleau, Winnipeg; Norm Beaudin, Winnipeg; Gary Veneruzzo, Los Angeles; Ron Anderson, Alberta; Bob Wall, Alberta; Wayne Connelly, Minnesota; Ted Hampson, Minnesota; Mike Byers, Los Angeles; Jim Harrison, Alberta; Ted Taylor, Houston; Gordon Labossiere, Houston; Jan Popiel, Chicago.

COACH
 Bobby Hull, Winnipeg. Assisted by Nick Mickoski, Winnipeg.
 *—Did not appear due to injury.

SCORE—EAST 6, WEST 2

FIRST PERIOD
1. West, Odrowski (Beaudin) 10:39
2. East, Jarrett (Ward) 10:51
 Penalties—Pleau (E) holding 4:43, Hanna (E) hooking 12:09, Harrison (W) tripping 19:23.

SECOND PERIOD
3. East, McKenzie (Carleton, Block) 3:37
4. East, Pleau (Webster, Caffery) 12:47
5. East, Dorey (Ward, Lawson) 19:43
 Penalties—none.

THIRD PERIOD
6. West, Hull (Connelly, Bordeleau) 3:05
7. East, Lawson (Jarrett, Tremblay) 7:29
8. East, Carleton (Charlebois, Dorey) 8:00
 Penalties—none.

SHOTS ON GOAL
West 18   14   15—47
East 8   13   12—33

GOALTENDERS: West—Wakely (first period), Norris (second period), Curran (third period). East—Cheevers (30 minutes), Smith (30 minutes).

REFEREE—Bill Friday. LINESMEN—Pierre Belanger, Ron Asselstine.

WINNING GOAL—Larry Pleau.

Attn. 5,435. (Two below zero/home television)

Distinction of scoring first World Hockey Association All-Star Game goal went to Los Angeles' Gerry Odrowski.

OVERTIME BREAKDOWN

	Total	Home	Road	East	West	Total Time	Avg. Time	Deci. Only Avg. Time
New England	5- 0- 2	2- 0- 1	3- 0- 1	3- 0- 1	2- 0- 1	50:34	7:13	6:07
Cleveland	5- 5- 3	4- 3- 2	1- 2- 1	2- 2- 2	3- 3- 1	76:20	5:52	4:38
Philadelphia	4- 3- 0	2- 2- 0	2- 1- 0	2- 1- 0	2- 2- 0	25:57	3:42	3:42
Ottawa	3- 3- 4	3- 1- 3	0- 2- 1	1- 2- 1	2- 1- 3	58:37	5:52	4:48
Quebec	2- 3- 5	1- 0- 5	1- 3- 0	2- 2- 3	0- 1- 2	73:33	7:21	4:43
New York	3- 4- 2	1- 2- 1	2- 2- 1	0- 3- 1	3- 1- 1	59:50	6:39	5:41
East Total	22-18-16	13- 8-12	9-10- 4	10-10- 8	12- 8- 8	344:51	6:10	4:37
Winnipeg	3- 4- 4	0- 0- 2	3- 4- 2	1- 2- 1	2- 2- 3	67:23	6:08	3:55
Houston	2- 4- 4	2- 2- 1	0- 2- 3	0- 4- 2	2- 0- 2	63:30	6:21	3:55
Los Angeles	4- 4- 6	1- 2- 1	3- 2- 5	2- 2- 4	2- 2- 2	95:03	6:47	4:23
Minnesota	7- 4- 3	4- 2- 1	3- 2- 2	4- 1- 0	3- 3- 3	81:56	5:51	4:43
Alberta	4- 5- 3	2- 1- 2	2- 4- 1	0- 2- 0	4- 3- 3	58:11	4:51	3:08
Chicago	3- 6- 2	2- 6- 0	1- 0- 2	1- 1- 1	2- 5- 1	69:07	6:17	5:27
West Total	23-27-22	11-13- 7	12-14-15	8-12- 8	15-15-14	435:10	6:03	4:18
WHA League Total	45-45-38	24-21-19	21-24-19	18-22-16	27-23-22	780:01	6:06	4:27

64 Games in overtime
45 Decisions
19 Ties

6:06 — Average time of overtime games
4:27 — Average time of decision in overtime games

44

TIME SPENT IN OVERTIME GAMES

Overtime Period Played	EAST						WEST					
	N.E.	Phil.	N.Y.	Otwa.	Clev.	Que.	Wpg.	Minn.	L.A.	Chi.	Hstn.	Alb.
1	5:27	1:23	6:09	10:00	6:09	10:00	4:53	10:00	1:56	10:00	10:00	4:53
2	10:00	1:59	1:56	1:11	5:27	0:23	10:00	1:23	10:00	9:27	4:03	10:00
3	2:43	0:30	2:35	4:32	10:00	2:35	4:03	6:42	9:27	7:01	4:32	6:42
4	10:00	2:38	10:00	0:23	4:44	0:48	10:00	1:11	4:44	4:10	10:00	1:59
5	7:57	5:45	9:41	10:00	0:30	10:00	3:15	7:01	10:00	10:00	10:00	10:00
6	6:57	9:42	10:00	10:00	3:15	10:00	0:29	4:10	10:00	4:00	6:06	1:06
7	7:30	4:00	7:41	5:58	2:29	9:42	10:00	2:29	10:00	5:04	10:00	2:38
8			4:18	0:48	6:06	10:00	6:07	10:00	1:57	2:36	2:43	1:48
9			7:30	5:45	0:29	10:00	7:41	10:00	1:06	6:57	1:48	1:25
10				10:00	10:00	10:00	10:00	1:57	9:41	9:57	4:18	5:04
11					7:57	1:05	0:55	5:58	6:07	0:55		2:36
12					10:00			1:25	10:00			10:00
13					9:43			9:57	1:05			
14								9:43	10:00			
Total Time	50:34	25:57	59:50	58:37	76:20	73:33	67:23	81:56	95:03	69:07	63:30	58:11
Avg. Time	7:13	3:42	6:39	5:52	5:52	7:21	6:08	5:51	6:47	6:17	6:21	4:51
Total Time of Decisions	30:34	25:57	39:50	18:37	46:20	23:33	27:23	51:56	35:03	49:07	23:30	28:11
Avg. Decision Time	6:07	3:42	5:41	3:06	4:38	4:43	3:55	4:43	4:23	5:27	3:55	3:08

Overtime Period Played

TEAM-BY-TEAM SCORING

CHICAGO COUGARS

Player	GP	G	A	Pts	PIM
B. Sicinski	77	25	63	88	18
R. Paiement	78	33	36	69	135
R. Fleming	75	23	45	68	93
J. Popiel	76	31	34	65	77
B. Whitlock	75	23	28	51	53
a) L. Mavety	67	9	40	49	73
R. Morris	76	31	17	48	84
D. Lodboa	58	15	18	33	16
B. Liddington	78	20	11	31	24
R. Anderson	74	3	26	29	34
B. Barber	75	4	19	23	39
b) J. Benzelock	43	9	12	21	23
D. Proceviat	53	4	14	18	33
R. Zaine	74	3	14	17	25
c) D. Sarrazin	33	3	8	11	2
D. Knibbs	41	3	8	11	0
L. Cahan	75	1	10	11	44
B. Glenwright	50	2	5	7	0
d) B. Blanchette	24	2	3	5	8
E. Hatoum	15	1	1	2	2
J. McLeod	54	0	1	1	2
P. Menard	1	0	0	0	0
J. Troolen	2	0	0	0	0
P. Viau	4	0	0	0	0
D. McGlynn	30	0	0	0	12
A. Gill	33	0	0	0	6
Cougar Totals	78	245	413	658	811

a—Also played 2 games with Los Angeles and 4 games with Philadelphia. b—Also played 26 games with Edmonton. c—Also played 35 games with New England. d—Also played 23 games with Edmonton.

KEY TO SCORING ABBREVIATIONS: GP—Games Played. G—Goals. A—Assists. Pts—Points. PIM—Penalty Minutes.

CLEVELAND CRUSADERS

Player	GP	G	A	Pts	PIM
R. Buchanan	75	37	44	81	20
G. Jarrett	77	40	39	79	79
J. Wiste	70	28	43	71	24
G. Pinder	78	30	36	66	21
P. Andrea	66	21	30	51	12
J. Hardy	72	17	33	50	80
P. Shmyr	73	5	43	48	169
R. Clearwater	78	11	36	47	41
G. Erickson	77	15	29	44	23
R. Pumple	77	21	20	41	45
T. Hodgson	74	15	23	38	93
D. Brindley	73	15	11	26	6
J. Hanna	66	6	20	26	68
S. Krake	26	9	10	19	61
B. Horton	74	2	17	19	55
B. Dillabough	72	8	8	16	8
W. Muloin	67	2	13	15	62
R. Hopiavuori	29	4	5	9	44
J. McMasters	74	1	7	8	37
A. Rycroft	7	0	2	2	0
G. Cheevers	52	0	1	1	30
B. Widden	26	0	0	0	5
Crusader Totals	78	287	470	757	1095

EDMONTON OILERS

Player	GP	G	A	Pts	PIM
J. Harrison	66	39	47	86	93
A. Hamilton	78	11	50	61	124
R. Perkins	71	21	37	58	19
R. Patenaude	77	29	27	56	59
R. Walters	78	28	26	54	37
B. Wall	78	16	29	45	20
V. Fonteyne	77	7	32	39	2
E. Joyal	71	22	16	38	16
B. Hicke	73	14	24	38	20
B. Carlin	65	12	22	34	6
D. Barrie	54	9	22	31	111
R. Anderson	73	14	15	29	43
K. Baird	75	14	15	29	112
B. Falkenberg	76	6	23	29	44
S. Carlyle	67	7	10	17	35
D. Kassian	50	6	7	13	14
B. McAneeley	51	5	7	12	24
a) B. Blanchette	23	5	4	9	2
R. Cote	61	3	5	8	46
J. Fisher	40	0	5	5	0
J. Norris	64	0	3	3	2
b) J. Benzelock	26	1	1	2	10
K. Brown	19	0	0	0	2
c) D. Harker	1	0	0	0	0
Oiler Totals	78	269	427	696	843

a—Also played 24 games with Chicago. b—Also played 43 games with Chicago. c—Also played 28 games with Philadelphia.

HOUSTON AEROS

Player	GP	G	A	Pts	PIM
G. Labossiere	78	36	60	96	56
T. Taylor	73	34	42	76	103
M. Hall	76	28	42	70	84
L. Lund	77	21	45	66	120
P. Popiel	74	16	48	64	158
D. Grierson	78	22	22	44	83
D. Harris	75	30	12	42	14
F. Hughes	76	22	19	41	41
B. McDonald	71	20	20	40	78
E. Hoekstra	78	11	28	39	12
L. Hale	68	4	26	30	65
K. Mortson	67	13	16	29	95
D. McCalium	69	9	20	29	112
J. Schella	77	2	24	26	239
J. Stanfield	71	8	12	20	8
B. Smith	48	7	6	13	19
R. Larose	67	1	10	11	25
G. Kannegiesser	45	0	10	10	32
B. Prentice	3	0	1	1	0
B. Hughes	2	0	0	0	2
W. Rutledge	36	0	0	0	11
D. McLeod	41	0	0	0	6
Aero Totals	78	284	463	747	1363

LOS ANGELES SHARKS

Player	GP	G	A	Pts	PIM
G. Veneruzzo	78	43	30	73	34
J. P. LeBlanc	77	19	50	69	49
B. Crashley	70	18	27	45	10
J. Szura	73	13	32	45	25
a) A. White	57	20	17	37	22
T. Serviss	73	11	26	37	32
G. Odrowski	78	6	31	37	89
b) M. Byers	56	19	17	36	20
T. Gilmore	71	17	18	35	191
E. Heiskala	70	12	17	29	150
J. Niekamp	78	7	22	29	155
c) B. Young	50	14	12	26	46
P. Slater	73	12	12	24	87
R. MacSweyn	78	0	23	23	39
T. McCaskill	73	11	11	22	150
J. Watson	75	5	15	20	123
S. Sutherland	44	11	6	17	98
d) F. Speck	28	3	13	16	22
e) M. Hyndman	19	8	7	15	11
B. MacNeil	42	4	7	11	48
f) B. Jones	20	2	7	9	8
H. Heggedal	8	2	1	3	0
g) L. Mavety	2	1	0	1	2
h) J. Krupicka	6	1	0	1	2
G. Gardner	50	0	1	1	2
B. Perreault	1	0	0	0	0
J. Zermiak	1	0	0	0	0
M. Jakubo	7	0	0	0	0
R. Gillow	38	0	0	0	6
Shark Totals	78	259	402	661	1477

a—Also played 13 games with New York. b—Also played 19 games with New England. c—Also played 23 games with Minnesota. d—Also played 47 games with Minnesota. e—Also played 59 games with New England. f—Also played 56 games with New York. g—Also played 4 games with Philadelphia and 67 games with Chicago. h—Also played 30 games with New York.

MINNESOTA FIGHTING SAINTS

Player	GP	G	A	Pts	PIM
W. Connelly	78	40	30	70	16
T. Hampson	77	17	45	52	20
B. Klatt	78	36	22	58	22
M. McMahon	75	12	39	51	87
K. Christiansen	64	12	30	42	24
G. Morrison	70	16	24	40	20
B. McMillan	75	13	27	40	48
T. Ball	76	6	34	40	66
M. Antonovich	75	20	19	39	46
J. Arbour	76	6	27	33	186
a) F. Speck	47	13	16	29	52
J. Johnson	33	9	14	23	12
L. Lilyholm	77	8	13	21	37
M. Pearson	70	8	12	20	12
T. Ryan	76	13	6	19	13
D. Paradise	77	3	15	18	189
F. Sanders	77	8	8	16	94
G. Konik	54	4	12	16	34
b) B. Young	23	5	6	11	20
C. Falkman	45	1	5	6	12
c) B. Rydman	29	0	1	1	65
M. Curran	43	0	1	1	26
C. Wetzel	1	0	0	0	0
J. McCartan	38	0	0	0	19
Team Totals	78	250	406	656	1134

a—Also played 28 games with Los Angeles. b—Also played 50 games with Los Angeles. c—Also played 2 games with New York.

NEW YORK RAIDERS
(NOW NEW YORK GOLDEN BLADES)

Player	GP	G	A	Pts	PIM
R. Ward	77	51	67	118	28
B. Sheehan	75	35	53	88	17
W. Rivers	75	37	40	77	47
G. Peacosh	67	37	34	71	25
N. Ferguson	56	28	40	68	8
K. Block	78	5	53	58	43
B. Bradley	78	22	33	55	20
M. Laughton	67	16	20	36	44
B. Perry	74	13	20	33	30
C. Reichmuth	73	13	14	27	127
B. Speer	69	3	23	26	40
H. Willis	74	3	21	24	159
a) B. Jones	56	11	12	23	24
K. Douglas	60	3	15	18	74
W. Olds	61	5	7	12	4
B. Winograd	52	0	12	12	23
J. Kennedy	54	5	6	10	11
G. Peters	23	2	7	9	24
B. Morenz	30	7	1	8	23
C. Chartre	12	2	3	5	0
b) A. White	13	1	4	5	2
T. Scharf	29	2	2	4	72
c) B. Brown	17	0	4	4	6
J. Gauthier	31	2	1	3	21
d) J. Krupicka	30	1	2	3	4
e) B. Rydman	2	0	0	0	4
I. Wilkie	6	0	0	0	0
G. Kurt	36	0	0	0	2
P. Donnelly	46	0	0	0	2
Team Totals	78	303	494	797	900

a—Also played 20 games with Los Angeles. b—Also played 57 games with Los Angeles. c—Also played 4 games with Philadelphia. d—Also played 6 games with Los Angeles. e—Also played 29 games with Minnesota.

NEW ENGLAND WHALERS

Player	GP	G	A	Pts	PIM
T. Webster	77	53	50	103	89
T. Caffery	74	39	61	100	14
L. Pleau	78	39	48	87	42
T. Sheehy	78	33	38	71	30
J. Dorey	75	7	56	63	95
J. French	74	24	35	59	43
T. Green	78	16	30	46	47
K. Ahearn	78	20	22	42	18
a) B. Selby	65	13	29	42	48
J. Danby	77	14	23	37	10
B. Selwood	75	13	21	34	114
T. Williams	69	10	21	31	14
R. Ley	76	3	27	30	108
T. Earl	77	10	13	23	4
b) H. Hyndman	59	4	14	18	21
P. Hurley	78	3	15	18	58
c) D. Sarrizin	35	4	7	11	0
d) M. Byers	19	6	4	10	4
J. Cunniff	33	3	5	8	16
G. Smith	23	3	3	6	6
R. Jordan	34	1	5	6	12
B. Landon	30	0	1	1	8
A. Smith	51	0	1	1	39
Team Totals	78	318	529	847	858

a—Also played 7 games with Quebec. b—Also played 19 games with Los Angeles. c—Also played 33 games with Chicago. d—Also played 56 games with Los Angeles.

OTTAWA NATIONALS
(NOW TORONTO TOROS)

Player	GP	G	A	Pts	PIM
W. Carleton	75	42	49	91	42
G. Kirk	78	28	40	68	54
B. Charlebois	78	24	40	64	28
G. Trottier	72	26	32	58	25
B. Leduc	77	22	33	55	71
S. King	69	18	34	52	28
T. Martin	75	19	27	46	27
B. Gibbons	73	7	35	42	62
R. Sentes	73	22	19	41	78
R. Cunningham	78	9	32	41	121
J. Gibson	59	22	13	35	48
R. Climie	31	12	19	31	2
B. Conacher	69	8	19	27	32
K. Stephanson	77	3	16	19	93
T. Simpson	57	10	7	17	44
M. Boland	41	1	15	16	44
M. Amodeo	60	1	14	15	77
S. Warr	71	3	8	11	79
C. Meloff	28	1	6	7	40
R. Riley	22	0	5	5	2
J. Donnelly	15	1	1	2	44
M. Haney	7	0	1	1	4
G. Gratton	50	0	1	1	10
F. Blum	2	0	0	0	0
L. Binkley	30	0	0	0	0
National Totals	78	279	466	745	1067

PHILADELPHIA BLAZERS
(NOW VANCOUVER BLAZERS)

Player	GP	G	A	Pts	PIM
A. Lacroix	78	50	74	124	83
D. Lawson	78	61	45	106	35
J. McKenzie	60	28	50	78	157
B. Campbell	75	25	48	73	85
D. Herriman	78	24	48	72	63
R. Plumb	78	10	41	51	66
D. Burgess	74	20	22	42	15
D. O'Donoghue	74	16	23	39	43
I. Spencer	54	2	27	29	43
J. Cardiff	78	3	24	27	185
M. Plante	70	13	12	25	35
R. Campeau	75	1	18	19	72
J. Migneault	54	10	8	18	38
M. Boudreau	33	7	7	14	4
C. LaPierre	24	5	9	14	2
J. Bennett	34	4	6	10	18
D. Sanderson	8	3	3	6	69
P. Henry	19	2	3	5	13
a) D. Harker	28	0	5	5	46
J. Gavel	8	1	3	4	0
N. Polano	17	0	3	3	24
D. Meloche	4	1	1	2	0
D. Hutchinson	28	0	2	2	34
C. St. Sauveur	2	1	0	1	0
P. Paiement	8	1	0	1	18
Y. Archambault	5	0	1	1	0
b) M. Rouleau	6	0	1	1	15
W. Mosdell	8	0	1	1	12
B. Parent	63	0	1	1	36
D. Sullivan	1	0	0	0	0
D. Mott	1	0	0	0	0
T. Cottringer	2	0	0	0	0
J. Chipchase	4	0	0	0	2
c) L. Mavety	4	0	0	0	14
d) B. Brown	4	0	0	0	2
S. Gellard	5	0	0	0	0
M. Myers	7	0	0	0	0
e) F. Golembrosky	8	0	0	0	0
M. Paille	14	0	0	0	0
Team Totals	78	288	486	774	1260

a—Also played 1 game with Alberta. b—Also played 52 games with Quebec. c—Also played 2 games with Los Angeles and 67 games with Chicago. d—Also played 17 games with New York. e—Also played 52 games with Quebec.

QUEBEC NORDIQUES

Player	GP	G	A	Pts	PIM
J. C. Tremblay	76	14	75	89	32
M. Parizeau	75	25	48	73	50
A. Gaudette	78	27	44	71	12
A. Caron	68	36	27	63	14
R. Guindon	71	28	28	56	31
R. Leclerc	60	24	28	52	111
J-G. Gendron	63	17	33	50	113
J. Payette	71	15	29	44	46
M. Archambault	57	12	25	37	36
Y. Bergeron	65	14	19	33	32
F. Lacombe	61	10	18	28	123
R. Giroux	59	10	12	22	41
a) M. Rouleau	52	7	14	21	142
b) F. Golembrosky	52	8	12	20	44
P. Roy	64	7	12	19	169
M. Harvey	40	6	13	19	14
P. Guite	65	10	8	18	136
J. Blain	69	1	10	11	78
K. Desejardine	38	2	6	8	36
P. Larose	28	0	7	7	7
G. Dufour	9	3	2	5	2
J. Yves Cartier	15	0	3	3	8
N. Descoteaux	2	0	1	1	0
c) B. Selby	7	0	1	1	4
J. Lemelin	9	0	1	1	0
A. Globensky	3	0	0	0	0
M. McNamara	19	0	0	0	5
R. Brodeur	24	0	0	0	4
S. Aubry	52	0	0	0	54
Team Totals	78	276	476	752	1354

a—Also played 6 games with Philadelphia.
b—Also played 8 games with Philadelphia.
c—Also played 65 games with New England.

WINNIPEG JETS

Player	GP	G	A	Pts	PIM
B. Hull	63	51	52	103	37
N. Beaudin	78	38	65	103	15
C. Bordeleau	78	47	54	101	12
L. Hornung	77	13	45	58	28
D. Johnson	76	19	23	43	17
A. McDonald	77	17	24	41	16
M. Black	77	18	16	34	31
W. Boyer	69	6	28	34	27
D. Bousseau	74	16	17	33	75
C. Swenson	76	7	21	28	19
J-G. Gratton	71	15	12	27	37
J. Zanussi	73	4	21	25	53
B. Sutherland	48	6	16	22	34
G. Rizzuto	61	10	10	20	32
S. Cuddie	77	7	13	20	121
B. Ash	74	3	14	17	39
D. Asmundsen	76	2	14	16	54
B. Cadle	56	4	4	8	39
B. Woytowich	62	2	4	6	47
J. Daley	29	0	1	1	10
G. Tumilson	3	0	0	0	0
J. Shmyr	7	0	0	0	2
E. Wakely	49	0	0	0	0
Team Totals	78	285	454	739	757

TEAM RECORDS

MOST POINTS, ONE SEASON:
94—New England Whalers, 1972-73, won 46, lost 30, tied 2.
FEWEST POINTS, ONE SEASON:
54—Chicago Cougars, 1972-73, won 26, lost 50, tied 2.
MOST WINS ONE SEASON:
46—New England Whalers, 1972-73, won 46, lost 30, tied 2.
FEWEST WINS, ONE SEASON:
26—Chicago Cougars, 1972-73, won 26, lost 50, tied 2.
MOST LOSSES, ONE SEASON:
50—Chicago Cougars, 1972-73, won 26, lost 50, tied 2.
FEWEST LOSSES, ONE SEASON:
30—New England Whalers, 1972-73, won 46, lost 30, tied 2.
MOST TIES, ONE SEASON:
6—Los Angeles Sharks, 1972-73.
LEAST TIES, ONE SEASON:
0—Philadelphia Blazers, 1972-73.
MOST HOME WINS, ONE SEASON:
30—New England Whalers, 1972-73.
MOST ROAD WINS, ONE SEASON:
19—Los Angeles Sharks, 1972-73.
MOST HOME LOSSES, ONE SEASON:
22—Chicago Cougars, 1972-73
MOST ROAD LOSSES, ONE SEASON:
28—Quebec Nordiques, 1972-73.
28—New York Raiders, 1972-73.
28—Chicago Cougars, 1972-73.
MOST HOME TIES, ONE SEASON:
5—Quebec Nordiques, 1972-73.
MOST ROAD TIES, ONE SEASON:
5—Los Angeles Sharks, 1972-73.
FEWEST HOME WINS, ONE SEASON:
17—Chicago Cougars, 1972-73.
FEWEST ROAD WINS, ONE SEASON:
9—Chicago Cougars, 1972-73.
FEWEST HOME LOSSES, ONE SEASON:
8—New England Whalers, 1972-73.
FEWEST ROAD LOSSES, ONE SEASON:
15—Los Angeles Sharks, 1972-73.
FEWEST HOME TIES, ONE SEASON:
0—Philadelphia Blazers, 1972-73.
0—Chicago Cougars, 1972-73.
FEWEST ROAD TIES, ONE SEASON:
0—Philadelphia Blazers, 1972-73.
LONGEST WIN STREAK, ONE SEASON:
10—Winnipeg Jets, Feb. 8, 1973 through March 6, 1973.
LONGEST UNDEFEATED STREAK:
10—Winnipeg Jets, Feb. 8, 1973 through March 6, 1973.
LONGEST HOME WIN STREAK:
9—New England Whalers, Feb. 15, 1973 to March 27, 1973.
9—New England Whalers, Nov. 18, 1972 to Dec. 17, 1972.
9—Ottawa Nationals, Feb. 25, 1973 to April 1, 1973.

49

LONGEST HOME UNDEFEATED STREAK:
14—New England Whalers, November 1, 1972 to December 17, 1972. 13 Wins, 1 Tie.
LONGEST HOME LOSING STREAK:
6—Chicago Cougars, Nov. 4, 1972 to Dec. 8, 1972.
LONGEST HOME WINLESS STREAK:
6—Chicago Cougars, Nov. 4, 1972 to Dec. 8, 1972. 6 Losses, no ties.
6—Quebec Nordiques, Feb. 11, 1973 to March 11, 1973. 4 losses, 2 ties.
LONGEST ROAD WIN STREAK:
5—Philadelphia Blazers, Dec. 31, 1972 to Jan. 28, 1973.
LONGEST ROAD UNDEFEATED STREAK:
6—Cleveland Crusaders, Nov. 15, 1972 to Nov. 14, 1972.
LONGEST ROAD LOSING STREAK:
9—Ottawa Nationals, Dec. 31, 1972 to Feb. 1, 1973.
LONGEST ROAD WINLESS STREAK:
11—Ottawa Nationals, Dec. 31, 1972 to Feb. 1, 1973.
LONGEST LOSING STREAK:
8—Alberta Oilers, Feb. 15, 1973 to March 6, 1973.
LONGEST WINLESS STREAK:
10—Ottawa Nationals, Jan. 19, 1973 to Feb. 6, 1973.
LONGEST NON-SHUTOUT RECORD:
78—Philadelphia Blazers, Entire 1972-73 season.
LONGEST TIME ONE TEAM WAS SHUTOUT:
138 Minutes, 53 Seconds—New York Raiders, from Dec. 26, 1972 to Jan. 4, 1973. Included two shutout games.
MOST TIMES SHUTOUT, ONE SEASON:
6—Philadelphia Blazers, 1972-73.
MOST SHUTOUTS, ONE SEASON:
5—Cleveland Crusaders, 1972-73.
5—Minnesota Fighting Saints, 1972-73.
MOST SHUTOUTS ON THE ROAD, ONE SEASON:
2—Philadelphia Blazers, 1972-73.
MOST SHUTOUTS AT HOME, ONE SEASON:
5—Minnesota Fighting Saints, 1972-73.
LONGEST SHUTOUT SEQUENCE, ONE SEASON:
153 Minutes, 5 Seconds—Cleveland Crusaders, from 10:24 of first period vs. Phil. on Oct. 25, 1972 until 3:29 of third period vs. Quebec on Oct. 29, 1972. Included shutout vs. Alberta on Oct. 27.
LEAST SHUTOUTS, ONE SEASON:
0—Ottawa Nationals, 1972-73.
FEWEST SHUTOUTS ON THE ROAD, ONE SEASON:
0—Minnesota Fighting Saints, Quebec Nordiques, New York Raiders, Chicago Cougars, Ottawa Nationals, Alberta Oilers, all in 1972-73 season.
FEWEST SHUTOUTS AT HOME, ONE SEASON:
0—Ottawa Nationals, 1972-73.
0—Houston Aeros, 1972-73.
0—Philadelphia Blazers, 1972-73.
MOST TIMES SHUTOUT ON THE ROAD, ONE SEASON:
6—Philadelphia Blazers, 1972-73.
LEAST TIMES SHUTOUT ON THE ROAD, ONE SEASON:
0—New York Raiders, 1972-73.
MOST TIMES SHUTOUT AT HOME, ONE SEASON:
2—New York Raiders, 1972-73. (Happened on consecutive nights—Dec. 31, 1972 and Jan. 1, 1973.)

LEAST TIMES SHUTOUT AT HOME, ONE SEASON:
0—Philadelphia Blazers, 1972-73.
0—Quebec Nordiques, 1972-73.
0—Winnipeg Jets, 1972-73.
0—Ottawa Nationals, 1972-73.
0—Minnesota Fighting Saints, 1972-73.
0—New England Whalers, 1972-73.
LEAST TIMES SHUTOUT, ONE SEASON:
1—Ottawa Nationals, 1972-73.
1—Minnesota Fighting Saints, 1972-73.
1—New England Whalers, 1972-73.
MOST GOALS SCORED, ONE SEASON:
318—New England Whalers, 1972-73.
FEWEST GOALS SCORED, ONE SEASON:
245—Chicago Cougars, 1972-73.
MOST GOALS ALLOWED, ONE SEASON:
334—New York Raiders, 1972-73.
FEWEST GOALS ALLOWED, ONE SEASON:
249—Winnipeg Jets, 1972-73.
MOST POWER PLAY GOALS, ONE SEASON:
71—Philadelphia Blazers, 1972-73.
MOST POWER PLAY GOALS ALLOWED, ONE SEASON:
64—Houston Aeros, 1972-73.
MOST SHORTHANDED GOALS SCORED, ONE SEASON:
13—Alberta Oilers, 1972-73.
MOST SHORTHANDED GOALS ALLOWED, ONE SEASON:
15—Quebec Nordiques, 1972-73.
MOST ASSISTS, ONE SEASON:
529—New England Whalers, 1972-73.
FEWEST ASSISTS, ONE SEASON:
402—Los Angeles Sharks, 1972-73.
MOST SCORING POINTS, ONE SEASON:
847—New England Whalers, 1972-73.
FEWEST SCORING POINTS, ONE SEASON:
656—Minnesota Fighting Saints, 1972-73. 250 goals, 406 assists.
MOST 50-OR-MORE-GOAL SCORERS, ONE TEAM, ONE SEASON:
2—Philadelphia Blazers, 1972-73. Andre Lacroix, 51; Danny Lawson, 61.
MOST 40-OR-MORE-GOAL SCORERS, ONE TEAM, ONE SEASON:
2—Philadelphia Blazers, 1972-73. Andre Lacroix, 51; Danny Lawson, 61.
2—Winnipeg Jets, 1972-73. Bobby Hull, 51; Chris Bordeleau, 47.
MOST 30-OR-MORE-GOAL SCORERS, ONE TEAM, ONE SEASON:
4—New England Whalers, 1972-73. Tom Webster, 53; Terry Caffery, 39; Larry Pleau, 39; Tim Sheehy, 33.
4—New York Raiders, 1972-73. Ron Ward, 51; Bobby Sheehan, 35; Wayne Rivers, 37; Gene Peacosh, 37.
MOST 20-OR-MORE-GOAL SCORERS, ONE TEAM, ONE SEASON:
8—Houston Aeros, 1972-73. Gordon Labossiere, 36; Ted Taylor, 34; Murray Hall, 28; Larry Lund, 21; Don Grierson, 22; Duke Harris, 30; Frank Hughes, 22; Brian McDonald, 20.
MOST 100-OR-MORE-POINT SCORERS, ONE TEAM, ONE SEASON:
3—Winnipeg Jets, 1972-73. Bobby Hull, 51 goals, 52 assists, 103 points; Norm Beaudin, 38 goals, 65 assists, 103 points; Chris Bordeleau, 47 goals, 54 assists, 101 points.

MOST PENALTY MINUTES, ONE TEAM, ONE SEASON:
1477—Los Angeles Sharks, 1972-73. 421 minors, 49 majors, 39 misconduct penalties.
LEAST PENALTY MINUTES, ONE TEAM, ONE SEASON:
757—Winnipeg Jets, 1972-73. 266 minors, 23 majors, 11 misconducts.
MOST GOALS, BOTH TEAMS, ONE GAME:
16—Philadelphia Blazers, New England Whalers, at Philadelphia, Dec. 16, 1972. New England won game 10-6.
MOST GOALS, ONE TEAM, ONE GAME:
11—Cleveland Crusaders, March 11, 1973, at Winnipeg. Crusaders defeated the Jets 11-2.
11—Philadelphia Blazers, March 9, 1973, at Philadelphia. Blazers defeated the Quebec Nordiques 11-3.
11—Houston Aeros, Jan. 23, 1973, at Houston. Aeros defeated the Ottawa Nationals 11-3.
11—Alberta Oilers, Jan. 30, 1973, at Edmonton. Oilers defeated the New York Raiders 11-3.
MOST CONSECUTIVE GOALS, ONE TEAM, ONE GAME:
9—New York Raiders, Dec. 13, 1972, at New York. Raiders defeated the Quebec Nordiques 9-1.
9—Los Angeles Sharks, Jan. 28, 1973, at Los Angeles. Sharks defeated the New York Raiders 9-2.
9—Philadelphia Blazers, Feb. 16, 1973, at Philadelphia. Blazers defeated the New York Raiders 9-2.
MOST POINTS, BOTH TEAMS, ONE GAME:
44—Philadelphia Blazers, New England Whalers, at Philadelphia, Dec. 16, 1973. Whalers won game 10-6. New England had 19 assists, Philadelphia had 9.
MOST POINTS, ONE TEAM, ONE GAME:
32—Alberta Oilers, Jan. 30, 1973, at Edmonton. Oilers defeated the New York Raiders 11-3, receiving 21 assists.
32—Philadelphia Blazers, March 9, 1973, at Winnipeg. Blazers defeated the Jets 11-2, receiving 21 assists.
MOST PENALTIES, BOTH TEAMS, ONE GAME:
29—Ottawa Nationals, Quebec Nordiques, at Ottawa Dec. 24, 1972. Ottawa received 11 minors, 2 majors. Quebec received 14 minors and 2 majors. Ottawa defeated Quebec 6-2.
29—Los Angeles Sharks, Quebec Nordiques, Feb. 24, 1973, at Los Angeles. The Sharks received 6 minors, 4 majors, 6 misconducts. Quebec received 7 minors, 4 majors, 2 misconducts. The Nordiques defeated the Sharks 5-3.
MOST PENALTY MINUTES, BOTH TEAMS, ONE GAME:
146—Los Angeles Sharks, Quebec Nordiques, Feb. 24, 1973, at Los Angeles. The Sharks received 6 minors, 4 majors, 6 misconducts. Quebec received 7 minors, 4 majors, 2 misconducts. The Nordiques defeated the Sharks 5-3.
MOST GOALS, BOTH TEAMS, ONE PERIOD:
9—Philadelphia Blazers, New England Whalers, at Philadelphia, Dec. 16, 1972, third period. Whalers scored five goals, the Blazers 4. New England won the game 10-6.
9—Ottawa Nationals, Quebec Nordiques, at Ottawa, Jan. 9, 1973, first period. Nationals scored 5 goals, Nordiques 4. Ottawa won the game 7-5.
MOST GOALS, ONE TEAM, ONE PERIOD:
6—Houston Aeros, December 2, 1972, at New York, second period during 7-2 win over the Raiders.
6—Minnesota Fighting Saints, Jan. 20, 1973, at Quebec, second period during a 10-5 win over the Nordiques.
6—Chicago Cougars, Jan. 25, 1973, third period, during 9-2 win over the New York Raiders in Chicago.
6—Alberta Oilers, Jan. 30, 1973 at Edmonton, during the third period of an 11-3 win over the New York Raiders.
6—Alberta Oilers, Feb. 11, 1973, at Edmonton, third period during a 7-5 win over the Minnesota Fighting Saints. The Oilers were down 5-0 in the second period and

52

scored 7 straight goals.
6—Philadelphia Blazers, Feb. 16, 1973, at Philadelphia, second period during 9-2 win over the New York Raiders.

FASTEST FIVE GOALS, BOTH TEAMS:
4 Minutes, 10 seconds—New York Raiders, Cleveland Crusaders, at New York, Feb. 25, 1973, third period. Scorers were: Norm Peacosh, N.Y. 3:59; Wayne Rivers, N.Y., 4:42; Ron Buchanan, Cleveland, 6:01; Gerry Pinder, Cleveland, 6:34; Wayne Rivers, N.Y., 8:09. New York won game 9-5.

FASTEST FIVE GOALS, ONE TEAM:
4 Minutes, 48 seconds—Alberta Oilers, at Edmonton, Jan. 30, 1973, third period. Scorers were Bernie Blanchette, 7:45; Rusty Patenaude, 10:48; Doug Barrie, 11:48; Steve Carlyle, 12:00; Jim Harrison, 12:33. Alberta won the game 11-3 over the New York Raiders.

FASTEST FOUR GOALS, BOTH TEAMS:
1 Minute, 3 seconds—New York, New England, at New York, Nov. 29, 1972, second period. Scorers were: John French, N.E., 12:53; Ron Ward, N.Y., 13:11; Ron Ward, N.Y., 13:20; Tom Earl, N.E., 13:56. New York won game 7-6.

FASTEST FOUR GOALS, ONE TEAM:
1 Minute, 45 seconds—Alberta Oilers, at Edmonton, Jan. 30, 1973, third period. Scorers were Rusty Patenaude, 10:48; Doug Barrie, 11:48; Steve Carlyle, 12:00; Jim Harrison, 12:33. Oilers defeated the New York Raiders 11-3.

FASTEST THREE GOALS, BOTH TEAMS:
27 Seconds—New York, New England, at New York, Nov. 29, 1972, second period. Scorers were: John French, N.E., 12:53; Ron Ward, N.Y. at 13:11 and 13:20. New York won game 7-6.

FASTEST THREE GOALS, ONE TEAM:
32 Seconds—Chicago, at Chicago, Dec. 19, 1972, third period. Scorers were: Paul Popiel at 18:46; Bob Sicinski at 19:02; Bob Liddington at 19:18. Chicago defeated Cleveland 6-1.

FASTEST TWO GOALS, BOTH TEAMS:
7 Seconds—Philadelphia Blazers, Winnipeg Jets, at Philadelphia, Dec. 15, 1972, third period. Scorers were: Brian Campbell, Phil. 19:36; Bobby Hull, Wpg., 19:43. Philadelphia won the game 6-4.
7 Seconds—Alberta Oilers, Minnesota Fighting Saints, at Edmonton, Dec. 1, 1972, first period. Scorers were: Billy Klatt, Minn., 13.22; Bob McAneely, Alb., 13:29. Minnesota won game 6-4.

FASTEST TWO GOALS, ONE TEAM:
4 Seconds—New England Whalers, Dec. 16, 1972, at Philadelphia, third period. Scorers were: Terry Caffery at 2:49; Brit Selby at 2:53. New England defeated the Blazers 10-6.

FASTEST THREE GOALS FROM THE START OF THE GAME, BOTH TEAMS:
2 Minutes, 21 seconds—Chicago Cougars, Minnesota Fighting Saints, at Chicago, March 15, 1973. Scorers were: Bill Klatt, Minn., 0:20; Wayne Connelly, Minnesota, 1:45; Bill Whitlock, Chicago, 2:21. Minnesota won game 7-4.

FASTEST THREE GOALS FROM START OF GAME, ONE TEAM:
4 Minutes, 48 seconds—Winnipeg Jets, Dec. 3, 1972, at Winnipeg. Danny Johnson at 2:21; Larry Hornung at 3:30; Bob Woytowitch at 4:48. Jets won game 5-1.

FASTEST TWO GOALS FROM THE START OF GAME, BOTH TEAMS:
55 Seconds—Chicago Cougars, Quebec Nordiques, at Chicago, Dec., 1972. Scorers were: Rick Morris, Chicago, 0:10; Alain Caron, Quebec, 0:55. Quebec won game 4-2.

FASTEST TWO GOALS FROM START OF GAME, ONE TEAM:
28 Seconds—Minnesota Fighting Saints, Feb. 17, 1973, at Cleveland. Scorers were: Mike McMahon at 0:19; George Morrison at 0:28. Minnesota won game 7-3.

FASTEST GOAL FROM START OF GAME:
10 Seconds—Chicago Cougars, Dec. 9, 1972, at Chicago. Scored by Rick Morris in the Cougars loss to the Quebec Nordiques by a score of 4-2.

INDIVIDUAL RECORDS

MOST GOALS, ONE SEASON:
61—Danny Lawson, Philadelphia Blazers, 1972-73.

MOST ASSISTS, ONE SEASON:
75—J. C. Tremblay, Quebec Nordiques, 1972-73.

MOST POINTS, ONE SEASON:
124—Andre Lacroix, Philadelphia Blazers, 1972-73, 50 goals and 74 assists.

MOST PENALTY MINUTES, ONE SEASON:
239—John Schella, Houston Aeros, 1972-73.

MOST SHUTOUTS BY A GOALTENDER, ONE SEASON:
5—Gerry Cheevers, Cleveland Crusaders, 1972-73.

MOST GAMES SCORING THREE OR MORE GOALS, ONE SEASON:
6—Danny Lawson, Philadelphia Blazers, 1972-73. (three three-goal nights and three four-goal nights).

MOST GAMES SCORING FOUR OR MORE GOALS, ONE SEASON:
3—Danny Lawson, Philadelphia Blazers, 1972-73.

MOST GAME WINNING GOALS, ONE SEASON:
11—Andre Lacroix, Philadelphia Blazers, 1972-73.

MOST POWER PLAY GOALS, ONE SEASON:
20—Danny Lawson, Philadelphia Blazers, 1972-73.

MOST SHORT-HANDED GOALS, ONE SEASON:
6—Jim Harrison, Alberta Oilers, 1972-73.
Bob Dillabough, Cleveland Crusaders, 1972-73.
Terry Ryan, Minnesota Fighting Saints, 1972-73.

LONGEST CONSECUTIVE GOAL-SCORING STREAK:
8 Games—Alain Caron, Quebec Nordiques, December 9, 1972 through December 23, 1972, 10 goals.

LONGEST CONSECUTIVE ASSIST-SCORING STREAK:
12 Games—Terry Caffery, New England Whalers, Dec. 11, 1972 through Dec. 31, 1972, 18 assists.

LONGEST CONSECUTIVE POINT-SCORING STREAK:
16 Games—Terry Caffery, New England Whalers, Dec. 7, 1972 through Jan. 13, 1973, 31 points (12 goals, 19 assists).

MOST GOALS, ONE GAME:
5—Ron Ward, New York Raiders, Jan. 4, 1973, at New York, Raiders defeated the Ottawa Nationals, 9-4.

MOST ASSISTS, ONE GAME:
7—Jim Harrison, Alberta Oilers, Jan. 30, 1973, at Edmonton, Oilers defeated the New York Raiders, 11-3.

MOST POINTS, ONE GAME:
10—Jim Harrison, Alberta Oilers, Jan. 30, 1973, at Edmonton, Oilers defeated the New York Raiders, 11-3. (3 goals, 7 assists).

MOST GOALS, ONE PERIOD:
3—Ron Ward, New York Raiders, Nov. 29, 1972, at N.Y., Raiders defeated the New England Whalers, 7-6. (2nd period).
Alton White, Los Angeles Sharks, Jan. 10, 1973, at Chicago, Sharks defeated the Cougars, 8-5. (2nd period).
Norm Beaudin, Winnipeg Jets, Feb. 25, 1973, at Winnipeg, Jets defeated the Philadelphia Blazers, 5-3. (3rd period).

MOST ASSISTS, ONE PERIOD:
4—Jim Harrison and Doug Barrie of the Alberta Oilers, both on Jan. 30, 1973, in Edmonton, in the third period of an Oilers' 11-3 win over the New York Raiders.

MOST POINTS, ONE PERIOD:
5—Jim Harrison and Doug Barrie of the Alberta Oilers, both on Jan. 30, 1973, in Edmonton, in the third period of an Oiler 11-3 win over the New York Raiders.

LONGEST SHUTOUT SEQUENCE BY A GOALTENDER:
143 Minutes, 32 Seconds—Bernie Parent, Philadelphia Blazers, from 14:02 of the first period, Dec. 31, 1972 against Los Angeles to 17:34, second period, Jan. 11, 1973 against New York Raiders. Streak included a shutout against the New York Raiders.

FASTEST TWO GOALS, ONE PLAYER, ONE GAME:
6 Seconds—Gary Veneruzzo, Los Angeles Sharks, Dec. 10, 1972, at L.A., at 15:24 and 15:30 of third period during a Shark 5-3 win over the Alberta Oilers.

FASTEST THREE GOALS, ONE PLAYER, ONE GAME:
6 Minutes, 44 Seconds—Ron Ward, New York Raiders, Nov. 29, 1972, at New York, at 13:11, 13:20 and 19:53 of second period during Raider 7-6 victory over the New England Whalers.

FASTEST FOUR GOALS, ONE PLAYER, ONE GAME:
19 Minutes, 22 Seconds—Brian McDonald, Houston Aeros, Dec. 19, 1972, at Houston, at 10:34 and 16:14 second period, and 9:46 and 9:56 of the third period during Aero 7-5 win over the Los Angeles Sharks.

FASTEST FIVE GOALS, ONE PLAYER, ONE GAME:
25 Minutes, 55 Seconds—Ron Ward, New York Raiders, Jan. 4, 1973, at New York, at 18:41 and 19:16 of first period, 13:46 and 19:01 of second period, and 4:34 of third period during New York 9-4 win over the Ottawa Nationals.

WORLD TROPHY PLAYOFFS

SERIES A (NEW ENGLAND VS. OTTAWA)

April 7 — New England 6, Ottawa 3 at Boston Garden (9,359).

April 8 — New England 4, Ottawa 3 — overtime — at Boston Garden (6,156).

April 10 — Ottawa 4, New England 2 at Maple Leaf Gardens, Toronto (4,879).

April 12 — New England 7, Ottawa 3 at Maple Leaf Gardens, Toronto (3,941).

April 14 — New England 5, Ottawa 4 — overtime — at Boston Garden (12,033).

(New England wins series, four games to one).

SERIES B (CLEVELAND VS. PHILADELPHIA)

April 4 — Cleveland 3, Philadelphia 2 — overtime — at Cleveland Arena (3,624).

April 7 — Cleveland 7, Philadelphia 1 at Cleveland Arena (8,262).

April 8 — Cleveland 3, Philadelphia 1 at Philadelphia Civic Center (4,023).

April 11 — Cleveland 6, Philadelphia 2 at Philadelphia Civic Center (3,211).

(Cleveland wins series, four games to none).

SERIES C (WINNIPEG VS. MINNESOTA)
April 6 — Winnipeg 3, Minnesota 1 at Winnipeg Arena (7,354).
April 8 — Winnipeg 5, Minnesota 2 at Winnipeg Arena (8,425).
April 10 — Minnesota 6, Winnipeg 4 at St. Paul Civic Center (5,151).
April 11 — Winnipeg 3, Minnesota 2 — overtime — at St. Paul Civic Center (6,982).
April 15 — Winnipeg 8, Minnesota 5 at Winnipeg Arena (8,852).
  (Winnipeg wins series, four games to one).

SERIES D (HOUSTON VS. LOS ANGELES)
April 5 — Houston 7, Los Angeles 2 at Sam Houston Coliseum (6,849).
April 7 — Los Angeles 4, Houston 2 at Sam Houston Coliseum (4,728).
April 11 — Los Angeles 3, Houston 2 at L.A. Sports Arena (6,181).
April 13 — Houston 3, Los Angeles 2 — overtime — at L.A. Sports Arena (7,773).
April 15 — Houston 6, Los Angeles 3 at Sam Houston Coliseum (6,118).
April 17 — Houston 3, Los Angeles 2 at L.A. Sports Arena (6,060).
  (Houston wins series, four games to two).

SERIES E (NEW ENGLAND VS. CLEVELAND) Eastern Division Finals
April 18 — New England 3, Cleveland 2 at Boston Garden (6,101).
April 19 — New England 3, Cleveland 2 at Boston Garden (7,119).
April 21 — New England 5, Cleveland 4 at Cleveland Arena (8,391).
April 22 — Cleveland 5, New England 2 at Cleveland Arena (4,183).
April 26 — New England 3, Cleveland 1 at Boston Garden (7,689).
  (New England wins series, four games to one).

SERIES F (WINNIPEG VS. HOUSTON) Western Division Finals
April 20 — Winnipeg 5, Houston 1 at Winnipeg Arena (7,044).
April 22 — Winnipeg 2, Houston 0 at Winnipeg Arena (5,029).
April 24 — Winnipeg 4, Houston 2 at Sam Houston Coliseum (6,722).
April 26 — Winnipeg 3, Houston 0 at Sam Houston Coliseum (6,362).
  (Winnipeg wins series, four games to none)

SERIES G (NEW ENGLAND VS. WINNIPEG) Avco World Trophy Championship
April 29 — New England 7, Winnipeg 2 at Boston Garden (6,526).
May 2 — New England 7, Winnipeg 4 at Winnipeg Arena (8,655).
May 3 — Winnipeg 4, New England 3 at Winnipeg Arena (7,200).
May 5 — New England 4, Winnipeg 2 at Boston Garden (13,697).
May 6 — New England 9, Winnipeg 6 at Boston Garden (11,186).
  (New England wins series, four games to one).

PLAYOFF SCORING

(1973—World Trophy Playoffs)

Player, Team	GP	G	A	Pts	PIM	PPG	WG	TC	PP	SH
N. Beaudin, Winnipeg	14	13	15	28	2	2.00	2	9	2	0
T. Webster, New Eng.	15	12	14	26	6	1.73	0	8	3	0
B. Hull, Winnipeg	14	9	16	25	16	1.78	3	6	2	0
T. Sheehy, New Eng.	15	9	14	23	13	1.53	3	8	2	0
L. Pleau, New Eng.	15	12	7	19	15	1.26	2	11	4	1
J. Dorey, New Eng.	15	3	16	19	41	1.26	0	2	1	0
T. Williams, New Eng.	15	6	11	17	2	1.13	1	4	2	0
B. Sutherland, Winnipeg	14	5	9	14	9	1.00	0	4	0	0
J. French, New Eng.	15	3	11	14	2	.93	1	2	0	0
C. Bordeleau, Winnipeg	12	5	8	13	4	1.08	0	5	1	0
G. Jarrett, Cleveland	9	8	3	11	19	1.22	1	5	3	0
M. Byers, New Eng.	12	6	5	11	6	.91	2	3	0	0
J. Wiste, Cleveland	9	3	8	11	13	1.22	1	1	1	0
G. Pinder, Cleveland	9	2	9	11	30	1.22	0	1	1	0
P. Popiel, Houston	10	2	9	11	23	1.10	0	2	1	0
L. Hornung, Winnipeg	14	2	9	11	0	.78	0	2	1	0
R. Buchanan, Cleveland	9	7	3	10	0	1.11	1	7	1	0
T. Caffery, New Eng.	8	3	7	10	0	1.25	0	0	0	0
L. Lund, Houston	10	3	7	10	24	1.00	1	2	0	0
R. Ley, New Eng.	15	3	7	10	24	.66	0	1	1	0
P. Andrea, Cleveland	9	2	8	10	2	1.11	0	2	1	0
M. Hall, Houston	10	4	4	8	18	.80	2	3	2	0
F. Hughes, Houston	10	4	4	8	2	.80	0	4	3	0
R. Pumple, Cleveland	9	3	5	8	11	.88	0	2	1	0
R. Selwood, New Eng.	15	3	5	8	22	.53	0	3	0	0
B. Selby, New Eng.	13	3	4	7	13	.53	1	3	1	0
J. Zanussi, Winnipeg	14	2	5	7	6	.50	1	2	0	0
A. McDonald, Winnipeg	14	2	5	7	2	.50	0	2	2	0
P. Hurley, New Eng.	15	0	7	7	14	.46	0	0	0	0
W. Boyer, Winnipeg	14	4	2	6	4	.42	2	3	1	0
W. Carleton, Ottawa	3	3	3	6	4	2.00	0	0	1	0
T. Green, New Eng.	12	1	5	6	25	.50	0	1	0	0
C. Swenson, Winnipeg	14	1	5	6	7	.42	0	1	1	0
D. Johnson, Winnipeg	14	4	1	5	0	.35	0	2	1	0
F. Speck, Los Angeles	6	3	2	5	2	.83	0	3	1	0
D. Rousseau, Winnipeg	14	3	2	5	2	.35	1	2	0	0
G. Kirk, Ottawa	5	2	3	5	12	.83	0	2	0	0
T. McCaskill, Los Angeles	6	2	3	5	12	.83	0	2	0	0
D. McCallum, Houston	10	2	3	5	6	.50	0	0	1	0
T. Earl, New Eng.	15	2	3	5	10	.33	2	2	0	0
G. Labossiere, Houston	6	1	4	5	8	.83	0	0	1	0
T. Martin, Ottawa	5	0	5	5	2	1.00	0	0	0	0
M. McMahon, Minnesota	5	0	5	5	2	1.00	0	0	0	0
J. P. LeBlanc, Los Angeles	6	0	5	5	2	.83	0	0	0	0
J. McKenzie, Phil.	4	3	1	4	8	1.00	0	2	1	0
R. Sentes, Ottawa	5	3	1	4	2	.80	0	2	1	0
T. Hampson, Minnesota	5	3	1	4	0	.80	0	1	0	0
T. Taylor, Houston	10	3	1	4	10	.40	1	1	1	0
B. Klatt, Minnesota	5	1	3	4	5	.80	0	1	1	0
B. Conacher, Ottawa	5	1	3	4	4	.80	0	1	0	0
W. Connelly, Minnesota	5	1	3	4	0	.80	0	1	0	0
T. Gilmore, Los Angeles	5	1	3	4	2	.80	0	1	0	0
P. Shmyr, Cleveland	8	1	3	4	19	.50	0	1	0	0
W. Muloin, Cleveland	9	1	3	4	14	.44	0	1	0	0
T. Hodgson, Cleveland	9	1	3	4	13	.44	0	1	1	0
B. Ash, Winnipeg	13	1	3	4	4	.30	1	0	0	0
M. Black, Winnipeg	14	1	3	4	2	.28	0	0	0	0

Player, Team	GP	G	A	Pts	PIM	PPG	WG	TC	PP	SH
G. Veneruzzo, Los Angeles	6	3	0	3	4	.50	1	3	1	0
Brian McDonald, Houston	10	3	0	3	16	.30	0	3	0	0
J. Johnson, Minnesota	5	2	1	3	2	.60	1	2	0	0
J. Niekamp, Los Angeles	6	2	1	3	10	.50	0	0	0	0
G. Erickson, Cleveland	9	2	1	3	2	.33	1	1	0	0
T. Ball, Minnesota	5	1	2	3	4	.60	0	1	1	0
B. Gibbon, Ottawa	5	1	2	3	12	.60	0	1	0	0
G. Trottier, Ottawa	5	1	2	3	0	.60	1	1	0	0
R. MacSweyn, Los Angeles	6	1	2	3	4	.50	0	1	0	0
G. Odrowski, Los Angeles	6	1	2	3	6	.50	1	1	0	0
S. Krake, Cleveland	9	1	2	3	27	.33	1	1	0	0
R. Clearwater, Cleveland	9	1	2	3	8	.33	0	1	0	0
E. Hoekstra, Houston	9	1	2	3	0	.33	0	0	0	0
L. Hale, Houston	10	1	2	3	2	.30	0	0	0	0
D. Asmundson, Winnipeg	12	1	2	3	8	.25	0	0	0	0
K. Ahearn, New Eng.	14	1	2	3	9	.21	0	1	0	0
B. MacMillan, Minnesota	5	0	3	3	0	.60	0	0	0	0
M. Hyndman, Los Angeles	6	0	3	3	17	.50	0	0	0	0
K. Mortson, Houston	10	0	3	3	16	.30	0	0	0	0
M. Pearson, Minnesota	5	2	0	2	0	.40	0	1	0	0
M. Antonovich, Minnesota	5	2	0	2	0	.40	0	2	0	0
G. Smith, New Eng.	11	2	0	2	4	.18	0	2	0	0
B. Charlebois, Ottawa	5	1	1	2	4	.40	1	1	0	0
R. Cunningham, Ottawa	5	1	1	2	2	.40	0	1	1	0
K. Stephanson, Ottawa	5	1	1	2	8	.40	0	1	1	0
E. Heiskala, Los Angeles	5	1	1	2	4	.40	0	1	1	0
B. Young, Minnesota	5	1	1	2	4	.40	0	1	0	0
G. Morrison, Minnesota	5	1	1	2	2	.40	0	1	0	0
D. Harris, Houston	10	1	1	2	4	.20	0	0	0	1
J.-G. Gratton, Winnipeg	12	1	1	2	4	.16	0	1	0	0
J. Cunniff, New Eng.	13	1	1	2	2	.15	0	1	0	0
B. Woytowich, Winnipeg	14	1	1	2	4	.14	0	1	0	0
C. LaPierre, Phil.	4	0	2	2	0	.50	0	0	0	0
A. Lacroix, Phil.	4	0	2	2	18	.50	0	0	0	0
R. Plumb, Phil.	4	0	2	2	13	.50	0	0	0	0
T. Ryan, Minnesota	5	0	2	2	0	.40	0	0	0	0
B. Leduc, Ottawa	5	0	2	2	4	.40	0	0	0	0
B. Crashley, Los Angeles	6	0	2	2	2	.33	0	0	0	0
S. Sutherland, Los Angeles	6	0	2	2	8	.33	0	0	0	0
Joe Hardy, Cleveland	7	0	2	2	0	.28	0	0	0	0
J. Schella, Houston	10	0	2	2	12	.20	0	0	0	0
B. Smith, Houston	10	0	2	2	0	.20	0	0	0	0
J. Gibson, Ottawa	1	1	0	1	5	1.00	0	1	0	0
J. Zermiak, Los Angeles	2	1	0	1	2	.50	0	0	0	0
D. Burgess, Phil.	4	1	0	1	0	.25	0	1	0	0
R. Campeau, Phil.	4	1	0	1	17	.25	0	0	1	0
D. Herriman, Phil.	4	1	0	1	14	.25	0	1	1	0
R. Climie, Ottawa	4	1	0	1	2	.25	0	1	1	0
L. Lilyholm, Minnesota	5	1	0	1	0	.20	0	1	0	0
K. Christiansen, Minnesota	5	1	0	1	0	.20	0	1	0	0
T. Simpson, Ottawa	5	1	0	1	0	.20	0	0	0	0
A. White, Los Angeles	6	1	0	1	0	.16	0	1	1	0
J. Stanfield, Houston	9	1	0	1	0	.11	0	1	0	0
B. Dillabough, Cleveland	9	1	0	1	0	.11	0	0	0	1
J. Shmyr, Winnipeg	3	0	1	1	2	.33	0	0	0	0
B. Campbell, Phil.	3	0	1	1	8	.33	0	0	0	0
D. O'Donoghue, Phil.	4	0	1	1	0	.25	0	0	0	0

Player, Team	GP	G	A	Pts	PIM	PPG	WG	TC	PP	SH
D. Lawson, Phil.	4	0	1	1	0	.25	0	0	0	0
J. McCartan, Minnesota	4	0	1	1	0	.25	0	0	0	0
F. Sanders, Minnesota	4	0	1	1	0	.25	0	0	0	0
J. Watson, Los Angeles	4	0	1	1	2	.25	0	0	0	0
D. Paradise, Minnesota	5	0	1	1	2	.20	0	0	0	0
J. Arbour, Minnesota	5	0	1	1	12	.20	0	0	0	0
S. King, Ottawa	5	0	1	1	7	.20	0	0	0	0
M. Amodeo, Ottawa	5	0	1	1	10	.20	0	0	0	0
R. Hopiavuori, Cleveland	8	0	1	1	6	.12	0	0	0	0
G. Kannegiesser, Houston	9	0	1	1	11	.11	0	0	0	0
B. Horton, Cleveland	9	0	1	1	10	.11	0	0	0	0
J. McMasters, Cleveland	9	0	1	1	6	.11	0	0	0	0
S. Cuddie, Winnipeg	12	0	1	1	10	.08	0	0	0	0
G. Rizzuto, Winnipeg	14	0	1	1	14	.07	0	0	0	0
A. Smith, New Eng.	15	0	1	1	12	.06	0	0	0	0
H. Heggedal, Los Angeles	1	0	0	0	0	.00	0	0	0	0
M. Boland, Ottawa	1	0	0	0	12	.00	0	0	0	0

POWER PLAY OPPORTUNITIES AND SHORTHANDED SITUATIONS

POWER PLAY	Opp.	GF	GA	Prof.	Freq.	SHORTHANDED	Sit.	GF	GA	Eff.	Freq.
Minnesota	11	4	0	36.4%	2.75	Houston	45	1	5	88.8%	9.00
Houston	27	9	1	33.3%	3.00	Cleveland	55	1	8	85.4%	6.87
Cleveland	39	9	0	23.0%	4.33	Winnipeg	33	0	6	81.8%	5.50
Winnipeg	48	11	2	22.9%	4.36	New England	64	1	13	79.6%	4.92
New England	75	14	0	18.6%	5.35	Philadelphia	17	0	4	76.5%	4.25
Ottawa	27	5	0	18.5%	5.40	Ottawa	30	0	8	73.3%	3.75
Los Angeles	25	4	0	16.0%	6.25	Los Angeles	20	1	9	55.0%	2.22
Philadelphia	25	4	1	16.0%	6.25	Minnesota	13	0	7	46.2%	1.86

Gerry Cheevers: Goaltender of the Year

INDIVIDUAL GOALTENDING STATISTICS
World Trophy Playoffs

Player, Team	Min.	GPI	W	L	SOG	GA	GAA
Gerry Cheevers, Cleveland	548	9	5	4	278	22	2.40
Bernie Parent, Philadelphia	70	1	0	1	42	3	2.57
Don McLeod, Houston	178	3	0	3	76	8	2.69
Wayne Rutledge, Houston	423	7	4	3	228	20	2.83
Russ Gillow, Los Angeles	247	5	1	2	115	12	2.91
Ernie Wakely, Winnipeg	420	7	4	3	210	22	3.14
Al Smith, New England	909	15	12	3	430	49	3.23
Joe Daley, Winnipeg	422	7	5	2	199	25	3.55
Jack McCartan, Minnesota	213	4	1	2	130	14	3.94
Yves Archambault, Phila.	153	3	0	2	66	11	4.31
Les Binkley, Ottawa	223	4	1	3	146	17	4.57
Gilles Gratton, Ottawa	86	2	0	1	73	7	4.84
George Gardner, Los Angeles	116	3	1	2	57	11	5.67
Mike Curran, Minnesota	90	2	0	2	61	9	5.97
Marcel Paille, Philadelphia	27	1	0	1	21	5	11.46

WHA OFFICIALS
1973-74

REFEREES:
1. Bill Friday
2. Bob Sloan
3. Ron Ego
4. Brent Casselman
6. Wayne Mundey
7. Darryl Havrelock
8. Ray Thomas
9. Bob Kolari
10. Pierre Belanger
11. Alan Glaspell
12. Ron Asselstine

LINESMEN:
18. Ron Asselstine
19. Wayne Mundey
20. Alan Glaspell
21. Pierre Belanger
22. Gene Kusy
23. Mike Entwistle
24. Ross Keenan
25. Eric Manship
26. Graham Hern
27. Tom Shamshak
28. Dennis Dahlman
29. Ken Pierce
30. Terry Kuliar

1973-'74 SCHEDULE

Sat.	Oct. 6	New York	at Cleveland
Sun.	Oct. 7	Chicago	at Toronto
		New England	at Quebec
Tues.	Oct. 9	New York	at Toronto
		Quebec	at New England
Wed.	Oct. 10	Winnipeg	at Vancouver
Thurs.	Oct. 11	Quebec	at Toronto
		Chicago	at New York
Fri.	Oct. 12	Winnipeg	at Edmonton
		Vancouver	at Minnesota
Sat.	Oct. 13	Houston	at Los Angeles
		Chicago	at New England (aft)
		Quebec	at Cleveland
Sun.	Oct. 14	Houston	at Edmonton
		Vancouver	at Winnipeg
		Minnesota	at Toronto
		New England	at New York (aft)
		Chicago	at Cleveland (aft)
Mon.	Oct. 15	Minnesota	at New England
Tues.	Oct. 16	Toronto	at Los Angeles
Wed.	Oct. 17	Houston	at Vancouver
		Winnipeg	at New England
Thurs.	Oct. 18	Chicago	at Los Angeles
		Toronto	at Quebec
		Winnipeg	at New York
Fri.	Oct. 19	Vancouver	at Edmonton
		New England	at Minnesota
Sat.	Oct. 20	Chicago	at Vancouver
		New York	at Quebec
		Toronto	at Cleveland
Sun.	Oct. 21	Chicago	at Edmonton
		Los Angeles	at Vancouver (aft)
		Minnesota	at Winnipeg
		Cleveland	at Houston
		New England	at Toronto
		Quebec	at New York (aft)
Mon.	Oct. 22	New York	at New England
Tues.	Oct. 23	Toronto	at Edmonton
		Cleveland	at Los Angeles
Wed.	Oct. 24	Toronto	at Vancouver
		Los Angeles	at Houston
		Minnesota	at New York
Thurs.	Oct. 25	Chicago	at Quebec
		New England	at New York
Fri.	Oct. 26	Toronto	at Winnipeg
		Quebec	at Minnesota
		Los Angeles	at Cleveland
Sat.	Oct. 27	Edmonton	at Vancouver
		Winnipeg	at Minnesota
		Los Angeles	at New England (aft)
		Houston	at Cleveland

Sun.	Oct. 28	Vancouver	at Edmonton
		Quebec	at Houston
		Chicago	at Toronto
		Los Angeles	at New York (aft)
Tues.	Oct. 30	Winnipeg	at Chicago
		Minnesota	at Houston
		Quebec	at Los Angeles
Wed.	Oct. 31	Winnipeg	at Cleveland
		Quebec	at Vancouver
Fri.	Nov. 2	Quebec	at Edmonton
		New York	at Winnipeg
		Minnesota	at Los Angeles
Sat.	Nov. 3	New York	at Vancouver
		Los Angeles	at Houston
		Toronto	at New England (aft)
		Chicago	at Cleveland
Sun.	Nov. 4	New York	at Vancouver (aft)
		Minnesota	at Edmonton
		Quebec	at Winnipeg
		Los Angeles	at Toronto
		Cleveland	at New England (aft)
Tues.	Nov. 6	New York	at Edmonton
		Winnipeg	at Quebec
		Los Angeles	at Chicago
Wed.	Nov. 7	Los Angeles	at Vancouver
		New York	at Minnesota
		Toronto	at Houston
		Winnipeg	at New England
Thurs.	Nov. 8	Edmonton	at Quebec
Fri.	Nov. 9	Vancouver	at Minnesota
		Toronto	at Los Angeles
Sat.	Nov. 10	Vancouver	at Houston
		Edmonton	at New England (aft)
		Quebec	at New York (aft)
		Winnipeg	at Cleveland
		Toronto	at Chicago
Sun.	Nov. 11	Los Angeles	at Winnipeg
		Cleveland	at Minnesota
		Edmonton	at Toronto
		New England	at Quebec
Mon.	Nov. 12	New York	at New England
Tues.	Nov. 13	Los Angeles	at Edmonton
		Houston	at Minnesota
		Cleveland	at Chicago
		Winnipeg	at Vancouver
Thurs.	Nov. 15	Minnesota	at Vancouver
		Houston	at Chicago
		New England	at Quebec
Fri.	Nov. 16	Edmonton	at Winnipeg
		Cleveland	at Los Angeles
Sat.	Nov. 17	Houston	at New York (aft)
		Quebec	at New England (aft)
		Toronto	at Chicago

63

Sun.	Nov. 18	Cleveland at Vancouver (aft)
		Minnesota at Edmonton
		New England at Los Angeles
		Winnipeg at Toronto
		Houston at Quebec
		Chicago at New York (aft)
Tues.	Nov. 20	Cleveland at Edmonton
		Minnesota at Los Angeles
Wed.	Nov. 21	Cleveland at Winnipeg
		New England at Houston
Thurs.	Nov. 22	Edmonton at Vancouver
		New England at Minnesota
		Chicago at Los Angeles
		Toronto at Quebec
Fri.	Nov. 23	Vancouver at Winnipeg
		Edmonton at Los Angeles
		Quebec at Cleveland
Sat.	Nov. 24	Chicago at Houston
		Toronto at Cleveland
Sun.	Nov. 25	Winnipeg at Minnesota
		Edmonton at Houston
		Vancouver at Toronto
		Quebec at New York (aft)
Mon.	Nov. 26	New York at New England
Tues.	Nov. 27	Winnipeg at Los Angeles
		Quebec at Toronto
Wed.	Nov. 28	Winnipeg at Houston
		Minnesota at Vancouver
Thurs.	Nov. 29	Cleveland at Quebec
		Houston at New England
		Edmonton at New York
Fri.	Nov. 30	Los Angeles at Winnipeg
		Toronto at Minnesota
Sat.	Dec. 1	Houston at Quebec
		Edmonton at Cleveland
		Los Angeles at Chicago
Sun.	Dec. 2	Quebec at Winnipeg
		Houston at Toronto
		Chicago at New England (aft)
		Minnesota at New York (aft)
		Edmonton at Cleveland (aft)
Tues.	Dec. 4	Los Angeles at Minnesota
		Edmonton at Chicago
Wed.	Dec. 5	Toronto at Vancouver
		Edmonton at Winnipeg
		New York at Houston
Thurs.	Dec. 6	Toronto at Edmonton
		Cleveland at New York
		Houston at Los Angeles (LB)
Fri.	Dec. 7	Toronto at Winnipeg
		Vancouver at Minnesota
Sat.	Dec. 8	Quebec at Minnesota
		New England at Cleveland
		New York at Chicago

Sun.	Dec. 9	Houston	at Vancouver (aft)
		New York	at Winnipeg
		Minnesota	at Toronto
		Chicago	at Quebec
		Cleveland	at New England
Tues.	Dec. 11	Minnesota	at Chicago
Wed.	Dec. 12	Quebec	at Vancouver
		Los Angeles	at Edmonton
		Houston	at Winnipeg
		Toronto	at New England
		New York	at Cleveland
Thurs.	Dec. 13	Cleveland	at Toronto
Fri.	Dec. 14	Quebec	at Edmonton
		Los Angeles	at Winnipeg
		Houston	at Minnesota
		New York	at New England
Sat.	Dec. 15	Los Angeles	at Vancouver
		Toronto	at Cleveland
		Houston	at Chicago
Sun.	Dec. 16	Minnesota	at Winnipeg
		Cleveland	at Houston
		Vancouver	at Los Angeles
		Quebec	at Toronto
		Chicago	at New England (aft)
		Edmonton	at New York (aft)
Tues.	Dec. 18	Vancouver	at Los Angeles
		New York	at Toronto
		Edmonton	at Quebec
		Winnipeg	at Chicago
Wed.	Dec. 19	Minnesota	at Vancouver
		Winnipeg	at Houston
		Edmonton	at New England
Fri.	Dec. 21	Vancouver	at Edmonton
		Los Angeles	at Minnesota
		Houston	at Toronto
Sat.	Dec. 22	Edmonton	at Vancouver
		Los Angeles	at Houston
		Toronto	at Quebec
		Winnipeg	at New England
		Chicago	at New York (aft)
		Minnesota	at Cleveland
Sun.	Dec. 23	Cleveland	at Minnesota
		Chicago	at Toronto
		Winnipeg	at New York (aft)
Mon.	Dec. 24	Vancouver	at New England (aft)
Wed.	Dec. 26	Chicago	at Winnipeg
		New England	at Houston
		Vancouver	at Cleveland
Thurs.	Dec. 27	Minnesota	at Edmonton
		New England	at Los Angeles
		Cleveland	at Quebec
Fri.	Dec. 28	Vancouver	at New York (aft)
		Quebec	at Chicago

65

Sat.	Dec. 29	New England	at Edmonton
		Toronto	at Minnesota
		Chicago	at Houston
		Winnipeg	at Quebec
		New York	at Cleveland
Sun.	Dec. 30	New England	at Vancouver (aft)
		Chicago	at Minnesota
		Houston	at Los Angeles
		Winnipeg	at Toronto
		Cleveland	at New York (aft)
Tues.	Jan. 1	Winnipeg	at Edmonton
		Cleveland	at Toronto
		Vancouver	at Chicago
Wed.	Jan. 2	Toronto	at New York
Thurs.	Jan. 3	ALL-STAR GAME IN ST. PAUL	
Fri.	Jan. 4	New England	at Winnipeg
		Edmonton	at Los Angeles
Sat.	Jan. 5	Vancouver	at Quebec
		Houston	at New York (aft)
		New England	at Cleveland
		Minnesota	at Chicago
Sun.	Jan. 6	Edmonton	at Minnesota
		Winnipeg	at Houston
		New York	at Toronto
		Chicago	at Quebec
		Vancouver	at Cleveland
Mon.	Jan. 7	Toronto	at New England
		Vancouver	at New York
Tues.	Jan. 8	Edmonton	at Houston
		Winnipeg	at Los Angeles
		Cleveland	at Chicago
Wed.	Jan. 9	Winnipeg	at Vancouver
		Edmonton	at Minnesota
Thurs.	Jan. 10	New England	at Toronto
		Los Angeles	at Quebec
Fri.	Jan. 11	Edmonton	at Winnipeg
Sat.	Jan. 12	Toronto	at Minnesota
		Quebec	at Houston
		Los Angeles	at Cleveland (aft)
Sun.	Jan. 13	Edmonton	at Vancouver (aft)
		Chicago	at Winnipeg
		New York	at Toronto
		Los Angeles	at New England
		Minnesota	at Cleveland (aft)
Tues.	Jan. 15	Minnesota	at Edmonton
		Quebec	at Los Angeles
Wed.	Jan. 16	Toronto	at Houston
		New York	at New England
Thurs.	Jan. 17	Vancouver	at Houston
		Chicago	at New England
Fri.	Jan. 18	New York	at Edmonton
		Cleveland	at Winnipeg
		Toronto	at Los Angeles

66

Sat.	Jan. 19	New York	at Vancouver
		Los Angeles	at Houston
		Minnesota	at New England
		Quebec	at Chicago
Sun.	Jan. 20	Cleveland	at Edmonton
		New York	at Winnipeg
		Vancouver	at Los Angeles
		New England	at Toronto
		Minnesota	at Quebec
Tues.	Jan. 22	New York	at Edmonton
		Los Angeles	at Houston
		New England	at Chicago
Wed.	Jan. 23	Cleveland	at Vancouver
		New York	at Minnesota
Thurs.	Jan. 24	Quebec	at Houston
		Cleveland	at Toronto
Fri.	Jan. 25	Winnipeg	at Edmonton
		Chicago	at Minnesota
		Quebec	at Los Angeles (LB)
Sat.	Jan. 26	Houston	at Vancouver
		Cleveland	at New England (aft)
Sun.	Jan. 27	Houston	at Edmonton
		Winnipeg	at Minnesota
		Vancouver	at Toronto
		Cleveland	at Quebec
		Los Angeles	at New York (aft)
Mon.	Jan. 28	Vancouver	at New England
Tues.	Jan. 29	Los Angeles	at Quebec
Wed.	Jan. 30	Chicago	at Vancouver
		Houston	at Cleveland
Thurs.	Jan. 31	Los Angeles	at Toronto
		Houston	at Quebec
		New England	at New York
Fri.	Feb. 1	Chicago	at Edmonton
		Los Angeles	at Winnipeg
		Toronto	at Quebec
Sat.	Feb. 2	Houston	at New England
		Minnesota	at Cleveland
Sun.	Feb. 3	Los Angeles	at Edmonton
		Chicago	at Winnipeg
		Minnesota	at Toronto
		New York	at Quebec
		New England	at Cleveland (aft)
Mon.	Feb. 4	Houston	at New York
Tues.	Feb. 5	Winnipeg	at Chicago
		New York	at Houston
		Cleveland	at Minnesota
		Edmonton	at Vancouver
Wed.	Feb. 6	Chicago	at Minnesota
		Quebec	at New England
Thurs.	Feb. 7	New York	at Los Angeles
Fri.	Feb. 8	Quebec	at Vancouver
		Houston	at Edmonton
		Minnesota	at Winnipeg
		New England	at Cleveland

67

Sat.	Feb. 9	Toronto	at Cleveland
		New York	at Chicago
Sun.	Feb. 10	Quebec	at Edmonton
		Houston	at Winnipeg
		Chicago	at Los Angeles (aft)
		Minnesota	at New England
		Toronto	at New York (aft)
Tues.	Feb. 12	Houston	at Minnesota
		Winnipeg	at Los Angeles
		Edmonton	at Chicago
		Quebec	at Toronto
Wed.	Feb. 13	New England	at Vancouver
		Edmonton	at Minnesota
		Winnipeg	at Houston
Thurs.	Feb. 14	Quebec	at Chicago
Fri.	Feb. 15	New England	at Edmonton
		Winnipeg	at Minnesota
		Houston	at Los Angeles
		Cleveland	at New York
Sat.	Feb. 16	Toronto	at Chicago
		Quebec	at Cleveland
Sun.	Feb. 17	Toronto	at Edmonton
		New England	at Winnipeg
		Minnesota	at Houston
		Vancouver	at Los Angeles (aft)
		Quebec	at New York
		Chicago	at Cleveland
Mon.	Feb. 18	Chicago	at New York
Tues.	Feb. 19	Toronto	at Vancouver
		Cleveland	at Quebec
Wed.	Feb. 20	Winnipeg	at Edmonton
		New York	at Houston
		New England	at Los Angeles
Thurs.	Feb. 21	Vancouver	at Chicago
Fri.	Feb. 22	Toronto	at Winnipeg
		Minnesota	at Quebec
Sat.	Feb. 23	Edmonton	at Houston
		Vancouver	at Cleveland
		New England	at Chicago
Sun.	Feb. 24	Chicago	at Winnipeg
		Vancouver	at Houston
		Edmonton	at Los Angeles
		New England	at Toronto
		New York	at Quebec
		Minnesota	at Cleveland (aft)
Mon.	Feb. 25	Toronto	at New York
Tues.	Feb. 26	Vancouver	at Houston
		Winnipeg	at Quebec
		Los Angeles	at Chicago
Wed.	Feb. 27	Los Angeles	at Minnesota
		Toronto	at New England

Thurs.	Feb. 28	Cleveland at Minnesota
		Winnipeg at Toronto
		Vancouver at Quebec
		New England at New York
		Houston at Chicago
Fri.	Mar. 1	Houston at Edmonton
		Minnesota at Winnipeg
		Cleveland at Chicago
Sat.	Mar. 2	Vancouver at New England (aft)
		Los Angeles at New York (aft)
Sun.	Mar. 3	Cleveland at Edmonton
		Quebec at Winnipeg
		Los Angeles at Minnesota
		New England at Houston
		Vancouver at New York (aft)
		Toronto at Chicago
Tues.	Mar. 5	Cleveland at Los Angeles
		New England at Chicago
Wed.	Mar. 6	New England at Minnesota
		Edmonton at Houston
Thurs.	Mar. 7	Cleveland at Vancouver
		Chicago at Quebec
Fri.	Mar. 8	Cleveland at Winnipeg
		Edmonton at Los Angeles
Sat.	Mar. 9	Quebec at Minnesota
		Toronto at Houston
		New England at New York (aft)
		Winnipeg at Chicago
Sun.	Mar. 10	Vancouver at Edmonton
		Minnesota at Los Angeles
		Cleveland at Toronto
		New York at Quebec
Mon.	Mar. 11	Winnipeg at New York
Tues.	Mar. 12	Los Angeles at Edmonton
		Minnesota at Houston
		New England at Chicago
Wed.	Mar. 13	Los Angeles at Vancouver
		Winnipeg at Cleveland
Thurs.	Mar. 14	New England at Vancouver
		Houston at Los Angeles
		Quebec at Toronto
		Minnesota at Chicago
Fri.	Mar. 15	New England at Edmonton
		Vancouver at Winnipeg
		Minnesota at New York
Sat.	Mar. 16	New York at Cleveland
		Quebec at Chicago
Sun.	Mar. 17	Vancouver at Edmonton
		New England at Winnipeg
		Cleveland at Houston
		Chicago at Toronto
		Minnesota at Quebec
Mon.	Mar. 18	Toronto at New York
Tues.	Mar. 19	Minnesota at Vancouver
		Cleveland at Chicago

Wed.	Mar. 20	New York	at Los Angeles
		Edmonton	at New England
		Houston	at Cleveland
Thurs.	Mar. 21	Houston	at Toronto
		Edmonton	at Quebec
		Vancouver	at Chicago
Fri.	Mar. 22	Minnesota	at Los Angeles
		Houston	at Winnipeg
Sat.	Mar. 23	Vancouver	at Quebec
		Edmonton	at Cleveland
		New York	at Chicago
Sun.	Mar. 24	Minnesota	at Houston
		*Winnipeg	at Los Angeles
		Vancouver	at Toronto
		New England	at Quebec
		Chicago	at Cleveland (aft)
Mon.	Mar. 25	Edmonton	at New York
Tues.	Mar. 26	Edmonton	at Chicago
Wed.	Mar. 27	New York	at Minnesota
		Houston	at Vancouver
		Los Angeles	at New England
		Quebec	at Cleveland
Thurs.	Mar. 28	Edmonton	at Toronto
		Los Angeles	at Quebec
		Cleveland	at New England
Fri.	Mar. 29	Chicago	at Vancouver
		Houston	at Winnipeg
		Edmonton	at Minnesota
Sat.	Mar. 30	Los Angeles	at Cleveland
		Toronto	at Quebec
Sun.	Mar. 31	Chicago	at Edmonton
		Vancouver	at Winnipeg
		Houston	at Minnesota
		Los Angeles	at Toronto
		Quebec	at New England
		Cleveland	at New York (aft)
Mon.	Apr. 1	Houston	at New England
Tues.	Apr. 2	Edmonton	at Toronto
		New York	at Chicago
Wed.	Apr. 3	Edmonton	at Winnipeg
		Vancouver	at Minnesota
		Chicago	at Houston
Thurs.	Apr. 4	Winnipeg	at Vancouver
		New York	at Los Angeles

All-Star Action with John McKenzie

WHA TRAVELOG

Approximate Air Mileage

	Chicago	Cleveland	Edmonton	Houston	Los Angeles	Minnesota	New England	New York	Quebec	Toronto	Vancouver	Winnipeg
Chicago	W	312	1646	932	1746	334	865	719	893	430	1850	834
Cleveland	312	O	1754	1104	2046	624	558	410	656	187	2150	1017
Edmonton	1646	1754	R	1864	1752	1252	2600	2457	2016	1671	503	835
Houston	932	1104	1864	L	1372	1046	1603	1416	1746	1299	2044	1469
Los Angeles	1746	2046	1752	1372	D	1940	2610	2454	2628	2175	1080	1990
Minnesota	334	624	1252	1046	1940		1385	1253	1227	780	1527	440
New England	865	558	2600	1603	2610	1385	H	186	403	463	2541	1765
New York	719	410	2457	1416	2454	1253	186	O	477	367	2445	1645
Quebec	893	656	2016	1746	2628	1227	403	477	C	462	2435	1277
Toronto	430	187	1671	1299	2175	780	463	367	462	K	2078	934
Vancouver	1850	2150	503	2044	1080	1527	2541	2445	2435	2078	E	1164
Winnipeg	834	1017	835	1469	1990	440	1765	1645	1277	934	1164	Y

CHRONOLOGICAL HISTORY

JANUARY, 1971
Dennis Murphy, co-founder with Gary L. Davidson of the American Basketball Association in 1968, conceives the idea for another major hockey league.

MARCH, 1971
Davidson and Murphy meet and explore the feasibility of a second major hockey league.

APRIL, 1971
The basketball season over, Murphy returns to California from Miami where he is general manager of the ABA Floridians and plans for the WHA are drawn.

JUNE, 1971
Articles of incorporation are filed in Delaware on June 10 for the World Hockey Association. Murphy meets with Jim Smith of Dayton, Ohio and Walt Marlow of the Los Angeles Herald-Examiner.

JULY, 1971
By-laws for the WHA are approved by the first Board of Trustees. Signatures on the document are Gary L. Davidson, Donald J. Regan and Dennis A. Murphy. Marlow advises W. D. (Bill) Hunter of Edmonton on the format of the new league, and in late July Hunter meets with Murphy for exploratory talks involving Canadian participation.

AUGUST, 1971
Davidson and Murphy start meeting with prospective franchise holders throughout North America.

SEPTEMBER, 1971
First formal meeting of the WHA is held Sept. 23-24 at the Century Plaza in Los Angeles, where interested ownership groups discuss the organization program.

OCTOBER, 1971
Davidson makes revolutionary announcement in Chicago on Oct. 20 that WHA player contracts WILL NOT contain a reserve clause and/or option clause.

NOVEMBER, 1971
The World Hockey Association, following two days of meetings at the Americana Hotel in New York, is formally organized on Nov. 1 with 10 franchises. The cities are Calgary, Chicago, Dayton, Edmonton, Los Angeles, Miami, New York, St. Paul, San Francisco and Winnipeg. Two additional franchises are granted Nov. 21 following a meeting in Tampa, Fla. to groups representing Ontario and New England. The following day (Nov. 22) Steve Arnold is named director of player personnel.

DECEMBER, 1971
The incredibility of a second major league has seized the imagination of the hockey fraternity throughout the world. J. Edward Fitkin, associated with the National Hockey League for 30 years, is named general manager of the San Francisco franchise. Post of publicity director and statistician is filled by Lee Meade of Hopkins, Minn.

JANUARY, 1972
Dennis Murphy, dividing his time between the league office and establishment of the Los Angeles franchise, on Jan. 7 announces the appointment of Terrence Slater as coach of the Sharks. A few days later, two of North America's foremost college coaches, Jack Kelley of Boston University and Glen Sonmor of the University of Minnesota, join the New England Whalers and Minnesota Fighting Saints respectively in the dual roles of general manager-coach. Vern Buffey, veteran National Hockey League official, accepts the post of referee-in-chief of the WHA. Richard I. (Dick) Wood and Seymour E. (Sy) Siegel, Trenton, New Jersey law partners, purchase the franchise rights for New York.

FEBRUARY, 1972
A group of Quebec City businessmen, led by Paul Racine, purchase the San Francisco franchise on the eve of the league's first historic player draft Feb. 12-13 in Anaheim, Calif. Fitkin becomes an official member of the league staff, presiding with Bill Hunter and Buffey over the draft which involved the selection of 1,081 amateurs and professionals. First player signed to a WHA contract was Steve Sutherland, by Gary Morrell of the Los Angeles Sharks in a Port Huron, Mich. motel room. First player of super star status to sign was Bernie Parent with the Miami franchise following negotiations with Lester Patrick, grandson of one of the NHL's founding fathers. The New England franchise, headed by Howard Baldwin, settled in Boston and the Ontario group, organized by Doug Michael, took up residence in Ottawa.

MARCH, 1972
Paul Deneau, owner of the Dayton, Ohio franchise, transfers to Houston and Jim Smith is named president and general manager of the Aeros. U.S. Olympic goaltender Mike Curran, one of 20 American-born players to ultimately dot WHA rosters, signs with Minnesota. A group of businessmen from suburban Oak Brook acquire the Chicago franchise. Fitkin is named assistant to President Gary L. Davidson, and Max Muhleman—a merchandising specialist with a strong record in major league auto racing—is named executive director of WHA Properties.

APRIL, 1972
Ten teams post $100,000 performance bonds at Continental Plaza Hotel in Chicago on April 14. Two teams, Calgary and Miami, are notified their franchises are in default and are given two weeks grace. On April 28, President Davidson cancels the franchises of Miami and Calgary.

MAY, 1972
James W. Browitt, a sports administrator of the first rank who formerly served as executive director of Freedom Hall in Louisville, accepts the post of league administrator and executive vice-president, succeeding Dennis Murphy who left the league office to devote all of his attention to the organization of the Los Angeles Sharks. New York Raiders sign lease with Madison Square Garden.

JUNE, 1972
James L. Cooper and Bernard A. Brown, a pair of New Jersey businessmen, obtain the 11th WHA franchise—name it the Blazers, and take over Parent's contract with Miami. Nick J. Mileti, a major league owner in baseball and basketball, is granted the WHA's 12th franchise for Cleveland. Jordon and Walter Kaiser, Chicago real estate developers, take over controlling interest in the Chicago franchise. John McKenzie is signed as player-coach of the Blazers. Then came the historic signing of Robert Marvin Hull by Ben Hatskin, owner of the Winnipeg Jets, on June 27. Hull received $1 million from WHA Properties and $1.75 million from the Jets, the contract extending over 10 years. Davidson presented Hull with the WHA check in St. Paul, and hours later the entourage flew to Winnipeg for the Jet signing.

JULY, 1972
With the acquisition of Hull, player signings became increasingly active. Twenty-eight are signed within the period of a week, among them J. C. Tremblay with the Quebec Nordiques, Gerry Cheevers with the Cleveland Crusaders, Bobby Sheehan with New York and Ted Green with New England. Quebec also announced signing of Maurice (Rocket) Richard as coach.

AUGUST, 1972
More than 300 players are now under contract, with the latest Derek Sanderson who agrees to 10 year pact with Philadelphia amounting to $2.325 million. Fitkin releases 78-game schedule.

SEPTEMBER, 1972
WHA teams begin training camp, with Philadelphia leading the way on Sept. 10. Rookie squads participate in first WHA action ever on Sept. 23.

OCTOBER, 1972
Professional contract players report to camp Oct. 1. President Davidson announces experimental program for usage of a colored puck. Red and blue are tried, but player protests result in return to conventional black. Shoot-out tie breaker following overtime period is also used in exhibition games, but is viewed with mixed emotions among players and coaches. Season opens Oct. 11 with Quebec at Cleveland and Edmonton at Ottawa. Edmonton's Ron Anderson scores first WHA regular-season goal. Court order kept Bobby Hull inactive.

NOVEMBER, 1972
Hull, after missing 14 games, is cleared for action following landmark ruling of Judge A. Leon Higginbotham, U.S. District Court for the Eastern Section of Pennsylvania. Decision rendered Nov. 8. The same night, Hull made official WHA debut in Quebec and assisted on winning goal as Jets edged Nordiques, 3-2.

DECEMBER, 1972
President Gary L. Davidson announces that scheduled exhibition series matching WHA all-star team against Czechoslovakia has been postponed due to fact that Czechs were unable to obtain sanction for the series from the Canadian Amateur Hockey Association. Donald J. Regan, WHA general counsel, repeated President Davidson's offer to the National Hockey League for settlement of differences out of court, at the same time predicting that cases currently on file will be resolved favorable to the WHA.

JANUARY, 1973
League's first all-star game in Quebec City Jan. 6 captured by East, 6-2, before a snow-bound crowd of 5,435. Game was locally televised. WHA Players' Association officially formed during All-Star break, with attorney Curt Leichner of Portland apointed general counsel. Opening of St. Paul Civic Arena attracts crowd of 11,701 New Year's Night. First CBS televised game, also in St. Paul, attracted crowd of 13,426 Jan. 7. Doug Harvey, 48, a 17-year star in the NHL, joins the Houston Aeros as assistant coach. Derek Sanderson, signed by the Blazers Aug. 4, is unsigned Jan. 17 and ultimately returns to the Boston Bruins of the NHL. Edmonton's Jim Harrison gets three goals and seven assists as Oilers trounce New York, 11-3.

FEBRUARY, 1973
Active only since Nov. 8, Bobby Hull finally cracks the WHA's top 10 scorers Feb. 19, rolling up 17 points in six games for a seasonal total of 74 and eighth place in the scoring derby. His goal output for 47 games was 38. Danny Lawson reached the 50-goal plateau Feb. 22 in Ottawa.

MARCH, 1973
On a rainy Sunday in Los Angeles (March 11) 12,804 people showed up at the Sports Arena for an 11 a.m. face-off between the Sharks and Ottawa Nationals. Cleveland owner Nick Mileti breaks ground March 16 for an $18 million arena on a 100-acre site in Richfield Township.

APRIL, 1973
New England (East) and Winnipeg (West) emerge divisional champions. Ottawa Nationals, following a rental contract dispute with the Ottawa Civic Center, move their playoff games to Maple Leaf Gardens in Toronto. Representatives of WHA and NHL meet secretly in New York (ex-officio) to discuss possible merger. President Gary L. Davidson later announces that WHA has rejected merger proposals and will continue to operate independently. "We believe the NHL's reserve clause to be wrong," said Davidson. "It would be impossible for us to consider any formal association with the NHL so long as they still have it." Goaltender Bernie Parent, after working the opening playoff game April 4, deserts the Philadelphia Blazers, who bow out in four straight defeats to Cleveland. Edmonton Oilers and Minnesota Fighting Saints, who finished in tie for fourth place in West, engaged in playoff April 4 on neutral ice (Calgary) with Saints winning, 4-2, before crowd of 6,400.

75

MAY, 1973
New England Whalers captured the World Trophy, besting Winnipeg Jets in series final, four games to one. New York franchise acquires new ownership, consisting of 14-man group headed by public relations executive Ralph Brent. Lee Matison is named vice-president. Team name is changed to Golden Blades. Ottawa Nationals are officially moved to Toronto with new ownership, Can Sports Ltd., a group of Toronto businessmen headed by John F. Bassett Jr., and Craig Eaton III. Team name changed to Toros. Philadelphia franchise sold to Canadian industrialist Jim Pattison, and relocated in Vancouver. Cincinnati group, headed by Brian Heekin III and William O. Dewitt Jr., granted franchise May 6 for the 1974-75 season.

JUNE, 1973
Gordie Howe, owner of more records than any man in the history of hockey, ends 21 months of retirement and signs with the Houston Aeros. Sons Marty, 19, and Mark, 18, also sign with Aeros, marking first time in history of major league sport that father plays alongside two sons.

JULY, 1973
Construction on schedule for three new buildings in league—Chicago, Edmonton and Cleveland. Pat Stapleton signs as playing-coach of the Chicago Cougars. Brian Shaw, one of Canada's premier junior coaches, named coach of Edmonton Oilers.

AUGUST, 1973
League general managers and coaches meet in Newport Beach. Announcement is made that official WHA puck will bear the signature of league president Gary L. Davidson.

SEPTEMBER, 1973
League membership increased to 15 teams with the awarding of franchises to Indianapolis (Dick Tinkham and John Weissert) and the Phoenix Roadrunners of the Western League, headed by Jim Wells. Along with Cincinnati, they'll become active for 1974-75 season. President Davidson announces the appointment of Walt Marlow as director of press relations.

OCTOBER, 1973
Season opens Oct. 6 with New York at Cleveland following a 40-game exhibition schedule with most of the attention focused on the Howe family. Winnipeg owner Ben Hatskin and Ed Fitkin named league vice-presidents. WHA reaches agreement with Canadian Amateur Hockey Association on drafting and signing of junior graduates.

The Exciting Difference

Hockey, it has been said, is a game combining all the elements—grace, speed, emotion, violence.

The purists said there just wasn't any room for improvement. But that was before the WHA came along.

World Hockey's rulebook, for the most part, duplicates that of any other professional league. There are, however, several innovations, that, in the league's inaugural season, proved extremely popular.

Take, for example, the WHA's overtime format.

There were 64 such situations last season, with 45 decisions rendered as against a mere 19 ties. The average elapsed time of the sudden death verdicts was 4:27, while the average time overall (64 OT's) was 6:06.

Beyond overtime and its attendant drama, other areas where WHA rules differ from other professional leagues are in ICING THE PUCK, OFFSIDE PASSES, CURVATURE OF THE STICK, and the THIRD MAN RULE.

THE ICING RULE

There is no shooting the puck down the ice with abandon by the shorthanded team. Icing is called and a resultant faceoff in the defending zone when the puck is cleared from inside the blueline the length of the rink—regardless of the manpower disadvantage. It has transformd penalty-killing into an art.

OFFSIDE PASS

In other leagues, a completed forward pass that crosses two lines is ruled offside unless the 'receiver' was in the same area of the ice as the 'passer' when the pass was made. In the WHA, a player may pass the puck from inside his own blueline to a teammate beyond the center red line, providing the puck precedes the player across the center red line and the receiver takes the puck ahead of his body. The rule is designed to bring about more quick breaks, but at the same time preventing a player from floating beyond the red line awaiting a breakaway pass.

STICK CURVATURE

The National League restricts the curvature of the stick blade to half an inch, mainly for the reason that goaltenders complain that curved blades represent an unfair advanage for the shooter adept at making the puck do tricks. The WHA has an allowable curvature of an inch and a quarter, resulting in more difficult shots for the goaltenders.

THIRD MAN RULE

The WHA's third man in a fight rule is somewhat more lax than in other leagues, where the man receives an automatic game misconduct penalty. In the WHA, he is given a 10-minute misconduct and assessed a $100 fine. If he violates the third-man-in rule a second time during a game, however, he has earned a game misconduct. The WHA rule was implemented to prevent bench-emptying brawls.

MINOR OFFICIALS

CHICAGO
SUPERVISOR
  Bill Rice
TIMEKEEPERS
  Frank Carriveau, Bill Marsh,
  Ralph Esposito
GOAL JUDGES
  Vince Hylka, Tony Schymanik
STATISTICIANS
  Bob Friedlander, John Marine
SCORERS
  Dick Bregnezer, Dean Summers

CLEVELAND
SUPERVISOR
  Earl Miller
TIMEKEEPERS
  Earl Miller, John Balunek
GOAL JUDGES
  Phil Simon, Howard Schleimer
SCORER
  Fred Heyer
STATISTICIAN
  Ed Hogan
STANDBY
  Ken Goss, Fred Heyer, Roger Hayda,
  Gary Nickerson, Tim Katrinak,
  Ray Liskay
  Ed Prokop

EDMONTON
TIMEKEEPER
  Bob Walker
GOAL JUDGES
  Ted McPhee, Dick Carreau
PUBLIC ADDRESS
  Bob Arnold

HOUSTON
OFFICIAL SCORER
  Dutch Keen
TIMEKEEPERS
  Joe Long, Ron Ellis
GOAL JUDGES
  Joe Chiswell, Leighton Young Jr.
STATISTICIAN
  Warren Hynes

LOS ANGELES
SUPERVISOR
  Frank Dunnigan
TIMEKEEPER
  Vince DiMarco
GOAL JUDGES
  Ben Cardas, Chuck Prince
STATISTICIANS
  Willie Mastin, Court Davis
SCORER
  Frank Dunnigan

MINNESOTA
SUPERVISOR
  Ron Vannelli
TIMEKEEPERS
  Eugene Gibbons, Joseph Birsch,
  James Killen
GOAL JUDGES
  Al Maki, John Jundt, Hank Frantzen
SCORER
  Arnie Bauer
STATISTICIANS
  Jack Kelly, Dan Gibbons
STANDBY
  Bill McClellan, Ron Smith,
  James Gibbons

NEW ENGLAND
SUPERVISOR
  Bill Henderson
TIMEKEEPERS
  Tony Nota, George Manning
GOAL JUDGES
  Robert Walsh, Edward Gibbons
STATISTICIAN
  Saul Weiss
SCORER
  Gerard McDermott
PUBLIC ADDRESS
  Weldon Haire
ATTENDANT
  James McDermott

NEW YORK
Frank Traverso   Dick Aslin
Jack Dillon   Russ Pagana
Nick Milos   Don Kessler
Charlie Joyce   Miltie Morse
Dick Gutwillig   Tony Daddario
Jeff Weintraub   Andy Desalvo
Leo Coar   Bill Kidder
Steve Foran   Robert Daddario
Don Webber   Robert Walsh

QUEBEC CITY
SUPERVISOR
  Adelard Morin
TIMEKEEPERS
  Claude Legare, Raymond Puchol
GOAL JUDGES
  Adrian Cloutier, Adelard Cloutier
SCORER
  Adelard Poulin
STATISTICIAN
  Michel Morin

VANCOUVER
SUPERVISOR
  Cal Pilkey
TIMEKEEPERS
  Cal Pilkey, G. Harley, L. Shevon
GOAL JUDGES
  J. MacGowan, S. MacGowan, J. Frizell
STATISTICIANS
  Fred Crane, Ed Starrick
PUBLIC ADDRESS
  Gerry Landa
SCORER
  K. Stein, T. Hull

TORONTO
SUPERVISOR
  Bruce Cameron
TIMEKEEPERS
  Connie Mandala, Bill Fry
GOAL JUDGES
  Gary Gordon, Pat Murphy
PUBLIC ADDRESS
  Darryl Wells
STATISTICIAN
  Jim Murchie
STANDBY
  Lorne Fellman

WINNIPEG
SUPERVISOR
  John MacLeod
TIMEKEEPERS
  Stanley Wolski, Bob Mick
GOAL JUDGES
  James Mair, James Witty, Dick Heaver
SCORERS
  Ted Barton, Dave Oakely
STATISTICIANS
  Stan Guptall, Sam Sanregret, Randy Huard

NEW TEAMS IN '74

CINCINNATI HOCKEY CLUB CORP.
3610 Carew Tower
Cincinnati, Ohio 45202
(513) 241-1818
PRESIDENT
Brian E. Heekin
EXECUTIVE VICE-PRESIDENT
William O. Dewitt, Jr.
CHAIRMAN OF THE BOARD
William O. Dewitt, Sr.

INDIANAPOLIS
IPS Management, Inc.
Suite 1650
Indiana National Bank Tower
Indianapolis, Ind. 46024
(317) 923-3636
John D. Weissert

PHOENIX PROFESSIONAL HOCKEY CLUB, INC.
1133 West Camelback Road
Phoenix, Arizona 85013

PRESIDENT
Jim Wells

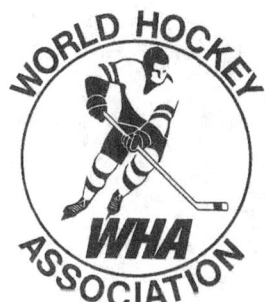

© WHA

HOUSTON AEROS: 1973-74 AVCO WORLD TROPHY CHAMPIONS

Top Row L to R: Bobby Brown, Trainer; Murray Hall; Ed Hoekstra; Marty Howe; Larry Lund; Joe Szura; Bill Prentice; Larry Hale; Don Grierson; Bobby Kincaid, Equipment Manager. **Middle Row:** Jim Sherrit; Frank Hughes; Jack Stanfield, Dunc McCallum; Gordon Kannegiesser; John Schella; Mark Howe; Andre Hinse; Doug Harvey, Assistant Coach. **Bottom Row:** Ron Grahame; Gordie Howe; Ted Taylor; Jim Smith, President and General Manager; Wayne Rutledge; Bill Dineen, Head Coach; Gordon Labossiere; Poul Popiel; Don McLeod.

1974-75 MEDIA GUIDE

EDITOR
WALT MARLOW

STATISTICIAN
FRANK POLNASZEK

CONTENTS

Team Effort	2
WHA Directory	3
Aeros	5
Blazers	7
Cougars	9
Crusaders	11
Fighting Saints	13
Jets	15
Mariners	17
Nordiques	19
Oilers	21
Racers	23
Roadrunners	25
Stags	27
Toros	29
Whalers	31
Stingers	32
Player Drafts	33
Abbreviations Code	37
Awards	38
Playoffs	39
Playoff Format	42
Playoff Records	43
Attendance	51
All Stars	52
'73-74 Statistics	54-68
Overtime Analysis	69
Team Statistics	71-77
WHA/NHL Records	79
WHA Records	81
Ind. Records	87
Travelog	92
WHA Chronology	93
WHA Officials	97
Rule Highlights	99
Media / Airlines	100
Schedule	104

THE COVER
*1973-74 ALL-STAR TEAM:
Clockwise - -
Paul Shmyr (Cleveland),
Gordie Howe (Houston),
Bobby Hull (Winnipeg),
Andre Lacroix (San Diego),
Pat Stapleton (Chicago),
Don McLeod (Vancouver).*

WHA PROPERTIES
705 Statler Office Building
Boston, Massachusetts 02116
Phone: (617) 426-3350
LARRY GORDON / Executive Director

Printed in USA — — — All Rights Reserved

DENNIS A. MURPHY
President

TRUSTEES

Chairman
BEN HATSKIN / Winnipeg

JORDON KAISER / Chicago
BILL DEWITT, Jr. / Cincinnati
NICK MILETI / Cleveland
W.D. (BILL) HUNTER / Edmonton
IRV KAPLAN / Houston
RICHARD TINKHAM / Indianapolis
CHARLES NOLTON / Michigan
WAYNE BELISLE / Minnesota
HOWARD BALDWIN / New England
BILL MACFARLAND / Phoenix
JOHN DACRES / Quebec
JOSEPH SCHWARTZ / San Diego
JOHN F. BASSETT, JR. / Toronto
BILL SLEEMAN / Vancouver

Team Effort

No single person established the World Hockey Association.

Nor is it ruled by a single person.

"My style is the team style," relates President Dennis Arthur Murphy, who, at 48, has left an indelible mark on the North American sports scene. "We function as a collective effort rather than individual. No man is bigger than the league."

That, in Murphy's analysis, is the premise on which the WHA was born and the reason, after a mere two seasons, that the league has been accorded complete credibility on the major league level.

Undeniably, it was Murphy, who, after launching the American Basketball Association, conceived the master plan for the WHA. But he doesn't view it as the act of a single man.

"There were a lot of people who contributed heavily to the formation of the WHA," reminds the Fullerton, California Irishman who took over as President in November, 1973. "Regardless of my role, or anyone else's, it remained for the franchises; in Canada and the U.S. to make the WHA a reality. No one can deny that they have succeeded."

Of the future, Murphy observes:

"My good friends of the mass media are making reference to the day when the National League, the Soviet Union, Czechoslovakia and the World Hockey Association will be part of a world tournament for the ultimate in hockey supremacy. I fully concur. It would be the greatest spectacle in sports."

WHA DIRECTORY

LEAGUE OFFICES
2082 Business Center Drive
Newport Beach, California 92664
Phone: (714) 833-9461

President
DENNIS A. MURPHY

Vice-Pres. / Administrator
JAMES W. BROWITT

Vice-Pres. / Director Hockey Operations
NORMAN "BUD" POILE

Director Public Relations
WALT MARLOW

General Counsel
CLAUDE YOUNG

Treasurer
PAUL RACINE

Asst. Treasurer / Controller
LINDA ZENK

Asst. to President
EDWARD FITKIN

Director WHA Properties
LARRY GORDON

Chief Supervisor Officials
VERN BUFFEY

League Statistician
FRANK POLNASZEK

Administrative Assistants
JOHN KANEL / CHRIS STOY

Executive Secretary
ELSIE HILL

Secretarial Staff
JANEEN BARBEE
JO ANNE KAKIMOTO
MARILYN LATHROP
SANDRA LEE

James W. Browitt

Norman "Bud" Poile

Walt Marlow

Claude Young

Paul Racine

Linda Zenk

Edward Fitkin

Vern Buffey

Larry Gordon

Frank Polnaszek

HOUSTON AEROS 1974-75 ROSTER

No.	Player	Pos.	S	Ht.	Wt.	Birth Date	1973-74 Club (League)	GP	G	A	TP	PIM
17	Larry Hale	D	L	6-1	180	10-9-41	Houston (WHA)	69	2	13	15	39
11	Murray Hall	RW	R	5-11	174	11-24-40	Houston (WHA)	78	30	28	58	18
16	Andre Hinse	LW	L	5-9	175	4-19-45	Houston (WHA)	72	34	42	76	25
9	Gordie Howe	RW	R	6-0	205	3-31-28	Houston (WHA)	70	31	69	100	46
4	Mark Howe	LW	L	5-11	180	5-28-55	Houston (WHA)	76	38	41	79	20
3	Marty Howe	D	L	6-1	185	2-18-54	Houston (WHA)	73	4	20	24	90
7	Frank Hughes	RW	R	5-10	180	10-1-49	Houston (WHA)	73	42	42	84	47
24	Glen Irwin	D	R	5-11	195	3-1-51	Fort Worth (CHL)	78	0	19	19	153
10	Gordon Labossiere	C	R	6-1	185	1-2-40	Houston (WHA)	67	19	36	55	30
27	Don Larway	RW	R	6-1	192	2-2-54	Swift Current (WCHL)	66	46	36	82	175
13	Larry Lund	C	R	6-0	190	9-9-40	Houston (WHA)	75	33	53	86	109
22	Bill Prentice	D	R	6-1	190	6-10-50	Houston (WHA)	55	1	2	3	35
21	Rich Preston	LW	R	6-0	185	5-22-52	Denver U. (WCHA)	38	20	25	45	36
6	Poul Popiel	D	L	5-10	176	2-28-43	Houston (WHA)	78	7	41	48	126
8	Terry Ruskowski	C	L	5-10	168	12-31-54	Swift Current (WCHL)	68	40	93	133	243
2	John Schella	D	R	6-0	180	5-9-47	Houston (WHA)	73	12	19	31	170
23	Jim Sherrit	C	R	5-7	170	9-29-48	Houston (WHA)	76	30	28	58	18
14	Ted Taylor	LW	L	6-0	175	2-25-42	Houston (WHA)	75	21	23	44	143

GOALTENDERS

No.	Player		S	Ht.	Wt.	Birth Date	1973-74 Club (League)	GP	MIN.	W-L-T	GA	AVG
29	Ron Grahame		L	5-11	175	6-7-50	Houston (WHA)	4	250	3-0-1	5	1.20
30	Wayne Rutledge		L	6-2	204	1-5-42	Houston (WHA)	25	1509	12-12-1	84	3.34
31	Glen Bueckert		L	5-9	183	8-25-54	Victoria (WCHL)	30	—	6-22-2	—	4.30

aeros

TELEX 77-5520

HOUSTON AEROS
HOCKEY CLUB, INC.
810 Bagby Street
Houston, Texas 77002   (713) 228-6437

Irvin Kaplan

Chairman of the Board	IRVIN KAPLAN
President/General Manager	JAMES S. SMITH
Head Coach	BILL DINEEN
Assistant Coach	DOUG HARVEY
Business Manager/ Public Relations Director	SONNY TATE
Club Attorney	HARRISON VICKERS
Head Trainer	BOBBY BROWN
Asst. Trainer/Equipment Mgr.	BOBBY KINCAID
Team Physician	DR. AL KNOLL
Orthopedic Specialist	DR. BILL RYLEE
Team Dentist	DR. GENE CRABTREE
Date Team Formed	APRIL 15, 1972
Home Arena	SAM HOUSTON COLISEUM, Civic Center, Downtown Houston.
Coliseum Capacity	9,874 (incl. standing room)
Coliseum Ice Surface	188 x 85
Press box location	West side (Top three Rows)
Club Colors	Navy Blue, Powder Blue, White
Training Camp	ICE HAUS (Town & Country Village).
Radio/Television	JERRY TRUPIANO (Play-by-Play) DAVE LUBESKI & SONNY TATE (color). All games home & away on KTRH-AM & eight road games televised on KHTV-39.
Ticket Prices	$6.50 / 5.50 / 4.50 / 4.00

James Smith

Bill Dineen

THE SUMMIT: New home of the Aeros commencing with the 1975-76 season. Construction of $18 million showplace, off S'West Freeway in Greenway Plaza, Started Feb. 1974. Capacity 16,000.

VANCOUVER BLAZERS 1974-75 ROSTER

No.	Player	Pos	S	Ht.	Wt.	Birth Date	1973-74 Club (League)	GP	G	A	TP	PIM
23	Serge Beaudoin	D	L	6-2	215	11-30-52	Vancouver (WHA)	26	1	11	12	37
6	Don McCulloch	D	L	6-2	190	3-23-51	Roanoke (SHL)	37	8	20	28	179
12	Peter McNamee	D		6-0	200		Richmond (AHL)	72	6	34	40	54
4	Mike Pelyk	D	L	6-1	190	9-29-47	Toronto (NHL)	68	5	46	51	154
3	Pat Price	D		6-2	200		Saskatoon (WCHL)	71	12	19	31	94
2	Duane Rupp	D	L	6-1	195	3-29-38	Hershey (AHL)	70	27	68	95	147
21	Paul Terbenche	D	L	5-10	175	9-16-45	Buffalo (NHL)	67	7	27	34	32
10	Rob Walton	D	R	5-9	165	9-3-49	Minnesota (WHA)	45	2	12	14	18
							Vancouver (WHA)	28	8	23	31	24
									8	15	23	2
14	Bryan Campbell	C	L	6-0	180	3-27-44	Vancouver (WHA)	76	27	62	89	50
7	Ron Chipperfield	C	L	5-11	180		Brandon (WCHL)	68	90	72	162	82
22	Claude St. Sauveur	C	L	6-1	175	8-15-52	Vancouver (WHA)	70	38	30	68	55
11	Danny Lawson	RW	R	5-11	185	10-30-47	Vancouver (WHA)	78	50	38	88	14
19	John McKenzie	RW	R	6-0	200	12-12-37	Vancouver (WHA)	45	14	38	52	71
17	Murray Myers	RW	L	6-0	185	7-28-47	Vancouver (WHA)	61	22	20	42	28
—	Don O'Donoghue	RW	L	6-0	190	9-27-49	Vancouver (WHA)	49	8	6	14	20
8	Don Burgess	LW	L	6-0	175	6-8-46	Vancouver (WHA)	78	30	36	66	8
18	John Migneault	LW	L	5-10	185	2-4-49	Vancouver (WHA)	74	21	26	47	27
—	Mike Chernoff	LW	L	5-10	175	6-13-46	Roanoke (SHL)	36	11	10	21	4
								4	2	4	5	7
5	Jim Cardiff	D	L	5-9	165	8-29-44	Vancouver (WHA)	78	1	21	22	188

GOALTENDERS

No.	Player	Pos	S	Ht.	Wt.	Birth Date	1973-74 Club (League)	GP	GA	SO	GAA
30	Peter Donnelly	G	L	5-8	160	6-14-48	Vancouver (WHA)	49	179	3	3.80
1	Don McLeod	G	L	6-1	190	8-24-46	Houston (WHA)	49	127	3	2.56

blazers

TELEX 045-086-18

VANCOUVER BLAZERS
Pacific Coliseum
Exhibition Park
Vancouver 6, B.C.   (604) 253-4181

Jim Pattison

President	JIM PATTISON
League Trustee	BILL SLEEMAN
General Manager/Coach	JOE CROZIER
Management Committee	
GUY LEWALL, FRED VANSTONE,	BILL SLEEMAN,
WILF RAY, STAN WHITTLE.	HARRY DUNBAR,
DON WALL, JIM PATTISON,	BUD EBERHARDT,
Asst. General Manager/Coach	ANDY BATHGATE
Public Relations Director	DENNY BOYD
Marketing Director	DON LEROSE
Ticket Manager	MILES DESHARNAIS
Controller	JOHN NEGLADUIK
Equipment Manager/Trainer	WARREN ELLIOTT
Chief Scout	AL MILLAR
Scouting Staff	MIKE SHABAGA (West)
	HAL SCHOOLEY (East)
	MARK REAUME (College).
	WARREN STRELOW
Training Camp	SASKATOON, SASK.
Radio/Television	RON OAKES (Play-by-Play)
	GARY RAIBLE & BERNIE PASCALL (Color)
	Radio: CJJC (800), CBC & BCTV.
Team Colors	ORANGE, YELLOW, BLACK
Date Team Formed	MAY 14,1973 (formerly Philadelphia Blazers)
Blazer Farm Teams	TULSA (CHL), CHARLOTTE (SHL)
Team Physician	DR. PETER WODYNSKI
Team Dentist	DR. BILL McCONNELL
Ticket Prices	$7.00 / 6.50 / 5.50 / 4.75 / 4.00

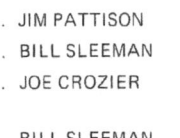
Joe Crozier

Andy Bathgate

PACIFIC COLISEUM:
Opened January 8, 1969.
Built at cost of $6 million.
Capacity 15, 569,
plus 1000 standing room.
Ice surface 200 by 85.
Press Box on West Side (100 seats)
Ten minutes from downtown.

CHICAGO COUGARS 1974-75 ROSTER

No.	Player	Pos.	S	Ht.	Wt.	Birth Date	1973-74 Club (League)	GP	G	A	TP	PIM
18	Bryon Baltimore	RD	R	6-2	196	8-26-52	Springfield Kings (AHL)	70	4	21	25	72
4	Darryl Maggs	RD	R	6-3	202	4-6-49	Chicago (WHA)	77	8	22	30	148
21	Larry Mavety	RD	R	5-11	196	5-29-42	Chicago (WHA)	77	15	36	51	157
23	Keith Kokkola	LD	L	6-3	204	5-4-49	Des Moines (IHL)	75	1	21	22	208
3	Dick Proceviat	LD	L	6-0	179	6-25-46	Chicago (WHA)	77	2	20	22	55
12	Pat Stapleton	LD	L	5-8	185	7-4-40	Chicago (WHA)	78	6	52	58	44
5	Jim Watson	LD	L	6-2	210	6-28-43	Los Angeles (WHA)	48	0	6	6	28
							Chicago (WHA)	23	0	5	5	22
14	Ralph Backstrom	C	L	5-10	180	9-18-37	Chicago (WHA)	78	33	50	83	26
11	Brian Coates	C	L	6-0	196	9-22-52	Long Island (NAHL)	14	10	15	25	39
							Chicago (WHA)	50	10	3	13	14
25	Joe Hardy	C	L	6-0	185	12-5-44	Chicago (WHA)	77	24	35	59	55
6	Gary MacGregor	C	L	5-11	176	9-21-54	Cornwall Jr. (QJHL)	66	100	74	174	82
8	Rod Zaine	C	L	5-10	171	5-18-46	Chicago (WHA)	77	5	13	18	17
22	Jim Benzelock	RW	R	5-11	187	6-21-47	Chicago (WHA)	55	6	7	13	19
16	Don Gordon	RW	R	5-11	184	4-17-48	Los Angeles (WHA)	29	8	6	14	24
							Chicago (WHA)	23	5	4	9	9
20	Duke Harris	RW	R	6-0	204	2-25-42	Chicago (WHA)	64	14	16	30	20
9	Rosaire Paiement	RW	R	5-11	183	8-12-45	Chicago (WHA)	78	30	43	73	87
24	Brian Glenwright	LW	L	6-3	206	10-8-49	Chicago (WHA)	15	3	2	5	0
7	Bobby Liddington	LW	L	6-0	179	9-14-48	Chicago (WHA)	72	26	21	47	20
10	Rick Morris	LW	L	5-11	176	7-5-46	Chicago (WHA)	77	17	16	33	140
19	Jan Popiel	LW	L	5-9	183	10-9-47	Chicago (WHA)	61	22	17	39	36
15	Francois Rochon	LW	L	5-11	181	4-18-53	Chicago (WHA)	70	12	11	23	27

GOALTENDERS								GP	GA	SO		GAA
1	Dave Dryden	G		6-2	186	9-5-41	Buffalo (NHL)	53	148	2		2.97
31	Andre Gill	G		5-7	175	9-19-41	Chicago (WHA)	13	46	1		3.44
							Long Island (NAHL)	19	50	2		2.63
30	Cam Newton	G	R	5-10	181	2-25-50	Chicago (WHA)	45	142	1		3.12

8

cougars

TELEX 253-357

CHICAGO COUGARS
HOCKEY CLUB INC.
Illinois Center
111 E. Wacker Drive
Chicago, Ill.   (312) 565-1900

Jordon Kaiser

Chairman of the Board	JORDON H. KAISER
President/General Manager	WALTER KAISER
Coach	PAT STAPLETON
Director of Player Personnel	JACQUES DEMERS
Head Scout	FLORENCE POTVIN
Scout	HENRY CAHAN
Director of Minor League Operations	GERRY LAMOUREAUX
Director of Sales/Marketing	KEN LA BUDA
News Media Director	MICHAEL HAGGERTY
Director of Ice Operations	MIKE HARDY
Head Trainer	EDDIE SWISS
Assistant Trainer	MIKE CAIRNS
Equipment Manager	IRA WILKS
Date Team Formed	JUNE, 1972
Training Camp	WHEATON-CAROL STREAM ICE-ARENA
Team Colors	JUNGLE GREEN, COUGAR GOLD
Television	26 road games on Channel 44 (Olympic Broadcasting) RED RUSH (Play-by-Play) LORN BROWN (color) DAN MULLALLY (commentary).
Radio	4 station network (WWMM-FM 92.7, WTAQ-AM 1300, WINR-FM 106.3, WGSB-AM 1480,) carries 39 home games and all playoff games. HOWARD BALSON (Play-by-Play) BUD KELLY (color).
Ticket Prices	$8.50 / 7.50 / 6.50 / 5.50 / 3.50

Walter Kaiser

Pat Stapleton

INTERNATIONAL AMPHITHEATRE:
4300 S. Halstead St.,
Capacity for hockey 9,000.
Home of the Cougars
since their inception.

CLEVELAND CRUSADERS 1974-75 ROSTER

No.	Player	Pos	S	Ht.	Wt.	Birth Date	1973-74 Club (League)	GP	G	A	Pts.	PM
4	Baxter, Paul	D	R	5-11	200	10-25-55	Winnipeg (WCHL)	63	10	30	40	384
6	Clearwater, Ray	D	L	5-11	175	11-10-42	Cleveland (WHA)	68	12	23	35	47
18	Edur, Tom	D	R	6-0	190	11-18-54	Cleveland (WHA)	77	7	31	38	26
2	Hillman, Larry	D	L	6-0	180	2-5-37	Cleveland (WHA)	44	5	21	26	37
8	Hillman, Wayne	D	L	6-0	205	11-13-38	Cleveland (WHA)	66	1	7	8	51
5	Muloin, Wayne	D	L	5-8	175	12-24-41	Cleveland (WHA)	76	3	7	10	39
3	Shmyr, Paul	D	L	5-11	175	1-28-46	Cleveland (WHA)	78	13	31	44	165
21	Andrea, Paul	RW	L	5-10	175	7-31-41	Cleveland (WHA)	69	15	18	33	14
25	Bartley, Mike	C-RW	R	5-9	178	7-28-50	Bowling Green (Col)	39	25	30	55	34
10	Buchanan, Ron	C	L	6-3	178	11-15-44	Cleveland (WHA)	49	18	27	45	2
11	Cardwell, Steve	LW	L	5-11	190	8-18-50	Minnesota (WHA)	77	23	23	46	100
16	Erickson, Grant	LW	L	5-9	165	4-28-47	Cleveland (WHA)	78	23	27	50	26
15	Heindl, Bill	LW	L	5-10	175	5-13-45	Cleveland (WHA)	67	4	14	18	4
20	Holbrook, Terry	RW	R	6-0	185	7-11-50	Minnesota (NHL)	22	1	3	4	4
12	Jarrett, Gary	LW	L	5-8	170	9-3-42	Cleveland (WHA)	75	31	39	70	68
17	Krake, Skip	RW	R	5-11	170	10-14-43	Cleveland (WHA)	69	20	36	56	94
22	Leduc, Rich	C	L	5-11	170	8-24-51	Boston (NHL)	28	3	3	6	12
							Boston (AHL)	29	7	11	18	60
14	McDonough, Al	RW	R	6-0	170	6-6-50	Pittsburgh (NHL)	37	14	22	36	12
							Atlanta (NHL)	35	10	9	19	15
29	Neale, Robbie	C	L	6-0	190	4-17-53	Cleveland (WHA)	43	8	9	17	30
7	Pinder, Gerry	LW	R	5-8	165	9-15-48	Cleveland (WHA)	73	23	33	56	90
19	Stewart, John	C	L	5-11	170	1-2-54	Bowling Green (Col)	39	27	43	70	50
28	Walker, Russ	RW	R	6-1	185	5-24-53	Cleveland (WHA)	76	15	14	29	117
24	Ward, Ron	C	R	5-11	175	9-12-44	Vancouver (WHA)	7	0	2	2	2
							Los Angeles (WHA)	40	14	19	33	16
							Cleveland (WHA)	23	19	7	26	7

GOALTENDERS	S.	Ht.	Wt.	Birth Date	1973-74 Club (League)	GP	GA	SO	GAA
30 Cheevers, Gerry	L	5-11	185	12-7-40	Cleveland (WHA)	59	180	4	3.03
1 Whidden, Bob	L	5-10	180	7-27-46	Cleveland (WHA)	22	80	1	3.90

10

crusaders

TELEX 985-376

CLEVELAND CRUSADERS LTD.

2923 Streetsboro Road
Richfield Township, Ohio   (216) 659-9100

Nick Mileti

President and Trustee	NICK J. MILETI
Alternate Trustee/Operations Manager	STEPHEN ZAYAC, Jr.
General Manager	JACK VIVIAN
Coach	JOHN HANNA
Chief Scout	BARRY FRASER
News Media Information Director	STEVE KLEIN
Promotions Director	BOB SCHMIDT
Trainer/Traveling Secretary	STEVE THOMAS
Trainer/Equipment Manager	DAVE SMITH
Team Physician	DR. ROBERT MACK
Team Dentist	DR. SHELDON KORMAN
Scouting Staff	BARRY FRASER, chief LES CUNNINGHAM, Staff ROGER ROY, Staff
Date Team Formed	JUNE 21, 1972
Training Camp	KENT STATE UNIVERSITY KSU Arena, Kent, Ohio
Radio/Play-by-Play	STEVE ALBERT 60 home and away games (WWWE-AM, 1100)
Television	14 Road (WUAB) STEVE ALBERT JOE TAIT PAUL WILCOX
Team Colors	CRUSADER PURPLE BLACK & WHITE
Press box location	CENTER ICE, EAST PLATFORM.
Ticket Prices	$7.50 / 6.00 / 5.00

Jack Vivian

John Hanna

THE COLISEUM: New, $20 million,
Coliseum Club, Telescreens.
18,500 capacity for hockey.
Ice surface 200 by 85
Owned by Ohio Sports Center Inc.
Nick Mileti, chairman of the board.

11

MINNESOTA FIGHTING SAINTS 1974-75 ROSTER

No.	Player	Pos	S	Ht.	Wt.	Birth Date	1973-74 Club (League)	GP	G	A	Pts.	PM
2	Dick Paradise	D	L	5-11	194	4-21-45	Minnesota (WHA)	67	2	7	9	71
3	Rick Smith	D	L	5-11	200	5-29-48	Minnesota (WHA)	71	10	28	38	98
15	Ron Busniuk	D-RW	R	5-11	180	8-13-48	Cincinnati (AHL)	68	7	24	31	146
							Buffalo (NHL)	5	0	3	3	4
24	Bob Boyd	D	R	6-1	190	11-27-51	Minnesota (WHA)	41	1	14	15	19
							Suncoast-WS (SHL)	39	5	21	26	21
17	John Arbour	D	L	5-11	194	9-28-45	Minnesota (WHA)	77	6	43	49	192
21	Terry Ball	D	R	5-9	165	11-29-44	Minnesota (WHA)	71	8	28	36	34
23	Mike McMahon	D	L	5-11	182	8-30-41	Minnesota (WHA)	71	10	35	45	82
6	Keith Christiansen	C	R	5-5	155	7-14-44	Minnesota (WHA)	74	11	25	36	36
10	Ted Hampson	C-LW	L	5-8	170	12-11-36	Minnesota (WHA)	77	17	38	55	9
12	*Mike Antonovich	C-LW	L	5-8	160	10-18-51	Minnesota (WHA)	68	21	29	50	4
20	Jim Johnson	C-LW	L	5-9	185	11-7-42	Minnesota (WHA)	71	15	39	54	30
25	Fran Huck	C	R	5-7	165	12-4-45	Winnipeg (WHA)	74	26	48	74	69
14	*Gary Gambucci	C-LW	L	5-9	175	9-27-46	Minnesota (NHL)	42	1	7	8	9
							New Haven (AHL)	2	2	1	3	2
							Portland (WHL)	21	11	15	26	20
22	Danny O'Shea	C	L	6-1	190	6-15-45	Out of hockey 73-74					
							St. Louis (NHL) 72-73	75	12	26	38	30
5	Don Tannahill	LW	L	5-11	175	2-21-49	Vancouver (NHL)	30	6	11	17	2
9	George Morrison	LW	L	6-1	175	12-24-48	Minnesota (WHA)	73	40	38	78	37
16	Gord Gallant	LW	L	5-11	178	10-27-50	Minnesota (WHA)	72	7	15	22	223
18	Bill Goldthorpe	LW	L	5-10	168	6-20-53	Syracuse (NAHL)	54	20	26	45	287
11	Murray Heatley	LW	L	5-8	185	11-7-48	Minnesota (WHA)	71	26	32	58	23
7	Wayne Connelly	RW	R	5-10	175	12-16-39	Minnesota (WHA)	78	42	53	95	16
8	*Bill Klatt	RW	R	5-10	180	10-16-47	Minnesota (WHA)	65	14	6	20	12
4	Mike Walton	RW	L	5-9	185	1-3-45	Minnesota (WHA)	78	57	60	117	88
26	Kevin O'Shea	RW	R	6-0	200	5-28-47	Phoenix (WHL)	54	24	21	45	40

GOALTENDERS		S	Ht.	Wt.	Birth Date	1973-74 Club (League)	GP	GA	SO	GAA
1	*Mike Curran		L	5-9	175	4-14-44	Minnesota (WHA)	40	130	2	3.27
30	*Jack McCartan		L	6-1	195	8-5-35	Minnesota (WHA)	2	5	1	7.14
35	John Garrett		L	5-8	170	5-17-51	Minnesota (WHA)	40	137	1	3.59

*American Born

fighting saints

TELEX 297-499

MINNESOTA FIGHTING SAINTS
St. Paul Civic Center
143 W. 4th Street
St. Paul, Minn. 55102   (612) 222-3040

Wayne Belisle

President/Trustee	WAYNE BELISLE
Alternate Trustee	JOHN IRVINE
General Manager	GLEN SONMOR
Coach	HARRY NEALE
Public Relations Director	MIKE LAMEY
Ticket Manager	TOM PERRAULT
Director of Advertising	DAVE BROOKS
Team Trainer	GLENN GOSTICK
Equipment Manager	DON NIEDERKORN
Team Physicians	DR. E. DUANE ENGSTROM
	DR. NORMAN HOLTE
	DR. LYLE O. JOHNSON
Western Canada Scout	ROY KELLY
Eastern Canada Scout	LLOYD GAIR
Team Formed	AUGUST 1, 1971
Training Camp	ST. PAUL CIVIC CENTER
Club Colors	ROYAL BLUE, WHITE, GOLD
Radio/Television	FRANK BUETEL (Play-by-Play).
Press Box	SOUTH SIDE
Biggest Crowd	APRIL 28, 1974 (17,211,) largest ever for hockey in State of Minnesota and a WHA record.
Ticket Prices	$6.50 / $5.00 / $4.00 / $3.00

Glen Sonmor

Harry Neale

CIVIC CENTER: Opened Jan. 1, 1973. Capacity 15, 705 plus standing room. Built at cost of $19 million. Only rink in North America with glass dasher boards. Ice surface 200 by 85.

13

WINNIPEG JETS 1974-75 ROSTER

No.	Player	Pos.	S	Ht.	Wt.	Birth Date	1973-74 Club (League)	GP	G	A	TP	PIM
21	Duke Asmundson	D	R	6-2	194	8-17-43	Winnipeg (WHA)	72	5	14	19	85
3	Mike Ford	D	R	6-1	180	7-26-52	Port Huron (IHL)	75	15	35	50	175
5	Larry Hornung	D	L	5-11	184	10-10-45	Winnipeg (WHA)	51	4	20	24	16
8	Perry Miller	D	L	6-1	194	6-24-52	Charlotte (SHL)	66	12	31	43	203
6	Heikki Riihiranta	D	L	5-11	190	10-4-48	Finalnd (European Amt'r)	--	-- RECORD UNLISTED --			--
4	Lars-Erik Sjoberg	D	L	5-8	179	4-5-44	Sweden (European Amt'r)	--	-- RECORD UNLISTED --			--
2	Bob Woytowich	D	R	5-11	197	8-18-41	Winnipeg (WHA)	72	6	28	34	45
7	Chris Bordeleau	C	L	5-9	172	9-23-47	Winnipeg (WHA)	75	26	49	75	22
12	Veli Pekka Ketola	C	L	6-3	207	3-28-48	Finland (European Amt'r)	--	-- RECORD UNLISTED --			--
14	Ulf Nilsson	C	R	5-11	176	5-11-50	Swedish Nationals (Eur. Amt.)	--	-- RECORD UNLISTED --			--
22	Danny Spring	C	R	6-0	180	10-13-51	Winnipeg (WHA)	66	8	16	24	8
18	Randy Andreachuk	RW	R	6-1	175	7-5-54	Kamloops Jrs. (BCJHL)	68	49	47	96	61
11	Norm Beaudin	RW	R	5-8	172	11-28-41	Winnipeg (WHA)	74	27	28	55	8
19	Milt Black	RW	R	5-10	179	6-20-49	Winnipeg (WHA)	47	6	9	15	14
16	Jean-Guy Gratton	RW	R	5-9	181	3-8-47	Winnipeg (WHA)	68	12	21	33	13
15	Anders Hedberg	RW	L	5-11	176	2-25-51	Sweden (European Amt'r)	--	-- RECORD UNLISTED --			--
20	Ron Snell	RW	R	5-10	171	8-11-48	Winnipeg (WHA)	70	24	25	49	30
10	Ron Ashton	LW	L	6-2	205	5-8-54	Saskatoon Jrs. (WCHL)	65	8	20	28	232
9	Bobby Hull	LW	L	5-10	191	1-3-39	Winnipeg (WHA)	75	53	42	95	36
17	Danny Johnson	LW	L	5-11	178	10-1-44	Winnipeg (WHA)	78	16	21	37	20

GOALTENDERS								GP	GA	SO	GAA	
1	Joe Daley	G	L	5-10	171	2-20-43	Winnipeg (WHA)	41	163	0	3.98	
24	Curt Larsson	G		5-10	171	12-11-44	Sweden (European Amt'r)	--	-- RECORD UNLISTED --			
30	Ernie Wakely	G		5-11	171	11-27-40	Winnipeg (WHA)	37	123	3	3.27	

jets

TELEX 075-87810

WINNIPEG HOCKEY CLUB, INC.
15-1430 Maroons Road
Winnipeg, Manitoba

(204) 772-9491

Bob Graham

President	BOB GRAHAM
Honorary Chairman of the Board	LT. GOV. JACK McKEAG
Trustee	BEN HATSKIN
Business Manager	RAY BAUSCHKE
Coach	RUDY PILOUS
Playing Coach	BOBBY HULL
Vice-President/Administration	BILL SHIELDS
Vice-President/Facilities	IVAN BERKOWITZ
Vice/President/League Relations	BEN HATSKIN
Vice-President/Marketing	OSCAR GRUBERT
Vice-President	ART COULTER
Vice-President	JIM BURNS
Vice-President	JACK WATTS
Director Player Personnel	BILL ROBINSON
Public Relations Director	J.D. BOYD
Trainer	BILL BOZAK
Equipment Manager	DOUG GUITTARD
Date Team Formed	DECEMBER 27, 1971
Training Camp	WINNIPEG ARENA
Team Colors	BLUE, RED & WHITE
Radio play-by-play	KEN NICHOLSON All home & Away Games (CJOB-680)
Color Commentators	BOB IRVING, VIC GRANT
Ticket Prices	$7.00 / 6.00 / 4.00

Ben Hatskin

Rudy Pilous

WINNIPEG ARENA
Opened Oct. 18, 1955.
Built at cost of $2 million.
Seating capacity 10,077 / standing room 11,000. Ice surface 200 by 85.
Arena phone (204) 783-4223.

SAN DIEGO MARINERS 1974-75 ROSTER

No.	Player	Pos	S	Ht.	Wt.	Birth Date	1973-74 Club (League)	GP	G	A	Pts.	PM
17	Ken Block	D	L	5-10	184	3-18-44	New Jersey (WHA)	74	3	43	46	22
6	Bob Falkenberg	D	L	6-0	195	1-1-46	Edmonton (WHA)	78	3	14	17	32
3	Harry Howell	D	L	6-1	200	12-28-32	New Jersey (WHA)	65	3	23	26	24
4	Kevin Morrison	D	L	5-11	202	10-28-49	New Jersey (WHA)	78	24	43	67	132
2	Ron Plumb	D	R	5-10	175	7-17-50	Vancouver (WHA)	75	6	32	38	40
26	Bill Speer	D	L	5-11	220	3-20-42	New Jersey (WHA)	66	1		4	30
28	Bob Wall	D	L	5-10	180	12-1-42	Edmonton (WHA)	74	6	31	37	46
10	Ray Adduono	C	L	5-9	160	1-21-47	Syracuse (AHL)	20	7	20	27	8
							Macon (SHL)	40	14	32	52	95
7	Andre Lacroix	C	L	5-8	175	6-5-45	New Jersey (WHA)	78	31	80	111	54
18	Mike Laughton	C	L	6-2	197	2-21-44	New Jersey (WHA)	71	20	18	38	34
15	Brian Morenz	C	L	5-10	185	5-11-49	New Jersey (WHA)	75	20	30	50	44
21	Tom Trevelyn	C	L	5-10	185	4-8-49	San Diego (WHL)	76	31	36	67	46
22	Jamie Bateman	RW	L	6-1	195	9-16-54	Quebec Jrs. (QJHL)	65	19	37	56	258
12	Wayne Rivers	RW	R	5-9	185	2-1-42	New Jersey (WHA)	73	30	27	57	20
20	Ted Scharf	RW	R	5-11	185	1-3-51	New Jersey (WHA)	63	4	2	6	107
8	Rick Sentes	RW	L	5-11	180	1-10-47	Toronto (WHA)	64	26	34	60	46
23	Doug Volmar	RW	R	6-1	215	1-9-45	Richmond (AHL)	47	24	12	36	30
16	Kevin Devine	LW	L	5-9	175	12-9-54	Toronto Jrs. (OHA)	67	40	29	69	218
9	Norm Ferguson	LW	R	5-8	173	10-16-45	New Jersey (WHA)	75	15	21	36	12
17	Lee Inglis	LW	L	5-10	175	8-31-47	Syracuse (NAHL)	55	30	40	70	32
25	Gene Peacosh	LW	L	5-11	180	9-28-48	New Jersey (WHA)	5	0	0	0	0
							New Jersey (WHA)	68	21	32	53	17
19	Brian Perry	LW	L	5-11	183	4-6-44	New Jersey (WHA)	71	20	11	31	19
11	Craig Reichmuth	LW	L	5-11	185	9-22-47	New Jersey (WHA)	72	10	8	18	114

GOALTENDERS

No.	Player	Pos	S	Ht.	Wt.	Birth Date	1973-74 Club (League)	GP	GA	SO	GAA
1	Russ Gillow	G	L	5-10	165	9-2-40	Los Angeles (WHA)	18	69	1	3.98
36	Joe Junkin	G	L	5-11	182	9-8-46	New Jersey (WHA)	53	197	1	3.79

mariners

TELEX 695-084

SAN DIEGO MARINERS
3500 Sports Arena Blvd.
San Diego, Calif. 92110

(714) 225-9633

Joseph Schwartz

President and Trustee	JOSEPH SCHWARTZ
Alternate Trustee	RICHARD SCHWARTZ
Executive Vice-President/ General Manager	HENRY (SKIP) FELDMAN
Coach	HARRY HOWELL
Director of Player Personnel	RON INGRAM
Business Manager	DANA LEWIS
Director of Sales & Marketing	JOHN MURPHY
Director of Public Relations	GABE De NUNZIO
Director of Promotion	GUS DIAMOND
Trainer	RALPH MITCHELL
Assistant Trainer	BOB SARNAS
Director of Group Sales	DON BUCHANAN
Chief Scout	LES CALDER
Scout	HERB ELK
Team Physicians	DR. DAN DENENBERG, DR. SAUL ROSS
Team Dentist	DR. ALAN GAYLE
Home Rink	San Diego Sports Arena
Press Box Location	North Side Loge
Public Address	JOHN De MOTT
Team Colors	Orange, Blue & White
Training Camp Site	La Mesa, California
Radio/Television	ROY STOREY (Play-by-Play) JERRY GROSS (Color) KOGO · · · All home and away games. Television package pending.
Ticket Prices	$7.00 / 5.00 / 3.50

Skip Feldman

Harry Howell

SPORTS ARENA:
Completed Nov. 17, 1966 at cost of $6.5 million. 33 acres of parking (4000 cars). 80 per cent of construction pre-cast concrete. Arena weighs 52 million pounds. Hockey capacity 13,700. Record crowd 13,752. Feb. 17, 1968 for WHL game. Four-sided electric scoreboard. Ice surface 200 x 85.

QUEBEC NORDIQUES 1974-75 ROSTER

No.	Player	Pos.	S	Ht.	Wt.	Birthdate	1973-74 Club (League)	GP	G	A	TP	PIM
2	Alain Beaule'	D	L	6-0	195	4-7-46	Quebec (WHA)	78	4	36	40	98
24	Jean Bernier	D	L	5-10	170	7-21-54	Shawinigan Jrs. (QJHL)	61	14	55	69	38
33	Dale Hoganson	D	L	5-10	190	7-8-49	Quebec (WHA)	62	8	33	41	23
20	Ric Jordon	D	L	6-3	200	3-31-50	Jacksonville (AHL)	45	8	8	16	54
							New England (WHA)	34	0	3	3	14
4	Francois Lacombe	D	L	5-10	188	2-24-48	Quebec (WHA)	71	9	27	36	37
10	Pierre Roy	D	L	6-0	175	3-12-52	Maine (NAHL)	39	4	21	25	116
3	J.C. Tremblay	D	L	5-10	185	1-22-39	Quebec (WHA)	44	2	7	9	8
							Quebec (WHA)	68	9	45	54	
21	Serge Bernier	C	R	6-1	190	4-29-47	Quebec (WHA)	74	37	49	86	101
16	Andre' Gaudette	C	L	5-7	165	12-16-47	Quebec (WHA)	78	24	44	68	14
17	Jeannot Gilbert	C	L	5-9	170	9-28-44	Quebec (WHA)	75	17	39	56	9
12	Michel Parizeau	C	L	5-9	165	4-9-48	Quebec (WHA)	78	26	34	60	35
27	Michel Rouleau	C	L	5-10	170	9-28-44	Maine (NAHL)	66	44	66	110	172
							Quebec (WHA)	4	0	4	4	2
19	Alain Caron	RW	R	5-9	180	4-27-38	Quebec (WHA)	59	31	15	46	8
9	Re'al Cloutier	RW	R	5-10	180	7-30-56	Quebec Jrs. (QJHL)	69	93	123	216	40
5	Rejean Houle	RW	L	5-11	165	10-25-49	Quebec (WHA)	69	27	35	62	24
15	Renald Leclerc	RW	R	5-11	165	11-12-47	Quebec (WHA)	58	17	26	43	77
14	Charles Constantin	LW	L	6-2	190	4-30-54	Quebec Jrs. (QJHL)	69	16	35	51	65
25	Robert Guindon	LW	L	5-8	160	11-6-51	Quebec (WHA)	77	31	39	70	25
6	Pierre Guite'	LW	L	6-1	192	4-17-52	Quebec (WHA)	72	14	20	34	114

GOALTENDERS

No.	Player	Pos.	S	Ht.	Wt.	Birthdate	1973-74 Club (League)	GP	GA	SO	GAA
1	Serge Aubry	G	L	5-9	165	1-2-42	Quebec (WHA)	26	90	1	3.87
30	Richard Brodeur	G	R	5-7	160	9-15-52	Quebec (WHA)	30	89	1	3.32
23	Michel Deguise	G	L	5-8	150	11-6-51	Quebec (WHA)	32	96	1	3.29

nordiques

TELEX 011-3068

QUEBEC NORDIQUES
LE CLUB DE HOCKEY LES NORDIQUES, INC.
Colisee De Quebec
Quebec City, Quebec
GIL 4W7   (418) 529-4161

John Dacres

Maurice Filion

Jean-Guy Gendron

Chairman of the Board	JEAN LESAGE
President / Trustee	JOHN DACRES
Vice-President	MAURICE TASCHEREAU
Alternate Trustee	PAUL RACINE
General Manager	MAURICE FILION
Coach	JEAN-GUY GENDRON
Chief Scout	YVAN PRUDHOMME
Director of Press Relations	DONALD D'AMOURS
Trainer	RENE' LACASSE
Team Physician	DR. ROBERT MEILLEUR
Director of Operations	PIERRE CHATEL
Public Address Announcer	YVES SABOURIN
Date Team Formed	JUNE 21, 1972
Training Camp	QUEBEC COLISEUM Quebec City, Quebec
Radio Play-by-Play	CLAUDE BEDARD 39 Road Games (CJRP-AM, 1060)
Television	FIVE STATION NETWORK, Reaching Sherbrooke, Hull, Chicoutimi, Quebec.
Team Colors	Red, White and Blue
Press box location	Top west of balconies
Ticket Prices	$8.00 / 6.50 / 6.00 / 3.50

THE COLISEE: Inaugurated Dec. 15, 1949. Capacity: 10,004 seating and 3,500 standees. First WHA Game Oct. 13, 1972 with Quebec defeating Alberta Oilers 6-0. On March 30, 1974, 13,346 witnessed Nordiques against Toronto Toros. Record Crowd 16,806 in March, 1951 for Quebec Citadelles-Barrie Flyers Memorial Cup Game. Ice surface 200 x85.

EDMONTON OILERS 1974-75 ROSTER

No.	Player	Pos.	S	Ht.	Wt.	Birth Date	1973-74 Club (League)	GP	G	A	TP	PIM
5	Doug Barrie	D	R	5-9	175	10-2-46	Edmonton (WHA)	69	4	27	31	216
20	Steve Carlyle	D	L	5-10	180	3-10-50	Edmonton (WHA)	50	2	13	15	18
27	Garry Cunningham	D	L	6-0	184	8-28-50	Winston-Salem (SHL)	64	5	9	14	33
3	Al Hamilton	D	R	6-1	195	8-20-46	Edmonton (WHA)	77	14	45	59	104
2	Barry Long	D	L	6-2	210	1-3-49	Los Angeles (NHL)	60	2	16	18	85
4	Ray McKay	D	L	6-4	183	8-22-46	California (NHL)	72	2	9	11	47
7	Jim Harrison	C	R	5-11	185	7-9-47	Edmonton (WHA)	46	24	45	69	99
16	Ed Joyal	C	L	6-0	180	5-8-40	Edmonton (WHA)	45	8	10	18	2
21	Bill Laing	C		6-2	190	3-24-53	Winston-Salem (SHL)	72	13	31	43	111
9	Ross Perkins	C	R	5-10	176	11-4-46	Edmonton (WHA)	78	16	40	56	43
18	Mike Rogers	C		5-9	170	11-24-54	Calgary Jrs. (WCHL)	—	67	73	140	32
11	Ron Climie	RW-LW	L	5-11	180	3-5-50	Edmonton (WHA)	76	38	36	74	22
14	Blair MacDonald	RW	R	5-9	180	11-17-53	Edmonton (WHA)	78	21	24	45	34
12	Bruce MacGregor	RW	R	5-10	180	4-26-41	New York (NHL)	66	17	26	43	6
6	Bill Morris	RW	L	6-0	185	6-26-49	Winston-Salem (SHL)	53	13	24	37	18
17	Rusty Patenaude	RW	R	5-9	175	11-17-49	Edmonton (WHA)	71	20	23	43	55
19	Ken Baird	LW	L	6-0	190	2-1-51	Edmonton (WHA)	68	17	19	36	115
25	Jack Gibson	LW	L	6-0	185	8-18-48	Toronto (WHA)	61	17	12	29	70
10	Tom Gilmore	LW	R	5-11	190	5-14-48	Edmonton (WHA)	57	19	23	42	164
8	Don Herriman	LW	L	5-10	165	1-2-46	New Jersey (WHA)	44	11	21	32	59
15	Bob Sheehan	LW	L	5-8	170	1-11-49	New Jersey (WHA)	10	1	3	4	6
							New Jersey (WHA)	50	12	8	20	8

GOALTENDERS

No.	Player	Pos.	S	Ht.	Wt.	Birth Date	1973-74 Club (League)	GP	GA	SO	GAA
30	Ken Brown	G	L	6-0	180	12-19-48	Winston-Salem (SHL)	29	145	0	5.53
30	Jacques Plante	G	L	6-0	175	1-17-29	Quebec (WHA)	—COACH & GENERAL MANAGER—			
1	Chris Worthy	G		6-0	186	10-23-47	Edmonton (WHA)	29	92	1	3.80

oilers

TELEX 037-3595

EDMONTON OILERS
EDMONTON WORLD HOCKEY
ENTERPRISES LIMITED
MacDonald Hotel
Edmonton, Alberta   (403) 426-4240

Zane Feldman

Chairman of the Board	DR. A.C. ALLARD
President	ZANE FELDMAN
Vice-President/General Manager	W.D. (BILL) HUNTER
Coach	BRIAN SHAW
Trustees	E.E. FITZGIBBONS A.F. GRIFFITHS HERB PINDER, Sr.
Secretary/Treasurer/Comptroller	R.L. BARTH
Director of Marketing	DOUG WENSCHLAG
Head Scout	ROBERT FREEMAN
Trainer	DICK BIELOUS
Equipment Manager	BARRY DEBENHAM
Date Team Formed	NOVEMBER, 1971
Radio	ROD PHILLIPS AL McCANN: All games home & away on Radio CFRN.
Team Colors	Royal Blue, Orange, White
Ticket Prices	$7.00 / 6.00 / 5.00 / 3.50

W.D. (Bill) Hunter

Brian Shaw

THE COLISEUM: Edmonton's new $13 million sports palace. Patterned after Pacific Coliseum in Vancouver. Circular in design, building has hockey capacity of 16,000, with provision of an additional 4,000. Located at 118th Ave. and 75th Street. Building and interior represents the height of luxury.

INDIANAPOLIS RACERS 1974-75 ROSTER

No.	Player	Pos	S	Ht.	Wt.	Birth Date	1973-74 Club (League)	GP	G	A	TP	PIM
3	Bob Ash	D	L	5-9	170	9-26-43	Winnipeg (WHA)	61	2	18	20	30
23	Roger Cote	D	L	5-9	184	12-22-39	Edmonton (WHA)	56	0	3	3	34
							Winston-Salem (SHL)	7	0	1	1	10
2	Ken Desjardine	D	L	6-0	180	8-23-47	Quebec (WHA)	69	2	9	11	46
5	Rick Fraser	D		5-9	165	7-11-54	Oshawa Jrs. (OHA)	69	4	18	22	25
4	Craig Hanmer	D		6-2	210	1-6-56	St. Paul Jrs. (MJHL)	84	5	19	24	119
6	Jim Hargreaves	D	R	5-11	195	5-2-50	Winnipeg (WHA)	54	1	4	5	50
26	Murray Kennett	D	L	5-11	185	6-28-52	San Diego (WHL)	76	6	25	31	35
16	Bob Fitchner	C	L	6-0	190	12-22-50	Edmonton (WHA)	31	1	2	3	23
							Winston-Salem (SHL)	31	16	16	32	107
15	Joe Robertson	C	L	5-11	180	3-10-48	Cincinnati (AHL)	55	21	30	51	101
22	John Sheridan	C		6-0	190	9-18-54	U of Minn. (WCHA)	38	24	14	38	42
17	Bob Sicinski	C		5-11	175	11-30-46	Chicago (WHA)	69	11	29	40	8
7	Bob Whitlock	C	L	5-10	175	7-16-49	Los Angeles (WHA)	66	20	29	49	30
20	Steve Andrascik	RW	R	5-11	190	11-6-48	Hershey (AHL)	70	23	43	66	36
19	Gary Bredin	RW	R	6-0	185	5-25-48	Rochester (AHL)	76	26	24	50	63
10	Nick Harbaruk	RW	R	5-11	195	8-16-43	St. Louis (NHL)	56	5	14	19	16
27	Rich Pumple	RW	L	6-3	200	11-2-48	Cleveland (WHA)	17	2	2	4	16
11	Ron Walters	RW	R	6-0	175	3-9-48	Los Angeles (WHA)	71	14	14	28	30
21	Kerry Bond	LW	L	6-0	190	7-18-45	Phoenix (WHL)	9	3	4	7	7
12	Brian McKenzie	LW	L	5-10	170	3-16-51	San Diego (WHL)	65	32	31	63	68
8	Steve Richardson	LW	L	6-1	185	5-4-49	Edmonton (WHA)	78	18	20	38	66
14	Jim Wiste	LW	L	5-10	180	2-18-46	Cincinnati (AHL)	63	13	29	42	58
							Cleveland (WHA)	76	23	35	58	24

GOALTENDERS

No.	Player	Pos	S	Ht.	Wt.	Birth Date	1973-74 Club (League)	GP	GA	SO	GAA
1	Andy Brown	G	L	6-0	185	2-15-44	Pittsburgh (NHL)	36	115	1	3.53
31	Ed Dyck	G	L	6-0	170	10-29-50	Vancouver (NHL)	12	45	0	4.63
							Seattle (WHL)	4	10	1	3.47

racers

TELEX 273-25

INDIANAPOLIS RACERS
IPS MANAGEMENT, INC.
Lower Concourse
Market Square Center
Indianapolis, Indiana 46204   (317) 635-3131

John Weissert

Chairman of the Board	L. CHARLES DE VOE
Trustee	RICHARD P. TINKHAM, Jr.
President/Alternate Trustee	JOHN D. WEISSERT
Coach	GERRY MOORE
Director of Operations	BILL ORWIG
Director of Playing Personnel	CHUCK CATTO
Public Relations Director	JOE VARGO
Trainer	BILL CARROLL
Assistant Trainer & Equipment Mgr.	FRASER GLEESON
Scouting Staff	FRANK MAHONEY DANNY SULLIVAN TOM HOOKWAY
Sales and Promotion Manager	TIM MILLER
Ticket Manager	MEL BROWN
Team Physicians	DR. JOSEPH RANDOLPH, DR. WILLIAM IRVINE
Team Dentist	DR. TOM LAPP
Press Box Location	North side of arena sections 6R & 7L
Team Colors	Red, White & Blue
Date Club Formed	SEPT. 14, 1973
Training Camp Site	Flint, Michigan
Radio	BOB LAMEY (all games) WIBC 1070-AM
Television	WTTV-Channel 4 (10 games)
Ticket Prices	$6.50 / 5.00 / 4.00 / 3.00

Bill Orwig

Gerry Moore

MARKET SQUARE ARENA:
New facility,
Built at cost of $22 million.
Ice level on third floor.
Capacity 16,500 (15,872 seats)
Ice surface 200 x 85.

PHOENIX ROADRUNNERS 1974-75 ROSTER

No.	Player	Pos.	S	Ht.	Wt.	Birth Date	1973-74 Club (League)	GP	G	A	TP	PIM
6	John Hughes	D	L	5-11	190	3-18-54	Toronto (OHA)	67	6	34	40	189
3	Al McLeod	D	L	5-11	195	5-17-49	Virginia (AHL)	54	1	13	14	52
5	Rick Newell	D	L	5-11	185	2-18-48	Virginia (AHL)	50	9	22	31	44
							Detroit (NHL)	3	0	0	0	0
18	Jim Niekamp	D	R	6-0	185	3-11-46	Los Angeles (WHA)	76	2	19	21	95
2	Jerry Odrowski	D	L	5-10	190	10-4-38	Los Angeles (WHA)	77	4	32	36	48
20	Mike Stevens	D		5-11	190	10-13-50	Denver (WHL)	71	3	25	28	67
14	Jim Boyd	C	L	5-9	180	6-4-49	Oklahoma City (CHL)	72	24	36	60	40
10	Robbie Ftorek	C	L	5-8	160	1-2-52	Virginia (AHL)	65	24	42	66	37
11	Murray Keogan	C	L	5-10	175	1-14-50	Detroit (NHL)	12	2	5	7	4
9	Dennis Sobchuk	C	L	6-2	180	1-12-54	Phoenix (WHL)	78	31	54	87	59
							Regina (WCHL)	66	68	78	146	78
22	Don Borgeson	RW	L	5-11	180	5-20-45	Providence (AHL)	72	21	29	50	28
17	Cam Connor	RW	L	6-2	210	8-10-54	Flin Flon (WCHL)	64	47	44	91	376
	Dave Gorman	RW	R	5-11	185	4-8-55	St. Catherines (OHA)	69	53	76	129	78
13	John Gray	RW	L	5-10	180	8-13-49	Oklahoma City (CHL)	59	25	35	60	155
8	Wayne Hicks	RW	R	5-11	185	4-9-37	Phoenix (WHL)	72	27	32	59	23
4	Howie Young	RW	R	6-0	200	8-2-37	Phoenix (WHL)	71	37	32	69	124
12	Bob Barlow	LW	L	5-10	175	6-17-35	Phoenix (WHL)	48	19	30	49	12
16	Michel Cormier	LW	L	5-9	170	12-22-45	Phoenix (WHL)	63	16	31	47	29
15	John Gofton	LW	L	5-10	180	11-27-53	Phoenix (WHL)	51	19	22	41	47
7	Hugh Harris	LW	L	6-0	190	6-7-48	New England (WHA)	75	24	28	52	78

GOALTENDERS

No.	Player	Pos.	S	Ht.	Wt.	Birth Date	1973-74 Club (League)	GP	GA	SO	GAA
30	Don Caley	G	L	5-10	170	10-9-45	Phoenix (WHL)	7	26	0	3.68
1	Gary Kurt	G	L	6-3	205	3-9-47	Syracuse (NAHL)	24	66		2.92
	Jack Norris	G	L	6-0	186	10-23-47	New Jersey (WHA)	20	75	0	4.13
							Edmonton (WHA)	53	158	2	3.21

roadrunners

TELEX 910-951-1557

PHOENIX ROADRUNNERS
1760 Valley Center
Phoenix, Arizona

(602) 257-5100

William McFarland

President and Trustee	WILLIAM H. MacFARLAND
Alternate Trustee/Chairman of the Board	BERT A. GETZ
Vice-President/Operations	JAMES G. WELLS
Directors	STEVEN W. CRAIG
	BERT A. GETZ
	H.J. LOUIS, M.D.
	KARL ELLER
	L.G. HOOKER, Jr.
	WM. H. MacFARLAND

Jim Wells

Business Manager	TERRY VIAR
Coach	SANDY HUCUL
Public Relations Director	DAVE WEISER
Player Personnel Director	E.I. "AL" ROLLINS
Western Scout	RUDY FILION
Eastern Scout	MURRAY COSTELLO
Legal Counsel	MIKE GALLAGHER
Promotions Manager	NORM SMITH
Team Physicians	ELI J. KRIGSTEN, M.D.
	THOMAS P. WHITE, M.D.
	DONALD A. CRYAN, M.D.
	ARTHUR C. STEVENSON, M.D.
Team Dentists	J. BARTON THOMPSON, D.D.S.
	REX E. UMBENAUER, D.D.S.
Trainers	JACK CURRAN, KEN FLEGER
Ticket Manager	MARY MILNER
Date WHA Team Formed	SEPTEMBER 18, 1973
Training Camp	BRANDON, MANITOBA
Radio / Television	JOE DAGGETT/MIKE LEONARD
	50 Games home & away
	KTAR. (620): 20 Road Games (KPHO-5)
Team Colors	Royal Blue, Gold, White
Arena	VETERANS MEMORIAL COLISEUM
	1826 W. McDowell Rd. (602) 252-6771
Ticket Prices	$7.50 / 6.00 / 5.00 / 4.00 / 3.00

Sandy Hucul

MEMORIAL COLISEUM:
Opened Oct. 21, 1967.
Capacity 12,600. Ice Surface 200 by 85.
Biggest crowd 12,155 Dec. 26, 1973 for
USSR vs. Roadrunners.
Roof has largest painting in world,
a representation of Bicentennial logo.

MICHIGAN STAGS 1974-75 ROSTER

No.	Player	Pos.	S	Ht.	Wt.	Birth Date	1973-74 Club (League)	GP	G	A	TP	PIM
15	Paul Curtis	D	L	6-0	185	9-29-47	Cincinnati-Providence (AHL)	66	3	21	24	37
	Bill Horton	D	L	6-0	185	9-5-46	Los Angeles (WHA)	60	0	9	9	46
3	Larry Johnston	D	R	6-0	195	7-30-43	Detroit (NHL)	65	2	12	14	139
25	Barry Legge	D	L	5-11	190	10-22-54	Winnipeg Jr. (WCHL)	66	13	34	47	198
2	Randy Legge	D	R	5-11	184	12-16-45	Providence (AHL)	75	4	21	25	121
21	John Miszuk	D	L	6-1	200	9-29-40	San Diego (WHL)	77	8	49	57	103
4	Bill Reed	D	R	5-11	190	5-25-54	Sault St. Marie Jr. (OHA)	63	13	43	56	240
	Jerry Zrymiak	D	R	6-0	195	10-19-46	Los Angeles (WHA)	27	2	8	10	8
							Greensboro (SHL)	54	3	29	32	95
10	J.P. LeBlanc	C	L	5-9	175	10-26-46	Los Angeles (WHA)	78	20	46	66	58
7	Jacques Locas	C	L	5-8	167	1-7-54	Quebec Jr. (QJHL)	63	99	107	206	87
17	Brian McDonald	C	R	5-11	190	3-23-45	Los Angeles (WHA)	56	22	30	52	56
20	Fred Speck	C	L	5-9	165	7-22-47	Los Angeles (WHA)	18	2	5	7	4
	Reg Thomas	C	L	5-10	180	4-21-43	Los Angeles (WHA)	72	14	21	35	22
16	Steve West	C	L	5-9	165	3-20-52	New Haven (AHL)	75	50	60	110	41
6	Bill Evo	LW	L	6-2	190	2-21-54	Peterborough Jr. (OHA)	82	28	34	62	193
8	Danny Gruen	LW	L	5-11	190	6-26-52	Detroit (NHL)	18	1	3	4	7
							Virginia (AHL)	57	25	27	52	64
19	Steve Sutherland	LW	L	6-0	172	9-1-46	Los Angeles (WHA)	72	20	12	32	182
9	Marc Tardif	LW	L	6-1	178	6-12-49	Los Angeles (WHA)	75	40	30	70	47
18	Gary Veneruzzo	LW	L	5-8	170	6-28-43	Los Angeles (WHA)	78	39	29	68	68
11	Len Fontaine	RW	R	5-8	168	2-25-48	Detroit (NHL)	7	0	1	1	4
							Virginia (AHL)	59	34	39	63	33
	Mike Hyndman	RW	L	5-11	205	12-8-45	Los Angeles (WHA)	8	0	1	1	0
							Greensboro (SHL)	12	4	6	10	9
22	Ed Johnstone	RW	R	5-9	175	3-2-54	Medicine Hat Jr. (WCHL)	68	64	54	118	164
24	Tom Serviss	RW	R	5-10	185	4-25-48	Los Angeles (WHA)	74	6	15	21	39
23	Alton White	RW	R	5-8	165	5-31-45	Los Angeles (WHA)	48	8	13	21	11
							Greensboro (SHL)	8	1	4	5	4

GOALTENDER

No.	Player	Pos.	S	Ht.	Wt.	Birth Date	1973-74 Club (League)	GP	GA	SO	GAA
1	Gerry Desjardins	G	L	5-11	185	7-22-44	New York Islanders (NHL)	36	101	0	3.12
30	Paul Hoganson	G	L	6-0	180	11-12-49	Los Angeles (WHA)	17	69	0	4.27
							Greensboro (SHL)	3	12	0	4.00
							Los Angeles (WHA)	17	69	0	4.27
	Jimmy McLeod	G	R	5-9	174	4-8-37	Jersey Knights (WHA)	10	36	0	4.18

stags

TELEX 230-238

MICHIGAN STAGS
30100 Telegraph Road
Birmingham, Mich. 48010   (313) 642-7200

Peter Shagena

Charles Nolton

John Wilson

Ownership/General Partners	PETER J. SHAGENA
	CHARLES H. NOLTON
Trustee	CHARLES H. NOLTON
General Manager/Coach	JOHN WILSON
Assistant to General Manager	GARY MORRELL
Business Manager	RICHARD L. COTE
Public Relations Director	GEORGE MASKIN
Team Trainer	NICK GAREN
Equipment Manager	JIM ZAPTON
Team Physicians	DR. PETER FORGATAS,
	DR. P.T. LEE
Team Dentist	DR. CHARLES REAUME
Team Colors	RED, BLACK & WHITE
Date Team Formed	JAN. 1972
	(formerly Los Angeles Sharks)
Radio / Television	GARY MORRELL (Play-by-Play)
	WWJ; All home & away except West Coast Games.
	TV-12; Road Games. NORM PLUMER (Color)
Training Camp	YOST FIELD HOUSE, ANN ARBOR, MICH.
Scouts	GORD HAIDY (Chief)
	JIM BAZDEL (West)
Starting Times	7:30 Tuesdays & Thursdays
	7:00 p.m. Sundays
Ticket Prices	$7.00 /6.00 / 5.00 / 4.00

COBO ARENA: Located in downtown Detroit, adjacent to Detroit River. Home of the Detroit Pistons of the NBA. Built 15 years ago. Capacity 10,200 for hockey. Ice surface 200 by 85.

TORONTO TOROS 1974-75 ROSTER

No.	Player	Pos.	S	Ht.	Wt.	Birth Date	1973-74 Club (League)	GP	G	A	TP	PIM
5	Mike Amodeo	D	L	5-10	195	6-22-52	Toronto (WHA)	76	0	11	11	82
4	Steve Cuddie	D	R	5-11	198	6-18-50	Toronto (WHA)	74	5	18	23	65
3	Rick Cunningham	D	L	5-10	190	3-3-51	Toronto (WHA)	75	2	19	21	88
6	Brian Gibbons	D	L	6-3	190	7-7-47	Toronto (WHA)	78	4	31	35	84
22	Gerard Gibbons	D	L	6-3	185	1-17-53	Toronto (WHA)	26	1	4	5	23
23	George Kuzmicz	D	L	6-1	200	5-24-52	Cornell (ECAC)	—	7	23	30	—
2	Jim Turkiewicz	D	L	5-10	185	4-13-55	Peterborough (OHA)	69	20	41	61	96
9	Wayne Dillon	C	L	6-0	180	5-24-55	Toronto (WHA)	71	30	35	56	13
32	Richard Dupras	C	L	6-0	184	1-1-50	Mohawk Valley (NAHL)	2	0	0	0	0
8	Richard Farda	C	L	5-9	175	11-8-45	Czechoslovakia	64	24	23	47	21
11	Gavin Kirk	C	L	5-10	175	12-6-51	Toronto (WHA)	78	20	48	68	44
20	Peter Marrin	C	R	5-10	175	8-8-53	Toronto (WHA)	31	1	4	5	4
14	Vaclav Nedomansky	C	L	6-1	210	3-14-44	Czechoslovakia	---RECORD UNLISTED---				
15	Brit Selby	C-LW	L	5-10	175	3-27-45	Toronto (WHA)	64	9	17	26	21
26	Tony Featherstone	RW	R	5-11	187	7-31-49	Minnesota (NHL)	54	9	12	21	4
25	Jeff Jacques	RW	R	5-11	180	4-4-52	Jacksonville (AHL)	73	18	25	43	83
17	Tom Martin	RW	R	5-9	175	10-16-47	Toronto (WHA)	74	25	32	57	14
12	Tom Simpson	RW	R	5-10	190	8-15-52	Toronto (WHA)	74	33	20	53	27
7	Guy Trottier	RW	R	5-8	170	4-1-41	Toronto (WHA)	71	27	35	62	58
10	Paul Henderson	LW	R	5-11	180	1-28-43	Toronto (WHA)	69	24	31	55	40
16	Pat Hickey	LW	L	6-1	185	5-14-53	Toronto (WHA)	78	26	29	55	52
19	Bob Leduc	LW	L	5-10	180	5-24-44	Toronto (WHA)	61	22	29	51	29
27	Frank Mahovlich	LW	L	6-1	205	1-10-38	Montreal (NHL)	71	31	49	80	47
21	Lou Nistico	LW-C	L	5-8	177	1-25-53	Toronto (WHA)	13	1	3	4	14
24	Gord Titcomb	LW	L	5-11	185	9-5-53	Jacksonville (AHL)	31	2	2	4	47

GOALTENDERS								GP	GA	SO	GAA	
30	Les Binkley	G	L	6-0	170	6-6-34	Toronto (WHA)	27	77	1½	3.27	
33	Gilles Gratton	G	R	5-11	155	7-28-52	Toronto (WHA)	57	188	2½	3.53	
1	Jim Shaw	G	L	6-1	185	10-18-45	Nova Scotia (AHL)	41	104	3	2.68	

toros

TELEX 06-23143

TORONTO TOROS
CAN SPORTS, INC.
14 Carlton St. (7th Floor)
Toronto, Ont.   (416) 595-1919

John F. Bassett

Board Chairman .... JOHN CRAIG EATON
President/Chief Executive Officer.... JOHN F. BASSETT, Jr.
Vice-President/Finance .... R.E. (BOB) GIROUX

Board of Directors

Ron Barbaro	John C. Eaton	Gordon C. Gray
John F. Bassett, Jr.	George Eaton	J. Chisholm Lyons
Allan Beattie	Peter Eby	Kenneth C. McGowen
Rudolph Bratty	John Finlay	Hugh McLelland
William Bremner	Allan Flood	Joseph Peters
Ronald E. Chisholm	Walter Fox	Harry Shier
George Cohon	Joseph J. Garwood	Steve Stavro
Douglas Creighton	Irving Gertstein	Nicholas Trbovich
		Ed Winkler

A.J. (Buck) Houle

General Manager .... A.J. (BUCK) HOULE
Coach .... BILLY HARRIS
Director Player Personnel .... GILLES LEGER
Director Media Relations .... R.G. (RICK) MATTHEW
Director Advertising, Promotions ... M.R. (MARTY) ZUCHOTZKI
Business/Ticket Manager .... MICHAEL McCLURE
Sales Managers .... PETER McASKILE
                              JOE WARWICK
Trainers .... FRANK VANDERHART,
                              LARRY ASHLEY
Team Doctors .... DR. M. BENT, DR. A. HART, DR. J. STARR
Team Dentist .... DR. T. McKEEN
Physiotherapist .... MERT PROPHET
Date Team Formed .... FEB., 1972 (Formerly Ottawa Nationals)
Training Camp .... OSHAWA, ONT.
Radio - Play-by-Play .... DAVE WRIGHT
                              Toros Network (6 stations) CHML-Hamilton,
                              CHEX- Peterborough, CKFW- Kitchener,
                              CKBB-Barrie, CKCB-Collingwood, CKQS-FM Oshawa
Television Play-by-Play .... MIKE ANSCOMBE, Global Network - 6 & 22.
Team Colors .... Blue, White, Red
Ticket Prices .... $9.00 / 7.00 / 6.00 / 4.50 / 3.00

Billy Harris

MAPLE LEAF GARDENS:
Opened Nov. 12, 1931.
Generally regarded as Canada's hockey shrine. Original construction cost $1.5 million. Building now reported to be worth $30 million. Original capacity 13,542. Present capacity including standees 16,485.

NEW ENGLAND WHALERS 1974-75 ROSTER

No.	Player	Pos.	S	Ht.	Wt.	Birth Date	1973-74 Club (League)	GP	G	A	TP	PIM
19	Thommy Abrahamsson	D	L	6-2	185	4-16-47	Swedish Nats.(European Amt'r)	RECORD UNLISTED				
10	Jim Dorey	D	L	6-1	190	8-17-47	New England (WHA)	77	6	40	46	134
6	Ted Green	D	R	5-10	210	3-23-40	New England (WHA)	74	7	26	33	42
5	Paul Hurley	D	R	5-11	195	7-12-46	New England (WHA)	52	3	11	14	21
2	Rick Ley	D	L	5-9	185	12-2-48	New England (WHA)	72	6	35	41	148
3	Brad Selwood	D	L	6-1	190	3-18-49	New England (WHA)	76	9	28	37	91
7	Terry Caffery	C	R	5-9	165	4-1-49	New England (WHA)	INJURED — DID NOT PLAY				
9	Wayne Carleton	C	L	6-3	215	8-4-46	Toronto (WHA)	78	37	55	92	31
4	Larry Pleau	C	L	6-1	185	5-29-47	New England (WHA)	77	26	48	69	35
20	Garry Swain	C	L	5-9	164	9-11-47	Baltimore (AHL)	12	2	7	9	10
21	Mike Byers	RW	R	5-10	185	9-11-46	New England (WHA)	78	29	21	50	6
27	Tom Earl	RW	R	5-11	180	1-27-47	New England (WHA)	78	10	10	20	29
16	Fred O'Donnell	RW	R	5-10	175	12-6-49	Boston (NHL)	42	5	5	10	48
15	Tim Sheehy	RW	R	6-1	185	9-3-48	New England (WHA)	77	29	29	58	22
8	Tom Webster	RW	R	5-10	185	10-4-48	New England (WHA)	64	43	27	70	28
22	Don Blackburn	LW	L	6-0	175	5-14-38	New England (WHA)	75	20	39	59	18
23	Nick Fotiu	LW	L	6-2	200	5-25-52	Cape Cod (NAHL)	72	12	24	36	379
11	John French	LW	L	5-11	175	8-25-50	New England (WHA)	75	24	48	72	31
14	Al Karlander	LW-C	L	5-8	170	11-5-46	New England (WHA)	77	20	41	61	46

GOALTENDERS

No.	Player	Pos.	S	Ht.	Wt.	Birth Date	1973-74 Club (League)	GP	GA	SO	GAA
27	Crister Abrahamsson	G		6-2	175	4-16-47	Swedish Nats.(European Amt'r)	— RECORD UNLISTED —			
1	Al Smith	G	R	6-1	200	11-10-45	New England (WHA)	55	164	2	3.08

whalers

TELEX 994 476

NEW ENGLAND WHALERS
HOCKEY CLUB, INC.
One Civic Center Plaza
Hartford, Conn. 06103   (203) 728-3366

Howard Baldwin

President / Trustee	HOWARD L. BALDWIN
Board of Directors	BOB CAPORALE HOWARD L. BALDWIN PETER SAVIN STAN SCHULTZ BLAKE IRONS
Executive Vice-President/ General Manager	JACK KELLEY
Vice-Pres. / Director Public Relations	KEVIN WALSH
Assistant to the President	GEORGE DUCHARME
Coach	RON RYAN
Asst. Coach / Director Player Personnel	JACK FERREIRA
Business Manager	DAVE ANDREWS
Media Relations Director	BOB NEUMEIER
Ticket Manager	BRIAN MacLEOD
Merchandising Manager	MIKE REDDY
Team Physicians	DR. VINCENT J. TURCO, DR. LOUIS PALOSKY
Chief Scout	RICHARD GREEN
Trainer	JOE ALTOTT
Equipment Manager	SKIP CUNNINGHAM
Date Team Formed	MARCH, 1972
Training Camp	WESLEYAN UNIVERSITY Middletown, Ct.
Team colors	GREEN, WHITE, BLACK
Home rinks	EASTERN STATES COLISEUM / Springfield, Phone: (413) 733-5101 14 games. Capacity 5516, Final 25 games HARTFORD CIVIC CENTER
Radio/Television	BILL RASMUSSEN (Play-by-Play) All home and away games on Springfield/Hartford Radio Network. Television: 13 games WFSB-TV (Channel 3)
Ticket Prices	$8.00 / 7.00 / 5.50 / 4.00

Jack Kelley

Ron Ryan

HARTFORD CIVIC CENTER:
$30 million convention center complex.
Whalers scheduled to take occupancy
January 15, 1975. Capacity 10,400
Ice Surface 200 x 85.

stingers

TELEX 214 - 286

CINCINNATI STINGERS
CINCINNATI HOCKEY CLUB CORP.
3610 Carew Tower
Cincinnati, Ohio 45202   (513) 241-1818

Brian Heekin

Bill DeWitt, Jr.

Terry Slater

Chairman of the Board	WILLIAM O. DEWITT
President	BRIAN E. HEEKIN
Executive Vice-President Chief Executive Officer	WILLIAM O. DEWITT, JR.
Vice-President/Treasurer	JAMES R. RAMMACHER
Coach	TERRENCE SLATER
Director of Sales/Promotions	WILLIAM R. BARRETT
Director of Player Personnel	JEROME M. RAFTER
Board of Directors	WILLIAM O. DEWITT
	WILLIAM O. DEWITT, JR.
	ALBERT E. HEEKIN, III
	BRIAN E. HEEKIN
	CHARLES L. HEEKIN
	LAWRENCE H. KYTE, JR.
	JAMES R. RAMMACHER
	PHILIP S. SMITH
Team Formed	1972 (Begins Play '75-76 Season)
Team Colors	Black, Yellow, White
Scouts	HARRY SOBCHUK (Western Canada)
	JACQUES LOCAS (Quebec region)

Players Under Contract and on Loan To:

Dennis Sobchuk (Phoenix)	Joe Robertson (Indianapolis)
Eugene Sobchuk (Phoenix)	Steve Andrascik (Indianapolis)
John Hughes (Phoenix)	Ralph Hopiavouri (Indianapolis)
Mike Pelyk (Vancouver)	Jacques Locas (Michigan)
Ned Yetten (Vancouver)	Ron Plumb (San Diego)
John Kiely (Vancouver)	Dick Spannbauer (Indianapolis)
	Brad Buetow (Unassigned)

RIVERFRONT COLISEUM:
To be completed in summer '75.
Cost Estimated at $20 million.
Capacity for hockey 16,500.
Ice surface 200 x 85.

32

draft

EXPANSION DRAFT

(Players Selected by Phoenix and Indianapolis at Toronto, Ontario May 30, 1974)

PHOENIX ROADRUNNERS		INDIANAPOLIS RACERS	
Gary Kurt/G	San Diego	Brian McKenzie/LW	Edmonton
Gerry Odrowski/D	Michigan	Bob Fitchner/C	Edmonton
Ted Hodgson/RW	Michigan	Bob Whitlock/C	Michigan
Bill Young/RW	Michigan	Bob Ash/D	Winnipeg
Rich Pumple/LW	Cleveland	Bob Sicinski/C	Chicago
Bob Jones/C	San Diego	Richard Campeau/D	Vancouver
Bernie Blanchette/RW	Edmonton	Roger Cote/D	Edmonton
Steve King/RW	Toronto	Jim Hargreaves/D	Winnipeg
Dick Sarrazin/RW	Chicago	M. Archambeault/LW	Quebec
Terry Ryan/C	Minnesota	Billy Orr/D	Toronto
Ron Anderson/D	Chicago	Cal Swenson/C	Winnipeg
Jack Gibson/LW	Toronto	Yves Bergeron/RW	Quebec
Jim McMasters/D	Cleveland	Pierre Henry/LW	Vancouver
Michel Plante/LW	Vancouver	Ken Desjardins/D	Quebec
Steve Warr/D	Toronto	Ron Morgan/LW	Cleveland
		Tom William/LW	New England

MAJOR LEAGUE DRAFT

OF CANADIAN AMATEURS (In Order of Selection)

Denotes Player Signed With WHA

No.	Name	Last Amateur Club	NHL Claim	WHA Claim
1. *	PRICE, Pat	Saskatoon Blades		Vancouver
2.	JOLY, Greg	Regina Pats	Washington	
3. *	WILL, Mike	Edmonton Oil Kings		Indianapolis
4. *	PAIEMENT, Wilfred	St. Catharines Hawks	Kansas	
5.	LARWAY, Don	Swift Current Broncos	Boston	Cincinnati
6. *	HAMPTON, Rick	St. Catharines Hawks	California	
7.	REED, Bill	S.S. Marie Greyhounds	Boston	Michigan
8.	GILLIES, Clark	Regina Pats	N.Y. Islanders	Edmonton
9. *	RHINESS, Brad	Kingston Canadians		San Diego
10.	CONNOR, Cam	Flin Flon Bombers	Montreal	Phoenix
11.	ANDRECHUK, Randy	Kamloops Chiefs	Philadelphia	Winnipeg
12. *	HICKS, Douglas	Flin Flon Bombers	Minnesota	
13.	SEETAERT, Douglas	Edmonton Oil Kings		Edmonton
14.	RISEBOROUGH, Douglas	Kitchener Rangers	Montreal	Cleveland
15. *	CLOUTIER, Real	Quebec Remparts		Quebec
16. *	LAROUCHE, Pierre	Sorel Eperviers	Pittsburgh	Houston
17.	McGREGOR, Gary	Cornwall Royals	Montreal	Chicago
18.	LOCHEAD, William	Oshawa Generals	Detroit	Indianapolis
19. *	BAXTER, Paul	Winnipeg Clubs		Cleveland
20.	CHARTRAW, Rick	Kitchener Rangers	Montreal	San Diego
21. *	TURKIEWICZ, Jim	Peterborough Petes		Toronto
22. *	FOGOLIN, Lee	Oshawa Generals	Buffalo	
23.	YOUNG, Tim	Ottawa 67's		New England
24. *	TREMBLAY, Mario	Montreal Bleu, Blanc, Rouge	Montreal	
25. *	BOUDREAU, Bruce	Toronto Marlboros		Minnesota
26. *	VALIQUETTE, Jack	S.S. Marie Greyhounds	Toronto	

No.	Name	Last Amateur Club	NHL Claim	WHA Claim
27. *	GORMAN, Dave	St. Catharines Hawks		Phoenix
28. *	MALONEY, Dave	Kitchener Rangers	New York	
29. *	TROTTIER, Brian	Swift Current Broncos	N.Y. Islanders	Cincinnati
30.	McTAVISH, Gordon	Sudbury Wolves	Montreal	Winnipeg
31. *	BLIGHT, Rick	Brandon Wheat Kings		Michigan
32. *	MULVEY, Grant	Calgary Centennials	Chicago	
33.	COSSETTE, Jacques	Sorel Eperviers	Pittsburgh	Vancouver
34.	CHIPPERFIELD, Ron	Brandon Wheat Kings	California	Vancouver
35.	DEVINE, Kevin	Toronto Marlboros	Toronto	San Diego
36. *	MARSAN, Mike	Sudbury Wolves	Washington	
37.	BURDON, Glen	Regina Pats	Kansas	Edmonton
38.	SEDLBAUER, Ron	Kitchener Rangers	Vancouver	Toronto
39.	CONSTANTIN, Charles	Quebec Remparts	Buffalo	Quebec
40.	NANTAIS, Richard	Quebec Remparts	Minnesota	Houston
41.	SIMMER, Charles	S.S. Marie Greyhounds	California	Cleveland
42. *	HOWE, Mark	Toronto Marlboros	Boston	
43.	LEMELIN, Roger	London Knights	Kansas	Toronto
44. *	HESS, Robert	New Westminster Bruins	St. Louis	
45.	LAIRD, Rob	Regina Pats	Pittsburgh	Minnesota
46. *	CHOUINARD, Guy	Quebec Remparts	Atlanta	
47.	WILLIAMS, David	Swift Current Broncos	Toronto	Cincinnati
48.	GARE, Dan	Calgary Centennials	Buffalo	Winnipeg
49.	GRESCHNER, Ron	New Westminster Bruins	N.Y. Rangers	Vancouver
50.	LUPIEN, Gilles	Montreal, Bleu, Blanc, Rouge	Montreal	Toronto
51.	DAIGLE, Alain	Trois-Rivieres Ducs	Chicago	Quebec
52.	McLEAN, Donald	Sudbury Wolves	Philadelphia	New England
53.	McINTOSH, Paul	Peterborough Petes	Buffalo	Chicago
54.	STURGEON, Peter	Kitchener Rangers	Boston	New England
55.	HUGHES, John	Toronto Marlboros	Vancouver	Houston
56.	PADDOCK, John	Brandon Wheat Kings	Washington	Minnesota
57.	KINSELLA, Brian	Oshawa Generals	Washington	Phoenix
58.	BOURNE, Robert	Saskatoon Blades	Kansas	Indianapolis
59.	INKPEN, Dave	Edmonton Oil Kings	N.Y. Islanders	Cincinnati
60.	ANDERSON, Brad	Victoria Cougars	N.Y. Islanders	Cincinnati
61.	ROGERS, Michael	Calgary Centennials	Vancouver	Edmonton
62.	BUYNAK, Gordon	Kingston Canadians	St. Louis	Phoenix
63.	HOLLAND, Jerry	Calgary Centennials	New York	Cincinnati
64.	MANDRYK, Dan	Calgary Centennials	Detroit	Phoenix
65.	EVO, Bill	Peterborough Petes	Detroit	Cincinnati
66.	DEZIEL, Michael	Sorel Eperviers	Buffalo	New England
67.	ASHTON, Ronald	Saskatoon Blades	Minnesota	Winnepeg
68.	HOWE, Marty	Toronto Marlboros	Montreal	
69.	PALMATEER, Mike	Toronto Marlboros	Toronto	Cincinnati
70.	MURRAY, Bob	Cornwall Royals	Chicago	Cincinnati
71.	RUSKOWSKI, Terry	Swift Current Broncos	Chicago	Houston
72.	SIROIS, Robert	Montreal, Bleu, Blanc, Rouge	Philadelphia	Houston
73.	WINTON, Brad	Toronto Marlboros	Los Angeles	Phoenix
74.	EDUR, Thomas	Toronto Marlboros	Boston	
75.	CLARKE, Jim	Toronto Marlboros	Vancouver	Phoenix
76.	NICHOLSON, Paul	London Knights	Washington	Michigan
77.	LOMENDA, Mark	Victoria Cougars	Kansas	Chicago
78.	PRICE, Tom	Ottawa 67's	California	Indianapolis
79.	LEGGE, Barry	Winnipeg Clubs	Montreal	Michigan

34

No.	Name	Last Amateur Club	NHL Claim	WHA Claim
80.	RIBBLE, Patrick	Oshawa Generals	Atlanta	Indianapolis
81.	DRISCOLL, Peter	Kingston Canadians	Toronto	Vancouver
82.	SNEPTS, Harold	Edmonton Oil Kings	Vancouver	Indianapolis
83.	McDOUGAL, Kim	Regina Pats	Minnesota	Winnipeg
84.	BERGERON, Michel	Sorel Eperviers	Detroit	Quebec
85.	LARIVIERE, Gary	St. Catherines Hawks	Buffalo	Chicago
86.	BOTTING, Cameron	Niagara Falls Flyers	Atlanta	Edmonton
87.	TORRESAN, Carlo	Sorel Eperviers	N.Y. Islanders	Toronto
88.	ANDERSON, Boyd	Medicine Hat Tigers	New York	Winnipeg
89.	ABERHARDT, Bruce	London Knights	Pittsburg	Phoenix
90.	McKEGNEY, Mike	Kitchener Rangers	Montreal	San Diego
91.	BATEMAN, James	Quebec Remparts	Boston	San Diego
92.	PATTERSON, Jack	Kamloops Chiefs	Washington	Indianapolis
93.	TREACY, Kevin	Cornwall Royals	New York	Edmonton
94.	BADIUK, Jerry	Kitchener Rangers	Atlanta	Houston
95.	BERNIER, Jean	Shawinigan Dynamos	Chicago	Quebec
96.	EVANS, Paul	Kitchener Rangers	Los Angeles	Chicago
97.	EMERSON, Derrick	Montreal, Bleu, Blanc, Rouge	Los Angeles	San Diego
98.	WHELDON, Don	London Knights	St. Louis	Indianapblis
99.	SMITH, Derek	Ottawa 67's	Buffalo	Houston
100.	LOGAN, David	Laval Nationals	Chicago	Quebec
101.	FINCK, Larry	St. Catherines Hawks	Pittsburg	Michigan
102.	SOBCHUK, Dennis	Regina Pats	Philadelphia	
103.	BOLAND, Mike	S.S. Marie Greyhounds	Kansas	San Diego
104.	PRYSUNKA, Sid	New Westminster Bruins	N.Y. Islanders	
105.	UHRICH, Rick	Regina Pats	Pittsburgh	Winnipeg
106.	SPRUCE, Andy	London Knights	Vancouver	Phoenix
107.	THOMPSON, Mike	Victoria Cougars	St. Louis	Cleveland
108.	MATHEWS, Marty	Flin Flon Bombers	Los Angeles	Edmonton
109.	WATT, Rob	Flin Flon Bombers	Vancourver	Phoenix
110.	HASSARD, Bill	Wexford Raiders	Toronto	Toronto
111.	JOHNSTONE, Ed	Medicine Hat Tigers	New York	Michigan
112.	VOLPE, Bob	Sudbury Wolves	Chicago	Indianapolis
113.	MALUTA, Ray	Flin Flon Bombers	Boston	San Diego
114.	FRIESEN, William	Swift Current Broncos	Philadelphia	
115.	ROOKE, Dave	Cornwall Royals	N.Y. Islanders	Winnipeg
116.	BEST, Bill	Sudbury Wolves	Boston	Indianapolis
117.	NOREAU, Bernard	Laval Nationals	Buffalo	Edmonton
118.	MALARCHUK, Garth	Calgary Centennials	Washington	Toronto
119.	DE MOISSAC, Emile	New Westminster Bruins		Chicago
120.	CASEY, Terry	St. Catherines Hawks	St. Louis	Michigan
121.	HILLIER, Al	Flin Flon Bombers		Minnesota
122.	STEWART, Harvey	Flin Flon Bombers	Los Angeles	Cleveland
123.	GASSOFF, Ken	Medicine Hat Tigers	New York	Houston
124.	MEMRYK, John	Winnipeg Clubs	New York	Winnipeg
125.	PRONCHUK, Ron	Brandon Wheat Kings	Washington	Michigan
126.	LEMELIN, Rejean	Sherbrooke Castors	Philadelphia	Chicago
127.	HOBIN, Michael	Hamilton Red Wings	Montreal	Vancouver
128.	NAZAR, John	Cornwall Royals	Washington	New England
129.	HOLST, Greg	Kingston Canadians	New York	San Diego
130.	McCABE, James	Welland Sabres	California	
131.	FERGUSON, Bob	Cornwall Royals	N.Y. Islanders	Winnipeg
132.	TORDOFF, Rod	Swift Current Broncos	St. Louis	Indianapolis
133.	CARUFEL, Denis	Sorel Eperviers	Kansas	Quebec

No.	Name	Last Amateur Club	NHL Claim	WHA Claim
134.	STEELE, Greg	Calgary Centennials	Detroit	Indianapolis
135.	BECK, Murray	New Westminster Bruins		Houston
136.	HELD, John	London Knights	Los Angeles	Vancouver
137.	TOULET, Mark	Moncton University		Indianapolis
138.	KEMP, Kevin	Ottawa 67's	Toronto	
139.	TOUZIN, Paul Andre	Shawinigan Dynamos	St. Louis	Michigan
140.	ST. CYR, Mike	Kitchener Rangers	Chicago	Indianapolis
141.	DUNCAN, John	Cornwall Royals	Washington	Winnipeg
142.	ERICKSON, Kelvin	Calgary Centennials	Washington	Indianapolis
143.	DUPUIS, Claude	Laval Nationals		Quebec
144.	KURLIAK, Brian	North Bay Trappers	Kansas	
145.	TRIVETT, Mark	Cornwall Royals		Chicago
146.	FOUBISTER, Jim	Victoria Cougars	N.Y. Islanders	
147.	McNEIL, Joe	St. Francis Xavier Univ.		Toronto
148.	STAFFEN, Dave	Ottawa 67's	Minnesota	New England
149.	MOORE, Richard	Montreal, Bleu, Blanc, Rouge		Minnesota
150.	CHICOYNE, James	Brandon Wheat Kings	Pittsburgh	Indianapolis
151.	DION, Michel	Montreal, Bleu, Blanc, Rouge		Indianapolis
152.	McLEOD, Glenn	Sudbury Wolves	Detroit	Cleveland
153.	BYE, Brian	Kitchener Rangers	N.Y. Islanders	San Diego
154.	HOPKINS, Larry	Toronto University	Atlanta	
155.	WILHELM, Wayne	Brandon Wheat Kings		Winnipeg
156.	JODZIA, Richard	Hamilton Red Wings	Buffalo	
157.	CHASE, Bob	Cornwall Royals		Chicago
158.	LESSARD, Mario	Sherbrooke Castors	Los Angeles	Quebec
159.	DAVIES, Jack	Thunder Bay Hurricanes		Toronto
160.	SYVRET, Dave	St. Catharines Hawks	Toronto	
161.	WANCHUK, Mike	Regina Pats		Winnipeg
162.	ARVISAIS, Claude	Shawinigan Dynamos	New York	Quebec
163.	FRIESON, Willy	Swift Current Broncos		Edmonton
164.	STEWARD, Gordon	Kamloops Chiefs	Montreal	Cleveland
165.	TRAER, Daryl	Thunder Bay Hurricanes		Chicago
166.	McKENZIE, Peter	St. Francis Xavier Univ.	Philadelphia	
167.	GAMELIN, Serge	Sorel Eperviers	Pittsburgh	Cleveland
168.	WHITE, Tony	Kitchener Rangers	Washington	New England
169.	DUNCOMBE, Reg	New Westminster Bruins		Minnesota
170.	ANDERSON, Brian	New Westminster Bruins	Minnesota	
171.	LUKSA, Charles	Kitchener Rangers	Montreal	Phoenix
172.	LORANGER, Louis	Shawinigan Dynamos	Atlanta	
173.	ROYER, Fermin	Sorel Eperviers		San Diego
174.	STOESZ, Andy	Selkirk Steelers	Toronto	
175.	DAVID, Pierre	Sorel Eperviers		Indianapolis
176.	DODD, Ken	New Westminster Bruins	New York	
177.	MABLEY, Scott	S.S. Marie Greyhounds	Washington	Indianapolis
178.	FRASER, Rick	Toronto University	Chicago	Indianapolis
179.	RILEY, John	Windsor Spitfires		Michigan
180.	LABROSSE, Marcel	Shawinigan Dynamos	Philadelphia	
181.	ELINSKY, Bob	Chatham Maroons		San Diego
182.	FLECK, Murray	Estevan Bruins	N.Y. Islanders	
183.	DUMAIS, Marcel	Sherbrooke Castors		Winnipeg
184.	BRAY, Duane	Flin Flon Bombers	Minnesota	
185.	HALL, Russell	Winnipeg Clubs	New York	Indianapolis
186.	BABIN, Mitch	North Bay Trappers	St. Louis	Indianapolis
187.	DUBOIS, Michel	Chicoutimi Sagueneens		Chicago

No.	Name	Last Amateur Club	NHL Claim	WHA Claim
188.	MONTGOMERY, Randy	Welland Sabres	Atlanta	
189.	ALLAN, Doug	New Westminster Bruins	St. Louis	Cleveland
190.	LOCAS, Jacques	Quebec Remparts	Los Angeles	
191.	HALL, Graham	Wexford Raiders		Indianapolis
192.	FESCHUK, Martin	Saskatoon Blades	Toronto	
193.	GIROUX, Mitch	Guelph Biltmores		San Diego
194.	KRENTZ, Ralph	Brandon Wheat Kings	New York	
195.	COUNTER, Doug	Aurora Tigers		Indianapolis
196.	McKEE, Dave	Oshawa Generals	Washington	
197.	BLANCHET, Robert	Kitchener Rangers	Washington	San Diego
198.	HAY, Don	New Westminster Bruins	Minnesota	Houston
199.	TIGHE, Peter	London Knights		New England
200.	PERRON, Richard	Quebec Remparts	Pittsburgh	
201.	PLOUFFE, Yves	Sorel Eperviers	Washington	Indianapolis
202.	GEOFFRION, Robert	Cornwall Royals	Buffalo	
203.	McPHEE, Ian	Swift Current Broncos		Houston
204.	JACQUES, Larry	Ottawa 67's	New York	Indianapolis
205.	BARKER, Brian	Sorel Eperviers		Indianapolis
206.	BYERS, Dwayne	Sherbrooke Castors	Chicago	New England
207.	WYNNE, Tom	Cornwall Royals		Winnipeg
208.	GUAY, Richard	Chicoutimi Sagueneens	Philadelphia	
209.	SMITH, Neil	Brockville Braves	N.Y. Islanders	
210.	PIZUNSKI, Edward	Peterborough Petes	Kansas	
211.	HINDMARCH, Richard	Calgary University	Pittsburgh	
212.	HOLDERNESS, Brian	Saskatoon Blades	Minnesota	
213.	ING, Glen	Victoria Cougars	Chicago	
214.	CASTLE, Tom	Peterborough Petes	New York	
215.	WING, Willie	Hamilton Red Wings	Kansas	
216.	PLANTE, Bernard	Trois-Rivieres Ducs	Wahsington	
217.	BRUBACHER, Eric	Kingston Canadians	New York	
218.	TAYLOR, Frank	Brandon Wheat Kings	Minnesota	
219.	BELL, Bill	Regina Pats	Washington	
220.	CHIASSON, Jacques	Drummondville Rangers	Washington	
221.	BOWER, John	Downsview	Washington	
222.	KRISKI, Bill	Winnipeg Clubs	New York	
223.	BOZACK, Terry	Pembroke Lumber Kings	Washington	
224.	BAST, Clifford	Medicine Hat Tigers	New York	
225.	COLE, Gordon	Brandon Wheat Kings	Washington	
226.	PHILLIPS, Ronald	St. Catharines Hawks	N.Y. Islanders	
227.	KERFOOT, Barry	Smiths Falls Bears	Washington	
228.	COSENTINO, Mike	Hamilton Red Wings	Washington	
229.	POOLE, Ronald	Kamloops Chiefs	Washington	

* *Exceptional players*

KEY TO ABBREVIATIONS:

Goaltending: Min. - - Minutes Played. GPI - - Games Played In. W - - Games Won. L - - Games Lost. T - - Games Tied. Pct. - - Percentage. SOG - - Shots on Goal. GA - - Goals Allowed. SVS - - Saves. GAA - - Goals Against Average for 60 minutes. EN - - Empty Net Goals. SA% - - Save percentage. GAF - - Goals Allowed Frequency (number of shots taken for each goal allowed). SG - - Shutout games. SP - - Shutout Periods.

Offensive: GP - - Games Played. G - - Goals. A - - Assists. PTS - - Total Points. PPG - - Average number of points per game. FG - - First Goal. PG - - Proximity Goal (one that brings a team within one goal of tying game). TG - - Tying Goal. TB - - Tie-breaking Goal. IG - - Insurance Goal (one that puts a team two goals ahead). WG - - Winning Goal. TC - - Total Clutch Goals. Pct. - - Percentage of Clutch Goals to Total Goals Scored. PP - - Power Play Goals. SHO - - Shorthanded Goals. MG - - Multiple Goal Games.

AWARDS

GARY L. DAVIDSON TROPHY
(Most Valuable Player)

Bobby Hull, Winnipeg Jets 1972-73
Gordie Howe, Houston Aeros 1973-74

W.D. (BILL) HUNTER TROPHY
(Scoring Champion)

Andre Lacroix, Philadelphia Blazers
Mike Walton, Minnesota Fighting Saints

DENNIS A. MURPHY AWARD
(Best Defenseman)

J.C. Tremblay, Quebec Nordiques .. 1972-73
Pat Stapleton, Chicago Cougars 1973-74

BEN HATSKIN TROPHY
(Best Goaltender)

Gerry Cheevers, Cleveland Crusaders
Don McLeod, Houston Aeros

LOU KAPLAN AWARD
(Rookie of the Year)

Terry Caffery, New England Whalers 1972-73
Mark Howe, Houston Aeros 1973-74

PAUL DENEAU AWARD
(Most Gentlemanly Player)

Ted Hampson, Minnesota Fighting Saints
Ralph Backstrom, Chicago Cougars

HOWARD BALDWIN AWARD
(Coach of the Year)

Jack Kelley, New England Whalers .. 1972-73
Billy Harris, Toronto Toros 1973-74

ALL-STAR GAME MVP

Wayne Carleton, Ottawa Nationals
Mike Walton, Minnesota Fighting Saints

WHA CASH AWARDS

INDIVIDUAL AWARDS
Most Valuable Player .... $ 4,000
Scoring Champion .... $ 4,000
Best Goaltender .... $ 4,000
Best Defenseman .... $ 4,000
Most Gentlemanly Player .... $ 4,000
Rookie of the Year .... $ 4,000
Coach of the Year .... $ 4,000

ALL-STAR GAME
Winning Team Share-per-Player . $ 300
Losing Team Share-per-Player .. $ 200

YEAR-END ALL-STARS
First Team Selectees .... $ 2,500
Second Team Selectees ..... $ 1,000

REGULAR SEASON DIVISION FINISH

1972-73/73-74
First Place Team $50,000
Second Place Team $25,000
Third Place Team $20,000
Fourth Place Team $10,000

1974-75
First Place Teams $50,000
Second Place Teams $25,000
Wild-Card Teams $20,000

playoffs

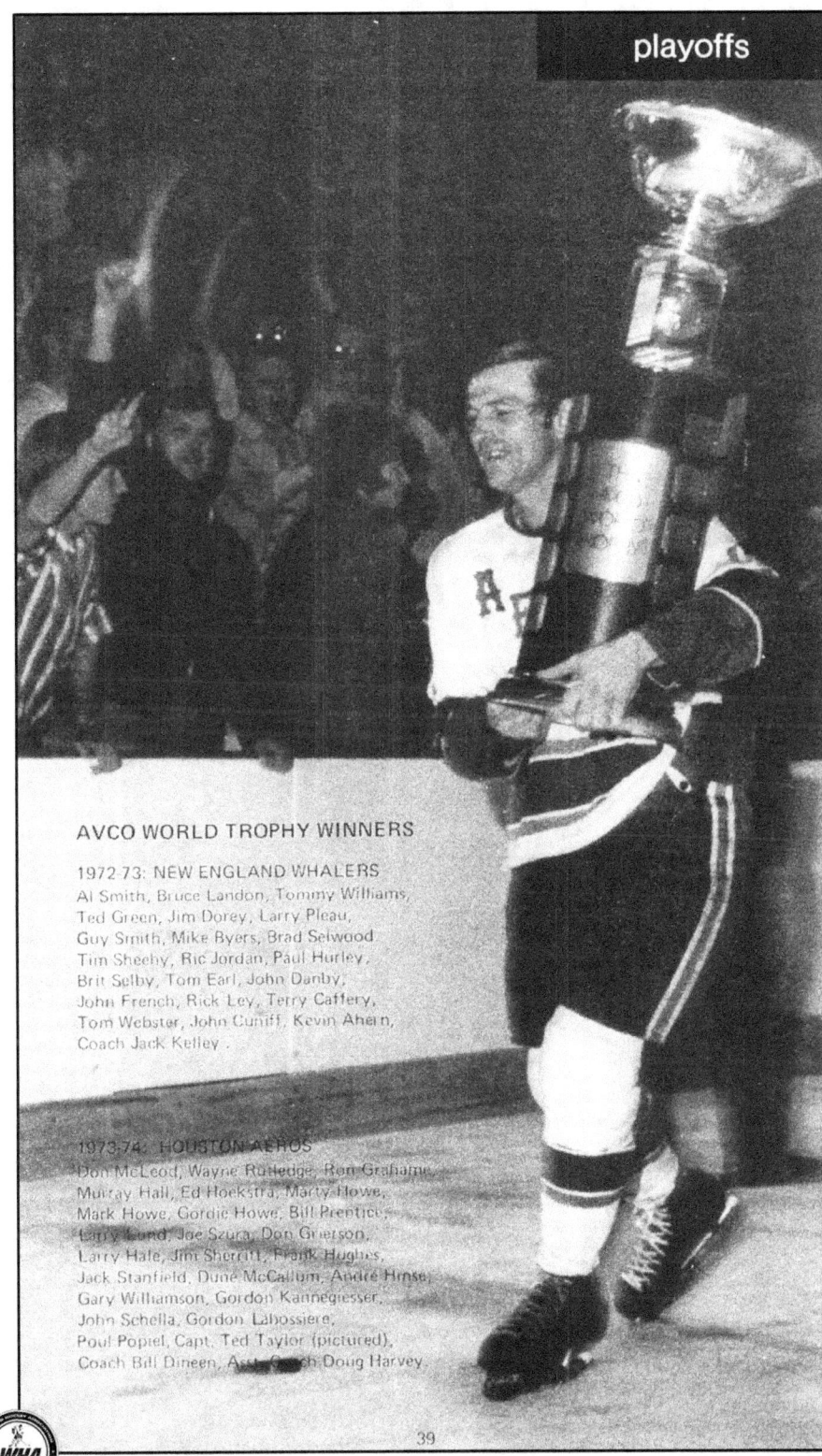

AVCO WORLD TROPHY WINNERS

1972-73: NEW ENGLAND WHALERS
Al Smith, Bruce Landon, Tommy Williams, Ted Green, Jim Dorey, Larry Pleau, Guy Smith, Mike Byers, Brad Selwood, Tim Sheehy, Ric Jordan, Paul Hurley, Brit Selby, Tom Earl, John Danby, John French, Rick Ley, Terry Caffery, Tom Webster, John Cuniff, Kevin Ahern, Coach Jack Kelley.

1973-74: HOUSTON AEROS
Don McLeod, Wayne Rutledge, Ron Graham, Murray Hall, Ed Hoekstra, Marty Howe, Mark Howe, Gordie Howe, Bill Prentice, Larry Lund, Joe Szura, Don Grierson, Larry Hale, Jim Sherritt, Frank Hughes, Jack Stanfield, Dune McCallum, André Hinse, Gary Williamson, Gordon Kannegiesser, John Schella, Gordon Labossiere, Poul Popiel, Capt. Ted Taylor (pictured), Coach Bill Dineen, Asst. Coach Doug Harvey.

```
┌─────────────────────────────────────────────────────┐
│         WHA PLAYOFF POOL 1974-75 SEASON             │
│                                                     │
│                       Winning Team    Losing Team   │
│       Quarter-Finals: ....... $60,000 ....... $40,000 │
│       Semi-Finals: ........... 60,000 ........ 40,000 │
│       Finals: ................ 80,000 ........ 60,000 │
└─────────────────────────────────────────────────────┘
```

AVCO WORLD TROPHY PLAYOFFS

1972-73

1973-74

SERIES "A" (QUARTER-FINAL ROUND)

(NEW ENGLAND vs OTTAWA)

April 7 — New England 6, Ottawa 3
April 8 — New England 4, Ottawa 3 (OT)
April 10 — Ottawa 4, New England 2
April 12 — New England 7, Ottawa 3
April 14 — New England 5, Ottawa 4 (OT)
(New England Wins Series, 4-1)

(HOUSTON vs WINNIPEG)

April 8 — Houston 5, Winnipeg 2
April 10 — Houston 3, Winnipeg 2
April 13 — Houston 10, Winnipeg 1
April 14 — Houston 5, Winnipeg 4
(Houston Wins Series, 4-0)

SERIES "B" (QUARTER-FINAL ROUND)

(CLEVELAND vs PHILADELPHIA)

April 4 — Cleveland 3, Philadelphia 2 (OT)
April 7 — Cleveland 7, Philadelphia 1
April 8 — Cleveland 3, Philadelphia 1
April 11 — Cleveland 6, Philadelphia 2
(Cleveland Wins Series, 4-0)

(MINNESOTA vs EDMONTON)

April 6 — Minnesota 2, Edmonton 1
April 7 — Minnesota 8, Edmonton 5
April 10 — Minnesota 6, Edmonton 2
April 12 — Edmonton 2, Minnesota 1
April 14 — Minnesota 5, Edmonton 4
(Minnesota Wins Series, 4-1)

SERIES "C" (QUARTER-FINAL ROUND)

(WINNIPEG vs MINNESOTA)

April 6 — Winnipeg 3, Minnesota 1
April 8 — Winnipeg 5, Minnesota 2
April 10 — Minnesota 4, Winnipeg 4
April 11 — Winnipeg 3, Minnesota 2 (OT)
April 15 — Winnipeg 8, Minnesota 5
(Winnipeg Wins Series, 4-1)

(CHICAGO vs NEW ENGLAND)

April 6 — New England 6, Chicago 4
April 7 — New England 4, Chicago 3 (OT)
April 9 — Chicago 8, New England 6
April 10 — Chicago 2, New England 1 (OT)
April 12 — Chicago 4, New England 2
April 14 — New England 2, Chicago 0
April 16 — Chicago 3, New England 2
(Chicago Wins Series, 4-3)

SERIES "D" (QUARTER-FINAL ROUND)

(HOUSTON vs LOS ANGELES)

April 5 — Houston 7, Los Angeles 2
April 7 — Los Angeles 4, Houston 2
April 11 — Los Angeles 3, Houston 2
April 13 — Houston 3, Los Angeles 2 (OT)
April 15 — Houston 6, Los Angeles 3
April 17 — Houston 3, Los Angeles 2
(Houston Wins Series, 4-2)

(TORONTO vs CLEVELAND)

April 7 — Toronto 4, Cleveland 0
April 9 — Toronto 4, Cleveland 3
April 12 — Toronto 4, Cleveland 2
April 13 — Cleveland 3, Toronto 2 (OT)
April 15 — Toronto 4, Cleveland 1
(Toronto Wins Series, 4-1)

1972-73

SERIES "E" (SEMI-FINAL ROUND)

(NEW ENGLAND vs CLEVELAND)

April 18 — New England 3, Cleveland 2
April 19 — New England 3, Cleveland 2
April 21 — New England 5, Cleveland 4
April 22 — Cleveland 5, New England 2
April 26 — New England 3, Cleveland 1
(New England Wins Series, 4-1)

SERIES "F" (SEMI-FINAL ROUND)

(WINNIPEG vs HOUSTON)

April 20 — Winnipeg 5, Houston 1
April 22 — Winnipeg 2, Houston 0
April 24 — Winnipeg 4, Houston 2
April 26 — Winnipeg 3, Houston 0
(Winnipeg Wins Series, 4-0)

1973-74

SERIES "E" (SEMI-FINAL ROUND)

(HOUSTON vs MINNESOTA)

April 18 — Minnesota 5, Houston 4 (OT)
April 20 — Houston 5, Minnesota 2
April 21 — Minnesota 4, Houston 1
April 28 — Houston 4, Minnesota 1
April 29 — Houston 9, Minnesota 4
May   1 — Houston 3, Minnesota 1
(Houston Wins Series, 4-2)

SERIES "F" (SEMI-FINAL ROUND)

(CHICAGO vs TORONTO)

April 19 — Toronto 6, Chicago 4
April 22 — Chicago 4, Toronto 3
April 28 — Chicago 3, Toronto 2
April 30 — Toronto 7, Chicago 6
May   1 — Toronto 5, Chicago 3
May   4 — Chicago 9, Toronto 2
May   6 — Chicago 5, Toronto 2

(Chicago Wins Series, 4-3)

SERIES "G" (FINAL ROUND)

(NEW ENGLAND vs WINNIPEG)

April 29 — New England 7, Winnipeg 2
May   2 — New England 7, Winnipeg 4
May   3 — Winnipeg 4, New England 3
May   5 — New England 4, Winnipeg 2
May   6 — New England 9, Winnipeg 6
(New England Wins Series, 4-1)

(HOUSTON vs CHICAGO)

May 12 — Houston 3, Chicago 2
May 15 — Houston 6, Chicago 1
May 17 — Houston 7, Chicago 2
May 19 — Houston 6, Chicago 2
(Houston Wins Series, 4-0)

TOP 10 PLAYOFF SCORERS

1972-73	GP	G	A	TP	PIM
1. Norm Beaudin, Wpg.	14	13	15	28	2
2. Tom Webster, N.E.	15	12	14	26	6
3. Bobby Hull, Wpg.	14	9	16	25	16
4. Tim Sheehy, N.E.	15	9	14	23	13
5. Larry Pleau, N.E.	15	12	7	19	15
6. Jim Dorey, N.E.	15	3	16	19	41
7. Tommy Williams, N.E.	15	6	11	17	2
8. Bill Sutherland, Wpg.	14	5	9	14	9
9. John French, N.E.	15	3	11	14	2
10. Chris Bordeleau, Wpg.	12	5	8	13	4

1973-74	GP	G	A	TP	PIM
1. Larry Lund, Hou.	14	9	14	23	56
2. Mark Howe, Hou.	14	9	10	19	4
3. Ralph Backstrom, Chi.	18	5	14	19	4
4. Mike Walton, Minn.	11	10	8	18	16
5. Andre Hinse, Hou.	14	8	9	17	18
6. Gordie Howe, Hou.	13	3	14	17	34
7. Gord Labossiere, Hou.	14	7	9	16	20
8. Murray Hall, Hou.	14	9	6	15	6
9. Rosaire Paiement, Chi.	18	9	6	15	16
10. Poul Popiel, Hou.	14	1	14	15	22

TOP 5 PLAYOFF GOALTENDERS

1972-73	MIN	SOG	GA	GAA
1. Gerry Cheevers, Clev.	548	278	22	2.40
2. Bernie Parent, Phil.	70	42	3	2.57
3. Don McLeod, Hou.	178	76	8	2.69
4. Wayne Rutledge, Hou.	.423	228	20	2.83
5. Russ Gillow, L.A.	247	115	12	2.91

1973-74	MIN	SOG	GA	GAA
1. Don McLeod, Hou.	842	386	35	2.49
2. Gilles Gratton, Tor.	539	287	25	2.78
3. Mike Curran, Minn.	289	161	14	2.91
4. Al Smith, N.E.	399	240	21	3.16
5. Chris Worthy, Edm.	146	72	8	3.29

PLAYOFF LEADERS

ALL-TIME WHA PLAYOFF SCORING LEADERS

NAME	TEAM	PY	GP	G	A	TP	PIM	PPG	GW	TC	PP	SH
1. Larry Lund	Hou.	2	24	12	21	33	80	1.38	2	6	1	2
2. Norm Beaudin	Wpg.	2	18	16	16	32	4	1.78	2	10	2	—
3. Tom Webster	N.E.	2	18	17	14	31	13	1.72	—	13	6	—
4. Tim Sheehey	N.E.	2	22	13	16	29	17	1.32	3	10	2	—
5. Bobby Hull	Wpg.	2	18	10	17	27	20	1.50	3	7	2	—
6. Poul Popiel	Hou.	2	24	3	23	26	45	1.08	—	3	2	—
7. Jim Dorey	N.E.	2	21	3	22	25	67	1.19	—	2	1	—
8. Murray Hall	Hou.	2	24	13	10	23	24	.96	5	9	4	—
9. Frank Hughes	Hou.	2	24	13	9	22	11	.92	1	8	6	—
10. Larry Pleau	N.E.	2	17	14	7	21	15	1.24	2	13	4	1
11. Gordon Labossiere	Hou.	2	20	8	13	21	28	1.05	2	4	4	—

GOALTENDING LEADERS (at least 500 minutes played)

GOALTENDER	TEAM	PY	MINS	GPI	W	L	SOG	GA	GAA
1. Don McLeod	Hou.	2	1,020	17	12	5	462	43	2.53
2. Gerry Cheevers	Clev.	2	851	14	6	8	274	40	2.82
3. Gilles Gratton	Otwa-Tor.	2	625	12	5	4	360	32	3.07
4. Joe Daley	Wpg.	2	641	9	5	4	256	33	3.09
5. Al Smith	N.E.	2	1,308	22	15	7	670	70	3.21
6. Andre Gill	Chi.	1	614	11	6	5	318	38	3.71

1974-75 PLAYOFF FORMAT

The first two finishers in each division automatically qualify, while the remaining two spots will be filled by the clubs with the best record from among the remaining eight. Pairings will be determined by the club with the highest number of points facing the "wild card club" with the fewest, next highest against the next fewest, and so on.

Following is an example:

HYPOTHETICAL FINISH OF LEAGUE STANDINGS

Canadian Division		East Division		West Division	
Edmonton	100	Chicago	91	San Diego	93
Winnipeg	90	Indianapolis	89	Houston	90
Toronto	88x	New England	78	Minnesota	87x
Vancouver	80	Cleveland	76	Michigan	73
Quebec	75			Phoenix	72

Edmonton, San Diego, Chicago, Winnipeg, Houston, Indianapolis automatically in.
x — 2 "Wild Card Teams" — Minnesota and Toronto

PLAYOFF PAIRINGS

Series "A" — Edmonton vs. Minnesota (Edmonton has Home-Ice advantage).
Series "B" — San Diego vs. Toronto (San Diego has Home-Ice advantage).
Series "C" — Chicago vs. Indianapolis (Chicago has Home-Ice advantage).
Series "D" — Winnipeg vs. Houston (Home-Ice advantage decided by Tie-breaking rules).
Series "E" — Winners of series' "A" and "D".
Series "F" — Winners of series' "B" and "C".
Series "G" — Winners of series "E" and "F".

TIE-BREAKING RULES

1. The club with the most wins.
2. The club with the fewest losses.
3. The club with the best goals-for and against average.

ALL SERIES BEST OF SEVEN

playoff leaders

TEAM PLAYOFF RECORDS

MOST GOALS, BOTH TEAMS, FOUR-GAME SERIES:
 32 — Houston Aeros, Winnipeg Jets, in 1974 Quarter-Final. Houston won series 4-0, outscoring Winnipeg 23-9.

MOST GOALS, ONE TEAM, FOUR-GAME SERIES:
 23 — Houston Aeros in 1974 Quarter-Final. Houston defeated Winnipeg Jets 4-0, outscoring Winnipeg 23-9.

MOST GOALS, BOTH TEAMS, FIVE-GAME SERIES:
 48 — New England Whalers, Winnipeg Jets in 1973 Final. New England won series 4-1, outscoring Winnipeg 30-18.

MOST GOALS, ONE TEAM, FIVE-GAMES SERIES:
 30 — New England in Final. New England defeated Winnipeg Jets 4-1, outscoring Winnipeg 30-18.

MOST GOALS, BOTH TEAMS, SIX-GAME SERIES:
 43 — Houston Aeros, Minnesota Fighting Saints in 1974 Semi-Final. Houston won series 4-2, outscoring Minnesota 26-17.

MOST GOALS, ONE TEAM, SIX-GAME SERIES:
 26 — Houston Aeros in 1974 Semi-Final. Houston defeated Minnesota Fighting Saints 4-2, outscoring Minnesota 26-17.

MOST GOALS, BOTH TEAMS, SEVEN-GAME SERIES:
 61 — Chicago Cougars, Toronto Toros in 1974 Semi-Final. Chicago won series 4-3, outscoring Toronto 34-27.

MOST GOALS, ONE TEAM, SEVEN-GAME SERIES:
 34 — Chicago Cougars in 1974 Semi-Final. Chicago defeated Toronto 4-3, outscoring Toronto 34-27.

FEWEST GOALS, BOTH TEAMS, FOUR-GAME SERIES:
 17 — Winnipeg Jets, Houston Aeros in 1973 Semi-Final. Winnipeg defeated Houston 4-0, outscoring Aeros 14-3.

FEWEST GOALS, ONE TEAM, FOUR-GAME SERIES:
 3 — Houston Aeros in 1973 Semi-Final. Houston was outscored by Winnipeg 14-3.

FEWEST GOALS, BOTH TEAMS, FIVE-GAME SERIES:
 27 — Toronto Toros, Cleveland Crusaders in 1974 Quarter-Final. Toronto won series 4-1, outscoring Cleveland 18-9.

FEWEST GOALS, ONE TEAM, FIVE-GAME SERIES:
 9 — Cleveland Crusaders in 1974 Quarter-Final. Cleveland outscored by Toronto 18-9.

FEWEST GOALS, BOTH TEAMS, SIX-GAME SERIES
 39 — Houston Aeros, Los Angeles Sharks in 1973 Quarter-Final. Houston won series 4-2, outscoring Los Angeles 23-16.

FEWEST GOALS, ONE TEAM, SIX-GAME SERIES
 16 — Los Angeles in 1973 Quarter-Final. Los Angeles was outscored by Houston 23-16.

FEWEST GOALS, BOTH TEAMS, SEVEN-GAME SERIES:
 47 — Chicago Cougars, New England Whalers in 1974 Quarter-Final. Chicago won series 4-3, outscoring New England 24-23.

WIDEST MARGIN OF VICTORY, SINGLE GAME:
 9 — Houston Aeros defeated Winnipeg 10-1, April 13, 1974. Houston won series 4-0.

MOST GOALS, BOTH TEAMS, ONE GAME:
 15 — New England Whalers, Winnipeg Jets, May 6, 1973, at Boston. Final Score: New England 9, Winnipeg 6. New England won the Final Series 4-1.

MOST GOALS, ONE TEAM, ONE GAME:
 10 — Houston Aeros at Houston, April 13, 1974. Final Score: Houston 10, Winnipeg 1. Houston won Quarter-Final Series 4-0.

MOST GOALS, BOTH TEAMS, ONE PERIOD:
 7 — Winnipeg Jets, Minnesota Fighting Saints at Winnipeg, April 15, 1973, in second period. Winnipeg, which won the game 8-5, scored 5 of the second period goals.
 — New England Whalers, Winnipeg Jets at Boston, May 6, 1973, in first period. New England, which won the game 9-6, scored five of the first period goals.
 — Minnesota Fighting Saints, Edmonton Oilers at St. Paul, April 7, 1974 in third period. Edmonton, which lost the game 8-5, scored four of the third period goals.
 — Chicago Cougars, New England Whalers at Chicago, April 9, 1974 in the second period. New England, which lost the game 8-6, scored four of the goals.
 — Chicago Cougars, Toronto Toros at Chicago, April 30, 1974, in the second period. Toronto, which won the game 7-6, scored five of the goals.

43

MOST GOALS, ONE TEAM, ONE PERIOD:
  5 — Winnipeg Jets at Winnipeg, April 15, 1973, in second period against Minnesota during 8-5 win.
   — New England Whalers at Winnipeg, May 2, 1973, in third period against Winnipeg during 7-4 win.
   — New England Whalers at Boston, May 6, 1973, in first period against Winnipeg during 9-6 win.
   — Chicago Cougars at Chicago, April 9, 1974, in first period against New England during 8-6 win.
   — Houston Aeros at Houston, April 13, 1974, in first period against Winnipeg during 10-1 win.
   — Toronto Toros at Chicago, April 30, 1974, in second period against Chicago during 7-6 win.

LONGEST OVERTIME:
  17:45 — Chicago Cougars, New England Whalers at Chicago, April 10, 1974. Chicago won game 2-1 on Ralph Backstrom's goal, and the series, 4-3.

SHORTEST OVERTIME:
  1:40 — Houston Aeros, Minnesota Fighting Saints at Houston, April 18, 1974. Minnesota won game on Mike Walton's goal, and Houston won the series 4-2.

MOST OVERTIME GAMES, QUARTER-FINAL SERIES:
  2 — New England Whalers, Ottawa Nationals in 1973. New England won series 4-1.
   — Chicago Cougars, New England Whalers in 1974. Chicago won series 4-3.

MOST OVERTIME GAMES, SEMI-FINAL SERIES:
  1 — Houston Aeros, Minnesota Fighting Saints in 1974. Houston won series 4-2.

MOST OVERTIME GAMES, FOUR-GAME SERIES:
  1 — Cleveland Crusaders, Philadelphia Blazers in 1973 series won by Cleveland.

MOST OVERTIME GAMES, FIVE-GAME SERIES:
  2 — New England Whalers, Ottawa Nationals in 1973 series won by New England 4-1.

MOST OVERTIME GAMES, SIX-GAME SERIES:
  1 — Houston Aeros, Los Angeles Sharks in 1973 series won by Houston 4-2.
   — Houston Aeros, Minnesota Fighting Saints in 1974 series won by Houston 4-2.

MOST OVERTIME GAMES, SEVEN-GAME SERIES:
  2 — Chicago Cougars, New England Whalers in 1974 series won by Chicago 4-3.

MOST OVERTIME PERIODS, ONE PLAYOFF YEAR, ONE TEAM:
  2 — New England in 1973, in 15 games. Both overtime periods came in the quarter-finals.
   — Ottawa Nationals in 1973, in 5 games, in the quarter-finals.
   — Chicago Cougars in 1974, in 18 games, both overtime periods coming in the quarter-finals.
   — New England Whalers in 1974, in 7 games, in the quarter-finals.

MOST CONSECUTIVE PLAYOFF GAME VICTORIES:
  7 — Houston Aeros. Streak began April 28, 1974, at St. Paul with a 4-1 win against the Minesota Fighting Saints in the 4th game of their semi-final series won by Houston 4-2. Houston swept the final series against Chicago Cougars 4-0.

LONGEST PLAYOFF LOSING STRING:
  6 — Winnipeg Jets lost the final two games of the 1973 Final Series against New England Whalers, beginning May 5, 1973, and lost four straight to the Houston Aeros in the 1974 Quarter-Final Series.

MOST SHUTOUTS, ONE PLAYOFF YEAR, ALL TEAMS:
  2 — 1973, in 34 games played. Both shutouts by Winnipeg.

MOST SHUTOUTS, ONE TEAM, ONE SERIES:
  2 — Winnipeg, in Semi-Final Series against Houston in 1973, won by Winnipeg 4-0.

MOST PENALTIES, BOTH TEAMS, ONE SERIES:
  116 — Houston Aeros, Minnesota Fighting Saints in 1974 Semi-Final Series won by Houston 4-2. Minnesota received 60 penalties, Houston received 56.

MOST PENALTY MINUTES, BOTH TEAMS, ONE SERIES:
  383 — Houston Aeros, Minnesota Fighting Saints in 1974 Semi-Final Series won by Houston 4-2. Minnesota received 213 minutes, Houston received 170.

MOST PENALTIES, ONE TEAM, ONE SERIES:
  60 — Minnesota Fighting Saints in 1974 Semi-Final Series against Houston Aeros won by Houston 4-2. Saints received 44 minors, 7 majors, 5 misconducts, 3 game misconducts, and 1 match penalty.

MOST PENALTY MINUTES, ONE TEAM, ONE SERIES:
213 — Minnesota Fighting Saints in 1974 Semi-Final Series won by Houston 4-2.

MOST PENALTIES, BOTH TEAMS, ONE GAME:
29 — Philadelphia Blazers, Cleveland Crusaders April 8, 1973, at Philadelphia. Philadelphia received 14 penalties, Cleveland 15. Cleveland won game 3-1.

MOST PENALTY MINUTES, BOTH TEAMS, ONE GAME:
98 — Minnesota Fighting Saints, Houston Aeros April 28, 1974 at St. Paul. Houston received 52 penalty minutes, Minnesota received 46 in game won by Houston 4-1.

MOST PENALTIES, ONE TEAM, ONE GAME:
17 — Toronto Toros, against Chicago Cougars at Toronto, May 1, 1974, in game won by Toronto 5-3.

MOST PENALTY MINUTES, ONE TEAM, ONE GAME:
65 — Chicago Cougars, April 16, 1974, at Springfield against New England Whalers in game won by Chicago 3-2.

MOST PENALTIES, BOTH TEAMS, ONE PERIOD:
17 — Minnesota Fighting Saints, Houston Aeros April 28, 1974 at St. Paul in the first period. Houston received 9 penalties, Minnesota 8 in game won by Aeros 4-1.

MOST PENALTY MINUTES, BOTH TEAMS, ONE PERIOD:
92 — Minnesota Fighting Saints, Houston Aeros April 28, 1974 at St. Paul in the first period. Houston 48 penalty minutes, Minnesota 44 in game won by Aeros 4-1.

MOST PENALTIES, ONE TEAM, ONE PERIOD:
10 — Chicago May 1, 1974, at Toronto in the third period of 5-3 loss to Toros.

MOST PENALTY MINUTES, ONE TEAM, ONE PERIOD:
55 — Chicago Cougars, April 16, 1974, at Springfield vs New England Whalers, in the third period of Cougars' 3-2 win.

FEWEST PENALTIES, BOTH TEAMS, ONE SERIES:
29 — Winnipeg Jets, Minnesota Fighting Saints in 1973 Quarter-Finals won by Winnipeg 4-1.

FEWEST PENALTIES, ONE TEAM, ONE SERIES:
13 — Winnipeg Jets, in 1973 Semi-Finals against Houston Aeros won by Houston 4-0.

MOST POWER PLAY GOALS, ONE TEAM, ONE PLAYOFF YEAR:
17 — Houston Aeros in 1974. 2 in Quarter-Finals against Winnipeg, 4 in Semi Finals against Minnesota, and 11 in Final Series against Chicago Cougars.

MOST POWER PLAY GOALS, BOTH TEAMS, ONE SERIES:
13 — New England Whalers, Ottawa Nationals in 1973 Quarter-Finals won by Whalers 4-1 New England had 8 Power Play Goals, Ottawa had 5.
— Houston Aeros, Los Angeles Sharks in 1973 Quarter-Finals won by Houston 4-2. Houston had 9 Power Play Goals, Los Angeles had 4.
— Houston Aeros, Chicago Cougars in 1974 Finals won by Houston 4-0. Houston had 11 Power Play Goals, Chicago had 2.

MOST POWER PLAY GOALS, ONE TEAM, ONE SERIES:
11 — Houston Aeros in 1974 Finals against Chicago won by Aeros 4-0.

MOST POWER PLAY GOALS, BOTH TEAMS, ONE GAME:
6 — Houston Aeros, Chicago Cougars, May 19, 1974 in Houston. Aeros had 5 Power Play Goals, Cougars had one. Houston won game 6-2.

MOST POWER PLAY GOALS, ONE TEAM, ONE GAME:
5 — Houston Aeros in 1974 Finals against Chicago, May 19, 1974 at Houston, in Aeros' 6-2 win.

MOST POWER PLAY GOALS, BOTH TEAMS, ONE PERIOD:
4 — Houston Aeros, Los Angeles Sharks, April 15, 1973, first period. Aeros had 2 Power Play Goals, Sharks had 2. Houston won game 6-3.

MOST POWER PLAY GOALS, ONE TEAM, ONE PERIOD:
3 — Houston Aeros against Chicago Cougars, May 19, 1974 at Houston in the second period of Aeros' 6-2 win.

MOST SHORT-HANDED GOALS, ONE TEAM, ONE PLAYOFF YEAR:
7 — Houston Aeros in 1974, with 3 against Winnipeg in the Quarter-Finals and 4 against Minnesota in the Semi-Finals.

MOST SHORT-HANDED GOALS, ONE TEAM, ONE SERIES:
4 — Houston Aeros in 1974 Semi-Final Series against Minnesota Fighting Saints won by Houston 4-2.

MOST SHORT-HANDED GOALS, ONE TEAM, ONE PERIOD:
2 — Houston Aeros, April 29, 1974 against Minnesota Fighting Saints at Houston, in the first period. Mark Howe and Gordie Howe scored in game won by Aeros 9-4.

FASTEST TWO GOALS, BOTH TEAMS:
    12 seconds — Houston Aeros, Minnesota Fighting Saints at Houston, April 20, 1974. Wayne Connelly scored for Minnesota at 18:31 of the second period, and Murray Hall scored at 18:43 of the second period for Houston. Aeros won the game 5-2.

FASTEST TWO GOALS, ONE TEAM:
    12 seconds — Toronto Toros, April 22, 1974 against Chicago at Toronto. Bob Leduc scored at 8:55 of the second period, and Tom Martin at 9:07 of the second period. Chicago won the game 4-3.

FASTEST THREE GOALS, BOTH TEAMS:
    56 seconds — Minnesota Fighting Saints, Edmonton Oilers, April 7, 1974 at St. Paul. Ted Hampson scored for Saints at 18:32 of the third period, Blair McDonald scored for Edmonton at 19:04, and Mike Walton scored an empty net goal for Minnesota at 19:28. Minnesota won the game 8-5.

FASTEST THREE GOALS, ONE TEAM:
    55 seconds — Cleveland Crusaders at Cleveland, April 7, 1973 against Philadelphia Blazers. Jim Wiste scored at 5:15 of the second period, Gerry Pinder at 5:51, and Gary Jarrett at 6:10. Cleveland won the game 7-1.

FASTEST FOUR GOALS, BOTH TEAMS:
    2 minutes, 18 seconds — Chicago Cougars, New England Whalers at Chicago, April 9, 1974. Jim Watson scored for Chicago at 7:35 of the second period, Don Blackburn for New England at 8:48, John Cunniff for New England at 9:23, and John French for New England at 9:53. Chicago won the game 8-6.

FASTEST TWO POWER PLAY GOALS, ONE TEAM:
    29 seconds — Minnesota Fighting Saints, April 6, 1974 at St. Paul against Edmonton Oilers. Murray Heatley scored at 9:09 of the second period, and Mike Walton scored at 9:38 in the Saints' 2-1 win.

FASTEST THREE POWER PLAY GOALS, ONE TEAM:
    3 minutes, 12 seconds — Houston Aeros, May 19, 1974 at Houston against Chicago Cougars in the Final Series. Andre Hinse scored at 12:40 of the second period, Gordon Labossiere scored at 13:58, and Larry Lund scored at 15:52 against Cougars goaltender Cam Newton in Aeros' 6-2 win.

FASTEST TWO SHORT-HANDED GOALS, ONE TEAM:
    42 seconds — Houston Aeros, April 29, 1974 against Minnesota Fighting Saints at Houston. Mark Howe scored at 15:48 of the first period, and Gordie Howe scored at 16:30 in Houston's 9-4 win.

INDIVIDUAL RECORDS

MOST CONSECUTIVE WINS BY GOALTENDER:
    7 — Don McLeod, Houston Aeros in 1974, with 3 wins in Semi-Finals against Minnesota and 4 wins in the Finals against Chicago.

MOST SHUTOUTS BY A GOALTENDER, ONE PLAYOFF YEAR:
    2 — Ernie Wakely, Winnipeg Jets, in 1973, during 7 games against Minnesota, Houston and New England.

MOST CONSECUTIVE SHUTOUTS:
    2 — Ernie Wakely, Winnipeg Jets, in 1973 Semi-Finals against Houston, won by Winnipeg 4-0. Wakely shutout Aeros 2-0 April 22, and 3-0 April 26.

LONGEST SHUTOUT SEQUENCE:
    145 minutes, 3 seconds — Ernie Wakely, Winnipeg Jets in 1973. Streak started at 14:43 of third period April 15 against Minnesota in a game won by Winnipeg 8-5; it continued April 22, with a 2-0 shutout of Houston, April 26 with a 3-0 shutout of Houston, and ended May 2 at 19:46 of the first period against New England on Tommy Williams' goal.

MOST POINTS, ONE PLAYOFF YEAR:
    28 — Norm Beaudin, Winnipeg Jets, in 1973. Beaudin had 13 goals and 15 assists in 14 games against Minnesota, Houston and New England.

MOST GOALS, ONE PLAYOFF YEAR:
    13 — Norm Beaudin, Winnipeg Jets in 1973, in 14 games against Minnesota, Houston and New England.

MOST ASSISTS, ONE PLAYOFF SEASON:
    16 — Bobby Hull, Winnipeg Jets, in 1973, in 14 games against Minnesota, Houston and New England.
    — Jim Dorey, New England Whalers, in 1973, in 15 games against Ottawa, Cleveland and Winnipeg.

playoff ind. record

MOST PENALTY MINUTES, ONE PLAYOFF SEASON:
  71 — Darryl Maggs, Chicago Cougars in 1974, in 18 games against New England, Toronto and Houston.

MOST POINTS BY DEFENSEMAN, ONE PLAYOFF YEAR:
  19 — Jim Dorey, New England in 1973. Dorey had 3 goals and 16 assists in 15 games against Ottawa, Cleveland and Winnipeg.

MOST GOALS BY A DEFENSEMAN, ONE PLAYOFF SEASON:
  4 — Larry Mavety, Chicago Cougars in 1974, with 2 goals in the Quarter-Finals against New England, 1 goal in the Semi-Finals against Toronto, and 1 goal in the Finals against Houston. Mavety played in 18 games.

MOST POINTS, ONE PLAYER, FOUR-GAME SERIES:
  9 — Gordie Howe, Houston Aeros in 1974 Finals against Chicago with 0 goals and 9 assists in series won by Houston 4-0.

MOST GOALS, FOUR-GAME SERIES:
  5 — Andre Hinse, Houston Aeros in 1974 Finals against Chicago won by Houston 4-0.

MOST ASSISTS, FOUR-GAME SERIES:
  9 — Gordie Howe, Houston Aeros in 1974 Finals against Chicago won by Houston 4-0.

MOST POINTS, FIVE-GAME SERIES:
  15 — Norm Beaudin, Winnipeg Jets in 1973, against Minnesota with 5 goals and 10 assists.

MOST GOALS, FIVE-GAME SERIES:
  7 — Tom Webster, New England Whalers in 1973 against Ottawa.

MOST ASSISTS, FIVE-GAME SERIES:
  10 — Norm Beaudin, Winnipeg Jets in 1973, against Minnesota.

MOST POINTS, SIX-GAME SERIES:
  10 — Poul Popiel, Houston Aeros in 1973 against Los Angeles with 2 goals and 8 assists.

MOST GOALS, SIX-GAME SERIES:
  5 — Mark Howe, Houston Aeros in 1974 Semi-Finals against Minnesota.

MOST ASSISTS, SIX-GAME SERIES:
  8 — Poul Popiel, Houston Aeros in 1973 against Los Angeles.

MOST POINTS, SEVEN-GAME SERIES:
  10 — Ralph Backstrom, Chicago Cougars in 1974 Semi-Finals against Toronto with 2 goals and 8 assists.
  — Rosaire Paiement, Chicago Cougars in 1974 Semi-Finals against Toronto with 7 goals and 3 assists.

MOST GOALS, SEVEN-GAME SERIES:
  7 — Rosaire Paiement, Chicago Cougars in 1974 Semi-Finals against Toronto.

MOST ASSISTS, SEVEN-GAME SERIES:
  8 — Ralph Backstrom, Chicago Cougars in 1974 Semi-Finals against Toronto.

MOST POINTS, QUARTER-FINAL SERIES:
  15 — Norm Beaudin, Winnipeg Jets in 1973 series against Minnesota won by Winnipeg 4-1.

MOST GOALS, QUARTER-FINAL SERIES:
  7 — Tom Webster, New England Whalers in 1973 series against Ottawa won by New England 4-1.

MOST ASSISTS, QUARTER-FINAL SERIES:
  10 — Norm Beaudin, Winnipeg Jets in 1973 series against Minnesota won by Winnipeg 4-1.

MOST POINTS, SEMI-FINAL SERIES:
  12 — Tim Sheehy, New England Whalers in 1973 against Cleveland with 6 goals and 6 assists in series won by Whalers 4-1.

MOST GOALS, SEMI-FINAL SERIES:
  7 — Rosaire Paiement, Chicago Cougars in 1974 against Toronto in 7 games.

MOST ASSISTS, SEMI-FINAL SERIES:
  8 — Ralph Backstrom, Chicago Cougars in 1974 against Toronto in 7 games.

MOST POINTS, FINAL SERIES:
  11 — Tom Webster, New England Whalers in 1973 against Winnipeg with 4 goals and 7 assists in series won by Whalers 4-1.
  — Tom Williams, New England Whalers in 1973 against Winnipeg with 2 goals and 9 assists in series won by Whalers 4-1.

MOST GOALS, FINAL SERIES:
  5 — Norm Beaudin, Winnipeg Jets in 1973 against New England.
  — Andre Hinse, Houston Aeros in 1974 against Chicago.

MOST ASSISTS, FINAL SERIES:
   9 — Tommy Williams, New England Whalers in 1973 against Winnipeg in series won by New England 4-1.
   — Gordie Howe, Houston Aeros in 1974 against Chicago in series won by Houston 4-0.

MOST POINTS, ONE GAME:
   7 — Norm Beaudin, Winnipeg Jets, April 15, 1973, against Minnesota at Winnipeg. Beaudin had 3 goals and 4 assists in Jets' 8-5 win.

MOST GOALS, ONE GAME:
   4 — Larry Lund, Houston Aeros, April 13, 1974 against Winnipeg in Aeros' 10-1 win. Elapsed time for the four goals was 43:50.

MOST ASSISTS, ONE GAME:
   4 — Record held by seven players.

MOST PENALTIES, ONE GAME:
   7 — Ted Taylor, Houston Aeros, April 28, 1974 at St. Paul against Minnesota. Taylor received 3 minors, 2 majors, and 2 misconducts in Aeros' 4-1 win.

MOST PENALTY MINUTES, ONE GAME:
   36 — Ted Taylor, Houston Aeros, April 28, 1974 at St. Paul against Minnesota in Aeros' 4-1 win.

MOST POINTS, ONE PERIOD:
   4 — Norm Beaudin, Winnipeg Jets, April 15, 1973 at Winnipeg against Minnesota. Beaudin had 2 goals and 2 assists in the second period of the Jets' 8-5 win.

MOST GOALS, ONE PERIOD:
   3 — Rick Sentes, Toronto Toros, April 12, 1974 at Cleveland in the second period of a 4-2 win. Elapsed time for the three goals was 8:42.

MOST ASSISTS, ONE PERIOD:
   3 — Wayne Dillon, Toronto Toros, April 30, 1974 at Chicago in the second period of the Toros' 7-6 win.
   3 — Poul Popiel, Houston Aeros, May 19, 1974 at Houston against Chicago in the second period of Aeros' 6-3 win.

MOST PENALTIES, ONE PERIOD:
   7 — Ted Taylor, Houston Aeros, April 28, 1974 at St. Paul against Minnesota in the first period of Aeros' 4-1 win. Taylor received 3 minors (including one double minor), 2 majors and 2 misconducts.

MOST PENALTY MINUTES, ON PERIOD:
   36 — Ted Taylor, Houston Aeros, April 28, 1974 at St. Paul against Minnesota in first period of Aeros' 4-1 win.

FASTEST GOAL FROM START OF GAME:
   21 Seconds — Tom Webster, New England Whalers, May 6, 1973 at Boston against Winnipeg. Webster scored against goaltender Joe Daley in Whalers' 9-6 win.

FASTEST TWO GOALS FROM START OF GAME:
   10:17 — Larry Lund, Houston Aeros, April 13, 1974 against Winnipeg at Houston. Lund scored against goaltender Frank Blum at 2:45 and 10:17 of the first period of Aeros' 10-1 win.

FASTEST GOAL FROM START OF PERIOD (OTHER THAN FIRST):
   7 Seconds — Mike Antonovich, Minnesota Fight Saints at Winnipeg, April 15, 1973. Antonovich scored against goaltender Ernie Wakely in the second period of Saints' 8-5 loss.

FASTEST TWO GOALS FROM START OF PERIOD (OTHER THAN FIRST):
   6:37 — Larry Lund, Houston Aeros April 13, 1974, against Winnipeg at Houston. Lund scored against goaltender Frank Blum at 2:18 and 6:37 of the third period of Aeros' 10-1 win.

FASTEST TWO GOALS:
   15 Seconds — Mike Walton, Minnesota Fighting Saints, April 14, 1974 against Edmonton at St. Paul. Walton scored at 19:05 and 19:20 of the first period against goaltender Chris Worthy in Saints' 5-4 win.

FASTEST THREE GOALS:
   8 minutes, 42 seconds — Rick Sentes, Toronto Toros, at Cleveland, April 12, 1974. Sentes scored in the second period at 10:41, 13:04 and 19:23 against goaltender Gerry Cheevers in the Toros' 4-2 win.

MOST CONSECUTIVE GAMES WITH POINTS:
   16 — Tim Sheehy, New England Whalers, beginning April 12, 1973 against Ottawa and ended April 12, 1974 against Chicago. In the streak, Sheehy had 15 goals and 16 assists.

MOST CONSECUTIVE GAMES WITH GOALS:
6 — Larry Pleau, New England Whalers beginning April 12, 1973 against Ottawa at Toronto, and ended April 27, 1973, at Boston against Cleveland. Pleau had 7 goals during the streak.

MOST CONSECUTIVE GAMES WITH ASSISTS:
9 — Tim Sheehy, New England Whalers, beginning April 12, 1973 against Ottawa at Toronto, and ended May 3, 1973, at Winnipeg. In the streak, Sheehy had 11 assists.

MOST GAME WINNING GOALS, ONE PLAYOFF YEAR:
3 — Bobby Hull, Winnipeg Jets, in 1973. 1 in Quarter-Finals, 1 in Semi-Finals, and 1 in Final Series
 — Tim Sheehy, New England Whalers, in 1973. 2 in Semi-Finals, 1 in Finals.
 — Mike Walton, Minnesota Fighting Saints, in 1974. 2 in Quarter-Finals, 1 in Semi-Finals.
 — Murray Hall, Houston Aeros, in 1974. 1 in Quarter-Finals, 1 in Semi-Finals, and 1 in Finals.

MOST OVERTIME GOALS, ONE PLAYOFF YEAR, ONE PLAYOFF SERIES:
1 — 9 players tied with 1.

MOST THREE-GOALS-OR-MORE GAMES, ONE PLAYOFF YEAR:
2 — Gary Jarrett, Cleveland Crusaders in 1973. Jarrett had 3 goals April 7 in Cleveland against Philadelphia in the Quarter-Finals, and 3 goals April 22 against New England in the Semi-Finals.

MOST POWER-PLAY GOALS, ONE PLAYOFF YEAR:
5 — Wayne Connelly, Minnesota Fighting Saints, in 1974. Connelly had 2 in the Quarter-Finals against Edmonton, and 2 in the Semi-Finals against Houston.

MOST POWER-PLAY GOALS, ONE SERIES:
4 — Andre Hinse, Houston Aeros in 1974 Finals against Chicago.

MOST POWER-PLAY GOALS, ONE GAME:
2 — 6 players tied with 2.

MOST POWER PLAY GOALS, ONE PERIOD:
2 — Tommy Williams, New England Whalers, April 12, 1973 against Ottawa in second period of 7-3 win.
 — Frank Hughes, Houston Aeros, April 15, 1973, against Los Angeles in first period of 6-3 win.
 — Tom Webster, New England Whalers, April 16, 1974, against Chicago in second period of 3-2 loss.
 — Andre Hinse, Houston Aeros, May 17, 1974, against Chicago in second period of 7-4 win.
 — Murray Hall, Houston Aeros, May 19, 1974, against Chicago in first period of 6-2 win.

MOST SHORT-HANDED GOALS, ONE PLAYOFF YEAR:
2 — Larry Lund, Houston Aeros, in 1974. 1 in Quarter-Finals, 1 in Semi-Finals.
 — Gordie Howe, Houston Aeros, in 1974. 1 in Quarter-Finals, 1 in Semi-Finals.
 — Mark Howe, Houston Aeros, in 1974. 2 in Semi-Finals.
 — Rod Zaine, Chicago Cougars, in 1974. 2 in Semi-Finals.

MOST SHORT-HANDED GOALS, ONE PLAYOFF SERIES:
2 — Mark Howe, Houston Aeros, in 1974 Semi-Finals against Minnesota.
 — Rod Zaine, Chicago Cougars, in 1974 Semi-Finals against Toronto.

MOST SHORT-HANDED GOALS, ONE PLAYOFF GAME:
1 — record held by many.

PENALTY SHOTS:
Wayne Dillon, Toronto Toros, April 19, 1974 against Chicago goaltender Cam Newton. Dillon scored in Toros' 6-4 win in Toronto. The only penalty shot awarded in WHA playoff competition.

PLAYOFF ATTENDANCE

2-YEAR TOTALS

TEAM	GP	1974 TOTALS	AVG.	GP	1973 TOTALS	AVG.	PER GAME CHANGE	PCT.	1974 CAPACITY	PCT.
EASTERN DIVISION										
New England	4	22,064	5,516	9	79,866	8,874	−3,358	− 37.8%	22,064	100.0%
Toronto	7	51,801	7,400	2	8,820	4,410	+2,990	+ 67.8%	112,805	45.9%
Cleveland	2	16,203	8,102	4	24,460	6,115	+1,987	+ 32.5%	18,600	87.1%
Chicago	8	25,093	3,137	—	—	—	—	—	42,000	59.7%
Quebec	—	—	—	—	—	—	—	—	—	—
New Jersey	—	—	—	—	—	—	—	—	—	—
EAST TOTALS	21	115,161	5,484	15	113,146	7,543	−2,059	− 27.3%	195,469	58.9%
WESTERN DIVISION										
Houston	7	65,356	9,337	5	33,098	6,620	+2,717	+ 41.0%	65,100	100.4%
Minnesota	6	81,569	13,595	2	12,133	6,067	+7,528	+124.1%	97,080	84.0%
Edmonton	2	9,806	4,903	—	—	—	—	—	10,400	94.3%
Winnipeg	2	17,138	8,569	7	52,559	7,508	+1,061	+ 14.1%	20,154	85.0%
Vancouver	—	—	—	2	7,234	3,617	—	—	—	—
Los Angeles	—	—	—	3	17,695	5,898	—	—	—	—
WEST TOTALS	17	173,869	10,228	19	122,719	6,459	+3,769	+ 58.4%	192,734	90.2%
WHA TOTALS	38	289,030	7,606	34	235,865	6,937	+ 669	+ 9.6%	388,203	74.5%

ALL-TIME TOP 5 WHA PLAYOFF CROWDS

	DATE	CROWD	SITE	FINAL SCORE
1.	4-28-74	17,211	St. Paul	Houston 4, Minnesota 1
2.	4-21-74	16,412	St. Paul	Minnesota 4, Houston 1
3.	5-5-73	13,697	Boston	New England 4, Winnipeg 2
4.	4-6-74	13,004	St. Paul	Minnesota 2, Edmonton 1
5.	5-1-74	12,422	St. Paul	Houston 3, Minnesota 1

TOP 15 CROWDS OF 1973-74 SEASON (Including Playoffs)

	DATE	CROWD	SITE	VISITING TEAM	FINAL SCORE		
1.	4-28-74	17,211	St. Paul	Houston	Houston -	4, Minnesota -	1
2.	4-21-74	16,412	St. Paul	Houston	Minnesota -	4, Houston -	1
3.	4- 1-74	14,7111	Boston	Houston	Houston -	4, New England -	1
4.	1-26-74	14,159	Vancouver	Houston	Houston -	4, Vancouver -	2
5.	3-30-74	13,699	Quebec	Toronto	Toronto -	3, Quebec -	1
6.	4- 6-74	13,004	St. Paul	Edmonton	Minnesota -	2, Edmonton -	1
7.	10-10-73	12,452	Vancouver	Winnipeg	Vancouver -	4, Winnipeg -	3
8.	5- 1-74	12,422	St. Paul	Houston	Houston -	3, Minnesota -	1
9.	10-17-73	12,186	Vancouver	Houston	Houston -	7, Vancouver -	2
10.	2-15-74	12,044	St. Paul	Winnipeg	Minnesota -	7, Winnipeg -	1
11.	4- 7-74	11,756	St. Paul	Edmonton	Minnesota -	8, Edmonton -	5
12.	3-31-74	11,734	St. Paul	Houston	Minnesota -	5, Houston -	2
13.	3-29-74	11,459	St. Paul	Edmonton	Edmonton -	3, Minnesota -	1
14.	3-27-74	11,332	Vancouver	Houston	Houston -	8, Vancouver -	1
15.	3- 9-74	11,072	St. Paul	Quebec	Minnesota -	9, Quebec -	5

attendance

REGULAR SEASON ATTENDANCE

HOME TEAM	GP	1973-74 TOTALS	1973-74 AVG.	1972-73 TOTALS	1972-73 AVG.	NET CHANGE	PCT.	1973-74 CAPACITY	PCT.
EASTERN DIVISION									
New England	39	232,814	5,970	272,255	6,981	−39,441	−14.5%	584,766	39.8%
Toronto	39	167,342	4,291	125,802	3,226	+41,540	+33.0%	227,700	73.5%
Cleveland	39	242,277	6,212	206,202	5,287	+36,075	+17.5%	362,700	66.8%
Chicago	39	192,048	4,924	178,960	4,589	+13,088	+ 7.3%	351,000	54.7%
Quebec	39	311,352	7,983	269,979	6,923	+41,373	+15.3%	390,000	79.8%
New Jersey	39	100,810	2,585	228,857	5,868	−128,047	−56.0%	334,500	30.1%
Eastern Totals	234	1,246,643	5,328	1,282,055	5,479	−35,412	− 2.7%	2,250,666	55.3%
WESTERN DIVISION									
Houston	39	265,622	6,811	180,037	4,616	+85,585	+47.5%	362,700	73.2%
Minnesota	39	256,772	6,584	228,360	5,855	+28,412	+12.4%	631,020	40.7%
Edmonton	39	172,737	4,429	149,280	3,828	+23,457	+15.7%	202,800	85.2%
Winnipeg	39	249,654	6,401	237,982	6,102	+11,672	+ 4.9%	393,003	63.5%
Vancouver	39	364,903	9,356	168,680	4,325	+196,223	+116.3%	607,191	60.1%
Los Angeles	39	208,175	5,338	233,285	5,982	−25,110	−10.8%	566,550	36.7%
Western Totals	234	1,517,863	6,487	1,197,624	5,118	+320,230	+26.7%	2,763,264	54.9%
WHA TOTALS	468	2,764,506	5,907	2,479,679	5,298	+284,827	+11.4%	5,013,930	55.1%

TEAM REGULAR SEASON DRAWING POWER

ROAD TEAM	GP	1973-74 TOTALS	1973-74 AVG.	1972-73 TOTALS	1972-73 AVG.	NET CHANGE	PCT.	1973-74 CAPACITY	PCT.
EASTERN DIVISION									
New England	39	228,516	5,859	195,412	5,011	+33,104	+16.9%	401,701	56.9%
Toronto	39	231,351	5,932	202,467	5,191	+28,884	+14.3%	418,254	55.3%
Cleveland	39	211,163	5,414	204,813	5,252	+ 6,350	+ 3.1%	410,934	51.4%
Chicago	39	221,851	5,688	193,075	4,951	+28,776	+14.9%	425,531	52.1%
Quebec	39	229,390	5,882	204,495	5,243	+24,895	+12.2%	426,379	53.8%
New Jersey	39	219,760	5,635	203,578	5,220	+16,182	+ 7.9%	420,448	52.3%
Eastern Totals	234	1,342,031	5,735	1,203,840	5,145	+138,191	+11.4%	2,503,247	53.6%
WESTERN DIVISION									
Houston	39	292,312	7,495	196,216	5,031	+96,096	+49.0%	435,511	67.1%
Minnesota	39	222,229	5,698	206,078	5,284	+16,151	+ 7.8%	401,466	55.4%
Edmonton	39	221,077	5,669	192,587	4,938	+28,490	+14.8%	443,466	49.8%
Winnipeg	39	263,803	6,746	286,623	7,349	−22,820	− 8.0%	430,078	61.3%
Vancouver	39	201,575	5,169	211,944	5,434	−10,369	− 4.9%	387,810	52.0%
Los Angeles	39	221,479	5,679	182,391	4,677	+39,088	+21.4%	411,886	53.8%
Western Totals	234	1,422,475	6,079	1,275,839	5,452	+146,636	+11.4%	2,510,683	56.6%
WHA TOTALS	468	2,764,506	5,907	2,479,679	5,298	+284,827	+11.4%	5,013,930	55.1%

TOP 15 WHA CROWDS
(REGULAR SEASON)

	DATE	CROWD	SITE	FINAL SCORE
1.	4- 1-74	14,711	Boston	Houston 4, New England 1
2.	10-12-72	14,772	Boston	New England 4, Philadelphia 3
3.	1-26-74	14,159	Vancouver	Houston 4, Vancouver 2
4.	3-30-74	13,699	Quebec	Toronto 3, Quebec 1
5.	2-25-73	13,674	New York	New York 9, Cleveland 5
6.	1- 7-73	13,426	St. Paul	Winnipeg 6, Minnesota 2
7.	3-11-73	12,804	Los Angeles	Los Angeles 4, Ottawa 2
8.	10-10-73	12,452	Vancouver	Vancouver 4, Winnipeg 3 (OT)
9.	3-30-74	12,216	Boston	New England 5, New York 4 (OT)
10.	10-17-73	12,186	Vancouver	Houston 7, Vancouver 2
11.	1-26-73	12,086	St. Paul	Minnesota 4, Ottawa 2
12.	2-15-74	12,044	St. Paul	Minnesota 7, Winnipeg 1
13.	10-13-72	11,792	Los Angeles	Houston 3, Los Angeles 2
14.	3-31-74	11,734	St. Paul	Minnesota 5, Houston 2
15.	3-29-74	11,459	St. Paul	Edmonton 3, Minnesota 1

WHA ALL STAR TEAMS
(Determined by Vote of News Media)

1972-73 FIRST TEAM		SECOND TEAM
Gerry Cheevers, Cleveland	GOAL	Bernie Parent, Philadelphia
J.C. Tremblay, Quebec	DEFENSE	Jim Dorey, New England
Paul Shmyr, Cleveland	DEFENSE	Larry Hornung, Winnipeg
Andre Lacroix, Philadelphia	CENTRE	Ron Ward, New York
Danny Lawson, Philadelphia	RIGHT WING	Tom Webster, New England
Bobby Hull, Winnipeg	LEFT WING	Gary Jarrett, Cleveland

1973-74 FIRST TEAM		SECOND TEAM
Don McLeod, Houston	GOAL	Gerry Cheevers, Cleveland
Pat Stapleton, Chicago	DEFENSE	J.C. Tremblay, Quebec
Paul Shmyr, Cleveland	DEFENSE	Al Hamilton, Edmonton
Andre Lacroix, New Jersey	CENTRE	Wayne Carleton, Toronto
Gordie Howe, Houston	RIGHT WING	Mike Walton, Minnesota
Bobby Hull, Winnipeg	LEFT WING	Mark Howe, Houston

MID-SEASON ALL-STAR GAME TEAMS (Determined by Vote of Players)

1972-73 EAST DIVISION
GOAL: Al Smith (New England), Gerry Cheevers (Cleveland), Serge Aubry (Quebec).
DEFENSE: Rick Ley (New England), J.C. Tremblay (Quebec), Paul Shmyr (Cleveland), Jim Dorey (New England), Ken Block (New York), John Hanna (Cleveland), Bob Charlebois (Ottawa).
CENTRE: Ron Ward (New York), Larry Pleau (New England), Terry Caffery (New England),
RIGHT WING: Tom Webster (New England), Danny Lawson (Philadelphia), Norm Ferguson (New York), John McKenzie (Philadelphia), Guy Trottier (Ottawa).
LEFT WING: Wayne Carleton (Ottawa), Gary Jarrett (Cleveland), Gerry Pinder (Cleveland), Michel Parizeau (Quebec), Ron Climie (Ottawa).

WEST DIVISION
GOAL: Mike Curran (Minnesota), Ernie Wakely (Winnipeg), Jack Norris (Alberta).
DEFENSE: Al Hamilton (Alberta), Larry Hornung (Winnipeg), Gerry Odrowski (Los Angeles), Ron Anderson (Chicago), Terry Ball (Minnesota), Mike McMahon (Minnesota), Bart Crashley (Los Angeles).
CENTRE: Chris Bordeleau (Winnipeg), Gordon Labossiere (Houston), Jim Harrison (Alberta), Ted Hampson (Minnesota).
RIGHT WING: Wayne Connelly (Minnesota), Norm Beaudin (Winnipeg), Mike Byers (Los Angeles), Gary Veneruzzo (Los Angeles).
LEFT WING: Bob Wall (Alberta), Bobby Hull (Winnipeg), Ted Taylor (Houston), Jan Popiel (Chicago).
OFFICIALS: Referee — Bill Friday. Linesmen — Pierre Belanger, Ron Asselstine.

GAME SITE: Quebec City, Quebec, January 6, 1973 (5,435)

EAST 6, WEST 2

FIRST PERIOD	1. WEST, Odrowski (Beaudin) 10:39
	2. EAST, Jarrett (Ward) 10:51
	PENALTIES — Pleau (E) (Holding) 4:43; Hanna (E) (Hooking) 12:09; Shmyr (E) (Holding) 17:25; Harrison (W) (Tripping) 9:23.
SECOND PERIOD	3. EAST, McKenzie (Carleton, Block) 3:37
	4. EAST, Pleau (Webster, Caffery) 12:47
	5. EAST, Dorey (Ward, Lawson) 19:43
	PENALTIES — None.
THIRD PERIOD	6. WEST, Hull (Connelly, Bordeleau) 3:05
	7. EAST, Lawson (Jarrett, Tremblay) 7:29
	8. EAST, Carleton (Charlebois, Dorey) 8:00
	PENALTIES — None.

SHOTS ON GOAL BY:
WEST.... 8 13 12 — 33
EAST ....18 14 15 — 47

COACH:
EAST, Jack Kelley (New England)
WEST, Bobby Hull and Nick Mickoski (Winnipeg)

all-stars

GOALTENDERS:
EAST: Al Smith, 30 Minutes, 1 goal against; Gerry Cheevers, 30 Minutes, 1 goal against.
WEST: Ernie Wakely, 20 Minutes, 1 goal against; Jack Norris, 20 Minutes, 3 goals against; Mike Curran, 20 minutes, 2 goals against.

1973-74 EAST DIVISION
GOAL: Gerry Cheevers (Cleveland), Gilles Gratton (Toronto), Al Smith (New England).
DEFENSE: Rick Ley (new England), J.C. Tremblay (Quebec), Pat Stapleton (Chicago), Paul Shmyr (Cleveland), Brad Selwood (New England), Jim Dorey (New England).
CENTRE: Larry Pleau (New England), Ralph Backstrom (Chicago), Andre Lacroix (New Jersey), Serge Bernier (Quebec).
RIGHT WING: Gerry Pinder (Cleveland), Tom Webster (New England), Rosaire Paiement (Chicago), Tom Simpson (Toronto).
LEFT WING: Rejean Houle (Quebec), Wayne Carleton (Toronto), Gary Jarrett (Cleveland), Hugh Harris (New England).
NAMED TO TEAM, But Unable To Participate Due To Injury: Bobby Sheehan (New Jersey), Dale Hoganson (Quebec).
SUITED But Not Playing: Gilles Gratton (Toronto).

WEST DIVISION
GOAL: Ernie Wakely (Winnipeg), Jack Norris (Edmonton), John Garrett (Minnesota).
DEFENSE: Rick Smith (Minnesota), Al Hamilton (Edmonton), Gerry Odrowski (Los Angeles), Poul Popiel (Houston), Bart Crashley (Los Angeles), Ralph MacSweyn (Vancouver).
CENTRE: Mike Walton (Minnesota), Larry Lund (Houston), Bryan Campbell (Vancouver), Fran Huck (Winnipeg), Ross Perkins (Edmonton).
RIGHT WING: Wayne Connelly (Minnesota), Gordie Howe (Houston), Danny Lawson (Vancouver), Frank Hughes (Houston).
LEFT WING: Bobby Hull (Winnipeg), Ron Climie (Edmonton), Marc Tardif (Los Angeles)
NAMED TO TEAM, But Unable To Participate Due To Injury:
Larry Hornung (Winnipeg), Jim Harrison (Edmonton).

OFFICIALS: Referee, Bob Sloan. Linesmen, Alan Glaspell and Gene Kusy.

GAME SITE: St. Paul Civic Center, January 3, 1974 (13,196)

EAST 8, WEST 4

FIRST PERIOD
1. EAST, R. Houle (S. Bernier, R. Paiement) 2:11
2. EAST, R. Backstrom (W. Carleton, P. Stapleton) 8:02(S.H.)
3. EAST, L. Pleau (Unassisted) 10:39
4. WEST, M. Walton (D. Lawson) 14:55
5. EAST, G. Pinder (A. Lacroix, P. Shmyr) 18:38
6. EAST, A. Lacroix (G. Pinder, G. Jarrett) 19:12
PENALTIES — R. Ley (E) (Interference) 6:34

SECOND PERIOD
7. WEST, M. Walton (B. Hull, M. Tardif) .... 7:27(P.P.)
8. EAST, R. Paiement (R. Backstrom) 9:15
9. WEST, M. Walton (A. Hamilton, R. Climie) .... 16:04(Hat Trick)
10. WEST, L. Lund (F. Hughes, A. Hamilton) 17:28
PENALTIES — T. Webster (E) (Tripping) 6:31

THIRD PERIOD
11. EAST, A. Lacroix (G. Jarrett, G. Pinder) 9:17
12. EAST, L. Pleau (H. Harris, T. Webster) 18:59
PENALTIES — R. Climie (W) (Hooking) 2:43

SHOTS ON GOAL BY:
EAST 10   12   10   — 32
WEST 10   13   7   — 30

COACH:
EAST, Jack Kelley (New England)
WEST, Bobby Hull and Nick Mickoski (Winnipeg)

GOALTENDERS:
EAST: Gerry Cheevers, 29 Minutes, 15 seconds, 2 goals; Gilles Gratton, 30 minutes, 45 seconds, 2 goals.
WEST: Jack Norris, 20 minutes, 5 goals; Ernie Wakely, 20 minutes, 1 goal; John Garrett, 20 minutes, 2 goals.

1973-74 FINAL STANDINGS

EASTERN DIVISION	GP	W	L	T	PTS	GF	GA	PCT
New England	78	43	31	4	90	291	260	.577
Toronto	78	41	33	4	86	304	272	.551
Cleveland	78	37	32	9	83	266	264	.532
Chicago	78	38	35	5	81	271	273	.519
Quebec	78	38	36	4	80	306	280	.513
New Jersey	78	32	42	4	68	268	313	.436

WESTERN DIVISION	GP	W	L	T	PTS	GF	GA	PCT
Houston	78	48	25	5	101	318	219	.647
Minnesota	78	44	32	2	90	332	275	.577
Edmonton	78	38	37	3	79	268	269	.506
Winnipeg	78	34	39	5	73	264	296	.468
Vancouver	78	27	50	1	55	278	345	.353
Los Angeles	78	25	53	0	50	239	339	.321

STANDINGS HOME-AND-AWAY

		At Home							On The Road				
W	L	T	PTS	GF	GA	PCT	EASTERN DIVISION	W	L	T	PTS	GF	GA	PCT
26	11	2	54	155	118	.692	New England Whalers	17	20	2	36	136	142	.462
25	11	3	53	167	118	.679	Toronto Toros	16	22	1	33	137	154	.423
27	8	4	58	147	105	.744	Cleveland Crusaders	10	24	5	25	119	159	.321
23	13	3	49	153	132	.628	Chicago Cougars	15	22	2	32	118	141	.410
25	10	4	54	179	115	.692	Quebec Nordiques	13	26	0	26	127	165	.333
22	16	1	45	161	139	.577	New Jersey Knights	10	26	3	23	107	174	.295
148	69	17	313	962	727	.669	......EAST TOTALS......	81	140	13	175	744	935	.374

W	L	T	PTS	GF	GA	PCT	WESTERN DIVISION	W	L	T	PTS	GF	GA	PCT
28	9	2	58	170	90	.744	Houston Aeros	20	16	3	43	148	129	.551
26	12	1	53	194	132	.679	Minnesota Saints	18	20	1	37	138	143	.474
24	14	1	49	152	120	.628	Edmonton Oilers	14	23	2	30	116	149	.385
26	11	2	54	164	109	.692	Winnipeg Jets	8	28	3	19	100	187	.244
19	20	0	38	154	152	.487	Vancouver Blazers	8	30	1	17	124	193	.218
17	22	0	34	126	153	.436	Los Angeles Sharks	8	31	0	16	113	186	.205
140	88	6	286	960	756	.611	......WEST TOTALS......	76	148	10	162	739	987	.346
288	157	23	599	1922	1483	.640	......WHA TOTALS......	157	288	23	337	1483	1922	.360

STANDINGS DIVISION-BY-DIVISION

		Against Own Division							Against Other Division				
W	L	T	PTS	GF	GA	PCT	EASTERN DIVISION	W	L	T	PTS	GF	GA	PCT
23	17	2	48	143	132	.571	New England Whalers	20	14	2	42	148	128	.583
18	21	3	39	154	154	.464	Toronto Toros	23	12	1	47	150	118	.653
17	18	5	39	127	138	.488	Cleveland Crusaders	20	14	4	44	139	126	.579
20	17	3	43	144	139	.538	Chicago Cougars	18	18	2	38	127	134	.500
21	20	1	43	154	142	.512	Quebec Nordiques	17	16	3	37	152	138	.514
16	22	4	36	138	155	.429	New Jersey Knights	16	20	0	32	130	158	.444
115	115	18	248	860	860	.500	......EAST TOTALS......	114	94	12	240	846	802	.545

W	L	T	PTS	GF	GA	PCT	WESTERN DIVISION	W	L	T	PTS	GF	GA	PCT
31	9	2	64	196	111	.762	Houston Aeros	17	16	3	37	122	108	.514
24	16	0	48	171	128	.600	Minnesota Saints	20	16	2	42	161	147	.553
19	23	0	38	139	155	.452	Edmonton Oilers	19	14	3	41	129	114	.569
15	23	2	32	124	165	.400	Winnipeg Jets	19	16	3	41	140	131	.539
18	24	0	36	145	167	.429	Vancouver Blazers	9	26	1	19	133	178	.264
15	27	0	30	122	171	.357	Los Angeles Sharks	10	26	0	20	117	168	.278
122	122	4	248	897	897	.500	......WEST TOTALS......	94	114	12	200	802	846	.455
237	237	22	496	1757	1757	.500	......WHA TOTALS......	208	208	24	440	1648	1648	.500

73-74 statistics

GOALTENDING 1973-74 REGULAR SEASON

	Min.	GPI	W	L	T	SOG	GA	SVS	GAA	SG	SP
HOUSTON	4730	78	48	25	5	2292	216	2076	2.74	4	101
Ron Grahame	250	4	3	0	1	123	5	118	1.20	1	9
Don McLeod	2971	49	33	13	3	1432	127	1305	2.56	3	66
Wayne Rutledge	1509	25	12	12	1	737	84	653	3.34	0	26
NEW ENGLAND	4759	78	43	31	4	2348	256	2092	3.23	2	100
Al Smith	3194	55	30	21	4	1569	164	1405	3.08	2	66
Bill Berglund	180	3	2	1	0	87	10	77	3.33	0	4
Bruce Landon	1386	24	11	9	2	692	82	610	3.55	0	30
CLEVELAND	4793	78	37	32	9	2591	260	2331	3.26	5	93
Gerry Cheevers	3562	59	30	20	6	1911	180	1731	3.03	4	73
Bob Whidden	1232	22	7	12	3	680	80	600	3.90	1	20
CHICAGO	4742	78	38	35	5	2398	264	2134	3.34	1	68
Cam Newton	2732	45	25	18	2	1352	143	1209	3.14	1	46
Andre Gill	803	13	4	7	2	418	46	372	3.44	0	9
Rich Coutu	1207	20	9	10	1	628	75	553	3.73	0	13
EDMONTON	4723	78	38	37	3	2578	263	2315	3.34	3	74
Jack Norris	2954	53	23	24	1	1546	158	1388	3.21	2	50
Ian Wilkie Edmonton Totals	256	5	3	1	1	128	9	119	2.11	0	7
Season Totals	1514	28	14	10	1	720	91	629	3.61	1	26
Chris Worthy	1453	29	11	12	1	866	92	774	3.80	1	17
Gary Doyle	60	1	1	0	0	38	4	34	4.00	0	0
TORONTO	4750	78	41	33	4	2635	270	2365	3.41	4	81
William Holden Toronto Totals	10	1	0	0	0	7	0	7	0.00	0	0
Season Totals	70	2	0	1	0	35	4	31	3.43	0	0
Frank Blum	131	5	1	0	0	66	5	61	2.29	0	2
Les Binkley	1412	27	14	9	1	776	77	699	3.27	1	21
Gilles Gratton	3200	57	26	24	3	1786	188	1598	3.53	2	58
MINNESOTA	4714	78	44	32	2	2884	272	2612	3.46	3	76
Mike Curran	2382	40	23	14	2	1444	130	1314	3.27	2	42
John Garrett	2290	40	21	18	0	1414	137	1277	3.59	1	34
Jack McCartan	42	2	0	0	0	26	5	21	7.14	0	0
QUEBEC	4749	78	38	36	4	2570	275	2295	3.47	3	75
Serge Aubry	1395	26	11	11	2	751	90	661	3.87	1	22
Michel Deguise	1750	32	12	13	1	919	96	823	3.29	1	29
Richard Brodeur	1607	30	15	12	1	900	89	811	3.32	1	24
WINNIPEG	4768	78	34	39	5	2614	290	2324	3.65	3	86
William Holden Winnipeg Totals	60	1	0	1	0	28	4	24	4.00	0	0
Season Totals	70	2	0	1	0	35	4	31	3.43	0	0
Ernie Wakely	2254	37	15	18	4	1184	123	1061	3.27	3	46
Joe Daley	2454	41	19	20	1	1402	163	1239	3.99	0	40
NEW JERSEY	4728	78	32	42	4	2624	308	2316	3.91	0	71
Joe Junkin	3121	53	21	25	4	1762	197	1565	3.79	1	48
Gary Kurt	1089	20	8	10	0	566	75	491	4.13	0	15
Jim McLeod	516	10	3	7	0	296	36	260	4.18	0	8
VANCOUVER	4739	78	27	50	1	2703	338	2365	4.28	3	68
Peter Donnelly	2824	49	22	24	0	1525	179	1346	3.80	3	52
George Gardner Van. Totals	1590	28	4	21	1	957	125	832	4.72	0	14
Season Totals	1710	30	4	23	1	1022	138	884	4.84	0	14
Yves Archambault	263	5	1	4	0	183	27	156	6.14	0	2
Danny Sullivan	60	1	0	1	0	38	7	31	7.00	0	0
LOS ANGELES	4693	78	25	53	0	2334	335	1997	4.28	3	56
Paul Hoganson	1308	26	6	16	0	711	102	609	4.68	0	11
Jim McLeod Los Angeles Total	969	17	4	13	0	481	69	412	4.27	1	10
Season Total	1485	27	7	20	0	777	105	672	4.24	1	18
TRADED PLAYERS											
George Gardner	120	2	0	2	0	65	13	52	6.50	0	0
Russ Gillow	1041	18	4	13	0	483	69	414	3.98	1	16
Ian Wilkie	1257	23	11	9	0	592	82	510	3.92	1	19

CHICAGO COUGARS 1973-74 FINAL STATISTICS

	GP	G	A	PTS	PIM	PPG	FG	PG	TG	TB	IG	WG	TC	PCT.	PP	SH	MG
Ralph Backstrom	78	33	50	83	26	1.06	5	3	7	4	9	8	23	.70	6	2	7
Rosaire Paiement	78	30	43	73	87	.94	5	3	8	6	5	3	27	.90	7	—	4
Joe Hardy	77	24	35	59	55	.77	4	2	3	6	2	2	18	.75	4	—	4
Pat Stapleton	78	6	52	58	44	.74	1	—	2	—	2	—	5	.83	2	1	1
Larry Mavety	77	15	36	51	157	.66	—	1	5	6	1	4	15	1.00	—	—	—
Bob Liddington	73	26	21	47	20	.64	3	4	5	7	5	2	24	.92	4	1	2
Bobby Sicinski	69	11	29	40	8	.58	3	3	7	3	3	1	10	1.00	4	—	—
Jan Popiel	63	22	17	39	36	.62	2	2	8	—	5	4	20	.91	1	—	4
Rick Morris	76	17	16	33	140	.43	2	1	3	1	2	2	13	.76	6	—	—
Duke Harris	64	14	16	30	20	.47	1	—	3	5	3	1	10	.71	1	—	2
Darryl Maggs	78	8	22	30	148	.38	4	—	1	3	3	—	6	.75	3	—	—
Don Gordon/Chicago Totals	23	5	4	9	9	.39	—	—	—	—	—	—	5	1.00	—	—	1
Season Totals	52	13	10	23	33	.44	1	1	2	2	1	1	9	.69	3	—	3
Frankie Rochon	71	12	11	23	27	.32	—	3	3	3	2	—	10	.83	4	1	1
Dick Proceviat	77	2	20	22	55	.29	—	—	2	—	2	—	2	1.00	1	—	—
Rod Zaine	78	5	13	18	17	.23	1	1	—	—	2	1	3	.60	—	1	—
Reg Fleming	45	2	12	14	49	.31	—	—	1	2	1	2	7	1.00	2	—	—
Brian Coates	50	10	3	13	14	.26	—	2	2	—	3	—	7	.70	—	1	1
Jim Benzelock	53	6	7	13	19	.25	—	4	1	1	1	—	5	.83	—	—	—
Jim Watson/Chicago Totals	23	0	5	5	22	.22	—	—	—	—	—	—	—	.00	—	—	—
Season Totals	71	0	11	11	50	.15	—	—	—	—	—	—	—	.00	—	—	—
Eric Nesterneko	29	2	5	7	8	.25	—	—	1	—	—	—	1	.50	1	—	—
Brian Glenwright	15	3	2	5	0	.33	1	—	—	—	1	1	3	1.00	—	—	—
John Shmyr	43	1	3	4	13	.09	—	—	—	—	—	—	1	1.00	1	—	—
Lorene Rombough	3	1	2	3	0	1.00	—	—	1	—	—	—	1	1.00	—	—	—
Curt Brackenbury	4	0	1	1	11	.25	—	—	—	—	—	—	—	.00	—	—	—
Gary Connelly	4	0	1	1	2	.25	—	—	—	—	—	—	—	.00	—	—	—
Dave Walter	4	0	1	1	0	.25	—	—	—	—	—	—	—	.00	—	—	—
Cam Newton	47	0	1	1	0	.02	—	—	—	—	—	—	—	.00	—	—	—
Jim Jones	1	0	0	0	0	.00	—	—	—	—	—	—	—	.00	—	—	—
Ron Anderson	2	0	0	0	0	.00	—	—	—	—	—	—	—	.00	—	—	—
Al MacKenzie	2	0	0	0	0	.00	—	—	—	—	—	—	—	.00	—	—	—
Larry Cahan	3	0	0	0	2	.00	—	—	—	—	—	—	—	.00	—	—	—
Andre Gill	13	0	0	0	0	.00	—	—	—	—	—	—	—	.00	—	—	—
Rich Coutu	20	0	0	0	0	.00	—	—	—	—	—	—	—	.00	—	—	—
a) Bobby Whitlock	52	16	19	35	44	.67	5	3	1	3	—	2	13	.81	6	1	2
TEAM TOTALS	78	271	447	718	1041	9.21	31	33	55	49	49	38	224	.83	51	7	30

a) traded to Los Angeles for Jim Watson and Don Gordon

CLEVELAND CRUSADERS 1973-74 FINAL STATISTICS

	GP	G	A	PTS	PIM	PFG	FG	PG	TG	TB	IG	WG	TC	PCT.	PP	SH	MG
Gary Jarrett	75	31	39	70	68	.93	8	3	8	4	4	4	28	.90	11	—	5
Ron Ward Cleveland Totals	23	19	7	26	7	1.13	3	1	4	6	4	4	18	.95	4	—	5
Season Totals	70	33	28	61	25	.87	3	3	9	9	4	6	28	.85	7	—	7
Jim Wiste	76	23	35	58	26	.76	6	—	3	3	7	7	20	.87	4	—	2
Gerry Pinder	73	23	33	56	90	.77	2	3	3	3	3	3	17	.74	3	1	2
Skip Krake	69	20	36	56	94	.81	4	4	6	5	5	3	16	.80	5	—	1
Grant Erickson	78	23	27	50	26	.64	4	6	—	6	5	5	23	1.00	3	2	2
Ron Buchanan	49	18	27	45	2	.92	4	3	4	4	3	3	15	.83	6	—	—
Paul Shmyr	78	13	31	44	165	.56	3	2	2	5	1	—	9	.69	3	—	2
Ray Clearwater	68	12	23	35	47	.51	5	3	4	—	1	1	8	.67	3	—	2
Tom Edur	76	7	31	38	26	.50	1	1	1	2	1	—	4	.57	1	—	—
Paul Andrea	69	15	18	33	14	.48	4	—	5	1	—	2	12	.80	6	3	1
Russ Walker	76	15	14	29	117	.38	—	3	3	3	6	2	12	.80	1	—	2
Larry Hillman	44	5	21	26	37	.59	—	1	2	3	1	—	3	.60	1	—	—
Doug Brindley	30	13	9	22	13	.73	3	—	2	2	4	1	12	.92	1	—	2
Billy Heindl	67	4	14	18	4	.27	1	—	1	—	—	1	6	.50	—	—	—
Rob Neale	43	8	9	17	30	.40	2	—	1	1	1	1	6	.75	—	—	1
Wayne Muloin	76	3	7	10	39	.13	—	—	—	—	1	—	1	1.00	1	—	—
Wayne Hillman	66	1	7	8	51	.12	—	1	—	2	—	—	2	.67	—	—	—
Norm Cournoyer	13	3	5	8	6	.62	—	—	—	—	2	—	2	.67	1	—	—
Dick Pumple	17	2	2	4	16	.24	1	1	—	—	—	—	2	1.00	—	—	—
Ralph Hopiavouri	13	0	2	2	6	.15	—	—	—	—	—	—	—	.00	—	—	—
Ron Morgan	4	0	1	1	7	.25	—	—	—	—	—	—	—	.00	—	—	—
Bob Whidden	22	0	1	1	2	.05	—	—	—	—	—	—	—	.00	—	—	—
Ray Adduono	2	0	0	0	0	.00	—	—	—	—	—	—	—	.00	—	—	—
Glen Shirton	4	0	0	0	0	.00	—	—	—	—	—	—	—	.00	—	—	—
Jim McMasters	9	0	0	0	4	.00	—	—	—	—	—	—	—	.00	—	—	—
Brad Buetow	25	0	0	0	4	.00	—	—	—	—	—	—	—	.00	—	—	—
Gerry Cheevers	59	0	0	0	30	.00	—	—	—	—	—	—	—	.00	—	—	—
a) Bill Young	53	8	9	17	70	.32	—	1	—	—	3	—	4	.50	—	—	1
a) Ted Hodgson	10	0	2	2	6	.20	—	—	—	—	—	—	—	.00	—	—	—
TEAM TOTALS	78	266	410	676	1007	8.67	46	27	46	44	48	37	216	.81	56	6	26

a) Traded to Los Angeles for Ron Ward

EDMONTON OILERS 1973-74 FINAL STATISTICS

	GP	G	A	PTS	PIM	PPG	FG	PG	TG	TB	IG	WG	TC	PCT.	PP	SH	MG
Ron Climie	76	38	36	74	22	.97	4	1	3	2	13	7	25	.66	9	—	8
Jim Harrison	46	24	45	69	99	1.50	4	—	3	5	7	7	19	.79	3	2	3
Al Hamilton	77	14	45	59	104	.77	1	1	4	5	2	2	12	.86	6	—	2
Ross Perkins	78	16	40	56	43	.72	3	—	2	—	3	3	11	.69	1	—	1
Len Lunde	71	26	22	48	8	.68	6	2	3	3	4	4	19	.73	7	2	1
Blair McDonald	78	21	24	45	34	.58	2	3	3	2	3	3	14	.67	7	—	—
Rusty Patenaude	71	20	23	43	55	.61	2	2	2	6	4	2	16	.80	5	—	1
Tom Gilmore	57	19	23	42	164	.74	5	1	3	2	4	2	13	.68	2	—	3
Brian McKenzie	78	18	20	38	66	.49	2	3	1	3	—	1	11	.61	2	—	3
Bob Wall	74	6	31	37	46	.50	2	2	—	—	—	—	4	.67	2	1	—
Ken Baird	68	17	19	36	115	.58	2	3	4	2	1	1	13	.76	2	—	1
Doug Barrie	69	4	27	31	214	.45	3	2	—	1	—	2	2	.50	—	—	—
Bobby Sheehan/Edmonton Total	10	1	3	4	6	.40	1	—	—	—	—	—	1	1.00	—	—	—
Season Total	60	13	11	24	14	.40	2	2	4	—	1	1	11	.85	6	—	1
Bob McAneeley	52	12	11	23	49	.44	2	2	2	1	—	1	7	.58	—	—	2
Val Fonteyne	72	9	13	22	2	.31	2	—	1	—	5	—	8	.89	—	4	—
Eddie Joyal	45	8	10	18	2	.40	2	—	2	2	1	1	7	.88	—	—	—
Bob Falkenberg	78	3	14	17	32	.22	1	—	1	—	—	—	2	.67	—	—	—
Steve Carlyle	50	2	13	15	18	.30	—	—	—	—	1	—	1	.50	—	—	—
Ron Anderson	19	5	2	7	6	.37	—	—	—	—	1	—	5	1.00	—	—	—
Jim McCrimmon	75	2	3	5	106	.07	—	2	1	—	3	1	2	1.00	—	—	—
Bob Fitchner	31	1	2	3	21	.10	—	—	—	—	1	—	—	.00	—	—	—
Jack Norris	53	0	3	3	0	.06	—	—	—	—	—	—	—	.00	—	—	—
Roger Cote	59	0	3	3	34	.05	—	—	—	—	—	—	—	.00	—	—	—
Jim Schraefel	34	1	1	2	0	.06	—	—	—	—	—	—	—	.00	—	—	—
Brian Carlin	5	1	0	1	2	.20	—	—	—	—	—	—	—	.00	—	—	—
Gary Doyle	1	0	0	0	0	.00	—	—	—	—	—	—	—	.00	—	—	—
Hal Colborne	2	0	0	0	0	.00	—	—	—	—	—	—	—	.00	—	—	—
Gary Cunningham	2	0	0	0	0	.00	—	—	—	—	—	—	—	.00	—	—	—
Ian Wilkie/Edmonton Total	5	0	0	0	2	.00	—	—	—	—	—	—	—	.00	—	—	—
Season Total	28	0	0	0	13	.00	—	—	—	—	—	—	—	.00	—	—	—
Chris Worthy	30	0	0	0	0	.00	—	—	—	—	—	—	—	.00	—	—	—
a) Wayne Zuk	2	0	0	0	0	.00	—	—	—	—	—	—	—	.00	—	—	—
TEAM TOTALS	78	268	433	701	1273	8.99	42	21	35	34	53	38	192	.72	40	9	25

a) traded to Los Angeles for Ian Wilkie

HOUSTON AEROS 1973-74 FINAL STATISTICS

	GP	G	A	PTS	PIM	PPG	FG	PG	TG	TB	IG	WG	TC	PCT.	PP	SH	MG
Gordie Howe	70	31	69	100	46	1.43	4	3	—	2	9	5	20	.65	9	3	3
Larry Lund	75	33	53	86	109	1.15	7	2	6	6	5	10	29	.88	7	2	3
Frank Hughes	73	42	42	84	47	1.15	8	—	7	3	4	3	24	.57	13	—	11
Andre Hinse	69	24	56	80	39	1.16	2	1	5	2	8	3	17	.71	10	—	4
Mark Howe	76	38	41	79	20	1.04	2	—	4	4	8	3	25	.66	5	5	8
Jim Sherrit	76	30	28	58	18	.76	7	3	4	2	2	2	13	.43	4	—	6
Murray Hall	78	30	28	58	25	.74	3	—	3	2	2	5	16	.55	8	2	5
Gordon Labossiere	67	19	36	55	30	.82	1	3	2	1	10	4	12	.63	4	—	2
Poul Popiel	78	7	41	48	126	.62	2	—	5	3	3	—	4	.57	1	—	—
Ted Taylor	75	21	23	44	143	.59	1	1	—	2	5	3	15	.71	1	3	1
John Schella	73	12	19	31	170	.42	2	1	2	2	5	3	12	1.00	—	2	1
Don Grierson	65	11	18	29	45	.45	2	1	2	—	1	2	6	.55	—	—	4
Marty Howe	73	4	20	24	90	.33	—	—	1	—	2	1	2	.50	—	—	—
Gordon Kannegeisser	78	0	20	20	26	.26	—	—	—	—	—	—	—	.00	—	—	—
Joe Szura	42	8	7	15	4	.36	1	—	1	2	1	3	5	.63	—	—	1
Larry Hale	69	2	14	16	39	.23	—	—	—	—	—	—	—	.00	—	—	—
Gary Williamson	9	2	6	8	0	.89	1	—	—	1	—	—	1	.50	1	—	—
Jack Stanfield	41	1	3	4	2	.10	—	—	—	—	—	—	—	.00	—	—	—
Bill Prentice	55	1	2	3	35	.05	—	—	—	—	1	—	1	1.00	—	—	—
Don McLeod	49	0	3	3	6	.06	—	—	—	—	—	—	—	.00	—	—	—
Ed Hoekstra	19	2	0	2	0	.11	—	—	1	1	—	1	2	1.00	—	—	—
Wayne Rutledge	26	0	1	1	14	.04	—	—	—	—	—	—	—	.00	—	—	—
Don Grahame	4	0	0	0	0	.00	—	—	—	—	—	—	—	.00	—	—	—
TEAM TOTALS	78	318	530	848	1038	10.87	45	13	39	32	64	48	204	.64	64	17	49

LOS ANGELES SHARKS 1973-74 FINAL STATISTICS (Now Michigan Stags)

	GP	G	A	PTS	PIM	PPG	FG	PG	TG	TB	IG	WG	TC	PCT.	PP	SH	MG
Marc Tardif	75	40	30	70	47	.93	5	6	6	8	7	3	32	.80	10	—	9
Gary Veneruzzo	78	39	29	68	68	.87	2	9	7	5	6	4	30	.77	5	—	5
J.P. LeBlanc	78	20	46	66	58	.85	4	3	1	6	3	—	17	.85	7	—	2
Brian McDonald	56	22	30	52	54	.93	3	4	6	3	3	3	19	.86	4	—	3
Bobby Whitlock/Los Angeles Total	14	4	10	14	4	1.00	—	1	—	1	—	—	3	.75	1	—	—
Season Total	66	20	29	49	30	.74	6	4	1	4	—	2	16	.80	7	1	2
Gerry Odrowski	77	4	32	36	48	.47	—	—	—	—	1	—	2	.50	2	—	—
Reg Thomas	72	14	21	35	22	.49	1	4	1	1	3	3	10	.71	1	—	—
Steve Sutherland	72	20	12	32	182	.44	6	2	3	5	3	4	19	.95	4	—	4
Bart Crashley	78	4	26	30	16	.38	—	1	—	1	2	1	4	1.00	2	—	—
Ron Walters	71	14	14	28	28	.39	4	—	6	—	2	3	13	.93	1	—	1
Bill Young/Los Angeles Total	16	1	3	4	4	.25	—	—	—	—	—	—	—	—	—	—	—
Season Total	69	9	12	21	74	.30	—	1	—	1	3	—	5	.56	—	—	1
Alton White	48	8	13	21	13	.44	2	—	2	2	2	1	7	.88	—	—	1
Tommy Serviss	74	6	15	21	37	.28	—	1	1	1	1	—	3	.50	2	—	—
Jim Niekamp	76	2	19	21	95	.28	—	—	—	—	—	—	2	1.00	—	—	—
Ron Garwasiuk	51	6	13	19	100	.37	1	—	—	1	2	1	5	.83	—	1	—
Ted Hodgson/Los Angeles Total	23	3	9	12	22	.52	—	—	—	—	1	—	1	.33	2	—	—
Season Total	33	3	11	14	22	.42	—	1	—	—	1	—	2	.33	2	—	—
Jerry Zrymiak	27	2	8	10	8	.37	—	—	—	—	—	1	2	1.00	—	—	—
Bill Horton	60	0	9	9	46	.15	—	—	—	—	—	—	—	—	—	—	—
Fred Speck	18	2	5	7	4	.39	—	1	1	—	—	—	1	.50	—	—	—
Earl Heiskala	24	2	6	8	45	.33	1	—	—	—	—	—	1	.50	—	—	—
Ted McCaskill	18	2	2	4	63	.22	—	—	—	—	—	—	—	—	—	1	—
Hal Willis	18	1	2	3	24	.17	—	1	—	—	—	—	1	1.00	—	—	—
Peter Slater	19	1	1	2	2	.11	—	—	—	—	—	—	—	.00	—	—	—
Kirk Bowman	10	0	2	2	0	.20	—	—	—	—	—	—	—	.00	—	—	—
Mike Hyndman	8	0	1	1	0	.13	—	—	—	—	—	—	—	.00	—	—	—
Brian Derkson	1	0	0	0	2	.00	—	—	—	—	—	—	—	.00	—	—	—
Paul Hoganson	27	0	0	0	0	.00	—	—	—	—	—	—	—	.00	—	—	—
Jimmy McLeod/Los Angeles Total	17	0	0	0	0	.00	—	—	—	—	—	—	—	.00	—	—	—
Season Total	27	0	0	0	2	.00	—	—	—	—	—	—	—	.00	—	—	—

PENALTIES
IN MINUTES BY TEAMS

1972-73 SEASON

		PIM	AVG.
1.	Los Angeles	1477	18.94
2.	Houston	1363	17.47
3.	Quebec	1354	17.36
4.	Philadelphia	1260	16.15
5.	Minnesota	1134	14.54
6.	Cleveland	1095	14.04
7.	Ottawa	1067	13.68
8.	New York	900	11.54
9.	New England	858	11.00
10.	Alberta	843	10.81
11.	Chicago	811	10.40
12.	Winnipeg	757	9.71
	TOTAL — —	12,919	27.60

1973-74 SEASON

		PIM	AVG.
1.	Edmonton	1273	16.32
2.	Minnesota	1243	15.94
3.	Los Angeles	1086	13.92
4.	Vancouver	1047	13.42
5.	Chicago	1041	13.35
6.	Houston	1038	13.31
7.	Cleveland	1007	12.91
8.	New Jersey	933	11.96
9.	Quebec	909	11.65
10.	New England	875	11.22
11.	Toronto	871	11.17
12.	Winnipeg	673	8.63
	TOTAL — —	11,996	25.63

TWO-YEAR TOTALS

		PIM	AVG.
1.	Los Angeles	2563	16.43
2.	Houston	2401	15.39
3.	Minnesota	2377	15.24
4.	Phil-Vancouver	2307	14.79
5.	Quebec	2263	14.51
6.	Alb-Edmonton	2116	13.56
7.	Cleveland	2102	13.47
8.	Otwa-Toronto	1938	12.42
9.	Chicago	1852	11.87
10.	New York / Jersey	1833	11.75
11.	New England	1733	11.11
12.	Winnipeg	1430	9.17
	TOTAL — —	24,915	26.62

TRADED PLAYERS

a)	George Gardner	2	0	0	0	0	0	.00							
a)	Ralph MacSweyn	13	0	3	3	6	23	.23						2	
b)	Russ Gillow	18	0	0	0	2	0	.00							
c)	Ron Ward	40	14	19	33	16	83	.83		10		3	1		2
d)	Jim Watson	48	0	6	6	28	13	.13				1			
d)	Don Gordon	29	8	6	14	24	48	.48		4					
e)	Ian Wilkie	23	0	0	0	2	0	.00							
	TEAM TOTALS	78	239	392	631	1086	8.09		25	37	42	37	187	4	29

a) Traded to Vancouver for Ron Ward
b) Traded with Rick Sentes to New Jersey for Jimmy McLeod
c) Traded to Cleveland for Bill Young and Ted Hodgson
d) Traded to Chicago for Bobby Whitlock
e) Traded to Edmonton for Wayne Zuk

MINNESOTA FIGHTING SAINTS 1973-74 FINAL STATISTICS

	GP	G	A	PTS	PIM	PPG	FG	PG	TG	TB	IG	WG	TC	PCT.	PP	SH	MG
Mike Walton	78	57	60	117	88	1.50	6	4	3	7	19	7	41	.72	9	9	13
Wayne Connelly	78	42	53	95	16	1.22	7	1	7	4	10	6	29	.69	15	—	7
George Morrison	73	40	38	78	37	1.07	6	3	1	9	7	3	26	.65	12	1	9
Murray Heatley	71	26	32	58	23	.82	5	—	4	3	9	5	22	.85	3	—	3
Ted Hampson	77	17	38	55	9	.71	—	2	3	3	4	4	12	.65	2	4	—
Jim Johnson	71	15	39	54	30	.76	3	3	5	—	1	4	12	.73	5	1	—
Mike Antonovich	68	21	29	50	4	.74	2	2	—	5	4	2	13	.62	2	1	1
John Arbour	77	6	43	49	192	.64	1	1	3	1	2	1	5	.83	1	—	2
Bob MacMillan	78	14	34	48	81	.62	3	1	3	2	1	—	10	.71	3	—	—
Steve Cardwell	77	23	23	46	100	.62	2	2	2	5	5	3	15	.65	1	1	5
Mike McMahon	71	10	35	45	82	.63	—	1	4	—	2	1	8	.80	1	—	1
Rick Smith	71	10	28	38	98	.54	3	—	1	1	1	3	7	.70	3	3	—
Keith Christiansen	74	11	25	36	36	.49	3	1	—	1	1	—	6	.45	4	1	—
Terry Ball	71	8	28	36	34	.51	3	—	1	1	—	2	6	.75	4	—	1
Gordon Gallant	72	7	15	22	223	.31	—	—	1	3	1	—	4	.57	—	—	—
Billy Klatt	65	14	6	20	12	.31	2	1	4	2	2	—	11	.79	3	—	1
Bob Boyd	41	1	14	15	14	.37	1	—	—	—	1	—	1	1.00	—	—	—
Dick Paradise	67	2	7	9	71	.13	—	1	1	—	—	—	2	1.00	—	—	—
Jack McCartan	2	0	0	0	0	.00	—	—	—	—	—	—	—	.00	—	—	—
Blaine Rydman	8	0	0	0	21	.00	—	—	—	—	—	—	—	.00	—	—	—
Mike Curran	41	0	0	0	6	.00	—	—	—	—	—	—	—	.00	—	—	—
John Garrett	42	0	0	0	10	.00	—	—	—	—	—	—	—	.00	—	—	—
TRADED PLAYERS																	
a) Rob Walton	45	8	23	31	24	.69	1	—	2	1	1	1	5	.63	1	—	—
TEAM TOTALS	78	332	570	902	1243	11.59	49	20	42	47	69	44	235	.71	61	20	43

(a) traded to Vancouver for Jean Tetreault

NEW ENGLAND WHALERS 1973-74 FINAL STATISTICS

	GP	G	A	PTS	PIM	PPG	FG	PG	TG	TB	IG	WG	TC	PCT.	PP	SH	MG
John French	77	24	48	72	31	.94	1	2	2	3	8	4	19	.79	5	1	3
Tom Webster	64	43	27	70	28	1.09	8	3	3	5	9	9	29	.67	5	—	7
Larry Pleau	77	26	43	69	35	.90	5	4	4	3	5	3	22	.85	6	—	2
Al Karlander	77	20	41	61	46	.77	5	4	2	2	2	1	14	.70	4	—	2
Don Blackburn	75	20	39	59	18	.79	3	1	3	5	4	2	16	.80	9	—	4
Tim Sheehy	77	29	29	58	22	.75	6	1	8	5	3	1	23	.79	2	—	3
Tommy Williams	70	21	37	58	6	.83	4	4	4	2	7	5	18	.86	3	—	2
Hugh Harris	75	24	28	52	78	.69	2	2	2	6	3	4	16	.67	1	—	4
Mike Byers	78	29	21	50	6	.64	5	1	4	4	3	4	20	.69	4	—	6
Jim Dorey	77	6	40	46	134	.60	—	—	—	—	1	—	3	.50	—	—	—
Rick Ley	72	6	35	41	148	.57	—	1	1	—	4	1	5	.83	3	—	—
Brad Selwood	76	9	28	37	91	.49	—	1	1	3	2	2	7	.78	3	—	1
Ted Green	75	7	26	33	42	.44	3	—	2	—	2	2	7	1.00	3	—	—
Tom Earl	78	10	10	20	29	.26	1	—	1	1	2	—	6	.60	2	—	1
Paul Hurley	52	3	11	14	21	.27	—	—	—	—	3	—	3	1.00	—	—	—
John Cunniff	30	7	5	12	14	.40	—	—	—	—	3	2	5	1.00	—	2	2
Bob Charlebois	74	4	7	11	6	.15	2	1	—	3	3	2	3	.71	—	—	—
Guy Smith	16	1	5	6	25	.38	—	—	—	1	1	1	3	.75	—	—	—
John Danby	72	2	2	4	6	.06	—	—	—	—	—	—	1	1.00	—	—	—
Ric Jordan	34	0	3	3	14	.09	—	—	—	—	1	—	1	.50	—	—	—
Al Smith	56	0	3	3	33	.05	—	—	—	—	—	—	—	.00	—	—	—
Mike Keeler	1	0	0	0	0	.00	—	—	—	—	—	—	—	.00	—	—	—
Bruce Landon	24	0	0	0	24	.00	—	—	—	—	—	—	—	.00	—	—	—
Bill Berglund	3	0	0	0	0	.00	—	—	—	—	—	—	—	.00	—	—	—
TEAM TOTALS	78	291	488	779	875	9.99	45	23	38	43	59	43	218	.75	47	3	36

JERSEY KNIGHTS 1973-74 FINAL STATISTICS Now San Diego Mariners

	GP	G	A	PTS	PIM	PPG	FG	PG	TG	TB	IG	WG	TC	PCT.	PP	SH	MG
Andre Lacroix	78	31	80	111	54	1.42	5	3	2	3	9	2	23	.74	11	—	4
Kevin Morrison	78	24	43	67	132	.86	2	3	2	2	2	—	11	.46	5	2	1
Wayne Rivers	73	30	27	57	20	.78	7	1	5	5	4	1	22	.73	5	—	8
Gene Peacosh	68	21	32	53	17	.78	3	—	—	4	3	4	11	.52	5	—	6
Brian Morenz	75	20	30	50	44	.67	1	2	—	3	6	5	13	.65	1	2	6
Ken Block	74	3	43	46	22	.62	—	—	—	—	—	—	1	.33	—	—	2
Bob Jones	78	17	28	45	20	.58	2	1	6	1	3	1	13	.76	6	—	1
Brian Bradley	78	15	23	38	12	.49	1	1	—	6	2	1	11	.73	3	1	3
Mike Laughton	71	20	18	38	34	.54	—	1	5	3	3	4	12	.60	3	—	1
Norm Ferguson	75	15	21	36	12	.48	3	3	2	3	3	4	15	1.00	3	1	1
Don Herriman	44	11	21	32	59	.73	2	—	1	2	4	1	7	.64	2	—	1
Brian Perry	71	20	11	31	19	.44	1	—	3	7	1	4	16	.80	3	1	3
Harry Howell	65	3	23	26	24	.40	—	1	—	1	—	2	2	.67	—	—	—
Bob Brown	59	7	13	20	38	.34	1	1	1	3	1	—	7	1.00	1	—	1
Craig Reichmuth	72	10	8	18	114	.25	3	1	—	1	1	1	5	.50	—	—	—
Gary Peters	34	2	5	7	18	.21	—	—	—	—	—	—	1	.50	1	—	—
Ted Scharf	63	4	2	6	107	.10	2	—	—	—	1	—	2	.50	—	—	—
Dean Boylan	61	1	5	6	112	.10	—	—	—	—	—	—	—	.00	—	—	—
Bill Speer	66	1	3	4	30	.06	—	—	1	—	—	—	1	1.00	—	—	—
Bob Winograd	7	1	0	1	0	.14	—	—	—	—	—	—	1	1.00	—	—	—
Ray Larose	18	0	1	1	20	.06	—	1	—	—	—	—	—	.00	—	—	—
Gary Kurt	21	0	1	1	0	.05	—	—	—	—	—	—	—	.00	—	—	—
Joe Junkin	52	0	1	1	7	.02	—	—	—	—	—	—	—	.00	—	—	—
Butch Barber	3	0	0	0	2	.00	—	—	—	—	—	—	—	.00	—	—	—
Claude Chartre	5	0	0	0	0	.00	—	—	—	—	—	—	—	.00	—	—	—
Lee Inglis	5	0	0	0	0	.00	—	—	—	—	—	—	—	.00	—	—	—
a) Jim McLeod	10	0	0	0	2	.00	—	—	—	—	—	—	—	.00	—	—	—
b) Bobby Sheehan	50	12	8	20	8	.40	1	2	4	1	1	1	10	.83	5	—	1
TEAM TOTALS	78	268	447	715	933	9.17	34	21	32	46	44	32	184	.69	52	7	33

a) Traded to Los Angeles for Russ Gillow and Rick Sentes
b) Traded to Edmonton for Bob Falkenberg

QUEBEC NORDIQUES 1973-74 FINAL STATISTICS

	GP	G	A	PTS	PIM	PPG	FG	PG	TG	TB	IG	WG	TC	PCT.	PP	SH	MG
Serge Bernier	74	37	49	86	107	1.16	3	3	5	6	7	8	26	.70	7	—	5
Robert Guindon	77	31	39	70	30	.91	7	1	5	2	6	4	23	.74	5	—	3
Andre Gaudette	78	24	44	68	16	.87	1	2	1	7	5	4	17	.75	3	1	3
Rejean Houle	69	27	35	62	17	.90	4	—	4	2	6	4	16	.59	6	—	5
Michel Parizeau	78	26	34	60	39	.77	3	1	8	2	6	3	20	.77	5	—	5
Jeannot Gilbert	75	17	39	56	20	.75	3	—	2	1	2	2	10	.59	4	—	1
J.C. Tremblay	68	9	44	53	10	.78	1	2	1	1	2	1	6	.67	4	—	—
Guy Dufour	74	27	23	50	30	.68	6	—	1	3	3	2	20	.74	6	—	2
Alain Caron	59	31	15	46	10	.78	1	3	7	4	5	1	22	.71	9	—	2
Renald Leclerc	58	17	27	44	84	.76	1	—	1	3	4	4	10	.59	2	—	10
Dale Hoganson	62	8	33	41	27	.66	—	—	2	5	—	2	7	.88	2	—	1
Alain Beaule	78	4	36	40	93	.51	—	1	2	—	1	—	3	.75	1	—	—
Francois Lacombe	71	9	26	35	41	.49	1	1	1	2	3	1	8	.89	4	—	—
Pierre Guite	72	14	20	34	106	.47	1	—	5	3	3	—	12	.86	—	—	4
Jean-Guy Gendron	64	11	8	19	42	.30	2	2	3	—	1	1	8	.73	1	—	1
Jean Payette	41	4	11	15	6	.37	—	—	—	—	—	—	1	.25	1	—	1
Rejean Giroux	12	5	6	11	14	.92	—	—	—	1	1	1	3	.60	—	—	1
Ken Desjardine	70	2	10	12	44	.17	—	—	—	1	1	1	2	1.00	1	—	—
Pierre Roy	44	2	7	9	137	.20	—	—	1	—	1	—	1	.50	—	—	—
Norm Descoteaux	35	1	6	7	6	.20	—	—	—	—	1	—	1	1.00	—	—	—
Mike Rouleau	4	0	4	4	2	1.00	—	—	—	—	—	—	—	.00	—	—	—
Serge Aubry	26	0	1	1	8	.04	—	—	—	—	—	—	—	.00	—	—	—
Richard Brodeur	30	0	1	1	0	.03	—	—	—	—	—	—	—	.00	—	—	—
Michel Deguise	32	0	1	1	0	.03	—	—	—	—	—	—	—	.00	—	—	—
Dave Balon	9	0	0	0	2	.00	—	—	—	—	—	—	—	.00	—	—	—
TEAM TOTALS	78	306	519	825	909	10.58	35	19	55	43	58	38	216	.71	61	1	43

TORONTO TOROS 1973-74 FINAL STATISTICS

	GP	G	A	PTS	PIM	PPG	FG	PG	TG	TB	IG	WG	TC	PCT.	PP	SH	MG
											—CLUTCH GOALS—						
Wayne Carleton	78	37	55	92	31	1.18	7	4	4	8	3	5	27	.73	5	—	5
Gavin Kirk	78	20	48	68	44	.87	2	4	4	5	1	2	16	.80	3	—	2
Wayne Dillon	78	30	35	65	13	.92	3	3	6	4	6	6	22	.73	7	—	5
Guy Trottier	71	27	35	62	58	.87	—	5	8	4	5	6	22	.81	4	—	4
Rick Sentes	64	26	34	60	46	.94	4	4	3	3	5	3	18	.69	6	—	6
Tom Martin	74	25	32	57	14	.77	2	1	—	4	9	3	19	.76	8	4	3
Pat Hickey	78	26	29	55	52	.71	4	—	4	5	3	—	16	.62	3	—	5
Tom Simpson	74	33	20	53	27	.72	7	2	5	4	3	4	26	.79	5	1	5
Bob Leduc	61	22	29	51	29	.84	1	2	3	4	7	2	15	.68	4	—	1
Steve King	67	14	22	36	26	.54	2	—	3	7	5	1	12	.86	4	—	1
Brian Gibbons	78	4	31	35	84	.45	1	—	5	4	4	—	3	.75	3	—	—
Brit Selby	64	9	17	26	21	.41	—	1	2	1	2	2	8	.89	1	—	1
Jack Gibson	61	16	9	25	60	.41	4	—	3	2	2	3	13	.81	4	—	—
Carl Brewer	77	2	23	25	42	.32	—	—	4	2	—	1	2	1.00	1	—	—
Steve Cuddie	74	5	18	23	65	.31	—	1	—	2	2	2	4	.80	—	—	—
Rick Cunningham	75	2	19	21	88	.28	1	1	—	2	—	—	2	1.00	1	—	—
Billy Orr	46	3	9	12	16	.26	2	—	—	—	1	—	3	1.00	—	—	—
Mike Amodeo	76	0	11	11	82	.14	—	—	—	—	—	—	—	—	—	—	—
Gerry Gibbons	26	1	4	5	23	.19	1	—	—	—	—	—	1	1.00	—	—	—
Peter Marrin	31	1	4	5	4	.16	—	—	—	—	—	—	—	—	—	—	—
Lou Nistico	13	1	3	4	14	.31	—	—	—	—	—	—	—	—	—	—	—
Gilles Gratton	59	0	4	4	28	.07	—	—	—	—	—	—	—	—	—	—	—
(a) William Holden	1	0	0	0	0	.00	—	—	—	—	—	—	—	.00	—	—	—
Richard Dupras	2	0	0	0	0	.00	—	—	—	—	—	—	—	.00	—	—	—
Frank Blum	5	0	0	0	0	.00	—	—	—	—	—	—	—	.00	—	—	—
Les Binkley	27	0	0	0	0	.00	—	—	—	—	—	—	—	.00	—	—	—
TEAM TOTALS	78	304	491	795	871	10.19	41	21	54	52	56	41	229	.75	60	5	38

(a) on loan to the Winnipeg Jets

VANCOUVER BLAZERS 1973-74 FINAL STATISTICS

	GP	G	A	PTS	PIM	PPG	FG	PG	TG	TB	IG	WG	TC	PCT.	PP	SH	MG
Bryan Campbell	76	27	62	89	50	1.17	2	—	5	5	2	3	14	.52	8	1	4
Danny Lawson	78	50	38	88	14	1.13	4	6	3	7	11	5	32	.64	10	—	10
Claude St. Sauveur	70	38	30	68	55	.97	5	4	9	7	7	5	33	.87	6	2	7
Don Burgess	78	30	36	66	8	.85	1	3	8	2	4	3	21	.70	5	3	5
Rob Walton/Vancouver Totals	28	8	15	23	2	.82	2	—	—	—	2	—	4	.50	1	—	1
Season Totals	73	16	38	54	26	.74	1	1	2	1	3	—	9	.56	2	—	1
John McKenzie	45	14	38	52	71	1.16	—	—	1	2	3	—	7	.50	2	—	1
John Migneault	74	21	26	47	27	.64	3	4	4	3	4	2	15	.71	3	—	4
Murray Meyers	61	22	20	42	28	.69	6	3	2	3	2	3	19	.86	2	2	1
Ron Plumb	75	6	32	38	40	.51	—	1	—	2	—	—	4	.67	1	—	—
Jim Adair	70	12	17	29	10	.41	2	2	4	3	—	2	10	.83	2	—	—
Colin Campbell	78	3	20	23	191	.29	2	1	—	—	—	—	2	.67	—	—	—
Ralph MacSweyn/Vancouver Total	56	2	18	20	52	.36	—	—	1	—	—	—	1	.50	—	—	—
Season Totals	72	2	21	23	58	.32	—	—	1	—	—	—	1	.50	—	—	—
Jim Cardiff	78	1	21	22	188	.28	—	—	—	—	—	—	—	.00	—	—	—
Mike Chernoff	36	11	10	21	4	.58	3	2	1	1	1	—	8	.73	—	1	2
Dennis Meloche	41	6	13	19	18	.46	1	2	3	—	—	—	6	1.00	—	—	—
Ed Hatoum	37	3	12	15	8	.41	—	—	—	2	—	—	2	.67	—	—	—
Don O'Donoghue	49	8	6	14	20	.29	—	2	2	2	1	—	7	.88	—	—	—
Dave Hutchison	69	0	13	13	151	.19	—	—	—	—	—	—	—	.00	—	—	—
Serge Beaudoin	26	1	11	12	37	.46	1	—	1	—	1	1	—	1.00	—	—	—
Sam Gellard	23	7	4	11	15	.48	2	2	—	—	—	—	5	.71	3	—	—
Jimmy Jones	18	3	2	5	23	.28	—	—	2	—	—	—	2	.67	2	—	—
Michel Plante	22	3	2	5	2	.23	—	—	1	2	—	1	3	1.00	—	—	—
Camille Lapierre	9	0	3	3	0	.33	—	—	—	—	—	—	—	.00	—	—	—
Michel Boudreau	3	1	0	1	0	.33	1	—	—	—	—	—	1	1.00	—	—	—
Irvin Spencer	19	0	1	1	6	.05	—	—	—	—	—	—	—	.00	—	—	—
Peter Donnelly	52	0	1	1	9	.02	—	—	—	—	—	—	—	.00	—	—	—
Peter McNamee	3	0	0	0	0	.00	—	—	—	—	—	—	—	.00	—	—	—
Yves Archambault	5	0	0	0	0	.00	—	—	—	—	—	—	—	.00	—	—	—
Rychard Campeau	7	0	0	0	2	.00	—	—	—	—	—	—	—	.00	—	—	—
George Gardner/Vancouver Total	28	0	0	0	0	.00	—	—	—	—	—	—	—	.00	—	—	—
Season Totals	30	0	0	0	0	.00	—	—	—	—	—	—	—	.00	—	—	—
a) Ron Ward	7	0	2	2	2	.29	—	—	—	—	—	—	—	.00	—	—	—
b) Jean Tetreault	6	1	1	2	0	.33	—	—	—	—	—	—	—	.00	—	—	—
TEAM TOTALS	78	278	454	732	1047	9.38	35	31	47	41	36	27	197	.71	47	7	37

a) Traded to Los Angeles for Ron Ward b) Traded to Minnesota for Rob Walton

WINNIPEG JETS 1973-74 FINAL STATISTICS

	GP	G	A	PTS	PIM	PPG	FG	PG	TG	TB	IG	WG	TC	PCT.	PP	SH	MG
Bobby Hull	75	53	42	95	38	1.27	9	2	8	9	11	9	41	.77	9	1	12
Chris Bordeleau	75	26	49	75	22	1.00	2	4	6	2	7	4	21	.81	5	1	2
Fran Huck	74	26	48	74	68	1.00	2	5	6	5	3	8	22	.85	2	2	3
Norm Beaudin	74	27	28	55	8	.74	7	6	3	1	7	2	24	.89	5	–	3
Ron Snell	70	24	25	49	32	.70	3	3	2	3	7	4	18	.75	5	–	3
Danny Johnson	78	16	21	37	20	.47	3	–	5	3	4	3	14	.88	2	–	3
Bob Woytowich	72	6	28	34	43	.47	2	2	–	2	1	1	5	.83	1	–	–
Jean-Guy Gratton	68	12	21	33	13	.49	2	1	–	3	1	–	8	.67	4	–	2
Ab McDonald	70	12	17	29	8	.41	–	1	4	2	1	–	8	.67	2	–	1
Joe Zanussi	76	3	22	25	53	.33	–	1	1	–	–	–	2	.67	–	–	–
Dan Spring	66	8	16	24	8	.36	1	1	1	2	2	2	6	.75	1	–	–
Larry Hornung	51	4	19	23	18	.45	–	1	–	1	1	–	3	.75	1	1	–
Bob Ash	60	2	18	20	30	.33	–	–	–	–	–	–	1	.50	–	–	–
Ted Hargreaves	74	7	12	19	15	.26	1	–	1	3	1	–	6	.86	–	2	–
Duke Asmundson	72	5	14	19	85	.26	–	–	–	1	–	–	3	.60	–	–	–
Dunc Rousseau	60	10	8	18	39	.30	3	1	2	–	–	1	6	.60	–	–	–
Milt Black	47	6	9	15	14	.32	1	–	1	1	–	–	3	.50	–	–	–
Bill Sutherland	12	4	5	9	6	.75	–	–	2	–	–	–	3	.50	–	–	–
Kelly Pratt	46	4	6	10	50	.22	1	–	1	1	–	–	2	.75	1	–	–
Cal Swenson	25	5	4	9	2	.36	–	–	2	–	–	–	3	.75	–	–	–
Garth Rizzuto	41	3	4	7	8	.17	–	1	1	2	–	–	2	.40	–	–	–
Ken Stephenson	29	0	7	7	24	.24	–	–	–	1	–	–	2	.67	1	1	–
Jim Hargreaves	53	1	4	5	50	.09	–	1	–	–	–	–	–	.00	–	–	–
Joe Daley	41	0	1	1	4	.02	–	–	–	–	–	–	1	1.00	–	–	–
a) William Holden	1	0	0	0	0	.00	–	–	–	–	–	–	–	.00	–	–	–
Ernie Wakely	37	0	0	0	9	.00	–	–	–	–	–	–	–	.00	–	–	–
TEAM TOTALS	78	264	428	692	673	8.87	34	32	44	41	47	34	201	.76	39	8	29

a) On loan from the Toronto Toros

1973-74 OVERTIME ANALYSIS

2-YEAR TOTALS	EASTERN DIVISION	73-74 TOTAL	73-74 AT HOME	73-74 ON ROAD	73-74 VS. EAST	73-74 VS. WEST	TOTAL 73-74 TIME	AVG. 73-74 TIME	DECISION ONLY 73-74 AVG. TIME
11 - 2 - 6	New England	6 - 2 - 4	3 - 0 - 2	3 - 2 - 2	3 - 1 - 2	3 - 1 - 2	82:39	6:53	5:20
7 - 5 - 8	Toronto	4 - 2 - 4	3 - 1 - 3	1 - 1 - 2	0 - 1 - 3	4 - 1 - 1	78:35	7:52	6:26
10 - 6 - 12	Cleveland	5 - 1 - 9	4 - 0 - 4	1 - 1 - 5	3 - 1 - 5	2 - 0 - 4	120:03	8:00	5:01
6 - 8 - 7	Chicago	3 - 2 - 5	2 - 1 - 3	1 - 1 - 2	1 - 1 - 3	2 - 1 - 2	72:19	7:14	4:28
5 - 7 - 9	Quebec	3 - 4 - 4	2 - 0 - 4	1 - 4 - 0	2 - 3 - 1	1 - 1 - 3	75:59	6:54	5:08
5 - 6 - 6	New Jersey	2 - 2 - 4	1 - 1 - 1	1 - 1 - 3	0 - 2 - 4	2 - 0 - 0	51:38	6:27	2:55
44 - 34 -48	TOTALS	23 - 13 - 30	15 - 3 - 17	8 - 10 - 13	9 - 9 - 18	14 - 4 - 12	481:13	7:17	5:02
	WESTERN DIVISION								
2 - 5 - 9	Houston	0 - 1 - 5	0 - 1 - 2	0 - 0 - 3	0 - 1 - 3	0 - 0 - 2	52:23	8:44	2:23
8 - 6 - 5	Minnesota	1 - 2 - 2	0 - 0 - 1	1 - 2 - 1	0 - 1 - 2	1 - 1 - 0	41:44	8:21	7:15
8 - 6 - 6	Edmonton	2 - 3 - 3	1 - 1 - 1	1 - 2 - 2	1 - 1 - 3	1 - 2 - 0	51:01	6:23	4:12
6 - 11 - 9	Winnipeg	3 - 7 - 5	2 - 5 - 2	1 - 2 - 3	0 - 2 - 3	3 - 5 - 2	95:16	6:21	4:32
9 - 9 - 1	Vancouver	5 - 6 - 1	3 - 2 - 0	2 - 4 - 1	2 - 5 - 1	3 - 1 - 0	65:45	5:29	5:04
6 - 8 - 6	Los Angeles	2 - 4 - 0	1 - 1 - 0	1 - 3 - 0	1 - 4 - 0	1 - 0 - 0	23:36	3:56	3:56
37 -47 -36	TOTALS	13 - 23 - 16	7 - 11 - 6	6 - 12 - 10	4 - 14 - 12	9 - 9 - 4	329:45	6:20	4:43
	1973-74 Totals	36 - 36 - 46	22 - 14 - 23	14 - 22 - 23	13 - 23 - 30	23 - 13 - 16	810:58	6:52	4:52
	Two-Year Totals	81 - 81 - 84	46 - 35 - 42	35 - 46 - 42	31 - 45 - 46	50 - 36 - 38	1590:59	6:42	4:38

1973-74: 59 games went into overtime (12.6% of all games).
36 games reached a decision in the overtime period (61.0% of overtime games; 8.5% of league decisions).
23 games remained tied after an overtime period (39.0% of overtime games; 4.9% of league games).

AFTER TWO SEASONS:
123 games have gone into overtime (13.1% of all games).
81 games reached a decision in the overtime period (65.9% of overtime games; 9.1% of league decisions).
42 games remained tied after an overtime period (34.1% of overtime games; 4.5% of league games).

THE SIXTH ATTACKER

(How Teams Did After Pulling Goaltender For Extra Forward)

1972-73 SEASON

	Times Pulled	Goals Scored	Pct.%	Freq.	E.N.G.'s Allowed	Pct.%	Freq.
New York	14	4	28.57%	3.50	2	14.29%	7.00
Winnipeg	8	2	25.00%	4.00	4	50.00%	2.00
New England	9	2	22.22%	4.50	1	11.11%	9.00
Los Angeles	12	2	16.67%	6.00	3	25.00%	4.00
Minnesota	11	1	9.09%	11.00	6	54.55%	1.83
Houston	12	1	8.33%	12.00	5	41.67%	2.40
Quebec	3	—	—	—	—	—	—
Cleveland	5	—	—	—	2	40.00%	2.50
Ottawa	9	—	—	—	5	55.56%	1.80
Philadelphia	11	—	—	—	8	72.73%	1.38
Alberta	16	—	—	—	4	25.00%	4.00
Chicago	19	—	—	—	6	31.58%	3.17
TOTALS	129	12	9.30%	10.75	46	35.66%	2.80

1973-74 SEASON

	Times Pulled	Goals Scored	Success Pct. %	Success Freq.	E.N.G.'s Allowed	Emp. Net Pct. %	Emp. Net Freq.
Los Angeles	18	3	16.67%	6.00	4	22.22%	4.50
Toronto	20	3	15.00%	6.67	2	10.00%	10.00
Edmonton	15	2	13.33%	7.50	6	40.00%	2.50
Minnesota	17	2	11.76%	8.50	3	17.65%	5.67
Houston	9	1	11.11%	9.00	3	33.33%	3.00
Winnipeg	12	1	8.33%	12.00	6	50.00%	2.00
Vancouver	13	1	7.69%	13.00	7	53.85%	1.86
Quebec	14	1	7.14%	14.00	5	35.71%	2.80
New Jersey	10	—	—	—	5	50.00%	2.00
New England	11	—	—	—	4	36.36%	2.75
Cleveland	12	—	—	—	4	33.33%	3.00
Chicago	19	—	—	—	9	47.37%	2.11
TOTALS	170	14	8.24%	12.14	58	34.12%	2.93

2-YEAR TOTALS

	Times Pulled	Goals Scored	Pct. %	Freq.	E.N.G.'s Allowed	Pct. %	Freq.
Los Angeles	30	5	16.67%	6.00	7	23.33%	4.29
New Jersey	24	4	16.67%	6.00	7	29.17%	3.43
Winnipeg	20	3	15.00%	6.67	10	50.00%	2.00
Minnesota	28	3	10.71%	9.33	9	32.14%	3.11
Toronto	29	3	10.34%	9.67	7	24.14%	4.14
New England	20	2	10.00%	10.00	5	25.00%	4.00
Houston	21	2	9.52%	10.50	8	38.10%	2.63
Edmonton	31	2	6.45%	15.50	10	32.26%	3.10
Quebec	17	1	5.88%	17.00	5	29.41%	3.40
Vancouver	24	1	4.17%	24.00	15	62.50%	1.60
Cleveland	17	—	—	—	6	35.29%	2.83
Chicago	38	—	—	—	15	39.47%	2.53
TOTALS	299	26	8.70%	11.50	104	34.78%	2.88

team statistics

TWO-YEAR TEAM TOTALS

TOTAL GAMES PLAYED (1972-73 / 1973-74)

	GP	W	L	T	Pts.	GF	GA	Pct.
NEW ENGLAND	156	89	61	6	184	609	523	.590
HOUSTON	156	87	60	9	183	602	488	.587
CLEVELAND	156	80	64	12	172	553	503	.551
MINNESOTA	156	82	69	5	169	582	544	.542
WINNIPEG	156	77	70	9	163	549	545	.522
*** TORONTO	156	76	72	8	160	583	573	.513
EDMONTON	156	76	74	6	158	537	525	.506
QUEBEC	156	71	76	9	151	582	593	.484
** NEW JERSEY	156	65	85	6	136	571	647	.436
CHICAGO	156	64	85	7	135	516	568	.433
**** VANCOUVER	156	65	90	1	131	566	650	.420
* LOS ANGELES	156	62	88	6	130	498	589	.417
TOTALS	936	894	894	84	1872	6748	6748	--

LIFETIME HOME RECORD

	GP	W	L	T	Pts.	GF	GA	Pct.
NEW ENGLAND	78	56	19	3	115	324	230	.737
CLEVELAND	78	53	19	6	112	311	220	.718
WINNIPEG	78	52	22	4	108	320	221	.692
HOUSTON	78	50	25	3	103	332	229	.660
QUEBEC	78	47	22	9	103	334	241	.660
MINNESOTA	78	50	26	2	102	321	248	.654
EDMONTON	78	49	26	3	101	313	236	.647
*** TORONTO	78	46	26	6	98	313	248	.628
** NEW JERSEY	78	45	31	2	92	337	283	.590
**** VANCOUVER	78	43	35	0	86	326	296	.551
CHICAGO	78	40	35	3	83	283	264	.532
* LOS ANGELES	78	35	42	1	71	243	275	.455
TOTALS	936	566	328	42	1174	3757	2991	.627

LIFETIME ROAD RECORD

	GP	W	L	T	Pts.	GF	GA	Pct.
HOUSTON	78	37	35	6	80	270	259	.513
NEW ENGLAND	78	33	42	3	69	285	293	.442
MINNESOTA	78	32	43	3	67	261	296	.429
*** TORONTO	78	30	46	2	62	270	325	.397
CLEVELAND	78	27	45	6	60	242	283	.385
* LOS ANGELES	78	27	46	5	59	255	314	.378
EDMONTON	78	27	48	3	57	224	289	.365
WINNIPEG	78	25	48	5	55	229	324	.353
CHICAGO	78	24	50	4	52	233	304	.333
QUEBEC	78	24	54	0	48	248	352	.308
**** VANCOUVER	78	22	55	1	45	240	354	.288
** NEW JERSEY	78	20	54	4	44	234	364	.282
TOTALS	936	328	566	42	698	2991	3757	.373

* Now Michigan
** Formerly New York, now San Diego
*** Formerly Ottawa
**** Formerly Philadelphia

CHICAGO COUGARS LIFETIME TOTALS

AT CHICAGO

AGAINST:	GP	W	L	T	Pts.	GF	GA	Pct.
Cleveland	7	2	4	1	5	21	23	.357
Edmonton	7	4	3	0	8	19	18	.571
Houston	7	3	4	0	6	20	29	.429
*Los Angeles	7	2	5	0	4	25	31	.286
Minnesota	8	3	5	0	6	32	37	.375
New England	7	3	4	0	6	23	23	.429
**New Jersey	7	6	1	0	12	36	16	.857
Quebec	7	5	2	0	10	32	21	.714
***Toronto	7	3	4	0	6	23	22	.429
****Vancouver	6	4	1	1	9	26	21	.750
Winnipeg	8	5	2	1	11	26	23	.687
TOTALS	78	40	35	3	83	283	264	.532

ON THE ROAD

GP	W	L	T	Pts.	GF	GA	Pct.
7	2	4	1	5	28	30	.357
7	1	5	1	3	15	27	.214
7	0	7	0	0	15	29	.000
7	5	2	0	10	26	15	.714
8	3	5	0	6	24	33	.375
7	2	5	0	4	19	25	.286
7	3	3	1	7	25	37	.214
7	4	2	1	9	16	25	.429
7	3	3	0	6	31	26	.643
6	0	8	0	0	22	24	.500
8	1	6	0	0	12	33	.000
78	24	50	4	52	233	304	.333

OVERALL TOTAL

GP	W	L	T	Pts.	GF	GA	Pct.
14	4	8	2	10	49	53	.357
14	5	8	1	11	34	45	.393
14	3	11	0	6	35	58	.214
14	7	7	0	14	51	46	.500
16	6	10	0	12	56	70	.375
14	5	9	0	10	42	48	.357
14	7	6	1	15	61	53	.536
14	8	6	0	16	48	46	.571
14	7	6	1	15	54	48	.536
12	7	4	1	15	48	45	.625
16	5	10	1	11	38	56	.344
156	64	85	7	135	516	568	.433

CLEVELAND CRUSADERS LIFETIME TOTALS

AT CLEVELAND

AGAINST:	GP	W	L	T	Pts.	GF	GA	Pct.
Chicago	7	4	2	1	9	30	28	.643
Edmonton	6	6	0	0	12	24	9	1.000
Houston	6	2	3	1	5	17	17	.417
*Los Angeles	6	4	1	1	9	21	18	.750
Minnesota	7	3	4	0	6	16	19	.429
New England	8	6	2	0	12	23	16	.750
**New Jersey	8	5	1	2	12	37	21	.750
Quebec	8	7	1	0	14	36	21	.875
***Toronto	8	6	1	1	13	31	23	.813
****Vancouver	8	5	3	0	10	51	30	.625
Winnipeg	6	5	1	0	10	25	18	.833
TOTALS	78	53	19	6	112	311	220	.718

ON THE ROAD

GP	W	L	T	Pts.	GF	GA	Pct.
7	4	2	1	9	23	21	.643
6	1	4	1	3	15	22	.250
6	3	2	1	7	18	12	.583
6	4	2	0	8	24	16	.667
7	2	4	1	5	25	30	.357
8	0	8	0	0	14	30	.000
8	3	5	0	6	24	35	.355
8	1	5	2	4	22	28	.250
8	3	5	0	6	22	29	.375
8	4	4	0	8	31	36	.500
6	2	4	0	4	24	24	.333
78	27	45	6	60	242	283	.385

OVERALL TOTAL

GP	W	L	T	Pts.	GF	GA	Pct.
14	8	4	2	18	53	49	.643
12	7	4	1	15	39	31	.625
12	5	5	2	12	35	29	.500
12	8	3	1	17	45	34	.708
14	5	8	1	11	41	49	.393
16	6	10	0	12	37	46	.375
16	8	6	2	18	61	56	.563
16	8	6	2	18	58	49	.563
16	9	6	1	19	53	52	.594
16	9	7	0	18	82	66	.563
12	7	5	0	14	49	42	.583
156	80	64	12	172	553	503	.551

*Now Michigan. **Formerly New York, now San Diego. ***Formerly Ottawa. ****Formerly Philadelphia.

EDMONTON OILERS LIFETIME TOTALS

AGAINST:	AT EDMONTON									ON THE ROAD									OVERALL TOTAL								
	GP	W	L	T	Pts	GF	GA	Pct.	GP	W	L	T	Pts	GF	GA	Pct.	GP	W	L	T	Pts	GF	GA	Pct.
Chicago	7	5	1	1	11	27	15	.786	7	3	4	0	6	18	19	.429	14	8	5	1	17	45	34	.607
Cleveland	6	4	1	1	9	22	15	.750	6	0	6	0	0	9	24	.000	12	4	7	1	9	31	39	.375
Houston	8	4	4	0	8	28	29	.500	8	2	6	0	4	22	31	.250	16	6	10	0	12	50	60	.375
* Los Angeles	8	6	2	0	12	40	24	.750	8	3	5	0	6	20	24	.375	16	9	7	0	18	60	48	.563
Minnesota	8	5	3	0	10	36	28	.625	8	4	4	0	8	31	29	.500	16	9	7	0	18	67	57	.563
New England	6	3	3	0	6	21	24	.500	6	2	3	1	5	18	21	.417	12	5	6	1	11	39	45	.458
** New Jersey	6	5	1	0	10	40	20	.833	6	3	3	0	6	22	25	.500	12	8	4	0	16	62	45	.667
Quebec	6	3	3	0	6	20	20	.500	6	2	3	1	5	20	27	.417	12	5	6	1	11	40	47	.458
*** Toronto	6	4	2	0	8	20	17	.667	6	3	3	0	6	22	19	.500	12	7	5	0	14	42	36	.583
**** Vancouver	8	5	3	0	10	24	17	.625	8	2	6	0	4	19	37	.250	16	7	9	0	14	43	54	.438
Winnipeg	9	5	3	1	11	35	27	.611	9	3	5	1	7	23	33	.389	18	8	8	2	18	58	60	.500
TOTALS	78	49	26	3	101	313	236	.647	78	27	48	3	57	224	289	.365	156	76	74	6	158	537	525	.506

HOUSTON AEROS LIFETIME TOTALS

AGAINST:	AT HOUSTON									ON THE ROAD									OVERALL TOTAL								
	GP	W	L	T	Pts	GF	GA	Pct.	GP	W	L	T	Pts	GF	GA	Pct.	GP	W	L	T	Pts	GF	GA	Pct.
Chicago	7	7	0	0	14	29	15	1.000	7	4	3	0	8	29	20	.571	14	11	3	0	22	58	35	.786
Cleveland	6	2	3	1	5	12	18	.417	6	3	2	1	7	17	17	.583	12	5	5	2	12	29	35	.500
Edmonton	8	6	2	0	12	31	22	.750	8	4	4	0	8	29	28	.500	16	10	6	0	20	60	50	.625
* Los Angeles	10	5	4	1	11	43	38	.550	10	6	4	0	12	35	33	.600	20	11	8	1	23	78	71	.575
Minnesota	8	5	3	0	10	32	23	.625	8	5	2	1	11	27	21	.688	16	10	5	1	21	59	44	.656
New England	6	2	4	0	4	21	24	.333	6	3	2	1	7	22	18	.583	12	5	6	1	11	43	42	.458
** New Jersey	6	4	2	0	8	27	16	.667	6	3	3	0	6	21	15	.500	12	7	5	0	14	48	31	.583
Quebec	6	3	3	0	6	22	16	.500	6	0	5	1	1	15	30	.167	12	3	8	1	7	37	46	.292
*** Toronto	6	5	1	0	10	35	16	.833	6	1	4	1	3	19	25	.250	12	6	5	1	13	54	41	.542
**** Vancouver	7	6	1	0	12	40	21	.857	7	6	1	0	12	35	17	.857	14	12	2	0	24	75	38	.857
Winnipeg	8	5	2	1	11	40	20	.688	8	2	5	1	5	21	35	.313	16	7	7	2	16	61	55	.500
TOTALS	78	50	25	3	103	332	229	.660	78	37	35	6	80	270	259	.513	156	87	60	9	183	602	488	.587

*Now Michigan. **Formerly New York, now San Diego. ***Formerly Ottawa. ****Formerly Philadelphia.

LOS ANGELES SHARKS LIFETIME TOTALS (Now Michigan Stags)

AGAINST:	AT LOS ANGELES								ON THE ROAD								OVERALL TOTAL							
	GP	W	L	T	Pts.	GF	GA	Pct.	GP	W	L	T	Pts.	GF	GA	Pct.	GP	W	L	T	Pts.	GF	GA	Pct.
Chicago	7	2	5	0	4	15	26	.286	7	5	2	0	10	31	25	.714	14	7	7	0	14	46	51	.500
Cleveland	6	2	4	0	4	16	24	.333	6	1	4	1	3	18	21	.250	12	3	8	1	7	34	45	.292
Edmonton	8	5	3	0	10	24	20	.625	8	2	6	0	4	24	40	.250	16	7	9	0	14	48	60	.437
Houston	10	4	6	0	8	33	35	.400	10	4	5	1	9	38	43	.450	20	8	11	1	17	71	78	.425
Minnesota	8	4	3	1	9	28	27	.562	8	3	5	0	6	28	32	.375	16	7	8	1	15	56	59	.469
* New England	6	3	3	0	6	16	21	.500	6	1	5	0	2	19	32	.167	12	4	8	0	8	35	53	.333
** New Jersey	6	3	3	0	6	30	27	.500	6	5	1	0	10	31	18	.833	12	8	4	0	16	61	45	.667
Quebec	6	4	2	0	8	22	19	.667	6	1	4	1	3	11	27	.250	12	5	6	1	11	33	46	.458
*** Toronto	6	3	3	0	6	18	19	.500	6	1	3	2	4	20	23	.333	12	4	6	2	10	38	42	.417
**** Vancouver	7	2	5	0	4	15	27	.286	7	3	4	0	6	24	23	.429	14	5	9	0	10	39	50	.357
Winnipeg	8	3	5	0	6	26	30	.375	8	1	7	0	2	11	30	.125	16	4	12	0	8	37	60	.250
TOTALS	78	35	42	1	71	243	275	.455	78	27	46	5	59	255	314	.378	156	62	88	6	130	498	589	.417

MINNESOTA FIGHTING SAINTS LIFETIME TOTALS

AGAINST:	AT ST. PAUL, MINNESOTA								ON THE ROAD								OVERALL TOTAL							
	GP	W	L	T	Pts.	GF	GA	Pct.	GP	W	L	T	Pts.	GF	GA	Pct.	GP	W	L	T	Pts.	GF	GA	Pct.
Chicago	8	5	3	0	10	33	24	.625	8	5	3	0	10	37	32	.625	16	10	6	0	20	70	56	.625
Cleveland	7	4	2	1	9	30	25	.643	7	4	3	0	8	19	16	.571	14	8	5	1	17	49	41	.607
Edmonton	8	4	4	0	8	29	31	.500	8	3	5	0	6	28	36	.375	16	7	9	0	14	57	67	.437
Houston	8	2	5	1	5	21	27	.312	8	3	5	0	6	23	32	.375	16	5	10	1	11	44	59	.343
* Los Angeles	8	5	3	0	10	32	28	.625	8	3	4	1	7	27	28	.438	16	8	7	1	17	59	56	.531
** New England	6	6	0	0	12	30	19	1.000	6	1	4	1	3	16	25	.250	12	7	4	1	15	46	44	.625
*** New Jersey	6	4	2	0	8	28	20	.667	6	2	4	0	4	16	23	.333	12	6	6	0	12	44	43	.500
Quebec	6	4	2	0	8	22	22	.667	6	3	3	0	6	37	26	.500	12	7	5	0	14	59	48	.583
*** Toronto	6	4	2	0	8	22	21	.667	6	1	5	0	2	16	32	.167	12	5	7	0	10	38	53	.417
**** Vancouver	7	6	1	0	12	23	13	.857	7	3	4	0	6	28	29	.439	14	9	5	0	18	56	42	.643
Winnipeg	8	6	2	0	12	40	18	.750	8	4	3	1	9	20	17	.562	16	10	5	1	21	60	35	.656
TOTALS	78	50	26	2	102	321	248	.654	78	32	43	3	67	261	296	.429	156	82	69	5	169	582	544	.542

*Now Michigan.   **Formerly New York, now San Diego.   ***Formerly Ottawa.   ****Formerly Philadelphia.

NEW ENGLAND WHALERS LIFETIME TOTALS

	AT BOSTON, MASSACHUSETTS								ON THE ROAD								OVERALL TOTAL							
AGAINST:	GP	W	L	T	Pts.	GF	GA	Pct.	GP	W	L	T	Pts.	GF	GA	Pct.	GP	W	L	T	Pts.	GF	GA	Pct.
Chicago	7	5	2	0	10	25	19	.714	7	4	3	0	8	23	23	.571	14	9	5	0	18	48	42	.643
Cleveland	8	8	0	0	16	30	14	1.000	8	2	6	0	4	16	23	.250	16	10	6	0	20	46	37	.625
Edmonton	6	3	2	1	7	21	18	.583	6	3	3	0	6	24	21	.500	12	6	5	1	13	45	39	.542
Houston	6	2	3	1	5	18	22	.417	6	4	2	0	8	24	21	.667	12	6	5	1	13	42	43	.542
* Los Angeles	6	5	1	0	10	32	19	.833	6	3	3	0	6	21	16	.500	12	8	4	0	16	53	35	.667
Minnesota	6	4	1	1	9	25	16	.750	6	0	6	0	0	19	30	.000	12	4	7	1	9	44	46	.375
** New Jersey	10	10	0	0	20	41	25	1.000	10	5	4	1	11	45	32	.550	20	15	4	1	31	86	57	.775
Quebec	8	4	4	0	8	29	29	.500	8	3	4	1	7	29	29	.438	16	7	8	1	15	58	58	.469
*** Toronto	8	5	3	0	10	40	33	.625	8	3	4	1	7	26	32	.438	16	8	7	1	17	66	65	.531
**** Vancouver	7	6	1	0	12	37	22	.857	7	2	5	0	4	34	38	.286	14	8	6	0	16	71	60	.571
Winnipeg	6	4	2	0	8	26	13	.667	6	4	2	0	8	24	28	.667	12	8	4	0	16	50	41	.667
TOTALS	78	56	19	3	115	324	230	.737	78	33	42	3	69	285	293	.442	156	89	61	6	184	609	523	.590

NEW JERSEY KNIGHTS LIFETIME TOTALS (Formerly New York, Now San Diego)

	AT NEW YORK & CHERRY HILL, NEW JERSEY								ON THE ROAD								OVERALL TOTAL							
AGAINST:	GP	W	L	T	Pts.	GF	GA	Pct.	GP	W	L	T	Pts.	GF	GA	Pct.	GP	W	L	T	Pts.	GF	GA	Pct.
Chicago	7	5	1	1	11	37	25	.786	7	1	6	0	2	16	36	.143	14	6	7	1	13	53	61	.464
Cleveland	8	5	3	0	10	35	24	.625	8	1	5	2	4	21	37	.250	16	6	8	2	14	56	61	.438
Edmonton	6	3	3	0	6	25	22	.500	6	1	5	0	2	20	40	.167	12	4	8	0	8	45	62	.333
Houston	6	3	3	0	6	15	21	.500	6	2	4	0	4	16	27	.333	12	5	7	0	10	31	48	.417
* Los Angeles	6	1	5	0	2	18	31	.167	6	3	3	0	6	27	30	.500	12	4	8	0	8	45	61	.333
Minnesota	6	4	2	0	8	23	16	.667	6	2	4	0	4	20	28	.333	12	6	6	0	12	43	44	.500
New England	10	4	5	1	9	32	45	.450	10	0	10	0	0	25	41	.000	20	4	15	1	9	57	86	.225
Quebec	8	7	1	0	14	47	22	.875	8	1	6	1	3	24	44	.188	16	8	7	1	17	71	66	.531
*** Toronto	8	6	2	0	12	50	33	.750	8	3	4	1	7	19	27	.438	16	9	6	1	19	69	60	.594
**** Vancouver	7	4	3	0	8	28	21	.571	7	5	2	0	10	27	22	.714	14	9	5	0	18	55	43	.643
Winnipeg	6	3	3	0	6	27	23	.500	6	1	5	0	2	19	32	.167	12	4	8	0	8	46	55	.333
TOTALS	78	45	31	2	92	337	283	.590	78	20	54	4	44	234	364	.282	156	65	85	6	136	571	647	.436

*Now Michigan. **Formerly New York, now San Diego. ***Formerly New York, Now San Diego. ***Formerly Ottawa. ****Formerly Philadelphia.

QUEBEC NORDIQUES LIFETIME TOTALS

	AT QUEBEC								ON THE ROAD								OVERALL TOTAL							
AGAINST:	GP	W	L	T	Pts.	GF	GA	Pct.	GP	W	L	T	Pts.	GF	GA	Pct.	GP	W	L	T	Pts.	GF	GA	Pct.
Chicago	7	4	3	0	8	25	16	.571	7	2	5	0	4	21	32	.286	14	6	8	0	12	46	48	.429
Cleveland	8	5	1	2	12	28	22	.750	8	1	7	0	2	21	36	.125	16	6	8	2	14	49	58	.437
Edmonton	6	3	2	1	7	27	20	.583	6	3	3	0	6	20	20	.500	12	6	5	1	13	47	40	.458
Houston	6	5	0	1	11	30	15	.833	6	3	3	0	6	16	22	.500	12	8	3	1	17	46	37	.708
* Los Angeles	6	4	1	1	9	27	11	.750	6	2	4	0	4	19	22	.333	12	6	5	1	13	46	33	.542
Minnesota	6	3	3	0	6	26	31	.500	6	2	4	0	4	22	28	.333	12	5	7	0	10	48	59	.417
New England	8	4	3	1	9	29	29	.562	8	4	4	0	8	29	29	.500	16	8	7	1	17	58	58	.531
** New Jersey	8	6	1	1	13	44	24	.813	8	1	7	0	2	22	47	.125	16	7	8	1	15	66	71	.469
*** Toronto	10	5	5	0	10	39	36	.500	10	3	7	0	6	33	45	.300	20	8	12	0	16	72	81	.400
**** Vancouver	7	6	1	0	12	38	19	.857	7	2	5	0	4	26	39	.286	14	8	6	0	16	64	58	.571
Winnipeg	6	2	2	2	6	21	18	.500	6	1	5	0	2	19	32	.167	12	3	7	2	8	40	50	.333
TOTALS	78	47	22	9	103	334	241	.660	78	24	54	0	48	248	352	.308	156	71	76	9	151	582	593	.484

TORONTO TOROS LIFETIME TOTALS (Formerly Ottawa Nationals)

	AT OTTAWA & TORONTO								ON THE ROAD								OVERALL TOTAL							
AGAINST:	GP	W	L	T	Pts.	GF	GA	Pct.	GP	W	L	T	Pts.	GF	GA	Pct.	GP	W	L	T	Pts.	GF	GA	Pct.
Chicago	7	2	4	1	5	26	31	.357	7	4	3	0	8	22	23	.571	14	6	7	1	13	48	54	.464
Cleveland	8	5	3	0	10	29	22	.625	8	1	6	1	3	23	31	.188	16	6	9	1	13	52	53	.406
Edmonton	6	3	3	0	6	19	22	.500	6	2	4	0	4	17	20	.333	12	5	7	0	10	36	42	.417
Houston	6	4	1	1	9	25	19	.750	6	1	5	0	2	16	35	.167	12	5	6	1	11	41	54	.458
* Los Angeles	6	3	1	2	8	23	20	.667	6	3	3	0	6	19	18	.500	12	6	4	2	14	42	38	.583
Minnesota	6	5	1	0	10	32	16	.833	6	2	4	0	4	21	22	.333	12	7	5	0	14	53	38	.583
** New England	8	4	3	1	9	32	26	.563	8	3	5	0	6	33	40	.375	16	7	8	1	15	65	66	.469
New Jersey	8	4	3	1	9	27	19	.563	8	2	6	0	4	33	50	.250	16	6	9	1	13	60	69	.406
***** Quebec	10	7	3	0	14	45	33	.700	10	5	5	0	10	36	39	.500	20	12	8	0	24	81	72	.600
Vancouver	7	5	2	0	10	31	25	.714	7	4	3	0	8	26	27	.571	14	9	5	0	18	57	52	.643
Winnipeg	6	4	2	0	8	24	15	.667	6	3	2	1	7	24	20	.583	12	7	4	1	15	48	35	.625
TOTALS	78	46	26	6	98	313	248	.628	78	30	46	2	62	270	325	.397	156	76	72	8	160	583	573	.513

*Now Michigan. **Formerly New York, now San Diego. ***Formerly Ottawa. ****Formerly Philadelphia.

VANCOUVER BLAZERS LIFETIME TOTALS (Formerly at Philadelphia)

AT PHILADELPHIA & VANCOUVER | ON THE ROAD | OVERALL TOTAL

AGAINST:	GP	W	L	T	Pts.	GF	GA	Pct.	GP	W	L	T	Pts.	GF	GA	Pct.	GP	W	L	T	Pts.	GF	GA	Pct.
Chicago	6	3	3	0	6	24	22	.500	6	1	4	1	3	21	26	.250	12	4	7	1	9	45	48	.375
Cleveland	8	4	4	0	8	36	31	.500	8	3	5	0	6	30	51	.375	16	7	9	0	14	66	82	.438
Edmonton	8	6	2	0	12	37	19	.750	8	3	5	0	6	17	24	.375	16	9	7	0	18	54	43	.563
Houston	7	1	6	0	2	17	35	.143	7	1	6	0	2	21	40	.143	14	2	12	0	4	38	75	.143
Los Angeles	7	4	3	0	8	23	28	.571	7	5	2	0	10	27	15	.714	14	9	5	0	18	50	39	.643
Minnesota	7	4	3	0	8	29	28	.571	7	1	6	0	2	13	28	.143	14	5	9	0	10	42	56	.357
New England	7	5	2	0	10	38	34	.714	7	1	6	0	2	22	37	.143	14	6	8	0	12	60	71	.429
New Jersey **	7	2	5	0	4	22	27	.286	7	3	4	0	6	21	28	.429	14	5	9	0	10	43	55	.357
Quebec	7	5	2	0	10	39	26	.714	7	1	6	0	2	19	38	.143	14	6	8	0	12	58	64	.429
Toronto ***	7	3	4	0	6	27	26	.429	7	2	5	0	4	25	31	.286	14	5	9	0	10	52	57	.357
Winnipeg	7	6	1	0	12	34	24	.857	7	1	6	0	2	24	36	.143	14	7	7	0	14	58	60	.500
TOTALS	78	43	35	0	86	326	296	.551	78	22	55	1	45	240	354	.288	156	65	90	1	131	566	650	.420

WINNIPEG JETS LIFETIME TOTALS

AT WINNIPEG | ON THE ROAD | OVERALL TOTAL

AGAINST:	GP	W	L	T	Pts.	GF	GA	Pct.	GP	W	L	T	Pts.	GF	GA	Pct.	GP	W	L	T	Pts.	GF	GA	Pct.
Chicago	8	8	0	0	16	33	12	1.000	8	2	5	1	5	23	26	.313	16	10	5	1	21	56	38	.656
Cleveland	6	4	2	0	8	24	24	.667	6	1	5	0	2	18	25	.167	12	5	7	0	10	42	49	.417
Edmonton	9	5	3	1	11	33	23	.611	9	3	5	1	7	27	35	.389	18	8	8	2	18	60	58	.500
Houston	8	5	2	1	11	35	21	.688	8	2	5	1	5	20	40	.313	16	7	7	2	16	55	61	.500
Los Angeles *	8	7	1	0	14	30	11	.875	8	5	3	0	10	30	26	.625	16	12	4	0	24	60	37	.750
Minnesota	8	3	4	1	7	17	20	.438	8	2	6	0	4	18	40	.250	16	5	10	1	11	35	60	.344
New England	6	2	4	0	4	28	24	.333	6	2	4	0	4	13	26	.333	12	4	8	0	8	41	50	.333
New Jersey **	6	5	1	0	10	32	19	.833	6	3	3	0	6	23	27	.500	12	8	4	0	16	55	46	.667
Quebec	6	5	1	0	10	32	19	.833	6	2	2	2	6	18	21	.500	12	7	3	2	16	50	40	.667
Toronto ***	6	2	3	1	5	20	24	.417	6	2	4	0	4	15	24	.333	12	4	7	1	9	35	48	.375
Vancouver ****	7	6	1	0	12	36	24	.857	7	1	6	0	2	24	34	.143	14	7	7	0	14	60	58	.500
TOTALS	78	52	22	4	108	320	221	.692	78	25	48	5	55	229	324	.353	156	77	70	9	163	549	545	.522

*Now Michigan. **Formerly New York, now San Diego. ***Formerly Ottawa. ****Formerly Philadelphia.

MAJOR LEAGUE RECORDS

TOTAL POINTS

No.	Player Team(s)	Seasons	Games Played	Goals	Assists	Total Points	Points per Game	Points per Season
1.	Gordie Howe, Detroit Red Wings – Houston Aeros	26	1,757	817	1,092	1,909	1.087	73.42
2.	Bobby Hull, Chicago Black Hawks – Winnipeg Jets	17	1,174	708	643	1.351	1.151	79.47
3.**	Alex Delvecchio, Detroit Red Wings	23	1,549	456	825	1,281	.827	55.70
4.**	Jean Beliveau, Montreal Canadiens	18	1,125	507	712	1,219	1.081	67.72
5.	Norm Ullman, Detroit Red Wings – Toronto Maple Leafs	19	1,330	481	713	1,194	.898	62.84
6.	Stan Mikita, Chicago Black Hawks	15	1,052	431	723	1,154	1.097	76.93
7.	John Bucyk, Detroit Red Wings – Boston Bruins	19	1,283	466	678	1,154	.892	60.21
8.	Frank Mahovlich, Toronto Maple Leafs – Detroit Red Wings – Montreal Canadiens	17	1,181	533	570	1,103	.934	64.88
9.	Phil Esposito, Chicago Black Hawks – Boston Bruins	11	769	466	577	1,043	1.356	94.82
10.	Henri Richard – Montreal Canadiens	18	1,165	336	642	978	.839	54.33

MOST GOALS

No.	Player Team(s)	Seasons Played	Games Played	Goals Scored	Goals Per Game	Goals per Season
1.	Gordie Howe, Detroit Red Wings – Houston Aeros	26	1,757	817	.465	31.42
2.	Bobby Hull, Chicago Black Hawks – Winnipeg Jets	17	1,174	708	.603	41.65
3.**	Maurice Richard, Montreal Canadiens	18	978	544	.556	30.22
4.	Frank Mahovlich, Toronto Maple Leafs – Detroit Red Wings – Montreal Canadiens	17	1,181	533	.451	31.35
5.**	Jean Beliveau, Montreal Canadiens	18	1,125	507	.451	28.17
6.	Norm Ullman, Detroit Red Wings – Toronto Maple Leafs	19	1,330	481	.362	25.32
7.	Phil Esposito, Chicago Black Hawks – Boston Bruins	11	769	466	.606	42.36
8.	John Bucyk, Detroit Red Wings – Boston Bruins	19	1,283	466	.363	24.53
9.	Alex Delvecchio, Detroit Red Wings	23	1,549	456	.294	19.83
10.	Stan Mikita, Chicago Black Hawks	15	1,052	431	.410	28.73

** – *No Longer Playing Professional Hockey.*

WHA/NHL records

MOST ASSISTS

No.	Player Team(s)	Seasons Played	Games Played	Total Assists	Assists per Game	Assists per Season
1.	Gordie Howe, Detroit Red Wings — Houston Aeros	26	1,757	1,092	.622	42.00
2.**	Alex Delvecchio, Detroit Red Wings...	23	1,549	825	.533	35.87
3.	Stan Mikita, Chicago Black Hawks	15	1,052	723	.687	48.20
4.	Norm Ullman, Detroit Red Wings — Toronto Maple Leafs	19	1,330	713	.536	37.53
5.	Jean Beliveau, Montreal Canadiens	18	1,125	712	.632	39.56
6.	John Bucyk, Detroit Red Wings — Boston Bruins	19	1,283	678	.528	35.68
7.	Bobby Hull, Chicago Black Hawks — Winnipeg Jets	17	1,174	643	.548	37.82
8.**	Henri Richard, Montreal Canadiens	18	1,165	642	.551	35.67
9.**	Andy Bathgate, New York Rangers — Toronto Maple Leafs — Detroit Red Wings — Pittsburgh Penguins	16	1,069	624	.584	39.00
10.	Phil Esposito, Chicago Black Hawks — Boston Bruins	11	769	577	.750	52.45

MOST PENALTY MINUTES

No.	Player Team(s)	Seasons Played	Games Played	Total Penalty Minutes	Avg. per Game	Avg. per Season
1.**	Ted Lindsay, Detroit Red Wings — Chicago Black Hawks	17	1,068	1,808	1.69	106.35
2.	Gordie Howe, Detroit Red Wings — Houston Aeros	26	1,757	1,688	.96	64.92
3.	Tim Horton, Toronto Maple Leafs — New York Rangers — Pittsburgh Penguins — Buffalo Sabres	22	1,446	1,611	1.11	73.23
4.	Reggie Fleming, Montreal Canadiens — Chicago Black Hawks — New York Rangers — Philadelphia Flyers — Chicago Cougars	13	869	1,610	1.85	123.85
5.	Bill Gadsby, Chicago Black Hawks — New York Rangers — Detroit Red Wings	20	1,248	1,539	1.23	76.95
6.**	Bob Baun, Toronto Maple Leafs — California Seals — Detroit Red Wings	17	964	1,493	1.55	87.82
7.	Eddie Shack, New York Rangers — Toronto Maple Leafs — Boston Bruins — Los Angeles Kings — Buffalo Sabres — Pittsburgh Penguins	16	1,021	1,426	1.40	89.13
8.**	Gus Mortson, Toronto Maple Leafs — Chicago Black Hawks — Detroit Red Wings	13	797	1,370	1.72	105.38
9.**	Fern Flaman, Boston Bruins — Toronto Maple Leafs	15	910	1,370	1.51	91.33
10.	Harry Howell, New York Rangers — California Seals — Los Angeles Kings — New York Golden Blades — New Jersey Knights	21	1,476	1,322	.90	62.95

** — No Longer Playing Professional Hockey.

WHA CAREER LEADERS (Two Seasons)

MOST POINTS

No.	Player, Team	Games Played	Goals	Assists	Total Points	Points Per Game
1.	Andre Lacroix, Phil., N.Y., N.J.	156	81	154	235	1.506
2.	Danny Lawson, Phil., Vancouver	156	111	95	206	1.321
3.	Bobby Hull, Winnipeg	138	104	94	198	1.435
4.	Wayne Carleton, Otwa., Toronto	153	79	104	183	1.196
5.	Ron Ward, N.Y., Van., L.A., Clev.	147	84	95	179	1.218
6.	Chris Bordeleau, Winnipeg	153	73	103	176	1.150
7.	Tom Webster, New England	141	96	77	173	1.227
8.	Wayne Connelly, Minnesota	156	82	83	165	1.058
9.	Bryan Campbell, Phil., Vancouver	151	52	110	162	1.073
10.	Norm Beaudin, Winnipeg	152	65	93	158	1.039

MOST GOALS

No.	Player, Team	Games Played	Goals	Goals Per Game
1.	Danny Lawson, Phil., Vancouver	156	111	.712
2.	Bobby Hull, Winnipeg	138	104	.754
3.	Tom Webster, New England	141	96	.681
4.	Ron Ward, N.Y., Van., L.A., Cleveland	147	84	.571
5.	Gary Veneruzzo, Los Angeles	156	82	.526
6.	Wayne Connelly, Minnesota	156	82	.526
7.	Andre Lacroix, Phil., N.Y., New Jersey	156	81	.519
8.	Wayne Carleton, Ottawa, Toronto	153	79	.516
9.	Chris Bordeleau, Winnipeg	153	73	.477
10.	Gary Jarrett, Cleveland	152	71	.467

MOST ASSISTS

No.	Player, Team	Games Played	Assists	Assists Per Game
1.	Andre Lacroix, Phil., N.Y., New Jersey	156	154	.987
2.	J.C. Tremblay, Quebec	144	119	.826
3.	Bryan Campbell, Phil., Vancouver	151	110	.728
4.	Wayne Carleton, Ottawa, Toronto	153	104	.680
5.	Chris Bordeleau, Winnipeg	153	103	.673
6.	Larry Lund, Houston	152	98	.645
7.	Gordon Labossiere, Houston	144	96	.667
8.	Ken Block, N.Y., New Jersey	152	96	.632
9.	Jim Dorey, New England	152	96	.632
10.	Jean-Paul LeBlanc, Los Angeles	155	96	.619

MOST PENALTY MINUTES

No.	Player, Team	Games Played	Penalty Minutes	Avg. Min's. Per Game
1.	John Schella, Houston	150	409	2.727
2.	John Arbour, Minnesota	153	380	2.484
3.	Jim Cardiff, Phil., Vancouver	156	373	2.391
4.	Tom Gilmore, L.A., Edmonton	128	355	2.773
5.	Paul Shmyr, Cleveland	151	334	2.212
6.	Doug Barrie, Edmonton	123	325	2.642
7.	Pierre Roy, Quebec	108	304	2.815
8.	Poul Popiel, Houston	152	284	1.868
9.	Steve Sutherland, Los Angeles	116	280	2.414
10.	Dick Paradise, Minnesota	144	260	1.806

career leaders

PENALTY SHOTS

Date	Player, Team	VS.	Goaltender, Team	Time	Per.	Result
1972-73 SEASON						
10-11-72	Bill Hicke, Alberta		Les Binkley, Ottawa	16:37	1	SCORED
11-29-72	Ron Ward, New York		Al Smith, New England	5:24	1	Failed
1-16-73	Rich Leduc, Quebec		Gilles Gratton, Ottawa	8:17	3	SCORED
1973-74 SEASON						
10-11-73	Andre Lacroix, New York		Cam Newton, Chicago	18:28	3	Failed
10-19-73	Denis Meloche, Vancouver		Jack Norris, Edmonton	15:19	3	Failed
10-25-73	Andre Lacroix, New York		Al Smith, New England	8:57	2	Failed
11- 3-73	Ron Buchanan, Cleveland		Andre Gill, Chicago	7:46	2	Failed
11-22-73	Wayne Connelly, Minnesota		Al Smith, New England	10:34	2	Failed
11-23-73	Marc Tardif, Los Angeles		Jack Norris, Edmonton	18:12	3	Failed
12-22-73	Gary Veneruzzo, Los Angeles		Don McLeod, Houston	15:08	3	Failed
12-29-73	Andre Lacroix, New Jersey		Gerry Cheevers, Clev	19:09	1	Failed
3- 1-74	Brian Carlin, Edmonton		Don McLeod, Houston	19:50	3	SCORED
3-10-74	Ron Garwasiuk, Los Angeles		Mike Curran, Minnesota	19:38	2	Failed
3-31-74	Brian Morenz, New Jersey		Gerry Cheevers, Clev	12:22	3	Failed
4- 1-74	Frank Hughes, Houston		Al Smith, New England	7:10	2	Failed

3-OR-MORE GOAL GAMES

(Regular Season Only — Two Year Totals)

Player	Team(s)	3- or More	4- or More	5 Goal	Player	Team	3- or More	4- or More	5 Goal
Danny Lawson	Phil-Van	9	3	—	Steve Cardwell	Minn.	1	—	—
Bobby Hull	Wpg.	8	2	—	Bryan Campbell	Van.	1	—	—
Mike Walton	Minn.	6	2	—	Wayne Connelly	Minn.	1	—	—
Ron Ward	NYR-LA-Clev.	5	1	1	Brian Coates	Chi.	1	—	—
Tom Webster	NE	4	—	—	Reg Fleming	Chi.	1	—	—
Andre Lacroix	Phil.	3	1	—	Jean-Guy Gratton	Wpg.	1	—	—
Claude St. Sauveur	Van.	3	—	—	Andre Gaudette	Que.	1	—	—
Frank Hughes	Hou.	3	—	—	Don Grierson	Hou.	1	—	—
John McKenzie	Phil-Van	3	—	—	Robert Guindon	Que.	1	—	—
Gene Peacosh	NYR-NJ	3	—	—	Rejean Giroux	Que.	1	—	—
Ron Buchanan	Clev.	2	1	—	Joe Hardy	Clev.	1	—	—
Chris Bordeleau	Wpg.	2	1	—	Ted Hodgson	Clev.	1	—	—
Tom Gilmore	LA-Edm.	2	1	—	Fran Huck	Wpg.	1	—	—
Gordie Howe	Hou.	2	1	—	Rejean Houle	Que.	1	—	—
Brian McDonald	LA	2	1	—	Mark Howe	Hou.	1	—	—
Alain Caron	Que.	2	—	—	Pat Hickey	Tor.	1	—	—
Don Herriman	Phil-NJ	2	—	—	Gavin Kirk	Otwa.	1	—	—
Jim Harrison	Edm.	2	—	—	Dan Lodboa	Chi.	1	—	—
Gord Labossiere	Hou.	2	—	—	Rick Morris	Chi.	1	—	—
J.P. Leblanc	LA	2	—	—	Murray Meyers	Van.	1	—	—
Jan Popiel	Chi.	2	—	—	Brian Morenz	NJ	1	—	—
Wayne Rivers	NYR	2	—	—	Kevin Morrison	NJ	1	—	—
Gary Veneruzzo	LA	2	—	—	Gerry Pinder	Clev.	1	—	—
Marc Tardif	LA	2	—	—	Larry Pleau	NE	1	—	—
Alton White	LA	2	—	—	Ross Perkins	Alb.	1	—	—
Ron Climie	Edm.	1	1	1	Rosaire Paiement	Chi.	1	—	—
Wayne Dillon	Tor.	1	1	—	Bobby Sheehan	NYR	1	—	—
John French	NE	1	1	—	Brit Selby	NE	1	—	—
Pat Hickey	Tor.	1	1	—	Tom Simpson	Tor.	1	—	—
George Morrison	Minn.	1	1	—	Ted Taylor	Hou.	1	—	—
Mike Antonovich	Minn.	1	—	—	Ron Walters	Alb.	1	—	—
Mike Byers	LA	1	—	—	Jim Wiste	Clev.	1	—	—
Norm Beaudin	Wpg.	1	—	—	Tommy Williams	NE	1	—	—
Wayne Carleton	Otwa.	1	—	—	Bill Young	Clev.	1	—	—
Terry Caffery	NE	1	—	—					

3-or more goal games includes games in which player scored 4 or 5 goals.
4-or more goal games includes games in which player scored 5 goals.
Teams shown are those player was with at the time of his multiple-scoring games.

TEAM RECORDS

MOST POINTS, ONE SEASON:
101 — Houston Aeros, 1973-74. Won 48, lost 25, tied 5.
FEWEST POINTS, ONE SEASON:
50 — Los Angeles Sharks, 1973-74. Won 25, lost 53, tied 0.
MOST WINS, ONE SEASON:
48 — Houston Aeros, 1973-74.
MOST HOME WINS, ONE SEASON:
30 — New England Whalers, 1972-73.
MOST ROAD WINS, ONE SEASON:
20 — Houston Aeros, 1973-74.
FEWEST WINS, ONE SEASON:
25 — Los Angeles Sharks, 1973-74.
FEWEST HOME WINS, ONE SEASON:
17 — Chicago Cougars, 1972-73.
17 — Los Angeles Sharks, 1973-74.
FEWEST ROAD WINS, ONE SEASON:
8 — Winnipeg Jets, 1973-74.
8 — Vancouver Blazers, 1973-74.
8 — Los Angeles Sharks, 1973-74.
MOST LOSSES, ONE SEASON:
53 — Los Angeles Sharks, 1973-74.
MOST HOME LOSSES, ONE SEASON:
22 — Chicago Cougars, 1972-73.
22 — Los Angeles Sharks, 1973-74.
MOST ROAD LOSSES, ONE SEASON:
31 — Los Angeles Sharks, 1973-74.
FEWEST LOSSES, ONE SEASON:
25 — Houston Aeros, 1973-74.
FEWEST HOME LOSSES, ONE SEASON:
8 — New England Whalers, 1972-73.
8 — Cleveland Crusaders, 1973-74.
FEWEST ROAD LOSSES, ONE SEASON:
15 — Los Angeles Sharks, 1972-73.
MOST TIES, ONE SEASON:
9 — Cleveland Crusaders, 1973-74.
MOST HOME TIES, ONE SEASON:
5 — Quebec Nordiques, 1972-73.
MOST ROAD TIES, ONE SEASON:
5 — Los Angeles Sharks, 1972-73.
5 — Cleveland Crusaders, 1973-74.
FEWEST TIES, ONE SEASON:
0 — Philadelphia Blazers, 1972-73.
0 — Los Angeles Sharks, 1973-74.
FEWEST HOME TIES, ONE SEASON:
0 — Philadelphia Blazers, 1972-73.
0 — Chicago Cougars, 1972-73.
0 — Vancouver Blazers, 1973-74.
0 — Los Angeles Sharks, 1973-74.
FEWEST ROAD TIES, ONE SEASON:
0 — Philadelphia Blazers, 1972-73.
0 — Quebec Nordiques, 1973-74.
0 — Los Angeles Sharks, 1973-74.
LONGEST UNDEFEATED STREAK:
11 Games — Edmonton Oilers, Oct. 21, 1973 to Nov. 16, 1973. 11 wins, no ties.
11 Games — Minnesota Fighting Saints, Feb. 13, 1974 to March 10, 1974. 10 wins, 1 tie.
LONGEST HOME UNDEFEATED STREAK:
14 Games — New England Whalers, Nov. 1, 1972 to Dec. 17, 1972. 13 wins, 1 tie.
LONGEST ROAD UNDEFEATED STREAK:
6 Games — Cleveland Crusaders, Oct. 15, 1972 to Nov. 14, 1972. 5 wins, 1 tie.
6 Games — Houston Aeros, Feb. 4, 1974 to March 1, 1974. 5 wins, 1 tie.
6 Games — Minnesota Fighting Saints, Feb. 8, 1974 to March 10, 1974. 6 wins.

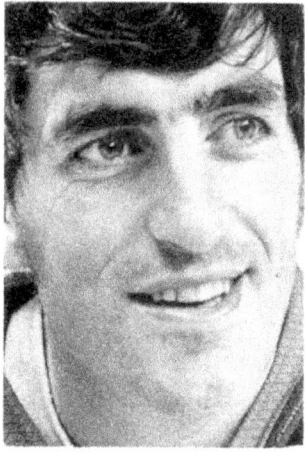

NORM BEAUDIN
Most Playoff Records (9)

JIM DOREY
Most Points by Defenseman (19)

LONGEST WINNING RECORD:
 11 Games — Quebec Nordiques, Jan. 5, 1974 to Feb. 22, 1974.

LONGEST HOME WINNING RECORD
 10 Games — Quebec Nordiques, Jan. 5, 1974 to Feb. 22, 1974.

LONGEST HOME WINNING RECORD INCLUDING PLAYOFFS:
 13 Games — New England Whalers, March 30, 1973 to Oct. 15, 1973. The Whalers won the final two games of the 1972-73 season, nine straight playoff games, and the first two games of the 1973-74 season.

LONGEST ROAD WINNING RECORD:
 6 Games — Minnesota Fighting Saints, Feb. 8, 1974 to March 10, 1974.

LONGEST LOSING STRING:
 10 Games — Vancouver Blazers, Oct. 21, 1973 to Nov. 13, 1973.

LONGEST HOME LOSING STRING:
 7 Games — Vancouver Blazers, Oct. 21, 1973 to Nov. 13, 1973.

LONGEST ROAD LOSING STRING:
 14 Games — Los Angeles Sharks, Jan. 29, 1974 to end of season. The Sharks have moved to Detroit where they have become the Michigan Stags.

LONGEST WINLESS RECORD:
 10 Games — Ottawa National, Jan. 19, 1973 to Feb. 6, 1973. 9 losses and 1 tie.
 10 Games — Vancouver Blazers, Oct. 21, 1973 to Nov. 10, 1973. 10 losses.

LONGEST HOME WINLESS RECORD:
 7 Games — Vancouver Blazers, Oct. 21, 1973 to Nov. 13, 1973. 7 losses.

LONGEST ROAD WINLESS RECORD:
 14 Games — Los Angeles Sharks, Jan. 29, 1974 to the end of the season. The Sharks lost the last 14 road games of the 1973-74 season.

ONE TEAM, ONE SEASON:
 71 — Philadelphia Blazers, 1972-73.

MOST POWER PLAY GOALS ALLOWED, ONE TEAM, ONE SEASON:
 66 — Vancouver Blazers, 1973-74.

MOST SHORTHANDED GOALS SCORED, ONE TEAM, ONE SEASON:
 20 — Minnesota Fighting Saints, 1973-74.

MOST SHORTHANDED GOALS ALLOWED, ONE TEAM, ONE SEASON:
 15 — Quebec Nordiques, 1972-73.
 15 — Winnipeg Jets, 1973-74.

MOST SCORING POINTS, ONE SEASON, ONE TEAM:
 902 — Minnesota Fighting Saints, 1973-74. 332 goals, 570 assists.

MOST GOALS SCORED, ONE TEAM, ONE SEASON:
 332 — Minnesota Fighting Saints, 1973-74 season.

FEWEST GOALS SCORED, ONE TEAM, ONE SEASON:
 239 — Los Angeles Sharks, 1973-74 season.

MOST GOALS ALLOWED, ONE TEAM, ONE SEASON:
 345 — Vancouver Blazers, 1973-74 season.

FEWEST GOALS ALLOWED, ONE TEAM, ONE SEASON:
 219 — Houston Aeros, 1973-74 season.

MOST ASSISTS, ONE TEAM, ONE SEASON:
 570 — Minnesota Fighting Saints, 1973-74 season.

FEWEST ASSISTS, ONE TEAM, ONE SEASON:
 392 — Los Angeles Sharks, 1973-74 season.

MOST 100-OR-MORE-POINT SCORERS, ONE TEAM, ONE SEASON:
 3 — Winnipeg Jets, 1972-73. Bobby Hull, 103 points; Norm Beaudin, 103 points; Chris Bordeleau, 101 points.

MOST 50-OR-MORE-GOAL SCORERS, ONE TEAM, ONE SEASON:
 2 — Philadelphia Blazers, 1972-73. Andre Lacroix, 50; Danny Lawson, 61.

MOST 40-OR-MORE-GOAL SCORERS, ONE TEAM, ONE SEASON:
 3 — Minnesota Fighting Saints, 1973-74. Mike Walton, 57; Wayne Connelly, 42; George Morrison, 40.

MOST 30-OR-MORE-GOAL SCORERS, ONE TEAM, ONE SEASON:
 6 — Houston Aeros, 1973-74. Frank Hughes, 42; Mark Howe, 38; Larry Lund, 33; Gordie Howe, 31; Jim Sherrit, 30; Murray Hall, 30.

MOST 20-OR-MORE-GOAL SCORERS, ONE TEAM, ONE SEASON:
 9 — New England Whalers, 1973-74. Tom Webster, 43; Mike Byers, 29; Tim Sheehy, 29; Larry Pleau, 26; John French, 24; Hugh Harris, 24; Tommy Williams, 21; Al Karlander, 20; Don Blackburn, 20.

MOST PENALTY MINUTES, ONE TEAM, ONE SEASON:
1477 Minutes — Los Angeles Sharks, 1972-73. (average of 18.9 minutes per game).

FEWEST PENALTY MINUTES, ONE TEAM, ONE SEASON:
671 Minutes — Winnipeg Jets, 1973-74. (average of 8.6 minutes per game).

MOST SHUTOUTS, ONE TEAM, ONE SEASON:
5 — Cleveland Crusaders, 1972-73. All by goaltender Gerry Cheevers.
5 — Minnesota Fighting Saints, 1972-73. Four by goaltender Mike Curran, one by goaltender Jack McCarten.
5 — Cleveland Crusaders, 1973-74. Four by goaltender Gerry Cheevers, one by goaltender Bob Whidden.

FEWEST SHUTOUTS, ONE TEAM, ONE SEASON:
0 — Ottawa National, 1972-73.

MOST SHUTOUTS AT HOME, ONE TEAM, ONE SEASON:
5 — Minnesota Fighting Saints, 1972-73. Four by goaltender Mike Curran, one by goaltender Jack McCarten.

FEWEST SHUTOUTS AT HOME, ONE TEAM, ONE SEASON:
0 — Ottawa Nationals, 1972-73.
0 — Houston Aeros, 1972-73.
0 — Philadelphia Blazers, 1972-73.
0 — New York Golden Blades-New Jersey Knights, 1973-74 (team moved to Cherry Hill New Jersey November 25, 1973).

MOST SHUTOUTS ON THE ROAD, ONE TEAM, ONE SEASON:
2 — Philadelphia Blazers, 1972-73. Both by goaltender Bernie Parent.
2 — Cleveland Crusaders, 1973-74. Both by goaltender Gerry Cheevers.
2 — Vancouver Blazers, 1973-74. Both by goaltender Peter Donnelly.

FEWEST SHUTOUTS ON THE ROAD, ONE TEAM, ONE SEASON:
0 — Minnesota Fighting Saints, 1972-73.
0 — Quebec Nordiques, 1972-73.
0 — New York Raiders, 1972-73.
0 — Chicago Cougars, 1972-73 and again in 1973-74.
0 — Ottawa Nationals, 1972-73.
0 — Alberta Oilers, 1972-73.

LONGEST SHUTOUT SEQUENCE BY A TEAM:
153 Minutes, 5 seconds — Cleveland Crusaders, from 10:24 of first period vs Philadelphia Blazers on Oct. 25, 1972 until 3:29 of the third period vs Quebec Nordiques on Oct. 29, 1972. Included a shutout of the Alberta Oilers Oct. 27.

MOST TIMES SHUTOUT, ONE TEAM, ONE SEASON:
8 — Los Angeles Sharks, 1973-74.

LEAST TIMES SHUTOUT, ONE TEAM, ONE SEASON:
0 — Minnesota Fighting Saints, 1973-74.
0 — Toronto Toros, 1973-74.

LONGEST TIME ONE TEAM WAS SHUTOUT:
169 Minutes, 39 Seconds — Chicago Cougars, from 12:44 of the third period in game vs Minnesota Fighting Saints on Jan. 5, 1974 until 12:23 of the second period of game vs Winnipeg on Jan. 13, 1974. Included two shutouts; by Quebec Nordiques, Jan. 6 and Cleveland Crusaders, Jan. 8

MOST TIMES SHUTOUT AT HOME, ONE TEAM, ONE SEASON:
5 — Los Angeles Sharks, 1973-74.

LEAST TIMES SHUTOUT AT HOME, ONE TEAM, ONE SEASON:
0 — Quebec Nordiques, 1972-73 and again in 1973-74.
0 — Ottawa Nationals, 1972-73 and again in 1973-74 as the Toronto Toros.
0 — Minnesota Fighting Saints, 1972-73 and again in 1973-74.
0 — Philadelphia Blazers, 1972-73.
0 — Winnipeg Jets, 1972-73.
0 — New England Whalers, 1972-73.
0 — Edmonton Oilers, 1973-74.
0 — Cleveland Crusaders, 1973-74.

MOST TIMES SHUTOUT ON THE ROAD, ONE TEAM, ONE SEASON:
6 — Philadelphia Blazers, 1972-73.

LEAST TIMES SHUTOUT ON THE ROAD, ONE TEAM, ONE SEASON:
0 — New York Raiders, 1972-73.
0 — Minnesota Fighting Saints, 1973-74.
0 — Houston Aeros, 1973-74.
0 — Toronto Toros, 1973-74.

SINGLE GAME RECORDS

MOST CONSECUTIVE GOALS, ONE TEAM, ONE GAME:
  10 — Houston Aeros, Dec. 19, 1973, at Houston. Defeated Winnipeg Jets, 10-0.
  10 — Minnesota Saints, Jan. 27, 1974, at St. Paul. Defeated Winnipeg Jets, 12-2.
  10 — Winnipeg Jets, March 17, 1974, at Winnipeg. Defeated New England, 10-1.

MOST GOALS, BOTH TEAMS, ONE GAME:
  16 — Philadelphia Blazers, New England Whalers, at Philadelphia, Dec. 16, 1972. Philadelphia was defeated by the Whalers, 10-6.
  16 — Toronto Toros, Vancouver Blazers, at Toronto, Jan. 27, 1974. Toronto defeated Vancouver, 9-7.
  16 — Jersey Knights, Toronto Toros, at Cherry Hill, New Jersey, March 18, 1974. Jersey defeated Toronto 11-5.

MOST GOALS, ONE TEAM, ONE GAME:
  12 — Minnesota Fighting Saints, Jan. 27, 1974, at St. Paul. Defeated Winnipeg, 12-2.

MOST GOALS, BOTH TEAMS, ONE PERIOD:
  9 — Philadelphia Blazers, New England Whalers, at Philadelphia, Dec. 16, 1972, third period. New England scored five goals, Philadelphia four. Whalers won, 10-6.
  9 — Ottawa Nationals, Quebec Nordiques, at Ottawa, Jan. 9, 1973, first period. Ottawa scored five goals, Quebec four. Nationals won, 7-5.
  9 — New England Whalers, Los Angeles Sharks, at Boston, Jan. 13, 1974, first period. New England scored five goals, Los Angeles four. Whalers won 9-6.
  9 — Winnipeg Jets, Houston Aeros, at Winnipeg, March 29, 1974, third period. Winnipeg scored six goals, Houston three. Jets defeated Aeros, 7-5.

MOST GOALS, ONE TEAM, ONE PERIOD:
  8 — Toronto Toros, Dec. 9, 1973, at Toronto. Toros defeated Minnesota 10-1 with eight goals in third period.

MOST POINTS, BOTH TEAMS, ONE GAME:
  45 — Toronto Toros, Vancouver Blazers, at Toronto, Jan. 27, 1974. Toronto had nine goals and 16 assists, the Blazers seven goals and 13 assists.

MOST POINTS, ONE TEAM, ONE GAME:
  34 — Minnesota Saints, January 27, 1974, at St. Paul. Defeated Winnipeg, 12-2.

MOST GOALS SCORED, TWO CONSECUTIVE GAMES, ONE TEAM:
  19 — Alberta Oilers defeated the New York Raiders 11-3 on Jan. 30, 1973 and again Feb. 1, 8-5.

MOST GOALS ALLOWED, TWO CONSECUTIVE GAMES, BY ONE TEAM:
  20 — New York Raiders were defeated by the Los Angeles Sharks 9-2 on Jan. 28, 1973 and the Alberta Oilers 11-3 on Jan. 30, 1973.

MOST GOALS SCORED, ONE TEAM, THREE CONSECUTIVE GAMES:
  24 — Vancouver Blazers defeated the Edmonton Oilers 8-0, Feb. 5, 1974; Quebec Nordiques 7-3 on Feb. 8, 1974; and New England Whalers 9-4 on Feb. 13.

MOST GOALS ALLOWED, ONE TEAM, THREE CONSECUTIVE GAMES:
  28 — New York Raiders were defeated by the Los Angeles Sharks 9-2 on Jan. 28, 1973 and by the Alberta Oilers by scores of 11-3 and 8-5 on Jan. 30 and Feb. 1.

MOST PENALTIES, BOTH TEAMS, ONE GAME:
  42 — Los Angeles Sharks, Quebec Nordiques, at Los Angeles, Jan. 15, 1974. Los Angeles received 11 minors, 5 majors, and 5 misconduct penalties. Quebec received 11 minors, 6 majors, 4 misconducts. Sharks won, 6-4.

MOST PENALTY MINUTES, BOTH TEAMS, ONE GAME:
  189 — Los Angeles Sharks, Quebec Nordiques, at Los Angeles, Jan. 15, 1974. Sharks received 11 minors, 5 majors, and 5 misconducts for a total of 97 Minutes. The Nordiques received 11 minors, 6 majors, and 4 misconduct penalties for a total of 92 Minutes. Sharks won, 6-4.

MOST PENALTIES, ONE TEAM, ONE GAME:
  21 — Quebec Nordiques, at Los Angeles, Jan. 15, 1974. Nordiques received 11 minors, 6 majors, and 4 misconducts.
  21 — Los Angeles Sharks, at Los Angeles, Jan. 15, 1974. Sharks received 11 minors, 5 majors, and 5 misconducts as they defeated Quebec, 6-4.

MOST PENALTY MINUTES, ONE TEAM, ONE GAME:
  97 — Los Angeles Sharks, at Los Angeles, Jan. 15, 1974. Sharks received 11 minors, 5 majors, and 5 misconducts.

85

MOST PENALTIES, BOTH TEAMS, ONE PERIOD: (and)
MOST PENALTY MINUTES, BOTH TEAMS, ONE PERIOD:
  25 Penalties, 143 Minutes — Los Angeles Sharks — Quebec at Los Angeles, Jan. 15, 1974. Sharks received 5 minors, 3 majors, and 5 misconducts for 75 minutes. Quebec received 4 minors, 4 majors and 4 misconducts for 68 minutes.

MOST PENALTIES, ONE TEAM, ONE PERIOD: (and)
MOST PENALTY MINUTES, ONE TEAM, ONE PERIOD:
  13 Penalties, 75 Penalty minutes — Los Angeles Sharks, Oct. 16, 1973, at Los Angeles, third period. Sharks received 5 minors, 3 majors and 5 misconducts as they were defeated by Toronto Toros, 3-0.
  13 Penalties, 75 Penalty minutes — Los Angeles Sharks, Jan. 15, 1974, at Los Angeles, first period. Sharks received 5 minors, 3 majors, and 5 misconducts in 6-4 defeat to Quebec.

FASTEST TWO GOALS FROM THE START OF GAME, BOTH TEAMS:
  52 Seconds — Winnipeg Jets, Minnesota Fighting Saints, at Winnipeg, Dec. 16, 1973. Scorers were Murry Heatley of Minnesota of 30 seconds, and Norm Beaudin of Winnipeg at 52 seconds. Minnesota Defeated Winnipeg, 3-2.

FASTEST TWO GOALS FROM THE START OF A GAME, ONE TEAM:
  28 Seconds — Minnesota Fighting Saints, at Cleveland, Feb. 17, 1973. Mike McMahon scored at 19 Seconds and George Morrison at 28 seconds. Minnesota won, 7-3.

FASTEST THREE GOALS FROM THE START OF A GAME, BOTH TEAMS:
  2 Minutes, 12 Seconds — Toronto Toros, Vancouver Blazers, Jan. 27, 1974, at Toronto. Mike Chernoff scored for Vancouver at 1:27; Wayne Dillon for Toronto at 1:58 and teammate Tom Simpson at 2:12. Toros won, 9-7.

FASTEST THREE GOALS FROM THE START OF GAME, ONE TEAM:
  2 Minutes, 45 Seconds — Edmonton Oilers, Oct. 14, 1973, at Edmonton. Jim Harrison scored at 13 seconds, Ron Climie at 35 seconds, and Ken Baird at 2:45. Oilers defeated Houston, 5-2.

FASTEST TWO GOALS FROM THE START OF A PERIOD OTHER THAN THE FIRST BY ONE TEAM:
  49 Seconds — Toronto Toros, Jan. 7, 1974, at Boston. Steve King scored at 22 seconds and Brit Selby at 49 seconds. Toronto defeated New England, 3-2.

FASTEST TWO GOALS, BOTH TEAMS:
  7 Seconds — Alberta Oilers, Minnesota Fight Saints, Dec. 1, 1972, at Edmonton. Billy Klatt scored for Minnesota at 13:22 and Bob McAneely for Alberta at 13:29. Minnesota won, 6-4.

FASTEST TWO GOALS, ONE TEAM:
  4 Seconds — New England Whalers, at Philadelphia, Dec. 16, 1972. Terry Caffery scored for the Whalers at 2:49 of the third period, Brit Selby at 2:53 as Whalers defeated Philadelphia, 10-6.

FASTEST THREE GOALS, BOTH TEAMS:
  27 Seconds — New York Raiders, New England Whalers, at New York, Nov. 29, 1972. John French scored for New England at 12:53 of the second period; Ron Ward for New York at 13:11 and 13:20. New York won, 7-6.

FASTEST THREE GOALS, ONE TEAM:
  32 Seconds — Chicago Cougars, Dec. 12, 1972, at Chicago. Poul Popiel scored at 18:46 of the third period, Bob Sicinski at 19:02 and Bob Liddington at 19:18 as Cougars defeated Cleveland, 6-1.

FASTEST FOUR GOALS, BOTH TEAMS:
  1 Minute, 3 Seconds — New York Raiders, New England Whalers, Nov. 29, 1972, at New York. John French scored for the Whalers at 12:53 of the second period; Ron Ward for the Raiders at 13:11 and again at 13:20; Tom Earl scored for the Whalers at 13:56. New York won, 7-6.

FASTEST FOUR GOALS, ONE TEAM:
  1 Minute, 15 Seconds — Alberta Oilers, Jan. 30, 1973, at Edmonton. Rusty Patenaude scored for Oilers at 10:48 of the third period; Doug Barrie at 11:48; Steve Carlyle at 12:00; and Jim Harrison at 12:33 as Alberta defeated New York, 11-3.

FASTEST FIVE GOALS, BOTH TEAMS:
  4 Minutes, 10 Seconds — New York Raiders, Cleveland Crusaders, Feb. 25, 1973, at New York. Norm Peacosh scored for Raiders at 3:59 of the third period; Wayne Rivers at 4:42 for the Raiders; Ron Buchanan at 6:01 and teammate Gerry Pinder at 6:34 for Cleveland; Wayne Rivers for New York at 8:09. Raiders won, 9-5.

FASTEST FIVE GOALS, ONE TEAM:
  4 Minutes, 48 Seconds — Alberta Oilers, Jan. 30, 1973, at Edmonton. Bernie

Blanchette scored for Oilers at 7:45, Rusty Patenaude at 10:48, Doug Barrie at 11:48, Steve Carlyle at 12:00, Jim Harrison at 12:33. Oilers 11-3 over New York.

MOST PROFICIENT POWER PLAY, ONE SEASON:
   28.7% — Houston Aeros, 1973-74 season. Aeros scored 64 power play goals in 223 power play opportunities.

MOST POWER PLAY OPPORTUNITIES, ONE SEASON:
   321 — Ottawa Nationals, 1972-73. Season. Nationals scored 59 power play goals for a proficiency of 18.3%.

MOST POWER PLAY OPPORTUNITIES, BOTH TEAMS, ONE GAME:
   20 — Houston Aeros, Vancouver Blazers, Feb. 26, 1974, at Houston. Both teams had 10 opportunities but only Vancouver scored a power play goal. However, the Aeros scored two goals while they were shorthanded and won, 3-2.

MOST POWER PLAY OPPORTUNITIES, ONE TEAM, ONE GAME:
   11 — Ottawa Nationals, Dec. 24, 1972, at Ottawa. The Nationals scored 1 power play goal in 6-2 victory over Quebec.
   11 — New York Raiders, Nov. 8, 1972, at Los Angeles. Raiders scored 1 power play goal in 2-1 defeat.
   11 — Minnesota Fighting Saints, Dec. 30, 1973, at St. Paul. Saints scored one power play goal in 5-3 loss to Chicago.

INDIVIDUAL RECORDS

MOST WHA SEASONS:
   2 — 275 players have played in both WHA seasons.

MOST GAMES, AND MOST CONSECUTIVE GAMES:
   176 — Rosaire Paiement, Chicago Cougars, 1972-73 through 1973-74.
   176 — Gary Veneruzzo, Los Angeles Sharks, 1972-73 through 0173-74.
   176 — Wayne Connelly, Minnesota Fighting Saints, 1972-73 through 1973-74.
   176 — Brian Bradley, New York Raiders — New York Golden Blades — New Jersey Knights, 1972-73 through 1973-74.
   176 — Gavin Kirk, Ottawa Nationals — Toronto Toros, 1972-73 through 1973-74.
   176 — Andre Lacroix, Philadelphia Blazers — New York Golden Blades — New Jersey Knights, 1972-73 through 1973-74.
   176 — Danny Lawson, Philadelphia Blazers — Vancouver Blazers, 1972-73 through 1973-74.
   176 — Jim Cardiff, Philadelphia Blazers — Vancouver Blazers, 1972-73 through 1973-74.
   176 — Andre Gaudette, Quebec Nordiques, 1972-73 through 1973-74.

MOST POINTS:
   235 — Andre Lacroix, Philadelphia Blazers — New York Golden Blades — New Jersey Knights, 176 games (81 goals, 154 assists).

MOST GOALS:
   111 — Danny Lawson, Philadelphia Blazers — Vancouver Blazers, 176 games.

MOST ASSISTS:
   154 — Andre Lacroix, Philadelphia Blazers — New York Golden Blades — New Jersey Knights, 176 games.

MOST PENALTY MINUTES:
   409 — John Schella, Houston Aeros, in two season, 150 games. (Avg. 2.73 Mins. per game).
   380 — John Arbour, Minnesota Fighting Saints, in two seasons, 153 games. (Avg. 2.48 Mins. per games).
   373 — Jim Cardiff, Philadelphia Blazers — Vancouver Blazers, in two seasons, 156 Games. (Avg. 2.39 Min's. per game).
   355 — Tom Gilmore, Los Angeles Sharks — Edmonton Oilers, in two seasons, 127 games. (Avg. 2.80 Min's per game).

MOST GAMES SCORING THREE OR MORE GOALS:
   9 — Danny Lawson, Philadelphia Blazers — Vancouver Blazers, in two seasons, six three-goal games, three four-goal games.
   8 — Bobby Hull, Winnipeg Jets, in two seasons, six three-goal games, two four-goal games.

MOST POINTS, ONE SEASON:
   124 — Andre Lacroix, Philadelphia Blazers, 1972-73, 78 games (50 goals, 74 assists).

87

MOST GOALS, ONE SEASON:
61 — Danny Lawson, Philadelphia Blazers, 1972-73, 78 games.

MOST ASSISTS, ONE SEASON:
80 — Andre Lacroix, New York Golden Blades — New Jersey Knights, 1973-74, 78 Games.

MOST POINTS, ONE SEASON, BY A DEFENSEMAN:
89 — J.C. Tremblay, Quebec Nordiques, 1972-73, 78 Games (14 goals, 75 assists).

MOST GOALS, ONE SEASON, BY A DEFENSEMAN:
24 — Kevin Morrison, New York Golden Blades — New Jersey Knights, 1973-74, 78 games (his rookie season).

MOST ASSISTS, ONE SEASON, BY A DEFENSEMAN:
75 — J.C. Tremblay, Quebec Nordiques, 1972-73, 78 games.

MOST POINTS, ONE SEASON, BY A CENTRE:
124 — Andre Lacroix, Philadelphia Blazers, 1972-73, 78 Games (50 goals, 74 assists).

MOST GOALS, ONE SEASON, BY A CENTRE:
51 — Ron Ward, New York Raiders, 1972-73, 78 games.

MOST ASSISTS, ONE SEASON, BY A CENTRE:
80 — Andre Lacroix, New York Golden Blades — New Jersey Knights, 1973-74, 78 games.

MOST POINTS, ONE SEASON, BY A RIGHT WINGER:
117 — Mike Walton, Minnesota Fighting Saints, 1973-74, 78 games (57 goals, 60 assists).

MOST GOALS, ONE SEASON, BY A RIGHT WINGER:
61 — Danny Lawson, Philadelphia Blazers, 1972-73, 78 games.

MOST ASSISTS, ONE SEASON, BY A RIGHT WINGER
69 — Gordie Howe, Houston Aeros, 1973-74, 78 games.

MOST POINTS, ONE SEASON, BY A LEFT WINGER:
103 — Bobby Hull, Winnipeg Jets, 1972-73, 78 games (51 goals, 52 assists).

MOST GOALS, ONE SEASON, BY A LEFT WINGER:
53 — Bobby Hull, Winnipeg Jets, 1973-74, 78 games.

MOST ASSISTS, ONE SEASON, BY A LEFT WINGER:
56 — Andre Hinse, Houston Aeros, 1973-74, 78 games (his rookie season).

MOST ASSISTS, ONE SEASON, BY A GOALTENDER:
4 — Gilles Gratton, Toronto Toros, 1973-74, Gratton played in 57 games.

MOST POINTS, ONE GAME:
10 — Jim Harrison, Alberta Oilers, Jan. 30, 1973, at Edmonton, 3 goals and 7 assists. The Oilers defeated the New York Raiders 11-3.

MOST GOALS, ONE GAME:
5 — Ron Ward, New York Raiders, Jan. 4, 1973, at New York where the Raiders defeated the Ottawa Nationals 9-4.
5 — Ron Climie, Edmonton Oilers, Nov. 6, 1973, at New York as the Oilers defeated the New York Golden Blades 8-0.

MOST ASSISTS, ONE GAME:
7 — Jim Harrison, Alberta Oilers, Jan. 30, 1973, at Edmonton. Alberta Oilers 11, New York Raiders 3.

MOST POINTS, ONE GAME, BY A DEFENSEMAN:
6 — Doug Barrie, Alberta Oilers, Jan. 30, 1973, at Edmonton. Alberta Oilers 11, New York Raiders 3.

MOST GOALS, ONE GAME, BY A DEFENSEMAN:
3 — Kevin Morrison, New Jersey Knights, March 18, 1974, at Cherry Hill, New Jersey, as the Knights defeated the Toronto Toros 11-5.

MOST ASSISTS, ONE GAME, BY A DEFENSEMAN:
5 — Doug Barrie, Alberta Oilers, Jan. 30, 1973, at Edmonton. Alberta Oilers 11, New York Raiders 3.

MOST POINTS, ONE GAME, BY A CENTRE:
10 — Jim Harrison, Alberta Oilers, Jan. 30, 1973, at Edmonton. Alberta Oilers 11, New York Raiders 3.

MOST GOALS, ONE GAME, BY A CENTRE:
5 — Ron Ward, New York Raiders, Jan. 4, 1973, at New York. New York Raiders 9, Ottawa Nationals 4.

MOST ASSISTS, ONE GAME, BY A CENTRE:
7 — Jim Harrison, Alberta Oilers, Jan. 30, 1973, at Edmonton. Alberta Oilers 11, New York Raiders 3.

MOST POINTS, ONE GAME, BY A RIGHT WINGER:
  7 — Danny Lawson, Philadelphia Blazers, Jan. 13, 1973, at Philadelphia. Blazers defeated Quebec, 9-4.

MOST GOALS, ONE GAME, BY A RIGHT WINGER:
  5 — Ron Climie, Edmonton Oilers, Nov. 6, 1973, at Edmonton. Oilers 8-0 over New York.

MOST ASSISTS, ONE GAME, BY A RIGHT WINGER:
  5 — Wayne Rivers, New York Raiders, jan. 4, 1973, at New York. New York Raiders 9, Ottawa 4.
  5 — Danny Lawson, Philadelphia Blazers, March 9, 1973, at Philadelphia. Blazers defeated Quebec, 11-3.
  5 — John McKenzie, Vancouver Blazers, Feb. 5, 1974, at Vancouver, in Blazer 8-0 win over Edmonton.
  5 — John French, New England Whalers, March 27, 1974, at Boston. Whalers lost to Los Angeles, 7-1.

MOST POINTS, ONE GAME, BY A LEFT WINGER:
  6 — Bobby Hull, Winnipeg Jets, Feb. 15, 1973, at Chicago in Winnipeg 7-2 win over Chicago.

MOST GOALS, ONE GAME, BY A LEFT WINGER:
  4 — Bobby Hull, Winnipeg Jets, Feb. 15, 1973, at Chicago. Winnipeg won, 7-2.
  4 — Bobby Hull, Winnipeg Jets, Nov. 4, 1973, at Winnipeg. Winnipeg 8, Quebec 2.
  4 — Gary Veneruzzo, Los Angeles Sharks, March 2, 1974, at Cherry Hill, New Jersey. New Jersey won, 8-7.
  4 — Marc Tardif, Los Angeles Sharks, March 24, 1974, at Los Angeles. Los Angeles 6, Winnipeg 3.
  4 — George Morrison, Minnesota Fighting Saints, April 3, 1974, at St. Paul. Minnesota 9, Vancouver 0.
  4 — Tom Gilmore, Edmonton Oilers, April 3, 1974, at Winnipeg. Gilmore scored in overtime to defeat Winnipeg, 6-5.

MOST ASSITS, ONE GAME, BY A LEFT WINGER:
  4 — Michel Parizeau, Quebec Nordiques, Dec. 31, 1972, at Quebec. Quebec Nordiques 8, Ottawa 4.
  4 — Bobby Hull, Winnipeg Jets, March 8, 1973, at Quebec. Winnipeg 7, Quebec 4.
  4 — Wayne Carleton, Toronto, Dec. 29, 1973, at St. Paul. Toros 9, Minnesota 3.
  4 — Don Herriman, Jersey Knights, Jan. 19, 1974, at Vancouver. Herriman assisted on overtime goal that defeated Vancouver, 5-4.

MOST POINTS, ONE PERIOD:
  5 — Jim Harrison, Alberta Oilers, Jan. 30, 1973, at Edmonton during the third period of Oiler 11-3 win over New York. (1 goal, 4 assists).
  5 — Doug Barrie, Alberta Oilers, Jan. 30, 1973, at Edmonton during the third period of Oiler 11-3 win over New York. (1 goal, 4 assists).

MOST GOALS, ONE PERIOD:
  4 — Ron Climie, Edmonton Oilers, Nov. 6, 1973, at Edmonton during third period of Oiler 8-0 shutout of New York.

MOST ASSISTS, ONE PERIOD:
  4 — Jim Harrison, Alberta Oilers, Jan. 30, 1973, at Edmonton during the third period of Oiler 11-3 win over New York.
  4 — Doug Barrie, Alberta Oilers, Jan. 30, 1973, at Edmonton during third period of Oiler 11-3 win over New York.

MOST PENALTY MINUTES, ONE SEASON:
  239 — John Schella, Houston, 1972-73.

MOST PENALTY MINUTES, ONE SEASON, BY A DEFENSEMAN:
  239 — John Schella, Houston, 1972-73.

MOST PENALTY MINUTES, ONE SEASON, BY A CENTRE:
  157 — Mike Rouleau, Quebec, 1972-73.

MOST PENALTY MINUTES, ONE SEASON, BY A RIGHT WINGER:
  157 — John McKenzie, Philadelphia, 1972-73.

MOST PENALTY MINUTES, ONE SEASON, BY A LEFT WINGER:
  223 — Gord Gallant, Minnesota, 1973-74, (rookie season).

MOST PENALTY MINUTES, ONE SEASON, BY A GOALTENDER:
  54 — Serge Aubry, Quebec, 1972-73, Aubry played in 52 games (rookie season).

MOST PENALTIES, ONE GAME:
  6 — Pierre Roy, Quebec Nordiques, Feb. 16, 1974, at Cleveland. Roy collected six minor penalties (also a WHA record). Cleveland defeated Quebec, 5-2.

- 6 — Pierre Roy, Quebec Nordiques, March 9, 1974, at St. Paul. Roy was called for five minors and a misconduct as Minnesota defeated Quebec, 9-5.
- 6 — Gord Gallant, Minnesota Fighting Saints, March 31, 1974, at Houston. Gallant collected two minors, three majors, and a game misconduct. Saints defeated Houston, 5-2.
- 6 — Derek Sanderson, Philadelphia Blazers, Oct. 24, 1972, at Winnipeg. Sanderson was assessed three minor penalties, two misconducts and a game misconduct as Blazers lost to Winnipeg, 5-3.
- 6 — Keke Mortson, Houston Aeros, Feb. 16, 1973, at Winnipeg. Mortson received three minors, a major, a misconduct, and a game misconduct. Winnipeg won, 7-0.
- 6 — Larry Hale, Houston Aeros, Feb. 25, 1973, at St. Paul. Hale was called for four minors, a major and a game misconduct. Houston over Minnesota, 4-1.

MOST PENALTY MINUTES, ONE GAME:
- 36 — Derek Sanderson, Philadelphia Blazers, Oct. 24, 1972, at Winnipeg. Sanderson was assessed three minors, two misconducts and a game misconduct. Blazers lost to Winnipeg, 5-3.

MOST PENALTIES, ONE PERIOD:
- 5 — John McKenzie, Philadelphia Blazers, Feb. 7, 1973, at Quebec, third period. McKenzie was called for two minors, a major, and two misconducts.
- 5 — Ted McCaskill, Los Angeles Sharks, Feb. 24, 1973, at Los Angeles, first period. McCaskill received two minors, a major, a misconduct and a game misconduct.
- 5 — Ted McCaskill, Los Angeles Sharks, Oct. 16, 1973, at Los Angeles, first period. McCaskill was assessed two minors, a major, a misconduct, a game misconduct.
- 5 — Ron Garwasiuk, Los Angeles Sharks, Jan. 15, 1974, at Los Angeles, first period. He was called for two minors, a major, a misconduct, and a game misconduct.

MOST MINOR PENALTIES, ONE PERIOD:
- 4 — Pierre Roy, Quebec Nordiques, Feb. 16, 1974, at Cleveland, third period.

MOST PENALTY MINUTES, ONE PERIOD:
- 30 — Doug Barrie, Edmonton Oilers, Feb. 13, 1974, at St. Paul, third period. Barrie received two majors and two misconducts.

MOST POWER PLAY GOALS, ONE SEASON:
- 20 — Danny Lawson, Philadelphia Blazers, 1972-73.

MOST SHORTHANDED GOALS, ONE SEASON:
- 9 — Mike Walton, Minnesota Fighting Saints, 1973-74.

LONGEST CONSECUTIVE POINT-SCORING STREAK:
- 16 Games — Terry Caffery, New England Whalers, Dec. 7, 1972 through Jan. 13, 1973. Caffery collected 31 points during his streak (12 goals, 19 assists).
- 16 Games — Mike Walton, Minnesota Fighting Saints, Feb. 5, 1974 through March 10, 1974. Walton collected 43 points (26 goals, 17 assists).

LONGEST CONSECUTIVE GOAL-SCORING STREAK:
- 9 Games — Danny Lawson, Vancouver Blazers, Dec. 26, 1973 through Jan. 17, 1974. Lawson collected 14 goals.

LONGEST CONSECUTIVE ASSIST-SCORING STREAK:
- 12 Games — Terry Caffery, New England Whalers, Dec. 11, 1972 through Dec. 31, 1972. Caffery collected 18 assists.

FASTEST GOAL FROM THE START OF A GAME:
- 10 seconds — Rick Morris, Chicago Cougars, Dec. 9, 1972, at Chicago. Morris scored at the 10-second mark of the first period against Quebec goaltender Jacques Lemelin. Quebec won, 4-2.

FASTEST TWO GOALS FROM THE START OF A GAME:
- 2 minutes, 27 seconds — Ross Perkins, Alberta Oilers, Nov. 24, 1972, at Boston. Perkins scored at 1:10 again at 2:27 of the first period. New England won, 7-2.

FASTEST THREE GOALS FROM THE START OF A GAME:
- 5 minutes, 8 seconds — Jim Wiste, Cleveland Crusaders, Feb. 16, 1974, at Cleveland. Wiste scored at 0:20, 4:51 and 5:03 of the first period. Crusaders 5, Quebec 2.

FASTEST GOAL FROM START OF A PERIOD (other than the first):
- 7 seconds — Wayne Connelly, Minnesota Fighting Saints, third period, Nov. 30, 1972, at New York. New York Raiders 5, Minnesota 2.
- 7 — Brian Bradley, Jersey Knights, second period, Dec. 23, 1973, at Cherry Hill. Jersey Knights 6, Winnipeg 3.
- 7 — Jim Wiste, Cleveland Crusaders, second period, Dec. 29, 1973, at Cleveland. Cleveland 3, Jersey Knights 0.

FASTEST TWO GOALS:
- 6 seconds — Gary Veneruzzo, Los Angeles Sharks, Dec. 10, 1972, third period at Los Angeles. Veneruzzo scored at 15:24 and 15:30. Sharks 5-3 over Alberta.

FASTEST THREE GOALS:
   43 seconds — George Morrison, Minnesota Fighting Saints, April 3, 1974. Morrison scored at 15:42, 15:56 and 16:25 of the second period. Saints 9, Vancouver 0.

FASTEST FOUR GOALS:
   12 minutes, 11 seconds — Ron Climie, Edmonton Oilers, Nov. 6, 1973, at Edmonton. Climie scored at 3:28, 4:01, 7:01 and 15:39 of the third period. Edmonton 8, New York 0.

FASTEST FIVE GOALS:
   25 minutes, 55 seconds — Ron Ward, New York Raiders, Jan. 4, 1973, at New York. Ward scored at 18:41 and 19:16 of the first period, 13:46, and 19:01 of the second period, and 4:34 of the third period. New York 9-4 over Ottawa.

MOST GAMES APPEARED IN BY A GOALTENDER, WHA CAREER:
   117 games — Jack Norris, Alberta and Edmonton Oilers, 1972-73 through 1973-74.
   111 games — Gerry Cheevers, Cleveland Crusaders, 1972-73 through 1973-74.
   108 games — Gilles Gratton, Ottawa Nationals-Toronto Toros, 1972-73 through 1973-74.
   106 games — Al Smith, New England Whalers, 1972-73 through 1973-74.

MOST SHUTOUTS, WHA CAREER:
   9 — Gerry Cheevers, Cleveland Crusaders, 2 seasons.
   6 — Mike Curran, Minnesota Fighting Saints, 2 season.
   5 — Al Smith, New England Whalers, 2 seasons.
   5 — Ernie Wakely, Winnipeg Jets, 2 seasons.

MOST SHUTOUTS, ONE SEASON:
   5 — Gerry Cheevers, Cleveland Crusaders, 1972-73.
   4 — Gerry Cheevers, Cleveland Crusaders, 1973-74.
   4 — Mike Curran, Minnesota Fighting Saints, 1972-73.

LONGEST SHUTOUT SEQUENCE BY A GOALTENDER:
   157 minutes, 37 seconds — Ernie Wakely, Winnipeg Jets, from 13:42 of the first period, Dec. 9, 1973 against Jersey Knights until 11:19 of the third period, Dec. 18, against Chicago. Streak included a shutout of Los Angeles Dec. 14, 1973.

MOST POINTS, ONE SEASON, BY A ROOKIE:
   100 — Terry Caffery, New England Whalers, 1972-73 (39 goals, 61 assists).
   88 — Bobby Sicinski, Chicago Cougars, 1972-73 (25 goals, 63 assists).
   81 — Ron Buchanan, Cleveland Crusaders, 1972-73 (37 goals, 44 assists).
   80 — Andre Hinse, Houston Aeros, 1973-74 (24 goals, 56 assists).
   79 — Mark Howe, Houston Aeros, 1973-74 (38 goals, 41 assists).

MOST GOALS, ONE SEASON, BY A ROOKIE:
   39 — Terry Caffery, New England Whalers, 1972-73.
   38 — Mark Howe, Houston Aeros, 1973-74.
   38 — Claude St. Sauveur, Vancouver Blazers, 1973-74.
   37 — Ron Buchanan, Cleveland Crusaders, 1972-73.
   36 — Billy Klatt, Minnesota Fighting Saints, 1972-73.

MOST ASSISTS, ONE SEASON, BY A ROOKIE:
   63 — Bobby Sicinski, Chicago Cougars, 1972-73.
   61 — Terry Caffery, New England Whalers, 1972-73.
   56 — Andre Hinse, Houston Aeros, 1973-74.
   53 — Ken Block, New York Raiders, 1972-73.

MOST PENALTY MINUTES, ONE SEASON, BY A ROOKIE:
   223 — Gordon Gallant, Minnesota Fighting Saints, 1973-74.
   191 — Tom Gilmore, Los Angeles Sharks, 1972-73.
   191 — Colin Campbell, Vancouver Blazers, 1973-74.
   185 — Jim Cardiff, Philadelphia Blazers, 1972-73.
   167 — Pierre Roy, Quebec Nordiques, 1972-73.
   159 — Hal Willis, New York Raiders, 1972-73.
   157 — Mike Rouleau, Quebec Nordiques, 1972-73.

FASTEST GOAL BY A ROOKIE:
   1 minute, 52 seconds — Larry Lund, Houston Aeros, scored his first WHA goal at 1:52 of the first period in his first WHA game, Oct. 12, 1972. Houston defeated Chicago, 3-2.

MOST GOALS, ONE GAME, BY A ROOKIE:
   4 — Pat Hickey, Toronto Toros, Dec. 9, 1973, at Toronto. Hickey scored all of his goals against Minnesota rookie goaltender John Garrett. Toros defeated Minnesota, 10-1.
   4 — Wayne Dillon, Toronto Toros, March 21, 1974, at Toronto. Dillon scored all of his goals against Houston goaltender Wayne Rutledge. Toros won, 6-3.

WHA TRAVELOG

Approximate Air Mileage

		Chicago	Cleveland	Indianapolis	New England	Houston	Michigan	Minnesota	Phoenix	San Diego	Edmonton	Quebec	Toronto	Vancouver	Winnipeg
EAST DIVISION	Chicago		312	167	777	932	238	344	1445	1729	1646	893	430	1850	744
	Cleveland	312		266	471	1104	94	624	1742	2031	1754	656	187	2150	1017
	Indianapolis	167	266		728	854	241	503	1489	1783	1741	924	431	2024	906
	New England	777	471	728		1512	540	1050	2213	2502	2044	430	373	2313	1510
	Houston	932	1104	854	1512		1095	1046	1015	1308	1864	1746	1299	2044	1469
WEST DIVISION	Michigan	238	94	241	540	1095		534	1681	1966	2102	677	206	2046	913
	Minnesota	344	624	503	1050	1046	534		1276	1532	1252	1227	780	1527	394
	Phoenix	1445	1742	1489	2213	1015	1681	1276		304	1962	2338	1878	1459	1679
	San Diego	1729	2031	1783	2502	1308	1966	1532	304		1694	2622	2179	1191	1873
CANADIAN DIVISION	Edmonton	1646	1754	1741	2044	1864	2102	1252	1962	1694		2016	1671	503	835
	Quebec	893	656	924	430	1746	677	1227	2338	2622	2016		462	2435	1277
	Toronto	430	187	431	373	1299	206	780	1878	2179	1671	462		2078	934
	Vancouver	1850	2150	2024	2313	2044	2046	1527	1459	1191	503	2435	2078		1164
	Winnipeg	744	1017	906	1510	1469	913	394	1679	1873	835	1277	934	1164	

WORLD HOCKEY KEY

WHA history

CHRONOLOGY

JANUARY, 1971
Dennis Murphy, co-founder with Gary L. Davidson of the American Basketball Association in 1968, conceives the idea for another major hockey league.

APRIL, 1971
The Basketball season over, Murphy returns to California from Miami where he is general manager of the ABA Floridians and plans for the WHA are drawn with Davidson.

JUNE, 1971
Articles of incorporation are filed in Delaware on June 10 for the World Hockey Association. Murphy meets with Jim Smith of Dayton, Ohio and Walt Marlow of the Los Angeles Herald-Examiner.

JULY, 1971
By-laws for the WHA are approved by the first Board of Trustees. Signatures on the document are Gary L. Davidson, Donald J. Regan and Dennis A. Murphy. Marlow advises W.D. (Bill) Hunter of Edmonton on the format of the new league, and in late July Hunter meets with Murphy for exploratory talks involving Canadian participation.

SEPTEMBER, 1971
First formal meeting of the WHA is held Sept. 23-24 at the Century Plaza in Los Angeles, whre interested ownership groups discuss the organization program.

OCTOBER, 1971
Revolutionary announcement is made in Chicago on Oct. 20 that WHA player contracts WILL NOT contain a reserve clause and/or option clause.

NOVEMBER, 1971
The World Hockey Association, following two days of meetings at the Americana Hotel in New York, is formally organized on Nov. 1 with 10 franchises. The cities are Calgary, Chicago, Dayton, Edmonton, Los Angeles, Miami, New York, St. Paul, San Francisco and Winnipeg. Two additional franchises are granted Nov. 21 following a meeting in Tampa, Fla. to groups representing Ontario and New England.

DECEMBER, 1971
The incredibility of a second major league has seized the imagination of the hockey fraternity throughout the world. J. Edward Fitkin, associated with the National Hockey League for 30 years, is named general manager of the San Francisco franchise.

JANUARY, 1972
Dennis Murphy, dividing his time between the league office and establishment of the Los Angeles franchise, on Jan. 7 announces the appointment of Terrence Slater as coach of the Sharks. A few days later, two of North America's foremost college coaches, Jack Kelley of Boston University and Glen Sonmor of the University of Minnesota, join the New England Whalers and Minnesota Fighting Saints respectively in the dual roles of general manager-coach. Vern Buffey, veteran National Hockey League official, accepts the post of referee-in-chief of the WHA. Richard I. (Dick) Wood and Seymour E. (Sy) Siegel, Trenton, New Jersey law partners, purchase the franchise rights for New York.

FEBRUARY, 1972
A group of Quebec City businessmen, led by Paul Racine, purchase the San Francisco franchise on the eve of the league's first historic player draft Feb. 12-13 in Anaheim, Calif. Fitkin becomes an official member of the league staff, presiding with Bill Hunter and Buffey over the draft which involved the selection of 1,081 amateurs and professionals. First player signed to WHA contract was Steve Sutherland, by Gary Morrell of the Los Angeles Sharks in a Port Huron, Mich. motel room. First player of super star status to sign was Bernie Parent with the Miami franchise following negotiations with Lester Patrick, grandson of one of the NHL's founding fathers. The New England franchise, headed by Howard Baldwin, settled in Boston and the Ontario group, organized by Doug Michel, took up residence in Ottawa.

MARCH, 1972
Paul Deneau, owner of the Dayton Ohio franchise, transfers to Houston and Jim Smith is named president and general manager of the Aeros. U.S. Olympic goaltender Mike Curran, one of 20 American-born players to ultimately dot WHA rosters, signs with Minnesota. A group of businessmen from suburban Oak Brook acquire the Chicago franchise. Fitkin is named assistant to President.

APRIL, 1972
Ten teams post $100,000 performance bonds at Continental Plaza Hotel in Chicago on April 14. Two teams, Calgary and Miami, are notified their franchises are in default and are given two weeks grace. On April 28, President Davidson cancels the franchises of Miami and Calgary.

MAY, 1972
James W. Browitt, sports administrator who formerly served as executive director of Freedom Hall in Louisville, accepts the post of league administrator and executive vice-president, succeeding Dennis Murphy who left the leauge office to devote all of his attention to the organization of the Los Angeles Sharks. New York Raiders sign lease with Madison Square Garden.

JUNE, 1972
James L. Cooper and Bernard A. Brown, a pair of New Jersey businessmen, obtain the 11th WHA franchise — name it the Blazers, and take over Parent's contract with Miami. Nick J. Mileti, a major league owner in baseball and basketball, is granted the WHA's 12th franchise for Cleveland. Jordon and Walter Kaiser, Chicago real estate developers, take over controlling interest in the Chicago franchise. John McKenzie is signed as player-coach of the Blazers. Then came the historic signing of Robert Marvin Hull by Ben Hatskin, owner of the Winnipeg Jets, on June 27. Hull received $1 million from WHA Properties and $1.75 million from the Jets, the contract extending over 10 years.

JULY, 1972
With the acquisition of Hull, player signings became increasingly active. Twenty-eight are signed within the period of a week, among them J.C. Tremblay with the Quebec Nordiques, Gerry Cheevers with the Cleveland Crusaders, Bobby Sheehan with New York and Ted Green with New England.

AUGUST, 1972
More than 300 players are now under contract, with the latest Derek Sanderson who agrees to 10-year pact with Philadelphia amounting to $2,325 million. Fitkin releases 78-game schedule.

SEPTEMBER, 1972
WHA teams begin training camp, with Philadelphia leading the way on Sept. 10. Rookie squads participate in first WHA action ever on Sept. 23.

OCTOBER, 1972
Professional contract players report to camp Oct. 1. League office announces experimental program for usage of a colored puck. Red and blue are tried, but player protests result in return to conventional black. Shoot-out tie breaker following overtime period is also used in exhibition games, but is viewed with mixed emotions among players and coaches. Season opens Oct. 11 with Quebec at Cleveland and Edmonton at Ottawa. Edmonton's Ron Anderson scores first WHA regular-season goal. Court order kept Bobby Hull inactive.

NOVEMBER, 1972
Hull, after missing 14 games, is cleared for action following landmark ruling of Judge A. Leon Higginbotham, U.S. District Court for the Eastern Section of Pennsylvania. Decision rendered Nov. 8. The same night, Hull made official WHA debut in Quebec and assisted on winning goal as Jets edged Nordiques, 3-2.

DECEMBER, 1972
Scheduled exhibition series matching WHA all-star team against Czechoslovakia was postponed when Czechs were unable to obtain sanction for the series from the Canadian Amateur Hockey Association.

JANUARY, 1973
League's first all-star game in Quebec City Jan. 6 captured by East, 6-2, before a snow-bound crowd of 5,435. Game was locally televised. WHA Players' Association officially formed during All-Star break, with attorney Curt Leichner of Portland appointed general counsel. Opening of St. Paul Civic Arena attracts crowd of 11,701 New Year's Night. First CBS televised game, also in St. Paul, attracted crowd of 13,426 Jan. 7. Doug Harvey, 48, a 17-year star in the NHL, joins the Houston Aeros as assistant coach. Derek Sanderson, signed by the Blazers Aug. 4, is unsigned Jan. 17 and ultimately returns to the Boston Bruins of the NHL.

FEBRUARY, 1973

Active only since Nov. 8, Bobby Hull finally cracks the WHA's top 10 scorers Feb. 19, rolling up 17 points in six games for a seasonal total of 74 and eighth place in the scoring derby. His goal output for 47 games was 38. Danny Lawson reached the 50-goal plateau Feb. 22 in Ottawa.

MARCH, 1973

On a rainy Sunday in Los Angeles (March 11) 12,804 people showed up at the Sports Arena for an 11 a.m. face-off between the Sharks and Ottawa Nationals. Cleveland owner Nick Mileti breaks ground March 16 for an $18 million arena on a 100-acre site in Richfield Township.

APRIL, 1973

New England (East) and Winnipeg (West) emerge divisional champions. Ottawa Nationals, following a rental contract dispute with the Ottawa Civic Center, move their playoff games to Maple Leaf Gardens in Toronto. Representatives of WHA and NHL meet secretly in New York (ex-officio) to discuss possible merger. WHA rejects merger proposals and will continue to operate independently. Goaltender Bernie Parent, after working the opening playoff game April 4, deserts the Philadelphia Blazers, who bow out in four straight defeats to Cleveland. Edmonton Oilers and Minnesota Fighting Saints, who finished in tie for fourth place in West, engaged in playoff April 4 on neutral ice (Calgary) with Saints winning, 4-2, before crowd of 6,400.

MAY, 1973

New England Whalers captured the World Trophy, besting Winnipeg Jets in series final, four games to one. New York franchise acquires new ownership, consisting of 14-man group. Team name is changed to Golden Blades. Ottawa Nationals are officially moved to Toronto with new ownership, Can Sports Ltd., a group of Toronto businessmen headed by John F. Bassett Jr., and Craig Eaton III. Team name changed to Toros. Philadelphia franchise sold to Canadian industrialist Jim Pattison, and relocated in Vancouver. Cincinnati group, headed by Brian Heekin III and William O. Dewitt Jr., granted franchise May 6 for the 1974-75 season.

JUNE, 1973

Gordie Howe, owner of more records than any man in history of hockey, ends 21 months of retirement and signs with the Houston Aeros. Sons Marty, 19, and Mark, 18, also sign with Aeros, marking first time in history of major league sport that father plays alongside two sons.

JULY, 1973

Pat Stapleton signs as playing-coach of the Chicago Cougars. Brian Shaw, one of Canada's premier junior coaches, named coach of Edmonton Oilers.

SEPTEMBER, 1973

League membership increased to 15 teams with the awarding of franchises to Indianapolis (Dick Tinkham and John Weissert) and Phoenix Roadrunners of Western League, headed by Jim Wells. Appointment of Walt Marlow as director of public relations announced. Legendary Gordie Howe, ending two years of retirement, made first professional appearance with sons Marty and Mark in New York exhibition game against New England Whalers. He scored 21 seconds into game with assist to son Mark.

OCTOBER, 1973

Franchise of New York Golden Blades is dissolved Oct. 18 and players become property of the league when WHA guarantees payroll. Gary Davidson, seized with outside interests, resigns WHA presidency Oct. 29 at board of trustees meeting in Chicago. A five-man committee, consisting of Davidson, Nick Mileti, Howard Baldwin, Tif Trimble and John Bassett, Jr., delegated to screen potential successor candidates.

NOVEMBER, 1973

Players of New York team are relocated in Cherry Hill, New Jersey Nov. 20 to form league-owned franchise. Team is named Jersey Knights. Dennis A. Murphy, who 34 months prior ignited the fuse that launched the WHA, resigns as president and general manager of Los Angeles Sharks to accept WHA presidency on interim basis Nov. 23. First goal involving entire Howe family Nov. 18 in Quebec, Mark scoring on assists from father, Gordie, and brother, Marty.

JANUARY, 1974

Purchase of Jersey franchise is announced Jan. 3 by Joseph Schwartz, Baltimore real estate developer. All-Star game in St. Paul on night of Jan. 3 attracts crowd of 13,196 as

East again defeats Wests 8-4. Howe scores 800th career goal Jan. 17 in Vancouver. Later in same game, son Mark got his 20th, with assist to Papa.

FEBRUARY, 1974

The 57-year-old National Hockey League and the two-year-old World Hockey Association settled $50 million case out of court Feb. 19 when both leagues signed agreement before U.S. District Judge A. Leon Higginbotham in Philadelphia. "Elimination of what was a perpetual reserve clause, without having to go to trial, represents a total victory for the WHA," Murphy said. Under the agreement, the WHA will be reimbursed by the NHL for legal expenses of $1.7 million. The decree also noted that on or before Jan. 1, 1975, committees of owners from both leagues would negotiate in good faith for scheduling of exhibition or interleague games, including an all-star game. New England Whalers announced Feb. 23 that team would move to Hartford, Ct., for the 1974-75 season.

MARCH, 1974

President Dennis Murphy, along with Attorney General Louis J. Lefkowitz of New York, announces March 20 that plans to refund season ticket purchasers of defunct New York Golden Blades Hockey Club have been completed. Murphy, on March 29, announces in Winnipeg that WHA and Canadian Amateur Hockey Association have reached agreement on signing of Canadian juniors.

APRIL, 1974

Charles Nolton and Peter Shagena, Detroit industrialists, announce transfer of Los Angeles Sharks franchise to Michigan on April 11. Biggest crowd in WHA's brief history, 17,211, established in St. Paul April 28 for fourth game of Houston-Minnesota semi-final series. Team Canada announces in Toronto April 29 that WHA will provide players for eight game series with Soviet Union in fall. Winnipeg's Ben Hatskin and Toronto's John Bassett, Jr. are WHA official representatives to Team Canada. Edmonton's Bill Hunter named manager and Toronto's Billy Harris is coach. Joseph Schwartz, owner of Jersey Knights, and President Dennis Murphy announce transfer of Knight's to San Diego April 30.

MAY, 1974

Houston Aeros capture Avco World Trophy in 14 games, losing only two to Minnesota while sweeping four straight from Winnipeg and Chicago. WHA expansion and amateur draft held in Toronto May 30-31. Junior draft results in 209 selections, of which more than 40 were to later sign.

JUNE, 1974

Norman R. "Bud" Poile, active in professional hockey since 1942 as player, coach and top level executive, is named vice-president in charge of hockey operations at board of trustees meeting June 6 at LaCosta, Calif. Highlight of three-day meetings was re-alignment of WHA clubs into three divisions, consisting of Canadian, West and East. "Wild Card" team playoff format adopted. Expansion teams Phoenix and Indianapolis placed in West and East divisions respectively. Cincinnati to become fifth Eastern Division club on entering league actively for 1975-76 season when new Riverfront Coliseum construction finalized. Toronto Toros announce signing of Frank Mahovlich June 19, marking third major super star to join league in as many years.

SEPTEMBER, 1974

WHA Team Canada reports to training camp in Edmonton for eight game series with Soviet Union. Selected players are: Gerry Cheevers, Don McLeod, Gilles Gratton (goal); Pat Stapleton, Paul Shmyr, J.C. Tremblay, Allan Hamilton, Brad Selwood, Rick Ley, Marty Howe, Pat Price, Rick Smith (defense); Gordie Howe, Bruce MacGregor, Tom Webster, Rejean Houle, John McKenzie (right wings); Ralph Backstrom, Andre Lacroix, Jim Harrison, Serge Bernier, Mike Walton (centers); Bobby Hull, Mark Howe, Frank Mahovlich, Paul Henderson, Marc Tardif (left wings). In first WHA game ever with National League team, Houston Aeros defeated St. Louis Blues, 5-3, Sept. 26, in Houston as rookie Don Larway scored two goals.   © 2018 WHA HOF / PCMP LLC

officials

WHA OFFICIALS

Chief Supervisor .... VERN BUFFEY
Supervisor .... BOB FRAMPTON

LEAGUE REFEREES

1. BILL FRIDAY
2. BOB SLOAN
3. RON EGO
4. BRENT CASSELMAN
6. WAYNE MUNDEY
9. BOB KOLARI
10. RON HARRIS
11. ALAN GLASPELL
12. RON ASSELSTINE

LINESMEN

18. Ron Asselstine
19. Wayne Mundey
20. Alan Glaspell
21. Pierre Belanger
22. Gene Kusy
23. Mike Entwistle
24. Ross Keenan
25. Eric Manship
26. Graham Hern
27. Dennis Dahlmann
28. Wayne Bonney
29. Joey Dame
30. Ron Foyt
31. Max Hansen
32. Tom Shamshak
33. Tom Marek
34. Glen Sherwood
36. Ken Pierce
38. Kevin Weatherby
40. Michel Chartre
42. Ron Rishagen
43. Michel Chee
44. Gord Kerr
46. Daryl Havrelock
47. Ron Renneberg
48. Paul Corcoran
56. Dick Haigh

MINOR OFFICIALS

CHICAGO — Bill Rice (supervisor); Dick Bregnezer (scorekeeper); Bob Friedlander (statistician); Vince Hylka, Dean Summers (goal judges); Frank Carriveau (timekeeper); Ralph Esposito, Bill Marsh (penalty timekeepers); Tony Shymanik (assistant scorekeeper); John Marine (assistant statistician).

CLEVELAND — Earl Miller (supervisor and timekeeper); Fred Hyer (scorekeeper); Ed Hogan, Ken Goss, Roger Hayda, Gary Nickerson (statisticians); Phil Simon, Howard Schleimer (goal judges); John Balunek (penalty timekeeper); Tim Katrinak, Ray Liskay (spares).

EDMONTON — Dick Carew (scorekeeper); Merv MacDonald (statistician); Ted McPhee, John Hess (goal judges); Bob Walker (timekeeper); Sandy Miller (assistant statistician); Gary Hill (spare).

HOUSTON — Dutch Keen (scorekeeper); Charles Toland (statistician); Joe Long (timekeeper); Ron Ellis (penalty timekeeper) Joe Chiswell, Leighton Young, Jr. (goal judges).

INDIANAPOLIS — Paul Minott (supervisor and scorekeeper); Don Lawless (statistician); Dale Hummel (timekeeper); Dennis Pope (penalty timekeeper); Lee Hummel, Bill Fuller, Tom Berry (goal judges); Bob Frazer, Bob Irwin, Ray Lord (spares).

MICHIGAN	Bob Love (scorekeeper); Morris Moorawniak (statistician); Larry Evo (timekeeper); Douglas J. Maskin (penalty timekeeper); Pat Kozlowski, Kurt Schneider, Tom Iszard (goal judges); Larry Pellicioni, Dick Polovich (assistant scorekeepers); Mel Hoberman (spare).
MINNESOTA	Ron Vannelli (supervisor); Arnie Bauer (scorekeeper); Jack Kelly (statistician); Joe Borsch (timekeeper); Jim Killen (penalty timekeeper); Al Maki, Bill McClellan, John Jundt, Rod Smith (goal judges); Paul Bauer (assistant scorekeeper); Ted Olson (assistant penalty timekeeper), Gene Gibbons, Dan Gibbons, Ted Greschner, Bud McGowen, Roger Pietrus, Bernie Colaizy, Randy Tollefson, Joe Fischler (spares).
NEW ENGLAND	Bill Henderson (supervisor); Bob Guarente (scorekeeper); Howard Holcomb (statistician); Dennis Cronin (timekeeper); Jim MacDonald (penalty timekeeper); Ray Cote, Bill Perry (goal judges); Bob Kaminski (penalty box); J.R. Chemalier (spare).
PHOENIX	Frank P. Austin (supervisor); John Moritz (scorekeeper); Frank Doyle, Ralph Henderson (penalty timekeepers); Arthur Cliff, Jack Flett, Herb Revans (goal judges); Joe Parks (assistant scorekeeper); James Winkle, Newton Bayless, Dick Corbo, Hal Wallace, Ron Sutherland (spares).
QUEBEC	Raymond Puchol (scorekeeper); Robert Marier (timekeeper); Claude Legare (penalty timekeeper); Adrien Cloutier, Gilles Poulin, James Cornell, Gaston Filion (goal judges); Adelard Poulin (away scores); Jean Cote (spare).
SAN DIEGO	Doug Zink (supervisor and timekeeper); Bill Brown (scorekeeper); Harry Lockwood (statistician); Manny Gomes (penalty timekeeper); Jim Koshley, Paul Kanegaly (goal judge); Jerry Davis, Al Krieger (penalty box); Sandy Fitzpatrick, Dick Klem, Bob Hughes (assistant scorekeepers and statisticians).
TORONTO	Bruce Cameron (supervisor and scorekeeper); Jim Murchie (statistician); Connie Mandala (timekeeper); Bill Fry (penalty timekeeper); Gary Gordon, Pat Murphy (goal judges); Lorne Fellman (spare).
VANCOUVER	Cal Pilkey (supervisor); Ken Stein (scorekeeper); William Swan (statistician); L. Shevon (timekeeper); G. Hartley (penalty timekeeper); Jim McGowan, Sid McGowan (goal judges); Trevor Hull, Ed Starick (spares).
WINNIPEG	R.W. Bell (supervisor); Dave Oakley (scorekeeper); R.M. Sanregret (assistant supervisor and statistician); Bob Mick (timekeeper); Dick Heaver (penalty timekeeper); James Witty, James Mier (goal judges); Ted Barton (public address announcer); G.R. Smith (assistant statistician); A.R. MacGilivray (assistant scorekeeper); R.K. Elson (assistant timekeeper); J. Schabler (spare).

rules

The Exciting Difference

Hockey, it has been said, is a game combining all the elements — grace, speed, emotion, violence.

The purists said there just wasn't any room for improvement. But that was before the WHA came along.

World Hockey's rulebook, for the most part, duplicates that of any other professional league. There have been, however, several innovations that give the WHA a distinctive flavor.

Take, for example, the WHA's overtime format.

Over two seasons, there have been 123 overtime games, with 81 decisions rendered as against a mere 42 ties. (See Page 69).

Beyond overtime and its attendant drama, other areas where WHA rules differ from other professional leagues are in ICING THE PUCK, OFFSIDE PASSES, CURVATURE OF THE STICK, and the THIRD MAN RULE.

THE ICING RULE

There is no shooting the puck down the ice with abandon by the shorthanded team. Icing is called and a resultant faceoff in the defending zone when the puck is cleared from inside the blueline the length of the rink — regardless of the manpower disadvantage. It has transformed penalty-killing into an art.

OFFSIDE PASS

In other leagues, a completed forward pass that crosses two lines is ruled offside unless the 'receiver' was in the same area of the ice as the 'passer' when the pass was made. In the WHA, a player may pass the puck from inside his own blueline to a teammate beyond the center red line, providing the puck precedes the player across the center red line and the receiver takes the puck ahead of his body. The rule is designed to bring about more quick breaks, but at the same time preventing a player from floating beyond the red line awaiting a breakaway pass.

STICK CURVATURE

The National League restricts the curvature of the stick blade to half an inch, mainly for the reason that goaltenders complain that curved blades represent an unfair advantage for the shooter adept at making the puck do tricks. The WHA has an allowable curvature of an inch and a quarter, resulting in more difficult shots for the goaltenders.

THIRD MAN RULE

The WHA's third man in a fight rule is somewhat more lax than in other leagues, where the man receives an automatic game misconduct penalty. In the WHA, he is given a 10-minute misconduct and assessed a $100 fine. If he violates the third-man-in rule a second time during a game, however, he has earned a game misconduct. The WHA rule was implemented to prevent bench-emptying brawls.

CHICAGO COUGARS

MICHAEL HAGGERTY, Public Relations Director (312) 565-1905

WRITERS REGULARLY ASSIGNED TO CLUB

ART DUNN, Chicago Tribune, 435 N. Michigan Ave., Chicago 60611, (312) 222-3475
DON EDWALDS, Chicago Sun-Times, 401 N. Wabash, Chicago 60611, (312) 321-2564
GEORGE VASS, Chicago Daily News, 401 N. Wabash, Chicago 60611, (312) 321-2814

MAJOR AIRLINES

AIR CANADA	(312) 527-3900	EASTERN	(312) 467-2900
ALLEGHENY	(312) 346-9020	NORTHWEST	(312) 346-4900
AMERICAN	(312) 372-8000	TWA	(312) 332-7600
CP AIR	(312) 565-0033	UNITED	(312) 569-3000

CINCINNATI STINGERS

BILL BARRETT, Public Relations Director (513) 241-1818

WRITERS REGULARLY ASSIGNED TO CLUB

JACK MURRAY, Cincinnati Enquirer, 617 Vine St., Cincinnati 45202, (513) 721-2700
BOB QUEENAN, Cincinnati Post, 800 Broadway, Cincinnati 45202, (513) 721-1111

CLEVELAND CRUSADERS

STEVE KLEIN, Public Relations Director (216) 659-9100

WRITERS REGULARLY ASSIGNED TO CLUB

BOB SCHLESINGER, Cleveland Press, 901 Lakeside Ave. Cleveland 44114, (216) 623-1111
RICH PASSAN, Cleveland Plain Dealer, 1801 Superior Ave. (216) 523-4371
JIM DERENDAL, Akron Beacon Journal, 44 E. Exchange St. Akron 44309, (216) 375-8050
STEVE LYTLE, Willoughby News Herald, Willoughby, Ohio (216) 942-2105

MAJOR AIRLINES

AIR CANADA	(216) 861-3757	NORTHWEST	(216) 267-0500
ALLEGHENY	(216) 696-8050	UNITED	(216) 333-3700

EDMONTON OILERS

DOUG WENSCHLAG, Director of Marketing, (403) 426-4240

WRITERS REGULARLY ASSIGNED TO CLUB

WAYNE OVERLAND, Edmonton Journal, 101 St. & 100 Ave., Edmonton, (403) 423-9597
JIM MATHESON, Edmonton Journal, 101 St. & 100 Ave., Edmonton, (403) 423-9597
JOHN SHORT, Canadian Press, 101 St. & 100 Ave. Edmonton (403) 424-6107

MAJOR AIRLINES

AIR CANADA	(403) 429-5461	PACIFIC WESTERN	(403) 452-4560
CP AIR	(403) 429-6371	TIME AIR	(403) 455-1015
HUGHES AIR WEST	(403) 429-4716		

media/airlines

HOUSTON AEROS

SONNY TATE, Public Relations Director and Business Manager (713) 228-2206

WRITERS REGULARLY ASSIGNED TO CLUB

RICH BURK, Houston Post, 4747 Southwest Fwy, Houston 77027, (713) 621-7000
TONY PEDERSON, Houston Chronicle, 512 Travis St. Houston 77002, (713) 220-7891

MAJOR AIRLINES

AMERICAN .... (713) 222-9873	DELTA .... (713) 623-6000
BRANIFF .... (713) 621-3111	EASTERN .... (713) 621-8100
CONTINENTAL ..... (713) 524-4711	NATIONAL .... (713) 224-9011

INDIANAPOLIS RACERS

JOE VARGO, Public Relations Director (317) 635-3131

WRITERS REGULARLY ASSIGNED TO CLUB

DAVE OVERPECK, Indianapolis Star, 307 N. Pennsylvania .... (317) 633-9180
DICK DENNY, Indianapolis News, 307 N. Pennsylvania .... (317) 633-1240

MAJOR AIRLINES

ALLEGHENY .... (317) 247-8101	EASTERN .... (317) 639-6611
AMERICAN .... (317) 637-1501	TWA .... (317) 635-4381
DELTA .... (317) 634-3200	

MINNESOTA FIGHTING SAINTS

MIKE LAMEY, Public Relations Director (612) 222-3040

WRITERS REGULARLY ASSIGNED TO CLUB

CHARLIE HALLMAN, St. Paul Pioneer Press-Dispatch, 55 E. Fourth St., St. Paul 55101
(612) 222-5011
BOB FOWLER, Minneapolis Star, 415 Portland Ave., Minneapolis 55415, (612) 372-4365
JOHN GILBERT, Minneapolis Tribune, 415 Portland Ave., Minn. 55415 (612) 372-4447
DAN STONEKING, Minneapolis Star, 415 Portland Ave., Minn. 55415, (612) 372-4365

MAJOR AIRLINES

ALLEGHENY .... (612) 338-5841	NORTHWEST .... (612) 726-1234
BRANIFF .... (612) 726-1200	OZARK .... (612) 333-3421
EASTERN .... (612) 335-9541	UNITED .... (612) 339-3671
NORTH CENTRAL .. (612) 726-7100	WESTERN .... (612) 726-4141

PHOENIX ROADRUNNERS

DAVE WEISER, Press Relations, Director (602) 257-5100

WRITERS REGULARLY ASSIGNED TO CLUB

FRANK GIANELLI, Arizona Republic, 120 E. Van Buren, Phoenix 85001 (602) 271-8250
DOUG McCONNELL, Phoenix Gazette, 120 E. Van Buren, Phoenix 85001 (602) 271-8641

MAJOR AIRLINES

AMERICAN .... (602) 264-2654	HUGHES .... (602) 273-9111
CONTINENTAL ..... (602) 258-8911	TWA .... (602) 252-7711
FRONTIER .... (602) 252-5041	WESTERN .... (602) 258-8881

101

MICHIGAN STAGS

GEORGE MASKIN, Public Relations Director (313) 642-7200

WRITERS REGULARLY ASSIGNED TO CLUB

CHARLES VINCENT, Detroit Free Press, 321 Lafayette, Detroit 48231 (313) 222-2260
JACK BERRY, Detroit News, 615 Lafayette, Detroit 48231 (313) 222-2260
JIM McKAY, Windsor Star, 167 Ferry St., Windsor, Ontario (519) 256-5533
JAN SHAFFER, Oakland Press, 48 W. Huron St., Box 9, Pontiac 48060 (313) 985-7171
JACK DULMAGE, Windsor Star, 167 Ferry St. Windsor, Ontario (519) 256-5533

MAJOR AIRLINES

AIR CANADA	(313) 833-3200	NORDAIR	(313) 965-4976
ALLEGHENY	(313) 965-9800	NORTH CENTRAL	(313) 964-6500
AMERICAN	(313) 965-1000	NORTHWEST	(313) 962-2002
BRANIFF	(313) 964-5710	TWA	(313) 962-8650
CP AIR	(313) 962-6025	UNITED	(313) 336-9000
DELTA	(313) 355-3200	WESTERN	(313) 965-4972

NEW ENGLAND WHALERS

BOB NEUMEIER, Media Relations Director (203) 728-3366

WRITERS REGULARLY ASSIGNED TO CLUB

TOM HINE, Hartford Courant, 285 Broad St., Hartford (203) 249-6411
BILL WINTERS, Hartford Times, 10 Prospect St., Hartford (203) 249-8211
DENNIS RANDALL, Hartford Times, 10 Prospect St., Hartford (203) 249-8211
GENE McCORMICK, Springfield News, 1860 Main St., Springfield 01101 (413) 787-2411
BOB BAINES, Springfield News, 1860 Main St., Springfield 01101 (413) 787-2411

MAJOR AIRLINES

ALLEGHENY	(203) 522-2161	EASTERN	(203) 525-0141
AMERICAN	(203) 527-5141	TWA	(203) 278-7710
DELTA	(203) 527-1811	UNITED	(203) 249-1311

QUEBEC NORDIQUES

DONALD D'AMOURS, Director of Public Relations (418) 529-4161

WRITERS REGULARLY ASSIGNED TO CLUB

CLAUDE BEDARD, Journal De Quebec, 450 Rue Bechard, Ville Vanier, Quebec City (418) 683-1573
CLAUDE CADORETTE, Journal De Quebec, 450 Rue Bechard, Ville Vanier, Quebec City (418) 683-1573
CLAUDE LAROCHELLE, Le Soleil, 390 Rue St. Vallier, Quebec City (418) 525-7134
JACQUES DRAPEAU, Le Soleil, 390 Rue St. Vallier, Quebec City (418) 525-7134
ANDRE BOUTHILLIER, Montreal-Matin, 2175 Blvd. Laurier, Sillery. (418) 653-3958

MAJOR AIRLINES

AIR CANADA (418) 692-0770   QUEBECAIR (418) 692-1031

SAN DIEGO MARINERS

GABE DENUNZIO, Director of Public Relations (714) 225-9633

WRITERS REGULARLY ASSIGNED TO CLUB

WAYNE LOCKWOOD, San Diego Union, P.O. Box 191, San Diego 92112 (714) 299-3131
PAUL COUR, Evening Tribune, P.O. Box 191, San Diego 92112 (714) 299-3131
MATT MITCHELL, El Cajon California , 613 W. Main St., El Cajon, (714) 442-4404

MAJOR AIRLINES

AIR CANADA	(800) 634-6631	EASTERN	(800) 252-0223
AMERICAN	(714) 235-7601	NATIONAL	(714) 239-3036
CP AIR	ZEnith 2-4209	UNITED	(714) 234-7171
DELTA	(714) 239-3431	WESTERN	(714) 234-0181

TORONTO TOROS

RICK MATTHEW, Public Relations Director (416) 595-1919

WRITERS REGULARLY ASSIGNED TO CLUB

JEFF GOODMAN, Toronto Globe & Mail, 444 Front St., Toronto (416) 361-5333
JIM KERNAGHAN, Toronto Star, 1 Yonge St., Toronto (416) 367-2000
RICK FRASER, Toronto Sun, 332 King St., West, Toronto (416) 366-9141
DENNIS PASSA, Canadian Press, 36 King St., E. Toronto (416) 364-0321

MAJOR AIRLINES

AIR CANADA	(416) 925-2311	EASTERN	(416) 362-7561
C.P. AIR	(416) 366-7531	NORTH CENTRAL	(416) 362-5392
ALLEGHENY	(416) 361-1560	TWA	(416) 366-2881
AMERICAN	(416) 925-4822	UNITED	(416) 368-2331

VANCOUVER BLAZERS

DENNY BOYD, Public Relations Director (604) 253-4181

WRITERS REGULARLY ASSIGNED TO CLUB

DENNIS FESER, Vancouver Sun, 2250 Granville St., Vancouver (604) 732-2395
TONY GALLAGHER, The Daily Province, 2250 Granville St., Vancouver (604) 732-2714
JACK LEONARD, The Daily Province, 2250 Granville St., Vancouver (604) 732-2714

MAJOR AIRLINES

AIR CANADA	(604) 683-7111	UNITED	(604) 683-7111
C.P. AIR	(604) 682-1411	WESTERN	(604) 682-5933

WINNIPEG JETS

J.D. BOYD, Public Relations Director (204) 772-9491

WRITERS REGULARLY ASSIGNED TO CLUB

REYN DAVIS, Winnipeg Free Press, 300 Carleton St., Winnipeg
VIC GRANT, Winnipeg Tribune, Smith & Graham, Winnipeg
JOHN KOROBANIK, Canadian Press, 300 Carleton St., Winnipeg

MAJOR AIRLINES

AIR CANADA	(204) 943-9361	MIDWEST	(204) 889-4450
C.P. AIR	(204) 957-1060	NORTHWEST	(204) 786-3481
FRONTIER	(204) 475-3330	TRANSAIR	(204) 889-4450

1974-75 WHA SCHEDULE

1974	1	Tues.	Oct. 15	Winnipeg ...... at Vancouver ....
	2			New England ... at Toronto ....
	3	Wed.	Oct. 16	San Diego ..... at Phoenix ....
	4			Houston ...... at Vancouver ....
	5	Thurs.	Oct. 17	Michigan ...... at Indianapolis ....
	6	Fri.	Oct. 18	Houston ...... at Phoenix ....
	7			Edmonton ..... at Winnipeg ....
	8			Chicago ...... at Vancouver ....
	9			Indianapolis ... at Toronto ....
	10	Sat.	Oct. 19	Cleveland ..... at Minnesota ....
	11			Michigan ...... at New England ....
	12			Houston ...... at San Diego ....
	13	Sun.	Oct. 20	Chicago .... at Vancouver ....
	14			Cleveland...... at Phoenix ....
	15			Michigan ..... at Toronto ....
	16			Indianapolis .... at Quebec ....
	17	Tues.	Oct. 22	Cleveland ..... at San Diego ....
	18			Minnesota ..... at Toronto ....
	19			Houston .... at Quebec.........
	20	Wed.	Oct. 23	Michigan ...... at Quebec ....
	21			Houston ...... at New England ......
	22			Cleveland ...... at Vancouver ....
	23	Thurs.	Oct. 24	Phoenix .... at San Diego ....
	24			Minnesota ..... at Indianapolis ......
	25	Fri.	Oct. 25	Winnipeg ...... at Toronto ....
	26	Sat.	Oct. 26	Minnesota ..... at Houston ....
	27			Phoenix .... at Quebec ....
	28			Indianapolis ... at New England ......
	29	Sun.	Oct. 27	Toronto ...... at Cleveland ....
	30			Quebec .... at Indianapolis ....
	31			Chicago ...... at Minnesota ....
	32			Michigan ...... at Winnipeg ....
	33	Mon.	Oct. 28	Phoenix ...... at Toronto ....
	34	Tues.	Oct. 29	Houston ...... at Chicago ....
	35			Minnesota ..... at Michigan ....
	36	Wed.	Oct. 30	Minnesota ..... at Cleveland ....
	37			Toronto....... at New England ......
	38			Phoenix ...... at Winnipeg ....
	39			Chicago ...... at Houston ....
	40			Edmonton ..... at Vancouver ....
	41	Thurs.	Oct. 31	Chicago ...... at San Diego ....
	42			New England ... at Indianapolis ....
	43			Cleveland ..... at Michigan ....
	44	Fri.	Nov. 1	Toronto ...... at Winnipeg ....
	45	Sat.	Nov. 2	Michigan ...... at Minnesota ....
	46			Phoenix ...... at Houston ....
	47			Edmonton ..... at Cleveland ....
	48			Toronto ...... at Chicago ....
	49			Quebec .... at New England ......
	50	Sun.	Nov. 3	Michigan ...... at Winnipeg ....
	51			Edmonton ..... at Indianapolis ....
	52			San Diego ..... at Vancouver ....
	53	Mon.	Nov. 4	Quebec .... at Toronto ....
	54	Tues.	Nov. 5	San Diego .... at Houston ....
	55			Phoenix ...... at Indianapolis ....
	56			Toronto ...... at Michigan ....
	57			Vancouver ..... at Chicago ....
	58			Minnesota ......at Winnipeg ....

104

schedule

#	Day	Date	Matchup
59	Wed.	Nov. 6	Vancouver at Quebec
60	Thurs.	Nov. 7	San Diego at Indianapolis
61	Fri.	Nov. 8	Cleveland at Vancouver
62			San Diego at New England
63	Sat.	Nov. 9	Toronto at Minnesota
64			Indianapolis at Houston
65			Phoenix at New England
66			Winnipeg at Vancouver
67	Sun.	Nov. 10	Phoenix at Minnesota
68			Cleveland at Edmonton
69			Indianapolis at Michigan
70			Toronto at Chicago
71			San Diego at Quebec
72	Tues.	Nov. 12	Quebec at Michigan
73			San Diego at Chicago
74			New England at Houston
75	Wed.	Nov. 13	Houston at Minnesota
76			Indianapolis at Quebec
77			Toronto at Vancouver
78			Winnipeg at Edmonton
79	Thurs.	Nov. 14	Cleveland at Phoenix
80			New England at San Diego
81			Chicago at Michigan
82	Fri.	Nov. 15	Toronto at Edmonton
83			Indianapolis at Winnipeg
84			Cleveland at San Diego
85	Sat.	Nov. 16	New England at Phoenix
86			Chicago at Houston
87			Michigan at Quebec
88	Sun.	Nov. 17	Indianapolis at Edmonton
89			Toronto at Winnipeg
90			New England at Michigan
91			Minnesota at Quebec
92			San Diego at Houston
93	Mon.	Nov. 18	Winnipeg at Edmonton
94	Tues.	Nov. 19	Houston at Indianapolis
95			New England at Chicago
96			Vancouver at San Diego
97	Wed.	Nov. 20	Edmonton at Quebec
98			Minnesota at Winnipeg
99			Indianapolis at Chicago
100	Thurs.	Nov. 21	New England at Indianapolis
101			Phoenix at Michigan
102			Cleveland at Quebec
103	Fri.	Nov. 22	Edmonton at Toronto
104			Houston at Vancouver
105			Michigan at Chicago
106	Sat.	Nov. 23	Toronto at Quebec
107			Chicago at New England
108			Houston at Vancouver
109			San Diego at Minnesota (1:30 pm)
110	Sun.	Nov. 24	Houston at Edmonton
111			Quebec at Cleveland
112			Phoenix at Winnipeg
113			Toronto at Indianapolis
114			Minnesota at Michigan
115			New England at Chicago
116	Tues.	Nov. 26	Phoenix at Houston
117			Winnipeg at Indianapolis

105

#	Day	Date	Game
118			Vancouver at Michigan
119			Minnesota at Toronto
120			Edmonton at San Diego
121			New England at Quebec
122	Wed.	Nov. 27	Chicago at Phoenix
123			Winnipeg at Cleveland
124	Thurs.	Nov. 28	Edmonton at Houston
125			Quebec at Indianapolis
126			Chicago at San Diego
127			Vancouver at Toronto
128	Fri.	Nov. 29	New England at Vancouver
129			Toronto at Phoenix
130			Indianapolis at Cleveland
131			Michigan at Winnipeg
132	Sat.	Nov. 30	Cleveland at Houston
133			Chicago at Minnesota
134	Sun.	Dec. 1	Phoenix at Minnesota
135			New England at Edmonton
136			Michigan at Cleveland
137			Quebec at Winnipeg
138			Houston at Indianapolis
139			Toronto at San Diego
140	Tues.	Dec. 3	New England at Michigan
141			Houston at Toronto
142			Phoenix at San Diego
143	Wed.	Dec. 4	San Diego at Phoenix
144			Minnesota at Quebec
145			New England at Cleveland
146			Houston at Winnipeg
147			Vancouver at Edmonton
148	Thurs.	Dec. 5	Chicago at Indianapolis
149			San Diego at Michigan
150			New England at Quebec
151	Fri.	Dec. 6	Edmonton at Phoenix
152			Winnipeg at Minnesota
153	Sat.	Dec. 7	San Diego at Cleveland
154			Michigan at Vancouver
155			Toronto at Chicago
156			Indianapolis at New England
157	Sun.	Dec. 8	Houston at Quebec
158			Michigan at Edmonton
159			Toronto at Phoenix
160			Chicago at Winnipeg
161			San Diego at Indianapolis
162			Minnesota at Vancouver
163	Tues.	Dec. 10	Vancouver at Cleveland
164			Winnipeg at Indianapolis
165			Minnesota at Toronto
166			Michigan at San Diego
167			Phoenix at Chicago
168	Wed.	Dec. 11	Vancouver at Houston
169			Edmonton at Quebec
170			Minnesota at New England
171	Thurs.	Dec. 12	Vancouver at Phoenix
172			Winnipeg at Michigan
173			Cleveland at Quebec
174	Fri.	Dec. 13	Edmonton at Minnesota
175			Cleveland at Toronto
176	Sat.	Dec. 14	Minnesota at Phoenix
177			Winnipeg at Houston
178			Indianapolis at San Diego
179			Michigan at Chicago
180			Quebec at New England

181	Sun.	Dec. 15	Edmonton	at Indianapolis
182			Quebec	at Minnesota
183			San Diego	at Houston
184			New England	at Winnipeg
185			Toronto	at Michigan
186			Cleveland	at Vancouver
187	Tues.	Dec. 17	Edmonton	at Houston
188			Vancouver	at Indianapolis
189			Winnipeg	at Toronto
190			Cleveland	at San Diego
191			Quebec	at Chicago
192			New England	at Michigan
193	Wed.	Dec. 18	Vancouver	at Phoenix
194			Winnipeg	at Quebec
195	Thurs.	Dec. 19	Vancouver	at Houston
196			Minnesota	at Indianapolis
197			Edmonton	at San Diego
198			Cleveland	at Michigan
199	Fri.	Dec. 20	Indianapolis	at Minnesota
200			Michigan	at Phoenix
201			New England	at Cleveland
202			Chicago	at Quebec
203	Sat.	Dec. 21	San Diego	at Vancouver
204			Edmonton	at Chicago
205			Houston	at New England
206	Sun.	Dec. 22	Phoenix	at Winnipeg
207			San Diego	at Edmonton
208			Chicago	at Toronto
209			Houston	at Cleveland
210			New England	at Indianapolis
211			Quebec	at Michigan
212	Mon.	Dec. 23	Cleveland	at Toronto
213	Thurs.	Dec. 26	Minnesota	at Edmonton
214			Michigan	at Vancouver
215			Winnipeg	at Phoenix
216			Cleveland	at Chicago
217	Fri.	Dec. 27	New England	at Minnesota
218			Quebec	at Cleveland
219			Chicago	at Toronto
220			Indianapolis	at Vancouver
221	Sat.	Dec. 28	New England	at Houston
222			Cleveland	at Phoenix
223			Winnipeg	at San Diego
224			Minnesota	at Chicago
225			Michigan	at Quebec
226	Sun.	Dec. 29	Cleveland	ar Minnesota
227			Indianapolis	at Edmonton
228			Chicago	at Michigan
229			Winnipeg	at Houston
230	Mon.	Dec. 30	Phoenix	at Quebec
231	Tues.	Dec. 31	Chicago	at Cleveland
232			Phoenix	at Michigan

1975

233	Wed.	Jan. 1	Indianapolis	at Quebec
234			Cleveland	at Minnesota
235			San Diego	at Edmonton
236	Thurs.	Jan. 2	Indianapolis	at Cleveland
237			Phoenix	at Vancouver
238			Michigan	at Houston
239	Fri.	Jan. 3	San Diego	at Minnesota
240			Phoenix	at Edmonton
241			New England	at Toronto

242	Sat.	Jan.	4	Michigan ...... at Houston ....
243				Toronto .... at Quebec ....
244				San Diego ..... at Cleveland ....
245				Indianapolis ... at Chicago ....
246				Vancouver ..... at New England ......
247	Sun.	Jan.	5	New England ... at Minnesota ....
248				Toronto .... at Cleveland ....
249				Phoenix .... at Indianapolis ....
250				Vancouver ..... at Michigan ....
251				Chicago .... at Edmonton ....
252	Tues.	Jan.	7	Minnesota ..... at Chicago ....
253				Winnipeg ...... at Cleveland ....
254				Vancouver .... at Indianapolis ......
255				Phoenix .... at Toronto ....
256				New England ... at San Diego ....
257				Quebec .... at Michigan ....
258	Wed.	Jan.	8	Vancouver ..... at Quebec ....
259	Thurs.	Jan.	9	New England ... at Phoenix ....
260				Winnipeg ...... at Michigan ....
261				Minnesota ..... at Edmonton ....
262	Fri.	Jan.	10	Indianapolis ... at Edmonton ....
263				Vancouver ..... at Cleveland ....
264				Quebec .... at Winnipeg ....
265				San Diego ..... at Toronto ....
266				Michigan ...... at Chicago ....
267	Sat.	Jan.	11	Phoenix .... at Houston ....
268				San Diego ..... at New England ......
269	Sun.	Jan.	12	Vancouver .... at Minnesota ....
270				Quebec .... at Edmonton ....
271				Toronto .... at Houston ....
272				Phoenix .... at Cleveland ....
273				Indianapolis ... at Winnipeg ....
274				San Diego ..... at Michigan ....
275	Tues.	Jan.	14	Indianapolis.... at Michigan ....
276				Toronto .... at San Diego ....
277				Quebec .... at Vancouver ....
278				Phoenix .... at Chicago ....
279	Wed.	Jan.	15	Toronto .... at Phoenix ....
280				Edmonton .... at Houston ....
281				Minnesota ..... at Cleveland ....
282				Vancouver ..... at Winnipeg ....
283				Chicago .... at New England ......
284	Thurs.	Jan.	16	Cleveland ..... at Indianapolis
285				Edmonton .... at San Diego ....
286				Chicago .... at Michigan ....
287	Fri.	Jan.	17	Edmonton ..... at Phoenix ....
288				Toronto .... at New England ......
289	Sat.	Jan.	18	Edmonton ..... at Phoenix ....
290				Houston ...... at San Diego ....
291				New England ... at Quebec ....
292				Minnesota ..... at Chicago ....
293				Michigan ...... at Cleveland ....
294	Sun.	Jan.	19	Cleveland ...... at Winnipeg ....
295				Indianapolis.... at Vancouver ....
296				Minnesota ..... at New England ......

ALL STAR GAME Tues. Jan. 21 Edmonton Coliseum

297	Wed.	Jan.	22	Vancouver ..... at Minnesota ....
298				Chicago .... at Phoenix ....
299				Indianapolis.... at Winnipeg ....
300	Thurs.	Jan.	23	Chicago .... at Indianapolis ....
301				Toronto .... at Michigan ....

108

302			Vancouver	at San Diego
303			Cleveland	at Quebec
304			Winnipeg	at Edmonton
305	Fri.	Jan. 24	Toronto	at Minnesota
306			Houston	at Edmonton
307			New England	at Phoenix
308			Winnipeg	at Vancouver
309	Sat.	Jan. 25	Chicago	at Quebec
310			Michigan	at Cleveland
311			New England	at San Diego
312	Sun.	Jan. 26	Michigan	at Minnesota
313			Toronto	at Edmonton
314			Indianapolis	at Phoenix
315			Houston	at Winnipeg
316			Vancouver	at Chicago
317	Mon.	Jan. 27	Cleveland	at New England
318	Tues.	Jan. 28	Minnesota	at Michigan
319			Quebec	at Toronto
320			Winnipeg	at San Diego
321			Cleveland	at Chicago
322			Phoenix	at Indianapolis
323			Houston	at Edmonton
324	Wed.	Jan. 29	Phoenix	at Cleveland
325			Michigan	at New England
326	Thurs.	Jan. 30	Winnipeg	at Phoenix
327			Toronto	at Indianapolis
328			Quebec	at Chicago
329	Fri.	Jan 31	Houston	at Minnesota
330			Cleveland	at Edmonton
331			Vancouver	at Toronto
332			Michigan	at New England
333	Sat.	Feb. 1	Michigan	at Phoenix
334			Quebec	at Indianapolis
335			Houston	at Chicago
336	Sun.	Feb. 2	Winnipeg	at Minnesota
337			Chicago	at Edmonton
338			Quebec	at Cleveland
339			Houston	at Michigan
340			Toronto	at Vancouver
341	Tues.	Feb. 4	Houston	at Indianapolis
342			Edmonton	at Michigan
343			Toronto	at San Diego
344			Quebec	at Chicago
345	Wed.	Feb. 5	Edmonton	at Minnesota
346			San Diego	at Phoenix
347			Toronto	at Houston
348			Winnipeg	at Cleveland
349			Chicago	at Vancouver
350	Thurs.	Feb. 6	Cleveland	at Michigan
351			Minnesota	at San Diego
352			Quebec	at Houston
353	Fri.	Feb. 7	Minnesota	at Phoenix
354			New England	at Winnipeg
355			Cleveland	at Toronto
356	Sat.	Feb. 8	Quebec	at Phoenix
357			Minnesota	at San Diego
358			New England	at Vancouver
359			Winnipeg	at Chicago
360			Michigan	at Houston
361	Sun.	Feb. 9	Phoenix	at Edmonton
362			Houston	at Cleveland
363			Chicago	at Winnipeg

109

364			Indianapolis	at Toronto
365			New England	at Vancouver
366	Mon.	Feb. 10	Chicago	at Indianapolis
367	Tues.	Feb. 11	Houston	at Michigan
368			Edmonton	at Toronto
369			Quebec	at San Diego
370			Indianapolis	at Chicago
371	Wed.	Feb. 12	Houston	at Minnesota
372			Chicago	at Cleveland
373			Toronto	at Winnipeg
374			Phoenix	at Vancouver
375			Edmonton	at New England
376	Thurs.	Feb. 13	Quebec	at Phoenix
377			San Diego	at Michigan
378	Fri.	Feb. 14	Quebec	at Minnesota
379			Toronto	at Edmonton
380			San Diego	at Cleveland
381			Indianapolis	at New England
382			Houston	at Winnipeg
383	Sat.	Feb. 15	Cleveland	at Winnipeg
384	Sun.	Feb. 16	San Diego	at Minnesota
385			Phoenix	at Edmonton
386			Toronto	at Vancouver
387			Winnipeg	at Chicago
388	Mon.	Feb. 17	Houston	at Quebec
389	Tues.	Feb. 18	Winnipeg	at Michigan
390			Phoenix	at San Diego
391			Vancouver	at Indianapolis
392			New England	at Edmonton
393	Wed.	Feb. 19	Quebec	at Houston
394			Minnesota	at Cleveland
395			Edmonton	at Winnipeg (7pm)
396	Thurs.	Feb. 20	Vancouver	at Michigan
397			Quebec	at San Diego
398			Chicago	at Toronto
399	Fri.	Feb. 21	New England	at Edmonton
400			Minnesota	at Indianapolis
401	Sat.	Feb. 22	Vancouver	at Houston
402			Toronto	at Cleveland
403	Sun.	Feb. 23	San Diego	at Quebec
404			Minnesota	at Edmonton
405			Toronto	at Houston
406			New England	at Winnipeg
407			Cleveland	at Indianapolis
408			Vancouver	at Chicago
409	Mon.	Feb. 24	San Diego	at Quebec
410	Tues.	Feb. 25	Indianapolis	at Michigan
411			San Diego	at Toronto
412			Edmonton	at Chicago
413			Vancouver	at New England
414			Minnesota	at Winnipeg
415	Wed.	Feb. 26	Indianapolis	at Minnesota
416			Cleveland	at Houston
417			Chicago	at New England
418	Thurs.	Feb. 27	Houston	at Phoenix
419			Edmonton	at Michigan
420			Minnesota	at New England
421			Vancouver	at Quebec
422	Fri.	Feb. 28	San Diego	at Winnipeg
423			Michigan	at Edmonton

424	Sat.	Mar.	1	Indianapolis	at Phoenix
425				Chicago	at Houston
426				Minnesota	at Quebec
427				Cleveland	at New England
428	Sun.	Mar.	2	Toronto	at Minnesota
429				Michigan	at Edmonton
430				San Diego	at Winnipeg
431				Vancouver	at New England
432				Indianapolis	at Houston
433				Chicago	at Phoenix
434	Tues.	Mar.	4	Michigan	at Toronto
435				Quebec	at San Diego
436				Cleveland	at Edmonton
437	Wed.	Mar.	5	New England	at Minnesota
438				Quebec	at Phoenix
439				Cleveland	at Winnipeg
440				Edmonton	at Vancouver
441	Thurs.	Mar.	6	Houston	at San Diego
442	Fri.	Mar.	7	Vancouver	at Edmonton
443				Winnipeg	at Phoenix
444				Quebec	at Toronto
445				Michigan	at Indianapolis
446	Sat.	Mar.	8	New England	at Houston
447				Cleveland	at Indianapolis
448				Winnipeg	at San Diego
449	Sun.	Mar.	9	Winnipeg	at Minnesota
450				Michigan	at Toronto
451				Phoenix	at Vancouver
452				Chicago	at Quebec
453	Tues.	Mar.	11	Phoenix	at Toronto
454				Minnesota	at San Diego
455				Edmonton	at Chicago
456				Winnipeg	at New England
457	Wed.	Mar.	12	Winnipeg	at Quebec
458				Minnesota	at Vancouver
459	Thurs.	Mar.	13	Toronto	at Indianapolis
460				Phoenix	at New England
461	Fri.	Mar.	14	Edmonton	at Cleveland
462				Quebec	at Winnipeg
463				Houston	ar Chicago
464				San Diego	at Toronto
465	Sat.	Mar.	15	Michigan	at Indianapolis
466				Quebec	at Vancouver
467				Edmonton	at New England
468	Sun.	Mar.	16	Toronto	at New England
469				Houston	at Cleveland
470				Edmonton	at Winnipeg
471				Quebec	at Vancouver
472				San Diego	at Chicago
473	Mon.	Mar.	17	Houston	at Toronto
474	Tues.	Mar.	18	Quebec	at Edmonton
475				Minnesota	at Vancouver
476				Phoenix	at Chicago
477	Wed.	Mar.	19	Indianapolis	at Houston
478				Phoenix	at Cleveland
479				Vancouver	at Winnipeg
480				San Diego	at New England
481	Thurs.	Mar.	20	Edmonton	at Indianapolis
482				Phoenix	at Michigan
483				Chicago	at San Diego
484				Quebec	at Houston

111

#	Day	Date	Matchup
485	Fri.	Mar. 21	Winnipeg at New England
486	Sat.	Mar. 22	Vancouver at Phoenix
487			Houston at New England
488			Indianapolis at San Diego
489			Winnipeg at Chicago
490			Edmonton at Cleveland
491	Sun.	Mar. 23	Edmonton at Minnesota
492			Indianapolis at Phoenix
493			Chicago at Winnipeg
494			Houston at Michigan
495			Vancouver at San Diego
496	Tues.	Mar. 25	Winnipeg at Indianapolis
497			Michigan at Minnesota
498			Vancouver at Toronto
499			San Diego at Chicago
500			Edmonton at New England
501	Wed.	Mar. 26	Houston at Phoenix
502			Chicago at Minnesota
503			Edmonton at Quebec
504			Vancouver at Cleveland
505	Thurs.	Mar. 27	San Diego at Indianapolis
506			Edmonton at Michigan
507			Clevleand at New England
508			Winnipeg at Houston
509	Fri.	Mar. 28	Minnesota at Phoenix
510			Edmonton at Toronto
511	Sat.	Mar. 29	Minnesota at Houston
512			Toronto at Quebec
513			Winnipeg at New England
514			San Diego at Vancouver
515			Indianapolis at Cleveland
516	Sun.	Mar. 30	San Diego at Edmonton
517			Chicago at Cleveland
518			Indianapolis at Minnesota
519			Michigan at Vancouver
520			New England at Toronto
521			Phoenix at Quebec
522	Tues.	Apr. 1	Vancouver at Minnesota
523			Indianapolis at Toronto
524			Cleveland at Chicago
525			Phoenix at New England
526			Michigan at San Diego
527			Quebec at Edmonton
528	Wed.	Apr. 2	Quebec at Minnesota
529			Cleveland at Houston
530			Vancouver at Winnipeg
531	Thurs.	Apr. 3	Quebec at New England
532			Michigan at San Diego
533	Fri.	Apr. 4	Vancouver at Edmonton
534			Phoenix at Minnesota
535			Winnipeg at Toronto
536			New England at Chicago
537	Sat.	Apr. 5	Edmonton at Vancouver
538			Winnipeg at Quebec
539			New England at Cleveland
540			Michigan at Phoenix
541			Indianapolis at San Diego
542			Minnesota at Houston
543	Sun.	Apr. 6	San Diego at Winnipeg
544			Houston at Toronto
545			Indianapolis at Vancouver
546			Chicago at Edmonton

Determination of who is hockey's greatest active goaltender may well have been established in the Team Canada / Soviet Union Summit II series. Here Gerry Cheevers of the Cleveland Crusaders makes one of several breathtaking saves as WHA Team Canada battled the powerful Soviets 1-1-2 through the Canadian segment of the series. While a Team Canada player is embroiled with a Russian, Pat Stapleton (12) of the Chicago Cougers moves to the aid of Cheevers. In the background, J.C. Tremblay of the Quebec Nordiques.

Photo by Michael Koster

4TH SEASON

1975-76

MEDIA GUIDE

EXECUTIVE EDITOR
LEO ORNEST

STATISTICIAN
FRANK POLNASZEK

CONTENTS

Chief Executive Officer/Trustees	2
WHA Directory	3
Calgary Cowboys	5
Cincinnati Stingers	7
Cleveland Crusaders	9
Denver Spurs	11
Edmonton Oilers	13
Houston Aeros	15
Indianapolis Racers	17
Minnesota Fighting Saints	19
New England Whalers	21
Phoenix Roadrunners	23
Quebec Nordiques	25
San Diego Mariners	27
Toronto Toros	29
Winnipeg Jets	31
WHA Officials	32
WHA Minor Officials	32
Bobby Hull	34
Avco World Trophy	36
Awards	37
All-Stars	38
History of League	40
Team Records	44
Single Game Records	47
Individual Records	51
Team Penalty Records	55
Major League Records	56
Career Leaders	58
Hat Tricks	59
Shutouts	59
Lifetime Team Totals	60
1974-75 Statistics	61-67
Individual Leaders/Trophies	68
Team Statistics	69-78
Goaltenders Records	79
Player Transactions	81
Attendance	82
Overtime Games	83
Power Play Statistics	84
Penalty Shots	85
Playoff Leaders	86
Penalty/Goaltending	89
Team Playoff Records	90
Playoff Records — Individual	93
Media/Airlines	96
Travelog	100
Differences	101
Schedule	102
Starting Times	112

THE COVER
Bobby Hull, Winnipeg Jets, WHA's most valuable player 1974-75. Hull scored 77 goals last season to set a major league goal scoring record. See pages 34-35.

PRINTED IN CANADA — ALL RIGHTS RESERVED — WORLD HOCKEY ASSOCIATION

BEN HATSKIN
Chairman of the Board / Chief Executive Officer
1328 Richardson Bldg.
One Lombard Place
Winnipeg, Manitoba R3B 0X3

Secretary: Rosemary De Laronde

TRUSTEES
William Sleeman/CALGARY
William O. DeWitt, Jr./CINCINNATI
Jay P. Moore/CLEVELAND
Ivan L. Mullinex/DENVER
W. D. (Bill) Hunter/EDMONTON
George Bolin/HOUSTON
Paul Deneau/INDIANAPOLIS
Wayne Belisle/MINNESOTA
Howard L. Baldwin/NEW ENGLAND
William H. MacFarland/PHOENIX
John Dacres/QUEBEC
Joseph Schwartz/SAN DIEGO
John F. Bassett, Jr./TORONTO
Oscar Grubert/WINNIPEG

ORGANIZED JUNE 10, 1971

DIRECTORY
WORLD HOCKEY ASSOCIATION

LEAGUE OFFICES
415 Yonge Street
Suite 1611
Toronto, Ontario, Canada M5B 2E7
Phone: (416) 366-4281
Telex: 06-22695

Executive Vice-President/
Hockey Operations
N. R. (BUD) POILE

Vice-President
HOWARD BALDWIN

Secretary
WAYNE BELISLE

Assistant Secretary/
Legal Counsel
A. J. MERCURY

Vice-President
Finance/Treasurer
JOHN GRAY

Executive Vice-President/
WHA Properties
LARRY GORDON

Vice-President/Director
of Communications
LEO ORNEST

Director of Information
& Statistics
FRANK POLNASZEK

Director of Officials
BOB FRAMPTON

Referee-In-Chief
BILL FRIDAY

N. R. (Bud) Poile

Howard Baldwin

Wayne Belisle

A. J. Mercury

John Gray

Larry Gordon

Leo Ornest

Frank Polnaszek

Bob Frampton

Bill Friday

CALGARY COWBOYS 1975-76 ROSTER

No.	FORWARDS	S	Ht.	Wt.	Born	1974-75 Club	League	GP	G	A	PTS	PIM
7	Chipperfield, Ron	R	5-11	180	3-28-54	Vancouver	(WHA)	78	19	20	39	30
15	Deadmarsh, Butch	L	5-11	186	4- 5-50	Vancouver	(WHA)	38	7	8	15	128
24	Driscoll, Peter	L	6- 0	190	10-27-54	Vancouver	(WHA)	21	3	2	5	40
17	Given, Dave (AB)		6- 1	185	7-19-54	Tulsa	(CHL)	56	9	10	19	183
25	Haas, Derek	L	6- 0	170	5- 1-55	Brown University	(ECAC)	22	10	20	30	14
18	Harris, Hugh	L	6- 0	190	6- 7-48	Vancouver	(WHA)	79	33	44	77	54
12	Israelson, Larry	L	6- 1	180	8- 2-52	Vancouver	(WHA)	46	12	9	21	10
						Tulsa	(CHL)	39	13	15	28	42
16	Jodzio, Rick	L	6- 1	185	6- 3-54	Vancouver	(WHA)	44	1	3	4	159
						Charlotte	(CHL)	37	9	8	17	109
11	Lawson, Danny	R	5-11	185	10-30-47	Vancouver	(WHA)	78	33	43	76	19
19	McLean, Denny	L	6- 2	195	7-30-55	Calgary	(WCHL)	68	39	44	83	85
9	Morrison, George	L	6- 1	175	12-24-48	Minnesota	(WHA)	76	31	29	60	30
8	Sentes, Rick	L	5-11	180	1-10-47	San Diego	(WHA)	74	44	41	85	52
5	Tannahill, Don	L	5-11	178	2-21-49	Minnesota	(WHA)	72	23	30	53	20
	DEFENSEMEN											
4	Evans, Chris	L	5- 9	181	9-14-46	St. Louis	(NHL)	22	0	3	3	4
6	Lacombe, Francois	L	5- 9	185	2- 2-48	Quebec	(WHA)	55	7	17	24	54
22	Olds, Wally (AB)	R	6- 2	200	8-17-49	Hampton	(SHL)	71	19	61	80	45
3	Reed, Bill	R	5-11	190	5-25-54	Mich./Balt.	(WHA)	32	3	6	9	40
2	Rupp, Duane	L	6- 1	195	3-29-38	Vancouver	(WHA)	73	3	26	29	45
21	Terbenche, Paul	L	5-10	170	9-16-45	Vancouver	(WHA)	60	3	14	17	10
	GOALTENDERS							GP	MIN	GA	SO	GAA
1	McLeod, Don	L	6- 1	190	8-24-46	Vancouver	(WHA)	71	4124	230	1	3.35
30	Wood, Wayne	L	6- 1	190	6- 5-51	Vancouver	(WHA)	11	512	30	0	3.52

AB – American Born.

Calgary

CALGARY COWBOYS
Calgary Cowboys Hockey Team, Ltd.
1418 Macleod Trail S.E.
Calgary, Alberta T2G 2N5   (403) 261-6990
                                 Telex: 03-822655

Jim Pattison

Bill Sleeman

President	JIM PATTISON
Trustee	BILL SLEEMAN
General Manager/Coach	JOE CROZIER
Vice-President Finance	ED PYRIK
Marketing Director	DON LeROSE
Equipment Manager/Trainer	JIM MURRAY
Chief Scout	AL MILLAR
Scouting Staff	HAL SCHOOLEY WARREN STRELOW
Training Camp	CALGARY, ALBERTA
Radio	CFAC-960 AM — all games ERIC BISHOP
Television	CFAC-Ch. 2 — 12 games
Team Colors	Red, White
Franchise Granted	June, 1972 (originally Philadelphia)
Ticket Prices	$9/7/6/5

Joe Crozier

STAMPEDE CORRAL:
Opened December 26, 1950. Built at cost of $5 million. Capacity 6,445 plus 1,500 standing room. Ice surface 200 by 80. 5 minutes from downtown. To undergo expansion to 15,000 capacity.

CINCINNATI STINGERS 1975-76 ROSTER

No.	FORWARDS	S	Ht.	Wt.	Born	1974-75 Club	League	GP	G	A	PTS	PIM
23	Andrascik, Steve		5-11	190	11- 6-48	Ind/Mich/Balt	(WHA)	77	6	11	17	58
12	Campbell, Bryan		6- 0	180	3-27-44	Vancouver	(WHA)	78	29	34	63	24
9	Dudley, Rick		6- 0	190	1-31-49	Buffalo	(NHL)	78	31	39	70	120
13	Guite, Pierre		6- 2	190	4-17-52	Baltimore	(WHA)	34	19	12	31	70
8	Larose, Claude		5-10	175	5-17-55	Sherbrooke	(QJHL)	74	69	76	145	12
18	Locas, Jacques		5- 9	175	1- 8-54	Hampton	(SHL)	15	12	4	16	10
16	MacNeil, Bernie		5-11	180	3- 7-50	Binghampton	(NAHL)	53	12	20	32	145
21	Myers, Murray		6- 0	185	2- 9-52	Vancouver	(WHA)	24	1	1	2	4
						Tulsa	(CHL)	25	8	8	16	16
26	Rombough, Lorne		5-11	190	4- 2-48	Hampton	(SHL)	69	52	39	91	18
17	Smedsmo, Dale (AB)		6- 1	205	4-23-51	Saginaw	(IHL)	20	5	0	5	48
						Hampton	(SHL)	43	13	6	19	145
14	Sobchuk, Dennis		6- 2	180	1-12-54	Oklahoma City	(CHL)	15	3	3	6	60
22	Sobchuk, Gene		5- 9	170	1- 2-51	Phoenix	(WHA)	78	32	45	77	36
						Tulsa	(CHL)	73	35	28	63	65
11	Veneruzzo, Gary		5- 8	175	6-28-43	Phoenix	(WHA)	3	1	0	1	0
						Mich./Balt.	(WHA)	77	33	27	60	57
	DEFENSEMEN											
5	Abbey, Bruce		6- 1	185	8-18-51	Michigan Tech	(WCHA)	36	3	14	17	83
10	Hughes, John		5-11	200	3-18-54	Phoenix	(WHA)	72	4	25	29	201
6	Inkpen, Dave		6- 0	185	9- 4-54	Flint-Des Moines	(IHL)	47	9	25	34	55
4	Pelyk, Mike		6- 1	190	9-29-47	Vancouver	(WHA)	75	14	26	40	121
2	Plumb, Ron		5-10	175	7-17-50	San Diego	(WHA)	78	10	38	48	56
7	Spannbauer, Dick (AB)		6- 3	210	3- 9-54	Mohawk Valley	(NAHL)	68	3	24	27	103

No.	GOALTENDERS	S	Ht.	Wt.	Born	1974-75 Club	League	GP	MIN	GA	SO	GAA
35	Aubry, Serge		5- 9	160	1- 2-42	Quebec	(WHA)	32	1762	109	0	3.71
31	Coutu, Rich		5-11	176	5- 3-51	Chicago	(WHA)	1	60	5	0	5.00
	LaPointe, Norm		6- 1	180	8-13-55	Long Island	(NAHL)	49	2835	153	—	3.24
1						Three Rivers	(QJHL)	72	4307	293	—	4.08

AB — American Born.

Cincinnati

CINCINNATI STINGERS
CINCINNATI HOCKEY CLUB CORP.
Riverfront Coliseum
Cincinnati, Ohio 45202

(513) 241-1818
Telex 214 286

Brian Heekin

Chairman of the Board	WILLIAM O. DeWITT
President	BRIAN E. HEEKIN
Executive Vice-President Chief Executive Officer/Trustee	WILLIAM O. DEWITT, JR.
Treasurer	ALBERT E. HEEKIN III
Secretary	LAWRENCE H. KYTE, JR.
Business Manager	RUDIE M. SCHAFFER
Coach	TERRENCE SLATER

Directors

CHARLES L. HEEKIN	WILLIAM O. DEWITT
LAWRENCE H. KYTE, JR.	WILLIAM O. DEWITT, Jr.
JAMES R. RAMMACHER	ALBERT E. HEEKIN, III
PHILIP S. SMITH	BRIAN E. HEEKIN

Bill DeWitt, Jr.

Director Player Personnel	JERRY M. RAFTER
Publicity Director	JOHN A. HEWIG
Director of Group Sales	BILL HARBOUR
Ticket Manager	HENRY A. ROYER
Chief Scout	FLORENCE POTVIN
Scouts	HARRY SOBCHUK, JACQUES LOCAS
Trainer	GLEN ERAMO
Assistant Trainer	ED ROTSCHILD
Franchise Granted	May 6, 1973
Radio	WLW-700 AM — all games ANDY MacWILLIAMS
Television	WLWT-Ch. 5 Cincinnati — 10 games WLWD-Ch. 2 Dayton — 5 games WLWC-Ch. 4 Columbus — 5 games
Team Colors	BLACK, YELLOW, WHITE
Training Camp	CINCINNATI
Ticket Prices	$8.25/7.25/6.25/4.25

Terry Slater

RIVERFRONT COLISEUM: Construction of $20 million facility started Nov. 12, 1973. Theatre seats, air conditioned, 35 private boxes. Ice surface 200 by 85. Capacity 15,820.

CLEVELAND CRUSADERS 1975-76 ROSTER

No.	FORWARDS	S	Ht.	Wt.	Born	1974-75 Club	League	GP	G	A	PTS	PIM
16	Erickson, Grant	L	5-9	165	4-28-47	Cleveland	(WHA)	78	12	16	28	24
23	Gruen, Dan	L	5-11	180	6-26-52	Mich/Wpg	(WHA)	66	19	28	47	94
15	Harrison, Jim	R	5-11	185	7- 9-47	Cleveland	(WHA)	60	20	22	42	106
20	Holbrook, Terry	R	6-0	185	7-11-50	Cleveland	(WHA)	78	10	13	23	7
12	Jarrett, Gary	L	5-8	170	9- 3-42	Cleveland	(WHA)	77	17	24	41	70
22	Leduc, Rich	L	5-11	170	8-24-51	Cleveland	(WHA)	77	35	31	66	122
14	McDonough, Al	R	6-0	170	6- 6-50	Cleveland	(WHA)	78	34	30	64	27
10	Moffat, Lyle	L	5-10	180	3-19-48	Toronto	(NHL)	21	2	7	9	13
						Oklahoma	(CHL)	39	17	19	36	87
7	Pinder, Gerry	R	5-8	165	9-15-48	Cleveland	(WHA)	73	13	27	40	61
17	Stewart, John A.	L	6-0	180	5-16-50	California	(NHL)	75	19	19	38	55
19	Stewart, John C.	L	5-11	170	1- 2-54	Cleveland	(WHA)	55	4	7	11	8
						Cape Cod	(NAHL)	13	5	11	16	14
28	Walker, Russ	R	6-1	185	5-24-53	Cleveland	(WHA)	65	14	11	25	80
24	Ward, Ron	R	5-11	175	9-12-44	Cleveland	(WHA)	73	30	32	62	18
	DEFENSEMEN											
21	Ball, Terry	R	5-9	165	11-29-44	Minnesota	(WHA)	76	8	37	45	36
4	Baxter, Paul	R	5-11	200	10-25-55	Cleveland	(WHA)	5	0	0	0	37
						Cape Cod	(NAHL)	2	1	0	1	11
6	Clearwater, Ray	L	5-11	175	11-10-42	Cleveland	(WHA)	66	4	18	22	51
18	Edur, Tom	R	6-0	190	11-18-54	Cleveland	(WHA)	62	3	21	24	28
26	Maxwell, Bryan	L	6-3	210	9- 7-55	Medicine Hat	(WCHL)	63	14	50	64	288
2	McKay, Ray	L	6-4	183	8-22-46	Edmonton	(WHA)	69	8	20	28	47
5	Muloin, Wayne	L	5-7	185	12-24-41	Cleveland	(WHA)	78	4	17	21	65
3	Shmyr, Paul	L	5-11	175	1-28-46	Cleveland	(WHA)	50	7	14	21	103
	GOALTENDERS							GP	MIN	GA	SO	GAA
30	Cheevers, Gerry	L	5-11	185	12- 7-40	Cleveland	(WHA)	52	3075	167	4	3.26
1	Whidden, Bob	L	5-10	180	7-27-46	Cleveland	(WHA)	29	1655	89	0	3.23

Cleveland

CLEVELAND CRUSADERS
CLEVELAND CRUSADERS, LTD.
2923 Streetsboro Road
Richfield Township, Ohio 44286   (216) 659-9100
Telex 985-376

President/Trustee	JAY P. MOORE
Vice-President	STEPHEN ZAYAC, JR.
General Manager/Alternate Trustee	JACK VIVIAN
Coach	JOHN WILSON
General Counsel	BINGHAM W. ZELLMER
Promotions Director	BOB SCHMIDT
Accountant	JACK GALLAGHER
Public Relations Director	JOE VARGO
Chief Scout	BARRY FRASER
Sales Manager	TOM BURNS
Team Physician	DR. ROBERT MACK
Team Dentist	DR. SHELDON KORMAN
Trainer/Traveling Secretary	STEVE THOMAS
Trainer/Equipment Manager	DAVE SMITH
Radio	WWWE — 1100 AM — 50 + games LEE HAMILTON
Television	Pending
Franchise Granted	JUNE 21, 1972
Training Camp	KENT ST. UNIVERSITY
Team Colors	PURPLE, BLACK, WHITE
Ticket Prices	$6.50/5/4.50

Jay Moore

Jack Vivian

John Wilson

THE COLISEUM: $20 million structure. Completed year ago. Telescreens, private boxes. Ice surface 200 by 85. Capacity 19,861.

DENVER SPURS 1975-76 ROSTER

No.	FORWARDS	S	Ht.	Wt.	Born	1974-75 Club	League	GP	G	A	PTS	PIM
14	Backstrom, Ralph		5-10	180	9-18-37	Chicago	(WHA)	70	15	24	39	28
11	Delorme, Ron		6-2½	182	9- 3-55	Lethbridge	(WCHL)	69	30	57	87	144
	Gassoff, Ken		5-10	185	10- 9-54	Salem	(SHL)	72	31	55	86	78
21	Lavender, Brian		6- 0	180	4-20-47	Calgary	(WCHL)	55	1	6	7	42
6	LeBlanc, J. P.		5- 9	175	10-20-46	Mich/Balt.	(WHA)	78	16	33	49	100
7	Liddington, Bob		5-11	179	9-15-48	Chicago	(WHA)	78	23	18	41	27
9	MacGregor, Gary		5-11	176	9-21-54	Chicago	(WHA)	78	44	34	78	26
23	Mara, Peter		5- 6	152	7- 5-47	Victoria	(WCHL)	67	17	21	38	16
	Martin, Rick		6- 2	200	2-17-55	Victoria	(WCHL)	70	21	24	45	110
11	Miazga, Greg		6- 1	195	5- 8-55	Chicago	(WCHL)	70	14	28	42	117
19	Popiel, Jan		5- 9	183	10- 9-47	Chicago	(WHA)	60	18	22	40	74
15	Rochon, Francois		5-11	181	4-18-53	Chicago	(WHA)	69	27	29	56	19
20	Zinger, Mal		6- 1	195	5- 5-55	Kamloops	(WCHL)	70	18	43	61	196
	DEFENSEMEN											
18	Baltimore, Bryon		6- 2	196	8-26-52	Chicago	(WHA)	77	8	12	20	110
2	Bignel, Larry		5-11	181	1-18-51	Hershey	(AHL)	74	8	26	34	206
5	Deslauriers, Denis		6- 1	190	5-29-52	Oklahoma	(CHL)	60	4	12	16	128
	Gibbons, Brian		6- 3	190	7- 7-47	Toronto	(WHA)	73	4	22	26	105
24	Kokkola, Keith		6- 3	210	5- 4-49	Chicago	(WHA)	33	0	2	2	69
3	Legge, Barry		6- 0	186	10-22-54	Mich/Balt.	(WHA)	36	3	18	21	20
	Maggs, Darryl		6- 3	202	4- 6-49	Chicago	(WHA)	77	6	27	33	137
4	Mavety, Larry		5-11	185	5-29-42	Chi/Tor	(WHA)	81	10	28	38	146
	Pearson, John		6- 0	200	11- 4-52	Univ. of Denver	(WCHA)			NO RECORD AVAILABLE		
	GOALTENDERS							GP	MIN	GA	SO	GAA
1	Grigg, Chris		6- 1	180	2- 2-53	Long Island	(NAHL)	33	1708	121	0	4.25
	Johnson, Bob		6- 1	185	11-12-48	Hershey Bears	(AHL)	31	1752	106	1	3.63
	Newton, Cameron		5-10	181	2-25-50	Chicago	(WHA)	32	1904	126	0	3.97
30	Sanza, Nick		5-11	178	2- 6-55	Sherbrooke	(QJHL)	66	3846	225	7	3.51

Denver

DENVER SPURS
DENVER PROFESSIONAL SPORTS, INC.
1635 Clay Street
Denver, Colo. 80204

(303) 629-7787
Telex 45-4384

Ivan Mullenix

John Henry

Jean-Guy Talbot

President/Trustee	IVAN L. MULLENIX
Vice-President/Alternate Trustee	JOHN H. HENRY
General Manager/Coach	JEAN-GUY TALBOT
Assistant to General Manager/Coach	BOB McCORD
Director Public Relations	J. B. (JAKE) BALDWIN, JR.
Assistant Director Public Relations	MS. SIDNEY CORNWALL
Trainer	TOBY WILSON
Assistant Trainer	JOHN CLAYTON
Team Physician	ROBERT G. FISHER, M.D.
Team Dentist	DAVID STONE, D.D.S.
Franchise Granted	JUNE, 1975
Radio	KOA — 850 AM — all games BOB MARTIN
Television	Pending
Team Colors	ORANGE, BLACK, WHITE
Training Camp	McNICHOLS SPORTS ARENA
Public Address Announcer	GENE PRICE
Ticket Prices	$8/6/5/4 (plus 10% city tax)

McNICHOLS SPORTS ARENA:
Ground breaking August 7, 1973. Named after current Denver Mayor William H. McNichols, Jr. Construction cost $13,500,000. Capacity 16,800.

EDMONTON OILERS 1975-76 ROSTER

No.	FORWARDS	S	Ht.	Wt.	Born	1974-75 Club	League	GP	G	A	PTS	PIM
19	Baird, Ken	L	6-0	190	2-1-51	Edmonton	(WHA)	77	30	28	58	151
5	Barrie, Doug	R	5-9	175	10-2-46	Edmonton	(WHA)	78	12	33	45	122
8	Evo, Bill	L	6-2	187	2-21-54	Mich/Balt	(WHA)	49	13	9	22	32
16	Joyal, Eddie	R	6-0	180	5-8-40	Edmonton	(WHA)	78	22	25	47	2
11	Krake, Skip	R	5-11	170	10-14-43	Cleveland	(WHA)	71	15	23	38	108
21	Laing, Bill	L	6-2	190	3-24-53	Edmonton	(WHA)	42	2	4	6	32
14	MacDonald, Blair	R	5-10	180	11-17-53	Edmonton	(WHA)	72	22	24	46	14
12	MacGregor, Bruce	R	5-10	180	4-26-41	Salt Lake	(CHL)	72	24	28	52	10
18	McAneeley, Bob	L	5-8	175	11-7-50	Victoria	(WCHL)	74	32	38	70	118
22	Morris, Peter	L	5-9	165	6-29-55	Edmonton	(WHA)	70	43	72	115	173
17	Patenaude, Rusty	R	5-9	175	10-17-49	Edmonton	(WHA)	56	20	16	36	38
7	Rogers, Mike	L	5-9	170	10-24-54	Sudbury	(OHA)	78	35	48	83	2
25	Russell, Bob	R	5-9	167	2-5-55	Edmonton	(WHA)	69	51	4	105	18
15	Sheehy, Tim (AB)	R	6-1	185	9-3-48	Omaha	(CHL)	81	28	33	61	22
10	Sutherland, Ali	L	5-8	170	9-25-48	Toronto	(NHL)	76	31	40	71	87
9	Ullman, Norm	L	5-10	185	12-26-35			80	9	26	35	8
	DEFENSEMEN											
20	Carlyle, Steve	L	5-10	180	3-10-50	Edmonton	(WHA)	73	4	25	29	46
3	Hamilton, Al	R	6-2	195	8-20-46	Edmonton	(WHA)	25	1	13	14	42
6	Kennett, Murray	L	5-10	175	6-28-52	Edmonton	(WHA)	78	5	17	22	25
4	Ketter, Kerry	L	6-1	200	9-20-47	Omaha	(CHL)	31	2	11	13	36
2	Long, Barry	L	6-2	210	1-3-49	Edmonton	(WHA)	78	20	40	60	116
13	McAneeley, Ted	L	5-9	185	11-7-50	Salt Lake	(CHL)	63	9	41	50	147

No.	GOALTENDERS	S	Ht.	Wt.	Born	1974-75 Club	League	GP	MIN	GA	SO	GAA
29	Dryden, Dave	L	6-1	186	9-5-41	Chicago	(WHA)	45	2728	176	1	3.87
30	Worthy, Chris	L	6-0	186	10-23-47	Edmonton	(WHA)	28	1660	99	1	3.58

AB—American Born.

Edmonton

EDMONTON OILERS
EDMONTON WORLD HOCKEY ENTERPRISES LTD.
EDMONTON COLISEUM
7424-118th Ave.,
Edmonton, Alta. T5B 4M9

(403) 474-8561
Telex 037-3595

Zane Feldman

Bill Hunter

Clare Drake

President/Chairman of the Board	ZANE FELDMAN
Vice-President/Trustee General Manager	W. D. (BILL) HUNTER
Vice-President	E. E. FITZGIBBONS
Directors	DR. A. C. ALLARD A. F. GRIFFITHS HERB PINDER, SR.
Secretary/Treasurer/Comptroller	R. L. BARTH
Director Marketing/Public Relations	DOUG T. WENSCHLAG
Coach	CLARE DRAKE
Chief Scout	ROBERT FREEMAN
Trainer/Physiotherapist	DAN DEVLIN
Equipment Manager	JOHN BLACKWELL
Franchise Granted	NOVEMBER, 1971
Radio	CFRN — 1260 AM — all games ROD PHILLIPS/AL McCANN
Television	ITV — Ch. 13 — 12 games
Team Colors	ROYAL BLUE, ORANGE, WHITE
Training Camp	EDMONTON COLISEUM
Ticket Prices	$8/7/5/4

THE COLISEUM: Canada's newest indoor arena. Cost $15 million. Excavation summer 1973, opened Nov. 10, 1974. Ice surface 200 by 85. Capacity 15,273. No standing room.

13

HOUSTON AEROS 1975-76 ROSTER

No.	FORWARDS	S	Ht.	Wt.	Born	1974-1975 Club	League	GP	G	A	PTS	PIM
11	Hall, Murray	R	5-11	174	11-24-40	Houston	(WHA)	78	18	29	47	40
19	Hansis, Ron	R	6-2	193	11-12-52	Mtl. Loyola	(ECCL)		NO RECORD AVAILABLE			
7	Hughes, Frank	R	5-10	180	10- 1-49	Houston	(WHA)	76	48	35	83	35
27	Larway, Don	R	6-1	192	2- 2-54	Houston	(WHA)	76	22	14	36	59
15	Peace, David	R	6-2	185	7-24-52	Cornell	(ECAC)	28	26	37	63	26
21	Preston, Rich	R	6-0	185	5-22-52	Houston	(WHA)	78	21	20	41	8
22	Borgeson, Don	L	5-11	180	5-20-45	Phoenix	(WHA)	74	29	28	57	38
16	Hinse, Andre	L	5-9	175	4-19-45	Houston	(WHA)	75	39	47	86	12
4	Howe, Mark, (AB)	L	5-11	180	5-28-55	Houston	(WHA)	74	36	40	76	30
14	Taylor, Ted	L	6-0	175	2-25-42	Houston	(WHA)	73	26	27	53	130
10	Labossiere, Gordon	L	6-1	185	1- 2-40	Houston	(WHA)	76	23	34	57	40
13	Lund, Larry	R	6-0	190	9-9-40	Houston	(WHA)	78	33	75	108	68
8	Ruskowski, Terry	L	5-11	168	12-31-54	Houston	(WHA)	71	10	37	47	134
23	Sherrit, Jim	R	5-7	170	9-29-48	Houston	(WHA)	77	22	25	47	25
	Tonelli, John	L	6-1	190	3-23-57	Toronto	(OHA)	70	49	86	135	85
18	West, Steve	L	5-9	165	3-20-52	Mich/Balt.	(WHA)	50	15	18	33	4
	DEFENSEMEN											
17	Hale, Larry	L	6-1	180	10- 9-41	Houston	(WHA)	76	2	18	20	40
3	Howe, Marty, (AB)	L	6-1	185	2-18-54	Houston	(WHA)	75	13	21	34	89
24	Irwin, Glen	R	5-11	195	3- 1-51	Houston	(WHA)	70	2	11	13	153
20	Mosdell, Wayne	R	6-3	195	4-12-44	Roanoke Vly.	(SHL)	72	21	51	72	71
6	Popiel, Poul	L	5-10	176	2-28-43	Houston	(WHA)	78	11	53	64	123
2	Schella, John	L	6-0	180	5- 9-47	Houston	(WHA)	78	10	42	52	176
5	Stevens, Mike	L	5-11	190	10-13-50	Phoenix	(WHA)	70	2	16	18	69
	GOALTENDERS							GP	MIN	GA	SO	GAA
1	Aberhart, Bruce	L	5-11	195	9-19-54	Tulsa	(CHL)	15	777	61	0	4.71
		L				Fort Wayne	(IHL)	13	647	57	0	5.29
29	Grahame, Ron	L	5-11	175	6- 7-50	Houston	(WHA)	43	2590	131	4	3.03
30	Rutledge, Wayne	L	6-2	200	1- 5-42	Houston	(WHA)	35	2098	113	2	3.23

AB—American Born.

Houston

HOUSTON AEROS
Houston Aeros Hockey Club, Inc.
The Summit
10 Greenway Plaza
Houston, Texas 77027

(713) 629-5555
Telex 77-5520

George Bolin

Chairman of the Board/Trustee	GEORGE BOLIN
Chairman Executive Committee	WALTER W. FONDREN III
President	GORDIE HOWE
Vice-President General Manager/Coach	BILL DINEEN
Vice-President Finance/Administration	BOB KELTIE
General Counsel/Alternate Trustee	HARRISON VICKERS
Assistant to General Manager	JACK STANFIELD
Director Media Relations	RICH BURK
Ticket Manager	BRYAN WINDHAM
Season Ticket Sales Director	BILL McCOWIN
Season Ticket Sales Co-ordinator	KEMPER KAISER
Trainer	BOBBY BROWN
Equipment Manager/Assistant Trainer	BOBBY KINCAID
Assistant Equipment Manager	BOB SKELTON
Team Physicians	DR. AL KNOLL/DR. BILL RYLEE
Team Dentist	DR. GENE CRABTREE
Franchise Granted	APRIL 15, 1972
Radio	KTRH-740 AM — all games JERRY TRUPIANO
Television	KVRL-Ch. 26 — 10 games.
Press Box Locations	LOWER CONCOURSE (north and south sides)
Team Colors	NAVY BLUE, POWDER BLUE, WHITE
Training Camp	SHARPSTOWN ICE CENTER (HOUSTON)
Ticket Prices	$10/8/7/5

Gordie Howe

Bill Dineen

THE SUMMIT: 10 Greenway Plaza. Underground parking for 6,000 cars. Construction cost $18.1 million. Excavation January, 1974. Ice surface 200 × 85. Capacity 14,906.

15

INDIANAPOLIS RACERS 1975-76 ROSTER

No.	FORWARDS	S	Ht.	Wt.	Born	1974-75 Club	League	GP	G	A	PTS	PIM
9	Buchanan, Ron		6-3	185	11-15-44	Ind/Edm/Clev	(WHA)	58	24	24	48	22
18	Coates, Brian		6-0	196	9-22-52	Long Island	(NAHL)	42	21	37	58	33
						Chicago	(WHA)	35	12	9	21	26
16	Fitchner, Bob		6-0	190	12-22-50	Indianapolis	(WHA)	77	11	19	30	114
10	Harbaruk, Nick		6-0	195	8-16-43	Indianapolis	(WHA)	78	20	23	43	52
26	Heatley, Murray		5-8	185	11-5-48	Ind/Minn	(WHA)	51	20	17	37	56
15	Karlander, Al		5-8	174	11-5-46	New England	(WHA)	51	7	14	21	2
20	Scharf, Ted		5-11	185	10-3-51	San Diego	(WHA)	67	3	1	4	94
22	Sheridan, John		6-1	190	9-18-54	Indianapolis	(WHA)	58	17	11	28	20
						Mohawk Valley	(NAHL)	15	8	7	15	22
17	Sicinski, Bob		5-9	175	11-13-46	Indianapolis	(WHA)	77	19	35	54	12
8	Thomas, Reg		5-10	170	4-21-53	Mich/Balt.	(WHA)	50	8	13	21	42
7	Whitlock, Bob		5-10	175	7-16-49	Indianapolis	(WHA)	74	31	26	57	56
14	Wiste, Jim		5-10	185	2-18-46	Indianapolis	(WHA)	75	13	28	41	30
6	Wyrozub, Randy		5-11	170	4-8-50	Richmond	(AHL)	71	21	32	53	31
	DEFENSEMEN											
24	Block, Ken		5-10	185	3-18-44	Ind/S.D.	(WHA)	73	1	28	29	30
4	Clackson, Kim		5-10	195	2-13-55	Victoria	(WCHL)	58	7	26	33	359
2	Prentice, Bill		6-0	190	8-3-50	Houston	(WHA)	17	0	3	3	19
						Tulsa	(CHL)	42	1	7	8	85
3	Proceviat, Dick		6-0	180	6-25-46	Ind/Chi	(WHA)	63	1	31	32	62
12	Stapleton, Pat		5-8	180	7-4-40	Chicago	(WHA)	68	4	30	34	38
5	Woytowich, Bob		5-11	197	8-18-41	Ind/Wpg	(WHA)	66	0	12	12	36
	GOALTENDERS							GP	MIN	GA	SO	GAA
1	Brown, Andy		6-0	185	2-15-44	Indianapolis	(WHA)	52	2979	206	2	4.15
30	Holmquist, Leif		5-11	175	9-22-42	National Team	(AIK)		NO RECORD AVAILABLE			

Indianapolis

INDIANAPOLIS RACERS
INDIANAPOLIS HOCKEY CLUB LTD.
Market Square Center
151 N. Delaware St.
Indianapolis, Ind. 46204   (317) 634-3131
                              Telex 273-25

Paul Deneau

Chairman of the Board/Trustee	PAUL H. DENEAU
President/General Manager Alternate Trustee	JAMES W. BROWITT
Vice-President	PER MOLLER
Secretary/Treasurer	JOHN L. EVANS
Coach	JACQUES DEMERS
Director Public Relations	WALT MARLOW
Head Trainer	EDDIE SWISS
Assistant Trainer	MICHEL CAIRNS
Sales/Promotion Manager	TIM MILLER
Ticket Manager	LARRY TAYLOR
Team Physicians	DR. JOSEPH RANDOLPH DR. WILLIAM IRVINE
Team Dentist	DR. TOM LAPP
Franchise Granted	SEPTEMBER 14, 1973
Radio	WIBC — 1070 AM — all games BOB LAMEY
Television	WTTV — Ch. 4 — 15 games 5 HOME, 10 AWAY
Team Colors	RED, WHITE, BLUE
Training Camp	CARMEL, IND.
Ticket Prices	$7.50/6/4

James Browitt

MARKET SQUARE ARENA:
Completed Sept. 14, 1974 at cost of $22 million. Ice surface (200 by 85) on third floor. Capacity 16,500 inc. standing room.

17

MINNESOTA FIGHTING SAINTS 1975-76 ROSTER

No.	FORWARDS	S	Ht.	Wt.	Born	1974-75 Club	League	GP	G	A	PTS	PIM
12	Antonovich, Mike (AB)	L	5-8	165	10-18-51	Minnesota	(WHA)	66	24	26	50	6
16	Boucha, Henry (AB)	R	6-0	185	6-1-51	Minnesota	(WHA)	51	15	14	29	23
19	Brackenbury, Curt	R	6-0	200	1-31-52	Hampton	(SHL)	6	0	0	0	22
20	Carlson, Jack (AB)	L	6-3	190	8-23-54	Minnesota	(WHA)	46	19	24	43	212
						Johnstown	(NAHL)	32	5	4	9	83
21	Carlson, Steve (AB)	L	6-3	180	8-26-55	Johnstown	(NAHL)	50	27	22	49	246
7	Connelly, Wayne	R	5-10	172	12-16-39	Minnesota	(WHA)	70	30	58	88	84
8	Gambucci, Gary (AB)	L	5-9	181	9-17-46	Minnesota	(WHA)	76	38	33	71	16
						Johnstown	(NAHL)	68	19	18	37	19
10	Hampson, Ted	L	5-8	172	11-11-36	Minnesota	(NAHL)	7	1	7	8	2
26	Hanson, Dave (AB)	L	6-0	193	4-12-54	Johnstown	(NAHL)	78	17	35	52	6
25	Huck, Fran	R	5-7	167	12-4-45	Minnesota	(WHA)	72	10	24	34	249
14	Keon, Dave	L	5-9	168	3-22-40	Toronto	(NHL)	78	22	44	66	26
19	McKenzie, John	R	5-9	178	12-12-37	Vancouver	(WHA)	78	16	43	59	4
4	Walton, Mike	L	5-9	180	1-3-45	Minnesota	(WHA)	74	23	37	60	84
								73	48	45	93	33
	DEFENSEMEN											
17	Arbour, John	L	6-0	217	9-28-45	Minnesota	(WHA)	71	12	43	55	67
5	Busniuk, Ron	R	5-11	194	8-13-48	Minnesota	(WHA)	73	2	21	23	176
2	Butters, Bill (AB)	R	5-10	185	1-1-51	Minnesota	(WHA)	31	2	2	4	58
15	Odrowski, Gerry	L	5-11	190	10-4-38	Okla. City	(CHL)	32	5	9	14	192
3	Smith, Rick	L	5-11	186	5-29-48	Phoenix	(WHA)	77	5	38	43	77
6	Westrum, Pat (AB)	L	5-10	185	3-3-48	Minnesota	(WHA)	78	9	29	38	112
						Johnstown	(NAHL)	22	0	3	3	46
23	Zyrmiak, Jerry	R	6-1	195	10-19-48	Baltimore	(WHA)	34	2	11	13	53
						Greensboro	(SHL)	48	3	9	12	53
								23	4	15	19	35

	GOALTENDERS							GP	MIN	GA	SO	GAA
1	Curran, Mike (AB)	L	5-9	177	4-14-44	Minnesota	(WHA)	27	1367	90	0	3.94
35	Garrett, John	L	5-8	176	5-17-51	Minnesota	(WHA)	55	3294	180	2	3.28

AB — American Born.

Minnesota

MINNESOTA FIGHTING SAINTS
MINNESOTA SAINTS, INC.
ST. PAUL CIVIC CENTER
143 W. 4th Street
St. Paul, Minn. 55102   (612) 222-3040
                          TELEX 297-499

Wayne Belisle

President/Trustee	WAYNE T. BELISLE
Alternate Trustee	JOHN IRVINE
General Manager	GLEN SONMOR
Coach	HARRY NEALE
Public Relations Director	MIKE LAMEY
Ticket Manager	TOM PERRAULT
Vice-President/Director Marketing	KEN BEIERSDORF
Trainer	GLENN GOSTICK
Equipment Manager	DON NIEDERKORN
Team Physicians	DR. E. DUANE ENGSTROM
	DR. NORMAN HOLTE
	DR. LYLE OL JOHNSON
Western Canada Scout	ROY KELLY
Eastern Canada Scout	LLOYD GAIR
Franchise Granted	AUGUST 1, 1971
Radio	WLOL – 1330 AM – all games
	FRANK BUETEL
Television	Pending
Club Colors	ROYAL BLUE, WHITE, GOLD
Press Box	SOUTH SIDE
Biggest Crowd	April 4, 1975 (17,312) largest ever for hockey in State of Minnesota and a WHA record.
Training Camp	ST. PAUL CIVIC CENTER
Ticket Prices	$7.50/$6.50/$5.50/$4.50/$3.50

Glen Sonmor

Harry Neale

CIVIC CENTER: Opened Jan. 1, 1973. Built at cost of $19 million. Only rink in North America with glass dasher boards. Ice surface 200 by 85. Capacity 15,705 plus standing room.

NEW ENGLAND WHALERS 1975-76 ROSTER

No.	FORWARDS	S	Ht.	Wt.	Born	1974-75 Club	League	GP	G	A	PTS	PIM
19	Arndt, Danny	L	5-10	175	3-26-55	Saskatoon	(WCHA)	57	44	34	78	19
21	Byers, Mike	R	5-10	195	9-11-46	New England	(WHA)	72	22	26	48	10
7	Caffery, Terry	R	5-9	170	4- 1-49	New England	(WHA)	65	15	37	52	12
9	Carleton, Wayne	L	6-3	215	8- 4-46	New England	(WHA)	73	35	39	74	50
18	Charlebois, Bob	L	5-11	180	5-27-44	Cape Cod	(NAHL)	8	1	0	1	0
						Edm/N.E.	(WHA)	60	24	57	81	54
15	Climie, Ron	L	5-11	180	3- 5-50	New England	(WHA)	74	23	31	54	27
23	Fotiu, Nick	L	6-2	200	5-25-52	New England	(WHA)	61	2	2	4	144
16	O'Donnell, Fred	R	5-10	180	12- 6-49	New England	(WHA)	76	21	15	36	84
12	Paiement, Rosaire	L	5-11	185	8-12-45	Chicago	(WHA)	78	26	48	74	97
4	Pleau, Larry	L	6-1	190	5-29-47	New England	(WHA)	78	30	34	64	50
20	Swain, Garry	L	5-9	170	9-11-47	New England	(WHA)	65	7	15	22	18
8	Webster, Tom	R	5-10	185	10- 4-48	New England	(WHA)	66	40	24	64	52
	DEFENSEMEN											
6	Abrahamsson, Thommy	L	6-2	190	4- 8-47	New England	(WHA)	76	8	23	31	44
10	Hangsleben, Alan	L	6-1	195	2-22-53	New England	(WHA)	26	0	6	6	8
						Cape Cod	(NAHL)	55	4	39	43	130
5	Hurley, Paul	R	5-11	195	7-12-46	New England	(WHA)	75	3	26	29	36
2	Ley, Rick	L	5-9	185	12- 2-48	New England	(WHA)	62	6	36	42	50
17	Roberts, Doug	R	6-2	200	10-28-42	Detroit	(NHL)	26	4	4	8	8
						Virginia	(AHL)	31	7	11	18	32
22	Roberts, Gordon	R	6-1	190	10- 2-57	Victoria	(WCHL)	53	19	45	64	145
3	Selwood, Brad	L	6-1	190	3-18-49	New England	(WHA)	77	4	35	39	117
	GOALTENDERS							GP	MIN	GA	SO	GAA
1	Abrahamsson, Christer		6-2	175	4- 8-47	New England	(WHA)	16	870	47	1	3.24
29	Hoganson, Paul		6-0	180	11-12-49	Baltimore	(WHA)	32	1776	122	2	4.12
30	Landon, Bruce		5-9	190	10- 5-49	New England	(WHA)	7	339	19	0	3.36
						Cape Cod	(NAHL)	3	214	12	0	3.36

New England

NEW ENGLAND WHALERS
NEW ENGLAND WHALERS HOCKEY CLUB, INC.
One Civic Center Plaza
Hartford, Ct. 06103   (203) 728-3366
                             Telex 994-476

Howard Baldwin

Managing General Partner/Trustee	HOWARD L. BALDWIN
General Manager/Coach	JACK KELLEY
Assistant to Managing General Partner	RON RYAN
Communications Director	BILL RASMUSSEN
Sales Manager	GEORGE DUCHARME
Public Relations Director	KEVIN WALSH
Business Manager	DAVE ANDREWS
Assistant General Manager	JACK FERREIRA
Media Relations Director	BOB NEUMEIER
Ticket Manager	BRIAN MACLEOD
Merchandising Manager	VAL CHAMBERLAIN
Trainer	JOE ALTOTT
Equipment Manager	SKIP CUNNINGHAM
Franchise Granted	NOVEMBER 21, 1971
Radio	WTIC 1080 AM Hartford - all games WARE 1250 AM — Ware, Mass. WSPR 1270 AM Springfield BOB NEUMEIER
Television	WFSB Ch. 3 — 6 games 5 Station CPTV Network — 12 games Ch. 24 Hartford Ch. 49 Bridgeport Ch. 53 Norwich Ch. 61 Waterbury Ch. 65 New Haven BILL RASMUSSEN/RON RYAN
Team Colors	GREEN, GOLD, WHITE
Training Camp	GLASTONBURY, CT.
Ticket Prices	$8.50/7/5

Jack Kelley

Ron Ryan

HARTFORD CIVIC CENTER:
Construction of $30 million Convention
Center complex started June, 1972.
Building opened Jan. 11, 1975. No
standing room. Ice surface 200 × 85.
Capacity 10,507.

21

PHOENIX ROADRUNNERS 1975-76 ROSTER

No.	FORWARDS	S	Ht.	Wt.	Born	1974-75 Club	League	GP	G	A	PTS	PIM
14	Boyd, Jim	L	5-10	180	6- 4-49	Phoenix	(WHA)	76	26	44	70	18
17	Connor, Cam	L	6- 2	205	8-10-54	Phoenix	(WHA)	57	9	19	28	168
16	Cormier, Michel	L	5- 9	175	12-22-45	Phoenix	(WHA)	78	36	38	74	26
21	Dean, Barry	L	6- 1	195	2-26-55	Medicine Hat	(WCHL)	64	40	75	115	159
8	Ftorek, Robbie (AB)	L	5- 9	160	1- 2-52	Phoenix	(WHA)	52	31	37	68	29
						Tulsa	(CHL)	11	6	10	16	14
15	Gray, John	L	5-10	180	8-13-49	Phoenix	(WHA)	75	35	33	68	107
9	Hall, Del	L	5-10	170	5- 7-49	Salt Lake	(CHL)	70	32	32	64	4
12	Huston, Ron	R	5-10	185	4- 8-45	California	(NHL)	56	12	21	33	8
11	Keogan, Murray	L	5-10	175	1-14-50	Phoenix	(WHA)	78	35	29	64	68
7	McNamee, Pete	L	5-11	200	9-11-50	Phx/Van	(WHA)	66	11	20	31	92
						Tulsa	(CHL)	13	2	7	9	50
18	Migneault, John	L	5-10	185	2- 4-49	Phx/Van	(WHA)	61	10	15	25	28
						Tulsa	(CHL)	8	5	3	8	0
24	Mononen, Lauri	L	6- 0	180	3-22-50	Finnish Nat'l	(Europe)	65	38	28	66	—
31	Sleep, Mike	R	6- 0	180	3-13-55	New Westminster	(WCHL)	70	28	34	62	91
33	Watt, Robbie	L	5-11	175	5- 8-54	Tulsa	(CHL)	33	8	9	17	11
	DEFENSEMEN											
38	Beaudoin, Serge	L	6- 2	215	10-30-52	Tulsa	(CHL)	37	6	31	37	139
26	Clarke, Jim	R	6- 3	215	8-11-54	Tulsa	(CHL)	67	3	8	11	74
4	Lariviere, Garry	R	6- 0	190	12- 6-54	Tulsa	(CHL)	76	15	38	53	168
						Phoenix	(WHA)	4	0	1	1	28
3	McLeod, Al	L	5-11	200	6-17-44	Phoenix	(WHA)	77	3	16	19	96
19	Niekamp, Jim (AB)	R	6- 1	185	3-11-46	Phoenix	(WHA)	71	2	26	28	66
19	Rautakallio, Pekka	L	5-11	185	7-25-53	Finnish Nat'l	(Europe)	66	10	18	28	29
6	Serafini, Ron (AB)	R	5-11	195	10-31-53	Denver	(CHL)	75	7	21	28	83

No.	GOALTENDERS	S	Ht.	Wt.	Born	1974-75 Club	League	GP	MIN	GA	SO	GAA
1	Kurt, Gary	R	6- 3	205	3- 9-47	Phoenix	(WHA)	47	2841	156	2	3.29
30	Norris, Jack	L	5-10	175	8- 5-42	Phoenix	(WHA)	33	1962	107	1	3.27

AB—American Born.

Phoenix

PHOENIX ROADRUNNERS
PHOENIX HOCKEY CLUB, INC.
1760 Valley Bank Center
Phoenix, Arizona 85073

(602) 257-5100
Telex 667-356

President and Trustee	WILLIAM H. MacFARLAND
Chairman of the Board/ Alternate Trustee	BERT A. GETZ
Vice-president/Operations	JAMES G. WELLS
Directors	STEPHEN W. CRAIG H. J. LOUIS, M.D. L. G. HOOKER, JR. BERT A. GETZ KARL ELLER WM. H. MacFARLAND
Business Manager	TERRY VIAR
Coach	SANDY HUCUL
Director of Sales	PORTER C. McKINNON, JR.
Director Public Relations	DAVE WEISER
Director Player Personnel	E. I. "AL" ROLLINS
Legal Counsel	MIKE GALLAGHER
Western Scout	RUDY FILION
Eastern Scout	MURRAY COSTELLO
Trainers	JACK CURRAN/KEN FLEGER
Team Physicians	ELI J. KRIGSTEAIN, M.D. THOMAS P. WHITE, M.D. DONALD A. CRYAN, M.D. ARTHUR C. STEVENSON, M.D.
Team Dentists	J. BARTON THOMPSON, D.D.S. REXE E. UMBENAUER, D.D.S.
Franchise Granted	SEPTEMBER 18, 1973
Training Camp	PHOENIX/TUCSON (Arizona)
Team Colors	ROYAL BLUE, GOLD, WHITE
Radio	KRUX — 1360 AM — all games JOE DAGGETT/MIKE LEONARD
Television	KPHO — Ch. 5 — 12 games
Ticket Prices	$8/5.50/4

William MacFarland

Bert Getz

Sandy Hucul

MEMORIAL COLISEUM:
Opened Oct. 21, 1967. Roof has largest painting in world, a representation of Bicentennial logo. Construction cost: $6,384,586.35. Ice surface 200 by 85. Capacity 12,600.

QUEBEC NORDIQUES 1975-76 ROSTER

No.	FORWARDS	S	Ht.	Wt.	Born	1974-75 Club	League	GP	G	A	PTS	PIM
7	Benzelock, Jim	R	5-11	187	6-21-47	Chicago	(WHA)	41	17	22	39	75
21	Bernier, Serge	R	6-1	190	4-29-47	Quebec	(WHA)	76	54	68	122	75
11	Bordeleau, Chris	L	5-8	152	9-23-47	Wpg/Que	(WHA)	71	23	41	64	24
9	Cloutier, Real	R	5-10	180	7-30-56	Quebec	(WHA)	67	26	27	53	38
14	Constantin, Charles	L	6-2	190	4-30-54	Minnesota	(WHA)	24	2	4	6	9
16	Gallant, Gordie	L	5-11	172	10-27-50	Maine	(NAHL)	64	10	13	23	205
2	Globensky, Allan	R	6-1	190	4-17-51	Quebec	(WHA)	39	7	8	15	42
5	Houle, Rejean	L	5-11	165	10-25-49	Quebec	(WHA)	65	40	52	92	37
15	Leclerc, Renald	R	5-11	165	11-12-47	Quebec	(WHA)	74	18	32	50	96
12	Parizeau, Michel	L	5-9	165	4-9-48	Quebec	(WHA)	78	28	46	74	67
17	Serviss, Tom	R	5-10	185	5-25-48	Michigan	(WHA)	65	12	18	30	20
19	Sutherland, Steve	L	6-10	172	9-1-46	Mich/Que	(WHA)	78	15	20	35	151
8	Tardif, Marc	L	6-1	178	6-12-49	Mich/Que	(WHA)	76	50	39	89	79
	DEFENSEMEN											
24	Bernier, Jean	L	5-10	170	7-21-54	Quebec	(WHA)	41	1	13	14	13
33	Hoganson, Dale	L	5-10	190	7-8-49	Quebec	(WHA)	77	9	34	43	47
20	Jordan, Rich	L	6-3	200	3-31-50	Quebec	(WHA)	69	6	8	14	68
6	Pronchuck, Ron	R	6-0	190	1-18-54	Syracuse	(NAHL)	58	2	25	27	90
10	Roy, Pierre	L	6-1	175	3-12-52	Quebec	(WHA)	78	1	18	19	120
3	Tremblay, J. C.	L	5-10	185	1-22-39	Quebec	(WHA)	69	16	56	72	18
4	Watson, Jim	L	6-2	210	6-28-43	Chicago	(WHA)	57	3	6	9	31
	GOALTENDERS							GP	MIN	GA	SO	GAA
30	Brodeur, Richard	R	5-7	160	9-15-52	Quebec	(WHA)	51	2938	188	0	3.84
23	Deguise, Michel	L	5-8	150	11-6-51	Quebec	(WHA)	---	--- DID NOT PLAY ---			---
1	Donnelly, Pete	R	5-8	160	6-14-48	Vancouver	(WHA)	---	--- DID NOT PLAY ---			---

Quebec

QUEBEC NORDIQUES
LE CLUB DE HOCKEY LES NORDIQUES, INC.
Colisee de Quebec
Quebec, P.Q. G1L 4W7

(418) 529-4161
Telex 011-3068

John Dacres

Chairman of the Board	JEAN LESAGE
President/Trustee	JOHN DACRES
Vice-President	MAURICE TASCHEREAU
General Manager	MAURICE FILLION
Coach	JEAN-GUY GENDRON
Chief Scout	YVAN PRUDHOMME
Director Public Relations	PAUL LeFRANCOIS
Trainer	RENE LACASSE
Team Physician	DR. ROBERT MEILLEUR
Public Address Announcer	YVES SABOURIN
Radio	CHRC — 800 AM Quebec City — all games Network: CKLM — 1570 AM — Montreal CKRS — 590 AM — Jonquiere CKCN — 560 AM — Sept-Iles CLAUDE BEDARD/ MARC SIMONEAU
Television	Five station Network — 10 games CFTM — Ch. 10 Montreal CFCN — Ch. 4 Quebec City CJPM — Ch. 6 Chicoutimi CHLT — Ch. 7 Sherbrooke CFVO — Cable 10 Hull JACQUES MOREAU/CLAUDE BEDARD
Team Colors	RED, WHITE, BLUE
Franchise Granted	JUNE 21, 1972
Training Camp	QUEBEC COLISEE
Ticket Prices	$8/6.50/6/3.50

Maurice Filion

Jean-Guy Gendron

THE COLISEE: Opened Dec. 15, 1949, cost of $4 million. Parking for 5000 cars. Air conditioned. Ice surface 200 by 85. Capacity 13,504. Seating for 10,004.

25

SAN DIEGO MARINERS 1975-76 ROSTER

No.	FORWARDS	S	Ht.	Wt.	Born	1974-75 Club	League	GP	G	A	PTS	PIM
10	Adduono, Ray	L	5-9	160	1-21-47	San Diego	(WHA)	78	15	59	74	23
8	Burgess, Don	L	6-0	170	6- 8-46	Vancouver	(WHA)	62	11	18	29	19
16	Devine, Kevin	L	5-9	175	12- 9-54	San Diego	(WHA)	46	4	10	14	48
						Syracuse	(NAHL)	27	11	12	23	23
9	Ferguson, Norm	R	5-8	173	10-16-45	San Diego	(WHA)	78	36	33	69	6
18	French, John	L	5-11	175	8-25-50	New England	(WHA)	75	12	41	53	28
	Goldthorpe, Bill	L	5-11	185	6-20-53	Syracuse	(NAHL)	2	0	0	0	0
						Baltimore	(WHA)	7	0	0	0	26
19	Inglis, Lee	L	5-10	175	8-31-47	Syracuse	(NAHL)	63	21	32	53	22
						San Diego	(WHA)	5	0	2	2	0
7	Lacroix, Andre	L	5-8	175	6- 5-45	San Diego	(WHA)	78	41	106	147	63
15	Morenz, Brian	L	5-10	185	5-11-49	San Diego	(WHA)	78	20	19	39	76
21	Noris, Joe	R	6-0	185	10-26-51	Syracuse	(AHL)	73	26	36	62	41
25	Peacosh, Gene	L	5-11	180	9-28-48	San Diego	(WHA)	78	43	36	79	22
12	Rivers, Wayne	R	5-9	185	2- 1-42	San Diego	(WHA)	78	54	53	107	52
27	Rouleau, Michel	L	5-10	170	9-28-44	San Diego	(WHA)	27	5	6	11	42
14	Tidey, Alex	R	6-0	182	1- 5 55	Lethbridge	(WCHL)	68	42	54	96	78
11	Walter, Dave	L	6-0	185	5- 6-52	Long Island	(NAHL)	62	38	42	80	75
	DEFENSEMEN											
6	Falkenberg, Bob	L	6-0	195	1- 1-46	San Diego	(WHA)	78	2	18	20	42
17	Hargreaves, Jim	R	5-11	195	5- 2-50	S.D./Ind	(WHA)	78	10	15	25	75
2	Hughes, Brent	L	6-0	205	6-17-43	Kansas City	(NHL)	66	1	18	19	43
23	McMahon, Mike	L	5-11	182	8-30-41	Minnesota	(WHA)	64	5	15	20	42
4	Morrison, Kevin	L	5-11	202	10-28-49	San Diego	(WHA)	78	20	61	81	143
5	Wall, Bob	L	5-10	185	12- 1-42	San Diego	(WHA)	33	0	9	9	15

No.	GOALTENDERS	S	Ht.	Wt.	Born	1974-75 Club	League	GP	MIN	GA	SO	GAA
1	Gillow, Russ	L	5-10	165	9- 2-40	San Diego	(WHA)	30	1653	94	1	3.41
						Syracuse	(NAHL)	2	129	4	0	1.86
31	Wakely, Ernie	L	5-11	170	11-27-40	Wpg/S.D.	(WHA)	41	2418	131	3	3.25

San Diego

Joseph Schwartz

Ron Ingram

SAN DIEGO MARINERS
Professional Sports Enterprises, Inc.
3500 Sports Arena Blvd.
San Diego, Ca. 92110   (714) 225-9633
                              Telex 695-084

President/Trustee	JOSEPH SCHWARTZ
General Manager/Coach	RONALD INGRAM
Business Manager/Public Relations	GABE DeNUNZIO
Director of Sales/Marketing	JOHN MURPHY
Promotions Director	GUS DIAMOND
Communications Director	ROY STOREY
Team Physician	DR. DAN DENENBERG
Team Dentist	DR. ALAN GAYLE
Trainer	RALPH MITCHELL
Chief Scout	LES CALDER
Scout	HERB ELK
Public Address Announcer	JOHN DeMOTT
Franchise Granted	JANUARY 3, 1974 (Formerly New Jersey)
Team Colors	ORANGE, BLUE, WHITE
Training Camp	MIRA MESA, CA.
Radio	KOGO-600 AM — all games ROY STOREY/JERRY GROSS
Television	Pending
Ticket Prices	$7.50/6.50/5.50/4.50/3.50

SPORTS ARENA: Completed Nov. 17, 1966, at cost of $6.5 million. 33 acres of parking (4,000 cars). Ice surface 200 by 85. Capacity 13,039.

27

TORONTO TOROS 1975-76 ROSTER

No.	FORWARDS	S	Ht.	Wt.	Born	1974-75 Club	League	GP	G	A	PTS	PIM
16	D'Alvise, Bob	L	5-11	180	12-23-52	Mich. Tech. Univ.	(WCHA)	42	37	47	84	4
8	Farda, Richard	L	5- 9	175	11- 8-45	Toronto	(WHA)	66	6	25	31	2
26	Featherstone, Tony	R	5-10	180	7-31-49	Toronto	(WHA)	77	25	39	64	25
19	Henderson, Paul	R	5-11	180	1-28-43	Toronto	(WHA)	58	30	33	63	20
25	Jacques, Jeff	R	5-11	190	4- 4-53	Mohawk Valley	(NAHL)	38	25	29	54	77
11	Kirk, Gavin	L	5-10	175	12- 6-51	Toronto	(WHA)	39	12	8	20	26
27	Mahovlich, Frank	L	5- 1	205	1-10-38	Toronto	(WHA)	78	15	58	73	69
20	Marrin, Peter	R	5-10	180	8- 8-53	Mohawk Valley	(NAHL)	73	38	44	82	30
							(WHA)	54	33	45	78	36
9	Napier, Mark	L	5-10	182	1-28-57	Toronto	(OHA)	4	3	1	4	0
14	Nedomansky, Vaclav	L	6- 1	210	3-14-44	Toronto	(WHA)	61	66	64	130	106
15	Nistico, Lou	L	5- 7	170	1-25-53	Mohawk Valley	(NAHL)	78	41	40	81	19
								42	21	27	48	103
28	Phaneuf, Jean Luc	R	5- 8	160	10-26-55	Montreal	(QJHL)	27	11	11	22	75
12	Simpson, Tom	R	5- 9	190	8-15-52	Toronto	(WHA)	71	51	100	151	13
								70	52	28	80	48
	DEFENSEMEN											
5	Amodeo, Mike	L	5- 8	185	6-22-52	Toronto	(WHA)	64	1	14	15	52
3	Cunningham, Rick	R	5-11	185	3- 3-51	Toronto	(WHA)	70	7	18	25	117
7	Dorey, Jim	L	6- 1	200	8-17-47	N.E./Tor	(WHA)	74	16	40	56	112
6	Foley, Rick	L	6- 4	218	9-22-45	Syracuse	(AHL)	69	13	40	53	306
22	Heaver, Paul	R	6- 1	195	2-15-55	Oshawa	(OHA)	67	10	24	34	163
10	Rollins, Jerry	R	6- 3	200	3-22-55	Winnipeg	(WCHL)	62	7	21	28	473
2	Turkiewicz, Jim	L	5-10	185	4-13-55	Toronto	(WHA)	78	3	27	30	28

No.	GOALTENDERS	S	Ht.	Wt.	Born	1974-75 Club	League	GP	MIN	GA	SO	GAA
1	Shaw, Jim		6- 1	185	10-18-45	Toronto	(WHA)	21	1055	71	0	4.04
33	Vien, Mario		5- 7	166	8- 7-55	Cornwall	(QJHL)	71	4211	280	1	3.99

Toronto

TORONTO TOROS

Toronto Toros Hockey Club
14 Carlton St.
Toronto, Ont. M5B 1K5

(416) 595-1919
Telex 06-23143

President/Trustee	JOHN F. BASSETT
Executive Vice-President	R. E. GIROUX
Assistant General Manager	GILLES LEGER
Coach	BOBBY BAUN
Director of Public Relations	JOE WARWICK
Director of Sales	PETE McASKILE
Ticket Manager	MICHAEL McCLURE
Assistant Ticket Manager	JOANNE LYDDON
Souvenir Manager	JOHN ARMOUR
Trainers	FRANK VANDERHART LARRY ASHLEY
Physiotherapist	MERT PROPHET
Medical Staff	DR. M. BENT DR. A. HART DR. J. STARR
Team Dentist	DR. T. McKEAN
Franchise Granted	February, 1972 (Ottawa Nationals)
Radio	Pending
Television	Global Network Ch. 6 & 22, Cable 3 — 22 games MIKE ANSCOMBE/CARL BREWER/BILL BIRD
Team Colors	BLUE, WHITE, RED
Training Camp	ORNSKOLDSVIK, SWEDEN
Ticket Prices	$10/8/6.50/5/3.50

John F. Bassett

Gilles Leger

Bob Baun

MAPLE LEAF GARDENS: Opened Nov. 12, 1931. Original construction cost $1.5 million. Ice surface 200 by 85. Capacity 16,507.

WINNIPEG JETS 1975-76 ROSTER

No.	FORWARDS	S	ht.	Wt.	Born	1974-75 Club	League	GP	G	A	PTS	PIM
11	Beaudin, Norm	R	5-8	172	11-28-41	Winnipeg	(WHA)	77	16	31	47	8
15	Hedberg, Anders	L	5-11	176	2-25-51	Winnipeg	(WHA)	65	53	47	100	45
9	Hull, Bobby	L	5-10	191	1-3-39	Winnipeg	(WHA)	78	77	65	142	41
12	Ketola, Veli-Pekka	L	6-3	207	3-28-48	Winnipeg	(WHA)	74	23	28	51	25
17	Lesuk, Bill	L	5-9	187	11-1-46	Washington	(NHL)	79	8	11	19	77
19	Lindh, Mats	L	6-1	180	9-12-47	Swedish Nationals (Europe)			NO RECORD AVAILABLE			
20	Lindstrom, Willy	L	6-0	180	5-5-51	Swedish Nationals (Europe)			NO RECORD AVAILABLE			
8	Miller, Perry	L	6-1	194	6-24-52	Winnipeg	(WHA)	67	9	19	28	133
14	Nilsson, Ulf	R	5-11	176	5-11-5	Winnipeg	(WHA)	78	26	94	120	79
10	Sullivan, Peter	R	5-9	170	7-25-51	Nova Scotia	(AHL)	75	44	60	104	50
	DEFENSEMEN											
21	Asmundson, Duke	R	6-2	200	8-17-43	Winnipeg	(WHA)	38	4	15	19	53
2	Bergman, Thommie	L	6-3	200	12-10-47	Winnipeg	(WHA)	49	4	15	19	70
3	Ford, Mike	R	6-1	180	7-26-52	Winnipeg	(WHA)	73	12	22	34	68
6	Green, Ted	R	5-10	190	3-23-40	New England	(WHA)	57	6	14	20	29
16	Hillman, Larry	L	5-11	185	2-5-37	Cleveland	(WHA)	77	0	16	16	83
5	Hornung, Larry	R	5-11	184	11-10-45	Winnipeg	(WHA)	69	7	25	32	21
7	Legge, Randy	R	5-11	185	12-16-45	Mich/Balt	(WHA)	78	1	14	15	69
18	Riihiranta, Hexi	L	5-11	190	10-4-48	Winnipeg	(WHA)	64	8	14	22	30
4	Sjoberg, Lars-Erik	L	5-8	179	4-5-44	Winnipeg	(WHA)	75	7	53	60	30
	GOALTENDERS							GP	MIN	GA	SO	GAA
1	Daley, Joe	L	5-10	171	2-20-43	Winnipeg	(WHA)	51	2902	175	1	3.62
30	Larsson, Curt	L	5-11	171	12-11-44	Winnipeg	(WHA)	26	1514	100	1	3.96

Winnipeg

WINNIPEG JETS
WINNIPEG HOCKEY CLUB, INC.
15-1430 Maroons Road
Winnipeg, Manitoba R3G 0L5

(204) 772-9491
Telex 075-87810

Bob Graham

President	R. G. (Bob) GRAHAM
Trustee	OSCAR GRUBERT
General Manager	RUDY PILOUS
Coaches	BOBBY KROMM/BOBBY HULL
Vice-Presidents	JACK McKEAG/JIM BURNS
Chief Scout	BILL ROBINSON
Director of Media Relations	NORMAN COSTON
Trainer	BILL BOZAK
Equipment Manager	KELLY PRUDEN
Franchise Granted	DECEMBER 27, 1971
Radio	CJOB — 680 AM — all games KEN NICOLSON/BOB IRVING ED DEARDEN
Television	Pending
Team Colors	BLUE, RED, WHITE
Training Camp	WINNIPEG ARENA
Ticket Prices	$8/6.50/4

Rudy Pilous

Bobby Kromm

WINNIPEG ARENA: Opened Oct. 18, 1955. Construction cost $2 million. Seating for 10,131. Arena phone (204) 783-4223. Ice Surface 200 × 85. Capacity 10,631.

WHA OFFICIALS

Director of Officials ....BOB FRAMPTON
Referee-In-Chief ....BILL FRIDAY

LEAGUE REFEREES

1. BILL FRIDAY
3. BOB KOLARI
4. WAYNE MUNDEY
5. RON HARRIS
6. PETER MOFFAT
10. ALLAN GLASPELL
11. RON ASSELSTINE

LINESMEN

12. Pierre Belanger
14. Ronald Fournier
20. Gene Kusy
21. Ross N. Keenan
22. Eric Manship
23. Graham Hern
24. Wayne Bonney
25. Joseph Dame
26. Ronald Foyt
27. Kenneth Pierce
28. Paul Corcoran

GAME OFFICIALS

CALGARY — Ernest Minhinnett (supervisor/game timekeeper), Jack Wafefield, Charles Marsh (goal judges), Bob Peltier, Joe Cassidy (scorers), Berto Pegoraro, Doug Young (penalty timekeepers), Stan Jaycock, Lou Soucier, Ed Soucier (statisticians), Daryl Janz (public address).

CINCINNATI — George Callies (supervisor/official scorer), Dennis White, Bruce Chamberlain (goal judges), Jay Rizzuto, Fred Heflin (timekeepers), Joe Minster, Don Fisher (statisticians), Dave Chamberlain, Terry Shutt (penalty box attendants), Bill Hagen, Steve Dick (alternates).

CLEVELAND — Earl Miller (supervisor/game timekeeper), Howard Schleimer, Philip Simon, Tim Katrinak (goal judges), Bob Carse, Ray Liskay (scorers), John Balunek, Ken Goss (penalty timekeepers), Roger Hayda, Gary Nickerson, Charles Kochy (statisticians), George Flynn, Tom Kimball (alternates), Howie Chizek (public address).

DENVER — Dan Polsby (supervisor/chief statistician), Gary Hart, Rod Lippman, Ed Fitzsimmons (goal judges), Hugh Gill, Joe Patrick (scorers), Fritz Carroll (game timekeeper), Bill Gill, Dick Coffenbow, Bill Haefle (penalty timekeepers), Danny Talbot (asst. statistician), Hugh Gill (alternate), Gene Price (public address).

officials

EDMONTON — Bob Walker (supervisor/game timekeeper), Ted McPhee, Gary Hill (goal judges), Sandy Miller, Don Whidden (scorers), Dick Carreau (penalty timekeeper), Merv McDonald, Bob Olynyk (statisticians), Grant Hill (alternate), Gordon Ross (public address).

HOUSTON — Charlie Toland (supervisor), Joe Chiswell, Andy Page (goal judges), Dutch Keen, Leighton Young (scorers), Joe Long, Ron Ellis, Jerry Raduziner (timekeepers), Ken Mays, Warren Hynes (statisticians), Terry Lieweke (public address).

INDIANAPOLIS — Paul Minott (supervisor/scorer), Lee Hummel, Bill Fuller, Tom Berry (goal judges), Ray Lord (asst. scorer), Dale Hummel, Dennis Pope, Bob Fraser (timekeepers), Don Lawless, Paul Minnott, Jr. (statisticians), Scott Starks, Bill Donnella (public address).

MINNESOTA — Ron Vanelli (supervisor), Rod Smith, Russ Miester, Bill McCellan, John Jundt, Al Maki (goal judges), Arnie Bauer, Paul Bauer (scorers), Joe Borsch, Jim Killen, Ted Olson (timekeepers), Jack Kelly, Dan Gibbons (statisticians), Jerry Hladky, Jim Essling (press box), Bud McGowan, Stan Persby, Roger Pietrus, Randy Tollefson, Joe Fischler, Bernie Coliazy (time table), Phil Mooney, Ted Greshner, Gene Gibbons (alternates).

NEW ENGLAND — John Richard (supervisor), Ray Cote, Bill Perry (goal judges), Bob Guarente (scorer), Jim MacDonald, Dennis Cronan (timekeepers), Howard Holcomb (statistician), Scott Rasmussen, Bob Kaminsky, J. R. Chevalier (penalty box attendants), John Pynchon (alternate), Floyd Richards (public address).

PHOENIX — Frank Austin (supervisor), Herb Revens, Ron Sutherland (goal judges), Newton Bayless, Jim Winkle (scorers), John Kline, Frank Doyle, Ralph Henderson (timekeepers), Joe Parks, Dick Corbo (statisticians), Art Cliff, Jack Flett, Hal Wallace, Creed Batson, Jr. (alternates), Dave Tunell (public address).

QUEBEC — Adrian Cloutier, Gilles Poulin, James Cornell, Gaston Filion, Adelard Cloutier (goal judges), Raymond Puchol, Adelard Poulin (scorers), Robert Marier, Claude Legare, Jean Cote (timekeepers), Marcel Beaudoin (statistician), Jean Gavel (public address).

SAN DIEGO — Doug Zink (supervisor/game timekeeper), Jerry Davis, Jim Koshley (goal judges), Bill Brown, Bruce Knight (scorers), Manny Gomes, Harry Lockwood (timekeepers), Bruce Binkowski (statistician), Ken Harwood, Bob Barlow, Nick Kochen, Dennis Rowden, Jake Gaston, Candy Shine, Bob Hughes, Vern Westcott, Jim Meyer, Stephen DeNunzio (alternates), John DeMott (public address).

TORONTO — Bruce Cameron (supervisor/scorer), Gary Gordon, Harold Clancy, Jack Schmidt (goal judges), Connie Mandala, Pat Murphy (timekeepers), Jim Murchie (statistician).

WINNIPEG — R. W. Bell (supervisor), James Witty, James Mier (goal judges), Dave Oakley, A. R. MacGilivray (scorers), Bob Mick, Dick Heaver, R. K. Elson (timekeepers), R. M. Sanregret, G. R. Smith (statisticians), J. Schabler (alternate), Ted Barton (public address).

BOBBY HULL: 77 Goals in 78 Games

A game-by-game account of Bobby Hull's 1974-75 season achievement of 77 goals in 78 games, most prolific single season goal production in the history of major league hockey.

Opp.	Date	Game No.	Goal Number	Sog	Vs. Goaltender	Final Score	
At Van.	10-15-74	1		5	Don McLeod	WPG 6	Van 2
Edm.	10-18	2		4	Ken Brown	WPG 4	Edm 0
At Tor.	10-25	3	1	8	Jim Shaw	Tor 3	WPG 1
Mich.	10-27	4	2	5	Gerry Desjardins	WPG 5	Mich 2
Phx.	10-30	5	3-4-5	10	Gary Kurt	WPG 6	Phx 5
Tor.	11- 1	6	6-7-8	6	Gilles Gratton	WPG 10	Tor 1
Mich.	11- 3	7	9	4	Jim McLeod		
			10	1	Gerry Desjardins	WPG 11	Mich 3
Minn.	11- 5	8	11	8	Mike Curran	WPG 6	Minn 4
At Van.	11- 9	9	12	7	Don McLeod	WPG 3	Van 3
At Edm.	11-13	10	13	7	Jacques Plante	Edm 5	WPG 3
Ind.	11-15	11		5	Ed Dyck	WPG 5	Ind 0
Tor.	11-17	12		5	Jim Shaw	Tor 3	WPG 1
At Edm.	11-18	13	14-15	4	Jacques Plante	Edm 5	WPG 3
Minn.	11-20	14	16-17	5	Mike Curran	WPG 3	Minn 1
Phx.	11-24	15		1	Jack Norris	Phx 3	WPG 1
At Ind.	11-26	16	18	6	Andy Brown	WPG 4	Ind 0
At Clev.	11-27	17	19	11	Gerry Cheevers	Clev 5	WPG 4
Mich.	11-29	18	20-21-22-23	15	Gerry Desjardins		
				2	Jim McLeod	WPG 7	Mich 6
Que.	12- 1	19		6	Richard Brodeur	WPG 3	Que 2
Hou.	12- 4	20		9	Ron Grahame	Hou 3	WPG 2
At Minn.	12- 6	21		4	Mike Curran	Minn 4	WPG 3
Chi.	12- 8	22		8	Cam Newton	WPG 5	Chi 2
At Ind.	12-10	23	24	5	Andy Brown	WPG 5	Ind 3
At Mich.	12-12	24	25	4	Gerry Desjardins	Micn 5	WPG 3
At Hou.	12-14	25	26	7	Ron Grahame	Hou 5	WPG 3
N.E.	12-15	26	27	7	Al Smith	N.E. 4	WPG 3
At Tor.	12-17	27	28-29	9	Gilles Gratton	WPG 4	Tor 1
At Que.	12-18	28		8	Richard Brodeur	Que 5	WPG 1
Phx.	12-22	29	30	12	Gary Kurt	Phx 4	WPG 2
At Phx.	12-26	30		6	Jack Norris	WPG 3	Phx 2
At S.D.	12-28	31	31	1	Joe Junkin		
			32	4	Russ Gillow	WPG 6	S.D. 4
At Hou.	12-29	32	33-34	6	Wayne Rutledge	Hou 6	WPG 3
At Clev.	1- 7-75	33	35	9	Gerry Cheevers	WPG 4	Clev 4
At Mich.	1- 9	34	36	10	Paul Hoganson	Mich 5	WPG 4
Que.	1-10	35		7	Richard Brodeur	Que 6	WPG 1
Van.	1-15	36		3	Don McLeod	Van 4	WPG 2
Clev.	1-19	37	37-38	9	Gerry Cheevers	WPG 9	Clev 4

Bobby Hull

Location	Date	Goal #	Multi	Assists	Goalie	Score			
Ind.	1-22	38	39	10	Andy Brown	Ind	3	WPG	1
At Edm.	1-23	39	40-41	6	Jacques Plante	Edm	7	WPG	3
At Van.	1-24	40		3	Don McLeod	Van	4	WPG	3
Hou.	1-26	41		4	Ron Grahame	Hou	3	WPG	1
At S.D.	1-28	42	42-43	10	Ernie Wakely	WPG	9	S.D.	7
At Phx.	1-30	43	44	3	Jack Norris	WPG	5	Phx	3
At Minn.	2- 2	44	45	6	John Garrett	Minn	5	WPG	4
At Clev.	2- 5	45		5	Gerry Cheevers	Clev	3	WPG	2
N.E.	2- 7	46	46	6	Al Smith	N.E.	5	WPG	4
At Chi.	2- 8	47	47	13	Dave Dryden	Chi	6	WPG	3
Chi.	2- 9	48		10	Dave Dryden	WPG	3	Chi	2
Tor.	2-12	49		6	Gilles Gratton	Tor	7	WPG	4
Hou.	2-14	50	48-49-50	10	Ron Grahame	WPG	5	Hou	3

Hull's 50th goal came with 1 minute 33 seconds remaining in 50th game.

Location	Date	Goal #	Multi	Assists	Goalie	Score			
Clev.	2-15	51		2	Bob Whidden	WPG	5	Clev	1
At Chi.	2-16	52		9	Cam Newton	WPG	6	Chi	3
At Balt.	2-18	53	51-52	8	Paul Hoganson	WPG	5	Balt	3
Edm.	2-19	54		8	Chris Worthy	WPG	4	Edm	1
N.E.	2-23	55		4	Al Smith	N.E.	2	WPG	1
Minn.	2-25	56	53	14	Mike Curran	Minn	6	WPG	6
S.D.	2-28	57	54-55	7	Ernie Wakely	WPG	4	S.D.	3
S.D.	3-02	58	56	10	Ernie Wakely	WPG	4	S.D.	4
Clev.	3-05	59	57	3	Gerry Cheevers	WPG	4	Clev	2
At Phx.	3-07	60	58-59	5	Gary Kurt	Phx	7	WPG	4
At S.D.	3-08	61		4	Ernie Wakely	S.D.	6	WPG	5
At Minn.	3-09	62	60	6	Mike Curran	WPG	6	Minn	5
At N.E.	3-11	63		7	Al Smith	N.E.	6	WPG	2
At Que.	3-12	64	61-62	6	Serge Aubry	Que	5	WPG	3
Que.	3-14	65	63	7	Richard Brodeur	WPG	4	Que	3
Edm.	3-16	66	64	3	Ken Brown				
			65-66	8	Chris Worthy	WPG	10	Edm	1
Van.	3-19	67	67-68	8	Don McLeod	WPG	8	Van	3
At N.E.	3-21	68	69	10	Al Smith	WPG	6	N.E.	3
At Chi.	3-22	69	70	12	Dave Dryden	WPG	4	Chi	2
Chi.	3-23	70		6	Dave Dryden	WPG	4	Chi	3
At Ind.	3-25	71	71-72	8	Andy Brown	WPG	4	Ind	3
At Hou.	3-27	72		5	Ron Grahame	Hou	8	WPG	0
At N.E.	3-29	73	73-74-75	10	Al Smith	WPG	9	N.E.	3
Ind.	3-31	74		1	Andy Brown				
				0	Ed Dyck	WPG	4	Ind	1
Van.	4-02	75		6	Don McLeod	Van	6	WPG	4
At Tor.	4-04	76		7	Jim Shaw	Tor	7	WPG	1
At Que.	4-05	77	76	18	Richard Brodeur	Que	9	WPG	5
S.D.	4-06	78	77	9	Russ Gillow	S.D.	5	WPG	5

THE AVCO WORLD TROPHY

WINNERS

1974-75: HOUSTON AEROS
Ron Grahame, Wayne Rutledge, Mark Howe, Gordie Howe, Marty Howe, Larry Lund, Gordon Labossiere, Frank Hughes, Poul Popiel, Murray Hall, Andre Hinse, John Schella, Bill Preston, Terry Ruskowski, Jim Sherrit, Don Larway, Larry Hale, Glen Irwin, Bill Prentice, Capt. Ted Taylor. Coach — Bill Dineen.

1973-74: HOUSTON AEROS
Don McLeod, Wayne Rutledge, Ron Grahame, Murray Hall, Ed Hoekstra, Mark Howe, Gordie Howe, Marty Howe, Bill Prentice, Larry Lund, Joe Szura, Don Grierson, Larry Hale, Jim Sherrit, Frank Hughes, Jack Stanfield, Dunc McCallum, Andre Hinse, Gary Williamson, Gordon Kannegiesser, John Schella, Gordon Labossiere, Poul Popiel, Capt. Ted Taylor. Coach — Bill Dineen.

1972-73: NEW ENGLAND WHALERS
Al Smith, Bruce Landon, Tommy Williams, Ted Green, Jim Dorey, Larry Pleau, Guy Smith, Mike Byers, Brad Selwood, Tim Sheehy, Ric Jordan, Paul Hurley, Brit Selby, Tom Earl, John Danby, John French, Rick Ley, Terry Caffery, Tom Webster, John Cuniff, Kevin Ahern. Coach — Jack Kelley.

DIVISION WINNERS

	WESTERN	EASTERN	CANADIAN
1974-75	Houston	New England	Quebec
1973-74	Houston	New England	
1972-73	Winnipeg	New England	

awards

INDIVIDUAL TROPHY

GORDIE HOWE TROPHY

CASH AWARDS

Most Valuable Player $4,000
Scoring Champion $4,000
Best Goaltender $4,000
Best Defenseman $4,000
Most Gentlemanly Player $4,000
Rookie of the Year $4,000
Coach of the Year $4,000

ALL-STAR GAME
Winning Team Share-per-Player $300
Losing Team Share-per-Player $200

YEAR-END ALL-STARS
First Team Selectees $2,500
Second Team Selectees $1,000

DIVISIONAL FINISHES: First Place Team $50,000, Second Place $25,000, Wild Card Qualifiers $7,500.

GORDIE HOWE TROPHY (Most Valuable Player)	W. D. (BILL) HUNTER TROPHY (Scoring Champion)
Bobby Hull/Winnipeg	..........1974-75 .... Andre Lacroix/San Diego
Gordie Howe/Houston	..........1973-74 .... Mike Walton/Minnesota
Bobby Hull/Winnipeg	..........1972-73 .... Andre Lacroix/Philadelphia

DENNIS A. MURPHY TROPHY (Best Defenseman)	BEN HATSKIN TROPHY (Best Goaltender)
J. C. Tremblay/Quebec	..........1974-75 .... Ron Grahame/Houston
Pat Stapleton/Chicago	..........1973-74 .... Don McLeod/Houston
J. C. Tremblay/Quebec	..........1972-73 .... Gerry Cheevers/Cleveland

LOU KAPLAN TROPHY (Rookie of the Year)	PAUL DENEAU TROPHY (Most Gentlemanly Player)
Anders Hedberg/Winnipeg	..........1974-75 .... Mike Rogers/Edmonton
Mark Howe/Houston	..........1973-74 .... Ralph Backstrom/Chicago
Terry Caffery/New England	..........1972-73 .... Ted Hampson/Minnesota

ROBERT SCHMERTZ MEMORIAL TROPHY (Coach of the Year)	ALL-STAR GAME MOST VALUABLE PLAYER
Sandy Hucul/Phoenix	..........1974-75 .... Rejean Houle/Quebec
Billy Harris/Toronto	..........1973-74 .... Mike Walton/Minnesota
Jack Kelley/New England	..........1972-73 .... Wayne Carleton/Ottawa

PLAYOFF MVP AWARD

1975 — Ron Grahame/Houston

WHA ALL-STAR TEAMS (Determined by Vote of News Media)

1974-75

FIRST TEAM		SECOND TEAM
Ron Grahame, Houston	GOAL	Gerry Cheevers, Cleveland
J. C. Tremblay, Quebec	DEFENSE	Poul Popiel, Houston
Kevin Morrison, S.D.	DEFENSE	Barry Long, Edmonton
Andre Lacroix, San Diego	CENTRE	Serge Bernier, Quebec
Bobby Hull, Winnipeg	LEFT WING	Marc Tardif, Quebec
Gordie Howe, Houston	RIGHT WING	Anders Hedberg, Winnipeg

1973-74

FIRST TEAM		SECOND TEAM
Don McLeod, Houston	GOAL	Gerry Cheevers, Cleveland
Pat Stapleton, Chicago	DEFENSE	J. C. Tremblay, Quebec
Paul Shmyr, Cleveland	DEFENSE	Al Hamilton, Edmonton
Andre Lacroix, New Jersey	CENTRE	Wayne Carleton, Toronto
Bobby Hull, Winnipeg	LEFT WING	Mark Howe, Houston
Gordie Howe, Houston	RIGHT WING	Mike Walton, Minnesota

1972-73

FIRST TEAM		SECOND TEAM
Gerry Cheevers, Cleveland	GOAL	Bernie Parent, Philadelphia
J. C. Tremblay, Quebec	DEFENSE	Jim Dorey, New England
Paul Shmyr, Cleveland	DEFENSE	Larry Hornung, Winnipeg
Andre Lacroix, Philadelphia	CENTRE	Ron Ward, New York
Bobby Hull, Winnipeg	LEFT WING	Gary Jarrett, Cleveland
Danny Lawson, Philadelphia	RIGHT WING	Tom Webster, New England

ALL-STAR GAME

The 1975-76 Game, to be played at the Coliseum in Cleveland Jan. 13, will be the World Hockey Association's 4th Annual. Invited to coach the teams will be the coaches of the 1974-75 Avco World Trophy finalists — Bill Dineen of the Houston Aeros and Jean-Guy Gendron of the Quebec Nordiques.

1974-75 GAME

Played at the Edmonton Coliseum, Jan. 21. The West scored its' first victory over the East, 6-4, before a sellout crowd of 15,326.

WEST DIVISION LINEUP:
Goal: Don McLeod (Vancouver), Wayne Rutledge (Houston), Joe Daley (Winnipeg).
Defense: Doug Barrie (Edmonton), John Schella (Houston), Barry Long (Edmonton), Gerry Odrowski (Phoenix), Poul Popiel (Houston), Lars-Erik Sjoberg (Winnipeg), Al Hamilton (Edmonton).
Forwards: Bobby Hull (Winnipeg), Gordie Howe (Houston), Mark Howe (Houston), Andre Lacroix (San Diego), Ulf Nilsson (Winnipeg), Larry Lund (Houston), Andre Hinse (Houston), Frank Hughes (Houston), Danny Lawson (Vancouver), Ted Taylor (Houston), Fran Huck (Minnesota), Mike Walton* (Minnesota).
*Injured. Did Not Play.

EAST DIVISION LINEUP:
Goal: Al Smith (New England), Gerry Cheevers (Cleveland), Andy Brown (Indianapolis).
Defense: Pat Stapleton (Chicago), Brad Selwood (New England), Rick Ley (New England), Dale Hoganson (Quebec), Jim Dorey (Toronto), J. C. Tremblay (Quebec), Paul Shmyr* (Cleveland).
Forwards: Serge Bernier (Quebec), Rejean Houle (Quebec), Marc Tardif (Quebec), Wayne Dillon (Toronto), Tom Simpson (Toronto), Paul Henderson (Toronto), Frank Mahovlich (Toronto), Ralph Backstrom (Chicago), Larry Pleau (New England), Tom Webster (New England), Gary Veneruzzo (Michigan), Pierre Guite* (Michigan).
*Injured. Did Not Play.

all-stars

SCORING SUMMARY

FIRST PERIOD:
1. West, Mark Howe (G. Howe, Lacroix) 7:08
2. West, Hinse (Lund, Hughes) 8:18
3. East, Tardif (Houle, Selwood) 13:32
4. East, Houle (Pleau, Dorey) 17:37
   Penalties — none.

SECOND PERIOD:
5. West, Hull (Lawson) 4:23
6. West, Hinse (Hughes, Odrowski) 6:35
7. West, Taylor (Lacroix, Schella) 10:07
8. West, G. Howe (Lacroix, Mark Howe) 11:53
9. East, Houle (Selwood, Dorey) 14:32
   Penalties — none.

THIRD PERIOD:
10. East, Bernier (Tardif, Houle) 11:20
    Penalties — none.

SHOTS ON GOAL BY:
WEST ... 7 11 12 — 30
EAST ....11 9 8 — 28

COACHES:
WEST, Bill Dineen (Houston)
EAST, Ron Ryan (New England)
GAME MVP — REJEAN HOULE (QUEBEC)

1972-73 GAME
Quebec, Jan. 6, 1973 (5,435)
EAST 6 WEST 2

FIRST PERIOD
1. West, Odrowski (Beaudin) 10:39
2. East, Jarrett (Ward) 10:51
   Penalties: Pleau (E) 4:43, Hanna (E) 12:09, Shmyr (E) 17:25, Harrison (W) 9:23.

SECOND PERIOD
3. East, McKenzie (Carleton, Block) 3:37
4. East, Pleau (Webster, Caffery) 12:47
5. East, Dorey, (Ward, Lawson) 19:43
   Penalties: none.

THIRD PERIOD
6. West, Hull (Connelly, Bordeleau) 3:05
7. East, Lawson (Jarrett, Tremblay) 7:29
8. East, Carleton (Charlebois, Dorey) 8:00
   Penalties: none

SHOTS ON GOAL BY:
WEST ... 8 13 12 — 33
EAST ....18 14 15 — 47

COACHES:
WEST, Bobby Hull (Winnipeg)
EAST, Jack Kelley (New England)
GAME MVP — Wayne Carleton (Ottawa)

1973-74 GAME
St. Paul, Jan. 3, 1974 (13,196)
EAST 8 WEST 4

FIRST PERIOD
1. East, Houle (Bernier, Paiement) 2:11
2. East, Backstrom (Carleton, Stapleton) 8:02
3. East, Pleau 10:39
4. West, Walton (Lawson) 14:55
5. East, Pinder (Lacroix, Shmyr) 18:38
6. East, Lacroix (Pinder, Jarrett) 19:12
   Penalties: Ley (E) 6:34

SECOND PERIOD
7. West, Walton (Hull, Tardif) 7:27
8. East, Paiement (Backstrom) 9:15
9. West, Walton (Hamilton, Climie) 16:04
10. West, Lund (Hughes, Hamilton) 17:28
    Penalties: Webster (E) 6:31

THIRD PERIOD
11. East, Lacroix (Jarrett, Pinder) 9:17
12. East, Pleau (Harris, Webster) 18:59
    Penalties: Climie (W) 2:43

SHOTS ON GOAL BY:
EAST ....10 12 10 — 32
WEST ...10 13 7 — 30

COACHES:
EAST, Jack Kelley (New England)
WEST, Bobby Hull (Winnipeg)
GAME MVP — Mike Walton (Minnesota)

CHRONOLOGY

1971

JANUARY
Dennis Murphy, co-founder with Gary L. Davidson of the American Basketball Association in 1968, conceives the idea for a second major hockey league.

APRIL
Murphy and Davidson formulate plans for the World Hockey Association.

JUNE
Articles of incorporation for the WHA are filed in Delaware June 10.

JULY
By-Laws for WHA are approved by League's first board of trustees. Signatures on document are those of Gary L. Davidson, President; Donald J. Regan and Dennis A. Murphy. Canadian participation launched when W. D. (Bill) Hunter, Edmonton, meets with league founders.

SEPTEMBER
First formal meeting of WHA held in Los Angeles where interested ownership groups gather Sept. 23-24.

OCTOBER
Revolutionary announcement made in Chicago Oct. 20 that WHA player contracts will not contain reserve and/or option clause.

NOVEMBER
WHA, following two days of meetings in New York, is formally organized Nov. 1 with establishment of 10 franchises — St. Paul, Chicago, Dayton, Edmonton, Los Angeles, Winnipeg, New York, Calgary, San Francisco and Miami. Two additional franchises granted Nov. 21 to Ontario and New England.

1972

JANUARY
First coach hired is Terrence Slater for Los Angeles Sharks, Jan. 7. His selection followed a few days later by naming of two of North America's foremost college coaches, Jack Kelley of Boston U for New England and Glen Sonmor of University of Minnesota for Minnesota Fighting Saints. Vern Buffey named referee-in-chief.

FEBRUARY
A group of Quebec City businessmen, led by Paul Racine, purchase the San Francisco franchise on the eve of the WHA's first player draft Feb. 12-13 in Anaheim, Calif. A total of 1,081 amateur and professional players selected. First player signed to WHA contract is Steve Sutherland by Los Angeles. New England franchise, headed by Howard Baldwin, settles in Boston and Ontario franchise, organized by Doug Michel, is based in Ottawa. Bernie Parent first player of major stature to sign with Miami franchise.

MARCH
Dayton franchise, headed by Paul Deneau, transfers to Houston. U.S. Olympic goaltender Mike Curran, one of 20 American-born players to ultimately join the WHA, signs with Minnesota. Edward Fitkin, veteran hockey executive, named assistant to the president.

APRIL
Ten franchises post $100,000 performance bonds in Chicago April 14.

MAY
Janes W. Browitt, formerly executive director of Freedom Hall in Louisville, appointed league administrator and executive vice-president, succeeding Dennis Murphy who took over active leadership of the Los Angeles franchise.

JUNE
James L. Cooper and Bernard A. Brown, New Jersey businessmen, established the WHA's 11th franchise in Philadelphia, and take over Parent's contract with Miami. Nick J. Mileti, a major league owner in baseball and basketball, is granted WHA's 12th franchise for Cleveland. Monumental $2.7 million signing of Bobby Hull by Ben Hatskin of Winnipeg Jets, June 27.

JULY
Player signings multiply with acquisition of Hull; J. C. Tremblay, Quebec Nordiques; Gerry Cheevers, Cleveland Crusaders; Bobby Sheehan, New York; Ted Green, New England.

WHA history

AUGUST
More than 300 players under contract. League divided into two divisions of six teams each with Cleveland Crusaders, New England Whalers, New York Raiders, Ottawa Nationals, Philadelphia Blazers and Quebec Nordiques in Eastern Division and Alberta Oilers, Chicago Cougars, Houston Aeros, Los Angeles Sharks, Minnesota Fighting Saints and Winnipeg Jets in Western Division. Adoption of 78 game schedule.

SEPTEMBER
Philadelphia first team to go to training camp on Sept. 10. Rookie squads participate in first ever WHA games Sept. 23.

OCTOBER
Professional contract players report to camps Oct. 1. Season opens Oct. 11 with Quebec at Cleveland and Alberta (Edmonton) at Ottawa. Ron Anderson of Alberta Oilers scores WHA's first regular season goal. Court order keeps Winnipeg's Hull inactive.

NOVEMBER
Hull, after missing 14 games, is cleared for action Nov. 8 following landmark ruling of Judge A. Leon Higginbotham, U.S. District Court for the Eastern Section of Pennsylvania. Hull made WHA debut same night and assisted on winning goal as Jets edged Nordiques, 3-2.

1973

JANUARY
League's first all-star game in Quebec City Jan. 6; East 6, West 2. Opening of new St. Paul Civic Arena, home of Minnesota Fighting Saints, attracts crowd of 11,701 New Year's Night. First CBS televised game, also in St. Paul, before crowd of 13,426, Jan. 7.

FEBRUARY
Danny Lawson, Philadelphia, first WHA player to score 50 goals, collecting 50th Feb. 22 in Ottawa.

MARCH
Cleveland owner Nick Mileti breaks ground for $18 million arena on 100 acre site in Richfield Township.

APRIL
New England (East) and Winnipeg (West) divisional champions. Ottawa Nationals move playoff games to Maple Leaf Gardens in Toronto. Representatives of WHA and NHL meet in New York (ex-officio) to discuss possible merger. WHA rejects proposal. Alberta Oilers and Minnesota, who deadlocked for fourth place in the West, play sudden-death playoff game April 4 on neutral ice (Calgary). Minnesota wins 4-2.

MAY
New England Whalers first winners of The Avco World Trophy, defeating Winnipeg Jets, four games to one. New York franchise acquires new ownership. Team name changed to Golden Blades. Ottawa Nationals move to Toronto with new ownership, Can Sports Ltd., a group of Toronto businessmen headed by John F. Bassett, Jr. and Craig Eaton III. Team name changed to Toros. Philadelphia franchise sold to Canadian industrialist Jim Pattison and re-located in Vancouver. Cincinnati group, headed by Brian Heekin III and William O. DeWitt Jr., granted franchise May 6. Cincinnati's first active season 1975-76.

JUNE
Gordie Howe, owner of more records than any man in history of hockey, ends 21 months retirement and signs with Houston Aeros. Sons Marty, 19, and Mark, 18, also sign with Aeros, marking first time in history of major league sport that father plays alongside two sons.

JULY
Pat Stapleton signs as player-coach of Chicago Cougars.

SEPTEMBER
League membership increases to 15 with awarding of franchises to Indianapolis (Dick Tinkham and John Weissert) and Phoenix Roadrunners of Western League, headed by Jim Wells. Walt Marlow, who aided in organizational structure of WHA, named director of public relations. Gordie Howe, ending two year retirement, makes first professional appearance with sons Marty and Mark Sept. 25 in New York exhibition game against New England Whalers. Howe scored 21 seconds into game with assist to son Mark.

OCTOBER
Franchise of New York Golden Blades dissolved Oct. 18. Players, property of league, reassembled as Jersey Knights. Gary Davidson resigns WHA presidency Oct. 29 at board of trustees meeting in Chicago.

NOVEMBER
League-owned Jersey Knights debut Nov. 20. Dennis Murphy named WHA interim president Nov. 23. Howe family combines for first goal Nov. 18 in Quebec, Mark scoring with assists to father Gordie and brother Marty.

1974

JANUARY
Purchase of Jersey Knights by Joseph Schwartz, Jan. 3. Second WHA All-Star game in St. Paul Jan. 3 attracts crowd of 13,196 as East again defeats West, 8-4. Howe scores 800th career goal Jan. 17 in Vancouver.

FEBRUARY
The 57-year-old National League and two-year-old WHA settle $50 million case out of court Feb. 19 when both leagues signed agreement before U.S. District Judge A. Leon Higginbotham. WHA reimbursed by NHL for legal expenses of $1.7 million.

MARCH
WHA and Canadian Amateur Hockey Association reach agreement March 29 in Winnipeg on signing of Canadian juniors.

APRIL
Los Angeles Sharks franchise transferred to Detroit and renamed Michigan Stags April 11 by team owners Charles Nolton and Pete Shagena. Biggest crowd in WHA's brief history, 17,211, in St. Paul April 28 for fourth game of Houston-Minnesota Avco World Trophy semi-final series. Team Canada announces in Toronto April 29 that WHA will provide players for eight-game series with Soviet Union. Ben Hatskin of Winnipeg and John Bassett, Jr., Toronto are WHA official representatives to Team Canada. Edmonton's Bill Hunter named Team manager and Toronto's Billy Harris coach. Transfer of Jersey Knights to San Diego announced April 30 by owner Joseph Schwartz.

MAY
Houston Aeros win The Avco World trophy and WHA 1974 championship in 14 games.

JUNE
Norman R. "Bud" Poile, active in professional hockey since 1942 as player, coach and top level executive, named vice-president in charge of hockey operations June 6. League divided into three divisions, Canadian, Eastern and Western. Divisions re-alignment: Edmonton, Toronto, Vancouver, Winnipeg and Quebec in Canadian Division; Houston, Michigan, Minnesota, Phoenix and San Diego in the West; Chicago, Cleveland, Indianapolis and New England in the East. Phoenix and Indianapolis are expansion teams, and Cincinnati becomes Eastern Division member in 1975-76. Toronto Toros sign Frank Mahovlich, June 19.

JULY
Larry Gordon, veteran sports executive, appointed executive vice-president of Properties.

SEPTEMBER
In first WHA game ever with NHL, Houston Aeros defeat St. Louis Blues, 5-3, Sept. 26 in Houston.

OCTOBER
WHA's third season opened Oct. 15 with new arenas in Cleveland, Edmonton, Indianapolis and later Hartford. Eight European stars debut in WHA — six Swedish, two Finnish and two Czechoslovakians.

NOVEMBER
WHA regular season record crowd of 15,326 established in Edmonton Nov. 10 with opening of new Coliseum.

DECEMBER
Paul H. Deneau, one of WHA's original architects, purchases the Indianapolis Racers Dec. 5. Deneau first owned the Houston Aeros. James Browitt, WHA vice-president, resigned Dec. 12 to become president and general manager of the Racers. A major league sports "first" realized Dec. 27 when Chicago Cougar players Pat Stapleton, Dave Dryden and Ralph Backstrom purchase the team.

1975

JANUARY
New England Whalers open new Hartford Civic Center Jan. 11 before sellout crowd of 10,570. Dennis Murphy announces resignation as president Jan. 20 effective June 1. WHA, at meeting in Edmonton for third annual all-star game Jan. 21, names Chairman of The Board Ben Hatskin chief executive officer. West Team captures its first all-star win, 6-4. League-operated Baltimore Blades, comprised of players from the defunct Michigan Stags, debut Jan. 29 in New England.

FEBRUARY
Winnipeg's Bobby Hull equals scoring record of Maurice Richard Feb. 14 with three goals against Houston — 50 goals in 50 games.

APRIL
Hull emerges major league hockey's greatest single season goal scorer ever with goal on final night of season, April 6, for an unprecedented 77 goals in 78 games. Regular season single game attendance record of 17,312 set in St. Paul April 4, Minnesota vs. Phoenix. Leo Ornest, veteran sports executive since 1948, named vice-president and director of communications.

MAY
Houston Aeros absorb only one defeat enroute to retaining The Avco World Trophy. Aero goaltender Ron Grahame first winner of Gordie Howe Trophy as MVP of playoffs. Jim Pattison, president of Vancouver Blazers, May 7 announced transfer of Blazer franchise to Calgary. Team name changed to Cowboys. Ivan L. Mullenix, owner of Denver Spurs, awarded WHA franchise May 19.

JUNE
League re-affirms Ben Hatskin as chief executive officer, and name Howard Baldwin of New England vice-president; Wayne Belisle of Minnesota secretary; Toronto's John Gray, vice-president of finance and treasurer and A. J. "Telly" Mercury of Winnipeg legal counsel. League's first ever intra-league draft held June 19 in Toronto. Houston realtor George Bolin announces group's purchase of Houston Aeros for $4.1 million. Gordie Howe named Aeros' president.

JULY
League office re-located in Toronto, Canada July 1. Eighty game schedule adopted.

SEPTEMBER
Toronto Toros and Winnipeg Jets first major league teams ever to establish training camps in Europe, Toronto in Sweden and Winnipeg in Finland.

DIVISIONAL LINEUP

CANADIAN	EASTERN	WESTERN
Calgary Cowboys	†Cincinnati Stingers	†Denver Spurs
Edmonton Oilers	Cleveland Crusaders	Houston Aeros
Quebec Nordiques	Indianapolis Racers	Minnesota Fighting Saints
Toronto Toros	New England Whalers	Phoenix Roadrunners
Winnipeg Jets		San Diego Mariners

© 2018 WHA HOF / PCMP LLC
†—Expansion franchises 1975-76 season.

LEAGUE SCHEDULE PAGE 102-112

TEAM — SEASON

MOST POINTS:
 106 — Houston, 1974-75.
MOST POINTS AT HOME:
 61 — New England, 1972-73. 30 wins, 8 losses, 1 tie.
MOST POINTS ON ROAD:
 50 — Houston, 1974-75.
FEWEST POINTS:
 39 — Indianapolis, 1974-75.
FEWEST POINTS AT HOME:
 26 — Indianapolis, 1974-75.
FEWEST POINTS ON ROAD:
 13 — Indianapolis, 1974-75.
  — Michigan/Baltimore, 1974-75.
MOST WINS:
 53 — Houston, 1974-75.
MOST HOME WINS:
 30 — New England, 1972-73.
MOST ROAD WINS:
 25 — Houston, 1974-75.
FEWEST WINS:
 18 — Indianapolis, 1974-75.
FEWEST HOME WINS:
 13 — Indianapolis, 1974-75.
FEWEST ROAD WINS:
 5 — Indianapolis, 1974-75.
MOST LOSSES:
 57 — Michigan/Baltimore, 1974-75.
MOST HOME LOSSES:
 26 — Indianapolis, 1974-75.
MOST ROAD LOSSES:
 32 — Michigan/Baltimore, 1974-75.
FEWEST LOSSES:
 25 — Houston, 1973-74 and 1974-75.
FEWEST HOME LOSSES:
 8 — New England, 1972-73 and 1974-75.
  — Cleveland, 1973-74.
FEWEST ROAD LOSSES:
 14 — Houston, 1974-75.
MOST TIES:
 9 — Cleveland, 1973-74.
MOST HOME TIES:
 5 — Quebec, 1972-73.
  — Phoenix, 1974-75.
MOST ROAD TIES:
 5 — Los Angeles, 1972-73.
  — Cleveland, 1973-74.
FEWEST TIES:
 0 — Philadelphia, 1972-73; Los Angeles, 1973-74; Quebec and Houston, 1974-75.
FEWEST HOME TIES:
 0 — Several teams.
FEWEST ROAD TIES:
 0 — Several teams.
LONGEST UNDEFEATED STREAK:
 12 — Toronto, March 22 — Oct. 28, 1974. 12 wins.
LONGEST UNDEFEATED STREAK (one season):
 11 — Edmonton, Oct. 21 — Nov. 16, 1973. 11 wins.
  — Minnesota, Feb. 13 — March 10, 1974. 10 wins, 1 tie.

WHA records

LONGEST HOME UNDEFEATED STREAK:
14 — New England, Nov. 1 — Dec. 17, 1972. 13 wins, 1 tie.

LONGEST ROAD UNDEFEATED STREAK:
9 — Houston, Oct. 29 — Dec. 4, 1974. 9 wins.

LONGEST WIN STREAK:
12 — Toronto, March 22 — Oct. 28, 1974.

LONGEST WIN STREAK (one season):
11 — Edmonton, Oct. 21 — Nov. 16, 1973.

LONGEST HOME WIN STREAK:
10 — Quebec, Jan. 5 — Feb. 22, 1974.

LONGEST ROAD WIN STREAK:
9 — Houston, Oct. 29 — Dec. 4, 1974.

LONGEST WINLESS STREAK:
13 — Indianapolis, Nov. 13 — Dec. 5, 1974. 13 losses.

LONGEST HOME WINLESS STREAK:
7 — Vancouver, Oct. 21 — Nov. 13, 1973.
 — Indianapolis, Nov. 19 — Dec. 5, 1974.
 — Baltimore, Feb. 2 — Feb. 20, 1975.

LONGEST ROAD WINLESS STREAK:
25 — Michigan/Baltimore, Oct. 19, 1974 — Feb. 1, 1975.

LONGEST LOSING STREAK:
13 games — Indianapolis — Nov. 13 — Dec. 5, 1974.

LONGEST HOME LOSING STREAK:
7 games — Vancouver, Oct. 21 — Nov. 13, 1973.
 — Indianapolis, Nov. 19 — Dec. 5, 1974.
 — Baltimore, Feb. 2 — Feb. 18, 1975.

LONGEST ROAD LOSING STREAK:
14 games — Los Angeles, Jan. 29 — March 31, 1974.

MOST POWER PLAY OPPORTUNITIES:
362 — Winnipeg, 1974-75.

MOST POWER PLAY GOALS:
74 — Winnipeg, 1974-75.

MOST GOALS ALLOWED WHILE ON POWER PLAY:
16 — Winnipeg, 1974-75.

MOST PROFICIENT POWER PLAY:
28.7% — Houston, 1973-74. 64 goals in 223 opportunities.

MOST SHORTHANDED SITUATIONS:
372 — Houston, 1974-75.

MOST GOALS SCORED WHILE SHORTHANDED:
20 — Minnesota, 1973-74.

MOST GOALS ALLOWED WHILE SHORTHANDED:
76 — Phoenix, 1974-75.

MOST EFFICIENT PENALTY KILLING:
86.5% — New England, 1974-75. 29 goals allowed in 215 situations.

MOST SCORING POINTS:
968 — Houston, 1974-75. 369 goals, 599 assists.

MOST GOALS SCORED:
369 — Houston, 1974-75.

MOST ASSISTS:
599 — Houston, 1974-75.

FEWEST SCORING POINTS:
540 — Michigan/Baltimore, 1974-75. 335 goals, 205 assists.

FEWEST GOALS SCORED:
205 — Michigan/Baltimore, 1974-75.

FEWEST ASSISTS:
335 — Michigan/Baltimore, 1974-75.

MOST GOALS ALLOWED:
345 — Vancouver, 1973-74.

FEWEST GOALS ALLOWED:
219 — Houston, 1973-74.

MOST 100-OR-MORE POINT SCORERS:
3 — Winnipeg, 1972-73. Bobby Hull (103); Norm Beaudin (103); Chris Bordeleau (101).
— Winnipeg, 1974-75. Bobby Hull (142); Ulf Nilsson (120); Anders Hedberg (100).

MOST 60-OR-MORE GOAL SCORERS:
1 — Philadelphia, 1972-73. (Danny Lawson-61).
— Winnipeg, 1974-75. (Bobby Hull-77).

MOST 50-OR-MORE GOAL SCORERS:
2 — Philadelphia, 1972-73. (Lawson-61; Andre Lacroix-50).
— Winnipeg, 1974-75. (Bobby Hull-77; Anders Hedberg-53).
— Quebec, 1974-75. (Serge Bernier-54; Marc Tardif-50).

MOST 40-OR-MORE GOAL SCORERS:
4 — San Diego, 1974-75. (Andre Lacroix-41; Wayne Rivers-54; Rick Sentes-44; Gene Peacosh-43).

MOST 30-OR-MORE GOAL SCORERS:
6 — Houston, 1973-74. (Frank Hughes-42); Mark Howe-38; Larry Lund-33; Gordie Howe-31; Jim Sherrit-30; Murray Hall-30).

MOST 20-OR-MORE GOAL SCORERS:
10 — Houston, 1974-75. (Hughes-48; Andre Hinse-39; Lund-33; G. Howe-34; Mark Howe-36; Ted Taylor-26; Rich Preston-20; Don Larway-22; Sherrit-22; Gord Labossiere-23).

MOST PENALTY MINUTES:
1477 — Los Angeles, 1972-73.

FEWEST PENALTY MINUTES:
671 — Winnipeg Jets, 1973-74.

MOST SHUTOUTS:
6 — Houston, 1974-75.

MOST SHUTOUTS AT HOME:
5 — Minnesota, 1972-73.

MOST SHUTOUTS ON ROAD:
3 — Houston, 1974-75.

FEWEST SHUTOUTS:
0 — Ottawa, 1972-73.
— Quebec, 1974-75.

FEWEST SHUTOUTS AT HOME:
0 — Ottawa, Houston, Philadelphia — 1972-73.
— New York/New Jersey — 1973-74.
— Quebec, 1974-75.

FEWEST SHUTOUTS ON ROAD:
0 — Several teams.

MOST TIMES SHUTOUT:
8 — Los Angeles, 1973-74.
— Indianapolis, 1974-75.

MOST TIMES SHUTOUT AT HOME:
5 — Los Angeles, 1973-74.
— Indianapolis, 1974-75.

MOST TIMES SHUTOUT ON ROAD:
6 — Philadelphia, 1972-73.

LEAST TIMES SHUTOUT:
0 — Toronto and Minnesota, 1973-74.
— Minnesota, Toronto, Houston and Quebec 1974-75.

LEAST TIMES SHUTOUT AT HOME:
0 — Several teams.

LEAST TIMES SHUTOUT ON ROAD:
0 — Several teams.

MOST CONSECUTIVE GAMES NOT SHUTOUT — (Regular season).
177 — Minnesota, since Feb. 9, 1973.

MOST CONSECUTIVE HOME GAMES NOT SHUTOUT:
117 — Quebec, Minnesota and Toronto (never been shutout at home).

MOST CONSECUTIVE ROAD GAMES NOT SHUTOUT:
  89 — Minnesota. Last shutout Feb. 9, 1973.
  87 — Houston. Last shutout Feb. 16, 1973.
  84 — Ottawa Nationals/Toronto Toros. Last shutout Feb. 15, 1973.
LONGEST SHUTOUT SEQUENCE BY A TEAM:
  153 Minutes, 5 Seconds — Cleveland, from 10:24 of first period vs. Philadelphia, Oct. 25 until 3:29 of period 3 vs. Quebec, Oct. 29, 1972. Streak included shutout of Alberta, Oct. 27.
LONGEST TIME ONE TEAM SHUTOUT:
  181 Min. 25 sec. — San Diego, 13:32 of second period vs. Houston, Nov. 5 until 14:57 of period two vs. Quebec Nov. 10, 1974. Included shutouts by Indianapolis and New England Nov. 7 & 8.
MOST TIMES PLAYERS HAD 3-OR-MORE GOAL NIGHTS:
  12 — Philadelphia, 1972-73.
MOST TIMES PLAYERS HAD 4-OR-MORE GOAL NIGHTS:
  4 — Philadelphia, 1972-73.
   — Toronto, 1974-75.

TEAM SINGLE GAME RECORDS

MOST GOALS, BOTH TEAMS, ONE GAME:
  16 — Dec. 16, 1972, New England 10 at Philadelphia 6.
   — Jan. 27, 1974, Vancouver 7 at Toronto 9.
   — Mar. 18, 1974, Toronto 5 at New Jersey 11.
   — Jan. 28, 1975, Winnipeg 9 at San Diego 7.
   — Feb. 27, 1975, Vancouver 7 at Quebec 9.
MOST GOALS, ONE TEAM, ONE GAME:
  12 — Jan. 27, 1974, Winnipeg 2 at Minnesota 12.
   — Mar. 1, 1975, Indianapolis 2 at Phoenix 12.
MOST MULTIPLE GOAL PERFORMANCES, ONE TEAM, ONE GAME:
  6 — Phoenix, Mar. 1, 1975. (Dennis Sobchuk, Robbie Ftorek, Dennis Boyd, Michel Cormier, John Gray, Bob Mowat scored two goals each). Phoenix 12, Indianapolis 2.
MOST POINTS, BOTH TEAMS, ONE GAME:
  45 — Jan. 27, 1973, Toronto 9, Vancouver 7 at Toronto. Toros 16 assists, Blazers 13.
MOST POINTS, ONE TEAM, ONE GAME:
  34 — Minnesota, Jan. 27, 1974 at St. Paul. Minn. 12, Winnipeg 2. Minn. had 22 assists.
MOST CONSECUTIVE GOALS, ONE TEAM, ONE GAME:
  10 — Dec. 19, 1973, Winnipeg 0 at Houston 10.
   — Jan. 27, 1974, Winnipeg 2 at Minnesota 12.
   — Mar. 17, 1974, New England 1 at Winnipeg 10.
   — Nov. 1, 1974, Toronto 1 at Winnipeg 10.
   — Nov. 19, 1974, Houston 10 at Indianapolis 0.
MOST CONSECUTIVE GOALS SCORED, ONE TEAM, MORE THAN ONE GAME:
  15 — Winnipeg scored final 10 goals in 10-1 vs. Toronto Nov. 1, the first five in 11-3 vs. Michigan Nov. 3, 1974.
   — Houston scored the last two in game won by San Diego 4-3 Nov. 17, all the goals 10-0 vs. Indianapolis Nov. 19, and the first three vs. Vancouver 4-1 Nov. 22, 1974.
MOST GOALS SCORED, TWO CONSECUTIVE GAMES, ONE TEAM:
  21 — Winnipeg defeated Toronto 10-1 Nov. 1 and Michigan 11-3 Nov. 3, 1974.
MOST GOALS SCORED, THREE CONSECUTIVE GAMES, ONE TEAM;
  27 — Winnipeg defeated Phoenix 6-5 Oct. 30, Toronto 10-1 Nov. 1 and Michigan 11-3 Nov. 3, 1974.
   — Winnipeg defeated Toronto 10-1 Nov. 1, Michigan 11-3 Nov. 3 and Minnesota 6-4 Nov. 5, 1974.
FEWEST GOALS SCORED, THREE CONSECUTIVE GAMES, ONE TEAM:
  1 — Indianapolis in losses to Winnipeg (5-0) Nov. 15, Edmonton (2-1) Nov. 17 and Houston (10-0) Nov. 19, 1974.
   — Chicago in losses to Quebec (4-0) Jan. 6, Cleveland (3-0) Jan. 8 and Winnipeg (3-1) Jan. 13, 1974.
   — Winnipeg in losses to Quebec (7-1) Feb. 26, Toronto (3-0) Feb. 28 and Minnesota (4-0) Mar. 1, 1974.

47

MOST GOALS ALLOWED, TWO CONSECUTIVE GAMES, ONE TEAM:
20 — New York in losses to Los Angeles (9-2) Jan. 28 and Alberta (11-3) Jan. 30, 1973.

MOST GOALS ALLOWED, THREE CONSECUTIVE GAMES, ONE TEAM:
28 — New York in losses to Los Angeles (9-2) Jan. 28, Alberta (11-3) Jan. 30 and (8-5) Feb. 1, 1973.

MOST PENALTIES, BOTH TEAMS, ONE GAME:
42 — Quebec at Los Angeles Jan. 15, 1974. L.A. 11 minors, 5 majors, 5 misconducts. Quebec 11 minors, 6 majors, 4 misconducts. L.A. Won 6-4.
— Cleveland at Indianapolis Mar. 8, 1975. Clev. 10 minors, 5 majors, 7 misconducts. Indianapolis 8 minors, 5 majors 7 misconducts. Clev. won 6-5.

MOST PENALTY MINUTES, BOTH TEAMS, ONE GAME:
228 — Cleveland at Indianapolis, Mar. 8, 1975. Cleveland had 11 minors, 5 majors and 7 misconducts for 117 minutes; Indianapolis 8 minors, 5 majors and 7 misconducts for 111 minutes. Clev. 6, Ind. 5.

MOST PENALTIES, ONE TEAM, ONE GAME: (and)
MOST PENALTY MINUTES, ONE TEAM, ONE GAME:
26 penalties, 137 min. — Phoenix, Feb. 7, 1975 vs. Minnesota at Phoenix. 11 minors, 7 majors, 8 misconducts. Phx. 4, Minn. 1.

MOST POWER PLAY OPPORTUNITIES, BOTH TEAMS, ONE GAME:
20 — Houston, Vancouver Blazers, Feb. 26, 1974, at Houston. 10 opportunities each. Vancouver scored one power play goal, Houston scored two shorthanded goals. Hou. 10. Van. 1.

MOST POWER PLAY OPPORTUNITIES, ONE GAME, ONE TEAM:
12 — Phoenix, Oct. 18, 1974, vs. Houston at Phoenix. Roadrunners had three power play goals, won game 6-4.
— Winnipeg, Jan. 26, 1975, vs. Houston at Winnipeg. Jets had no power play goals. Houston won, 3-1.

MOST SHORTHANDED GOALS, ONE GAME, ONE TEAM:
3 — Minnesota Mar. 6, 1974, vs. New England at St. Paul. Minn. 8, N.E. 6.
— Winnipeg, Nov. 1, 1974, vs. Toronto at Winnipeg, Wpg. 10, Tor. 1.
— Phoenix, Jan. 22, 1975, vs. Chicago at Phoenix. Phx. 8, Chi. 5.
— Houston, Mar. 27, 1975, vs. Winnipeg at Houston, Hou. 8, Wpg. 0.

MOST SHOTS ON GOAL, BOTH TEAMS, ONE GAME:
107 — Michigan at Winnipeg, Nov. 29, 1974. Jets 54-53. Wpg. 7, Mich 6.
— San Diego at Toronto, Mar. 14, 1975. Toros 59-48. S.D. 6, Tor. 4.

MOST SHOTS ON GOAL, ONE TEAM, ONE GAME:
59 — Toronto. Mar. 14, 1975, vs. San Diego at Toronto. S.D. 6, Tor. 4.

MOST GOALS, BOTH TEAMS, ONE PERIOD:
9 — New England (5) Philadelphia (4) at Philadelphia Dec. 16, 1972. Third period, New England, 10-6.
— Ottawa (5) Quebec (4) at Ottawa Jan. 9, 1973. First period. Ottawa, 7-5.
— New England (5) Los Angeles (4) at Boston Jan. 13, 1974.
— Winnipeg (6) Houston (3) at Winnipeg Mar. 29, 1974. Third period. Winnipeg, 7-5.

MOST GOALS, ONE TEAM, ONE PERIOD:
8 — Toronto Dec. 9, 1973 at Toronto vs. Minnesota. Third period. Toronto, 10-1.

MOST PENALTIES, BOTH TEAMS, ONE PERIOD: (and)
MOST PENALTY MINUTES, BOTH TEAMS, ONE PERIOD:
32 penalties, 192 min. — Cleveland at Indianapolis, Mar. 8, 1975. Second period. Cleveland 7 minors, 4 majors, 6 misconducts for 94 minutes; Indianapolis 4 minors, 4 majors. 7 misconducts for 98 minutes. Cleveland, 6-5.

MOST PENALTIES, ONE TEAM, ONE PERIOD: (and)
MOST PENALTY MINUTES, ONE TEAM, ONE PERIOD:
20 penalties, 111 min. — Phoenix, Feb. 7, 1975, vs. Minnesota. Third period. 8 minors, 5 majors, 7 misconducts. Roadrunners, 4-1.

FASTEST TWO GOALS, BOTH TEAMS:
5 sec. — Winnipeg at San Diego, Jan. 28, 1975. First period. Bobby Hull (Wpg) at 19:41, Norm Ferguson (S.D.) at 1946. Wpg. 9, S.D. 7.

FASTEST THREE GOALS, BOTH TEAMS:
27 sec. — New England at New York, Nov. 29, 1972. Second period. John French (N.E.) 12:53, Ron Ward (NY) 13:11 and 13:20. N.Y. 7, N.E. 6.

FASTEST FOUR GOALS, TWO TEAMS:
1 min., 3 sec. — New England at New York, Nov. 29, 1972. Second period. John French (NE) 12:53, Ron Ward (NY) 13:11 and 13:20, Tom Earl (NE) 13:56. N.Y. 7, N.E. 6.

FASTEST FIVE GOALS, TWO TEAMS:
4 min., 10 sec. — Cleveland at New York, 3rd period, Feb. 25, 1973. Norm Peacosh (NY) 3:59; Wayne Rivers (NY) 4:42; Ron Buchanan (C) 6:01; Gerry Pinder (C) 6:34; Wayne Rivers (NY) 8:09. NY 9, Clev. 5.

FASTEST TWO GOALS, ONE TEAM:
4 sec. — New England, period 3, Dec. 16, 1972 at Philadelphia. Terry Caffery, 2:49 and Brit Selby, 2:53. N.E. 10, Phil. 6.

FASTEST THREE GOALS, ONE TEAM:
32 sec. — Chicago, period 3, Dec. 19, 1972 vs. Cleveland at Chicago. Paul Popiel, 1846, Bob Sicinski 19:02, Bob Liddington 19:18. Chi. 6, Clev. 1.

FASTEST FOUR GOALS, ONE TEAM:
1 min., 45 sec. — Alberta Oilers, period 3, Jan. 30, 1973, vs. New York at Edmonton. Rusty Patenaude 10:48, Doug Barrie 11:48, Steve Carlyle 12:00, Jim Harrison 12:33. Alta. 11, N.Y. 3.

FASTEST FIVE GOALS, ONE TEAM:
4 min., 48 sec — Alberta Oilers, period 3, Jan. 30, 1973, vs. New York at Edmonton. Bernie Blanchette 7:45, Rusty Patenaude 10:48, Doug Barrie 11:48, Steve Carlyle 12:00, Jim Harrison 12:33. Alta. 11, N.Y. 3.

FASTEST TWO GOALS, FROM START OF GAME, BOTH TEAMS:
43 sec. — Phoenix at New England, Mar. 13, 1975. Robbie Ftorek (P) 0:12, Don Blackburn (NE) 0:43. Phx. 5, N.E. 5.

FASTEST THREE GOALS FROM THE START OF GAME, BOTH TEAMS:
2 min., 12 sec. — Vancouver at Toronto, Jan. 27, 1974. Mike Chernoff (V) 1:27, Wayne Dillon (T) 1:58, Tom Simpson (T) 2:12. Tor. 9, Van. 7.

FASTEST FOUR GOALS FROM START OF GAME, BOTH TEAMS:
4 min., 13 sec. — Michigan at Winnipeg, Nov. 29, 1974. Tom Serviss (M) 0:28, Perry Miller (W) 3:02, Hexi Riihiranta (W) 3:15, Bobby Hull (W) 4:13. Wpg. 7, Mich. 6.

FASTEST FIVE GOALS, FROM START OF GAME, BOTH TEAMS:
8 min., 53 sec. — Winnipeg at Chicago, Feb. 8, 1975. Ulf Nilsson (W) 0:23, Peter Mara (C) 4:25, Gary MacGregor (C) 6:00, Bobby Hull (W) 6:21, Rick Morris (C) 8:53. Chi. 6, Wpg. 3.

FASTEST TWO GOALS FROM START OF SECOND PERIOD, BOTH TEAMS:
58 sec. — Houston at Los Angeles, Feb. 15, 1974. Jim Sherrit (H) 0:24, Gary Veneruzzo (LA) 0:58. Hou. 6, L.A. 4.

FASTEST THREE GOALS FROM START OF SECOND PERIOD, BOTH TEAMS:
2 min., 2 sec. — New England at Philadelphia, Dec. 16, 1972. Danny Lawson (P) 0:30, John French (NE) 1:16, John McKenzie (P) 2:02. N.E. 10, Phil. 6.

FASTEST FOUR GOALS FROM START OF SECOND PERIOD, BOTH TEAMS:
5 min., 15 sec. — Minnesota at Quebec, Jan. 20, 1973. Terry Ryan (M) 1:10 and 1:27, Jean-Guy Gendron (Q) 2:17 and 5:15, Minn. 10, Que. 5.

FASTEST FIVE GOALS FROM START OF SECOND PERIOD, BOTH TEAMS:
6 min., 48 sec. — Minnesota at Quebec, Jan. 20, 1973. Terry Ryan (M) 1:10 and 1:27, Jean-Guy Gendron (Q) 2:17 and 5:15, Frank Sanders (M) 6:48. Minn. 10, Que. 5.

FASTEST TWO GOALS FROM START OF THIRD PERIOD, BOTH TEAMS:
45 sec. — Quebec at Cleveland, Dec. 27, 1974. Rich Leduc (C) 0:27, Serge Bernier (Q) 0:45. Clev. 4, Que. 3.

FASTEST THREE GOALS FROM START OF THIRD PERIOD, BOTH TEAMS:
2 min., 59 sec. — Edmonton at Quebec, March 21, 1974. Rejean Giroux (Q) 2:03, Ron Climie (E) 2:31, Len Lunde (E) 2:59. Que. 5, Edm. 5.

FASTEST FOUR GOALS FROM START OF THIRD PERIOD, BOTH TEAMS:
3 min., 17 sec. — New England at Philadelphia, Dec. 16, 1972. Larry Pleau (NE) 1:03, Terry Caffery (NE) 2:49, Brit Selby (NE) 2:53, Danny Lawson (P) 3:17. N.E. 10, Phil. 6.

FASTEST FIVE GOALS FROM START OF THIRD PERIOD, BOTH TEAMS:
 4 min., 51 sec. — New England at Philadelphia, Dec. 16, 1972. Larry Pleau (NE) 1:03, Terry Caffery (NE) 2:49, Brit Selby (NE) 2:53, Danny Lawson (P) 3:17, Michel Plante (P) 4:51. N.E. 10, Phil. 6.

FASTEST TWO GOALS FROM START OF GAME, ONE TEAM:
 28 sec. — Minnesota, Feb. 17, 1973, at Cleveland. Mike McMahon 0:19, George Morrison 0:28. Minn. 7, Clev. 3.

FASTEST THREE GOALS FROM START OF GAME, ONE TEAM:
 2 min., 45 sec. — Edmonton, Oct. 14, 1973, vs. Houston at Edmonton. Jim Harrison 0:13, Ron Climie 0:35, Ken Baird 2:45. Edm. 5, Hou. 2.

FASTEST FOUR GOALS FROM START OF GAME, ONE TEAM:
 6 min., 39 sec. — Quebec, Oct. 20, 1973, vs. New York at Quebec. Jean-Guy Gendron 1:37, Michel Parizeau 2:27, J. C. Tremblay 4:28, Parizeau 6:39. Que. 8, N.Y. 1.

FASTEST FIVE GOALS FROM START OF GAME, ONE TEAM:
 11 min, 5 sec. — Winnipeg, Nov. 1, 1974, vs. Toronto at Winnipeg. Perry Ford 3:36, Danny Spring 5:21, Bobby Hull 7:20, Chris Bordeleau 9:01 and 11:05. Wpg. 10, Tor. 1.

FASTEST TWO GOALS FROM START OF SECOND PERIOD, ONE TEAM:
 1 min., — New England, March 26, 1973, at Cleveland. Terry Caffery 0:39, Brad Selwood 1:00. Clev. 7, N.E. 5.

FASTEST THREE GOALS FROM START OF SECOND PERIOD, ONE TEAM:
 3 min., 11 sec. — Toronto, Mar. 10, 1974, vs. Cleveland at Toronto. Gavin Kirk 0:54, Rick Sentes 1:36, Pat Hickey 3:11. Tor. 8, Clev. 3.

FASTEST FOUR GOALS FROM START OF SECOND PERIOD, ONE TEAM:
 5 min., 54 sec. — Houston, Mar. 27, 1974, at Vancouver. Frank Hughes 3:26, Jim Sherrit 4:01, Don Grierson 4:46, Murray Hall 5:54. Hou. 8, Van. 1.

FASTEST FIVE GOALS FROM START OF SECOND PERIOD, ONE TEAM:
 10 min., 8 sec. — Minnesota, Jan. 5, 1975, vs. New England at St. Paul. Mike Walton 2:43, Fran Huck 5:18 & 6:02, George Morrison 9:03, Wayne Connelly 10:08. Minn. 9, N.E. 3.

FASTEST TWO GOALS FROM START OF THIRD PERIOD, ONE TEAM:
 47 sec. — Toronto, Nov. 9, 1974, at Minnesota. Paul Henderson 0:23 and 0:47. Tor. 7, Minn. 4.

FASTEST THREE GOALS FROM START OF THIRD PERIOD, ONE TEAM:
 2 min., 29 sec. — Houston, Jan. 15, 1975, vs. Edmonton at Houston. Gordie Howe 0:27, Andre Hinse 1:17 & 2:29. Hou. 9, Edm. 2.

FASTEST FOUR GOALS FROM START OF THIRD PERIOD, ONE TEAM:
 3 min., 51 sec. — Philadelphia, Dec. 13, 1972, vs. Winnipeg at Philadelphia. Danny Lawson 1:32, Michel Plante 2:02, 2:54, Bryon Campbell 3:51. Phil. 7, Wpg. 4.

FASTEST FIVE GOALS FROM START OF THIRD PERIOD, ONE TEAM:
 10 min., 15 sec. — New England, Dec. 16, 1972, at Philadelphia. Larry Pleau 1:03, Terry Caffery 2:49, Brit Selby 2:53, 8:14, Tom Earl 10;15. N.E. 10, Phil. 6.

FORWARD LINE RECORDS

MOST POINTS BY A FORWARD LINE, ONE SEASON:
 362 — Ulf Nilsson, Anders Hedberg, Bobby Hull (156 goals, 206 assists) for Winnipeg, 1974-75. (Avg. 4.64 points per game).

MOST GOALS BY A FORWARD LINE, ONE SEASON:
 156 — Ulf Nilsson, Anders Hedberg, Bobby Hull, Winnipeg 1974-75. (Avg. 2.00 goals per game).

MOST ASSISTS FORWARD LINE, ONE SEASON:
 206 — Ulf Nilsson, Anders Hedberg, Bobby Hull, Winnipeg, 1974-75. (Avg. 2.64 per game, 1.64 per goal).

MOST SHOTS ON GOAL BY FORWARD LINE, ONE SEASON:
 974 — Ulf Nilsson, Anders Hedberg, Bobby Hull, Winnipeg, 1974-75. (Avg. 12.4 shots per game).

INDIVIDUAL

MOST SEASONS:
  3 — Held by several players.
MOST GAMES:
  236 — Tim Sheehy, New England and Edmonton.
  234 — Rosaire Paiement, Chicago Cougars.
    — Gavin Kirk, Ottawa Nationals-Toronto Toros.
    — Andre Lacroix, Philadelphia, New York, New Jersey, San Diego.
    — Danny Lawson, Philadelphia, Vancouver.
MOST POINTS:
  382 — Andre Lacroix, Philadelphia, New York, New Jersey, San Diego.
    In three seasons has 122 goals, 260 assists and two scoring championships.
MOST GOALS:
  181 — Bobby Hull, Winnipeg.
MOST ASSISTS:
  260 — Andre Lacroix, Philadelphia, New York, New Jersey, San Diego.
MOST PENALTY MINUTES:
  585 — John Schella, Houston.
MOST THREE-OR-MORE-GOAL NIGHTS:
  14 — Bobby Hull, Winnipeg. (11 three-goal 3 four-goal)
MOST FOUR-OR-MORE-GOAL NIGHTS:
  3 — Danny Lawson, Philadelphia.
    — Bobby Hull, Winnipeg.
    — Tom Simpson, Toronto.
MOST FIVE-OR-MORE-GOAL NIGHTS:
  1 — Ron Climie, Edmonton.
    — Ron Ward, New York.
    — Andre Hinse, Houston.
MOST GAMES PLAYED-IN BY A GOALTENDER:
  165 — Al Smith, New England.
  163 — Gerry Cheevers, Cleveland.
  161 — Don McLeod, Houston, Vancouver.
  160 — Gilles Gratton, Ottawa, Toronto.
MOST SHUTOUTS:
  13 — Gerry Cheevers, Cleveland.
  8 — Ernie Wakely, Winnipeg, San Diego.
MOST CONSECUTIVE GAMES PLAYED:
  234 — Rosaire Paiement, Chicago, 1972-75.
    — Gavin Kirk, Ottawa-Toronto, 1972-75.
    — Andre Lacroix, Philadelphia, New York Blades-New Jersey, San Diego, 1972-75.
    — Danny Lawson, Philadelphia-Vancouver, 1972-75.

INDIVIDUAL SINGLE SEASON

MOST GAMES:
  81 — Tim Sheehy, New England, Edmonton, 1974-75.
MOST POINTS:
  147 — Andre Lacroix, San Diego, 1974-75 (41 goals, 106 assists).
MOST GOALS:
  77 — Bobby Hull, Winnipeg, 1974-75
MOST ASSISTS:
  106 — Andre Lacroix, San Diego, 1974-75.
MOST POINTS, BY A CENTRE:
  147 — Andre Lacroix, San Diego, 1974-75.
MOST GOALS, BY A CENTRE:
  54 — Serge Bernier, Quebec, 1974-75.
MOST ASSISTS, BY A CENTRE:
  106 — Andre Lacroix, San Diego, 1974-75.

MOST POINTS, BY A RIGHT WINGER:
117 — Mike Walton, Minnesota, 1973-74.
MOST GOALS, BY A RIGHT WINGER:
61 — Danny Lawson, Philadelphia, 1972-73.
MOST ASSISTS, BY A RIGHT WINGER:
69 — Gordie Howe, Houston, 1973-74.
MOST POINTS, BY A LEFT WINGER:
142 — Bobby Hull, Winnipeg, 1974-75.
MOST GOALS, BY A LEFT WINGER:
77 — Bobby Hull, Winnipeg, 1974-75.
MOST ASSISTS, BY A LEFT WINGER:
65 — Bobby Hulll, Winnipeg, 1974-75.
MOST POINTS, BY A DEFENCEMAN:
89 — J. C. Tremblay, Quebec, 1972-73.
MOST GOALS, BY A DEFENCEMAN:
24 — Kevin Morrison, New York/New Jersey, 1973-74 (rookie season).
MOST ASSISTS, BY A DEFENCEMAN:
75 — J. C. Tremblay, Quebec, 1972-73.
MOST POINTS, BY A GOALTENDER: (and)
MOST ASSISTS, BY A GOALTENDER:
8 — Don McLeod, Vancouver, 1974-75.
MOST PENALTY MINUTES:
239 — John Schella, Houston, 1972-73.
MOST PENALTY MINUTES, BY A CENTRE:
157 — Michel Rouleau, Quebec, 1972-73.
MOST PENALTY MINUTES, BY A RIGHT WINGER:
168 — Can Connor, Phoenix, 1974-75 (rookie).
MOST PENALTY MINUTES, BY A LEFT WINGER:
223 — Gord Gallant, Minnesota, 1973-74 (rookie).
MOST PENALTY MINUTES, BY A DEFENCEMAN:
239 — John Schella, Houston, 1972-73.
MOST PENALTY MINUTES, BY A GOALTENDER:
75 — Andy Brown, Indianapolis, 1974-75.
MOST POWER PLAY GOALS:
27 — Bobby Hull, Winnipeg, 1974-75.
MOST SHORTHANDED GOALS:
9 — Mike Walton, Minnesota, 1973-74.
MOST GAMES PLAYED IN, BY A GOALTENDER:
72 — Don McLeod, Vancouver, 1974-75.
64 — Jack Norris, Alberta, 1972-73.
MOST CONSECUTIVE GAMES PLAYED IN, BY A GOALTENDER:
41 — Don McLeod, Vancouver, between Dec. 26, 1974, and Mar. 25, 1975.
MOST SHUTOUTS:
5 — Gerry Cheevers, Cleveland, 1972-73.
MOST SHUTOUTS, AT HOME:
4 — Mike Curran, Minnesota, 1972-73 (rookie).
  — Gerry Cheevers, Cleveland, 1972-73.
MOST SHUTOUTS ON ROAD:
3 — Ron Grahame, 1974-75 (rookie).
FASTEST 20 GOALS:
18 games — Bobby Hull, Winnipeg, 1974-75.
FASTEST 30 GOALS:
29 games — Bobby Hull, Winnipeg, 1974-75.
FASTEST 40 GOALS:
41 games — Bobby Hull, Winnipeg, 1974-75.
FASTEST 50 GOALS:
50 games — Bobby Hull, Winnipeg, 1974-75.
FASTEST 60 GOALS:
62 games — Bobby Hull, Winnipeg, 1974-75.

FASTEST 70 GOALS:
69 games — Bobby Hull, Winnipeg, 1974-75.
LONGEST CONSECUTIVE POINT-SCORING STREAK:
32 games — Andre Lacroix, San Diego, between Nov. 19, 1974, to Feb. 13, 1975, (17 goals, 53 assists).
LONGEST CONSECUTIVE GOAL-SCORING STREAK:
11 games — Serge Bernier, Quebec, between Dec. 5 and Dec. 22, 1974 (16 goals).
LONGEST CONSECUTIVE ASSIST-SCORING STREAK:
16 games — Andre Lacroix, San Diego, between Jan. 18 and Feb. 25, 1975 (32 assists).
LONGEST SHUTOUT SEQUENCE BY A GOALTENDER:
157 min., 37 sec. — Ernie Wakely, Winnipeg, between 13:42 of the first period Dec. 9 vs. New Jersey and 11:19 of the third period vs. Chicago Dec. 18, 1973. Included shutout of Los Angeles.

INDIVIDUAL — SINGLE GAME

MOST POINTS:
10 — Jim Harrison, Alberta, Jan. 30, 1973, 3 goals, 7 assists.
MOST GOALS:
5 — Ron Ward, New York, Jan. 4, 1973, vs. Ottawa.
— Ron Climie, Edmonton, Nov. 6, 1973, vs. New York.
— Andre Hinse, Houston, Jan. 15, 1975, vs. Edmonton.
MOST ASSISTS:
7 — Jim Harrison, Alberta, Jan. 30, 1973, vs. New York.
MOST POINTS, BY A CENTRE:
10 — Jim Harrison, Alberta, Jan. 30, 1973, vs. New York.
MOST GOALS, BY A CENTRE:
5 — Ron Ward, New York Raiders, Jan. 4, 1973, vs. Ottawa.
MOST ASSISTS, BY A CENTRE:
7 — Jim Harrison, Alberta, Jan. 30, 1973 vs New York.
MOST POINTS, BY A RIGHT WINGER:
7 — Danny Lawson, Philadelphia, Jan. 13, 1973, vs. Quebec (3 goals, 4 assists).
MOST GOALS, BY A RIGHT WINGER:
5 — Ron Climie, Edmonton, Nov. 6, 1973, vs. New York.
MOST ASSISTS, BY A RIGHT WINGER:
5 — Wayne Rivers, New York, Jan. 4, 1973, vs. Ottawa.
— Danny Lawson, Philadelphia, Mar. 9, 1973, vs. Quebec.
— John McKenzie, Vancouver, Feb. 5, 1974, vs. Edmonton.
— John French, New England, Mar. 27, 1974, vs. Los Angeles.
MOST POINTS, BY A LEFT WINGER:
6 — Bobby Hull, Winnipeg, Feb. 15, 1973, at Chicago (4 goals, 2 assists).
MOST GOALS, BY A LEFT WINGER:
5 — Andre Hinse, Houston, Jan. 15, 1975, vs. Edmonton.
MOST ASSISTS, BY A LEFT WINGER:
4 — Michel Parizeau, Quebec, Dec. 31, 1972, vs. Ottawa.
— Bobby Hull, Winnipeg, Mar. 8, 1973, at Quebec.
— Wayne Carleton, Toronto, Dec. 29, 1973, at Minnesota.
— Don Herriman, New Jersey, Jan. 19, 1974, at Vancouver (last assist in overtime).
— Gerry Pinder, Cleveland, Oct. 20, 1974, at Phoenix.
— Andre Hinse, Houston, Nov. 5, 1974, vs. San Diego.
— Michel Cormier, Phoenix, Jan. 22, 1975, vs. Chicago.
MOST POINTS, BY A DEFENCEMAN:
6 — Doug Barrie, Alberta, Jan. 30, 1973, vs. New York (1 goal, 5 assists).
MOST GOALS, BY A DEFENCEMAN:
3 — Kevin Morrison, New Jersey, Mar. 18, 1974, vs. Toronto.
MOST ASSISTS, BY A DEFENCEMAN:
5 — Doug Barrie, Alberta, Jan. 30, 1973, vs. New York.
— Kevin Morrison, San Diego, Mar. 4, 1975, vs. Quebec.
MOST POINTS, BY A GOALTENDER (and)
MOST ASSISTS, BY A GOALTENDER:
2 — Don McLeod, Vancouver, Feb. 9, 1975, vs. New England.

FASTEST TWO GOALS, BY ONE PLAYER:
 6 sec. — Gary Veneruzzo, Los Angeles, Dec. 10, 1972, scored at 15:24 and 15:30 of the third period, vs. Alberta.

FASTEST THREE GOALS:
 43 sec. — George Morrison, Minnesota, Apr. 3, 1974, scored at 15:42, 15:56 and 16:25 of the second period, vs. Vancouver.

FASTEST FOUR GOALS:
 12 min., 11 sec. — Ron Climie, Edmonton, Nov. 6, 1973, scored at 3:28, 4:01, 7:10 and 15:39 of the third period, vs. New York.

FASTEST FIVE GOALS:
 25 min., 55 sec. — Ron Ward, New York, Jan. 4, 1973, scored at 18:41 and 19:16 of the first period, 13:46, 19:01 of the second period and 4:34 of the third period, vs. Ottawa.

MOST SHOTS ON GOAL:
 18 — Bobby Hull, Winnipeg, Apr. 5, 1975 (1 goal), at Quebec.
 17 — Bobby Hull, Winnipeg, Nov. 29, 1974 (4 goals), vs. Michigan.

MOST PENALTIES:
 6 — Held by the following: Pierre Roy, Quebec (twice); Gord Gallant, Minnesota; Derek Sanderson, Philadelphia; Keke Mortson, Houston; Larry Hale, Houston; Poul Popiel, Houston; John Hughes, Phoenix; Jack Carlson, Minnesota.

MOST PENALTY MINUTES:
 36 — Derek Sanderson, Philadelphia, Oct. 24, 1972 (3 minors, 3 misconducts), at Winnipeg.

MOST SAVES, BY A WINNING GOALTENDER:
 53 — John Garrett, Minnesota, Dec. 26, 1974, at Edmonton.

MOST POINTS, ONE PERIOD:
 5 — Jim Harrison, Alberta, Jan. 30, 1973 (1 goal, 4 assists, third period), vs. New York.
 — Doug Barrie, Alberta, Jan. 30, 1973 (1 goal, 4 assists, third period), vs. New York.

MOST GOALS, ONE PERIOD:
 4 — Ron Climie, Edmonton, Nov. 6, 1973, third period, vs. New York.

MOST ASSISTS, ONE PERIOD:
 4 — Jim Harrison, Alberta, Jan. 30, 1973, third period, vs. New York.
 — Doug Barrie, Alberta, Jan. 30, 1973, third period, vs. New York.

MOST PENALTIES, ONE PERIOD:
 5 — Held by the following: John McKenzie, Philadelphia; Ted McCaskill, Los Angeles; Jack Carlson, Minnesota; Peter McNamee, Phoenix.

MOST PENALTY MINUTES, ONE PERIOD:
 30 — Doug Barrie, Edmonton, Feb. 13, 1974, third period, vs. Minnesota (2 misconducts, 2 majors).

ROOKIE RECORDS

MOST POINTS:
 120 — Ulf Nilsson, Winnipeg, 1974-75.

MOST GOALS:
 53 — Anders Hedberg, Winnipeg, 1974-75.

MOST ASSISTS:
 94 — Ulf Nilsson, Winnipeg, 1974-75.

MOST PENALTY MINUTES:
 223 — Gord Gallant, Minnesota, 1973-74.

MOST 3-OR-MORE-GOAL NIGHTS:
 3 — Claude St. Sauveur, Vancouver, 1973-74.
 — Anders Hedberg, Winnipeg, 1974-75.

MOST 4-OR-MORE-GOAL NIGHTS:
 5 players have had 4-goal nights in their rookie season.

MOST POWER PLAY GOALS:
 20 — Anders Heberg, Winnipeg, 1974-75.

MOST SHORTHANDED GOALS:
 6 — Terry Ryan, Minnesota, 1972-73.

MOST SHUTOUTS:
4 — Mike Curran, Minnesota, 1972-73.
— Ron Grahame, Houston, 1974-75.
MOST HOME SHUTOUTS:
4 — Mike Curran, Minnesota, 1972-73.
MOST ROAD SHUTOUTS:
3 — Ron Grahame, Houston, 1974-75.
FASTEST GOAL BY A ROOKIE:
51 sec. — Ed Johnstone, Michigan, Oct. 17, 1974, in first Major League game.
FASTEST THREE GOALS BY A ROOKIE:
46 min., 2 sec. — Jeff Jacques, Toronto, Jan. 12, 1975, scored at 18:41 of the first period, 5:06 and 6:02 of third period of first Major League game.
FASTEST FOUR GOALS, BY A ROOKIE:
53 min., 49 sec. — Jeff Jacques, Toronto, Jan. 12, 1975, scored at 18:41 of first period, 5:06, 6:02 and 13:49 of third period in first Major League game.
EARLIEST SHUTOUT, BY A ROOKIE GOALTENDER:
First game — Bob Blanchet, at San Diego, Dec. 14, 1974, San Diego 2, Indianapolis 0 (14 saves).

TEAM LIFETIME PENALTY MINUTES

		SEASONS	GP	PIM	Average Game	Average Season
1.	Houston	3	234	3658	15.63	1219
2.	Minnesota	3	234	3610	15.43	1203
3.	Quebec	3	234	3395	14.51	1132
4.	Calgary	3	234	3382	14.15	1127
5.	Cleveland	3	234	3375	14.42	1125
6.	Edmonton	3	234	3012	12.87	1004
7.	San Diego	3	234	2891	12.35	964
8.	Toronto	3	234	2821	12.06	940
9.	New England	3	234	2600	11.11	867
10.	Winnipeg	3	234	2299	9.82	766
11.	Phoenix	1	78	1388	17.79	1388
12.	Indianapolis	1	78	970	12.44	970
	Defunct Teams	—	468	6605	14.11	1101
	Total	3	1482	40,006	13.50	1053

PENALTIES IN MINUTES
(BY TEAMS)
1974-75 SEASON

		PIM	GA
1.	Phoenix	1388	17.79
2.	Cleveland	1273	16.32
3.	Houston	1257	16.12
4.	Minnesota	1233	15.81
5.	Quebec	1132	14.51
6.	Mich/Balt	1104	14.15
7.	Chicago	1086	13.92
8.	Vancouver	1075	13.78
9.	San Diego	1058	13.56
10.	Indianapolis	970	12.44
11.	Edmonton	896	11.49
12.	Toronto	883	11.32
13.	Winnipeg	869	11.14
14.	New England	867	11.12
	Total	15,091	13.82

MAJOR LEAGUE RECORDS

TOTAL POINTS

		League	Seasons	GP	G	A	PTS	Avg. Game	Avg. Season
1.	Gordie Howe, Detroit .	(NHL)							
	Houston	(WHA)	27	1832	851	1157	2008	1.096	74.37
2.	Bobby Hull, Chicago ..	(NHL)							
	Winnipeg .	(WHA)	18	1252	785	708	1493	1.192	82.94
3.	A. Delvecchio, Detroit	(NHL)	23	1549	456	825	1281	.827	55.70
4.	Stan Mikita, Chicago ..	(NHL)	16	1131	467	773	1240	1.096	77.50
5.	Norm Ullman, Det/Tor	(NHL)	20	1410	490	739	1229	.872	61.45
6.	John Bucyk, Det/Bos	(NHL)	20	1361	495	730	1225	.900	61.25
7.	J. Beliveau, Montreal .	(NHL)	18	1125	507	712	1219	1.081	67.72
8.	F. Mahovlich Tor/Det/Mon	(NHL)							
	Toronto	(WHA)	18	1254	571	614	1185	.945	65.83
9.	Phil Esposito, Chi/Bos	(NHL)	12	848	527	643	1170	1.380	97.50
10.	H. Richard, Montreal ..	(NHL)	19	1256	358	688	1046	.833	55.05

MOST GOALS

		League	Seasons	GP	Goals	Avg. Game	Avg. Season
1.	Gordie Howe, Detroit	(NHL)					
	Houston	(WHA)	27	1832	851	.465	31.52
2.	Bobby Hull, Chicago	(NHL)					
	Winnipeg	(WHA)	18	1252	785	.627	43.61
3.	Frank Mahovlich, Tor/Det/Mon	(NHL)					
	Toronto	(WHA)	18	1254	571	.455	31.72
4.	Maurice Richard, Montreal	(NHL)	18	978	544	.556	30.22
5.	Phil Esposito, Chicago/Boston	(NHL)	12	848	527	.621	43.92
6.	Jean Beliveau, Montreal	(NHL)	18	1125	507	.451	28.17
7.	John Bucyk, Detroit/Boston	(NHL)	20	1361	495	.364	24.75
8.	Norm Ullman, Detroit/Toronto	(NHL)	20	1410	490	.348	24.50
9.	Stan Mikita, Chicago	(NHL)	16	1131	467	.413	29.19
10.	Alex Delvecchio, Detroit	(NHL)	23	1549	456	.294	19.83

MOST ASSISTS

		League	Seasons	GP	Total Assists	Per Game	Per Season
1.	Gordie Howe, Detroit	(NHL)					
	Houston	(WHA)	27	1832	1157	.632	42.85
2.	Alex Delvecchio, Detroit	(NHL)	23	1549	825	.533	35.87
3.	Stan Mikita, Chicago	(NHL)	16	1131	783	.692	48.94
4.	Norman Ullman, Detroit/Toronto ...	(NHL)	20	1410	739	.524	36.95
5.	John Bucyk, Detroit/Boston	(NHL)	20	1361	730	.536	36.50
6.	Jean Beliveau, Montreal	(NHL)	18	1125	712	.633	39.56
7.	Bobby Hull, Chicago	(NHL)					
	Winnipeg	(WHA)	18	1252	708	.565	39.33
8.	Henri Richard, Montreal	(NHL)	19	1256	688	.548	36.22
9.	Phil Esposito, Chicago/Boston	(NHL)	12	848	643	.758	53.58
10.	Andy Bathgate, NY/Tor/Det/Pitt...	(NHL)					
	Vancouver	(WHA)	17	1080	630	.583	37.06

56

major league

MOST PENALTY MINUTES

		League	Seasons	Games	Total PIM	Avg. Game	Avg. Season
1.	Ted Lindsay, Detroit/Chicago	(NHL)	17	1068	1808	1.69	106.35
2.	Gordie Howe, Detroit	(NHL)					
	Houston	(WHA)	27	1832	1772	.97	65.63
3.	Tim Horton, Tor/NY/Pitt/Buff	(NHL)	22	1446	1611	1.11	73.23
4.	Reg Fleming, Mon/Chi/NY/Phil	(NHL)	13	869	1610	1.85	123.85
5.	Bryan Watson, Mon/Det/Cal/Pitt/St.L.	(NHL)	9	630	1557	2.47	173.00
6.	Bill Gadsby, Chi/NY/Det	(NHL)	20	1248	1539	1.23	76.95
7.	Bob Baun, Tor/Cal/Det	(NHL)	17	964	1493	1.55	87.85
8.	Ed Shack NY/Tor/Bos/LA/Buff/Pitt	(NHL)	18	1047	1437	1.37	79.83
9.	Fern Flaman, Boston/Toronto	(NHL)	15	910	1370	1.51	91.33
9.	Gus Mortson, Tor/Chi/Det	(NHL)	13	797	1370	1.72	105.38

THE AMAZING HOWE

To give added perspective to Gordie Howe's record 2,008 points, the following chart shows when other current Major Leaguers could hit the 2,000 points plateau. This is based on their current averages and they would have to maintain those averages over several 80-game seasons.

	ADD'L GAMES NEEDED	ADD'L SEASONS NEEDED	AT WHAT AGE	DURING WHAT SEASON
BOBBY HULL	432	5.4	41	1979-80
STAN MIKITA	701	8.6	43	1982-83
NORM ULLMAN	893	11.2	50	1985-86
JOHN BUCYK	870	10.9	50	1984-85
FRANK MAHOVLICH	823	10.3	47	1984-85
PHIL ESPOSITO	607	7.6	41	1981-82
BOBBY ORR	810	10.1	37	1984-85
ANDRE LACROIX	1361	17.0	47	1991-92

WHA CAREER LEADERS (THREE SEASONS)

MOST POINTS

		TM	GP	G	A	PTS	Avg. Season	Avg. Game
1.	Andre Lacroix	S.D.	234	122	260	382	127.3	1.632
2.	Bobby Hull	Wpg	216	181	159	340	113.3	1.574
3.	Danny Lawson	Calg	234	144	126	270	90.0	1.154
4.	Larry Lund	Hou	230	87	173	260	86.7	1.130
5.	Wayne Carleton	N.E.	226	114	143	257	85.7	1.137
6.	Wayne Rivers	S.D.	226	121	120	241	80.3	1.066
6.	Ron Ward	Cle	220	114	127	241	80.3	1.095
8.	Chris Bordeleau	Que	224	96	144	240	80.0	1.071
9.	Tom Webster	N.E.	207	136	102	238	79.3	1.150
10.	Wayne Connelly	Min	232	120	116	236	78.7	1.017

MOST GOALS

		TM.	YRS	GP	G	Avg. Season	Avg. Game
1.	Bobby Hull	Wpg	3	216	181	60.33	.838
2.	Danny Lawson	Calg	3	234	144	48.00	.615
3.	Tom Webster	N.E.	3	207	136	45.33	.657
4.	Wayne Rivers	S.D.	3	226	122	40.67	.540
5.	Andre Lacroix	S.D.	3	234	121	40.33	.517
6.	Wayne Connelly	Min	3	232	120	40.00	.517
7.	Ron Ward	Cle	3	220	114	38.00	.518
7.	Wayne Carleton	N.E.	3	226	114	38.00	.504
9.	Frank Hughes	Hou	3	225	112	37.33	.498
10.	Mike Walton	Min	2	153	105	52.50	.686

MOST ASSISTS

		TM.	YRS.	GP	A	Avg. Season	Avg. Game
1.	Andre Lacroix	S.D.	3	234	260	86.67	1.111
2.	J. C. Tremblay	Que	3	212	175	58.33	.825
3.	Larry Lund	Hou	3	230	173	57.67	.752
4.	Bobby Hull	Wpg	3	216	159	53.00	.736
5.	Gavin Kirk	Tor	3	234	146	48.67	.624
6.	Chris Bordeleau	Que	3	224	144	48.00	.643
6.	Bryan Campbell	Cin	3	229	144	48.00	.629
8.	Wayne Carleton	N.E.	3	226	143	47.67	.633
9.	Jim Dorey	Tor	3	226	136	45.33	.602
10.	Gordie Howe	Hou	2	145	134	67.00	.924

MOST PENALTY MINUTES

		TM.	YRS.	GP	PIM	Avg. Season	Avg. Game
1.	John Schella	Hou	3	229	585	195.0	2.555
2.	Doug Barrie	Edm	3	201	447	149.0	2.224
3.	John Arbour	Min	3	224	445	148.3	1.987
4.	Tom Gilmore	Edm	3	202	439	146.3	2.173
5.	Paul Shmyr	Cle	3	200	437	145.7	2.185
6.	Steve Sutherland	Que	3	194	431	143.7	2.222
7.	Gord Gallant	Que	2	138	426	213.0	3.087
8.	Pierre Roy	Que	3	169	424	141.3	2.509
9.	Jim Cardiff	Van	3	200	398	132.7	1.990
10.	Larry Mavety	Tor	3	224	396	132.0	1.768

58

career leaders

3-OR-MORE GOAL GAMES

Player, Team	Hat Tricks	Goal Nights 3	4	5
Bobby Hull, Winnipeg	14	11	3	—
Danny Lawson, Vancouver	10	7	3	—
Mike Walton, Minnesota	7	5	2	—
Ron Ward, Cleveland	5	4	—	1
Tom Simpson, Toronto	5	2	3	—
Frank Hughes, Houston	5	5	—	—
Gene Peacosh, San Diego	5	5	—	—
Rick Sentes, San Diego	4	3	1	—
Wayne Rivers, San Diego	4	4	—	—
Claude St. Sauveur, Van.	4	4	—	—
Marc Tardif, Quebec	4	4	—	—
Tom Webster, New England	4	4	—	—
Anders Hedberg, Winnipeg	3	2	1	—
Andre Lacroix, San Diego	3	2	1	—
Larry Pleau, New England	3	3	—	—
John McKenzie, Vancouver	3	3	—	—
Andre Hinse, Houston	2	1	—	1
Chris Bordeleau, Quebec	2	1	1	—
Ron Buchanan, Indianapolis	2	1	1	—
Tom Gilmore, Edmonton	2	1	1	—
Pat Hickey, Toronto	2	1	1	—
Gordie Howe, Houston	2	1	1	—
Brian McDonald, Indianapolis	2	1	1	—
George Morrison, Minnesota	2	1	1	—
Don Borgeson, Phoenix	2	2	—	—
Terry Caffery, New England	2	2	—	—
Bryan Campbell, Vancouver	2	2	—	—
Wayne Carleton, New England	2	2	—	—
Alain Caron, Baltimore	2	2	—	—
Real Cloutier, Quebec	2	2	—	—
Jim Harrison, Cleveland	2	2	—	—
Don Herriman, Edmonton	2	2	—	—
Rejean Houle, Quebec	2	2	—	—
Mark Howe, Houston	2	2	—	—
Fran Huck, Minnesota	2	2	—	—
Gord Labossiere, Houston	2	2	—	—
J. P. Leblanc, Baltimore	2	2	—	—
Larry Lund, Houston	2	2	—	—
Frank Mahovlich, Toronto	2	2	—	—
Jan Popiel, Chicago	2	2	—	—
Francois Rochon, Chicago	2	2	—	—
Ted Taylor, Houston	2	2	—	—
Gary Veneruzzo, Baltimore	2	2	—	—
Alton White, Baltimore	2	2	—	—
Ron Climie, New England	1	—	—	1
Jeff Jacques, Toronto	1	—	1	—
Wayne Dillon, Toronto	1	—	1	—
John French, New England	1	—	1	—
Mike Antonovich, Minnesota	1	1	—	—
Ken Baird, Edmonton	1	1	—	—
Norm Beaudin, Winnipeg	1	1	—	—
Don Blackburn, New England	1	1	—	—
Mike Byers, New England	1	1	—	—
Steve Cardwell, Cleveland	1	1	—	—
Brian Coates, Indianapolis	1	1	—	—
Wayne Connelly, Minnesota	1	1	—	—
Michel Cormier, Phoenix	1	1	—	—
Reg Fleming, Chicago	1	1	—	—
Robbie Ftorek, Phoenix	1	1	—	—
Gary Gambucci, Minnesota	1	1	—	—
Andre Gaudette, Quebec	1	1	—	—
Rejean Giroux, Quebec	1	1	—	—
Jean Guy Gratton, Winnipeg	1	1	—	—
Don Grierson, Houston	1	1	—	—
Robert Guindon, Quebec	1	1	—	—
Pierre Guite, Baltimore	1	1	—	—
Joe Hardy, San Diego	1	1	—	—
Hugh Harris, Vancouver	1	1	—	—
Paul Henderson, Toronto	1	1	—	—
Ted Hodgson, Cleveland	1	1	—	—
Danny Johnson, Winnipeg	1	1	—	—
Gavin Kirk, Toronto	1	1	—	—
Rich Leduc, Cleveland	1	1	—	—
Dan Lodboa, Chicago	1	1	—	—
Gary MacGregor, Chicago	1	1	—	—
Peter Mara, Chicago	1	1	—	—
Brian McDonald, Indianapolis	1	1	—	—
Al McDonough, Cleveland	1	1	—	—
Murray Meyers, Vancouver	1	1	—	—
Brian Morenz, San Diego	1	1	—	—
Rick Morris, Chicago	1	1	—	—
Kevin Morrison, San Diego	1	1	—	—
Vaclav Nedomansky, Toronto	1	1	—	—
Fred O'Donnell, New England	1	1	—	—
Rosaire Paiement, New England	1	1	—	—
Michel Parizeau, Quebec	1	1	—	—
Ross Perkins, Edmonton	1	1	—	—
Gerry Pinder, Cleveland	1	1	—	—
Mike Rogers, Edmonton	1	1	—	—
Brit Selby, Toronto	1	1	—	—
Bobby Sheehan, Edmonton	1	1	—	—
Steve Sutherland, Quebec	1	1	—	—
Ron Walters, Edmonton	1	1	—	—
Bob Whitlock, Indianapolis	1	1	—	—
Steve West, Baltimore	1	1	—	—
Jim Wiste, Indianapolis	1	1	—	—
Tommy Williams, New England	1	1	—	—
Bill Young, Cleveland	1	1	—	—

MOST SHUTOUTS

		TEAM	YRS.	GP	SO	FREQ.
1.	Gerry Cheevers	Cle	3	163	13	12.54
2.	Ernie Wakely	S.D.	3	127	8	15.88
3.	Mike Curran	Min	3	110	7	15.71
3.	Al Smith	N.E.	3	165	7	23.57
5.	Ron Grahame	Hou	2	47	5	9.40
5.	Peter Donnelly	Que	2	96	5	19.20
5.	Don McLeod	Calg	3	161	5	32.20
8.	Russ Gillow	S.D.	3	86	4	21.50
8.	Jack Norris	Phx	3	150	4	37.50
8.	Gilles Gratton	Tor	3	160	4	40.00

LIFETIME TEAM TOTALS

STANDINGS

	GP	W	L	T	PTS	GF	GA	PCT
Houston	234	140	85	9	289	971	735	.618
New England	234	132	91	11	275	883	802	.588
Minnesota	234	124	102	8	256	890	823	.547
(c) Toronto	234	119	105	10	248	932	877	.530
Cleveland	234	115	104	15	245	789	761	.524
Winnipeg	234	115	105	14	244	871	838	.521
Quebec	234	117	108	9	243	913	892	.519
Edmonton	234	112	112	10	234	816	804	.500
(b) San Diego	234	108	116	10	226	897	915	.483
(a) Calgary	234	102	129	3	207	822	920	.442
Phoenix	78	39	31	8	86	300	265	.551
Indianapolis	78	18	57	3	39	216	338	.250
(d) Defunct Teams	468	177	273	18	372	1480	1810	.397
Totals	1482	1418	1418	64	2964	10,780	10,780	.500

LIFETIME HOME

	GP	W	L	T	PTS	GF	GA	PCT
New England	117	84	27	6	174	481	348	.744
Houston	117	78	36	3	159	537	349	.679
Cleveland	117	76	34	7	159	441	329	.679
Winnipeg	117	75	35	7	157	491	342	.671
Quebec	117	74	34	9	157	518	381	.671
Minnesota	117	76	39	2	154	497	384	.658
Edmonton	117	74	38	5	153	487	366	.654
(b) San Diego	117	71	42	4	146	529	409	.624
(c) Toronto	117	70	41	6	146	488	387	.624
(a) Calgary	117	68	47	2	138	464	411	.590
Phoenix	39	23	11	5	51	170	115	.654
Indianapolis	39	13	26	0	26	106	149	.333
(d) Defunct Teams	234	108	118	8	224	767	834	.479
Totals	1482	890	528	64	1844	5976	4804	.622

LIFETIME ROAD

	GP	W	L	T	PTS	GF	GA	PCT
Houston	117	62	49	6	130	434	386	.556
(c) Toronto	117	49	64	4	102	444	490	.436
Minnesota	117	48	63	6	102	393	439	.436
New England	117	48	64	5	101	402	454	.432
Winnipeg	117	40	70	7	87	380	496	.372
Quebec	117	43	74	0	86	395	511	.368
Cleveland	117	39	70	8	86	348	432	.368
Edmonton	117	38	74	5	81	329	438	.346
(b) San Diego	117	37	74	6	80	368	506	.342
(a) Calgary	117	34	82	1	69	358	509	.295
Phoenix	39	16	20	3	35	130	150	.449
Indianapolis	39	5	31	3	13	110	189	.167
(d) Defunct Teams	234	69	155	10	148	713	976	.316
Totals	1482	528	890	64	1120	4804	5976	.378

(a) *Formerly Philadelphia / Vancouver* (b) *Formerly New York / New Jersey*
(c) *Formerly Ottawa* (d) *Formerly Chicago / Los Angeles / Michigan / Baltimore*

CALGARY COWBOYS LIFETIME TOTALS (formerly Philadelphia & Vancouver Blazers)

AGAINST:	AT PHILADELPHIA/VANCOUVER								ON ROAD								OVERALL							
	GP	W	L	T	PTS	GF	GA	PCT	GP	W	L	T	PTS	GF	GA	PCT	GP	W	L	T	PTS	GF	GA	PCT
Cleveland	11	6	5	0	12	43	35	.545	11	4	7	0	8	40	64	.364	22	10	12	0	20	83	99	.455
Edmonton	11	9	2	0	18	54	27	.818	11	3	8	0	6	23	39	.273	22	12	10	0	24	77	66	.545
Houston	10	1	9	0	2	20	49	.100	10	3	7	0	6	30	48	.300	20	4	16	0	8	50	97	.200
Indianapolis	3	2	0	1	5	10	5	.833	3	2	1	0	4	14	8	.667	6	4	1	1	9	24	13	.750
Minnesota	10	6	4	0	12	40	37	.600	10	2	8	0	4	20	40	.200	20	8	12	0	16	60	77	.400
New England	10	8	2	0	16	52	37	.800	10	1	9	0	2	28	48	.100	20	9	11	0	18	80	85	.450
Phoenix	3	3	0	0	6	12	9	1.000	3	0	3	0	0	7	13	.000	6	3	3	0	6	19	22	.500
Quebec	10	7	3	0	14	52	38	.700	10	1	9	0	2	32	56	.100	20	8	12	0	16	84	94	.400
(b) San Diego	10	3	7	0	6	29	41	.300	10	3	7	0	6	24	38	.300	20	6	14	0	12	53	79	.300
(c) Toronto	10	4	6	0	8	38	40	.400	10	3	7	0	6	35	47	.300	20	7	13	0	14	73	87	.350
Winnipeg	10	7	2	1	15	43	36	.750	10	3	7	0	6	37	50	.300	20	10	9	1	21	80	86	.525
(d) Defunct Teams	19	12	7	0	24	71	57	.632	19	9	9	1	19	68	58	.500	38	21	16	1	43	139	115	.566
TOTALS	117	68	47	2	138	464	411	.590	117	34	82	1	69	358	509	.295	234	102	129	3	207	822	920	.442

CLEVELAND CRUSADERS LIFETIME TOTALS

AGAINST:	AT CLEVELAND								ON ROAD								OVERALL							
	GP	W	L	T	PTS	GF	GA	PCT	GP	W	L	T	PTS	GF	GA	PCT	GP	W	L	T	PTS	GF	GA	PCT
(a) Calgary	11	7	4	0	14	64	40	.636	11	5	6	0	10	35	43	.455	22	12	10	0	24	99	83	.545
Edmonton	9	8	1	0	16	34	14	.889	9	3	5	1	7	21	27	.389	18	11	6	1	23	55	41	.639
Houston	9	2	6	1	5	19	26	.278	9	4	4	1	9	34	32	.500	18	6	10	2	14	53	58	.389
Indianapolis	3	3	0	0	6	15	8	1.000	3	1	2	0	2	8	15	.333	6	4	2	0	8	23	23	.667
Minnesota	10	3	7	0	6	22	30	.300	10	3	6	1	7	30	43	.350	20	6	13	1	13	52	73	.325
New England	11	8	3	0	17	33	21	.727	11	0	10	1	1	21	41	.045	22	8	13	1	17	54	62	.386
Phoenix	3	3	0	0	6	15	8	1.000	3	1	1	1	3	8	8	.500	6	4	1	1	9	23	16	.750
Quebec	11	9	2	0	18	46	29	.818	11	2	7	2	6	31	39	.273	22	11	9	2	24	77	68	.545
(b) San Diego	11	7	2	2	16	43	26	.727	11	4	7	0	8	34	51	.364	22	11	9	2	24	77	77	.545
(c) Toronto	11	7	3	1	15	43	36	.682	11	4	7	0	8	33	41	.364	22	11	10	1	23	76	77	.523
Winnipeg	9	7	1	1	15	37	28	.833	9	2	7	0	4	31	42	.222	18	9	8	1	19	68	70	.528
(d) Defunct Teams	19	12	5	2	26	70	63	.684	19	10	8	1	21	62	50	.553	38	22	13	3	47	132	113	.618
TOTALS	117	76	34	7	159	441	329	.679	117	39	70	8	86	348	432	.368	234	115	104	15	245	789	761	.524

(a) Formerly Philadelphia/Vancouver (b) Formerly New York/New Jersey
(c) Formerly Ottawa (d) Formerly Chicago/Los Angeles/Michigan/Baltimore

EDMONTON OILERS LIFETIME TOTALS (formerly Alberta)

AGAINST:	AT EDMONTON								ON ROAD								OVERALL							
	GP	W	L	T	PTS	GF	GA	PCT	GP	W	L	T	PTS	GF	GA	PCT	GP	W	L	T	PTS	GF	GA	PCT
(a) Calgary	11	8	3	0	16	39	23	.727	11	2	9	0	4	27	54	.182	22	10	12	0	20	66	77	.455
Cleveland	9	5	3	1	11	27	21	.611	9	1	8	0	2	14	34	.111	18	6	11	1	13	41	55	.361
Houston	11	6	5	0	12	45	43	.545	11	2	9	0	4	26	49	.182	22	8	14	0	16	71	92	.364
Indianapolis	3	2	0	1	5	10	8	.833	3	2	1	0	4	7	5	.667	6	4	1	1	9	17	13	.750
Minnesota	11	7	4	0	14	46	39	.636	11	5	6	0	10	40	41	.455	22	12	10	0	24	86	80	.545
New England	9	5	4	0	10	37	35	.556	9	2	5	2	6	26	34	.333	18	7	9	2	16	63	69	.444
Phoenix	3	0	2	1	1	11	14	.167	3	1	2	0	2	9	7	.333	6	1	4	1	3	20	21	.250
Quebec	9	4	5	0	8	32	33	.444	9	3	5	1	7	31	39	.389	18	7	10	1	15	63	72	.417
(b) San Diego	9	7	2	0	14	51	30	.778	9	4	5	0	8	32	39	.444	18	11	7	0	22	83	69	.611
(c) Toronto	9	6	3	0	12	38	32	.667	9	4	5	0	8	37	30	.444	18	10	8	0	20	75	62	.556
Winnipeg	12	8	3	1	17	52	36	.708	12	3	8	1	7	25	51	.292	24	11	11	2	24	77	87	.500
(d) Defunct Teams	21	16	4	1	33	99	52	.786	21	9	11	1	19	55	55	.452	42	25	15	2	52	154	107	.619
TOTALS	117	74	38	5	153	487	366	.654	117	38	74	5	81	329	438	.346	234	112	112	10	234	816	804	.500

HOUSTON AEROS LIFETIME TOTALS

AGAINST:	AT HOUSTON								ON ROAD								OVERALL							
	GP	W	L	T	PTS	GF	GA	PCT	GP	W	L	T	PTS	GF	GA	PCT	GP	W	L	T	PTS	GF	GA	PCT
(a) Calgary	10	7	3	0	14	48	30	.700	10	9	1	0	18	49	20	.900	20	16	4	0	32	97	50	.800
Cleveland	9	4	4	1	9	32	34	.500	9	6	2	1	13	26	19	.722	18	10	6	2	22	58	53	.611
Edmonton	11	9	2	0	18	49	26	.818	11	5	6	0	10	43	45	.455	22	14	8	0	28	92	71	.636
Indianapolis	3	2	1	0	4	14	13	.667	3	3	0	0	6	21	6	1.000	6	5	1	0	10	35	19	.833
Minnesota	11	8	3	0	16	51	29	.727	11	7	3	1	15	39	31	.682	22	15	6	1	31	90	60	.705
New England	9	4	5	0	8	37	31	.444	9	5	3	1	11	36	29	.611	18	9	8	1	19	73	60	.528
Phoenix	3	2	1	0	4	18	12	.667	3	1	2	0	2	12	10	.333	6	3	3	0	6	30	22	.500
Quebec	9	5	4	0	10	40	27	.556	9	1	7	1	3	23	42	.167	18	6	11	1	13	63	69	.361
(b) San Diego	9	5	4	0	10	42	27	.556	9	3	6	0	6	31	33	.333	18	8	10	0	16	73	60	.444
(c) Toronto	9	7	2	0	14	49	26	.778	9	3	5	1	7	33	36	.389	18	10	7	1	21	82	62	.583
Winnipeg	11	8	2	1	17	59	26	.773	11	4	6	1	9	30	43	.409	22	12	8	2	26	89	69	.591
(d) Defunct Teams	23	17	5	1	35	98	68	.761	23	15	8	0	30	91	72	.652	46	32	13	1	65	189	140	.707
TOTALS	117	78	36	3	159	537	349	.679	117	62	49	6	130	434	386	.556	234	140	85	9	289	971	735	.618

(a) Formerly Philadelphia/Vancouver (b) Formerly New York/New Jersey
(c) Formerly Ottawa (d) Formerly Chicago/Los Angeles/Michigan/Baltimore

INDIANAPOLIS RACERS LIFETIME TOTALS

AGAINST:	AT INDIANAPOLIS								ON ROAD								OVERALL							
	GP	W	L	T	PTS	GF	GA	PCT	GP	W	L	T	PTS	GF	GA	PCT	GP	W	L	T	PTS	GF	GA	PCT
(a) Calgary	3	1	2	0	2	8	14	.333	3	0	2	1	1	5	10	.167	6	1	4	1	3	13	24	.250
Cleveland	3	2	1	0	4	15	8	.667	3	0	3	0	0	8	15	.000	6	2	4	0	4	23	23	.333
Edmonton	3	1	2	0	2	5	7	.333	3	0	2	1	1	8	10	.167	6	1	4	1	3	13	17	.250
Houston	3	0	3	0	0	6	21	.000	3	1	2	0	2	13	14	.333	6	1	5	0	2	19	35	.167
Minnesota	3	1	2	0	2	7	11	.333	3	0	3	0	0	10	15	.000	6	1	5	0	2	17	26	.167
New England	3	1	2	0	2	3	11	.333	3	0	3	0	0	7	16	.000	6	1	5	0	2	10	27	.167
Phoenix	3	0	3	0	0	2	8	.000	3	0	3	0	0	5	23	.000	6	0	6	0	0	7	31	.000
Quebec	3	1	2	0	2	11	12	.333	3	0	3	0	0	7	20	.000	6	1	5	0	2	18	32	.167
(b) San Diego	3	2	1	0	4	10	8	.667	3	0	3	0	0	6	16	.000	6	2	4	0	4	16	24	.333
(c) Toronto	3	1	2	0	2	9	16	.333	3	0	3	0	0	7	17	.000	6	1	5	0	2	16	33	.167
Winnipeg	3	0	3	0	0	6	13	.000	3	1	2	0	2	4	10	.333	6	1	5	0	2	10	23	.167
(d) Defunct Teams	6	3	3	0	6	24	20	.500	6	3	2	1	7	30	23	.583	12	6	5	1	13	54	43	.542
TOTALS	39	13	26	0	26	106	149	.333	39	5	31	3	13	110	189	.167	78	18	57	3	39	216	338	.250

MINNESOTA FIGHTING SAINTS LIFETIME TOTALS

AGAINST:	AT ST. PAUL								ON ROAD								OVERALL							
	GP	W	L	T	PTS	GF	GA	PCT	GP	W	L	T	PTS	GF	GA	PCT	GP	W	L	T	PTS	GF	GA	PCT
(a) Calgary	10	8	2	0	16	40	20	.800	10	4	6	0	8	37	40	.400	20	12	8	0	24	77	60	.600
Cleveland	10	6	3	1	13	43	30	.650	10	7	3	0	14	30	22	.700	20	13	6	1	27	73	52	.675
Edmonton	11	6	5	0	12	41	40	.545	11	4	7	0	8	39	46	.364	22	10	12	0	20	80	86	.455
Houston	11	3	7	1	7	31	39	.318	11	3	8	0	6	29	51	.273	22	6	15	1	13	60	90	.295
Indianapolis	3	3	0	0	6	15	10	1.000	3	2	0	1	4	11	7	.667	6	5	0	1	10	26	17	.833
New England	9	9	0	0	18	50	28	1.000	9	2	6	1	5	22	34	.278	18	11	6	1	23	72	62	.639
Phoenix	3	2	1	0	4	15	9	.667	3	0	2	1	1	6	10	.167	6	2	3	1	5	21	19	.417
Quebec	9	5	4	0	10	40	38	.556	9	6	3	0	12	48	31	.667	18	11	7	0	22	88	69	.611
(b) San Diego	9	5	4	0	10	37	29	.556	9	3	5	1	7	28	37	.389	18	8	9	1	17	65	66	.472
(c) Toronto	9	6	3	0	12	38	36	.667	9	3	6	0	6	28	47	.333	18	9	9	0	18	66	83	.500
Winnipeg	11	8	3	0	16	54	30	.727	11	4	5	2	10	31	32	.455	22	12	8	2	26	85	62	.591
(d) Defunct Teams	22	15	7	0	30	93	75	.682	22	10	11	1	21	84	82	.477	44	25	18	1	51	177	157	.580
TOTALS	117	76	39	2	154	497	384	.658	117	48	63	6	102	393	439	.436	234	124	102	8	256	890	823	.547

(a) *Formerly Philadelphia/Vancouver* (b) *Formerly New York/New Jersey*
(c) *Formerly Ottawa* (d) *Formerly Chicago/Los Angeles/Michigan/Baltimore*

NEW ENGLAND WHALERS LIFETIME TOTALS

AGAINST:	AT BOSTON/HARTFORD									ON ROAD									OVERALL								
	GP	W	L	T	PTS	GF	GA	PCT	GP	W	L	T	PTS	GF	GA	PCT	GP	W	L	T	PTS	GF	GA	PCT
(a) Calgary	10	9	1	0	18	48	28	.900	10	2	8	0	4	37	52	.200	20	11	9	0	22	85	80	.550
Cleveland	11	10	0	1	21	41	21	.955	11	3	8	0	6	21	33	.273	22	13	8	1	27	62	54	.614
Edmonton	9	5	2	2	12	34	26	.667	9	4	5	0	8	35	37	.444	18	9	7	2	20	69	63	.556
Houston	9	3	5	1	7	29	36	.389	9	5	4	0	10	31	37	.556	18	8	9	1	17	60	73	.472
Indianapolis	3	3	0	0	6	16	7	1.000	3	2	1	0	4	11	3	.667	6	5	1	0	10	27	10	.833
Minnesota	9	6	2	1	13	34	22	.722	9	0	9	0	0	28	50	.000	18	6	11	1	13	62	72	.361
Phoenix	3	1	1	1	3	12	12	.500	3	0	2	1	1	5	11	.167	6	1	3	2	4	17	23	.333
Quebec	11	7	4	0	14	46	36	.636	11	4	6	1	9	37	50	.409	22	11	10	1	23	83	86	.523
(b) San Diego	13	12	1	0	24	49	34	.923	13	6	6	1	13	57	45	.500	26	18	7	1	37	106	79	.712
(c) Toronto	11	8	3	0	16	54	41	.727	11	5	5	1	11	37	44	.500	22	13	8	1	27	91	85	.617
Winnipeg	9	5	4	0	10	38	30	.556	9	7	2	0	14	35	36	.778	18	12	6	0	24	73	66	.667
(d) Defunct Teams	19	15	4	0	30	80	55	.789	19	10	8	1	21	68	56	.553	38	25	12	1	51	148	111	.671
TOTALS	117	84	27	6	174	481	348	.744	117	48	64	5	101	402	454	.432	234	132	91	11	275	883	802	.588

PHOENIX ROADRUNNERS LIFETIME TOTALS

AGAINST:	AT PHOENIX									ON ROAD									OVERALL								
	GP	W	L	T	PTS	GF	GA	PCT	GP	W	L	T	PTS	GF	GA	PCT	GP	W	L	T	PTS	GF	GA	PCT
(a) Calgary	3	3	0	0	6	13	7	1.000	3	0	3	0	0	9	12	.000	6	3	3	0	6	22	19	.500
Cleveland	3	1	1	1	3	8	8	.500	3	0	3	0	0	8	15	.000	6	1	4	1	3	16	23	.250
Edmonton	3	2	1	0	4	7	9	.667	3	2	0	1	5	14	11	.833	6	4	1	1	9	21	20	.750
Houston	3	2	1	0	4	10	12	.667	3	1	2	0	2	12	18	.333	6	3	3	0	6	22	30	.500
Indianapolis	3	3	0	0	6	23	5	1.000	3	0	0	3	6	8	2	1.000	6	3	0	3	12	31	7	1.000
Minnesota	3	2	0	1	5	10	6	.833	3	3	0	0	6	9	15	.333	6	5	0	1	11	19	21	.583
New England	3	2	1	0	4	11	5	.833	3	1	1	1	3	12	12	.500	6	3	2	1	7	23	17	.667
Quebec	3	1	2	0	2	12	12	.333	3	1	2	0	2	12	13	.333	6	2	4	0	4	24	25	.333
(b) San Diego	3	2	1	0	4	17	6	.667	3	1	2	0	2	6	13	.333	6	3	3	0	6	23	19	.500
(c) Toronto	3	0	1	2	2	11	14	.333	3	1	2	0	2	10	16	.333	6	1	3	2	4	21	30	.333
Winnipeg	3	1	2	0	2	12	12	.333	3	2	1	0	4	12	9	.667	6	3	3	0	6	24	21	.500
(d) Defunct Teams	6	4	2	0	8	36	19	.667	6	3	2	1	7	18	14	.583	12	7	4	1	15	54	33	.625
TOTALS	39	23	11	5	51	170	115	.654	39	16	20	3	35	130	150	.449	78	39	31	8	86	300	265	.551

(a) *Formerly Philadelphia/Vancouver* (b) *Formerly New York/New Jersey*
(c) *Formerly Ottawa* (d) *Formerly Chicago/Los Angeles/Michigan/Baltimore*

QUEBEC NORDIQUES LIFETIME TOTALS

	AT QUEBEC CITY								ON ROAD								OVERALL						
AGAINST:	GP	W	L	T	PTS	GF	GA	PCT	GP	W	L	T	PTS	GF	GA	PCT	GP	W	L	T	PTS	GF	GA	PCT
(a) Calgary	10	9	1	0	18	56	32	.900	10	3	7	0	6	38	52	.300	20	12	8	0	24	94	84	.600
Cleveland	11	7	2	2	16	39	31	.727	11	2	9	0	4	29	46	.182	22	9	11	2	20	68	77	.455
Edmonton	9	5	3	1	11	39	31	.611	9	5	4	0	10	33	32	.278	18	10	7	1	21	72	63	.583
Houston	9	7	1	1	15	42	23	.833	9	4	5	0	8	27	40	.444	18	11	6	1	23	69	63	.639
Indianapolis	3	3	0	0	6	20	7	1.000	3	2	1	0	4	12	11	.667	6	5	1	0	10	32	18	.833
Minnesota	9	3	6	0	6	31	48	.333	9	4	5	0	8	38	40	.444	18	7	11	0	14	69	88	.389
New England	11	6	4	1	13	50	37	.591	11	4	7	0	8	36	46	.364	22	10	11	1	21	86	83	.477
Phoenix	3	2	1	0	4	13	12	.667	3	2	1	0	4	12	12	.667	6	4	2	0	8	25	24	.667
(b) San Diego	11	8	2	1	17	58	35	.773	11	1	10	0	2	28	69	.091	22	9	12	1	19	86	104	.432
(c) Toronto	13	6	7	0	12	48	51	.462	13	5	8	0	10	46	55	.385	26	11	15	0	22	94	106	.423
Winnipeg	9	5	2	2	12	40	27	.667	9	2	7	0	4	30	40	.222	18	7	9	2	16	70	67	.444
(d) Defunct Teams	19	13	5	1	27	82	47	.711	19	9	10	0	18	66	68	.474	38	22	15	1	45	148	115	.592
TOTALS	117	74	34	9	157	518	381	.671	117	43	74	0	86	395	511	.368	234	117	108	9	243	913	892	.519

SAN DIEGO MARINERS LIFETIME TOTALS (Formerly New Jersey/New York)

	AT S.D/NEW JERSEY/NEW YORK								ON ROAD								OVERALL						
AGAINST:	GP	W	L	T	PTS	GF	GA	PCT	GP	W	L	T	PTS	GF	GA	PCT	GP	W	L	T	PTS	GF	GA	PCT
(a) Calgary	10	7	3	0	14	38	24	.700	10	7	3	0	14	41	29	.700	20	14	6	0	28	79	53	.700
Cleveland	11	7	4	0	14	51	34	.318	11	2	7	2	6	26	43	.273	22	9	11	2	20	77	77	.455
Edmonton	9	5	4	0	10	39	32	.556	9	2	7	0	4	30	51	.222	18	7	11	0	14	69	83	.389
Houston	9	6	3	0	12	33	31	.667	9	4	5	0	8	27	42	.444	18	10	8	0	20	60	73	.556
Indianapolis	3	3	0	0	6	16	61	.000	3	1	2	0	2	8	10	.333	6	4	2	0	8	24	16	.667
Minnesota	9	5	3	1	11	37	28	.611	9	4	5	0	8	29	37	.444	18	9	8	1	19	66	65	.528
New England	13	6	6	1	13	45	57	.500	13	1	12	0	2	34	49	.077	26	7	18	1	15	79	106	.288
Phoenix	3	2	1	0	4	13	6	.667	3	1	2	0	2	6	17	.333	6	3	3	0	6	19	23	.500
Quebec	11	10	1	0	20	69	28	.909	11	2	8	1	5	35	58	.227	22	12	9	1	25	104	86	.568
(c) Toronto	11	8	3	0	16	65	44	.727	11	4	6	1	9	32	41	.409	22	12	9	1	25	97	85	.568
Winnipeg	9	4	5	0	8	44	43	.444	9	1	6	2	4	31	45	.222	18	5	11	2	12	75	88	.333
(d) Defunct Teams	19	8	9	2	18	79	76	.474	19	8	11	0	16	69	84	.421	38	16	20	2	34	148	160	.447
TOTALS	117	71	42	4	146	529	409	.624	117	37	74	6	80	368	506	.342	234	108	116	10	226	897	915	.483

(a) Formerly Philadelphia/Vancouver (b) Formerly New York/New Jersey
(c) Formerly Ottawa (d) Formerly Chicago/Los Angeles/Michigan/Baltimore

TORONTO TOROS LIFETIME TOTALS — Formerly Ottawa Nationals

AGAINST:	AT TORONTO/OTTAWA								ON ROAD								OVERALL							
	GP	W	L	T	PTS	GF	GA	PCT	GP	W	L	T	PTS	GF	GA	PCT	GP	W	L	T	PTS	GF	GA	PCT
(a) Calgary	10	7	3	0	14	47	35	.700	10	6	4	0	12	40	38	.600	20	13	7	0	26	87	73	.650
Cleveland	11	7	4	0	14	41	33	.636	11	3	7	1	7	36	43	.318	22	10	11	1	21	77	76	.477
Edmonton	9	5	4	0	10	30	37	.556	9	3	6	0	6	32	38	.333	18	8	10	0	16	62	75	.444
Houston	9	5	3	1	11	36	33	.611	9	2	7	0	4	26	49	.222	18	7	10	1	15	62	82	.417
Indianapolis	3	3	0	0	6	17	7	1.000	3	2	1	0	4	16	9	.667	6	5	1	0	10	33	16	.833
Minnesota	9	6	3	0	12	47	28	.677	9	3	6	0	6	36	38	.333	18	9	9	0	18	83	66	.500
New England	11	5	5	1	11	44	37	.500	11	4	8	0	8	41	54	.273	22	9	13	1	17	85	91	.386
Phoenix	3	2	1	0	4	16	10	.667	3	1	0	2	2	14	11	.667	6	3	1	2	8	30	21	.667
Quebec	13	8	5	0	16	55	46	.615	13	7	6	0	14	51	48	.538	26	15	11	0	30	106	94	.577
(b) San Diego	11	6	4	1	13	41	32	.591	11	3	8	0	6	44	65	.273	22	9	12	1	19	85	97	.432
Winnipeg	9	6	3	0	12	35	21	.667	9	5	3	1	11	35	35	.611	18	11	6	1	23	70	56	.639
(d) Defunct Teams	19	10	6	3	23	79	68	.605	19	11	8	0	22	73	62	.579	38	21	14	3	45	152	130	.592
TOTALS	117	70	41	6	146	488	387	.624	117	49	64	4	102	444	490	.436	234	119	105	10	248	932	877	.430

WINNIPEG JETS LIFETIME TOTALS

AGAINST:	AT WINNIPEG								ON ROAD								OVERALL							
	GP	W	L	T	PTS	GF	GA	PCT	GP	W	L	T	PTS	GF	GA	PCT	GP	W	L	T	PTS	GF	GA	PCT
(a) Calgary	10	7	3	0	14	50	37	.700	10	2	7	1	5	36	43	.250	20	9	10	1	19	86	80	.475
Cleveland	9	7	2	0	14	42	31	.778	9	2	7	0	3	28	37	.167	18	9	9	0	17	70	68	.472
Edmonton	12	8	3	1	17	51	25	.708	12	3	8	1	7	36	52	.292	24	11	11	2	24	87	77	.500
Houston	11	6	4	1	13	43	30	.591	11	2	8	1	5	26	59	.227	22	8	12	2	18	69	89	.409
Indianapolis	3	2	1	0	4	10	4	.667	3	3	0	0	6	13	6	1.000	6	5	1	0	10	23	10	.833
Minnesota	11	5	4	2	12	32	31	.545	11	3	8	0	6	30	54	.273	22	8	12	2	18	62	85	.409
New England	9	2	7	0	4	36	35	.222	9	4	5	0	8	30	38	.444	18	6	12	0	12	66	73	.333
Phoenix	3	1	2	0	2	9	12	.333	3	2	1	0	4	12	12	.667	6	3	3	0	6	21	24	.500
Quebec	9	7	2	0	14	40	30	.778	9	2	5	2	6	27	40	.333	18	9	7	2	20	67	70	.556
(b) San Diego	9	6	1	2	14	45	31	.778	9	5	4	0	10	43	44	.556	18	11	5	2	24	88	75	.667
(c) Toronto	9	3	5	1	7	35	35	.389	9	3	6	0	6	21	35	.333	18	6	11	1	13	56	70	.361
(d) Defunct Teams	22	21	1	0	42	98	41	.955	22	10	11	1	21	78	76	.477	44	31	12	1	63	176	117	.716
TOTALS	117	75	35	7	157	491	342	.671	117	40	70	7	87	380	496	.372	234	115	105	14	244	871	838	.521

(a) *Formerly Philadelphia / Vancouver* (b) *Formerly New York / New Jersey*
(c) *Formerly Ottawa* (d) *Formerly Chicago / Los Angeles / Michigan / Baltimore.*

74-75 statistics

1974-75 FINAL STANDINGS

CANADIAN DIVISION	GP	W	L	T	PTS	GF	GA	PCT
Quebec	78	46	32	0	92	331	299	.590
Toronto	78	43	33	2	88	349	304	.564
Winnipeg	78	38	35	5	81	322	293	.519
Vancouver	78	37	39	2	76	256	270	.487
Edmonton	78	36	38	4	76	279	279	.487
EASTERN DIVISION								
New England	78	43	30	5	91	274	279	.583
Cleveland	78	35	40	3	73	236	258	.468
Chicago	78	30	47	1	61	261	312	.391
Indianapolis	78	18	57	3	39	216	338	.250
WESTERN DIVISION								
Houston	78	53	25	0	106	369	247	.679
San Diego	78	43	31	4	90	326	268	.577
Minnesota	78	42	33	3	87	308	279	.558
Phoenix	78	39	31	8	86	300	265	.551
Baltimore	78	21	53	4	46	205	341	.295

HOME AND ROAD RECORDS

HOME								ROAD						
W	L	T	PTS	GF	GA	PCT	CANADIAN	W	L	T	PTS	GF	GA	PCT
27	12	0	54	184	140	.692	Quebec	19	20	0	38	147	159	.487
24	15	0	48	175	139	.613	Toronto	19	18	2	40	174	165	.513
23	13	3	49	171	121	.628	Winnipeg	15	22	2	32	151	172	.410
25	12	2	52	138	115	.667	Vancouver	12	27	0	24	118	155	.308
25	12	2	52	174	130	.667	Edmonton	11	26	2	24	105	149	.308
124	64	7	255	842	645	.654	TOTALS	76	113	6	158	695	800	.405
							EASTERN							
28	8	3	59	157	118	.756	New England	15	22	2	32	117	161	.410
23	15	1	47	130	109	.603	Cleveland	12	25	2	26	106	149	.333
18	20	1	37	138	153	.474	Chicago	12	27	0	24	123	159	.308
13	26	0	26	106	149	.333	Indianapolis	5	31	3	13	110	189	.167
82	69	5	169	531	529	.542	TOTALS	44	105	7	95	456	658	.304
							WESTERN							
28	11	0	56	205	120	.718	Houston	25	14	0	50	164	127	641
26	11	2	54	192	126	.692	San Diego	17	20	2	36	134	142	.462
26	13	0	52	176	136	.667	Minnesota	16	20	3	35	132	143	.449
23	11	5	51	170	115	.654	Phoenix	16	20	3	35	130	150	.449
15	21	3	33	103	142	.679	Baltimore	6	32	1	13	102	199	167
118	67	10	246	846	639	.631	TOTALS	80	106	9	169	662	761	.433
324	200	22	670	2219	1813	.614	WHA TOTALS	200	324	22	422	1813	2219	.386

W. D. (BILL) HUNTER TROPHY

(Individual Point Leaders — 1974-75)

		TM	GP	G	A	PTS	PIM	SOG	SC%
1.	André Lacroix	S.D.	78	41	106	147	63	275	.15
2.	Bobby Hull	Wpg	78	77	65	142	41	556	.14
3.	Serge Bernier	Que	76	54	68	122	75	335	.16
4.	*Ulf Nilsson	Wpg	78	26	94	120	79	147	.18
5.	Larry Lund	Hou	78	33	75	108	68	188	.18
6.	Wayne Rivers	S.D.	78	54	53	107	52	323	.17
7.	*Anders Hedberg	Wpg	65	53	47	100	45	271	.20
8.	Gordie Howe	Hou	75	34	65	99	84	255	.13
9.	Wayne Dillon	Tor	77	29	66	95	22	250	.12
10.	Mike Walton	Minn	75	48	45	93	33	300	.16
11.	Réjean Houle	Que	64	40	52	92	37	275	.15
12.	Marc Tardif	Que	76	50	39	89	79	286	.17
13.	Andre Hinse	Hou	75	39	47	86	12	190	.21
14.	Rick Sentes	S.D.	74	44	41	85	52	217	.20
15.	Frank Hughes	Hou	76	48	35	83	35	306	.23
15.	*Mike Rogers	Edm	78	35	48	83	2	189	.19
17.	Frank Mahovlich	Tor	73	38	44	82	27	268	.14
18.	*Vaclav Nedomansky	Tor	78	41	40	81	19	306	.13
18.	Kevin Morrison	S.D.	78	20	61	81	143	280	.07
20.	Tom Simpson	Tor	70	52	28	80	48	228	.23
21.	Gene Peacosh	S.D.	78	43	36	79	22	269	.16
22.	*Gary MacGregor	Chi	78	44	34	78	26	269	.16
23.	Hugh Harris	Van	80	33	44	77	64	239	.14
23.	*Dennis Sobchuk	Phx	78	32	45	77	36	242	.13
25.	Mark Howe	Hou	74	36	40	76	30	256	.14
25.	Danny Lawson	Van	78	33	43	76	19	298	.11
27.	*Michel Cormier	Phx	78	36	38	74	26	242	.15
27.	Wayne Carleton	N.E.	73	35	39	74	50	323	.11
27.	Michel Parizeau	Que	78	28	46	74	69	145	.19
27.	Rosaire Paiement	Chi	78	26	48	74	97	256	.10
27.	*Ray Addouno	S.D.	78	15	59	74	23	129	.12

* — Rookie (15 or fewer major league games)

SCORING, PENALTY RECORDS BY TEAMS 1974-75 SEASON

CHICAGO COUGARS

	GP	G	A	PTS	PIM	SOG	SC%
*Gary MacGregor	78	44	34	78	26	269	.16
Rosaire Paiement	78	26	48	74	97	256	.10
Francois Rochon	69	27	29	56	19	160	.17
*Mark Lomenda	69	16	33	49	21	128	.13
Bob Liddington	78	23	18	41	27	155	.15
Jan Popiel	60	18	22	40	74	97	.19

	GP	G	A	PTS	PIM	SOG	SC%
Ralph Backstrom	70	15	24	39	28	161	.09
*Peter Mara	57	17	21	38	16	90	.19
Pat Stapleton	68	4	30	34	38	105	.04
Darrly Maggs	77	6	27	33	137	213	.03
Rick Morris	78	15	13	28	110	115	.13
Duke Harris	54	9	19	28	18	109	.08
Brian Coates	35	12	9	21	26	62	.19
*Bryon Baltimore	77	8	12	20	110	104	.08
Dunc McCallum	31	0	10	10	24	28	.00
Don Gordon	42	4	5	9	10	49	.08
Jim Watson	57	3	6	9	31	62	.05
Rod Zaine	68	3	6	9	16	28	.11
Lou Angotti	26	2	5	7	9	14	.14
Jim Benzelock	10	0	2	2	14	5	.00
*Keith Kokkola	33	0	2	2	69	47	.00
Dave Walter	6	1	0	1	2	14	.07
Dave Dryden	45	0	1	1	4	0	.00
*Rich Dumas	1	0	0	0	0	0	.00
Rich Coutu	1	0	0	0	0	0	.00
*Jim Pritchard	2	0	0	0	0	2	.00
Cam Newton	32	0	0	0	0	0	.00
Cougars	78	261	409	670	1086	2494	.10
Opponents	78	312	496	808	1042	2844	.11

CLEVELAND CRUSADERS

	GP	G	A	PTS	PIM	SOG	SC%
Rich Leduc	78	34	31	65	122	299	.11
Al McDonough	78	34	30	64	27	257	.13
Ron Ward	73	30	32	62	18	208	.14
Jim Harrison	60	20	22	42	106	152	.13
Gary Jarrett	77	17	24	41	70	233	.07
Gerry Pinder	74	13	28	41	71	180	.07
Skip Krake	71	15	23	38	108	157	.10
Grant Erickson	78	12	15	27	24	128	.10
Russ Walker	66	14	11	25	80	131	.11
Terry Holbrook	78	10	13	23	7	86	.12
Toomas Edur	61	3	20	23	28	107	.03
Steve Cardwell	75	9	13	22	127	110	.08
Ray Clearwater	66	4	18	22	51	104	.04
Paul Shmyr	49	7	14	21	103	87	.08
Wayne Moulin	78	4	17	21	65	89	.04
Larry Hillman	77	0	16	16	83	151	.00
*John Stewart	59	4	7	11	8	52	.08
Wayne Hillman	60	2	9	11	37	30	.07
Ron Anderson	39	0	9	9	10	34	.00
Gerry Cheevers	52	0	1	1	59	0	.00
Paul Baxter	5	0	0	0	37	3	.00
Bob Whidden	29	0	0	0	2	0	.00
Crusaders	78	236	356	592	1273	2628	.09
Opponents	78	258	414	672	1150	2695	.10

EDMONTON OILERS

	GP	G	A	PTS	PIM	SOG	SC%
*Mike Rogers	78	35	48	83	2	189	.19
Tim Sheehy: N.E.	52	20	13	33	18	131	.15
Edm.	29	8	20	28	4	81	.10
Totals	81	28	33	61	22	212	.13
Barry Long	78	20	40	60	116	167	.12
Ken Baird	77	30	28	58	151	173	.17
Bob Sheehan	77	19	39	58	8	178	.11
Bruce MacGregor	72	24	28	52	10	151	.16
Ed Joyal	78	22	25	47	2	183	.12
Blair MacDonald	72	22	24	46	14	155	.14
Doug Barrie	78	12	33	45	122	152	.08
Rusty Patenaude	56	20	16	36	38	92	.22
Tom Gilmore	74	12	19	31	84	140	.09
Steve Carlyle	73	4	25	29	46	118	.03
Ray McKay	69	8	20	28	47	208	.04
Ross Perkins	76	7	16	23	33	89	.08
*Murray Kennett: Ind.	28	1	3	4	8	9	.11
Edm.	50	4	14	18	17	47	.09
Totals	78	5	17	22	25	56	.09
Al Hamilton	25	1	13	14	42	49	.02
*Bill Morris	36	4	8	12	6	34	.12
*Bill Laing	43	2	4	6	32	26	.08
Jim McCrimmon	34	1	5	6	50	27	.04
*Doug Kerslake	10	4	0	4	10	17	.24
Don Herriman	33	1	2	3	21	24	.04
Jacques Plante	31	0	1	1	2	0	.00
Ken Brown	33	0	1	1	2	0	.00
Chris Worthy	29	0	0	0	7	0	.00
Oilers	78	279	470	749	896	2429	.11
Opponents	78	279	438	717	939	2575	.11

HOUSTON AEROS

	GP	G	A	PTS	PIM	SOG	SC%
Larry Lund	78	33	75	108	68	188	.18
Gordie Howe	75	34	65	99	84	255	.13
Andre Hinse	75	39	47	86	12	190	.21
Frank Hughes	76	48	35	83	35	206	.23
Mark Howe	74	36	40	76	30	256	.14
Paul Popiel	78	11	53	64	22	236	.05
Gordon Labossiere	76	23	34	57	40	171	.13
Ted Taylor	73	26	27	53	130	201	.13
John Schella	78	10	42	52	176	222	.05
Jim Sherrit	77	22	25	47	25	135	.15
Murray Hall	78	18	29	47	28	127	.14
*Terry Ruskowski	71	10	36	46	134	105	.10
*Bill Preston	78	20	21	41	10	137	.15
*Don Larway	76	21	13	34	59	140	.15
Marty Howe	75	13	21	34	89	158	.08

	GP	G	A	PTS	PIM	SOG	SC%
Larry Hale	76	2	18	20	40	51	.04
*Glen Irwin	70	2	11	13	153	61	.03
Bill Prentice	17	0	3	3	19	13	.00
*Ron Grahame	43	0	1	1	6	0	.00
Wayne Rutledge	33	0	0	0	0	0	.00
Aeros	**78**	**369**	**599**	**968**	**1257**	**2851**	**.13**
Opponents	**78**	**247**	**402**	**649**	**1012**	**2334**	**.11**

INDIANAPOLIS RACERS

		GP	G	A	PTS	PIM	SOG	SC%
Bobby Whitlock		73	31	26	57	56	290	.11
Bobby Sicinski		77	19	34	53	12	206	.09
Ron Buchanan:	Clev.	4	2	0	2	2	6	.33
	Edm.	22	6	9	15	4	60	.10
	Ind.	32	16	15	31	16	89	.15
	Totals	58	24	24	48	22	155	.15
Nick Harbaruk		78	20	23	43	52	157	.13
Jim Wiste		75	13	28	41	30	114	.11
*Kerry Bond		71	22	15	37	23	204	.11
*Murray Heatley:	Minn.	22	5	9	14	31	27	.19
	Ind.	29	15	8	23	25	83	.18
	Totals	51	20	17	37	56	110	.18
Brian McDonald:	Mich.	18	3	5	8	15	39	.08
	Ind	47	14	15	29	19	104	.13
	Totals	65	17	20	37	34	143	.12
Dick Proceviat:	Chi.	11	0	3	3	11	11	.00
	Ind.	52	1	28	29	51	65	.01
	Totals	63	1	31	32	62	76	.01
Bob Fitchner		78	11	19	30	96	108	.10
Ken Block:	S.D.	36	1	11	12	12	43	.02
	Ind.	37	0	17	17	18	48	.00
	Totals	73	1	28	29	30	91	.01
*John Sheridan		58	17	11	28	20	137	.12
Jim Johnson:	Minn.	11	1	3	4	0	16	.06
	Ind.	42	7	15	22	12	62	.11
	Totals	53	8	18	26	12	78	.10
Bob Ash		64	1	14	15	19	53	.02
Rich Pumple		34	4	8	12	29	72	.06
Bob Woytowich:	Wpg.	24	0	4	4	8	11	.00
	Ind.	42	0	8	8	28	30	.00
	Totals	66	0	12	12	36	41	.00
Bill Horton		59	2	9	11	30	42	.04
Ralph Hopiavouri		28	2	8	10	21	64	.03
Ken Desjardine		46	0	8	8	68	60	.00
*Ross Smith		15	1	6	7	19	23	.04

	GP	G	A	PTS	PIM	SOG	SC%
*Jacques Locas: Mich.	12	1	4	5	4	18	.06
Ind.	11	0	1	1	2	8	.00
Totals	23	1	5	6	6	26	.04
Roger Cote	36	0	6	6	24	33	.00
Gordon Kannegiesser	4	1	4	5	4	6	.17
Ron Walters	17	2	1	3	9	18	.11
Brian McKenzie	9	1	0	1	6	9	.11
*Craig Hanmer	27	1	0	1	15	28	.04
Andy Brown	52	0	1	1	75	0	.00
*Michel Dione	1	0	0	0	0	0	.00
*Rick Fraser	4	0	0	0	2	5	.00
Ed Dyck	32	0	0	0	6	0	.00
Racers	**78**	**216**	**371**	**587**	**970**	**2398**	**.09**
Opponents	**78**	**338**	**540**	**878**	**1046**	**2503**	**.14**

MICHIGAN STAGS/BALTIMORE BLADES

	GP	G	A	PTS	PIM	SOG	SC%
Gary Veneruzzo	77	33	27	60	57	244	.15
J. P. LeBlanc	78	16	33	49	100	207	.08
*Gary Bredin: Ind.	10	3	2	5	8	12	.25
Mich./Balt.	67	15	21	36	29	113	.13
Totals	77	18	23	41	37	125	.14
*Steve West	50	15	18	33	4	116	.13
Pierre Guite: Que.	22	14	8	22	59	50	.28
Mich./Balt.	13	5	4	9	11	36	.14
Totals	35	19	12	31	70	86	.22
*Steve Richardson: Ind.	19	1	4	5	16	39	.03
Mich./Balt.	47	8	18	26	58	107	.07
Totals	66	9	22	31	74	146	.06
Tom Serviss	61	12	17	29	18	134	.09
Alain Caron: Que.	21	7	3	10	2	35	.20
Mich./Balt.	47	8	5	13	4	98	.08
Totals	68	15	8	23	6	133	.11
*Bill Evo	49	13	9	22	32	99	.13
Alton White	27	9	12	21	8	52	.18
Reggie Thomas	50	8	13	21	42	147	.05
*Barry Legge	36	3	18	21	20	66	.05
John Miszuk	66	2	19	21	56	98	.02
Paul Curtis	76	4	15	19	32	110	.04
*Steve Andrascik: Ind.	20	2	4	6	16	56	.04
Mich./Balt.	57	4	7	11	42	118	.02
Totals	77	6	11	17	58	174	.03
*Randy Legge	78	1	14	15	69	73	.01

	GP	G	A	PTS	PIM	SOG	SC%
Guy Trottier: Tor.	6	2	2	4	2	5	.40
Mich.	17	5	4	9	2	34	.15
Totals	23	7	6	13	4	39	.18
Fred Speck	30	4	8	12	18	65	.30
Jerry Zrymiak	49	3	9	12	53	45	.06
Len Fontaine	21	1	8	9	6	28	.04
Larry Johnston	49	0	9	9	93	51	.00
*Ed Johnstone	23	4	4	8	43	43	.09
Craig Reichmuth: S.D.	28	2	1	3	58	35	.06
Mich./Balt.	16	0	2	2	23	18	.00
Totals	44	2	3	5	81	53	.04
Paul Larose	5	1	1	2	2	5	.20
*Gary Sittler	5	1	1	2	14	10	.10
Bob Jones	5	0	1	1	8	10	.00
Gerry Desjardins	41	0	1	1	13	0	.00
Claude Chartre	1	0	0	0	0	2	.00
*Bill Goldthorpe	7	0	0	0	26	6	.00
*Bill Reed	11	0	0	0	12	14	.00
Jim McLeod	16	0	0	0	0	0	.00
Paul Hoganson	32	0	0	0	12	0	.00
Blades	**78**	**205**	**335**	**540**	**1104**	**2430**	**.08**
Opponents	**78**	**341**	**565**	**906**	**1101**	**2797**	**.12**

MINNESOTA FIGHTING SAINTS

	GP	G	A	PTS	PIM	SOG	SC%
Mike Walton	75	48	45	93	33	300	.16
Wayne Connelly	76	38	33	71	16	260	.15
Fran Huck	78	22	45	67	26	184	.12
George Morrison	76	31	29	60	30	177	.18
John Arbour	71	11	43	54	67	220	.05
Don Tannahill	72	23	30	53	20	141	.16
Ted Hampson	78	17	36	53	6	117	.15
Mike Antonovich	67	24	26	50	20	147	.16
Terry Ball	76	8	37	45	36	143	.06
Danny O'Shea	76	16	25	41	47	161	.10
Rick Smith	78	9	29	38	112	158	.06
Gary Gambucci	67	19	18	37	19	121	.16
Gord Gallant	66	10	13	23	203	91	.11
*Ron Busniuk	73	2	21	23	176	76	.03
Kevin O'Shea	68	10	10	20	42	106	.10
Mike McMahon	54	5	15	20	42	78	.06
*Joe Robertson: Ind	18	4	4	8	23	31	.13
Minn.	11	1	4	5	4	7	.14
Totals	29	5	8	13	27	38	.13
*Jack Carlson	32	5	5	10	85	50	.10
*Bill Butters	24	2	2	4	58	16	.13
*Pat Westrum	23	0	3	3	48	10	.00

	GP	G	A	PTS	PIM	SOG	SC%
Jack McCartan	2	0	0	0	0	0	.00
*Curt Brackenbury	7	0	0	0	22	0	.00
Bob Boyd	13	0	0	0	21	9	.00
Mike Curran	26	0	0	0	18	0	.00
John Garrett	56	0	0	0	6	0	.00
Fighting Saints	**78**	**308**	**482**	**790**	**1233**	**2589**	**.12**
Opponents	**78**	**279**	**475**	**754**	**1226**	**2749**	**.10**

NEW ENGLAND WHALERS

	GP	G	A	PTS	PIM	SOG	SC%
Wayne Carleton	73	35	39	74	50	323	.11
Tom Webster	66	40	24	64	52	212	.19
Larry Pleau	78	30	34	64	50	208	.15
Ron Climie: Edm.	49	15	27	42	15	90	.17
N.E.	25	8	4	12	12	43	.19
Totals	74	23	31	54	27	133	.17
John French	75	12	41	53	28	140	.09
Terry Caffery	67	15	37	52	12	133	.11
Don Blackburn	50	18	32	50	10	78	.23
Mike Byers	72	22	26	48	10	157	.14
Rick Ley	62	6	36	42	50	125	.05
Brad Selwood	77	4	35	39	117	148	.03
Fred O'Donnell	76	21	15	36	84	131	.15
*T. Abrahamsson	76	8	22	30	46	151	.05
Paul Hurley	75	3	26	29	36	149	.02
*Garry Swain	66	7	15	22	18	71	.10
Al Karlander	48	7	14	21	2	64	.11
Ted Green	57	6	14	20	29	75	.08
Tom Earl	72	3	8	11	20	52	.06
*Nick Fotiu	61	2	2	4	144	40	.05
*Allan Hangsleben	26	0	4	4	8	25	.00
Bob Charlebois	8	1	0	1	0	6	.17
*Gerry Methe	5	0	1	1	4	2	.00
*Bill Berglund	2	0	0	0	0	0	.00
Bruce Landon	7	0	0	0	0	0	.00
*Christer Abrahamsson	16	0	0	0	0	0	.00
Al Smith	59	0	0	0	18	0	.00
Whalers	**78**	**274**	**460**	**734**	**867**	**2558**	**.11**
Opponents	**78**	**279**	**452**	**731**	**788**	**2493**	**.11**

PHOENIX ROADRUNNERS

	GP	G	A	PTS	PIM	SOG	SC%
*Dennis Sobchuk	78	32	45	77	36	242	.13
*Michel Cormier	78	36	38	74	26	242	.15
*Jim Boyd	76	26	44	70	18	188	.14
*John Gray	75	35	33	68	107	155	.23
*Robbie Ftorek	53	31	37	68	29	155	.20
*Murray Keogan	78	35	29	64	68	225	.16
*Don Borgeson	74	29	28	57	38	205	.14

	GP	G	A	PTS	PIM	SOG	SC%
Gerry Odrowski	77	5	38	43	77	143	.03
*Peter McNamee: Van.	11	2	1	3	15	6	.33
Phx.	55	9	19	28	77	90	.10
Totals	66	11	20	31	92	96	.11
*John Hughes	72	4	25	29	201	91	.04
*Cam Connor	57	9	19	28	168	91	.10
Jim Niekamp	71	2	26	28	66	78	.03
Bob Barlow	51	6	20	26	8	94	.06
John Migneault: Van.	14	4	2	6	12	16	.25
Phx.	47	6	13	19	16	63	.10
Totals	61	10	15	25	28	79	.13
*Bob Mowat	53	9	10	19	34	56	.16
*Wendell Bennett	67	4	15	19	92	58	.07
*Al McLeod	77	3	16	19	98	75	.04
*Mike Stevens	70	2	16	18	69	86	.02
*Dave Gorman	13	3	5	8	10	15	.20
*Rick Newell	25	0	4	4	39	24	.00
Gary Kurt	47	0	2	2	2	0	.00
*Gene Sobchuk	3	1	0	1	0	9	.11
*Gary Lariviere	4	0	1	1	28	14	.00
Jack Norris	33	0	1	1	2	0	.00
Serge Beaudoin: Van.	4	0	0	0	2	1	.00
Phx.	0	0	0	0	0	0	.00
Totals	4	0	0	0	2	1	.00
Roadrunners	**78**	**300**	**506**	**806**	**1388**	**2454**	**.12**
Opponents	**78**	**265**	**440**	**705**	**1233**	**2339**	**.11**

QUEBEC NORDIQUES

	GP	G	A	PTS	PIM	SOG	SC%
Serge Bernier	76	54	68	122	75	335	.16
Rejean Houle	64	40	52	92	37	275	.15
Marc Tardif: Mich.	23	12	5	17	9	79	.15
Que.	53	38	34	72	70	207	.18
Totals	76	50	39	89	79	286	.17
Michel Parizeau	78	28	46	74	69	145	.19
J. C. Tremblay	68	16	56	72	18	176	.09
Chris Bordeleau: Wpg.	18	8	8	16	0	52	.15
Que.	53	15	33	48	24	187	.08
Totals	71	23	41	64	24	239	.10
*Real Cloutier	63	26	27	53	36	154	.17
Renald Leclerc	73	18	32	50	85	206	.09
Dale Hoganson	78	9	35	44	47	221	.04
S. Sutherland: Mich.	22	1	5	6	37	25	.04
Que.	56	14	15	29	114	110	.13
Totals	78	15	20	35	151	135	.11

	GP	G	A	PTS	PIM	SOG	SC%
Robert Guindon	69	12	18	30	23	134	.09
Jeannot Gilbert	58	7	21	28	12	46	.15
Andre Gaudette	67	10	17	27	6	88	.11
Francois Lacombe	55	7	17	24	54	109	.06
Pierre Roy	61	1	18	19	118	57	.02
Ric Jordan	56	6	8	14	75	79	.08
*Jean Bernier	34	1	13	14	13	55	.02
*Charles Constantin	20	2	4	6	9	14	.07
*Jean-Claude Garneau	17	0	5	5	27		
*Denis Patry	3	1	2	3	2	4	.25
Richard Brodeur	51	0	2	2	13	0	.00
Serge Aubry	32	0	1	1	22	0	.00
*Allan Globensky	5	0	0	0	5	2	.00
Nordiques	**78**	**331**	**552**	**883**	**1132**	**2708**	**.12**
Opponents	**78**	**299**	**482**	**781**	**1177**	**2753**	**.11**

SAN DIEGO MARINERS

	GP	G	A	PTS	PIM	SOG	SC%
Andre Lacroix	78	41	106	147	63	275	.15
Wayne Rivers	78	54	53	107	52	323	.17
Rick Sentes	74	44	41	85	52	217	.20
Kevin Morrison	78	20	61	81	143	280	.07
Gene Peacosh	78	43	36	79	22	269	.16
*Ray Addouno	78	15	59	74	23	129	.12
Norm Ferguson	78	36	33	69	6	227	.16
Ron Plumb	78	10	38	48	56	215	.05
Brian Morenz	78	20	19	39	76	133	.15
Joe Hardy: Chi.	17	1	6	7	8	14	.07
Ind.	32	2	17	19	36	64	.03
S.D.	12	2	3	5	22	6	.33
Totals	61	5	26	31	66	84	.06
Jim Hargreaves: Ind.	37	2	5	7	30	63	.03
S.D.	41	8	10	18	45	52	.15
Totals	78	10	15	25	75	115	.09
Mike Rouleau: Que.	19	1	7	8	63	21	.05
Mich.	7	0	3	3	25	14	.00
S.D.	27	5	6	11	42	42	.12
Totals	53	6	16	22	130	77	.08
Bob Falkenberg	78	2	18	20	42	95	.02
Mike Laughton	65	7	9	16	22	92	.07
*Kevin Devine	46	4	10	14	48	60	.07
Harry Howell	74	4	10	14	28	78	.05
Brian Bradley	34	4	5	9	6	40	.10
Bob Wall	33	0	9	9	15	39	.00
Ted Scharf	67	3	1	4	94	37	.08
*Jamie Bateman	24	0	3	3	96	17	.00
Lee Inglis	5	0	2	2	0	11	.00

	GP	G	A	PTS	PIM	SOG	SC%
*Tom Trevelyn	20	0	2	2	4	17	.00
Doug Volmar	10	0	1	1	4	17	.00
Joe Junkin	16	0	1	1	2	0	.00
Russ Gillow	30	0	1	1	4	0	.00
*Reg Krezanski	2	0	0	0	2	2	.00
Bob Blanchet	3	0	0	0	0	0	.00
Dean Boylan	3	0	0	0	10	1	.00
Ernie Wakely: Wpg.	6	0	0	0	0	0	.00
S.D.	35	0	0	0	0	0	.00
Totals	41	0	0	0	0	0	.00
Mariners	**78**	**326**	**549**	**875**	**1058**	**2690**	**.12**
Opponents	**78**	**268**	**426**	**694**	**916**	**2441**	**.11**

TORONTO TOROS

	GP	G	A	PTS	PIM	SOG	SC%
Wayne Dillon	77	29	66	95	22	250	.12
Frank Mahovlich	73	38	44	82	27	268	.14
*Vaclav Nedomansky	78	41	40	81	19	306	.13
Tom Simpson	70	52	28	80	48	228	.23
Gavin Kirk	78	15	58	73	69	149	.10
Pat Hickey	74	34	34	68	50	215	.16
Paul Henderson	58	30	33	63	18	146	.21
Tony Featherstone	76	25	38	63	26	194	.13
Jim Dorey: N.E.	31	5	17	22	43	85	.06
Tor.	43	11	23	34	69	114	.10
Totals	74	16	40	56	112	199	.08
Larry Mavety: Chi.	57	10	22	32	126	169	.06
Tor.	17	0	9	9	24	28	.00
Totals	74	10	31	41	150	197	.05
Tom Martin	64	14	17	31	18	184	.08
*Richard Farda	66	6	25	31	2	85	.07
*Jim Turkiewicz	78	3	27	30	28	113	.03
Brian Gibbons	73	4	22	26	105	103	.04
Rick Cunningham	71	7	18	25	117	113	.06
*Lou Nistico	29	11	11	22	75	68	.16
Steve Cuddie	70	5	16	21	49	92	.05
*Jeff Jacques	39	12	8	20	26	54	.22
Mike Amodeo	64	1	13	14	50	55	.02
*George Kuzmicz	34	0	12	12	22	27	.00
Bob Leduc	19	3	4	7	9	31	.10
Brit Selby	17	1	4	5	0	14	.07
Peter Marrin	4	3	1	4	0	6	.50
Gilles Gratton	53	0	4	4	8	1	.00
*Gord Titcomb	2	0	1	1	0	5	.00
Les Binkley	17	0	0	0	0	0	.00
*Jim Shaw	20	0	0	0	0	0	.00
Toros	**78**	**349**	**561**	**910**	**883**	**2902**	**.12**
Opponents	**78**	**304**	**497**	**801**	**1094**	**2674**	**.11**

VANCOUVER BLAZERS

	GP	G	A	PTS	PIM	SOG	SC%
Hugh Harris: Phx.	22	10	10	20	15	53	.19
Van.	58	23	34	57	49	186	.12
Totals	80	33	44	77	64	239	.14
Danny Lawson	78	33	43	76	19	298	.11
Bryan Campbell	78	29	34	63	24	251	.12
John McKenzie	74	23	37	60	82	107	.21
Rob Walton	75	24	33	57	28	159	.15
Claude St. Sauveur	76	24	23	47	32	200	.12
Mike Pelyk	75	14	26	40	121	167	.08
*Ron Chipperfield	78	19	20	39	30	238	.08
*Pat Price	69	5	29	34	54	96	.05
Don Burgess	62	11	18	29	19	131	.08
Duane Rupp	72	3	26	29	45	101	.03
*Larry Isrealson	46	12	9	21	10	63	.19
Jim Jones	63	11	7	18	39	98	.11
Paul Terbenche	60	3	14	17	10	81	.04
Ernest Deadmarsh	38	7	8	15	128	44	.16
*Don McCulloch	51	1	9	10	42	93	.01
Arnie Brown: Mich.	50	3	4	7	27	63	.05
Van.	10	0	1	1	13	14	.00
Totals ...	60	3	5	8	40	77	.04
Don McLeod	72	0	8	8	14	3	.00
Andy Bathgate	11	1	6	7	2	12	.08
*John Shmyr	39	1	5	6	43	13	.08
*Peter Driscoll	21	3	2	5	40	18	.17
*Rick Jodzio	44	1	3	4	159	22	.05
Murray Myers	24	1	1	2	4	18	.06
Jim Cardiff	44	0	2	2	25	15	.00
*Bud Gulka	5	1	0	1	10	1	1.00
Dan Givens	1	0	0	0	0	0	.00
Mike Chernoff	3	0	0	0	0	3	.00
*Ray Di Lorenzi	3	0	0	0	0	4	.00
Dan O'Donoghue	4	0	0	0	0	4	.00
*Wayne Wood	11	0	0	0	0	0	.00
Blazers	78	256	401	657	1075	1441	.10
Opponents	78	270	451	721	1100	2366	.11

WINNIPEG JETS

	GP	G	A	PTS	PIM	SOG	SC%
Bobby Hull	78	77	65	142	41	556	.14
*Ulf Nilsson	78	26	94	120	79	147	.18
*Anders Hedberg	65	53	47	100	45	271	.20
*Lars-Erik Sjoberg	75	7	53	60	30	123	.06
*Veli Pekka Ketola	74	23	28	51	25	154	.15
Danny Gruen: Mich. ...	34	10	16	26	73	92	.11
Wpg.	32	9	12	21	21	64	.14
Totals ..	66	19	28	47	94	156	.12

	GP	G	A	PTS	PIM	SOG	SC%
Norm Beaudin	77	16	31	47	8	202	.08
Danny Spring	60	19	24	43	22	123	.15
Howie Young: Phx.	30	3	12	15	44	46	.07
Wpg.	42	13	10	23	42	81	.16
Totals	72	16	22	38	86	127	.13
*Mike Ford	73	12	22	31	68	205	.06
Danny Johnson	78	18	14	32	25	111	.16
Larry Hornung	69	7	25	32	21	80	.09
*Perry Miller	67	9	19	28	133	99	.09
Alain Beaule: Que.	22	4	7	11	19	29	.14
Wpg.	54	0	14	14	24	36	.00
Totals	76	4	21	25	43	65	.06
*Heikki Riihiranta	64	8	14	22	30	102	.08
Duke Asmundson	38	4	15	19	53	49	08
Thommie Bergman	49	4	15	19	70	85	.04
Jean-Guy Gratton	49	4	8	12	2	57	.08
Milt Black	65	4	6	10	10	37	.11
Robbie Neale: Clev.	9	1	3	4	4	13	.08
Wpg.	7	0	2	2	4	14	.00
Totals	16	1	5	6	8	27	.04
*Ron Ashton	36	1	3	4	66	36	.03
*Curt Larsson	26	0	1	1	4	0	.00
Joe Daley	51	0	1	1	6	0	.00
Ron Snell	20	0	0	0	8	15	.00
Jets	**78**	**322**	**536**	**858**	**869**	**2666**	**.12**
Opponents	**78**	**293**	**493**	**786**	**1208**	**2659**	**.11**

GOALTENDING 1974-75 REGULAR SEASON

	Min.	GPI	W	L	T	SOG	GA	GAA	GAF	SO
HOUSTON	4688	78	53	25	0	2352	244	3.12	9.64	6
°Ron Grahame	2590	43	33	10	0	1307	131	3.03	9.98	4
Wayne Rutledge	2092	35	20	15	0	1045	113	3.24	9.25	2
OPPONENT	4681	78	25	53	0	2847	365	4.68	7.80	0
CLEVELAND	4727	78	35	40	3	2681	256	3.25	10.47	4
Bob Whidden	1654	29	9	16	1	918	89	3.23	10.31	0
Gerry Cheevers	3076	52	26	24	2	1763	167	3.26	10.56	4
OPPONENT	4722	78	40	35	3	2632	231	2.94	11.39	7
PHOENIX	4803	78	39	31	8	2355	263	3.29	8.95	3
Jack Norris	1962	33	14	15	4	979	107	3.27	9.24	1
Gary Kurt	2841	47	25	16	4	1356	156	3.29	8.69	2
OPPONENT	4800	78	31	39	8	2448	291	3.64	8.41	2
SAN DIEGO	4735	78	43	31	4	2427	262	3.32	9.26	5
°Bob Blanchet	179	3	2	1	0	70	7	2.35	10.00	1
Ernie Wakely										
San Diego Totals	2062	35	20	12	2	1091	115	3.35	9.49	2
Season Totals	2418	41	23	15	2	1304	131	3.25	9.95	3
Joe Junkin	839	15	6	7	0	416	46	3.29	9.04	1
Russ Gillow	1653	30	15	11	2	864	94	3.41	9.19	1
OPPONENT	4731	78	31	43	4	2765	325	4.12	8.51	2

	Min.	GPI	W	L	T	SOG	GA	GAA	GAF	SO
VANCOUVER	4696	78	37	39	2	2386	263	3.36	9.07	1
Don McLeod	4124	71	32	35	2	2106	230	3.35	9.16	1
Wayne Wood	512	11	4	4	0	263	30	3.52	8.77	0
OPPONENT	4712	78	39	37	2	2439	254	3.23	9.60	4
NEW ENGLAND	4758	78	43	30	5	2488	274	3.46	9.08	3
°Crister Abrahamsson	870	16	8	6	1	504	47	3.24	10.72	1
Bruce Landon	339	7	2	3	0	190	19	3.36	10.00	0
Al Smith	3494	59	33	21	4	1725	202	3.47	8.54	2
Bill Berglund	36	2	0	0	0	16	3	5.00	5.33	0
°Ted Ouimet	20	1	0	0	0	13	3	9.00	4.33	0
OPPONENT	4757	78	30	43	5	2547	272	3.43	9.36	1
EDMONTON	4740	78	36	38	4	2579	273	3.46	9.45	4
Jacques Plante	1592	40	15	14	1	803	88	3.32	9.13	1
Ken Brown	1466	32	11	11	0	844	85	3.48	9.93	2
Chris Worthy	1660	28	11	13	3	929	99	3.58	9.38	1
OPPONENT	4739	78	38	36	4	2422	272	3.44	8.90	5
MINNESOTA	4722	78	42	33	3	2745	275	3.49	9.98	2
John Garrett	3294	58	30	23	2	1890	180	3.28	10.50	2
Mike Curran	1367	26	11	10	1	836	87	3.82	9.61	0
Mick McCartan	61	2	1	0	0	38	5	4.92	7.60	0
OPPONENT	4724	78	33	42	3	2623	303	3.85	8.66	0
WINNIPEG	4771	78	38	35	5	2647	291	3.66	9.10	3
Joe Daley	2902	51	23	21	4	1550	175	3.62	8.86	1
°Curt Larsson	1514	26	12	11	1	887	100	3.96	8.87	1
Departed Goalies	355	6	3	3	0	213	16	2.70	13.31	1
OPPONENT	4872	78	35	38	5	2689	316	3.89	8.51	1
QUEBEC	4700	78	46	32	0	2691	297	3.79	9.06	0
Serge Aubry	1762	31	17	11	0	959	109	3.71	8.80	0
Richard Brodeur	2938	51	29	21	0	1737	191	3.90	9.09	0
OPPONENT	4700	78	32	46	0	2766	327	4.17	8.46	0
TORONTO	4708	78	43	33	2	2644	302	3.85	8.75	2
Les Binkley	772	17	6	4	0	419	47	3.65	8.91	0
Gilles Gratton	2881	52	30	20	1	1632	185	3.85	8.82	2
°Jim Shaw	1055	22	7	9	1	611	70	3.91	8.73	0
OPPONENT	4711	78	33	43	2	2853	345	4.39	8.27	0
CHICAGO	4704	78	30	47	1	2911	307	3.92	9.48	1
°Rich Dumas	1	1	0	0	0	000	000	0.00	0.00	0
Dave Dryden	2728	45	18	26	1	1679	176	3.87	9.54	1
Cam Newton	1905	32	12	20	0	1196	126	3.97	9.49	0
Rich Coutu	60	1	0	1	0	36	5	5.00	7.20	0
OPPONENT	4701	78	47	30	1	2461	258	3.29	9.54	4
MICHIGAN/BALTIMORE	4754	78	21	53	4	2821	336	4.21	8.40	2
Paul Hoganson	1776	32	9	19	2	1010	122	4.12	8.28	2
Gerry Desjardins	2282	41	9	28	1	1391	162	4.26	8.59	0
Jim McLeod	694	16	3	6	1	421	53	4.58	7.94	0
OPPONENT	4753	78	53	21	4	2427	201	2.54	12.07	4
INDIANAPOLIS	4731	78	18	57	3	2580	333	4.22	7.75	2
Michel Dione	59	1	0	1	0	38	4	4.00	9.50	0
Andy Brown	2979	52	15	35	0	1627	206	4.15	7.90	2
Ed Dyck	1692	32	3	21	3	913	127	4.50	7.19	0
OPPONENT	4735	78	57	18	3	2384	213	2.70	11.19	8

GOALTENDING ABBREVIATIONS: Min — minutes played (**odd seconds are rounded off to nearest minute**). GPI — games played in. W — won. L — lost. T — tied. SOG — shots on goal. GA — goals allowed. GAA — goals against average for 60 minutes. GAF — goals allowed frequency (**number of shots taken for each goal allowed**). SO — shutouts.

° — Rookie.

WHA PLAYER TRANSACTIONS
1974-75 SEASON

OCT.
26 — JIM HARRISON, Edmonton, traded to Cleveland for RON BUCHANAN.

NOV.
7 — GUY TROTTIER, Toronto Toros sold to Michigan.
10 — GARY BREDIN, Indianapolis, traded to Michigan for BILL HORTON.
27 — JACQUES LOCAS and BRIAN McDONALD, Michigan traded to Indianapolis for STEVE ANDRASCIK and STEVE RICHARDSON.
 — BUTCH DEADMARSH, Kansas City Scouts of National League acquired on waivers by Vancouver Blazers for $30,000.
30 — JOE ROBERTSON, Indianapolis, traded to Minnesota Saints for JIM JOHNSON.

DEC.
6 — CHRIS BORDELEAU, Winnipeg, traded to Quebec for ALAIN BEAULE.
7 — MARC TARDIF and STEVE SUTHERLAND, Michigan, traded to Quebec for PIERRE GUITE, ALAIN CARON and MICHEL ROULEAU.
 — HUGH HARRIS and JOHN TAFT, Phoenix, traded to Vancouver Blazers for PETER McNAMEE, JOHN MIGNEAULT and SERGE BEAUDOIN.
 — DICK PROCEVIAT, Chicago Cougars, traded to Indianapolis for future considerations.
12 — JOE HARDY, Chicago Cougars, traded to Indianapolis for future considerations.
23 — THOMMIE BERGMAN, Detroit Red Wings of the National League acquired on waivers by Winnipeg Jets for $30,000.
27 — BOB WOYTOWICH, Winnipeg, sold to Indianapolis.
31 — MURRAY KENNETT, Indianapolis, traded to Edmonton for future considerations.
 — JIM DOREY, New England, sent to Toronto to fulfill 'future consideration' in WAYNE CARLETON trade of Sept. '74. Toronto also received a New England second round draft pick.
 — MICHEL ROULEAU, Michigan, traded to San Diego for CRAIG REICHMUTH.

JAN.
6 — ERNIE WAKELY, Winnipeg, sold to San Diego.
8 — KEN BLOCK, San Diego, traded to Indianapolis for JIM HARGREAVES.
17 — HOWIE YOUNG, Phoenix, sold to Winnipeg.
23 — RON BUCHANAN, Edmonton, sent to Indianapolis as 'future consideration' in MURRAY KENNETT deal of Dec. 31.

FEB.
1 — DANNY GRUEN, Baltimore, traded to Winnipeg for future considerations. Returned to Baltimore at end of season.
2 — MURRAY HEATLEY, Minnesota, traded to Indianapolis for future considerations.
5 — BILL GOLDTHORPE, Minnesota, sold to Baltimore.
7 — ROBBIE NEALE, Cleveland, traded to Winnipeg for cash and future considerations.
15 — TIM SHEEHY, New England, traded to Edmonton for RON CLIMIE.
27 — LARRY MAVETY, Chicago Cougars, traded to Toronto Toros for 2nd round draft picks in 75 and 76 amateur drafts.

MAR.
1 — ARNIE BROWN and GERRY DESJARDINS, Baltimore, made free agents.
10 — JOE HARDY, Indianapolis, traded to San Diego for future considerations.
 — ARNIE BROWN acquired as free agent by Vancouver Blazers.

REGULAR SEASON ATTENDANCE

Canadian Division	GP	1974-75 Totals	1974-75 Average	1973-74 Totals	1973-74 Average	Net Change	Pct. Change	1974-75 Capacity	Pct.
Edmonton	39	418,150	10,722	172,737	4,429	+ 245,413	142.1	597,714	70.0
Quebec	39	366,848	9,406	311,352	7,983	+ 55,496	17.8	390,156	94.0
Toronto	39	407,006	10,436	167,432	4,291	+ 239,664	143.2	628,485	64.8
Vancouver	39	312,563	8,014	364,903	9,356	− 52,340	− 14.3	607,191	51.5
Winnipeg	39	334,857	8,586	249,654	6,401	+ 85,203	34.1	393,003	85.2
TOTALS	195	1,839,424	9,433	1,265,988	6,492	+ 573,436	45.3	2,616,549	70.3
Eastern Division									
Chicago	39	123,543	3,168	192,048	4,924	− 68,505	− 35.7	351,000	35.2
Cleveland	39	270,304	6,931	242,277	6,212	+ 28,027	11.6	721,500	37.5
Indianapolis	39	309,005	7,923					619,008	49.9
New England	39	305,959	7,845	232,814	5,970	+ 73,145	31.4	344,890	88.7
TOTALS	156	1,008,811	6,467	667,139	4,277	+ 341,672	51.2	2,036,398	49.5
Western Division									
Houston	39	265,230	6,801	265,622	6,811	− 392	− .01	351,000	75.6
Michigan-Balt.	39	127,072	3,258	208,175	5,338	− 81,103	− 39.0	416,925	30.5
Minnesota	39	327,979	8,410	256,772	6,584	+ 71,207	27.7	612,495	53.5
Phoenix	39	290,277	7,443					487,500	59.5
San Diego	39	237,118	6,080	100,810	2,585	+ 136,308	135.2	508,521	46.6
TOTALS	195	1,247,676	6,398	831,379	4,263	+ 416,297	50.1	2,376,441	52.5
14 Team Totals	546	4,095,911	7,502	2,764,506	5,907	+ 1,331,045	48.2	7,029,388	58.3
12 Original Teams	468	3,496,629	7,471	2,764,506	5,907	+ 732,123	26.5	5,922,880	59.0

DRAWING POWER ON THE ROAD

Canadian Division	GP	1974-75 Totals	1974-75 Average	1973-74 Totals	1973-74 Average	Net Change	Pct Change	1974-75 Road Capacity
Edmonton	39	286,770	7,353	221,077	5,669	+ 65,693	29.7	501,639
Quebec	39	297,326	7,624	229,390	5,882	+ 67,936	29.6	504,248
Toronto	39	307,873	7,894	231,351	5,932	− 76,522	33.1	492,031
Vancouver	39	258,978	6,640	201,575	5,169	+ 57,403	28.5	493,669
Winnipeg	39	356,187	9,133	263,803	6,746	+ 92,384	35.0	515,136
TOTALS	195	1,507,134	7,729	1,147,196	5,883	+ 359,938	31.4	2,506,723
Eastern Division								
Chicago	39	271,642	6,965	221,851	5,688	+ 49,791	22.4	513,376
Cleveland	39	287,036	7,360	211,163	5,414	+ 75,873	35.9	489,867
Indianapolis	39	267,981	6,871	—	—	—	—	490,019
New England	39	279,580	7,169	228,516	5,859	+ 51,064	22.3	512,721
TOTALS	156	1,106,239	7,091	661,530	5,654	+ 444,709	67.2	2,005,983
Western Division								
Houston	39	363,047	9,309	292,312	7,495	+ 70,735	24.2	510,635
Mich./Balt.	39	284,170	7,286	221,479	5,679	+ 62,691	28.3	508,651
Minnesota	39	280,989	7,205	222,229	5,698	+ 58,760	26.4	492,136
Phoenix	39	274,904	7,049	—	—	—	—	502,876
San Diego	39	279,428	7,165	219,760	5,635	+ 59,668	27.2	502,384
TOTALS	195	1,482,538	7,603	955,780	6,127	+ 526,758	55.1	2,516,682
14 Team Totals	546	4,095,911	7,502	2,764,506	5,907	+ 1,331,405	48.2	7,029,388
12 Original Teams	468	3,553,026	7,592	2,764,506	5,907	+ 788,520	28.5	6,036,493

1974-75 OVERTIME ANALYSIS

overtime

3-Year Totals		Total	At Home	On Road	vs. Can.	vs. East	vs. West	Total '74-75 Time	Avg. '74-75 Time	Dec. Only '74-75 Avg. Time
	CANADIAN DIVISION									
9-10- 9	Quebec	4- 3- 0	2- 2- 0	2- 1- 0	1- 1- 0	0- 1- 0	3- 1- 0	24:26	3:29	3:29
9- 6-10	Toronto	2- 1- 2	1- 0- 0	1- 1- 2	1- 0- 0	1- 1- 0	0- 0- 2	31:30	6:18	3:50
9-17-14	Winnipeg	3- 6- 5	1- 2- 3	2- 4- 2	0- 1- 2	1- 3- 1	2- 2- 2	98:29	7:02	5:43
11-11- 3	Vancouver	2- 2- 2	2- 0- 2	0- 2- 0	1- 0- 1	0- 1- 1	1- 1- 0	29:03	4:51	1:49
11-11-10	Edmonton	5- 3- 4	3- 1- 2	2- 2- 2	0- 1- 0	2- 1- 3	3- 1- 1	63:39	5:18	2:57
49- 55- 46	TOTALS	16- 15- 13	9- 5- 7	7- 10- 6	3- 3- 3	4- 7- 5	9- 5- 5	247:07	5:37	3:47
	EASTERN DIVISION									
18- 2-11	New England	7- 0- 5	4- 0- 3	3- 0- 2	4- 0- 1	1- 0- 1	2- 0- 3	84:15	7:01	4:54
12- 9-15	Cleveland	2- 3- 3	1- 0- 1	1- 3- 2	1- 1- 1	0- 1- 1	1- 1- 1	58:31	7:19	5:42
10-10- 8	Chicago	4- 2- 1	4- 0- 1	0- 2- 0	2- 1- 0	2- 0- 1	0- 1- 0	32:03	4:35	3:04
1- 8- 3	Indianapolis	1- 8- 3	0- 3- 0	1- 5- 3	0- 2- 2	0- 2- 1	1- 4- 0	61:17	5:06	3:29
41- 29- 37	TOTALS	14- 13- 12	9- 3- 5	5- 10- 7	7- 4- 4	3- 3- 4	4- 6- 4	236:06	6:03	4:18
	WESTERN DIVISION									
5- 7- 9	Houston	3- 2- 0	1- 1- 0	2- 1- 0	1- 0- 0	2- 1- 0	0- 1- 0	11:22	2:16	2:16
7-10-10	San Diego	2- 4- 4	2- 2- 2	0- 2- 2	1- 2- 2	0- 1- 0	1- 1- 2	61:37	6:10	3:36
12- 8- 8	Minnesota	4- 2- 3	3- 1- 0	1- 1- 3	1- 1- 1	2- 0- 0	1- 1- 2	52:52	5:52	3:49
2- 6- 8	Phoenix	2- 6- 8	1- 3- 5	1- 3- 3	0- 4- 3	1- 1- 3	1- 1- 2	129:24	8:05	6:11
11-12-10	Mich/Balt	5- 4- 4	3- 3- 3	2- 1- 1	2- 2- 1	1- 1- 1	2- 1- 2	81:08	6:14	4:34
37- 43- 45	TOTALS	16- 18- 19	10- 10- 10	6- 8- 9	5- 9- 7	6- 4- 4	5- 5- 8	336:23	6:21	4:18
127- 127- 128	1974-75 TOTALS	46- 46- 44	28- 18- 22	18- 28- 22	15- 16- 14	13- 14- 13	18- 16- 17	819:36	6:02	4:08

1974-75: 68 games went into overtime (12.6% of all games)
46 games reached a decision in overtime periods (67.6% of overtime games; 8.8% of League Decisions)
22 games remained tied after overtime periods (32.4% of overtime periods; 4.0% of all games)

AFTER THREE SEASONS:
191 games went into overtime (12.9% of all games)
127 games reached decisions in overtime periods (66.5% of overtime games; 9.0% of League Decisions)
64 games remained tied after an overtime period (33.5% of overtime games; 4.3% of all games)

THE SIXTH ATTACKER
(How Teams Did After Pulling Goaltender for Extra Forward)

1974-75 SEASON

	Times Pulled	Goals Scored	Success Pct.	Freq.	E.N.G's Allowed	E.N.G. Pct.	E.N.G. Freq.
1. Quebec	8	2	25.00%	4.00	2	25.00%	4.00
2. Minnesota	14	2	14.29%	7.00	4	28.57%	3.50
3. Winnipeg	9	1	11.11%	9.00	2	22.22%	4.50
4. Cleveland	19	2	10.53%	9.50	2	10.53%	9.50
5. Phoenix	10	1	10.00%	10.00	2	20.00%	5.00
6. San Diego	12	1	8.33%	12.00	6	50.00%	2.00
6. Houston	12	1	8.33%	12.00	3	25.00%	4.00
8. Mich/Balt	17	1	5.88%	17.00	5	29.41%	3.40
9. New England	10	0	—	—	5	50.00%	2.00
9. Toronto	12	0	—	—	2	16.67%	6.00
9. Edmonton	12	0	—	—	6	50.00%	2.00
9. Vancouver	15	0	—	—	7	46.67%	2.14
9. Indianapolis	17	0	—	—	5	29.41%	3.40
9. Chicago	22	0	—	—	5	22.73%	4.40
TOTALS	189	11	5.82%	17.18	56	29.63%	3.38

3-YEAR TOTALS

	Times Pulled	Goals Scored	Success Pct.	Freq.	E.N.G's Allowed	E.N.G. Pct.	E.N.G. Freq.
1. NY/NJ/SD	36	5	13.89%	7.20	13	36.11%	2.77
2. Winnipeg	29	4	13.79%	7.25	12	41.38%	2.42
3. L.A./Mich/Balt	47	6	12.77%	7.83	12	25.53%	3.92
4. Quebec	25	3	12.00%	8.33	7	28.00%	3.57
5. Minnesota	42	5	11.90%	8.40	13	30.95%	3.23
6. Phoenix	10	1	10.00%	10.00	2	20.00%	5.00
7. Houston	33	3	9.09%	11.00	11	33.33%	3.00
8. Ottawa/Toronto	41	3	7.32%	13.67	9	21.95%	4.56
9. New England	30	2	6.67%	15.00	10	33.33%	3.00
10. Cleveland	36	2	5.56%	18.00	8	22.22%	4.50
11. Edmonton	43	2	4.65%	21.50	16	37.21%	2.69
12. Phil/Van	39	1	2.56%	39.00	22	56.41%	1.77
13. Indianapolis	17	0	—	—	5	29.41%	3.40
14. Chicago	60	0	—	—	20	33.33%	3.00
TOTALS	488	37	7.58%	13.19	160	32.79%	3.05

POWER PLAY OPPORTUNITIES 1974-75

	GP	OPNT. PIM	AVG. PIM	OPPR	GF	GA	PROF.	FREQ.
1. Houston	78	1012	12.97	254	71	6	28.0%	3.58
2. San Diego	78	916	11.74	218	60	8	27.5%	3.63
3. Minnesota	78	1226	15.72	228	53	7	23.2%	4.30
4. Quebec	78	1177	15.09	284	62	12	21.8%	4.58
5. Vancouver	78	1100	14.10	271	59	7	21.8%	4.59
6. Winnipeg	78	1208	15.49	362	74	16	20.4%	4.89
7. Toronto	78	1094	14.03	285	57	9	20.0%	5.00
8. Chicago	78	1042	13.36	237	46	11	19.4%	5.15
9. Baltimore	78	1101	14.12	279	52	12	18.6%	5.37
10. New England	78	788	10.10	225	38	5	16.9%	5.92
11. Cleveland	78	1150	14.74	226	38	6	16.8%	5.95
12. Phoenix	78	1233	15.81	304	50	6	16.4%	6.08
13. Indianapolis	78	1046	13.41	290	45	14	15.5%	6.44
14. Edmonton	78	939	12.04	262	40	4	15.3%	6.55
TOTALS	546	15032	13.77	3722	745	123	20.0%	5.00

PENALTY SHOTS

Date	Player, Team	V.S. Goaltender, Team	Time	Per.	Result
1972-73 SEASON					
10-11-72	Bill Hicke, Alberta	Les Binkley, Ottawa	16:37	1	**SCORED**
11-29-72	Ron Ward, New York	Al Smith, New England	5:24	1	failed
1-16-73	Renald Leclerc, Quebec	Gilles Gratton, Ottawa	8:17	3	**SCORED**
3-25-73	Renald Leclerc, Quebec	Jack Norris, Alberta	6:15	3	**SCORED**
1973-74 SEASON					
10-11-73	Andre Lacroix, New York	Cam Newton, Chicago	18:28	3	failed
10-19-73	Denis Meloche, Vancouver	Jack Norris, Edmonton	15:19	3	failed
10-25-73	Andre Lacroix, New York	Al Smith, New England	8:57	2	failed
11- 3-73	Ron Buchanan, Cleveland	Andre Gill, Chicago	7:46	2	failed
11-22-73	Wayne Connelly, Minnesota	Al Smith, New England	10:34	2	failed
11-23-73	Marc Tardif, Los Angeles	Jack Norris, Edmonton	18:12	3	failed
12-22-73	Gary Veneruzzo, Los Angeles	Don McLeod, Houston	15:08	3	failed
12-29-73	Andre Lacroix, New Jersey	Gerry Cheevers, Clev.	19:09	1	failed
3- 1-74	Brian Carlin, Edmonton	Don McLeod, Houston	19:50	3	**SCORED**
3-10-74	Ron Garwasiuk, Los Angeles	Mike Curran, Minnesota	19:38	2	failed
3-14-74	Tom Martin, Toronto	Cam Newton, Chicago	3:39	2	failed
3-31-74	Brian Morenz, New Jersey	Gerry Cheevers, Clev.	12:22	3	failed
4- 1-74	Frank Hughes, Houston	Al Smith, New England	7:10	2	failed
1974-75 SEASON					
10-24-74	Wayne Connelly, Minnesota	Andy Brown, Ind.	11:44	1	failed
11-12-74	Gary MacGregor, Chicago	Joe Junkin, San Diego	10:19	1	failed
12- 4-74	Ed Joyal, Edmonton	Don McLeod, Vancouver	6:45	2	**SCORED**
12-26-74	Wayne Connelly, Minnesota	Jacques Plante, Edm.	7:44	1	failed
1- 4-75	Danny Lawson, Vancouver	Al Smith, New England	19:42	3	**SCORED**
1- 5-75	Bob Leduc, Toronto	Bob Whidden, Cleveland	9:49	1	failed
1 28 75	Norm Ferguson, San Diego	Joe Daley, Winnipeg	12:46	3	failed
2-11-75	Rejean Houle, Quebec	Ernie Wakely, San Diego	8:30	2	**SCORED**
3- 1-75	Bob Mowat, Phoenix	Andy Brown, Ind.	19:36	2	**SCORED**
3-12-75	Jim Harrison, Cleveland	Paul Hoganson, Balt.	5:34	2	failed

AFTER THREE SEASONS: 27 shots, 8 scored. Success ratio of 29.63 per cent.

SHORTHANDED SITUATIONS 1974-75

		GP	PIM	AVG	SITS.	GF	GA	EFFIC.	FREQ.
1.	New England	78	867	11.12	215	6	29	86.5%	7.41
2.	Winnipeg	78	869	11.14	221	11	37	83.3%	5.97
3.	Houston	78	1257	16.12	372	18	64	82.8%	5.81
4.	Baltimore	78	1104	14.15	278	4	50	82.0%	5.56
5.	Minnesota	78	1233	15.81	256	16	47	81.6%	5.45
6.	San Diego	78	1058	13.56	275	11	53	80.7%	5.19
7.	Chicago	78	1086	13.92	282	6	58	79.4%	4.86
8.	Toronto	78	883	11.32	233	7	50	78.5%	4.66
9.	Quebec	78	1132	14.51	237	11	51	78.5%	4.65
10.	Indianapolis	78	970	12.44	256	4	55	78.5%	4.65
11.	Edmonton	78	896	11.49	236	10	52	78.0%	4.54
12.	Cleveland	78	1273	16.32	275	4	61	77.8%	4.51
13.	Vancouver	78	1075	13.78	267	8	62	76.8%	4.31
14.	Phoenix	78	1388	17.79	315	7	76	75.9%	4.14
	TOTALS	546	15032	13.77	3722	123	745	80.0%	5.00

ABBREVIATIONS: OP'NT PM — Opponent penalty minutes; AVG PIM — average penalty minutes; OPPR — opportunities; GF — goals for; GA — goals against; PROF. — proficiency; FREQ. — frequency; SITS. — situations; EFF. — efficiency.

AVCO WORLD TROPHY PLAYOFFS

1975
QUARTER-FINALS

SERIES A
(CLEVELAND vs. HOUSTON)
April 10 — Houston 8 Cleveland 5
April 12 — Houston 5 Cleveland 3
April 13 — Cleveland 3 Houston 1
April 15 — Houston 7 Cleveland 2
April 17 — Houston 3 Cleveland 1
(Houston Wins Series 4-1)

SERIES B
(PHOENIX vs. QUEBEC)
April 8 — Quebec 5 Phoenix 2
April 10 — Quebec 6 Phoenix 2
April 12 — Quebec 3 Phoenix 0
April 15 — Phoenix 6 *Quebec 5
April 17 — Quebec 4 Phoenix 2
* Overtime: Michel Cormier 7:27.
(Quebec Wins Series 4-1)

SERIES C
(MINNESOTA vs. NEW ENGLAND)
April 9 — Minnesota 6 New England 5
April 11 — New England 3 *Minnesota 2
April 13 — Minnesota 8 New England 3
April 15 — New England 5 Minnesota 2
April 18 — Minnesota 4 New England 0
April 19 — Minnesota 6 New England 1
* Overtime: Rick Ley 6:46.
(Minnesota Wins Series 4-2)

SERIES D
(TORONTO vs. SAN DIEGO)
April 9 — San Diego 5 Toronto 3
April 12 — San Diego 7 Toronto 6
April 14 — Toronto 5 San Diego 2
April 16 — Toronto 6 San Diego 5
April 18 — San Diego 4 Toronto 3
April 21 — San Diego 6 Toronto 4
(San Diego Wins Series 4-2)

SEMI-FINALS

SERIES E
(SAN DIEGO vs. HOUSTON)
April 25 — Houston 4 San Diego 0
April 27 — Houston 2 San Diego 1
April 29 — Houston 6 San Diego 0
May 1 — Houston 5 *San Diego 4
* Overtime: Jim Sherrit 0:27.
(Houston Wins Series 4-0)

SERIES F
(MINNESOTA vs. QUEBEC)
April 22 — Quebec 4 Minnesota 1
April 24 — Minnesota 5 Quebec 3
April 26 — Quebec 6 Minnesota 1
April 27 — Minnesota 4 Quebec 2
April 29 — Quebec 6 Minnesota 3
May 1 — Quebec 4 Minnesota 2
(Quebec Wins Series 4-2)

FINALS

SERIES G
(QUEBEC vs. HOUSTON)
May 3 — Houston 6 Quebec 2
May 6 — Houston 5 Quebec 3
May 10 — Houston 2 Quebec 0
May 12 — Houston 7 Quebec 2
(Houston Wins Avco Trophy 4-0)

LEADING GOALTENDERS

	TM	MIN	SOG	GA	GAA	SO
*Ron Grahame	Hou	.780	439	26	2.00	3
Richard Brodeur	Que	.906	550	48	3.18	1
John Garrett	Min	.726	406	41	3.39	1
Garry Kurt	Phx	.207	81	12	3.48	0
Russ Gillow	S.D.	.79	56	5	3.80	0

* Selected MVP of playoffs and winner of Gordie Howe Trophy.

TOP 10 SCORERS

	TM	GP	G	A	PTS	PIM
Mark Howe	Hou	13	10	12	22	0
Marc Tardif	Que	15	10	11	21	10
Gordie Howe	Hou	13	8	12	20	20
Larry Lund	Hou	13	5	13	18	13
Mike Walton	Min	12	10	7	17	10
Rejean Houle	Que	15	10	6	16	2
Serge Bernier	Que	16	8	8	16	6
Fran Huck	Min	12	3	13	16	6
C. Bordeleau	Que	15	2	13	15	2
R. LeClerc	Que	14	7	7	14	41
Ray Addounone	S.D.	10	5	9	14	13
G. Morrison	Min	12	5	9	14	0

playoffs

1973   1974

SERIES "A" (QUARTER-FINALS)

(NEW ENGLAND vs. OTTAWA)

April 7 — New England 6 Ottawa 3
April 8 — New England 4 *Ottawa 3
April 10 — Ottawa 4 New England 2
April 12 — New England 7 Ottawa 3
April 14 — New England 5 *Ottawa 4
* Overtime: Brit Selby 3:37.
          Mike Byers 5:47.
(New England Wins Series 4-1)

(HOUSTON vs. WINNIPEG)

April 8 — Houston 5 Winnipeg 2
April 10 — Houston 3 Winnipeg 2
April 13 — Houston 10 Winnipeg 1
April 14 — Houston 5 Winnipeg 4
(Houston Wins Series 4-0)

SERIES "B" (QUARTER-FINALS)

(CLEVELAND vs. PHILADELPHIA)

April 4 — Cleveland 3 *Philadelphia 2
April 7 — Cleveland 7 Philadelphia 1
April 8 — Cleveland 3 Philadelphia 1
April 11 — Cleveland 6 Philadelphia 2
* Overtime: Ron Buchanan 9:49.
(Cleveland Wins Series 4-0)

(MINNESOTA vs. EDMONTON)

April 6 — Minnesota 2 Edmonton 1
April 7 — Minnesota 8 Edmonton 5
April 10 — Minnesota 6 Edmonton 2
April 12 — Edmonton 2 Minnesota 1
April 14 — Minnesota 5 Edmonton 4
(Minnesota Wins Series 4-1)

SERIES "C" (QUARTER-FINALS)

(WINNIPEG vs. MINNESOTA)

April 6 — Winnipeg 3 Minnesota 1
April 8 — Winnipeg 5 Minnesota 2
April 10 — Minnesota 4 Winnipeg 4
April 11 — Winnipeg 3 *Minnesota 2
April 15 — Winnipeg 8 Minnesota 5
* Overtime: Norm Beaudin 3:12.
(Winnipeg Wins Series 4-1)

(CHICAGO vs. NEW ENGLAND)

April 6 — New England 6 Chicago 4
April 7 — New England 4 *Chicago 3
April 9 — Chicago 8 New England 5
April 10 — Chicago 2 *New England 1
April 12 — Chicago 4 New England 2
April 14 — New England 2 Chicago 0
April 16 — Chicago 3 New England 2
* Overtime: John French 2:51.
          Ralph Backstrom 17:45.
(Chicago Wins Series 4-3)

SERIES "D" (QUARTER-FINALS)

(HOUSTON vs. LOS ANGELES)

April 5 — Houston 7 Los Angeles 2
April 7 — Los Angeles 4 Houston 2
April 11 — Los Angeles 3 Houston 2
April 13 — Houston 3 *Los Angeles 2
April 15 — Houston 6 Los Angeles 3
April 17 — Houston 3 Los Angeles 2
* Overtime: Murray Hall 3:38.
(Houston Wins Series 4-2)

(TORONTO vs. CLEVELAND)

April 7 — Toronto 4 Cleveland 0
April 9 — Toronto 4 Cleveland 3
April 12 — Toronto 4 Cleveland 2
April 13 — Cleveland 3 Toronto 1
April 15 — Toronto 4 Cleveland 1
* Overtime: Wayne Muloin 4:17.
(Toronto Wins Series 4-1)

SERIES "E" (SEMI-FINALS)

(NEW ENGLAND vs. CLEVELAND)

April 18 — New England 3 Cleveland 2
April 19 — New England 3 Cleveland 2
April 21 — New England 5 Cleveland 4
April 22 — Cleveland 5 New England 2
April 26 — New England 3 Cleveland 1
(New England Wins Series 4-1)

(HOUSTON vs. MINNESOTA)

April 18 — Minnesota 5* Houston 4
April 20 — Houston 5 Minnesota 2
April 21 — Minnesota 4 Houston 1
April 28 — Houston 4 Minnesota 1
April 29 — Houston 9 Minnesota 4
May 1 — Houston 3 Minnesota 1
* Overtime: Mike Walton 1:40.
(Houston Wins Series 4-2)

SERIES "F" (SEMI-FINALS)

(WINNIPEG vs. HOUSTON)
April 20 — Winnipeg 5 Houston 1
April 22 — Winnipeg 2 Houston 0
April 24 — Winnipeg 4 Houston 2
April 26 — Winnipeg 3 Houston 0
(Winnipeg Wins Series 4-0)

(CHICAGO vs. TORONTO)
April 19 — Toronto 6 Chicago 4
April 22 — Chicago 4 Toronto 3
April 28 — Chicago 3 Toronto 2
April 30 — Toronto 7 Chicago 6
May 1 — Toronto 5 Chicago 3
May 4 — Chicago 9 Toronto 2
May 6 — Chicago 5 Toronto 2
(Chicago Wins Series 4-3)

SERIES "G" (FINAL ROUND)

(NEW ENGLAND vs. WINNIPEG)
April 29 — New England 7 Winnipeg 2
May 2 — New England 7 Winnipeg 4
May 3 — Winnipeg 4 New England 3
May 5 — New England 4 Winnipeg 2
May 6 — New England 9 Winnipeg 6
(New England Wins Series 4-1)

(HOUSTON vs. CHICAGO)
May 12 — Houston 3 Chicago 2
May 15 — Houston 6 Chicago 1
May 17 — Houston 7 Chicago 4
May 19 — Houston 6 Chicago 2
(Houston Wins Series 4-0)

TOP 10 SCORERS

1973

	TM	GP	G	A	PTS	PIM
Norm Beaudin	Wpg	14	13	15	28	2
Tom Webster	N.E.	15	12	14	26	6
Bobby Hull	Wpg	14	9	16	25	16
Tim Sheehy	N.E.	15	9	14	23	13
Larry Pleau	N.E.	15	12	7	19	15
Jim Dorey	N.E.	15	3	16	19	41
Tom Williams	N.E.	15	6	11	17	2
B. Sutherland	Wpg	14	5	9	14	9
John French	N.E.	15	3	11	14	2
C. Bordeleau	Wpg	12	5	8	13	4

1974

	TM	GP	G	A	PTS	PIM
Larry Lund	Hou	14	9	14	23	56
Mark Howe	Hou	14	9	10	19	4
R. Backstrom	Chi	18	5	14	19	4
Mike Walton	Min	11	10	8	18	16
Andre Hinse	Hou	14	8	9	17	18
Gordie Howe	Hou	13	3	14	17	34
G. Labessiere	Hou	14	7	9	16	20
Murray Hall	Hou	14	9	6	15	6
R. Paiement	Chi	18	9	6	15	16
Poul Popiel	Hou	14	1	14	15	22

PLAYOFF LEADERS (ALL-TIME)

SCORING

		TM.	PY	GP	G	A	PTS.	PIM	PPG	WG	IP	PP	SH
1.	Larry Lund	Hou	3	37	17	34	51	93	1.38	7	29	1	2
2.	Mark Howe	Hou	2	27	19	22	41	4	1.52	3	28	4	3
3.	Gordie Howe	Hou	2	26	11	26	37	54	1.42	2	23	3	2
3.	Poul Popiel	Hou	3	37	4	33	37	79	1.00	—	22	2	—
5.	Mike Walton	Min	2	23	20	25	35	26	1.52	5	21	6	1
6.	Frank Hughes	Hou	3	37	19	15	34	13	.92	2	18	9	—
6.	Gord Labossiere	Hou	3	33	14	20	34	32	1.03	3	24	4	—
8.	Tom Webster	N.E.	3	21	18	19	33	13	1.57	—	25	6	—
8.	Murray Hall	Hou	3	37	20	13	33	32	.89	7	23	5	—
8.	Chris Bordeleau	Wpg/Que	3	30	10	23	33	6	1.10	1	22	1	—
8.	Jim Dorey	N.E./Tor	3	27	5	28	33	69	1.22	—	27	1	—

PENALTY LEADERS

		TM.	PY.	GP	PIM	AVG. GAME
1.	Larry Lund	Hou	3	37	93	2.51
2.	Ted Taylor	Hou	3	35	92	2.63
3.	Poul Popiel	Hou	3	37	79	2.14
4.	Rick Ley	N.E.	3	28	74	2.64
5.	Darryl Maggs	Chi	1	18	71	3.94
6.	Jim Dorey	N.E./Tor	3	27	69	2.56
7.	Gord Gallant	Minn	2	12	67	5.58
8.	John Schella	Hou	3	37	66	1.78
8.	Skip Krake	Clev	2	14	66	4.71
10.	Paul Shmyr	Clev	3	18	65	3.61

GOALTENDING (at Least 750 minutes played)

	TM.	PY.	MINS.	GPI	W	L	SOG	GA	GAA	SO
Ron Grahame	Hou	1	780	13	12	1	439	26	2.00	3
Don McLeod	Hou	2	1020	17	12	5	462	43	2.53	0
Gerry Cheevers	Cle	3	1151	19	7	12	455	63	3.28	0
Al Smith	N.E.	3	1674	28	17	11	862	98	3.51	1
John Garrett	Min	2	1098	19	10	8	662	66	3.61	1

3-YEAR PLAYOFF ATTENDANCE

	1975			1974			1973		
CANADIAN DIVISION	GP	TOTAL	AVG.	GP	TOTAL	AVG.	GP	TOTAL	AVG.
Quebec	8	77,788	9,724	—	—	—	—	—	—
Toronto	3	28,162	9,387	7	51,801	7,400	2	8,820	4,410
Edmonton	—	—	—	2	9,806	4,903	—	—	—
Winnipeg	—	—	—	2	17,138	8,569	7	52,559	7,508
Vancouver	—	—	—	—	—	—	2	7,234	3,617
	11	105,950	9,632	11	78,745	7,159	11	68,613	6,238
Eastern Division									
New England	3	30,521	10,174	4	22,064	5,516	9	79,866	8,874
Cleveland	2	13,784	6,892	2	16,203	8,102	4	24,460	6,115
Chicago	—	—	—	8	25,093	3,137	—	—	—
Indianapolis	—	—	—	—	—	—	—	—	—
	5	44,305	8,861	14	63,360	4,526	13	104,326	8,025
Western Division									
Houston	7	52,938	7,563	7	65,356	9,337	5	33,098	6,620
Minnesota	6	63,177	10,530	6	81,569	13,595	2	12,133	6,067
San Diego	5	54,906	10,981	—	—	—	—	—	—
Phoenix	2	14,767	7,384	—	—	—	—	—	—
Baltimore	—	—	—	—	—	—	3	17,695	5,898
	20	185,788	9,289	13	146,925	11,302	10	62,926	6,293
	36	336,043	9,335	38	289,000	7,606	34	235,865	6,937

WHA PLAYOFF RECORDS
TEAM

MOST GOALS, BOTH TEAMS, FOUR GAME SERIES:
  32 — Houston/Winnipeg, 1974 quarter-finals. Houston won series 4-0, outscoring Winnipeg 23-9.

MOST GOALS, ONE TEAM, FOUR GAME SERIES:
  23 — Houston, 1974 quarter-finals. Houston won series, outscored Winnipeg 23-9.

MOST GOALS, BOTH TEAMS, FIVE GAME SERIES:
  48 — New England/Winnipeg, 1973 final. New England won series 4-1, outscoring Winnipeg, 30-18.

MOST GOALS, ONE TEAM, FIVE GAME SERIES:
  30 — New England, 1973 final. N.E. defeated Winnipeg 4-0, outscored Jets 30-18.

MOST GOALS, BOTH TEAMS, SIX GAME SERIES:
  56 — San Diego/Toronto, 1975 quarter finals. San Diego defeated Toronto 4-2, outscored Toros, 29-27.

MOST GOALS, ONE TEAM, SIX GAME SERIES:
  29 — San Diego, 1975 quarter-finals. San Diego defeated Toronto 4-2, outscored Toros 29-27.

MOST GOALS, BOTH TEAMS, SEVEN GAME SERIES:
  61 — Chicago/Toronto, 1974 semi-finals. Chicago defeated Toronto 4-2, outscoring them 34-27.

MOST GOALS, ONE TEAM, SEVEN GAME SERIES:
  34 — Chicago, 1974 semi-finals. Cougars defeated Toronto 4-3, outscored them 34-27.

FEWEST GOALS, BOTH TEAMS, FOUR GAME SERIES:
  17 — Winnipeg/Houston, 1973 semi-finals. Winnipeg won series 4-0, outscored Houston 14-3.

FEWEST GOALS, ONE TEAM, FOUR GAME SERIES:
  3 — Houston, 1973 semi-finals. Lost series to Winnipeg 4-0, outscored 14-3.

FEWEST GOALS, BOTH TEAMS, FIVE GAME SERIES:
  27 — Toronto/Cleveland, 1974 quarter-finals. Toronto won series 4-1, outscored Cleveland 18-9.

FEWEST GOALS, ONE TEAM, FIVE GAME SERIES:
  9 — Cleveland, 1974 quarter-finals. Lost to Toronto 4-1, outscored 18-9.

FEWEST GOALS, BOTH TEAMS, SIX GAME SERIES:
  39 — Houston/Los Angeles, 1973 quarter-final series. Houston won series 4-2, outscored Los Angeles 23-16.

FEWEST GOALS, ONE TEAM, SIX GAME SERIES:
  16 — Los Angeles, 1973 quarter-finals. Lost to Houston 4-2, outscored 23-16.
  — Minnesota, 1975 semi-finals. Lost to Quebec 4-2, outscored 25-16.

FEWEST GOALS, BOTH TEAMS, SEVEN GAME SERIES:
  47 — Chicago/New England, 1974 quarter-finals. Chicago won series 4-3, outscored New England 24-23.

FEWEST GOALS, ONE TEAM, SEVEN GAME SERIES:
  23 — New England, 1974 quarter-finals. Chicago won 4-3, outscored N.E. 24-23.

WIDEST MARGIN OF VICTORY, ONE GAME:
  9 goals — Houston defeated Winnipeg 10-1, April 13, 1974. Houston won series 4-0.

MOST GOALS, BOTH TEAMS, ONE GAME:
  15 — New England/Winnipeg, May 6, 1973, at Boston. Final game of final series. New England won 9-6 and series 4-1.

MOST GOALS, ONE TEAM, ONE GAME:
  10 — Houston, April 13, 1974, Winnipeg 1 at Houston 10.

MOST GOALS, BOTH TEAMS, ONE PERIOD:
  7 — in 6 different games.

MOST GOALS, ONE TEAM, ONE PERIOD:
  5 — by seven teams.

SHORTEST OVERTIME:
  27 sec. — San Diego at Houston, May 1, 1975. Jim Sherrit of Houston. Assists to Mark Howe and John Schella.

playoff records

LONGEST OVERTIME:
17 minutes, 45 seconds — New England at Chicago, April 10, 1974. Ralph Backstrom scored to give Chicago 2-1 decision. Assist to Duke Harris.

MOST OVERTIME GAMES, QUARTER-FINAL SERIES:
2 — New England/Ottawa, 1973, New England won both.
— New England/Chicago, 1974, teams split.

MOST OVERTIME GAMES, SEMI-FINAL SERIES:
1 — Houston/Minnesota, 1974. Minnesota won.
— Houston/San Diego, 1975. Houston won.

MOST OVERTIME GAMES IN FINAL SERIES:
0 — No final round game has gone into overtime.

MOST OVERTIME GAMES, FOUR GAME SERIES:
1 — Cleveland/Philadelphia, 1973, won by Cleveland.
— Houston/San Diego, 1975, won by Houston.

MOST OVERTIME GAMES IN FIVE GAME SERIES:
2 — New England/Ottawa, 1973, both won by New England.

MOST OVERTIME GAMES, SIX GAME SERIES:
1 — Houston/Los Angeles, 1973, game won by Houston.
— Houston/Minnesota, 1974, game won by Minnesota.
— New England/Minnesota, 1975, game won by New England.

MOST OVERTIME GAMES, SEVEN GAME SERIES:
2 — Chicago/New England, 1974, each team won an overtime game.

MOST OVERTIME PERIODS, ONE TEAM, ONE PLAYOFF YEAR:
2 — New England, 1973, 1974.
— Ottawa, 1973.
— Chicago, 1974.

MOST CONSECUTIVE PLAYOFF GAME VICTORIES:
10 — Houston. Won final 10 games 1975 playoffs.

LONGEST PLAYOFF LOSING STREAK:
6 — Winnipeg. Lost final two games to New England in 1973 and four straight to Houston in 1974.

MOST SHUTOUTS, ONE PLAYOFF YEAR, ALL TEAMS:
5 — 1975, three by Houston, one each by Minnesota and Quebec.

MOST SHUTOUTS, ONE TEAM, ONE PLAYOFF YEAR:
3 — Houston, 1975.

MOST SHUTOUTS, ONE TEAM, ONE SERIES:
2 — Winnipeg, 1973, shutout Houston twice in semi-final round won by Winnipeg 4-0.
— Houston, 1975, shutout San Diego twice in semi-finals won by Houston 4-0.

MOST PENALTIES, BOTH TEAMS, ONE SERIES: (and) MOST PENALTY MINUTES, BOTH TEAMS, ONE SERIES:
116 penalties, 383 min. — Houston/Minnesota, 1974 semi-finals. Houston had 56 penalties for 170 minutes, Minnesota 60 for 213 minutes. Houston won series 4-2.

MOST PENALTIES, ONE TEAM, ONE SERIES: (and) MOST PENALTY MINUTES, ONE TEAM, ONE SERIES:
60 penalties, 213 min. — Minnesota, 1974 semi-final series vs. Houston. Houston won series 4-2.

FEWEST PENALTIES, BOTH TEAMS, ONE SERIES: (and) FEWEST PENALTY MINUTES, BOTH TEAMS, ONE SERIES:
29 penalties, 74 min. — Winnipeg/Minnesota, 1973, quarter-finals, Minnesota received 14 minors, 1 major. Winnipeg 12 minors, 1 major and 1 misconduct. Winnipeg won series, 4-1.

FEWEST PENALTIES, ONE TEAM, ONE SERIES: (and) FEWEST PENALTY MINUTES, ONE TEAM, ONE SERIES:
13 penalties, 29 min. — Winnipeg, 1973 semi-finals vs. Houston. Series won by Winnipeg 4-0.

MOST PENALTIES, BOTH TEAMS, ONE GAME: (and) MOST PENALTY MINUTES, BOTH TEAMS, ONE GAME:
41 penalties, 217 min. — Minnesota at New England, April 11, 1975. New England had 21 penalties for 116 minutes, Minnesota 20 for 101 minutes. New England won game 3-2 and Minnesota won series 4-2.

MOST PENALTIES, ONE TEAM, ONE GAME: (and) MOST PENALTY MINUTES, ONE TEAM, ONE GAME:
 21 penalties, 116 min. — New England, April 11, 1975, vs. Minnesota at Hartford, Conn. New England won game 3-2, Minnesota son series 4-2.

MOST PENALTIES, BOTH TEAMS, ONE PERIOD: (and) MOST PENALTY MINUTES, BOTH TEAMS, ONE PERIOD:
 34 penalties, 189 minutes — Minnesota at New England, April 11, 1975, second period. Minnestoa had 16 penalties for 82 minutes, New England had 18 penalties for 107 minutes. New England won game 3-2.

MOST PENALTIES, ONE TEAM, ONE PERIOD: (and) MOST PENALTY MINUTES, ONE TEAM, ONE PERIOD:
 18 penalties, 107 min. — New England, April 11, 1975, vs. Minnesota at Hartford. New England won game 3-2.

MOST POWER PLAY GOALS, ONE TEAM, ONE PLAYOFF YEAR:
 17 — Houston, 1974.

MOST POWER PLAY GOALS, BOTH TEAMS, ONE SERIES:
 14 — San Diego/Toronto, 1975 quarter-final series won by San Diego 4-2. San Diego scored 8 power play goals, Toronto 6.

MOST POWER PLAY GOALS, ONE TEAM, ONE SERIES:
 11 — Houston, 1974, final series vs. Chicago. Houston won series 4-0.

MOST POWER PLAY GOALS, BOTH TEAMS, ONE GAME:
 6 — April 15, 1973, Los Angeles at Houston. Houston had 3, L.A. 2. Houston won game 6-3 and the series 4-2.
 — May 19, 1974, Chicago at Houston. Houston had 5, Chicago 1. Houston won game 6-2 and series 4-0.
 — April 13, 1975, New England at Minnestoa. Minnestoa had 4, New England 2. Minnestoa won game 8-3 and the series 4-2.

MOST POWER PLAY GOALS, ONE TEAM, ONE GAME:
 5 — Houston, May 19, 1974 vs. Chicago at Houston. Houston won game 6-2, series 4-0.

MOST POWER PLAY GOALS, BOTH TEAMS, ONE PERIOD:
 4 — Los Angeles at Houston, April 15, 1973. First period, each team scored two power play goals. Houston won game 6-3, series 4-2.

MOST POWER PLAY GOALS, ONE TEAM, ONE PERIOD:
 3 — Houston vs. Chicago, May 19, 1974, final round. Houston won game 6-2, series 4-2. Second period.
 — Minnesota, April 13, 1975, quarter-final round, first period. Minnesota won game, 8-3, series 4-2.

MOST POWER PLAY OPPORTUNITIES, ONE TEAM, ONE GAME:
 10 — Philadelphia, April 8, 1973, vs. Cleveland. Lost game 3-1, series 4-0.

MOST POWER PLAY OPPORTUNITIES, BOTH TEAMS, ONE GAME:
 17 — Cleveland 7, at Philadelphia 10, April 8, 1973.

MOST POWER PLAY OPPORTUNITIES, ONE TEAM, ONE SERIES:
 30 — New England, 1973 quarter final vs. Ottawa. N.E. won series, 4-1.

MOST POWER PLAY OPPORTUNITIES, BOTH TEAMS, ONE SERIES:
 57 — New England/Ottawa, 1973 quarter final.

MOST SHORTHANDED GOALS, ONE TEAM, ONE PLAYOFF YEAR:
 7 — Houston, 1974, in 10 games.

MOST SHORTHANDED GOALS, ONE TEAM, ONE SERIES:
 4 — Houston, 1974 semi-final vs. Minnesota, 6 games. Houston won series, 4-2.

MOST SHORTHANDED GOALS, ONE TEAM, ONE GAME: (and)
MOST SHORTHANDED GOALS, ONE TEAM, ONE PERIOD:
 2 — Houston, April 29, 1974 vs. Minnesota. First period. Houston won game 9-4, series 4-2.
 — New England, April 15, 1975 at Minnesota, third period. New England, 5-2. Minnesota won series 4-2.

FASTEST TWO GOALS, BOTH TEAMS, ONE GAME:
 8 sec. — Minnesota at Quebec, April 29, 1975. Mike Walton scored for Minnesota at 8:53, Marc Tardif for Quebec at 9:01 of second period. Quebec won game 6-3, series 4-2.

FASTEST TWO GOALS, ONE TEAM:
 12 sec. — Toronto vs. Chicago, April 22, 1974, Bob Leduc scored at 8:55, Tom Martin at 9:07. Chicago won game 4-3, series 4-3.

FASTEST THREE GOALS, BOTH TEAMS:
 56 sec. — Edmonton at Minnesota, April 7, 1974, third period. Ted Hampson scored for Minnestoa at 18:32, Blair McDonald for Edmonton at 19:04, Mike Walton into an empty net at 19:28. Minnesota won game 8-5, series 4-1.

FASTEST THREE GOALS, ONE TEAM:
 55 sec. — Cleveland vs. Philadelphia, April 7, 1973. Jim Wiste 5:15, Garry Pinder 5:51 and Gary Jarrett at 6:10 of the second period. Cleveland won game 7-1, series 4-0.

FASTEST TWO POWER PLAY GOALS, ONE TEAM:
 29 sec. — Minnesota, April 6, 1974 vs. Edmonton. Murray Heatley at 9:09, Mike Walton at 9:38 of second period.

FASTEST THREE POWER PLAY GOALS, ONE TEAM:
 3 minutes, 12 sec. — Houston, May 19, 1974, vs. Chicago. Andre Hinse 12:40, Gord Labossiere 13:58, Larry Lund 15:52 in final game of final series. Houston won game, 6-2, series 4-0.

FASTEST TWO SHORTHANDED GOALS, ONE TEAM:
 42 sec. — Houston, April 29, 1974, semi-final vs. Minnesota. Mark Howe 15:48, Gordie Howe 16:30 of first period.

INDIVIDUAL

MOST POINTS, ONE PLAYOFF YEAR:
 28 — Norm Beaudin, Winnipeg, 1973. 13 goals, 15 assists (14 games).

MOST GOALS, ONE PLAYOFF YEAR:
 13 — Norm Beaudin, Winnipeg, 1973 (14 games).

MOST ASSISTS, ONE PLAYOFF YEAR:
 16 — Bobby Hull, Winnipeg, 1973 (14 games).
 — Jim Dorey, New England, 1974 (15 games).

MOST PENALTY MINUTES, ONE PLAYOFF YEAR:
 71 — Darryl Maggs, Chicago, 1974 (18 games).
 67 — Gord Gallant, Minnesota, 1974 (10 games).

MOST POINTS, BY A DEFENCEMAN, ONE PLAYOFF YEAR:
 19 — Jim Dorey, New England, 1973, 3 goals, 16 assists (15 games).

MOST GOALS, BY A DEFENCEMAN, ONE PLAYOFF YEAR:
 4 — Larry Mavety, Chicago, 1974 (18 games).

MOST ASSISTS, BY A DEFENCEMAN, ONE PLAYOFF YEAR:
 16 — Jim Dorey, New England, 1973 (15 games).

MOST POINTS, FOUR GAME SERIES:
 9 — Gordie Howe, Houston, 1974 vs. Chicago. 9 assists.

MOST GOALS, FOUR GAME SERIES:
 5 — Andre Hinse, Houston, 1974 vs. Chicago.
 — Gordie Howe, Houston, 1975 vs. Quebec.

MOST ASSISTS, FOUR GAME SERIES:
 9 — Gordie Howe, Houston, 1974 vs. Chicago.

MOST POINTS IN FIVE GAME SERIES:
 15 — Norm Beaudin, Winnipeg, 1973 vs. Minnesota. 5 goals, 10 assists.

MOST GOALS, FIVE GAME SERIES:
 8 — Mark Howe, Houston, 1975 vs. Cleveland.

MOST ASSISTS, FIVE GAME SERIES:
 10 — Norm Beaudin, Winnipeg, 1973 vs. Minnesota.

MOST POINTS, SIX GAME SERIES:
 12 — Fran Huck, Minnesota, 1975 vs. New England. 2 goals, 10 assists.
 — Ray Addouno, San Diego, 1975 vs. Toronto. 4 goals, 8 assists.

MOST GOALS, SIX GAME SERIES:
 7 — Gene Peacosh, San Diego, 1975 vs. Toronto.

MOST ASSISTS, SIX GAME SERIES:
 10 — Fran Huck, Minnesota, 1975 vs. New England.

MOST POINTS, SEVEN GAME SERIES:
 10 — Ralph Backstrom, Chicago, 1974, vs. Toronto. 2 goals, 8 assists.
 — Rosaire Paiement, Chicago, 1974 vs. Toronto. 7 goals, 3 assists.

MOST GOALS, SEVEN GAME SERIES:
 7 — Rosaire Paiement, Chicago, 1974 vs. Toronto.

MOST ASSISTS, SEVEN GAME SERIES:
 8 — Ralph Backstrom, Chicago, 1974 vs. Toronto.

MOST POINTS, QUARTER FINAL SERIES:
 15 — Norm Beaudin, Winnipeg 1973 vs. Minnesota. 5 goals, 10 assists.
MOST GOALS, QUARTER FINAL SERIES:
 8 — Mark Howe, Houston 1975 vs. Cleveland.
MOST ASSISTS, QUARTER FINAL SERIES:
 10 — Norm Beaudin, Winnipeg, 1973, vs. Minnesota.
  — Fran Huck, Minnesota, 1975 vs. New England.
MOST POINTS, SEMI-FINAL SERIES:
 12 — Tim Sheehy, New England, 1973 vs. Cleveland. 6 goals, 6 assists.
MOST GOALS, SEMI-FINAL SERIES:
 7 — Rosaire Paiement, Chicago, 1974 vs. Toronto.
MOST ASSISTS, SEMI-FINAL SERIES:
 8 — Ralph Backstrom, Chicago, 1974 vs. Toronto.
MOST POINTS, FINAL SERIES:
 11 — Tom Webster, New England, 1973 vs. Winnipeg. 4 goals, 7 assists.
  — Tommy Williams, New England, 1973 vs. Winnipeg. 2 goals, 9 assists.
MOST GOALS, FINAL SERIES:
 5 — Norm Beaudin, Winnipeg, 1973 vs. New England.
  — Andre Hinse, Houston, 1974 vs. Chicago.
  — Gordie Howe, Houston, 1975 vs. Quebec.
MOST ASSISTS, FINAL SERIES:
 9 — Tommy Williams, New England, 1973 vs. Winnipeg.
  — Gordie Howe, Houston, 1974 vs. Chicago.
MOST CONSECUTIVE GAMES WITH POINTS:
 16 — Tim Sheehy, New England, Apr. 12, 1973 to Apr. 12, 1974. 13 goals, 16 assists.
MOST CONSECUTIVE GAMES WITH GOALS:
 6 — Larry Pleau, New England. Apr. 12, to Apr. 26, 1973.
MOST CONSECUTIVE GAMES WITH ASSISTS:
 9 — Tim Sheehy, New England. Apr. 12 to May 3, 1973.
MOST GAME WINNING GOALS, ONE PLAYOFF YEAR:
 3 — Bobby Hull, Winnipeg, 1973.
  — Tim Sheehy, New England, 1973.
  — Mike Walton, Minnesota, 1974.
  — Murray Hall, Houston, 1974.
MOST POWER PLAY GOALS, ONE PLAYOFF YEAR:
 5 — Wayne Connelly, Minnesota, 1974.
MOST POWER PLAY GOALS, ONE PLAYOFF SERIES:
 4 — Andre Hinse, Houston 1974 vs. Chicago, 4 games.
MOST POWER PLAY GOALS, ONE GAME:
 2 — Tom Webster (New England — twice); Andre Hinse (Houston — twice); Tommy Williams (New England); Frank Hughes (Houston); Tom Martin (Toronto); Murray Hall (Houston); Mark Howe (Houston); Rejean Houle (Quebec).
MOST POWER PLAY GOALS, ONE PERIOD:
 2 — Tommy Williams (N.E.); Frank Hughes (Hou); Tom Webster (N.E.); Andre Hinse (Hou); Murray Hall (Hou).
MOST SHORTHANDED GOALS, ONE PLAYOFF YEAR:
 2 — Larry Lund, Houston, 1974.
  — Gordie Howe, Houston, 1974.
  — Mark Howe, Houston, 1974.
  — Rod Zaine, Chicago, 1974.
MOST SHORTHANDED GOALS, ONE SERIES:
 2 — Mark Howe, Houston, 1974 vs. Minnesota.
  — Rod Zaine, Chicago, 1974 vs. Toronto.
MOST SHORTHANDED GOALS, ONE GAME:
 1 — No player has scored more than one. There have been 19 in WHA history.
MOST OVERTIME GOALS, ONE PLAYOFF YEAR: (and)
MOST OVERTIME GOALS, ONE PLAYOFF SERIES:
 1 — No player has scored more than 1. There have been 12 overtime games.
MOST THREE-OR-MORE GOAL GAMES, ONE PLAYOFF YEAR:
 2 — Gary Jarrett, Cleveland 1973.
  — Mark Howe, Houston 1975.

MOST CONSECUTIVE WINS BY A GOALTENDER:
   10 — Ron Grahame, Houston 1975. Has won the last ten games in which he has appeared.
MOST SHUTOUTS, ONE PLAYOFF YEAR, BY A GOALTENDER:
   3 — Ron Grahame, Houston, 1975.
LONGEST SHUTOUT SEQUENCE:
   145 mins., 3 sec. — Ernie Wakely, Winnipeg. Streak started at 14:13 of third period vs. Minnesota Apr. 15 and ended May 2, 1973 at 19:46 of third period vs. New England. Included shutouts of Houston Apr. 22, Apr. 26.
MOST CONSECUTIVE SHUTOUTS:
   2 — Ernie Wakely, Winnipeg, 1973 vs. Houston Apr. 22 and Apr. 26.
MOST POINTS, ONE GAME:
   7 — Norm Beaudin, Winnipeg Apr. 15, 1973 (3 goals, 4 assists) vs. Minnesota.
MOST GOALS, ONE GAME:
   4 — Larry Lund, Houston, Apr. 13, 1974 vs. Winnipeg.
MOST ASSISTS, ONE GAME:
   4 — Jim Dorey, New England, Apr. 7, 1973 vs. Ottawa.
     — Bobby Hull, Winnipeg, Apr. 15, 1973 vs. Minnesota.
     — Bill Sutherland, Winnipeg, Apr. 15, 1973 vs. Minnesota.
     — Norm Beaudin, Winnipeg, Apr. 15, 1973 vs. Minnesota.
     — Tommy Williams, New England, May 6, 1973 vs. Winnipeg.
     — Poul Popiel, Houston, May 19, 1974, vs. Chicago.
     — Gordie Howe, Houston, May 19, 1974 vs. Chicago.
     — Marc Tardif, Quebec, Apr. 10, 1975 vs. Phoenix.
     — Larry Lund, Houston, May 12, 1975 at Quebec.
MOST PENALTIES, ONE GAME: (and) MOST PENALTY MINUTES, ONE GAME:
   7 penalties, 36 min. — Ted Taylor, Houston, Apr. 28, 1974, at Minnesota. 3 minors, 2 majors, 2 misconducts.
MOST POINTS, ONE PERIOD:
   4 — Norm Beaudin, Winnipeg, Apr. 15, 1973 vs. Minnesota. (2 goals, 2 assists).
     — Robbie Ftorek, Phoenix, Apr. 15, 1975 vs. Quebec. (1 goal, 3 assists)
     — Mike Walton, Minnesota, Apr. 24, 1975 at Quebec. (2 goals, 2 assists).
MOST GOALS, ONE PERIOD:
   3 — Rick Sentes, Toronto, Apr. 12, 1974 at Cleveland.
MOST ASSISTS, ONE PERIOD:
   3 — Wayne Dillon, Toronto, Apr. 30, 1974 at Chicago.
     — Poul Popiel, Houston, May 19, 1974 vs. Chicago.
     — Marc Tardif, Quebec, Apr. 10, 1975, vs. Phoenix.
     — Ray Addouno, San Diego, Apr. 12, 1975, vs. Toronto.
     — Robbie Ftorek, Phoenix, Apr. 15, 1975, vs. Quebec.
     — Al McLeod, Phoenix, Apr. 15, 1975, vs. Quebec.
MOST PENALTIES, ONE PERIOD: (and) MOST PENALTY MINUTES, ONE PERIOD:
   7 penalties, 36 min. — Ted Taylor, Houston, Apr. 28, 1974 at Minnesota (3 minors, 2 majors, 2 misconducts).
FASTEST GOAL FROM START OF GAME:
   15 sec. — Jim Harrison, Cleveland, Apr. 10, 1975, at Houston.
FASTEST TWO GOALS, FROM START OF GAME:
   9 mins., 39 sec. — Dennis Sobchuk, Phoenix, Apr. 15, 1975, vs. Quebec.
FASTEST GOAL FROM THE START OF PERIOD, OTHER THAN THE FIRST:
   7 sec. — Mike Antonovich, Minnesota, Apr. 15, 1973 at Winnipeg. 2nd period.
FASTEST TWO GOALS FROM START OF PERIOD, OTHER THAN FIRST:
   6 mins., 37 sec. — Larry Lund, Houston, Apr. 13, 1974, third period vs. Winnipeg.
FASTEST TWO GOALS:
   15 sec. — Mike Walton, Minnesota, Apr. 14, 1974, vs. Edmonton. 19:05 and 19:20 of first period.
FASTEST THREE GOALS:
   8 min. 42 sec. — Rick Sentes, Toronto, Apr. 12, 1974 at Cleveland. 10:41, 13:04 and 19:23 of second period.
PENALTY SHOT GOALS:
   1 — Wayne Dillon, Toronto, Apr. 19, 1974 vs. Cam Newton, Chicago. (Only one awarded in three years). Toronto won game 6-4.

CALGARY COWBOYS

Don LeROSE, Director of Marketing/Public Relations (403) 261-6990

WRITERS REGULARLY ASSIGNED TO CLUB

GEORGE BILYCH, Calgary Herald, 206-7th Ave. S.W., Calgary
DICK CHUBEY, Calgary Albertan, 830-10th Ave. S.W., Calgary

MAJOR AIRLINES

AIR CANADA	(403) 265-9555	PACIFIC WESTERN	(403) 265-0790
CP AIR	(403) 265-8300	TIME AIR	(403) 277-8596
HUGHES AIR WEST	(403) 277-0755	WESTERN	(403) 277-0176

CINCINNATI STINGERS

JOHN A. HEWIG, Publicity Director (513) 241-1818

WRITERS REGULARLY ASSIGNED TO CLUB

DAVE FUSELIER, Cincinnati Enquirer, 617 Vine Street, Cincinnati, Ohio 45202 .... (513) 721-2700
BOB QUEENAN, Cincinnati Post, 800 Broadway, Cincinnati, Ohio 45202 .... (513) 721-1111

MAJOR AIRLINES

AIR CANADA	(513) 232-7780	DELTA	(513) 721-7000
ALLEGHENY	(513) 621-9220	AMERICAN	(513) 621-6200
TWA	(513) 381-1600	EASTERN	(513) 241-6800

CLEVELAND CRUSADERS

JOE VARGO, Public Relations Director (216) 659-9100

WRITERS REGULARLY ASSIGNED TO CLUB

BOB SCHLESINGER, Cleveland Press, 901 Lakeside Ave., Cleveland 44114 .... (216) 623-1111
RICH PASSAN, Cleveland Plain Dealer, 1801 Superior Ave. .... (216) 523-4371
JIM DERENDAL, Akron Beacon Journal, 44E. Exchange St., Akron 44309 .... (216) 375-8050
STEVE LYTLE, Willoughby News Herald, Willoughby, Ohio .... (216) 942-2105

MAJOR AIRLINES

AIR CANADA	(216) 861-3757	NORTHWEST	(216) 267-0500
ALLEGHENY	(216) 696-8050	UNITED	(216) 333-3700

DENVER SPURS

JAKE BALDWIN, Public Relations Director (303) 629-7787

WRITERS REGULARLY ASSIGNED TO CLUB

TERRY ANDERSON, Denver Post, 650-15th St., Denver .... (303) 297-1010
FRED PIETLA, Rocky Mountain News, 400 W. Colfax, Denver .... (303) 892-5000
TRACY RINGOLSBY, United Press International .... (303) 255-1428
JOHN MOSSMAN, Associated Press .... (303) 825-0123

MAJOR AIRLINES

CONTINENTAL	(303) 398-3000	UNITED	(303) 398-4171
WESTERN	(303) 398-3400	FRONTIER	(303) 399-0808
TWA	(303) 292-6620	BRANIFF	(303) 825-1111
TEXAS INTERNATIONAL	(303) 398-5500		

media/airlines

EDMONTON OILERS

DOUG WENSCHLAG, Director of Marketing (403) 474-8561

WRITERS REGULARLY ASSIGNED TO CLUB

WAYNE OVERLAND, Edmonton Journal, 101 St. & 100 Ave., Edmonton .... (403) 423-9597
JIM MATHESON, Edmonton Journal, 101 St. & 100 Ave., Edmonton .... (403) 423-9597
JOHN SHORT, Canadian Press, 101 St. & 100 Ave., Edmonton .... (403) 424-6107

MAJOR AIRLINES

AIR CANADA	(403) 429-5461	PACIFIC WESTERN	(403) 452-4560
CP AIR	(403) 429-6371	TIME AIR	(403) 455-1015
	HUGHES AIR WEST	(403) 429-4716	

HOUSTON AEROS

RICH BURK, Public Relations Director (713) 623-8321

WRITERS REGULARLY ASSIGNED TO CLUB

DALE ROBERTSON, Houston Post, 4747 Southwest Fwy, Houston 77027 .... (713) 621-7000
HERB HOLLAND, Houston Chronicle, 512 Travis St., Houston 77002 .... (713) 220-7891

MAJOR AIRLINES

AMERICAN	(713) 222-9873	DELTA	(713) 623-6000
BRANIFF	(713) 621-3111	EASTERN	(713) 621-8100
CONTINENTAL	(713) 524-4711	NATIONAL	(713) 224-9011

INDIANAPOLIS RACERS

BILL MARVEL, Public Relations Director (317) 635-3131

WRITERS REGULARLY ASSIGNED TO CLUB

DAVE OVERPECK, Indianapolis Star, 307 N. Pennsylvana .... (317) 633-9180
DICK DENNY, Indianapolis News, 307 N. Pennsylvania .... (317) 633-1240

MAJOR AIRLINES

ALLEGHENY	(317) 247-8101	EASTERN	(317) 639-6611
AMERICAN	(317) 637-1501	TWA	(317) 635-4381
	DELTA	(317) 634-3200	

MINNESOTA FIGHTING SAINTS

MIKE LAMEY, Public Relations Director (612) 222-3040

WRITERS REGULARLY ASSIGNED TO CLUB

CHARLIE HALLMAN, St. Paul Pioneer Press-Dispatch, 55 E. Fourth St., St. Paul 55101 (612) 222-5011
BOB FOWLER, Minneapolis Star, 415 Portland Ave., Minneapolis 55415 .... (612) 372-4365
JOHN GILBERT, Minneapolis Tribune, 415 Portland Ave., Minn. 55415 .... (612) 372-4447

MAJOR AIRLINES

ALLEGHENY	(612) 338-5841	NORTHWEST	(612) 726-1234
BRANIFF	(612) 726-1200	OZARK	(612) 333-3421
EASTERN	(612) 335-9541	UNITED	(612) 339-3671
NORTH CENTRAL	(612) 726-7100	WESTERN	(612) 726-4141

NEW ENGLAND WHALERS

BOB NEUMEIER, Media Relations Director (203) 728-3366

WRITERS REGULARLY ASSIGNED TO CLUB

TOM HINE, Hartford Courant, 285 Broad St., Hartford .... (203) 249-6411
BILL WINTERS, Hartford Times, 10 Prospect St., Hartford .... (203) 249-8211
DENNIS RANDALL, Hartford Times, 10 Prospect St., Hartford .... (203) 249-8211
KEVIN McGUIRK, Springfield News, 1860 Main St., Springfield 01101 .... (413) 787-2411

MAJOR AIRLINES

ALLEGHENY	(203) 522-2161	EASTERN	(203) 525-0141
AMERICAN	(203) 527-5141	TWA	(203) 278-7710
DELTA	(203) 527-1811	UNITED	(203) 249-1311

PHOENIX ROADRUNNERS

DAVE WEISER, Press Relations Director (602) 257-5100

WRITERS REGULARLY ASSIGNED TO CLUB

FRANK GIANELLI, Arizona Republic, 120 E. Van Buren, Phoenix 85001 .... (602) 271-8250
DOUG McCONNELL, Phoenix Gazette, 120 E. Van Buren, Phoenix 85001 .... (602) 271-8641

MAJOR AIRLINES

AMERICAN	(602) 264-2654	HUGHES	(602) 273-9111
CONTINENTAL	(602) 258-8911	TWA	(602) 252-7711
FRONTIER	(602) 252-5041	WESTERN	(602) 258-8881

QUEBEC NORDIQUES

PAUL LE FRANCOIS, Director of Public Relations (418) 529-4161

WRITERS REGULARLY ASSIGNED TO CLUB

CLAUDE BEDARD, Journal De Quebec, 450 Rue Bechard, Ville Vanier, Quebec City .... (418) 683-1573
CLAUDE CADORETTE, Journal De Quebec, 450 Rue Bechard, Ville Vanier, Quebec City (418) 683-1573
CLAUDE LAROCHELLE, Le Soleil, 390 Rue St. Vallier, Quebec City .... (418) 525-7134
MAURICE DUMAS, Le Soleil, 390 Rue St. Vallier, Quebec City .... (418) 525-7134

MAJOR AIRLINES

AIR CANADA	(418) 692-0770	QUEBECAIR	(418) 692-1031

SAN DIEGO MARINERS

GABE DENUNZIO, Director of Public Relations (714) 225-9633

WRITERS REGULARLY ASSIGNED TO CLUB

WAYNE LOCKWOOD, San Diego Union, P.O. Box 191, San Diego 92112 .... (714) 299-3131
PAUL COUR, Evening Tribune, P.O. Box 191, San Diego 92112 .... (714) 299-3131
MATT MITCHELL, El Cajon California, 613 W. Main St., El Cajon .... (714) 442-4404

MAJOR AIRLINES

AIR CANADA	(800) 634-6631	EASTERN	(800) 252-0223
AMERICAN	(714) 235-7601	NATIONAL	(714) 239-3036
CP AIR	Zenith 2-4209	UNITED	(714) 234-7171
DELTA	(714) 239-3431	WESTERN	(714) 234-0181

TORONTO TOROS

JOE WARWICK, Public Relations Director (416) 595-1919

WRITERS REGULARLY ASSIGNED TO CLUB

DON RAMSAY, Toronto Globe & Mail, 444 Front St., Toronto .... (416) 361-5333
JIM KERNAGHAN, Toronto Star, 1 Yonge St., Toronto .... (416) 367-2000
RICK FRASER, Toronto Sun, 332 King St. West, Toronto .... (416) 366-9141
IAN MacLAINE, Canadian Press, 36 King St. E., Toronto .... (416) 364-0321

MAJOR AIRLINES

AIR CANADA	(416) 925-2311	EASTERN	(416) 362-7561
CP AIR	(416) 366-7531	NORTH CENTRAL	(416) 362-5392
ALLEGHENY	(416) 361-1560	TWA	(416) 366-2881
AMERICAN	(416) 925-4822	UNITED	(416) 368-2331

WINNIPEG JETS

NORMAN COSTON, Public Relations Director (204) 772-9491

WRITERS REGULARLY ASSIGNED TO CLUB

REYN DAVIS, Winnipeg Free Press, 300 Carleton St., Winnipeg
ED DEARDEN, Winnipeg Tribune, Smith & Graham, Winnipeg
JOHN KOROBANIK, Canadian Press, 300 Carleton St., Winnipeg

MAJOR AIRLINES

AIR CANADA	(204) 943-9361	MIDWEST	(204) 889-4450
CP AIR	(204) 957-1060	NORTHWEST	(204) 786-3481
FRONTIER	(204) 475-3330	TRANSAIR	(204) 889-4450

WIRE SERVICE CONTACTS

ASSOCIATED PRESS, 50 Rockefeller Plaza, New York, N.Y. 10020, (212) 262-6080. Murray Rose, Hal Bock, Frank Brown, Ben Olan, Will Grimsley.

CANADIAN PRESS, 36 King Street East, Toronto, Canada (416) 364-0321. Ian MacLaine, Dennis Passen.

UNITED PRESS INTERNATIONAL, 220 East 42nd Street, New York, N.Y. Joe Marrinelli, Martin Lader, 171 Yonge St., Suite 50, Toronto, Canada (416) 363-8834. Monty Charness.

MAGAZINES

SPORTS ILLUSTRATED, Time-Life Building, New York, N.Y. (212) 586-1212. Mark Mulvoy, Ken Rudeen, Jerry Kirshenbaum, Angel Reyes.

THE SPORTING NEWS, 1212 N. Lindberg Blvd., St. Louis, Mo. (314) 997-7111. Larry Wigge.

THE HOCKEY NEWS, 1434 St. Catherine St. W., Montreal, P.Q. (514) 866-4841. Ken McKenzie, Charlie Halpin.

NATIONAL SPORTS PUBLICATIONS, 39-58 65th Place, Queens, N.Y. Norm McLean.

NATIONAL STAR, 730 Third Avenue, New York (212) 557-9200. Pete Bodo, Steve Williams.

HOCKEY ILLUSTRATED, 333 Johnson Ave., Brooklyn, New York (212) 456-8600. Jim McNally.

1975-76 SEASON
WORLD HOCKEY ASSOCIATION TRAVELOG

APPROXIMATE AIR MILEAGE	CAL.	CIN.	CLEV.	DVR.	EDM.	HOU.	IND.	MINN.	N.E.	PHX.	QUE.	S.D.	TOR.	WPG.
Calgary		1658	1681	903	1040	1729	1569	1049	2088	1262	1932	1337	1688	835
Cincinnati	1958		226	1081	1678	879	98	596	661	1569	870	1865	408	993
Cleveland	1681	226		907	1754	1104	266	624	471	1742	656	2031	187	1017
Denver	903	1081	907		1021	875	989	693	1684	589	1794	840	1332	940
Edmonton	1040	1678	1754	1021		1864	1741	1252	2044	1962	2016	1694	1671	835
Houston	1729	879	1104	875	1864		854	1046	1512	1015	1746	1308	1299	1469
Indianapolis	1569	98	266	989	1741	854		503	728	1489	924	1783	431	906
Minnesota	1049	596	624	693	1252	1046	503		1050	1276	1227	1532	780	394
New England	2088	861	471	1684	2044	1512	728	1050		2213	430	2502	373	1510
Phoenix	1262	1569	1742	589	1962	1015	1489	1276	2213		2338	304	1878	1679
Quebec	1932	870	856	1794	2016	1746	924	1227	430	2338		2622	462	1277
San Diego	1337	1865	2031	840	1694	1308	1783	1532	2502	304	2622		2179	1873
Toronto	1688	408	187	1332	1671	1299	431	780	373	1878	462	2179		934
Winnipeg	835	993	1017	940	835	1469	906	394	1510	1679	1277	1873	934	

The Exciting Difference

Hockey, it has been said, is a game combining all the elements — grace, speed, emotion, violence.

The purists said there just wasn't any room for improvement. But that was before the WHA came along.

World Hockey's rulebook, for the most part, duplicates that of any other professional league. There have been, however, several innovations that give the WHA a distinctive flavor.

Take, for example, the WHA's overtime format.

Over three seasons, there have been 191 overtime games, with 127 decisions rendered as against a mere 64 ties.

Beyond overtime and its attendant drama, other areas where WHA rules differ from other professional leagues are in OFFSIDE PASSES, CURVATURE OF THE STICK, and the THIRD MAN RULE.

OFFSIDE PASS

In other leagues, a completed forward pass that crosses two lines is ruled offside unless the 'receiver' was in the same area of the ice as the 'passer' when the pass was made. In the WHA, a player may pass the puck from inside his own blueline to a teammate beyond the center red line, providing the puck precedes the player across the center red line and the receiver takes the puck ahead of his body. The rule is designed to bring about more quick breaks, but at the same time preventing a player from floating beyond the red line awaiting a breakaway pass.

STICK CURVATURE

The National League restricts the curvature of the stick blade to half an inch, mainly for the reason that goaltenders complain that curved blades represent an unfair advantage for the shooter adept at making the puck do tricks. The WHA has an allowable curvature of an inch and a quarter, resulting in more difficult shots for the goaltenders.

THIRD MAN RULE

The WHA's "third man rule in an altercation" is somewhat more realistic than in other leagues where an automatic game misconduct is issued.

Depending on the actions of the "third man" WHA officials have the option of issuing NO PENALTY, A TWO-MINUTE MINOR, FIVE-MINUTE MAJOR or 10-MINUTE MISCONDUCT. A game misconduct applies to second time violators in a single game.

WHA 1975-76 SCHEDULE

1975

1	Thurs.	Oct.	9	Winnipeg	at	Quebec
2	Fri.	Oct.	10	San Diego	at	Phoenix
3				Minnesota	at	Edmonton
4				Indianapolis	at	Denver
5	Sat.	Oct.	11	Houston	at	New England
6				Cincinnati	at	Cleveland
7				Phoenix	at	San Diego
8				Toronto	at	Quebec
9	Sun.	Oct.	12	Indianapolis	at	Edmonton
10				Winnipeg	at	Phoenix
11				Minnesota	at	Calgary
12	Tues.	Oct.	14	Indianapolis	at	Calgary
13				Houston	at	Toronto
14				Edmonton	at	Quebec
15	Wed.	Oct.	15	Edmonton	at	New England
16				Cleveland	at	Minnesota
17	Thurs.	Oct.	16	Indianapolis	at	San Diego
18				Winnipeg	at	Denver
19	Fri.	Oct.	17	Cincinnati	at	Calgary
20				Denver	at	Phoenix
21				Edmonton	at	Toronto
22	Sat.	Oct.	18	Toronto	at	New England
23				Denver	at	Indianapolis
24				Houston	at	Quebec
25				Edmonton	at	Minnesota
26				Winnipeg	at	San Diego
27	Sun.	Oct.	19	Houston	at	Cleveland
28				Cincinnati	at	Edmonton
29				Winnipeg	at	Phoenix
30	Tues.	Oct.	21	New England	at	Quebec
31				Cincinnati	at	Winnipeg
32				Minnesota	at	Indianapolis
33	Wed.	Oct.	22	Denver	at	Calgary
34	Thurs.	Oct.	23	Edmonton	at	Cincinnati
35				Houston	at	Indianapolis
36				Minnesota	at	San Diego
37	Fri.	Oct.	24	New England	at	Toronto
38				Phoenix	at	Calgary
39				Denver	at	Winnipeg
40	Sat.	Oct.	25	Edmonton	at	Cleveland
41				Houston	at	Cincinnati
42				Minnesota	at	San Diego
43				Toronto	at	Quebec
44	Sun.	Oct.	26	Calgary	at	New England
45				Edmonton	at	Indianapolis
46				Phoenix	at	Winnipeg
47	Tues.	Oct.	28	Phoenix	at	Edmonton
48				Quebec	at	Toronto

schedule

49	Wed.	Oct. 29	Quebec	at	New England
50			Calgary	at	Cleveland
51			Cincinnati	at	Minnesota
52	Thurs.	Oct. 30	Cincinnati	at	Winnipeg
53			Calgary	at	Indianapolis
54			Phoenix	at	Denver
55			Houston	at	San Diego
56	Fri.	Oct. 31	New England	at	Edmonton
57			Quebec	at	Cleveland
58	Sat.	Nov. 1	Quebec	at	Indianapolis
59			Calgary	at	Cincinnati
60			Phoenix	at	Minnesota
61			Houston	at	Denver
62	Sun.	Nov. 2	Quebec	at	Winnipeg
63			New England	at	Calgary
64			San Diego	at	Edmonton
65			Phoenix	at	Cleveland
66	Tues.	Nov. 4	New England	at	Winnipeg
67			Quebec	at	Edmonton
68			San Diego	at	Calgary
69			Toronto	at	Indianapolis
70			Cleveland	at	Denver
71	Wed.	Nov. 5	Quebec	at	Calgary
72			Minnesota	at	Houston
73	Thurs.	Nov. 6	Quebec	at	Denver
74			Cincinnati	at	New England
75	Fri.	Nov. 7	Toronto	at	Edmonton
76			San Diego	at	Denver
77			Phoenix	at	Houston
78			Cleveland	at	Calgary
79	Sat.	Nov. 8	Indianapolis	at	Quebec
80			Toronto	at	Minnesota
81			San Diego	at	Cincinnati
82			Phoenix	at	New England
83	Sun.	Nov. 9	Toronto	at	Winnipeg
84			*Phoenix	at	Quebec
85			Cleveland	at	Edmonton
86			Denver	at	Houston
87			New England	at	Cincinnati
88	Tues.	Nov. 11	Cleveland	at	Winnipeg
89			Minnesota	at	Quebec
90			Edmonton	at	Calgary
91			Toronto	at	Houston
92	Wed.	Nov. 12	Houston	at	New England
93	Thurs.	Nov. 13	Winnipeg	at	Calgary
94			Toronto	at	Denver
95			Cleveland	at	San Diego
96	Fri.	Nov. 14	Edmonton	at	Winnipeg
97			Toronto	at	Phoenix
98	Sat.	Nov. 15	Quebec	at	New England
99			Toronto	at	San Diego
100			Houston	at	Cincinnati
101			Indianapolis	at	Minnesota
102			Cleveland	at	Denver

*—Denotes afternoon game.

103

103	Sun.	Nov.	16	Indianapolis	at	Winnipeg
104				Houston	at	Calgary
106				Cleveland	at	Phoenix
107				Minnesota	at	Cincinnati
108	Mon.	Nov.	17	Indianapolis	at	Toronto
105				San Diego	at	Edmonton
109	Tues.	Nov.	18	Houston	at	Winnipeg
110				Cincinnati	at	Quebec
111				San Diego	at	Calgary
112				Edmonton	at	Denver
113	Wed.	Nov.	19	Minnesota	at	Cleveland
114				New England	at	Indianapolis
115	Thurs.	Nov.	20	Winnipeg	at	Quebec
116				Edmonton	at	Phoenix
117				Denver	at	San Diego
118				Minnesota	at	New England
119	Fri.	Nov.	21	Calgary	at	Denver
120				Edmonton	at	Houston
121				Cincinnati	at	Toronto
122	Sat.	Nov.	22	Winnipeg	at	Cleveland
123				Quebec	at	Cincinnati
124				Calgary	at	Minnesota
125				Edmonton	at	San Diego
126				Phoenix	at	New England
127	Sun.	Nov.	23	Winnipeg	at	New England
128				Quebec	at	Houston
129				Cincinnati	at	Denver
130	Tues.	Nov.	25	Edmonton	at	San Diego
131				Cleveland	at	Toronto
132				Indianapolis	at	Houston
133				New England	at	Minnesota
134	Wed.	Nov.	26	Winnipeg	at	Cincinnati
135				Denver	at	Cleveland
136	Thurs.	Nov.	27	Winnipeg	at	Indianapolis
137				Quebec	at	San Diego
138				Calgary	at	Phoenix
139				Cincinnati	at	Minnesota
140	Fri.	Nov.	28	Winnipeg	at	Toronto
141				Edmonton	at	Houston
142				Denver	at	New England
143				Indianapolis	at	Cleveland
144	Sat.	Nov.	29	Quebec	at	Phoenix
145				Calgary	at	San Diego
146				Toronto	at	Cincinnati
147				Indianapolis	at	New England
148	Sun.	Nov.	30	Denver	at	Indianapolis
149				Minnesota	at	Winnipeg
150				Quebec	at	Phoenix
151				Calgary	at	Edmonton
152				Toronto	at	Cleveland
153				San Diego	at	Houston
154	Tues.	Dec.	2	New England	at	Houston
155				Winnipeg	at	Denver
156				Cleveland	at	Quebec
157				Toronto	at	Edmonton

158	Wed.	Dec.	3	Cincinnati	at	Cleveland
159				Toronto	at	Calgary
160	Thurs.	Dec.	4	New England	at	Phoenix
161				Winnipeg	at	San Diego
162				Cincinnati	at	Indianapolis
163	Fri.	Dec.	5	Denver	at	Minnesota
164				Winnipeg	at	Houston
165				Edmonton	at	Calgary
166				Quebec	at	Toronto
167	Sat.	Dec.	6	Houston	at	Phoenix
168				New England	at	San Diego
169				Denver	at	Cincinnati
170				Cleveland	at	Indianapolis
171	Sun.	Dec.	7	New England	at	Denver
172				Cleveland	at	Cincinnati
173				Calgary	at	Edmonton
174				Quebec	at	Winnipeg
175	Tues.	Dec.	9	Minnesota	at	Toronto
176				Cleveland	at	Denver
177				Quebec	at	Calgary
178				Cincinnati	at	Houston
179	Wed.	Dec.	10	Minnesota	at	New England
180				Indianapolis	at	Phoenix
181				Toronto	at	Winnipeg
182				Quebec	at	Edmonton
183	Thurs.	Dec.	11	Indianapolis	at	San Diego
184				Edmonton	at	Calgary
185	Fri.	Dec.	12	Minnesota	at	Cleveland
186				Indianapolis	at	Houston
187				Cincinnati	at	Phoenix
188				Calgary	at	Winnipeg
189				Quebec	at	Toronto
190	Sat.	Dec.	13	Houston	at	Minnesota
191				Phoenix	at	Denver
192				Cincinnati	at	San Diego
193				Cleveland	at	New England
194				Toronto	at	Quebec
195	Sun.	Dec.	14	Houston	at	Cleveland
196				San Diego	at	Phoenix
197				New England	at	Indianapolis
198				Calgary	at	Toronto
199				Winnipeg	at	Edmonton
200	Tues.	Dec.	16	San Diego	at	Houston
201				Cincinnati	at	Denver
202				Edmonton	at	Indianapolis
203				Calgary	at	Quebec
204				Winnipeg	at	Toronto
205	Wed.	Dec.	17	New England	at	Minnesota
206				Edmonton	at	Cleveland
207	Thurs.	Dec.	18	Indianapolis	at	Phoenix
208				Cincinnati	at	San Diego
209				Winnipeg	at	Quebec
210	Fri.	Dec.	19	Cleveland	at	Indianapolis
211				Edmonton	at	New England
212				Calgary	at	Toronto
213				San Diego	at	Denver

214	Sat.	Dec.	20	Winnipeg	at	Minnesota
215				Houston	at	Phoenix
216				Indianapolis	at	Cleveland
217				New England	at	Cincinnati
218				Calgary	at	Quebec
219	Sun.	Dec.	21	Minnesota	at	Winnipeg
220				Houston	at	San Diego
221				Phoenix	at	Indianapolis
222				*Quebec	at	Cincinnati
223				Toronto	at	Edmonton
224	Mon.	Dec.	22	New England	at	Cleveland
225	Tues.	Dec.	23	Minnesota	at	Denver
226				Phoenix	at	Cincinnati
227				Quebec	at	San Diego
228				Toronto	at	Calgary
229				Winnipeg	at	Edmonton
230	Fri.	Dec.	26	Denver	at	Houston
231				Cincinnati	at	New England
232				Calgary	at	Winnipeg
233				Edmonton	at	Toronto
234				Phoenix	at	San Diego
235	Sat.	Dec.	27	Minnesota	at	Houston
236				Denver	at	Phoenix
237				Cincinnati	at	Indianapolis
238				Toronto	at	Cleveland
239				Edmonton	at	Quebec
240	Sun.	Dec.	28	San Diego	at	Minnesota
241				Phoenix	at	Denver
242				Indianapolis	at	Cincinnati
243				Cleveland	at	New England
244				Winnipeg	at	Calgary
245				Quebec	at	Toronto
246	Tues.	Dec.	30	Quebec	at	Minnesota
247				San Diego	at	New England
248				Indianapolis	at	Denver
249				Edmonton	at	Toronto
250				Winnipeg	at	Houston

1976

251	Thurs.	Jan.	1	Edmonton	at	Calgary
252	Fri.	Jan.	2	San Diego	at	Indianapolis
253				Denver	at	Cincinnati
254				Quebec	at	Cleveland
255				Calgary	at	Edmonton
256				Phoenix	at	Toronto
257	Sat.	Jan.	3	Indianapolis	at	Minnesota
258				San Diego	at	Cincinnati
259				Cleveland	at	New England
260				Winnipeg	at	Calgary
261				Phoenix	at	Quebec
262				Denver	at	Houston
263	Sun.	Jan.	4	New England	at	Indianapolis
264				Phoenix	at	Cleveland
265				Winnipeg	at	Edmonton
266				Denver	at	Minnesota
267	Tues.	Jan.	6	Indianapolis	at	Edmonton
268				Cincinnati	at	Houston

*—Denotes afternoon game.

269				New England	at	Denver
270				Winnipeg	at	Calgary
271				San Diego	at	Toronto
272	Wed.	Jan.	7	San Diego	at	Cleveland
273				Toronto	at	Winnipeg
274				Phoenix	at	Minnesota
275	Thurs.	Jan.	8	Indianapolis	at	Calgary
276				Cincinnati	at	Phoenix
277				New England	at	Denver
278	Fri.	Jan.	9	Indianapolis	at	Winnipeg
279				Cleveland	at	Houston
280				San Diego	at	New England
281				Toronto	at	Edmonton
282	Sat.	Jan.	10	San Diego	at	Quebec
283				Houston	at	Minnesota
284				Denver	at	Phoenix
285	Sun.	Jan.	11	*Indianapolis	at	Cleveland
286				Minnesota	at	Cincinnati
287				San Diego	at	New England
288				*Calgary	at	Toronto
289				Denver	at	Winnipeg
290				Houston	at	Edmonton

ALL STAR GAME Tues., Jan. 13 Cleveland Coliseum

291	Wed.	Jan.	14	Houston	at	Winnipeg
292	Thurs.	Jan.	15	Cleveland	at	Indianapolis
293				Cincinnati	at	New England
294				Calgary	at	Quebec
295				Minnesota	at	San Diego
296	Fri.	Jan.	16	New England	at	Cleveland
297				Edmonton	at	Winnipeg
298				Minnestoa	at	Phoenix
299				Houston	at	Denver
300	Sat.	Jan.	17	Cincinnati	at	Indianapolis
301				Houston	at	Calgary
302				Toronto	at	Quebec
303				Minnestoa	at	Phoenix
304				Denver	at	San Diego
305	Sun.	Jan.	18	New England	at	Winnipeg
306	Tues.	Jan.	20	Indianapolis	at	Quebec
307				New England	at	Phoenix
308				Toronto	at	Houston
309				Denver	at	Edmonton
310	Wed.	Jan.	21	Cleveland	at	Cincinnati
311				New England	at	Houston
312				Calgary	at	Winnipeg
313				San Diego	at	Minnesota
314	Thurs.	Jan.	22	Calgary	at	Denver
315				Toronto	at	Phoenix
316	Fri.	Jan.	23	Denver	at	Indianapolis
317				New England	at	Cleveland
318				Calgary	at	Houston
319				Edmonton	at	Winnipeg
320				San Diego	at	Minnesota

*—Denotes afternoon game.

321	Sat.	Jan.	24	New England	at	Cincinnati
322				Toronto	at	San Diego
323				Phoenix	at	Denver
324	Sun.	Jan.	25	*Cleveland	at	Indianapolis
325				*Calgary	at	Houston
326				Edmonton	at	Quebec
327				Toronto	at	Minnestoa
328				San Diego	at	Phoenix
329	Tues.	Jan.	27	Cincinnati	at	Quebec
330				Edmonton	at	Toronto
331				Phoenix	at	San Diego
332	Wed.	Jan	28	Cleveland	at	Cincinnati
333				Denver	at	New England
334				Calgary	at	Phoenix
335				Winnipeg	at	Minnesota
336				Houston	at	Edmonton
337	Thurs.	Jan.	29	Minnesota	at	Indianapolis
338				Calgary	at	San Diego
339	Fri.	Jan.	30	Houston	at	Indianapolis
340				Cleveland	at	Phoenix
341				Winnipeg	at	New England
342				Denver	at	Toronto
343	Sat.	Jan.	31	Winnipeg	at	Cincinnati
344				Cleveland	at	San Diego
345				Denver	at	Quebec
346				Houston	at	Minnesota
347	Sun.	Feb.	1	*Winnipeg	at	Indianapolis
348				Cincinnati	at	Edmonton
349				*New England	at	Toronto
350				Cleveland	at	Minnesota
351	Tues.	Feb.	3	Cincinnati	at	Calgary
352				Winnipeg	at	Quebec
353				New England	at	Edmonton
354				Minnesota	at	Houston
355	Wed.	Feb.	4	Cleveland	at	Phoenix
356				Minnesota	at	San Diego
357	Thurs.	Feb.	5	New England	at	Calgary
358				Quebec	at	Indianapolis
359				Edmonton	at	Phoenix
360				Cleveland	at	San Diego
361				Minnesota	at	Denver
362	Fri.	Feb.	6	Winnipeg	at	Toronto
363				Edmonton	at	Cincinnati
364				Indianapolis	at	Houston
365	Sat.	Feb.	7	Quebec	at	Calgary
366				Winnipeg	at	Cleveland
367				Edmonton	at	Denver
368				Toronto	at	New England
369				Cincinnati	at	Indianapolis
370				Minnesota	at	Phoenix
371	Sun.	Feb.	8	Calgary	at	Winnipeg
372				Quebec	at	Edmonton
373				Cleveland	at	New England
374				San Diego	at	Houston
375				Minnesota	at	Phoenix

*—Denotes afternoon game.

376	Tues.	Feb. 10	Toronto	at	Calgary
377			Houston	at	Denver
378			San Diego	at	Minnesota
379	Wed.	Feb. 11	Quebec	at	Winnipeg
380			Cincinnati	at	Cleveland
381	Thurs.	Feb. 12	Quebec	at	Minnesota
382			Houston	at	Phoenix
383			Denver	at	San Diego
384	Fri.	Feb. 13	Calgary	at	Indianapolis
385			Quebec	at	Denver
386			Toronto	at	Edmonton
387			Cincinnati	at	New England
388	Sat.	Feb. 14	Indianapolis	at	Cincinnati
389			Houston	at	San Diego
390			Phoenix	at	Minnesota
391	Sun.	Feb. 15	Calgary	at	Cincinnati
392			Toronto	at	Winnipeg
393			Quebec	at	Houston
394			Phoenix	at	Edmonton
395			San Diego	at	Indianapolis
396			New England	at	Cleveland
397			*Denver	at	Minnesota
398	Tues.	Feb. 17	Winnipeg	at	Edmonton
399			San Diego	at	Quebec
400			Minnesota	at	Toronto
401			New England	at	Houston
402	Wed.	Feb. 18	Calgary	at	Cleveland
403			Phoenix	at	Winnipeg
404	Thurs.	Feb. 19	New England	at	Indianapolis
405			Cleveland	at	Houston
406	Fri.	Feb. 20	Minnesota	at	Calgary
407			Edmonton	at	Winnipeg
408			San Diego	at	Toronto
409			Phoenix	at	Cincinnati
410	Sat.	Feb. 21	Toronto	at	Denver
411			Indianapolis	at	Cleveland
412			San Diego	at	Cincinnati
413	Sun.	Feb. 22	Toronto	at	Calgary
414			New England	at	Quebec
415			Minnesota	at	Edmonton
416			*Phoenix	at	Indianapolis
417			*Houston	at	Cleveland
418	Tues.	Feb. 24	Calgary	at	Edmonton
419			Houston	at	Quebec
420			Cincinnati	at	Toronto
421			San Diego	at	Denver
422	Wed.	Feb. 25	Edmonton	at	Calgary
423			Cleveland	at	Winnipeg
424			New England	at	Cincinnati
425			San Diego	at	Minnesota
426	Thurs.	Feb. 26	Houston	at	New England
427			Phoenix	at	Denver
428	Fri.	Feb. 27	Cleveland	at	Calgary

*—Denotes afternoon game.

109

429				Edmonton	at	Winnipeg
430				Houston	at	Toronto
431				San Diego	at	Phoenix
432	Sat.	Feb.	28	Winnipeg	at	Quebec
433				Indianapolis	at	New England
434				Minnesota	at	Cincinnati
435				Denver	at	San Diego
436	Sun.	Feb.	29	Phoenix	at	Calgary
437				*Winnipeg	at	Toronto
438				Cleveland	at	Edmonton
439				Indianapolis	at	Cincinnati
440				Houston	at	Minnesota
441				San Diego	at	Denver
442	Tues.	Mar.	2	New England	at	San Diego
443				Indianapolis	at	Phoenix
444				Denver	at	Calgary
445				Quebec	at	Toronto
446	Wed.	Mar.	3	Houston	at	Minnesota
447				Cleveland	at	Cincinnati
448				Calgary	at	Edmonton
449	Thurs.	Mar.	4	New England	at	San Diego
450				Minnesota	at	Denver
451				Cincinnati	at	Indianapolis
452				Quebec	at	Calgary
453	Fri.	Mar.	5	Phoenix	at	Houston
454				Quebec	at	Edmonton
455	Sat.	Mar.	6	*Cleveland	at	Houston
456				New England	at	Phoenix
457				Minnesota	at	Denver
458				Indianapolis	at	Cincinnati
459	Sun.	Mar.	7	Denver	at	Cincinnati
460				Cleveland	at	Indianapolis
461				Calgary	at	Winnipeg
462				Quebec	at	Edmonton
463	Tues.	Mar.	9	Minnesota	at	Houston
464				Denver	at	Toronto
465				Quebec	at	Calgary
466	Wed.	Mar.	10	Phoenix	at	New England
467				Cincinnati	at	Minnesota
468				Denver	at	Cleveland
469				Quebec	at	Winnipeg
470	Thurs.	Mar.	11	Houston	at	San Diego
471				Toronto	at	Indianapolis
472				Edmonton	at	Calgary
473	Fri.	Mar.	12	Phoenix	at	Toronto
474				Indianapolis	at	Cincinnati
475				Cleveland	at	New England
476				Quebec	at	Winnipeg
477	Sat.	Mar.	13	Houston	at	San Diego
478				Phoenix	at	Indianapolis
479				Calgary	at	Minnesota
480				New England	at	Cincinnati
481	Sun.	Mar.	14	San Diego	at	Winnipeg
482				Phoenix	at	Cleveland

*—Denotes afternoon game.

483				Indianapolis	at	Denver
484				Toronto	at	Quebec
485	Tues.	Mar.	16	Minnesota	at	Quebec
486				Cleveland	at	Toronto
487				Calgary	at	Edmonton
488	Wed.	Mar.	17	Houston	at	Phoenix
489				Minnesota	at	New England
490				Toronto	at	Cincinnati
491				Calgary	at	Winnipeg
492	Thurs.	Mar.	18	San Diego	at	Indianapolis
493	Fri.	Mar.	19	San Diego	at	Houston
494				Denver	at	Phoenix
495				Cincinnati	at	New England
496				Winnipeg	at	Edmonton
497				Quebec	at	Toronto
498	Sat.	Mar.	20	Houston	at	Cincinnati
499				Denver	at	San Diego
500				Minnesota	at	Cleveland
501				Indianapolis	at	New England
502				Calgary	at	Quebec
503	Sun.	Mar.	21	Phoenix	at	Houston
504				Denver	at	Edmonton
505				*Cincinnati	at	Cleveland
506				New England	at	Minnesota
507				*Winnipeg	at	Toronto
508	Tues.	Mar.	23	Indianapolis	at	San Diego
509				Cleveland	at	Quebec
510				Calgary	at	Toronto
511	Wed.	Mar.	24	Cincinnati	at	Phoenix
512				Indianapolis	at	Minnesota
513				Denver	at	Cleveland
514				Edmonton	at	Winnipeg
515				Calgary	at	New England
516	Thurs.	Mar.	25	Cincinnati	at	San Diego
517				Denver	at	Quebec
518				Minnesota	at	Indianapolis
519	Fri.	Mar.	26	Cincinnati	at	Houston
520				San Diego	at	Phoenix
521				Indianapolis	at	Cleveland
522				Denver	at	New England
523				Edmonton	at	Toronto
524	Sat.	Mar.	27	Phoenix	at	San Diego
525				Cleveland	at	Minnesota
526				Calgary	at	Quebec
527	Sun.	Mar.	28	Phoenix	at	Houston
528				San Diego	at	Winnipeg
529				*Edmonton	at	Minnesota
530				Cincinnati	at	Denver
531				Indianapolis	at	New England
532				*Calgary	at	Toronto
533	Tues.	Mar.	30	Denver	at	Houston
534				Toronto	at	Calgary
535				Edmonton	at	Quebec
536				Phoenix	at	Cincinnati

*—Denotes afternoon game.

537	Wed.	Mar.	31	Denver	at	Minnesota ....
538				New England	at	Cleveland ....
539				Toronto	at	Winnipeg ....
540	Thurs.	Apr.	1	Houston	at	Indianapolis ....
541				Minnesota	at	Denver ....
542				Edmonton	at	
543	Fri.	Apr.	2	Indianapolis	at	Toronto ....
544				Cleveland	at	Cincinnati ....
545				Winnipeg	at	Calgary ....
546	Sat.	Apr.	3	Houston	at	Denver ....
547				Minnesota	at	Phoenix ....
548				New England	at	Indianapolis ....
549				Toronto	at	Quebec ....
550				San Diego	at	Cleveland ....
551	Sun.	Apr.	4	Denver	at	Houston ....
552				Phoenix	at	Minnesota ....
553				Indianapolis	at	New England ....
554				*Cincinnati	at	Cleveland ....
555				Winnipeg	at	Edmonton ....
556				*Quebec	at	Toronto ....
557	Tues.	Apr.	6	Winnipeg	at	Calgary ....
558				Toronto	at	Quebec ....
559				San Diego	at	Cleveland ....
560				Phoenix	at	Houston ....

*—Denotes afternoon game.

WHA STARTING TIMES (All times local)

CALGARY (Mountain Time)
P.M.
Sunday Nights 7:05
Week Nights 8:05

CINCINNATI (Eastern Time)
Sunday, Dec. 21 .... 5:30
Sunday Nights 7:05
Week Nights 7:35

CLEVELAND (Eastern Time)
Sundays: Jan. 11, Feb. 22,
Mar. 21, Apr. 4 .... 2:00
Sunday Nights 7:30
Week Nights 7:30

DENVER (Mountain Time)
Sundays: Feb. 29, Mar. 28 .... 4:00
Sunday Nights 7:35
Week Nights 7:35

EDMONTON (Mountain Time)
Sunday Nights 7:30
Week Nights 8:00

HOUSTON (Central Time)
Sunday, Jan. 25; Sat., Mar. 6 .... 2:00
Week Nights 7:30

INDIANAPOLIS (Eastern Time)
Sundays: Jan. 25, Feb. 1, Feb. 22 2:00
Sunday Nights 7:00
Week Nights 8:00

MINNESOTA (Central Time)
Sundays: Feb. 15, Mar. 28 .... 2:00
Saturdays Nights 8:00
Sunday Nights 7:30
Week Nights 7:30

NEW ENGLAND (Eastern Time)
All Games 7:30

PHOENIX (Mountain Time)
Sundays 4:00
Week Nights 8:00

QUEBEC (Eastern Time)
Sunday Afternoons 2:05
Week Nights 8:05

SAN DIEGO (Pacific Time)
All Games 7:30

TORONTO (Eastern Time)
Sunday Nights: Dec. 14, Dec. 28 . 7:30
Sunday Afternoons 2:00
Week Nights 8:00

WINNIPEG (Central Time)
Tuesday, Nov. 11; Fri., Dec. 26 ... 7:30
Sunday Nights 7:30
Week Nights 8:00

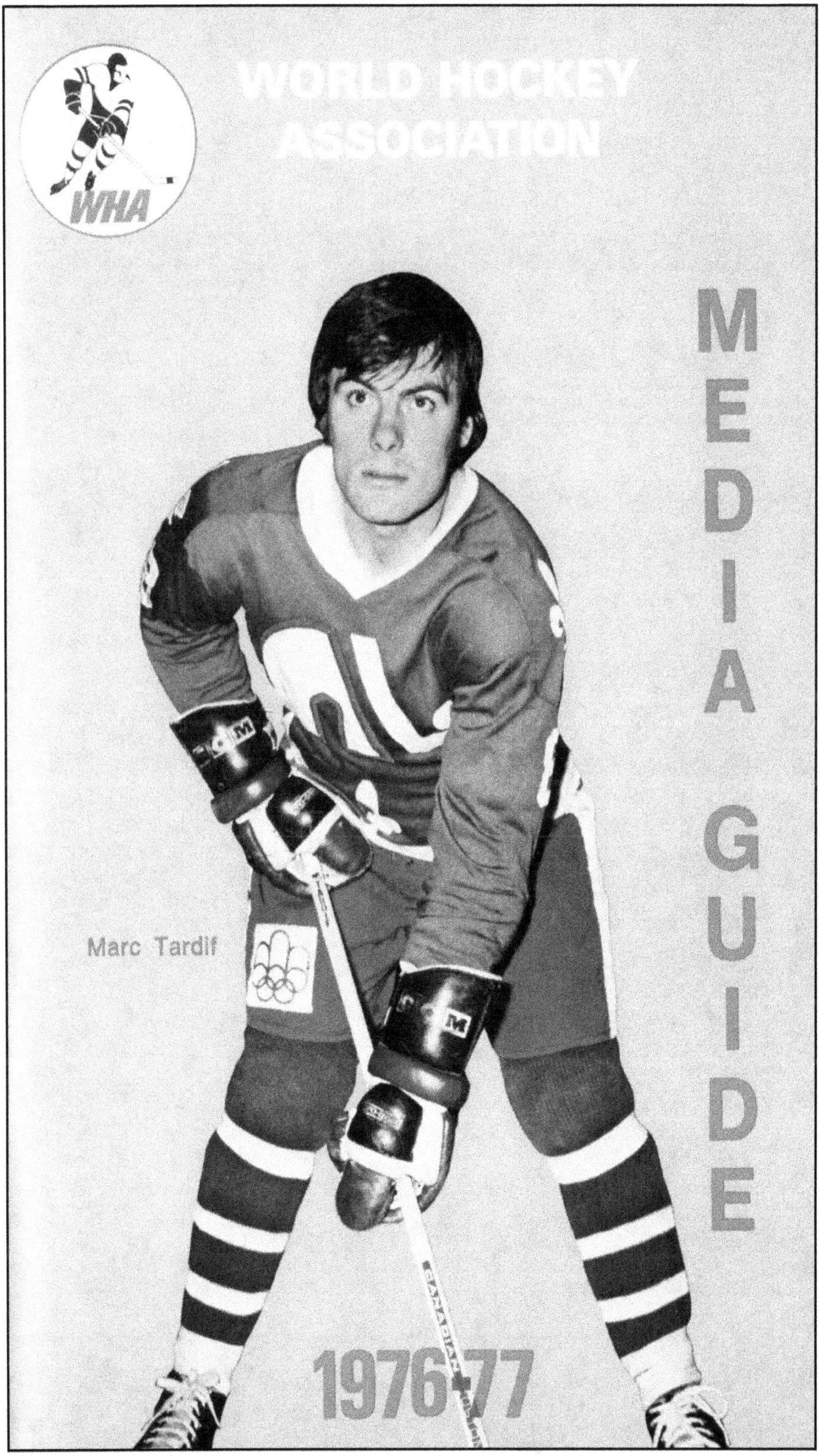

WORLD HOCKEY ASSOCIATION

Marc Tardif

MEDIA GUIDE

1976-77

5TH SEASON

1976-77

MEDIA GUIDE

EXECUTIVE EDITOR
LEO ORNEST

STATISTICIAN
FRANK POLNASZEK

CONTENTS

Chief Executive Officer/Trustees	2
President	3
WHA Directory	4
Avco Trophy/O'Keefe Cup	5
Birmingham Bulls	6-7
Calgary Cowboys	8-9
Cincinnati Stingers	10-11
Edmonton Oilers	12-13
Houston Aeros	14-15
Indianapolis Racers	16-17
Minnesota Fighting Saints	18-19
New England Whalers	20-21
Phoenix Roadrunners	22-23
Quebec Nordiques	24-25
San Diego Mariners	26-27
Winnipeg Jets	28-29
Hall-of-Fame	30-21
WHA Referees/Linesmen	32
WHA Minor Game Officials	32-33
The Avco World Trophy Winners	34
Trophy/Award Winners	35
All-Star Teams	36
All-Star Games/Results	37-38
History of League	39-43
League Season Attendance	43
Team Records	44-50
Single Game Records	51-55
Penalty Records	55
Major League Records	56-57
WHA Career Leaders	58-59
Hat Tricks	60
Lifetime Team Totals	61-67
1975-76 Statistics	68-80
Goaltenders Records, 1975-76	81-82
Overtime Games	83
Power Play Statistics	84-85
Penalty Shots	85
Player Transactions	86
WHA Playoffs/Results	87-90
Penalty Leaders	90
Travelog	91
Team Playoff Records	92-95
Individual Playoff Records	95-97
Media/Airlines	98-101
The Differences	101
Arena Seating Capacities	101
League Schedule, 1976-77	102-112
International Series	112
Starting Times	112

THE COVER:

Marc Tardif, Quebec Nordiques, WHA's Most Valuable Player, leading scorer and all-star left wing, 1975-76. Tardif had 148 points on 71 goals and 77 assists.

PRINTED IN CANADA — ALL RIGHTS RESERVED — WORLD HOCKEY ASSOCIATION

BEN HATSKIN
Chairman of the Board / Chief Executive Officer
1328 Richardson Bldg.
One Lombard Place
Winnipeg, Canada R3B 0X3

Secretary: Rosemary De Laronde

TRUSTEES

Birmingham	John F. Bassett, Jr.
Calgary	William Sleeman
Cincinnati	William O. DeWitt, Jr.
Edmonton	Mitch Klimove
Houston	George R. Bolin
Indianapolis	Harold A. Ducote, Jr.
Minnesota	Nick J. Mileti
New England	Howard L. Baldwin
Phoenix	Karl Eller
Quebec	John Dacres
San Diego	Ballard F. Smith
Winnipeg	Oscar Grubert

ORGANIZED JUNE 10, 1971

WILLIAM H. MacFARLAND
President
Chief Operating Officer
415 Yonge Street
Suite 1611
Toronto, Canada M5B 2E7

MEMBER CLUBS

DIRECTORY
WORLD HOCKEY ASSOCIATION

LEAGUE OFFICES
415 Yonge Street
Suite 1611
Toronto, Ontario, Canada M5B 2E7
Phone: (416) 366-4281
Telex: 06-22695

Executive Vice-President/Marketing
LARRY GORDON

Vice-President
HOWARD BALDWIN

Secretary/Legal Counsel
A. J. MERCURY

Controller
JOHN GRAY

Communications
LEO ORNEST

Chief Statistician
FRANK POLNASZEK

Public Relations
GARY CLARK

Chief-of-Officials
BOB FRAMPTON

Referee-in-Chief
BILL FRIDAY

Larry Gordon

Howard Baldwin

A. J. Mercury

John Gray

Leo Ornest

Frank Polnaszek

Gary Clark

Bob Frampton

Bill Friday

Winnipeg Jets first Canadian team to win the World Hockey Association Championship and The Avco World Trophy. Shown holding The Avco World Trophy are, left to right: Ben Hatskin, Chairman of the Board and Chief Executive Officer of the WHA; and from the Winnipeg Jets, R. G. (Bob) Graham, President; Lars-Erik Sjoberg, Captain; and Bobby Kromm, Coach.

Winnipeg Jets win The O'Keefe Cup. Awarded to the Canadian champions of the WHA. Ben Hatskin, Chairman of the Board and Chief Executive Officer of the World Hockey Association, and Wendell Waddell, General Manager Carling O'Keefe Breweries, Manitoba, present The O'Keefe Cup to Lars-Erik Sjoberg, Captain of the Winnipeg Jets. Julian Klymkiw, Sales Promotion Manager Carling O'Keefe Breweries, Manitoba, holds the plaque which was presented to each member of the Winnipeg Jets.

BIRMINGHAM BULLS 1976-77 ROSTER

No.	FORWARDS	S	Ht.	Wt.	Birthplace	Date	1975-76 Club	Lea.	GP	G	A	PTS	PIM
16	D'Alvise, Bob	L	5-11	170	Etobicoke, Ont.	12-23-52	Buffalo	NAHL	19	13	15	28	2
8	Farda, Richard	L	5-9	175	Brno, Czech.	11-8-45	Toronto	WHA	59	5	8	13	10
18	Gorman, Dave	R	5-11	180	Oshawa, Ont.	4-8-55	Toronto	WHA	63	19	35	54	8
19	Henderson, Paul	R	5-11	180	Kincardine, Ont.	1-28-43	Phoenix	WHA	67	11	20	31	28
25	Jacques, Jeff	R	5-11	190	Preston, Ont.	4-4-53	Toronto	WHA	65	26	29	55	22
11	Kirk, Gavin	L	5-10	175	London, Eng.	12-6-51	Toronto	WHA	81	17	33	50	113
27	Mahovlich, Frank	L	6-1	205	Timmins, Ont.	1-10-38	Tor/Cgy	WHA	77	35	46	81	46
20	Marrin, Peter	R	5-10	160	Toronto, Ont.	8-8-53	Toronto	WHA	75	34	55	89	14
9	Napier, Mark	L	5-10	182	Toronto, Ont.	1-28-57	Toronto	WHA	64	22	16	38	16
14	Nedomansky, Vaclav	L	6-1	210	Hodonin, Czech.	3-14-44	Toronto	WHA	78	43	50	93	20
15	Nistico, Lou	L	5-7	170	Thunder Bay, Ont.	1-25-53	Buffalo	NAHL	81	56	42	98	8
							Toronto	WHA	10	9	5	14	49
28	Phaneuf, Jean-Luc	R	5-8	160	Montreal, Que.	10-26-55	Buffalo	NAHL	65	12	22	34	120
							Toronto	WHA	2	0	1	1	0
							Toronto	WHA	48	8	8	16	4
12	Simpson, Tom	R	5-9	190	Bowmanville, Ont.	8-15-52	Toronto	WHA	73	20	21	41	15
DEFENSEMEN													
21	Ball, Terry	R	5-9	165	Selkirk, Man.	11-29-44	Clev/Cinn	WHA	59	5	29	34	30
3	Cunningham, Rick	R	5-11	185	Toronto, Ont.	3-3-51	Buffalo	NAHL	1	1	0	1	2
							Toronto	WHA	36	5	14	19	57
22	Heaver, Paul	R	6-1	190	London, Eng.	2-15-55	Toronto	WHA	66	2	12	14	83
							Buffalo	NAHL	11	2	5	7	21
33	Hoganson, Dale	L	5-10	190	N. Battleford, Sask.	7-8-49	Quebec	WHA	45	3	14	17	18
26	Lagace, Jean-Guy	R	5-8	175	L'Abord-A-Plouffe, Que.	2-5-45	Kansas City	NHL	69	3	10	13	108
10	Syvret, Dave	L	6-0	190	Hamilton, Ont.	10-28-54	Buffalo	NAHL	33	3	26	29	40
							Toronto	WHA	30	1	11	12	14
2	Turkiewicz, Jim	L	5-10	185	Hamilton, Ont.	4-13-55	Toronto	WHA	77	10	30	40	55
GOALTENDERS									GP	MIN	GA	SO	GAA
35	Garrett, John	L	5-9	170	Toronto, Ont.	5-17-51	Minn/Tor	WHA	61	3730	210	3	3.38
1	Wood, Wayne	L	6-1	190	Toronto, Ont.	6-5-51	Cgy/Tor	WHA	32	1661	107	1	3.87

Birmingham

ALABAMA HOCKEY
Birmingham Bulls
One Civic Center Plaza
Birmingham, Ala. 35203

(205) 251-2855
Telex 59-747

John F. Bassett

President/Trustee	JOHN F. BASSETT, JR.
Executive Vice-President	PETER McASKILE
Comptroller	JAMES C. BRASHER
General Manager/Coach	GILLES LEGER
Director of Public Relations	JIM FINKS, JR.
Program and Souveniers	WAYNE GRUBB
Ticket Manager	BOB LOCHAMY
Trainers	FRANK VANDERHART LARRY ASHLEY
Medical Staff	DR. DON AUTREY DR. LOUIS LEMACK DR. GORDON ROBINSON
Team Dentist	DR. GORDON MOXLEY
Franchise Granted	FEBRUARY, 1972 (Ottawa Nationals) MAY, 1973 Toronto Toros
Radio	WAPI — 94.5 FM — all games GARY SANDERS
Television	PENDING
Team Colors	BLUE, WHITE, RED
Training Camp	BIRMINGHAM
Ticket Prices	$8/6.50/5
Game Times	SUN.-THUR. 7:30 P.M. FRI. & SAT. 8:00 P.M. SUN., JAN. 23 2:00 P.M. SUN., MAR. 20 2:00 P.M.

Gilles Leger

JEFFERSON COUNTY CIVIC CENTER:
Opened September 21, 1976. Bulls defeated Atlanta (N.H.L.), 7-6, overtime. $68 million complex, arena $28 million. Ice surface 200 x 85. Capacity 16,759.

7

CALGARY COWBOYS 1976-77 ROSTER

No.	FORWARDS	S	Ht.	Wt.	Birthplace	Date	1975-76 Club	Lea.	GP	G	A	PTS	PIM
7	Chipperfield, Ron	R	5-11	180	Brandon, Man.	3-28-54	Calgary	WHA	75	42	41	83	32
12	Connelly, Wayne	R	5-10	175	Rouyn, Que.	12-16-39	Minn/Clev	WHA	71	29	25	54	23
24	Driscoll, Peter	L	6-0	190	Kingston, Ont.	10-27-54	Calgary	WHA	75	16	18	34	127
18	Jodzio, Rick	L	6-1	185	Edmonton, Alta.	6-3-54	Springfield	AHL	24	2	3	5	37
							Calgary	WHA	47	10	7	17	137
11	Lawson, Danny	R	5-11	185	Toronto, Ont.	10-30-47	Calgary	WHA	80	44	52	96	46
15	Lemieux, Richard	L	5-8	165	Temiscamingue, Que.	4-19-51	KC/Atl	NHL	3	0	1	1	0
							Nova Scotia	AHL	60	25	23	48	37
17	Miller, Warren*	R	5-10	170	St. Paul, Minn.		U. of Minn	WCHA	44	26	31	57	52
							Calgary	WHA	3	0	0	0	0
9	Morrison, George	L	6-1	175	Toronto, Ont.	12-24-48	Calgary	WHA	79	25	32	57	13
10	Powis, Lynn	L	6-0	185	Saskatoon, Sask.	4-19-49	Providence	AHL	52	39	31	61	54
							Calgary	WHA	21	4	10	14	2
16	St. Sauveur, Claude	L	6-0	170	Sherbrooke, Que.	1-2-52	Atlanta	NHL	79	24	24	48	23
8	Sentes, Rick	L	5-11	180	Regina, Sask.	1-10-47	Calgary	WHA	72	25	24	49	33
5	Tannahill, Don	L	5-11	178	Penetang, Ont.	2-21-49	Calgary	WHA	78	25	24	49	10
DEFENSEMEN													
4	Evans, Chris	L	5-9	181	Toronto, Ont.	9-14-46	Calgary	WHA	75	3	20	23	50
3	Ford, Mike	R	6-1	180	Ottawa, Ont.	7-26-52	Winnipeg	WHA	81	13	43	56	70
6	Hurley, Paul*	R	5-11	180	Melrose, Mass.	7-12-46	NE/Edm	WHA	42	1	18	19	34
23	Miszuk, John	L	6-2	200	Naliboki, Poland	9-29-40	Calgary	WHA	69	2	21	23	66
2	Pesut, George	L	6-1	185	Saskatoon, Sask.	6-17-53	Salt Lake	CHL	7	2	0	2	10
							California	NHL	45	3	9	12	57
21	Terbenche, Paul	L	5-10	170	Port Hope, Ont.	9-16-45	Calgary	WHA	58	2	14	16	22
GOALTENDERS									GP	MIN	GA	SO	GAA
29	Bromley, Gary	L	5-10	160	Edmonton, Alta.	1-19-50	Buffalo	NHL	1	60	7	0	7.00
							Providence	AHL	7	405	30	0	4.44
1	McLeod, Don	L	6-1	190	Trail, B.C.	8-24-46	Calgary	WHA	63	3534	207	1	3.51

* American Born

Calgary

CALGARY COWBOYS
Calgary Cowboys Hockey Team, Ltd.
1418 Macleod Trail S.E.
Calgary, Alberta T2G 2N5   (403) 261-6990
                                   Telex: 03-821-667

President	BILL HAY
Trustee	BILL SLEEMAN
Alternate Trustee	JOE KRYCZKA
General Manager/Coach	JOE CROZIER
Vice-President/Administration	ED PYRIK
Marketing Director	DON LeROSE
Controller	COLIN CATLEY
Equipment Manager/Trainer	JIM MURRAY
Chief Scout	AL MILLAR
Scouting Staff	HAL SCHOOLEY WARREN STRELOW
Franchise Granted	JUNE, 1972 (originally Philadelphia)
Radio	CFAC — 960 AM — all games ERIC BISHOP
Television	CFAC — Ch. 2; CABLE 7
Team Colors	RED, WHITE
Training Camp	CALGARY
Ticket Prices	$9/7/6/5
Game Times	SUN. 7:00 P.M. WEEK NIGHTS 8:00 P.M. SUN., DEC. 26 2:00 P.M. SAT., JAN. 1 2:00 P.M.

Bill Hay

Bill Sleeman

Joe Crozier

STAMPEDE CORRAL:
Opened December 26, 1950. Built at cost of $5 million. Seats: 6,445 plus 1,500 standing room. Capacity 7,945. Ice Surface 200 x 80.

CINCINNATI STINGERS 1976-77 ROSTER

No.	FORWARDS	S	Ht.	Wt.	Birthplace	Date	1975-76 Club	Lea.	GP	G	A	PTS	PIM
15	Abgrall, Dennis	R	6-0	180	Mooseomin, Sask.	4-24-53	Ft. Worth	CHL	64	21	36	57	37
26	Carroll, Gregg	L	6-1	185	Edmonton, Alta.	11-12-56	Los Angeles	NHL	14	0	2	2	4
9	Dudley, Rick	L	6-0	190	Toronto, Ont.	1-31-49	Medicine Hat	WCHL	64	60	112	172	156
13	Guite, Pierre	L	6-2	190	Montreal, Que.	4-17-52	Cincinnati	WHA	74	43	38	81	80
24	Hislop, Jamie	R	5-10	180	Sarnia, Ont.	1-20-54	U. New Hamp	ECAC	52	20	24	44	
8	Larose, Claude	L	5-10	175	St. Jean, Que.	5-17-55	Cincinnati	WHA	31	23	43	66	15
25	Leduc, Richard	L	5-11	170	Ile Perrot, Que.	8-24-51	Cleveland	WHA	79	28	24	52	76
11	Locas, Jacques	L	5-9	175	St. Jerome, Que.	1-8-54	Cincinnati	WHA	79	36	22	58	70
18	Marsh, Peter	L	6-1	180	Halifax, N.S.	12-21-56	Sherbrooke	QJHL	80	27	46	73	102
14	Sobchuk, Dennis	L	6-2	180	Lang, Sask.	1-12-54	Cincinnati	WHA	69	75	81	156	74
22	Sobchuk, Gene	L	5-9	170	Lang, Sask.	1-2-51	Cincinnati	WHA	77	32	40	72	39
12	Steele, Billy	R	5-9	165	Edinburgh, Scotland	11-13-52	Tidewater	SHL	78	24	19	43	81
							Buffalo	NAHL	65	33	29	62	4
17	Stoughton, Blaine	R	5-10	185	Gilbert Plains, Man.	3-13-53	Toronto	NHL	10	7	8	15	8
							Okla City	CHL	43	6	11	17	24
	DEFENSEMEN								30	14	22	36	
10	Hughes, John	L	5-11	200	Charlottetown, PEI	3-18-53	Cincinnati	WHA	79	3	34	37	204
5	Inkpen, Dave	R	6-0	185	Edmonton, Alta.	9-4-54	Cincinnati	WHA	80	4	24	28	95
21	Legge, Barry	L	6-0	187	Winnipeg, Man.	10-22-54	Den/Clev	WHA	75	6	15	21	37
6	Maxwell, Bryan	L	6-3	210	Lethbridge, Alta.	9-7-55	Cleveland	WHA	73	3	14	17	177
23	Ouimet, Francois	L	5-10	175	Montreal, Que.	10-14-51	Minnesota	NAHL	9	0	2	2	73
							Johnstown	NAHL	58	7	50	57	
2	Plumb, Ron	R	5-10	175	Kingston, Ont.	7-17-50	Cincinnati	WHA	80	10	36	46	31
	GOALTENDERS								GP	MIN	GA	SO	GAA
1	Hoganson, Paul		6-3	180	Toronto, Ont.	11-12-49	NE/Cinn	WHA	50	2616	161	2	3.69
30	LaPointe, Norm		6-1	180	Laval, Que.	8-13-55	Cincinnati	WHA	12	641	55	0	5.15
							Hampton	SHL	33	1917	86	0	2.69

* American Born

Cincinnati

CINCINNATI STINGERS
CINCINNATI HOCKEY CLUB CORP.
Riverfront Coliseum
Cincinnati, Ohio 45202   (513) 241-1818
                                Telex 214-286

Chairman of the Board	WILLIAM O. DeWITT
President	BRIAN E. HEEKIN
Executive Vice-President Chief Executive Officer/Trustee	WILLIAM O. DeWITT, JR.
Treasurer	ALBERT E. HEEKIN III
Secretary	LAWRENCE H. KYTE, JR.
Business Manager	DORI LOEPP
Coach	TERRENCE SLATER
Director Player Personnel	JERRY M. RAFTER

Brian Heekin

Directors
CHARLES L. HEEKIN   WILLIAM O. DeWITT
LAWRENCE H. KYTE, JR.   WILLIAM O. DeWITT, JR.
JAMES R. RAMMACHER   ALBERT E. HEEKIN, III
PHILIP S. SMITH   BRIAN E. HEEKIN

Bill DeWitt, Jr.

Publicity Director	JOHN A. HEWIG
Director of Group Sales	BILL HARBOUR
Ticket Manager	HENRY A. ROYER
Chief Scout	FLO POTVIN
Trainer	DON NIEDERKORN
Assistant Trainer	TIM RINGLER
Equipment Manager	ED ROTHSCHILD
Franchise Granted	MAY 6, 1973
Radio	WLW — 700 AM — all games ANDY MacWILLIAMS
Television	WLWT — Ch. 5 Cincinnati WLWD — Ch. 2 Dayton WLWC — Ch. 4 Columbus PHIL SAMP
Team Colors	STINGER YELLOW, BUMBLEBEE BLACK, WHITE
Training Camp	CINCINNATI
Ticket Prices	$8.25/7.25/5.25/3.25
Game Times	SUN. 7:05 P.M. WEEK NIGHTS 7:35 P.M. SUN., FEB. 13 2:05 P.M. SUN., MAR. 6 2:05 P.M. SUN., MAR. 13 2:05 P.M.

Terry Slater

RIVERFRONT COLISEUM:
Construction of $20 million facility started Nov. 12, 1973. First game Oct. 23, 1975, Stingers 6, Edmonton 4. Attendance 10,628. Theatre seats, air conditioned, 35 private boxes. Ice surface 200 by 85. Capacity 15,820.

EDMONTON OILERS 1976-77 ROSTER

No.	FORWARDS	S	Ht.	Wt.	Birthplace	Date	1975-76 Club	Lea.	GP	G	A	PTS	PIM
19	Beaton, Frank	L	5-11	170	Antigonish, N.S.	3-28-53	Cincinnati	WHA	29	2	3	5	61
							Hampton	SHL	45	17	14	31	276
21	Campbell, Bryan	L	6-0	175	Sudbury, Ont.	3-27-44	Cincinnati	WHA	77	22	50	72	24
20	Laframboise, Peter	L	6-2	185	Ottawa, Ont.	1-18-50	Hershey	AHL	69	18	47	65	88
11	Merrell, Barry	R	6-1	178	Dauphin, Man.	5-16-45	Rochester	AHL	70	28	41	69	20
22	Morris, Peter	L	5-8	165	Edmonton, Alta.	6-29-55	Edmonton	WHA	75	7	13	20	34
7	Morris, Rick	L	5-11	175	Hamilton, Ont.	7-5-46	Edmonton	WHA	74	20	21	41	110
8	Nevin, Bob	R	6-0	190	So. Porcupine, Ont.	3-18-38	Los Angeles	NHL	77	13	42	55	14
17	Patenaude, Rusty	R	5-9	175	Williams Lake, B.C.	10-17-49	Edmonton	WHA	78	42	30	72	86
25	Russell, Bob	L	5-9	167	Toronto, Ont.	2-5-55	Greensboro	SHL	19	11	9	20	4
							Edmonton	WHA	58	13	18	31	19
14	Sather, Glen	L	5-11	180	High River, Alta.	9-2-43	Minnesota	NHL	72	9	10	19	94
15	Sheehy, Tim	R	6-1	185	Ft. Frances, Ont.	9-3-48	Edmonton	WHA	81	34	31	65	17
9	Ullman, Norm	L	5-10	185	Provost, Alta.	12-26-35	Edmonton	WHA	78	31	56	87	12
12	Williams, Warren*	R	5-11	190	Duluth, Minn.	9-11-52	Salt Lake	CHL	56	31	42	73	155
	DEFENSEMEN												
5	Barrie, Doug	R	5-9	175	Edmonton, Alta.	10-2-46	Edmonton	WHA	79	4	21	25	81
3	Hamilton, Al	R	6-2	195	Flin Flon, Man.	8-20-46	Edmonton	WHA	54	2	32	34	78
4	Hornung, Larry	L	6-0	190	Weyburn, Sask.	11-10-45	Winnipeg	WHA	76	3	18	21	26
26	Langevin, Dave*	L	6-2	200	St. Paul, Minn.	5-15-54	U.of Minn.	WCHA	34	19	26	45	82
23	Patterson, Dennis	L	5-8	175	Peterborough, Ont.	1-9-50	Kansas City	NHL	69	5	16	21	28
6	Wilkins, Barry	L	6-0	190	Toronto, Ont.	2-28-47	Pittsburgh	NHL	75	0	27	27	106

No.	GOALTENDERS	S	Ht.	Wt.	Birthplace	Date	1975-76 Club	Lea.	GP	MIN	GA	SO	GAA
1	Broderick, Ken	R	5-11	175	Toronto, Ont.	2-16-42	Rochester	AHL	42	2541	136	2	3.21
28	Dryden, Dave	L	6-1	186	Hamilton, Ont.	9-5-41	Edmonton	WHA	62	3567	235	1	2.95

*American Born

12

Edmonton

EDMONTON OILERS
EDMONTON WORLD HOCKEY ENTERPRISES LTD.
EDMONTON COLISEUM
7424-118th Ave.,
Edmonton, Alta. T5B 4M9

(403) 474-8561
Telex 037-3595

Nelson Skalbania

President/Trustee	MITCH KLIMOVE
Secretary-Treasurer/Trustee	NELSON SKALBANIA
General Manager/Coach	ARMAND (BEP) GUIDOLIN
Assistant General Manager	GORDIE ROBSON
Directors	NELSON SKALBANIA PETER POCKLANGTON ZANE FELDMAN DR. A. C. ALLARD GORDIE ROBSON
Director Marketing/Public Relations	DOUG T. WENSCHLAG
Comptroller	IRENE HONSTEIN
Chief Scout	ROBERT FREEMAN
Trainer	JOHN BLACKWELL
Team Physicians	DR. JOHN HARVEY DR. ROBERT LEFEBRE
Team Dentist	DR. BRIAN NORD
Franchise Granted	NOVEMBER, 1971
Radio	CFRN — 1260 AM — all games ROD PHILLIPS/AL McCANN
Television	CITV — Ch. 13
Team Colors	ROYAL BLUE, ORANGE, WHITE
Training Camp	EDMONTON
Ticket Prices	$8/7/5/4
Game Times	SUN. 7:30 P.M. WEEK NIGHTS 8:00 P.M.

Mitch Klimove

Bep Guidolin

THE COLISEUM: Canada's newest indoor arena. Cost $15 million. Excavation summer 1973, opened Nov. 10, 1974. Ice surface 200 × 85. Capacity 15,273. No standing room.

HOUSTON AEROS 1976-77 ROSTER

No.	FORWARDS	S	Ht.	Wt.	Birthplace	Date	1975-76 Club	Lea.	GP	G	A	PTS	PIM
15	Connor, Cam	L	6-2	205	Winnipeg, Man.	8-10-54	Phoenix	WHA	73	18	21	39	295
16	Hinse, Andre	L	5-9	175	Three Rivers, Que.	4-19-45	Houston	WHA	70	35	39	74	6
9	Howe, Gordie	R	6-0	203	Floral, Sask.	3-31-28	Houston	WHA	78	32	70	102	72
4	Howe, Mark*	L	5-11	180	Detroit, Mich.	5-28-55	Houston	WHA	72	39	37	76	38
7	Hughes, Frank	R	5-10	195	Fernie, B.C.	1-10-49	Houston	WHA	80	32	45	77	26
27	Larway, Don	R	6-1	195	Oak Lake, Man.	2-12-54	Houston	WHA	80	30	20	50	45
12	Lukowich, Morris	L	5-9	170	Spears, Sask.	6-1-56	Medicine Hat	WCHL	72	65	77	142	195
13	Lund, Larry	R	6-0	190	Penticton, B.C.	9-9-40	Houston	WHA	73	24	39	73	50
21	Preston, Rich	R	6-0	185	Regina, Sask.	5-22-52	Houston	WHA	77	22	34	56	37
8	Ruskowski, Terry	L	5-9	170	Prince Albert, Sask.	12-31-54	Houston	WHA	65	14	35	49	95
14	Taylor, Ted	L	6-0	175	Oak Leaf, Man.	2-25-42	Houston	WHA	68	25	25	40	78
18	Tonelli, John	L	6-1	195	Hamilton, Ont.	3-23-57	Houston	WHA	78	17	15	32	68
	DEFENSEMEN												
17	Hale, Larry	L	6-1	180	Summerland, B.C.	10-9-41	Houston	WHA	77	1	14	15	32
3	Howe, Marty	L	6-1	185	Detroit, Mich.	2-18-54	Houston	WHA	79	14	23	37	81
24	Irwin, Glen	R	5-11	190	Edmonton, Alta.	3-1-51	Houston	WHA	72	3	8	11	116
6	Popiel, Poul	L	5-10	175	Sollested, Denmark	2-28-43	Houston	WHA	77	10	36	46	71
2	Schella, John	R	6-0	180	Port Arthur, Ont.	5-9-47	Houston	WHA	75	6	32	38	106

	GOALTENDERS	S	Ht.	Wt.	Birthplace	Date	1975-76 Club	Lea.	GP	MIN	GA	SO	GAA
29	Grahame, Ron		5-11	175	Victoria, B.C.	6-7-59	Houston	WHA	57	3343	182	3	3.27
30	Rutledge, Wayne		6-2	200	Barrie, Ont.	1-5-42	Houston	WHA	25	1456	77	1	3.16

* American Born

HOUSTON AEROS
Houston Aeros Hockey Club, Inc.
The Summit
10 Greenway Plaza
Houston, Texas 77046

(713) 629-5555
Telex 77-5520

Houston

George Bolin

Chairman of the Board/Trustee	GEORGE R. BOLIN
Chairman Executive Committee	WALTER W. FONDREN III
President/General Counsel	HARRISON VICKERS
Vice-President Hockey Operations/General Manager/Coach	BILL DINEEN
Vice-President Finance/Administration	ROBERT C. KELTIE
Assistant General Manager/Coach	JACK STANFIELD
Director of Sales	BRYAN WINDHAM
Director of Ticket Sales	KEMPER KAISER
Director Media Relations	RICH BURK
Trainer	BOBBY BROWN
Equipment Manager/Assistant Trainer	BOBBY KINCAID
Assistant Equipment Manager	BOB SKELTON
Team Physicians	STAFF, ST. LUKE'S METHODIST HOSPITAL
Team Dentist	DR. GENE CRABTREE
Franchise Granted	APRIL 15, 1972
Radio	KTRH — 740 AM — all games JERRY TRUPIANO/JACK STANFIELD
Television	KPRC — Ch. 2 JERRY TRUPIANO/JACK STANFIELD
Team Colors	NAVY BLUE, POWDER BLUE, WHITE
Training Camp	HOUSTON
Ticket Prices	$10/8/7/5/3
Game Times	ALL GAMES 7:35 P.M. SUN., MAR. 27 2:05 P.M.

Harrison Vickers

Bill Dineen

THE SUMMIT: 10 Greenway Plaza. Underground parking for 6,000 cars. Construction cost $18.1 million. Excavation January, 1974. First game Nov. 5, 1976, Aeros 6, Minnesota 4. Attendance 12,053. Ice surface 200 X 85. Capacity 15,256.

INDIANAPOLIS RACERS 1976-77 ROSTER

No.	FORWARDS	S	Ht.	Wt.	Birthplace	Date	1975-76 Club	Lea.	GP	G	A	PTS	PIM
10	Harbaruk, Nick	R	6-0	195	Drohiczyn, Poland	8-16-43	Indianapolis	WHA	75	23	19	42	26
7	Harris, Hugh	L	6-0	190	Toronto, Ont.	6-7-48	Cgy/Ind	WHA	70	17	37	54	42
15	Karlander, Al	L	5-8	175	Lac La Hache, B.C.	11-5-46	Indianapolis	WHA	76	16	28	44	36
8	Leclerc, Renald	R	5-11	170	Ville de Vanier, Que.	12-12-47	Que/Ind	WHA	82	33	38	71	87
25	Lomenda, Mark	R	6-0	186	Esterhazy, Sask.	4-14-54	Dvr/Ind	WHA	39	6	17	23	11
14	MacDonald, Blair	R	5-10	180	Cornwall, Ont.	11-17-53	Edm/Ind	WHA	85	26	16	42	22
11	McDonald, Brian	R	5-11	190	Toronto, Ont.	3-23-45	Mohawk Val	NAHL	10	5	9	14	17
							Indianapolis	WHA	63	16	17	33	58
6	Paiement, Rosaire	R	5-11	185	Earlton, Ont.	8-12-45	New England	WHA	80	28	43	71	89
16	Parizeau, Michel	L	5-10	165	Montreal, Que.	4-9-48	Que/Ind	WHA	75	25	42	67	44
22	Peacosh, Gene	L	5-11	180	Sherridon, Man.	9-28-48	San Diego	WHA	79	37	33	70	35
19	Rochon, Francois	L	5-11	181	Montreal, Que.	4-18-53	Dvr/Ind	WHA	59	17	12	29	41
9	Thomas, Reg	L	5-10	180	Lambeth, Que.	4-21-53	Indianapolis	WHA	80	23	17	40	23
23	Zuke, Mike	R	6-0	180	Sault Ste. Marie, Ont.	4-16-54	Mich Tech	WCHA	43	47	57	104	42
	DEFENSEMEN												
5	Baltimore, Bryon	L	6-2	190	Whitehorse, Yukon	8-26-52	Dvr/Ind	WHA	78	2	18	20	62
24	Block, Ken	L	5-10	185	Steinbach, Man.	3-18-44	Indianapolis	WHA	79	1	25	26	28
4	Clackson, Kim	R	5-11	195	Saskatoon, Sask.	2-13-55	Indianapolis	WHA	77	1	12	13	351
2	Maggs, Darryl	R	6-1	195	Victoria, B.C.	4-6-49	Dvr/Ind	WHA	78	9	39	48	82
3	Procéviat, Dick	L	6-0	180	Whitemouth, B.C.	6-25-46	Indianapolis	WHA	72	7	13	20	31
12	Stapleton, Pat	L	5-8	180	Sarnia, Ont.	7-4-40	Indianapolis	WHA	80	5	40	45	48

No.	GOALTENDERS	S	Ht.	Wt.	Birthplace	Date	1975-76 Club	Lea.	GP	MIN	GA	SO	GAA
1	Brown, Andy	L	6-0	185	Hamilton, Ont.	2-15-44	Indianapolis	WHA	24	1368	82	1	3.60
31	Dion, Michel	L	5-10	170	Granby, Que.	2-11-54	Mohawk Val	NAHL	22	1295	83	0	3.84
							Mohawk Val	NAHL	38	2245	164	0	4.38
28	Park, Jim	R	6-1	190	Toronto, Ont.	6-22-52	Indianapolis	WHA	11	578	23	0	2.41

Indianapolis

INDIANAPOLIS RACERS
Hockey Management Inc.
Market Square Center
151 N. Delaware St.
Indianapolis, Ind. 46204

(317) 635-3131
Telex 273-25

President/Trustee	HAROLD A. DUCOTE, JR.
Chairman	PAUL H. DENEAU
Vice-President	PER MOLLER
Secretary	JOHN L. EVANS
Treasurer	EDWARD (BUD) SULLIVAN
Coach/Dir. Player Personnel	JACQUES DEMERS
General Manager/Business Op.	BRIAN CONACHER
Director Public Relations	WALT MARLOW
Head Trainer	EDDIE SWISS
Assistant Trainer	MICHEL CAIRNS
Sales/Promotion Manager	JOHN L. SALTER
Ticket Manager	LARRY TAYLOR
Team Physicians	DR. JOSEPH RANDOLPH DR. WILLIAM IRVINE
Team Dentists	DR. TOM LAPP DR. DAVID PHILLIPS
Franchise Granted	SEPTEMBER 14, 1973
Radio	WIBC — 1070 AM — all games BOB LAMEY
Television	WTTV — Ch. 4 LEE HAMILTON
Team Colors	RED, WHITE, BLUE
Training Camp	CARMEL, IND.
Ticket Prices	$7.50/6/4
Game Times	SUN. 7:00 P.M. WEEK NIGHTS 8:00 P.M. SUN., JAN. 2 2:00 P.M. SUN., MAR. 20 3:00 P.M.

Jacques Demers

MARKET SQUARE ARENA:
Completed Sept. 14, 1974 at cost of $22 million. Ice surface (200 × 85) on third floor. Seats: 15,873. Capacity 16,040 with standing room.

MINNESOTA FIGHTING SAINTS 1976-77 ROSTER

No.	FORWARDS	S	Ht.	Wt.	Birthplace	Date	1975-76 Club	Lea.	GP	G	A	PTS	PIM
10	Adduono, Ray	L	5-9	170	Fort William, Ont.	1-21-47	San Diego	WHA	80	23	67	90	22
12	Antonovich, Mike*	L	5-8	165	Calumet, Minn.	10-18-51	Minnesota	NHL	12	0	2	2	8
							Minnesota	WHA	57	25	21	46	18
20	Carlson, Jack*	L	6-3	200	Virginia, Minn.	8-23-54	Minn/Edm	WHA	68	9	11	20	220
25	Carlson, Steve*	L	6-3	180	Virginia, Minn.	8-26-55	Johnstown	NAHL	40	22	24	46	55
							Minnesota	WHA	10	0	1	1	23
15	Deadmarsh, Butch	L	6-0	193	Trail, B.C.	4-5-50	Calgary	WHA	79	26	28	54	196
16	Gallant, Gord	L	5-11	175	Shediac, N.B.	10-27-50	Quebec	WHA	64	4	15	19	297
23	Gruen, Dan	L	5-11	175	Thunder Bay, Ont.	6-26-52	Cleveland	WHA	80	26	24	50	72
14	Keon, Dave	L	5-9	167	Noranda, Que.	3-22-40	Minn/Ind	WHA	69	29	46	75	6
26	McDonough, Al	R	6-0	170	St. Catharines, Ont.	6-6-50	Cleveland	WHA	80	23	22	45	19
19	McKenzie, John	R	5-7	175	High River, Alta.	12-12-37	Minn/Cinn	WHA	69	24	36	60	54
9	Patrick, Craig*	L	6-0	185	Detroit, Mich.	5-20-46	Kansas City	NHL	80	17	18	35	14
7	Stewart, John A.	L	6-0	182	Eriksdale, Man.	5-16-50	Cleveland	WHA	79	12	21	33	43
24	Ward, Ron	R	5-10	183	Cornwall, Ont.	9-12-44	Cleveland	WHA	75	32	50	82	24
	DEFENSEMEN												
17	Arbour, John	L	5-11	200	Niagara Falls, Ont.	9-28-45	Dvr/Minn	WHA	41	2	17	19	63
2	Butters, Bill	R	5-10	192	St. Paul, Minn.	1-10-51	Minn/Hou	WHA	73	0	19	19	188
5	Hanson, Dave*	R	6-0	193	Cumberland, Wis.	4-12-54	Johnstown	NAHL	66	8	21	29	311
4	McKay, Ray	L	6-5	202	Edmonton, Alta.	8-22-45	Syracuse	NAHL	3	1	1	2	0
							Cleveland	WHA	68	3	10	13	44
8	Zrymiak, Jerry	R	6-1	195	Regina, Sask.	10-19-48	Johnstown	NAHL	42	5	30	35	53
							Minn/Tor	WHA	56	0	18	18	58
6	Westrum, Pat*	L	5-10	182	Minneapolis, Minn.	3-3-48	Minn/Cgy	WHA	63	3	12	15	0
	GOALTENDERS								GP		MIN	GA SO	GAA
1	Curran, Mike*	R	5-8	170	Int'l Falls, Minn.	4-14-44	Minnesota	WHA	5		240	22 0	5.50
30	Levasseur, Louis	R	5-10	160	Noranda, Que.	6-16-49	Minnesota	WHA	4		193	60 0	3.11
							Johnstown	NAHL	30		1757	89 1	3.04

* American Born

Minnesota

MINNESOTA FIGHTING SAINTS
ST. PAUL HOCKEY CLUB, LTD.
ST. PAUL CIVIC CENTER
143 W. 4th Street
St. Paul, Minn. 55102

(612) 221-0123
TELEX •

Nick Mileti

Trustee	NICK J. MILETI
President/Alternate Trustee	ROBERT D. BROWN
General Manager/Coach	GLEN SONMOR
Assistant Coach/Dir. Player Personnel	JACK McCARTAN
Director of Marketing/Communication	LEE MEADE
Media Information Director	KEN RESNICK
Ticket Manager	MARK FITZGERALD
Group Sales Director	JACK BLESI
Controller	PETER KIRCHERT
Trainer	GLENN GOSTICK
Equipment Manager	BUDDY KESSELL
Franchise Granted	JUNE 21, 1972
Biggest Crowd	April 4, 1975 (17,312) largest ever for hockey in State of Minnesota and a WHA record.
Radio	PENDING
Television	PENDING
Team Colors	SCARLET, LIGHT GOLD, WHITE
Training Camp	ST. PAUL CIVIC CENTER
Ticket Prices	$8/6/4.50/3.50
Game Times	SUN. 7:35 P.M. WEEK NIGHTS 8:05 P.M. SUN., FEB. 20 2:05 P.M. SUN., MAR. 13 2:05 P.M.

Bob Brown

Glen Sonmor

CIVIC CENTER:
Opened Jan. 1, 1973. Built at cost of $19 million. Only rink in North America with glass dasher boards. Ice surface 200 × 85. Capacity 15,594 plus standing room.

19

NEW ENGLAND WHALERS 1976-77 ROSTER

No.	FORWARDS	S	Ht.	Wt.	Birthplace	Date	1975-76 Club	Lea.	GP	G	A	PTS	PIM
19	Arndt, Danny	L	5-10	175	Saskatoon, Sask.	3-26-55	Cape Cod	NAHL	7	0	2	2	2
9	Backstrom, Ralph	L	5-10	170	Krikland Lake, Ont.	9-18-37	New England	WHA	69	8	8	16	10
21	Bolduc, Danny*	L	5-10	180	Waterville, Maine	4- 6-53	Dvr/NE	WHA	80	35	48	83	20
22	Callighen, Brent	L	5-11	175	Toronto, Ont.	5-15-53	New England	IHL	14	2	5	7	14
15	Climie, Ron	L	5-11	180	Hamilton, Ont.	3- 5-50	Kalamazoo	WHA	72	25	33	58	104
27	Earl, Tom	R	6- 0	180	Niagara Falls, Ont.	6-10-47	New England	WHA	65	25	20	45	17
10	Hangsleben, Alan*	L	6- 1	195	Warroad, Minn.	2-22-53	Cape Cod	NAHL	66	8	11	19	26
							New England	WHA	1	0	0	0	9
11	Hynes, David*	L	5- 9	182	Cambridge, Mass.	4-17-51	Rochester	AHL	78	2	23	25	62
16	Lyle, George	L	6- 2	205	Vancouver, B.C.	11-24-53	Mich Tech	WCHA	63	37	30	67	20
12	MacGregor, Gary	L	5- 9	170	Kingston, Ont.	9-21-54	Dvr/Clev	WHA	43	47	41	88	42
4	Pleau, Larry*	L	6- 1	190	Lynn, Mass.	5-29-47	New England	WHA	83	21	17	38	24
17	Rogers, Mike	L	5- 9	170	Calgary, Alta.	10-24-54	Edm/NE	WHA	75	29	45	74	21
8	Webster, Tom	R	5-10	185	Kirkland Lake, Ont.	10- 4-48	New England	WHA	70	30	29	59	20
									55	33	50	83	24
	DEFENSEMEN												
6	Abrahamsson, Thommy	L	6- 2	190	Umea, Sweden	4- 8-47	New England	WHA	63	14	21	35	47
5	Busniuk, Ron	R	6- 0	190	Fort William, Ont.	9-22-47	Minn/NE	WHA	71	2	14	16	205
2	Ley, Rick	L	5- 9	185	Orillia, Ont.	12- 2-48	New England	WHA	67	8	30	38	78
14	Roberts, Doug*	R	6- 2	200	Detroit, Mich.	10-28-42	New England	WHA	76	4	13	17	51
7	Roberts, Gordie*	L	6- 1	190	Detroit, Mich.	10- 2-57	New England	WHA	77	3	19	22	102
3	Selwood, Brad	L	6- 0	200	Leamington, Ont.	3-18-48	New England	WHA	40	2	10	12	28

	GOALTENDERS								GP	MIN	GA	SO	GAA
1	Abrahamsson, Christer		6- 2	175	Umea, Sweden	4- 8-47	New England	WHA	41	2385	136	2	3.42
30	Landon, Bruce		5- 9	190	Kingston, Ont.	10- 5-49	New England	WHA	38	2181	126	0	3.47

* American Born

New England

NEW ENGLAND WHALERS
NEW ENGLAND WHALERS HOCKEY CLUB, INC.
One Civic Center Plaza
Hartford, Ct. 06103   (203) 728-3366
                           Telex 994-476

Howard Baldwin

Managing General Partner/Trustee	HOWARD L. BALDWIN
General Manager	RON RYAN
Coach	HARRY NEALE
Business Manager	DAVE ANDREWS
Assistant General Manager	JACK FERREIRA
Assistant to General Manager	DON BLACKBURN
Communications Director	BILL RASMUSSEN
Public Relations Director	DENNIS RANDALL
Media Relations Director	BOB NEUMEIER
Ticket Manager	BRIAN MacLEOD
Accountant	RON RONSTROM
Merchandise Manager	GEORGE DUCHARME
Trainer	JOE ALTOTT
Equipment Manager	SKIP CUNNINGHAM
Franchise Granted	NOVEMBER 21, 1971
Radio	WTIC — 1080 AM — Hartford — All games
	WSPR — 1270 AM — Springfield BOB NEUMEIER
Television	WHCT — Ch. 18 — Hartford BILL RASMUSSEN
Team Colors	GREEN, GOLD, WHITE
Training Camp	GLASTONBURY, CT.
Ticket Prices	$8.50/7/5
Game Times	ALL GAMES 7:30 P.M. SUN., JAN. 23 2:00 P.M. SUN., MAR. 27 2:00 P.M.

Ron Ryan

Harry Neale

HARTFORD CIVIC CENTER:
Construction of $30 million Convention Center complex started June, 1972. Building opened Jan. 11, 1975. No standing room. Ice surface 200 × 85. Capacity 10,507.

21

PHOENIX ROADRUNNERS 1976-77 ROSTER

No.	FORWARDS	S	Ht.	Wt.	Birthplace	Date	1975-76 Club	Lea.	GP	G	A	PTS	PIM
16	Cormier, Michel	L	5-9	175	Three Rivers, Que.	12-22-45	Phoenix	WHA	46	21	15	36	4
8	Florek, Robbie*	L	5-9	160	Needham, Mass.	1-2-52	Phoenix	WHA	80	41	72	113	109
15	Gray, John	L	5-10	180	Little Current, Ont.	8-13-49	Phoenix	WHA	79	35	45	80	136
9	Hall, Del	L	5-10	170	Peterborough, Ont.	5-7-49	Phoenix	WHA	80	47	44	91	10
20	Hobin, Mike	L	5-11	180	Sarnia, Ont.	2-21-54	Tucson	CHL	66	27	39	66	31
							Phoenix	WHA	9	1	1	2	2
12	Huston, Ron	R	5-10	185	Manitou, Man.	4-8-45	Phoenix	WHA	79	22	44	66	6
7	Liddington, Bob	L	5-11	175	Calgary, Alta.	9-15-48	Tucson	CHL	23	12	12	24	20
							Dvr/Ott/Hou	WHA	36	7	8	15	18
24	Mononen, Lauri	L	6-0	185	Joensuu, Finland	3-22-50	Phoenix	WHA	75	15	21	36	19
22	Repo, Seppo	R	5-10	180	Turku, Finland	9-21-47	TPS	FIN	35	33	22	55	32
27	Sleep, Mike	R	6-0	180	Montreal, Que.	3-13-55	Tucson	CHL	69	23	30	53	46
							Phoenix	WHA	9	2	0	2	0
23	Tamminen, Juhani	L	5-11	185	Turku, Finland	5-26-50	Cleveland	WHA	65	7	14	21	0

No.	DEFENSEMEN	S	Ht.	Wt.	Birthplace	Date	1975-76 Club	Lea.	GP	G	A	PTS	PIM
5	Beaudoin, Serge	L	6-2	215	Montreal, Que.	10-30-52	Phoenix	WHA	76	0	21	21	102
4	Lariviere, Garry	R	6-0	190	St. Catharines, Ont.	12-6-54	Phoenix	WHA	79	7	17	24	98
3	McLeod, Al	L	5-11	210	Medicine Hat, Alta.	6-17-49	Phoenix	WHA	80	2	18	20	82
2	Niekamp, Jim*	R	6-1	185	Detroit, Mich.	3-11-46	Phoenix	WHA	79	4	15	19	79
19	Rautakallio, Pekka	L	5-11	185	Pori, Finland	7-25-53	Phoenix	WHA	73	11	39	50	8
6	Rollins, Jerry	R	6-2	195	New Westminster, B.C.	3-22-55	Toronto	WHA	52	5	7	12	185

No.	GOALTENDERS	S	Ht.	Wt.	Birthplace	Date	1975-76 Club	Lea.	GP	MIN	GA	SO	GAA
1	Kurt, Gary		6-3	205	Kitchener, Ont.	3-9-47	Phoenix	WHA	40	2369	147	1	3.72
25	Hebenton, Clay		5-10	185	Victoria, B.C.	2-20-53	Tucson	CHL	7	379	40	0	6.33
							Phoenix	WHA	2	80	9		6.75

* American Born

Phoenix

PHOENIX ROADRUNNERS
PHOENIX ROADRUNNERS HOCKEY CLUB, INC.
5350 North 16th St., Suite 106
Phoenix, Arizona 85016   (602) 263-7828
                                Telex: 667-356

Chairman of the Board/Trustee	KARL ELLER
President	BRIAN O'NEILL
Director of Operations	ROBERT GOLDWATER
Directors	KARL ELLER BRIAN O'NEILL STEPHEN W. CRAIG
Business Manager	TERRY VIAR
General Manager/Coach	E. I. (AL) ROLLINS
Director of Sales/Promotions	PORTER C. McKINNON, JR.
Director Public Relations	DAVE WEISER
Legal Counsel	STEPHEN W. CRAIG
Trainers	JACK CURRAN/KEN FLEGER
Team Physicians	ELI J. KRIGSTEN, M.D. THOMAS P. WHITE, M.D. DONALD A. CRYAN, M.D. ARTHUR C. STEVENSON, M.D.
Team Dentists	DR. J. BARTON THOMPSON DR. REX E. UMBENAUER
Franchise Granted	SEPTEMBER 18, 1973
Team Colors	PEACOCK BLUE, GOLD, WHITE
Radio	KRUX — 1360 AM KXTC — 92.3 FM JOE DAGGETT
Television	PENDING
Training Camp	TAMPERE, FINLAND
Ticket Prices	$8.50/6.50/5.50/4/3
Game Times	SUN. 7:00 P.M. WEEK NIGHTS 7:30 P.M. SUN., FEB. 27 2:00 P.M.

Karl Eller

Brian O'Neill

Al Rollins

MEMORIAL COLISEUM:
Opened Oct. 21, 1967. Roof has largest painting in world, a representation of Bicentennial logo. Construction cost: $6,384,586.35. Ice surface 200 by 85. Capacity 12,474.

QUEBEC NORDIQUES 1976-77 ROSTER

FORWARDS

No.		S	Ht.	Wt.	Birthplace	Date	1975-76 Club	Lea.	GP	G	A	PTS	PIM
21	Bernier, Serge	R	6-1	190	Padoue, Que.	4-29-47	Quebec	WHA	70	34	68	102	89
11	Bordeleau, Chris	L	5-8	152	Noranda, Que.	9-23-47	Quebec	WHA	73	37	72	109	44
17	Bordeleau, Paulin	L	5-9	155	Noranda, Que.	1-29-53	Vancouver	NHL	48	5	12	17	6
							Tulsa	CHL	14	5	9	14	11
18	Boudrias, Andre	L	5-8	165	Montreal, Que.	9-19-43	Vancouver	NHL	71	7	31	38	10
15	Brackenbury, Curt	L	5-10	190	Kapuskasing, Ont.	1-31-52	Minn/Que	WHA	74	8	14	22	361
9	Cloutier, Real	R	5-10	180	Quebec, Que.	7-30-56	Quebec	WHA	80	60	55	115	27
14	Constantin, Charles	L	6-2	190	Montreal, Que.	4-30-54	Quebec	WHA	44	8	8	16	77
							Maine	NAHL	8	1	1	2	40
12	Fitchner, Bob	L	6-0	190	Sudbury, Ont.	12-22-50	Ind/Que	WHA	75	22	25	47	129
16	Grenier, Richard	L	5-11	170	Montreal, Que.	9-18-52	Beauce	NAHL	73	77	83	160	82
19	Sutherland, Steve	L	6-0	172	Noranda, Que.	9-1-46	Quebec	WHA	75	22	19	41	202
8	Tardif, Marc	L	6-1	178	Granby, Que.	6-12-49	Quebec	WHA	81	71	77	148	91

DEFENSEMEN

No.		S	Ht.	Wt.	Birthplace	Date	1975-76 Club	Lea.	GP	G	A	PTS	PIM
4	Baxter, Paul	R	5-11	200	Winnipeg, Man.	10-25-55	Cleveland	WHA	67	3	7	10	201
							Syracuse	NAHL	3	1	2	3	9
24	Bernier, Jean	L	5-10	170	St-Hyacinthe, Que.	7-21-54	Quebec	WHA	81	4	26	30	12
7	Dorey, Jim	L	6-1	192	Kingston, Ont.	8-17-47	Toronto	WHA	74	9	51	60	134
22	Lacombe, Francois	L	5-9	185	Montreal, Que.	2-2-48	Calgary	WHA	71	3	28	31	62
10	Roy, Pierre	L	6-1	175	Amos, Que.	3-12-52	Quebec	WHA	79	6	30	36	258
3	Tremblay, Jean-Claude	L	5-10	185	Bagotville, Que.	1-22-39	Quebec	WHA	81	12	77	89	16
2	Weir, Wally	R	6-1	205	Verdun, Que.	6-3-54	Flint	IHL	7	0	0	0	4
							Beauce	NAHL	56	6	20	26	180

GOALTENDERS

No.		S	Ht.	Wt.	Birthplace	Date	1975-76 Club	Lea.	GP	MIN	GA	SO	GAA
25	Aubry, Serge	L	5-9	160	Montreal, Que.	1-2-42	Cincinnati	WHA	12	549	38	1	4.15
1	Brodeur, Richard	R	5-7	160	Longueuil, Que.	9-15-52	Quebec	WHA	69	3967	244	2	3.69

Quebec

QUEBEC NORDIQUES
LE CLUB DE HOCKEY LES NORDIQUES, INC.
Colisee de Quebec
Quebec, P.Q. G1L 4W7   (418) 529-4161
                             Telex: 051-3068

John Dacres

Chairman of the Board	JEAN LESAGE
President/Trustee	JOHN DACRES
Vice-President	MAURICE TASCHEREAU
General Manager	MAURICE FILLION
Coach	MARC BOILEAU
Chief Scout	YVAN PRUDHOMME
Director Public Relations	PAUL LEFRANCOIS
Trainer	RENE LACASSE
Assistant Trainer	CLAUDE LANGLOIS
Team Physician	DR. ROBERT MEILLEUR
Physiotherapist	GEORGES MORRISET
Franchise Granted	JUNE 21, 1972
Radio	CHRC — 800 AM — Quebec City — All games CLAUDE BEDARD/MARC SIMONEAU
Television	PENDING
Team Colors	RED, WHITE, BLUE
Training Camp	QUEBEC COLISEE
Ticket Prices	$10/7.50/5.00
Game Times	ALL GAMES 7:00 P.M.

Maurice Fillion

Marc Boileau

THE COLISEE:
Opened Dec. 15, 1949, cost of $4 million. Parking for 5,000 cars. Air conditioned. Ice surface 200 × 85. Capacity: 13,512. Seating for 10,012.

25

SAN DIEGO MARINERS 1976-77 ROSTER

No.	FORWARDS	S	Ht.	Wt.	Birthplace	Date	1975-76 Club	Lea.	GP	G	A	PTS	PIM
8	Burgess, Don	L	6-0	170	Port Edward, Ont.	6-8-46	San Diego	WHA	73	14	11	25	35
16	Devine, Kevin	L	5-9	175	Toronto, Ont.	12-9-54	San Diego	WHA	80	21	28	49	102
19	Dobek, Bob*	L	6-0	182	Detroit, Mich.	10-4-52	San Diego	WHA	14	3	1	4	2
9	Ferguson, Norm	R	5-8	177	Sydney, N.S.	10-16-45	San Diego	WHA	79	37	37	74	12
11	French, John	L	5-11	175	Orillia, Ont.	8-25-50	San Diego	WHA	76	25	39	64	16
7	Lacroix, Andre	L	5-8	175	Lauzon, Que.	6-5-45	San Diego	WHA	80	29	72	101	52
21	Noris, Joe*	R	6-0	185	Denver, Colo.	10-26-51	San Diego	WHA	80	28	40	68	24
14	Pinder, Gerry	R	5-8	168	Saskatoon, Sask.	9-15-48	Cleveland	WHA	79	21	30	51	118
10	Rhiness, Brad	L	5-9	170	Huntsville, Ont.	11-6-56	Kingston	OHA	65	52	60	112	28
12	Rivers, Wayne	R	5-9	185	Hamilton, Ont.	2-1-42	San Diego	WHA	71	19	25	44	24
17	Veneruzzo, Gary	L	5-8	175	Fort William, Ont.	6-28-43	Cinn/Phx	WHA	75	22	26	48	35
	DEFENSEMEN												
18	Boddy, Greg	L	6-2	200	Ponoka, Alta.	3-19-49	Vancouver	NHL	34	5	6	11	33
							Tulsa	CHL	24	0	9	9	12
6	Falkenberg, Bob	L	6-0	205	Stettler, Alta.	1-1-46	San Diego	WHA	79	3	13	16	31
2	Hughes, Brent	L	6-0	205	Bowmanville, Ont.	6-17-43	San Diego	WHA	78	7	28	35	63
5	Legge, Randy	R	5-11	185	Newmarket, Ont.	12-16-45	Mohawk Val	NAHL	24	1	12	13	50
							Wpg/Clev	WHA	45	1	8	9	28
4	Morrison, Kevin	L	5-11	202	Sydney, N.S.	10-28-49	San Diego	WHA	80	22	43	65	56
3	Shmyr, Paul	L	5-11	175	Cudworth, Sask.	1-28-46	Cleveland	WHA	70	6	44	50	101

No.	GOALTENDERS	S	Ht.	Wt.	Birthplace	Date	1975-76 Club	Lea.	GP	MIN	GA	SO	GAA
1	Lockett, Ken	L	6-0	180	Toronto, Ont.	8-30-47	Vancouver	NHL	30	1436	83	0	3.47
31	Wakely, Ernie	L	5-11	175	Flin Flon, Man.	11-27-40	San Diego	WHA	67	3824	208	3	3.26

* American Born

San Diego

SAN DIEGO MARINERS
San Diego Mariners, Inc.
3500 Sports Arena Blvd.
San Diego, CA 92110

(714) 225-9633
Telex: 695-084

Ray Kroc

Chairman of the Board	RAY A. KROC
President	E. J. BAVASI
V-P/General Manager/Trustee	BALLARD F. SMITH
Vice-President/Legal Counsel	DONALD G. LUBIN
Coach/Director of Player Personnel	RON INGRAM
Business Manager/Public Relations	GABE DeNUNZIO
Director of Sales/Promotions	DON BUCHANAN
Director of Broadcasting	RON OAKES
Chief Scout	LES CALDER
Trainer	RALPH MITCHELL
Assistant Trainer	HANK ROBB
Team Physicians	DR. H. PAUL BAUER
	DR. RICHARD RICHLEY
	DR. LEROY RHEIN
Team Dentist	DR. ALAN GALE
Franchise Granted	JANUARY 3, 1974 (formerly New Jersey)
Radio	KOGO — 600 AM — all games
	RON OAKES
Television	PENDING
Team Colors	ORANGE, BLUE, WHITE
Training Camp	MIRA MESA, CA
Ticket Prices	$7.50/5.50/3
Game Times	ALL GAMES 7:00 P.M.

Ballard Smith

Ron Ingram

SPORTS ARENA:
Completed Nov. 17, 1966, at cost of $6.5 million. 33 acres of parking (4,000 cars). Ice surface 200 × 85. Capacity: 13,029.

WINNIPEG JETS 1976-77 ROSTER

No.	FORWARDS	S	Ht.	Wt.	Birthplace	Date	1975-76 Club	Lea.	GP	G	A	PTS	PIM
18	Guindon, Bob	L	5-9	170	Labelle, Que.	11-19-50	Winnipeg	WHA	29	3	3	6	14
15	Hedberg, Anders	L	5-11	176	Ornskoldsvik, Sweden	2-25-51	Winnipeg	WHA	75	50	55	105	46
9	Hull, Bobby	L	5-10	191	Point Anne, Ont.	1-3-39	Winnipeg	WHA	80	53	70	123	29
12	Ketola, Veli-Pekka	L	6-3	207	Pori, Finland	3-28-48	Winnipeg	WHA	80	32	36	68	32
21	Labraaten, Dan	R	6-0	185	Arvika, Sweden	6-9-51	Leksand	IF	16	13	9	22	6
17	Lesuk, Bill	L	5-9	187	Moose Jaw, Sask.	11-1-46	Winnipeg	WHA	81	15	21	36	92
19	Lindh, Mats	L	6-1	180	Orsa, Sweden	9-12-47	Winnipeg	WHA	65	19	15	34	12
20	Lindstrom, Willy	L	6-0	180	Grunns, Sweden	5-5-51	Winnipeg	WHA	81	23	35	58	32
25	Miller, Perry	L	6-1	194	Winnipeg, Man.	6-24-52	Minn/Wpg	WHA	60	8	10	18	48
22	Moffat, Lyle	L	5-10	185	Calgary, Alta.	3-19-48	Winnipeg	WHA	74	17	15	32	52
14	Nilsson, Ulf	R	5-11	176	Nynashamn, Sweden	5-11-50	Winnipeg	WHA	78	38	76	114	89
23	Ruhnke, Kent	R	6-1	180	Toronto, Ont.	9-18-52	U. of Tor.	OUC	43	51	29	82	22
10	Sullivan, Peter	R	5-9	170	Toronto, Ont.	7-25-51	Winnipeg	WHA	78	32	39	71	22
	DEFENSEMEN												
2	Bergman, Thommie	L	6-3	200	Munkfors, Sweden	12-10-47	Winnipeg	WHA	81	11	30	41	111
8	Dunn, Dave	L	6-3	200	Moosomin, Sask.	8-19-48	Toronto	NHL	42	0	8	8	84
							Oklahoma	CHL	9	1	7	8	10
6	Green, Ted	R	5-10	190	St. Boniface, Man.	3-23-40	Winnipeg	WHA	79	5	23	28	73
3	Long, Barry	L	6-2	210	Red Deer, Alta.	1-3-49	Edmonton	WHA	78	10	32	42	66
5	Riihiranta, Hexi	L	5-11	190	Helsinki, Finland	10-4-48	Winnipeg	WHA	70	1	8	9	27
4	Sjoberg, Lars-Erik	L	5-8	179	Falun, Sweden	4-5-44	Winnipeg	WHA	81	5	36	41	12

No.	GOALTENDERS	S	Ht.	Wt.	Birthplace	Date	1975-76 Club	Lea.	GP	MIN	GA	SO	GAA
1	Daley, Joe	L	5-10	171	E. Kildonan, Man.	2-20-43	Winnipeg	WHA	62	3612	171	5	2.84
30	Larsson, Curt	L	5-11	171	Nykoping, Sweden	12-11-44	Winnipeg	WHA	23	1287	83	0	3.87

Winnipeg

WINNIPEG JETS
WINNIPEG HOCKEY CLUB, INC.
15-1430 Maroons Road
Winnipeg, Manitoba R3G 0L5

(204) 772-9491
Telex 075-87810

Jack McKeag

Chairman of the Board	R. G. (BOB) GRAHAM
President	JACK McKEAG
Trustee	OSCAR GRUBERT
Vice-Presidents	JIM BURNS/DR. GERRY WILSON
Treasurer	BILL SHIELDS
General Manager	RUDY PILOUS
Coach	BOBBY KROMM
Chief Scout	BILL ROBINSON
Director of Media Relations	NORMAN COSTON
Ticket Manager	BOB BELL
Trainer	BILL BOZAK
Equipment Manager	KELLY PRUDEN
Franchise Granted	DECEMBER 27, 1971
Radio	CJOB — 680 AM — all games KEN NICOLSON/BOB IRVING ED DEARDEN
Television	CKND — Ch. 9 ANDY ARNOT
Team Colors	BLUE, RED, WHITE
Training Camp	WINNIPEG
Ticket Prices	$9/7.50/4.25
Game Times	SUN. 7:30 P.M. WEEK NIGHTS 8:00 P.M.

Rudy Pilous

Bobby Kromm

WINNIPEG ARENA:
Opened Oct. 18, 1955. Construction cost $2 million. Seating for 10,140. Arena phone (204) 783-4223. Ice surface 200 × 85. Capacity 10,390.

THE WHA AT THE HALL OF FAME

It was an historic day — August 7, 1976 — at the opening of the World Hockey Association's display in the International Hockey Hall of Fame and Museum located in Kingston, Canada, when the legendary Gordie Howe, the game's greatest all-time star, was the feature attraction.

Howe, the 48-year-old superstar, who was born in Floral, Sask., Canada March 31, 1928, and who continues to amaze everybody with his incomparable play, is in his 29th season of major professional league championship competition. Gordie played 25 seasons with the Detroit Red

Shown above, left to right: Gordie Howe; Johnnie Kelly, president of the International Hockey Hall of Fame and Museum; Larry Gordon, executive vice-president, World Hockey Association. In the background is The Avco World Trophy, emblematic of WHA hockey supremacy; and the bronze statue behind Kelly's right shoulder is the Gordie Howe Trophy, awarded annually to the MVP in the World Hockey Association.

Howe's fans are all ages. Miss Bessie Dehaney of Kingston, who has been a sports fan all of her life, lined up to talk to and get the autograph of the Houston Aeros' superstar, who holds virtually every scoring record in major professional hockey.

INTERNATIONAL HOCKEY AND MUSEUM

Wings of the NHL, and this is his 4th season with the Houston Aeros of the WHA.

Howe is the only athlete to ever play on the same team and to compete in a major pro league with his two sons — Marty and Mark.

It was a full day for Gordie Howe, WHA executive vice-president Larry Gordon, International Hockey Hall of Fame President Johnnie Kelly, vice-president and curator Josh Nichols, and directors E. H. Hare, Bill Fitsell, Peter Radley and David Bourque.

Howe & Co. started the day with a tour of the sites of the 1976 summer Olympics. Then a luncheon where Howe and Gordon spoke.

The afternoon belonged to an overflow crowd of more than 2,000 who came to the Hall to welcome, talk to and get the autograph of the holder of more records than anyone in the game — No. 9 of the Houston Aeros.

"I'll stay as long as this takes" smiled the personable Howe who chatted with the fans as he signed all autographs on a first name basis. There was awe in the faces of the youngsters. Many had never seen Howe play but they knew they were in the company of the greatest.

Howe's fans are of all ages. Miss Bessie Dehaney of Kingston, who is a "young 80" and who has been a sports fan for all her life, lined up to talk to and get Howe's autograph.

The tremendous respect and excitement Howe generates wherever he appears is vividly illustrated in the photos on this page, which were taken at the Hall.

August 7 was "WHA Day" at the hockey shrine. Several WHA trophies were on public display for the first time, including The AVCO World Trophy, emblematic of WHA league supremacy, The O'Keefe Cup, The Gordie Howe Trophy, and several individual trophies. Also, the original sweaters Howe and his two sons, Mark and Marty wore during the first

season they played for the Aeros, drew a lot of attention.

Howe started the season with 965 career goals, and he could become the first player to reach the "impossible" 1,000 goals!

The International Hockey Hall of Fame and Museum is the original shrine for amateur and professional hockey. It features sticks, skates, sweaters, pads, and just about everything connected with hockey.

The word "Hockey" is derived from the French word "Hoquet."

It all started over 120 years ago in Kingston, Canada. Kingston is recognized as the "Birthplace of Hockey." The first organized league hockey was played in Kingston in the season of 1885-86. Baseball has its Cooperstown (N.Y.). Football has its Canton (Ohio). And Hockey has its Kingston.

WHA OFFICIALS

Chief-of-Officials .... BOB FRAMPTON
Referee-in-Chief .... BILL FRIDAY

REFEREES

1. BILL FRIDAY
2. RON EGO
3. BOB KOLARI
6. RON HARRIS
7. PETER MOFFAT
8. STEVE DOWLING
9. WAYNE MUNDEY
10. ALAN GLASPELL
11. RON FOURNIER

LINESMEN

15. Ron Asselstine
16. Ross Keenan
17. Graham Hern
18. Wayne Bonney
19. Ron Foyt
20. Joey Dame
25. Ken Pierce
26. Steve Barry
27. Dave Madsen
28. Gord Kerr
29. Michel Chartre
30. Frank Larochelle
31. Jim Brunelle
33. Bob McPherson
34. Dennis Fonteyne
35. Darryl Havrelock
36. Ron Renneberg

GAME OFFICIALS

BIRMINGHAM L. Hawkins (timekeeper), B. Miller (penalty timekeeper), D. Haldefer, F. Watrus (goal judges), E. McDonald (scorer), John Rolerad (statistician), Tony Bruno, Jim Christian (public address).

EDMONTON Bob Walker (supervisor/game timekeeper), Ted McPhee, Gary Hill, K. Schultz (goal judges), Sandy Miller, Don Whidden (scorers), Dick Curreau, Grant Hill (timekeepers), Merv McDonald, Bob Olynyk (statisticians), Gordon Ross (public address).

HOUSTON Charlie Toland (supervisor), Joe Chiswell, Phil Brand (goal judges), L. M. "Dutch" Keen (official scorer), Joe Long, Ron Ellis (timekeepers), Ken May (statistician), George Patterson, Peter Bryant (alternates), Terry Leiweke (public address).

CALGARY Ernest Minhinnett (supervisor/game timekeeper), Jack Wakefield, Charles Marsh (goal judges), Don Young, Bob Peltier, Joe Cassidy (scorers), Berto Pegeraro, Doug Young (penalty timekeepers), Stan Jaycock, Lou Soucier, Ed Soucier (statisticians), Daryl Janz (public address).

officials

CINCINNATI — George Callies (supervisor/official scorer), Dennis White, Bruce Chamberlain (goal judges), Jay Rizzuto, Fred Heflin (timekeepers), Joe Minster, Don Fisher (statisticians), Dave Chamberlain, Terry Shutt (penalty box attendants), Bill Hagen, Steve Dick, Ron Kissinger (alternates).

INDIANAPOLIS — Paul Minott, Sr. (supervisor/scorer), Bill Fuller, Ed Kikendall, Paul Minott, Jr. (goal judges), Pete Lederer, Dennis Pope (timekeepers), Don Lawless, (statistician), Ray Lord, Don Kouns, Garth Hayes, (alternates), Bob Richards (public address).

MINNESOTA — Ron Vanelli (supervisor), Rod Smith, Russ Miester, Bill McCellan, John Jundt, Al Maki (goal judges), Arnie Bauer, Paul Bauer (scorers), Joe Borsch, Ted Olson (timekeepers), Jack Kelly, Dan Gibbons (statisticians), Phil Mooney, Ted Gershner, Gene Gibbons (alternates).

NEW ENGLAND — Bill Henderson (supervisor/statistician), Ray Cote, Bill Perry (goal judges), Bob Guarante (scorer), Jim MacDonald, Dennis Cornan (timekeepers), Bob Kaminsky, J. R. Chevalier, John Richards (penalty box attendants), Floyd Richards (public address).

PHOENIX — Frank Austin (supervisor), Herb Revans, Art Cliff (goal judges), Newton Bayless (scorer), John Kline, Frank Doyle, Ralph Henderson (timekeepers), Joe Parks, Jim Winkles (statisticians), Jack Flett, Hal Wallace, Ron Sutherland, Dick Corbo, Duane Two, Irv Sloboda (alternates), Bob Baker (public address).

QUEBEC — Raymond Puchol (supervisor), Adrien Cloutier, Michel Marier, James Coernell, Gaston Filion, Adelard Cloutier (goal judges), Raymond Puchol, Gilles Poulin (scorer), Robert Marier, Claude Legare, Jean Cote (timekeepers), Marcel Beaudoin (statistician), Jean Gavel (public address).

SAN DIEGO — Doug Zink (supervisor/game timekeeper), Jerry Davis, Jim Koshley (goal judges), Gary Gerwig, Kay Moore, Stephen DeNunzio (scorers), Manny Gomes, Bob Barlow, Vern Westlott (timekeepers), Harry Lockwood, Jim Meyer, Jim Lockwood (statisticians), Ken Harwood, Nick Kochen, Dennis Rowden, Bob Sexton, Al Lopez, (alternates), Bruce Binkowski (public address).

WINNIPEG — R. W. Sanregret (supervisor), Len Amey, James Mier (goal judges), Earl Nernberg (scorers), Bob Mick, George Orbell (timekeepers), Jim Amey (statistician), John Schabler, John Ablett (alternates) Don Kirton (public address).

THE AVCO WORLD TROPHY

WINNERS

1975-76: WINNIPEG JETS
Joe Daley, Curt Larsson, Ulf Nilsson, Bobby Hull, Anders Hedberg, Peter Sullivan, Thommie Bergman, Mike Ford, Veli-Pekka Ketola, Willy Lindstrom, Lyle Moffat, Robert Guindon, Duke Asmundson, Norm Beaudin, Mats Lindh, Bill Lesuk, Hexi Riihiranta, Larry Hornung, Ted Green, Larry Hillman, Gerry Odrowski. Capt. Lars-Erik Sjoberg. Coach Bobby Kromm; Gen. Mgr. Rudy Pilous.

1974-75: HOUSTON AEROS
Ron Grahame, Wayne Rutledge, Mark Howe, Gordie Howe, Marty Howe, Larry Lund, Gordon Labossiere, Frank Hughes, Poul Popiel, Murray Hall, Andre Hinse, John Schella, Bill Preston, Terry Ruskowski, Jim Sherrit, Don Larway, Larry Hale, Glen Irwin, Bill Prentice, Capt. Ted Taylor. Gen. Mgr./Coach — Bill Dineen.

1973-74: HOUSTON AEROS
Don McLeod, Wayne Rutledge, Ron Grahame, Murray Hall, Ed Hoekstra, Mark Howe, Gordie Howe, Marty Howe, Bill Prentice, Larry Lund, Joe Szura, Don Grierson, Larry Hale, Jim Sherrit, Frank Hughes, Jack Stanfield, Dunc McCallum, Andre Hinse, Gary Williamson, Gordon Kannegiesser, John Schella, Gordon Labossiere, Poul Popiel, Capt. Ted Taylor. Gen. Mgr./Coach — Bill Dineen.

1972-73: NEW ENGLAND WHALERS
Al Smith, Bruce Landon, Tommy Williams, Ted Green, Jim Dorey, Larry Pleau, Guy Smith, Mike Byers, Brad Selwood, Tim Sheehy, Ric Jordan, Paul Hurley, Brit Selby, Tom Earl, John Danby, John French, Rick Ley, Terry Caffery, Tom Webster, John Cuniff, Kevin Ahern. Gen. Mgr./Coach — Jack Kelley.

DIVISION WINNERS

	WESTERN	EASTERN	CANADIAN
1975-76	Houston	Indianapolis	Winnipeg
1974-75	Houston	New England	Quebec
1973-74	Houston	New England	
1972-73	Winnipeg	New England	

awards

INDIVIDUAL TROPHY

GORDIE HOWE TROPHY

	SEASON	
GORDIE HOWE TROPHY (Most Valuable Player)		**W. D. (BILL) HUNTER TROPHY** (Scoring Champion)
Marc Tardif/Quebec	1975-76	Marc Tardif/Quebec
Bobby Hull/Winnipeg	1974-75	Andre Lacroix/San Diego
Gordie Howe/Houston	1973-74	Mike Walton/Minnesota
Bobby Hull/Winnipeg	1972-73	Andre Lacroix/Philadelphia
DENNIS A. MURPHY TROPHY (Best Defenceman)		**BEN HATSKIN TROPHY** (Best Goaltender)
Paul Shmyr/Cleveland	1975-76	Michel Dion/Indianapolis
J. C. Tremblay/Quebec	1974-75	Ron Grahame/Houston
Pat Stapleton/Chicago	1973-74	Don McLeod/Houston
J. C. Tremblay/Quebec	1972-73	Gerry Cheevers/Cleveland
LOU KAPLAN TROPHY (Rookie of the Year)		**PAUL DENEAU TROPHY** (Most Gentlemanly Player)
Mark Napier/Toronto	1975-76	Vaclav Nedomansky/Toronto
Anders Hedberg/Winnipeg	1974-75	Mike Rogers/Edmonton
Mark Howe/Houston	1973-74	Ralph Backstrom/Chicago
Terry Caffery/New England	1972-73	Ted Hampson/Minnesota
ROBERT SCHMERTZ MEMORIAL TROPHY (Coach of the Year)		**ALL-STAR GAME MOST VALUABLE PLAYER**
Bobby Kromm/Winnipeg	1975-76 }	Real Cloutier/Quebec Paul Shmyr/Cleveland
Sandy Hucul/Phoenix	1974-75	Rejean Houle/Quebec
Billy Harris/Toronto	1973-74	Mike Walton/Minnesota
Jack Kelley/New England	1972-73	Wayne Carleton/Ottawa

PLAYOFF MVP AWARD
1976 — Ulf Nilsson/Winnipeg
1975 — Ron Grahame/Houston

WHA ALL-STAR TEAMS
(Determined by Vote of News Media)

1975-76

FIRST TEAM		SECOND TEAM
Joe Daley, Winnipeg	GOAL	Ron Grahame, Houston
Paul Shmyr, Cleveland	DEFENSE	Kevin Morrison, San Diego
J. C. Tremblay, Quebec	DEFENSE	Pat Stapleton, Indianapolis
Ulf Nilsson, Winnipeg	CENTRE	Robbie Ftorek, Phoenix
Marc Tardif, Quebec	LEFT WING	Bobby Hull, Winnipeg
Anders Hedberg, Winnipeg	RIGHT WING	Real Cloutier, Quebec

1974-75

FIRST TEAM		SECOND TEAM
Ron Grahame, Houston	GOAL	Gerry Cheevers, Cleveland
J. C. Tremblay, Quebec	DEFENSE	Poul Popiel, Houston
Kevin Morrison, S.D.	DEFENSE	Barry Long, Edmonton
Andre Lacroix, San Diego	CENTRE	Serge Bernier, Quebec
Bobby Hull, Winnipeg	LEFT WING	Marc Tardif, Quebec
Gordie Howe, Houston	RIGHT WING	Anders Hedberg, Winnipeg

1973-74

FIRST TEAM		SECOND TEAM
Don McLeod, Houston	GOAL	Gerry Cheevers, Cleveland
Pat Stapleton, Chicago	DEFENSE	J. C. Tremblay, Quebec
Paul Shmyr, Cleveland	DEFENSE	Al Hamilton, Edmonton
Andre Lacroix, New Jersey	CENTRE	Wayne Carleton, Toronto
Bobby Hull, Winnipeg	LEFT WING	Mark Howe, Houston
Gordie Howe, Houston	RIGHT WING	Mike Walton, Minnesota

1972-73

FIRST TEAM		SECOND TEAM
Gerry Cheevers, Cleveland	GOAL	Bernie Parent, Philadelphia
J. C. Tremblay, Quebec	DEFENSE	Jim Dorey, New England
Paul Shmyr, Cleveland	DEFENSE	Larry Hornung, Winnipeg
Andre Lacroix, Philadelphia	CENTRE	Ron Ward, New York
Bobby Hull, Winnipeg	LEFT WING	Gary Jarrett, Cleveland
Danny Lawson, Philadelphia	RIGHT WING	Tom Webster, New England

ALL-STAR GAME

The 1976-77 Game, to be played at the Civic Center in Hartford, Conn., Jan. 18, 1977 will be the World Hockey Association's 5th Annual. It will be between the Eastern Division and the Western Division all-stars.

all-stars

Game No. 4 **1975-76 GAME**

Played at the Cleveland Coliseum, Jan. 13, 1976. The Canadian all-stars defeated the United States, 6-1. Attendance: 15,491.

CANADIAN DIVISION LINEUP:
Coach: Jean-Guy Gendron (Quebec)
Goal: *Joe Daley (Winnipeg), Don McLeod (Calgary), Jim Shaw (Toronto)
Defense: Lars-Erik Sjoberg (Winnipeg), *J. C. Tremblay (Quebec), Barry Long (Edmonton), Larry Hornung (Winnipeg), Thommie Bergman (Winnipeg), John Miszuk (Calgary), Paul Terbenche (Calgary).
Forwards: Vaclav Nedomansky (Toronto), Bobby Hull (Winnipeg), Anders Hedberg (Winnipeg), Ulf Nilsson (Winnipeg), Marc Tardif (Quebec), Real Cloutier (Quebec), Serge Bernier (Quebec), Chris Bordeleau (Quebec), Frank Mahovlich (Toronto), Rejean Houle (Quebec), Danny Lawson (Calgary), Rusty Patenaude (Edmonton).
*Injured. Did not play.

UNITED STATES DIVISIONS LINEUP:
Coach: Bill Dineen (Houston)
Goal: Gerry Cheevers (Cleveland), Christer Abrahamsson (New England).
Defense: Paul Shmyr (Cleveland), Pat Stapleton (Indianapolis), Kevin Morrison (San Diego), John Schella (Houston), Marty Howe (Houston), Rick Ley (New England).
Forwards: Andre Lacroix (San Diego), Gene Peacosh (San Diego), Gordie Howe (Houston), Dave Keon (Minnesota), Claude Larose (Cincinnati), Mike Walton (Minnesota), Robbie Ftorek (Phoenix), Wayne Carleton (New England), Mark Howe (Houston), Ralph Backstrom (Denver), Tom Webster (New England), Don Borgeson (Denver).

SCORING SUMMARY

FIRST PERIOD: No scoring.
Penalties: Ley (US) :29, Schella (US) 8:37, Hull (C) 8:37, Patenaude (C) 12:48.

SECOND PERIOD: 1. C. Cloutier (Tardif) 1:45
2. C. Mahovlich (Bergman) 11:50
3. C. Cloutier (Sjoberg, Bordeleau) 16:44
Penalties: Backstrom (US) 14:56, Long (C) 18:03.

THIRD PERIOD: 4. C. Lawson 3:50
5. US. Lacroix (Ley) 13:26
6. C. Nilsson (Hedberg, Miszuk) 15:33
7. C. Cloutier (Bordeleau, Tardif) 18:04
Penalties: Nedomansky (C) 3:32, Long (C) 18:45.

SHOTS ON GOAL BY:
CANADA 8   9   13   — 30
UNITED STATES 9   9   7   — 25

REFEREE: Bill Friday. Linesmen: Ross Keenan, Graham Hern.
GAME MVPs: Canadian Team — Real Cloutier
          U.S.A. Team — Paul Shmyr

Game No. 3 **1974-75 GAME**
Edmonton, Jan. 21, 1975 (15,326)
WEST 6, EAST 4

FIRST PERIOD: 1. West, Mark Howe (G. Howe, Lacroix) 7:08
2. West, Hinse (Lund, Hughes) 8:18
3. East, Tardif (Houle, Selwood) 13:32
4. East, Houle (Pleau, Dorey) 17:37
. Penalties — none.

SECOND PERIOD: 5. West, Hull (Lawson) 4:23
6. West, Hinse (Hughes, Odrowski) 6:35
7. West, Taylor (Lacroix, Schella) 10:07
8. West, G. Howe (Lacroix, Mark Howe) 11:53
9. East, Houle (Selwood, Dorey) 14:32
Penalties — none.

THIRD PERIOD: 10. East, Bernier (Tardif, Houle) 11:20
Penalties — none.

SHOTS ON GOAL BY:
WEST ... 7 11 12 — 30
EAST ....11 9 8 — 28

COACHES:
WEST, Bill Dineen (Houston)
EAST, Ron Ryan (New England)
GAME MVP — Rejean Houle (Quebec)

Game No. 2 | 1973-74 GAME
St. Paul, Jan. 3, 1974 (13,196)
EAST 8, WEST 4

FIRST PERIOD
1. East, Houle (Bernier, Paiement) 2:11
2. East, Backstrom (Carleton, Stapleton) 8:02
3. East, Pleau 10:39
4. West, Walton (Lawson) 14:55
5. East, Pinder (Lacroix, Shmyr) 18:38
6. East, Lacroix (Pinder, Jarrett) 19:12
Penalties: Ley (E) 6:34

SECOND PERIOD
7. West, Walton (Hull, Tardif) 7:27
8. East, Paiement (Backstrom) 9:15
9. West, Walton (Hamilton, Climie) 16:04
10. West, Lund (Hughes, Hamilton) 17:28
Penalties: Webster (E) 6:31

THIRD PERIOD
11. East, Lacroix (Jarrett, Pinder) 9:17
12. East, Pleau (Harris, Webster) 18:59
Penalties: Climie (W) 2:43

SHOTS ON GOAL BY:
EAST ....10 12 10 — 32
WEST ...10 13 7 — 30

COACHES:
EAST, Jack Kelley (New England)
WEST, Bobby Hull (Winnipeg)
GAME MVP — Mike Walton (Minnesota)

Game No. 1 | 1972-73 GAME
Quebec, Jan. 6, 1973 (5,435)
EAST 6, WEST 2

FIRST PERIOD
1. West, Odrowski (Beaudin) 10:39
2. East, Jarrett (Ward) 10:51
Penalties: Pleau (E) 4:43, Hanna (E) 12:09, Shmyr (E) 17:25, Harrison (W) 9:23.

SECOND PERIOD
3. East, McKenzie (Carleton, Block) 3:37
4. East, Pleau (Webster, Caffery) 12:47
5. East, Dorey, (Ward, Lawson) 19:43
Penalties: none.

THIRD PERIOD
6. West, Hull (Connelly, Bordeleau) 3:05
7. East, Lawson (Jarrett, Tremblay) 7:29
8. East, Carleton (Charlebois, Dorey) 8:00
Penalties: none

SHOTS ON GOAL BY:
WEST ... 8 13 12 — 33
EAST ....18 14 15 — 47

COACHES:
WEST, Bobby Hull (Winnipeg)
EAST, Jack Kelley (New England)
GAME MVP — Wayne Carleton (Ottawa)

WORLD HOCKEY ASSOCIATION 1976-77 SEASON

EASTERN DIVISION	WESTERN DIVISION
Birmingham Bulls	Calgary Cowboys
Cincinnati Stingers	Edmonton Oilers
Indianapolis Racers	Houston Aeros
Minnesota Fighting Saints	Phoenix Roadrunners
New England Whalers	San Diego Mariners
Quebec Nordiques	Winnipeg Jets

WHA history

CHRONOLOGY

1971

JANUARY
Dennis Murphy, co-founder with Gary L. Davidson of the American Basketball Association in 1968, conceives the idea for a second major hockey league.

APRIL
Murphy and Davidson formulate plans for the World Hockey Association.

JUNE
Articles of incorporation for the WHA are filed in Delaware June 10.

JULY
By-Laws for WHA are approved by League's first board of trustees. Signatures on document are those of Gary L. Davidson, President; Donald J. Regan and Dennis A. Murphy. Canadian participation launched when W. D. (Bill) Hunter, Edmonton, meets with league founders.

SEPTEMBER
First formal meeting of WHA held in Los Angeles Sept. 23-24.

OCTOBER
Revolutionary announcement made in Chicago Oct. 20 that WHA player contracts will not contain reserve and/or option clause.

NOVEMBER
WHA, following two days of meetings in New York, is formally organized Nov. 1 with establishment of 10 franchises — St. Paul, Chicago, Dayton, Edmonton, Los Angeles, Winnipeg, New York, Calgary, San Francisco and Miami. Two additional franchises granted Nov. 21 to Ontario and New England.

1972

JANUARY
First coach hired is Terrence Slater for Los Angeles Sharks, Jan. 7. His selection followed a few days later by naming of two of North America's foremost college coaches, Jack Kelley of Boston U for New England and Glen Sonmor of U. of Minnesota for Minnesota Fighting Saints. Vern Buffey named referee-in-chief.

FEBRUARY
A group of Quebec City businessmen, led by Paul Racine, purchase the San Francisco franchise on the eve of the WHA's first player draft Feb. 12-13 in Anaheim, Calif. A total of 1,081 amateur and professional players selected. First player signed to WHA contract is Steve Sutherland by Los Angeles. New England franchise, headed by Howard Baldwin, settles in Boston and Ontario franchise, organized by Doug Michel, is based in Ottawa. Bernie Parent, first player of major stature, signs with Miami.

MARCH
Dayton franchise, headed by Paul Deneau, transfers to Houston. U.S. Olympic goaltender Mike Curran, one of 20 American-born players to ultimately join the WHA, signs with Minnesota. Edward Fitkin, veteran hockey executive, named assistant to the president.

APRIL
Ten franchises post $100,000 performance bonds in Chicago April 14.

MAY
Janes W. Browitt, formerly executive director of Freedom Hall in Louisville, appointed league administrator and executive vice-president, succeeding Dennis Murphy who took over active leadership of the Los Angeles franchise.

JUNE
James L. Cooper and Bernard A. Brown, New Jersey businessmen, established the WHA's 11th franchise in Philadelphia, and take over Parent's contract with Miami. Nick J. Mileti, a major league owner in baseball and basketball, is granted WHA's 12th franchise for Cleveland. Monumental $2.7 million signing of Bobby Hull by Ben Hatskin of Winnipeg Jets, June 27.

JULY
Player signings multiply with acquisition of Hull; J. C. Tremblay, Quebec Nordiques; Gerry Cheevers, Cleveland Crusaders; Bobby Sheehan, New York; Ted Green, New England.

AUGUST

More than 300 players under contract. League divided into two divisions of six teams each with Cleveland Crusaders, New England Whalers, New York Raiders, Ottawa Nationals, Philadelphia Blazers and Quebec Nordiques in Eastern Division and Alberta Oilers, Chicago Cougars, Houston Aeros, Los Angeles Sharks, Minnesota Fighting Saints and Winnipeg Jets in Western Division. Adoption of 78 game schedule.

SEPTEMBER

Philadelphia first team to go to training camp on Sept. 10. Rookie squads participate in first ever WHA games Sept. 23.

OCTOBER

Professional contract players report to camps Oct. 1. Season opens Oct. 11 with Quebec at Cleveland and Alberta (Edmonton) at Ottawa. Ron Anderson of Alberta Oilers scores WHA's first regular season goal. Court order keeps Winnipeg's Hull inactive.

NOVEMBER

Hull, after missing 14 games, is cleared for action Nov. 8 following landmark ruling of Judge A. Leon Higginbotham, U.S. District Court for the Eastern Section of Pennsylvania. Hull made WHA debut same night and assisted on winning goal as Jets beat Quebec, 3-2.

1973

JANUARY

League's first all-star game in Quebec City Jan. 6; East 6, West 2. Opening of new St. Paul Civic Arena, home of Minnesota Fighting Saints, attracts crowd of 11,701 New Year's Night. First CBS televised game, also in St. Paul, before crowd of 13,426, Jan. 7.

FEBRUARY

Danny Lawson, Philadelphia, first WHA player to score 50 goals, collecting 50th Feb. 22 in Ottawa.

MARCH

Cleveland owner Nick Mileti breaks ground for $18 million arena on 100 acre site in Richfield Township.

APRIL

New England (East) and Winnipeg (West) divisional champions. Ottawa Nationals move playoff games to Maple Leaf Gardens in Toronto. Representatives of WHA and NHL meet in New York (ex-officio) to discuss possible merger. WHA rejects proposal. Alberta Oilers and Minnesota, who deadlocked for fourth place in the West, play sudden-death playoff game April 4 on neutral ice (Calgary). Minnesota wins 4-2.

MAY

New England Whalers first winners of The Avco World Trophy, defeating Winnipeg Jets, four games to one. New York franchise acquires new ownership. Team name changed to Golden Blades. Ottawa Nationals move to Toronto with new ownership, Can Sports Ltd., a group of Toronto businessmen headed by John F. Bassett, Jr. and Craig Eaton III. Team name changed to Toros. Philadelphia franchise sold to Canadian industrialist Jim Pattison and re-located in Vancouver. Cincinnati group, headed by Brian Heekin III and William O. DeWitt Jr., granted franchise May 6. Cincinnati's first active season 1975-76.

JUNE

Gordie Howe, owner of more records than any man in history of hockey, ends 21 months retirement and signs with Houston Aeros. Sons Marty, 19, and Mark, 18, also sign with Aeros, marking first time in history of major league sport that father plays alongside two sons.

JULY

Pat Stapleton signs as player-coach of Chicago Cougars.

SEPTEMBER

League membership increases to 15 with awarding of franchises to Indianapolis (Dick Tinkham and John Weissert) and Phoenix Roadrunners of Western League, headed by Jim Wells. Walt Marlow who aided in organizational structure of WHA, named director of public relations. Gordie Howe, ending two year retirement, makes first professional appearance with sons Marty and Mark Sept. 25 in New York exhibition game against New England Whalers. Howe scored 21 seconds into game with assist to son Mark.

OCTOBER
Franchise of New York Golden Blades dissolved Oct. 18. Players, property of league, reassembled as Jersey Knights. Gary Davidson resigns WHA presidency Oct. 29 at trustees' meeting in Chicago.

NOVEMBER
League-owned Jersey Knights debut Nov. 20. Dennis Murphy named WHA interim president Nov. 23. Howe family combines for first goal Nov. 18 in Quebec, Mark scoring with assists to father Gordie and brother Marty.

1974

JANUARY
Purchase of Jersey Knights by Joseph Schwartz, Jan. 3. Second WHA All-Star game in St. Paul Jan. 3 attracts crowd of 13,196 as East again defeats West, 8-4. Howe scores 800th career goal Jan. 17 in Vancouver.

FEBRUARY
The 57-year-old National League and two-year-old WHA settle $50 million case out of court Feb. 19 when both leagues signed agreement before U.S. District Judge A. Leon Higginbotham. WHA reimbursed by NHL for legal expenses of $1.7 million.

MARCH
WHA and Canadian Amateur Hockey Association reach agreement March 29 in Winnipeg on signing of Canadian juniors.

APRIL
Los Angeles Sharks franchise transferred to Detroit and renamed Michigan Stags April 11 by team owners Charles Nolton and Pete Shagena. Biggest crowd in WHA's brief history, 17,211, in St. Paul April 28 for fourth game of Houston-Minnesota Avco World Trophy semi-final series. Team Canada announces in Toronto April 29 that WHA will provide players for eight-game series with Soviet Union. Ben Hatskin of Winnipeg and John Bassett, Jr., Toronto are WHA official representatives to Team Canada. Edmonton's Bill Hunter named Team manager and Toronto's Billy Harris coach. Transfer of Jersey Knights to San Diego announced April 30 by owner Joseph Schwartz.

MAY
Houston Aeros win The Avco World trophy and WHA 1974 championship.

JUNE
Norman R. "Bud" Poile, active in professional hockey since 1942 as player, coach and top level executive, named vice-president in charge of hockey operations June 6. League divided into three divisions, Canadian, Eastern and Western. Divisions re-alignment: Edmonton, Toronto, Vancouver, Winnipeg and Quebec in Canadian Division; Houston, Michigan, Minnesota, Phoenix and San Diego in the West; Chicago, Cleveland, Indianapolis and New England in the East. Phoenix and Indianapolis are expansion teams, and Cincinnati becomes Eastern Division member in 1975-76. Toronto Toros sign Frank Mahovlich, June 19.

JULY
Larry Gordon, veteran sports executive, appointed executive vice-president of Properties.

SEPTEMBER
In first WHA game ever with NHL, Houston Aeros defeat St. Louis Blues, 5-3, Sept. 26 in Houston.

OCTOBER
WHA's third season opened Oct. 15 with new arenas in Cleveland, Edmonton, Indianapolis and later Hartford. Eight European stars debut in WHA — six Swedish, two Finnish and two Czechoslovakians.

NOVEMBER
WHA regular season record crowd of 15,326 established in Edmonton Nov. 10 with opening of new Coliseum.

DECEMBER
Paul H. Deneau, one of WHA's original architects, purchases the Indianapolis Racers Dec. 5. Deneau first owned the Houston Aeros. James Browitt, WHA vice-president, resigned Dec. 12 to become president and general manager of the Racers. A major league sports "first" realized Dec. 27 when Chicago Cougar players Pat Stapleton, Dave Dryden and Ralph Backstrom purchase the team.

1975

JANUARY
New England Whalers open new Hartford Civic Center Jan. 11 before sellout crowd of 10,570. Dennis Murphy announces resignation as president Jan. 20 effective June 1. WHA, at meeting in Edmonton for third annual all-star game Jan. 21, names Chairman of The Board Ben Hatskin chief executive officer. West Team wins its first all-star game, 6-4. League-operated Baltimore Blades, comprised of players from the defunct Michigan Stags, debut Jan. 29 in New England.

FEBRUARY
Winnipeg's Bobby Hull equals scoring record of Maurice Richard Feb. 14 with three goals against Houston — 50 goals in 50 games.

APRIL
Hull emerges major league hockey's greatest single season goal scorer ever with goal on final night of season, April 6, for an unprecedented 77 goals in 78 games. Regular season single game attendance record of 17,312 set in St. Paul April 4, Minnesota vs. Phoenix. Leo Ornest, veteran sports executive since 1948, named vice-president and director of communications.

MAY
Houston Aeros absorb only one defeat enroute to retaining The Avco World Trophy. Aero goaltender Ron Grahame chosen MVP of playoffs. Jim Pattison, president of Vancouver Blazers, May 7 announced transfer of Blazer franchise to Calgary. Team name changed to Cowboys. Ivan L. Mullenix, owner of Denver Spurs, awarded WHA franchise May 19.

JUNE
League re-affirms Ben Hatskin as chief executive officer, and name Howard Baldwin of New England vice-president; Wayne Belisle of Minnesota secretary; Toronto's John Gray, vice-president of finance and treasurer and A. J. "Telly" Mercury of Winnipeg legal counsel. League's first ever intra-league draft held June 19 in Toronto. Houston realtor George Bolin announces group's purchase of Houston Aeros for $4.1 million. Gordie Howe named Aeros' president.

JULY
League office re-located in Toronto, Canada July 1. Eighty game schedule adopted.

SEPTEMBER
Toronto Toros and Winnipeg Jets first major league teams ever to establish training camps in Europe, Toronto in Sweden and Winnipeg in Finland.

OCTOBER
Denver Spurs host Indianapolis Oct. 10 in first WHA league game at new McNichols Sports Arena. Calgary Cowboys (formerly Vancouver Blazers) host Minnesota Oct. 12 in first WHA league game at Stampede Corral. Cincinnati hosts Edmonton Oct. 23 in first WHA league game at new Riverfront Coliseum.

NOVEMBER
Houston opens new arena, The Summit, Nov. 5, vs. Minnesota.

DECEMBER
Bobby Hull, Winnipeg Jets, first WHA player to score 200 goals in league play, Dec. 14.

1976

JANUARY
Denver Spurs become Ottawa Civics, Jan. 2. Ottawa hosts New England in Ottawa at the Civic Centre before 9,467, Jan. 7. Fourth WHA All-Star Game at the Coliseum in Cleveland, Jan. 13. Canada defeats U.S.A. 6 to 1; attendance 15,491. Game telecast nationally in the U.S.A. on PBS network and in Canada on WHA network. Ottawa plays last game in WHA vs. Houston in Ottawa, Jan. 15.

FEBRUARY
Gordie Howe, Houston Aeros, records his 1,200th career assist at Phoenix, Feb. 12. WHA league attendance again passes the three million mark, Feb. 25. Minnesota Fighting Saints suspend operations, Feb. 28.

APRIL
Houston has best overall percentage (.663) with 53 wins and 106 points in 80 games vs. runner-up Winnipeg (.654) with 52 wins and 106 points in 81 games. Marc Tardif sets new

scoring record with 148 points (71 goals, 77 assists). New WHA league season attendance record of 4,123,121.

MAY

Bud Poile resigns as executive vice-president, hockey operations. Winnipeg Jets lose only one game in becoming first Canadian team to win both Canadian championship (The O'Keefe Cup) and WHA championship (The AVCO World Trophy). Winnipeg centre Ulf Nilsson named MVP of playoffs. Playoff attendance records: 445,924, marking first time more than 400,000 watched WHA playoffs, including 15 sellouts, also a new high.

JUNE

League realigned into 2 divisions — eastern and western. Toronto Toros move to Birmingham, Alabama and named Birmingham Bulls. International 3rd period rule adopted. Teams change goals at the 10-minute mark. More than 30 WHA players, coaches and officials invited to participate in 1976 Canada Cup Series.

JULY

New violence rules recommended by the violence committee of the WHA and the WHA Players Association, in Toronto July 22.

AUGUST

San Diego franchise purchased by Ray A. Kroc. WHA approves transfer of Cleveland franchise, headed by Nick J. Miletti, to St. Paul, Minnesota. New violence rules adopted by trustees Aug. 9.

SEPTEMBER

William H. MacFarland appointed president and chief operating officer of the WHA. O'Keefe Breweries Company purchases controlling interest in Quebec Nordiques.

HOME ATTENDANCES
LEAGUE SEASON 1975-76

	GP	1975-76 Totals	1975-76 Average	1974-75 Totals	1974-75 Average	Net Change	Pct Change	1975-76 Capacity	Pct.
Canadian Division									
Edmonton	40	317,234	7,931	418,150	10,722	− (100,916)	− (24.1)	610,920	51.9
Quebec	40	395,383	9,885	366,848	9,406	+ 28,353	+ 7.8	400,160	98.8
Toronto	40	359,305	8,983	407,006	10,436	− (47,401)	− (11.6)	652,280	55.1
Calgary	40	197,913	4,948	312,563	8,014	− (114,650)	− (36.7)	257,800	76.8
Winnipeg	40	347,838	8,696	334,857	8,586	+ 12,981	+ 3.9	405,240	85.8
TOTALS	200	1,617,637	8,088	1,839,424	9,433	− (221,751)	− (12.1)	2,326,400	69.5
Eastern Division									
Cincinnati	40	309,630	7,741	-	-	-	-	632,800	48.9
Cleveland	40	254,224	6,356	270,304	6,931	− (16,080)	− (5.9)	746,440	34.1
Indianapolis	40	351,127	8,778	309,005	7,932	+ 42,122	+ 13.6	634,880	55.3
New England	40	372,334	9,308	305,959	7,845	+ 66,375	+ 21.7	420,280	88.6
TOTALS	160	1,287,315	8,046	1,008,811	6,467	+ 278,504	+ 27.6	2,434,400	52.9
Western Division									
Houston	40	367,187	9,180	265,230	6,801	+ 101,957	+ 38.4	596,240	61.6
Denver/Ottawa	23	99,394	4,321	-	-	-	-	371,400	26.8
Minnesota	29	243,488	8,396	327,979	8,410	− (84,491)	− (25.8)	455,445	53.5
Phoenix	40	258,576	6,464	290,277	7,443	− (31,701)	− (10.9)	504,000	51.3
San Diego	40	249,488	6,237	237,118	6,080	+ 12,370	+ 5.2	521,560	47.8
TOTALS	172	1,218,133	7,082	1,247,676	6,398	− (29,543)	− (2.4)	2,448,645	49.7
14 Team Totals	532	4,123,121	7,750	4,095,911	7,502	+ 27,210	+ 0.7	7,209,445	57.2

TEAM — SEASON

MOST POINTS:
106 — Houston, 1974-75/1975-76; Winnipeg, 1975-76

FEWEST POINTS:
39 — Indianapolis, 1974-75

MOST POINTS AT HOME:
66 — Houston; Quebec; 1975-76. 33 wins, 7 losses

FEWEST POINTS AT HOME:
26 — Indianapolis, 1974-75

MOST POINTS ON ROAD:
50 — Houston, 1974-75

FEWEST POINTS ON ROAD:
13 — Indianapolis; Michigan/Baltimore; 1974-75

MOST WINS:
53 — Houston, 1974-75/1975-76

FEWEST WINS:
18 — Indianapolis, 1974-75

MOST HOME WINS:
33 — Houston; Quebec; 1975-76

FEWEST HOME WINS:
13 — Indianapolis, 1974-75

MOST ROAD WINS:
25 — Houston, 1974-75

FEWEST ROAD WINS:
5 — Indianapolis, 1974-75

MOST LOSSES:
57 — Indianapolis, 1974-75

FEWEST LOSSES:
25 — Houston, 1973-74/1974-75

MOST HOME LOSSES:
26 — Indianapolis, 1974-75

FEWEST HOME LOSSES:
7 — Houston; Quebec; 1975-76

MOST ROAD LOSSES:
32 — Michigan/Baltimore, 1974-75 (40 games); Edmonton and Toronto 1975-76 (41 games)

FEWEST ROAD LOSSES:
14 — Houston, 1974-75

MOST TIES:
9 — Cleveland, 1973-74

FEWEST TIES:
0 — Philadelphia (1972-73); Los Angeles (1973-74); Quebec (1974-75); Houston (1974-75/1975-76)

MOST HOME TIES
6 — Phoenix, 1975-76 (40 games)
5 — Phoenix, 1974-75; Quebec, 1972-73 (39 games)

FEWEST HOME TIES:
0 — By 13 teams

MOST ROAD TIES:
5 — Los Angeles, 1972-73; Cleveland 1973-74 (39 games); N.E., 1975-76 (40 games)

FEWEST ROAD TIES:
0 — By nine teams

MOST GOALS SCORED:
371 — Quebec, 1975-76 (81 games)

44

WHA records

MOST GOALS ALLOWED:
398 — Toronto, 1975-76 (81 games)
FEWEST GOALS SCORED:
205 — Michigan/Baltimore, 1974-75
FEWEST GOALS ALLOWED:
219 — Houston, 1973-74
MOST SCORING POINTS:
999 — Quebec, 1975-76. 371 goals, 628 assists (81 games)
FEWEST SCORING POINTS:
540 — Michigan/Baltimore, 1974-75
MOST ASSISTS:
628 — Quebec, 1975-76 (81 games)
FEWEST ASSISTS:
335 — Michigan/Baltimore, 1974-75
MOST SHUTOUTS:
6 — Houston, 1974-75
FEWEST SHUTOUTS:
0 — Ottawa, 1972-73; Quebec, 1974-75
MOST TIMES SHUTOUT:
8 — Los Angeles, 1973-74; Indianapolis, 1974-75
LEAST TIMES SHUTOUT:
0 — Seven teams
MOST CONSECUTIVE GAMES NOT SHUTOUT:
200 — Minnesota. Feb. 9, 1973 to Dec. 12, 1975
MOST SHUTOUTS AT HOME:
5 — Minnesota, 1972-73
FEWEST SHUTOUTS AT HOME:
0 — Five teams
MOST TIMES SHUTOUT AT HOME:
5 — Los Angeles, 1973-74, Indianapolis, 1974-75
LEAST TIMES SHUTOUT AT HOME:
0 — 24 teams
MOST CONSECUTIVE HOME GAMES NOT SHUTOUT:
157 — Quebec and Toronto (Birmingham) have never been shutout at home
MOST SHUTOUTS ON THE ROAD:
3 — Houston, 1974-75.
FEWEST SHUTOUTS ON THE ROAD:
0 — 17 teams
MOST TIMES SHUTOUT ON ROAD:
6 — Philadelphia, 1972-73
LEAST TIMES SHUTOUT ON ROAD:
0 — 10 teams.
MOST CONSECUTIVE ROAD GAMES NOT SHUTOUT:
106 — Ottawa/Toronto. Feb. 15, 1973 to Dec. 27, 1975
LONGEST SHUTOUT SEQUENCE:
228 Minutes, 10 Seconds — Winnipeg, from 8:25 of first period vs. Denver Oct. 24 until 16:35 of third period vs. Quebec Nov. 2, 1975. Streak included shutouts of Phoenix, Oct. 26 and Cincinnati, Oct. 30
LONGEST TIME ONE TEAM SHUTOUT:
181 minutes, 25 seconds — San Diego, from 13:32 of second period vs. Houston Nov. 5 until 14:57 of second period vs. Quebec Nov. 10, 1974. Included shutouts by Indianapolis, Nov. 7 and New England, Nov. 8
MOST PENALTY MINUTES:
1654 — Quebec, 1975-76
FEWEST PENALTY MINUTES:
671 — Winnipeg, 1973-74

MOST POWERPLAY OPPORTUNITIES:
394 — Winnipeg, 1975-76

MOST POWER PLAY GOALS:
77 — Houston, 1975-76 (80 games); Quebec, 1975-76 (81 games)

MOST GOALS ALLOWED WHILE ON POWERPLAY:
16 — Winnipeg, 1974-75

MOST PROFICIENT POWER PLAY:
30.9% — Quebec, 1975-76. 77 goals in 249 opportunities

MOST SHORTHANDED SITUATIONS:
372 — Houston, 1974-75

MOST GOALS SCORED WHILE SHORTHANDED:
20 — Minnesota, 1973-74

MOST GOALS ALLOWED WHILE SHORTHANDED:
89 — Phoenix, 1975-76

MOST EFFICIENT PENALTY KILLING:
86.5% — New England, 1974-75

MOST 100-OR-MORE POINT SCORERS:
5 — Quebec, 1975-76. M. Tardif (148); R. Cloutier (114); C. Bordeleau (109); R. Houle (103); S. Bernier (102)

MOST 60-OR-MORE GOAL SCORERS:
2 — Quebec, 1975-76. M. Tardif (71); R. Cloutier (60)

MOST 50-OR-MORE GOAL SCORERS:
3 — Quebec, 1975-76. M. Tardif (71); R. Cloutier (60); R. Houle (51)

MOST PLAYERS WITH 4-OR-MORE GOAL NIGHTS:
4 — Philadelphia, 1972-73. A. Lacroix (2); D. Lawson (2)
— Toronto, 1974-75. T. Simpson (3); J. Jacques (1)

MOST PLAYERS WITH 3-OR-MORE GOAL NIGHTS: (HAT TRICK)
12 — Philadelphia, 1972-73. D. Lawson (6); A. Lacroix (3); J. McKenzie (2); D. Herriman (1)
— Quebec, 1975-76. R. Houle (5); R. Cloutier (4); S. Bernier, M. Tardif, T. Serviss (1 each)

LONGEST UNDEFEATED STREAK:
12 — Toronto, March 22-Oct. 28, 1974. 12 wins

LONGEST UNDEFEATED STREAK: (One Season)
11 — Edmonton, Oct. 21-Nov. 16, 1973. 11 wins
— Minnesota, Feb. 13-March 10, 1974. 10 wins, 1 tie

LONGEST WIN STREAK:
12 — Toronto, March 22-Oct. 28, 1974

LONGEST WIN STREAK: (One Season)
11 — Edmonton, Oct. 21-Nov. 16, 1973

LONGEST LOSING STREAK:
13 — Indianapolis, Nov. 13-Dec. 5, 1974

LONGEST WINLESS STREAK:
17 — Toronto, Jan. 22-Feb. 29, 1976. 15 losses, 2 ties

LONGEST HOME WIN STREAK: (Including Playoffs)
22 — Houston, March 19-Dec. 3, 1975

LONGEST HOME WIN STREAK: (Regular Season)
15 — Houston, March 19-Dec. 3, 1975

LONGEST HOME WINNING STREAK: (One Season)
10 — Quebec, Jan. 5-Feb. 22, 1974

LONGEST HOME LOSING STREAK:
7 — Vancouver, Oct. 21-Nov. 13, 1973
— Indianapolis, Nov. 19-Dec. 5, 1974
— Baltimore, Feb. 2-Feb. 18, 1975

LONGEST HOME WINLESS STREAK:
8 — Denver, Oct. 10-Nov. 18, 1975. 7 losses, 1 tie

LONGEST ROAD UNDEFEATED STREAK:
9 — Indianapolis, March 6, 1976 to April 4, 1976. 7 wins, 2 ties
— Houston, Oct. 29-Dec. 4, 1974. 9 wins

LONGEST ROAD WIN STREAK:
9 — Houston, Oct. 29-Dec. 4, 1974
LONGEST ROAD LOSING STREAK:
14 — Los Angeles, Jan. 29-March 31, 1974
LONGEST ROAD WINLESS STREAK:
25 — Michigan/Baltimore, Oct. 19, 1974 to Feb. 1, 1975. 24 losses, 1 tie
MOST CONSECUTIVE TIE GAMES:
3 — Indianapolis, March 18-March 23, 1976
MOST CONSECUTIVE OVERTIME GAMES:
4 — Alberta, Feb. 28-March 10, 1973. Won 2, lost 2
— Chicago, March 5-March 10, 1973. Won 1, lost 2, tied 1
— Indianapolis, March 18-March 25, 1976. Won 1, tied 3

TEAM SINGLE GAME RECORDS

MOST GOALS, BOTH TEAMS, ONE GAME:
19 — Nov. 13/75, Toronto 11 at Denver 8; Nov. 30/75, Toronto 9 at Cleveland 10
MOST GOALS, ONE TEAM, ONE GAME:
12 — Jan. 27/74, Winnipeg 2 at Minnesota 12; Mar. 1/75, Indianapolis 2 at Phoenix 12
MOST MULTIPLE GOAL PERFORMANCES, ONE TEAM, ONE GAME:
6 — Phoenix, March 1/75, (Dennis Sobchuk, Robbie Ftorek, Dennis Boyd, Michel Cormier, John Gray, Bob Mowat scored two goals each). Indy 2 at Phoenix 12
MOST CONSECUTIVE GOALS, ONE TEAM, ONE GAME:
10 — Dec. 19/73, Winnipeg 0 at Houston 10
— Jan. 27/74, Winnipeg 2 at Minnesota 12
— Mar. 17/74, New England 1 at Winnipeg 10
— Nov. 1/74, Toronto 1 at Winnipeg 10
— Nov. 19/74, Houston 10 at Indianapolis 0
MOST CONSECUTIVE GOALS BY ONE TEAM MORE THAN ONE GAME:
15 — Houston. Last 2 vs. San Diego Nov. 17, all 10 vs. Indianapolis Nov. 19 and first 3 at Vancouver Nov. 22/74
— Winnipeg. Last 10 vs. Toronto Nov. 1 and first 5 vs. Michigan Nov. 3/75
MOST GOALS SCORED, TWO CONSECUTIVE GAMES, ONE TEAM:
21 — Winnipeg defeated Toronto 10-1, Nov. 1 and Michigan 11-3, Nov. 3/74
MOST GOALS SCORED, THREE CONSECUTIVE GAMES, ONE TEAM:
27 — Winnipeg 6-Phoenix 5, Oct. 30; Winnipeg 10-Toronto 1, Nov. 1; Winnipeg 11-Michigan 3, Nov. 3/74
— Winnipeg 10-Toronto 1, Nov. 1; Winnipeg 11-Michigan 3, Nov. 3; Winnipeg 6-Minnesota 4, Nov. 5/75
MOST GOALS SCORED BY A LOSING TEAM:
9 — Toronto 9 at Cleveland 10, Nov. 30, 1975
MOST GOALS, BOTH TEAMS, ONE PERIOD:
9 — Five games, 10 teams
MOST GOALS, ONE TEAM, ONE PERIOD:
8 — Toronto third period Dec. 9, 1973 vs. Minnesota. Toronto 10, Minnesota 1
MOST POWERPLAY GOALS, ONE TEAM, ONE GAME:
6 — Indianapolis Dec. 4, 1975 vs. Cincinnati. Indianapolis 7, Cincinnati 1
— Calgary March 9, 1976 vs. Quebec. Calgary 7, Quebec 4
— Winnipeg March 10, 1976 vs. Quebec. Winnipeg 10, Quebec 3
MOST POWERPLAY GOALS SCORED IN TWO CONSECUTIVE GAMES:
11 — Winnipeg, 6 vs. Quebec March 10, 1976, and 5 vs. Quebec March 12, 1976
MOST POINTS, BOTH TEAMS, ONE GAME:
50 — Toronto 11 at Denver 8, Nov. 13, 1975. Toronto 19 assists, Denver 12
— Cleveland 10 vs. Toronto 9, Nov. 30, 1975. Cleveland 17 assists, Toronto 14
MOST POINTS, ONE TEAM, ONE GAME:
34 — Minnesota 12 vs. Winnipeg 8, Jan. 27, 1974. Minnesota 22 assists

MOST GOALS ALLOWED, TWO CONSECUTIVE GAMES, ONE TEAM:
21 — Quebec lost to Cincinnati 11-7, Dec. 21, and to San Diego 10-4, Dec. 23, 1975

FEWEST GOALS SCORED, THREE CONSECUTIVE GAMES:
1 — Several teams

MOST PENALTIES, BOTH TEAMS, ONE GAME:
45 — Cleveland at Minnesota Oct. 15, 1975. Cleveland 16 minors, 4 majors, 4 misconducts. Minnesota 13 minors, 4 majors, 4 misconducts. Clev. won 8-4

MOST PENALTY MINUTES, BOTH TEAMS, ONE GAME:
228 — Cleveland at Indianapolis March 8, 1975. Cleveland 11 minors, 5 majors, 7 misconducts for 117 minutes. Indianapolis 8 minors, 5 majors, 7 misconducts for 111 minutes. Clev. won 6-5

MOST PENALTIES, ONE TEAM, ONE GAME: (and)
MOST PENALTY MINUTES, ONE TEAM, ONE GAME:
26 penalties, 137 minutes — Phoenix Feb. 7, 1975 vs. Minnesota. Phoenix 11 minors, 7 majors, 5 misconducts, 3 game misconducts. Phoenix won, 4-1

MOST PENALTIES, BOTH TEAMS, ONE PERIOD: (and)
MOST PENALTY MINUTES, BOTH TEAMS, ONE PERIOD:
32 penalties, 192 minutes — Cleveland at Indianapolis March 8, 1975. Indianapolis 7 minors, 4 majors, 6 misconducts for 98 minutes. Cleveland 4 minors, 4 majors, 7 misconducts for 94 minutes in the second period. Cleveland won 6-5

MOST PENALTIES, ONE TEAM, ONE PERIOD: (an)
MOST PENALTY MINUTES, ONE TEAM, ONE PERIOD:
20 penalties, 111 minutes Phoenix Feb. 7, 1975 vs. Minnesota. Phoenix 8 minors, 5 majors, 7 misconducts in the third period. Phoenix won 4-1

MOST POWERPLAY OPPORTUNITIES, BOTH TEAMS, ONE GAME:
21 — Cincinnati (9) at Indianapolis (12) Dec. 4, 1975. Indy won 7-1

MOST POWERPLAY OPPORTUNITIES, ONE TEAM, ONE GAME:
13 — Winnipeg Oct. 21, 1975 vs. Cincinnati. Winnipeg scored 3 p.p. goals; won 7-0
— Winnipeg March 10, 1976 vs. Quebec. Winnipeg scored 6 p.p. goals; won 10-3

MOST SHORTHANDED GOALS, ONE GAME, ONE TEAM:
3 — Minnesota March 6, 1974 vs. New England. Minnesota won 8-6
— Winnipeg Nov. 1, 1974 vs. Toronto. Winnipeg won 10-1
— Phoenix Jan. 22, 1975 vs. Chicago. Phoenix won 8-5
— Houston March 27, 1975 vs. Winnipeg. Houston won 8-0

MOST GOALS ALLOWED WHILE SHORTHANDED, ONE TEAM, TWO GAMES:
12 — Quebec allowed 6 at Calgary March 9; and 6 at Winnipeg March 10, 1976

MOST GOALS ALLOWED WHILE SHORTHANDED, ONE TEAM, THREE GAMES:
17 — Quebec allowed 6 at Calgary, March 9; 6 at Winnipeg March 10; and 5 at Winnipeg March 12, 1976

FASTEST TWO GOALS, BOTH TEAMS:
5 seconds — Winnipeg at San Diego Jan. 28, 1975. First period. Bobby Hull (Winnipeg) at 19:41; Norm Ferguson (San Diego) at 19:46 Wpg. won 9-7

FASTEST THREE GOALS, BOTH TEAMS:
27 seconds — New England at New York, Nov. 29, 1972. Second period. John French (N.E.) 12:53; Ron Ward (NY)13:11 and 13:20. N.Y. won 7-6

FASTEST FOUR GOALS, TWO TEAMS:
1 min. 2 sec. — San Diego at Cincinnati Nov. 8, 1975. Second period. Gene Peacosh (SD) 14:50; Kevin Devine (SD) 15:14; Dave Inkpen (Cin) 15:32; and Andre Lacroix (SD) 15:52. Cin. won 7-4

FASTEST FIVE GOALS, TWO TEAMS:
3 min. 5 sec. — San Diego at Toronto Feb. 20, 1976. Second period. John French (SD) 6:55; Vaclav Nedomansky (Tor) 7:12; Brian Morenz (SD) 8:22; Kevin Devine (SD) 8:42; and Gene Peacosh (SD) 10:00. S.D. won 6-4

FASTEST TWO GOALS, ONE TEAM:
4 sec. — New England. Third period. Dec. 16, 1972 at Philadelphia. Terry Caffery 2:49; and Brit Selby 2:53. N.E. won 10-6

FASTEST THREE GOALS, ONE TEAM:
32 sec. — Chicago. Third period. Dec. 19, 1972 vs. Cleveland. Poul Popiel 18:46; Bob Sicinski 19:02; and Bob Liddington 19:18. Chicago won 6-1

FASTEST FOUR GOALS, ONE TEAM:
  1 min. 45 sec. — Alberta Oilers. Third period. Jan. 30, 1973 vs. N.Y. Raiders. Rusty Patenaude 10:48; Doug Barrie 11:48; Steve Carlyle 12:00; and Jim Harrison 12:33. Alberta won 11-3

FASTEST FIVE GOALS, ONE TEAM:
  4 min. 48 sec. — Alberta Oilers. Third period. Jan. 30, 1973 vs. New York at Edmonton. Bernie Blanchette 7:45; Rusty Patenaude 10:48; Doug Barrie 11:48; Steve Carlyle 12:00; Jim Harrison 12:33. Alta. won 11-3

FASTEST THREE POWERPLAY GOALS, ONE TEAM:
  1 min. 46 sec. — Indianapolis. Oct. 30, 1975 vs. Calgary. Randy Wyrozub 18:42 and 19:02 in second period and 0:28 in third period. Calgary won 7-5

FASTEST TWO GOALS FROM THE START OF GAME, BOTH TEAMS:
  43 sec. — Phoenix at New England March 13, 1975. Robbie Ftorek (Phx) 0:12; and Don Blackburn (NE) 0:43.

FASTEST THREE GOALS FROM START OF GAME, BOTH TEAMS:
  2 min. 12 sec. — Vancouver at Toronto Jan. 27, 1974. Mike Chernoff (Van) 1:27; Wayne Dillon (Tor) 1:58; and Tom Simpson (Tor) 2:12. Tor. won 9-7

FASTEST FOUR GOALS FROM START OF GAME, BOTH TEAMS:
  3 min. 44 sec. — New England at Winnipeg Oct. 10, 1976. Ulf Nilsson (Wpg) 0:35; Rosaire Paiement (NE) 1:55; Ulf Nilsson (Wpg) 2:34; and Dan Bolduc (NE) 3:44. Wpg. won 5-2

FASTEST FIVE GOALS FROM START OF GAME, BOTH TEAMS:
  6 min. 1 sec. — Winnipeg at Denver Oct. 16, 1975. Willy Lindstrom (Wpg) 1:00; Veli-Pekka Ketola (Wpg) 1:59 and 3:10; Bill Lesuk (Wpg) 5:27; and Francois Rochon (Dvr) 6:01. Wpg. won 7-3

FASTEST TWO GOALS FROM START OF SECOND PERIOD, BOTH TEAMS:
  58 sec. — Houston at Los Angeles Feb. 15, 1974. Jim Sherrit (Hou) 0:24; and Gary Veneruzzo (LA) 0:58. Houston won 6-4

FASTEST TWO GOALS FROM START OF THIRD PERIOD, BOTH TEAMS:
  45 sec. — Quebec at Cleveland Dec. 27, 1974. Rich Leduc (Clv) 0:27; Serge Bernier (Que) 0:45. Clev. won 4-3

FASTEST TWO GOALS FROM START OF GAME, ONE TEAM:
  28 sec. — Minnesota Feb. 17, 1973 at Cleveland. Mike McMahon 0:19; and George Morrison 0:28. Minn. won 7-3

FASTEST THREE GOALS FROM START OF GAME, ONE TEAM:
  2 min. 45 sec. — Edmonton Oct. 14, 1973 vs. Houston. Jim Harrison 0:13; Ron Climie 0:35; and Ken Baird 2:45. Edm. won 5-2

FASTEST FOUR GOALS FROM START OF GAME, ONE TEAM:
  5 min. 27 sec. — Winnipeg Oct. 16, 1975 at Denver. Willy Lindstrom 1:00; Veli-Pekka Ketola 1:59 and 3:10; and Bill Lesuk 5:27. Wpg. won 7-3

FASTEST FIVE GOALS FROM START OF GAME, ONE TEAM:
  11 min. 5 sec. — Winnipeg Nov. 1, 1974 vs. Toronto. Perry Ford 3:36; Danny Spring 5:21; Bobby Hull 7:20; and Chris Bordeleau 9:01 and 11:05. Wpg. won 10-1

FASTEST TWO GOALS FROM START OF SECOND PERIOD, ONE TEAM:
  20 sec. — Cincinnati Oct. 23, 1975 vs. Edmonton. Rick Dudley 0:12 and 0:20. Cin. 6-4

FASTEST TWO GOALS FROM START OF THIRD PERIOD, ONE TEAM:
  47 sec. — Toronto Nov. 9, 1974 at Minnesota. Paul Henderson 0:23 and 0:47. Tor. 7-4

MOST SHOTS ON GOAL, BOTH TEAMS, ONE GAME:
  107 — Michigan (53) at Winnipeg (54) Nov. 29, 1974. Wpg. won 7-6
  — San Diego (48) at Toronto (59) March 14, 1975. S.D. won 6-4

MOST SHOTS ON GOAL, ONE TEAM, ONE GAME:
  64 — San Diego Dec. 23, 1975 vs. Quebec. S.D. won 10-4

MOST SHOTS ON GOAL IN A LOSING EFFORT:
  59 — Toronto March 14, 1975 vs. San Diego. S.D. won 6-4

MOST SHOTS ON GOAL, ONE PERIOD, BOTH TEAMS:
  41 — Indianapolis (17) at Toronto (24) Feb. 9, 1975 second period. Tor. won 7-5

MOST SHOTS ON GOAL, ONE PERIOD, ONE TEAM:
  32 — San Diego Dec. 23, 1975 first period vs. Quebec. S.D. won 10-4

FEWEST SHOTS ON GOAL, BOTH TEAMS, ONE GAME:
    35 — New England (14) at Cleveland (21) Nov. 17, 1972. Clev. won 3-0

FEWEST SHOTS ON GOAL, ONE TEAM, ONE GAME:
    11 — Indianapolis Dec. 18, 1975 at Phoenix. Phx. won 7-1

FEWEST SHOTS ON GOAL, ONE PERIOD, BOTH TEAMS:
    7 — Cleveland (2) at Los Angeles (5) second period Nov. 16, 1973. Clev. won 4-3

FEWEST SHOTS ON GOAL, ONE PERIOD, ONE TEAM:
    0 — New York Raiders first period Nov. 5, 1972 at Winnipeg
    — Indianapolis second period March 23, 1976 at San Diego

FEWEST SHOTS ON GOAL BY A WINNING TEAM:
    13 — New England Dec. 14, 1972 at Los Angeles. N.E. won 5-2

FORWARD LINE RECORDS

MOST POINTS BY A FORWARD LINE, ONE SEASON:
    371 — Chris Bordeleau (109), Real Cloutier (114), Marc Tardif (148). Quebec, 1975-76. (Avg. 4.58 points per game). 81 games
    362 — Ulf Nilsson (120), Anders Hedberg (100), Bobby Hull (142). Winnipeg, 1974-75. (Avg. 4.64 points per game). 78 games

MOST GOALS BY A FORWARD LINE, ONE SEASON:
    168 — Chris Bordeleau (37), Real Cloutier (60), Marc Tardif (71). Quebec, 1975-76 (Avg. 2.07 goals per game). 81 games
    156 — Ulf Nilsson (26), Anders Hedberg (53), Bobby Hull (77). Winnipeg, 1974-75. (Avg. 2.00 goals per game). 78 games

MOST ASSISTS BY A FORWARD LINE, ONE SEASON:
    206 — Ulf Nilsson (94), Anders Hedberg (47), Bobby Hull (65). Winnipeg, 1974-75. (Avg. 2.64 per game, 1.32 per goal)

MOST SHOTS ON GOAL BY A FORWARD LINE, ONE SEASON:
    974 — Ulf Nilsson (147), Anders Hedberg (271), Bobby Hull (556). Winnipeg, 1974-75. (Avg. 12.4 per game)

INDIVIDUAL CAREER

MOST SEASONS:
    4 — Several players

MOST GAMES:
    317 — Tim Sheehy; New England, Edmonton

MOST CONSECUTIVE GAMES PLAYED:
    314 — Rosaire Paiement; Chicago, New England. (Has never missed a WHA game)
    — Andre Lacroix; Philadelphia, New York, New Jersey, San Diego. (Has never missed a WHA game)
    — Danny Lawson; Philadelphia, Vancouver, Calgary. (Has never missed a WHA game)
    311 — Gavin Kirk; Ottawa, Toronto, Calgary. (Has never missed a WHA game)

MOST POINTS:
    483 — Andre Lacroix; Philadelphia, New York, New Jersey, San Diego. 151 goals, 332 assists and two scoring championships

MOST GOALS:
    234 — Bobby Hull, Winnipeg

MOST ASSISTS:
    332 — Andre Lacroix; Philadelphia, New York, New Jersey, San Diego

MOST PENALTY MINUTES:
    723 — Gord Gallant; Minnesota, Quebec

MOST THREE-OR-MORE GOAL GAMES:
    16 — Bobby Hull, Winnipeg. 13 three goal, 3 four goal games

MOST FOUR-OR-MORE GOAL GAMES:
3 — Bobby Hull, Winnipeg
  — Danny Lawson; Philadelphia, Vancouver, Calgary
  — Tom Simpson, Toronto

MOST FIVE GOAL GAMES:
2 — Ron Ward; New York, Cleveland

MOST GAMES APPEARED IN, BY A GOALTENDER:
224 — Don McLeod; Houston, Vancouver, Calgary

MOST SHUTOUTS:
13 — Gerry Cheevers, Cleveland

INDIVIDUAL — SINGLE SEASON

MOST GAMES:
81 — 11 Players

MOST POINTS:
148 — Marc Tardif, Quebec, 1975-76 (71 goals, 77 assists)
147 — Andre Lacroix, San Diego, 1974-75 (41 goals, 106 assists)

MOST GOALS:
77 — Bobby Hull, Winnipeg, 1974-75

MOST ASSISTS:
106 — Andre Lacroix, San Diego, 1974-75

MOST POINTS BY A CENTRE:
147 — Andre Lacroix, San Diego, 1974-75

MOST GOALS BY A CENTRE:
56 — Vaclav Nedomansky, Toronto, 1975-76

MOST ASSISTS BY A CENTRE:
106 — Andre Lacroix, San Diego, 1974-75

MOST POINTS BY A RIGHT WING:
117 — Mike Walton, Minnesota, 1973-74 (57 goals, 60 assists)

MOST GOALS BY A RIGHT WING:
61 — Danny Lawson, Philadelphia, 1972-73

MOST ASSISTS BY A RIGHT WING:
69 — Gordie Howe, Houston, 1973-74

BOBBY HULL

MOST POINTS BY A LEFT WING:
148 — Marc Tardif, Quebec, 1975-76 (71 goals, 77 assists)

MOST GOALS BY A LEFT WING:
77 — Bobby Hull, Winnipeg, 1974-75

MOST ASSISTS BY A LEFT WING:
77 — Marc Tardif, Quebec, 1975-76

MOST POINTS BY A DEFENCEMAN:
89 — J. C. Tremblay, Quebec, 1972-73. (14 goals, 75 assists)
  — J. C. Tremblay, Quebec 1975-76. (12 goals, 77 assists)

MOST GOALS BY A DEFENCEMAN:
24 — Kevin Morrison, New Jersey, 1973-74

MOST ASSISTS BY A DEFENCEMAN:
77 — J. C. Tremblay, Quebec, 1975-76

MOST POINTS AND ASSISTS BY A GOALTENDER:
13 — Don McLeod, Calgary, 1975-76

MOST PENALTY MINUTES:
365 — Curt Brackenbury, Minnesota, Quebec, 1975-76

MOST PENALTY MINUTES BY A CENTRE:
157 — Mike Rouleau, Quebec, 1972-73

MOST PENALTY MINUTES BY A RIGHT WINGER:
365 — Curt Brackenbury, Minnesota, Quebec, 1975-76

MOST PENALTY MINUTES BY A LEFT WING:
297 — Gord Gallant, Minnesota, Quebec, 1975-76

MOST PENALTY MINUTES BY A DEFENCEMAN:
351 — Kim Clackson, Indianapolis, 1975-76

MOST PENALTY MINUTES BY A GOALTENDER:
75 — Andy Brown, Indianapolis, 1974-75
MOST POWER PLAY GOALS:
27 — Bobby Hull, Winnipeg, 1974-75
MOST SHORTHANDED GOALS:
9 — Mike Walton, Minnesota, 1973-74
LONGEST CONSECUTIVE POINT STREAK:
32 games — Andre Lacroix, San Diego. Between Nov. 19, 1974 and Feb. 13, 1975. (17 goals, 53 assists, 70 points)
LONGEST CONSECUTIVE GOAL STREAK:
11 games — Serge Bernier, Quebec. 16 goals between Dec. 5 and Dec. 22, 1974
LONGEST CONSECUTIVE ASSIST STREAK:
16 games — Andre Lacroix, San Diego. 32 assists between Jan. 18 and Feb. 25, 1975
FASTEST 20 GOALS:
18 games — Bobby Hull, Winnipeg, 1974-75
FASTEST 30 GOALS:
29 games — Bobby Hull, Winnipeg, 1974-75
FASTEST 40 GOALS:
41 games — Bobby Hull, Winnipeg, 1974-75
FASTEST 50 GOALS:
50 games — Bobby Hull, Winnipeg, 1974-75
FASTEST 60 GOALS:
62 games — Bobby Hull, Winnipeg, 1974-75
FASTEST 70 GOALS:
69 games — Bobby Hull, Winnipeg, 1974-75

INDIVIDUAL — SINGLE GAME

MOST POINTS:
10 — Jim Harrison, Alberta, Jan. 30, 1973 vs. New York Raiders. 3 goals, 7 assists
MOST GOALS:
5 — Ron Ward, N.Y. Raiders vs. Ottawa Nationals, Jan. 4, 1973
— Ron Ward, Cleveland vs. Toronto, Nov. 30, 1975
— Ron Climie, Edmonton vs. N.Y. Golden Blades. Nov. 6, 1973
— Andre Hinse, Houston vs. Edmonton, Jan. 15, 1975
— Vaclav Nedomansky, Toronto vs. Denver, Nov. 13, 1975
— Wayne Connelly, Minnesota vs. Cincinnati, Nov. 27, 1975
MOST ASSISTS:
7 — Jim Harrison, Alberta vs. N.Y. Raiders, Jan. 30, 1973
— Jim Harrison, Cleveland vs. Toronto, Nov. 30, 1975
MOST POINTS BY A RIGHT WING:
7 — Danny Lawson, Philadelphia vs. Quebec, Jan. 13, 1973. 3 goals, 4 assists
— Ron Ward, Cleveland vs. Toronto, Nov. 30, 1975. 5 goals, 2 assists
MOST GOALS BY A RIGHT WING:
5 — Ron Climie, Edmonton vs. N.Y. Golden Blades. Nov. 6, 1973
— Ron Ward, Cleveland vs. Toronto, Nov. 30, 1975
MOST ASSISTS BY A RIGHT WING:
5 — Wayne Rivers, N.Y. Raiders vs. Ottawa Nationals, Jan. 4, 1974
— Danny Lawson, Philadelphia vs. Ottawa Nationals, March 9, 1973
— John McKenzie, Vancouver vs. Edmonton, Feb. 5, 1974
— John French, New England vs. Los Angeles, March 27, 1974
MOST POINTS BY A CENTRE:
10 — Jim Harrison, Alberta vs. N.Y. Raiders, Jan. 30, 1973. 3 goals, 7 assists
MOST GOALS BY A CENTRE:
5 — Ron Ward, N.Y. Raiders vs. Ottawa Nationals, Jan. 4, 1973
— Vaclav Nedomansky, Toronto vs. Denver, Nov. 13, 1975
MOST ASSISTS BY A CENTRE:
7 — Jim Harrison, Alberta vs. N.Y. Raiders, Jan 30, 1973
— Jim Harrison, Cleveland vs. Toronto, Nov. 30, 1975

MOST POINTS BY A LEFT WING:
6 — Bobby Hull, Winnipeg at Chicago, Feb. 15, 1973. 4 goals, 2 assists
— Marc Tardif, Quebec vs. Edmonton, Oct. 14, 1975. 2 goals, 4 assists

MOST GOALS BY A LEFT WING:
5 — Andre Hinse, Houston vs Edmonton, Jan. 15, 1975

MOST ASSISTS BY A LEFT WING:
4 — Eight players

MOST POINTS BY A DEFENCEMAN:
6 — Doug Barrie, Alberta vs. N.Y. Raiders, Jan. 30, 1973. 1 goal, 5 assists
— Pat Stapleton, Indianapolis vs. Cincinnati, Dec. 4, 1975. 6 assists

MOST GOALS BY A DEFENCEMAN:
3 — Kevin Morrison, New Jersey vs. Toronto, March 18, 1974

MOST ASSISTS BY A DEFENCEMAN:
6 — Pat Stapleton, Indianapolis vs. Cincinnati, Dec. 4, 1975

MOST POINTS AND ASSISTS BY A GOALTENDER:
2 — Don McLeod, Vancouver vs. New England, Feb. 9, 1975
— Don McLeod, Calgary vs. Edmonton, Dec. 5, 1975

MOST SHOTS-ON-GOAL:
18 — Bobby Hull, Winnipeg at Quebec, April 5, 1975

MOST POINTS, ONE PERIOD:
5 — Jim Harrison, Alberta vs. N.Y. Raiders, Jan. 30, 1973. Third period. 1 goal, 4 assists
— Doug Barrie, Alberta vs. N.Y. Raiders, Jan. 30, 1973. Third period. 1 goal, 4 assists
— Jim Harrison, Cleveland vs. Toronto, Nov. 30, 1975. Third period. 5 assists

MOST GOALS, ONE PERIOD:
4 — Ron Climie, Edmonton vs. N.Y. Golden Blades, Nov. 6, 1973. Third period

MOST ASSISTS, ONE PERIOD:
5 — Jim Harrison, Cleveland vs. Toronto, Nov. 30, 1975. Third period

FASTEST TWO GOALS:
6 seconds — Gary Veneruzzo, Los Angeles vs. Alberta, Dec. 10, 1972. Goals at 15:24 and 15:30 of third period

FASTEST THREE GOALS:
43 seconds — George Morrison, Minnesota vs. Vancouver, April 3, 1974. Goals at 15:42, 15:56 and 16:25 of second period

FASTEST THREE POWER PLAY GOALS:
1 minute, 46 seconds — Randy Wyrozub, Indianapolis vs. Calgary, Oct. 30, 1975. Goals at 18:42 and 19:02 of second period, and 0:28 of third period

FASTEST TWO POWER PLAY GOALS:
20 seconds — Randy Wyrozub, Indianapolis vs. Calgary, Oct. 30, 1975. Goals at 18:42 and 19:02 of second period

FASTEST GOAL FROM THE START OF GAME:
5 seconds — Russ Walker, Cleveland vs. Minnesota, Feb. 19, 1975

FASTEST TWO GOALS FROM THE START OF GAME:
1 minute, 24 seconds — Doug Kerslake, Edmonton vs. Quebec, March 18, 1975. Goals at 1:12 and 1:24

FASTEST GOAL FROM THE START OF SECOND PERIOD:
5 seconds — Skip Krake, Cleveland vs. San Diego, Dec. 7, 1974

FASTEST GOAL FROM THE START OF THIRD PERIOD:
7 seconds — Wayne Connelly, Minnesota at N.Y. Raiders, Nov. 30, 1972

FASTEST GOAL IN OVERTIME:
4 seconds — John French, New England at Quebec, Nov. 26, 1973

MOST PENALTIES:
8 — Kim Clackson, Indianapolis vs. Denver, Nov. 30, 1975. (4 minors, 3 majors, 1 misconduct for 33 minutes)

MOST PENALTY MINUTES:
39 — Curt Brackenbury, Minnesota vs. Phoenix, Jan. 17, 1976. (2 minors, 1 major and 3 misconduct penalties)

MOST PENALTIES AND PENALTY MINUTES ONE PERIOD:
6 penalties, 39 minutes — Curt Brackenbury, Minnesota vs. Phoenix, Jan 17, 1976. (2 minors, 1 major and 3 misconducts)

GOALTENDER RECORDS

MOST GAMES:
69 — Richard Brodeur, Quebec 1975-76
MOST CONSECUTIVE GAMES APPEARED IN:
41 — Don McLeod, Vancouver. Between Dec. 26/74 and March 25/75
MOST SHUTOUTS:
5 — Joe Daley, Winnipeg, 1975-76; Gerry Cheevers, Cleveland, 1972-73
MOST SHUTOUTS AT HOME:
4 — Mike Curran, Minnesota, 1972-73
 — Gerry Cheevers, Cleveland, 1972-73
 — Joe Daley, Winnipeg, 1975-76
MOST SHUTOUTS ON ROAD:
3 — Ron Grahame, Houston, 1974-75
LONGEST UNDEFEATED STREAK:
12 games — Gary Kurt, Phoenix. Between Nov. 26 and Dec. 30, 1974. (11 wins, 1 tie)
LONGEST WINNING STREAK:
11 games — Ron Grahame, Houston. Between Dec. 1, 1974 and Jan. 15, 1975
LONGEST LOSING STREAK:
12 games — George Gardner, Vancouver. Between Nov. 25, 1973 and March 21, 1975
LONGEST WINLESS STREAK:
16 games — George Gardner, Vancouver. Between Nov. 25, 1973 and end of 1974-75 season. (15 losses, 1 tie)
 — Ed Dyck, Indianapolis. Between Nov. 15, 1974 and March 13, 1975. (13 losses, 3 ties)
LONGEST HOME UNDEFEATED STREAK:
12 games — Gerry Cheevers, Cleveland. Between Nov. 24, 1973 and Jan. 30, 1975. (11 wins, 1 tie)
LONGEST HOME WINNING STREAK:
10 games — Gerry Cheevers, Cleveland. Between Dec. 1, 1973 and Jan. 30, 1974
 — Richard Brodeur, Quebec. Between Jan. 10 and Feb. 24, 1976
 — Christer Abrahamsson, N.E. Between Dec. 10, 1975 and Jan. 28, 1976
LONGEST HOME WINLESS AND LOSING STREAK:
8 games — Andre Gill, Chicago. From Dec. 14, 1972 to March 28, 1973
 — Ed Dyck, Indianapolis. From Nov. 5, 1974 to Jan. 19, 1975
LONGEST ROAD WINLESS AND LOSING STREAK:
19 games — Paul Hoganson; Los Angeles, Michigan, Baltimore. From Nov. 11, 1973 to March 4, 1975. (19 losses)
MOST SAVES BY A WINNING GOALTENDER:
53 — John Garrett, Minnesota at Edmonton, Dec. 26, 1974
LONGEST SHUTOUT SEQUENCE BY A GOALTENDER:
228 minutes, 10 seconds — Joe Daley, Winnipeg. Between 8:25 of first period vs. Denver Oct. 24, 1975 and 16:35 of third period vs. Quebec Nov. 2, 1975. Included shutouts of Phoenix and Cincinnati

ROOKIE RECORDS

MOST POINTS:
120 — Ulf Nilsson, Winnipeg, 1974-75. 26 goals, 94 assists
MOST GOALS:
53 — Anders Hedberg, Winnipeg, 1974-75
MOST ASSISTS:
94 — Ulf Nilsson, Winnipeg, 1974-75
MOST PENALTY MINUTES:
351 — Kim Clackson, Indianapolis, 1975-76
FASTEST HAT TRICK AND FOUR GOAL GAME:
33 minutes, 8 seconds — Jeff Jacques, Toronto, scored 4 goals in his first game, Jan. 12, 1975 at Houston. Goals at 18:41 of first period; 5:06, 6:02 and 13:49 of third period

MOST THREE-OR-MORE GOAL GAMES:
3 — Claude St. Sauveur, Vancouver 1973-74
  — Anders Hedberg, Winnipeg, 1974-75

FASTEST GOAL:
51 seconds — Ed Johnstone, Michigan, in his first game Oct. 17, 1974 at Indianapolis

MOST GOALS:
4 — Pat Hickey, Toronto vs. Minnesota, Dec. 9, 1973
  — Wayne Dillon, Toronto vs. Houston, March 21, 1973
  — Jeff Jacques, Toronto at Houston, Jan. 12, 1975

MOST POWER PLAY GOALS:
20 — Anders Hedberg, Winnipeg, 1974-75

MOST SHUTOUTS:
4 — Mike Curran, Minnesota, 1972-73
  — Ron Grahame, Houston, 1974-75

TEAM LIFETIME PENALTY MINUTES

		SEASONS	GP	PIM	AVERAGE GAME	AVERAGE SEASON
1.	Quebec Nordiques	4	315	5049	16.03	1262
2.	Houston Aeros	4	314	4751	15.13	1188
3.	Cleveland Crusaders	4	314	4731	15.07	1183
4.	Calgary Cowboys	4	314	4446	14.16	1112
5.	Edmonton Oilers	4	315	4003	12.71	1001
6.	Toronto Toros	4	315	3920	12.44	980
7.	New England Whalers	4	314	3612	11.50	903
8.	San Diego Mariners	4	314	3607	11.49	902
9.	Winnipeg Jets	4	315	3239	10.28	810
10.	Phoenix Roadrunners	2	158	2680	16.96	1340
11.	Indianapolis Racers	2	158	2271	14.37	1136
12.	Cincinnati Stingers	1	80	1344	16.80	1344
	Defunct Teams	10¼	802	12105	16.09	1181
	Totals	4	2014	55758	13.84	1088

PENALTIES IN MINUTES
(BY TEAMS)

1975-76 SEASON

		GP	PIM	AVG
1.	Quebec	81	1654	20.42
2.	Cleveland	80	1356	16.95
3.	Cincinnati	80	1344	16.80
4.	Indianapolis	80	1301	16.26
5.	Phoenix	80	1292	16.15
6.	Toronto	81	1099	13.57
7.	Houston	80	1093	13.66
8.	Calgary	80	1064	13.30
9.	New England	80	1012	12.65
10.	Edmonton	81	991	12.23
11.	Winnipeg	81	940	11.60
12.	San Diego	80	716	8.95
	Defunct Teams	100	2070	20.70
	Totals	532	15932	14.97

MAJOR LEAGUE RECORDS

TOTAL POINTS

	Player	Teams	Lea	Sea	GP	G	A	Pts	Average Game	Average Season
1.	G. Howe	Detroit	NHL	25	1687	786	1023	1809	1.072	72.36
		Houston	WHA	3	223	97	204	301	1.350	100.33
				28	1910	883	1227	2110	1.105	75.36
2.	B. Hull	Chicago	NHL	15	1036	604	549	1153	1.113	76.87
		Winnipeg	WHA	4	296	234	229	463	1.564	115.75
				19	1332	838	778	1616	1.213	85.05
3.	N. Ullman	Det/Tor	NHL	20	1410	490	739	1229	.872	61.45
		Edmonton	WHA	1	77	31	56	87	1.130	87.00
				21	1487	521	795	1316	.885	62.67
4.	J. Bucyk	Det/Bos	NHL	21	1438	531	777	1308	.910	62.29
5.	S. Mikita	Chicago	NHL	17	1179	483	814	1297	1.100	76.29
6.	A. Delvecchio	Detroit	NHL	23	1549	456	825	1281	.827	55.70
7.	F. Mahovlich	Tor/Det/Mtl	NHL	17	1181	533	570	1103	.934	64.88
		Toronto	WHA	2	148	72	99	171	1.155	85.50
				19	1329	605	669	1274	.959	67.05
8.	P. Esposito	Chi/Bos/NYR	NHL	13	922	562	691	1253	1.359	96.38
9.	J. Beliveau	Montreal	NHL	18	1125	507	712	1219	1.084	67.72
10.	H. Richard	Montreal	NHL	18	978	358	688	1046	1.070	58.11

MOST GOALS

	Player	Teams	Lea	Sea	GP	Goals	Average Game	Average Season
1.	G. Howe	Detroit	NHL	25	1687	786	.466	31.44
		Houston	WHA	3	223	97	.435	32.33
				28	1910	883	.462	31.54
2.	B. Hull	Chicago	NHL	15	1036	604	.583	40.27
		Winnipeg	WHA	4	296	234	.791	58.50
				19	1332	838	.629	44.11
3.	F. Mahovlich	Tor/Det/Mtl	NHL	17	1181	533	.451	31.35
		Toronto	WHA	2	148	72	.486	36.00
				19	1329	605	.455	31.84
4.	P. Esposito	Chi/Bos/NYR	NHL	13	922	562	.610	43.23
5.	M. Richard	Montreal	NHL	18	978	544	.556	30.22
6.	J. Bucyk	Det/Bos	NHL	21	1438	531	.369	25.29
7.	N. Ullman	Det/Tor	NHL	20	1410	490	.348	24.50
		Edmonton	WHA	1	77	31	.403	31.00
				21	1487	521	.350	24.81
8.	J. Beliveau	Montreal	NHL	18	1125	507	.451	28.17
9.	S. Mikita	Chicago	NHL	17	1179	483	.410	28.41
10.	A. Delvecchio	Detroit	NHL	23	1549	456	.294	19.83
11.	D. Keon	Toronto	NHL	15	1062	365	.344	24.33
		Minn/Indy	WHA	1	69	29	.420	29.00
				16	1131	394	.348	24.63

major league

MOST ASSISTS

	Player	Teams	Lea	Sea	Games	Assists	Average Game	Average Season
1.	G. Howe	Detroit	NHL	25	1687	1023	.606	40.92
		Houston	WHA	3	223	204	.915	68.00
				28	1910	1227	.642	43.82
2.	A. Delvecchio	Detroit	NHL	23	1549	825	.533	35.87
3.	S. Mikita	Chicago	NHL	17	1179	814	.690	47.88
4.	N. Ullman	Det/Tor	NHL	20	1410	739	.524	36.95
		Edmonton	WHA	1	77	56	.727	56.00
				21	1487	795	.535	37.86
5.	B. Hull	Chicago	NHL	15	1036	549	.530	36.60
		Winnipeg	WHA	4	296	229	.774	57.25
				19	1332	778	.584	40.95
6.	J. Bucyk	Det/Bos	NHL	21	1438	777	.540	37.00
7.	J. Beliveau	Montreal	NHL	18	1125	712	.633	39.56
8.	P. Esposito	Chi/Bos/NYR	NHL	13	922	691	.749	53.15
9.	H. Richard	Montreal	NHL	18	978	688	.703	38.22
10.	F. Mahovlich	Tor/Det/Mtl	NHL	17	1181	570	.483	33.53
		Toronto	WHA	2	148	99	.669	49.50
				19	1329	669	.503	35.21

MOST PENALTY MINUTES

	Player	Teams	Lea	Sea	GP	PIM	Average Game	Average Season
1.	Bryan Watson	Mtl/Cal/Pitt St. Lou/Det	NHL	10	709	1879	2.650	187.90
2.	Gordie Howe	Detroit	NHL	25	1687	1643	.974	65.72
		Houston	WHA	3	223	206	.924	68.67
				28	1910	1849	.968	66.04
3.	Ted Lindsay	Det/Chi	NHL	17	1068	1808	1.693	106.35
4.	Tim Horton	Tor/NYR/Pitt/Buf	NHL	22	1446	1611	1.114	73.23
5.	Reg Fleming	Mtl/Chi/NYR/Phil	NHL	11	749	1468	1.960	133.45
		Chicago	WHA	2	120	142	1.183	71.00
				13	869	1610	1.853	123.85
6.	Bill Gadsby	Chi/NYR/Det	NHL	20	1248	1539	1.233	76.95
7.	Bob Baun	Tor/Cal/Det	NHL	17	964	1493	1.549	87.85
8.	Ed Shack	NYR/Tor/Bos LA/Buf/Pitt	NHL	18	1047	1437	1.372	79.83
9.	Dave Schultz	Phil	NHL	5	297	1386	4.667	277.20
10.	Gus Mortson	Tor/Chi/Det	NHL	13	797	1370	1.719	105.38
11.	Fern Flaman	Bos/Tor	NHL	15	910	1370	1.505	91.33

WHA CAREER LEADERS

MOST POINTS

	Player	Teams	Seasons	GP	G	A	TP
1.	Andre Lacroix	Philadelphia	1	78	50	74	124
		NY/NJ/SD	3	236	101	258	359
			4	314	151	332	483
2.	Bobby Hull	Winnipeg	4	296	234	229	463
3.	Danny Lawson	Phil/Van/Cgy	4	314	188	178	366
4.	Chris Bordeleau	Winnipeg	2¼	171	81	111	192
		Quebec	1¾	127	52	105	157
			4	298	133	216	349
5.	Larry Lund	Houston	4	303	111	222	333
6.	Ron Ward	New York	1	77	51	67	118
		Vancouver	⅒	7	0	2	2
		Los Angeles	⅗	40	14	19	33
		Cleveland	2³⁄₁₀	50	81	89	170
			4	274	146	177	323
7.	Tom Webster	New England	4	262	169	152	321
8.	Wayne Carleton	Ott/Tor	2	153	79	104	183
		New England	1⅗	107	47	60	107
		Edmonton	⅖	26	5	16	21
			4	286	131	180	311
9.	Serge Bernier	Quebec	3	220	125	185	310
10.	Marc Tardiff	LA/Mich	1³⁄₁₀	98	52	35	87
		Quebec	1⁷⁄₁₀	134	109	111	220
			3	232	161	146	307
11.	J. C. Tremblay	Quebec	4	292	51	252	303
12.	Gordie Howe	Houston	3	223	97	204	301

MOST GOALS

	Player	Team	Seasons	GP	G	Average Game	Average Season
1.	Bobby Hull	Winnipeg	4	296	234	.791	58.50
2.	Danny Lawson	Phil/Van/Cgy	4	314	188	.599	47.00
3.	Tom Webster	New England	4	262	169	.645	42.25
4.	Marc Tardiff	LA/Mich/Que	3	232	161	.694	53.67
5.	Andre Lacroix	Phil/NY/NJ/SD	4	314	151	.481	37.75
6.	Wayne Connelly	Minn/Clev	4	303	149	.492	37.25
7.	Ron Ward	NY/Van/LA/Clev	4	274	146	.533	36.50
8.	Frank Hughes	Houston	4	305	143	.469	35.75
9.	Wayne Rivers	NY/NJ/SD	4	297	140	.471	35.00
10.	Gene Peacosh	NY/NJ/SD	4	292	138	.473	34.50

58

career leaders

MOST ASSISTS

	Player	Teams	Sea	GP	PIM	Average Season	Average Game
1.	Andre Lacroix	Phil/NY/NJ/SD	4	314	332	83.00	1.057
2.	J. C. Tremblay	Quebec	4	292	252	63.00	.863
3.	Bobby Hull	Winnipeg	4	296	229	57.25	.774
4.	Larry Lund	Houston	4	303	222	55.50	.733
5.	Chris Bordeleau	Wpg/Que	4	298	216	54.00	.725
6.	Gordie Howe	Houston	3	223	204	68.00	.915
7.	Brian Campbell	Phil/Van/Cin	4	306	194	48.50	.634
8.	Gavin Kirk	Ott/Tor/Cgy	4	311	192	48.00	.617
9.	John McKenzie	Phil/Van/Min/Cin	4	248	191	47.75	.770
10.	Jim Dorey	NE/Tor	4	300	187	46.75	.623
11.	Serge Bernier	Quebec	3	220	185	61.67	.841

MOST PENALTY MINUTES

	Player	Teams	Sea	GP	PIM	Average Game	Average Season
1.	Gord Gallant	Minn/Que	3	202	723	3.58	241.00
2.	John Schella	Houston	4	302	691	2.29	172.75
3.	Pierre Roy	Quebec	4	247	682	2.76	170.50
4.	S. Sutherland	LA/Mich/Que	4	268	638	2.38	159.50
5.	Paul Shmyr	Cleveland	4	270	538	1.99	134.50
6.	Doug Barrie	Edmonton	4	280	528	1.89	132.00
7.	John Arbour	Minn/Dvr	4	264	508	1.92	127.00
8.	Jim Dorey	NE/Tor	4	300	474	1.58	118.50
9.	Ken Baird	Edmonton	4	268	465	1.74	116.25
10.	Ted Taylor	Houston	4	209	464	1.61	116.00
11.	Cam Connor	Phoenix	2	130	463	3.56	231.50

MOST SHUTOUTS

		TEAM	YRS.	GP	SO
1.	Gerry Cheevers	Cleveland	4	191	14
2.	Ernie Wakely	WPG/SD	4	194	11
3.	Joe Daley	Winnipeg	4	183	8
3.	Ron Grahame	Houston	3	104	8
3.	Mike Curran	Minnesota	4	115	8
6.	Al Smith	New England	3	165	7
7.	Don McLeod	Hou/Van/Cal	4	122	6
7.	John Garrett	Minn/Tor	3	159	6
9.	Jack Norris	Edm/Phx	4	191	5
9.	Peter Donnelly	Van/Que	2	100	5
11.	Serge Aubry	Que/Cin	4	121	4
11.	Paul Hoganson	LA/Mich/Balt/Cin	3	108	4
11.	Russ Gillow	LA/SD	3	109	4
11.	Gilles Gratton	Ott/Tor	3	160	4

3-OR-MORE GOAL GAMES

Player	Teams	Hat Tricks	Goal Games 3	4	5	Player	Teams	Hat Tricks	Goal Games 3	4	5
Bobby Hull	Winnipeg	16	13	3	0	Murray Myers	Van/Cin	3	3	0	0
Danny Lawson	Phil/Van/Cgy	12	9	3	0	Michel Cormier	Phoenix	3	3	0	0
Rejean Houle	Quebec	7	6	1	0	Andre Hinse	Houston	2	1	0	1
Mike Walton	Minnesota	7	5	2	0	Chris Bordeleau	Winnipeg	2	1	1	0
Ron Ward	NY/LA/Clev	6	4	0	2	Ron Buchanan	Cleveland	2	1	1	0
Tom Simpson	Toronto	6	3	3	0	Tom Gilmore	LA/Edm	2	1	1	0
Real Cloutier	Quebec	6	5	1	0	Pat Hickey	Toronto	2	1	1	0
Mark Howe	Houston	6	6	0	0	Brian McDonald	Hou/LA	2	1	1	0
Marc Tardif	LA/Que	5	4	1	0	Terry Caffery	New England	2	2	0	0
Frank Hughes	Houston	5	5	0	0	Bryan Campbell	Vancouver	2	2	0	0
Gene Peacosh	NY/NJ/SD	5	5	0	0	Wayne Carleton	Ott/NE	2	2	0	0
Tom Webster	New England	5	5	0	0	Alain Caron	Quebec	2	2	0	0
Larry Pleau	New England	5	5	0	0	Jim Harrison	Edmonton	2	2	0	0
Andre Lacroix	Phil/SD	4	3	1	0	Don Herriman	Phil/NJ	2	2	0	0
Rick Sentes	San Diego	4	3	1	0	Fran Huck	Wpg/Minn	2	2	0	0
Anders Hedberg	Winnipeg	4	3	1	0	J. P. Leblanc	Los Angeles	2	2	0	0
Wayne Rivers	NY/SD	4	4	0	0	Jan Popiel	Chicago	2	2	0	0
Claude St. Sauveur	Vancouver	4	4	0	0	Francois Rochon	Chicago	2	2	0	0
Wayne Connelly	Minn/Clev	4	3	0	1	Ted Taylor	Houston	2	2	0	0
Vaclav Nedomansky	Toronto	4	3	0	1	Alton White	Los Angeles	2	2	0	0
Ron Climie	Edm/NE	3	2	0	1	Ralph Backstrom	New England	2	2	0	0
Gordie Howe	Houston	3	1	2	0	Ron Chipperfield	Calgary	2	2	0	0
George Morrison	Wpg/Cgy	3	2	1	0	Murray Hall	Houston	2	2	0	0
Gary Veneruzzo	LA/Phx	3	2	1	0	Paul Henderson	Toronto	2	2	0	0
Tom Martin	Ott/Tor	3	2	1	0	Rich Leduc	Cleveland	2	2	0	0
Larry Lund	Houston	3	3	0	0	Rosaire Paiement	Chi/NE	2	2	0	0
John McKenzie	Phil/Van	3	3	0	0	Michel Parizeau	Que/Ind	2	2	0	0
Don Borgeson	Phx/Dvr	3	3	0	0	Peter Sullivan	Winnipeg	2	2	0	0
Frank Mahovlich	Toronto	3	3	0	0	Tim Sheehy	Edmonton	1	0	1	0
Gord Labossiere	Houston	3	3	0	0	Jeff Jacques	Toronto	1	0	1	0
Robbie Ftorek	Phoenix	3	3	0	0	Wayne Dillon	Toronto	1	0	1	0
						John French	New England	1	0	1	0

(Team(s) shown is who player was with when he scored 3-or-more goals in a game).

NOTE: During the first four seasons of the WHA, 64 players scored a hat trick, 3 goals in a game, including Sheehy, Jacques, Dillon and French, who each scored 4 goals in a game.

SUMMARY

In the first four seasons of league competition 121 different players scored 3-or-more goals in a league game. Bobby Hull, Winnipeg, leads with 16, followed by Danny Lawson, Calgary, with 12.

The feat of scoring 4-goals-in a league game has been recorded by 23 different players. There is a three-way tie for the lead amongst Hull, Lawson and Tom Simpson, Toronto, now with Birmingham, who have each done it three times.

Five players have scored five goals in a game. Ron Ward, Minnesota, has done it twice. Wayne Connelly, Calgary; Vaclav Nedomansky, Birmingham; Ron Climie, New England; and Andre Hinse, Houston; have each done it once.

© 2018 WHA HOF / PCMP LLC

LIFETIME TEAM TOTALS

STANDINGS

	GP	W	L	T	PTS	GF	GA	PCT
Houston	314	193	112	9	395	1312	998	.629
Winnipeg	315	167	132	16	350	1216	1092	.556
New England	314	165	131	18	348	1138	1092	.554
Quebec	315	167	135	13	347	1284	1208	.551
Phoenix	158	78	66	14	170	602	552	.538
(c) Minnesota	314	150	144	20	320	1062	1040	.510
(d) San Diego	314	144	154	16	304	1200	1205	.484
(a) Birmingham	315	143	157	15	301	1267	1275	.478
(b) Calgary	314	143	164	7	293	1129	1202	.467
Edmonton	315	139	161	15	293	1084	1149	.465
Cincinnati	80	35	44	1	71	285	340	.444
Indianapolis	158	53	96	9	115	461	585	.364
(e) Defunct Teams	802	345	426	31	721	2715	3017	.450
Totals	2014	1922	1922	92	2014	14755	14755	.500

LIFETIME HOME

	GP	W	L	T	PTS	GF	GA	PCT
Houston	157	111	43	3	225	744	475	.717
Quebec	157	107	41	9	223	734	512	.710
New England	157	106	43	8	220	629	478	.701
Winnipeg	157	104	46	7	215	667	448	.685
(c) Minnesota	157	99	49	9	207	586	441	.659
Cincinnati	40	26	14	0	52	170	152	.650
(d) San Diego	157	95	54	8	198	700	519	.631
Edmonton	157	94	55	8	196	638	511	.624
Phoenix	79	43	25	11	97	333	250	.614
(b) Calgary	157	93	60	4	190	626	531	.605
(a) Birmingham	157	86	61	10	182	672	567	.580
Indianapolis	79	34	43	2	70	233	266	.443
(e) Defunct Teams	403	208	182	13	429	1454	1419	.532
Totals	2014	1206	716	92	2504	8186	6569	.622

LIFETIME ROAD

	GP	W	L	T	PTS	GF	GA	PCT
Houston	157	82	69	6	170	568	523	.540
Phoenix	79	35	41	3	73	269	302	.462
Winnipeg	158	63	86	9	135	549	644	.427
New England	157	59	88	10	128	509	614	.408
Quebec	158	60	94	4	124	550	696	.392
(a) Birmingham	158	57	96	5	119	595	708	.377
(c) Minnesota	157	51	95	11	113	476	599	.360
(d) San Diego	157	49	100	8	106	500	686	.331
(b) Calgary	157	50	104	3	103	503	671	.328
Edmonton	158	45	106	7	97	446	638	.307
Indianapolis	79	19	53	7	45	228	319	.285
Cincinnati	40	9	30	1	19	115	188	.238
(e) Defunct Teams	399	137	244	18	292	1261	1598	.366
Totals	2014	716	1206	92	1524	6569	8186	.378

(a) *Formerly Ottawa/Toronto;* (b) *Formerly Philadelphia/Vancouver;*
(c) *Formerly Cleveland;* (d) *Formerly New York/New Jersey;*
(e) *Formerly Chicago/Los Angeles/Michigan/Baltimore/Denver-Ottawa/Minnesota.*

BIRMINGHAM BULLS LIFETIME TOTALS (formerly Ottawa Nationals/Toronto Toros)

	AT OTTAWA/TORONTO								ON ROAD								OVERALL						
AGAINST	GP	W	L	T	PTS	GF	GA	PCT	GP	W	L	T	PTS	GF	GA	PCT	GP	W	L	T	PTS	GF	GA	PCT
(b) Calgary	15	9	5	1	19	68	55	.633	15	7	8	0	14	52	65	.467	30	16	13	1	33	120	120	.550
Cincinnati	2	1	1	0	2	14	16	.500	2	1	1	0	2	13	10	.500	4	2	2	0	4	27	26	.500
Edmonton	14	8	4	2	18	59	57	.643	14	4	10	0	8	48	62	.286	28	12	14	2	26	107	119	.464
Houston	11	6	4	1	13	48	43	.591	11	3	8	0	6	37	59	.273	22	9	12	1	19	85	102	.432
Indianapolis	5	3	2	0	6	20	16	.600	5	2	3	0	4	20	16	.400	10	5	5	0	10	40	32	.500
(c) Minnesota	13	8	5	0	16	50	37	.615	14	4	9	1	9	51	63	.321	27	12	14	1	25	101	100	.463
New England	13	5	7	1	11	53	49	.423	13	3	10	0	6	45	64	.231	26	8	17	1	17	98	113	.327
Phoenix	5	3	2	0	6	22	16	.600	5	1	1	3	5	20	19	.500	10	4	3	3	11	42	35	.550
Quebec	21	12	8	1	25	90	78	.595	21	8	13	0	16	76	92	.381	42	20	21	1	41	166	170	.488
(d) San Diego	13	7	5	1	15	51	42	.577	13	4	9	0	8	54	75	.308	26	11	14	1	23	105	117	.442
Winnipeg	15	8	7	0	16	65	51	.533	14	5	8	1	11	54	66	.393	29	13	15	1	27	119	117	.466
(e) Defunct Teams	30	16	11	3	35	132	107	.583	31	15	16	0	30	125	117	.484	61	31	27	3	65	257	224	.533
Totals	157	86	61	10	182	672	567	.580	158	57	96	5	119	595	708	.377	315	143	147	15	301	1267	1275	.4788

CALGARY COWBOYS LIFETIME TOTALS (formerly Vancouver/Philadelphia)

	AT CALGARY/VANC/PHIL								ON ROAD								OVERALL						
AGAINST	GP	W	L	T	PTS	GF	GA	PCT	GP	W	L	T	PTS	GF	GA	PCT	GP	W	L	T	PTS	GF	GA	PCT
(a) Birmingham	15	8	7	0	16	65	52	.533	15	5	9	1	11	55	68	.367	30	13	16	1	27	120	120	.450
Cincinnati	2	1	1	0	2	5	9	.500	2	0	2	0	0	6	8	.000	4	1	3	0	2	11	16	.250
Edmonton	18	15	3	0	30	88	42	.833	18	7	10	1	15	54	63	.417	36	22	13	1	45	142	105	.625
Houston	12	3	9	0	6	29	54	.250	12	3	9	0	6	33	55	.250	24	6	18	0	12	62	109	.500
Indianapolis	5	4	0	1	9	18	9	.900	5	4	1	0	8	25	16	.800	10	8	1	1	17	43	25	.850
(c) Minnesota	13	8	5	0	16	53	41	.615	13	5	8	0	10	43	69	.385	26	13	13	0	26	96	110	.500
New England	12	9	3	0	18	60	46	.750	13	2	11	0	4	37	61	.154	25	11	14	0	22	97	107	.440
Phoenix	5	3	2	0	6	17	18	.600	5	1	4	0	2	12	19	.200	10	4	6	0	8	29	37	.400
Quebec	15	11	3	1	23	75	50	.767	15	2	13	0	4	57	89	.133	30	13	16	1	27	132	139	.450
(d) San Diego	12	3	8	1	7	35	51	.292	12	4	8	0	8	29	43	.333	24	7	16	1	15	64	94	.625
Winnipeg	16	10	5	1	21	66	56	.656	16	4	12	0	8	52	76	.250	32	14	17	1	29	118	132	.453
(e) Defunct Teams	32	18	14	0	36	115	104	.563	31	13	17	1	27	100	104	.435	63	31	31	1	63	215	208	.500
Totals	157	93	60	4	190	626	531	.605	157	50	104	3	103	503	671	.328	314	143	164	7	293	1129	1202	.467

(a) Formerly Ottawa/Toronto; (b) Formerly Philadelphia/Vancouver;
(c) Formerly Cleveland; (d) Formerly New York/New Jersey;
(e) Formerly Chicago/Los Angeles/Michigan/Baltimore/Denver-Ottawa/Minnesota.

CINCINNATI STINGERS LIFETIME TOTALS

		AT CINCINNATI								ON ROAD								OVERALL					
AGAINST	GP	W	L	T	PTS	GF	GA	PCT	GP	W	L	T	PTS	GF	GA	PCT	GP	W	L	T	PTS	GF	GA	PCT
(a) Birmingham	2	1	1	0	2	10	13	.500	2	1	1	0	2	16	14	.500	4	2	2	0	4	26	27	.500
(b) Calgary	2	2	0	0	4	8	4	1.000	2	1	1	0	2	8	5	.500	4	3	1	0	6	16	11	.750
Edmonton	2	2	0	0	4	13	4	1.000	2	0	2	0	0	4	9	.000	4	2	2	0	4	17	13	.500
Houston	4	3	1	0	6	19	14	.750	3	0	3	0	0	8	18	.000	7	3	4	0	6	27	32	.429
Indianapolis	5	2	3	0	4	14	17	.400	6	1	5	0	2	11	21	.167	11	3	8	0	6	25	38	.273
(c) Minnesota	5	4	1	0	8	24	14	.800	6	2	4	0	4	14	22	.333	11	6	5	0	12	38	36	.545
New England	6	5	1	0	10	25	17	.833	5	1	4	0	2	18	24	.200	11	6	5	0	12	43	41	.545
Phoenix	3	1	2	0	2	9	13	.333	3	2	1	0	4	10	13	.667	6	3	3	0	6	19	26	.500
Quebec	2	1	1	0	2	17	16	.500	2	0	2	0	0	5	15	.000	4	1	3	0	2	22	31	.250
(d) San Diego	3	3	0	0	6	15	9	1.000	3	0	2	1	1	7	19	.167	6	3	2	1	7	22	28	.583
Winnipeg	2	0	2	0	0	5	16	.000	2	0	2	0	0	0	11	.000	4	0	4	0	0	5	27	.000
(e) Defunct Teams	4	2	2	0	4	11	13	.500	4	1	3	0	2	14	17	.250	8	3	5	0	6	25	30	.375
Totals	40	26	14	0	52	170	152	.650	40	9	30	1	19	115	188	.238	80	35	44	1	71	285	340	.444

EDMONTON OILERS LIFETIME TOTALS (formerly Alberta)

		AT EDMONTON								ON ROAD								OVERALL					
AGAINST	GP	W	L	T	PTS	GF	GA	PCT	GP	W	L	T	PTS	GF	GA	PCT	GP	W	L	T	PTS	GF	GA	PCT
(a) Birmingham	14	10	4	0	20	62	48	.714	14	4	8	2	10	57	59	.357	28	14	12	2	30	119	107	.536
(b) Calgary	18	10	7	1	21	63	54	.583	18	3	15	0	6	42	88	.167	36	13	22	1	27	105	142	.375
Cincinnati	2	2	0	0	4	9	4	1.000	2	0	2	0	0	4	13	.000	4	2	2	0	4	13	17	.500
Houston	13	6	7	0	12	53	54	.462	13	2	11	0	4	32	60	.154	26	8	18	0	16	85	114	.308
Indianapolis	5	4	0	1	9	19	13	.900	5	3	2	0	6	13	10	.600	10	7	2	1	15	32	23	.750
(c) Minnesota	11	6	4	1	13	33	27	.591	11	2	9	0	4	19	41	.182	22	8	13	1	17	52	68	.386
New England	11	6	4	1	13	43	37	.591	11	2	7	2	6	32	43	.273	22	8	11	3	19	75	80	.432
Phoenix	5	1	3	1	3	20	21	.300	5	1	4	0	2	11	15	.200	10	2	7	1	5	31	36	.250
Quebec	15	6	9	0	12	57	59	.400	15	3	11	1	7	55	82	.233	30	9	20	1	19	112	141	.317
(d) San Diego	11	9	2	0	18	62	36	.818	11	5	6	0	10	37	48	.455	22	14	8	0	28	99	84	.636
Winnipeg	18	10	6	2	22	67	60	.611	19	5	13	1	11	43	76	.289	37	15	19	3	33	110	136	.446
(e) Defunct Teams	34	24	9	1	49	150	98	.721	34	15	18	1	31	101	103	.456	68	39	27	2	80	251	201	.588
Totals	157	94	55	8	196	638	511	.624	158	45	106	7	97	446	638	.307	315	139	161	15	293	1084	1149	.465

(a) Formerly Ottawa/Toronto; (b) Formerly Philadelphia/Vancouver;
(c) Formerly Cleveland; (d) Formerly New York/New Jersey;
(e) Formerly Chicago/Los Angeles/Michigan/Baltimore/Denver-Ottawa/Minnesota.

HOUSTON AEROS LIFETIME TOTALS

AGAINST	AT HOUSTON								ON ROAD								OVERALL							
	GP	W	L	T	PTS	GF	GA	PCT	GP	W	L	T	PTS	GF	GA	PCT	GP	W	L	T	PTS	GF	GA	PCT
(a) Birmingham	11	8	3	0	16	59	37	.727	11	4	6	1	9	43	48	.409	22	12	9	1	25	102	85	.568
(b) Calgary	12	9	3	0	18	55	33	.750	12	9	3	0	18	54	29	.750	24	18	6	0	36	109	62	.750
Cincinnati	3	3	0	0	6	18	8	1.000	4	1	3	0	2	14	19	.250	7	4	3	0	8	32	27	.571
Edmonton	13	11	2	0	22	60	32	.423	13	7	6	0	14	54	53	.538	26	18	8	0	36	114	85	.692
Indianapolis	6	5	1	0	10	26	19	.833	7	4	3	0	8	29	17	.571	13	9	4	0	18	55	36	.692
(c) Minnesota	12	6	5	1	13	47	47	.542	13	9	3	1	19	40	31	.731	25	15	8	2	32	87	78	.640
New England	12	6	6	0	12	52	42	.500	12	7	4	1	15	47	35	.625	24	13	10	1	27	99	77	.563
Phoenix	8	7	1	0	14	48	30	.875	8	5	3	0	10	40	26	.625	16	12	4	0	24	88	56	.750
Quebec	11	6	5	0	12	46	31	.545	11	1	9	1	3	26	49	.136	22	7	14	1	15	72	80	.341
(d) San Diego	16	10	6	0	20	82	48	.625	14	5	9	0	10	41	49	.357	30	15	15	0	30	123	97	.500
Winnipeg	13	9	3	1	19	67	35	.731	13	4	7	2	10	34	49	.423	26	13	10	3	29	101	84	.577
(e) Defunct Teams	40	31	8	1	63	184	113	.788	39	25	13	1	51	146	118	.654	79	56	21	2	114	330	231	.722
Totals	157	111	43	3	25	744	475	.717	157	82	69	6	170	568	523	.540	314	193	112	9	395	1312	998	.629

INDIANAPOLIS RACERS LIFETIME TOTALS

AGAINST	AT INDIANAPOLIS								ON ROAD								OVERALL							
	GP	W	L	T	PTS	GF	GA	PCT	GP	W	L	T	PTS	GF	GA	PCT	GP	W	L	T	PTS	GF	GA	PCT
(a) Birmingham	5	3	2	0	6	16	20	.600	5	2	3	0	4	16	20	.400	10	5	5	0	10	32	40	.500
(b) Calgary	5	1	4	0	2	16	25	.200	5	0	4	1	1	9	18	.100	10	1	8	1	3	25	43	.150
Cincinnati	6	5	1	0	10	21	11	.833	5	3	2	0	6	17	14	.600	11	8	3	0	16	38	25	.727
Edmonton	5	2	3	0	4	10	13	.400	5	0	4	1	1	13	19	.100	10	2	7	1	5	23	32	.250
Houston	7	3	4	0	6	17	29	.429	6	1	5	0	2	19	26	.167	13	4	9	0	8	36	55	.308
(c) Minnesota	8	5	3	0	10	29	24	.625	8	2	6	0	4	22	30	.250	16	7	9	0	14	51	54	.438
New England	8	4	3	1	9	23	24	.563	10	4	4	2	10	31	34	.500	18	8	7	3	19	54	58	.528
Phoenix	6	2	4	0	4	15	19	.333	6	1	5	0	2	10	36	.167	12	3	9	0	6	25	55	.250
Quebec	5	2	3	0	4	17	19	.400	5	0	5	0	0	11	26	.000	10	2	8	0	4	28	45	.200
(d) San Diego	6	2	3	1	5	16	17	.417	6	0	4	2	2	17	30	.167	12	2	7	3	7	33	47	.292
Winnipeg	5	1	4	0	2	10	16	.200	5	2	3	0	4	7	13	.400	10	3	7	0	6	17	29	.300
(e) Defunct Teams	13	4	9	0	8	43	49	.308	13	4	8	1	9	56	53	.346	26	8	17	1	17	99	102	.327
Totals	79	34	43	2	70	233	266	.443	79	19	53	7	45	228	319	.285	158	53	96	9	115	461	585	.364

(a) Formerly Ottawa/Toronto; (b) Formerly Philadelphia/Vancouver;
(c) Formerly Cleveland; (d) Formerly New York/New Jersey;
(e) Formerly Chicago/Los Angeles/Michigan/Baltimore/Denver-Ottawa/Minnesota.

MINNESOTA FIGHTING SAINTS LIFETIME TOTALS (formerly Cleveland)

AGAINST	AT CLEVELAND								ON ROAD								OVERALL							
	GP	W	L	T	PTS	GF	GA	PCT	GP	W	L	T	PTS	GF	GA	PCT	GP	W	L	T	PTS	GF	GA	PCT
(a) Birmingham	14	9	4	1	19	63	51	.679	13	5	8	0	10	37	50	.385	27	14	12	1	29	100	101	.537
(b) Calgary	13	8	5	0	16	69	43	.615	13	5	8	0	10	41	53	.385	26	13	13	0	26	110	96	.500
Cincinnati	6	4	2	0	8	22	14	.667	5	1	4	0	2	14	24	.200	11	5	6	0	10	36	38	.455
Edmonton	11	9	2	0	18	41	19	.818	11	4	6	1	9	27	33	.409	22	13	8	1	27	68	52	.614
Houston	13	3	9	1	7	31	40	.269	12	5	6	1	11	47	47	.458	25	8	15	2	18	78	87	.360
Indianapolis	8	6	2	0	12	30	22	.750	8	3	5	0	6	24	29	.375	16	9	7	0	18	54	51	.563
New England	16	10	5	1	21	47	34	.656	16	14	2	0	1	35	62	.094	32	11	19	2	24	82	96	.375
Phoenix	6	5	1	0	10	25	15	.833	7	2	2	3	7	23	26	.500	13	7	3	3	17	48	41	.654
Quebec	13	11	2	0	22	57	35	.846	13	3	8	2	8	36	49	.308	26	14	10	2	30	93	84	.577
(d) San Diego	14	9	3	2	18	57	34	.643	14	4	10	0	8	41	62	.286	28	13	13	2	28	98	96	.500
Winnipeg	11	8	1	2	18	47	35	.818	11	3	8	0	6	36	49	.273	22	11	9	2	24	83	84	.545
(e) Defunct Teams	32	17	13	2	36	97	99	.563	34	15	16	3	33	115	115	.485	66	32	29	5	69	212	214	.523
Totals	157	99	49	9	207	586	441	.659	157	51	95	11	113	476	599	.360	314	150	144	20	320	1062	1040	.510

NEW ENGLAND WHALERS LIFETIME TOTALS

AGAINST	AT BOSTON/SPRINGFIELD/HARTFORD								ON ROAD								OVERALL							
	GP	W	L	T	PTS	GF	GA	PCT	GP	W	L	T	PTS	GF	GA	PCT	GP	W	L	T	PTS	GF	GA	PCT
(a) Birmingham	13	10	3	0	20	64	45	.769	13	7	5	1	15	49	53	.577	26	17	8	1	35	113	98	.673
(b) Calgary	13	11	2	0	22	61	37	.846	12	3	9	0	6	46	60	.250	25	14	11	0	28	107	97	.560
Cincinnati	5	4	1	0	8	24	18	.800	6	1	5	0	2	17	25	.167	11	5	6	0	10	41	43	.455
Edmonton	11	7	2	2	16	43	32	.727	11	4	6	1	9	37	43	.409	22	11	8	3	25	80	75	.568
Houston	12	4	7	1	9	35	47	.375	12	6	6	0	12	42	52	.500	24	10	13	1	21	77	99	.438
Indianapolis	10	4	4	2	10	34	31	.500	8	3	4	1	7	24	23	.438	18	7	8	3	17	58	54	.472
(c) Minnesota	16	14	1	1	29	62	35	.906	16	5	10	1	11	34	47	.344	32	19	11	2	40	96	82	.625
Phoenix	6	2	3	1	5	23	23	.417	6	1	3	2	4	18	23	.333	12	3	6	3	9	41	46	.375
Quebec	13	8	5	0	16	51	41	.615	14	4	9	1	9	39	65	.321	27	12	14	1	25	90	106	.463
(d) San Diego	16	14	2	0	28	65	46	.875	16	7	8	1	15	64	60	.469	32	21	10	1	43	129	106	.672
Winnipeg	11	5	6	0	10	43	39	.455	11	7	4	0	14	37	47	.636	22	12	10	0	24	80	86	.545
(e) Defunct Teams	31	23	7	1	47	124	84	.758	32	11	19	2	24	102	116	.375	63	34	26	3	71	226	200	.563
Totals	157	106	43	8	220	629	478	.701	157	59	88	10	128	509	614	.408	314	165	131	18	348	1138	1092	.554

(a) Formerly Ottawa/Toronto; (b) Formerly Philadelphia/Vancouver;
(c) Formerly Cleveland; (d) Formerly New York/New Jersey;
(e) Formerly Chicago/Los Angeles/Michigan/Baltimore/Denver-Ottawa/Minnesota.

PHOENIX ROADRUNNERS LIFETIME TOTALS

	AGAINST	GP	W	L	T	PTS	GF	GA	PCT		GP	W	L	T	PTS	GF	GA	PCT		GP	W	L	T	PTS	GF	GA	PCT
		AT PHOENIX									**ON ROAD**									**OVERALL**							
(a)	Birmingham	5	1	1	3	5	19	20	.500		5	2	3	0	4	16	22	.400		10	3	4	3	9	35	42	.450
(b)	Calgary	5	4	1	0	8	19	12	.800		5	2	3	0	4	18	17	.400		10	6	4	0	12	37	29	.600
	Cincinnati	3	1	2	0	2	13	10	.333		3	2	1	0	4	13	9	.667		6	3	3	0	6	26	19	.500
	Edmonton	5	4	1	0	8	15	11	.800		5	3	1	1	7	21	20	.700		10	7	2	1	15	36	31	.750
	Houston	8	3	5	0	6	26	40	.375		8	1	7	0	2	30	48	.125		16	4	12	0	8	56	88	.250
	Indianapolis	6	5	1	0	10	36	10	.833		6	4	2	0	8	19	15	.667		12	9	3	0	18	55	25	.750
(c)	Minnesota	7	2	2	3	7	26	23	.500		6	1	5	0	2	15	25	.167		13	3	7	3	9	41	48	.346
	New England	6	3	1	2	8	23	18	.667		6	3	2	1	7	23	23	.583		12	6	3	3	15	46	41	.625
	Quebec	5	1	3	1	3	17	18	.300		5	2	3	0	4	19	21	.400		10	3	6	1	7	36	39	.350
(d)	San Diego	8	7	1	0	14	41	22	.875		10	5	5	0	10	28	38	.500		18	12	6	0	24	69	60	.667
	Winnipeg	5	2	3	0	4	18	21	.400		5	2	3	0	4	15	18	.400		10	4	6	0	8	33	39	.400
(e)	Defunct Teams	16	10	4	2	22	80	45	.688		15	8	6	1	17	52	46	.567		31	18	10	3	39	132	91	.629
	Totals	79	43	25	11	97	333	250	.614		79	35	41	3	73	269	302	.462		158	78	66	14	170	602	552	.538

QUEBEC NORDIQUES LIFETIME TOTALS

	AGAINST	GP	W	L	T	PTS	GF	GA	PCT		GP	W	L	T	PTS	GF	GA	PCT		GP	W	L	T	PTS	GF	GA	PCT
		AT QUEBEC CITY									**ON ROAD**									**OVERALL**							
(a)	Birmingham	21	13	8	0	26	92	76	.619		21	8	12	1	17	78	90	.405		42	21	20	1	43	170	166	.512
(b)	Calgary	15	13	2	0	26	89	57	.867		15	3	11	1	7	50	75	.233		30	16	13	1	33	139	132	.550
	Cincinnati	2	2	0	0	4	15	5	1.000		2	1	1	0	2	16	17	.500		4	3	1	0	6	31	22	.750
	Edmonton	15	11	3	1	23	82	55	.767		15	9	6	0	18	59	57	.600		30	20	9	1	41	141	112	.683
	Houston	11	9	1	1	19	49	26	.864		11	5	6	0	10	31	46	.455		22	14	7	1	29	80	72	.659
	Indianapolis	5	5	0	0	10	26	11	1.000		5	3	2	0	6	19	17	.600		10	8	2	0	16	45	28	.800
(c)	Minnesota	13	8	3	2	18	49	36	.692		13	2	11	0	4	35	58	.154		26	10	14	2	22	84	94	.423
	New England	14	9	4	1	19	65	39	.679		13	5	8	0	10	41	50	.385		27	14	12	1	29	106	89	.537
	Phoenix	5	3	2	0	6	21	19	.600		5	3	1	1	7	18	17	.700		10	6	3	1	13	39	36	.650
(d)	San Diego	13	10	2	1	21	67	40	.808		13	1	12	0	2	33	84	.077		26	11	14	1	23	100	124	.442
	Winnipeg	14	7	5	2	16	58	47	.571		14	6	8	0	12	53	64	.429		28	13	13	2	28	111	111	.500
(e)	Defunct Teams	29	17	11	1	35	121	101	.603		31	14	16	1	29	117	121	.468		60	31	27	2	64	238	222	.533
	Totals	157	107	41	9	223	734	512	.710		158	60	94	4	124	550	696	.392		315	167	135	13	347	1284	1208	.551

(a) Formerly Ottawa/Toronto; (b) Formerly Philadelphia/Vancouver;
(c) Formerly Cleveland; (d) Formerly New York/New Jersey;
(e) Formerly Chicago/Los Angeles/Michigan/Baltimore/Denver-Ottawa/Minnesota.

SAN DIEGO MARINERS LIFETIME TOTALS (formerly New Jersey/New York)

AGAINST	AT SAN DIEGO/NJ/NY								ON ROAD								OVERALL							
	GP	W	L	T	PTS	GF	GA	PCT	GP	W	L	T	PTS	GF	GA	PCT	GP	W	L	T	PTS	GF	GA	PCT
(a) Birmingham	13	9	4	0	18	75	54	.692	13	5	7	1	11	42	51	.423	26	14	11	1	29	117	105	.558
(b) Calgary	12	8	4	0	16	43	29	.667	12	8	3	1	17	51	35	.708	24	16	7	1	33	94	64	.688
Cincinnati	3	2	0	1	5	19	7	.833	3	0	3	0	0	9	15	.000	6	2	3	1	5	28	22	.417
Edmonton	11	6	5	0	12	48	37	.545	11	2	9	0	4	36	62	.182	22	8	14	0	16	84	99	.364
Houston	14	9	5	0	18	49	41	.643	16	6	10	0	12	48	82	.375	30	15	15	0	30	97	123	.500
Indianapolis	6	4	0	2	10	30	17	.833	6	3	2	1	7	17	16	.583	12	7	2	3	17	47	33	.708
(c) Minnesota	14	10	4	0	20	62	41	.714	14	3	9	2	8	34	57	.286	28	13	13	2	28	96	98	.500
New England	16	8	7	1	17	60	64	.531	16	5	11	0	10	46	65	.313	32	13	18	1	27	106	129	.328
Phoenix	10	5	5	0	10	38	28	.500	8	1	7	0	2	22	41	.125	18	6	12	0	12	60	69	.333
Quebec	13	12	1	0	24	84	32	.923	13	2	10	1	5	40	67	.192	26	14	11	1	29	124	99	.558
Winnipeg	11	5	6	0	10	50	50	.455	10	1	7	2	4	32	51	.200	21	6	13	2	14	82	101	.333
(e) Defunct Teams	34	17	13	4	38	142	119	.559	35	16	19	0	32	123	144	.457	69	33	32	4	70	265	263	.507
Totals	157	95	54	8	198	700	519	.631	157	49	100	8	106	500	686	.331	314	144	154	16	304	1200	1205	.484

WINNIPEG JETS LIFETIME TOTALS

AGAINST	AT WINNIPEG								ON ROAD								OVERALL							
	GP	W	L	T	PTS	GF	GA	PCT	GP	W	L	T	PTS	GF	GA	PCT	GP	W	L	T	PTS	GF	GA	PCT
(a) Birmingham	14	8	5	1	17	66	54	.607	15	7	8	0	14	51	65	.467	29	15	13	1	31	117	119	.534
(b) Calgary	16	12	4	0	24	76	52	.750	16	5	10	1	11	56	66	.344	32	17	14	1	35	132	118	.547
Cincinnati	2	2	0	0	4	11	0	1.000	2	2	0	0	4	16	5	1.000	4	4	0	0	8	27	5	1.000
Edmonton	19	13	5	1	27	76	43	.711	18	6	10	2	14	60	67	.438	37	19	15	3	41	136	110	.554
Houston	13	7	5	1	15	49	34	.577	13	3	9	1	7	35	67	.269	26	10	14	2	22	84	101	.423
Indianapolis	5	3	2	0	6	13	7	.600	5	4	1	0	8	16	10	.800	10	7	3	0	14	29	17	.700
(c) Minnesota	11	8	3	0	16	49	36	.727	11	1	8	2	4	35	47	.182	22	9	11	2	20	84	83	.455
Phoenix	11	4	7	0	8	47	37	.364	11	6	5	0	12	39	43	.545	22	10	12	0	20	86	80	.455
New England	5	3	2	0	6	18	15	.600	5	3	2	0	6	21	18	.600	10	6	4	0	12	39	33	.600
Quebec	14	8	5	1	16	64	53	.571	14	5	7	2	12	47	58	.429	28	13	13	2	28	111	111	.500
(d) San Diego	10	7	1	2	16	51	32	.800	11	6	5	0	12	49	50	.545	21	13	6	2	28	100	82	.667
(e) Defunct Teams	37	29	6	2	60	147	85	.811	37	15	21	1	31	124	148	.419	74	44	27	3	91	271	233	.615
Totals	157	104	46	7	215	667	448	.685	158	63	86	9	135	549	644	.427	315	167	132	16	350	1216	1092	.556

(a) Formerly Ottawa/Toronto; (b) Formerly Philadelphia/Vancouver;
(c) Formerly Cleveland; (d) Formerly New York/New Jersey;
(e) Formerly Chicago/Los Angeles/Michigan/Baltimore/Denver-Ottawa/Minnesota.

1975-76 FINAL STANDINGS

CANADIAN DIVISION	GP	W	L	T	PTS	GF	GA	PCT
Winnipeg Jets	81	52	27	2	106	345	254	.654
Quebec Nordiques	81	50	27	4	104	371	316	.642
Calgary Cowboys	80	41	35	4	86	307	282	.538
Edmonton Oilers	81	27	49	5	59	268	345	.364
Toronto Toros	81	24	52	5	53	335	398	.327

EASTERN DIVISION	GP	W	L	T	PTS	GF	GA	PCT
Indianapolis Racers	80	35	39	6	76	245	247	.475
Cleveland Crusaders	80	35	40	5	75	273	279	.469
New England Whalers	80	33	40	7	73	255	290	.460
Cincinnati Stingers	80	35	44	1	71	285	340	.444

WESTERN DIVISION	GP	W	L	T	PTS	GF	GA	PCT
Houston Aeros	80	53	27	0	106	341	263	.663
Phoenix Roadrunners	80	39	35	6	84	302	287	.525
San Diego Mariners	80	36	38	6	78	303	290	.488
Minnesota Fighting Saints	59	30	25	4	64	211	212	.542
Denver Spurs/Ottawa Civics	41	14	26	1	29	134	172	.354

HOME AND ROAD RECORDS

HOME									ROAD						
W	L	T	PTS	GF	GA	PCT	CANADIAN	W	L	T	PTS	GF	GA	PCT
29	11	0	58	176	106	.725	Winnipeg	23	16	2	48	169	148	.585
33	7	0	66	216	131	.825	Quebec	17	20	4	38	155	185	.463
25	13	2	52	162	120	.650	Calgary	16	22	2	34	145	162	.425
20	17	3	43	151	145	.538	Edmonton	7	32	2	16	117	200	.195
16	20	4	36	184	180	.450	Toronto	8	32	1	17	151	218	.207
123	68	9	255	889	682	.638	TOTALS	71	122	11	153	737	913	.375
							EASTERN							
21	17	2	44	127	117	.550	Indianapolis	14	22	4	32	118	130	.400
23	15	2	48	145	112	.600	Cleveland	12	25	3	27	128	167	.338
22	16	2	46	148	130	.575	New England	11	24	5	27	107	160	.338
26	14	0	52	170	152	.650	Cincinnati	9	30	1	19	115	188	.238
92	62	6	190	590	511	.597	TOTALS	46	101	13	105	468	645	.328
							WESTERN							
33	7	0	66	207	126	.825	Houston	20	20	0	40	134	137	.500
20	14	6	46	163	135	.575	Phoenix	19	21	0	38	139	152	.475
24	12	4	52	171	110	.650	San Diego	12	26	2	26	132	180	.325
16	11	2	34	111	108	.586	Minnesota	14	14	2	30	100	104	.500
8	14	1	17	79	93	.370	Denver/Ottawa	6	12	0	12	55	79	.333
101	58	13	215	731	572	.625	TOTALS	71	73	4	146	560	652	.435
316	188	28	660	2210	1765	.620	WHA TOTALS	188	316	28	404	1765	2210	.380

75-76 statistics

W. D. (BILL) HUNTER TROPHY

Individual Point Leaders — 1975-76 Season

		TM	GP	G	A	PTS	PIM	SOG	SC%
1.	Marc Tardif	Que	81	71	77	148	79	359	.20
2.	Bobby Hull	Wpg	80	53	70	123	30	416	.13
3.	Real Cloutier	Que	80	60	54	114	27	246	.24
3.	Ulf Nilsson	Wpg	78	38	76	114	84	152	.25
5.	Robbie Ftorek	Phx	80	41	72	113	109	232	.18
6.	Chris Bordeleau	Que	74	37	72	109	42	243	.15
7.	Anders Hedberg	Wpg	76	50	55	105	48	271	.18
8.	Rejean Houle	Que	81	51	52	103	61	256	.20
9.	Serge Bernier	Que	70	34	68	102	91	283	.12
9.	Gordie Howe	Hou	78	32	70	102	76	241	.13
11.	Andre Lacroix	S.D.	80	29	72	101	42	274	.11
12.	Vaclav Nedomansky	Tor	81	56	42	98	8	328	.17
13.	Danny Lawson	Cgy	80	44	52	96	46	381	.12
14.	Mark Napier	Tor	78	43	50	93	20	245	.18
15.	Del Hall	Phx	80	47	44	91	10	249	.19
16.	Ray Adduono	S.D.	80	23	67	90	22	92	.25
17.	Frank Mahovlich	Tor	75	34	55	89	14	239	.14
17.	J. C. Tremblay	Que	80	12	77	89	16	161	.07
19.	Norm Ullman	Edm	77	31	56	87	12	158	.19
20.	Ron Chipperfield	Cgy	75	42	41	83	32	228	.18
20.	Ralph Backstrom	Dvr/Ott/N.E.	79	35	48	83	20	236	.15
20.	Tom Webster	N.E.	55	33	50	83	24	195	.17
23.	Gavin Kirk	Tor/Cgy	77	36	46	82	46	179	.20
23.	Ron Ward	Clev	75	32	50	82	24	172	.19
25.	Rick Dudley	Cin	74	43	38	81	156	218	.20
26.	John Gray	Phx	79	35	45	80	136	192	.18
27.	Mark Howe	Hou	72	39	37	76	38	270	.14
27.	Frank Hughes	Hou	80	31	45	76	26	165	.19

* Rookie (20 or fewer major league games and born 1952 or later)

SCORING, PENALTY RECORDS BY TEAMS 1975-76 SEASON

CALGARY COWBOYS

	GP	G	A	Pts	PIM	SOG	SC%
Danny Lawson	80	44	52	96	46	381	.12
Ron Chipperfield	75	42	41	83	32	228	.18
Gavin Kirk: Tor	62	29	38	67	32	142	.20
Cgy	15	7	8	15	14	37	.19
Totals	77	36	46	82	46	179	.20
George Morrison	79	25	32	57	13	145	.17
Butch Deadmarsh	79	26	28	54	196	215	.12
Rick Sentes	72	25	24	49	33	139	.18
Don Tannahill	78	25	24	49	10	174	.14

	GP	G	A	Pts	PIM	SOG	SC%
Bob Leiter	51	17	17	34	8	94	.18
Peter Driscoll	75	16	18	34	127	118	.14
Larry Israelson	57	10	22	32	26	69	.14
Francois Lacombe	71	3	28	31	62	100	.03
Steve Hull	58	11	15	26	6	81	.14
Chris Evans	75	3	20	23	50	146	.02
John Miszuk	69	2	21	23	66	77	.03
*Ray Delorenzi	39	8	12	20	4	56	.14
Murray Keogan: Phx	8	0	2	2	4	14	.00
Cgy	38	7	11	18	19	61	.11
Totals	46	7	13	20	23	75	.09
Terry Caffery: NE	2	0	0	0	0	2	.00
Cgy	21	5	13	18	4	38	.13
Totals	23	5	13	18	4	40	.13
Rick Jodzio	47	10	7	17	137	44	.23
Duane Rupp	42	0	16	16	33	61	.00
Pat Westrum: Minn	54	3	10	13	98	55	.05
Cgy	9	0	2	2	23	8	.00
Totals	63	3	12	15	121	63	.05
*Derek Haas	30	5	9	14	6	34	.15
Lynn Powis	21	4	10	14	2	63	.06
Don McLeod	63	0	13	13	4	6	.00
Bernie Lukowich	15	5	2	7	18	24	.21
Paul Terbenche	58	2	14	6	22	58	.03
Wally Olds	28	0	5	5	6	17	.00
*Bill Reed	29	0	5	5	14	29	.00
Harry Howell	31	0	3	3	6	26	.00
Bill Gratton	6	0	1	1	2	4	.00
Dave Gilmour	1	0	0	0	0	0	.00
Ken Desjardine	1	0	0	0	0	0	.00
Rob Walton	2	0	0	0	0	1	.00
Warren Miller	3	0	0	0	0	4	.00
Vic Mercredi	3	0	0	0	29	1	.00
Yvon Bilodeau	4	0	0	0	2	2	.00
Jim McCrimmon	5	0	0	0	2	0	.00
*Ed Humphreys	8	0	0	0	0	0	.00
Cowboys	80	307	481	788	1064	2588	.12
Opponents	80	282	474	756	1008	2274	.12

CINCINNATI STINGERS

	GP	G	A	Pts	PIM	SOG	SC%
Rick Dudley	74	43	38	81	156	218	.20
Jacques Locas	80	27	46	73	70	200	.14
Dennis Sobchuk	79	32	40	72	74	254	.13
Bryan Campbell	77	22	50	72	24	191	.12
John McKenzie: Minn	57	21	26	47	48	125	.16
Cin	12	3	10	13	6	17	.18
Totals	69	24	36	60	54	142	.17

	GP	G	A	Pts	PIM	SOG	SC%
*Claude Larose	79	28	24	52	19	195	.14
Ron Plumb	80	10	36	46	31	287	.03
Pierre Guite	52	20	24	44	80	114	.18
Gene Sobchuk	78	24	19	42	37	184	.13
John Hughes	79	3	34	37	204	171	.02
Terry Ball: Clev	23	2	15	17	18	62	.03
Cin	36	3	14	17	12	63	.05
Totals	59	5	29	34	30	125	.04
Mike Pelyk	75	10	23	33	117	176	.06
Murray Myers	56	14	15	29	12	108	.13
*Dave Inkpen	80	4	24	28	95	120	.03
Bernie MacNeil	77	15	12	27	83	122	.12
Dale Smedsmo	66	8	14	22	187	67	.12
Mike Byers: NE	21	4	3	7	0	25	.13
Cin	20	3	3	6	0	42	.07
Totals	41	7	6	13	0	67	.10
*Pat Donnelly	23	5	7	12	4	54	.09
Don O'Donoghue	20	1	8	9	0	11	.09
Steve Andrascik	20	3	2	5	21	44	.07
*Frank Beaton	29	2	3	5	61	19	.11
Billy Steele	3	2	0	2	0	4	.50
Ron Serafini	16	0	2	2	15	15	.00
Paul Hoganson: NE	4	0	1	1	0	0	.00
Cin	45	0	1	1	4	0	.00
Totals	49	0	2	2	4	0	.00
Bruce Abbey	17	1	0	1	12	2	.50
Serge Aubry	12	0	1	1	4	0	.00
*John Kiely	22	0	1	1	6	0	.00
Rich Coutu	3	0	0	0	0	0	.00
*Norm LaPointe	12	0	0	0	2	0	.00
*Dan Justin	17	0	0	0	2	19	.00
Traded Players	14	3	2	5	8	32	.09
Stingers	**80**	**285**	**452**	**737**	**1344**	**2738**	**.10**
Opponents	**80**	**340**	**562**	**902**	**1248**	**2606**	**.13**

CLEVELAND CRUSADERS

	GP	G	A	Pts	PIM	SOG	SC%
Ron Ward	75	32	50	82	24	172	.19
Jim Harrison	59	34	38	72	62	216	.16
Rich Leduc	79	36	22	58	76	286	.13
Wayne Connelly, Minn	59	24	23	47	19	203	.11
Clev	12	5	2	7	4	39	.13
Totals	71	29	25	54	23	242	.12
Gerry Pinder	79	21	30	51	118	201	.10
Danny Gruen	80	26	24	50	72	173	.15
Paul Shmyr	70	6	44	50	101	165	.04
Al McDonough	80	23	22	45	19	229	.10

	GP	G	A	Pts	PIM	SOG	SC%
Russ Walker	72	23	15	38	122	161	.14
Gary MacGregor, Dvr	38	16	14	30	18	127	.13
Clev	35	5	3	8	6	45	.11
Totals	73	21	17	38	24	172	.12
Tom Edur	80	7	28	35	62	151	.05
Gary Jarrett	69	16	17	33	22	128	.13
John A. Stewart	79	12	21	33	43	166	.07
Juhani Tamminen	65	7	14	21	0	101	.07
Barry Legge, Dvr	40	6	8	14	15	59	.14
Clev	35	0	7	7	22	28	.00
Totals	75	6	15	21	37	87	.07
*Bryan Maxwell	73	3	14	17	177	67	.05
Ray McKay	68	3	10	13	44	50	.06
John C. Stewart	42	2	9	11	15	68	.03
*Paul Baxter	67	3	7	10	201	65	.05
Bill Evo, Edm	8	0	4	4	0	4	.03
Clev	40	1	5	6	32	30	.03
Totals	48	1	9	10	32	34	.03
Randy Legge, Wpg	1	0	0	0	0	0	.03
Clev	44	1	8	9	28	41	.03
Totals	45	1	8	9	28	41	.03
Terry Holbrook	15	1	2	3	6	17	.06
Mike Conroy	4	0	1	1	0	0	.00
Cam Newton, Dvr	11	0	0	0	0	0	.00
Clev	15	0	1	1	0	0	.00
Totals	26	0	1	1	0	0	.00
Bob Johnson, Dvr	24	0	1	1	7	0	.00
Clev	18	0	0	0	2	0	.00
Totals	42	0	1	1	9	0	.00
John Voss	0	0	0	0	0	0	.00
Jacques Caron	2	0	0	0	0	0	.00
*Brian Bowles	3	0	0	0	0	0	.00
Bob Whidden	21	0	0	0	2	0	.00
Gerry Cheevers	28	0	0	0	15	0	.00
Traded Players	33	4	7	11	33	56	.13
Crusaders	**80**	**273**	**423**	**696**	**1356**	**2730**	**.10**
Opponents	**80**	**279**	**462**	**741**	**1339**	**2632**	**.11**

DENVER SPURS/OTTAWA CIVICS

	GP	G	A	Pts	PIM	SOG	SC%
Jim Sherrit	40	11	19	30	16	91	.12
Larry Bignell	41	5	5	10	43	40	.13
Peter Mara	40	3	7	10	8	41	.07
J. P. LeBlanc	15	1	5	6	25	26	.04
Ron Delorme	22	1	3	4	28	10	.10
Larry Mavety	14	0	4	4	14	20	.00

	GP	G	A	Pts	PIM	SOG	SC%
Keith Kokkola	16	0	3	3	40	26	.00
Brian Lavender	37	2	0	2	7	7	.29
*Bill Goldthorpe: S.D.	14	1	0	1	30	12	.10
Dvr.	12	0	0	0	31	7	.00
Totals	26	1	0	1	61	19	.05
Lynn Zimmerman	8	0	1	1	0	0	.00
*Nick Sanza	1	0	0	0	0	0	.00
*Ed Pizunski	1	0	0	0	0	0	.00
Brian Gibbons	2	0	0	0	0	0	.00
Chris Grigg	2	0	0	0	0	0	.00
Spurs/Civics	**41**	**134**	**210**	**344**	**536**	**1261**	**.11**
Opponents	**41**	**172**	**295**	**467**	**519**	**1339**	**.13**

EDMONTON OILERS

	GP	G	A	Pts	PIM	SOG	SC%
Norm Ullman	77	31	56	87	12	158	.19
Rusty Patenaude	77	42	30	72	88	202	.20
Tim Sheehy	81	24	31	65	17	223	.15
Wayne Careton: N.E.	35	12	21	33	6	107	.12
Edm	26	5	16	21	6	86	.06
Totals	61	17	37	54	12	193	.09
Barry Long	78	10	32	42	66	214	.05
Rick Mooris: Dvr	40	9	16	25	58	75	.12
Edm	33	11	15	26	52	89	.12
Totals	74	20	21	41	110	164	.12
Ken Baird	48	13	24	37	87	93	14
Al Hamilton	54	2	32	34	78	83	.02
*Bob Russell	58	13	18	31	19	118	.11
Bob McAneeley	71	12	16	28	60	84	.14
Doug Barrie	79	4	21	25	81	109	.04
Bruce MacGregor	63	13	10	23	13	65	.20
Dan Spring	75	12	11	23	8	72	.17
Jack Carlson: Minn	58	8	10	18	189	68	.14
Edm	10	1	1	2	31	13	.08
Totals	68	9	11	20	220	81	.11
Bill Laing	54	8	12	20	67	62	.13
*Peter Morris	75	7	13	20	34	62	.11
Ted McAneeley	79	2	17	19	71	63	.25
Paul Hurley: N.E.	16	0	14	14	20	98	.00
Edm	26	1	4	5	14	47	.02
Totals	42	1	18	19	34	145	.01
*John Rogers	44	9	8	17	34	59	.15
Skip Krake	41	8	8	16	55	64	.13
Steve Carlyle	28	0	11	11	10	27	.00
Kerry Ketter	48	1	9	10	20	48	.02
Ed Joyal	45	5	4	9	6	53	.09
Murray Kennett	28	3	4	7	14	22	.14

	GP	G	A	Pts	PIM	SOG	SC%
Wayne Muloin: Clev.	27	0	5	5	12	16	.00
Edm	10	1	1	2	0	2	.50
Totals	37	1	6	7	12	18	.06
Doug Kerslake	13	1	1	2	4	4	.25
Dave Dryden	62	0	2	2	2	0	.00
Frank Turnbull	3	0	0	0	0	0	.00
Chris Worthy	24	0	0	0	2	0	.00
Oilers	**81**	**268**	**433**	**701**	**991**	**2284**	**.12**
Opponents	**81**	**345**	**547**	**892**	**1149**	**2706**	**.13**

HOUSTON AEROS

	GP	G	A	Pts	PIM	SOG	SC%
Gordie Howe	78	32	70	102	76	241	.13
Mark Howe	72	39	37	76	38	270	.14
Frank Hughes	80	31	45	76	26	165	.19
Andre Hinse	70	35	38	73	6	158	.22
Larry Lund	73	24	49	73	50	146	.16
Gordon Labossiere	80	24	32	56	18	151	.16
Rich Preston	77	22	33	55	33	159	.14
Don Larway	79	30	20	50	56	196	.15
Terry Ruskowski	65	14	35	49	100	105	.13
Murray Hall	80	20	26	46	18	118	.17
Poul Popiel	78	10	36	46	71	162	.06
Ted Taylor	68	15	26	41	88	130	.12
John Schella	74	6	32	38	106	193	.03
Marty Howe	80	14	23	37	81	179	.08
*John Tonelli	79	17	14	31	66	123	.14
Bill Butters: Minn	59	0	15	15	170	82	.00
Hou	14	0	4	4	18	11	.00
Totals	73	0	19	19	188	93	.00
Bob Liddington: Dvr	35	7	8	15	14	63	.11
Hou	2	0	0	0	2	1	.00
Totals	37	7	8	15	16	64	.11
Larry Hale	77	2	12	14	30	49	.04
Jan Popiel: Dvr	1	0	0	0	0	0	.00
Hou	67	4	7	11	59	68	.06
Totals	68	4	7	11	59	68	.06
Glen Irwin	72	3	8	11	116	59	.05
Ron Grahame	57	0	1	1	22	0	.00
Mike Stevens	6	0	0	0	2	7	.00
Wayne Rutledge	25	0	0	0	6	0	.00
Aeros	**80**	**341**	**555**	**896**	**1093**	**2680**	**.13**
Opponents	**80**	**263**	**407**	**670**	**933**	**2536**	**.10**

INDIANAPOLIS RACERS

	GP	G	A	Pts	PIM	SOG	SC%
Dave Keon: Minn	57	26	38	64	4	144	.24
Ind	12	3	7	10	2	40	.08
Totals	69	29	45	74	6	184	.16

	GP	G	A	Pts	PIM	SOG	SC%
Renald Leclerc: Que	42	15	17	32	35	100	.15
Ind	40	18	21	39	52	152	.12
Totals	82	33	38	71	87	252	.13
Michel Parizeau: Que	58	12	27	39	20	79	.14
Ind	23	13	15	28	22	58	.22
Totals	81	25	42	67	42	137	.18
Hugh Harris: Cal	30	5	9	14	19	66	.07
Ind	41	12	27	39	23	166	.07
Totals	71	17	36	53	42	232	.07
Darryl Maggs: Dvr	42	4	23	27	42	98	.06
Ind	36	5	16	21	40	90	.06
Totals	78	9	39	48	82	188	.05
Al Karlander	79	19	26	45	36	121	.16
Pat Stapleton	80	4	40	44	48	205	.02
Blair MacDonald: Edm	29	7	5	12	8	72	.14
Ind	56	20	11	31	14	142	.14
Totals	85	27	16	43	22	214	.13
Bob Sicinski	70	9	34	43	4	140	.06
Nick Harbaruk	76	23	19	42	24	170	.14
Reg Thomas	80	23	17	40	23	192	.12
Brian McDonald	62	15	18	33	54	117	.13
Francois Rochon: Dvr	41	11	10	21	10	78	.05
Ind	19	6	2	8	31	21	.29
Totals	60	17	12	29	41	99	.17
Brian Coates	59	11	16	27	24	72	.15
Ken Block	79	1	25	26	28	104	.01
Randy Wyrozub	55	11	14	25	8	79	.14
Bob Whitlock	30	7	15	22	16	111	.06
Mark Lomenda: Dvr	37	6	16	22	11	66	.18
Ind	2	0	0	0	0	4	.00
Totals	39	6	16	22	11	70	.09
Ted Scharf	74	7	14	21	56	90	.08
Dick Proceviat	73	7	13	20	31	65	.11
Bryon Baltimore: Dvr	41	1	8	9	32	47	.02
Ind	37	1	10	11	30	44	.02
Totals	78	2	18	20	62	91	.02
*Kim Clackson	77	1	12	13	351	71	.01
Ron Buchanan	23	4	7	11	4	60	.07
Bob Woytowich	42	1	7	8	14	23	.04
Murray Heatley	34	2	5	7	7	46	.04
John Sheridan	11	1	2	3	0	9	.11
Kerry Bond	15	2	0	2	9	20	.10
Jim Wiste	7	0	2	2	0	3	.00

	GP	G	A	Pts	PIM	SOG	SC%
*Jim Park	11	0	1	1	2	0	.00
Andy Brown	24	0	1	1	0	0	.00
Bob Rosselle	1	0	0	0	0	1	.00
Bob Jones	2	0	0	0	0	3	.00
Glen Critch	3	0	0	0	0	0	.00
Leif Holmquist	19	0	0	0	2	0	.00
*Michel Dion	31	0	0	0	2	0	.00
Traded Players	123	21	20	41	298	150	.14
Racers	**80**	**245**	**420**	**665**	**1301**	**2566**	**.10**
Opponents	**80**	**247**	**408**	**655**	**1309**	**2515**	**.10**

MINNESOTA FIGHTING SAINTS

	GP	G	A	Pts	PIM	SOG	SC%
Mike Walton	58	31	40	71	27	210	.15
Fran Huck	59	17	32	49	27	115	.15
Mike Antonovich	57	25	21	46	18	166	.15
Henry Boucha	36	15	20	35	47	85	.18
Rick Smith	51	1	32	33	50	101	.01
*Paul Holmgren	51	14	16	30	121	97	.14
John Arbour: Dvr	34	2	13	15	49	62	.06
Minn	7	0	4	4	14	15	.00
Totals	41	2	17	19	63	77	.03
Gary Gambucci	45	10	6	16	14	92	.11
*Bruce Boudreau	30	3	6	9	4	36	.08
Francois Ouimet	9	0	2	2	2	3	.00
*Jeff Carlson	7	0	1	1	14	10	.00
*Steve Carlson	10	0	1	1	23	7	.00
Craig Sarner	1	0	0	0	0	1	.00
*Jean Tetreault	3	0	0	0	0	1	.00
Louis Levasseur	4	0	0	0	0	0	.00
Mike Curran	6	0	0	0	2	0	.00
Saints	**59**	**211**	**363**	**574**	**1354**	**1927**	**.11**
Opponents	**59**	**212**	**360**	**572**	**1210**	**1976**	**.00**

NEW ENGLAND WHALERS

	GP	G	A	Pts	PIM	SOG	SC%
Ralph Backstrom: Dvr	41	21	29	50	14	142	.15
NE	38	14	19	33	6	94	.15
Totals	79	35	48	83	20	236	.15
Tom Webster	55	33	50	83	24	195	.17
Larry Pleau	75	29	45	74	21	192	.15
Rosaire Paiement	80	28	43	71	89	200	.14
Mike Rogers: Edm	44	12	15	27	10	96	.12
NE	36	18	14	32	10	88	.20
Totals	80	30	29	59	20	184	.16
Don Borgeson: Dvr	40	21	16	37	26	119	.19
NE	31	9	8	17	4	62	.15
Totals	71	30	24	54	30	181	.17
Ron Climie	65	25	20	45	17	118	.21
Rick Ley	67	8	30	38	78	130	.06

	GP	G	A	Pts	PIM	SOG	SC%
T. Abrahamsson	63	14	21	35	47	150	.09
Garry Swain	79	10	16	26	46	118	.09
Alan Hangsleben	78	2	23	25	62	118	.02
Fred O'Donnell	79	11	11	22	81	100	.11
*Gordon Roberts	77	3	19	22	102	115	.03
Tom Earl	66	8	11	19	26	63	.13
Doug Roberts	76	4	13	17	51	109	.04
*Danny Arndt	69	8	8	16	10	89	.09
Ron Busniuk: Minn	60	2	11	13	150	76	.04
NE	11	0	3	3	55	18	.00
Totals	71	2	14	16	205	94	.02
Bob McManama	37	3	10	13	28	39	.08
Brad Selwood	40	2	10	12	28	55	.04
Dan Boldoc	14	2	5	7	14	27	.07
Bob Charlebois	28	3	3	6	0	19	.16
Nick Fotiu	49	3	2	5	94	44	.07
Don Blackburn	21	2	3	5	6	15	.13
*John Gateman	12	0	1	1	6	6	.00
Bruce Landon	38	0	1	1	0	0	.00
C. Abrahamsson	40	0	1	1	6	0	.00
John Danby	1	0	0	0	0	0	.00
*Cap Raeder	3	0	0	0	0	0	.00
Steve Richardson	6	0	0	0	0	5	.00
*James Troy	14	0	0	0	43	7	.00
Traded Players	80	12	35	47	26	199	.06
Whalers	80	255	424	679	1012	2390	.11
Opponents	80	290	469	759	1072	2472	.12

PHOENIX ROADRUNNERS

	GP	G	A	Pts	PIM	SOG	SC%
Robert Ftorek	80	41	72	113	109	232	.18
Del Hall	80	47	44	91	10	249	.19
John Gray	79	35	45	80	136	192	.18
Ron Huston	79	22	44	66	4	185	.12
Jim Boyd	80	23	34	57	44	189	.12
*Pekka Rautakallio	73	11	39	50	8	191	.06
Gary Venruzzo: Cin	14	3	2	5	8	30	.13
Phx	61	19	24	43	27	130	.15
Totals	75	22	26	48	35	160	.14
Cam Connor	73	18	21	39	295	153	.12
Michel Cormier	46	21	15	36	4	120	.18
Lauri Mononen	75	15	21	36	19	135	.11
*Barry Dean	71	9	25	34	110	126	.07
*Dave Gorman	67	11	20	31	28	120	.09
*Garry Lariviere	79	7	17	24	100	102	.07
Serge Beaudoin	76	0	21	21	102	96	.00
John Migneault	68	8	12	20	14	69	.12
Al McLeod	80	2	17	19	82	83	.02
Jim Niekamp	79	4	14	18	77	87	.05
*Jim Clarke	59	1	9	10	57	56	.02

	GP	G	A	Pts	PIM	SOG	SC%
Grant Erickson	33	4	4	8	6	64	.06
Gary Kurt	40	0	4	4	2	1	.00
Dave Walter: SD	16	1	2	3	6	13	.16
Phx	0	0	0	0	0	0	.00
Totals	16	1	2	3	6	13	.08
*Mike Sleep	9	2	0	2	0	5	.40
*Mike Hobin	9	1	1	2	2	13	.08
Jack Norris	41	0	2	2	6	0	.00
Clay Hebenton	2	0	0	0	0	0	.00
Traded Players	15	1	2	3	32	19	.05
Roadrunners	**80**	**302**	**514**	**816**	**1292**	**2730**	**.11**
Opponents	**80**	**287**	**480**	**767**	**1124**	**2390**	**.12**
QUEBEC NORDIQUES							
Marc Tardif	81	71	77	148	79	359	.20
Real Cloutier	80	60	54	114	27	246	.24
Chris Bordeleau	74	37	72	109	42	243	.15
Rejean Houle	81	51	52	103	61	256	.20
Serge Bernier	70	34	68	102	91	283	.12
J. C. Tremblay	80	12	77	89	16	161	.07
Bob Fitchner: Ind	52	15	16	31	112	74	.19
Que	21	7	9	16	22	34	.21
Totals	73	22	25	47	134	108	.20
Steve Sutherland	74	22	19	41	197	159	.14
Pierre Roy	78	6	30	36	258	100	.06
Ted Hampson: Minn	59	5	15	20	14	46	.08
Que	14	4	10	14	2	18	.22
Totals	73	9	25	34	16	84	.11
Jean Bernier	81	4	26	30	10	111	.04
Tom Serviss	71	7	19	26	12	76	.09
Curt Brackenbury: Minn	59	4	9	13	254	52	.05
Que	15	4	5	9	111	24	.17
Totals	74	8	14	22	365	76	.11
Gord Gallant	64	4	15	19	297	90	.04
Dale Hoganson	45	3	14	17	18	64	.05
Charles Constantin	41	8	7	15	77	60	.13
Bill Prentice: Ind	38	4	2	6	92	47	.09
Que	21	2	5	7	89	22	.09
Totals	59	6	7	13	181	69	.09
Ric Jordan	54	4	7	11	75	49	.08
Jim Benzelock	34	2	5	7	6	37	.06
*Michel Dubois: Ind	34	2	2	4	104	29	.08
Que	21	0	3	3	23	13	.00
Totals	55	2	5	7	127	42	.04
Allan Globensky	34	1	2	3	13	7	.13
Richard Brodeur	69	0	3	3	2	0	.00

	GP	G	A	Pts	PIM	SOG	SC%
Florent Fortier	4	1	1	2	0	2	.50
Michel Deguise	18	0	1	1	0	0	.00
Jim Watson	28	0	1	1	24	17	.00
Gary Grisdale	2	0	1	1	5	0	.00
John Cunniff	2	0	0	0	5	0	.00
Pete Donnelly	4	0	0	0	0	0	.00
Traded Players	100	27	44	71	59	181	.15
Nordiques	81	371	628	999	1654	2603	.14
Opponents	81	316	503	819	1389	2742	.12

SAN DIEGO MARINERS

	GP	G	A	Pts	PIM	SOG	SC%
Andre Lacroix	80	29	72	101	42	274	.11
Ray Adduono	80	23	67	90	22	92	.25
Norm Ferguson	79	37	37	74	12	253	.15
Gene Peacosh	79	37	33	70	35	214	.17
Joe Norris	80	28	40	68	24	194	.14
Kevin Morrison	80	22	43	65	56	334	.07
John French	76	25	39	64	16	110	.23
Kevin Devine	80	21	28	49	102	109	.19
Wayne Rivers	71	19	25	44	24	188	.10
Brent Hughes	78	7	28	35	63	104	.07
*Alex Tidey	74	16	11	27	46	160	.10
Don Burgess	73	14	11	25	35	122	.11
Bob Wall	68	1	20	21	32	73	.01
Gary Bredin: Dvr	16	4	3	7	2	25	.15
SD	50	4	5	9	10	55	.07
Totals	67	8	8	16	12	70	.11
Bob Falkenberg	79	3	13	16	31	71	.04
Mike McMahon	69	2	12	14	38	79	.03
Brian Morenz	40	6	7	13	22	38	.16
Peter McNamee: Phx	14	1	2	3	32	22	.04
SD	51	1	3	4	27	52	.02
Totals	65	2	5	7	59	70	.03
Bob Dobek	14	3	1	4	2	23	.13
Jim Hargreaves	43	1	1	2	26	34	.03
Ernie Wakely	67	0	2	2	6	1	.00
Jamie Bateman	7	1	0	1	4	6	.17
*Bob Blanchet	1	0	0	0	0	0	.00
*Brian Bye	1	0	0	0	0	1	.00
*Rick Lalonde	2	0	0	0	0	0	.00
Gary Jacquith	2	0	0	0	0	0	.00
Russ Gillow	23	0	0	0	0	0	.00
Mariners	80	303	501	804	716	2617	.12
Opponents	80	290	483	773	900	2576	.11

TORONTO TOROS

	GP	G	A	Pts	PIM	SOG	SC%
Vaclav Nedomansky	81	56	42	98	8	328	.17
*Mark Napier	78	43	50	93	20	245	.18
Frank Mahovlich	75	34	55	89	14	239	.14

	GP	G	A	Pts	PIM	SOG	SC%
Jim Dorey	74	9	51	60	134	163	.06
Paul Henderson	65	26	29	55	22	179	.15
Richard Farda	63	19	35	54	8	109	.17
Jeff Jacques	81	17	33	50	113	101	.17
Tom Simpson	73	20	21	41	15	159	.13
Peter Marrin	64	22	16	38	16	105	.21
Jim Turkiewicz	77	9	29	38	55	111	.08
Lou Nistico	65	12	22	34	120	154	.08
Rick Cunningham	36	5	14	19	57	58	.09
*Jean-Luc Phaneuf	48	8	8	16	4	65	.12
*Paul Heaver	66	2	12	14	83	42	.05
*Bob D'Alvise	59	5	8	13	10	61	.08
Jerry Zyrmiak: Minn	22	0	8	8	16	18	.00
Tor	17	0	5	5	21	13	.00
Totals	39	0	13	13	37	31	.00
*Jerry Rollins	52	5	7	12	185	59	.08
Mike Amodeo	31	4	8	12	35	33	.12
Dave Syvret	50	1	11	12	14	36	.03
Tony Featherstone	32	4	7	11	5	33	.12
*Peter Folco	19	1	8	9	15	18	.06
Steve Atkinson	52	2	6	8	22	35	.06
Rick Foley	11	1	2	3	6	15	.07
Gerard Gibbons	5	1	0	1	7	3	.33
*Gilles Bilodeau	14	0	1	1	38	5	.00
*Greg Neeld	17	0	1	1	18	10	.00
Wayne Wood: Cal	19	0	0	0	4	0	.00
Tor	13	0	1	1	0	0	.00
Totals	32	0	1	1	4	0	.00
John Garrett: Minn	52	0	0	0	6	0	.00
Tor	9	0	1	1	0	0	.00
Totals	61	0	1	1	6	0	.00
George Kuzmicz	1	0	0	0	0	0	.00
John Van Horlick	2	0	0	0	12	0	.00
Jack Gibson	2	0	0	0	0	5	.00
Paul Crowley	4	0	0	0	0	5	.00
Les Binkley	7	0	0	0	0	0	.00
Jim Shaw	16	0	0	0	0	0	.00
Dave Tataryn	23	0	0	0	2	0	.00
*Mario Vien	25	0	0	0	2	0	.00
Traded Players	62	28	38	66	32	142	.20
Toros	**81**	**335**	**523**	**858**	**1099**	**2573**	**.13**
Opponents	**81**	**398**	**647**	**1045**	**1086**	**3159**	**.13**

WINNIPEG JETS

	GP	G	A	Pts	PIM	SOG	SC%
Bobby Hull	80	53	70	123	30	416	.13
Ulf Nilsson	78	38	76	114	84	152	.25
Anders Hedberg	76	50	55	105	48	271	.18
Peter Sullivan	78	32	39	71	22	161	.20

	GP	G	A	PTS	PIM	SOG	PCT
Veli-P. Ketola	80	32	36	68	32	339	.09
Willy Lindstrom	81	23	36	59	32	151	.15
Mike Ford	81	13	43	56	70	245	.05
Norm Beaudin	80	16	31	47	38	155	.10
Thommie Bergman	81	11	30	41	111	183	.06
Lars-E. Sjoberg	81	5	36	41	12	120	.04
Bill Lesuk	81	15	21	36	92	120	.13
Mats Lindh	65	19	15	34	12	99	.19
Lyle Moffat: Clev	33	4	7	11	33	57	.08
Wpg	42	13	9	22	44	61	.21
Totals	75	17	16	33	77	118	.14
Ted Green	79	5	23	28	73	61	.08
Larry Hornung	76	3	18	21	26	50	.06
Perry Miller: Minn	13	1	4	5	7	15	.11
Wpg	47	7	6	13	41	42	.17
Totals	60	8	10	18	48	57	.14
Duke Asmundson	72	5	11	16	19	50	.10
Gerry Odrowski: Minn	37	1	12	13	10	69	.02
Wpg	13	0	1	1	6	13	.00
Totals	50	1	13	14	16	82	.01
Larry Hillman	71	1	12	13	62	67	.01
Hexi Riihiranta	70	1	8	9	26	38	.03
Robert Guindon	29	3	3	6	14	26	.12
Curt Larsson	23	0	1	1	0	0	.00
Joe Daley	62	0	1	1	17	0	.00
Traded Players	1	0	0	0	0	0	.00
Jets	81	345	581	926	940	2733	.13
Opponents	81	254	418	672	1469	2406	.11

GOALTENDING 1975-76 REGULAR SEASON

	GPI	MIN	W	L	T	SOG	GA	GAA	GAF	SO
INDIANAPOLIS	80	4879	35	39	6	2512	244	3.00	10.30	1
*Michel Dion	31	1860	14	15	1	942	85	2.74	11.08	0
*Jim Park	11	572	6	4	0	297	23	2.41	12.91	0
Leif Holmquist	19	1079	6	9	3	522	54	3.00	9.67	0
Andy Brown	24	1368	9	11	2	751	82	3.60	9.16	1
OPPONENTS	80	4880	39	35	6	2562	241	2.96	10.63	4
WINNIPEG	81	4898	52	27	2	2406	254	3.11	9.47	5
Joe Daley	62	3612	41	17	1	1771	171	2.84	10.36	5
Curt Larsson	23	1287	11	10	1	635	83	3.87	7.65	0
OPPONENTS	81	4897	27	52	2	2731	343	4.20	7.96	2
HOUSTON	80	4.801	53	27	0	2532	259	3.24	9.78	4
Ron Grahame	57	3343	39	17	0	1752	182	3.27	9.63	3
Wayne Rutledge	25	1456	14	10	0	780	77	3.17	10.13	1
OPPONENTS	80	4799	27	53	0	2679	340	4.25	7.88	1
CLEVELAND	80	4869	35	40	5	2630	277	3.41	9.49	3
Cam Newton										
Cleveland Totals	15	896	7	7	1	468	48	3.21	9.75	0
Season Totals	25	1469	11	13	1	72	83	3.39	9.42	1
Bob Whidden	21	1230	7	11	2	650	70	3.41	9.29	1
Gerry Cheevers	28	1570	11	14	1	834	95	3.58	8.78	1
Bob Johnson										
Cleveland Totals	18	1043	9	8	0	601	56	3.22	10.73	1
Season Totals	42	2388	16	21	1	1290	144	3.62	8.96	1
Jacques Caron	2	130	1	0	1	77	8	3.69	9.63	0
OPPONENTS	80	4871	40	35	5	2726	269	3.31	10.13	4

	GPI	MIN	W	L	T	SOG	GA	GAA	GAF	SO
NEW ENGLAND	80	4890	33	40	7	2469	286	3.51	8.63	2
Bruce Landon	38	2181	14	19	5	1094	126	3.47	8.68	0
C. Abrahamsson	41	2385	18	18	2	1221	136	3.42	8.98	2
°Cap Raeder	2	100	0	1	0	46	8	4.80	5.75	0
Paul Hoganson	4	224	1	2	0	108	16	4.29	6.75	0
OPPONENTS	80	4885	40	33	7	2384	249	3.06	9.51	6
MINNESOTA	59	3711	30	25	4	1973	209	3.38	9.44	3
Louis Levasseur	4	193	2	1	0	87	10	3.11	8.70	0
Mike Curran	5	240	2	2	0	153	22	5.50	6.95	1
OPPONENTS	59	3609	25	30	4	1926	210	3.49	9.17	3
CALGARY	80	4855	41	35	4	2270	278	3.44	8.17	2
Don McLeod	63	3534	30	27	3	1600	207	3.51	7.73	1
°Ed Humphreys	8	441	2	5	0	255	27	3.67	9.44	0
Traded Players	19	880	9	3	1	415	45	3.07	922	1
OPPONENTS	80	4857	35	41	4	2596	305	3.77	8.51	4
PHOENIX	80	4859	39	35	6	2387	284	3.51	8.40	2
Jack Norris	41	2412	21	14	4	1177	128	3.18	9.20	1
Gary Kurt	40	2369	18	20	2	1162	147	3.72	7.90	1
Clay Hebenton	2	80	0	1	0	48	9	6.75	5.33	0
OPPONENTS	80	4864	35	39	6	2627	299	3.69	8.79	2
SAN DIEGO	80	4894	36	38	6	2572	286	3.51	8.99	3
Ernie Wakely	67	3824	35	27	4	1980	208	3.25	9.52	3
Russ Gillow	23	1037	1	10	2	568	74	4.28	7.68	0
Bob Blanchet	1	32	0	1	0	24	4	7.50	6.00	0
OPPONENTS	80	4902	38	36	6	2615	301	3.68	8.69	0
QUEBEC	81	4932	50	27	4	2740	314	3.82	8.73	2
Richard Brodeur	69	3967	44	21	2	2216	244	3.69	9.06	2
Michel Deguise	18	835	6	5	2	460	60	4.35	7.67	0
Peter Donnelly	4	129	0	1	0	65	10	4.65	6.50	0
OPPONENTS	81	4924	27	50	4	2598	366	4.46	7.10	1
OTTAWA	41	2506	14	26	1	1339	172	4.12	7.78	1
Lynn Zimmerman	8	495	2	6	1	301	31	3.76	9.71	0
Chris Grigg	2	80	0	0	0	59	13	9.75	4.54	0
°Nick Sanza	1	20	0	0	0	12	5	15.00	2.40	0
OPPONENTS	41	2508	26	14	1	1259	132	3.16	9.54	1
CINCINNATI	80	4817	35	44	1	2599	333	4.15	7.80	3
Paul Hoganson	50	2616	20	26	0	1378	161	3.69	8.56	2
Serge Aubry	12	549	6	4	0	267	38	4.15	7.03	1
°John Kiely	22	1087	6	8	1	604	78	4.31	7.74	0
°Norm LaPointe	12	641	4	6	0	377	55	5.15	6.85	0
Rich Coutu	3	149	0	0	0	81	17	6.85	4.76	0
OPPONENTS	80	4815	44	35	1	2735	282	3.51	9.70	2
EDMONTON	81	4927	27	49	5	2703	342	4.16	7.90	2
Dave Dryden	62	3567	22	34	5	1927	235	3.95	8.20	1
Chris Worthy	24	1256	5	14	0	711	98	4.68	7.20	0
Frank Turnbull	3	106	0	1	0	65	9	5.09	7.22	0
OPPONENTS	81	4930	49	27	5	2281	265	3.23	8.61	2
TORONTO	81	4931	24	52	5	3156	395	4.81	7.99	1
John Garrett										
Toronto Totals	9	551	3	6	0	349	33	3.59	10.58	1
Season Totals	61	3730	29	28	4	2022	210	3.38	9.63	3
Wayne Wood										
Toronto Totals	13	781	6	7	0	474	62	4.76	7.65	0
Season Totals	32	1661	14	10	1	889	107	3.87	8.31	1
Dave Tataryn	23	1261	7	12	1	786	100	4.76	7.86	0
Jim Shaw	16	777	4	7	1	506	63	4.86	8.03	0
°Mario Vien	26	1228	4	14	3	830	105	5.13	7.91	0
Les Binkley	7	335	0	6	0	212	32	5.73	6.63	0
OPPONENTS	81	4935	52	24	5	2570	332	4.04	7.74	1

GOALTENDING ABBREVIATIONS: Min — minutes played (**odd seconds are rounded off to nearest minute**). GPI — games played in. W — won. L — lost. T — tied. SOG — shots on goal. GA — goals allowed. GAA — goals against average for 60 minutes. GAF — goals allowed frequency (**number of shots taken for each goal allowed**). SO — shutouts.

° Rookie.

overtime

1975-76 OVERTIME ANALYSIS

4-Year Totals	CANADIAN DIVISION	Total	At Home	On Road	vs. Can.	vs. East	vs. West	Total '75-76 Time	Avg. '75-76 Time	Dec. Only '75-76 Avg. Time
15-18-16	Winnipeg	6- 1- 2	3- 1- 0	3- 0- 2	3- 0- 1	1- 1- 1	2- 0- 0	46:02	5:07	4:20
15-13-13	Quebec	6- 3- 4	3- 2- 0	3- 1- 4	4- 2- 2	1- 1- 0	1- 0- 2	74:03	5:42	3:47
15-13- 7	Calgary	4- 2- 4	1- 0- 2	3- 2- 2	1- 1- 3	2- 1- 0	1- 0- 1	63:02	6:18	3:50
13-14-15	Edmonton	2- 3- 5	1- 2- 3	1- 1- 2	1- 2- 4	0- 1- 1	1- 0- 0	74:05	7:24	4:49
10-13-15	Toronto	1- 7- 5	1- 4- 4	0- 3- 1	1- 5- 4	0- 1- 0	0- 1- 1	79:48	5:42	3:47
68-71-66	TOTALS	19-16-20	9- 9- 9	10- 7-11	10-10-14	4- 5- 2	5- 1- 4	337:00	6:08	3:55
	EASTERN DIVISION									
4-12- 9	Indianapolis	3- 4- 6	2- 2- 2	1- 2- 4	1- 2- 0	1- 0- 3	1- 2- 3	88:59	6:51	4:08
16-14-20	Cleveland	4- 5- 5	2- 2- 2	2- 3- 3	2- 0- 1	0- 2- 1	2- 3- 3	78:42	5:37	3:11
20- 5-18	New England	2- 3- 7	2- 0- 2	0- 3- 5	1- 2- 1	1- 0- 4	0- 1- 2	96:04	8:00	5:13
2- 2- 1	Cincinnati	2- 2- 1	2- 0- 0	0- 2- 1	1- 0- 0	1- 1- 0	0- 1- 1	25:03	5:01	3:01
42-33-48	TOTALS	11-14-19	8- 4- 6	3-10-13	5- 4- 2	3- 3- 8	3- 7- 9	288:48	6:34	3:57
	WESTERN DIVISION									
7- 9- 9	Houston	2- 2- 0	0- 0- 0	2- 2- 0	1- 0- 0	0- 1- 0	1- 1- 0	8:07	2:02	2:02
6- 8-14	Phoenix	4- 2- 6	1- 1- 6	3- 1- 0	0- 0- 3	1- 1- 3	3- 1- 1	71:06	5:56	1:51
11-16-16	San Diego	4- 6- 6	1- 4- 4	3- 2- 2	0- 3- 1	1- 0- 4	3- 3- 1	101:34	6:21	4:09
16-11-12	Minnesota	4- 3- 4	3- 1- 2	1- 2- 2	0- 0- 1	2- 1- 1	2- 2- 2	74:22	6:46	4:55
3- 4- 1	Denver/Ottawa	3- 4- 1	3- 3- 1	0- 1- 0	3- 2- 0	0- 0- 1	0- 2- 0	49:50	6:14	5:41
43-48-52	TOTALS	17-17-17	8- 9-13	9- 8- 4	1- 5- 4	7- 3- 9	9- 9- 4	304:59	5:59	3:58
174-174-92	TOTALS	47-47-28	25-22-28	22-25-28	16-19-20	14-11-19	17-17-17	930:47	6:12	3:57

1975-76 (532 Games): 75 games went into overtime (14.1% of all games)
47 games reached a decision in overtime periods (62.7% of overtime games; 9.3% of league decisions)
28 games remained tied after overtime periods (37.3% of overtime games; 5.3% of all games)

AFTER 4 SEASONS (2,014 games):
266 games went into overtime (13.2% of all games)
174 games reached a decision in overtime periods (65.4% of overtime games; 9.1% of league decisions)
92 games remained tied after overtime periods (34.6% of overtime games; 4.6% of all games)

THE SIXTH ATTACKER
(How Teams Did After Pulling Goaltender for Extra Forward)

1975-76 SEASON

	Times Pulled	Goals Scored	Success Pct.	Success Freq.	E.N.G.'s Allowed	E.N.G. Pct.	E.N.G. Freq.
1. San Diego	13	3	23.08%	4.33	4	30.77%	3.25
2. Quebec	5	1	20.00%	5.00	2	40.00%	2.50
3. Houston	12	2	16.67%	6.00	4	33.33%	3.00
4. New England	13	2	15.38%	6.50	4	30.77%	3.25
5. Cincinnati	16	2	12.50%	8.00	7	43.75%	2.29
6. Edmonton	14	1	7.14%	14.00	3	21.43%	4.67
6. Calgary	14	1	7.14%	14.00	4	28.57%	3.50
8. Cleveland	20	1	5.00%	20.00	2	10.00%	10.00
9. Winnipeg	11	0	—	—	0	—	—
9. Phoenix	11	0	—	—	3	27.21%	3.67
9. Toronto	13	0	—	—	3	23.08%	4.33
9. Indianapolis	15	0	—	—	3	20.00%	5.00
Defunct Teams	13	3	23.08%	4.33	3	23.08%	4.33
TOTALS	170	16	9.41%	10.63	42	24.71%	4.05

4-YEAR TOTALS

	Times Pulled	Goals Scored	Success Pct.	Success Freq.	E.N.G.'s Allowed	E.N.G. Pct.	E.N.G. Freq.
1. NY/NJ/SD	49	8	16.33%	6.13	17	34.69%	2.88
2. Quebec	30	4	13.33%	7.50	9	30.00%	3.33
3. Cincinnati	16	2	12.50%	8.00	7	43.75%	2.29
4. Houston	45	5	11.11%	9.00	15	33.33%	3.00
5. Winnipeg	40	4	10.00%	10.00	12	30.00%	3.33
6. New England	43	4	9.30%	10.75	14	32.56%	3.07
7. Ottawa/Toronto	54	3	5.56%	18.00	12	22.22%	4.50
8. Cleveland	56	3	5.36%	18.67	10	17.86%	5.60
9. Edmonton	57	3	5.26%	19.00	19	33.33%	3.00
10. Phoenix	21	1	4.76%	21.00	5	23.81%	4.20
11. Phil/Van/Clgy	53	2	3.77%	26.50	26	49.06%	2.04
12. Indianapolis	32	0	—	—	8	25.00%	4.00
Defunct Teams	162	14	8.64%	11.57	48	29.63%	3.38
TOTALS	658	53	8.05%	12.42	202	30.70%	3.26

POWER PLAY OPPORTUNITIES 1975-76

	GP	OPNT. PIM	AVG. PIM	OPP	GF	GA	PROF.	FREQ.
1. Quebec	81	1389	17.1	249	77	10	30.9%	3.23
2. Houston	80	933	11.7	254	77	10	30.3%	3.30
3. Cleveland	80	1339	16.7	292	69	14	23.6%	4.23
4. Indianapolis	80	1309	16.4	254	59	9	23.2%	4.31
5. San Diego	80	900	11.1	287	66	10	23.0%	4.35
6. Calgary	80	1008	12.6	271	59	13	21.8%	4.59
7. Minnesota	59	1210	20.5	185	40	9	21.6%	4.63
8. Phoenix	80	1124	14.1	276	57	3	20.7%	4.84
9. Toronto	81	1086	13.4	279	54	7	19.4%	5.17
10. Edmonton	81	1149	14.2	293	53	10	18.1%	5.53
11. New England	80	1072	13.4	259	46	4	17.8%	5.63
12. Winnipeg	81	1469	18.1	394	68	8	17.3%	5.79
13. Cincinnati	80	1248	15.6	317	54	8	17.0%	5.87
14. Denver/Ott.	41	519	12.7	149	25	6	16.8%	5.96
TOTALS	532	15755	14.8	3759	804	121	21.5%	4.81

PENALTY SHOTS

Date	Player, Team	V.S. Goaltender, Team	Time	Per.	Result
1972-73 SEASON					
10-11-72	Bill Hicke, Alberta	Les Binkley, Ottawa	16:37	1	**SCORED**
11-29-72	Ron Ward, New York	Al Smith, New England	5:24	1	failed
1-16-73	Renald Leclerc, Quebec	Gilles Gratton, Ottawa	8:17	3	**SCORED**
3-25-73	Renald Leclerc, Quebec	Jack Norris, Alberta	6:15	3	**SCORED**
1973-74 SEASON					
10-11-73	Andre Lacroix, New York	Cam Newton, Chicago	18:28	3	failed
10-19-73	Denis Meloche, Vancouver	Jack Norris, Edmonton	15:19	3	failed
10-25-73	Andre Lacroix, New York	Al Smith, New England	8:57	2	failed
11-3-73	Ron Buchanan, Cleveland	Andre Gill, Chicago	7:46	2	failed
11-22-73	Wayne Connelly, Minnesota	Al Smith, New England	10:34	2	failed
11-23-73	Marc Tardif, Los Angeles	Jack Norris, Edmonton	18:12	3	failed
12-22-73	Gary Veneruzzo, Los Angeles	Don McLeod, Houston	15:08	3	failed
12-29-73	Andre Lacroix, New Jersey	Gerry Cheevers, Clev.	19:09	1	failed
3-1-74	Brian Carlin, Edmonton	Don McLeod, Houston	19:50	3	**SCORED**
3-10-74	Ron Garwasiuk, Los Angeles	Mike Curran, Minnesota	19:38	2	failed
3-14-74	Tom Martin, Toronto	Cam Newton, Chicago	3:39	2	failed
3-31-74	Brian Morenz, New Jersey	Gerry Cheevers, Clev.	12:22	3	failed
4-1-74	Frank Hughes, Houston	Al Smith, New England	7:10	2	failed
1974-75 SEASON					
10-24-74	Wayne Connelly, Minnesota	Andy Brown, Ind.	11:44	1	failed
11-12-74	Gary MacGregor, Chicago	Joe Junkin, San Diego	10:19	1	failed
12-4-74	Ed Joyal, Edmonton	Don McLeod, Vancouver	6:45	2	**SCORED**
12-26-74	Wayne Connelly, Minnesota	Jacques Plante, Edm.	7:44	1	failed
1-4-75	Danny Lawson, Vancouver	Al Smith, New England	19:42	3	**SCORED**
1-5-75	Bob Leduc, Toronto	Bob Whidden, Cleveland	9:49	1	failed
1-28-75	Norm Ferguson, San Diego	Joe Daley, Winnipeg	12:46	3	failed
2-11-75	Rejean Houle, Quebec	Ernie Wakely, San Diego	8:30	2	**SCORED**
3-1-75	Bob Mowat, Phoenix	Andy Brown, Ind.	19:36	2	**SCORED**
3-12-75	Jim Harrison, Cleveland	Paul Hoganson, Balt.	5:34	2	failed
1975-76 SEASON					
10-10-75	Kevin Devine, San Diego	Gary Kurt, Phoenix	6:01	2	failed
10-28-75	Serge Bernier, Quebec	Mario Vien, Toronto	13:45	1	**SCORED**
2-6-76	Mark Napier, Toronto	Joe Daley, Winnipeg	13:43	3	**SCORED**
2-18-76	Al McDonough, Cleveland	Don McLeod, Calgary	2:48	3	failed
2-18-76	Dave Gruen, Cleveland	Don McLeod, Calgary	11:47	3	failed
3-2-76	Rick Morris, Edmonton	Don McLeod, Calgary	18:33	1	**SCORED**
3-20-76	Chris Bordeleau, Quebec	Don McLeod, Calgary	8:46	1	failed
3-20-76	Rejean Houle, Quebec	Don McLeod, Calgary	10:21	1	failed
3-30-76	Florent Fortier, Quebec	Chris Worthy, Edm.	14:46	3	failed

AFTER FOUR SEASONS: 36 shots, 11 scored. Success ratio of 32.73 per cent.

SHORTHANDED SITUATIONS 1975-76

		GP	PIM	AVG.	SIT.	GF	GA	EFF.	FREQ.
1.	Houston	80	1093	13.7	301	13	43	85.7%	7.00
2.	Cleveland	80	1356	17.0	294	11	49	83.3%	6.00
3.	Winnipeg	81	940	11.6	251	10	45	82.1%	5.58
4.	San Diego	80	716	9.0	220	6	42	80.9%	5.24
5.	Indianapolis	80	1301	16.3	252	6	52	79.4%	4.85
6.	New England	80	1012	12.7	271	15	56	79.3%	4.84
7.	Denver/Ott.	41	536	13.1	148	2	31	79.1%	4.77
8.	Edmonton	81	991	12.2	273	8	58	78.8%	4.71
9.	Quebec	81	1654	20.4	305	5	69	77.4%	4.42
10.	Toronto	81	1099	13.6	251	9	59	76.5%	4.25
11.	Calgary	80	1064	13.3	297	15	70	76.4%	4.24
12.	Minnesota	59	1354	22.9	245	5	58	76.3%	4.22
13.	Cincinnati	80	1344	16.8	321	8	83	74.1%	3.87
14.	Phoenix	80	1292	16.2	330	8	89	73.0%	3.71
	TOTALS	532	15755	14.8	3759	121	804	78.5%	4.81

ABBREVIATIONS: OPNT PIM — Opponent penalty minutes; AVG PIM — average penalty minutes; OPPR — opportunities; GF — goals for; GA — goals against; PROF. — proficiency; FREQ. — frequency; SIT — situations; EFF. — efficiency.

WHA PLAYER TRANSACTIONS
1975-76 SEASON

OCTOBER/1975
26 — DON BORGESON and JIM SHERRIT, Houston, traded to Denver for JAN POPIEL.
15 — JOHN FRENCH, New England, traded to San Diego for future consideration.
28 — TERRY CAFFERY, New England, traded to Calgary for future consideration.
29 — MURRAY KEOGAN, Phoenix, sold to Calgary.
— JOHN ARBOUR, Minnesota, traded to Denver for 1st round draft choice and future consideration.

NOVEMBER
2 — GRANT ERICKSON, Cleveland, traded to Phoenix for ROBBIE WATT and RICK NEWELL.
24 — GARY BREDIN, Denver, traded to San Diego for BILL GOLDTHORPE.
— GARY VENERUZZO, Cincinnati, traded to Phoenix for RON SERAFINI.

DECEMBER
8 — BLAIR MacDONALD, Edmonton, traded to Indianapolis for draft choice.
12 — PETER McNAMEE, Phoenix, traded to San Diego for DAVE WALTER.
14 — PAUL HOGANSON acquired as a free agent by Cincinnati.

JANUARY/1976
2 — LYLE MOFFAT, Cleveland, traded to Winnipeg for RANDY LEGGE and future consideration.
4 — WAYNE MULOIN, Cleveland, traded to Edmonton for BILL EVO and future consideration.
8 — REMALD LECLERC, Quebec, traded to Indianapolis for BILL PRENTICE.
— HUGH HARRIS, Calgary, traded to Indianapolis for future consideration.
15 — GARY MacGREGOR and BARRY LEGGE, Ottawa, sold to Cleveland.
— DON BORGESON and RALPH BACKSTROM, Ottawa, sold to New England.
18 — DARRYL MAGGS, FRANCOIS ROCHON, MARK LOMENDA, BRYON BALTIMORE, Ottawa, sold to Indianapolis.
20 — All Ottawa players declared free agents.
— WAYNE CARLETON, New England, traded to Edmonton for MIKE ROGERS and future consideration.
— TERRY BALL, Cleveland, traded to Cincinnati for future consideration.
22 — RICK MORRIS signed as a free agent by Edmonton.
24 — PERRY MILLER, Winnipeg, traded to Minnesota for GERRY ODROWSKI.
31 — CAM NEWTON and BOB JOHNSON signed as free agents by Cleveland.

FEBRUARY
2 — KERRY KETTER, STEVE CARLYLE, Edmonton, traded to New England for PAUL HURLEY, and future consideration.
17 — JOHN ARBOUR, signed as a free agent by Minnesota.
18 — MICHEL PARIZEAU, Quebec, traded to Indianapolis for MICHEL DUBOIS and BOB FITCHNER.
24 — MIKE BYERS signed as a free agent by Cincinnati.
26 — BOB LIDDINGTON signed as a free agent by Houston.
— WAYNE WOOD, Calgary, traded to Toronto for future consideration.

MARCH
3 — Minnesota players made free agents.
4 — GAVIN KIRK, Toronto, sent to Calgary to complete WAYNE WOOD trade of Feb. 26.
5 — JOHN GARRETT signed as a free agent by Toronto.
9 — RON BUSNIUK signed as a free agent by New England.
10 — JERRY ZRYMIAK signed as a free agent by Toronto.
— CURT BRACKENBURY signed as a free agent by Quebec.
11 — TED HAMPSON signed as a free agent by Quebec.
— JOHN McKENZIE signed as a free agent by Cincinnati.
12 — PERRY MILLER signed as a free agent by Winnipeg.
— DAVE KEON signed as a free agent by Indianapolis.
13 — BILL BUTTERS signed as a free agent by Houston.
15 — WAYNE CONNELLY signed as a free agent by Cleveland.
— JACK CARLSON signed as a free agent by Edmonton.
16 — PAT WESTRUM signed as a free agent by Calgary.

playoffs

WORLD HOCKEY ASSOCIATION CHAMPIONSHIP
THE AVCO WORLD TROPHY

1976

SERIES "A" (Canadian Semi-Finals)
April 9 — Edmonton 3 at Winnipeg 7
April 11 — Edmonton 4 at Winnipeg 5
April 14 — Winnipeg 3 at Edmonton 2
April 16 — Winnipeg 7 at Edmonton 2
(Winnipeg Wins 4-0)

SERIES "B" (Canadian Semi-Finals)
April 10 — Calgary 3 at Quebec 1
April 11 — Calgary 8 at Quebec 4
April 14 — Quebec 2 at Calgary 3
April 16 — Quebec 4 at Calgary 0
April 18 — Calgary 6 at Quebec 4
(Calgary Wins 4-1)

SERIES "C" (USA Preliminary Round)
April 9 — Cleveland 3 at New England 5
April 10 — New England 6 at Cleveland 1
April 11 — New England 3 at Cleveland 2
(New England Wins 3-0)

SERIES "D" (USA Preliminary Round)
April 9 — San Diego 1 at Phoenix 3
April 10 — Phoenix 2 at San Diego 4
April 13 — San Diego 4 at Phoenix 6
April 15 — Phoenix 1 at San Diego 5
April 17 — San Diego 2 at Phoenix 1
(San Diego Wins 3-2)

SERIES "E" (Canadian Finals)
April 23 — Calgary 1 at Winnipeg 6
April 25 — Calgary 2 at Winnipeg 3
April 28 — Winnipeg 6 at Calgary 3
April 30 — Winnipeg 3 at Calgary 7
May 2 — Calgary 0 at Winnipeg 4
(Winnipeg Wins O'Keefe Cup 4-1)

1975

SERIES "A" (Quarter-Finals)

CLEVELAND vs. HOUSTON
April 10 — Houston 8 Cleveland 5
April 12 — Houston 5 Cleveland 3
April 13 — Cleveland 3 Houston 1
April 15 — Houston 7 Cleveland 2
April 17 — Houston 3 Cleveland 1
(Houston Wins 4-1)

SERIES "B" (Quarter-Finals)

PHOENIX vs. QUEBEC
April 8 — Quebec 5 Phoenix 2
April 10 — Quebec 6 Phoenix 2
April 12 — Quebec 3 Phoenix 0
* April 15 — Phoenix 6 Quebec 5
April 17 — Quebec 4 Phoenix 2
* Overtime: Michel Cormier 7:27.
(Quebec Wins 4-1)

SERIES "C" (Quarter-Finals)

MINNESOTA vs. NEW ENGLAND
April 9 — Minnesota 6 New England 5
*April 11 — New England 3 Minnesota 2
April 13 — Minnesota 8 New England 3
April 15 — New England 5 Minnesota 2
April 18 — Minnesota 4 New England 0
April 19 — Minnesota 6 New England 1
* Overtime: Rick Ley 6:46.
(Minnesota Wins 4-2)

SERIES "D" (Quarter-Finals)

TORONTO vs. SAN DIEGO
April 9 — san Diego 5 Toronto 3
April 12 — San Diego 7 Toronto 6
April 14 — Toronto 5 San Diego 2
April 16 — Toronto 6 San Diego 5
April 18 — San Diego 4 Toronto 3
April 21 — San Diego 6 Toronto 4
(San Diego Wins 4-2)

1976

SERIES "F" (USA Quarter-Finals)
April 16 — New England 4 at Indianapolis 1
April 17 — New England 0 at Indianapolis 4
April 21 — Indianapolis 0 at New England 3
April 23 — Indianapolis 1 at New England 2
April 24 — New England 0 at Indianapolis 4
April 27 — Indianapolis 5 at New England 3
April 29 — New England 6 at Indianapolis 0
(New England Wins 4-3)

SERIES "G" (USA Quarter-Finals)
April 21 — San Diego 6 at Houston 8
April 23 — San Diego 1 at Houston 3
April 25 — Houston 8 at San Diego 4
April 27 — Houston 2 at San Diego 3
April 28 — San Diego 3 at Houston 2
April 30 — Houston 3 at San Diego 2
(Houston Wins 4-2)

SERIES "H" (USA Semi-Finals)
May 5 — New England 4 at Houston 2
May 7 — New England 2 at Houston 5
May 9 — Houston 1 at New England 4
May 11 — Houston 4 at New England 3
May 13 — New England 2 at Houston 4
May 15 — Houston 1 at New England 6
May 16 — New England 0 at Houston 2
(Houston Wins 4-3)

SERIES "I" (Finals)
May 20 — Winnipeg 4 at Houston 3
May 23 — Winnipeg 5 at Houston 4
May 25 — Houston 3 at Winnipeg 6
May 27 — Houston 1 at Winnipeg 9
(Winnipeg Wins Avco World Trophy 4-0)

TOP 12 SCORERS

	TM	GP	G	A	PTS	PIM
*Ulf Nilsson	Wpg	13	7	9	26	6
Bobby Hull	Wpg	13	12	11	23	4
Anders Hedberg	Wpg	13	13	6	19	15
Tom Webster	N.E.	17	10	9	19	6
Terry Ruskowski	Hou	16	6	10	16	64
Mark Howe	Hou	17	6	10	16	18
Rosaire Paiement	N.E.	17	4	11	15	41
John Tonelli	Hou	17	7	7	14	18
Peter Sullivan	Wpg	13	6	7	13	0
Mike Rogers	N.E.	17	5	8	13	2
Thommie Bergman	Wpg	13	3	10	13	8
Mike Ford	Wpg	12	1	12	13	8

*Voted MVP of playoffs and winner of Gordie Howe Trophy.

LEADING GOALTENDERS

	TM	MIN	SOG	GA	GAA	SO
Bruce Landon	N.E.	197	104	7	2.13	0
Cap Raeder	N.W.	819	409	31	2.37	2
Michel Dion	Ind	126	73	5	2.38	0
Jim Park	Ind	294	156	12	2.45	2
Joe Dailey	Wpg	671	255	29	2.59	1
Wayne Rutledge	Hou	200	103	10	3.00	0

1975

SERIES "E" (Semi-Finals)
SAN DIEGO vs. HOUSTON
April 25 — Houston 4 San Diego 0
April 27 — Houston 2 San Diego 1
April 29 — Houston 6 San Diego 0
*May 1 — Houston 5 San Diego 4
° Overtime: Jim Sherrit 0:27.
(Houston Wins 4-0)

SERIES "F" (Semi-Finals)
MINNESOTA vs. QUEBEC
April 22 — Quebec 4 Minnesota 1
April 24 — Minnesota 5 Quebec 3
April 26 — Quebec 6 Minnesota 1
April 27 — Minnesota 4 Quebec 2
April 29 — Quebec 6 Minnesota 3
May 1 — Quebec 4 Minnesota 2
(Quebec Wins 4-2)

SERIES "G" (Finals)
QUEBEC vs. HOUSTON
May 3 — Houston 6 Quebec 2
May 6 — Houston 5 Quebec 3
May 10 — Houston 2 Quebec 0
May 12 — Houston 7 Quebec 2
(Houston Wins Avco World Trophy 4-0)

TOP 10 SCORERS

	TM	GP	G	A	PTS	PIM
Mark Howe	Hou	13	10	12	22	0
Marc Tardif	Que	15	10	11	21	10
Gordie Howe	Hou	13	8	12	20	20
Larry Lund	Hou	13	5	13	18	13
Mike Walton	Min	12	10	7	17	10
Rejean Houle	Que	15	10	6	16	2
Serge Bernier	Que	16	8	8	16	6
Fran Huck	Min	12	3	13	16	6
C. Bordeleau	Que	15	2	13	15	2
Rey Leclerc	Que	14	7	7	14	41
Ray Adduono	S.D.	10	5	9	14	13
G. Morrison	Min	12	5	9	14	0

LEADING GOALTENDERS

	TM	MIN	SOG	GA	GAA	SO
*Ron Grahame	Hou	.780	439	26	2.00	3
Richard Brodeur	Que	.906	550	48	3.18	1
John Garrett	Min	.726	406	41	3.39	1
Garry Kurt	Phx	.207	81	12	3.48	0
Russ Gillow	S.D.	.79	56	5	3.80	0

* Selected MVP of playoffs and winner of Gordie Howe Trophy.

1973   1974
SERIES "A" (QUARTER-FINALS)

NEW ENGLAND vs. OTTAWA

April 7 — New England 6 Ottawa 3
*April 8 — New England 4 Ottawa 3
April 10 — Ottawa 4 New England 2
April 12 — New England 7 Ottawa 3
*April 14 — New England 5 Ottawa 4
* Overtime: Brit Selby 3:37.
           Mike Byers 5:47.
  (New England Wins 4-1)

HOUSTON vs. WINNIPEG

April 8 — Houston 5 Winnipeg 2
April 10 — Houston 3 Winnipeg 2
April 13 — Houston 10 Winnipeg 1
April 14 — Houston 5 Winnipeg 4
  (Houston Wins 4-0)

SERIES "B" (QUARTER-FINALS)

CLEVELAND vs. PHILADELPHIA

*April 4 — Cleveland 3 Philadelphia 2
April 7 — Cleveland 7 Philadelphia 1
April 8 — Cleveland 3 Philadelphia 1
April 11 — Cleveland 6 Philadelphia 2
* Overtime: Ron Buchanan 9:49.
  (Cleveland Wins 4-0)

MINNESOTA vs. EDMONTON

April 6 — Minnesota 2 Edmonton 1
April 7 — Minnesota 8 Edmonton 5
April 10 — Minnesota 6 Edmonton 2
April 12 — Edmonton 2 Minnesota 1
April 14 — Minnesota 5 Edmonton 4
  (Minnesota Wins 4-1)

SERIES "C" (QUARTER-FINALS)

WINNIPEG vs. MINNESOTA

April 6 — Winnipeg 3 Minnesota 1
April 8 — Winnipeg 5 Minnesota 2
April 10 — Minnesota 4 Winnipeg 3
*April 11 — Winnipeg 3 Minnesota 2
April 15 — Winnipeg 8 Minnesota 5
* Overtime: Norm Beaudin 3:12.
  (Winnipeg Wins 4-1)

CHICAGO vs. NEW ENGLAND

April 6 — New England 6 Chicago 4
*April 7 — New England 4 Chicago 3
April 9 — Chicago 8 New England 6
*April 10 — Chicago 2 New England 1
April 12 — Chicago 4 New England 2
April 14 — New England 2 Chicago 0
April 16 — Chicago 3 New England 2
* Overtime: John French 2:51.
           Ralph Backstrom 17:45.
  (Chicago Wins 4-3)

SERIES "D" (QUARTER-FINALS)

HOUSTON vs. LOS ANGELES

April 5 — Houston 7 Los Angeles 2
April 7 — Los Angeles 4 Houston 2
April 11 — Los Angeles 3 Houston 2
*April 13 — Houston 3 Los Angeles 2
April 15 — Houston 6 Los Angeles 3
April 17 — Houston 3 Los Angeles 2
* Overtime: Murray Hall 3:38.
  (Houston Wins 4-2)

TORONTO vs. CLEVELAND

April 7 — Toronto 4 Cleveland 0
April 9 — Toronto 4 Cleveland 3
April 12 — Toronto 4 Cleveland 2
*April 13 — Cleveland 3 Toronto 2
April 15 — Toronto 4 Cleveland 1
* Overtime: Wayne Muloin 4:17.
  (Toronto Wins 4-1)

SERIES "E" (SEMI-FINALS)

NEW ENGLAND vs. CLEVELAND

April 18 — New England 3 Cleveland 2
April 19 — New England 3 Cleveland 2
April 21 — New England 5 Cleveland 4
April 22 — Cleveland 5 New England 2
April 26 — New England 3 Cleveland 1
  (New England Wins 4-1)

HOUSTON vs. MINNESOTA

*April 18 — Minnesota 5 Houston 4
April 20 — Houston 5 Minnesota 2
April 21 — Minnesota 4 Houston 1
April 28 — Houston 4 Minnesota 1
April 29 — Houston 9 Minnesota 4
May 1 — Houston 3 Minnesota 1
* Overtime: Mike Walton 1:40.
  (Houston Wins 4-2)

SERIES "F" (SEMI-FINALS)

1973
WINNIPEG vs. HOUSTON
April 20 — Winnipeg 5 Houston 1
April 22 — Winnipeg 2 Houston 0
April 24 — Winnipeg 4 Houston 2
April 26 — Winnipeg 3 Houston 0
(Winnipeg Wins 4-0)

1974
CHICAGO vs. TORONTO
April 19 — Toronto 6 Chicago 4
April 22 — Chicago 4 Toronto 3
April 28 — Chicago 3 Toronto 2
April 30 — Toronto 7 Chicago 6
May 1 — Toronto 5 Chicago 3
May 4 — Chicago 9 Toronto 2
May 6 — Chicago 5 Toronto 2
(Chicago Wins 4-3)

SERIES "G" (FINALS)

1973
NEW ENGLAND vs. WINNIPEG
April 29 — New England 7 Winnipeg 2
May 2 — New England 7 Winnipeg 4
May 3 — Winnipeg 4 New England 3
May 5 — New England 4 Winnipeg 2
May 6 — New England 9 Winnipeg 6
(New England Wins 4-1)

1974
HOUSTON vs. CHICAGO
May 12 — Houston 3 Chicago 2
May 15 — Houston 6 Chicago 1
May 17 — Houston 7 Chicago 4
May 19 — Houston 6 Chicago 2
(Houston Wins 4-0)

TOP 10 SCORERS

1973

	TM	GP	G	A	PTS	PIM
Norm Beaudin	Wpg	14	13	15	28	2
Tom Webster	N.E.	15	12	14	26	6
Bobby Hull	Wpg	14	9	16	25	16
Tim Sheehy	N.E.	15	9	14	23	13
Larry Pleau	N.E.	15	12	7	19	15
Jim Dorey	N.E.	15	3	16	19	41
Tom Williams	N.E.	15	6	11	17	2
B. Sutherland	Wpg	14	5	9	14	9
John French	N.E.	15	3	11	14	2
C. Bordeleau	Wpg	12	5	8	13	4

1974

	TM	GP	G	A	PTS	PIM
Larry Lund	Hou	14	9	14	23	56
Mark Howe	Hou	14	9	10	19	4
R. Backstrom	Chi	18	5	14	19	4
Mike Walton	Min	11	10	8	18	16
Andre Hinse	Hou	14	8	9	17	18
Gordie Howe	Hou	13	3	14	17	34
G. Labessiere	Hou	14	7	9	16	20
Murray Hall	Hou	14	9	6	15	6
R. Paiement	Chi	18	9	6	15	16
Poul Popiel	Hou	14	1	14	15	22

PLAYOFF LEADERS (ALL-TIME)

SCORING

		TM	PY	GP	G	A	PTS.	PIM	WG	IP	PP	SH
1.	Mark Howe	Houston	3	44	25	32	57	22	3	41	5	4
2.	Larry Lund	Houston	4	42	18	35	53	97	7	30	2	2
3.	Tom Webster	N. England	4	38	28	28	52	19	0	39	9	0
4.	Gordie Howe	Houston	3	43	15	34	49	85	2	30	4	2
5.	Bobby Hull	Winnipeg	3	31	21	26	47	20	4	33	8	0
6.	Poul Popiel	Houston	4	54	7	38	45	95	1	30	4	0
7.	Gord Labossiere	Houston	4	50	16	28	44	46	3	31	5	0
8.	Frank Hughes	Houston	4	54	24	16	40	49	3	22	10	0
9.	Murray Hall	Houston	4	54	21	17	38	32	8	27	5	0
10.	Chris Bordeleau	Wpg./Que.	4	35	11	24	35	10	1	23	1	0
10.	Mike Walton	Minnesota	2	23	20	25	35	26	5	21	6	1
12.	Jim Dorey	N.E./Tor	3	27	5	28	33	69	0	27	1	0

ALL-TIME PENALTY LEADERS

		TEAM	PY	GP	PIM	AVG. GAME
1.	Rick Ley	New England	4	45	123	2.73
2.	Ted Taylor	Houston	4	52	109	2.10
3.	John Schella	Houston	4	54	104	1.93
4.	Gord Gallant	Minn/Que	3	17	98	5.76
5.	Larry Lund	Houston	4	42	97	2.30
6.	Poul Popiel	Houston	4	54	95	1.76
7.	Darryl Maggs	Chi/Clev	2	21	91	4.33
8.	Gordie Howe	Houston	3	43	85	1.98
9.	Terry Ruskowski	Houston	2	30	79	2.63
10.	Jim Dorey	N.E./Tor	3	27	69	2.56

WORLD HOCKEY ASSOCIATION TRAVELOG/1976-77

APPROXIMATE AIR MILEAGE	BIR.	CGY.	CIN.	EDM.	HOU.	IND.	MIN.	N.E.	PHX.	QUE.	S.D	WPG.
Birmingham	—	1831	432	1831	599	522	996	949	1497	1226	1801	996
Calgary	1831	—	1658	104	1729	1569	1049	2088	1262	1932	1337	835
Cincinnati	432	1658	—	1678	873	98	596	661	1569	870	1865	993
Edmonton	1831	104	1678	—	1864	1741	1252	2044	1962	2016	1694	835
Houston	599	1729	879	1864	—	854	1046	1512	1015	1746	1308	1469
Indianapolis	522	1569	98	1741	854	—	503	728	1489	924	1783	906
Minnesota	996	1049	596	1252	1046	503	—	1050	1270	1227	1532	394
New England	949	2088	661	2044	1512	728	1050	—	2213	430	2502	1510
Phoenix	1497	1262	1569	1962	1015	1489	1270	2213	—	2338	304	1679
Quebec	1226	1932	870	2016	1746	924	1227	430	2338	—	2622	1362
San Diego	1801	1337	1865	1694	1308	1783	1532	2502	304	2622	—	1873
Winnipeg	996	835	993	835	1469	906	394	1510	1679	1362	1873	—

WHA PLAYOFF RECORDS
TEAM

MOST GOALS, BOTH TEAMS, FOUR GAME SERIES:
35 — Houston/Winnipeg, 1976 finals. Winnipeg won series 4-0, outscored Houston 24-11.

MOST GOALS, ONE TEAM, FOUR GAME SERIES:
24 — Winnipeg, 1976 finals. Winnipeg won series 4-0, outscored Houston 24-11.

MOST GOALS, BOTH TEAMS, FIVE GAME SERIES:
48 — New England/Winnipeg, 1973 final. New England won series 4-1, outscored Winnipeg, 30-18.

MOST GOALS, ONE TEAM, FIVE GAME SERIES:
30 — New England, 1973 final. N.E. defeated Winnipeg 4-0, outscored Jets 30-18.

MOST GOALS, BOTH TEAMS, SIX GAME SERIES:
56 — San Diego/Toronto, 1975 quarter finals. San Diego defeated Toronto 4-2, outscored Toros, 29-27.

MOST GOALS, ONE TEAM, SIX GAME SERIES:
29 — San Diego, 1975 quarter-finals. San Diego defeated Toronto 4-2, outscored Toros 29-27.

MOST GOALS, BOTH TEAMS, SEVEN GAME SERIES:
61 — Chicago/Toronto, 1974 semi-finals. Chicago defeated Toronto 4-2, outscored Toros 34-27.

MOST GOALS, ONE TEAM, SEVEN GAME SERIES:
34 — Chicago, 1974 semi-finals. Cougars defeated Toronto 4-3, outscored Toros 34-27.

FEWEST GOALS, BOTH TEAMS, FOUR GAME SERIES:
17 — Winnipeg/Houston, 1973 semi-finals. Winnipeg won series 4-0, outscored Houston 14-3.

FEWEST GOALS, ONE TEAM, FOUR GAME SERIES:
3 — Houston, 1973 semi-finals. Lost series to Winnipeg 4-0, outscored 14-3.

FEWEST GOALS, BOTH TEAMS, FIVE GAME SERIES:
27 — Toronto/Cleveland, 1974 quarter-finals. Toronto won series 4-1, outscored Cleveland 18-9.

FEWEST GOALS, ONE TEAM, FIVE GAME SERIES:
9 — Cleveland, 1974 quarter-finals. Lost to Toronto 4-1, outscored 18-9.

FEWEST GOALS, BOTH TEAMS, SIX GAME SERIES:
39 — Houston/Los Angeles, 1973 quarter-final series. Houston won series 4-2, outscored Los Angeles 23-16.

FEWEST GOALS, ONE TEAM, SIX GAME SERIES:
16 — Los Angeles, 1973 quarter-finals. Lost to Houston 4-2, outscored 23-16.
— Minnesota, 1975 semi-finals. Lost to Quebec 4-2, outscored 25-16.

FEWEST GOALS, BOTH TEAMS, SEVEN GAME SERIES:
33 — New England/Indianapolis, 1976 quarter-finals. N.E. won series 4-3, outscored Indianapolis 18-15.

FEWEST GOALS, ONE TEAM, SEVEN GAME SERIES:
15 — Indianapolis, 1976 quarter-finals. New England won series 4-3, outscored Indianapolis 18-15.

WIDEST MARGIN OF VICTORY, ONE GAME:
9 goals — Houston defeated Winnipeg 10-1, April 13, 1974. Houston won series 4-0.

MOST GOALS, BOTH TEAMS, ONE GAME:
15 — New England/Winnipeg, May 6, 1973, at Boston. Final game of final series. New England won 9-6 and series 4-1.

MOST GOALS, ONE TEAM, ONE GAME:
10 — Houston, April 13, 1974, Winnipeg 1 at Houston 10.

MOST GOALS, BOTH TEAMS, ONE PERIOD:
8 — Houston/San Diego, April 21, 1976. First period. Houston 6, San Diego 2.

MOST GOALS, ONE TEAM, ONE PERIOD:
6 — Calgary/Quebec, April 11, 1976. Third period. Calgary 6.
— Houston/San Diego, April 21, 1976. First period. Houston 6.

SHORTEST OVERTIME:
27 — San Diego at Houston, May 1, 1975. Goal, Jim Sherrit of Houston. Assists, Mark Howe and John Schella.

playoff records

LONGEST OVERTIME:
  17 minutes, 45 seconds — New England at Chicago, April 10, 1974. Ralph Backstrom scored to give Chicago 2-1 decision. Assist to Duke Harris.

MOST OVERTIME GAMES, QUARTER-FINAL SERIES:
  2 — New England/Ottawa, 1973, New England won both.
  — New England/Chicago, 1974, teams split.

MOST OVERTIME GAMES, SEMI-FINAL SERIES:
  1 — Houston/Minnesota, 1974. Minnesota won.
  — Houston/San Diego, 1975. Houston won.
  — Winnipeg/Edmonton, 1976, won by Winnipeg.

MOST OVERTIME GAMES IN FINAL SERIES:
  0 — No final series game has gone into overtime.

MOST OVERTIME GAMES, FOUR GAME SERIES:
  1 — Cleveland/Philadelphia, 1973, won by Cleveland.
  — Houston/San Diego, 1975, won by Houston.

MOST OVERTIME GAMES IN FIVE GAME SERIES:
  2 — New England/Ottawa, 1973, both won by New England.

MOST OVERTIME GAMES, SIX GAME SERIES:
  1 — Houston/Los Angeles, 1973, game won by Houston.
  — Houston/Minnesota, 1974, game won by Minnesota.
  — New England/Minnesota, 1975, game won by New England.

MOST OVERTIME GAMES, SEVEN GAME SERIES:
  2 — Chicago/New England, 1974, each team won an overtime game.

MOST OVERTIME PERIODS, ONE TEAM, ONE PLAYOFF YEAR:
  2 — New England, 1973, 1974.
  — Ottawa, 1973.
  — Chicago, 1974.

MOST CONSECUTIVE PLAYOFF GAME VICTORIES:
  13 — Houston won final 10 games, 1975 playoffs and first 3 games, 1976 playoffs.

LONGEST PLAYOFF LOSING STREAK:
  6 — Winnipeg. Lost final two games to New England in 1973 and four straight to Houston in 1974.

MOST SHUTOUTS, ONE PLAYOFF YEAR, ALL TEAMS:
  6 — 1976. Two each by New England and Indianapolis; one each by Winnipeg and Houston.

MOST SHUTOUTS, ONE TEAM, ONE PLAYOFF YEAR:
  3 — Houston, 1975.

MOST SHUTOUTS, ONE TEAM, ONE SERIES:
  2 — Winnipeg, 1973, shutout Houston twice in semi-finals, won by Winnipeg 4-0.
  — Houston, 1975, shutout San Diego twice in semi-finals, won by Houston 4-0.
  — New England, 1976 shutout Indianapolis twice in quarter-finals, won by N.E. 4-3.
  — Indianapolis, 1976, shutout New England twice in quarter-finals, won by N.E. 4-3.

MOST PENALTIES, BOTH TEAMS, ONE SERIES: (and) MOST PENALTY MINUTES, BOTH TEAMS, ONE SERIES:
  116 penalties, 383 min. — Houston/Minnesota, 1974 semi-finals. Houston had 56 penalties for 170 minutes, Minnesota 60 for 213 minutes. Houston won series 4-2.

MOST PENALTIES, ONE TEAM, ONE SERIES: (and) MOST PENALTY MINUTES, ONE TEAM, ONE SERIES:
  60 penalties, 213 min. — Minnesota, 1974 semi-final series vs. Houston. Houston won series 4-2.

FEWEST PENALTIES, BOTH TEAMS, ONE SERIES: (and) FEWEST PENALTY MINUTES, BOTH TEAMS, ONE SERIES:
  29 penalties, 74 min. — Winnipeg/Minnesota, 1973, quarter-finals, Minnesota received 14 minors, 1 major. Winnipeg 12 minors, 1 major and 1 misconduct. Winnipeg won series 4-1.

FEWEST PENALTIES, ONE TEAM, ONE SERIES: (and) FEWEST PENALTY MINUTES, ONE TEAM, ONE SERIES:
  13 penalties, 29 min. — Winnipeg, 1973 semi-finals vs. Houston. Series won by Winnipeg 4-0.

MOST PENALTIES, BOTH TEAMS, ONE GAME: (and) MOST PENALTY MINUTES, BOTH TEAMS, ONE GAME:
  41 penalties, 217 min. — Minnesota at New England, April 11, 1975. New England had

21 penalties for 116 minutes, Minnesota 20 for 101 minutes. New England won game 3-2 and Minnesota won series 4-2.

MOST PENALTIES, ONE TEAM, ONE GAME: (and) MOST PENALTY MINUTES, ONE TEAM, ONE GAME:
21 penalties, 116 Min. — New England, April 11, 1975, vs. Minnesota at Hartford, Conn. New England won game 3-2, Minnesota won series 4-2.

MOST PENALTIES, BOTH TEAMS, ONE PERIOD: (and) MOST PENALTY MINUTES, BOTH TEAMS, ONE PERIOD:
34 penalties, 189 minutes — Minnesota at New England, April 11, 1975, second period. Minnesota had 16 penalties for 82 minutes, New England had 18 penalties for 107 minutes. New England won game 3-2.

MOST PENALTIES, ONE TEAM, ONE PERIOD: (and) MOST PENALTY MINUTES, ONE TEAM, ONE PERIOD:
18 penalties, 107 min. — New England, April 11, 1975, vs. Minnesota at Hartford, New England won game 3-2.

MOST POWER PLAY GOALS, ONE TEAM, ONE PLAYOFF YEAR:
17 — Houston, 1974.

MOST POWER PLAY GOALS, BOTH TEAMS, ONE SERIES:
16 — Houston/New England, 1976 quarter-finals series won by Houston 4-3. Each team scored 8 power play goals.

MOST POWER PLAY GOALS, ONE TEAM, ONE SERIES:
11 — Houston, 1974, final series vs. Chicago. Houston won series 4-0.

MOST POWER PLAY GOALS, BOTH TEAMS, ONE GAME:
6 — April 15, 1973, Los Angeles at Houston. Houston had 3, L.A. 2. Houston won game 6-3 and the series 4-2.
— May 19, 1974, Chicago at Houston. Houston had 5, Chicago 1, Houston won game 6-2 and series 4-0.
— April 13, 1975, New England at Minnesota. Minnesota had 4, New England 2. Minnesota won game 8-3 and the series 4-2.

MOST POWER PLAY GOALS, ONE TEAM, ONE GAME:
5 — Houston, May 19, 1974 vs. Chicago at Houston. Houston won game 6-2, series 4-0.

MOST POWER PLAY GOALS, BOTH TEAMS, ONE PERIOD:
4 — Los Angeles at Houston, April 15, 1973. First period, each team scored two power play goals. Houston won game 6-3, series 4-2.

MOST POWER PLAY GOALS, ONE TEAM, ONE PERIOD:
3 — Houston vs. Chicago, May 19, 1974, final round. Houston won game 6-2, series 4-2. Second period.
— Minnesota, April 13, 1975, quarter-final round, first period. Minnesota won game, 8-3, series 4-2.

MOST POWER PLAY OPPORTUNITIES, ONE TEAM, ONE GAME:
13 — San Diego, April 21, 1976, vs. Houston. Lost game 8-6, series 4-2.

MOST POWER PLAY OPPORTUNITIES, BOTH TEAMS, ONE GAME:
20 — San Diego 13, at Houston 7. April 21, 1976. Houston won 8-6.

MOST POWER PLAY OPPORTUNITIES, ONE TEAM, ONE SERIES:
43 — Houston, 1976 quarter-finals vs. New England. Houston won series 4-3.

MOST POWER PLAY OPPORTUNITIES, BOTH TEAMS, ONE SERIES:
73 — Houston/New England, 1976 semi-finals. Houston 43, N.E. 30.

MOST SHORTHANDED GOALS, ONE TEAM, ONE PLAYOFF YEAR:
7 — Houston, 1974, in 10 games.

MOST SHORTHANDED GOALS, ONE TEAM, ONE SERIES:
4 — Houston, 1974 semi-final vs. Minnesota, 6 games. Houston won series, 4-2.

MOST SHORTHANDED GOALS, ONE TEAM, ONE GAME: (and)
MOST SHORTHANDED GOALS, ONE TEAM, ONE PERIOD:
2 — Houston, April 29, 1974 vs. Minnesota. First period. Houston won game 9-4, series 4-2.
— New England, April 15, 1975 at Minnesota. Third period. New England, 5-2. Minnesota won series 4-2.
— Houston, April 21, 1976, at Houston. First period. Houston 8-6. Houston won series 4-2.

FASTEST TWO GOALS, BOTH TEAMS, ONE GAME:
8 sec — Minnesota at Quebec, April 29, 1975. Mike Walton scored for Minnesota at 8:53, Marc Tardif for Quebec at 9:01 of second period. Quebec won game 6-3, series 4-2.

FASTEST TWO GOALS, ONE TEAM:
  3 sec. — Calgary vs. Winnipeg, April 28, 1976. Calgary's Lynn Powis scored at 4:08 and Don Tannahill at 4:11. Winnipeg won game 6-3, series 4-1.

FASTEST THREE GOALS, BOTH TEAMS:
  52 sec. — Winnipeg at Calgary, April 30, 1976. First period. Danny Lawson scored for Calgary at 3:12 and Gavin Kirk at 3:52; and Anders Hedberg for Winnipeg at 4:04. Calgary won game 7-3, Winnipeg won series 4-1.

FASTEST THREE GOALS, ONE TEAM:
  55 sec. — Cleveland vs. Philadelphia, April 7, 1973. Jim Wiste 5:15, Garry Pinder 5:51 and Gary Jarrett at 6:10 of the second period. Cleveland won game 7-1, series 4-0.

FASTEST TWO POWER PLAY GOALS, ONE TEAM:
  29 sec. — Minnesota, April 6, 1974 vs. Edmonton. Murray Heatley at 9:09, Mike Walton at 9:38 of second period.

FASTEST THREE POWER PLAY GOALS, ONE TEAM:
  3 minutes, 12 sec. — Houston, May 19, 1974, vs. Chicago. Andre Hinse 12:40, Gord Labossiere 13:58, Larry Lund 15:52 in final game of final series. Houston won game, 6-2, series 4-0.

FASTEST TWO SHORTHANDED GOALS, ONE TEAM:
  39 sec. — Houston, April 21, 1976, quarter-finals vs. San Diego. Rich Preston, Houston, at 4:52 and 5:31, first period.

INDIVIDUAL

MOST POINTS, ONE PLAYOFF YEAR:
  28 — Norm Beaudin, Winnipeg, 1973. 13 goals, 15 assists (14 games).

MOST GOALS, ONE PLAYOFF YEAR:
  13 — Norm Beaudin, Winnipeg, 1973 (14 games).
  — Anders Hedberg, Winnipeg, 1976 (13 games).

MOST ASSISTS, ONE PLAYOFF YEAR:
  19 — Ulf Nilsson, Winnipeg, 1976 (13 games).

MOST PENALTY MINUTES, ONE PLAYOFF YEAR:
  71 — Darryl Maggs, Chicago, 1974 (18 games).

MOST POINTS, BY A DEFENCEMAN, ONE PLAYOFF YEAR:
  19 — Jim Dorey, New England, 1973, 3 goals, 16 assists (15 games).

MOST GOALS, BY A DEFENCEMAN, ONE PLAYOFF YEAR:
  5 — Chris Evans, Calgary, 1976 (10 games).

MOST ASSISTS, BY A DEFENCEMAN, ONE PLAYOFF YEAR:
  16 — Jim Dorey, New England, 1973 (15 games).

MOST POINTS, FOUR GAME SERIES:
  9 — Gordie Howe, Houston, 1974 vs. Chicago, 9 assists.
  6 — Ulf Nilsson, Winnipeg, 1976, vs. Houston. 3 goals, 6 assists.

MOST GOALS, FOUR GAME SERIES:
  6 — Anders Hedberg, Winnipeg, 1976 vs. Houston.

MOST ASSISTS, FOUR GAME SERIES:
  9 — Gordie Howe, Houston, 1974 vs. Chicago.

MOST POINTS IN FIVE GAMES SERIES:
  15 — Norm Beaudin, Winnipeg, 1973 vs. Minnesota. 5 goals, 10 assists.

MOST GOALS, FIVE GAME SERIES:
  8 — Mark Howe, Houston, 1975 vs. Cleveland.

MOST ASSISTS, FIVE GAME SERIES
  10 — Norm Beaudin, Winnipeg, 1973 vs. Minnesota.

MOST POINTS, SIX GAME SERIES:
  12 — Fran Huck, Minnesota, 1975 vs. New England 2 goals, 10 assists.
  — Ray Addouno, San Diego, 1975 vs. Toronto. 4 goals, 8 assists.

MOST GOALS, SIX GAME SERIES:
  7 — Gene Peacosh, San Diego, 1975 vs. Toronto.

MOST ASSISTS, SIX GAME SERIES:
  10 — Fran Huck, Minnesota, 1975 vs. New England.

MOST POINTS, SEVEN GAME SERIES:
  10 — Ralph Backstrom, Chicago, 1974, vs. Toronto. 2 goals, 8 assists.

— Rosaire Paiement, Chicago, 1974 vs. Toronto. 7 goals, 3 assists.
— Tom Webster, New England, 1976 vs. Houston. 7 goals, 3 assists.

MOST GOALS, SEVEN GAMES SERIES:
7 — Rosaire Paiement, Chicago, 1974 vs. Toronto.
— Tom Webster, New England, 1976 vs. Houston.

MOST ASSISTS, SEVEN GAME SERIES:
8 — Ralph Backstrom, Chicago, 1974 vs. Toronto.

MOST POINTS, QUARTER FINAL SERIES:
15 — Norm Beaudin, Winnipeg 1973 vs. Minnesota. 5 goals, 10 assists.

MOST GOALS, QUARTER FINAL SERIES:
8 — Mark Howe, Houston 1975 vs. Cleveland.

MOST ASSISTS, QUARTER FINAL SERIES:
10 — Norm Beaudin, Winnipeg, 1973 vs. Minnesota.
— Fran Huck, Minnesota, 1975 vs. New England.

MOST POINTS, SEMI-FINAL SERIES:
12 — Tim Sheehy, New England, 1973 vs. Cleveland. 6 goals, 6 assists.

MOST GOALS, SEMI-FINAL SERIES:
7 — Rosaire Paiement, Chicago, 1974 vs. Toronto.
— Tom Webster, New England, 1976 vs. Houston.

MOST ASSISTS, SEMI-FINAL SERIES:
8 — Ralph Backstrom, Chicago, 1974 vs. Toronto.

MOST POINTS, FINAL SERIES:
11 — Tom Webster, New England, 1973 vs. Winnipeg. 4 goals, 7 assists.
— Tommy Williams, New England, 1973 vs. Winnipeg. 2 goals, 9 assists.

MOST GOALS, FINAL SERIES:
6 — Anders Hedberg, Winnipeg, 1976 vs. Houston.

MOST ASSISTS, FINAL SERIES:
9 — Tommy Williams, New England, 1973 vs. Winnipeg.
— Gordie Howe, Houston, 1974 vs. Chicago.

MOST CONSECUTIVE GAMES WITH POINTS:
16 — Tim Sheehy, New England, Apr. 12, 1973 to Apr. 12, 1974. 13 goals, 16 assists.

MOST CONSECUTIVE GAMES WITH GOALS:
8 — Bobby Hull, Winnipeg, April 14 to April 28, 1976.
— Anders Hedberg, Winnipeg, April 25 to May 27, 1976.

MOST CONSECUTIVE GAMES WITH ASSISTS:
11 — Ulf Nilsson, Winnipeg, April 8 to May 25, 1976.

MOST GAME WINNING GOALS, ONE PLAYOFF YEAR:
3 — Bobby Hull, Winnipeg, 1973.
— Tim Sheehy, New England, 1973.
— Mike Walton, Minnesota, 1974.
— Murray Hall, Houston, 1974.

MOST POWER PLAY GOALS, ONE PLAYOFF YEAR:
5 — Wayne Connelly, Minnesota, 1974.
— Bobby Hull, Winnipeg, 1976.

MOST POWER PLAY GOALS, ONE PLAYOFF SERIES:
4 — Andre Hinse, Houston 1974 vs. Chicago, 4 games.

MOST POWER PLAY GOALS, ONE GAME:
2 — Tom Webster (New England — twice); Andre Hinse (Houston — twice); Tommy Williams (New England); Frank Hughes (Houston); Tom Martin (Toronto); Murray Hall, Mark Howe and Poul Popiel (Houston); Rejean Houle (Quebec).

MOST POWER PLAY GOALS, ONE PERIOD:
2 — Tommy Williams (N.E.); Frank Hughes (Hou); Tom Webster (N.E.) Andre Hinse (Hou); Murray Hall (Hou).

MOST SHORTHANDED GOALS, ONE PLAYOFF YEAR:
2 — Larry Lund, Houston, 1974.   — Rich Preston, Houston, 1976.
— Gordie Howe, Houston, 1974.   — Chris Evans, Calgary, 1976
— Mark Howe, Houston, 1974.
— Rod Zaine, Chicago, 1974

MOST SHORTHANDED GOALS, ONE SERIES:
2 — Mark Howe, Houston, 1974 vs. Minnesota.   — Rich Preston, Houston, 1976.
— Rod Zaine, Chicago, 1974 vs. Toronto.   — Chris Evans, Calgary, 1976

MOST SHORTHANDED GOALS, ONE GAME:
1 — No player has scored more than one. There have been 23 in WHA history.

MOST OVERTIME GOALS, ONE PLAYOFF YEAR: (and)
MOST OVERTIME GOALS, ONE PLAYOFF SERIES:
1 — No player has scored more than 1. There have been 14 overtime games.

MOST THREE-OR-MORE GOAL GAMES, ONE PLAYOFF YEAR:
2 — Gary Jarrett, Cleveland 1973.
— Mark Howe, Houston 1975.

MOST CONSECUTIVE WINS BY A GOALTENDER:
13 — Ron Grahame, Houston. Won the last 10 games 1975, and first 3 games vs. San Diego in 1976.

MOST SHUTOUTS, ONE PLAYOFF YEAR, BY A GOALTENDER:
3 — Ron Grahame, Houston, 1975.

LONGEST SHUTOUT SEQUENCE:
145 mins., 3 sec — Ernie Wakely, Winnipeg. Streak started at 14:13 of third period vs. Minnesota Apr. 15 and ended May 2, 1973 at 19:46 of third period vs. New England. Included shutouts of Houston Apr. 22, Apr. 26.

MOST CONSECUTIVE SHUTOUTS:
2 — Ernie Wakely, Winnipeg, 1973 vs. Houston Apr. 22 and Apr. 26.

MOST POINTS, ONE GAME:
7 — Norm Beaudin, Winnipeg Apr. 15, 1973 (3 goals, 4 assists) vs. Minnesota.

MOST GOALS, ONE GAME:
4 — Larry Lund, Houston, Apr. 13, 1974 vs. Winnipeg.

MOST ASSISTS, ONE GAME:
4 — 13 different players.

MOST PENALTIES, ONE GAME: (and) MOST PENALTY MINUTES, ONE GAME:
7 penalties, 36 min. — Ted Taylor, Houston, Apr. 28, 1974 at Minnesota. 3 minors, 2 majors, 2 misconducts.

MOST POINTS, ONE PERIOD:
4 — Norm Beaudin, Winnipeg, Apr. 15, 1973 vs. Minnesota. (2 goals, 2 assists).
— Robbie Ftorek, Phoenix, Apr. 15, 1975 vs. Quebec. (1 goal, 3 assists).
— Mike Walton, Minnesota, Apr. 24, 1975 at Quebec. (2 goals, 2 assists).

MOST GOALS, ONE PERIOD:
3 — Rick Sentes, Toronto, Apr. 12, 1974 at Cleveland.

MOST ASSISTS, ONE PERIOD:
3 — 9 different players.

MOST PENALTIES, ONE PERIOD: (and) MOST PENALTY MINUTES, ONE PERIOD:
7 penalties, 36 min. — Ted Taylor, Houston, Apr. 28, 1974 at Minnesota (3 minors, 2 majors, 2 misconducts).

FASTEST GOAL FROM START OF GAME:
15 sec. — Jim Harrison, Cleveland, Apr. 10, 1975, at Houston.

FASTEST TWO GOALS, FROM START OF GAME:
5 mins., 31 sec. — Rich Preston, Houston, April 21, 1976 vs. San Diego.

FASTEST GOAL FROM THE START OF PERIOD, OTHER THAN THE FIRST:
7 sec — Mike Antonovich, Minnesota, Apr. 15, 1973 at Winnipeg. 2nd period.

FASTEST TWO GOALS FROM START OF PERIOD, OTHER THAN FIRST:
6 mins., 37 sec. — Larry Lund, Houston, Apr. 13, 1974, third period vs. Winnipeg.

FASTEST TWO GOALS:
15 sec. — Mike Walton, Minnesota, Apr. 14, 1974, vs. Edmonton. 19:05 and 19:20 of first period.

FASTEST THREE GOALS:
8 min. 42 sec. — Rich Sentes, Toronto, Apr. 12, 1974 at Cleveland. 10:41, 13:04 and 19:23 of second period.

PENALTY SHOT GOALS:
1 — Wayne Dillon, Toronto, Apr. 19, 1974 vs. Cam Newton, Chicago. (Only one awarded in three years). Toronto won game 6-4.
2 — Gord Labossiere, Houston, April 21, 1975 vs. Ernie Wakely, San Diego. Houston won game 8-6.
3 — Tom Earl, New England, May 5, 1976 vs. Ron Grahame, Houston. N.E. won game 4-2.

BIRMINGHAM BULLS

JIM FINKS, Director of Public Relations (205) 251-2855

WRITERS REGULARLY ASSIGNED TO CLUB

JIMMY BRYAN, Birmingham News, Box 2553, Birmingham 35202 .... (205) 325-2405
JOHN CARGILE, Birmingham Post Herald, Box 2553, Birmingham 35202 .... (205) 325-2420

MAJOR AIRLINES

Delta	(205) 328-2000	United	(205) 323-7731
Eastern	(205) 328-9851	Southern	(205) 252-4124

CALGARY COWBOYS

Don LeROSE, Director of Marketing/Public Relations (403) 261-6990

WRITERS REGULARLY ASSIGNED TO CLUB

GEORGE BILYCH, Calgary Herald, 206-7th Ave. S.W., Calgary .... (403) 263-3220
DICK CHUBEY, Calgary Albertan, 830-10th Ave. S.W., Calgary .... (403) 263-7730

MAJOR AIRLINES

AIR CANADA	(403) 265-9555	PACIFIC WESTERN	(403) 265-0790
CP AIR	(403) 265-8300	TIME AIR	(403) 277-8596
HUGHES AIR WEST	(403) 277-0755	WESTERN	(403) 277-0176

CINCINNATI STINGERS

JOHN A. HEWIG, Publicity Director (513) 241-1818

WRITERS REGULARLY ASSIGNED TO CLUB

TERRY FLYNN, Cincinnati Enquirer, 617 Vine Street, Cincinnati, Ohio 45202 .... (513) 721-2700
GREG NOBLE, Cincinnati Post, 800 Broadway, Cincinnati, Ohio 45202 .... (513) 721-1111

MAJOR AIRLINES

AIR CANADA	(513) 232-7780	DELTA	(513) 721-7000
ALLEGHENY	(513) 621-9220	AMERICAN	(513) 621-6200
TWA	(513) 381-1600	EASTERN	(513) 241-6800

EDMONTON OILERS

DOUG WENSCHLAG, Director of Marketing (403) 474-8561

WRITERS REGULARLY ASSIGNED TO CLUB

JIM MATHESON, Edmonton Journal, 101 St. & 100 Ave., Edmonton .... (403) 423-9597
JOHN SHORT, Canadian Press, 101 St. & 100 Ave., Edmonton .... (403) 424-6107

MAJOR AIRLINES

AIR CANADA	(403) 429-5461	PACIFIC WESTERN	(403) 452-4560
CP AIR	(403) 429-6371	TIME AIR	(403) 455-1015
HUGHES AIR WEST	(403) 429-4716		

media/airlines

HOUSTON AEROS

RICH BURK, Public Relations Director   (713) 623-8321

WRITERS REGULARLY ASSIGNED TO CLUB

CHUCK MYERS, Houston Post, 4747 Southwest Fwy, Houston 77027 .... (713) 621-7000
DICK PEEBLES, Houston Chronicle, 512 Travis St., Houston 77002 .... (713) 220-7891

MAJOR AIRLINES

AMERICAN	(713) 222-9873	DELTA	(713) 623-6000
BRANIFF	(713) 621-3111	EASTERN	(713) 621-8100
CONTINENTAL	(713) 524-4711	NATIONAL	(713) 224-9011

INDIANAPOLIS RACERS

WALT MARLOW, Public Relations Director   (317) 635-3131

WRITERS REGULARLY ASSIGNED TO CLUB

DAVE OVERPECK, Indianapolis Star, 307 N. Pennsylvana .... (317) 633-9180
DICK DENNY, Indianapolis News, 307 N. Pennsylvania .... (317) 633-1240

MAJOR AIRLINES

ALLEGHENY	(317) 247-8101	EASTERN	(317) 639-6611
AMERICAN	(317) 637-1501	TWA	(317) 635-4381
	DELTA	(317) 634-3200	

MINNESOTA FIGHTING SAINTS

KEN RESNICK, Media Information Director   (612) 221-0123

WRITERS REGULARLY ASSIGNED TO CLUB

CHARLIE HALLMAN, St. Paul Pioneer Press-Dispatch, 55 E. Fourth St., St. Paul 55101 (612) 222-5011
BOB FOWLER, Minneapolis Star, 415 Portland Ave., Minneapolis 55415 .... (612) 372-4365
JOHN GILBERT, Minneapolis Tribune, 415 Portland Ave., Minn. 55415 .... (612) 372-4447

MAJOR AIRLINES

ALLEGHENY	(612) 338-5841	NORTHWEST	(612) 726-1234
BRANIFF	(612) 726-1200	OZARK	(612) 333-3421
EASTERN	(612) 335-9541	UNITED	(612) 339-3671
NORTH CENTRAL	(612) 726-7100	WESTERN	(612) 726-4141

NEW ENGLAND WHALERS

DENNIS RANDALL, Public Relations Director   (203) 728-3366

WRITERS REGULARLY ASSIGNED TO CLUB

HOWIE HOLCOMB, Hartford Times, 10 Prospect St., Hartford .... (203) 249-8211
KEVIN McGUIRK, Springfield News, 1860 Main St., Springfield 01101 .... (413) 787-2411
GENE McCORMACK, Springfield Union, 1860 Main St., Springfield 01101 .... (413) 787-2411

MAJOR AIRLINES

ALLEGHENY	(203) 522-2161	EASTERN	(203) 525-0141
AMERICAN	(203) 527-5141	TWA	(203) 278-7710
DELTA	(203) 527-1811	UNITED	(203) 249-1311

PHOENIX ROADRUNNERS

DAVE WEISER, Press Relations Director   (602) 257-5100

WRITERS REGULARLY ASSIGNED TO CLUB

FRANK GIANELLI, Arizona Republic, 120 E. Van Buren, Phoenix 85001 .... (602) 271-8250
DOUG McCONNELL, Phoenix Gazette, 120 E. Van Buren, Phoenix 85001 .... (602) 271-8641

MAJOR AIRLINES

AMERICAN	(602) 264-2654	HUGHES	(602) 273-9111
CONTINENTAL	(602) 258-8911	TWA	(602) 252-7711
FRONTIER	(602) 252-5041	WESTERN	(602) 258-8881

QUEBEC NORDIQUES

PAUL LE FRANCOIS, Director of Public Relations   (418) 529-4161

WRITERS REGULARLY ASSIGNED TO CLUB

CLAUDE BEDARD, Journal De Quebec, 450 Rue Bechard, Ville Vanier, Quebec City .... (418) 683-1573
CLAUDE CADORETTE, Journal De Quebec, 450 Rue Bechard, Ville Vanier, Quebec City .... (418) 683-1573
CLAUDE LAROCHELLE, Le Soleil, 390 Rue St. Vallier, Quebec City .... (418) 525-7134
MAURICE DUMAS, Le Soleil, 390 Rue St. Vallier, Quebec City .... (418) 525-7134

MAJOR AIRLINES

AIR CANADA .... (418) 692-0770   QUEBECAIR .... (418) 692-1031

SAN DIEGO MARINERS

GABE DENUNZIO, Director of Public Relations/Business Manager   (714) 225-9633

WRITERS REGULARLY ASSIGNED TO CLUB

WAYNE LOCKWOOD, San Diego Union, P.O. Box 191, San Diego 92112 .... (714) 299-3131
PAUL COUR, Evening Tribune, P.O. Box 191, San Diego 92112 .... (714) 299-3131
MATT MITCHELL, El Cajon California, 613 W. Main St., El Cajon .... (714) 442-4404

MAJOR AIRLINES

AIR CANADA	(800) 634-6631	EASTERN	(800) 252-0223
AMERICAN	(714) 235-7601	NATIONAL	(714) 239-3036
CP AIR	Zenith 2-4209	UNITED	(714) 234-7171
DELTA	(714) 239-3431	WESTERN	(714) 234-0181

WINNIPEG JETS

NORMAN COSTON, Director of Media Relations   (204) 772-9491

WRITERS REGULARLY ASSIGNED TO CLUB

REYN DAVIS, Winnipeg Free Press, 300 Carleton St., Winnipeg .... (204) 943-9331
ED DEARDEN, Winnipeg Tribune, Smith & Graham, Winnipeg .... (204) 985-4631
JOHN KOROBANIK, Canadian Press, 300 Carleton St., Winnipeg .... (204) 942-8188

MAJOR AIRLINES

AIR CANADA	(204) 943-9361	MIDWEST	(204) 889-4450
CP AIR	(204) 957-1060	NORTHWEST	(204) 786-3481
FRONTIER	(204) 475-3330	TRANSAIR	(204) 889-4450

100

The Exciting Difference

Hockey, it has been said, is a game combining all the elements — grace, speed, emotion, violence.

The purists said there just wasn't any room for improvement. But that was before the WHA came along.

The World Hockey Association's rulebook, for the most part, duplicates that of any other professional league. There have been, however, several innovations that give the WHA a distinctive flavor.

OVERTIME

Over four seasons, there have been 266 overtime games, with 174 decisions, against 92 ties in league games.

Beyond overtime and its attendant drama, other areas where WHA rules differ from other professional leagues are in OFFSIDE PASSES AND CURVATURE OF THE STICK.

OFFSIDE PASS

In other leagues, a completed forward pass that crosses two lines is ruled offside unless the 'receiver' was in the same area of the ice as the 'passer' when the pass was made. In the WHA, a player may pass the puck from inside his own blueline to a teammate beyond the center red line, providing the puck precedes the player across the center red line and the receiver takes the puck ahead of his body. The rule is designed to bring about more quick breaks, but at the same time preventing a player from floating beyond the red line awaiting a breakaway pass.

STICK CURVATURE

The National League restricts the curvature of the stick blade to half an inch, mainly for the reason that goaltenders complain that curved blades represent an unfair advantage for the shooter adept at making the puck do tricks. The WHA has an allowable curvature of an inch and a quarter, resulting in more difficult shots for the goaltenders.

WIRE SERVICE CONTACTS

ASSOCIATED PRESS, 50 Rockefeller Plaza, New York, N.Y. 10020 (212) 262-6080. Murray Rose, Hal Bock, Frank Brown, Ben Olan, Will Grimsley.

CANADIAN PRESS, 36 King Street East, Toronto, Canada (416) 364-0321. Ian MacLaine, Chuck Svoboda.

UNITED PRESS INTERNATIONAL, 220 East 42nd Street, New York, N.Y. Joe Marrinelli, Martin Lader, 171 Yonge St., Suite 50, Toronto, Canada (416) 363-8834. Ken Becker.

MAGAZINES

SPORTS ILLUSTRATED, Time-Life Building, New York N.Y. (212) 586-1212. Mark Mulvoy, Peter Gammons, Angel Reyes.

THE SPORTING NEWS, 1212 N. Lindberg Blvd., St. Louis, Mo. (314) 997-7111. Larry Wigge.

THE HOCKEY NEWS, 1434 St. Catherine St. W., Montreal, P.Q. (514) 866-4841. Ken McKenzie, Charlie Halpin.

NATIONAL SPORTS PUBLICATIONS, 39-58 65th Place, Queens, N.Y. Norm McLean.

NATIONAL STAR, 730 Third Avenue, New York (212) 557-9200. Pete Bodo, Steve Williams.

HOCKEY ILLUSTRATED, 333 Johnson Ave., Brooklyn, New York (212) 456-8600. Jim McNally.

WHA 1976-77 SCHEDULE

1976

1	Thu.	Oct.	7	Minnesota	at	Cincinnati
2	Fri.	Oct.	8	Calgary	at	Winnipeg
3				Houston	at	Birmingham
4				New England	at	Edmonton
5				Cincinnati	at	Phoenix
6				Minnesota	at	Indianapolis
7	Sat.	Oct.	9	Calgary	at	Quebec
8				Phoenix	at	Houston
9				Cincinnati	at	San Diego
10	Sun.	Oct.	10	Birmingham	at	Quebec
11				New England	at	Winnipeg
12				Indianapolis	at	Minnesota
13	Tue.	Oct.	12	Calgary	at	Birmingham
14				San Diego	at	Quebec
15	Wed.	Oct.	13	Calgary	at	Houston
16	Thu.	Oct.	14	Cincinnati	at	Birmingham
17				Minnesota	at	Phoenix
18	Fri.	Oct.	15	San Diego	at	Minnesota
19				Winnipeg	at	Edmonton
20				Cincinnati	at	Indianapolis
21	Sat.	Oct.	16	Calgary	at	San Diego
22				Birmingham	at	Houston
23				Quebec	at	New England
24				Winnipeg	at	Phoenix
25	Sun.	Oct.	17	Birmingham	at	Minnesota
26				Indianapolis	at	Edmonton
27				Winnipeg	at	San Diego
28				Cincinnati	at	Quebec
29	Tue.	Oct.	19	New England	at	Houston
30				Indianapolis	at	Winnipeg
31				Quebec	at	Birmingham
32				Phoenix	at	Edmonton
33				Cincinnati	at	Minnesota
34	Thu.	Oct.	21	Indianapolis	at	San Diego
35				Quebec	at	Calgary
36				Houston	at	Birmingham
37	Fri.	Oct.	22	Calgary	at	Minnesota
38				Houston	at	New England
39				Phoenix	at	Winnipeg
40	Sat.	Oct.	23	Birmingham	at	Indianapolis
41				Houston	at	Quebec
42				Cincinnati	at	New England
43	Sun.	Oct.	24	Birmingham	at	Winnipeg
44				San Diego	at	Calgary
45				Phoenix	at	Edmonton

46	Tue.	Oct.	26	Edmonton	at Houston
47				Birmingham	at Calgary
48				San Diego	at Minnesota
49				Phoenix	at Quebec
50				Cincinnati	at New England
51	Wed.	Oct.	27	San Diego	at Indianapolis
52	Thu.	Oct.	28	Edmonton	at Birmingham
53				Minnesota	at Houston
54	Fri.	Oct.	29	San Diego	at Cincinnati
55				Quebec	at Indianapolis
56				Phoenix	at New England
57				Edmonton	at Winnipeg
58	Sat.	Oct.	30	Birmingham	at New England
59				Houston	at Calgary
60				Minnesota	at Quebec
61				Phoenix	at Cincinnati
62	Sun.	Oct.	31	Houston	at Edmonton
63				San Diego	at Winnipeg
64	Tue.	Nov.	2	San Diego	at Birmingham
65				Minnesota	at Calgary
66				Phoenix	at Quebec
67				Houston	at Winnipeg
68	Wed.	Nov.	3	Minnesota	at Edmonton
69				Indianapolis	at Cincinnati
70	Thu.	Nov.	4	Phoenix	at Birmingham
71				Cincinnati	at Indianapolis
72				Edmonton	at Calgary
73	Fri.	Nov.	5	New England	at Edmonton
74				Minnesota	at Winnipeg
75				Phoenix	at Houston
76	Sat.	Nov.	6	Birmingham	at Quebec
77				Houston	at San Diego
78				Winnipeg	at Cincinnati
79	Sun.	Nov.	7	Edmonton	at Winnipeg
80				New England	at Calgary
81				Indianapolis	at San Diego
82				Phoenix	at Minnesota
83	Tue.	Nov.	9	Birmingham	at Quebec
84				New England	at Winnipeg
85				Indianapolis	at Houston
86	Wed.	Nov.	10	Edmonton	at Cincinnati
87				Indianapolis	at Phoenix
88	Thu.	Nov.	11	San Diego	at Birmingham
89				New England	at Minnesota
90				Winnipeg	at Calgary
91	Fri.	Nov.	12	New England	at Phoenix
92				San Diego	at Houston

103

93	Sat.	Nov.	13	Edmonton	at	Birmingham
94				Minnesota	at	Quebec
95				Indianapolis	at	Cincinnati
96	Sun.	Nov.	14	San Diego	at	Phoenix
97				Winnipeg	at	Calgary
98				Indianapolis	at	Quebec
99	Tue.	Nov.	16	Calgary	at	Houston
100				Edmonton	at	Phoenix
101				New England	at	Birmingham
102				Quebec	at	Winnipeg
103				Cincinnati	at	Indianapolis
104	Wed.	Nov.	17	Edmonton	at	San Diego
105				Birmingham	at	New England
106	Thu.	Nov.	18	Calgary	at	Phoenix
107				Quebec	at	Minnesota
108	Fri.	Nov.	19	Houston	at	San Diego
109				Quebec	at	Calgary
109				Winnipeg	at	New England
111				Cincinnati	at	Edmonton
112				Birmingham	at	Indianapolis
113	Sat.	Nov.	20	Houston	at	Phoenix
114				Winnipeg	at	Indianapolis
115				Minnesota	at	New England
116	Sun.	Nov.	21	Calgary	at	Minnesota
117				San Diego	at	Birmingham
118				Quebec	at	Edmonton
119				Cincinnati	at	Winnipeg
120	Tue.	Nov.	23	Calgary	at	Birmingham
121				Edmonton	at	Houston
122				New England	at	Indianapolis
123				Winnipeg	at	Quebec
124				Cincinnati	at	Minnesota
125	Wed.	Nov.	24	Edmonton	at	San Diego
126				Indianapolis	at	Cincinnati
127				Calgary	at	Phoenix
128	Thu.	Nov.	25	New England	at	Birmingham
129				Quebec	at	Indianapolis
130	Fri.	Nov.	26	Edmonton	at	Phoenix
131				Winnipeg	at	Houston
132				Quebec	at	Minnesota
133	Sat.	Nov.	27	San Diego	at	Calgary
134				Indianapolis	at	Quebec
135				Birmingham	at	Cincinnati
136				Minnesota	at	New England
137	Sun.	Nov.	28	San Diego	at	Edmonton
138				Indianapolis	at	New England
139				Phoenix	at	Winnipeg
140				Minnesota	at	Birmingham

141	Tue.	Nov.	30	New England	at	Quebec
142				Phoenix	at	Edmonton
143				Cincinnati	at	Birmingham
144				San Diego	at	Winnipeg
145	Wed.	Dec.	1	Calgary	at	New England
146	Thu.	Dec.	2	Calgary	at	Indianapolis
147				Phoenix	at	San Diego
148				Edmonton	at	Birmingham
149	Fri.	Dec.	3	Calgary	at	Cincinnati
150				Edmonton	at	Houston
151				Quebec	at	New England
152				Winnipeg	at	Minnesota
153	Sat.	Dec.	4	Edmonton	at	Indianapolis
154				San Diego	at	Phoenix
155				Winnipeg	at	New England
156	Sun.	Dec.	5	Edmonton	at	Minnesota
157				Houston	at	Cincinnati
158				Winnipeg	at	Quebec
159				Phoenix	at	Calgary
160	Tue.	Dec.	7	Edmonton	at	Quebec
161				New England	at	Minnesota
162				Phoenix	at	Winnipeg
163				Indianapolis	at	Birmingham
164	Wed.	Dec.	8	Houston	at	New England
165				San Diego	at	Cincinnati
166				Winnipeg	at	Calgary
167	Thu.	Dec.	9	Quebec	at	Phoenix
168	Fri.	Dec.	10	Calgary	at	Minnesota
169				Birmingham	at	Winnipeg
170				Houston	at	Cincinnati
171				San Diego	at	Indianapolis
172	Sat.	Dec.	11	San Diego	at	New England
173				Houston	at	Quebec
174				Edmonton	at	Calgary
176	Sun	Dec.	12	Birmingham	at	Edmonton
176				Houston	at	Indianapolis
177				New England	at	Quebec
178				San Diego	at	Minnesota
179				Phoenix	at	Cincinnati
180	Tue.	Dec.	14	New England	at	Quebec
181				San Diego	at	Edmonton
182				Phoenix	at	Houston
183	Wed.	Dec.	15	Birmingham	at	Phoenix
184				Minnesota	at	Cincinnati
185	Thu.	Dec.	16	Edmonton	at	San Diego
186				Minnesota	at	Indianapolis
187	Fri.	Dec.	17	Edmonton	at	Phoenix

105

188			Indianapolis	at	New England
189			Birmingham	at	Houston
190	Sat.	Dec. 18	Birmingham	at	New England
191			Houston	at	San Diego
192			Quebec	at	Calgary
193			Cincinnati	at	Minnesota
194	Sun.	Dec. 19	Houston	at	Phoenix
195			Quebec	at	San Diego
196			Cincinnati	at	Edmonton
197			Birmingham	at	Indianapolis
198	Tue.	Dec. 21	Calgary	at	Edmonton
199			New England	at	Houston
200			Quebec	at	Birmingham
201	Wed.	Dec. 22	Birmingham	at	Cincinnati
202			San Diego	at	Phoenix
203			Quebec	at	Minnesota
204	Thu.	Dec. 23	New England	at	San Diego
205			Cincinnati	at	Houston
206			Minnesota	at	Calgary
207	Sun.	Dec. 26	Houston	at	Birmingham
208			Minnesota	at	New England
209			Indianapolis	at	San Diego
210			Quebec	at	Winnipeg
211			*Cincinnati	at	Calgary
212	Tue.	Dec. 28	Indianapolis	at	Phoenix
213			Quebec	at	Edmonton
214			Winnipeg	at	Houston
215			New England	at	Minnesota
216	Thu.	Dec. 30	New England	at	Cincinnati
217			Minnesota	at	Birmingham
218			Winnipeg	at	San Diego

1977

219	Sat.	Jan. 1	*Edmonton	at	Calgary
220	Sun.	Jan. 2	Birmingham	at	Minnesota
221			Houston	at	Winnipeg
222			Cincinnatti	at	New England
223			*Phoenix	at	Indianapolis
224	Tue.	Jan. 4	Houston	at	Edmonton
225			New England	at	Quebec
226			Indianapolis	at	Winnipeg
227			Phoenix	at	Birmingham
228	Wed.	Jan. 5	Houston	at	Calgary
229			San Diego	at	New England
230	Fri.	Jan. 7	Birmingham	at	Cincinnati
231			Calgary	at	Edmonton
232			Houston	at	Minnesota
233			Quebec	at	New England

* Afternoon Game

234	Sat.	Jan.	8	San Diego .... at Cincinnati ....
235				Edmonton .... at Minnesota ....
236				Indianapolis .... at Calgary ....
237				Phoenix .... at New England ....
238	Sun.	Jan.	9	Birmingham .... at Winnipeg ....
239				San Diego .... at Quebec ....
240				Indianapolis .... at Edmonton ....
241	Tue.	Jan.	11	Edmonton .... at Quebec ....
242				New England .... at Cincinnati ....
243				San Diego .... at Houston ....
244				Indianapolis .... at Calgary ....
245				Phoenix .... at Winnipeg ....
246	Wed.	Jan.	12	Birmingham .... at Minnesota ....
247				Houston .... at Phoenix ....
248	Thu.	Jan.	13	New England .... at Indianapolis ....
249				Cincinnati .... at San Diego ....
250	Fri.	Jan.	14	Birmingham .... at Houston ....
251				Edmonton .... at New England ....
252				Cincinnati .... at Phoenix ....
253				Winnipeg .... at Calgary ....
254				Indianapolis .... at Minnesota ....
255	Sat.	Jan.	15	Calgary .... at San Diego ....
256				Edmonton .... at Indianapolis ....
257				Minnesota .... at Quebec ....
258	Sun.	Jan.	16	Calgary .... at Phoenix ....
259				Edmonton .... at Houston ....
260				Minnesota .... at New England ....
261				Cincinnati .... at Winnipeg ....
262				Birmingham .... at San Diego ....

Tue. Jan 18 ALL STAR GAME at HARTFORD, CONN.

263	Wed.	Jan.	19	Quebec .... at Birmingham ....
264	Thu.	Jan.	20	Edmonton .... at San Diego ....
265				Quebec .... at New England ....
266				Cincinnati .... at Phoenix ....
267	Fri.	Jan.	21	Calgary .... at Indianapolis ....
268				Minnesota .... at Houston ....
269				Cincinnati .... at Winnipeg ....
270	Sat.	Jan.	22	Calgary .... at Quebec ....
271				Edmonton .... at Phoenix ....
272				Minnesota .... at San Diego ....
273	Sun.	Jan.	23	Calgary .... at Winnipeg ....
274				San Diego .... at Houston ....
275				*Indianapolis .... at Birmingham ....
276				*Cincinnati .... at New England ....
277				Phoenix .... at Edmonton ....

* Afternoon Game

278	Tue.	Jan.	25	New England	at	Cincinnati
279				Indianapolis	at	Quebec
280				Phoenix	at	Calgary
281				Winnipeg	at	Houston
282	Wed.	Jan.	26	Phoenix	at	Minnesota
283	Thu.	Jan.	27	New England	at	San Diego
284				Winnipeg	at	Birmingham
285	Fri.	Jan.	28	Houston	at	Edmonton
286				New England	at	Phoenix
287				Minnesota	at	Indianapolis
288	Sat.	Jan.	29	Houston	at	Calgary
289				Indianapolis	at	Minnesota
290				Cincinnati	at	Quebec
291				Winnipeg	at	San Diego
292	Sun.	Jan.	30	Calgary	at	Edmonton
293				New England	at	Indianapolis
294				Minnesota	at	Birmingham
295				Winnipeg	at	Phoenix
296	Tue.	Feb.	1	Phoenix	at	San Diego
297				Calgary	at	Houston
298				New England	at	Birmingham
299				Minnesota	at	Quebec
300				Winnipeg	at	Edmonton
301	Wed.	Feb.	2	Birmingham	at	Cincinnati
302				Calgary	at	San Diego
303				Minnesota	at	Indianapolis
304	Thu.	Feb.	3	Houston	at	Phoenix
305	Fri.	Feb.	4	New England	at	Houston
306				San Diego	at	Winnipeg
307	Sat.	Feb.	5	Birmingham	at	Indianapolis
308				Calgary	at	Phoenix
309				Minnesota	at	Cincinnati
310	Sun.	Feb.	6	Calgary	at	Winnipeg
311				San Diego	at	Edmonton
312				Minnesota	at	New England
313				Cincinnati	at	Quebec
314	Tue.	Feb.	8	Houston	at	Indianapolis
315				San Diego	at	Edmonton
316				Winnipeg	at	Quebec
317	Wed.	Feb.	9	Birmingham	at	Phoenix
318				Indianapolis	at	Cincinnati
319	Thu.	Feb.	10	Winnipeg	at	New England
320				Houston	at	Minnesota
321	Fri.	Feb.	11	Edmonton	at	Calgary
322				Quebec	at	Indianapolis
323				Winnipeg	at	Cincinnati
324				San Diego	at	Phoenix

325	Sat.	Feb.	12	Birmingham	at	San Diego
326				Indianapolis	at	New England
327				Quebec	at	Houston
328				Cincinnati	at	Minnesota
329	Sun.	Feb.	13	Calgary	at	Edmonton
330				*New England	at	Cincinnati
331				Phoenix	at	San Diego
332				Winnipeg	at	Indianapolis
333	Tue.	Feb.	15	Calgary	at	Winnipeg
334				Indianapolis	at	Minnesota
335				Cincinnati	at	Edmonton
336				Quebec	at	Houston
337	Wed.	Feb.	16	Quebec	at	San Diego
338				Cincinnati	at	Calgary
339				Phoenix	at	Birmingham
340	Thu.	Feb.	17	Phoenix	at	New England
341				Indianapolis	at	Winnipeg
342	Fri.	Feb.	18	Birmingham	at	New England
343				San Diego	at	Houston
344				Quebec	at	Minnesota
345				Cincinnati	at	Calgary
346				Winnipeg	at	Edmonton
347	Sat.	Feb.	19	Quebec	at	Cincinnati
348				Phoenix	at	Indianapolis
349	Sun.	Feb.	20	Edmonton	at	Winnipeg
350				*Houston	at	Minnesota
351				New England	at	Calgary
352				Indianapolis	at	Birmingham
353				Phoenix	at	Cincinnati
354	Tue.	Feb.	22	Houston	at	Winnipeg
355				New England	at	Edmonton
356				Indianapolis	at	Quebec
357				Cincinnati	at	Birmingham
358	Wed.	Feb.	23	Houston	at	Calgary
359				Winnipeg	at	Phoenix
360	Thu.	Feb.	24	Quebec	at	Birmingham
361				Minnesota	at	San Diego
362	Fri.	Feb.	25	New England	at	Calgary
363				Indianapolis	at	Edmonton
364				Quebec	at	Cincinnati
365				Minnesota	at	Phoenix
366	Sat.	Feb.	26	Birmingham	at	Quebec
367				Houston	at	San Diego
368				Winnipeg	at	Cincinnati
369	Sun.	Feb.	27	Houston	at	Phoenix
370				New England	at	Winnipeg
371				Indianapolis	at	Calgary
372				Minnesota	at	Edmonton

* Afternoon Game

109

373	Tue.	Mar.	1	Quebec	at	Edmonton
374				Minnesota	at	Calgary
375				Phoenix	at	Houston
376	Wed.	Mar.	2	San Diego	at	New England
377				Quebec	at	Winnipeg
378	Thu.	Mar.	3	Birmingham	at	Calgary
379				Minnesota	at	Edmonton
380	Fri.	Mar.	4	Houston	at	New England
381				San Diego	at	Indianapolis
382				Minnesota	at	Winnipeg
383	Sat.	Mar.	5	San Diego	at	Quebec
384				Indianapolis	at	Cincinnati
385				Winnipeg	at	Phoenix
386	Sun.	Mar.	6	Birmingham	at	Edmonton
387				*Houston	at	Cincinnati
388				San Diego	at	Calgary
389				Quebec	at	New England
390				Phoenix	at	Indianapolis
391				Winnipeg	at	Minnesota
392	Tue.	Mar.	8	San Diego	at	Winnipeg
393				Phoenix	at	Quebec
394				Minnesota	at	Houston
395	Wed.	Mar.	9	Edmonton	at	Cincinnati
396				San Diego	at	Calgary
397				Minnesota	at	Birmingham
398	Thu.	Mar.	10	Edmonton	at	Indianapolis
399	Fri.	Mar.	11	New England	at	Birmingham
400				Minnesota	at	Winnipeg
401				Cincinnati	at	Houston
402	Sat.	Mar.	12	Birmingham	at	Indianapolis
403				Calgary	at	Cincinnati
404				Edmonton	at	Quebec
405				Phoenix	at	San Diego
406	Sun.	Mar.	13	Birmingham	at	Cincinnati
407				Edmonton	at	Winnipeg
408				*New England	at	Minnesota
409				Indianapolis	at	Houston
410	Tue.	Mar.	15	Calgary	at	Indianapolis
411				Edmonton	at	Minnesota
412				Quebec	at	Houston
413				Cincinnati	at	Birmingham
414				Phoenix	at	San Diego
415	Wed.	Mar.	16	Calgary	at	Cincinnati
416	Thu.	Mar.	17	Quebec	at	Phoenix
417				Indianapolis	at	Birmingham
418				Winnipeg	at	Edmonton
419	Fri.	Mar.	18	Calgary	at	New England
420				Minnesota	at	Cincinnati
421				Phoenix	at	Houston
422				Winnipeg	at	Indianapolis

* Afternoon Game

423	Sat.	Mar.	19	Calgary	at	Quebec
424				Minnesota	at	Phoenix
425	Sun.	Mar.	20	Calgary	at	New England
426				*Houston	at	Indianapolis
427				Minnesota	at	San Diego
428				*Winnipeg	at	Birmingham
429	Tue.	Mar.	22	Calgary	at	Birmingham
430				Edmonton	at	Winnipeg
431				Houston	at	Quebec
432				Cincinnati	at	Indianapolis
433	Wed.	Mar.	23	Birmingham	at	Phoenix
434				Quebec	at	Cincinnati
435				New England	at	Minnesota
436	Thu.	Mar.	24	Quebec	at	Indianapolis
437				Birmingham	at	San Diego
438				Edmonton	at	New England
439	Fri.	Mar.	25	Calgary	at	Houston
440				Edmonton	at	Cincinnati
441				San Diego	at	Phoenix
442	Sat.	Mar.	26	Indianapolis	at	New England
443				Cincinnati	at	Quebec
444				Phoenix	at	Minnesota
445				Calgary	at	San Diego
446	Sun.	Mar.	27	Edmonton	at	New England
447				Indianapolis	at	Birmingham
448				*Winnipeg	at	Houston
449				Phoenix	at	Calgary
450				Minnesota	at	Quebec
451	Tue.	Mar.	29	Houston	at	Winnipeg
452				New England	at	San Diego
453				Phoenix	at	Calgary
454				Cincinnati	at	Birmingham
455	Wed.	Mar.	30	Houston	at	Edmonton
456				Quebec	at	Minnesota
457				Cincinnati	at	Indianapolis
458	Thu.	Mar.	31	New England	at	Phoenix
459				Winnipeg	at	San Diego
460	Fri.	Apr.	1	Calgary	at	Edmonton
461				Cincinnati	at	Houston
462	Sat.	Apr.	2	Edmonton	at	Calgary
463				New England	at	Indianapolis
464				Quebec	at	Phoenix
465				Cincinnati	at	San Diego
466				Winnipeg	at	Birmingham
467	Sun.	Apr.	3	Birmingham	at	Minnesota
468				Calgary	at	Winnipeg
469				Quebec	at	San Diego
470				Indianapolis	at	Houston
471	Mon.	Apr.	4	Winnipeg	at	Edmonton

*Afternoon Game

472	Tue.	Apr.	5	Birmingham	at	Calgary
473				New England	at	Quebec
474				San Diego	at	Houston
475	Wed.	Apr.	6	Birmingham	at	Edmonton
476				Houston,	at	San Diego
477				Indianapolis	at	Phoenix
478				Quebec	at	Cincinnati
479				Winnipeg	at	Minnesota
480	Thu.	Apr.	7	Winnipeg	at	Calgary

INTERNATIONAL SERIES

1	Sun.	Dec.	12	Czechoslovakia	at	Winnipeg
2	Mon.	Dec.	13	Czechoslovakia	at	Edmonton
3	Wed.	Dec.	15	Czechoslovakia	at	Calgary
4	Fri.	Dec.	17	Czechoslovakia	at	Minnesota
5	Mon.	Dec.	20	Czechoslovakia	at	New England
6	Wed.	Dec.	22	Czechoslovakia	at	Indianapolis
7	Mon.	Dec.	27	Soviets	at	New England
8	Tue.	Dec.	28	Soviets	at	Cincinnati
9	Thu.	Dec.	30	Soviets	at	Houston
10	Sat.	Jan.	1	Soviets	at	Indianapolis
11	Mon.	Jan.	3	Soviets	at	San Diego
12	Wed.	Jan.	5	Soviets	at	Edmonton
13	Thu.	Jan.	6	Soviets	at	Winnipeg
14	Sat.	Jan.	8	Soviets	at	Quebec

WHA STARTING TIMES (All Times Local)

BIRMINGHAM (Central Time)
P.M.
Sundays: Jan. 23, Mar. 20 .... 2:00
Sun. thru Thur. Nights 7:30
Fri. and Sat. Nights 8:00

CALGARY (Mountain Time)
Sun. Dec. 26; Sat. Jan. 1 .... 2:00
Sunday Nights 7:00
Week Nights 8:00

CINCINNATI (Eastern Time)
Sundays: Feb. 13, Mar. 6, 13 ..... 2:05
Sunday Nights 7:05
Week Nights 7:35

EDMONTON (Mountain Time)
Sunday Nights 7:30
Week Nights 8:00

HOUSTON (Central Time)
Sunday, Mar. 27 .... 2:05
All Other Games 7:35

INDIANAPOLIS (Eastern Time)
Sunday, Jan. 2 .... 2:00
Sunday, Mar. 20 .... 3:00
Sunday Nights 7:00
Week Nights 8:00

MINNESOTA (Central Time)
P.M.
Sundays: Feb. 20, Mar. 13 .... 2:05
Sunday Nights 7:35
Week Nights 8:05

NEW ENGLAND (Eastern Time)
Sundays: Jan. 23, Mar. 27 .... 2:00
All Other Games 7:30

PHOENIX (Mountain Time)
Sunday, Feb. 27 .... 2:00
Sunday Nights 7:00
Week Nights 7:30

QUEBEC (Eastern Time)
All Games 8:00

SAN DIEGO (Pacific Time)
All Games 7:00

WINNIPEG (Central Time)
Sunday Nights 7:30
Week Nights 8:00

DAYLIGHT SAVING TIME
ENDS: Sunday, October 31, 1976
STARTS: Sunday, April 24, 1977

NOTE: Indianapolis and Phoenix remain on Standard Time

1977-78 MEDIA GUIDE

WORLD HOCKEY ASSOCIATION MVP

ROBBIE FTOREK

WORLD HOCKEY ASSOCIATION

6TH SEASON

1977-78 MEDIA GUIDE

EDITOR
GARY CLARK

STATISTICIAN
FRANK POLNASZEK

Printed in USA
All Rights Reserved
World Hockey Association

CONTENTS

Directory
- League Directory 2-3
- Team Directories 4-11
- Team Rosters 12-15

Pre-Season '77
- Game Results 16

1976-77
- Final Standings 17
- Leading Individual Scorers and Goaltenders 18
- Complete Scoring and Penalty Statistics 19-24
- Complete Goaltending Statistics 24
- Power Play, Shorthanded Efficiency and Extra Attacker Statistics 25
- Overtime Analysis 26

International Series '78
- Schedule 27
- International Series '77 28

WHA History
- Ftorek Wins Howe Trophy 29
- Individual Trophy Winners 30
- All-Star Teams 31
- Lifetime Team Totals 32
- Team Yearly Records 33
- Team vs. Team 34-37
- Penalty Shots 38
- Career Hat Tricks 39
- Career Leaders 40-41
- Hedberg Breaks Rocket's Record 42
- Regular Season Records . 43-50

All-Star Game
- 1977 Game Summary 51
- All-time Statistics 52

Playoffs
- Avco Trophy Winners 53
- All-time Game Results 54-58
- Complete Goaltending Statistics 59
- 1977 Complete Scoring Statistics 60-63
- Playoff Records 64-69

Travelogue 70

Schedule
- 1977-78 Schedule 71-78

DIRECTORY

WORLD HOCKEY ASSOCIATION

BEN HATSKIN

Chairman of the Board
BEN HATSKIN
175 Hargrave Street
Winnipeg, Manitoba
Telephone 204-944-8267
Telex 075-7116 WHA WPG

President
HOWARD L. BALDWIN
One Civic Center Plaza
Hartford, Connecticut
06103
Telephone 203-728-3366
Telex 966-485 WHA A HFD

Trustees
HOWARD L. BALDWIN
JOHN F. BASSETT, JR.
HARRISON VICKERS
JOHN DACRES
WILLIAM O. DEWITT, JR.
OSCAR GRUBERT
PETER POCKLINGTON
NELSON SKALBANIA

HOWARD L. BALDWIN

WORLD HOCKEY ASSOCIATION

Operating Offices
Suite 1700
One Financial Plaza
Hartford, Connecticut
06103
Telephone 203-278-4240
Telex 966-485 WHA A HFD

Executive Director
LARRY GORDON

General Counsel
BILL MacFARLAND

Public Relations Director
GARY CLARK

Chief Statistician
FRANK POLNASZEK

Business Manager
W. DAVID ANDREWS III

Director of Officials
BOB FRAMPTON

Supervisor of Officials
ART SKOV

Referees
BILL FRIDAY
RON EGO
RON HARRIS
PETER MOFFAT
ALAN GLASPELL
RON FOURNIER

Linesmen
RON ASSELSTINE
WAYNE BONNEY
RON FOYT
JOE DAME
STEVE BARRY
DAVE MADSEN
MICKEY JASKUL
TIM McCONAGHY
MICHEL CHARTRE
GORD KERR
DARRYL HAVRELOCK

LARRY GORDON — BILL MacFARLAND

GARY CLARK — FRANK POLNASZEK

W. DAVID ANDREWS III — BOB FRAMPTON

BIRMINGHAM BULLS

Alabama Hockey, Ltd.
One Civic Center Plaza
Birmingham, Alabama
35203
Telephone 205-251-2855
Telex 59-747 BHAM BULLS BHM

President
JOHN F. BASSETT, JR.

Executive Vice-President
PETER McASKILE

General Manager
GILLES LEGER

Coach
GLEN SONMOR

Director of Public Relations
JOE REID

Comptroller
JAMES C. BRASHER

Director of Ticket Operations
MIKE RUSSELL

Trainers
FRANK VANDERHART
LARRY ASHLEY

Supervisor of Minor Officials
EDEN McDONALD

Home Arena
Jefferson County Civic Center

Seating Capacity
16,753

Ticket Prices
8.00, 6.50, 5.00

Broadcasting Radio Station
WAPI-AM (1070)

Announcers
GARY SANDERS
TOM ROBERTS

Team Colors
Blue, Red

John Bassett

Gilles Leger

Glen Sonmor

4

CINCINNATI STINGERS

Cincinnati Hockey Club, Inc.
Riverfront Coliseum
Cincinnati, Ohio
45202
Telephone 513-241-1818
Telex 214-286 SPORTS INC CIN

Chairman of the Board
WILLIAM O. DEWITT, SR.

President
BRIAN E. HEEKIN

Executive Vice-President
WILLIAM O. DEWITT, JR.

Vice-President
LEFTY McFADDEN

Director of Player Personnel
JERRY RAFTER

Coach
JACQUES DEMERS

Bill DeWitt, Jr.

Director of Public Relations
JOHN A. HEWIG

Business Manager
BRENDA VERTUCCA

Ticket Manager
HENRY ROYER

Head Scout
FLORENT POTVIN

Trainers
BILL CONNELLY
TIM RINGLER

Supervisor of Minor Officials
GEORGE CALLIES

Jerry Rafter

Home Arena
Riverfront Coliseum

Seating Capacity
15,820

Ticket Prices
8.25, 7.25, 6.25, 4.25

Broadcasting Radio Station
WLW-AM (700)

Announcer
ANDY MacWILLIAMS

Team Colors
Stinger Yellow, Bumblebee Black

Jacques Demers

5

EDMONTON OILERS

Edmonton World Hockey Enterprises, Ltd.
Edmonton Coliseum
Edmonton, Alberta
T5B 4M9
Telephone 403-474-8561
Telex 037-3595 HOCKEY EDM

Owner
PETER POCKLINGTON

General Manager
BRIAN CONACHER

Director of Hockey Operations
Coach
GLEN SATHER

Director of Player Personnel
BRUCE MacGREGOR

Director of Publicity/Marketing
DOUG WENSCHLAG

Comptroller
IRENE HONSTEIN

Scout
BOB FREEMAN

Trainers
JOHN BLACKWELL
BILL SNOW

Supervisors of Minor Officials
SANDY MILLER
DICK CARREAU

Home Arena
Edmonton Coliseum

Seating Capacity
15,248

Ticket Prices
8.00, 5.50, 4.00

Broadcasting Radio Station
CFRN-AM (1260)

Announcers
ROD PHILLIPS
AL McCANN

Team Colors
Blue, Orange

Peter Pocklington

Brian Conacher

Glen Sather

6

HOUSTON AEROS

Hockey Ventures, Inc.
10 Greenway Plaza
Houston, Texas
77046
Telephone 713-629-5555
Telex 775-520 AEROS HSN

President
HARRISON VICKERS

General Manager
Coach
BILL DINEEN

Assistant General Manager
Vice-President/Marketing
JACK STANFIELD

Public Relations Director
TERRY LEIWEKE

Business Manager
BRYAN WINDHAM

Director of Sales
KEMPER KAISER

Head Scout
BARRY FRASER

Trainers
BOBBY BROWN
BOBBY KINCAID

Supervisor of Minor Officials
CHARLES TOLLAND

Home Arena
The Summit

Seating Capacity
15,256

Ticket Prices
10.50, 8.50, 5.50, 3.00

Broadcasting Radio Station
KTRH-AM (740)

Announcer
JERRY TRUPIANO

Team Colors
Royal Blue, Powder Blue

Harrison Vickers

Bill Dineen

Jack Stanfield

7

INDIANAPOLIS RACERS

Indianapolis Racers 1977, Inc.
151 North Delaware Street
Market Square Center
Indianapolis, Indiana
46204
Telephone 317-635-3131
Telex 27-325 WHA RACERS IND

General Partner
NELSON SKALBANIA

Executive Vice-President
DONALD LeROSE

Director of Player Personnel
Coach
RON INGRAM

Assistant Coach
RON BUCHANAN

Nelson Skalbania

Director of Marketing/Public Relations
DON WAHLE

Comptroller
FRANCES LAWYER

Trainers
BILL CARROLL
ED ROTHSCHILD

Supervisor of Minor Officials
PAUL MINOT, SR.

Home Arena
Market Square Arena

Don LeRose

Seating Capacity
16,042

Ticket Prices
8.00, 7.50, 6.00, 4.00

Broadcasting Radio Stations
WIBC-AM (1070)
WNON-FM (100.9)

Announcers
MIKE FORNES
CHET COPPOCK

Team Colors
Blue, Red

Ron Ingram

8

NEW ENGLAND WHALERS

New England Whalers Hockey Club, Ltd.
One Civic Center Plaza
Hartford, Connecticut
06103
Telephone 203-728-3366
Telex 994-476 NE WHALERS HFD

Managing General Partner
HOWARD L. BALDWIN

Director of Hockey Operations
JACK KELLEY

Director of Marketing
BILL BARNES

Director of Player Personnel
RON RYAN

Coach
HARRY NEALE

Assistant Coach
DON BLACKBURN

Public Relations Director
DENNIS RANDALL

Business Manager
W. DAVID ANDREWS III

Communications Director
BILL RASMUSSEN

Ticket Manager
BRIAN McLEOD

Trainers
JOE ALTOTT
SKIP CUNNINGHAM

Supervisor of Minor Officials
BILL HENDERSON

Home Arena
Hartford Civic Center

Seating Capacity
10,507

Ticket Prices
9.75, 8.00, 6.00

Broadcasting Radio Station
WTIC-AM (1080)

Announcers
BOB NEUMEIER
GARRY SWAIN

Team Colors
Green, Gold

Howard Baldwin

Jack Kelley

Harry Neale

9

QUEBEC NORDIQUES

Le Club de Hockey les Nordiques, Inc.
Colisee de Quebec
Quebec City, Quebec
G1L 4W7
Telephone 418-529-4161
Telex 051-3068 NORDIQUES QBC

Chairman of the Board
HON. JEAN LESAGE

President
JOHN DACRES

Vice-President
MAURICE TASCHEREAU

Director of Hockey
MAURICE FILION

Coach
MARC BOILEAU

Legal Counsel
Treasurer
MARCEL AUBUT

Administrative Director
JACQUES DESMEULES

Comptroller
LAURENT CARRIER

Head Scout
YVAN PRUD'HOMME

Trainers
RENE LACASSE
CLAUDE LANGLOIS

Supervisor of Minor Officials
RAYMOND PUCHOL

Home Arena
Colisee de Quebec

Seating Capacity
10,012

Ticket Prices
10.00, 7.50, 5.00

Broadcasting Radio Station
CHRC-AM (800)

Announcer
CLAUDE BEDARD

Team Colors
Blue, Red

John Dacres

Maurice Filion

Marc Boileau

10

WINNIPEG JETS

Winnipeg Jets Hockey Club, Inc.
15-1430 Maroons Road
Winnipeg, Manitoba
R3G 0L5
Telephone 204-772-9491
Telex 075-87810 HOCKEY WPG

Chairman of the Board
R. G. GRAHAM

President
HON. J. W. McKEAG

General Manager
RUDY PILOUS

Coach
LARRY HILLMAN

Director of Public Relations
BOB BELL

Comptroller
Administration Manager
DON FASO

Head Scout
BILL ROBINSON

Trainers
BILL BOZAK
KELLY PRUDEN

Supervisor of Minor Officials
SAM SANREGRET

Home Arena
Winnipeg Arena

Seating Capacity
10,151

Ticket Prices
10.00, 9.50, 9.00, 8.00, 5.50, 4.25

Broadcasting Radio Station
CJOB-AM (680)

Announcers
KEN NICHOLSON
ED DEARDEN

Team Colors
Blue, Red

Hon. J. W. McKeag

Rudy Pilous

Larry Hilman

11

BIRMINGHAM BULLS ROSTER

PLAYER	POS	S	HT	WT	BIRTHPLACE	BIRTHDATE
Garrett, John	G		5-9	170	Toronto, Ont.	May 17 51
Mio, Ed	G		5-10	181	Windsor, Ont.	Jan 31 54
Wood, Wayne	G		6-1	190	Toronto, Ont.	Jun 5 51
Evans, Chris	D	L	5-9	181	Toronto, Ont.	Sep 14 46
Hoganson, Dale	D	L	5-11	190	North Battleford, Sask.	Jul 8 49
Hughes, Brent	D	L	6-0	205	Bowmanville, Ont.	Jun 17 43
Lagace, Jean Guy	D	R	5-8	175	L'Abord Plouffe, Que.	Feb 5 45
Langway, Rod	D	L	6-3	210	Randolph, Mass.	May 3 57
Terbenche, Paul	D	L	5-10	170	Port Hope, Ont.	Sep 16 45
Turkiewicz, Jim	D	L	5-10	185	Hamilton, Ont.	Apr 13 55
Westrum, Pat	D	L	5-10	185	Minneapolis, Minn.	Mar 3 48
Alley, Steve	LW	L	6-0	185	Anoka, Minn.	Dec 19 53
Arndt, Danny	LW	L	5-10	170	Saskatoon, Sask.	Mar 26 55
Bilodeau, Gilles	LW	L	6-1	215	St. Prime, Que.	Jul 31 55
Cassolato, Tony	RW	R	5-11	180	Guelph, Ont.	May 7 56
Gorman, Dave	RW	R	5-11	180	London, Ont.	Apr 8 55
Henderson, Paul	LW	R	5-11	180	Kincardine, Ont.	Jan 28 43
Linseman, Ken	C	L	5-10	175	Kingston, Ont.	Aug 11 58
Mahovlich, Frank	LW	L	6-1	205	Timmons, Ont.	Jan 10 38
Marrin, Peter	C	R	5-10	160	Toronto, Ont.	Aug 8 53
Napier, Mark	RW	R	5-10	185	Toronto, Ont.	Jan 28 57
Nedomansky, Vaclav	C	L	6-1	210	Hodonin, Czechoslovakia	Mar 14 44
Noris, Joe	C	R	6-0	185	Denver, Col.	Oct 26 51
Sheehy, Tim	RW	R	6-1	185	Internat'l Falls, Minn.	Sep 3 48
Stewart, JC	C	L	5-11	170	Toronto, Ont.	Jan 2 54

CINCINNATI STINGERS ROSTER

PLAYER	POS	S	HT	WT	BIRTHPLACE	BIRTHDATE
Dion, Michel	G		5-10	170	Granby, Que.	Feb 11 54
LaPointe, Norm	G		6-1	180	Laval, Que.	Aug 13 55
Liut, Mike	G		6-2	180	Weston, Ont.	Jan 7 56
Wakely, Ernie	G		5-11	175	Flin Flon, Man.	Nov 27 40
Beaudoin, Serge	D	L	6-2	215	Montreal, Que.	Oct 30 52
Lahache, Floyd	D	R	5-10	175	Caughnawage, Que.	Sep 17 57
Legge, Barry	D	L	6-0	185	Winnipeg, Man.	Oct 22 54
Marotte, Gilles	D	L	5-9	195	Montreal, Que.	Jan 7 45
Melrose, Barry	D	R	6-2	200	Kelvington, Sask.	Jul 15 56
Norwich, Craig	D	L	5-11	175	Edina, Minn.	Dec 15 55
Plumb, Ron	D	R	5-10	175	Kingston, Ont.	Jul 17 50
Abgrall, Dennis	RW	R	6-0	180	Mooseomin, Sask.	Apr 24 53
Dudley, Rick	LW	L	6-0	190	Toronto, Ont.	Jan 31 49
Ftorek, Robbie	C	L	5-8	150	Needham, Mass.	Jan 2 52
Gilligan, Bill	RW	R	5-11	175	Beverly, Mass.	Aug 5 54
Hall, Del	LW	L	5-10	170	Peterborough, Ont.	May 7 49
Hislop, Jamie	RW	R	5-10	180	Sarnia, Ont.	Jan 20 54
Larose, Claude	LW	L	5-10	175	St. Jean, Que.	May 17 55
Leduc, Rich	C	L	5-11	170	Ile Perrot, Que.	Aug 24 51
Locas, Jacques	C	L	5-8	170	St. Jerome, Que.	Jan 7 54
Marsh, Peter	LW	L	6-1	180	Halifax, Nova Scotia	Dec 21 56
Sobchuk, Dennis	C	L	6-2	180	Lang, Sask.	Jan 12 54
Sobchuk, Gene	LW	L	5-9	170	Lang, Sask.	Jan 2 51
Stoughton, Blaine	RW	R	5-10	185	Gilbert Plains, Man.	Mar 13 53

EDMONTON OILERS ROSTER

PLAYER	POS	S	HT	WT	BIRTHPLACE	BIRTHDATE
Broderick, Ken	G		5-11	175	Toronto, Ont.	Feb 16 42
Dryden, Dave	G		6-2	185	Hamilton, Ont.	Sep 5 41
Turnbull, Frank	G		5-8	155	Trenton, Ont.	Jan 13 53
Busniuk, Ron	D	R	6-1	190	Fort William, Ont.	Sep 22 47
Hamilton, Al	D	R	6-2	195	Flin Flon, Man.	Aug 20 46
Inkpen, Dave	D	R	6-0	185	Edmonton, Alta.	Sep 4 54
Langevin, Dave	D	L	6-2	200	St. Paul, Minn.	May 15 54
Micheletti, Joe	D	L	6-0	185	Hibbing, Minn.	Oct 24 54
Shmyr, Paul	D	L	5-11	175	Cudworth, Sask.	Jan 28 46
Baird, Ken	LW	L	6-0	190	Flin Flon, Man.	Feb 1 51
Callighen, Brett	LW	L	5-11	175	Toronto, Ont.	May 15 53
Campbell, Bryan	C	L	6-0	175	Sudbury, Ont.	Mar 27 44
Chipperfield, Ron	C	R	5-11	180	Brandon, Man.	Mar 28 54
Deadmarsh, Butch	LW	L	5-11	185	Trail, B.C.	Apr 5 50
Ferguson, Norm	RW	R	5-8	177	Sydney, Nova Scotia	Oct 16 45
Flett, Bill	RW	R	6-1	207	Vermillion, Alta.	Jul 21 43
Holland, Jerry	LW	L	5-10	180	Beaverlodge, Alta.	Aug 25 54
MacDonald, Blair	RW	R	5-10	180	Cornwall, Ont.	Nov 17 53
MacGregor, Gary	C	L	5-9	170	Kingston, Ont.	Sep 21 54
Miller, Warren	RW	R	5-11	180	St. Paul, Minn.	Jan 1 54
Morris, Rick	LW	L	5-11	175	Hamilton, Ont.	Jul 5 46
Rota, Randy	LW	L	5-8	170	Creston, B.C.	Aug 16 50
Semenko, Dave	LW	L	6-3	200	Winnipeg, Man.	Jul 12 57
Tannahill, Don	LW	L	5-11	178	Penetang, Ont.	Feb 21 49
Widing, Juha	C	L	6-1	190	Uleaborg, Finland	Jul 4 47
Zuke, Mike	C	R	5-11	175	Sault Ste. Maire, Ont.	Apr 16 54

HOUSTON AEROS ROSTER

PLAYER	POS	S	HT	WT	BIRTHPLACE	BIRTHDATE
Hebenton, Clay	G		5-10	185	Victoria, B.C.	Feb 20 53
Rutledge, Wayne	G		6-2	200	Barrie, Ont.	Jan 5 42
Zimmerman, Lynn	G		5-7	155	Fort Erie, Ont.	Jul 13 42
Campbell, Scott	D	L	6-2	205	Toronto, Ont.	Jun 22 57
Chicoyne, Jim	D	R	6-1	205	Winnipeg, Man.	Sep 19 54
Hale, Larry	D	L	6-1	180	Summerland, B.C.	Oct 9 41
Hughes, John	D	L	5-11	200	Charlottetown, P.E.I.	Mar 18 54
Irwin, Glen	D	R	5-11	190	Edmonton, Alta.	Mar 1 51
McLeod, Al	D	L	5-11	210	Medicine Hat, Alta.	Jun 17 49
Popiel, Poul	D	L	5-10	175	Sollestad, Denmark	Feb 28 43
Schella, John	D	R	6-0	180	Port Arthur, Ont.	May 9 47
Connor, Cam	LW	L	6-2	200	Winnipeg, Man.	Aug 10 54
Gray, John	RW	L	5-10	180	Little Current, Ont.	Aug 13 49
Hansis, Ron	RW	R	6-2	193	Brownsville, Tex.	Nov 12 52
Hughes, Frank	RW	R	5-10	180	Fernie, B.C.	Jan 10 49
LaCroix, Andre	C	L	5-8	175	Lauzon, Que.	Jun 5 45
Larway, Don	RW	R	6-1	195	Oak Lake, Man.	Feb 12 54
Liddington, Bob	LW	L	5-11	175	Calgary, Alta.	Sep 15 48
Lukowich, Morris	LW	L	5-9	170	Saskatoon, Sask.	Jun 1 56
Lund, Larry	C	R	6-0	190	Penticton, B.C.	Sep 9 40
Preston, Rich	RW	R	6-0	185	Regina, Sask.	May 22 52
Ruskowski, Terry	C	L	5-9	170	Prince Albert, Sask.	Dec 31 54
Taylor, Ted	LW	L	6-0	175	Oak Lake, Man.	Feb 25 42
Tonelli, John	C	L	6-1	195	Hamilton, Ont.	Mar 23 57
West, Steve	C	L	5-8	150	Peterborough, Ont.	Mar 20 52

INDIANAPOLIS RACERS ROSTER

PLAYER	POS	S	HT	WT	BIRTHPLACE	BIRTHDATE
Inness, Gary	G		6-0	195	Toronto, Ont.	May 28 49
McDuffe, Peter	G		5-10	180	Milton, Ont.	Feb 16 48
Park, Jim	G		6-1	190	Toronto, Ont.	Jun 22 52
Baltimore, Bryon	D	L	6-2	190	Whitehorse, Yukon	Aug 26 52
Block, Ken	D	L	5-10	185	Steinbach, Man.	Mar 18 44
Fortier, Dave	D	L	5-11	190	Sudbury, Ont.	Jun 17 51
Maggs, Darryl	D	R	6-1	195	Victoria, B.C.	Apr 6 49
Morrison, Kevin	D	L	5-11	205	Sydney, Nova Scotia	Oct 28 49
Prentice, Bill	D	L	6-0	190	Lindsay, Ont.	Aug 3 50
Wilkins, Barry	D	L	6-0	190	Toronto, Ont.	Feb 28 47
Burgess, Don	LW	L	6-0	170	Port Edward, Ont.	Jun 8 46
Devine, Kevin	LW	L	5-9	175	Toronto, Ont.	Dec 9 54
French, John	LW	L	5-11	175	Orillia, Ont.	Aug 26 50
Harris, Hugh	LW	L	6-0	190	Toronto, Ont.	Jun 7 48
Leclerc, Renald	RW	R	5-11	170	Ville de Vanier, Que.	Dec 12 47
Paiement, Rosaire	RW	R	5-11	185	Earlton, Ont.	Aug 12 45
Parizeau, Michel	C	L	5-10	165	Montreal, Que.	Apr 9 48
Patenaude, Rusty	RW	R	5-9	175	Williams Lake, B.C.	Oct 17 49
Powis, Lynn	C	L	6-0	185	Saskatoon, Sask.	Apr 19 49
Rhiness, Brad	C	L	5-9	170	Huntsville, Ont.	Nov 6 56
St. Sauveur, Claude	C	L	6-0	170	Sherbrooke, Que.	Jan 2 52
Sheehan, Bobby	C	L	5-8	170	Weymouth, Mass.	Jan 11 49
Smedsmo, Dale	LW	L	6-1	195	Roseau, Minn.	Apr 23 51
Spring, Frank	RW	R	6-3	210	Cranbrook, B.C.	Oct 19 49
Thomas, Reg	LW	L	5-10	180	Lambeth, Ont.	Apr 21 53

NEW ENGLAND WHALERS ROSTER

PLAYER	POS	S	HT	WT	BIRTHPLACE	BIRTHDATE
Levasseur, Lou	G		5-10	160	Noranda, Que.	Jun 16 49
Raeder, Cap	G		5-11	170	Needham, Mass.	Oct 8 53
Smith, Al	G		6-1	200	Toronto, Ont.	Nov 10 45
Butters, Bill	D	R	5-10	190	St. Paul, Minn.	Jan 10 51
Hangsleben, Alan	D	L	6-1	195	Warroad, Minn.	Feb 22 53
Howe, Marty	D	L	6-1	185	Detroit, Mich.	Feb 18 54
Ley, Rick	D	L	5-9	185	Orillia, Ont.	Dec 2 48
Maxwell, Bryan	D	L	6-2	210	Lethbridge, Alta.	Sep 7 55
Roberts, Gordie	D	L	6-1	190	Detroit, Mich.	Oct 2 57
Selwood, Brad	D	L	6-1	200	Leamington, Ont.	Mar 18 48
Antonovich, Mike	LW	L	5-8	165	Calumet, Minn.	Oct 18 51
Bolduc, Danny	RW	L	5-10	175	Waterville, Maine	Apr 6 53
Carlson, Jack	LW	L	6-3	200	Virginia, Minn.	Aug 23 54
Carlson, Steve	C	L	6-2	171	Virginia, Minn.	Aug 26 55
Carroll, Greg	C	L	6-0	180	Edmonton, Alta.	Nov 12 56
Howe, Gordie	RW	R	6-0	203	Floral, Sask.	Mar 31 28
Howe, Mark	LW	L	5-11	180	Detroit, Mich.	May 28 55
Keon, Dave	C	R	5-9	167	Noranda, Que.	Mar 22 40
Lyle, George	LW	L	6-2	210	Vancouver, B.C.	Nov 24 53
Mayer, Jim	RW	R	6-0	190	Capreol, Ont.	Oct 30 54
McKenzie, John	RW	R	5-7	175	High River, Alta.	Feb 12 37
Peloffy, Andre	C	L	5-8	160	Sete, France	Feb 25 51
Pleau, Larry	C	L	6-1	190	Lynn, Mass.	Jun 29 47
Rogers, Mike	C	L	5-9	170	Calgary, Alta.	Oct 24 54
Webster, Tom	RW	R	5-10	195	Kirland Lake, Ont.	Oct 4 48

QUEBEC NORDIQUES ROSTER

PLAYER	POS	S	HT	WT	BIRTHPLACE	BIRTHDATE
Brodeur, Richard	G		5-7	160	Longueuil, Que.	Sep 15 52
Corsi, Jim	G		5-8	173	Montreal, Que.	Jun 19 54
McLeod, Don	G		6-1	190	Trail, B.C.	Aug 24 46
Baxter, Paul	D	R	5-11	200	Winnipeg, Man.	Oct 25 55
Bernier, Jean	D	L	5-10	180	St. Hyancinthe, Que.	Jul 21 54
Dorey, Jim	D	L	6-1	192	Kingston, Ont.	Aug 17 47
Lacombe, Francois	D	L	5-9	185	Montreal, Que.	Feb 2 48
Lariviere, Garry	D	R	6-0	190	St. Catharines, Ont.	Dec 6 54
Tremblay, JC	D	L	5-10	185	Bagotville, Que.	Jan 22 39
Weir, Wally	D	R	6-2	200	Verdun, Que.	Jun 3 54
Bernier, Serge	C	R	6-1	190	Padoue, Que.	Apr 29 47
Bordeleau, Christian	C	L	5-8	155	Noranda, Que.	Sep 23 47
Bordeleau, Paulin	RW	R	5-9	155	Noranda, Que.	Jan 29 53
Boudrias, Andre	C	L	5-8	165	Montreal, Que.	Sep 19 43
Brackenbury, Curt	RW	R	5-10	190	Kapuskasing, Ont.	Jan 31 52
Cloutier, Real	RW	L	5-10	180	Quebec City, Que.	Jul 30 56
Constantin, Charles	LW	L	6-2	190	Montreal, Que.	Apr 30 54
Cote, Alain	LW	L	5-11	207	Matane, Que.	May 3 57
Driscoll, Peter	LW	L	6-0	190	Kingston, Ont.	Oct 27 54
Dube, Norm	LW	L	5-11	185	Sherbrooke, Que.	Sep 12 51
Fitchner, Bob	C	L	6-0	190	Sudbury, Ont.	Dec 22 52
Guite, Pierre	LW	L	6-2	190	Montreal, Que.	Apr 17 52
Lagace, Pierre	C	L	6-2	205	Montreal, Que.	Oct 27 57
Sutherland, Steve	LW	L	6-0	172	Noranda, Que.	Sep 1 46
Tardif, Marc	LW	L	6-1	178	Granby, Que.	Sep 23 47

WINNIPEG JETS ROSTER

PLAYER	POS	S	HT	WT	BIRTHPLACE	BIRTHDATE
Bromley, Gary	G		5-10	160	Edmonton, Alta.	Jan 19 50
Daley, Joe	G		5-10	171	Kildonan, Man.	Feb 20 43
Mattsson, Markus	G		6-2	183	Tampere, Finland	Jul 30 57
Bergman, Thommie	D	L	6-3	200	Munkfors, Sweden	Dec 10 47
Clackson, Kim	D	R	5-11	195	Saskatoon, Sask.	Feb 13 55
Davis, Bill	D	L	6-1	190	Lindsay, Ont.	Aug 22 54
Dunn, Dave	D	L	6-3	200	Mosseomin, Sask.	Aug 19 48
Green, Ted	D	R	5-10	190	St. Boniface, Man.	Mar 23 40
Hornung, Larry	D	L	6-0	190	Weyburn, Sask.	Nov 10 45
Long, Barry	D	L	6-2	210	Red Deer, Alta.	Jan 3 49
Sjoberg, Lars Erik	D	L	5-8	179	Falun, Sweden	Apr 5 44
Guindon, Bobby	LW	L	5-9	175	Labelle, Que.	Nov 19 50
Hedberg, Anders	RW	L	5-11	176	Ornskoldsvik, Sweden	Feb 25 51
Huck, Fran	C	R	5-7	165	Regina, Sask.	Dec 4 45
Hull, Bobby	LW	L	5-10	191	Point Anne, Ont.	Jan 3 39
Kryskow, Dave	LW	L	5-10	175	Edmonton, Alta.	Dec 25 51
Labraaten, Danny	LW	R	6-0	185	Arvika, Sweden	Jun 9 51
Lesuk, Bill	LW	L	5-9	187	Moose Jaw, Sask.	Nov 1 46
Lindstrom, Willy	RW	L	6-0	180	Grunns, Sweden	May 5 51
Moffat, Lyle	LW	L	5-10	185	Calgary, Alta.	Mar 19 48
Nilsson, Kent	C	L	6-1	185	Nynashamn, Sweden	Aug 31 56
Nilsson, Ulf	C	R	5-11	176	Leksand, Sweden	May 11 50
Ruhnke, Kent	RW	R	6-1	180	Toronto, Ont.	Sep 18 52
Sullivan, Peter	C	R	5-9	170	Toronto, Ont.	Jul 25 51

PRE-SEASON '77

"The World Hockey Association is capable of playing hockey at any level in the world. We have proven it in past International competition, and now we have proven it again."

Such was the reaction of President Howard Baldwin to the WHA's impressive 13 win, 6 loss, 2 tie Pre-Season '77 record against National Hockey League opponents.

"We proved that, game in and game out, our teams can play with their teams. And we proved it indisputably."

WORLD HOCKEY ASSOCIATION PRE-SEASON RECORD VS NATIONAL HOCKEY LEAGUE

WHA TEAM	GP	W	L	T	PTS	GF	GA	PCT
Birmingham Bulls	2	0	2	0	0	0	6	.000
Cincinnati Stingers	1	1	0	0	2	4	2	1.000
Edmonton Oilers	3	2	1	0	4	10	10	.667
Houston Aeros	1	0	1	0	0	3	5	.000
Indianapolis Racers	—	—	—	—	—	—	—	—
New England Whalers	7	5	1	1	11	32	22	.786
Quebec Nordiques	2	1	0	1	3	9	8	.750
Winnipeg Jets	5	4	1	0	8	15	7	.800
TOTALS	21	13	6	2	28	73	60	.667

GAME RESULTS

DATE	SCORE	RESULT
Sep 25	New England Whalers 2, Chicago Black Hawks 2	t*
Sep 28	New England Whalers 5, Washington Capitals 4	w*
	Minnesota North Stars 2, Winnipeg Jets 1	l*
Sep 30	New England Whalers 7, New York Rangers 4	w
	Atlanta Flames 4, Birmingham Bulls 0	l
Oct 1	Boston Bruins 5, New England Whalers 0	l
	Winnipeg Jets 4, Minnesota North Stars 3	w
Oct 3	Edmonton Oilers 3, St. Louis Blues 2	w*
Oct 4	New England Whalers 5, Atlanta Flames 4	w
Oct 5	Atlanta Flames 5, Houston Aeros 3	l
	Winnipeg Jets 6, St. Louis Blues 2	w
Oct 6	Cincinnati Stingers 4, Washington Capitals 2	w
	Winnipeg Jets 3, St. Louis Blues 0	w
Oct 7	New England Whalers 9, Pittsburgh Penguins 0	w
	St. Louis Blues 4, Birmingham Bulls 0	l
Oct 8	Quebec Nordiques 5, New York Rangers 5	t*
	Edmonton Oilers 5, Detroit Red Wings 4	w
Oct 9	New England Whalers 4, Atlanta Flames 3	w
	Winnipeg Jets 1, Detroit Red Wings 0	w
	Cleveland Barons 4, Edmonton Oilers 2	l
Oct 10	Quebec Nordiques 4, Washington Capitals 3	w*

*OVERTIME GAME

1976-77

FINAL STANDINGS

EASTERN DIVISION	GP	W	L	T	PTS	GF	GA	PCT
Quebec Nordiques	81	47	31	3	97	353	295	.599
Cincinnati Stingers	81	39	37	5	83	354	303	.512
Indianapolis Racers	81	36	37	8	80	276	305	.494
New England Whalers	81	35	40	6	76	275	290	.469
Birmingham Bulls	81	31	46	4	66	289	309	.407
Minnesota Fighting Saints	42	19	18	5	43	136	129	.512
TOTALS	447	207	209	31	445	1683	1631	.498

WESTERN DIVISION	GP	W	L	T	PTS	GF	GA	PCT
Houston Aeros	80	50	24	6	106	320	241	.663
Winnipeg Jets	80	46	32	2	94	366	291	.588
San Diego Mariners	81	40	37	4	84	284	283	.519
Edmonton Oilers	81	34	43	4	72	243	304	.444
Calgary Cowboys	81	31	43	7	69	252	296	.426
Phoenix Roadrunners	80	28	48	4	60	281	383	.375
TOTALS	483	229	227	27	485	1746	1798	.502

HOME RECORDS

TEAM	GP	W	L	T	PTS	GF	GA	PCT
Houston Aeros	40	33	3	4	70	180	88	.875
Winnipeg Jets	40	30	9	1	61	207	119	.763
Cincinnati Stingers	40	29	10	1	59	207	115	.738
Quebec Nordiques	40	29	10	1	59	186	117	.738
San Diego Mariners	40	26	10	4	56	164	122	.700
Calgary Cowboys	40	26	12	2	54	160	117	.675
Indianapolis Racers	40	24	13	3	51	157	134	.638
Minnesota Fighting Saints	25	14	8	3	31	94	69	.620
Edmonton Oilers	40	24	15	1	49	148	131	.613
Birmingham Bulls	40	22	15	3	47	117	131	.588
New England Whalers	40	20	16	4	44	150	133	.550
Phoenix Roadrunners	40	20	18	2	42	164	159	.525
TOTALS	465	297	139	29	623	1994	1435	.670

ROAD RECORDS

TEAM	GP	W	L	T	PTS	GF	GA	PCT
Quebec Nordiques	41	18	21	2	38	167	178	.463
Houston Aeros	40	17	21	2	36	140	153	.450
Winnipeg Jets	40	16	23	1	33	159	172	.413
New England Whalers	41	15	24	2	32	125	157	.390
Indianapolis Racers	41	12	24	5	29	119	171	.354
Minnesota Fighting Saints	17	5	10	2	12	42	60	.353
San Diego Mariners	41	14	27	0	28	120	161	.341
Cincinnati Stingers	41	10	27	4	24	147	188	.293
Edmonton Oilers	41	10	28	3	23	95	173	.280
Birmingham Bulls	41	9	31	1	19	112	178	.232
Phoenix Roadrunners	40	8	30	2	18	117	224	.225
Calgary Cowboys	41	5	31	5	15	92	179	.183
TOTALS	465	139	297	29	307	1435	1994	.330

THIRTY LEADING INDIVIDUAL SCORERS

PLAYER	TEAM	GP	G	A	PTS	PIM	EGR	EG%
Cloutier, Real	Quebec	76	66	75	141	39	+47	+.11
Hedberg, Anders	Winnipeg	68	70	61	131	48	+48	+.16
Nilsson, Ulf	Winnipeg	71	39	85	124	89	+57	+.17
Ftorek, Robbie	Phoenix	80	46	71	117	86	+26	+.21
LaCroix, Andre	San Diego	81	32	82	114	79	-2	+.04
Tardif, Marc	Quebec	62	49	60	109	65	+29	+.07
Leduc, Rich	Cincinnati	81	52	55	107	75	+28	+.03
Bordeleau, Chris	Quebec	72	32	75	107	34	+28	+.05
Stoughton, Blaine	Cincinnati	81	52	52	104	39	+24	+.00
Napier, Mark	Birmingham	80	60	36	96	24	+16	+.09
Sobchuk, Dennis	Cincinnati	81	44	52	96	38	+14	-.01
Bernier, Serge	Quebec	74	43	53	96	94	+0	-.06
Noris, Joe	San Diego	73	35	57	92	30	+2	+.06
Keon, Dave	Min-Ngd	76	27	63	90	10	+38	+.11
Dudley, Rick	Cincinnati	77	41	47	88	102	+25	+.02
Webster, Tom	New England	70	36	49	85	43	+18	+.06
Ruskowski, Terry	Houston	80	24	60	84	146	+31	+.04
Bordeleau, Paulin	Quebec	80	42	41	83	52	+7	-.02
Sullivan, Peter	Winnipeg	78	31	52	83	18	+11	-.01
Rogers, Mike	New England	78	25	57	82	10	+11	+.06
Lindstrom, Willy	Winnipeg	79	44	36	80	37	-2	-.05
Hall, Del	Phoenix	80	38	41	79	30	+6	+.13
Preston, Rich	Houston	80	38	41	79	54	+37	+.07
Larose, Claude	Cincinnati	81	30	46	76	8	+18	+.00
Howe, Mark	Houston	57	23	52	75	46	+41	+.07
Lyle, George	New England	75	39	33	72	62	+30	+.15
Antonovich, Mike	Min-Ngd	75	40	31	71	38	+28	+.07
Ferguson, Norm	San Diego	77	39	32	71	5	-5	+.02
Maggs, Darryl	Indianapolis	81	16	55	71	114	+4	+.08
Sheehy, Tim	Edm-Bhm	78	41	29	70	48	-9	-.03

TEN LEADING INDIVIDUAL GOALTENDERS

PLAYER	TEAM	GAA	GP	MINS	SO	SV%	W	L	T
Grahame, Ron	Houston	2.74	39	2345	4	.901	27	10	2
Caron, Jacques	Cincinnati	2.83	24	1292	3	.892	13	6	2
Wakely, Ernie	San Diego	3.09	46	2506	3	.896	22	18	3
Raeder, Cap	New England	3.12	26	1328	2	.902	12	10	1
Rutledge, Wayne	Houston	3.15	42	2512	3	.898	23	14	4
Landon, Bruce	New England	3.17	23	1118	1	.896	8	8	1
Daley, Joe	Winnipeg	3.24	65	3818	3	.892	39	23	2
Dryden, Dave	Edmonton	3.26	24	1416	1	.889	10	13	0
Dion, Michel	Indianapolis	3.36	42	2286	1	.891	17	19	3
Levasseur, Lou	Min-Edm	3.40	51	2928	2	.898	21	23	5

COMPLETE INDIVIDUAL SCORING AND PENALTY STATISTICS

PLAYER	TEAM	GP	G	A	PTS	PIM	EGR	EG%
Abgrall, Dennis	Cincinnati	80	23	39	62	22	+26	+.04
Abrahamsson, Christer	New England	45	0	1	1	12	—	—
Abrahamsson, Thommy	New England	64	6	24	30	33	+6	-.01
Adduono, Ray	Min-Sdg	53	6	24	30	22	-13	-.10
Antonovich, Mike	Min-Edm-Ngd	75	40	31	71	38	+28	+.07
Arbour, John	Min-Cgy	70	4	34	38	60	-12	-.04
Ardnt, Danny	Ngd-Edm	47	8	14	22	11	-15	-.06
Aubry, Serge	Quebec	21	0	1	1	0	—	—
Backstrom, Ralph	New England	77	17	31	48	30	+1	evn
Baird, Ken	Edm-Cgy	9	1	2	3	2	evn	evn
Ball, Terry	Birmingham	23	1	6	7	8	+2	+.12
Baltimore, Bryon	Indianapolis	55	0	15	15	63	-22	-.10
Barrie, Doug	Edmonton	70	8	19	27	92	-4	+.04
Baxter, Paul	Quebec	66	6	17	23	244	+14	evn
Beaton, Frank	Edmonton	68	4	9	13	274	-12	-.04
Beaudoin, Serge	Phoenix	77	6	24	30	136	-11	+.06
Bergman, Thommie	Winnipeg	42	2	24	26	37	+3	evn
Bernier, Jean	Quebec	72	2	13	15	23	+2	-.04
Bernier, Serge	Quebec	74	43	53	96	94	evn	-.06
Bilodeau, Gilles	Birmingham	34	2	6	8	133	+1	evn
Block, Ken	Indianapolis	52	3	10	13	25	-12	-.03
Boddy, Greg	Sdg-Edm	64	2	19	21	60	+5	+.09
Bolduc, Danny	New England	33	8	3	11	15	-13	-.11
Bordeleau, Chris	Quebec	72	32	75	107	34	+28	+.05
Bordeleau, Paulin	Quebec	80	42	41	83	52	+7	-.02
Boudrias, Andre	Quebec	74	12	31	43	12	+3	-.02
Boyd, Jim	Calgary	13	0	2	2	6	-7	-.14
Brackenbury, Curt	Quebec	77	16	13	29	146	+2	-.03
Bray, Duane	Phoenix	46	2	6	8	62	-41	-.13
Broderick, Ken	Edmonton	40	0	3	3	2	—	—
Brodeur, Richard	Quebec	53	0	1	1	0	—	—
Bromley, Gary	Calgary	28	0	0	0	2	—	—
Brown, Andy	Indianapolis	10	0	0	0	0	—	—
Burchell, Randy	Indianapolis	5	0	1	1	0	—	—
Burgess, Don	San Diego	77	20	22	42	8	-8	-.01
Busniuk, Ron	Ngd-Edm	84	3	11	14	224	-10	evn
Butters, Bill	Min-Edm-Ngd	75	1	17	18	215	+16	evn
Callighen, Brett	Ngd-Edm	62	15	26	41	89	+5	+.08
Campbell, Bryan	Indianapolis	74	13	46	59	24	-18	-.02
Carleton, Wayne	Birmingham	3	1	0	1	0	-2	-.21
Carlson, Jack	Min-Ngd	71	11	8	19	139	-3	-.07
Carlson, Steve	Min-Ngd	52	9	17	26	48	+3	-.02
Caron, Jacques	Cincinnati	24	0	1	1	0	—	—
Carroll, Greg	Cincinnati	77	15	39	54	53	+16	+.02
Cassolato, Tony	San Diego	43	13	12	25	26	+9	+.07
Chipperfield, Ron	Calgary	81	27	27	54	32	-10	-.01
Clackson, Kim	Indianapolis	71	3	8	11	168	-9	-.03
Clearwater, Ray	Minnesota	2	0	0	0	2	-3	-.37
Climie, Ron	New England	3	0	0	0	0	-1	-.09
Cloutier, Real	Quebec	76	66	75	141	39	+47	+.11
Coates, Brian	Indianapolis	16	1	5	6	4	-2	+.05
Cole, Jim	Winnipeg	2	0	1	1	0	-1	-.09
Connelly, Wayne	Cgy-Edm	63	18	21	39	22	-2	evn
Connor, Cam	Houston	76	35	32	67	224	+23	+.03
Constantin, Charles	Quebec	77	14	19	33	93	+1	-.02
Cormier, Michel	Phoenix	58	13	16	29	22	-26	-.06

PLAYER	TEAM	GP	G	A	PTS	PIM	EGR	EG%
Cournoyer, Norm	San Diego	19	1	2	3	8	-14	-.17
Cunningham, Rick	Birmingham	63	0	8	8	75	-18	-.04
Curran, Mike	Minnesota	16	0	0	0	6	—	—
Daley, Joe	Winnipeg	65	0	4	4	6	—	—
Davidson, Blair	Phoenix	2	0	0	0	2	-1	-.07
Deadmarsh, Butch	Min-Cgy	73	22	21	43	128	-10	-.06
Deschamps, Andre	Calgary	9	1	2	3	19	-2	+.01
Devine, Kevin	San Diego	81	30	20	50	114	-12	-.01
Dion, Michel	Indianapolis	42	0	0	0	0	—	—
Dobek, Bob	San Diego	58	7	17	24	17	-9	-.04
Donaldson, Gary	Houston	5	0	0	0	6	-3	-.23
Dorey, Jim	Quebec	73	13	34	47	102	+26	+.04
Driscoll, Peter	Calgary	76	23	29	52	120	-8	+.01
Dryden, Dave	Edmonton	24	0	2	2	0	—	—
Dube, Norm	Quebec	39	15	18	33	8	+11	+.06
Dubois, Michel	Quebec	4	0	0	0	0	evn	-.12
Dudley, Rick	Cincinnati	77	41	47	88	102	+25	+.02
Dunn, Dave	Winnipeg	40	3	11	14	129	-1	-.06
Earl, Tom	New England	54	9	14	23	37	-7	-.02
Evans, Chris	Calgary	81	7	27	34	60	+12	+.12
Falkenberg, Bob	San Diego	64	0	6	6	34	-11	-.08
Farda, Richard	Birmingham	48	9	26	35	2	-23	-.09
Fedorko, Mike	Houston	4	0	0	0	0	-4	-.24
Ferguson, Norm	San Diego	77	39	32	71	5	-5	+.02
Fitchner, Bob	Quebec	81	9	30	39	105	+1	-.03
Flett, Bill	Edmonton	48	34	20	54	20	+7	+.10
Folco, Peter	Birmingham	2	0	0	0	0	-3	-.23
Ford, Mike	Calgary	76	8	34	42	34	+6	-.03
Fortunato, Joe	Edmonton	1	0	0	0	0	evn	evn
French, John	San Diego	44	14	21	35	6	-3	-.01
Ftorek, Robbie	Phoenix	80	46	71	117	86	+26	+.21
Gallant, Gord	Minnesota	71	10	16	26	126	+7	evn
Garrett, John	Birmingham	65	0	3	3	21	—	—
Gorman, Dave	Phx-Bhm	57	9	13	22	38	evn	evn
Grahame, Ron	Houston	39	0	0	0	0	—	—
Gray, John	Phx-Hsn	75	31	30	61	84	+21	+.02
Green, Ted	Winnipeg	70	4	21	25	45	+12	-.01
Greig, Bruce	Calgary	7	1	1	2	10	-1	+.01
Grenier, Richard	Quebec	34	11	9	20	4	-6	-.11
Gruen, Dan	Min-Cgy	35	11	9	20	19	+9	+.01
Guindon, Bob	Winnipeg	69	10	17	27	19	-12	-.09
Guite, Pierre	Cin-Qbc	62	12	14	26	99	-5	-.07
Hale, Larry	Houston	67	0	14	14	18	+9	-.06
Hall, Del	Phoenix	80	38	41	79	30	+6	+.13
Hamilton, Al	Edmonton	81	8	37	45	60	-19	evn
Hangsleben, Alan	New England	74	13	9	22	79	-24	-.12
Hansis, Ron	Houston	22	4	3	7	6	-4	-.07
Hanson, Dave	Min-Ngd	8	0	2	2	44	-9	-.29
Harbaruk, Nick	Indianapolis	27	2	2	4	2	-16	-.17
Harris, Hugh	Indianapolis	46	21	35	56	21	+10	+.13
Hart, Richard	Birmingham	4	0	0	0	0	+1	+.10
Heaver, Paul	Birmingham	5	0	0	0	0	evn	evn
Hebenton, Clay	Phoenix	56	0	0	0	2	—	—
Hedberg, Anders	Winnipeg	68	70	61	131	48	+48	+.16
Henderson, Paul	Birmingham	81	23	25	48	30	-9	-.02
Hinse, Andre	Hsn-Phx	42	4	10	14	12	-16	-.09
Hislop, Jamie	Cincinnati	46	7	19	26	6	+11	+.01
Hobin, Mike	Phoenix	68	17	18	35	14	-43	-.11
Hoganson, Dale	Birmingham	81	7	48	55	48	+1	+.03

PLAYER	TEAM	GP	G	A	PTS	PIM	EGR	EG%
Hoganson, Paul	Cin-Ind	28	0	0	0	2	—	—
Hornung, Larry	Edm-Sdg	79	6	10	16	8	-13	-.01
Howe, Gordie	Houston	62	24	44	68	57	+27	+.03
Howe, Mark	Houston	57	23	52	75	46	+41	+.07
Howe, Marty	Houston	80	17	28	45	103	+29	+.02
Huck, Fran	Winnipeg	12	2	2	4	10	-1	-.04
Hughes, Frank	Hsn-Phx	75	27	37	64	22	evn	+.07
Hughes, Brent	San Diego	62	4	13	17	48	-3	+.02
Hughes, John	Cincinnati	79	3	27	30	113	+15	-.01
Hull, Bobby	Winnipeg	34	21	32	53	14	+16	+.10
Hull, Steve	Calgary	2	0	2	2	0	+1	+.15
Humphreys, Ed	Quebec	22	0	1	1	0	—	—
Hurley, Paul	Calgary	34	0	6	6	32	-8	-.11
Huston, Ron	Phoenix	80	20	39	59	10	-57	-.12
Hynes, David	New England	22	5	4	9	4	+5	+.10
Inkpen, Dave	Cin-Ind	80	7	26	33	81	+16	+.04
Irwin, Glen	Houston	44	2	4	6	168	-12	-.16
Israelson, Larry	Calgary	2	0	0	0	0	-2	-.29
Jacques, Jeff	Birmingham	79	21	27	48	92	-1	+.01
Jodzio, Rick	Calgary	46	4	6	10	61	-13	-.06
Jordan, Ric	Calgary	5	0	0	0	4	-9	-.36
Justin, Dan	Cincinnati	6	0	2	2	4	+3	+.07
Karlander, Al	Indianapolis	65	17	28	45	23	+5	+.07
Keon, Dave	Min-Ngd	76	27	63	90	10	+38	+.11
Ketola, Veli Pekka	Wpg-Cgy	81	29	35	64	61	-30	-.10
Kirk, Gavin	Bhm-Edm	81	17	46	63	50	-10	+.03
Kokkola, Keith	Birmingham	5	0	0	0	21	-3	+.05
Kryskow, Dave	Calgary	45	16	17	33	47	-14	+.00
Kurt, Gary	Phoenix	33	0	3	3	6	—	—
Labraaten, Dan	Winnipeg	64	24	27	51	21	-11	-.07
Lacombe, Francois	Quebec	81	5	22	27	86	+17	+.00
Lacroix, Andre	San Diego	81	32	82	114	79	-2	+.04
Laframboise, Peter	Edmonton	17	0	5	5	12	-6	-.06
Lagace, Jean Guy	Birmingham	78	2	25	27	110	-8	+.00
Landon, Bruce	New England	23	0	0	0	4	—	—
Langevin, Dave	Edmonton	77	7	16	23	94	-16	-.01
LaPointe, Norm	Cincinnati	52	0	0	0	2	—	—
Lariviere, Garry	Phx-Qbc	76	7	26	33	56	-12	+.01
Larose, Claude	Cincinnati	81	30	46	76	8	+18	+.00
Larsson, Curt	Winnipeg	19	0	1	1	4	—	—
Larway, Don	Houston	75	11	13	24	112	+5	-.05
Lawson, Danny	Cgy-Wpg	78	30	26	56	28	-13	-.09
Leclerc, Renald	Indianapolis	68	25	30	55	43	-7	-.01
Leduc, Rich	Cincinnati	81	52	55	107	75	+28	+.03
Legge, Barry	Min-Cin	76	7	22	29	39	+19	-.02
Legge, Randy	San Diego	69	1	9	10	69	-18	-.04
Lemieux, Richard	Calgary	33	6	11	17	9	-4	-.06
Lesuk, Bill	Winnipeg	78	14	27	41	85	+23	+.07
Levasseur, Louis	Min-Edm	51	0	1	1	4	—	—
Ley, Rick	New England	55	2	21	23	102	-6	-.08
Liddington, Bob	Phoenix	80	20	24	44	28	-22	+.00
Lindh, Mats	Winnipeg	73	14	17	31	2	-13	-.09
Lindskog, Doug	Calgary	2	0	0	0	2	-1	-.20
Lindstrom, Willy	Winnipeg	79	44	36	80	37	-2	-.05
Locas, Jacques	Cin-Cgy	67	21	17	38	29	-5	-.02
Lockett, Ken	San Diego	45	0	0	0	15	—	—
Lomenda, Mark	Indianapolis	56	9	12	21	14	-11	-.05
Long, Barry	Edm-Wpg	73	9	39	48	56	-5	-.04
Long, Ted	Cincinnati	1	0	0	0	0	-1	-.25

PLAYER	TEAM	GP	G	A	PTS	PIM	EGR	EG%
Lukowich, Bernie	Calgary	6	0	1	1	0	+2	+.44
Lukowich, Morris	Houston	62	27	18	45	67	+20	+.01
Lund, Larry	Houston	80	29	38	67	36	+20	-.02
Lyle, George	New England	75	39	33	72	62	+30	+.15
MacDonald, Blair	Indianapolis	81	34	30	64	28	+10	+.09
MacGregor, Gary	Ngd-Ind	46	8	13	21	8	-25	-.12
Maggs, Darryl	Indianapolis	81	16	55	71	114	+4	+.08
Mahovlich, Frank	Birmingham	17	3	20	23	12	-1	+.04
Marrin, Peter	Birmingham	79	23	37	60	36	-1	-.02
Marsh, Jim	Birmingham	1	0	0	0	0	-3	-.50
Marsh, Peter	Cincinnati	76	23	28	51	52	+11	-.01
Mavety, Larry	Indianapolis	10	2	2	4	8	-1	+.04
Maxwell, Bryan	Cincinnati	34	1	8	9	29	+2	-.02
Mayer, Jim	Calgary	21	2	3	5	0	-9	-.08
McDonald, Brian	Indianapolis	50	15	13	28	48	-20	-.08
McDonough, Al	Minnesota	42	9	21	30	6	+13	+.07
McKay, Ray	Min-Bhm	61	2	10	12	39	+14	+.00
McKenzie, John	Min-Ngd	74	28	32	60	77	+24	+.04
McLeod, Al	Phx-Hsn	70	8	26	34	55	+9	-.06
McLeod, Don	Calgary	67	0	9	9	2	—	—
McNamee, Peter	San Diego	41	3	6	9	38	-7	-.03
Melrose, Barry	Cincinnati	29	1	4	5	8	-22	-.23
Merrell, Barry	Edmonton	10	1	3	4	0	-2	+.11
Micheletti, Joe	Calgary	14	3	3	6	10	-5	+.13
Milani, Tom	Minnesota	2	0	0	0	0	-2	-1.0
Miller, Perry	Winnipeg	74	14	31	45	124	+27	+.06
Miller, Warren	Calgary	80	23	32	55	51	+11	+.11
Miszuk, John	Calgary	79	2	26	28	57	+5	+.09
Moffat, Lyle	Winnipeg	74	13	11	24	90	-7	-.05
Mononen, Lauri	Phoenix	67	21	29	50	0	-20	+.00
Morin, Wayne	Calgary	13	2	0	2	25	-3	+.14
Morris, Peter	Edmonton	3	0	0	0	2	-2	-.22
Morris, Rick	Edmonton	79	18	17	35	76	-1	+.07
Morrison, George	Calgary	63	11	19	30	10	-10	-.03
Morrison, Kevin	San Diego	75	8	30	38	68	-30	-.07
Mott, Morris	Winnipeg	2	0	1	1	5	+1	+.08
Napier, Mark	Birmingham	80	60	36	96	24	+16	+.09
Nedomansky, Vaclav	Birmingham	81	36	33	69	10	-13	-.03
Nevin, Bob	Edmonton	13	3	2	5	0	-8	-.11
Nilsson, Ulf	Winnipeg	71	39	85	124	89	+57	+.17
Niekamp, Jim	Phoenix	79	1	15	16	91	-32	-.02
Nistico, Lou	Birmingham	79	20	36	56	166	-9	-.02
Noris, Joe	San Diego	73	35	57	92	30	+2	+.06
O'Connell, Tim	San Diego	16	0	3	3	4	-12	-.22
Ouimet, Francois	Cincinnati	16	1	8	9	10	+12	+.12
Paiement, Rosaire	Ngd-Ind	80	23	27	50	103	-1	-.01
Parizeau, Michel	Indianapolis	75	18	37	55	39	+6	+.06
Park, Jim	Indianapolis	31	0	1	1	6	—	—
Patenaude, Rusty	Edmonton	73	25	16	41	57	-23	-.07
Patrick, Craig	Minnesota	30	6	11	17	6	+4	-.01
Patrick, Glenn	Edmonton	23	0	4	4	62	-10	-.16
Patterson, Dennis	Edmonton	23	0	2	2	2	-18	-.22
Peacosh, Gene	Edm-Ind	75	27	30	57	35	+1	+.03
Pentland, Dwayne	Houston	29	1	2	3	6	+3	-.07
Pesut, George	Calgary	17	2	0	2	2	-7	-.13
Phaneuf, Jean-Luc	Birmingham	30	2	7	9	2	-4	+.00
Pinder, Gerry	San Diego	44	6	13	19	36	-24	-.18
Pleau, Larry	New England	78	11	21	32	22	-17	-.09
Plumb, Ron	Cincinnati	79	11	58	69	52	+64	+.16

22

PLAYER	TEAM	GP	G	A	PTS	PIM	EGR	EG%
Popiel, Jan	Phoenix	28	3	2	5	8	-24	-.19
Popiel, Poul	Houston	80	12	56	68	87	+53	+.10
Powis, Lynn	Calgary	63	30	30	60	40	+4	+.06
Prentice, Bill	Edmonton	3	0	0	0	2	+2	+.29
Preston, Rich	Houston	80	38	41	79	54	+37	+.07
Proceviat, Dick	Indianapolis	55	2	12	14	33	-7	+.02
Raeder, Cap	New England	26	0	0	0	2	—	—
Rautakallio, Pekka	Phoenix	78	4	31	35	8	-24	+.03
Repo, Seppo	Phoenix	80	29	31	60	10	-35	-.03
Rhiness, Brad	San Diego	58	9	14	23	14	-17	-.06
Riihiranta, Hexi	Winnipeg	53	1	16	17	28	-1	-.07
Rivers, Wayne	San Diego	60	18	31	49	40	+5	+.08
Roberts, Doug	New England	64	3	18	21	33	-6	-.03
Roberts, Gordie	New England	77	13	33	46	169	+16	+.10
Rochon, Francois	Indianapolis	57	15	8	23	8	-13	-.03
Rogers, Mike	New England	78	25	57	82	10	+11	+.06
Rollins, Jerry	Bhm-Phx	71	4	10	14	186	-27	-.03
Rota, Randy	Edmonton	40	9	6	15	8	-10	-.05
Roy, Pierre	Qbc-Cin	68	6	17	23	176	+29	+.05
Ruhnke, Kent	Winnipeg	51	11	11	22	2	-12	-.08
Ruskowski, Terry	Houston	80	24	60	84	146	+31	+.04
Russell, Bob	Edmonton	57	7	6	13	41	-10	-.02
Rutledge, Wayne	Houston	42	0	3	3	6	—	—
St. Sauveur, Claude	Cgy-Edm	32	5	10	15	4	-2	-.01
Sather, Glen	Edmonton	81	19	34	53	77	-17	+.01
Scharf, Ted	Edmonton	5	0	2	2	14	-1	-.04
Schella, John	Houston	20	0	6	6	28	+8	+.09
Schneider, Buzz	Birmingham	4	0	0	0	2	-2	-.13
Selwood, Brad	New England	41	4	12	16	71	-8	-.09
Sentes, Rick	Cgy-Sdg	53	20	25	45	24	+24	+.15
Serviss, Tom	Calgary	8	2	1	3	2	-1	-.07
Sheehy, Tim	Edm-Bhm	78	41	29	70	48	-9	-.03
Shmyr, Paul	San Diego	81	13	37	50	103	-4	+.04
Sicinski, Bob	Indianapolis	60	12	24	36	14	-8	-.05
Simpson, Tom	Bhm-Edm	40	10	8	18	26	-10	-.01
Sjoberg, Lars Erik	Winnipeg	52	2	38	40	31	+9	+.00
Sleep, Mike	Phoenix	13	2	2	4	6	-3	-.03
Smedsmo, Dale	Ngd-Cin	38	2	5	7	97	-13	-.10
Sobchuk, Dennis	Cincinnati	81	44	52	96	38	+14	-.01
Stapleton, Pat	Indianapolis	81	8	45	53	29	-28	-.07
Steele, Billy	Cincinnati	81	9	22	31	21	+11	+.00
Stewart, John A.	Min-Bhm	16	3	3	6	2	-6	-.24
Stewart, JC	Birmingham	52	17	24	41	33	+11	+.05
Stewart, Paul	Edmonton	2	0	0	0	2	+00	+.00
Stoughton, Blaine	Cincinnati	81	52	52	104	39	+24	+.00
Sullivan, Peter	Winnipeg	78	31	52	83	18	+11	-.01
Sutherland, Steve	Quebec	36	6	9	15	34	+6	+.04
Swain, Garry	New England	26	5	2	7	6	-6	-.08
Syvret, Dave	Birmingham	8	0	0	0	0	-4	-.04
Tamminen, Juhani	Phoenix	65	10	29	39	22	-23	-.02
Tannahill, Don	Calgary	72	10	22	32	4	-9	-.04
Tardif, Marc	Quebec	62	49	60	109	65	+29	+.07
Taylor, Ted	Houston	78	16	35	51	90	+29	+.05
Terbenche, Paul	Calgary	80	9	24	33	30	-14	+.00
Thomas, Reg	Indianapolis	79	25	30	55	34	-9	+.00
Tonelli, John	Houston	80	24	31	55	109	+14	-.03
Tremblay, JC	Quebec	53	4	31	35	16	+2	-.08
Troy, Jamie	New England	7	0	0	0	7	-3	-.15
Turkiewicz, Jim	Birmingham	80	6	25	31	54	+5	+.05

PLAYER	TEAM	GP	G	A	PTS	PIM	EGR	EG%
Ullman, Norm	Edmonton	67	16	27	43	28	-23	-.07
Veneruzzo, Gary	San Diego	40	14	11	25	18	+4	+.06
Wakely, Ernie	San Diego	46	0	1	1	0	—	—
Walsh, Brian	Calgary	5	0	2	2	12	-3	+.17
Ward, Ron	Min-Wpg-Cgy	64	24	33	57	8	+9	+.06
Webster, Tom	New England	70	36	49	85	43	+18	+.06
Weir, Wally	Quebec	69	3	17	20	197	+13	+.00
West, Steve	Houston	3	0	0	0	2	-3	-.26
Westrum, Pat	Min-Bhm	74	2	20	22	90	+23	+.03
Wilkins, Barry	Edmonton	51	4	24	28	75	-7	+.10
Williams, Butch	Edmonton	29	3	10	13	16	-9	-.07
Winograd, Bob	San Diego	1	0	0	0	0	+1	+1.0
Wood, Wayne	Birmingham	22	0	0	0	0	—	—
Young, Howie	Phoenix	26	1	3	4	23	-8	+.00
Zrymiak, Jerry	Minnesota	40	2	10	12	14	+7	+.00
Zuke, Mike	Indianapolis	15	3	4	7	2	-2	-.03

COMPLETE INDIVIDUAL GOALTENDING STATISTICS

PLAYER	TEAM	GAA	GP	MINS	SO	SV%	W	L	T
Abrahamsson, Christer	New England	3.84	45	2484	0	.889	15	22	4
Aubrey, Serge	Quebec	3.98	21	769	1	.862	6	5	0
Broderick, Ken	Edmonton	3.49	40	2301	4	.878	18	18	1
Brodeur, Richard	Quebec	3.45	53	2906	2	.880	29	18	2
Bromley, Gary	Calgary	3.83	28	1237	0	.873	6	9	2
Brown, Andy	Indianapolis	3.63	10	430	0	.867	1	4	1
Burchell, Randy	Indianapolis	3.53	5	136	0	.910	1	0	0
Caron, Jacques	Cincinnati	2.83	24	1292	3	.892	13	6	2
Curran, Mike	Minnesota	3.54	16	848	0	.895	4	7	3
Daley, Joe	Winnipeg	3.24	64	3818	3	.892	39	23	2
Dion, Michel	Indianapolis	3.36	42	2286	1	.891	17	19	3
Dryden, Dave	Edmonton	3.26	24	1416	1	.889	10	13	0
Garrett, John	Birmingham	3.53	65	3803	4	.899	24	34	4
Grahame, Ron	Houston	2.74	39	2345	4	.901	27	10	2
Hebenton, Clay	Phoenix	4.22	56	3129	0	.875	17	29	3
Hoganson, Paul	Cin-Ind	4.33	28	1218	1	.853	8	8	1
Humphreys, Ed	Quebec	3.58	22	1240	1	.880	12	8	1
Kurt, Gary	Phoenix	5.55	33	1752	0	.838	11	19	1
Larsson, Curt	Winnipeg	4.83	19	1019	0	.850	7	9	0
Landon, Bruce	New England	3.17	23	1118	1	.896	8	8	1
LaPointe, Norm	Cincinnati	3.73	52	2817	2	.878	21	25	2
Levasseur, Louis	Min-Edm	3.40	51	2928	2	.898	21	23	5
Lockett, Ken	San Diego	3.70	45	2397	1	.871	18	19	1
McLeod, Don	Calgary	3.40	66	3701	3	.879	25	34	5
Park, Jim	Indianapolis	3.96	31	1727	1	.873	14	12	4
Raeder, Cap	New England	3.12	26	1328	2	.902	12	10	1
Rutledge, Wayne	Houston	3.15	42	2512	3	.898	23	14	4
Wakely, Ernie	San Diego	3.09	46	2506	3	.896	22	18	3
Wood, Wayne	Birmingham	4.13	23	1132	0	.883	7	12	0

POWER PLAY PROFICIENCY

TEAM	GP	OPNT PIM	OPP	GF	GA	PROF	FREQ
Houston	80	1172	227	64	4	.282	3.55
Quebec	81	1212	258	70	6	.271	3.69
San Diego	81	981	257	69	6	.268	3.72
Winnipeg	80	1432	370	90	11	.243	4.11
Indianapolis	81	837	259	57	2	.220	4.54
Edmonton	81	1194	242	50	11	.207	4.84
Minnesota	42	526	107	22	7	.206	4.86
Birmingham	81	1250	261	50	7	.192	5.22
New England	81	1186	245	47	10	.192	5.21
Cincinnati	81	1054	283	54	7	.191	5.24
Phoenix	80	972	246	47	10	.191	5.23
Calgary	81	875	258	38	10	.147	6.79
TOTALS	465	12,691	3013	658	91	.218	4.58

SHORTHANDED EFFICIENCY

TEAM	GP	PIM	AVG	SIT	GF	GA	EFF	FREQ
Houston	80	1432	17.9	361	11	61	.831	5.92
Calgary	81	832	10.3	228	8	47	.794	4.85
Edmonton	81	1319	16.3	278	1	58	.791	4.79
Quebec	81	1485	18.3	316	16	66	.791	4.79
San Diego	81	834	10.3	204	11.	43	.789	4.74
Winnipeg	80	991	12.4	231	9	49	.788	4.71
Cincinnati	81	970	12.0	259	6	58	.776	4.47
New England	81	1254	15.5	281	8	65	.769	4.32
Birmingham	81	1179	14.6	231	6	54	.766	4.28
Indianapolis	81	880	10.9	251	7	62	.753	4.05
Minnesota	42	600	14.3	130	3	33	.748	3.97
Phoenix	80	915	11.4	243	5	62	.745	3.92
TOTALS	465	12,691	13.6	3013	91	658	.782	4.58

EXTRA ATTACKER RESULTS

TEAM	GOALIE PULLED	SUCCESS X			BACKFIRE		
		GF	PCT	FREQ	GA	PCT	FREQ
Phoenix	12	3	.250	4.00	1	.083	12.00
Birmingham	23	5	.217	4.60	7	.304	3.29
Indianapolis	19	3	.158	6.33	5	.263	3.80
New England	19	2	.105	9.50	3	.158	6.33
Quebec	10	1	.100	10.00	3	.300	3.33
Minnesota	12	1	.083	12.00	1	.083	12.00
Winnipeg	13	1	.077	13.00	3	.231	4.33
Calgary	17	1	.059	17.00	7	.412	2.43
Houston	8	0	.000	0.00	2	.250	4.00
Cincinnati	9	0	.000	0.00	3	.333	3.00
Edmonton	11	0	.000	0.00	5	.455	2.20
San Diego	12	0	.000	0.00	6	.500	2.00
TOTALS	165	17	.103	9.71	46	.279	3.59

25

OVERTIME ANALYSIS

5-YEAR TOTALS

TEAM	OVERTIME RECORD	AT HOME	ON ROAD	AVG DURATION	1	2	3	4	5	6	7	8	9	10	TIES
11- 22- 19 Birmingham	1- 9- 4	1- 5- 3	0- 4- 1	6:02	3	1	1	—	—	—	1	2	1	1	4
16- 14- 14 Calgary	1- 1- 7	0- 1- 2	1- 0- 5	9:40	—	1	—	—	—	—	1	1	1	1	7
2- 9- 6 Cincinnati	0- 7- 5	0- 1- 1	0- 6- 4	6:31	—	2	—	1	2	—	2	2	—	—	5
19- 15- 19 Edmonton	6- 1- 4	3- 1- 1	3- 0- 3	6:48	1	—	1	—	1	—	2	2	—	—	4
8- 9- 15 Houston	1- 0- 6	1- 0- 4	0- 0- 2	8:43	—	1	—	—	—	—	—	—	—	—	6
11- 14- 17 Indianapolis	7- 2- 8	3- 1- 3	4- 1- 5	7:23	1	—	1	—	3	1	—	2	1	—	8
16- 14- 25 Minnesota	0- 0- 5	0- 0- 3	0- 0- 2	10:00	—	—	—	—	—	1	—	—	—	—	5
22- 8- 24 New England	2- 3- 6	1- 1- 4	1- 2- 2	7:21	1	1	1	—	1	1	—	1	1	—	6
9- 14- 18 Phoenix	3- 6- 4	2- 3- 2	1- 3- 2	6:17	2	1	2	1	—	—	—	—	2	1	4
19- 15- 16 Quebec	4- 2- 3	2- 1- 1	2- 1- 2	6:25	1	—	2	—	1	—	—	1	—	2	3
14- 17- 20 San Diego	3- 1- 4	1- 1- 4	2- 0- 0	6:21	2	—	1	1	—	—	1	—	—	1	4
19- 18- 18 Winnipeg	4- 0- 2	3- 0- 1	1- 0- 1	7:07	1	—	—	—	—	—	—	—	1	—	2
40- 37- 31 — Other Clubs —															
206-206-121	32-32-29	17-15-29	15-17-29	7:10	6	3	4	1	4	1	3	4	3	3	29
					9.8	4.9	6.6	1.6	6.6	1.6	4.9	6.6	4.9	4.9	47.5
										PCT.					

1976-77 TOTALS: 61 OVERTIME GAMES (13.1% of all games)
32 GAMES DECIDED (52.5% of overtime games, 6.9% of all games)
29 GAMES REMAINED TIED (47.5% of overtime games, 6.2% of all games)

5 SEASON TOTALS: 327 OVERTIME GAMES (13.2% of all games)
206 GAMES DECIDED (63.0% of overtime games, 8.3% of all games)
121 GAMES REMAINED TIED (37.0% of overtime games, 4.9% of all games)

WHA-INTERNATIONAL

INTERNATIONAL SERIES '78

1977-78 will mark the second successive season that the World Hockey Association has established itself as the absolute leader in the growth of top level International competition. International Series '78 is the most comprehensive confrontation ever scheduled between a North American major league and Europe's leading hockey powers. Sixteen of the thirty-four games to be played in WHA arenas will count in the regular season standings, another first for the WHA.

The complete schedule:

CZECHOSLOVAKIA
Fri. Dec. 9 at Indianapolis
Sun. Dec. 11 at Quebec
Tue. Dec. 13 at Winnipeg
Wed. Dec. 14 at Edmonton
Fri. Dec. 16 at New England
Sun. Dec. 18 at Houston
Tue. Dec. 20 at Cincinnati
Wed. Dec. 21 at Birmingham

SOVIET ALL-STARS
Wed. Dec. 14 at New England
Sat. Dec. 17 at Cincinnati
Sun. Dec. 18 at Indianapolis
Tue. Dec. 20 at Winnipeg
Wed. Dec. 21 at Edmonton
Fri. Dec. 23 at Houston
Mon. Dec. 26 at Birmingham
Wed. Dec. 28 at Houston
Sun. Jan. 1 at Indianapolis
Tue. Jan. 3 at Quebec

SOVIET NATIONALS
Wed. Jan. 4 at Edmonton
Thu. Jan. 5 at Winnipeg
Sat. Jan. 7 at Quebec
Sun. Jan. 8 at Cincinnati
Tue. Jan. 10 at Indianapolis
Wed. Jan. 11 at New England

SWEDEN
Fri. Mar. 17 at Indianapolis
Sun. Mar. 19 at New England
Tue. Mar. 21 at Houston
Sun. Mar. 26 at Cincinnati
Tue. Mar. 28 at Birmingham

FINLAND
Sat. Mar. 18 at Birmingham
Sun. Mar. 19 at Houston
Wed. Mar. 22 at Indianapolis
Sat. Mar. 25 at Cincinnati
Sun. Mar. 26 at New England

IZVESTIA CUP TOURNAMENT
Dec. 15 - Dec. 22 Quebec Nordiques at Moscow

JAPAN EXHIBITION TOUR
Dec. 29 - Jan. 1 Winnipeg vs. Soviet Nationals

INTERNATIONAL SERIES '77
GAME BY GAME RESULTS

SOVIET NATIONALS

Monday, December 27	New England Whalers 5, Soviet Nationals 2
Tuesday, December 28	Soviet Nationals 7, Cincinnati Stingers 5
Thursday, December 30	Soviet Nationals 10, Houston Aeros 1
Saturday, January 1	Soviet Nationals 5, Indianapolis Racers 2
Monday, January 3	Soviet Nationals 6, San Diego Mariners 3
Wednesday, January 5	Soviet Nationals 3, Edmonton Oilers 2
Thursday, January 6	Soviet Nationals 3, Winnipeg Jets 2
Saturday, January 8	Quebec Nordiques 6, Soviet Nationals 1

CZECHOSLOVAKIA

Sunday, December 12	Winnipeg Jets 6, Czechoslovakia 5
Monday, December 13	Edmonton Oilers 6, Czechoslovakia 4
Wednesday, December 15	Czechoslovakia 5, Calgary Cowboys 4
Friday, December 17	Minnesota Fighting Saints 3, Czechoslovakia 2 (ot)
Monday, December 20	Czechoslovakia 4, New England Whalers 1
Wednesday, December 22	Indianapolis Racers 3, Czechoslovakia 2

IZVESTIA CUP TOURNAMENT

Thursday, December 16	Czechoslovakia 3, Winnipeg Jets 2
Friday, December 17	Winnipeg Jets 4, Sweden 4
Sunday, December 19	Soviet Nationals 6, Winnipeg Jets 4
Tuesday, December 21	Winnipeg Jets 2, Finland 1

SOVIET NATIONALS
COMPLETE SCORING STATISTICS

PLAYER	GP	G	A	TP	PIM
Vladimir Petrov	6	6	5	11	0
Aleksandr Yakushev	7	7	1	8	6
Helmut Balderis	7	4	4	8	10
Aleksandr Maltsev	7	3	4	7	4
Victor Shalimov	7	2	5	7	0
Valeri Kharlamov	7	1	6	7	4
Aleksandr Golikov	7	3	3	6	0
Sergei Babinov	7	1	4	5	8
Boris Mikhailov	5	3	1	4	6
Vasiliy Pervukhin	8	1	3	4	6
Vladimir Lutchenko	8	0	4	4	2
Aleksandr Bilialetdinov	8	0	4	4	12
Vladimir Krikunov	7	2	1	3	2
Vladimir Shadrin	7	0	3	3	4
Valeri Kovin	5	1	1	2	4
Gennadi Tsygankov	4	0	2	2	4
Petr Prirodin	2	1	0	1	0
Boris Aleksandrov	3	1	0	1	0
Yuri Liapkin	7	1	0	1	0
Vladimir Vikilov	5	0	1	1	0
Victor Zhluktov	3	0	0	0	0
Vladimir Repniov	4	0	0	0	0
Vladislav Tretiak	5	0	0	0	0
Aleksandr Sidelnikov	5	0	0	0	4
Valeri Vasiljev	6	0	0	0	4
Totals	8	37	52	89	84

SOVIET NATIONALS
COMPLETE GOALTENDING STATISTICS

PLAYER	GAA	GP	MIN	W	L	T
Aleksandr Sidelnikov	2.57	5	210	3	0	0
Vladislav Tretiak	3.78	5	270	3	2	0
Totals	3.25	8	480	6	2	0

CZECHOSLOVAKIA
COMPLETE SCORING STATISTICS

PLAYER	GP	G	A	TP	PIM
Marian Stastny	6	5	3	8	2
Milan Novy	6	1	7	8	2
Eduard Novak	6	5	1	6	0
Jaroslav Pouzar	6	3	3	6	2
Peter Stastny	6	0	6	6	2
Lubomir Bauer	6	2	1	3	4
Otakar Vejvoda	6	1	2	3	0
Vaclav Sykora	6	1	2	3	0
Miroslav Kravacek	6	0	3	3	0
Frantisek Kaberle	6	1	1	2	0
Frantisek Pospisil	6	0	2	2	7
Jan Neliba	5	1	0	1	8
Zdenek Muller	6	1	0	1	0
Antonin Melc	4	1	0	1	2
Jaroslav Vins	5	0	1	1	4
Vladimir Dzurilla	5	0	1	1	0
Frantisek Cermek	6	0	1	1	6
Jaroslav Novotny	1	0	0	0	0
Miroslav Termer	1	0	0	0	0
Miroslav Krasa	1	0	0	0	0
Zdenek Nedved	1	0	0	0	0
Ladislav Vysusil	4	0	0	0	0
Milan Skrbec	5	0	0	0	0
Totals	6	22	35	57	47

CZECHOSLOVAKIA
COMPLETE GOALTENDING STATISTICS

PLAYER	GAA	GP	MIN	W	L	T
Vladimir Dzurilla	.339	5	301	2	3	0
Miroslav Termer	4.44	1	54	0	1	0
Miroslav Krasa	20.00	1	6	0	0	0
Totals	3.82	6	361	2	4	0

WHA HISTORY

FTOREK WINS GORDIE HOWE TROPHY, BECOMES FIRST AMERICAN-BORN MVP

On Monday, May 23, 1977, Robert Brian "Robbie" Ftorek earned a permanent place in the history of the World Hockey Association, and a very large place in the history of North American Hockey.

On that sunny spring afternoon, before a packed press gathering atop the World Trade Center in New York City, Robbie Ftorek was presented the Gordie Howe Trophy for being WHA Most Valuable Player for 1976-77.

Ftorek, a native of Needham, Massachusetts, thus became the first American ever to win a major league hockey MVP award.

Bill MacFarland, then President of the WHA, heralded Robbie's selection as "the most significant individual accomplishment in the history of United States hockey."

During Ftorek's rise to stardom, he epitomized the emergence of the American hockey player.

In 1975-76, he became the first American ever to score 100 points in a single major league season by accounting for 113 points on 41 goals and 72 assists. That season he also became only the sixth big league player ever to hit the century mark in both points and penalty minutes. His 113 points were accompanied by 109 minutes of penalty time.

In September of 1976, at the first Canada Cup Tournament, Ftorek led Team USA, comprised of the most talented group of professional players ever assembled on one American team, to a surprisingly strong showing against the world's top hockey powers. Robbie was the tournament scoring leader for the Americans, and he was named Team USA's Most Valuable Player.

Ftorek's Canada Cup brilliance continued throughout 1976-77. He repeated his 100 point accomplishment of the previous season by scoring 46 goals and 71 assists, good for a career high 117 points. He was "plus 26" on a team that allowed 102 more goals than it scored. He was on the ice for 47 percent of the goals that his team scored and only 26 percent of the goals that it allowed. The difference between those figures, 21 percent, was far greater than that recorded by any other player in the WHA.

So Robbie Ftorek earned the privilege to stand in hockey's spotlight on a spring afternoon in New York, and to hear the "Living Legend" himself, Gordie Howe say, "Robbie, you have given hope to every American youngster who dreams of playing major league hockey."

INDIVIDUAL TROPHY WINNERS

HOWE TROPHY
(Most Valuable Player)
Robbie Ftorek	1976-77
Marc Tardif	1975-76
Bobby Hull	1974-75
Gordie Howe	1973-74
Bobby Hull	1972-73

HATSKIN TROPHY
(Best Goaltender)
Ron Grahame	1976-77
Michel Dion	1975-76
Ron Grahame	1974-75
Don McLeod	1973-74
Gerry Cheevers	1972-73

HUNTER TROPHY
(Scoring Champion)
Real Cloutier	1976-77
Marc Tardif	1975-76
Andre LaCroix	1974-75
Mike Walton	1973-74
Andre LaCroix	1972-73

OUTSTANDING DEFENSEMAN
Ron Plumb	1976-77
Paul Shmyr	1975-76
JC Tremblay	1974-75
Pat Stapleton	1973-74
JC Tremblay	1972-73

ROOKIE OF THE YEAR
George Lyle	1976-77
Mark Napier	1975-76
Anders Hedberg	1974-75
Mark Howe	1973-74
Terry Caffery	1972-73

MOST GENTLEMANLY PLAYER
Dave Keon	1976-77
Vaclav Nedomansky	1975-76
Mike Rogers	1974-75
Ralph Backstrom	1973-74
Ted Hampson	1972-73

SCHMERTZ TROPHY
(Coach of the Year)
Bill Dineen	1976-77
Bobby Kromm	1975-76
Sandy Hucul	1974-75
Billy Harris	1973-74
Jack Kelley	1972-73

The Howe Trophy

The Individual Trophy

OFFICIAL END OF SEASON ALL-STAR TEAMS

1976-77

FIRST TEAM	POSITION	SECOND TEAM
John Garrett	GOAL	Joe Daley
Darryl Maggs	DEFENSE	Poul Popiel
Ron Plumb	DEFENSE	Mark Howe
Robbie Ftorek	CENTER	Ulf Nilsson
Anders Hedberg	RIGHT WING	Real Cloutier
Marc Tardif	LEFT WING	Rick Dudley

1975-76

FIRST TEAM	POSITION	SECOND TEAM
Joe Daley	GOAL	Ron Grahame
Paul Shmyr	DEFENSE	Kevin Morrison
JC Tremblay	DEFENSE	Pat Stapleton
Ulf Nilsson	CENTER	Robbie Ftorek
Anders Hedberg	RIGHT WING	Real Cloutier
Marc Tardif	LEFT WING	Bobby Hull

1974-75

FIRST TEAM	POSITION	SECOND TEAM
Ron Grahame	GOAL	Gerry Cheevers
JC Tremblay	DEFENSE	Poul Popiel
Kevin Morrison	DEFENSE	Barry Long
Andre LaCroix	CENTER	Serge Bernier
Gordie Howe	RIGHT WING	Anders Hedberg
Bobby Hull	LEFT WING	Marc Tardif

1973-74

FIRST TEAM	POSITION	SECOND TEAM
Don McLeod	GOAL	Gerry Cheevers
Pat Stapleton	DEFENSE	JC Tremblay
Paul Shmyr	DEFENSE	Al Hamilton
Andre LaCroix	CENTER	Wayne Carleton
Gordie Howe	RIGHT WING	Mike Walton
Bobby Hull	LEFT WING	Mark Howe

1972-73

FIRST TEAM	POSITION	SECOND TEAM
Gerry Cheevers	GOAL	Bernie Parent
JC Tremblay	DEFENSE	Jim Dorey
Paul Shmyr	DEFENSE	Larry Hornung
Andre LaCroix	CENTER	Ron Ward
Danny Lawson	RIGHT WING	Tom Webster
Bobby Hull	LEFT WING	Gary Jarrett

LIFETIME TEAM TOTALS

LIFETIME OVERALL STANDINGS

	GP	W	L	T	PTS	GF	GA	PCT
Houston Aeros	394	243	136	15	501	1632	1239	.636
Winnipeg Jets	395	213	164	18	444	1582	1383	.562
Quebec Nordiques	396	214	166	16	444	1637	1503	.561
New England Whalers	395	200	171	24	424	1413	1382	.537
Cincinnati Stingers	161	74	81	6	154	639	643	.478
Birmingham Bulls	396	174	203	19	367	1556	1584	.463
Edmonton Oilers	396	173	204	19	365	1327	1453	.461
Indianapolis Racers	239	89	133	17	195	737	890	.408

LIFETIME HOME STANDINGS

	GP	W	L	T	PTS	GF	GA	PCT
Houston Aeros	197	144	46	7	295	924	563	.749
Quebec Nordiques	197	136	51	10	282	920	629	.716
Winnipeg Jets	197	134	55	8	276	874	567	.701
Cincinnati Stingers	80	55	24	1	111	377	267	.694
New England Whalers	197	126	59	12	264	779	611	.670
Edmonton Oilers	197	118	79	9	245	786	642	.622
Birmingham Bulls	197	108	76	13	›229	849	698	.581
Indianapolis Racers	119	58	56	5	121	390	400	.508

LIFETIME ROAD STANDINGS

	GP	W	L	T	PTS	GF	GA	PCT
Houston Aeros	197	99	90	8	206	708	676	.523
Winnipeg Jets	198	79	109	10	168	708	816	.424
Quebec Nordiques	199	78	115	6	162	717	874	.407
New England Whalers	198	74	112	12	160	634	771	.404
Birmingham Bulls	199	66	127	6	138	707	886	.347
Indianapolis Racers	120	31	77	12	74	347	490	.308
Edmonton Oilers	199	55	134	10	120	541	811	.302
Cincinnati Stingers	81	19	57	5	43	262	376	.265

YEARLY RECORDS / CURRENT WHA TEAMS

BIRMINGHAM BULLS

	GP	W	L	T	PTS	GF	GA	POSITION	PLAYOFF RESULT
1976-77	81	31	46	4	66	289	309	5th East Div.	
1975-76	81	24	52	5	53	335	398	5th Can. Div.	
1974-75	78	43	33	2	88	349	304	2nd Can. Div.	Lost Qrtr-Fnls
1973-74	78	41	33	4	86	304	272	2nd East Div.	Lost Semi-Fnls
1972-73	78	35	39	4	74	279	301	4th East Div.	Lost Qrtr-Fnls

CINCINNATI STINGERS

	GP	W	L	T	PTS	GF	GA	POSITION	PLAYOFF RESULT
1976-77	81	39	37	5	83	354	303	2nd East Div.	Lost Qrtr-Fnls
1975-76	80	35	44	1	71	285	340	4th East Div.	

EDMONTON OILERS

	GP	W	L	T	PTS	GF	GA	POSITION	PLAYOFF RESULT
1976-77	81	34	43	4	72	243	304	4th West Div.	Lost Qrtr-Fnls
1975-76	81	27	49	5	59	268	345	4th Can. Div.	Lost Qrtr-Fnls
1974-75	78	36	38	4	76	279	279	5th Can. Div.	
1973-74	78	38	37	3	79	268	269	3rd West Div.	Lost Qrtr-Fnls
1972-73	78	38	37	3	79	269	256	5th West Div.	

HOUSTON AEROS

	GP	W	L	T	PTS	GF	GA	POSITION	PLAYOFF RESULT
1976-77	80	50	24	6	106	320	241	1st West Div.	Lost Semi-Fnls
1975-76	80	53	27	0	106	341	263	1st West Div.	Lost Finals
1974-75	78	53	25	0	106	369	247	1st West Div.	WON AVCO TROPHY
1973-74	78	48	25	5	101	318	219	1st West Div.	WON AVCO TROPHY
1972-73	78	39	35	4	82	284	269	2nd West Div.	Lost Semi-Fnls

INDIANAPOLIS RACERS

	GP	W	L	T	PTS	GF	GA	POSITION	PLAYOFF RESULT
1976-77	81	36	37	8	80	276	305	3rd East Div.	Lost Semi-Fnls
1975-76	80	35	39	6	76	245	247	1st East Div.	Lost Qrtr-Fnls
1974-75	78	18	57	3	39	216	338	4th East Div.	

NEW ENGLAND WHALERS

	GP	W	L	T	PTS	GF	GA	POSITION	PLAYOFF RESULT
1976-77	81	35	40	6	76	275	290	4th East Div.	Lost Qrtr-Fnls
1975-76	80	33	40	7	73	255	290	3rd East Div.	Lost Semi-Fnls
1974-75	78	43	30	5	91	274	279	1st East Div.	Lost Qrtr-Fnls
1973-74	78	43	31	4	90	291	260	1st East Div.	Lost Qrtr-Fnls
1972-73	78	46	30	2	94	318	263	1st East Div.	WON AVCO TROPHY

QUEBEC NORDIQUES

	GP	W	L	T	PTS	GF	GA	POSITION	PLAYOFF RESULT
1976-77	81	47	31	3	97	353	295	1st East Div.	WON AVCO TROPHY
1975-76	81	50	27	4	104	371	316	2nd Can. Div.	Lost Qrtr-Fnls
1974-75	78	46	32	0	92	331	299	1st Can. Div.	Lost Finals
1973-74	78	38	36	4	80	306	280	5th East Div.	
1972-73	78	33	40	5	71	276	313	5th East Div.	

WINNIPEG JETS

	GP	W	L	T	PTS	GF	GA	POSITION	PLAYOFF RESULT
1976-77	80	46	32	2	94	366	291	2nd West Div.	Lost Finals
1975-76	81	52	27	2	106	345	254	1st Can. Div.	WON AVCO TROPHY
1974-75	78	38	35	5	81	322	293	3rd Can. Div.	
1973-74	78	34	39	5	73	264	296	4th West Div.	Lost Qrtr-Fnls
1972-73	78	43	31	4	90	285	249	1st West Div.	Lost Finals

LIFETIME TEAM VS. TEAM

BIRMINGHAM BULLS

AGAINST	AT HOME								ON ROAD								OVERALL							
	GP	W	L	T	PTS	GF	GA	PCT	GP	W	L	T	PTS	GF	GA	PCT	GP	W	L	T	PTS	GF	GA	PCT
Cincinnati	8	4	2	2	10	41	35	.625	7	3	4	0	6	28	30	.429	15	7	6	2	16	69	65	.533
Edmonton	17	8	7	2	18	67	68	.529	18	5	13	0	10	61	78	.278	35	13	20	2	28	128	146	.400
Houston	14	9	4	1	19	66	52	.679	15	4	11	0	8	45	76	.267	29	13	15	1	27	111	128	.466
Indianapolis	10	5	4	1	11	39	31	.550	10	3	7	0	6	29	36	.300	20	8	11	1	17	68	67	.425
New England	18	8	9	1	17	74	68	.472	17	4	13	0	8	58	83	.235	35	12	22	1	25	132	151	.357
Quebec	25	15	9	1	31	115	92	.620	25	8	17	0	16	90	111	.320	50	23	26	1	47	205	203	.470
Winnipeg	18	9	9	0	18	76	61	.500	17	6	10	1	13	61	80	.382	35	15	19	1	31	137	141	.443
Other Clubs	87	50	32	5	105	371	291	.603	90	33	52	5	71	335	392	.394	177	83	84	10	176	706	683	.497
TOTALS	197	108	76	13	229	849	698	.581	199	66	127	6	138	707	886	.347	396	174	203	19	367	1556	1584	.463

CINCINNATI STINGERS

AGAINST	AT HOME								ON ROAD								OVERALL							
	GP	W	L	T	PTS	GF	GA	PCT	GP	W	L	T	PTS	GF	GA	PCT	GP	W	L	T	PTS	GF	GA	PCT
Birmingham	7	4	3	0	8	30	28	.571	8	2	4	2	6	35	41	.375	15	6	7	2	14	65	69	.467
Edmonton	5	4	1	0	8	25	13	.800	5	1	4	0	2	16	21	.200	10	5	5	0	10	41	34	.500
Houston	7	5	2	0	10	35	25	.714	6	0	6	0	0	17	34	.000	13	5	8	0	10	52	59	.385
Indianapolis	10	6	4	0	12	48	28	.600	11	4	9	1	3	27	45	.136	21	10	13	1	15	75	73	.357
New England	11	8	3	0	16	53	35	.727	9	2	7	0	4	28	36	.222	20	10	10	0	20	81	71	.500
Quebec	7	4	2	1	9	38	30	.643	7	2	5	0	4	19	38	.286	14	6	7	1	13	57	68	.464
Winnipeg	5	2	3	0	4	22	27	.400	5	2	3	0	4	15	23	.400	10	4	6	0	8	37	50	.400
Other Clubs	28	22	6	0	44	126	81	.786	30	9	19	2	20	105	138	.333	58	31	25	2	64	231	219	.552
TOTALS	80	55	24	1	111	377	267	.694	81	19	57	5	43	262	376	.265	161	74	81	6	154	639	643	.478

EDMONTON OILERS

AGAINST	GP	W	L	T	PTS	GF	GA	PCT	GP	W	L	T	PTS	GF	GA	PCT	GP	W	L	T	PTS	GF	GA	PCT
			AT HOME								ON ROAD									OVERALL				
Birmingham	18	13	5	0	26	78	61	.722	17	7	8	2	16	68	67	.471	35	20	13	2	42	146	128	.600
Cincinnati	5	4	1	0	8	21	16	.800	5	1	4	0	2	13	25	.200	10	5	5	0	10	34	41	.500
Houston	17	7	10	0	14	65	67	.412	18	2	15	1	5	40	76	.139	35	9	25	1	19	105	143	.271
Indianapolis	8	6	1	1	13	33	21	.813	8	2	4	2	6	23	24	.500	16	8	5	3	19	56	45	.656
New England	14	8	5	1	17	52	44	.607	14	4	8	2	10	44	55	.357	28	12	13	3	27	96	99	.482
Quebec	18	7	11	0	14	69	72	.389	18	5	11	2	12	67	91	.333	36	12	22	2	26	136	163	.361
Winnipeg	24	14	8	2	20	87	88	.625	25	5	19	1	11	56	120	.220	49	19	27	3	41	143	208	.418
Other Clubs	93	59	29	5	123	381	273	.661	94	27	65	2	56	230	353	.298	187	86	94	7	179	611	626	.479
TOTALS	197	118	79	9	245	786	642	.622	199	55	134	10	120	541	811	.302	396	173	204	19	365	1327	1453	.461

HOUSTON AEROS

AGAINST	GP	W	L	T	PTS	GF	GA	PCT	GP	W	L	T	PTS	GF	GA	PCT	GP	W	L	T	PTS	GF	GA	PCT
			AT HOME								ON ROAD									OVERALL				
Birmingham	15	11	4	0	22	76	45	.733	14	4	9	1	9	52	66	.321	29	15	13	1	31	128	111	.534
Cincinnati	6	6	0	0	12	34	17	1.000	7	2	5	0	4	25	35	.286	13	8	5	0	16	59	52	.615
Edmonton	18	15	2	1	31	76	40	.861	17	10	7	0	20	67	65	.588	35	25	9	1	51	143	105	.729
Indianapolis	9	7	2	0	14	41	28	.778	10	6	3	1	13	44	25	.650	19	13	5	1	27	85	53	.711
New England	15	8	6	1	17	64	47	.567	15	7	7	1	15	52	48	.500	30	15	13	2	32	116	95	.533
Quebec	14	9	5	0	18	61	39	.643	14	1	12	1	3	31	65	.107	28	10	17	1	21	92	104	.375
Winnipeg	17	11	4	2	24	82	46	.706	17	7	9	1	15	46	60	.441	34	18	13	3	39	128	106	.574
Other Clubs	103	77	23	3	157	490	301	.762	103	62	38	3	127	391	312	.617	206	139	61	6	284	881	613	.689
TOTALS	197	144	46	7	295	924	563	.749	197	99	90	8	206	708	676	.523	394	243	136	15	501	1632	1239	.636

INDIANAPOLIS RACERS

		AT HOME							ON ROAD							OVERALL					
AGAINST	GP	W	L	T	PTS	GF	GA	PCT	GP	W	L	T	PTS	GF	GA	PCT	GP	W	L	T	PTS	GF	GA	PCT
Birmingham	10	7	3	0	14	36	29	.700	10	4	5	1	9	31	39	.450	20	11	8	1	23	67	68	.575
Cincinnati	11	9	1	1	19	45	27	.864	10	4	6	0	8	28	48	.400	21	13	7	1	27	73	75	.643
Edmonton	8	4	4	0	8	24	23	.500	8	1	6	1	3	21	33	.188	16	5	10	1	11	45	56	.344
Houston	10	3	6	1	7	25	44	.350	9	2	7	0	4	28	41	.222	19	5	13	1	11	53	85	.289
New England	12	7	4	1	15	38	31	.625	16	8	4	4	20	57	52	.625	28	15	8	5	35	95	83	.461
Quebec	11	5	6	0	10	39	47	.455	10	2	8	0	4	29	40	.200	21	7	14	0	14	68	87	.333
Winnipeg	8	2	6	0	4	28	34	.250	8	2	6	0	4	11	25	.250	16	4	12	0	8	39	59	.250
Other Clubs	49	21	26	2	44	155	165	.449	49	8	35	6	22	142	212	.224	98	29	61	8	66	297	377	.337
TOTALS	119	58	56	5	121	390	400	.508	120	31	77	12	74	347	490	.308	239	89	133	17	195	737	890	.408

NEW ENGLAND WHALERS

		AT HOME							ON ROAD							OVERALL					
AGAINST	GP	W	L	T	PTS	GF	GA	PCT	GP	W	L	T	PTS	GF	GA	PCT	GP	W	L	T	PTS	GF	GA	PCT
Birmingham	17	13	4	0	26	83	58	.765	18	9	8	1	19	68	74	.528	35	22	12	1	45	151	132	.643
Cincinnati	9	7	2	0	14	36	28	.777	11	3	8	0	6	35	53	.273	20	10	10	0	20	71	81	.500
Edmonton	14	8	4	2	18	55	44	.643	14	5	8	1	11	44	53	.393	28	13	12	3	29	99	96	.518
Houston	15	7	7	1	15	48	52	.500	15	6	8	1	13	47	64	.433	30	13	15	2	28	95	116	.467
Indianapolis	16	4	8	4	12	52	57	.375	12	4	7	1	9	31	38	.375	28	8	15	5	21	83	95	.375
Quebec	18	9	8	1	19	71	68	.528	20	5	14	1	11	52	90	.275	38	14	22	2	30	123	158	.395
Winnipeg	14	6	8	0	12	54	55	.429	14	8	6	0	16	46	59	.571	28	14	14	0	28	100	114	.500
Other Clubs	94	72	18	4	148	380	249	.787	94	34	53	7	75	311	341	.399	188	106	71	11	223	691	590	.593
TOTALS	197	126	59	12	264	779	611	.670	198	74	112	12	160	634	771	.404	395	200	171	24	424	1413	1382	.537

QUEBEC NORDIQUES

AGAINST	AT HOME								ON ROAD								OVERALL							
	GP	W	L	T	PTS	GF	GA	PCT	GP	W	L	T	PTS	GF	GA	PCT	GP	W	L	T	PTS	GF	GA	PCT
Birmingham	25	17	8	0	34	111	90	.680	25	9	15	1	19	92	115	.380	50	26	23	1	53	203	205	.530
Cincinnati	7	5	2	0	10	38	19	.714	7	2	4	1	5	30	38	.357	14	7	6	1	15	68	57	.536
Edmonton	18	11	5	2	24	91	67	.667	18	11	7	0	22	72	69	.611	36	22	12	2	46	163	136	.639
Houston	14	12	2	1	25	65	31	.893	14	5	9	0	10	39	61	.357	28	17	10	1	35	104	92	.625
Indianapolis	10	8	2	0	16	40	29	.800	11	6	5	0	12	47	39	.273	21	14	7	0	28	87	68	.667
New England	20	14	5	1	29	90	52	.725	18	8	9	1	17	68	70	.472	38	22	14	2	46	158	122	.605
Winnipeg	17	9	6	2	20	73	62	.588	17	7	10	0	14	72	79	.412	34	16	16	2	34	145	141	.500
Other Clubs	86	60	22	4	124	412	279	.721	89	30	56	3	63	297	403	.354	175	90	78	7	187	709	682	.534
TOTALS	197	136	51	10	282	920	629	.716	199	78	115	6	162	717	874	.407	396	214	166	16	444	1637	1503	.561

WINNIPEG JETS

AGAINST	AT HOME								ON ROAD								OVERALL							
	GP	W	L	T	PTS	GF	GA	PCT	GP	W	L	T	PTS	GF	GA	PCT	GP	W	L	T	PTS	GF	GA	PCT
Birmingham	17	10	6	1	21	80	61	.618	18	9	9	0	18	61	76	.500	35	19	15	1	39	141	137	.557
Cincinnati	5	3	2	0	6	23	15	.600	5	3	2	0	6	27	22	.600	10	6	4	0	12	50	37	.600
Edmonton	25	19	5	1	39	120	56	.780	24	8	14	2	18	88	87	.375	49	27	19	3	57	208	143	.582
Houston	17	9	7	1	19	60	46	.559	17	4	11	2	10	46	82	.294	34	13	18	3	29	106	128	.426
Indianapolis	8	6	2	0	12	25	11	.750	8	6	2	0	12	34	28	.750	16	12	4	0	24	59	39	.750
New England	14	6	8	0	12	59	46	.429	14	8	6	0	16	55	54	.571	28	14	14	0	28	114	100	.500
Quebec	17	10	7	0	20	79	72	.588	17	6	9	2	14	62	73	.412	34	16	16	2	34	141	145	.500
Other Clubs	94	71	18	5	147	428	260	.782	95	35	56	4	74	335	394	.389	189	106	74	9	221	763	654	.585
TOTALS	197	134	55	8	276	874	567	.701	198	79	109	10	168	708	816	.424	395	213	164	18	444	1582	1383	.562

PENALTY SHOTS

DATE	SHOOTER	DEFENDING GOALIE	PER	TIME	RESULT
1972-73 Season					
Oct 11 72	Billy Hicke	Les Binkley	1	16:37	SCORED
Nov 29 72	Ron Ward	Al Smith	1	5:24	failed
Jan 16 73	Renald Leclerc	Gilles Gratton	3	8:17	SCORED
Mar 25 73	Renald Leclerc	Jack Norris	3	6:15	SCORED
1973-74 Season					
Oct 11 73	Andre LaCroix	Cam Newton	3	18:28	failed
Oct 19 73	Denis Meloche	Jack Norris	3	15:19	failed
Oct 25 73	Andre LaCroix	Al Smith	2	8:57	failed
Nov 3 73	Ron Buchanan	Andre Gill	2	7:46	failed
Nov 22 73	Wayne Connelly	Al Smith	2	10:34	failed
Nov 23 73	Marc Tardif	Jack Norris	3	18:12	failed
Dec 22 73	Gary Veneruzzo	Don McLeod	3	15:08	failed
Dec 29 73	Andre LaCroix	Gerry Cheevers	1	19:09	failed
Mar 1 74	Brian Carlin	Don McLeod	3	19:50	SCORED
Mar 10 74	Ron Garwasiuk	Mike Curran	2	19:38	failed
Mar 14 74	Tom Martin	Cam Newton	2	3:39	failed
Mar 31 74	Brian Morenz	Gerry Cheevers	3	12:22	failed
Apr 1 74	Frank Hughes	Al Smith	2	7:10	failed
1974-75 Season					
Oct 24 74	Wayne Connelly	Andy Brown	1	11:44	failed
Nov 12 74	Gary MacGregor	Joe Junkin	1	10:19	failed
Dec 4 74	Eddie Joyal	Don McLeod	2	6:45	SCORED
Dec 26 74	Wayne Connelly	Jacques Plante	1	7:44	failed
Jan 4 75	Danny Lawson	Al Smith	3	19:42	SCORED
Jan 5 75	Bobby Leduc	Bob Whidden	1	9:49	failed
Jan 28 75	Norm Ferguson	Joe Daley	3	12:46	failed
Feb 11 75	Rejean Houle	Ernie Wakely	2	8:30	SCORED
Mar 1 75	Bob Mowat	Andy Brown	2	19:36	SCORED
Mar 12 75	Jim Harrison	Paul Hoganson	2	5:34	failed
1975-76 Season					
Oct 10 75	Kevin Devine	Gary Kurt	2	6:01	failed
Oct 28 75	Serge Bernier	Mario Vien	1	13:45	SCORED
Feb 6 76	Mark Napier	Joe Daley	3	13:43	SCORED
Feb 18 76	Al McDonough	Don McLeod	3	2:48	failed
Feb 18 76	Danny Gruen	Don McLeod	3	11:47	failed
Mar 2 76	Rick Morris	Don McLeod	1	18:33	SCORED
Mar 20 76	Chris Bordeleau	Don McLeod	1	8:46	failed
Mar 20 76	Rejean Houle	Don McLeod	1	10:21	failed
Mar 30 76	Florent Fortier	Chris Worthy	3	14:46	failed
1976-77 Season					
Oct 17 76	Danny Gruen	Wayne Wood	2	6:49	failed
Nov 11 76	Danny Lawson	Curt Larsson	2	14:30	failed
Dec 17 76	Robbie Ftorek	Ken Broderick	1	17:53	failed
Dec 26 76	Mark Napier	Wayne Rutledge	3	17:44	SCORED
Jan 20 77	Frank Hughes	Paul Hoganson	3	15:56	failed
Feb 18 77	Bruce Greig	Norm LaPointe	2	16:46	SCORED

Five Season Totals: 42 Attempts, 13 Scores, .310 Success Ratio

CAREER HAT TRICKS

Listed are eighty-one players who have scored 3 or more goals in a single game at least two times, or who have scored 4 or more goals in a single game at least one time, in their WHA careers.

Player	Hat Tricks	3 Goal Games	4 Goal Games	5 Goal Games	Player	Hat Tricks	3 Goal Games	4 Goal Games	5 Goal Games
Bobby Hull	17	14	3	0	Chris Bordeleau	2	1	1	0
Real Cloutier	14	12	1	1	Ron Buchanan	2	1	1	0
Danny Lawson	12	9	3	0	Rick Dudley	2	1	1	0
Anders Hedberg	9	5	4	0	Tom Gilmore	2	1	1	0
Marc Tardif	8	6	2	0	Pat Hickey	2	1	1	0
Ron Ward	7	5	0	2	Tim Sheehy	2	1	1	0
Mike Walton	7	5	2	0	Blaine Stoughton	2	1	1	0
Rejean Houle	7	6	1	0	Ralph Backstrom	2	2	0	0
Frank Hughes	7	6	1	0	Serge Bernier	2	2	0	0
Tom Simpson	6	3	3	0	Terry Caffery	2	2	0	0
Mark Howe	6	6	0	0	Bryan Campbell	2	2	0	0
Gene Peacosh	6	6	0	0	Wayne Carleton	2	2	0	0
Tom Webster	6	6	0	0	Alain Caron	2	2	0	0
Andre LaCroix	5	4	1	0	Ron Chipperfield	2	2	0	0
Larry Lund	5	5	0	0	Bill Flett	2	2	0	0
Larry Pleau	5	5	0	0	Pierre Guite	2	2	0	0
Wayne Connelly	4	3	0	1	Murray Hall	2	2	0	0
Vaclav Nedomansky	4	3	0	1	Jim Harrison	2	2	0	0
Rick Sentes	4	3	1	0	Paul Henderson	2	2	0	0
Gary Veneruzzo	4	3	1	0	Don Herriman	2	2	0	0
Mike Antonovich	4	4	0	0	Fran Huck	2	2	0	0
Robbie Ftorek	4	4	0	0	Al Karlander	2	2	0	0
Rich Leduc	4	4	0	0	Veli Pekka Ketola	2	2	0	0
John McKenzie	4	4	0	0	JP LeBlanc	2	2	0	0
Wayne Rivers	4	4	0	0	Willy Lindstrom	2	2	0	0
Claude St. Sauveur	4	4	0	0	Blair MacDonald	2	2	0	0
Ron Climie	3	2	0	1	Gary MacGregor	2	2	0	0
Gordie Howe	3	1	2	0	Peter Marsh	2	2	0	0
Tom Martin	3	2	1	0	Michel Parizeau	2	2	0	0
Brian McDonald	3	2	1	0	Rusty Patenaude	2	2	0	0
George Morrison	3	2	1	0	Jan Popiel	2	2	0	0
Don Borgeson	3	3	0	0	Francois Rochon	2	2	0	0
Michel Cormier	3	3	0	0	Peter Sullivan	2	2	0	0
Del Hall	3	3	0	0	Ted Taylor	2	2	0	0
Gord Labossiere	3	3	0	0	Alton White	2	2	0	0
Frank Mahovlich	3	3	0	0	Wayne Dillon	1	0	1	0
Murray Myers	3	3	0	0	John French	1	0	1	0
Mark Napier	3	3	0	0	Jeff Jacques	1	0	1	0
Ulf Nilsson	3	3	0	0	Perry Miller	1	0	1	0
Rosaire Paiement	3	3	0	0	Terry Ruskowski	1	0	1	0
Andre Hinse	2	1	0	1					

Sixty-one additional players have scored 3 goals in a single game one time in their WHA careers.

CAREER LEADERS

POINTS SCORED

	PLAYER	77-78 TEAM	SP	GP	G	A	PTS	AVG/GP	AVG/SP
1.	Andre LaCroix	Houston	5	395	183	414	597	1.51	119.4
2.	Bobby Hull	Winnipeg	5	330	255	261	516	1.56	103.2
3.	Chris Bordeleau	Quebec	5	370	165	291	456	1.23	91.2
4.	Danny Lawson		5	392	218	204	422	1.08	84.4
5.	Marc Tardif	Quebec	4	294	210	206	416	1.42	104.0
6.	Serge Bernier	Quebec	4	294	168	238	406	1.38	101.5
7.	Tom Webster	New England	5	332	205	201	406	1.22	81.2
8.	Larry Lund	Houston	5	383	140	260	400	1.04	80.0
9.	Ron Ward		5	338	170	210	380	1.12	76.0
10.	Gordie Howe	New England	4	285	121	248	369	1.30	92.3
11.	Ulf Nilsson	Winnipeg	3	227	103	255	358	1.58	119.3
12.	Bryan Campbell	Edmonton	5	380	116	240	356	.94	71.2
13.	Gavin Kirk		5	392	116	238	354	.90	70.8
14.	Frank Hughes	Houston	5	380	170	178	348	.92	69.6
15.	JC Tremblay	Quebec	5	345	55	283	338	.98	67.6

GOALS SCORED

	PLAYER	77-78 TEAM	SP	GP	G	AVG/GP	AVG/SP
1.	Bobby Hull	Winnipeg	5	330	255	.773	51.0
2.	Danny Lawson		5	392	218	.556	43.6
3.	Marc Tardif	Quebec	4	294	210	.714	52.5
4.	Tom Webster	New England	5	332	205	.617	41.0
5.	Andre LaCroix	Houston	5	395	183	.463	36.6
6.	Anders Hedberg	Winnipeg	3	209	173	.828	57.7
7.	Tim Sheehy	Birmingham	5	395	171	.433	34.2
8.	Ron Ward		5	338	170	.503	34.0
9.	Frank Hughes	Houston	5	380	170	.447	34.0
10.	Serge Bernier	Quebec	4	294	168	.571	42.0
11.	Wayne Connelly		5	369	167	.453	33.4
12.	Gene Peacosh		5	364	165	.453	33.0
13.	Chris Bordeleau	Quebec	5	370	165	.446	33.0
14.	Wayne Rivers		5	357	158	.443	31.6
15.	Norm Ferguson	Edmonton	5	365	155	.425	31.0

ASSISTS SCORED

	PLAYER	77-78 TEAM	SP	GP	A	AVG/GP	AVG/SP
1.	Andre LaCroix	Houston	5	395	414	1.048	82.8
2.	Chris Bordeleau	Quebec	5	370	291	.786	58.2
3.	JC Tremblay	Quebec	5	345	283	.820	56.6
4.	Bobby Hull	Winnipeg	5	330	261	.791	52.2
5.	Larry Lund	Houston	5	383	260	.679	52.0
6.	Ulf Nilsson	Winnipeg	3	227	255	1.123	85.0
7.	Gordie Howe	New England	4	285	248	.870	62.0
8.	Bryan Campbell	Edmonton	5	380	240	.632	48.0
9.	Serge Bernier	Quebec	4	294	238	.810	59.5
10.	Gavin Kirk		5	392	238	.607	47.6
11.	Poul Popiel	Houston	5	387	234	.605	46.8
12.	John McKenzie	New England	5	322	223	.693	44.6
13.	Jim Dorey	Quebec	5	373	221	.592	44.2
14.	Ron Plumb	Cincinnati	5	390	215	.551	43.0
15.	Michel Parizeau	Indianapolis	5	387	207	.535	41.4

PENALTY MINUTES ASSESSED

PLAYER	77-78 TEAM	SP	GP	PIM	AVG/GP	AVG/SP
1. Pierre Roy		5	315	858	2.72	171.6
2. Gord Gallant		4	273	849	3.11	212.3
3. John Schella	Houston	5	322	719	2.23	143.8
4. Cam Connor	Houston	3	206	687	3.34	229.0
5. Steve Sutherland	Quebec	5	304	672	2.21	134.4
6. Paul Shmyr	Edmonton	5	351	641	1.83	128.2
7. Doug Barrie		5	350	620	1.77	124.0
8. Ron Busniuk	Edmonton	3	227	605	2.67	201.7
9. Jim Dorey	Quebec	5	373	576	1.54	115.2
10. John Arbour		5	334	568	1.70	113.6
11. Ted Taylor		5	367	554	1.51	110.8
12. Rick Morris	Edmonton	5	383	520	1.36	104.0
13. John Hughes	Houston	3	230	518	2.25	172.7
14. Rosaire Paiement	Indianapolis	5	394	511	1.30	102.2
15. Rick Ley	New England	5	333	496	1.49	99.2

GAMES PLAYED

PLAYER	77-78 TEAM	GP
1. Tim Sheehy	Birmingham	395
Andre LaCroix	Houston	395
3. Rosaire Paiement	Indianapolis	394
4. Gavin Kirk		392
Danny Lawson		392
6. Ron Plumb	Cincinnati	390
7. Poul Popiel	Houston	387
8. Larry Pleau	New England	386
9. Rick Morris	Edmonton	385
10. Larry Lund	Houston	383
Jim Niekamp		383
12. Frank Hughes	Houston	381
13. Bryan Campbell	Edmonton	380
14. Jim Dorey	Quebec	373
15. Chris Bordeleau	Quebec	370

GAMES PLAYED / GOALTENDER

PLAYER	77-78 TEAM	GP
1. Don McLeod	Quebec	306
2. Joe Daley	Winnipeg	248
3. Richard Brodeur	Quebec	227
4. Ernie Wakely	Cincinnati	240
5. John Garrett	Birmingham	224
6. Gerry Cheevers		191
Jack Norris		191
8. Gary Kurt		176
9. Al Smith	New England	165
10. Wayne Rutledge	Houston	164

GOALS AGAINST AVERAGE
(minimum 70 games played)

PLAYER	77-78 TEAM	GAA	W	L	T	SV%	SO
1. Ron Grahame		2.99	102	37	3	.900	12
2. Michel Dion	Cincinnati	3.10	31	35	4	.899	1
3. Gerry Cheevers		3.12	99	78	9	.905	14
4. Wayne Rutledge	Houston	3.16	90	65	7	.896	6
5. Jack Norris		3.17	86	82	12	.897	5
6. Ernie Wakely	Cincinnati	3.21	121	97	16	.896	14
7. Al Smith	New England	3.25	94	61	7	.892	7
8. Don McLeod	Quebec	3.30	139	129	14	.887	9
9. Joe Daley	Winnipeg	3.30	139	91	9	.892	11
10. John Garrett	Birmingham	3.44	104	103	10	.901	10

HEDBERG SCORES 51 GOALS IN 47 GAMES, ESTABLISHES ALL-TIME HOCKEY RECORD

Anders Hedberg has authored a long list of records and accomplishments in three seasons of World Hockey Association play. On February 6, 1977, he completed a record that may etch him indelible in the annals of hockey history.

On that night, the Swedish right winger scored goals 49, 50, and 51 to lead Winnipeg Jets to a 6-4 win over Calgary Cowboys. The game was the Jets' 49th of the 1976-77 season, and it was only the 47th that Hedberg had played in.

Hedberg therefore broke the record that had been established 32 seasons previous by the immortal Maurice "Rocket" Richard, and matched just two seasons previous by the equally immortal Bobby Hull.

In 1944-45, Richard became the first player to score 50 goals in a season by netting number 50 in the final game of what was then a 50 game NHL season. In 1974-75, Hull scored a dramatic hat trick for goals number 48, 49, and 50 in the Jets' 50th game of the season. Hull went on to score a season-record 77 goals.

Hedberg's onslaught was even more dramatic. The 25 year old Hedberg was playing with a cracked rib, but had scored eight goals in his previous two games to literally come from nowhere in his bid for immortality.

After 43 games, Hedberg had 40 goals and a rib injury that was supposed to sideline him indefinitely. He missed but two games. In his first game upon returning to action, he was "held" to one assist. Then the record-setting spree began.

In a game at Edmonton, the "Swedish Express" scored four times to bring his season goal total to 44. Returning home to the Winnipeg Arena against San Diego, he scored four more, numbers 45, 46, 47, and 48.

Stepping onto the ice for the Calgary game, Hedberg said, "I got a very special feeling from the fans — I knew that they expected something special from me."

In the second period, with the score tied 2-2, and with Calgary defenseman John Miszuk serving a double minor, Hedberg started working on "something special." At 13:42, Hedberg carried the puck down the boards, behind the net, and jammed it home between the post and Goaltender Gary Bromley's stick side. Goal Number 49.

Less than 40 seconds later, however, it appeared the dream might be over. Still skating on the power play, Hedberg attempted to vault the Calgary defense, but instead fell heavily to the ice.

He was removed to the Jets' dressing room where he was examined by the team doctor. The doctor's verdict: stretched knee ligaments.

The Jets went to the dressing room for the second intermission with a 4-2 lead. When they returned to the ice for Period Three, Hedberg did not return with them.

Hedberg refused to surrender. His knee heavily taped, he returned to the Jets' bench shortly into the period. Even Hedberg, though, doubted his own chances. "After I was hurt I did not think I could get the record, I knew I couldn't skate as well as I should."

But get the record he did. Midway in the period, Hedberg took the ice on a line change, just seconds later gathered in a pass from Bill Lesuk, fired towards Bromley, and scored number 50. At 11:21 of Period Three, the third year pro had completed a feat that no major league player had ever before accomplished.

He added lustre to his mark by scoring still another goal, an empty-netter with one second remaining on a pass from linemate and countryman Ulf Nilsson.

Anders Hedberg had scored 11 goals in three consecutive games, a record. He had added his third four goal game of the season, a record. He had scored fifty goals in each of his first three major league seasons, a record. And he had scored 51 goals in 49 or 47 games, pick the one you like. They are both records.

WHA
REGULAR SEASON RECORDS

TEAM — SINGLE SEASON

MOST POINTS:
   106   Houston, 1974-75 and 1975-76 and 1976-77
         Winnipeg, 1975-76

FEWEST POINTS:
   39   Indianapolis, 1974-75

MOST WINS:
   53   Houston, 1974-75 and 1975-76

FEWEST WINS:
   18   Indianapolis, 1974-75

MOST LOSSES:
   57   Indianapolis, 1974-75

FEWEST LOSSES:
   24   Houston, 1976-77

MOST TIES:
   9   Cleveland, 1973-74

MOST CONSECUTIVE NON-TIE GAMES, CONSECUTIVE SEASONS:
   187   Houston, Feb 10 74 - Oct 19 76

MOST CONSECUTIVE TIE GAMES:
   3   Indianapolis, Mar 18 76 - Mar 23 76

MOST CONSECUTIVE OVERTIME GAMES:
   4   Edmonton, Feb 28 73 - Mar 10 73 (two wins, two losses)
         Chicago, Mar 5 73 - Mar 10 73 (one win, two losses, one tie)
         Indianapolis, Mar 18 76 - Mar 25 76 (one win, three ties)

MOST CONSECUTIVE GAMES UNDEFEATED:
   11   Edmonton, Oct 21 73 - Nov 16 73 (eleven wins)
         Minnesota, Feb 13 74 - Mar 10 74 (ten wins, one tie)

MOST CONSECUTIVE GAMES, NO WINS:
   17   Toronto, Jan 22 76 - Feb 29 76 (fifteen losses, two ties)

MOST CONSECUTIVE LOSSES:
   13   Indianapolis, Nov 13 74 - Dec 5 74

MOST GOALS SCORED:
   371   Quebec, 1975-76

MOST GOALS ALLOWED:
   398   Toronto, 1975-76

FEWEST GOALS SCORED:
   205   Baltimore, 1974-75

FEWEST GOALS ALLOWED:
   219   Houston, 1973-74

MOST SCORING POINTS:
   999   Quebec, 1975-76 (371 goals, 628 assists)

FEWEST SCORING POINTS:
   540   Baltimore, 1974-75 (205 goals, 335 assists)

MOST CONSECUTIVE GOALS SCORED:
   17   Cincinnati, Dec 10 76 (3) - Dec 12 76 (8) -
         Dec 15 76 (5) - Dec 19 76 (1)

MOST GOALS SCORED, TWO CONSECUTIVE GAMES:
   21   Winnipeg, Nov 1 74 (10) - Nov 3 74 (11)

43

MOST GOALS ALLOWED, TWO CONSECUTIVE GAMES:
  21   Quebec, Dec 21 75 (11) - Dec 23 75 (10)
MOST SHUTOUTS:
  7   Houston, 1976-77
FEWEST SHUTOUTS:
  0   Ottawa, 1972-73
      Quebec, 1974-75
      Phoenix, 1976-77
LONGEST SHUTOUT SEQUENCE:
  228:10   Winnipeg, Oct 24 75 - Nov 2 75
LONGEST SEQUENCE, ONE TEAM SHUTOUT:
  190:21   Calgary, Mar 18 77 - Mar 22 77
MOST GAMES ONE TEAM SHUTOUT:
  8   Los Angeles, 1973-74
      Indianapolis, 1974-75
MOST CONSECUTIVE GAMES NOT SHUTOUT, CONSECUTIVE SEASONS:
  200   Minnesota, Feb 9 73 - Dec 12 75
MOST PENALTY MINUTES:
  1654   Quebec, 1975-76
FEWEST PENALTY MINUTES:
  673   Winnipeg, 1973-74
MOST POWER PLAY GOALS SCORED:
  90   Winnipeg, 1976-77
MOST GOALS ALLOWED WHILE ON POWER PLAY:
  16   Winnipeg, 1974-75
MOST SHORTHANDED GOALS SCORED:
  20   Minnesota, 1973-74
MOST GOALS ALLOWED WHILE SHORTHANDED:
  89   Phoenix, 1975-76
MOST 100 POINT SCORERS:
  5   Quebec, 1975-76
MOST 60 GOAL SCORERS:
  2   Quebec, 1975-76
MOST 50 GOAL SCORERS:
  3   Quebec, 1975-76
MOST 40 GOAL SCORERS:
  4   San Diego, 1974-75
      Cincinnati, 1976-77
      Quebec, 1976-77
MOST 30 GOAL SCORERS:
  6   Houston, 1973-74
MOST 20 GOAL SCORERS:
  10   Houston, 1974-75
MOST HAT TRICKS:
  14   Quebec, 1976-77
MOST GOALS SCORED, ONE TEAM:
  12   Minnesota, Jan 27 74 v Winnipeg
       Phoenix, Mar 1 74 v Indianapolis
       Quebec, Dec 26 76 v Winnipeg

MOST GOALS SCORED, BOTH TEAMS:
   19   Toronto 11, at Denver 8, Nov 13 75
         Cleveland 10, at Toronto 9, Nov 30 75

FEWEST GOALS SCORED, BOTH TEAMS:
    0   Cleveland at Chicago, Jan 8 74
         New England at Minnesota, Dec 17 75
         Edmonton at Houston, Dec 3 76

MOST CONSECUTIVE GOALS SCORED:
   11   Winnipeg, Feb 1 77

MOST POINTS SCORED, ONE TEAM:
   34   Minnesota, Jan 27 74

MOST POINTS SCORED, BOTH TEAMS:
   50   Toronto, Denver, Nov 13 75
         Cleveland, Toronto, Nov 30 75

MOST PENALTIES, ONE TEAM:
MOST PENALTY MINUTES, ONE TEAM:
   26   Phoenix, Feb 7 75 (11 minors, 7 majors, 8 misconducts)
   137

MOST PENALTIES, BOTH TEAMS:
   45   Cleveland (24) and Minnesota (21), Oct 15 75

MOST PENALTY MINUTES, BOTH TEAMS:
   228 Cleveland (117) and Indianapolis (111), Mar 8 75

MOST POWER PLAY GOALS SCORED, ONE TEAM:
    6   Indianapolis, Dec 4 75 v Cincinnati
         Calgary, Mar 9 76 v Quebec
         Winnipeg, Mar 10 76 v Quebec

MOST SHORTHANDED GOALS SCORED, ONE TEAM:
    3   By six teams

MOST POWER PLAY OPPORTUNITIES, ONE TEAM:
   13   Winnipeg, Oct 21 75
         Winnipeg, Mar 10 76
         Winnipeg, Mar 27 77

MOST POWER PLAY OPPORTUNITIES, BOTH TEAMS:
   21   Cincinnati (9) and Indianapolis (12), Dec 4 75

MOST SHOTS ON GOAL, ONE TEAM:
   64   San Diego, Dec 23 75 v Quebec

MOST SHOTS ON GOAL, BOTH TEAMS:
   107 Winnipeg (54) and Michigan (53), Nov 29 74
         San Diego (48) and Toronto (59), Mar 14 75

FEWEST SHOTS ON GOAL, ONE TEAM:
   11   Indianapolis, Dec 18 75 v Phoenix
         Edmonton, Dec 16 76 v San Diego

FEWEST SHOTS ON GOAL, BOTH TEAMS:
   33   Winnipeg (14) and San Diego (19), Oct 17 76

FEWEST SHOTS ON GOAL, WINNING TEAM:
   13   New England, Dec 14 72 v Los Angeles (5-2 win)

MOST SHOTS ON GOAL, LOSING TEAM:
   59   Toronto, Mar 14 75 v San Diego (6-4 loss)

TEAM — SINGLE PERIOD

MOST GOALS SCORED, ONE TEAM:
  8   Toronto, Period 3, Dec 9 73 v Minnesota

MOST GOALS SCORED, BOTH TEAMS:
  9   By five teams

FASTEST TWO GOALS, ONE TEAM:
  :04   New England, Period 3, Dec 16 72 v Philadelphia
         Caffery 2:49, Selby 2:53

FASTEST THREE GOALS, ONE TEAM:
  :32   Chicago, Period 3, Dec 19 72 v Cleveland
         Popiel 18:46, Sicinski 19:02, Liddington 19:18

FASTEST FOUR GOALS, ONE TEAM:
  1:45   Edmonton, Period 3, Jan 30 73 v New York
         Patenaude 10:48, Barrie 11:48, Carlyle 12:00, Harrison 12:33

FASTEST TWO GOALS, BOTH TEAMS:
  :04   Calgary at San Diego, Period 3, Mar 26 77
         Ward (C) 4:22, Rivers (SD) 4:26

FASTEST THREE GOALS, BOTH TEAMS:
  :27   New England at New York, Period 2, Nov 29 72
         French (NE) 12:53, Ward (NY) 13:11, Ward (NY) 13:20

FASTEST FOUR GOALS, BOTH TEAMS:
  1:02   San Diego at Cincinnati, Period 2, Nov 8 75
         Peacosh (SD) 14:50, Devine (SD) 15:14,
         Inkpen (C) 15:32, LaCroix (SD) 15:52

FASTEST FIVE GOALS, BOTH TEAMS:
  3:05   San Diego at Toronto, Period 2, Feb 20 76
         French (SD) 6:55, Nedomansky (T) 7:12, Morenz (SD) 8:22,
         Devine (SD) 8:42, Peacosh (SD) 10:00

MOST PENALTIES, ONE TEAM:
MOST PENALTY MINUTES, ONE TEAM:
  20   Phoenix, Period 3, Feb 7 75 v Minnesota
  111   (8 minors, 5 majors, 7 misconducts)

MOST PENALTIES, BOTH TEAMS:
MOST PENALTY MINUTES BOTH TEAMS:
  32   Cleveland (17,94) at Indianapolis (15,98), Period 2, Mar 8 75
  192

MOST SHOTS ON GOAL, ONE TEAM:
  32   San Diego, Period 1, Dec 23 75 v Quebec

MOST SHOTS ON GOAL, BOTH TEAMS:
  41   Indianapolis (17) at Toronto (24), Period 2, Feb 9 75

FEWEST SHOTS ON GOAL, ONE TEAM:
  0   New York, Period 1, Nov 5 72 v Winnipeg
       Indianapolis, Period 2, Mar 23 76 v San Diego

FEWEST SHOTS ON GOAL, TWO TEAMS:
  7   Cleveland (2) at Los Angeles (5), Period 2, Nov 16 73

INDIVIDUAL — SINGLE SEASON

MOST POINTS:
148   Marc Tardif, 1975-76
MOST GOALS:
77   Bobby Hull, 1974-75
MOST ASSISTS:
106   Andre LaCroix, 1974-75
MOST POINTS BY A CENTER:
147   Andre LaCroix, 1974-75
MOST GOALS BY A CENTER:
56   Vaclav Nedomansky, 1975-76
MOST ASSISTS BY A CENTER:
106   Andre LaCroix, 1974-75
MOST POINTS BY A RIGHT WING:
141   Real Cloutier, 1976-77
MOST GOALS BY A RIGHT WING:
70   Anders Hedberg, 1976-77
MOST ASSISTS BY A RIGHT WING:
75   Real Cloutier, 1976-77
MOST POINTS BY A LEFT WING:
148   Marc Tardif, 1975-76
MOST GOALS BY A LEFT WING:
77   Bobby Hull, 1974-75
MOST ASSISTS BY A LEFT WING:
77   Marc Tardif, 1975-76
MOST POINTS BY A DEFENSEMAN:
89   JC Tremblay, 1972-73 and 1975-76
MOST GOALS BY A DEFENSEMAN:
24   Kevin Morrison, 1973-74
MOST ASSISTS BY A DEFENSEMAN:
77   JC Tremblay, 1975-76
MOST ASSISTS BY A GOALTENDER:
13   Don McLeod, 1975-76
MOST POINTS BY A ROOKIE:
120   Ulf Nilsson, 1974-75
MOST GOALS BY A ROOKIE:
53   Anders Hedberg, 1974-75
MOST ASSISTS BY A ROOKIE:
94   Ulf Nilsson, 1974-75
MOST PENALTY MINUTES:
365   Curt Brackenbury, 1975-76
       (45 minors, 29 majors, 13 misconducts)
MOST PENALTY MINUTES BY A CENTER:
157   Michel Rouleau, 1972-73
MOST PENALTY MINUTES BY A RIGHT WING:
365   Curt Brackenbury, 1975-76
MOST PENALTY MINUTES BY A LEFT WING:
297   Gord Gallant, 1975-76
MOST PENALTY MINUTES BY A DEFENSEMAN:
351   Kim Clackson, 1975-76

MOST PENALTY MINUTES BY A GOALTENDER:
   75   Andy Brown, 1974-75
MOST PENALTY MINUTES BY A ROOKIE:
   351   Kim Clackson, 1975-76
MOST POWER PLAY GOALS:
   27   Bobby Hull, 1974-75
MOST SHORTHANDED GOALS:
   9   Mike Walton, 1973-74
FEWEST GAMES, START OF SEASON, 20 GOALS SCORED:
   18   Bobby Hull, 1974-75
          Real Cloutier, 1976-77
FEWEST GAMES, START OF SEASON, 30 GOALS SCORED:
   29   Bobby Hull, 1974-75
FEWEST GAMES, START OF SEASON, 40 GOALS SCORED:
   41   Bobby Hull, 1974-75
FEWEST GAMES, START OF SEASON, 50 GOALS SCORED:
   47   Anders Hedberg, 1976-77
FEWEST GAMES, START OF SEASON, 60 GOALS SCORED:
   57   Anders Hedberg, 1976-77

GOALTENDER — SINGLE SEASON

MOST GAMES PLAYED:
   69   Richard Brodeur, 1975-76
MOST MINUTES PLAYED:
   4124 Don McLeod, 1974-75
MOST CONSECUTIVE GAMES PLAYED:
   41   Don McLeod, Dec 26 74 - Mar 25 75
MOST SHUTOUTS:
   5   Gerry Cheevers, 1972-73
       Joe Daley, 1975-76
MOST SHUTOUTS ON ROAD:
   3   Ron Grahame, 1974-75
MOST CONSECUTIVE GAMES WON:
MOST CONSECUTIVE GAMES UNDEFEATED:
   16   Ron Grahame, Jan 16 77 - Apr 9 77
MOST CONSECUTIVE GAMES LOST:
   12   George Gardner, Nov 25 73 - Mar 21 75
MOST CONSECUTIVE GAMES WINLESS:
   16   George Gardner, Nov 25 73 - Apr 4 75
          Ed Dyck, Nov 15 74 - Mar 13 75
LONGEST CONSECUTIVE SHUTOUT SEQUENCE:
228:10 Joe Daley, Oct 24 75 - Nov 2 75
         (includes two complete shutouts)

INDIVIDUAL — SINGLE GAME

MOST POINTS:
   10   Jim Harrison, Jan 30 73
        (3 goals, 7 assists)

MOST GOALS:
   5   Ron Ward, Jan 4 73
        Ron Climie, Nov 6 73
        Andre Hinse, Jan 15 75
        Vaclav Nedomansky, Nov 13 75
        Wayne Connelly, Nov 27 75
        Ron Ward, Nov 30 75
        Real Cloutier, Oct 26 76

MOST ASSISTS:
   7   Jim Harrison, Jan 30 73
        Jim Harrison, Nov 30 75

MOST POINTS BY A RIGHT WING:
   7   Danny Lawson, Jan 13 73
        (3 goals, 4 assists)
        Ron Ward, Nov 30 75
        (5 goals, 2 assists)

MOST GOALS BY A RIGHT WING:
   5   Ron Climie, Nov 6 73
        Ron Ward, Nov 30 75
        Real Cloutier, Oct 26 76

MOST ASSISTS BY A RIGHT WING:
   5   Wayne Rivers, Jan 4 74
        Danny Lawson, Mar 9 73
        John McKenzie, Feb 5 74
        John French, Mar 27 74

MOST POINTS BY A CENTER:
   10   Jim Harrison, Jan 30 73

MOST GOALS BY A CENTER:
   5   Ron Ward, Jan 4 73
        Vaclav Nedomansky, Nov 13 75

MOST ASSISTS BY A CENTER:
   7   Jim Harrison, Jan 30 73
        Jim Harrison, Nov 30 75

MOST POINTS BY A LEFT WING:
   6   Bobby Hull, Feb 15 73
        Marc Tardif, Oct 14 75

MOST GOALS BY A LEFT WING:
   5   Andre Hinse, Jan 15 75

MOST ASSISTS BY A LEFT WING:
   4   By eight players

MOST POINTS BY A DEFENSEMAN:
   6   Doug Barrie, Jan 30 73
        Pat Stapleton, Dec 4 75

MOST GOALS BY A DEFENSEMAN:
   3   Kevin Morrison, Mar 18 74
        Perry Miller, Feb 1 77

MOST ASSISTS BY A DEFENSEMAN:
    6   Pat Stapleton, Dec 4 75

MOST ASSISTS BY A GOALTENDER:
    3   Gary Kurt, Jan 20 77

MOST SHOTS ON GOAL:
    18   Bobby Hull, Apr 5 75

FASTEST TWO GOALS:
    :06   Gary Veneruzzo, Period 3, Dec 10 72
    Goals at 15:24 and 15:30

FASTEST THREE GOALS:
    :43   George Morrison, Period 2, Apr 3 74
    Goals at 15:42, 15:56, and 16:25

FASTEST GOAL, START OF GAME:
    :05   Russ Walker, Feb 19 75

FASTEST TWO GOALS, START OF GAME:
    1:24   Doug Kerslake, Mar 18 75

FASTEST GOAL, START OF PERIOD TWO:
    :05   Skip Krake, Dec 7 74

FASTEST GOAL, START OF PERIOD THREE:
    :07   Wayne Connelly, Nov 30 72

FASTEST OVERTIME GOAL:
    :04   John French, Nov 26 73

MOST PENALTIES:
    8   Kim Clackson, Nov 30 75
    (4 minors, 3 majors, 1 misconduct)
    Paul Baxter, Nov 2 76
    (6 minors, 1 major, 1 misconduct)
    Wally Weir, Dec 12 76
    (7 minors, 1 major)

MOST PENALTY MINUTES:
    39   Curt Brackenbury, Jan 17 76
    (2 minors, 1 major, 3 misconducts)

ALL-STAR GAME

1978 WHA ALL-STAR GAME
JANUARY 17, 1978, QUEBEC CITY

The World Hockey Association's sixth annual All-Star Game, scheduled for January 17 at Quebec City, will reestablish a traditional All-Star format that has been absent from the major leagues for several seasons.

The defending Avco World Trophy Champions, Quebec Nordiques, will be challenged by the WHA All-Stars, as selected from the seven other League teams. The first twelve members of the All-Stars will again be chosen by a vote of the WHA News Media, while the remainder of the stellar squad will be chosen by All-Star Coach Bill Dineen.

1977 WHA ALL-STAR GAME
JANUARY 18, 1977, HARTFORD
EASTERN DIVISION 4, WESTERN DIVISION 2

LINEUPS:
Western Division
Coach: Bobby Kromm
Goaltenders: Wayne Rutledge, Joe Daley
Defensemen: Thommie Bergman, Paul Shmyr, Kevin Morrison, Barry Wilkins, Poul Popiel, Paul Terbenche
Forwards: Bobby Hull, Ulf Nilsson, Anders Hedberg, Andre LaCroix, Robbie Ftorek, Gordie Howe, Norm Ferguson, Danny Lawson, Cam Connor, Del Hall, Willy Lindstrom, Joe Noris

Eastern Division
Coach: Jacques Demers
Goaltenders: Lou Levasseur, John Garrett
Defensemen: Pat Stapleton, JC Tremblay, Ron Plumb, Gordie Roberts, John Hughes, Thommy Abrahamsson
Forwards: Serge Bernier, Real Cloutier, Marc Tardif, Michel Parizeau, Hugh Harris, Mark Napier, Mike Rogers, Blair MacDonald, George Lyle, Dennis Sobchuk, Rich Leduc, Ralph Backstrom

ALL-STAR GAME RESULTS

1. January 6, 1973 at Quebec   East 6, West 2
2. January 3, 1974 at St. Paul   East 8, West 4
3. January 21, 1975 at Edmonton   West 6, East 4
4. January 13, 1976 at Cleveland   Canada 6, United States 1
5. January 18, 1977 at Hartford   East 4, West 2

ALL-STAR GAME MOST VALUABLE PLAYERS

1977	Lou Levasseur	1975	Rejean Houle
	Willy Lindstrom	1974	Mike Walton
1976	Real Cloutier	1973	Wayne Carleton
	Paul Shmyr		

CAREER ALL-STAR STATISTICS
ALL ACTIVE WHA PLAYERS

SCORING, PENALTY STATISTICS

PLAYER	GP	G	A	PTS	PIM	PLAYER	GP	G	A	PTS	PIM
Bergman, Thommie	2	0	1	1	0	Long, Barry	2	0	0	0	4
Bernier, Serge	4	1	2	3	0	Lund, Larry	2	1	1	2	0
Block, Ken	1	0	1	1	0	Lyle, George	1	1	0	1	0
Bordeleau, Chris	2	0	3	3	0	MacDonald, Blair	1	0	0	0	0
Campbell, Bryan	1	0	0	0	0	Mahovlich, Frank	2	1	0	1	0
Cloutier, Real	2	4	0	4	2	McKenzie, John	1	1	0	1	0
Connor, Cam	1	0	0	0	0	McLeod, Don	2	0	0	0	0
Daley, Joe	2	0	0	0	0	Morrison, Kevin	2	0	0	0	0
Dorey, Jim	3	1	3	4	0	Napier, Mark	1	0	0	0	0
Ferguson, Norm	2	0	0	0	0	Nedomansky, Vaclav	1	0	0	0	2
Ftorek, Robbie	2	0	0	0	0	Nilsson, Ulf	3	1	0	1	0
Garrett, John	2	0	0	0	0	Noris, Joe	1	0	0	0	0
Hall, Del	1	0	0	0	0	Paiement, Rosaire	1	1	1	2	0
Hamilton, Al	2	0	2	2	0	Parizeau, Michel	2	0	0	0	0
Harris, Hugh	2	0	1	1	0	Patenaude, Rusty	1	0	0	0	2
Hedberg, Anders	2	0	1	1	0	Pleau, Larry	3	3	1	4	2
Henderson, Paul	1	0	0	0	0	Plumb, Ron	1	0	0	0	0
Hoganson, Dale	1	0	0	0	0	Popiel, Poul	3	0	0	0	0
Hornung, Larry	2	0	0	0	0	Roberts, Gordie	1	0	0	0	0
Howe, Gordie	4	1	1	2	0	Rogers, Mike	1	0	1	1	0
Howe, Mark	2	1	1	2	0	Rutledge, Wayne	2	0	0	0	0
Howe, Marty	1	0	0	0	0	Schella, John	2	0	1	1	2
Huck, Fran	2	0	0	0	0	Selwood, Brad	2	0	2	2	0
Hughes, Frank	2	0	3	3	0	Shmyr, Paul	4	1	1	2	2
Hughes, John	1	0	1	1	0	Sjoberg, Lars Erik	2	0	1	1	0
Hull, Bobby	5	2	1	3	2	Smith, Al	1	0	0	0	0
Keon, Dave	1	0	0	0	0	Sobchuk, Dennis	1	0	1	1	0
LaCroix, Andre	4	3	5	8	0	Stapleton, Pat	4	0	2	2	0
Larose, Claude	1	0	0	0	0	Tardif, Marc	4	2	5	7	0
Levasseur, Lou	1	0	0	0	0	Terbenche, Paul	2	0	0	0	0
Ley, Rick	4	0	1	1	4	Tremblay, JC	4	1	1	2	0
Lindstrom, Willy	1	1	1	2	0	Wakely, Ernie	2	0	0	0	0
Leduc, Rich	1	0	1	1	0	Webster, Tom	4	0	2	2	2
						Wilkins, Barry	1	0	1	1	0

SCORING:
Period One
1. E Tremblay (Sobchuk, Leduc) 11:17
2. W Shmyr (LaCroix, Lindstrom) 11:58
3. E Tardif (Bernier, Stapleton) 14:56

Period Two
No Scoring

Period Three
3. W Lindstrom (Wilkins) 4:07
4. E Cloutier (Tardif, Hughes) 7:57
6. E Lyle (Abrahamsson, Rogers) 8:35

PENALTIES:
Period One
Cloutier 15:29

Periods Two, Three
No Penalties

SHOTS ON GOAL:
West 18 20 13 - 51
East   7 11   9 - 27

SCORE BY PERIODS:
West 1 0 1 - 2
East 2 0 2 - 4

REFEREE: Ron Harris
LINESMEN: Alan Glaspell, Ron Fournier
ATTENDANCE: 10,337

AVCO WORLD TROPHY

1977 — QUEBEC NORDIQUES
General Manager Maurice Filion,
Coach Marc Boileau,
Captain Marc Tardif, Serge Aubry,
Paul Baxter, Jean Bernier, Serge Bernier,
Chris Bordeleau, Paulin Bordeleau,
Andre Boudrias, Curt Brackenbury,
Richard Brodeur, Real Cloutier,
Charles Constantin, Jim Dorey,
Norm Dube, Bob Fitchner, Pierre Guite,
Ed Humphreys, Francois Lacombe,
Garry Lariviere, Steve Sutherland,
JC Tremblay, Wally Weir.

1976 — WINNIPEG JETS
General Manager Rudy Pilous,
Coach Bobby Kromm,
Captain Lars-Erik Sjoberg,
Duke Asmundson, Norm Beaudin,
Thommie Bergman, Joe Daley, Mike Ford,
Ted Green, Bobby Guindon,
Larry Hillman, Anders Hedberg,
Larry Hornung, Bobby Hull,
Veli Pekka Ketola, Curt Larsson,
Bill Lesuk, Mats Lindh,
Willy Lindstrom, Lyle Moffat, Ulf Nilsson,
Gerry Odrowski, Heikki Riihiranta,
Peter Sullivan.

1975 — HOUSTON AEROS
General Manager-Coach Bill Dineen,
Captain Ted Taylor, Ron Grahame,
Larry Hale, Murray Hall, Andre Hinse,
Gordie Howe, Mark Howe, Marty Howe,
Frank Hughes, Glen Irwin,
Gord Labossiere, Don Larway,
Larry Lund, Poul Popiel, Bill Prentice,
Rich Preston, Terry Ruskowski,
Wayne Rutledge, John Schella,
Jim Sherrit.

1974 — HOUSTON AEROS
General Manager-Coach Bill Dineen,
Captain Ted Taylor, Ron Grahame,
Don Grierson, Larry Hale, Murray Hall,
Andre Hinse, Gordie Howe, Mark Howe,
Marty Howe, Frank Hughes,
Gord Kannegeisser, Gord Labossiere,
Larry Lund, Dunc McCallum,
Don McLeod, Poul Popiel, Bill Prentice,
Wayne Rutledge, John Schella,
Jim Sherrit, Jack Stanfield, Joe Szura,
Gary Williamson.

1973 — NEW ENGLAND WHALERS
General Manager-Coach Jack Kelley,
Captain Ted Green, Kevin Ahearn,
Mike Byers, Terry Caffery, John Cuniff,
Jack Danby, Jim Dorey, Tom Earl,
John French, Paul Hurley,
Bruce Landon, Rick Ley, Larry Pleau,
Brit Selby, Brad Selwood, Tim Sheehy,
Al Smith, Guy Smith, Tom Webster,
Tommy Williams.

53

1977 AVCO WORLD TROPHY GAME RESULTS

FINALS

QUEBEC / WINNIPEG

Date	Away	Score	Home	Score
May 11	Winnipeg	2	QUEBEC	1
May 15	QUEBEC	6	Winnipeg	1
May 18	WINNIPEG	6	Quebec	1
May 20	Quebec	4	WINNIPEG	2
May 22	QUEBEC	8	Winnipeg	3
May 24	WINNIPEG	12	Quebec	3
May 26	QUEBEC	8	Winnipeg	2

(Quebec wins, four games to three)

SEMI-FINALS

QUEBEC / INDIANAPOLIS

April 23	QUEBEC	3	Indianapolis	1
April 25	QUEBEC	8	Indianapolis	3
April 28	Quebec	6	INDIANAPOLIS	5*
April 30	INDIANAPOLIS	2	Quebec	0

(Quebec wins, four games to one)

WINNIPEG / HOUSTON

April 26	WINNIPEG	4	Houston	3
April 28	Houston	7	WINNIPEG	2
April 30	WINNIPEG	4	Houston	3
May 1	WINNIPEG	6	Houston	4
May 3	HOUSTON	3	Winnipeg	2
May 5	WINNIPEG	6	Houston	3

(Winnipeg wins, four games to two)

QUARTER-FINALS

QUEBEC / NEW ENGLAND

April 9	QUEBEC	5	New England	2
April 12	QUEBEC	7	New England	3
April 14	Quebec	4	NEW ENGLAND	3*
April 16	NEW ENGLAND	6	Quebec	4
April 19	QUEBEC	3	New England	0

(Quebec wins, four games to one)

HOUSTON / EDMONTON

April 13	HOUSTON	4	Edmonton	3*
April 15	HOUSTON	6	Edmonton	2
April 17	EDMONTON	7	Houston	2
April 20	Houston	4	EDMONTON	1
April 22	HOUSTON	4	Edmonton	3

(Houston wins, four games to one)

CINCINNATI / INDIANAPOLIS

April 9	Indianapolis	4	CINCINNATI	3*
April 12	Indianapolis	7	CINCINNATI	2
April 14	INDIANAPOLIS	5	Cincinnati	3
April 16	INDIANAPOLIS	3	Cincinnati	1

(Indianapolis wins, four games to none)

WINNIPEG / SAN DIEGO

April 10	WINNIPEG	5	San Diego	1
April 12	WINNIPEG	4	San Diego	1
April 16	SAN DIEGO	5	Winnipeg	4
April 17	SAN DIEGO	6	Winnipeg	4
April 20	WINNIPEG	3	San Diego	0
April 22	SAN DIEGO	3	Winnipeg	1
April 24	WINNIPEG	7	San Diego	3

(Winnipeg wins, four games to three)

CAPITAL LETTERS DENOTE HOME TEAMS
*Games decided in overtime

1976 AVCO WORLD TROPHY
GAME RESULTS

FINALS

WINNIPEG / HOUSTON

May 20 Winnipeg	4	HOUSTON	3
May 23 Winnipeg	5	HOUSTON	4
May 25 WINNIPEG	6	Houston	3
May 27 WINNIPEG	9	Houston	1

(Winnipeg wins, four games to none)

SEMI-FINALS

HOUSTON / NEW ENGLAND

May 5 New England	4	HOUSTON	2
May 7 HOUSTON	5	New England	2
May 9 NEW ENGLAND	4	Houston	1
May 11 Houston	4	NEW ENGLAND	3
May 13 HOUSTON	4	New England	2
May 15 NEW ENGLAND	6	Houston	1
May 16 HOUSTON	2	New England	0

(Houston wins, four games to three)

CALGARY / WINNIPEG

April 23 WINNIPEG	6	Calgary	1
April 25 WINNIPEG	3	Calgary	2
April 28 Winnipeg	6	CALGARY	3
April 30 CALGARY	7	Winnipeg	3
May 2 WINNIPEG	4	Calgary	0

(Winnipeg wins, four games to one)

QUARTER-FINALS

NEW ENGLAND / INDIANAPOLIS

April 16 New England	4	INDIANAPOLIS	1
April 17 INDIANAPOLIS	4	New England	0
April 21 NEW ENGLAND	3	Indianapolis	0
April 23 NEW ENGLAND	2	Indianapolis	1
April 24 INDIANAPOLIS	4	New England	0
April 27 Indianapolis	5	NEW ENGLAND	3
April 29 New England	6	INDIANAPOLIS	0

(New England wins, four games to three)

HOUSTON / SAN DIEGO

April 21 HOUSTON	8	San Diego	6
April 23 HOUSTON	3	San Diego	1
April 25 Houston	8	SAN DIEGO	4
April 27 SAN DIEGO	3	Houston	2
April 28 San Diego	3	HOUSTON	2
April 30 Houston	3	SAN DIEGO	2

(Houston wins, four games to two)

CALGARY / QUEBEC

April 10 Calgary	3	QUEBEC	1
April 11 Calgary	8	QUEBEC	4
April 14 CALGARY	3	Quebec	2
April 16 Quebec	4	CALGARY	3
April 18 Calgary	6	QUEBEC	4

(Calgary wins, four games to one)

WINNIPEG / EDMONTON

April 9 WINNIPEG	7	Edmonton	3
April 11 WINNIPEG	5	Edmonton	4
April 14 Winnipeg	3	EDMONTON	2
April 16 Winnipeg	7	EDMONTON	2

(Winnipeg wins, four games to none)

PRELIMINARY ROUND

NEW ENGLAND / CLEVELAND

April 9 NEW ENGLAND	5	Cleveland	3
April 10 New England	6	CLEVELAND	1
April 11 New England	3	CLEVELAND	2

(New England wins, three games to none)

SAN DIEGO / PHOENIX

April 9 PHOENIX	3	San Diego	1
April 10 SAN DIEGO	4	Phoenix	2
April 13 PHOENIX	6	San Diego	4
April 15 SAN DIEGO	5	Phoenix	1
April 17 San Diego	2	PHOENIX	1

(San Diego wins, three games to two)

CAPITAL LETTERS DENOTE HOME TEAMS
*Games decided in overtime

1975 AVCO WORLD TROPHY GAME RESULTS

FINALS

HOUSTON / QUEBEC

May 3	HOUSTON	6 Quebec	2
May 6	HOUSTON	5 Quebec	3
May 10	Houston	2 QUEBEC	0
May 12	Houston	7 QUEBEC	2

(Houston wins, four games to none)

SEMI-FINALS

QUEBEC / MINNESOTA

April 22	QUEBEC	4 Minnesota	1
April 24	Minnesota	5 QUEBEC	3
April 26	Quebec	6 MINNESOTA	1
April 27	MINNESOTA	4 Quebec	2
April 29	QUEBEC	6 Minnesota	3
May 1	Quebec	4 MINNESOTA	2

(Quebec wins, four games to two)

HOUSTON / SAN DIEGO

April 25	Houston	4 SAN DIEGO	0
April 27	Houston	2 SAN DIEGO	1
April 29	HOUSTON	6 San Diego	0
May 1	HOUSTON	5 San Diego	4*

(Houston wins, four games to none)

QUARTER-FINALS

SAN DIEGO / TORONTO

April 9	SAN DIEGO	5 Toronto	3
April 12	SAN DIEGO	7 Toronto	6
April 14	TORONTO	5 San Diego	2
April 16	TORONTO	6 San Diego	5
April 18	SAN DIEGO	4 Toronto	3
April 21	San Diego	6 TORONTO	4

(San Diego wins, four games to two)

MINNESOTA / NEW ENGLAND

April 9	Minnesota	6 NEW ENGLAND	5
April 11	NEW ENGLAND	3 Minnesota	2*
April 13	MINNESOTA	8 New England	3
April 15	New England	5 MINNESOTA	2
April 18	Minnesota	4 NEW ENGLAND	0
April 19	MINNESOTA	6 New England	1

(Minnesota wins, four games to two)

QUEBEC / PHOENIX

April 8	QUEBEC	5 Phoenix	2
April 10	QUEBEC	6 Phoenix	2
April 12	Quebec	3 PHOENIX	0
April 15	PHOENIX	6 Quebec	5*
April 17	QUEBEC	4 Phoenix	2

(Quebec wins four games to one)

HOUSTON / CLEVELAND

April 10	HOUSTON	8 Cleveland	5
April 12	HOUSTON	5 Cleveland	3
April 13	CLEVELAND	3 Houston	1
April 15	Houston	7 CLEVELAND	2
April 17	HOUSTON	3 Cleveland	1

(Houston wins four games to one)

CAPITAL LETTERS DENOTE HOME TEAMS
*Games decided in overtime

1974 AVCO WORLD TROPHY GAME RESULTS

FINALS

HOUSTON / CHICAGO

May 12	Houston	3	CHICAGO	2
May 15	Houston	6	CHICAGO	1
May 17	HOUSTON	7	Chicago	4
May 19	HOUSTON	6	Chicago	2

(Houston wins, four games to none)

SEMI-FINALS

CHICAGO / TORONTO

April 19	TORONTO	6	Chicago	4
April 22	Chicago	4	TORONTO	3
April 28	CHICAGO	3	Toronto	2
April 30	Toronto	7	CHICAGO	6
May 1	TORONTO	5	Chicago	3
May 4	CHICAGO	9	Toronto	2
May 6	Chicago	5	TORONTO	2

(Chicago wins, four games to three)

HOUSTON / MINNESOTA

April 18	Minnesota	5	HOUSTON	4
April 20	HOUSTON	5	Minnesota	2
April 21	MINNESOTA	4	Houston	1
April 28	Houston	4	MINNESOTA	1
April 29	HOUSTON	9	Minnesota	4
May 1	Houston	3	MINNESOTA	1

(Houston wins, four games to two)

QUARTER-FINALS

CHICAGO / NEW ENGLAND

April 6	NEW ENGLAND	6	Chicago	4
April 7	NEW ENGLAND	4	Chicago	3*
April 9	CHICAGO	8	New England	6
April 10	CHICAGO	2	New England	1*
April 12	Chicago	4	NEW ENGLAND	2
April 14	New England	2	CHICAGO	0
April 16	Chicago	3	NEW ENGLAND	2

(Chicago wins, four games to three)

TORONTO / CLEVELAND

April 7	TORONTO	4	Cleveland	0
April 9	TORONTO	4	Cleveland	3
April 12	Toronto	4	CLEVELAND	2
April 13	CLEVELAND	3	Toronto	2
April 15	TORONTO	4	Cleveland	1

(Toronto wins, four games to one)

MINNESOTA / EDMONTON

April 6	MINNESOTA	2	Edmonton	1
April 7	MINNESOTA	8	Edmonton	5
April 10	Minnesota	6	EDMONTON	2
April 12	EDMONTON	2	Minnesota	1
April 14	MINNESOTA	5	Edmonton	4

(Minnesota wins, four games to one)

HOUSTON / WINNIPEG

April 8	Houston	5	WINNIPEG	2
April 10	Houston	3	WINNIPEG	2
April 13	HOUSTON	10	Winnipeg	1
April 14	HOUSTON	5	Winnipeg	4

(Houston wins, four games to none)

CAPITAL LETTERS DENOTE HOME TEAMS
*Games decided in overtime

1973 AVCO WORLD TROPHY GAME RESULTS

FINALS

NEW ENGLAND / WINNIPEG

April 29	NEW ENGLAND 7	Winnipeg	2
May 2	New England 7	WINNIPEG	4
May 3	WINNIPEG 4	New England	3
May 5	NEW ENGLAND 4	Winnipeg	2
May 6	NEW ENGLAND 9	Winnipeg	6

(New England wins, four games to one)

SEMI-FINALS

NEW ENGLAND / CLEVELAND

April 18	NEW ENGLAND 3	Cleveland	2
April 19	NEW ENGLAND 3	Cleveland	2
April 21	New England 5	CLEVELAND	4
April 22	CLEVELAND 5	New England	2
April 26	NEW ENGLAND 3	Cleveland	1

(New England wins, four games to one)

WINNIPEG / HOUSTON

April 20	WINNIPEG 5	Houston	1
April 22	WINNIPEG 2	Houston	0
April 24	Winnipeg 4	HOUSTON	2
April 26	Winnipeg 3	HOUSTON	0

(Winnipeg wins, four games to none)

QUARTER-FINALS

WINNIPEG / MINNESOTA

April 6	WINNIPEG 3	Minnesota	1
April 8	WINNIPEG 5	Minnesota	2
April 10	MINNESOTA 4	Winnipeg	4
April 11	Winnipeg 3	MINNESOTA	2
April 15	WINNIPEG 8	Minnesota	5

(Winnipeg wins, four games to one)

HOUSTON / LOS ANGELES

April 5	HOUSTON 7	Los Angeles	2
April 7	Los Angeles 4	HOUSTON	2
April 11	LOS ANGELES 3	Houston	2
April 13	Houston 3	LOS ANGELES	2*
April 15	HOUSTON 6	Los Angeles	3
April 17	Houston 3	LOS ANGELES	2

(Houston wins, four games to two)

NEW ENGLAND / OTTAWA

April 7	NEW ENGLAND 6	Ottawa	3
April 8	NEW ENGLAND 4	Ottawa	3*
April 10	OTTAWA 4	New England	2
April 12	New England 7	OTTAWA	3
April 14	NEW ENGLAND 5	Ottawa	4*

(New England wins, four games to one)

CLEVELAND / PHILADELPHIA

April 4	CLEVELAND 3	Philadelphia	2*
April 7	CLEVELAND 7	Philadelphia	1
April 8	Cleveland 3	PHILADELPHIA	1
April 11	Cleveland 6	PHILADELPHIA	2

(Cleveland wins, four games to none)

CAPITAL LETTERS DENOTE HOME TEAMS
*Games decided in overtime

1977 AVCO WORLD TROPHY
COMPLETE GOALTENDING STATISTICS

PLAYER	GAA	GP	MINS	W	L	PCT	SOG	GA	SV%
Cincinnati Stingers									
Norm LaPointe	3.52	4	273	0	3	.000	124	16	.871
Jacques Caron	12.86	1	14	0	1	.000	6	3	.500
Team Totals	3.96	4	288	0	4	.000	130	19	.854
Opponents' Goaltending	1.87	4	289	4	0	1.000	150	9	.940
Edmonton Oilers									
Ken Broderick	3.35	3	719	1	2	.333	82	10	.878
Louis Levasseur	4.51	2	133	0	2	.000	74	10	.865
Team Totals	3.83	5	313	1	4	.200	156	20	.872
Opponents' Goaltending	3.07	5	313	4	1	.800	145	16	.890
Houston Aeros									
Wayne Rutledge	2.00	2	120	2	0	1.000	54	4	.926
Ron Grahame	3.85	9	561	4	5	.444	265	36	.864
Team Totals	3.52	11	681	6	5	.545	319	40	.875
Opponents' Goaltending	3.79	11	680	5	6	.455	338	43	.873
Indianapolis Racers									
Paul Hoganson	2.93	5	348	3	2	.600	179	17	.905
Michel Dion	4.16	4	245	2	2	.500	140	17	.878
Team Totals	3.44	9	593	5	4	.556	319	34	.893
Opponents' Goaltending	3.34	9	592	4	5	.444	273	33	.879
New England Whalers									
Christer Abrahamsson	3.33	2	90	0	1	.000	51	5	.902
Bruce Landon	4.34	3	152	1	2	.333	75	11	.853
Cap Raeder	7.00	1	60	0	1	.000	34	7	.794
Team Totals	4.57	5	302	1	4	.200	610	23	.856
Opponents' Goaltending	2.79	5	301	4	1	.800	137	14	.898
Quebec Nordiques									
Richard Brodeur	3.28	17	1007	12	5	.706	465	55	.882
Serge Aubry	3.33	3	18	—	—	—	465	1	.900
Team Totals	3.28	17	1025	12	5	.706	475	56	.882
Opponents' Goaltending	4.62	17	1026	5	12	.294	530	79	.879
San Diego Mariners									
Ernie Wakely	4.38	3	160	2	1	.667	75	9	.880
Ken Lockett	4.38	5	260	1	3	.250	146	19	.870
Team Totals	4.00	7	420	3	4	.429	221	28	.873
Opponents' Goaltending	2.58	7	418	4	3	.571	192	18	.906
Winnipeg Jets									
Curt Larsson	3.00	1	20	—	—	—	6	1	.833
Joe Daley	3.59	20	1186	11	9	.550	569	71	.875
Team Totals	3.58	20	1206	11	9	.550	575	72	.873
Opponents' Goaltending	3.98	20	1207	9	11	.450	590	80	.864

1977 AVCO WORLD TROPHY
COMPLETE SCORING STATISTICS

CINCINNATI STINGERS

PLAYER	GP	G	A	PTS	SOG	PIM	+/-	+/-%
Rich Leduc	4	1	3	4	13	16	-9	-.25
Claude Larose	4	2	1	3	12	0	-1	+.25
Ron Plumb	4	1	2	3	18	0	-3	+.12
Greg Carroll	4	1	2	3	6	0	+0	+.11
Blaine Stoughton	4	0	3	3	15	2	-5	+.00
Peter Marsh	4	2	0	2	15	0	-4	-.05
Dennis Abgrall	4	2	0	2	8	5	-3	+.02
Dale Smedsmo	2	0	1	1	6	0	+0	+.15
Dennis Sobchuk	3	0	1	1	8	2	-1	-.08
Pierre Roy	3	0	1	1	5	7	-3	+.29
Rick Dudley	4	0	1	1	9	7	-7	-.44
Jamie Hislop	4	0	1	1	5	4	+1	+.17
Jacques Caron	1	0	0	0	0	0	-3	—
Barry Melrose	2	0	0	0	4	2	+0	+.30
Billy Steele	2	0	0	0	1	0	-1	-.17
John Hughes	4	0	0	0	8	8	-5	+.00
Norm LaPointe	4	0	0	0	0	0	-7	—
Barry Legge	4	0	0	0	10	0	-7	-.23
Bryan Maxwell	4	0	0	0	5	29	-3	-.19
STINGER TOTALS	4	9	16	25	150	82	-10	
OPPONENT TOTALS	4	19	34	53	130	66	+10	

EDMONTON OILERS

PLAYER	GP	G	A	PTS	SOG	PIM	+/-	+/-%
Brett Callighen	5	4	1	5	10	7	+1	+.13
Randy Rota	5	3	2	5	11	0	+2	+.26
Bryan Campbell	5	3	1	4	11	0	-4	-.37
Al Hamilton	5	0	4	4	20	4	+1	+.16
Dave Langevin	5	2	1	3	15	9	-6	-.34
Gregg Boddy	4	1	2	3	14	14	+2	+.27
Norm Ullman	5	0	3	3	4	0	-2	-.11
Glen Sather	5	1	1	2	7	2	-3	-.18
Frank Beaton	5	0	2	2	4	21	+2	+.18
Ron Busniuk	5	0	2	2	3	37	-4	-.19
Bill Flett	5	0	2	2	15	2	-3	-.18
Gavin Kirk	5	1	0	1	6	4	+5	+.45
Claude St.Sauveur	5	1	0	1	4	0	-3	-.20
Barry Wilkins	4	0	1	1	0	2	+2	+.25
Wayne Connelly	5	0	1	1	4	0	-4	-.27
Rick Morris	5	0	1	1	11	4	-4	-.25
Bob Russell	1	0	0	0	0	0	+1	+.50
Louis Levasseur	2	0	0	0	0	2	-4	—
Rusty Patenaude	2	0	0	0	3	8	+0	-.05
Glenn Patrick	2	0	0	0	0	0	-1	-.25
Ken Broderick	3	0	0	0	0	0	+1	—
Doug Barrie	4	0	0	0	3	0	+0	+.06
OILER TOTALS	5	16	24	40	145	114	-3	
OPPONENT TOTALS	5	20	34	54	156	136	+3	

INDIANAPOLIS RACERS

PLAYER	GP	G	A	PTS	SOG	PIM	+/-	+/-%
Reg Thomas	9	7	9	16	31	4	+8	+.34
Blair MacDonald	9	7	8	15	30	4	+11	+.45
Michel Parizeau	8	3	6	9	15	8	+7	+.35
Pat Stapleton	9	2	6	8	20	0	-1	-.03
Brian McDonald	9	3	4	7	22	33	-5	-.18
Gene Peacosh	9	3	3	6	24	2	-2	-.07
Darryl Maggs	9	1	4	5	26	4	-3	-.11
Rosaire Paiement	9	0	5	5	15	15	-3	-.11
Mark Lomenda	9	3	1	4	16	17	-3	-.11
Al Karlander	6	2	1	3	9	0	+0	+.10
Bob Sicinski	9	0	3	3	12	4	-5	-.19
Nick Harbaruk	6	1	1	2	3	0	-1	-.07
Renald Leclerc	9	1	1	2	21	4	-7	-.27
Ken Block	9	0	2	2	6	6	+4	+.18
Dave Inkpen	9	0	2	2	3	8	-4	-.15
Paul Hoganson	5	0	1	1	0	0	-5	—
Francois Rochon	5	0	1	1	5	0	-1	-.09
Kim Clackson	9	0	1	1	10	24	+2	+.09
Hugh Harris	2	0	0	0	3	0	-1	-.17
Michel Dion	4	0	0	0	0	0	+4	—
Bryon Baltimore	9	0	0	0	3	5	+1	+.06
RACER TOTALS	9	33	59	92	273	140	-1	
OPPONENT TOTALS	9	34	54	88	319	160	+1	

HOUSTON AEROS

PLAYER	GP	G	A	PTS	SOG	PIM	+/-	+/-%
Terry Ruskowski	11	6	11	17	24	67	+8	+.24
Mark Howe	11	4	10	14	46	2	+3	+.04
Morris Lukowich	11	6	4	10	29	19	+4	+.10
Larry Lund	11	2	8	10	14	17	-2	-.11
Gordie Howe	11	5	3	8	24	11	+1	-.01
Ted Taylor	11	4	4	8	19	28	-2	-.11
Rich Preston	11	3	5	8	37	10	+6	+.17
Cam Connor	11	3	4	7	34	47	-1	-.08
John Tonelli	11	3	4	7	18	12	-1	-.08
Poul Popiel	11	0	7	7	18	10	+4	+.08
Marty Howe	11	3	1	4	31	10	-3	-.17
Al McLeod	10	1	3	4	8	9	-2	-.11
John Schella	6	1	2	3	13	6	+1	+.05
Ron Hansis	8	1	1	2	3	4	+0	-.02
Larry Hale	11	0	2	2	4	6	+5	+.13
Don Larway	3	1	0	1	1	0	+0	-.02
John Gray	6	0	1	1	7	8	-3	-.20
Ron Grahame	9	0	1	1	0	2	+2	—
Dwayne Pentland	2	0	0	0	0	0	+0	.+.00
Wayne Rutledge	2	0	0	0	0	0	+2	—
Steve West	6	0	0	0	8	0	+1	+.05
AERO TOTALS	11	43	71	114	336	273	+4	
OPPONENT TOTALS	11	40	70	110	319	198	-4	

© 2018 WHA HOF / PCMP LLC

NEW ENGLAND WHALERS

PLAYER	GP	G	A	PTS	SOG	PIM	+/-	+/-%
Dave Keon	5	3	1	4	10	0	+4	+.47
Mike Antonovich	5	2	2	4	21	4	+5	+.53
Gordie Roberts	5	2	2	4	9	6	-2	+.03
Rick Ley	5	0	4	4	7	4	+1	+.27
John McKenzie	5	2	1	3	6	8	+4	+.47
Thommy Abrahamsson	5	0	3	3	13	0	-3	-.07
Jack Carlson	5	1	1	2	5	9	-2	-.03
Mike Rogers	5	1	1	2	6	2	-4	-.17
Tom Webster	5	1	1	2	15	0	-5	-.27
George Lyle	5	1	0	1	9	4	-4	-.17
Larry Pleau	5	1	0	1	10	0	-4	-.23
Bruce Landon	3	0	1	1	0	0	-1	—
Bill Butters	5	0	1	1	5	15	-1	+.07
Tom Earl	1	0	0	0	0	0	+0	+.00
Dave Hanson	1	0	0	0	1	0	+0	+.00
Cap Raeder	1	0	0	0	0	0	-2	—
Chris Abrahamsson	2	0	0	0	0	0	-3	—
Doug Roberts	2	0	0	0	2	0	-1	-.25
Garry Swain	2	0	0	0	1	0	+0	+.00
Ralph Backstrom	3	0	0	0	3	0	-1	-.14
Alan Hangsleben	4	0	0	0	2	9	-1	-.08
Steve Carlson	5	0	0	0	9	9	-2	-.07
Brad Selwood	5	0	0	0	3	2	-1	+.03
WHALER TOTALS	5	14	18	32	137	72	-5	
OPPONENT TOTALS	5	23	38	61	160	98	+5	

QUEBEC NORDIQUES

PLAYER	GP	G	A	PTS	SOG	PIM	+/-	+/-%
Serge Bernier	17	14	22	36	67	10	+16	+.13
Real Cloutier	17	14	13	27	63	10	+11	+.04
Paulin Bordeleau	16	12	9	21	51	12	+12	+.07
Norm Dube	14	3	12	15	22	11	+12	+.15
Andre Boudrias	17	3	12	15	18	6	+5	+.00
Marc Tardif	12	4	10	14	32	8	+5	-.04
JC Tremblay	17	2	9	11	25	2	+8	-.03
Garry Lariviere	17	0	10	10	24	10	+13	+.04
Chris Bordeleau	8	4	5	9	22	0	+3	-.03
Curt Brackenbury	17	3	5	8	22	51	-1	-.12
Francois Lacombe	17	4	3	7	27	16	+6	-.06
Bob Fitchner	17	3	3	6	26	16	+1	-.05
Wally Weir	17	1	5	6	16	13	+3	-.04
Pierre Guite	17	5	0	5	21	9	+1	-.04
Steve Sutherland	17	5	0	5	54	16	-4	-.17
Paul Baxter	12	2	2	4	17	35	+1	-.10
Jean Bernier	9	0	2	2	2	0	+3	-.01
Jim Dorey	10	0	2	2	18	28	+10	+.21
Michel Dubois	2	0	1	1	2	0	+1	+.25
Charles Constantin	15	0	1	1	13	15	+4	+.05
Serge Aubry	3	0	0	0	0	0	+0	—
Richard Brodeur	17	0	0	0	0	2	+22	—
NORDIQUE TOTALS	17	79	125	204	430	274	+22	
OPPONENT TOTALS	17	56	86	142	475	209	-22	

SAN DIEGO MARINERS

PLAYER	GP	G	A	PTS	SOG	PIM	+/-	+/-%
Andre Lacroix	7	1	6	7	20	6	-1	+.09
Norm Ferguson	7	2	4	6	21	0	+2	+.21
Ray Addouno	7	3	2	5	8	19	+0	+.10
John French	7	2	3	5	13	2	+1	+.17
Brent Hughes	7	1	4	5	5	0	+5	+.46
Rick Sentes	5	4	0	4	12	12	-3	-.08
Don Burgess	7	2	2	4	9	0	-2	+.02
Kevin Devine	7	1	3	4	12	14	-5	-.13
Kevin Morrison	7	1	3	4	26	8	+6	+.50
Joe Noris	7	2	1	3	28	6	-5	-.13
Wayne Rivers	7	1	1	2	9	2	-4	-.10
Paul Shmyr	7	0	2	2	12	8	-12	-.42
Brad Rhiness	5	0	1	1	2	0	+1	+.08
Bob Falkenberg	2	0	0	0	0	0	+0	+.00
Peter McNamee	2	0	0	0	2	2	-1	-.11
Tony Cassolato	3	0	0	0	1	4	-4	-.36
Ernie Wakely	3	0	0	0	0	0	+0	—
Bob Dobek	5	0	0	0	1	4	-2	-.12
Ken Lockett	5	0	0	0	0	0	-8	—
Larry Hornung	6	0	0	0	4	0	-12	-.54
Randy Legge	7	0	0	0	0	18	-6	-.23
Gary Veneruzzo	7	0	0	0	7	0	-1	-.02
MARINER TOTALS	7	19	32	51	192	107	-8	
OPPONENT TOTALS	7	28	48	76	221	115	+8	

WINNIPEG JETS

PLAYER	GP	G	A	PTS	SOG	PIM	+/-	+/-%
Anders Hedberg	20	13	16	29	63	13	+6	+.09
Ulf Nilsson	20	6	21	27	46	33	+5	+.08
Dan Labraaten	20	7	17	24	36	15	+8	+.13
Bobby Hull	20	13	9	22	79	2	+6	+.10
Peter Sullivan	20	7	12	19	41	2	+5	+.08
Mike Ford	20	3	13	16	42	12	+7	+.11
Willy Lindstrom	20	9	6	15	48	22	+5	+.08
Perry Miller	20	4	6	10	37	27	-6	-.10
Mats Lindh	20	2	7	9	20	2	+0	+.00
Dave Dunn	20	4	4	8	24	23	-7	-.12
Bobby Guindon	20	4	4	8	21	9	-4	-.07
Danny Lawson	13	2	4	6	45	6	-9	-.15
Barry Long	20	1	5	6	34	10	-1	-.02
Lars-Erik Sjoberg	20	0	6	6	10	22	+11	+.18
Ted Green	20	1	3	4	15	12	-4	-.07
Bill Lesuk	18	2	1	3	16	22	-7	-.14
Lyle Moffat	17	2	0	2	11	6	-6	-.18
Fran Huck	7	0	2	2	2	6	-1	-.02
Joe Daley	20	0	1	1	0	0	+1	—
Curt Larsson	1	0	0	0	0	0	+0	—
JET TOTALS	20	80	137	217	590	262	+1	
OPPONENT TOTALS	20	73	118	191	574	342	-1	

AVCO WORLD TROPHY PLAYOFF RECORDS

TEAM — SINGLE SERIES, SINGLE PLAYOFF YEAR

MOST GOALS SCORED, ONE TEAM, FOUR GAME SERIES:
24   Winnipeg, 1976 Finals

MOST GOALS SCORED, BOTH TEAMS, FOUR GAME SERIES:
35   Winnipeg (24) and Houston (11), 1976 Finals

MOST GOALS SCORED, ONE TEAM, FIVE GAME SERIES:
30   New England, 1973 Finals

MOST GOALS SCORED, BOTH TEAMS, FIVE GAME SERIES:
48   New England (30) and Winnipeg (18), 1973 Finals

MOST GOALS SCORED, ONE TEAM, SIX GAME SERIES:
29   San Diego, 1975 Quarter-Finals

MOST GOALS SCORED, BOTH TEAMS, SIX GAME SERIES:
56   San Diego (29) and Toronto (27), 1975 Quarter-Finals

MOST GOALS SCORED, ONE TEAM, SEVEN GAME SERIES:
34   Chicago, 1974 Semi-Finals

MOST GOALS SCORED, BOTH TEAMS, SEVEN GAME SERIES:
61   Chicago (34) and Toronto (27), 1974 Semi-Finals

FEWEST GOALS SCORED, ONE TEAM, FOUR GAME SERIES:
3   Houston, 1973 Semi-Finals

FEWEST GOALS SCORED, BOTH TEAMS, FOUR GAME SERIES:
17   Winnipeg (14) and Houston (3), 1973 Semi-Finals

FEWEST GOALS SCORED, ONE TEAM, FIVE GAME SERIES:
9   Cleveland, 1974 Semi-Finals

FEWEST GOALS SCORED, BOTH TEAMS, FIVE GAME SERIES:
27   Toronto (18) and Cleveland (9), 1974 Semi-Finals

FEWEST GOALS SCORED, ONE TEAM, SIX GAME SERIES:
16   Los Angeles, 1973 Quarter-Finals
     Minnesota, 1975 Semi-Finals

FEWEST GOALS SCORED, BOTH TEAMS, SIX GAME SERIES:
39   Houston (23) and Los Angeles (16), 1973 Quarter-Finals

FEWEST GOALS SCORED, ONE TEAM, SEVEN GAME SERIES:
15   Indianapolis, 1976 Quarter-Finals

FEWEST GOALS SCORED, BOTH TEAMS, SEVEN GAME SERIES:
33   New England (18) and Indianapolis (15), 1976 Quarter-Finals

MOST OVERTIME GAMES, ONE SERIES:
2   New England and Ottawa, 1973 Quarter-Finals
    Chicago and New England, 1974 Quarter-Finals

MOST CONSECUTIVE WINS:
13   Houston, 1975 (10) and 1976 (3)

MOST CONSECUTIVE LOSSES:
7   Edmonton, 1974 (1), 1976 (4), and 1977 (2)

MOST PENALTIES, ONE TEAM, ONE SERIES:
60   Minnesota, 1974 Semi-Finals
     Houston, 1977 Semi-Finals

MOST PENALTY MINUTES, ONE TEAM, ONE SERIES:
213   Minnesota, 1974 Semi-Finals

MOST PENALTIES, BOTH TEAMS, ONE SERIES:
MOST PENALTY MINUTES, BOTH TEAMS, ONE SERIES:
   116   Houston (56,170) and Minnesota (60,213), 1974 Semi-Finals
   383
FEWEST PENALTIES, ONE TEAM, ONE SERIES:
   13   Winnipeg, 1973 Semi-Finals
FEWEST PENALTY MINUTES, ONE TEAM, ONE SERIES:
   29   Winnipeg, 1973 Semi-Finals
FEWEST PENALTIES, BOTH TEAMS, ONE SERIES:
FEWEST PENALTY MINUTES, BOTH TEAMS, ONE SERIES:
   29   Winnipeg (14,41) and Minnesota (15,33), 1973 Quarter-Finals
   74
MOST POWER PLAY OPPORTUNITIES, ONE TEAM, ONE SERIES:
   43   Houston, 1976 Semi-Finals
MOST POWER PLAY OPPORTUNITIES, BOTH TEAMS, ONE SERIES:
   73   Houston (43) and New England (30), 1976 Semi-Finals
MOST POWER PLAY OPPORTUNITIES, ONE TEAM, ONE PLAYOFF YEAR:
   96   Winnipeg, 1977
MOST POWER PLAY GOALS, ONE TEAM, ONE SERIES:
   11   Houston, 1974 Finals
MOST POWER PLAY GOALS, BOTH TEAMS, ONE SERIES:
   16   Houston (8) and New England (8), 1976 Semi-Finals
MOST POWER PLAY GOALS, ONE TEAM, ONE PLAYOFF YEAR:
   19   Winnipeg, 1977
MOST SHORTHANDED GOALS, ONE TEAM, ONE SERIES:
   4   Houston, 1974 Semi-Finals
MOST SHORTHANDED GOALS, ONE TEAM, ONE PLAYOFF YEAR:
   7   Houston, 1974 Semi-Finals

TEAM — SINGLE GAME
MOST GOALS SCORED, ONE TEAM:
   12   Winnipeg, May 24 77
MOST GOALS SCORED, BOTH TEAMS:
   15   New England (9) and Winnipeg (6), May 6 73
          Winnipeg (12) and Quebec (3), May 24 77
LARGEST MARGIN OF VICTORY:
   9   Houston (10) and Winnipeg (1), Apr 13 74
         Winnipeg (12) and Quebec (3), May 24 77
MOST PENALTIES, ONE TEAM:
MOST PENALTY MINUTES, ONE TEAM:
   21   New England, Apr 11 75
   116   Calgary, Apr 11 76
MOST PENALTIES, BOTH TEAMS:
MOST PENALTY MINUTES, BOTH TEAMS:
   41   Minnesota (20,101) and New England (21,116), Apr 11 75
   217
MOST POWER PLAY OPPORTUNITIES, ONE TEAM:
   13   San Diego, Apr 21 76
MOST POWER PLAY OPPORTUNITIES, BOTH TEAMS:
   20   San Diego (13) at Houston (7), Apr 21 76

MOST POWER PLAY GOALS, ONE TEAM:
 5   Houston, May 19 74
MOST POWER PLAY GOALS, BOTH TEAMS:
 6   Chicago (1) at Houston (5), May 19 74
     New England (2) at Minnesota (4), Apr 13 75
     Houston (3) at New England (3), May 11 76

TEAM — SINGLE PERIOD

MOST GOALS SCORED, ONE TEAM:
 6   Calgary, Period 3, Apr 11 76
     Houston, Period 1, Apr 21 76
     Quebec, Period 2, May 26 77
MOST GOALS SCORED, BOTH TEAMS:
 8   Houston (6) and San Diego (2), Period 1, Apr 21 76
FASTEST TWO GOALS, ONE TEAM:
 :03 Calgary, Period 2, Apr 28 76
      Powis 4:08, Tannahill 4:11
FASTEST THREE GOALS, ONE TEAM:
 :55 Cleveland, Period 2, Apr 7 73
      Wiste 5:15, Pinder 5:51, Jarrett 6:10
FASTEST TWO GOALS, BOTH TEAMS:
 :08 Minnesota at Quebec, Period 2, Apr 29 75
      Walton (M) 8:53, Tardif (Q) 9:01
FASTEST THREE GOALS, BOTH TEAMS:
 :52 Winnipeg at Calgary, Period 1, Apr 30 76
      Lawson (C) 3:12, Kirk (C) 3:52, Hedberg (W) 4:04
FASTEST FOUR GOALS, BOTH TEAMS:
 2:18 New England at Chicago, Period 2, Apr 9 74
      Watson (C) 7:35, Blackburn (NE) 8:48, Cunniff (NE) 9:23
      French (NE) 9:53
FASTEST TWO POWER GOALS, ONE TEAM:
 :29 Minnesota, Period 2, Apr 6 74
      Heatley 9:09, Walton 9:38
FASTEST TWO SHORTHANDED GOALS, ONE TEAM:
 :39 Houston, Period 1, Apr 21 76
      Preston 4:52, Preston 5:31
MOST POWER PLAY GOALS, ONE TEAM:
 3   Houston, Period 2, May 19 74
     Minnesota, Period 1, Apr 13 75
MOST POWER PLAY GOALS, BOTH TEAMS:
 4   Los Angeles (2) at Houston (2), Period 1, Apr 15 73
     Quebec (2) at New England (2), Period 1, Apr 16 77
     Minnesota at Houston, Period 2, Apr 20 74
     Connelly (M) 8:53, Tardif

INDIVIDUAL — SINGLE SERIES, SINGLE PLAYOFF YEAR

MOST POINTS, ONE PLAYOFF YEAR:
39   Serge Bernier, 1977

MOST GOALS, ONE PLAYOFF YEAR:
14   Serge Bernier, 1977
     Real Cloutier, 1977

MOST ASSISTS, ONE PLAYOFF YEAR:
22   Serge Bernier, 1977

MOST PENALTY MINUTES, ONE PLAYOFF YEAR:
71   Darryl Maggs, 1974

MOST POINTS BY A DEFENSEMAN: (and)
MOST ASSISTS BY A DEFENSEMAN, ONE PLAYOFF YEAR:
19 points, 16 assists — Jim Dorey, 1973

MOST GOALS, BY A DEFENSEMAN, ONE PLAYOFF YEAR:
5   Chris Evans, 1976

MOST POINTS, FOUR GAME SERIES:
9   Gordie Howe, 1974
    Ulf Nilsson, 1976
    Reg Thomas, 1977

MOST GOALS, FOUR GAME SERIES:
6   Anders Hedberg, 1976

MOST ASSISTS, FOUR GAME SERIES:
9   Gordie Howe, 1974

MOST POINTS, FIVE GAME SERIES:
15   Norm Beaudin, 1973

MOST GOALS, FIVE GAME SERIES:
8   Mark Howe, 1975

MOST ASSISTS, FIVE GAME SERIES:
10   Norm Beaudin, 1973

MOST POINTS, SIX GAME SERIES:
12   Fran Huck, 1975
     Ray Addouno, 1975
     Ulf Nilsson, 1977

MOST GOALS, SIX GAME SERIES:
7   Gene Peacosh, 1975

MOST ASSISTS, SIX GAME SERIES:
10   Fran Huck, 1975
     Ulf Nilsson, 1977

MOST POINTS, SEVEN GAME SERIES:
13   Serge Bernier, 1977

MOST GOALS, SEVEN GAME SERIES:
7   Rosaire Paiement, 1974
    Tom Webster, 1976
    Bobby Hull, 1977

MOST ASSISTS, SEVEN GAME SERIES:
8   Ralph Backstrom, 1974
    Serge Bernier, 1977

MOST POINTS, QUARTER-FINAL SERIES:
15   Norm Beaudin, 1973

MOST GOALS, QUARTER-FINAL SERIES:
8   Mark Howe, 1975

67

MOST ASSISTS, QUARTER-FINAL SERIES:
   10   Norm Beaudin, 1973
         Fran Huck, 1975

MOST POINTS, SEMI-FINAL SERIES:
   12   Tim Sheehy, 1973
         Serge Bernier, 1977
         Ulf Nilsson, 1977

MOST GOALS, SEMI-FINAL SERIES:
    7   Rosaire Paiement, 1974
         Tom Webster, 1976

MOST ASSISTS, SEMI-FINAL SERIES:
   10   Ulf Nilsson, 1977

MOST POINTS, FINAL SERIES:
   13   Serge Bernier, 1977

MOST GOALS, FINAL SERIES:
    6   Anders Hedberg, 1976

MOST ASSISTS, FINAL SERIES:
    9   Gordie Howe, 1974

MOST GAME WINNING GOALS, ONE PLAYOFF YEAR:
    4   Paulin Bordeleau, 1977

MOST POWER PLAY GOALS, ONE PLAYOFF YEAR:
    5   Bobby Hull, 1976
         Anders Hedberg, 1977

MOST POWER PLAY GOALS, ONE SERIES:
    4   Andre Hinse, 1974

MOST SHORTHANDED GOALS, ONE SERIES:
    2   Mark Howe, 1974
         Rod Zaine, 1974
         Rich Preston, 1976
         Chris Evans, 1976

MOST CONSECUTIVE POINT SCORING GAMES:
   15   Ulf Nilsson, Apr 9 76 - Apr 12 77

MOST CONSECUTIVE GOAL SCORING GAMES:
    9   Anders Hedberg, Apr 25 76 - Apr 12 77

MOST CONSECUTIVE ASSIST SCORING GAMES:
   11   Ulf Nilsson, Apr 9 76 - May 25 76

INDIVIDUAL — SINGLE GAME

MOST POINTS:
    7   Norm Beaudin, Apr 15 73
MOST GOALS:
    4   Larry Lund, Apr 13 74
MOST ASSISTS:
    4   By sixteen players
MOST PENALTIES:
MOST PENALTY MINUTES:
    7   Ted Taylor, Apr 28 74
    36
FASTEST GOAL, START OF GAME:
    :15   Jim Harrison, Apr 10 75
FASTEST TWO GOALS, START OF GAME:
    5:31   Rich Preston, Apr 21 76
FASTEST TWO GOALS:
    :15   Mike Walton, Apr 14 74
FASTEST THREE GOALS:
    8:42   Rick Sentes, Apr 12 74
FASTEST OVERTIME GOAL:
    :27   Jim Sherrit, May 1 75

INDIVIDUAL — SINGLE PERIOD

MOST POINTS:
    4   Norm Beaudin, Period 2, Apr 15 73
         Robbie Ftorek, Period 1, Apr 15 75
         Mike Walton, Period 2, Apr 24 75
MOST GOALS:
    3   Rick Sentes, Period 2, Apr 12 74
MOST ASSISTS:
    3   By nine players
MOST PENALTIES:
MOST PENALTY MINUTES:
    7   Ted Taylor, Period 1, Apr 28 74
    36

WORLD HOCKEY ASSOCIATION TRAVELOG 1977-78

APPROXIMATE AIR MILEAGE

	BIR.	CIN.	EDM.	HOU.	IND.	N.E.	QUE.	WPG.
Birmingham	—	432	1831	599	522	949	1226	996
Cincinnati	432	—	1678	879	98	661	870	993
Edmonton	1831	1678	—	1864	1741	2044	2016	835
Houston	599	879	1864	—	854	1512	1746	1469
Indianapolis	522	98	1741	854	—	728	924	906
New England	949	661	2044	1512	728	—	430	1510
Quebec	1226	870	2016	1746	924	430	—	1362
Winnipeg	996	993	835	1469	906	1510	1362	—

SCHEDULE

OFFICIAL 1977-78 WHA SCHEDULE

Regular season games are numbered 1-328.
International Exhibitions are not numbered.

1	Wed	Oct 12	New England	.....	at Houston	.....
2			Winnipeg	.....	at Edmonton	.....
3			Indianapolis	.....	at Cincinnati	.....
4	Thu	Oct 13	Quebec	.....	at Winnipeg	.....
5	Fri	Oct 14	Houston	.....	at Birmingham	.....
6			Quebec	.....	at Edmonton	.....
7	Sat	Oct 15	Winnipeg	.....	at Cincinnati	.....
8			Indianapolis	.....	at Houston	.....
9			Edmonton	.....	at Quebec	.....
10			Birmingham	.....	at New England	.....
11	Sun	Oct 16	Indianapolis	.....	at Winnipeg	.....
12			New England	.....	at Cincinnati	.....
13	Tue	Oct 18	New England	.....	at Indianapolis	.....
14			Cincinnati	.....	at Quebec	.....
15	Wed	Oct 19	New England	.....	at Edmonton	.....
16	Fri	Oct 21	Quebec	.....	at Indianapolis	.....
17			Cincinnati	.....	at Houston	.....
18			New England	.....	at Winnipeg	.....
19	Sat	Oct 22	Birmingham	.....	at Quebec	.....
20	Sun	Oct 23	Birmingham	.....	at Winnipeg	.....
21	Tue	Oct 25	Indianapolis	.....	at Birmingham	.....
22	Wed	Oct 26	Winnipeg	.....	at Indianapolis	.....
23			Edmonton	.....	at Houston	.....
24			Quebec	.....	at New England	.....
25	Fri	Oct 28	Edmonton	.....	at Birmingham	.....
26			Cincinnati	.....	at Winnipeg	.....
27	Sat	Oct 29	Birmingham	.....	at Indianapolis	.....
28			Houston	.....	at New England	.....
29	Sun	Oct 30	Houston	.....	at Quebec	.....
30			Edmonton	.....	at Winnipeg	.....
31	Tue	Nov 1	Houston	.....	at Indianapolis	.....
32			New England	.....	at Quebec	.....
33	Wed	Nov 2	Winnipeg	.....	at Edmonton	.....
34			Birmingham	.....	at Houston	.....

35	Fri	Nov 4	Winnipeg	.....	at Birmingham	.....
36			Quebec	.....	at Houston	.....
37			Cincinnati	.....	at New England	.....
38			Indianapolis	.....	at Edmonton	.....
39	Sat	Nov 5	Quebec	.....	at Birmingham	.....
40			Winnipeg	.....	at Cincinnati	.....
41	Sun	Nov 6	New England	.....	at Cincinnati	.....
42			Houston	.....	at Edmonton	.....
43	Tue	Nov 8	New England	.....	at Birmingham	.....
44			Edmonton	.....	at Quebec	.....
45	Wed	Nov 9	Birmingham	.....	at Cincinnati	.....
46			Houston	.....	at Winnipeg	.....
47	Thu	Nov 10	Edmonton	.....	at New England	.....
48	Fri	Nov 11	Edmonton	.....	at Cincinnati	.....
49			Indianapolis	.....	at Houston	.....
50			Quebec	.....	at Winnipeg	.....
51	Sat	Nov 12	Edmonton	.....	at Birmingham	.....
52			Indianapolis	.....	at New England	.....
53			Cincinnati	.....	at Quebec	.....
54	Sun	Nov 13	Cincinnati	.....	at Winnipeg	.....
55	Tue	Nov 15	New England	.....	at Indianapolis	.....
56			Winnipeg	.....	at Quebec	.....
57	Wed	Nov 16	Cincinnati	.....	at Edmonton	.....
58			Birmingham	.....	at Winnipeg	.....
59	Fri	Nov 18	Cincinnati	.....	at Edmonton	.....
60			Quebec	.....	at Houston	.....
61			Birmingham	.....	at Indianapolis	.....
62			Winnipeg	.....	at New England	.....
63	Sat	Nov 19	Houston	.....	at Birmingham	.....
64			Winnipeg	.....	at Indianapolis	.....
65	Sun	Nov 20	New England	.....	at Edmonton	.....
66			Indianapolis	.....	at Quebec	.....
67			Cincinnati	.....	at Winnipeg	.....
68	Tue	Nov 22	New England	.....	at Quebec	.....
69			Winnipeg	.....	at Edmonton	.....
70	Wed	Nov 23	Quebec	.....	at Cincinnati	.....
71			Birmingham	.....	at Houston	.....
72			Indianapolis	.....	at New England	.....
73	Thu	Nov 24	Cincinnati	.....	at Birmingham	.....
74			Edmonton	.....	at Indianapolis	.....
75	Fri	Nov 25	Quebec	.....	at New England	.....
76			Cincinnati	.....	at Houston	.....
77	Sat	Nov 26	Cincinnati	.....	at Indianapolis	.....
78			Edmonton	.....	at New England	.....
79			Birmingham	.....	at Quebec	.....
80	Sun	Nov 27	Birmingham	.....	at Winnipeg	.....
81	Tue	Nov 29	Cincinnati	.....	at Quebec	.....
82	Wed	Nov 30	Indianapolis	.....	at Cincinnati	.....

83			Birmingham	.....	at Edmonton	.....
84			New England	.....	at Houston	.....
85	Thu	Dec 1	Quebec	.....	at Indianapolis	.....
86	Fri	Dec 2	Birmingham	.....	at Edmonton	.....
87			Indianapolis	.....	at Houston	.....
88			Winnipeg	.....	at New England	.....
89	Sat	Dec 3	Cincinnati	.....	at New England	.....
90			Winnipeg	.....	at Quebec	.....
91	Sun	Dec 4	Indianapolis	.....	at Birmingham	.....
92			Houston	.....	at Cincinnati	.....
93			Edmonton	.....	at Winnipeg	.....
94	Tue	Dec 6	New England	.....	at Indianapolis	.....
95			Houston	.....	at Quebec	.....
96	Wed	Dec 7	Houston	.....	at Winnipeg	.....
97			New England	.....	at Birmingham	.....
98			Cincinnati	.....	at Edmonton	.....
99	Fri	Dec 9	New England	.....	at Birmingham	.....
100			Houston	.....	at Edmonton	.....
101			Czechoslovakia	.....	at Indianapolis	.....
102	Sat	Dec 10	Indianapolis	.....	at Quebec	.....
103	Sun	Dec 11	Houston	.....	at Edmonton	.....
104			Indianapolis	.....	at Winnipeg	.....
105			Czechoslovakia	.....	at Quebec	.....
106	Tue	Dec 13	Birmingham	.....	at Houston	.....
107			Czechoslovakia	.....	at Winnipeg	.....
108	Wed	Dec 14	Indianapolis	.....	at Cincinnati	.....
109			Sov. All-Stars	.....	at New England	.....
110			Czechoslovakia	.....	at Edmonton	.....
111	Thu	Dec 15	Cincinnati	.....	at Birmingham	.....
112			Houston	.....	at Indianapolis	.....

Quebec at Izvestia Cup at Moscow December 15 - December 22

113	Fri	Dec 16	Czechoslovakia	.....	at New England	.....
115	Sat	Dec 17	Winnipeg	.....	at New England	.....
116			Sov. All-Stars	.....	at Cincinnati	.....
117	Sun	Dec 18	Edmonton	.....	at Birmingham	.....
118			New England	.....	at Winnipeg	.....
122			Sov. All-Stars	.....	at Indianapolis	.....
120			Czechoslovakia	.....	at Houston	.....
121	Tue	Dec 20	Edmonton	.....	at Houston	.....
114			Sov. All-Stars	.....	at Winnipeg	.....
123			Czechoslovakia	.....	at Cincinnati	.....
124	Wed	Dec 21	Winnipeg	.....	at Houston	.....
125			Czechoslovakia	.....	at Birmingham	.....
126			Sov. All-Stars	.....	at Edmonton	.....
127	Thu	Dec 22	Cincinnati	.....	at Indianapolis	.....
128	Fri	Dec 23	Winnipeg	.....	at Cincinnati	.....
129			Indianapolis	.....	at New England	.....
135			Sov. All-Stars	.....	at Houston	.....

131	Mon Dec 26	Quebec	.....	at Winnipeg	.....
130		Sov. All-Stars	.....	at Birmingham	.....
132	Tue Dec 27	Quebec	.....	at Edmonton	.....
133		Birmingham	.....	at New England	.....
134	Wed Dec 28	Indianapolis	.....	at Cincinnati	.....
		Sov. All-Stars	.....	at Houston	.....
136	Thu Dec 29	Houston	.....	at Indianapolis	.....
137		Birmingham	.....	at Cincinnati	.....

Winnipeg vs. Soviet Nationals at Japan December 29 - January 1

138	Fri Dec 30	Indianapolis	.....	at Edmonton	.....
139		Cincinnati	.....	at Houston	.....
140		Birmingham	.....	at New England	.....
141		Sov. All-Stars	.....	at Quebec	.....

— 1978 —

142	Sun Jan 1	New England	.....	at Cincinnati	.....
143		Houston	.....	at Edmonton	.....
144		Quebec	.....	at Birmingham	.....
145	Tue Jan 3	Indianapolis	.....	at Quebec	.....
146	Wed Jan 4	Houston	.....	at Cincinnati	.....
147		Birmingham	.....	at Indianapolis	.....
148		Quebec	.....	at New England	.....
		Sov. Nationals	.....	at Edmonton	.....
	Thu Jan 5	Sov. Nationals	.....	at Winnipeg	.....
149	Fri Jan 6	Houston	.....	at Birmingham	.....
150		Quebec	.....	at Cincinnati	.....
151		Winnipeg	.....	at Edmonton	.....
152		New England	.....	at Indianapolis	.....
153	Sat Jan 7	Indianapolis	.....	at Houston	.....
154		Cincinnati	.....	at New England	.....
		Sov. Nationals	.....	at Quebec	.....
155	Sun Jan 8	Edmonton	.....	at Houston	.....
156		Birmingham	.....	at New England	.....
157		Indianapolis	.....	at Winnipeg	.....
		Sov. Nationals	.....	at Cincinnati	.....
158	Tue Jan 10	Birmingham	.....	at Quebec	.....
		Sov. Nationals	.....	at Indianapolis	.....
159	Wed Jan 11	Edmonton	.....	at Cincinnati	.....
160		Quebec	.....	at Indianapolis	.....
161		Birmingham	.....	at Winnipeg	.....
		Sov. Nationals	.....	at New England	.....
162	Fri Jan 13	Winnipeg	.....	at Houston	.....
163		Edmonton	.....	at New England	.....
164	Sat Jan 14	Birmingham	.....	at Cincinnati	.....

74

165			Winnipeg	.....	at Indianapolis	.....
166			Houston	.....	at New England	.....
167			Edmonton	.....	at Quebec	.....
168	Sun	Jan 15	Edmonton	.....	at Winnipeg	.....
169			Cincinnati	.....	at Quebec	.....
	Tue	Jan 17	ALL-STAR GAME AT QUEBEC			
170	Wed	Jan 18	Cincinnati	.....	at Birmingham	.....
171			New England	.....	at Edmonton	.....
172			Quebec	.....	at Winnipeg	.....
173	Fri	Jan 20	Edmonton	.....	at Birmingham	.....
174			Quebec	.....	at Cincinnati	.....
175			Houston	.....	at Indianapolis	.....
176			New England	.....	at Winnipeg	.....
177	Sat	Jan 21	Cincinnati	.....	at Houston	.....
178			Edmonton	.....	at Indianapolis	.....
179			New England	.....	at Quebec	.....
180	Sun	Jan 22	Edmonton	.....	at Cincinnati	.....
181			Birmingham	.....	at Houston	.....
182			Quebec	.....	at New England	.....
183			Indianapolis	.....	at Winnipeg	.....
184	Tue	Jan 24	Houston	.....	at Quebec	.....
185	Wed	Jan 25	Winnipeg	.....	at Birmingham	.....
186			New England	.....	at Cincinnati	.....
187			Indianapolis	.....	at Edmonton	.....
188	Thu	Jan 26	New England	.....	at Houston	.....
189	Fri	Jan 27	Winnipeg	.....	at Birmingham	.....
190			Quebec	.....	at Edmonton	.....
191	Sat	Jan 28	New England	.....	at Birmingham	.....
192			Winnipeg	.....	at Houston	.....
193			Cincinnati	.....	at Indianapolis	.....
194	Sun	Jan 29	Winnipeg	.....	at Cincinnati	.....
195			Quebec	.....	at Edmonton	.....
196			New England	.....	at Houston	.....
197	Tue	Jan 31	Houston	.....	at Birmingham	.....
198			Edmonton	.....	at Indianapolis	.....
199			Winnipeg	.....	at Quebec	.....
200	Wed	Feb 1	Indianapolis	.....	at Cincinnati	.....
201			Edmonton	.....	at New England	.....
202	Thu	Feb 2	Quebec	.....	at Birmingham	.....
203	Fri	Feb 3	Houston	.....	at Cincinnati	.....
204			Quebec	.....	at Indianapolis	.....
205			Edmonton	.....	at New England	.....
206	Sat	Feb 4	Indianapolis	.....	at Birmingham	.....
207			Winnipeg	.....	at Cincinnati	.....
208			New England	.....	at Houston	.....
209			Edmonton	.....	at Quebec	.....
210	Sun	Feb 5	Birmingham	.....	at Indianapolis	.....
211			Cincinnati	.....	at New England	.....

212			Edmonton	.....	at Winnipeg	.....
213	Tue	Feb 7	Birmingham	.....	at Quebec	.....
214	Wed	Feb 8	Cincinnati	.....	at Edmonton	.....
215			Quebec	.....	at New England	.....
216			Birmingham	.....	at Winnipeg	.....
217	Thu	Feb 9	Quebec	.....	at Houston	.....
218	Fri	Feb 10	Indianapolis	.....	at New England	.....
219			Cincinnati	.....	at Winnipeg	.....
220	Sat	Feb 11	New England	.....	at Cincinnati	.....
221			Quebec	.....	at Houston	.....
222			Winnipeg	.....	at Indianapolis	.....
223	Sun	Feb 12	Quebec	.....	at Cincinnati	.....
224			Birmingham	.....	at Edmonton	.....
225			Winnipeg	.....	at Houston	.....
226	Tue	Feb 14	Birmingham	.....	at Edmonton	.....
227	Wed	Feb 15	Houston	.....	at Cincinnati	.....
228			Edmonton	.....	at Winnipeg	.....
229			Quebec	.....	at Indianapolis	.....
230	Thu	Feb 16	Birmingham	.....	at Houston	.....
231	Fri	Feb 17	Indianapolis	.....	at Birmingham	.....
232			Quebec	.....	at Edmonton	.....
233			Cincinnati	.....	at Houston	.....
234			Winnipeg	.....	at New England	.....
235	Sat	Feb 18	Houston	.....	at Birmingham	.....
236			Winnipeg	.....	at Cincinnati	.....
237			New England	.....	at Indianapolis	.....
238	Sun	Feb 19	Birmingham	.....	at Cincinnati	.....
239			Indianapolis	.....	at Edmonton	.....
240			Quebec	.....	at Winnipeg	.....
241	Tue	Feb 21	New England	.....	at Quebec	.....
242	Wed	Feb 22	Houston	.....	at Edmonton	.....
243			New England	.....	at Winnipeg	.....
244	Thu	Feb 23	Quebec	.....	at Birmingham	.....
245	Fri	Feb 24	Houston	.....	at Edmonton	.....
246			New England	.....	at Winnipeg	.....
247	Sat	Feb 25	Indianapolis	.....	at Quebec	.....
248			Cincinnati	.....	at Birmingham	.....
249	Sun	Feb 26	Indianapolis	.....	at Birmingham	.....
250			New England	.....	at Edmonton	.....
251			Houston	.....	at Winnipeg	.....
252	Tue	Feb 28	Houston	.....	at Quebec	.....
253	Wed	Mar 1	Winnipeg	.....	at Birmingham	.....
254			Cincinnati	.....	at Edmonton	.....
255			Houston	.....	at Indianapolis	.....
256			Quebec	.....	at New England	.....
257	Fri	Mar 3	Indianapolis	.....	at Edmonton	.....
258			Houston	.....	at New England	.....
259			Cincinnati	.....	at Winnipeg	.....

260	Sat	Mar 4	Winnipeg	.....	at Indianapolis	.....
261			Birmingham	.....	at New England	.....
262			Houston	.....	at Quebec	.....
263	Sun	Mar 5	Edmonton	.....	at Birmingham	.....
264			Cincinnati	.....	at Indianapolis	.....
265			New England	.....	at Quebec	.....
266			Houston	.....	at Winnipeg	.....
267	Tue	Mar 7	Edmonton	.....	at Houston	.....
268			Cincinnati	.....	at Quebec	.....
269	Wed	Mar 8	Quebec	.....	at Indianapolis	.....
270	Thu	Mar 9	Quebec	.....	at Birmingham	.....
271			Edmonton	.....	at Cincinnati	.....
272			New England	.....	at Houston	.....
273			Indianapolis	.....	at Winnipeg	.....
274	Fri	Mar 10	New England	.....	at Birmingham	.....
275	Sat	Mar 11	Edmonton	.....	at Cincinnati	.....
276			Houston	.....	at Indianapolis	.....
277			Winnipeg	.....	at Quebec	.....
278	Sun	Mar 12	Indianapolis	.....	at Houston	.....
279			Birmingham	.....	at Winnipeg	.....
280	Tue	Mar 14	Edmonton	.....	at Quebec	.....
281	Wed	Mar 15	Birmingham	.....	at Cincinnati	.....
282			Indianapolis	.....	at New England	.....
283			Edmonton	.....	at Winnipeg	.....
			Sweden	.....	at Houston	.....
284	Fri	Mar 17	New England	.....	at Cincinnati	.....
285			Birmingham	.....	at Houston	.....
286			Winnipeg	.....	at Edmonton	.....
			Sweden	.....	at Indianapolis	.....
287	Sat	Mar 18	Indianapolis	.....	at Cincinnati	.....
288			New England	.....	at Quebec	.....
			Finland	.....	at Birmingham	.....
289	Sun	Mar 19	Indianapolis	.....	at Birmingham	.....
290			Cincinnati	.....	at Edmonton	.....
291			Quebec	.....	at Winnipeg	.....
			Finland	.....	at Houston	.....
			Sweden	.....	at New England	.....
292	Tue	Mar 21	Birmingham	.....	at Quebec	.....
			Sweden	.....	at Houston	.....
293	Wed	Mar 22	Houston	.....	at Cincinnati	.....
294			Birmingham	.....	at Edmonton	.....
295			Winnipeg	.....	at New England	.....
			Finland	.....	at Indianapolis	.....
296	Fri	Mar 24	Quebec	.....	at Birmingham	.....
297			Indianapolis	.....	at Edmonton	.....
298			Houston	.....	at New England	.....
299	Sat	Mar 25	Winnipeg	.....	at Birmingham	.....
300			Quebec	.....	at Houston	.....

			Finland	.....	at Cincinnati	.....
	Sun	Mar 26	Finland	.....	at New England	.....
			Sweden	.....	at Cincinnati	.....
301	Tue	Mar 28	Edmonton	.....	at Indianapolis	.....
302			Winnipeg	.....	at Houston	.....
303			Cincinnati	.....	at Quebec	.....
			Sweden	.....	at Birmingham	.....
304	Wed	Mar 29	Cincinnati	.....	at New England	.....
305	Thu	Mar 30	Edmonton	.....	at Houston	.....
306			Winnipeg	.....	at Indianapolis	.....
307	Fri	Mar 31	Edmonton	.....	at Birmingham	.....
308			Indianapolis	.....	at New England	.....
309	Sat	Apr 1	Cincinnati	.....	at Birmingham	.....
310			Edmonton	.....	at Indianapolis	.....
311			Houston	.....	at New England	.....
312			Winnipeg	.....	at Quebec	.....
313	Sun	Apr 2	Houston	.....	at Quebec	.....
314	Tue	Apr 4	Edmonton	.....	at Quebec	.....
315			Winnipeg	.....	at Houston	.....
316	Wed	Apr 5	Birmingham	.....	at Cincinnati	.....
317			New England	.....	at Edmonton	.....
318	Thu	Apr 6	New England	.....	at Winnipeg	.....
319	Fri	Apr 7	Cincinnati	.....	at Indianapolis	.....
320			Winnipeg	.....	at Edmonton	.....
321			Houston	.....	at Birmingham	.....
322	Sat	Apr 8	Cincinnati	.....	at Houston	.....
323			Birmingham	.....	at New England	.....
324			Indianapolis	.....	at Quebec	.....
325	Sun	Apr 9	Quebec	.....	at Cincinnati	.....
326			Birmingham	.....	at Indianapolis	.....
327			Edmonton	.....	at New England	.....
328			Houston	.....	at Winnipeg	.....

WORLD HOCKEY ASSOCIATION
1978-79 MEDIA GUIDE

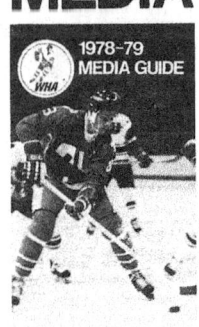

ON THE COVER
MARC TARDIF, THE WHA'S MOST VALUABLE PLAYER FOR THE 1977-78 REGULAR SEASON

EDITOR
JOHN A. HEWIG

STATISTICIAN
FRANK POLNASZEK

Photo Credits:
COVER: JOE BLACK
INSIDE: JORY LEVINGTON
   SUE MacMASTER

Printed in USA
All Rights Reserved
World Hockey Association

CONTENTS

WHA Directory	2-3
Club Directories	4-16
Team Rosters	5-17
1977-78 Regular Season	**18-29**
Final Standings	19
Top Thirty Scorers	20
Top Ten Goaltenders	20
Individual Statistics	21-24
Goaltending Statistics	25-26
Three or more goal nights	27-28
Power-Play Proficiency/ Short-handed Efficiency	28
Overtime Analysis and Extra Attacker	28-29
1977-78 AVCO World Trophy Playoffs	**30-36**
Game Results	32
Play-off Statistics	33-35
Goaltending Statistics	36
1977-78 Award Winners	**37-40**
Biographies	38-40
1977-78 All-Star Team	40
1978-79 Career Records of Active Players	**41-142**
Regular Season History	**143-194**
All-time WHA Player Listing and Statistics, including Play-Offs	144-155
All-time WHA Goaltending Statistics	156-157
Team Records	158-171
Individual Records	171-182
Club Records	183-184
Career Leaders	185-186
Career Hat Tricks	186-188
Penalty Shots	189
Goaltending Leaders	190-191
Career Shut-outs	192
Trophy Winners	192-193
1972-78 All-Star teams	194
AVCO Play-Off History	**195-224**
AVCO Champions	196
AVCO Standings	197
Team Records	197-213
Individual Records	213-218
Club vs. Club Records	218-221
Career Leaders	222-223
Goaltending Leaders	223-224
Penalty Shots	224
1978-79 Schedule	**225-232**

WHA DIRECTORY

BEN HATSKIN
Chairman of the Board

HOWARD L. BALDWIN
President

LEAGUE TRUSTEES

BIRMINGHAM — JOHN F. BASSETT

CINCINNATI — WILLIAM O. DEWITT, JR.

EDMONTON — PETER POCKLINGTON

INDIANAPOLIS — NELSON SKALBANIA

NEW ENGLAND — HOWARD L. BALDWIN

QUEBEC — MARCEL AUBUT

WINNIPEG — MICHAEL GOBUTY

WORLD HOCKEY ASSOCIATION
FRONT OFFICE

RONALD K. RYAN
Executive Director

GARY C. CLARK
Director of Administration

JOHN A. HEWIG
Director of Public Relations

FRANK POLNASZEK
Statistician

ROBERT RONSTROM
Accountant

ROBERT FRAMPTON
Director of Officials

Secretary/Bookkeeper
ANNE BAXTER

Executive Secretary
GINNY KELLEY

WHA OPERATING OFFICES

ONE FINANCIAL PLAZA
SUITE 1700
HARTFORD, CONNECTICUT 06103

TELEPHONE 203-278-4240
TELEX 966-485 WHA A HTF

BIRMINGHAM BULLS

Alabama Hockey, Ltd.
One Civic Center Plaza
Birmingham, Alabama
35203
Telephone 205-251-2855
Telex 59-747 BHAM BULLS BHM

John F. Bassett

Gilles Leger

John Brophy

President
JOHN F. BASSETT

Executive Vice-President
PETER McASKILE

General Manager
GILLES LEGER

Coach
JOHN BROPHY

Director of Marketing
JOE W. REID, JR.

*Broadcaster/
Director of Public Relations*
ELI GOLD

*Assistant to Public Relations/
Marketing*
P. J. BRYAN

Director of Ticket Operations
MIKE RUSSELL

Director of Season Tickets
STEPHANIE SEAY

Comptroller
PHOEBE LIMBAUGH

Administrative Assistant
BRENDA HAWKINS

Trainer
LARRY ASHLEY

Equipment Manager
BO DODD

Team Physicians
DR. DON AUTREY
DR. GORDON ROBINSON
DR. BRUCE NEWELL

Home Arena
Birmingham Jefferson County Coliseum

Seating Capacity
16,753

Broadcasting Radio Station
WAPI-AM (1070)

Announcer
ELI GOLD

Team Colors
Red, White, Blue

4

BIRMINGHAM BULLS ROSTER — 1978-79

GOALTENDERS

PLAYER	POS	HT	WT	PLACE OF BIRTH	DATE	1977-78 CLUB	GP	MINS	GA	SO	GAA
Riggin, Pat	G	5-9	163	Kincardine, Ont	5-26-59	London (OHA)	37	2266	140	0	3.65
Szabo, Rick	G	5-7	160	Hamilton, Ont.	8-16-55	Philadelphia (AHL)	5	305	27	0	5.31
						Saginaw (IHL)	30	1486	106	0	4.28
Wood, Wayne	G	6-1	195	Toronto, Ont.	6-05-51	Birmingham	32	1551	99	1	3.83

FORWARDS

PLAYER	POS	HT	WT	PLACE OF BIRTH	DATE	1977-78 CLUB	GP	G	A	PTS	PIM
Adduono, Rick	C	5-10	170	Ft. William, Ont.	1-25-55	Rochester (AHL)	76	38	60	98	34
Alley, Steve	LW	6-0	185	Anoka, Minn.	12-19-53	Birmingham	27	8	12	20	11
						Hampton (AHL)	30	6	3	9	27
						Springfield (AHL)	1	0	0	0	0
Cassolato, Tony	RW	5-11	182	Guelph, Ont.	5-07-56	Birmingham	77	18	25	43	59
Crowder, Keith	RW	6-0	190	S. Porcupine, Ont.	1-06-59	Peterborough (OHA)	58	30	30	60	139
Gorman, Dave	LW	5-11	180	Oshawa, Ont.	4-08-55	Birmingham	63	19	21	40	93
						Hampton (AHL)	2	0	0	0	12
Goulet, Michel	RW	6-1	195	Peribonqa, Ont	4-21-60	Quebec (QMJHL)	72	73	62	135	109
Henderson, Paul	LW	5-11	180	Kincardine, Ont.	1-28-43	Birmingham	80	37	29	66	22
Kirk, Gavin	C	5-10	165	London, England	12-06-51	Philadelphia (AHL)	59	21	26	47	32
Marrin, Peter	C	5-10	185	Toronto, Ont.	8-08-53	Birmingham	80	28	43	71	53
O'Neil, Paul	C	6-1	185	Charlestown, Ma.	8-24-53	Hampton (AHL)	36	17	27	44	9
						San Diego (PHL)	17	11	9	20	0
Roberto, Phil	RW	6-1	190	Niagara Falls, Ont.	1-01-49	Birmingham (WHA)	53	8	20	28	91
Sleigher, Louis	RW	5-11	195	Nouvelle, Que.	10-23-58	Chicoutimi (QMJHL)	71	65	54	119	125
Stephenson, Bob	RW	6-1	187	Saskatoon, Sask.	2-01-54	Birmingham	39	7	6	13	33
						Hampton (AHL)	1	0	0	0	0
						Flint (IHL)	6	2	5	7	7
Stewart, John C.	C	6-0	180	Toronto, Ont.	1-02-54	Tulsa (CHL)	9	1	1	2	7
						Birmingham	48	13	26	39	52
						Philadelphia (AHL)	24	11	13	24	44
Vaive, Rick	RW	6-0	180	Ottawa, Ont.	5-14-59	Sherbrooke (QMJHL)	68	76	79	155	199

DEFENSEMEN

PLAYER	POS	HT	WT	PLACE OF BIRTH	DATE	1977-78 CLUB	GP	G	A	PTS	PIM
Beaudoin, Serge	D	6-2	215	Montreal, Que.	11-30-52	Birmingham	64	8	25	33	105
						Cincinnati	13	0	1	1	10
Bolonchuk, Larry	D	5-10	190	Winnipeg, Man.	2-26-52	Washington (NHL)	49	3	8	11	79
						Hampton (AHL)	14	1	1	2	8
						Hershey (AHL)	19	0	7	7	12
Gingras, Gaston	D	6-0	191	North Bay, Ont.	2-13-59	Hamilton (OHA)	29	11	19	30	37
						Kitchener (OHA)	32	13	24	37	31
Hartsburg, Craig	D	6-1	190	Stratford, Ont.	6-29-59	Slt. St. Marie (OHA)	36	15	42	57	101
Hughes, Brent	D	6-0	205	Bowmanville, Ont.	6-17-43	Birmingham	80	9	35	44	48
Ramage, Rob	D	6-2	195	Byron, Ont.	1-11-59	London (OHA)	59	17	47	64	162
Tebbutt, Greg	D	6-3	215	Vancouver, BC	5-11-57	Flin Flon (WCHL)	55	28	46	74	270
Turkiewicz, Jim	D	5-10	175	Peterborough, Ont.	4-13-55	Birmingham	78	3	21	24	45

CINCINNATI STINGERS

Cincinnati Hockey Club, Inc.
Riverfront Coliseum
Cincinnati, Ohio 45202
Telephone 513-241-1818
Telex 214-286 SPORTS INC CIN

Brian E. Heekin

Chairman of the Board
WILLIAM O. DEWITT, SR.

President
BRIAN E. HEEKIN

Executive Vice-President
WILLIAM O. DEWITT, JR.

Vice-President
WILLIAM BARRETT

Vice-President
LEFTY McFADDEN

Director of Player Personnel/Coach
FLOYD SMITH

Head Scout
FLO POTVIN

Western Scout
JIM BAZDELL

Director of Media Relations
BOB FIRESTONE

Director of Promotions
MIKE MARTAUS

Director of Sales
JIM McVAY

Director of Group Sales
BILL HARBOUR

Trainer
BILL CONNELLY

Equipment Manager
TIM RINGLER

Supervisor of Minor Officials
GEORGE CALLIES

Home Arena
Cincinnati Riverfront Coliseum

Seating Capacity
15,794

Ticket Prices
8.25, 7.25, 5.50, 3.50

Broadcasting Radio Station
WLW-AM (700)

Announcer
DICK CARLSON

Team Colors
Stinger Yellow, Bumblebee Black

William O. Dewitt, Jr.

Floyd Smith

CINCINNATI STINGERS ROSTER — 1978-79

GOALTENDERS

PLAYER	POS	HT	WT	PLACE OF BIRTH	DATE	1977-78 CLUB	GP	MINS	GA	SO	GAA
Dion, Michel	G	5-10	170	Granby, Que.	2-11-54	Cincinnati (WHA)	45	2356	140	4	3.57
Liut, Mike	G	6-2	180	Weston, Ont.	1-07-56	Cincinnati (WHA)	27	1215	86	0	4.25
Raeder, Cap	G	6-0	175	Needham, Mass.	10-08-53	Philadelphia (AHL)	9	472	38	0	4.83

FORWARDS

PLAYER	POS	HT	WT	PLACE OF BIRTH	DATE	1977-78 CLUB	GP	G	A	PTS	PIM
Clark, Gordie	RW	5-10	180	St. John, N.B.	5-31-52	Rochester (AHL)	75	37	51	88	18
Debol, Dave	C	5-11	175	St. Clair Shores, Mich.	3-27-56	Cincinnati (WHA)	9	3	2	5	2
Dudley, Rick	LW	6-0	190	Toronto, Ont.	1-31-49	Cincinnati (WHA)	72	30	42	72	156
Ftorek, Robbie	C	5-8	160	Needham, Mass.	1-02-52	Cincinnati (WHA)	80	59	50	109	54
Gartner, Mike	RW	6-0	180	Ottawa, Ont.	10-29-59	Niagara Falls (OHA)	64	41	49	90	56
Gilbert, Ed	C	5-11	185	Hamilton, Ont.	3-12-52	Did not play					
Gilligan, Bill	C	5-11	175	Beverly, Mass.	8-05-54	Cincinnati (WHA)	54	10	14	24	59
Harris, Hugh	LW	6-0	201	Toronto, Ont.	6-07-48	Indianapolis (WHA)	19	1	7	8	6
Hislop, Jamie	RW	5-10	180	Sarnia, Ont.	1-20-54	Cincinnati (WHA)	45	11	23	34	30
Marsh, Peter	LW	6-0	170	Halifax, Nova Scotia	12-21-56	Cincinnati (WHA)	80	24	43	67	17
Shutt, Byron	LW	6-1	195	Toronto, Ont.	10-26-55	Bowling Green (CCHA)	74	25	25	50	123
Stewart, Paul	LW	6-1	205	Boston, Mass.	3-21-54	Cincinnati (WHA)	39	12	31	43	106
Thomas, Reg	LW	5-10	185	Lambeth, Ont.	4-21-53	Indianapolis (WHA)	40	1	5	6	241
						Cincinnati (WHA)	49	15	16	31	44
							18	4	2	6	12

DEFENSEMEN

PLAYER	POS	HT	WT	PLACE OF BIRTH	DATE	1977-78 CLUB	GP	G	A	PTS	PIM
Baltimore, Bryon	D	6-2	2'3	Whitehorse, Yukon	8-26-52	Indianapolis (WHA)	22	1	7	8	23
						Cincinnati (WHA)	28	2	9	11	47
Davis, Kelly	D	6-0	198	Grand Prairie, Alta.	9-23-58	Flin Flon (WCHL)	67	22	61	83	210
Dornseif, Dave	D	6-3	205	Edina, Minn.		Providence Coll. (ECAC)	3	0	1	1	0
Lahache, Floyd	D	5-10	185	Caughnawaga, Que.	9-17-57	Cincinnati (WHA)	11	0	3	3	13
Legge, Barry	D	6-0	186	Winnipeg, Man.	10-22-54	Cincinnati (WHA)	78	7	17	24	114
Luksa, Chuck	D	6-1	190	Toronto, Ont	2-19-54	Nova Scotia (AHL)	66	3	23	26	89
Melrose, Barry	D	6-2	205	Kelvington, Sask.	7-15-56	Cincinnati (WHA)	69	2	9	11	113
Norwich, Craig	D	5-11	175	Edina, Minn.	12-15-55	Cincinnati (WHA)	65	7	23	30	48

EDMONTON OILERS

Edmonton World Hockey Enterprises, Ltd.
Edmonton Coliseum
Edmonton, Alberta
T5B 4M9
Telephone 403-474-8561
Telex 037-3595 HOCKEY EDM

President
PETER POCKLINGTON

General Manager
L. D. GORDON

Director of Player Personnel
BRUCE MacGREGOR

Coach
GLEN SATHER

Head Scout
BARRY FRASER

Scouts
BOB FREEMAN
BOB WALL

Director of Marketing
DOUG WENSCHLAG

Director of Public Relations
JOHN SHORT

Trainers
JOHN BLACKWELL
PETER MILLAR

Supervisor of Minor Officials
DICK CARREAU

Home Arena
Edmonton Coliseum

Seating Capacity
15,248

Ticket Prices
10.00, 9.00, 7.00, 6.00, 4.50

Broadcasting Radio Station
CFRN-AM (1260)

Announcer
ROD PHILLIPS

Team Colors
Royal Blue, Orange, White

Peter Pocklington

L. D. Gordon

Glen Sather

8

EDMONTON OILERS ROSTER — 1978-79

GOALTENDERS

PLAYER	POS	HT	WT	PLACE OF BIRTH	DATE	1977-78 CLUB	GP	MIN	GA	SO	GAA
Dryden, David	G	6-1½	186	Hamilton, Ont.	9-05-41	Edmonton (WHA)	48	2578	150	2	3.49
Hendrick, Larry	G	6-0	155	Edmonton, Alta	9-23-55	Binghamton (AHL)	14	752	49	0	3.91
						Phoenix (CHL)	5	255	26	0	6.12
Walsh, Ed	G	5-10	180	Arlington, Mass.	8-18-51	Nova Scotia (AHL)	5	360	20	0	4.00
						Binghamton (AHL)	18	914	76	0	4.98
						Springfield (AHL)	13	744	64	0	5.16

FORWARDS

PLAYER	POS	HT	WT	PLACE OF BIRTH	DATE	1977-78 CLUB	GP	G	A	PTS	PIM
Berry, Doug	C	6-1	190	New Westminster, B.C.	6-03-57	Univ. of Denver (WCHA)	32	25	39	64	34
Buat, George	RW	6-0	190	Calgary, Alta.	1-06-58	Seattle (WCHL)	71	40	54	94	127
Callighen, Brett	LW	5-11	175	Toronto, Ont.	5-15-53	Edmonton (WHA)	80	20	30	50	112
Carlson, Steve	C	6-2	175	Virginia, Minn.	8-26-55	New England (WHA)	38	6	7	13	11
						Springfield (AHL)	37	21	15	36	48
Carter, Ron	RW	6-1	205	Chateauguay, Que.	3-14-58	Sherbrooke (QJMHL)	71	88	86	174	28
Chipperfield, Ron	C	5-11	180	Brandon, Man.	3-28-54	Edmonton (WHA)	80	33	52	85	48
Flett, Bill	RW	6-1	207	Vermilion, Alta.	7-21-43	Edmonton (WHA)	74	41	28	69	34
George, Wes	LW	6-2	220	Young, Sask.	9-26-58	Saskatoon (WCHL)	70	38	40	78	205
Goldsworthy, Bill	RW	6-1	190	Kitchener, Ont.	8-24-44	Indianapolis (WHA)	32	8	10	18	10
						New Haven (AHL)	4	1	2	3	4
						New York (NHL)	7	0	1	1	12
Guite, Pierre	RW	6-2	190	Montreal, Que.	4-17-52	Edmonton (WHA)	60	12	21	33	71
						Quebec (WHA)	18	4	5	9	15
Hunter, Dave	LW	5-11	195	Petrolia, Ont.	1-01-58	Sudbury (OHA)	68	44	44	88	197
MacDonald, Blair	RW	5-10	180	Cornwall, Ont.	11-17-53	Edmonton (WHA)	80	34	34	68	11
Mayer, Jim	RW	6-0	190	Capreol, Ont.	10-30-54	New England (WHA)	51	11	9	20	21
Semenko, Dave	LW	6-3	210	Winnipeg, Man.	7-12-57	Edmonton (WHA)	65	6	6	12	140
Sobchuk, Dennis	C	6-2	176	Lang, Sask.	1-12-54	Edmonton (WHA)	13	6	3	9	4
						Cincinnati (WHA)	23	5	9	14	22
Weir, Stan	C	6-1	170	Ponoka, Alta.	3-17-52	Toronto (NHL)	30	12	5	17	4
						Tulsa (CHL)	42	24	33	57	38

DEFENSEMEN

PLAYER	POS	HT	WT	PLACE OF BIRTH	DATE	1977-78 CLUB	GP	G	A	PTS	PIM
Alexander, Claire	D	5-10	180	Collingwood, Ont.	6-16-45	Vancouver (NHL)	32	8	18	26	6
						Tulsa (CHL)	46	14	42	56	22
Hamilton, Al	D	6-2	195	Flin Flon, Man	8-20-46	Edmonton (WHA)	59	11	43	54	46
Langevin, David	D	6-2	200	St. Paul, Minn.	5-15-54	Edmonton (WHA)	62	6	22	28	90
Micheletti, Joe	D	6-0	185	Hibbing, Minn.	10-24-54	Edmonton (WHA)	56	14	34	48	56
Neilson, Jim	D	6-2	200	Big River, Sask.	11-11-40	Cleveland (NHL)	68	2	21	23	20
Sandbeck, Cal	D	6-1	218	Int'l. Falls, Minn.	1-28-56	Edmonton (WHA)	11	1	2	3	39
Shmyr, Paul	D	5-11	175	Cudworth, Sask.	1-28-46	Edmonton (WHA)	80	9	40	49	100

INDIANAPOLIS RACERS

Indianapolis Racers 1977, Inc.
137 East Ohio Street
Indianapolis, Indiana 46204
Telephone 317-635-3131
Telex 27-325 WHA RACERS IND

Chairman of the Board
NELSON SKALBANIA

President
ROBERT JOHNSTON

Executive Vice-President/Marketing
DONALD M. LEROSE

General Manager/Coach
PATRICK STAPLETON

Assistant General Manager
ROD ZAINE

Director of Hockey Operations
BILL NEAL

*Director of Player Personnel
Head Scout*
AL KARLANDER

Director of Public Relations
CHARLIE BEAL

Ticket Manager
DIANE COREY

Trainers
LOUIE GREENWALD
JOHN CAREY

Supervisor of Minor Officials
PAUL MINOT

Home Arena
MARKET SQUARE ARENA

Actual Seating Capacity
15,861

Ticket Prices
8.50, 8.00, 6.50, 5.00

Broadcasting Radio Stations
WIBC-AM (1070)
WIBC-FM (100.9)

Announcers
MIKE FORNES
AL KARLANDER

Team Colors
Red, White, Blue

Nelson Skalbania

Donald M. LeRose

Patrick Stapleton

INDIANAPOLIS RACERS ROSTER — 1978-79

GOALTENDERS

PLAYER	POS	HT	WT	PLACE OF BIRTH	DATE	1977-78 CLUB	GP	GA	GAA
Inness, Gary	G	6-0	190	Toronto, Ont.	5-28-49	Indianapolis (WHA)	52	200	4.21
Mio, Ed	G	5-10	180	Windsor, Ont.	1-31-54	Indianapolis (WHA)	17	64	4.27
Park, Jim	G	6-1	190	Toronto, Ont.	6-22-52	Indianapolis (WHA)	54	41	4.21
Smith, Gary	G	6-4	215	Ottawa, Ont.	2-04-44				

FORWARDS

PLAYER	POS	HT	WT	PLACE OF BIRTH	DATE	1977-78 CLUB	GP	G	A	PTS	PIM
Burgess, Don	LW	6-0	170	Pt. Edward, Ont.	9-19-53	Indianapolis (WHA)	79	11	12	23	2
Driscoll, Peter	LW	6-0	190	Kingston, On.	10-27-54	Indianapolis (WHA)	56	25	21	46	130
Greig, Bruce	LW	6-2	220	High River, Alta	5-09-53	Cincinnati (WHA)					
Gretzky, Wayne	C	5-11	165	Brantford, Ont.	1-26-61	S:t. St. Marie (OMJL)	64	70	111	181	
Larose, Claude	LW	5-11	170	St. Jean, Que.	5-17-55	Cincinnati (WHA)	28	14	16	30	12
Larway, Don	RW	6-1	195	Oak Lake, Man.	2-12-54	Houston (WHA)	51	11	20	31	6
Leduc, Richard	C	5-11	170	Ile Perrot, Que.	8-24-51	Indianapolis (WHA)	80	9	18	27	41
Leroux, Gerry	LW	5-7	160	St. Bernardin, Ont.	6-09-58	Cincinnati (WHA)	28	10	15	25	38
Magee, Dean	LW	6-1	210	Banff, Alta.	4-29-55	Windsor (OHL)	54	27	31	58	44
Moretto, Angelo	C	6-3	212	Toronto, Ont.	9-18-53	Colorado (WCHA)	68	57	66	123	85
Nugent, Kevin	RW	6-5	235	Edina, Minn.	1956	Phoenix (CHL)	25	13	15	28	50
Parizeau, Michel	C&LW	5-10	165	Montreal, Que.	4-09-48	Univ. of Notre Dame	14	1	6	7	22
St. Sauveur, Claude	LW	6-0	170	Sherbrooke, Que.	1-02-52	Indianapolis (WHA)	39	22	28	50	32
Stoughton, Blaine	RW	5-10	185	Gilbert Plains, Man.	3-13-53	Indianapolis (WHA)	70	13	27	40	47
						Indianapolis (WHA)	72	36	42	78	24
						Cincinnati (WHA)	47	13	13	26	28
							30	6	13	19	36

DEFENSEMEN

PLAYER	POS	HT	WT	PLACE OF BIRTH	DATE	1977-78 CLUB	GP	G	A	PTS	PIM
Block, Ken	D	5-10	191	Steinbach, Man.	3-18-44	Indianapolis (WHA)	77	1	25	26	34
Fortier, Dave	D	5-11	189	Sudbury, Ont.	6-17-51	Indianapolis (WHA)	54	1	15	16	86
Hughes, John	D	5-11	200	Charlottetown, PEI	3-18-54	Houston (WHA)	79	3	25	28	130
Inkpen, Dave	D	6-0	195	Edmonton, Alta.	9-04-54	Houston (WHA)	24	1	9	10	24
						Edmonton (WHA)	19	0	1	1	16
						Quebec (WHA)	24	0	1	1	20
Irwin, Glen	D	5-11	195	Edmonton, Alta.	3-01-51	Indianapolis (WHA)	20	0	0	0	72
						Houston (WHA)	3	0	0	0	0
						Binghampton (AHL)	51	0	12	12	191
Morrison, Kevin	D	5-11	202	Sydney, N.S.	10-28-49	Indianapolis (WHA)	75	17	40	57	49

NEW ENGLAND WHALERS

New England Whalers Hockey Club, Ltd.
One Civic Center Plaza
Hartford, Connecticut 06103
Telephone 203-728-3366
Telex 994-476 NE WHALERS HFD

Managing General Partner
HOWARD L. BALDWIN

Director of Hockey Operations
JACK KELLEY

Assistant to Director of Hockey Operations
BOB CROCKER

Head Coach
BILL DINEEN

Assistant Coach
LARRY PLEAU

Head Scout
DON BLACKBURN

Scouts
BOB CHARLEBOIS
JACK McCARTAN

Director of Marketing
WILLIAM E. BARNES

Business Manager
W. DAVID ANDREWS III

Director of Public Relations
DENNIS RANDALL

Ticket Manager
BRIAN MacLEOD

Advertising/Sales Manager
JAY WOODS

Merchandise Manager
MIKE REDDY

Director of New Ticket Sales
BILL HENDERSON

Controller
ROBERT L. KELLEY

Trainer
JOE ALTOTT

Assistant Trainer
SKIP CUNNINGHAM

Supervisor of Minor Officials
BILL HENDERSON

Home Arena
Springfield Civic Center

Seating Capacity: 7,625

Ticket Prices: 9.75, 6.50

Radio: WTIC-AM (1080)

Announcers
BOB NEUMEIER
LARRY PLEAU

Team Colors: Green, White, Gold

Howard L. Baldwin

Jack Kelley

Bill Dineen

NEW ENGLAND WHALERS ROSTER — 1978-79

GOALTENDERS

PLAYER	POS	HT	WT	PLACE OF BIRTH	DATE	1977-78 CLUB	GP	MINS	GA	SO	GAA
Garrett, John	G	5-8	175	Trenton, Ont.	6-17-51	Birmingham	58	3306	210	2	3.81
O'Toole, Tom	G	6-0	180	Kingston, Ont.	8-12-55	San Francisco (PHL)	21	1201	65	0	3.24
Smith, Al	G	6-1	200	Toronto, Ont.	11-10-45	New England (WHA)	55	3246	174	2	3.22

FORWARDS

PLAYER	POS	HT	WT	PLACE OF BIRTH	DATE	1977-78 CLUB	GP	G	A	PTS	PIM
Antonovich, Mike	LW	5-8	165	Calumet, Minn.	10-18-51	New England (WHA)	75	32	35	67	32
Brubaker, Jeff	LW	6-2	210	Hagerstown, Md.	2-24-58	Peterborough (OHA)	68	20	24	44	307
Carlson, Jack	LW	6-3	200	Virginia, Minn.	8-23-54	New England (WHA)	67	9	20	29	192
Douglas, Jordy	C	6-0	195	Winnipeg, Man.	1-20-58	Flin Flon (WCHL)	71	60	56	116	131
Howe, Gordie	C	6-0	203	Floral, Sask.	3-31-28	New England (WHA)	76	34	62	96	85
Howe, Mark	LW	5-11	180	Detroit, Mich.	5-28-55	New England (WHA)	70	30	61	91	32
Keon, Dave	C	5-9	167	Noranda, Que.	3-22-40	New England (WHA)	78	24	38	62	2
Lacroix, Andre	C	5-8	175	Lauzon, Que.	6-05-45	Houston (WHA)	78	36	77	113	57
Lyle, George	LW	6-2	210	Edmonton, Alta.	11-24-53	New England (WHA)	68	30	24	54	74
McKenzie, John	RW	5-7	175	High River, Alta.	12-12-37	New England (WHA)	79	27	29	56	61
Miller, Warren	RW	5-11	180	St. Paul, Minn.	1-1-54	Edmonton (WHA)	18	2	4	6	18
						Quebec (WHA)	60	14	24	38	47
Peloffy, Andre	C	5-8	160	Sete, France	2-25-51	New England (WHA)	10	2	0	2	2
						Springfield (AHL)	67	33	55	88	73
Rogers, Mike	C	5-9	170	Calgary, Alta.	10-24-54	New England (WHA)	80	28	43	71	46
Sheehy, Tim	RW	6-1	185	Int'l. Falls, Minn.	9-03-48	New England (WHA)	25	8	11	19	14
						Detroit (NHL)	15	0	0	0	0
						Birmingham (WHA)	13	4	2	6	5
Warner, Jim	RW	5-11	180	St. Paul, Minn.	3-26-54	Colorado Coll. (WCHA)	33	24	36	60	46

DEFENSEMEN

PLAYER	POS	HT	WT	PLACE OF BIRTH	DATE	1977-78 CLUB	GP	G	A	PTS	PIM
Hangsleben, Alan	D	6-1	195	Warroad, Minn.	2-22-53	New England (WHA)	79	11	18	29	140
Howe, Marty	D	6-1	185	Detroit, Mich.	2-18-54	New England (WHA)	75	10	10	20	66
Ley, Rick	D	5-9	185	Orillia, Ont.	12-02-48	New England (WHA)	73	3	41	44	95
Plumb, Ron	D	5-10	175	Kingston, Ont.	7-17-50	Cincinnati (WHA)	27	1	9	10	18
						New England (WHA)	54	13	34	47	47
Roberts, Gordie	D	6-1	190	Detroit, Mich.	10-02-57	New England (WHA)	78	15	46	61	118
Selwood, Brad	D	6-1	200	Leamington, Ont.	3-18-48	New England (WHA)	80	6	25	31	88

QUEBEC NORDIQUES

Le Club de Hockey les Nordiques, Inc.
Colisee de Quebec
Quebec City, Quebec
G1L 4W7
Telephone 418-529-4161
Telex 051-3068 NORDIQUES QBC

Chairman of the Board
JEAN LESAGE

President
MARCEL AUBUT

Executive Vice-President
REJEAN BERGERON

Vice-President
Director of Hockey Operations
MAURICE FILION

Coach
JACQUES DEMERS

Head Scout
YVAN PRUD'HOMME

Director of Promotions
ROBERT MARTIMBEAULT

Ticket Manager
LUCIEN BOUTET

Trainers
RENE LACASSE
CLAUDE LANGLOIS
BRIAN TURPIN

Supervisor of Minor Officials
RAYMOND PUCHOL

Home Arena
Quebec Coliseum

Seating Capacity
10,004

Ticket Prices
12.00, 9.00, 5.75

Broadcasting Radio Station
CKCV-AM (1280)

Announcers
ANDRE COTE
MICHEL VILLENEUVE

Team Colors
Blue, Red, White

Marcel Aubut

Maurice Filion

Jacques Demers

14

QUEBEC NORDIQUES ROSTER — 1978-79

GOALTENDERS

PLAYER	POS	HT	WT	PLACE OF BIRTH	DATE	1977-78 CLUB	GP	MINS	GA	SO	GAA
Brodeur, Richard	G	5-7	175	Montreal, Que.	9-15-52	Quebec (WHA)	37	1962	123	0	3.70
Corsi, Jim	G	5-8	173	Montreal, Que.	6-19-54	Quebec (WHA)	22	1089	80	0	4.52
Levasseur, Louis	G	5-10	160	Noranda, Que.	6-16-49	New England (WHA)	27	1655	91	3	3.30

FORWARDS

PLAYER	POS	HT	WT	PLACE OF BIRTH	DATE	1977-78 CLUB	GP	G	A	PTS	PIM
Bernier, Serge	C	6-1	205	Padoue, Que.	4-29-47	Quebec (WHA)	74	26	52	78	48
Bilodeau, Gilles	LW	6-1	220	St. Prime, Que.	6-31-55	Birmingham (WHA)	59	2	2	4	258
						Binghamton (AHL)	4	1	2	3	7
Bordeleau, Christian	C	5-8	160	Noranda, Que.	9-23-47	Quebec (WHA)	26	9	22	31	30
Bordeleau, Paulin	RW	5-9	155	Noranda, Que.	1-29-53	Quebec (WHA)	78	42	23	65	29
Brackenbury, Curt	RW	5-10	190	Kapuskasing, Que.	1-31-52	Quebec (WHA)	32	4	9	13	52
Cloutier, Real	RW	5-10	185	St. Emile, Que	7-30-56	Quebec (WHA)	72	56	73	119	19
Cote, Alain	LW	5-10	203	Matane, Que.	5-03-57	Quebec (WHA)	40	3	5	8	8
						Hampton (AHL)	36	15	17	32	38
David, Richard	LW	6-2	205	N.D. de la Salette, Que.	4-08-58	ThreeRivers (QJMHL)	69	50	61	111	81
Dube, Normand	LW	5-11	185	Sherbrooke, Que	9-12-51	Quebec (WHA)	47	16	31	47	76
Fitchner, Bob	C	6-0	190	Sudbury, Ont	12-22-50	Quebec (WHA)	72	15	28	43	76
Geoffrion, Danny	RW	5-10	185	Montreal, Que.	1-24-58	Cornwall (OJMHL)	71	68	75	143	183
Lagace, Pierre	C	6-2	210	L'Abord-A-Plouffe, Que.	10-27-57	Hampton (AHL)	17	2	4	6	4
						Quebec (WHA)	22	2	3	5	4
Tardif, Marc	LW	6-1	190	Granby, Que.	6-12-49	Quebec (WHA)	78	65	89	154	50

DEFENSEMEN

PLAYER	POS	HT	WT	PLACE OF BIRTH	DATE	1977-78 CLUB	GP	G	A	PTS	PIM
Baxter, Paul	D	5-11	200	Winnipeg, Man.	10-28-55	Quebec (WHA)	76	6	29	35	239
Dorey, Jim	D	6-1	192	Kingston, On.	8-17-47	Quebec (WHA)	28	1	9	20	23
Hoganson, Dale	D	5-10	190	North Battleford, Sask.	7-08-49	Birmingham (WHA)	43	1	12	13	29
Lacombe, Francois	D	5-10	188	Montreal, Que.	2-24-48	Quebec (WHA)	26	1	7	8	12
Lariviere, Gary	D	6-0	190	St. Catharines, Ont.	12-06-54	Quebec (WHA)	80	7	49	56	76
Tremblay, J.C.	D	5-9	187	Bagotville, Que.	1-22-39	Quebec (WHA)	54	5	37	42	26
Weir, Wally	D	6-2	195	Verdun, Que.	6-03-54	Quebec (WHA)	13	0	0	0	47

WINNIPEG JETS

Winnipeg Jets Hockey Club, Inc.
15-1430 Maroons Road
Winnipeg, Manitoba R3G 0L5
Telephone 204-772-9491
Telex 075-87810 HOCKEY WPG

President
MICHAEL GOBUTY

Executive Vice-President
R. M. (BOBBY) HULL

Executive Director of Marketing and Administration
ROBERT BELL

Executive Director Hockey Operations
RUDY PILOUS

Coach
LARRY HILLMAN

Chief Scout
BILL ROBINSON

Eastern Scout
NORM DEFELICE

Assistant Director of Marketing
KEN FENSON

Trainer
BILL BOZAK

Equipment Manager
KELLY PRUDEN

Supervisor of Minor Officials
R. M. (SAM) SANREGRET

Home Arena
Winnipeg Arena

Seating Capacity
10,151

Ticket Prices
10.00, 9.50, 8.00, 5.50, 4.25

Broadcasting Radio Station
CJOB-AM (680)

Announcer
KEN NICHOLSEN

Team Colors:
Red, White, Blue

Michael Gobuty

Rudy Pilous

Larry Hillman

16

WINNIPEG JETS ROSTER — 1978-79

GOALTENDERS

PLAYER	POS	HT	WT	PLACE OF BIRTH	DATE	1977-78 CLUB	GP	MIN	GA	SO	GAA
Daley, Joe	G	5-10	171	Kildonan, Man.	2-20-43	Winnipeg (WHA)	37	2075	114	1	3.30
Mattsson, Markus	G	6-0	180	Tampere, Finland	7-30-57	Winnipeg (WHA)	10	511	30	0	3.52
						Quebec (WHA)	6	266	30	0	6.77

FORWARDS

PLAYER	POS	HT	WT	PLACE OF BIRTH	DATE	1977-78 CLUB	GP	G	A	PTS	PIM
Gray, John	RW	5-10	180	Little Current, Ont.	8-13-49	Houston (WHA)	77	35	23	58	80
Guindon, Bob	C	5-9	175	Labelle, Que.	11-19-50	Winnipeg (WHA)	77	20	22	42	18
Hicks, Glenn	LW	5-10½	177	Red Deer, Alta.	8-29-58	Flin Flon (WCL)	72	50	69	119	225
Hull, Bobby	LW	5-10	191	Point Anne, Ont.	1-03-39	Winnipeg (WHA)	77	46	71	117	23
Lesuk, Bill	LW	5-9	187	Moose Jaw, Sask.	11-01-46	Winnipeg (WHA)	80	9	18	27	41
Lindstrom, Willy	RW	6-0	180	Grums, Sweden	5-05-51	Winnipeg (WHA)	77	30	30	60	42
Lukowich, Morris	LW	5-9	170	Saskatoon, Sask.	6-01-56	Houston (WHA)	80	40	35	75	131
Moffat, Lyle	LW	5-10	185	Calgary, Alta.	3-19-48	Winnipeg (WHA)	57	9	16	25	39
Nilsson, Kent	C	6-1	185	Nynasham, Sweden	8-31-56	Winnipeg (WHA)	80	42	65	107	8
Preston, Rich	RW	6-0	185	Regina, Sask.	5-22-52	Houston (WHA)	73	25	25	0	52
Ruskowski, Terry	C	5-9	170	Prince Albert, Sask.	12-31-54	Houston (WHA)	78	15	57	72	170
Sullivan, Peter	C	5-9	170	Toronto, Ont.	7-25-51	Winnipeg (WHA)	77	16	39	55	43
West, Steve	C	5-8	150	Peterborough, Ont.	3-20-52	Houston (WHA)	71	11	21	32	23
Yakiwchuk, Dale	C	6-4	205	Calgary, Alta.	10-17-58	Portland (WCL)	62	34	51	85	312

DEFENSEMEN

PLAYER	POS	HT	WT	PLACE OF BIRTH	DATE	1977-78 CLUB	GP	G	A	PTS	PIM
Amodeo, Mike	D	5-10	190	Toronto, Ont.	6-22-57	Sweden (SIHF)	unavailable				
						Winnipeg (WHA)	3	1	1	2	3
Clackson, Kim	D	5-11	195	Saskatoon, Sask.	2-13-55	Winnipeg (WHA)	52	2	7	9	203
Campbell, Scott	D	6-2	205	Toronto, Ont.	6-22-57	Houston (WHA)	75	8	29	37	116
Davis, Bill	D	6-1	190	Lindsay, Ont.	8-22-54	Winnipeg (WHA)	12	0	0	0	2
Green, Ted	D	5-11	195	St. Boniface, Man.	3-23-40	Winnipeg (WHA)	73	4	22	26	52
Long, Barry	D	6-2	210	Red Deer, Ont.	1-31-49	Winnipeg (WHA)	78	7	24	31	42
MacKinnon, Paul	D	6-0	190	Brantford, Ont.	11-06-58	Peterborough (OHA)	60	1	26	27	80
Sjoberg, Lars-Erik	D	5-8	179	Falun, Sweden	4-05-44	Winnipeg (WHA)	78	11	39	50	72
Terbenche, Paul	D	5-10	190	Trail, B.C.	9-16-45	Birmingham (WHA)	11	1	0	1	0

1977-78 REGULAR SEASON

New England Whaler Johnny "Pie" McKenzie enters his seventh WHA season this year. For McKenzie's career record, see page 108.

WORLD HOCKEY ASSOCIATION FINAL STANDINGS 1977-78 SEASON

TEAM	GP	W	L	T	PTS	GF	GA	PCT
Winnipeg Jets	80	50	28	2	102	381	270	.638
New England Whalers	80	44	31	5	93	335	269	.581
Houston Aeros	80	42	34	4	88	296	302	.550
Quebec Nordiques	80	40	37	3	83	349	347	.519
Edmonton Oilers	80	38	39	3	79	309	307	.494
Birmingham Bulls	80	36	41	3	75	287	314	.469
Cincinnati Stingers	80	35	42	3	73	298	332	.456
Indianapolis Racers	80	24	51	5	53	267	353	.331
Soviet All-Stars	8	3	4	1	7	27	36	.438
Czechoslovakia	8	1	6	1	3	21	40	.188

HOME RECORDS

TEAM	GP	W	L	T	PTS	GF	GA	PCT
Quebec Nordiques	41	29	10	2	60	210	150	.732
Winnipeg Jets	41	28	11	2	58	213	124	.707
Houston Aeros	41	26	13	2	54	165	139	.659
New England Whalers	41	26	14	1	53	180	120	.646
Edmonton Oilers	41	24	15	2	50	186	147	.610
Birmingham Bulls	41	23	16	2	48	171	127	.585
Cincinnati Stingers	41	21	19	1	43	163	154	.524
Indianapolis Racers	41	17	21	3	37	159	162	.451
TOTALS	328	194	119	15	403	1447	1123	.614

ROAD RECORDS

TEAM	GP	W	L	T	PTS	GF	GA	PCT
Winnipeg Jets	39	22	17	0	44	168	146	.564
New England Whalers	39	18	17	4	40	155	149	.513
Houston Aeros	39	16	21	2	34	131	163	.436
Cincinnati Stingers	39	14	23	2	30	135	178	.385
Edmonton Oilers	39	14	24	1	29	123	160	.372
Birmingham Bulls	39	13	25	1	27	116	187	.346
Quebec Nordiques	39	11	27	1	23	139	197	.295
Indianapolis Racers	39	7	30	2	16	108	191	.205
CCCP/CSSR	16	4	10	2	10	48	76	.313
TOTALS	328	119	194	15	253	1123	1447	.386

TOP THIRTY INDIVIDUAL SCORERS

	PLAYER	TEAM	GP	G	A	PTS	PIM	EGR	EG%
1.	Tardif, Marc	Que	78	65	89	154	50	+15	+.08
2.	Cloutier, Real	Que	73	56	73	129	19	+14	+.09
3.	Nilsson, Ulf	Wpg	73	37	89	126	89	+41	+.08
4.	Hedberg, Anders	Wpg	77	63	59	122	60	+60	+.14
5.	Hull, Bobby	Wpg	77	46	71	117	23	+55	+.12
6.	Lacroix, Andre	Hou	78	36	77	113	57	+ 8	evn
7.	Ftorek, Robbie	Cin	80	59	50	109	54	+31	+.16
8.	Nilsson, Kent*	Wpg	80	42	65	107	8	+27	+.03
9.	Howe, Gordie	NE	76	34	62	96	85	+46	+.14
10.	Howe, Mark	NE	70	30	61	91	32	+30	+.03
11.	Chipperfield, Ron	Edm	80	33	52	85	48	+ 1	+.01
12.	Leduc, Rich	Cin/Ind	82	37	46	83	82	-43	-.09
13.	St. Sauveur, Claude	Ind	72	36	42	78	24	- 5	+.09
13.	Bernier, Serge	Que	58	26	52	78	48	- 1	-.02
15.	Linseman, Ken*	Bir	71	38	38	76	126	+ 6	evn
16.	Lukowich, Morris	Hou	80	40	35	75	131	+13	+.04
17.	Ruskowski, Terry	Hou	78	15	57	72	170	+13	+.04
18.	Dudley, Rick	Cin	72	30	41	71	156	- 1	+.02
18.	Marrin, Peter	Bir	80	28	43	71	53	+ 9	+.04
18.	Rogers, Mike	NE	80	28	43	71	46	+22	+.02
21.	Flett, Bill	Edm	74	41	28	69	34	+ 9	+.04
22.	MacDonald, Blair	Edm	80	34	34	68	11	-12	-.05
23.	Antonovich, Mike	NE	75	32	35	67	32	+17	-.01
23.	Hislop, Jamie	Cin	80	24	43	67	17	+20	+.11
25.	Henderson, Paul	Bir	80	37	29	66	22	+ 4	+.01
26.	Bordeleau, Paulin	Que	77	42	23	65	29	-13	-.02
26.	Napier, Mark	Bir	79	33	32	65	90	-11	-.05
28.	Tonelli, John	Hou	65	23	41	64	103	+13	+.04
29.	Keon, Dave	NE	77	24	38	62	2	- 4	-.10
30.	Larose, Claude	Cin/Ind	79	25	36	61	18	-26	-.04
30.	Roberts, Gordie	NE	78	15	46	61	118	+17	-.05

TOP TEN INDIVIDUAL GOALTENDERS

	PLAYER	TEAM	GAA	GP	MINS	SO	SV%	W	L	T
1.	Smith, Al	NE	3.22	55	3246	2	.885	30	20	3
2.	Daley, Joe	Wpg	3.30	37	2075	1	.883	21	11	1
2.	Levasseur, Louis	NE	3.30	27	1655	3	.886	14	11	2
2.	Bromley, Gary	Wpg	3.30	39	2252	1	.886	25	12	1
5.	Wakely, Ernie	Cin/Hou	3.41	57	3381	2	.891	28	23	4
6.	Dryden, Dave	Edm	3.49	48	2578	2	.879	21	23	2
7.	Dion, Michel	Cin	3.57	45	2356	4	.885	21	17	1
8.	McLeod, Don	Que/Edm	3.67	40	2126	2	.865	17	14	1
9.	Brodeur, Richard	Que	3.70	36	1962	0	.892	18	15	2
10.	Garrett, John	Bir	3.81	58	3306	2	.877	24	31	1

INDIVIDUAL SCORING AND PENALTY STATISTICS

PLAYER	POS	TEAM	GP	G	A	PT.	PIM	EG	EG%
Abgrall, Dennis	LW	Cin	65	13	11	24	13	- 2	+.03
Addouno, Ray	C	Ind	8	1	2	3	0	- 5	-.14
Ahrens, Chris	D	Edm	4	0	0	0	15	- 5	-.31
Allen, Jeff	D	Cin	2	0	0	0	0	evn	evn
Alley, Steve	LW	Bir	27	8	12	20	11	+17	+.26
Amodeo, Mike	D	Wpg	3	1	1	2	0	+ 3	+.25
Antonovich, Mike	LW	NE	75	32	35	67	32	+17	-.01
Arndt, Danny	LW	Bir	4	0	1	1	0	+ 1	+.11
Baird, Ken	LW	Edm/Wpg	55	16	11	27	31	+ 5	-.01
Baltimore, Bryon	D	Ind/Cin	50	3	16	19	70	- 9	+.02
Baxter, Paul	D	Que	76	6	29	35	240	-37	-.12
Beaton, Frank	LW	Bir	56	6	9	15	279	- 8	-.07
Beaudoin, Serge	D	Cin/Bir	77	8	26	34	115	+ 3	evn
Bergman, Thommie	D	Wpg	65	5	28	33	43	+22	-.01
Bernier, Jean	D	Que	74	10	32	42	4	+22	+.13
Bernier, Serge	C	Que	58	26	52	78	48	- 1	-.02
Bilodeau, Gilles	LW	Bir	59	2	2	4	258	-14	-.09
Block, Ken	D	Ind	77	1	25	26	34	-39	-.06
Bolduc, Danny	RW	NE	41	5	5	10	22	+ 6	+.03
Bordeleau, Chris	C	Que	26	9	22	31	28	+ 6	+.05
Bordeleau, Paulin	RW	Que	77	42	23	65	29	-13	-.02
Boudrias, Andre	C	Que	66	10	17	27	22	+ 4	+.04
Brackenbury, Curt	RW	Que	33	4	9	13	54	+ 4	-.01
Broderick, Ken	G	Edm/Que	33	0	0	0	0	—	—
Brodeur, Richard	G	Que	36	0	2	2	0	—	—
Bromley, Gary	G	Wpg	39	0	1	1	4	—	—
Burgess, Don	LW	Ind	79	11	12	23	2	-30	-.08
Busniuk, Ron	D	Edm	59	2	18	20	157	- 8	-.02
Butters, Bill	D	NE	45	1	13	14	69	+21	+.03
Callighen, Brett	LW	Edm	80	20	30	50	112	+ 5	+.02
Campbell, Bryan	C	Edm	53	7	13	20	12	-17	-.11
*Campbell, Scott	D	Hou	75	8	29	37	116	+10	+.02
Carlson, Jack	LW	NE	67	9	20	29	192	+ 9	-.03
Carlson, Steve	C	NE	38	6	7	13	11	+ 7	+.05
Carroll, Greg	C	NE/Cin	74	15	27	42	63	+ 6	-.01
Cassolato, Tony	RW	Bir	77	18	25	43	59	- 3	-.01
Chipperfield, Ron	C	Edm	80	33	52	85	48	+ 1	+.01
Clackson, Kim	D	Wpg	52	2	7	9	203	+ 6	-.04
Cloutier, Real	RW	Que	73	56	73	129	19	+14	+.09
Coates, Brian	LW	Cin	42	8	10	18	18	+ 7	+.05
Connor, Cam	LW	Hou	68	21	16	37	217	+ 4	evn
Constantin, Charles	LW	Que/Ind	54	4	5	9	50	- 2	evn
*Corsi, Jim	G	Que	23	0	1	1	2	—	—
*Cote, Alain	LW	Que	27	3	5	8	8	- 9	-.06
*Cross, Jim	D	Edm	2	0	0	0	0	- 3	-.43
Daley, Joe	G	Wpg	37	0	2	2	2	—	—
Davis, Bill	D	Wpg	12	0	0	0	2	- 9	-.21
Deadmarsh, Butch	LW	Edm/Cin	65	8	9	17	118	+ 5	+.02
Debol, Dave	C	Cin	9	3	2	5	2	+ 2	+.09
Demarco, Ab	D	Edm	47	6	8	14	20	- 7	-.07
Devine, Kevin	LW	Ind	76	19	23	42	141	-24	evn
Dion, Michel	G	Cin	45	0	0	0	26	—	—
Dorey, Jim	D	Que	26	1	9	10	23	- 5	-.07
*Dornseif, Dave	D	Ind	3	0	1	1	0	+ 1	+.28
Driscoll, Peter	LW	Que/Ind	77	28	28	56	158	- 1	+.06
Dryden, Dave	G	Edm	48	0	1	1	0	—	—

PLAYER	POS	TEAM	GP	G	A	PT.	PIM	EG	EG%
Dryden, Dave	G	Edm	48	0	1	1	0	—	—
Dube, Norm	LW	Que	73	16	31	47	17	-10	-.01
Dudley, Rick	LW	Cin	72	30	41	71	156	- 1	+.02
Dunn, Dave	D	Wpg	66	6	20	26	79	+20	-.01
Durbano, Steve	D	Bir	45	6	4	10	284	-12	-.11
Evans, Chris	D	Bir/Que	48	1	4	5	26	-11	-.02
Falkenberg, Bob	D	Edm	2	0	0	0	0	- 1	-.09
Ferguson, Norm	RW	Edm	71	26	21	47	2	+14	+.06
Fitchner, Bob	D	Que	72	15	28	43	76	- 5	-.01
Flett, Bill	RW	Edm	74	41	28	69	34	+ 9	+.04
Ford, Mike	D	Wpg	3	0	0	0	0	- 5	-.45
Fortier, Dave	D	Ind	54	1	15	16	86	-17	+.01
French, John	LW	Ind	74	9	8	17	6	-25	-.07
Ftorek, Robbie	C	Cin	80	59	50	109	54	+31	+.16
Garrett, John	G	Bir	58	0	3	3	26	—	—
*Gilligan, Bill	RW	Cin	54	10	14	24	59	-13	-.08
Goldsworthy, Bill	RW	Ind	32	8	10	18	10	+ 2	+.13
Gorman, Dave	LW	Bir	63	19	21	40	93	+18	+.08
Gray, John	LW	Hou	77	35	23	58	80	+15	+.05
Green, Ted	D	Wpg	73	4	22	26	52	+19	evn
Greig, Bruce	LW	Cin	32	3	1	4	57	- 1	-.01
Guindon, Robert	C/RW	Wpg	77	20	22	42	18	- 1	-.06
Guite, Pierre	LW	Que/Edm	78	16	26	42	86	- 1	-.03
Hagman, Matti	C	Que	53	25	31	56	16	-14	-.02
Hale, Larry	D	Hou	56	2	11	13	22	+ 4	evn
Hall, Del	LW	Cin/Edm	26	4	3	7	4	- 3	-.01
Hamilton, Al	D	Edm	59	11	43	54	46	+24	+.10
Handrahan, Alf	RW	Cin	14	1	3	4	42	+ 2	-.02
Hangsleben, Alan	D/LW	NE	79	11	18	29	140	+17	-.02
Hansis, Ron	R/LW	Hou	78	13	9	22	51	evn	-.01
*Hanson, Dave	LW	Bir	42	7	16	23	241	+10	+.06
Harris, Hugh	LW/C	Ind/Cin	64	12	30	42	36	- 3	evn
Hedberg, Anders	RW	Wpg	77	63	59	122	60	+60	+.14
Henderson, Paul	LW	Bir	80	37	29	66	22	+ 4	+.01
Hislop, Jamie	RW	Cin	80	24	43	67	17	+20	+.11
Hoganson, Dale	D	Bir	43	1	12	13	29	- 6	-.06
Hoganson, Paul	G	Cin	7	0	0	0	0	—	—
*Holland, Jerry	LW	Edm	22	2	1	3	14	- 1	-.05
Hornung, Larry	D	Wpg	19	1	4	5	2	+17	+.21
Howe, Gordie	C	NE	76	34	62	96	85	+46	+.14
Howe, Mark	LW	NE	70	30	61	91	32	+30	+.03
Howe, Marty	D	NE	75	10	10	20	66	+10	-.04
Huck, Fran	C	Wpg	5	0	0	0	2	- 2	-.25
Hughes, Brent	D	Bir	80	9	35	44	48	+12	+.06
Hughes, Frank	RW	Hou	11	3	2	5	2	-10	-.19
Hughes, John	D	Hou	79	3	25	28	130	+20	+.06
Hull, Bobby	LW	Wpg	77	46	71	117	23	+55	+.12
Inkpen, Dave	D	Edm/Que/Ind	67	1	11	12	60	-17	-.01
Inness, Gary	G	Ind	52	0	0	0	42	—	—
Irwin, Glen	D	Hou/Ind	23	0	0	0	72	- 3	+.01
Jarry, Pierre	LW	Edm	18	4	10	14	4	- 1	+.07
Keon, Dave	C	NE	77	24	38	62	2	- 4	-.10
Kryskow, Dave	LW	Wpg	71	20	21	41	16	+12	+.01
Labraaten, Dan	LW	Wpg	47	18	16	34	30	+ 7	-.04
Lacombe, Francois	D	Que	22	1	7	8	12	+ 1	-.04
Lacroix, Andre	C	Hou	78	36	77	113	57	+ 8	evn
*Lagace, Pierre	C	Que	17	2	4	6	2	+ 1	+.09
Lahache, Floyd	D	Cin	11	0	3	3	13	- 6	-.04
Langevin, Dave	D	Edm	62	6	22	28	90	+11	+.05

PLAYER	POS	TEAM	GP	G	A	PT.	PIM	EG	EG%
*Langway, Rod	LW	Bir	52	3	18	21	52	+10	+.08
LaPointe, Norm	G	Cin	13	0	1	1	4	—	—
Lariviere, Garry	D	Que	80	7	49	56	78	+ 3	+.04
Larose, Claude	LW	Cin/Ind	79	25	36	61	18	-26	-.04
Larway, Don	RW	Hou	69	24	35	59	52	+ 1	-.02
Leclerc, Rene	RW	Ind	60	12	15	27	31	- 7	+.06
Leduc, Rich	C	Cin/Ind	82	37	46	83	82	-43	-.09
Legge, Barry	D	Cin	78	7	17	24	114	- 7	-.01
Lesuk, Bill	LW	Wpg	80	9	18	27	48	- 4	-.07
Levasseur, Louis	G	NE	27	0	0	0	2	—	—
Ley, Rick	D	NE	73	3	41	44	95	+36	+.05
Lindstrom, Willy	RW	Wpg	77	30	30	60	42	+ 4	-.04
*Linseman, Ken	C	Bir	71	38	38	76	126	+ 6	evn
*Liut, Mike	G	Cin	27	0	1	1	0	—	—
*Lloyd, Owen	D	Edm	3	0	1	1	4	- 1	+.20
Locas, Jacques	C	Cin	17	0	2	2	6	- 7	-.10
Long, Barry	D	Wpg	78	7	24	31	42	+10	-.06
Lukowich, Morris	LW	Hou	80	40	35	75	131	+13	+.04
Lund, Larry	C	Hou	76	9	17	26	36	-22	-.12
Lyle, George	RW	NE	68	30	24	54	74	+12	-.02
MacDonald, Blair	RW	Edm	80	34	34	68	11	-12	-.05
MacGregor, Gary	C	Edm	37	11	2	13	29	- 2	-.03
Maggs, Darryl	D	Ind/Cin	62	8	20	28	37	-18	-.01
Mahovlich, Frank	LW	Bir	72	14	24	38	22	- 5	-.05
Marotte, Gilles	D	Cin/Ind	73	3	20	23	76	-23	evn
Marrin, Peter	C	Bir	80	28	43	71	53	+ 9	+.04
Marsh, Peter	RW	Cin	74	25	25	50	123	-17	-.05
*Mattsson, Markus	G	Que/Wpg	16	0	0	0	2	—	—
Maxwell, Bryan	D	NE	17	2	1	3	11	+ 9	+.09
Mayer, Jim	RW	NE	51	11	9	20	21	+ 1	-.03
*Mazur, John	LW	Hou	1	0	0	0	0	- 1	-.33
McDuffe, Peter	G	Ind	12	0	0	0	0	—	—
McKay, Ray	D	Edm	14	1	4	5	4	+ 3	+.18
McKenzie, John	RW	NE	79	27	29	56	61	+15	-.01
McLeod, Al	D	Hou	80	2	22	24	54	+18	+.05
McLeod, Don	G	Que/Edm	40	0	10	10	2	—	—
McMullen, Dale	LW	Edm	1	0	0	0	0	evn	evn
Melrose, Barry	D	Cin	69	2	9	11	113	-10	-.04
*Micheletti, Joe	D/LW	Edm	56	14	34	48	56	+ 8	evn
Miller, Warren	RW	Edm/Que	78	16	28	44	68	-25	-.07
*Mio, Ed	G	Ind	17	0	0	0	0	—	—
Moffat, Lyle	LW	Wpg	57	9	16	25	39	- 6	-.07
Morris, Rick	RW	Edm/Que	30	1	6	7	47	- 6	-.01
Morrison, Kevin	D	Ind	75	17	40	57	49	-32	evn
Mortson, Keke	C	Hou	6	0	1	1	7	- 1	-.04
Napier, Mark	RW	Bir	79	33	32	65	90	-11	-.05
Nedomansky, Vaclav	C	Bir	12	2	3	5	6	- 9	-.18
*Nilsson, Kent	C	Wpg	80	42	65	107	8	+27	+.03
Nilsson, Ulf	C	Wpg	73	37	*89	126	89	+41	+.08
Noris, Joe	C	Bir	45	9	19	28	6	- 9	-.04
*Norwich, Craig	D	Cin	65	7	23	30	48	+ 3	+.05
Paiement, Rosaire	RW	Ind	61	6	24	30	81	-23	-.02
Parizeau, Michel	C	Ind	70	13	27	40	47	-13	+.02
Park, Jim	G	Ind	12	0	0	0	6	—	—
Patenaude, Rusty	RW	Ind	76	23	19	42	71	- 2	+.02
Peloffy, Andre	C	NE	10	2	0	2	2	- 2	-.06
Pinder, Gerry	LW	Edm	5	0	1	1	0	- 1	+.01
Pleau, Larry	LW	NE	54	16	18	34	4	+12	-.02
Plumb, Ron	D	Cin/NE	81	14	43	57	63	-12	-.02

PLAYER	POS	TEAM	GP	G	A	PT.	PIM	EG	EG%
Popiel, Poul	D	Hou	80	6	31	37	53	- 6	-.06
Powis, Lynn	C	Ind/Wpg	69	16	25	41	18	- 3	-.01
Prentice, Bill	D/LW	Ind	21	1	1	2	28	- 4	+.01
Preston, Rich	RW	Hou	73	25	25	50	52	+ 3	evn
*Primeau, Kevin	RW	Edm	7	0	1	1	2	- 1	evn
Rhiness, Brad	C	Ind	12	3	3	6	2	- 4	-.02
Roberto, Phil	RW	Bir	53	8	20	28	91	+ 7	+.03
Roberts, Gordie	D	NE	78	15	46	61	118	+17	-.05
Rogers, Mike	C	NE	80	28	43	71	46	+22	+.02
Rota, Randy	LW	Edm	53	8	22	30	12	+11	+.05
Ruhnke, Kent	RW	Wpg	21	8	9	17	2	+ 9	+.03
Ruskowski, Terry	C	Hou	78	15	57	72	170	+13	+.04
Rutledge, Wayne	G	Hou	12	0	0	0	2	—	—
*Sandbeck, Cal	D	Edm	11	1	2	3	39	+ 1	+.08
St. Sauveur, Claude	C	Ind	72	36	42	78	24	- 5	+.09
Schella, John	D	Hou	63	9	20	29	125	- 2	-.04
Selwood, Brad	D	NE	80	6	25	31	88	+11	-.05
*Semenko, Dave	LW	Edm	65	6	6	12	140	- 4	-.02
Sheehan, Bobby	C	Ind	29	8	7	15	6	-19	-.11
Sheehy, Tim	RW	Bir/NE	38	12	13	25	17	-16	-.18
Shmyr, Paul	D	Edm	80	9	40	49	100	- 9	-.03
Sjoberg, Lars-Erik	D	Wpg	78	11	39	50	72	+60	+.13
Smedsmo, Dale	LW	Ind	6	0	3	3	7	+ 3	+.30
Smith, Al	G	NE	55	0	3	3	4	—	—
Sobchuk, Dennis	C	Cin/Edm	36	11	12	23	26	-15	-.10
Spring, Frank	RW	Ind	13	2	4	6	2	+ 1	+.08
Stapleton, Pat	D	Cin	65	4	45	49	28	+ 6	+.04
*Stephenson, Bob	RW	Bir	39	7	6	13	33	- 2	-.01
Stewart, John C.	C	Bir	48	13	26	39	52	+13	+.06
Stewart, Paul	D	Cin	40	1	5	6	241	- 7	-.07
Stoughton, Blaine	RW	Cin/Ind	77	19	26	45	64	-37	-.08
Sullivan, Peter	C	Wpg	77	16	39	55	43	-12	-.13
Sutherland, Steve	LW	Que	75	23	10	33	143	-15	-.05
Tardif, Marc	LW	Que	78	65	89	154	50	+15	+.08
Taylor, Ted	LW	Hou	54	11	11	22	46	+ 8	+.03
Terbenche, Paul	D	Bir/Hou	11	1	0	1	0	+ 1	+.11
Thomas, Reg	LW	Ind/Cin	67	19	18	37	56	-16	evn
Tonelli, John	C/LW	Hou	65	23	41	64	103	+13	+.04
Topolnisky, Craig	D	Edm	10	0	2	2	4	- 1	+.03
Tremblay, J.C.	D	Que	54	5	37	42	26	-14	-.03
Trognitz, Willie	LW	Cin	29	2	1	3	94	- 3	-.01
Troy, Jim	RW	Edm	47	2	0	2	124	-11	-.07
Turkiewicz, Jim	D	Bir	78	3	21	24	45	+10	-.05
Turnbull, Frank	G	Edm	1	0	0	0	0	—	—
Wakely, Ernie	G	Cin/Hou	57	0	4	4	2	—	—
Webster, Tom	RW	NE	20	15	5	20	5	+ 8	+.05
Weir, Wally	D	Que	13	0	0	0	47	- 5	-.16
West, Steve	LW	Hou	71	11	21	32	23	+ 4	evn
Westrum, Pat	D	Bir	77	2	10	12	97	- 7	-.03
Widing, Juha	C	Edm	71	18	24	42	8	+10	+.05
Wilkins, Barry	D	Ind	79	2	21	23	79	-35	-.03
Wood, Wayne	G	Bir	32	0	3	3	22	—	—
Zimmerman, Lynn	G	Hou	20	0	0	0	4	—	—
*Zuke, Mike	C	Edm	71	23	34	57	47	+ 1	+.02

*Rookie

INDIVIDUAL GOALTENDING STATISTICS

	GAA	GP	MIN	W	L	T	PCT	SOG	SAA	GA	SVS	SV%	SO
NEW ENGLAND WHALERS	3.24	80	4900	44	31	5	.581	2306	28.2	265	2041	.885	5
Al Smith	3.22	55	3246	30	20	3	.594	1510	27.9	174	1336	.885	2
Louis Levasseur	3.30	27	1655	14	11	2	.536	796	28.9	91	705	.886	3
OPPONENT GOALTENDING	4.02	80	4893	31	44	5	.419	2579	31.6	328	2251	.873	2
WINNIPEG JETS	3.32	80	4837	50	28	2	.638	2318	28.8	268	2050	.884	2
Joe Daley	3.30	37	2075	21	11	1	.652	971	28.1	114	857	.883	1
Gary Bromley	3.30	39	2252	25	12	1	.671	1090	29.0	124	966	.886	1
Markuss Mattsson:													
Quebec	6.77	6	266	1	3	0	.250	166	37.4	30	136	.819	—
Winnipeg	3.52	10	511	4	5	0	.444	423	30.1	30	227	.883	—
SEASON TOTALS	4.63	16	777	5	8	0	.385	423	32.7	60	363	.858	—
OPPONENT GOALTENDING	4.67	80	4836	28	50	2	.363	2486	30.8	376	2110	.849	—
HOUSTON AEROS	3.66	80	4870	42	34	4	.550	2609	32.1	297	2312	.886	2
Ernie Wakely:													
Cincinnati	5.02	6	311	0	5	0	.000	146	28.2	26	120	.822	—
Houston	3.24	51	3070	28	18	4	.600	1608	31.4	166	1442	.897	2
SEASON TOTALS	3.41	57	3381	28	23	4	.545	1754	31.1	192	1562	.891	2
Lynn Zimmerman	4.32	20	1166	10	9	0	.526	641	33.0	84	557	.869	—
Wayne Rutledge	4.45	12	634	4	7	0	.364	360	34.1	47	313	.869	—
OPPONENT GOALTENDING	3.63	80	4864	34	42	4	.450	2219	27.4	294	1925	.868	3
EDMONTON OILERS	3.71	80	4858	38	39	3	.494	2218	27.4	300	1918	.865	4
Dave Dryden	3.49	48	2578	21	23	2	.478	1239	28.8	150	1089	.879	2
Don McLeod:													
Quebec	4.17	7	403	2	4	0	.333	215	32.0	28	187	.870	—
Edmonton	3.55	33	1723	15	10	1	.596	750	26.1	102	648	.864	2
SEASON TOTALS	3.67	40	2126	17	14	1	.547	965	27.2	130	835	.865	2
Frank Turnbull	6.00	1	60	0	1	0	.000	24	24.0	6	18	.750	—
TRADED GOALTENDER:													
Ken Broderick	5.07	9	497	2	5	0	.286	206	24.9	42	164	.796	—
OPPONENT GOALTENDING	3.72	80	4865	39	38	3	.506	2855	35.2	302	2553	.894	2

*WHA Rookie

	GAA	GP	MIN	W	L	T	PCT	SOG	SAA	GA	SVS	SV%	SO
BIRMINGHAM BULLS	3.82	80	4857	36	41	3	.469	2508	31.0	309	2199	.877	3
John Garrett	3.81	58	3306	24	31	1	.438	1714	31.1	210	1504	.877	2
Wayne Wood	3.83	32	1551	12	10	2	.542	794	30.7	99	695	.875	1
OPPONENT GOALTENDING	3.47	80	4854	41	36	3	.531	2252	27.8	281	1971	.875	4
CINCINNATI STINGERS	4.03	80	4854	35	42	3	.456	2527	31.2	326	2201	.871	4
Michel Dion	3.57	45	2356	21	17	1	.551	1220	31.1	140	1080	.885	4
*Mike Liut	4.25	27	1215	8	12	0	.400	663	32.7	86	577	.870	—
Paul Hoganson	4.42	7	326	1	2	1	.375	153	28.2	24	129	.843	—
Norm LaPointe	4.64	13	647	5	6	1	.458	345	32.0	50	295	.855	—
TRADED GOALTENDER:													
Ernie Wakely	5.02	6	311	0	5	0	.000	146	28.2	26	120	.822	—
OPPONENT GOALTENDING	3.63	80	4858	42	35	3	.544	2464	30.4	294	2170	.881	3
INDIANAPOLIS RACERS	4.24	80	4873	24	51	5	.331	2649	32.6	344	2305	.870	—
Gary Inness	4.21	52	2850	14	30	4	.333	1543	32.5	200	1343	.870	—
Jim Park	4.21	12	584	3	7	0	.300	323	33.2	41	282	.873	—
*Ed Mio	4.27	17	900	6	8	0	.429	470	31.3	64	406	.864	—
Peter McDuffe	4.34	12	539	1	6	1	.188	313	34.8	39	274	.875	—
OPPONENT GOALTENDING	3.26	80	4873	51	24	5	.669	2335	28.8	265	2070	.887	5
QUEBEC NORDIQUES	4.25	80	4860	40	37	3	.519	2738	33.8	344	2394	.874	—
Richard Brodeur	3.70	36	1962	18	15	2	.543	1120	34.3	121	999	.892	—
*Jim Corsi	4.52	23	1089	10	7	0	.588	647	35.6	82	565	.873	—
Ken Broderick:													
Edmonton	5.07	9	497	2	5	0	.286	206	24.9	42	164	.796	—
Quebec	4.37	24	1140	9	8	1	.528	590	31.1	83	507	.859	—
SEASON TOTALS	4.58	33	1637	11	31	1	.460	796	29.2	125	671	.843	—
TRADED GOALTENDERS:													
Markus Mattsson	6.77	6	266	1	3	0	.250	166	37.4	30	136	.819	—
Don McLeod	4.17	7	403	2	4	0	.333	215	32.0	28	187	.870	—
OPPONENT GOALTENDING	4.23	80	4863	37	40	3	.481	2714	33.5	343	2371	.874	—

*WHA Rookie

1977-78 THREE-OR-MORE GOAL NIGHTS

DATE	PLAYER	TEAM	OPPONENT	ELAPSED TIME	VS. GOALTENDER
Oct. 12/77	Hull, Bobby	Wpg	7, at Edm 3	36:51	Ken Broderick
Oct. 15/77	Lukowich, Morris	at Hou	5, Ind 1	20:41	Gary Inness
Oct. 19/77	Webster, Tom	NE	6, at Edm 3	22:41	Frank Turnbull
Oct. 23/77	Hull, Bobby	at Wpg	10, Bir 3	14:39	John Garrett
Oct. 26/77	St. Sauveur, Claude	at Ind	5, Wpg 3	26:46	*Markus Mattsson
Oct. 28/77	Campbell, Bryan	Edm	3, at Bir 2	27:32	John Garrett
Oct. 29/77	Sheehan, Bobby	at Ind	6, Bir 2	19:55	John Garrett
Oct. 30/77	Gray, John	Hou	4, at Que 5	45:35	Richard Brodeur
Nov. 12/77	Ftorek, Robbie	Cin	6, at Que 5	36:24	Don McLeod
Nov. 15/77	Antonovich, Mike	NE	6, at Ind 4	57:47	Gary Inness
Nov. 18/77	Tardif, Marc	Que	5, at Hou 6	48:04	Lynn Zimmerman
Nov. 20/77	Bordeleau, Paulin	at Que	5, Ind 2	42:35	Peter McDuffe
Nov. 24/77	Patenaude, Rusty	at Ind	5, Edm 4	(51:04)	Dave Dryden
Dec. 1/77	Tardif, Marc	Que	4, at Ind 5	46:02	Peter McDuffe-(2) Gary Inness-(1)
Dec. 9/77	Richter, Pavel	CSSR	5, at Ind 3	30:26	Gary Inness
Dec. 11/77	Baird, Ken	at Wpg	7, Ind 1	21:40	Gary Inness
Dec. 17/77	Carlson, Jack	at NE	3, Wpg 6	52:29	Gary Bromley
Dec. 21/77	Widing, Juha	at Edm	5, Sov. All-Stars 2	24:28	Gergej Barbariko
Dec. 29/77	Napier, Mark	Bir	7, at Cin 1	42:39	Michel Dion-(2) Norm Lapointe-(1)
Dec. 30/77	Sobchuk, Dennis	at Edm	8, Ind 5	45:24	Peter McDuffe-(2) Gary Inness-(1)
Jan. 10/78	*Linseman, Ken	Bir	4, at Que 6	31:38	Ken Broderick
Jan. 27/78	*Zuke, Mike	at Edm	9, Que 6	2:18	*Markus Mattsson
Jan. 28/78	Henderson, Paul	at Bir	8, Wpg 5	2:16	Joe Daley
Jan. 31/78	Nilsson, Ulf	Wpg	7, at Que 2	16:49	Ken Broderick-(2) *Jim Corsi-(1)
Feb. 1/78	Abgrall, Dennis	at Cin	8, Ind 0	40:06	Gary Inness
Feb. 7/78	Hagman, Matti	at Que	8, Bir 3	18:37	Wayne Wood
Feb. 8/78	Marsh, Peter	Cin	6, at Edm 6	15:00	Don McLeod
Feb. 8/78	Hedberg, Anders	at Wpg	9, Bir 0	33:09	John Garrett
Feb. 11/78	*Nilsson, Kent	Wpg	5, at Ind 3	29:58	Gary Inness
Feb. 15/78	Bordeleau, Paulin	Que	6, at Ind 9	13:07	Ed Mio
Feb. 17/78	Henderson, Paul	at Bir	5, Ind 4	(26:02)	Ed Mio
Feb. 23/78	Henderson, Paul	at Bir	7, Que 3	35:06	*Jim Corsi
Feb. 24/78	MacDonald, Blair	at Edm	5, Hou 4	(45:07)	Ernie Wakely
Feb. 26/78	Gray, John	Hou	6, at Wpg 9	45:10	Joe Daley-(1) Gary Bromley-(2)
Feb. 28/78	Cloutier, Real	at Que	5, Hou 2	54:10	Ernie Wakely
Mar. 3/78	Ftorek, Robbie	Cin	5, at Wpg 1	37:16	Gary Bromley
Mar. 11/78	*Nilsson, Kent	Wpg	7, at Que 4	37:46	Richard Brodeur
Mar. 14/78	Cloutier, Real	at Que	6, Edm 3	45:59	Don McLeod-(+EN)
Mar. 15/78	Antonovich, Mike	at NE	7, Ind 0	49:15	Gary Inness
Mar. 15/78	Ferguson, Norm	at Edm	6, Wpg 2	26:13	Gary Bromley
Mar. 22/78	Dudley, Rick	at Cin	9, Hou 2	22:22	Ernie Wakely
Mar. 25/78	Tardif, Marc	Que	3, at Hou 4	40:45	Lynn Zimmerman
Mar. 26/78	Howe, Mark	at NE	5, Edm 3	42:22	Don McLeod
Mar. 29/78	Rogers, Mike	at NE	6, Cin 1	21:15	Michel Dion-(1) Paul Hoganson-(2)
Apr. 2/78	Tardif, Marc	at Que	7, Hou 1	42:48	Ernie Wakely
Apr. 3/78	McKenzie, John	at NE	8, Hou 6	48:09	Lynn Zimmerman
Apr. 5/78	Demarco, Ab	at Edm	4, NE 4	7:35	Louis Levasseur
Arp. 9/78	Alley, Steve	Bir	9, at Ind 7	11:08	Jim Park
Apr. 9/78	Gorman, Dave	Bir	9, at Ind 7	15:08	Jim Park

4-GOAL NIGHTS

DATE	PLAYER	TEAM	OPPONENT	ELAPSED TIME	VS. GOALTENDER
Oct. 12/77	Leduc, Rich	at Cin	4, Ind 5	45:05	Gary Inness
Dec. 10/77	Hagman, Matti	at Que	5, Ind 3	26:46	Peter McDuffe
Dec. 14/77	Flett, Bill	at Edm	6, CSSR 1	23:08	Miroslav Kapoun
Dec. 26/77	Hedberg, Anders	at Wpg	9, Que 4	53:14	*Jim Corsi-(2) Ken Broderick-(2)
Jan. 1/78	Cloutier, Real	Que	5, at Bir 2	35:44	Wayne Wood
Feb. 3/78	MacDonald, Blair	Edm	6, at NE 3	46:49	Louis Levasseur
Feb. 18/78	Hedberg, Anders	Wpg	4, at Cin 0	35:58	Paul Hoganson

*Indicates player involved is a Rookie. Elapsed Time in Brackets ( ) indicates final goal scored in overtime.

POWER PLAY PROFICIENCY

WHA CLUBS	GP	MINS	AVG	OPP	GF	GA	PROF	FREQ
1. Quebec Nordiques	80	1216	15.2	277	79	10	28.5%	3.51
2. New England Whalers	80	1129	14.1	239	62	4	25.9%	3.85
3. Winnipeg Jets	80	1189	14.9	330	78	8	23.6%	4.23
4. Edmonton Oilers	80	1447	18.1	283	62	8	21.9%	4.56
5. Cincinnati Stingers	80	1528	19.1	295	62	10	21.0%	4.76
5. Birmingham Bulls	80	1949	24.4	286	60	13	21.0%	4.77
7. Houston Aeros	80	1331	16.6	270	56	8	20.7%	4.82
8. Indianapolis Racers	80	1512	18.9	317	56	13	17.7%	5.66

SHORTHANDED EFFICIENCY

WHA CLUBS	GP	PIM	PIM AVG	SIT	GF	GA	EFF	FREQ
1. Winnipeg Jets	80	988	12.4	233	16	44	81.1%	5.30
2. Edmonton Oilers	80	1296	16.2	292	11	60	79.5%	4.87
3. New England Whalers	80	1255	15.7	315	9	65	79.4%	4.85
4. Houston Aeros	80	1543	19.3	366	6	77	79.0%	4.75
5. Indianapolis Racers	80	1189	14.9	241	6	51	78.8%	4.73
6. Quebec Nordiques	80	1185	14.8	269	11	60	77.7%	4.48
7. Birmingham Bulls	80	2177	27.2	355	8	84	76.3%	4.23
8. Cincinnati Stingers	80	1701	21.3	256	7	76	70.3%	3.37

WORLD HOCKEY ASSOCIATION OVERTIME ANALYSIS 1972 - 1978

	77/78 OVERALL			77/78 AT HOME			77/78 ON ROAD			SIX YEAR OVERTIME TOTALS				
	W	L	T	W	L	T	W	L	T	O/P	O/W	O/L	O/T	O/PCT
Birmingham	3	4	3	2	3	2	1	1	1	62	14	26	22	.403
Cincinnati	6	3	3	3	1	1	3	2	2	29	8	12	9	.431
Edmonton	7	3	3	4	1	2	3	2	1	66	26	18	22	.561
Houston	5	4	4	3	2	2	2	2	2	45	13	13	19	.500
Indianapolis	3	5	5	2	2	3	1	3	2	55	14	19	22	.455
New England	4	6	5	0	4	1	4	2	4	69	26	14	29	.587
Quebec	7	5	2	3	2	1	4	3	1	64	26	20	18	.547
Winnipeg	1	6	2	0	4	2	1	2	0	64	20	24	20	.469
Czechoslovakia	0	0	1	—	—	—	0	0	1	1	0	0	1	.500
Other Clubs	—	—	—	—	—	—	—	—	—	299	95	96	108	.498
TOTALS	36	36	14	17	19	14	19	17	14	377	242	242	135	.500

EXTRA ATTACKER RESULTS 1977-78

	TIMES PULLED	TIMES WORKED	— SUCCESS — PCT.	FREQ.	TIMES BACKFIRED	— BACKFIRE — PCT.	FREQ.
Birmingham	15	-0-	—	—	5	33.3%	3.00
Cincinnati	17	2	11.8%	8.50	6	35.3%	2.83
Edmonton	22	3	13.6%	7.33	7	31.8%	3.14
Houston	11	-0-	—	—	4	36.4%	2.75
Indianapolis	17	3	17.6%	5.66	9	52.9%	1.89
New England ...	12	-0-	—	—	4	33.3%	3.00
Quebec	15	4	26.7%	3.75	3	20.0%	5.00
Winnipeg	8	-0-	—	—	2	25.0%	4.00
TOTALS	117	12	10.3%	9.75	40	34.2%	2.93

Winnipeg's Bobby Hull averaged over a point per game as the Jets captured the Avco World Trophy for the second time. For Hull's career record, see page 89.

1978 AVCO WORLD TROPHY GAME RESULTS

FINALS

WINNIPEG / NEW ENGLAND

May 12	WINNIPEG	4 New England	1
May 14	WINNIPEG	5 New England	2
May 19	New England	2 WINNIPEG	10
May 22	New England	3 WINNIPEG	5

(Winnipeg wins, four games to none)

SEMI-FINALS

NEW ENGLAND / QUEBEC

April 28	Quebec	1 NEW ENGLAND	5
April 30	QUEBEC	3 New England	2
May 3	NEW ENGLAND	5 Quebec	4
May 5	NEW ENGLAND	7 Quebec	3
May 7	Quebec	3 NEW ENGLAND	6

(New England wins, four games to one)

QUARTER FINALS

QUEBEC / HOUSTON

April 16	Quebec	3 HOUSTON	4*
April 18	QUEBEC	5 Houston	4*
April 20	Houston	1 QUEBEC	5
April 21	Houston	0 QUEBEC	3
April 23	Quebec	2 HOUSTON	5
April 26	Houston	2 QUEBEC	11

(Quebec wins, four games to two)

NEW ENGLAND / EDMONTON

April 14	Edmonton	4 NEW ENGLAND	6
April 16	Edmonton	1 NEW ENGLAND	4
April 19	New England	0 EDMONTON	2
April 21	NEW ENGLAND	9 Edmonton	1
April 23	Edmonton	1 NEW ENGLAND	4

(New England wins, four games to one)

WINNIPEG / BIRMINGHAM

April 14	Birmingham	3 WINNIPEG	9
April 16	Birmingham	3 WINNIPEG	8
April 19	Winnipeg	2 BIRMINGHAM	3
April 21	WINNIPEG	5 Birmingham	1
April 23	Birmingham	2 WINNIPEG	5

(Winnipeg wins, four games to one)

© 2018 WHA HOF / PCMP LLC
CAPITAL LETTERS DENOTE HOME TEAMS
*Games decided in overtime

1978 AVCO WORLD TROPHY PLAYOFF STATISTICS

BIRMINGHAM BULLS

PLAYER	GP	G	A	PTS	PIM	+/-	+/-%
Linseman, Ken	5	2	2	4	15	+1	+.20
Marrin, Peter	5	0	3	3	2	-2	evn
Beaton, Frank	5	2	0	2	10	-2	evn
Mahovlich, Frank	3	1	1	2	0	+2	+.29
Gorman, Dave	4	1	1	2	0	-2	-.06
Henderson, Paul	5	1	1	2	0	-4	-.20
Stewart, John C.	5	1	1	2	6	-3	-.13
Turkiewicz, Jim	5	1	1	2	0	-2	-.07
Durbano, Steve	4	0	2	2	16	evn	+.15
Napier, Mark	5	0	2	2	14	+2	+.27
Roberto, Phil	4	1	0	1	20	-2	-.06
Alley, Steve	5	1	0	1	5	-3	-.20
Beaudoin, Serge	5	1	0	1	46	-2	evn
Westrum, Pat	3	0	1	1	—	+1	+.17
Hanson, Dave	5	0	1	1	48	-1	-.03
Wood, Wayne	1	0	0	0	0	—	—
Bilodeau, Gilles	3	0	0	0	27	+1	+.17
Cassolato, Tony	4	0	0	0	4	-2	-.13
Langway, Rod	4	0	0	0	9	-2	-.18
Garrett, John	5	0	0	0	0	—	—
Hoganson, Dale	5	0	0	0	7	-1	+.07
Hughes, Brent	5	0	0	0	12	-3	-.07
BULL TOTALS	5	12	16	28	243	-5	
OPPONENT TOTALS	5	29	51	80	172	+5	

EDMONTON OILERS

PLAYER	GP	G	A	PTS	PIM	+/-	+/-%
Zuke, Mike	5	2	3	5	0	-2	+.21
Shmyr, Paul	5	1	3	4	11	-3	+.13
Chipperfield, Ron	5	1	1	2	0	-1	+.02
Guite, Pierre	5	1	1	2	20	-3	-.05
Rota, Randy	5	1	1	2	4	-1	+.02
MacDonald, Blair	5	1	1	2	0	-2	+.21
Callighen, Brett	5	0	2	2	16	-1	+.02
Langevin, Dave	5	0	2	2	10	-4	-.13
Micheletti, Joe	5	0	2	2	4	evn	+.09
Jarry, Pierre	5	1	0	1	4	-3	-.23
Sobchuk, Dennis	5	1	0	1	4	-2	-.15
McKay, Ray	4	0	1	1	4	-1	+.13
Widing, Juha	5	0	1	1	0	-4	-.21
Demarco, Ab	1	0	0	0	0	-1	-.34
Dryden, Dave	2	0	0	0	0	—	—
Primeau, Kevin	2	0	0	0	2	-2	-.29
Troy, Jim	2	0	0	0	0	evn	evn
McLeod, Don	4	0	0	0	0	—	—
Busniuk, Ron	5	0	0	0	18	-2	-.06
Ferguson, Norm	5	0	0	0	0	-2	-.15
Sandbeck, Cal	5	0	0	0	10	-1	+.19
Semenko, Dave	5	0	0	0	8	-1	+.02
OILER TOTALS	5	9	18	27	115	-7	
OPPONENT TOTALS	5	23	38	61	99	+7	

HOUSTON AEROS

PLAYER	GP	G	A	PTS	PIM	+/-	+/-%
Taylor, Ted	6	3	1	4	10	+2	+.18
Lacroix, Andre	6	2	2	4	0	-4	-.13
Tonelli, John	6	1	3	4	8	-4	-.10
Larway, Don	6	1	2	3	4	-3	-.11
Lukowich, Morris	6	1	2	3	17	-3	-.08
Gray, John	6	0	3	3	10	+2	+.18
Ruskowski, Terry	4	1	1	2	5	-1	-.02
Campbell, Scott	6	1	1	2	8	-2	-.01
Hansis, Ron	6	1	1	2	4	evn	+.08
Hughes, John	6	1	1	2	6	+2	+.20
Terbenche, Paul	6	1	1	2	0	evn	+.03
Lund, Larry	6	0	2	2	2	-1	evn
Popiel, Poul	6	0	2	2	13	+4	+.32
Connor, Cam	2	1	0	1	22	+1	+.11
McLeod, Al	6	1	0	1	2	-9	-.38
West, Steve	6	1	0	1	0	+2	+.14
Mortson, Keke	2	0	1	1	0	+1	+.20
Schella, John	6	0	1	1	33	-8	-.32
Zimmerman, Lynn	4	0	0	0	6	—	—
Rutledge, Wayne	3	0	0	0	2	—	—
AERO TOTALS	6	16	24	40	152	-5	
OPPONENT TOTALS	6	29	50	79	189	+5	

NEW ENGLAND WHALERS

PLAYER	GP	G	A	PTS	PIM	+/-	+/-%
Antonovich, Mike	14	10	7	17	4	+1	-.01
Keon, Dave	14	5	11	16	4	+2	+.02
Howe, Mark	14	8	7	15	18	evn	-.03
McKenzie, John	14	6	6	12	16	-2	-.08
Rogers, Mike	14	5	6	11	8	-2	-.08
Howe, Gordie	14	5	5	10	15	evn	-.02
Pleau, Larry	14	5	4	9	8	-2	-.08
Carlson, Steve	13	2	7	9	2	+4	+.07
Ley, Rick	14	1	8	9	4	+2	evn
Bolduc, Dan	14	2	4	6	4	+1	-.01
Plumb, Ron	14	1	5	6	16	+2	+.04
Hangsleben, Alan	14	1	4	5	37	+2	+.01
Roberts, Gordie	14	0	5	5	29	+1	-.01
Sheehy, Tim	13	1	3	4	9	+1	+.01
Lyle, George	12	2	1	3	13	+5	+.11
Selwood, Brad	14	0	3	3	8	+4	+.07
Carlson, Jack	9	1	1	2	14	-2	-.06
Howe, Marty	14	1	1	2	13	-2	-.08
Levasseur, Louis	12	0	1	1	2	—	—
Mayer, Jim	0	—	—	—	—	—	—
Peloffy, Andre	2	0	0	0	0	-1	-.13
Smith, Al	3	0	0	0	0	—	—
WHALER TOTALS	14	56	89	145	224	+4	
OPPONENT TOTALS	14	47	81	128	250	-4	

QUEBEC NORDIQUES

PLAYER	GP	G	A	PTS	PIM	+/-	+/-%
Cloutier, Real	10	9	7	16	15	evn	+.07
Tardif, Marc	11	6	9	15	11	-2	-.11
Bernier, Serge	11	4	10	14	17	-1	+.03
Baxter, Paul	11	4	7	11	42	evn	+.06
Bordeleau, Paulin	11	4	6	10	2	+1	+.07
Bernier, Jean	10	3	4	7	2	+2	+.05
Fitchner, Bob	11	1	6	7	10	-3	-.07
Bordeleau, Chris	10	1	5	6	6	evn	+.01
Lariviere, Garry	11	3	2	5	4	-7	-.17
Lacombe, Francois	10	1	4	5	2	evn	-.01
Dube, Norm	10	2	2	4	6	+4	+.15
Cote, Alain	11	1	2	3	0	-3	-.09
Weir, Wally	11	1	2	3	50	-4	-.07
Dorey, Jim	11	0	3	3	34	-2	-.01
Sutherland, Steve	11	2	0	2	37	-4	-.10
Brackenbury, Curt	10	1	1	2	31	-2	-.07
Boudrias, Andre	11	0	2	2	4	-2	-.05
Miller, Warren	11	0	2	2	0	-3	-.09
Tremblay, J. C.	1	0	1	1	0	-2	-.33
Brodeur, Richard	11	0	1	1	0	—	—
Corsi, Jim	0	—	—	—	—	—	—
Lagace, Pierre	1	0	0	0	0	-1	-.20
Broderick, Ken	2	0	0	0	0	—	—
NORDIQUE TOTALS	11	43	76	119	273	-5	
OPPONENT TOTALS	11	41	61	102	224	+5	

WINNIPEG JETS

PLAYER	GP	G	A	PTS	PIM	+/-	+/-%
Hedberg, Anders	9	9	6	15	2	+5	-.04
Nilsson, Ulf	9	1	13	14	12	+5	-.04
Guindon, Bob	9	8	5	13	5	+9	+.13
Moffat, Lyle	9	5	7	12	9	+3	-.09
Hull, Bobby	9	8	3	11	12	+5	-.04
Nilsson, Kent	9	2	8	10	10	+2	-.04
Sjoberg, Lars-Erik	9	0	9	9	4	+8	+.02
Kryskow, Dave	9	4	4	8	2	+1	-.10
Lindstrom, Willy	8	3	4	7	17	+3	-.02
Sullivan, Peter	9	3	4	7	4	+3	-.01
Lesuk, Bill	9	2	5	7	12	+9	+.16
Long, Barry	9	0	5	5	6	+11	+.22
Amodeo, Mike	7	1	3	4	19	-2	-.42
Baird, Ken	7	0	4	4	7	+1	-.08
Powis, Lynn	3	2	1	3	7	+2	+.04
Dunn, Dave	9	1	2	3	0	+8	+.05
Ruhnke, Kent	5	2	0	2	0	-2	-.23
Labraaten, Dan	4	1	1	2	8	+4	+.11
Green, Ted	8	0	2	2	2	+4	-.10
Ford, Mike	2	1	0	1	0	-1	-.33
Daley, Joe	5	0	1	1	20	—	—
Clackson, Kim	9	0	1	1	61	+6	+.11
Mattsson, Markus	0	—	—	—	—	—	—
Bromley, Gary	5	0	0	0	2	—	—
JET TOTALS	9	53	88	141	223	+18	
OPPONENT TOTALS	9	20	30	50	296	-18	

1978 AVCO WORLD TROPHY GOALTENDING STATISTICS

PLAYER	GAA	GP	MIN	W	L	PCT	SOG	GA	SV%
Winnipeg Jets									
Bromley, Gary	1.57	5	268	4	0	1.000	115	7	.939
Daley, Joe	2.87	5	271	4	1	.800	110	13	.882
Team Totals	2.22	9	539	8	1	.889	225	20	.911
Opponents' Goaltending	5.67	9	539	1	8	.111	287	51	.822
New England Whalers									
Levasseur, Louis	2.59	12	719	8	4	.667	332	31	.907
Smith, Al	7.00	3	120	0	2	.000	60	14	.767
Team Totals	3.22	14	839	8	6	.571	392	45	.885
Opponents' Goaltending	3.94	14	838	6	8	.429	467	55	.882
Quebec Nordiques									
Broderick, Ken	2.50	2	48	0	1	.000	12	2	.833
Brodeur, Richard	3.67	11	622	5	5	.500	366	38	.896
Team Totals	3.58	11	670	5	6	.455	378	40	.894
Opponents' Goaltending	3.85	11	670	6	5	.545	338	43	.873
Edmonton Oilers									
Dryden, Dave	3.94	2	91	0	1	.000	51	6	.882
McLeod, Don	4.64	4	207	1	3	.250	114	16	.860
Team Totals	4.43	5	298	1	4	.200	165	22	.867
Opponents' Goaltending	1.80	5	300	4	1	.800	132	9	.932
Houston Aeros									
Rutledge, Wayne	3.65	3	131	1	2	.333	75	8	.893
Zimmerman, Lynn	5.28	4	239	1	2	.333	119	21	.824
Team Totals	4.70	6	370	2	4	.333	194	29	.851
Opponents' Goaltending	2.43	6	370	4	2	.667	190	15	.921
Birmingham Bulls									
Garrett, John	5.76	5	271	1	4	.200	152	26	.829
Wood, Wayne	6.15	1	29	—	—	—	19	3	.842
Team Totals	5.80	5	300	1	4	.200	171	29	.830
Opponents' Goaltending	2.40	5	299	4	1	.800	111	12	.892

1977-78 AWARD WINNERS

Quebec's Marc Tardif accepts the Gordie Howe Trophy as the 1977-78 MVP in the World Hockey Association from Robbie Ftorek (1976-77 winner) and Gordie Howe (1973-74 winner). Sitting in the foreground is WHA Chairman of the Board Ben Hatskin. For career record of Marc Tardif, see page 135.

MARC TARDIF WINS GORDIE HOWE TROPHY AS WHA MOST VALUABLE PLAYER

Marc Tardif, 30-year-old left winger of the Quebec Nordiques, captured the Howe Trophy as the World Hockey Association's Most Valuable Player for 1977-78, the second time in three years that he has done so.

In winning the award, Tardif becomes the second player in the six year history of the WHA to have won the Howe Trophy twice. Winnipeg's Bobby Hull was the recipient in 1972-73 and again in 1974-75.

At 6'0", 180 lbs., Tardif first won the award two years ago following a record-breaking point total of 148, including a personal high of 71 goals while playing in 81 regular season games (71 goals, 77 assists, 148 points).

Now, two short years later, Tardif is once again in the hockey spotlight as the WHA's Most Valuable Player, again after breaking the league record for most points in one season. He surpassed his own record by six points as he scored 65 goals and added 89 assists for a total of 154 points last year.

In winning the award, the Granby, Quebec native outdistanced second place finisher Ulf Nilsson by 63 points as he received 153 total points in the balloting of members of the media throughout all WHA cities.

Tardif registered at least one point in 66 of the 78 games that he played in during the 1977-78 regular season, including a streak of nine straight games at the end of the year. His largest point production in one game came February 7 in Quebec when he tallied one goal and four assists in a winning effort by the Nordiques. In addition, the Quebec captain enjoyed four point nights on twelve different occasions throughout the year.

Of his 65 goals, he had seven game winners (2 in overtime), four hat tricks and 10 two goal games.

During the five years that Tardif has played in the World Hockey Association, he is currently third in career point production with 570. Andre Lacroix is first with 710 points and Bobby Hull is second with 633 points, but both Lacroix and Hull have played one more year than Tardif.

Prior to joining the WHA in June of 1973 Marc spent three full years with the NHL Montreal Canadiens where he scored 75 goals and assisted on 77 others.

Jacques Demers, newly appointed Coach of the Nordiques, said recently that "Marc is perhaps the most explosive player in the game today. After four years of worrying about how he can beat you in so many ways, it's going to be a pleasure to have him on my team. Every coach in hockey would like to have Marc Tardif play for him."

BILL DINEEN WINS SCHMERTZ TROPHY SECOND STRAIGHT YEAR

Forty-five year old **Bill "Foxy" Dineen** won the Coach of the Year Award in the World Hockey Association last year for the second straight season.

Dineen, who guided the Houston Aeros to third place behind Winnipeg and New England, enters the '78-'79 season as the winningest coach in the WHA with a six year record of 285-170-19. This season he is the new head coach of the New England Whalers.

Prior to the start of the 1977-78 season, the Houston Aeros were pegged by many hockey experts as a team that probably would finish out of the playoffs when April rolled around, especially with the Howe family signing with the New England Whalers. Dineen's Aeros, however, had different ideas. With a tight checking system used effectively both at home and away, Houston finished with the third best record overall with 42 wins, 34 losses and 4 ties, good for 88 total points.

After finishing in second place in the Western Division in 1972-73, Dineen had guided the Aeros to four consecutive divisional titles before finishing third this past season.

KENT NILSSON VOTED ROOKIE OF THE YEAR

Kent Nilsson, the slick 20-year-old center from Nynashamn, Sweden won the Rookie of the Year honors, making him the second Swedish born player to earn this distinction in the past four years. Anders Hedberg received the Award for his performance during the 1974-75 season.

Nilsson, who exploded for 20 points in his first nine games, completed the regular season with 42 goals and 65 assists for 107 points while accumulating only 8 minutes in penalties.

Nilsson, who stands 6'1" and weighs 185 lbs., is no relation to Ulf Nilsson, who has played in North America for the past four years.

This past year, Kent was one of seven Swedish players to play with the AVCO Champion Winnipeg Jets. The Jets pioneered importing Swedish players four years ago and during this time period Winnipeg has gone to AVCO Cup Finals three times.

LARS-ERIK SJOBERG WINS OUTSTANDING DEFENSEMAN AWARD

Winnipeg Jet captain **Lars-Erik Sjoberg** received the Outstanding Defenseman Award for the 1977-78 season. Sjoberg, who was born in Falun, Sweden on April 5, 1944, has completed four years in the World Hockey Association. He is 34 years old.

The 5'8", 179 lb. Sjoberg enjoyed his best season point-wise in the WHA last year by scoring 11 goals and 39 assists for 50 total points while leading all WHA players with a plus-minus total of +60. Similarly, last year's winner of the Outstanding Defenseman Award, Ron Plumb, led the entire league in plus-minus with a +64. At the time, Plumb was with the Cincinnati Stingers but he has since been dealt to the New England Whalers.

Sjoberg's winning of the Outstanding Defenseman Award last year coincided with his being named to the first team All-Star selection. It was also the first time that Sjoberg had been voted to the All-Star team in his four years with Winnipeg.

AL SMITH WINS HATSKIN TROPHY AS TOP GOALTENDER

Thirty-three-year-old **Al Smith** has been voted the top goaltender of the World Hockey Association for the 1977-78 season. Smith, who rejoined the New England Whalers after two years with the Buffalo Sabres of the National Hockey League, led all goaltenders in the league with a 3.22 goals against average while recording two shutouts.

Smith, who was born in Toronto, Ontario, stands 6'1" and weighs 200 lbs., was an original New England Whaler back in 1972-73 and played three seasons with New England prior to joining the Buffalo team in 1975.

"Smitty" was the only goaltender in the league to record 30 or more victories last year, finishing with a 30-20-3 won-loss-tie record. Remarkably, Smith has never finished a WHA season with less than 30 victories.

In 55 games, he was one of three WHA goaltenders to toil over 3000 minutes last year, along with Houston's Ernie Wakely and Birmingham's John Garrett.

DAVE KEON CAPTURES
MOST GENTLEMANLY PLAYER AWARD

For the second straight season, center **Dave Keon** of the New England Whalers was selected as the Most Gentlemanly Player in the World Hockey Association.

Keon, who spent 15 seasons with the Toronto Maple Leafs prior to joining the WHA for the 1975-76 season, spent only two minutes in the penalty box all season long, with those two minutes coming in the Whalers' 77th game of the year. While staying out of the penalty box, Keon also managed to score 24 goals and also add 38 assists for a total of 62 points.

In his first three seasons with the WHA, Dave has spent only 18 total minutes in the penalty box. Over his 18 year major league career, the shifty center has spent a total of only 93 minutes in the sin bin.

Keon also won the Lady Byng Memorial Trophy twice while with the Maple Leafs, during the 1961-62 season and again the following year.

BOB GUINDON NAMED
AVCO CUP PLAYOFF MOST VALUABLE PLAYER

Consistent **Bob Guindon** of the Winnipeg Jets was voted the Most Valuable Player Trophy for the 1978 AVCO Cup playoffs. Guindon, who is 27 and stands only 5'9" with a weight of 160 lbs., scored 8 goals and added 5 assists as the Jets won 8 of 9 games on their way to the AVCO Trophy. Interestingly enough, the only game that Guindon did not register at least one point was in the 3-2 loss to Birmingham in the opening round of the playoffs.

Guindon, who was born in Labelle, Quebec on November 19, 1950, has been in the World Hockey Association all seven years of its existence. He played with the Quebec Nordiques for the first three years before being traded to the Jets prior to the 1975-76 season.

Guindon, who shoots left and played on the left side in Quebec, split his ice-time between center and right wing with Winnipeg last season.

Prior to joining the WHA, Bob spent two years with the Fort Worth Wings of the CHL after being drafted in the second round of the amateur draft by Detroit in 1970.

OFFICIAL END OF SEASON
ALL-STAR TEAMS

1977-78

FIRST TEAM	POSITION	SECOND TEAM
Al Smith	GOAL	Ernie Wakely
Lars-Erik Sjoberg	DEFENSE	Rick Ley
Al Hamilton	DEFENSE	Barry Long
Ulf Nilsson	CENTER	Robbie Ftorek
Anders Hedberg	RIGHT WING	Real Cloutier
Marc Tardif	LEFT WING	Bobby Hull

CAREER RECORDS OF ACTIVE PLAYERS

Winnipeg's Morris Lukowich eyes his third season in the WHA. For career record of Lukowich, see page 103.

Listed below is the phonetic key to all players affiliated with the World Hockey Association this year. Included are players now on assignment to a minor league affiliate. Please refer to this key if you are not positive on the pronunciation of a player listed in this section.

A = cat	OH = go
AH = ability	OO = too
AW = applaud	OR = pour
AY = able	OW = ouch
E = bed	OY = point
EE = feel	S = pacific
EW = too	UH = puff, touch, son
F = phone	UR = term
I = tin	Y = time
J = george	YOU = few
K = cat	ZH = rouge

ADDUONO, RICK
ah - DOON - oh

CENTER
Height: 5'10"
Weight: 170 lbs.
Birthdate: January 25, 1955
Birthplace: Ft. William, Ontario
Shoots: Left

REGULAR SEASON CAREER

SEASON	CLUB	LEAGUE	GP	G	A	PTS	PIM
1973-74	St. Catharines	Jr. "A" OHA	70	51	84	135	24
1974-75	St. Catharines	Jr. "A" OHA	55	27	39	66	31
1975-76	Binghamton	NAHL	2	2	0	2	0
	Rochester	AHL	68	11	23	34	24
	Boston	NHL	1	0	0	0	0
1976-77	Rochester	AHL	77	29	45	74	38
1977-78	Rochester	AHL	76	38	60	98	34

ALEXANDER, CLAIRE
AHL - ex - AHN - dur

DEFENSE
Height: 5'10"
Weight: 180 lbs.
Birthdate: June 16, 1945
Birthplace: Collingwood, Ontario
Shoots: Right

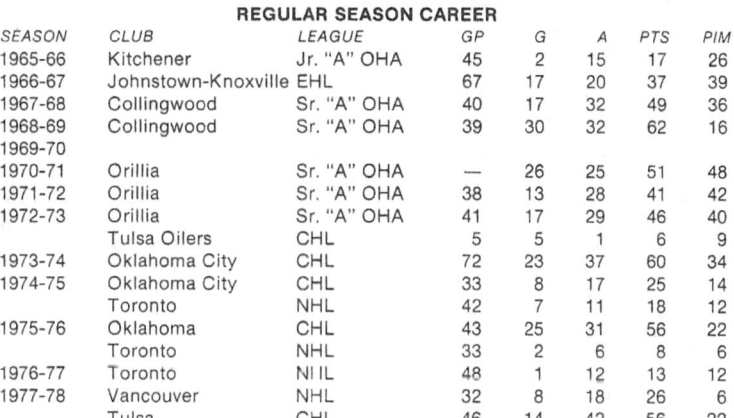

REGULAR SEASON CAREER

SEASON	CLUB	LEAGUE	GP	G	A	PTS	PIM
1965-66	Kitchener	Jr. "A" OHA	45	2	15	17	26
1966-67	Johnstown-Knoxville	EHL	67	17	20	37	39
1967-68	Collingwood	Sr. "A" OHA	40	17	32	49	36
1968-69	Collingwood	Sr. "A" OHA	39	30	32	62	16
1969-70							
1970-71	Orillia	Sr. "A" OHA	—	26	25	51	48
1971-72	Orillia	Sr. "A" OHA	38	13	28	41	42
1972-73	Orillia	Sr. "A" OHA	41	17	29	46	40
	Tulsa Oilers	CHL	5	5	1	6	9
1973-74	Oklahoma City	CHL	72	23	37	60	34
1974-75	Oklahoma City	CHL	33	8	17	25	14
	Toronto	NHL	42	7	11	18	12
1975-76	Oklahoma	CHL	43	25	31	56	22
	Toronto	NHL	33	2	6	8	6
1976-77	Toronto	NHL	48	1	12	13	12
1977-78	Vancouver	NHL	32	8	18	26	6
	Tulsa	CHL	46	14	42	56	22

ALLEY, STEVE
AHL - lee

LEFT WING
Height: 6'0"
Weight: 185 lbs.
Birthdate: December 29, 1953
Birthplace: Anoka, Minnesota
Shoots: Left

REGULAR SEASON CAREER

SEASON	CLUB	LEAGUE	GP	G	A	PTS	PIM
1972-73	U. of Wisconsin	WCHA	40	8	15	23	12
1973-74	U. of Wisconsin	WCHA	36	12	19	31	16
1974-75	U. of Wisconsin	WCHA	38	23	25	48	84
1975-76	U.S. National Team		64	29	33	62	67
	U.S. Olympic Team		6	1	1	2	4
1976-77	U. of Wisconsin	WCHA	45	32	31	63	50
1977-78	Hampton	SHL	30	6	3	9	27
	Birmingham	**WHA**	**27**	**8**	**12**	**20**	**11**
WHA TOTALS			**27**	**8**	**12**	**20**	**11**

WHA PLAYOFFS

YEAR	CLUB	GP	G	A	PTS	PIM
1978	Birmingham	5	1	0	1	5

AMODEO, MIKE
a - MOHD - ee - o

DEFENSE
Height: 5'10"
Weight: 190 lbs.
Birthdate: June 22, 1952
Birthplace: Toronto, Ontario
Shoots: Left

REGULAR SEASON CAREER

SEASON	CLUB	LEAGUE	GP	G	A	PTS	PIM
1969-70	Toronto Marlboros	Jr. "A" OHA	54	5	11	16	161
1970-71	Toronto Marlboros	Jr. "A" OHA	11	0	3	3	31
	Niagara Falls Flyers	Jr. "A" OHA	3	0	0	0	2
	Oshawa Generals	Jr. "A" OHA	24	0	12	12	65
1971-72	Oshawa Generals	Jr. "A" OHA	63	6	34	40	130
1972-73	**Ottawa Nationals**	**WHA**	**61**	**1**	**14**	**15**	**77**
1973-74	**Toronto Toros**	**WHA**	**77**	**0**	**11**	**11**	**82**
1974-75	**Toronto Toros**	**WHA**	**64**	**1**	**13**	**14**	**50**
1975-76	Rochester Americans	AHL	10	0	2	2	4
	Toronto Toros	**WHA**	**31**	**4**	**8**	**12**	**35**
1976-77	Orebro Sweden		34	5	3	8	38
1977-78	Orebro Sweden		colspan unavailable				
	Winnipeg	**WHA**	**3**	**1**	**1**	**2**	**0**
WHA TOTALS			**236**	**7**	**47**	**54**	**244**

WHA PLAYOFFS

YEAR	CLUB	GP	G	A	PTS	PIM
1973	Ottawa	5	0	1	1	10
1974	Toronto	12	0	2	2	26
1975	Toronto	3	0	1	1	4
1978	Winnipeg	7	1	3	4	19
TOTALS		**27**	**1**	**7**	**8**	**59**

ANTONOVICH, MIKE
an - TOH - noh - vich

LEFT WING
Height: 5'8"
Weight: 165 lbs.
Birthdate: October 18, 1951
Birthplace: Calumet, Minnesota
Shoots: Left

REGULAR SEASON CAREER

SEASON	CLUB	LEAGUE	GP	G	A	PTS	PIM
1970-71	U. of Minn.	WCHA	24	10	14	24	20
1971-72	U. of Minn.	WCHA	13	8	2	10	19
1972-73	Minnesota	WHA	75	20	19	39	46
1973-74	Minnesota	WHA	68	21	29	50	4
1974-75	Minnesota	WHA	67	24	26	50	20
1975-76	Minnesota	WHA	57	25	21	46	18
	Minnesota	NHL	12	0	2	2	8
1976-77	Minnesota	WHA	42	27	21	48	28
	Edmonton	WHA	7	1	1	2	0
	New England	WHA	26	12	9	21	10
1977-78	New England	WHA	75	32	35	67	32
WHA TOTALS			417	162	161	323	158

WHA PLAYOFFS

YEAR	CLUB	GP	G	A	PTS	PIM
1973	Minnesota	5	2	0	2	0
1974	Minnesota	11	1	4	5	4
1975	Minnesota	12	1	4	5	2
1977	New England	5	2	2	4	4
1978	New England	14	10	7	17	4
TOTALS		47	16	17	33	14

BALTIMORE, BRYON
BAWL - ti - mor

DEFENSE
Height: 6'2"
Weight: 203 lbs.
Birthdate: August 26, 1952
Birthplace: Whitehorse, Yukon
Shoots: Left

REGULAR SEASON CAREER

SEASON	CLUB	LEAGUE	GP	G	A	PTS	PIM
1972-73	Springfield	AHL	73	15	12	27	36
1973-74	Springfield	AHL	68	4	21	25	72
1974-75	Chicago	WHA	77	8	12	20	110
1975-76	Denver/Ottawa	WHA	41	1	8	9	32
	Indianapolis	WHA	37	1	10	11	30
1976-77	Indianapolis	WHA	55	0	15	15	63
1977-78	Indianapolis	WHA	22	1	7	8	23
	Cincinnati	WHA	28	2	9	11	47
WHA TOTALS			260	13	61	74	305

WHA PLAYOFFS

YEAR	CLUB	GP	G	A	PTS	PIM
1976	Indianapolis	7	0	1	1	4
1977	Indianapolis	9	0	0	0	5
TOTALS		16	0	1	1	9

BAXTER, PAUL
BAX - tur

DEFENSE
Height: 5'11"
Weight: 200 lbs.
Birthdate: October 25, 1955
Birthplace: Winnipeg, Manitoba
Shoots: Right

REGULAR SEASON CAREER

SEASON	CLUB	LEAGUE	GP	G	A	PTS	PIM
1973-74	Winnipeg	WCHL	63	10	30	40	384
1974-75	Cape Cod	NAHL	2	1	0	1	11
	Cleveland	WHA	5	0	0	0	37
1975-76	Cleveland	WHA	67	3	7	10	201
1976-77	Quebec	WHA	66	6	17	23	244
1977-78	Quebec	WHA	76	6	29	35	240
WHA TOTALS			**214**	**15**	**53**	**68**	**722**

WHA PLAYOFFS

YEAR	CLUB	GP	G	A	PTS	PIM
1976	Cleveland	3	0	0	0	10
1977	Quebec	12	2	2	4	35
1978	Quebec	11	4	7	11	42
TOTALS		**26**	**6**	**9**	**15**	**87**

BEAUDOIN, SERGE
boh - DWAHN

DEFENSE
Height: 6'2"
Weight: 215 lbs.
Birthdate: November 30, 1952
Birthplace: Montreal, Quebec
Shoots: Left

REGULAR SEASON CAREER

SEASON	CLUB	LEAGUE	GP	G	A	PTS	PIM
1971-72	Three Rivers	QMJHL	61	17	50	67	244
1972-73	Roanoke Valley	EHL	76	10	43	53	221
1973-74	Roanoke Valley	SHL	37	8	20	28	179
	Vancouver	WHA	26	1	11	12	37
1974-75	Tulsa	CHL	37	6	31	37	139
	Vancouver	WHA	4	0	0	0	2
1975-76	Phoenix	WHA	76	0	21	21	102
1976-77	Phoenix	WHA	77	6	24	30	136
1977-78	Cincinnati	WHA	13	0	1	1	10
	Birmingham	WHA	64	8	25	33	105
WHA TOTALS			**260**	**15**	**82**	**97**	**392**

WHA PLAYOFFS

YEAR	CLUB	GP	G	A	PTS	PIM
1976	Phoenix	5	1	0	1	10
1978	Birmingham	5	1	0	1	46
TOTALS		**10**	**2**	**0**	**2**	**56**

BERNIER, SERGE
burn - YAY

CENTER
Height: 6'1"
Weight: 190 lbs.
Birthdate: April 29, 1947
Birthplace: Padoue, Quebec
Shoots: Right

REGULAR SEASON CAREER

SEASON	CLUB	LEAGUE	GP	G	A	PTS	PIM
1967-68	Quebec	AHL	33	7	11	18	56
1968-69	Quebec	AHL	70	27	32	59	118
	Philadelphia	NHL	1	0	0	0	2
1969-70	Philadelphia	NHL	1	0	1	1	0
	Quebec	AHL	70	22	48	70	88
1970-71	Philadelphia	NHL	77	23	28	51	77
1971-72	Philadelphia	NHL	44	12	11	23	51
	Los Angeles	NHL	26	11	11	22	12
1972-73	Los Angeles	NHL	75	22	46	68	43
1973-74	**Quebec**	**WHA**	74	37	49	86	107
1974-75	**Quebec**	**WHA**	76	54	68	122	75
1975-76	**Quebec**	**WHA**	70	34	68	102	91
1976-77	**Quebec**	**WHA**	74	43	53	96	94
1977-78	**Quebec**	**WHA**	58	26	52	78	48
WHA TOTALS			**352**	**194**	**290**	**484**	**415**

WHA PLAYOFFS

YEAR	CLUB	GP	G	A	PTS	PIM
1975	Quebec	16	8	8	16	6
1976	Quebec	5	2	6	8	6
1977	Quebec	17	14	22	36	10
1978	Quebec	11	4	10	14	17
TOTALS		**49**	**28**	**46**	**74**	**39**

47

BERRY, DOUG
BEHR - ree

CENTER
Height: 6'1"
Weight: 190 lbs.
Birthdate: June 3, 1957
Birthplace: New Westminster, British Columbia
Shoots: Left

REGULAR SEASON CAREER

SEASON	CLUB	LEAGUE	GP	G	A	PTS	PIM
1975-76	Denver Univ.	WCHA	39	12	28	40	32
1976-77	Denver Univ.	WCHA	40	17	41	58	42
1977-78	Denver Univ.	WCHA	32	25	39	64	34

BILODEAU, GILLES
bi - lah - DOH

LEFT WING
Height: 6'1"
Weight: 220 lbs.
Birthdate: July 31, 1955
Birthplace: St. Prime, Quebec
Shoots: Left

REGULAR SEASON CAREER

SEASON	CLUB	LEAGUE	GP	G	A	PTS	PIM
1974-75	Sorel	QMJHL	66	6	9	15	377
1975-76	Beauce	NAHL	58	8	17	25	451
	Toronto	**WHA**	**14**	**0**	**1**	**1**	**38**
1976-77	Charlotte	SHL	28	3	6	9	242
	Birmingham	**WHA**	**34**	**2**	**6**	**8**	**133**
1977-78	**Birmingham**	**WHA**	**59**	**2**	**2**	**4**	**258**
WHA TOTALS			**107**	**4**	**9**	**13**	**429**

WHA PLAYOFFS

YEAR	CLUB	GP	G	A	PTS	PIM
1978	Birmingham	3	0	0	0	27
TOTALS		**3**	**0**	**0**	**0**	**27**

BLOCK, KEN
BLAHK

DEFENSE
Height: 5'10"
Weight: 191 lbs.
Birthdate: March 18, 1944
Birthplace: Steinbach, Manitoba
Shoots: Left

REGULAR SEASON CAREER

SEASON	CLUB	LEAGUE	GP	G	A	PTS	PIM
1963-64	Flin Flon	MJHL	62	14	43	57	59
1964-65	New York	EHL	70	5	31	36	51
	Baltimore	AHL	5	0	2	2	2
1965-66	Baltimore	AHL	37	2	8	10	6
	Minnesota	CPHL	30	0	6	6	8
1966-67	Omaha	CPHL	10	0	4	4	6
	Vancouver	WHL	62	8	22	30	16
1967-68	Rochester	AHL	24	1	1	2	0
	Memphis	CPHL	18	5	5	10	24
	Vancouver	WHL	17	2	6	8	4
1968-69	Vancouver	WHL	22	1	2	3	6
	Rochester	AHL	45	4	15	19	10
1969-70	Rochester	AHL	69	9	35	44	51
1970-71	Rochester	AHL	71	5	33	38	38
	Vancouver	NHL	1	0	0	0	0
1971-72	Rochester	AHL	71	4	29	33	69
1972-73	New York	WHA	78	5	53	58	43
1973-74	Jersey	WHA	74	3	43	46	22
1974-75	San Diego	WHA	36	1	11	12	12
	Indianapolis	WHA	37	0	17	17	18
1975-76	Indianapolis	WHA	79	1	25	26	28
1976-77	Indianapolis	WHA	52	3	10	13	25
1977-78	Indianapolis	WHA	77	1	25	26	34
WHA TOTALS			433	14	184	198	182

WHA PLAYOFFS

YEAR	CLUB	GP	G	A	PTS	PIM
1976	Indianapolis	7	0	4	4	2
1977	Indianapolis	9	0	2	2	6
TOTALS		16	0	6	6	8

BOLONCHUK, LARRY
boh - LUN - chuhk

DEFENSE
Height: 5'10"
Weight: 190 lbs.
Birthdate: February 26, 1952
Birthplace: Winnipeg, Manitoba
Shoots: Right

REGULAR SEASON CAREER

SEASON	CLUB	LEAGUE	GP	G	A	PTS	PIM
1970-71	Winnipeg	WCHL	66	4	31	35	140
1971-72	Winnipeg	WCHL	67	7	32	39	175
1972-73	Seattle	WHL	59	2	9	11	97
	Vancouver	NHL	15	0	0	0	6
1973-74	Des Moines	IHL	71	6	27	33	166
	Seattle	WHL	3	0	2	2	4
1974-75	Dayton	IHL	58	9	21	30	139
1975-76	Dayton	IHL	77	4	39	43	174
	Washington	NHL	1	0	1	1	0
1976-77	Dayton	IHL	71	2	21	23	124
	Washington	NHL	9	0	0	0	12
1977-78	Hampton	AHL	14	1	1	2	38
	Washington	NHL	49	3	8	11	79
	Hershey	AHL	19	0	7	7	12

BORDELEAU, CHRIS
BOR - deh - loh

CENTER
Height: 5'8"
Weight: 172 lbs.
Birthdate: September 23, 1947
Birthplace: Noranda, Quebec
Shoots: Left

REGULAR SEASON CAREER

SEASON	CLUB	LEAGUE	GP	G	A	PTS	PIM
1966-67	Montreal	Jr. "A" OHA	33	8	19	27	30
1967-68	Houston	CHL	68	23	28	51	22
1968-69	Houston	CHL	54	21	36	57	33
	Montreal	NHL	13	1	3	4	4
1969-70	Montreal	NHL	48	2	13	15	18
1970-71	St. Louis	NHL	78	21	32	53	48
1971-72	St. Louis	NHL	41	8	9	17	6
	Chicago	NHL	25	6	8	14	6
1972-73	**Winnipeg**	**WHA**	78	47	54	101	12
1973-74	**Winnipeg**	**WHA**	75	26	49	75	22
1974-75	**Winnipeg**	**WHA**	18	8	8	16	0
	Quebec	**WHA**	53	15	33	48	24
1975-76	**Quebec**	**WHA**	74	37	72	109	42
1976-77	**Quebec**	**WHA**	72	32	75	107	34
1977-78	**Quebec**	**WHA**	26	9	22	31	28
WHA TOTALS			396	174	313	487	162

WHA PLAYOFFS

YEAR	CLUB	GP	G	A	PTS	PIM
1973	Winnipeg	12	5	8	13	4
1974	Winnipeg	3	3	2	5	0
1975	Quebec	15	2	13	15	2
1976	Quebec	5	1	1	2	4
1977	Quebec	8	4	5	9	0
1978	Quebec	10	1	5	6	6
TOTALS		53	16	34	50	16

BORDELEAU, PAULIN
BOR - deh - loh

RIGHT WING
Height: 5'9"
Weight: 163 lbs.
Birthdate: January 29, 1953
Birthplace: Noranda, Quebec
Shoots: Right

REGULAR SEASON CAREER

SEASON	CLUB	LEAGUE	GP	G	A	PTS	PIM
1972-73	Toronto	Jr. "A" OHA	56	54	43	97	26
1973-74	Vancouver	NHL	68	11	13	24	20
1974-75	Vancouver	NHL	67	17	31	48	21
1975-76	Vancouver	NHL	48	5	12	17	6
1976-77	**Quebec**	**WHA**	80	42	41	83	52
1977-78	**Quebec**	**WHA**	77	42	23	65	29
WHA TOTALS			157	84	64	148	81

WHA PLAYOFFS

YEAR	CLUB	GP	G	A	PTS	PIM
1977	Quebec	16	12	9	21	12
1978	Quebec	11	4	6	10	2
TOTALS		27	16	15	31	14

BRACKENBURY, CURT
BRAK - en - BEHR - ree

RIGHT WING
Height: 5'10"
Weight: 197 lbs.
Birthdate: January 31, 1952
Birthplace: Kapuskasing, Ontario
Shoots: Right

REGULAR SEASON CAREER

SEASON	CLUB	LEAGUE	GP	G	A	PTS	PIM
1972-73	Jersey	EHL	68	17	27	44	66
1973-74	Des Moines	IHL	13	1	5	6	4
	Long Island	NAHL	45	8	20	28	194
	Chicago	**WHA**	**4**	**0**	**1**	**1**	**11**
1974-75	Hampton	SHL	46	19	24	43	212
	Minnesota	**WHA**	**7**	**0**	**0**	**0**	**22**
1975-76	**Minnesota**	**WHA**	**59**	**4**	**9**	**13**	**255**
	Quebec	**WHA**	**15**	**4**	**5**	**9**	**110**
1976-77	**Quebec**	**WHA**	**77**	**16**	**13**	**29**	**146**
1977-78	**Quebec**	**WHA**	**33**	**4**	**9**	**13**	**54**
WHA TOTALS			**195**	**28**	**37**	**65**	**598**

WHA PLAYOFFS

YEAR	CLUB	GP	G	A	PTS	PIM
1975	Minnesota	12	0	2	2	59
1976	Quebec	5	0	0	0	18
1977	Quebec	17	3	5	8	51
1978	Quebec	10	1	1	2	31
TOTALS		**44**	**4**	**8**	**12**	**159**

BRODEUR, RICHARD
broh - DUR

GOALTENDER
Height: 5'7"
Weight: 160 lbs.
Birthdate: September 15, 1952
Birthplace: Longueuil, Quebec
Shoots: Left

REGULAR SEASON CAREER

SEASON	CLUB	LEAGUE	GP	GA	SO	GAA
1971-72	Cornwall	QJHL	58	170	5	2.93
1972-73	Quebec	WHA	24	102	0	4.75
1973-74	Quebec	WHA	30	89	1	3.32
	Maine	NAHL	16	47	0	3.04
1974-75	Quebec	WHA	51	188	0	3.84
1975-76	Quebec	WHA	69	244	2	3.69
1976-77	Quebec	WHA	53	167	2	3.45
1977-78	Quebec	WHA	36	121	0	3.70
WHA TOTALS			263	911	5	3.73

WHA PLAYOFFS

YEAR	CLUB	GP	GA	SO	GAA
1975	Quebec	15	48	1	3.18
1976	Quebec	5	22	0	4.41
1977	Quebec	17	55	1	3.28
1978	Quebec	11	38	1	3.67
TOTALS		48	163	3	3.45

BRUBAKER, JEFF
BROU - bah - kur

LEFT WING
Height: 6'2"
Weight: 210 lbs.
Birthdate: February 24, 1958
Birthplace: Hagerstown, Maryland
Shoots: Left

REGULAR SEASON CAREER

SEASON	CLUB	LEAGUE	GP	G	A	PTS	PIM
1976-77	Peterborough	OHA	26	0	5	5	143
1977-78	Peterborough	OHA	68	20	24	44	307

BUAT, GEORGE
BOH - t

RIGHT WING
Height: 6'0"
Weight: 190 lbs.
Birthdate: January 6, 1958
Birthplace: Calgary, Alberta
Shoots: Right

REGULAR SEASON CAREER

SEASON	CLUB	LEAGUE	GP	G	A	PTS	PIM
1976-77	Portland	WCHL	60	14	14	28	29
1977-78	Seattle	WCHL	71	40	54	94	127

BURGESS, DON
BUR - ges

LEFT WING
Height: 6'0"
Weight: 170 lbs.
Birthdate: June 8, 1946
Birthplace: Pt. Edward, Ontario
Shoots: Left

REGULAR SEASON CAREER

SEASON	CLUB	LEAGUE	GP	G	A	PTS	PIM
1966-67	St. Catharines	Jr. "A" OHA	42	6	11	17	30
1967-68	Greensboro	EHL	72	30	37	67	59
1968-69	Greensboro	EHL	72	44	51	95	18
1969-70	Greensboro	EHL	74	36	49	85	26
1970-71	Greensboro	EHL	72	41	76	117	18
1971-72	Greensboro	EHL	73	39	58	97	29
1972-73	**Philadelphia**	**WHA**	74	20	22	42	15
1973-74	**Vancouver**	**WHA**	78	30	36	66	8
1974-75	Tulsa	CHL	12	6	5	11	4
	Vancouver	**WHA**	62	11	18	29	19
1975-76	**San Diego**	**WHA**	73	14	11	25	35
1976-77	**San Diego**	**WHA**	77	20	22	42	8
1977-78	**Indianapolis**	**WHA**	79	11	12	23	2
WHA TOTALS			**443**	**106**	**121**	**228**	**87**

WHA PLAYOFFS

YEAR	CLUB	GP	G	A	PTS	PIM
1973	Philadelphia	4	1	0	1	0
1976	San Diego	11	1	7	8	4
1977	San Diego	7	2	2	4	0
TOTALS		**22**	**4**	**9**	**13**	**4**

CALLIGHEN, BRETT
KAL - li - gen

CENTER
Height: 5'11"
Weight: 182 lbs.
Birthdate: May 15, 1953
Birthplace: Toronto, Ontario
Shoots: Left

REGULAR SEASON CAREER

SEASON	CLUB	LEAGUE	GP	G	A	PTS	PIM
1974-75	Flint-Kalamazoo	IHL	71	9	31	40	120
	Dallas	CHL	5	0	1	1	2
1975-76	Kalamazoo	IHL	72	25	33	58	104
1976-77	**New England**	**WHA**	33	6	10	16	41
	Edmonton	WHA	29	9	16	25	48
1977-78	**Edmonton**	**WHA**	80	20	30	50	112
WHA TOTALS			142	35	56	91	201

WHA PLAYOFFS

YEAR	CLUB	GP	G	A	PTS	PIM
1977	Edmonton	5	4	1	5	7
1978	Edmonton	5	0	2	2	16
TOTALS		10	4	3	7	23

CAMPBELL, SCOTT
KAM - bel

DEFENSE
Height: 6'3"
Weight: 205 lbs.
Birthdate: June 22, 1957
Birthplace: Toronto, Ontario
Shoots: Left

REGULAR SEASON CAREER

SEASON	CLUB	LEAGUE	GP	G	A	PTS	PIM
1974-75	London	Jr. "A" OHA	68	4	15	19	52
1975-76	London	Jr. "A" OHA	62	6	25	31	66
1976-77	London	Jr. "A" OHA	60	23	44	67	86
1977-78	**Houston**	**WHA**	75	8	29	37	116
WHA TOTALS			75	8	29	37	116

WHA PLAYOFFS

YEAR	CLUB	GP	G	A	PTS	PIM
1978	Houston	6	1	1	2	8

CARLSON, JACK
KAHRL - suhn

RIGHT WING
Height: 6'3"
Weight: 205 lbs.
Birthdate: August 23, 1954
Birthplace: Virginia, Minnesota
Shoots: Left

REGULAR SEASON CAREER

SEASON	CLUB	LEAGUE	GP	G	A	PTS	PIM
1973-74	Marquette	USHL	55	42	29	71	175
1974-75	Johnstown	NAHL	50	27	22	49	248
	Minnesota	WHA	32	5	5	10	85
1975-76	Minnesota	WHA	58	8	10	18	189
	Edmonton	WHA	10	1	1	2	31
1976-77	Minnesota	WHA	36	4	3	7	55
	New England	WHA	35	7	5	12	81
1977-78	New England	WHA	67	9	20	29	192
WHA TOTALS			238	34	44	78	633

WHA PLAYOFFS

YEAR	CLUB	GP	G	A	PTS	PIM
1975	Minnesota	10	1	2	3	41
1976	Edmonton	4	0	0	0	4
1977	New England	5	1	1	2	9
1978	New England	9	1	1	2	14
TOTALS		28	3	4	7	68

CARLSON, STEVE
KAHRL - suhn

CENTER
Height: 6'2"
Weight: 175 lbs.
Birthdate: August 26, 1955
Birthplace: Virginia, Minnesota
Shoots: Right

REGULAR SEASON CAREER

SEASON	CLUB	LEAGUE	GP	G	A	PTS	PIM
1973-74	Marquette	USHL	42	34	45	79	77
1974-75	Johnstown	NAHL	70	30	58	88	84
1975-76	Minnesota	WHA	10	0	1	1	23
	Johnstown	NAHL	40	22	24	46	55
1976-77	Minnesota	WHA	21	5	8	13	8
	New England	WHA	31	4	9	13	40
1977-78	New England	WHA	38	6	7	13	11
	Springfield	AHL	37	21	15	36	48
WHA TOTALS			100	15	25	40	82

56

WHA PLAYOFFS

YEAR	CLUB	GP	G	A	PTS	PIM
1977	New England	5	0	0	0	9
1978	New England	13	2	7	9	2
TOTALS		**18**	**2**	**7**	**9**	**11**

CARTER, RON
KAHR - tur

RIGHT WING
Height: 6'1"
Weight: 205 lbs.
Birthdate: March 14, 1958
Birthplace: Chateauguay, Quebec
Shoots: Left

REGULAR SEASON CAREER

SEASON	CLUB	LEAGUE	GP	G	A	PTS	PIM
1975-76	Sherbrooke	QMJHL	68	34	36	70	12
1976-77	Sherbrooke	QMJHL	72	77	50	127	18
1977-78	Sherbrooke	QMJHL	71	88	86	174	28

CASSOLATO, TONY
KAS - soh - LAH - toh

RIGHT WING
Height: 5'11"
Weight: 180 lbs.
Birthdate: May 7, 1956
Birthplace: Guelph, Ontario
Shoots: Right

REGULAR SEASON CAREER

SEASON	CLUB	LEAGUE	GP	G	A	PTS	PIM
1975-76	Peterborough	Jr. "A" OHA	60	26	39	65	59
1976-77	Charlotte	SHL	19	9	10	19	18
	San Diego	**WHA**	**43**	**13**	**12**	**25**	**26**
1977-78	**Birmingham**	**WHA**	**77**	**18**	**25**	**43**	**59**
WHA TOTALS			**120**	**31**	**37**	**68**	**85**

WHA PLAYOFFS

YEAR	CLUB	GP	G	A	PTS	PIM
1977	San Diego	3	0	0	0	4
1978	Birmingham	4	0	0	0	4
TOTALS		**7**	**0**	**0**	**0**	**8**

CHIPPERFIELD, RON
CHIP - pur - feeld

CENTER
Height: 5'11"
Weight: 186 lbs.
Birthdate: March 28, 1954
Birthplace: Brandon, Manitoba
Shoots: Right

REGULAR SEASON CAREER

SEASON	CLUB	LEAGUE	GP	G	A	PTS	PIM
1973-74	Brandon	WCHL	66	90	72	162	82
1974-75	Vancouver	WHA	78	19	20	39	30
1975-76	Calgary	WHA	75	42	41	83	32
1976-77	Calgary	WHA	81	27	27	54	32
1977-78	Edmonton	WHA	80	33	52	85	48
WHA TOTALS			314	121	140	261	142

WHA PLAYOFFS

YEAR	CLUB	GP	G	A	PTS	PIM
1976	Calgary	10	5	4	9	6
1978	Edmonton	5	1	1	2	0
TOTALS		15	6	5	11	6

CLACKSON, KIM
KLAK - suhn

DEFENSE
Height: 5'11"
Weight: 195 lbs.
Birthdate: February 13, 1955
Birthplace: Saskatoon, Saskatchewan
Shoots: Right

REGULAR SEASON CAREER

SEASON	CLUB	LEAGUE	GP	G	A	PTS	PIM
1974-75	Victoria	WCHL	58	7	26	33	359
1975-76	Indianapolis	WHA	77	1	12	13	351
1976-77	Indianapolis	WHA	71	3	8	11	168
1977-78	Winnipeg	WHA	52	2	7	9	203
WHA TOTALS			200	6	27	33	722

WHA PLAYOFFS

YEAR	CLUB	GP	G	A	PTS	PIM
1976	Indianapolis	6	0	0	0	25
1977	Indianapolis	9	0	1	1	24
1978	Winnipeg	9	0	1	1	61
TOTALS		24	0	2	2	110

CLARK, GORDIE
KLAHRK

RIGHT WING
Height: 5'10"
Weight: 180 lbs.
Birthdate: May 31, 1952
Birthplace: St. John, New Brunswick
Shoots: Right

REGULAR SEASON CAREER

SEASON	CLUB	LEAGUE	GP	G	A	PTS	PIM
1971-72	U. of New Hampshire	ECAC	30	27	30	57	46
1972-73	U. of New Hampshire	ECAC	29	24	28	52	52
1973-74	U. of New Hampshire	ECAC	31	25	28	53	20
1974-75	Rochester	AHL	65	22	42	64	34
	Boston	NHL	1	0	0	0	0
1975-76	Rochester	AHL	72	30	49	79	7
	Boston	NHL	7	0	1	1	0
1976-77	Rochester	AHL	58	34	38	72	50
1977-78	Rochester	AHL	75	37	51	88	18

CLOUTIER, REAL
klew - tee - AY

RIGHT WING
Height: 5'10"
Weight: 185 lbs.
Birthdate: July 30, 1956
Birthplace: St. Emile, Quebec
Shoots: Right

REGULAR SEASON CAREER

SEASON	CLUB	LEAGUE	GP	G	A	PTS	PIM
1974-75	Quebec	WHA	63	26	27	53	36
1975-76	Quebec	WHA	80	60	54	114	27
1976-77	Quebec	WHA	76	66	75	141	39
1977-78	Quebec	WHA	73	56	73	129	19
WHA TOTALS			292	208	229	437	121

WHA PLAYOFFS

YEAR	CLUB	GP	G	A	PTS	PIM
1975	Quebec	12	4	3	7	2
1976	Quebec	5	4	5	9	0
1977	Quebec	17	14	13	27	10
1978	Quebec	10	9	7	16	15
TOTALS		44	31	28	59	27

CORSI, JIM
KOR - see

GOALTENDER
Height: 5'10"
Weight: 180 lbs.
Birthdate: June 19, 1954
Birthplace: Montreal, Quebec
Shoots: Left

REGULAR SEASON CAREER

SEASON	CLUB	LEAGUE	GP	GA	SO	GAA
1976-77	Maine	NAHL	54	181	1	3.57
1977-78	Quebec	WHA	23	82	0	4.52
WHA TOTALS			23	82	0	4.52

COTE, ALAIN
koh - TAY

LEFT WING
Height: 5'10"
Weight: 203 lbs.
Birthdate: May 3, 1957
Birthplace: Matane, Quebec
Shoots: Left

REGULAR SEASON CAREER

SEASON	CLUB	LEAGUE	GP	G	A	PTS	PIM
1974-75	Chicoutimi	QMJHL	57	15	29	44	43
1975-76	Chicoutimi	QMJHL	72	35	49	84	93
1976-77	Chicoutimi	QMJHL	56	42	45	87	86
1977-78	Hampton	SHL	36	15	17	32	38
	Quebec	WHA	27	3	5	8	8
WHA TOTALS			27	3	5	8	8

WHA PLAYOFFS

YEAR	CLUB	GP	G	A	PTS	PIM
1978	Quebec	11	1	2	3	0
TOTALS		11	1	2	3	0

CROWDER, KEITH
KROW - der

RIGHT WING
Height: 6'0"
Weight: 190 lbs.
Birthdate: January 6, 1959
Birthplace: South Porcupine, Ontario
Shoots: Right

REGULAR SEASON CAREER

SEASON	CLUB	LEAGUE	GP	G	A	PTS	PIM
1976-77	Peterborough	OHA	58	13	19	32	99
1977-78	Peterborough	OHA	58	30	30	60	139

DALEY, JOE
DAY - lee

GOALTENDER
Height: 5'10"
Weight: 170 lbs.
Birthdate: February 20, 1943
Birthplace: Kildonan, Manitoba
Shoots: Left

REGULAR SEASON CAREER

SEASON	CLUB	LEAGUE	GP	GA	SO	GAA
1962-63	Weyburn	SJHL	—	—	—	—
1963-64	Johnstown	EHL	66	221	4	3.35
	Pittsburgh	AHL	2	7	0	3.50
	Cincinnati	CPHL	1	3	0	3.00
1964-65	Johnstown	EHL	69½	168	6	2.42
1965-66	Memphis	CPHL	67⅓	202	2	3.15
	San Francisco	WHL	7	17	2	2.43
1966-67	Pittsburgh	AHL	16	43	0	2.72
	Memphis	CPHL	49	169	0	3.34
1967-68	Baltimore	AHL	56	192	2	3.49
1968-69	Pittsburgh	NHL	29	87	2	3.23
1969-70	Baltimore	AHL	34	107	0	3.44
	Pittsburgh	NHL	9	26	0	2.95
1970-71	Buffalo	NHL	38	128	1	3.70
1971-72	Detroit	NHL	29	85	0	3.14
1972-73	**Winnipeg**	**WHA**	29	83	2	2.89
1973-74	**Winnipeg**	**WHA**	41	163	0	3.99
1974-75	**Winnipeg**	**WHA**	51	175	1	3.62
1975-76	**Winnipeg**	**WHA**	62	171	5	2.84
1976-77	**Winnipeg**	**WHA**	65	206	3	3.24
1977-78	**Winnipeg**	**WHA**	37	114	1	3.30
WHA TOTALS			285	912	12	3.30

WHA PLAYOFFS

YEAR	CLUB	GP	GA	SO	GAA
1973	Winnipeg	7	25	0	3.55
1974	Winnipeg	2	8	0	4.03
1976	Winnipeg	12	29	1	2.59
1977	Winnipeg	20	71	1	3.59
1978	Winnipeg	5	13	0	2.87
TOTALS		46	146	2	3.32

DAVID, RICHARD
dah - VEED

LEFT WING
Height: 6'2"
Weight: 205 lbs.
Birthdate: April 8, 1958
Birthplace: Notre Dame, De La Sallette, Quebec
Shoots: Left

REGULAR SEASON CAREER

SEASON	CLUB	LEAGUE	GP	G	A	PTS	PIM
1976-77	Three Rivers	QJMHL	60	52	58	110	103
1977-78	Three Rivers	QJMHL	69	50	61	111	81

DAVIS, BILL
DAY - vis

DEFENSE
Height: 6'1"
Weight: 180 lbs.
Birthdate: August 22, 1954
Birthplace: Lindsay, Ontario
Shoots: Left

REGULAR SEASON CAREER

SEASON	CLUB	LEAGUE	GP	G	A	PTS	PIM
1973-74	Colgate	ECAC	28	2	6	8	26
1974-75	Colgate	ECAC	26	5	29	34	54
1975-76	Colgate	ECAC	25	6	15	21	38
1976-77	Colgate	ECAC	28	6	20	26	62
1977-78	Philadelphia	NAHL	58	3	14	17	27
	Winnipeg	**WHA**	12	0	0	0	2
WHA TOTALS			12	0	0	0	2

DAVIS, KELLY
DAY - vis

DEFENSE
Height: 6'0"
Weight: 198 lbs.
Birthdate: September 23, 1958
Birthplace: Grand Prairie, Alberta
Shoots: Left

REGULAR SEASON CAREER

SEASON	CLUB	LEAGUE	GP	G	A	PTS	PIM
1976-77	Flin Flon	WCHL	72	5	44	49	150
1977-78	Flin Flon	WCHL	67	22	61	83	210

DEBOL, DAVE
DEE - bawl

CENTER
Height: 5'11"
Weight: 175 lbs.
Birthdate: March 27, 1956
Birthplace: St. Clair Shores, Michigan
Shoots: Right

REGULAR SEASON CAREER

SEASON	CLUB	LEAGUE	GP	G	A	PTS	PIM
1974-75	U. of Michigan	WCHA	33	18	18	36	0
1975-76	U. of Michigan	WCHA	42	39	22	61	22
1976-77	U. of Michigan	WCHA	45	43	56	99	40
1977-78	U. of Michigan	WCHA	46	20	38	58	16
	Cincinnati	**WHA**	9	3	2	5	2
WHA TOTALS			9	3	2	5	2

DION, MICHEL
dee - AHN

GOALTENDER
Height: 5'10"
Weight: 170 lbs.
Birthdate: February 11, 1954
Birthplace: Granby, Quebec
Shoots: Right

REGULAR SEASON CAREER

SEASON	CLUB	LEAGUE	GP	GA	SO	GAA
1973-74	Montreal	QMJHL	31	135	0	4.41
1974-75	Mohawk Valley	NAHL	28	96	0	3.90
	Indianapolis	**WHA**	1	4	0	4.00
1975-76	Mohawk Valley	NAHL	22	83	0	3.84
	Indianapolis	**WHA**	31	85	0	2.74
1976-77	**Indianapolis**	**WHA**	42	128	1	3.36
1977-78	**Cincinnati**	**WHA**	45	140	4	3.57
WHA TOTALS			119	357	5	3.26

WHA PLAYOFFS

YEAR	CLUB	GP	GA	SO	GAA
1976	Indianapolis	3	5	0	3.26
1977	Indianapolis	4	17	0	4.16
TOTALS		7	22	0	3.56

DOREY, JIM
DOR - ee

DEFENSE
Height: 6'1"
Weight: 190 lbs.
Birthdate: August 17, 1947
Birthplace: Kingston, Ontario
Shoots: Left

REGULAR SEASON CAREER

SEASON	CLUB	LEAGUE	GP	G	A	PTS	PIM
1963-64	Niagara Falls	OHA	21	1	0	1	0
1964-65	—	—	—	—	—	—	—
1965-66	London	Jr. "A" OHA	47	5	20	25	168
1966-67	London	Jr. "A" OHA	48	8	41	49	196
1967-68	Tulsa	CHL	35	4	24	28	81
	Phoenix	WHL	4	0	0	0	2
	Rochester	AHL	20	0	3	3	16
1968-69	Toronto	NHL	61	8	22	30	200
1969-70	Toronto	NHL	46	6	11	17	99
1970-71	Toronto	NHL	74	7	22	29	198
1971-72	Toronto	NHL	50	4	19	23	56
	New York	NHL	1	0	0	0	0
1972-73	New England	WHA	75	7	56	63	95
1973-74	New England	WHA	77	6	40	46	134
1974-75	New England	WHA	31	5	17	22	43
	Toronto	WHA	43	11	23	34	69
1975-76	Toronto	WHA	74	9	51	60	134
1976-77	Quebec	WHA	73	13	34	47	102
1977-78	Quebec	WHA	26	1	9	10	23
WHA TOTALS			**399**	**52**	**230**	**282**	**600**

WHA PLAYOFFS

YEAR	CLUB	GP	G	A	PTS	PIM
1973	New England	15	3	16	19	41
1974	New England	6	0	6	6	26
1975	Toronto	6	2	6	8	2
1977	Quebec	10	0	2	2	28
1978	Quebec	11	0	3	3	34
TOTALS		**48**	**5**	**33**	**38**	**131**

DORNSEIF, DAVE
DOHRN - sef

DEFENSE
Height: 6'3"
Weight: 205 lbs.
Birthdate: August 12, 1956
Birthplace: Edina, Minnesota
Shoots: Left

REGULAR SEASON CAREER

SEASON	CLUB	LEAGUE	GP	G	A	PTS	PIM
1974-75	Providence	ECAC	26	6	26	32	29
1975-76	Providence	ECAC	28	3	19	22	14
1976-77	Providence	ECAC	22	3	23	26	21
1977-78	Providence	ECAC	34	7	35	42	48
	Indianapolis	WHA	3	0	1	1	0
WHA TOTALS			3	0	1	1	0

DOUGLAS, JORDY
DUGH - las

LEFT WING
Height: 6'0"
Weight: 195 lbs.
Birthdate: January 20, 1958
Birthplace: Winnipeg, Manitoba
Shoots: Left

REGULAR SEASON CAREER

SEASON	CLUB	LEAGUE	GP	G	A	PTS	PIM
1976-77	Flin Flon	WCHL	59	40	23	63	71
1977-78	Flin Flon	WCHL	71	60	56	116	131

DRISCOLL, PETER
DRIS - kuhl

LEFT WING
Height: 6'0"
Weight: 190 lbs.
Birthdate: October 27, 1954
Birthplace: Kingston, Ontario
Shoots: Left

REGULAR SEASON CAREER

SEASON	CLUB	LEAGUE	GP	G	A	PTS	PIM
1974-75	Tulsa	CHL	56	9	10	19	183
	Vancouver	WHA	21	3	2	5	40
1975-76	Calgary	WHA	75	16	18	34	127
1976-77	Calgary	WHA	76	23	29	52	120
1977-78	Quebec	WHA	21	3	7	10	28
	Indianapolis	WHA	56	25	21	46	130
WHA TOTALS			249	70	77	147	445

WHA PLAYOFFS

YEAR	CLUB	GP	G	A	PTS	PIM
1976	Calgary	10	2	5	7	41
TOTALS		10	2	5	7	41

DRYDEN, DAVE
DRY - den

GOALTENDER
Height: 6'1"
Weight: 186 lbs.
Birthdate: September 5, 1941
Birthplace: Hamilton, Ontario
Shoots: Left

REGULAR SEASON CAREER

SEASON	CLUB	LEAGUE	GP	GA	SO	GAA
1958-59	Aurora	Jr. "B" OHA	—	—	—	—
1959-60	Toronto	Jr. "A" OHA	12	39	1	3.25
1960-61	Toronto	Jr. "A" OHA	18	66	1	3.67
1961-62	Rochester	AHL	1	2	0	2.00
	New York	NHL	1	3	0	3.00
	Toronto	Jr. "A" OHA	31⅓	99	3	3.16
1962-63	Galt	Sr. "A" OHA	40	174	2	4.35
1963-64	Galt	Sr. "A" OHA	39	141	0	3.61
1964-65	Galt	Sr. "A" OHA	34	106	1	3.10
	Buffalo	AHL	4	6	1	1.50
1965-66	Chicago	NHL	11	23	0	3.00
1966-67	St. Louis	CPHL	48	158	2	3.29
1967-68	Chicago	NHL	27	69	1	3.03
1968-69	Chicago	NHL	30	79	3	3.20
1969-70	Dallas	CHL	2	6	0	3.00
1970-71	Salt Lake	WHL	8	34	0	5.64
	Buffalo	NHL	10	23	1	3.37
1971-72	Buffalo	NHL	20	68	0	3.97
1972-73	Buffalo	NHL	37	89	3	2.65
1973-74	Buffalo	NHL	53	148	1	2.97
1974-75	**Chicago**	**WHA**	**45**	**176**	**1**	**3.87**
1975-76	**Edmonton**	**WHA**	**62**	**235**	**1**	**3.95**
1976-77	**Edmonton**	**WHA**	**24**	**77**	**1**	**3.26**
1977-78	**Edmonton**	**WHA**	**48**	**150**	**2**	**3.49**
WHA TOTALS			**179**	**638**	**5**	**3.72**

WHA PLAYOFFS

YEAR	CLUB	GP	GA	SO	GAA
1976	Edmonton	3	15	0	5.00
1978	Edmonton	2	6	0	3.94
TOTALS		**5**	**21**	**0**	**4.55**

DUBE, NORM
DOO - bay

LEFT WING
Height: 5'11"
Weight: 176 lbs.
Birthdate: September 12, 1951
Birthplace: Sherbrooke, Quebec
Shoots: Left

REGULAR SEASON CAREER

SEASON	CLUB	LEAGUE	GP	G	A	PTS	PIM
1970-71	Sherbrooke	QMJHL	62	72	66	138	17
1971-72	U. of Sherbrooke	QUAA	32	25	30	55	24
1972-73	Springfield	AHL	66	30	30	60	21
1973-74	Springfield	AHL	48	32	21	53	10
1974-75	Providence	AHL	14	5	0	5	4
	Kansas City	NHL	56	8	10	18	54
1975-76	Springfield	AHL	67	31	38	69	28
	Kansas City	NHL	1	0	0	0	0
1976-77	Beauce	NAHL	29	20	32	52	12
	Quebec	**WHA**	39	15	18	33	8
1977-78	**Quebec**	**WHA**	73	16	31	47	17
WHA TOTALS			112	31	49	80	25

WHA PLAYOFFS

YEAR	CLUB	GP	G	A	PTS	PIM
1977	Quebec	14	3	12	15	11
1978	Quebec	10	2	2	4	6
TOTALS		24	5	14	19	17

DUDLEY, RICK
DUHD - lee

LEFT WING
Height: 6'0"
Weight: 190 lbs.
Birthdate: January 31, 1949
Birthplace: Toronto, Ontario
Shoots: Left

REGULAR SEASON CAREER

SEASON	CLUB	LEAGUE	GP	G	A	PTS	PIM
1968-69	Dixie	Jr. "B" OHA	—	—	—	—	—
	St. Catharines	Jr. "A" OHA	26	8	7	15	43
1969-70	Iowa	CHL	26	3	3	6	36
1970-71	Cleveland	AHL	16	1	0	1	2
	Flint	IHL	15	1	5	6	30
1971-72	Cincinnati	AHL	51	6	23	29	272
1972-73	Cincinnati	AHL	64	40	44	84	159
	Buffalo	NHL	6	0	1	1	7
1973-74	Buffalo	NHL	67	13	13	26	71
1974-75	Buffalo	NHL	78	31	39	70	116
1975-76	**Cincinnati**	**WHA**	74	43	38	81	156
1976-77	**Cincinnati**	**WHA**	77	41	47	88	102
1977-78	**Cincinnati**	**WHA**	72	30	41	71	156
WHA TOTALS			223	114	126	240	414

WHA PLAYOFFS

YEAR	CLUB	GP	G	A	PTS	PIM
1977	Cincinnati	4	0	1	1	7
TOTALS		4	0	1	1	7

FITCHNER, BOB
FICH - nur

CENTER
Height: 6'0"
Weight: 190 lbs.
Birthdate: December 22, 1950
Birthplace: Sudbury, Ontario
Shoots: Left

REGULAR SEASON CAREER

SEASON	CLUB	LEAGUE	GP	G	A	PTS	PIM
1969-70	Brandon	WCHL	60	20	44	64	119
1970-71	Amarillo	CHL	70	9	10	19	49
1971-72	Hershey	AHL	3	0	0	0	0
	Fort Wayne	IHL	52	11	17	28	106
1972-73	Fort Wayne	IHL	73	26	37	63	157
1973-74	Winston-Salem	SHL	31	16	16	32	107
	Edmonton	WHA	31	1	2	3	21
1974-75	Indianapolis	WHA	78	11	19	30	96
1975-76	Indianapolis	WHA	52	15	16	31	112
	Quebec	WHA	21	7	9	16	22
1976-77	Quebec	WHA	81	9	30	39	105
1977-78	Quebec	WHA	72	15	28	43	76
WHA TOTALS			**335**	**58**	**104**	**162**	**432**

WHA PLAYOFFS

YEAR	CLUB	GP	G	A	PTS	PIM
1976	Quebec	5	1	0	1	8
1977	Quebec	17	3	3	6	16
1978	Quebec	11	1	6	7	10
TOTALS		**33**	**5**	**9**	**14**	**34**

FLETT, BILL
FLET

RIGHT WING
Height: 6'1"
Weight: 207 lbs.
Birthdate: July 21, 1943
Birthplace: Vermilion, Alberta
Shoots: Right

REGULAR SEASON CAREER

SEASON	CLUB	LEAGUE	GP	G	A	PTS	PIM
1962-63	Melville	SJHL	44	31	54	85	80
1963-64	Charlotte	EHL	41	26	21	47	48
	Rochester	AHL	1	0	0	0	0
1964-65	Victoria	WHL	23	1	7	8	14
	Tulsa	CPHL	39	8	22	30	58
1965-66	Tulsa	CPHL	55	23	23	46	83
1966-67	Tulsa	CPHL	62	16	28	44	108
1967-68	Los Angeles	NHL	73	26	20	46	97
1968-69	Los Angeles	NHL	72	24	25	49	53
1969-70	Springfield	AHL	5	2	6	8	6
	Los Angeles	NHL	69	14	18	32	70
1970-71	Los Angeles	NHL	64	13	24	37	57
1971-72	Los Angeles	NHL	45	7	12	19	18
	Philadelphia	NHL	31	11	10	21	26
1972-73	Philadelphia	NHL	69	43	31	74	53
1973-74	Philadelphia	NHL	67	17	27	44	51
1974-75	Toronto	NHL	77	15	25	40	38
1975-76	Atlanta	NHL	78	23	17	40	30
1976-77	Atlanta	NHL	0	0	0	0	0
	Edmonton	WHA	48	34	20	54	20
1977-78	Edmonton	WHA	74	41	28	69	34
WHA TOTALS			**122**	**75**	**48**	**123**	**54**

WHA PLAYOFFS

YEAR	CLUB	GP	G	A	PTS	PIM
1977	Edmonton	5	0	2	2	2
TOTALS		**5**	**0**	**2**	**2**	**2**

FORTIER, DAVE
for - tee - AY

DEFENSE
Height: 5'11"
Weight: 189 lbs.
Birthdate: June 17, 1951
Birthplace: Sudbury, Ontario
Shoots: Left

REGULAR SEASON CAREER

SEASON	CLUB	LEAGUE	GP	G	A	PTS	PIM
1970-71	St. Catharines	Jr. "A" OHA	60	8	16	24	196
1971-72	Tulsa	CHL	71	7	20	27	217
1972-73	Tulsa	CHL	50	2	20	22	148
	Toronto	NHL	23	1	4	5	63
1973-74	Oklahoma City	CHL	72	10	38	48	200
1974-75	New York	NHL	65	6	12	18	79
1975-76	New York	NHL	59	0	2	2	68
1976-77	Vancouver	NHL	58	1	3	4	125
1977-78	Indianapolis	WHA	54	1	15	16	86
WHA TOTALS			**54**	**1**	**15**	**16**	**86**

FTOREK, ROBBIE
fah - TOR - ik

CENTER
Height: 5'8"
Weight: 155 lbs.
Birthdate: January 2, 1952
Birthplace: Needham, Massachusetts
Shoots: Left

REGULAR SEASON CAREER

SEASON	CLUB	LEAGUE	GP	G	A	PTS	PIM
1970-71	Halifax	MJHL					
1971-72	USA Olympic Team						
1972-73	Virginia	AHL	55	17	42	59	36
	Detroit	NHL	3	0	0	0	0
1973-74	Virginia	AHL	65	24	42	66	37
	Detroit	NHL	12	2	5	7	4
1974-75	Tulsa	CHL	11	6	10	16	14
	Phoenix	WHA	53	31	37	68	29
1975-76	Phoenix	WHA	80	41	72	113	109
1976-77	Phoenix	WHA	80	46	71	117	86
1977-78	Cincinnati	WHA	80	59	50	109	54
WHA TOTALS			293	177	230	407	278

WHA PLAYOFFS

YEAR	CLUB	GP	G	A	PTS	PIM
1975	Phoenix	5	2	5	7	2
1976	Phoenix	5	1	3	4	2
TOTALS		10	3	8	11	4

GARRETT, JOHN
GEHR - ret

GOALTENDER
Height: 5'8"
Weight: 175 lbs.
Birthdate: June 17, 1951
Birthplace: Trenton, Ontario
Shoots: Left

REGULAR SEASON CAREER

SEASON	CLUB	LEAGUE	GP	GA	SO	GAA
1969-70	Peterborough	OHA	47	142	3	2.99
1970-71	Peterborough	OHA	51	151	5	2.96
1971-72	Kansas City	CHL	35	121	3	3.55
1972-73	Richmond	AHL	37	117	0	3.26
	Portland	WHL	17	52	2	3.28
1973-74	**Minnesota**	**WHA**	40	137	1	3.59
1974-75	**Minnesota**	**WHA**	58	180	2	3.28
1975-76	**Minnesota**	**WHA**	52	177	2	3.34
	Toronto	WHA	9	33	1	3.59
1976-77	**Birmingham**	**WHA**	65	224	4	3.53
1977-78	**Birmingham**	**WHA**	58	210	2	3.81
WHA TOTALS			282	961	12	3.51

WHA PLAYOFFS

YEAR	CLUB	GP	GA	SO	GAA
1974	Minnesota	7	25	0	4.04
1975	Minnesota	12	41	1	3.39
1978	Birmingham	5	26	0	5.76
TOTALS		24	92	1	4.03

GARTNER, MIKE
GAHRT - nur

RIGHT WING
Height: 6'0"
Weight: 180 lbs.
Birthdate: October 29, 1959
Birthplace: Ottawa, Ontario
Shoots: Right

REGULAR SEASON CAREER

SEASON	CLUB	LEAGUE	GP	G	A	PTS	PIM
1976-77	Niagara Falls	OHA	62	33	42	75	125
1977-78	Niagara Falls	OHA	64	41	49	90	56

GEOFFRION, DANNY
JEF - re - OHN

RIGHT WING
Height: 5'10"
Weight: 185 lbs.
Birthdate: January 24, 1958
Birthplace: Montreal, Quebec
Shoots: Right

REGULAR SEASON CAREER

SEASON	CLUB	LEAGUE	GP	G	A	PTS	PIM
1976-77	Cornwall	QMJHL	65	39	57	96	148
1977-78	Cornwall	QMJHL	71	68	75	143	183

GEORGE, WES
JORJ

LEFT WING
Height: 6'2"
Weight: 220 lbs.
Birthdate: September 26, 1958
Birthplace: Young, Saskatchewan
Shoots: Left

REGULAR SEASON CAREER

SEASON	CLUB	LEAGUE	GP	G	A	PTS	PIM
1976-77	Saskatoon	WCHL	39	14	19	33	107
1977-78	Saskatoon	WCHL	70	38	40	78	205

GILBERT, ED
GIL - bert

CENTER
Height: 5'11"
Weight: 185 lbs.
Birthdate: March 12, 1952
Birthplace: Hamilton, Ontario
Shoots: Left

REGULAR SEASON CAREER

SEASON	CLUB	LEAGUE	GP	G	A	PTS	PIM
1969-70	Hamilton	Jr. "B" OHA	—	13	9	22	15
	Hamilton	Jr. "A" OHA	43	8	17	25	10
1971-72	Hamilton	Jr. "A" OHA	57	20	35	55	28
	Hamilton	Jr. "A" OHA	62	33	41	74	40
1972-73	Nova Scotia	AHL	72	21	18	39	20
1973-74	Nova Scotia	AHL	75	30	44	74	40
1974-75	Kansas City	NHL	80	16	22	38	14
1975-76	Kansas City	NHL	41	4	8	12	8
	Pittsburgh	NHL	38	1	1	2	0
1976-77	Hershey	AHL	68	20	29	49	12
	Pittsburgh	NHL	7	0	0	0	0
1977-78	Did Not Play						

72

GILLIGAN, BILL
GIL - i - gan

CENTER
Height: 5'11"
Weight: 175 lbs.
Birthdate: August 5, 1954
Birthplace: Beverly, Massachusetts
Shoots: Right

REGULAR SEASON CAREER

SEASON	CLUB	LEAGUE	GP	G	A	PTS	PIM
1973-74	Brown Univ.	ECAC	19	35	36	71	10
1974-75	Brown Univ.	ECAC	25	20	22	42	12
1975-76	Brown Univ.	ECAC	30	25	54	79	10
1976-77	Brown Univ.	ECAC	26	23	36	59	39
1977-78	**Cincinnati**	**WHA**	**54**	**10**	**14**	**24**	**59**
	Hampton	AHL	18	10	11	21	18
WHA TOTALS			**54**	**10**	**14**	**24**	**59**

GINGRAS, GASTON
jin - GRAH

DEFENSE
Height: 6'0"
Weight: 191 lbs.
Birthdate: February 13, 1959
Birthplace: North Bay, Ontario
Shoots: Left

REGULAR SEASON CAREER

SEASON	CLUB	LEAGUE	GP	G	A	PTS	PIM
1975-76	Kitchener	OHA	66	13	31	44	94
1976-77	Kitchener	OHA	59	13	62	75	134
1977-78	Kitchener	Jr. "A" OHA	32	13	24	37	31
	Hamilton	Jr. "A" OHA	29	11	19	30	37

GOLDSWORTHY, BILL
GOHLDZ - wur - the

RIGHT WING
Height: 6'1"
Weight: 190 lbs.
Birthdate: August 24, 1944
Birthplace: Kitchener, Ontario
Shoots: Right

REGULAR SEASON CAREER

SEASON	CLUB	LEAGUE	GP	G	A	PTS	PIM
1964-65	Niagara Falls	Jr. "A" OHA	54	28	27	55	
	Boston	NHL	2	0	0	0	0
1965-66	Oklahoma City	CPHL	22	2	5	7	65
	Boston	NHL	13	3	1	4	6
1966-67	Oklahoma City	CPHL	11	4	1	5	14
	Buffalo	AHL	22	9	11	20	42
	Boston	NHL	18	3	5	8	21
1967-68	Minnesota	NHL	68	14	19	33	68
1968-69	Memphis	CHL	6	4	0	4	6
	Minnesota	NHL	68	14	10	24	110
1969-70	Minnesota	NHL	75	36	29	65	89
1970-71	Minnesota	NHL	77	34	31	65	85
1971-72	Minnesota	NHL	78	31	31	62	59
1972-73	Minnesota	NHL	75	27	33	60	97
1973-74	Minnesota	NHL	74	48	26	74	73
1974-75	Minnesota	NHL	71	37	35	72	77
1975-76	Minnesota	NHL	68	24	22	46	47
1976-77	Minnesota	NHL	16	2	3	5	6
	New York	NHL	61	10	12	22	43
1977-78	**Indianapolis**	**WHA**	**32**	**8**	**10**	**18**	**10**
WHA TOTALS			**32**	**8**	**10**	**18**	**10**

GORMAN, DAVE
GOR - man

RIGHT WING
Height: 5'11"
Weight: 185 lbs.
Birthdate: April 8, 1955
Birthplace: Oshawa, Ontario
Shoots: Right

REGULAR SEASON CAREER

SEASON	CLUB	LEAGUE	GP	G	A	PTS	PIM
1973-74	St. Catharines	Jr. "A" OHA	69	53	76	129	78
1974-75	Phoenix	WHA	13	3	5	8	10
	Tulsa	CHL	58	19	21	40	96
1975-76	Phoenix	WHA	67	11	20	31	28
1976-77	Phoenix	WHA	5	0	0	0	0
	Birmingham	WHA	52	9	13	22	38
1977-78	Birmingham	WHA	63	19	21	40	93
	Hampton	AHL	2	0	0	0	12
WHA TOTALS			200	42	59	101	169

WHA PLAYOFFS

YEAR	CLUB	GP	G	A	PTS	PIM
1976	Phoenix	5	0	2	2	24
1978	Birmingham	4	1	1	2	0
TOTALS		9	1	3	4	24

GOULET, MICHEL
goo - LAY

RIGHT WING
Height: 6'1"
Weight: 195 lbs.
Birthdate: April 21, 1960
Birthplace: Peribonqa, Quebec
Shoots: Right

REGULAR SEASON CAREER

SEASON	CLUB	LEAGUE	GP	G	A	PTS	PIM
1976-77	Quebec	QMJHL	37	17	18	35	9
1977-78	Quebec	QMJHL	72	73	62	135	109

75

GRAY, JOHN
GRAY

RIGHT WING
Height: 5'10"
Weight: 180 lbs.
Birthdate: August 13, 1949
Birthplace: Little Current, Ontario
Shoots: Left

REGULAR SEASON CAREER

SEASON	CLUB	LEAGUE	GP	G	A	PTS	PIM
1972-73	Tulsa	CHL	68	15	25	40	147
1973-74	Oklahoma City	CHL	59	25	35	60	155
1974-75	**Phoenix**	**WHA**	75	35	33	68	107
1975-76	**Phoenix**	**WHA**	79	35	45	80	136
1976-77	**Phoenix**	**WHA**	28	10	10	20	59
	Houston	WHA	47	21	20	41	25
1977-78	Houston	WHA	77	35	23	58	80
WHA TOTALS			306	136	131	267	407

WHA PLAYOFFS

YEAR	CLUB	GP	G	A	PTS	PIM
1975	Phoenix	5	2	3	5	12
1976	Phoenix	5	1	1	2	7
1977	Phoenix	6	0	1	1	8
1978	Houston	6	0	3	3	10
TOTALS		22	3	8	11	37

GREEN, TED
GREEN

DEFENSE
Height: 5'11"
Weight: 195 lbs.
Birthdate: March 23, 1940
Birthplace: St. Boniface, Manitoba
Shoots: Right

REGULAR SEASON CAREER

SEASON	CLUB	LEAGUE	GP	G	A	PTS	PIM
1959-60	Winnipeg	WHL	70	8	20	28	109
1960-61	Kingston	EPHL	11	1	5	6	30
	Boston	NHL	1	0	0	0	2
	Winnipeg	WHL	57	1	18	19	127
1961-62	Boston	NHL	66	3	8	11	116
1962-63	Boston	NHL	70	1	11	12	117
1963-64	Boston	NHL	70	4	10	14	145
1964-65	Boston	NHL	70	8	27	35	156
1965-66	Boston	NHL	27	5	13	18	113
1966-67	Boston	NHL	47	6	10	16	67
1967-68	Boston	NHL	72	7	36	43	133
1968-69	Boston	NHL	65	8	38	46	99
1969-70	Did not play						
1970-71	Boston	NHL	78	5	37	42	60
1971-72	Boston	NHL	54	1	16	17	21
1972-73	New England	WHA	78	16	30	46	47
1973-74	New England	WHA	75	7	26	33	42
1974-75	New England	WHA	57	6	14	20	29
1975-76	Winnipeg	WHA	79	5	23	28	73
1976-77	Winnipeg	WHA	70	4	21	25	45
1977-78	Winnipeg	WHA	73	4	22	26	52
WHA TOTALS			**438**	**42**	**136**	**178**	**288**

WHA PLAYOFFS

YEAR	CLUB	GP	G	A	PTS	PIM
1973	New England	12	1	5	6	25
1974	New England	7	0	4	4	2
1975	New England	3	0	0	0	2
1976	Winnipeg	11	0	2	2	16
1977	Winnipeg	20	1	3	4	12
1978	Winnipeg	8	0	2	2	2
TOTALS		**61**	**2**	**16**	**18**	**59**

GREIG, BRUCE
GREG

LEFT WING
Height: 6'2"
Weight: 220 lbs.
Birthdate: May 9, 1953
Birthplace: High River, Alberta
Shoots: Left

REGULAR SEASON CAREER

SEASON	CLUB	LEAGUE	GP	G	A	PTS	PIM
1971-72	Medicine Hat	WCHL	17	3	3	6	11
1972-73	Vancouver	WCHL	24	3	3	6	79
1973-74	Salt Lake City	WHL	13	1	2	3	36
	California	NHL	1	0	0	0	4
1974-75	California	NHL	8	0	1	1	42
1975-76	Salt Lake City	WHL	1	0	0	0	11
	Flint	IHL	10	0	5	5	77
1976-77	Greensboro	SHL	33	10	14	24	68
	Tidewater	SHL	2	0	0	0	2
	Calgary	**WHA**	**7**	**1**	**1**	**2**	**10**
1977-78	**Cincinnati**	**WHA**	**32**	**3**	**1**	**4**	**57**
WHA TOTALS			**39**	**4**	**2**	**6**	**67**

GRETZKY, WAYNE
GRETZ - kee

CENTER
Height: 5'11"
Weight: 165 lbs.
Birthdate: January 26, 1961
Birthplace: Brantford, Ontario
Shoots: Left

REGULAR SEASON CAREER

SEASON	CLUB	LEAGUE	GP	G	A	PTS	PIM
1977-78	Sault St. Marie	OHA	64	70	112	182	14

GUINDON, BOB
geen - DOH

CENTER
Height: 5'9"
Weight: 175 lbs.
Birthdate: November 19, 1950
Birthplace: Labelle, Quebec
Shoots: Left

REGULAR SEASON CAREER

SEASON	CLUB	LEAGUE	GP	G	A	PTS	PIM
1969-70	Montreal	Jr. "A" OHA	53	43	51	94	62
1970-71	Fort Worth	CHL	61	12	13	25	15
1971-72	Fort Worth	CHL	72	22	26	48	36
1972-73	**Quebec**	**WHA**	**71**	**28**	**28**	**56**	**31**
1973-74	**Quebec**	**WHA**	**77**	**31**	**39**	**70**	**30**
1974-75	**Quebec**	**WHA**	**69**	**12**	**18**	**30**	**23**
1975-76	**Winnipeg**	**WHA**	**29**	**3**	**3**	**6**	**14**
1976-77	**Winnipeg**	**WHA**	**69**	**10**	**17**	**27**	**19**
1977-78	**Winnipeg**	**WHA**	**77**	**20**	**22**	**42**	**18**
WHA TOTALS			**392**	**104**	**127**	**231**	**135**

WHA PLAYOFFS

YEAR	CLUB	GP	G	A	PTS	PIM
1975	Quebec	15	7	6	13	10
1976	Winnipeg	13	3	3	6	9
1977	Winnipeg	20	4	4	8	9
1978	Winnipeg	9	8	5	13	5
TOTALS		**57**	**22**	**18**	**40**	**33**

GUITE, PIERRE
GEE - TAY

RIGHT WING
Height: 6'2"
Weight: 190 lbs.
Birthdate: April 17, 1952
Birthplace: Montreal, Quebec
Shoots: Left

REGULAR SEASON CAREER

SEASON	CLUB	LEAGUE	GP	G	A	PTS	PIM
1969-70	St. Catharines	Jr. "A" OHA	51	31	30	61	162
1970-71	St. Catharines	Jr. "A" OHA	56	25	14	39	113
1972-73	Quebec	WHA	66	10	8	18	136
1973-74	Quebec	WHA	68	14	20	34	106
1974-75	Quebec	WHA	22	14	8	22	59
	Michigan	WHA	13	5	4	9	11
1975-76	Cincinnati	WHA	52	20	24	44	80
1976-77	Cincinnati	WHA	27	10	8	18	32
	Quebec	WHA	35	2	6	8	67
1977-78	Quebec	WHA	18	4	5	9	15
	Edmonton	WHA	60	12	21	33	71
WHA TOTALS			**361**	**91**	**104**	**195**	**577**

WHA PLAYOFFS

YEAR	CLUB	GP	G	A	PTS	PIM
1977	Quebec	17	5	0	5	9
1978	Edmonton	5	1	1	2	20
TOTALS		**22**	**6**	**1**	**7**	**29**

HAMILTON, AL
HAM - mil - tuhn

DEFENSE
Height: 6'2"
Weight: 195 lbs.
Birthdate: August 20, 1946
Birthplace: Flin Flon, Manitoba
Shoots: Right

REGULAR SEASON CAREER

SEASON	CLUB	LEAGUE	GP	G	A	PTS	PIM
1964-65	St. Paul	CPHL	3	0	2	2	0
1965-66	Edmonton	ASHL	58	15	22	37	99
	New York	NHL	4	0	0	0	0
1966-67	Omaha	CHL	68	11	25	36	96
1967-68	Buffalo	AHL	72	9	21	30	82
	New York	NHL	2	0	0	0	0
1968-69	Buffalo	AHL	41	4	14	18	61
	New York	NHL	16	0	0	0	8
1969-70	New York	NHL	59	0	5	5	54
1970-71	Buffalo	NHL	69	2	28	30	71
1971-72	Buffalo	NHL	76	4	30	34	105
1972-73	**Alberta**	**WHA**	**78**	**11**	**50**	**61**	**124**
1973-74	**Edmonton**	**WHA**	**78**	**14**	**45**	**59**	**104**
1974-75	**Edmonton**	**WHA**	**25**	**1**	**13**	**14**	**42**
1975-76	**Edmonton**	**WHA**	**54**	**2**	**32**	**34**	**78**
1976-77	**Edmonton**	**WHA**	**81**	**8**	**37**	**45**	**60**
1977-78	**Edmonton**	**WHA**	**59**	**11**	**43**	**54**	**46**
WHA TOTALS			**375**	**47**	**220**	**267**	**454**

WHA PLAYOFFS

YEAR	CLUB	GP	G	A	PTS	PIM
1974	Edmonton	4	1	1	2	15
1976	Edmonton	4	0	1	1	6
1977	Edmonton	5	0	4	4	4
TOTALS		**13**	**1**	**6**	**7**	**25**

HANGSLEBEN, ALAN
HANGS - lay - ben

DEFENSE
Height: 6'1"
Weight: 195 lbs.
Birthdate: February 22, 1953
Birthplace: Warroad, Minnesota
Shoots: Left

REGULAR SEASON CAREER

SEASON	CLUB	LEAGUE	GP	G	A	PTS	PIM
1972-73	Univ. No. Dak.	WCHA	36	15	18	33	77
1973-74	Univ. No. Dak.	WCHA	24	9	16	25	56
1974-75	New England	WHA	26	0	5	5	8
	Cape Cod	NAHL	55	4	39	43	130
1975-76	Cape Cod	NAHL	1	0	0	0	9
	New England	WHA	78	2	23	25	62
1976-77	New England	WHA	74	13	9	22	79
1977-78	New England	WHA	79	11	18	29	140
WHA TOTALS			257	26	55	81	289

WHA PLAYOFFS

YEAR	CLUB	GP	G	A	PTS	PIM
1975	New England	6	0	3	3	19
1976	New England	13	2	3	5	20
1977	New England	4	0	0	0	9
1978	New England	14	1	4	5	37
TOTALS		37	3	10	13	85

HARRIS, HUGH
HEHR - ris

LEFT WING
Height: 6'0"
Weight: 201 lbs.
Birthdate: June 7, 1948
Birthplace: Toronto, Ontario
Shoots: Left

REGULAR SEASON CAREER

SEASON	CLUB	LEAGUE	GP	G	A	PTS	PIM
1967-68	Muskegon	IHL	63	16	19	35	72
1968-69	Muskegon	IHL	71	33	39	72	83
1969-70	Muskegon	IHL	48	31	25	56	35
1970-71	Muskegon	IHL	63	39	47	86	86
1971-72	Cincinnati	AHL	71	18	24	42	70
1972-73	Cincinnati	AHL	14	7	7	14	37
	Buffalo	NHL	60	12	26	38	17
1973-74	New England	WHA	75	24	28	52	78
1974-75	Phoenix	WHA	22	10	10	20	15
	Vancouver	WHA	58	23	34	57	49
1975-76	Calgary	WHA	30	5	9	14	19
	Indianapolis	WHA	41	12	27	39	23
1976-77	Indianapolis	WHA	46	21	35	56	21
1977-78	Indianapolis	WHA	19	1	7	8	6
	Cincinnati	WHA	45	11	23	34	30
WHA TOTALS			336	107	173	280	241

WHA PLAYOFFS

YEAR	CLUB	GP	G	A	PTS	PIM
1974	New England	7	0	4	4	11
1976	Indianapolis	7	2	5	7	8
1977	Indianapolis	2	0	0	0	0
TOTALS		16	2	9	11	19

HARTSBURG, CRAIG
HAHRTS - burg

DEFENSE
Height: 6'1"
Weight: 190 lbs.
Birthdate: June 29, 1959
Birthplace: Stratford, Ontario
Shoots: Left

REGULAR SEASON CAREER

SEASON	CLUB	LEAGUE	GP	G	A	PTS	PIM
1975-76	Sault St. Marie	Jr. "A" OHA	64	9	19	28	105
1976-77	Sault St. Marie	Jr. "A" OHA	61	29	64	93	142
1977-78	Sault St. Marie	Jr. "A" OHA	36	15	42	57	101

HENDERSON, PAUL
HEN - dur - suhn

LEFT WING
Height: 5'10"
Weight: 180 lbs.
Birthdate: January 28, 1943
Birthplace: Kincardine, Ontario
Shoots: Right

REGULAR SEASON CAREER

SEASON	CLUB	LEAGUE	GP	G	A	PTS	PIM
1962-63	Hamilton	Jr. "A" OHA	48	49	27	76	24
	Detroit	NHL	2	0	0	0	9
1963-64	Pittsburgh	AHL	38	10	14	24	18
	Detroit	NHL	32	3	3	6	14
1964-65	Detroit	NHL	70	8	13	21	30
1965-66	Detroit	NHL	69	22	24	46	34
1966-67	Detroit	NHL	46	21	19	40	10
1967-68	Detroit	NHL	50	13	20	33	35
	Toronto	NHL	13	5	6	11	8
1968-69	Toronto	NHL	74	27	32	59	16
1969-70	Toronto	NHL	67	20	22	42	18
1970-71	Toronto	NHL	72	30	30	60	34
1971-72	Toronto	NHL	73	38	19	57	32
1972-73	Toronto	NHL	40	18	16	34	18
1973-74	Toronto	NHL	69	24	31	55	40
1974-75	**Toronto**	**WHA**	**58**	**30**	**33**	**63**	**18**
1975-76	**Toronto**	**WHA**	**65**	**26**	**29**	**55**	**22**
1976-77	**Birmingham**	**WHA**	**81**	**23**	**25**	**48**	**30**
1977-78	**Birmingham**	**WHA**	**80**	**37**	**29**	**66**	**22**
WHA TOTALS			**284**	**116**	**116**	**232**	**92**

WHA PLAYOFFS

YEAR	CLUB	GP	G	A	PTS	PIM
1978	Birmingham	5	1	1	2	0
TOTALS		**5**	**1**	**1**	**2**	**0**

HENDRICKS, LARRY
HEND - riks

GOALTENDER
Height: 6'0"
Weight: 155 lbs.
Birthdate: September 23, 1955
Birthplace: Edmonton, Alberta
Shoots: Left

REGULAR SEASON CAREER

SEASON	CLUB	LEAGUE	GP	GA	SO	GAA
1970-71	Edmonton	AJHL	29	134	0	4.63
	Edmonton	WCHL	1	0	0	0.00
1971-72	Edmonton	WCHL	46	137	3	3.47
1972-73	Edmonton	WCHL	38	102	1	3.13
1973-74	Edmonton	WCHL	35	134	1	4.25
1974-75	Calgary	WCHL	62	326	0	5.51
1975-76	Toledo	IHL	23	90	0	4.09
	Salt Lake City	CHL	16	71	1	4.59
1976-77	Salt Lake City	CHL	33	124	2	4.05
1977-78	Binghamton	AHL	14	49	0	3.91
	Phoenix	CHL	5	26	0	6.12

HICKS, GLENN
HICKS

LEFT WING
Height: 5'10"
Weight: 177 lbs.
Birthdate: August 28, 1958
Birthplace: Red Deer, Alberta
Shoots: Left

REGULAR SEASON CAREER

SEASON	CLUB	LEAGUE	GP	G	A	PTS	PIM
1976-77	Flin Flon	WCHL	71	28	31	59	175
1977-78	Flin Flon	WCHL	72	50	69	119	225

HISLOP, JAMIE
HIS - luhp

RIGHT WING
Height: 5'10"
Weight: 180 lbs.
Birthdate: January 20, 1954
Birthplace: Sarnia, Ontario
Shoots: Right

REGULAR SEASON CAREER

SEASON	CLUB	LEAGUE	GP	G	A	PTS	PIM
1971-72	Stratford	Jr. "B" OHA	38	26	30	56	—
1972-73	U. of New Hampshire	ECAC	26	5	16	21	—
1973-74	U. of New Hampshire	ECAC	31	21	35	56	30
1974-75	U. of New Hampshire	ECAC	31	28	38	66	12
1975-76	U. of New Hampshire	ECAC	31	23	43	66	20
1976-77	Hampton	SHL	37	16	17	33	11
	Cincinnati	WHA	46	7	19	26	6
1977-78	Cincinnati	WHA	80	24	43	67	17
WHA TOTALS			126	31	62	93	23

WHA PLAYOFFS

YEAR	CLUB	GP	G	A	PTS	PIM
1977	Cincinnati	4	0	1	1	4
TOTALS		4	0	1	1	4

HOGANSON, DALE
HOH - gan - suhn

DEFENSE
Height: 5'11"
Weight: 190 lbs.
Birthdate: July 8, 1949
Birthplace: North Battleford, Saskatchewan
Shoots: Left

REGULAR SEASON CAREER

SEASON	CLUB	LEAGUE	GP	G	A	PTS	PIM
1968-69	Estevan	WCHL	54	16	44	60	67
1969-70	Los Angeles	NHL	49	1	7	8	37
	Springfield	AHL	19	2	5	7	43
1970-71	Los Angeles	NHL	70	4	10	14	52
1971-72	Los Angeles	NHL	10	1	2	3	14
	Nova Scotia	AHL	13	3	4	7	11
	Montreal	NHL	21	0	0	0	2
1972-73	Montreal	NHL	25	0	2	2	2
1973-74	Quebec	WHA	62	8	33	41	27
1974-75	Quebec	WHA	78	9	35	44	47
1975-76	Quebec	WHA	45	3	14	17	18
1976-77	Birmingham	WHA	81	7	48	55	48
1977-78	Birmingham	WHA	43	1	12	13	29
WHA TOTALS			309	28	142	170	169

WHA PLAYOFFS

YEAR	CLUB	GP	G	A	PTS	PIM
1975	Quebec	13	1	3	4	4

1976	Quebec		5	1	3	4	2
1978	Birmingham		5	0	0	0	7
TOTALS			23	2	6	8	13

HOWE, GORDIE
HOW

RIGHT WING
Height: 6'0"
Weight: 203 lbs.
Birthdate: March 31, 1928
Birthplace: Floral, Saskatchewan
Shoots: Right

REGULAR SEASON CAREER

SEASON	CLUB	LEAGUE	GP	G	A	PTS	PIM
1945-46	Omaha	USHL	51	22	26	48	53
1946-47	Detroit	NHL	58	7	15	22	52
1947-48	Detroit	NHL	60	16	28	44	63
1948-49	Detroit	NHL	40	12	25	37	57
1949-50	Detroit	NHL	70	35	33	68	69
1950-51	Detroit	NHL	70	43	43	86	74
1951-52	Detroit	NHL	70	47	39	86	78
1952-53	Detroit	NHL	70	49	46	95	57
1953-54	Detroit	NHL	70	33	48	81	109
1954-55	Detroit	NHL	64	29	33	62	68
1955-56	Detroit	NHL	70	38	41	79	100
1956-57	Detroit	NHL	70	44	45	89	72
1957-58	Detroit	NHL	64	33	44	77	40
1958-59	Detroit	NHL	70	32	45	78	57
1959-60	Detroit	NHL	70	28	45	73	45
1960-61	Detroit	NHL	64	23	49	72	30
1961-62	Detroit	NHL	70	33	44	77	54
1962-63	Detroit	NHL	70	38	48	86	100
1963-64	Detroit	NHL	69	26	47	73	70
1964-65	Detroit	NHL	70	29	47	76	104
1965-66	Detroit	NHL	70	29	46	75	83
1966-67	Detroit	NHL	69	25	40	65	53
1967-68	Detroit	NHL	74	39	43	82	53
1968-69	Detroit	NHL	76	44	59	103	58
1969-70	Detroit	NHL	76	31	40	71	58
1970-71	Detroit	NHL	63	23	29	52	38
1973-74	**Houston**	**WHA**	**70**	**31**	**69**	**100**	**46**
1974-75	**Houston**	**WHA**	**75**	**34**	**65**	**99**	**84**
1975-76	**Houston**	**WHA**	**78**	**32**	**70**	**102**	**76**
1976-77	**Houston**	**WHA**	**62**	**24**	**44**	**68**	**57**
1977-78	**New England**	**WHA**	**76**	**34**	**62**	**96**	**85**
WHA TOTALS			361	155	310	465	348

WHA PLAYOFFS

YEAR	CLUB	GP	G	A	PTS	PIM
1974	Houston	13	3	14	17	34
1975	Houston	13	8	12	20	20
1976	Houston	17	4	8	12	31
1977	Houston	11	5	3	8	11
1978	New England	14	5	5	10	15
TOTALS		68	25	42	67	111

85

HOWE, MARK
HOW

LEFT WING
Height: 5'11"
Weight: 180 lbs.
Birthdate: May 28, 1955
Birthplace: Detroit, Michigan
Shoots: Left

REGULAR SEASON CAREER

SEASON	CLUB	LEAGUE	GP	G	A	PTS	PIM
1972-73	Toronto	Jr. "A" OHA	60	38	66	104	27
1973-74	Houston	WHA	76	38	41	79	20
1974-75	Houston	WHA	74	36	40	76	30
1975-76	Houston	WHA	72	39	37	76	38
1976-77	Houston	WHA	57	23	52	75	46
1977-78	New England	WHA	70	30	61	91	32
WHA TOTALS			349	166	231	397	166

WHA PLAYOFFS

YEAR	CLUB	GP	G	A	PTS	PIM
1974	Houston	14	9	10	19	4
1975	Houston	13	10	12	22	0
1976	Houston	17	6	10	16	18
1977	Houston	10	4	10	14	2
1978	New England	14	8	7	15	18
TOTALS		68	37	49	86	42

HOWE, MARTY
HOW

DEFENSE
Height: 6'1"
Weight: 185 lbs.
Birthdate: February 18, 1954
Birthplace: Detroit, Michigan
Shoots: Left

REGULAR SEASON CAREER

SEASON	CLUB	LEAGUE	GP	G	A	PTS	PIM
1972-73	Toronto	Jr. "A" OHA	38	11	17	28	81
1973-74	Houston	WHA	73	4	20	24	90
1974-75	Houston	WHA	75	13	21	34	89
1975-76	Houston	WHA	80	14	23	37	81
1976-77	Houston	WHA	80	17	28	45	103
1977-78	New England	WHA	75	10	10	20	66
WHA TOTALS			383	58	102	160	429

WHA PLAYOFFS

YEAR	CLUB	GP	G	A	PTS	PIM
1974	Houston	14	1	5	6	31
1975	Houston	11	0	2	2	11
1976	Houston	16	4	4	8	12
1977	Houston	11	3	1	4	10
1978	New England	14	1	1	2	13
TOTALS		66	9	13	22	77

HUGHES, BRENT
HYOUZ

DEFENSE
Height: 6'0"
Weight: 205 lbs.
Birthdate: June 17, 1943
Birthplace: Bowmanville, Ontario
Shoots: Left

REGULAR SEASON CAREER

SEASON	CLUB	LEAGUE	GP	G	A	PTS	PIM
1959-60	Toronto	Jr. "A" OHA	16	0	1	1	—
1961-62	St. Catharines	Jr. "A" OHA	41	1	7	8	—
1962-63	St. Catharines	Jr. "A" OHA	50	9	18	27	49
1963-64	New Haven	EHL	53	6	25	31	100
1964-65	Minneapolis	CPHL	68	2	16	18	79
1965-66	Memphis	CPHL	70	4	21	25	50
1966-67	Memphis	CPHL	52	3	15	18	49
	Pittsburgh	AHL	5	2	4	6	4
1967-68	Springfield	AHL	25	5	14	19	30
	Los Angeles	NHL	44	4	10	14	36
1968-69	Los Angeles	NHL	72	2	19	21	73
1969-70	Los Angeles	NHL	52	1	7	8	108
	Springfield	AHL	3	0	0	0	10
1970-71	Quebec	AHL	25	4	20	24	34
	Philadelphia	NHL	30	1	10	11	21
1971-72	Baltimore	AHL	10	2	4	6	6
	Philadelphia	NHL	63	2	20	22	35
1972-73	Philadelphia	NHL	29	2	11	13	32
	St. Louis	NHL	8	1	1	2	0
1973-74	St. Louis	NHL	2	0	0	0	0
	Detroit	NHL	69	1	21	22	92
1974-75	Kansas City	NHL	66	1	18	19	43
1975-76	**San Diego**	**WHA**	78	7	28	35	63
1976-77	**San Diego**	**WHA**	62	4	13	17	48
1977-78	**Birmingham**	**WHA**	80	9	35	44	48
WHA TOTALS			220	20	76	96	159

WHA PLAYOFFS

YEAR	CLUB	GP	G	A	PTS	PIM
1976	San Diego	10	1	5	6	6
1977	San Diego	7	1	4	5	0
1978	Birmingham	5	0	0	0	12
TOTALS		22	2	9	11	18

HUGHES, JOHN
HYOUZ

DEFENSE
Height: 5'11"
Weight: 200 lbs.
Birthdate: March 18, 1954
Birthplace: Charlottetown, P.E.I.
Shoots: Left

REGULAR SEASON CAREER

SEASON	CLUB	LEAGUE	GP	G	A	PTS	PIM
1973-74	Toronto	Jr. "A" OHA	67	6	34	40	189
1974-75	Phoenix	WHA	72	4	25	29	201
1975-76	Cincinnati	WHA	79	3	34	37	204
1976-77	Cincinnati	WHA	79	3	27	30	113
1977-78	Houston	WHA	79	3	25	28	130
WHA TOTALS			309	13	111	124	648

WHA PLAYOFFS

YEAR	CLUB	GP	G	A	PTS	PIM
1975	Phoenix	0	0	0	0	0
1977	Cincinnati	4	0	0	0	8
1978	Houston	6	1	1	2	6
TOTALS		10	1	1	2	14

HULL, BOBBY
HUHL

LEFT WING
Height: 5'10"
Weight: 191 lbs.
Birthdate: January 3, 1939
Birthplace: Point Anne, Ontario
Shoots: Left

REGULAR SEASON CAREER

SEASON	CLUB	LEAGUE	GP	G	A	PTS	PIM
1956-57	St. Catharines	Jr. "A" OHA	52	33	28	61	—
1957-58	Chicago	NHL	70	13	34	47	62
1958-59	Chicago	NHL	70	18	32	50	50
1959-60	Chicago	NHL	70	39	42	81	68
1960-61	Chicago	NHL	67	31	25	56	43
1961-62	Chicago	NHL	70	50	34	84	35
1962-63	Chicago	NHL	65	31	31	62	27
1963-64	Chicago	NHL	70	43	44	87	50
1964-65	Chicago	NHL	61	39	32	71	32
1965-66	Chicago	NHL	65	54	43	97	70
1966-67	Chicago	NHL	66	52	28	80	52
1967-68	Chicago	NHL	71	44	31	75	39
1968-69	Chicago	NHL	74	58	49	107	48
1969-70	Chicago	NHL	61	38	29	67	8
1970-71	Chicago	NHL	78	44	52	96	32
1971-72	Chicago	NHL	78	50	43	93	24
1972-73	**Winnipeg**	**WHA**	**63**	**51**	**52**	**103**	**37**
1973-74	**Winnipeg**	**WHA**	**75**	**53**	**42**	**95**	**38**
1974-75	**Winnipeg**	**WHA**	**78**	**77**	**65**	**142**	**41**
1975-76	**Winnipeg**	**WHA**	**80**	**53**	**70**	**123**	**30**
1976-77	**Winnipeg**	**WHA**	**34**	**21**	**32**	**53**	**14**
1977-78	**Winnipeg**	**WHA**	**77**	**46**	**71**	**117**	**23**
WHA TOTALS			**407**	**301**	**332**	**633**	**183**

WHA PLAYOFFS

YEAR	CLUB	GP	G	A	PTS	PIM
1973	Winnipeg	14	9	16	25	16
1974	Winnipeg	4	1	1	2	4
1976	Winnipeg	13	12	8	20	4
1977	Winnipeg	20	13	9	22	2
1978	Winnipeg	9	8	3	11	12
TOTALS		**60**	**43**	**37**	**80**	**38**

HUNTER, DAVE
HUHNT - ur

LEFT WING
Height: 5'11"
Weight: 195 lbs.
Birthdate: January 1, 1958
Birthplace: Petrolia, Ontario
Shoots: Left

REGULAR SEASON CAREER

SEASON	CLUB	LEAGUE	GP	G	A	PTS	PIM
1975-76	Sudbury	OHA	53	7	21	28	147
1976-77	Sudbury	OHA	62	30	56	86	140
1977-78	Sudbury	Jr. "A" OHA	68	44	44	88	196

INKPEN, DAVE
INK - pen

DEFENSE
Height: 6'0"
Weight: 195 lbs.
Birthdate: September 4, 1954
Birthplace: Edmonton, Alberta
Shoots: Right

REGULAR SEASON CAREER

SEASON	CLUB	LEAGUE	GP	G	A	PTS	PIM
1971-72	Edmonton	WCHL	52	3	11	14	42
1972-73	Edmonton	WCHL	68	5	30	35	172
1973-74	Edmonton	WCHL	57	11	42	53	141
1974-75	Flint-Des Moines	IHL	47	9	23	32	55
	Fort Worth	CHL	5	0	0	0	5
1975-76	**Cincinnati**	**WHA**	**80**	**4**	**24**	**28**	**95**
1976-77	**Cincinnati**	**WHA**	**48**	**3**	**14**	**17**	**61**
	Indianapolis	**WHA**	**32**	**4**	**12**	**16**	**20**
1977-78	**Edmonton**	**WHA**	**19**	**0**	**1**	**1**	**16**
	Quebec	**WHA**	**24**	**0**	**1**	**1**	**20**
	Indianapolis	**WHA**	**24**	**1**	**9**	**10**	**24**
WHA TOTALS			**227**	**12**	**61**	**73**	**236**

WHA PLAYOFFS

YEAR	CLUB	GP	G	A	PTS	PIM
1977	Indianapolis	9	0	2	2	8
TOTALS		**9**	**0**	**2**	**2**	**8**

INNESS, GARY
IN - nes

GOALTENDER
Height: 6'0"
Weight: 190 lbs.
Birthdate: May 28, 1949
Birthplace: Toronto, Ontario
Shoots: Right

REGULAR SEASON CAREER

SEASON	CLUB	LEAGUE	GP	GA	SO	GAA
1973-74	Hershey	AHL	20	56	1	2.90
	Pittsburgh	NHL	20	56	0	3.26
1974-75	Pittsburgh	NHL	57	161	2	3.09
1975-76	Hershey	AHL	2	9	0	4.54
	Pittsburgh	NHL	23	82	0	4.06
	Philadelphia	NHL	2	3	0	1.50
1976-77	Philadelphia	NHL	6	9	0	2.57
1977-78	**Indianapolis**	**WHA**	**52**	**200**	**0**	**4.21**
WHA TOTALS			**52**	**200**	**0**	**4.21**

IRWIN, GLEN
UR - win

DEFENSE
Height: 5'11"
Weight: 195 lbs.
Birthdate: March 1, 1951
Birthplace: Edmonton, Alberta
Shoots: Right

REGULAR SEASON CAREER

SEASON	CLUB	LEAGUE	GP	G	A	PTS	PIM
1970-71	Estevan	WCHL	64	8	26	34	261
1971-72	Richmond	AHL	18	0	2	2	16
	San Diego	WHL	9	0	1	1	22
	Seattle	WHL	7	0	0	0	10
	Flint	IHL	17	1	2	3	48
1972-73	Richmond	AHL	15	0	0	0	36
1973-74	Fort Worth	CHL	68	0	13	13	135
1974-75	**Houston**	**WHA**	**70**	**2**	**11**	**13**	**153**
1975-76	**Houston**	**WHA**	**72**	**3**	**8**	**11**	**116**
1976-77	Oklahoma City	CHL	24	1	2	3	70
	Houston	**WHA**	**44**	**2**	**4**	**6**	**168**
1977-78	**Houston**	**WHA**	**3**	**0**	**0**	**0**	**0**
	Binghamton	AHL	51	0	12	12	191
	Indianapolis	**WHA**	**20**	**0**	**0**	**0**	**72**
WHA TOTALS			**209**	**7**	**23**	**30**	**509**

WHA PLAYOFFS

YEAR	CLUB	GP	G	A	PTS	PIM
1975	Houston	13	0	2	2	8
1976	Houston	5	0	0	0	9
TOTALS		**18**	**0**	**2**	**2**	**17**

KEON, DAVE
KEE- ahn

CENTER
Height: 5'9"
Weight: 167 lbs.
Birthdate: March 22, 1940
Birthplace: Noranda, Quebec
Shoots: Right

PLAYING CAREER

SEASON	CLUB	LEAGUE	GP	G	A	PTS	PIM
1960-61	Toronto	NHL	70	20	25	45	6
1961-62	Toronto	NHL	64	26	35	61	2
1962-63	Toronto	NHL	68	28	28	56	2
1963-64	Toronto	NHL	70	23	37	60	6
1964-65	Toronto	NHL	65	21	29	50	10
1965-66	Toronto	NHL	69	24	30	54	4
1966-67	Toronto	NHL	66	19	33	52	2
1967-68	Toronto	NHL	67	11	37	48	4
1968-69	Toronto	NHL	75	27	34	61	12
1969-70	Toronto	NHL	72	32	30	62	6
1970-71	Toronto	NHL	76	38	38	76	4
1971-72	Toronto	NHL	72	18	30	48	4
1972-73	Toronto	NHL	76	37	36	73	2
1973-74	Toronto	NHL	74	25	28	53	7
1974-75	Toronto	NHL	78	16	43	59	4
1975-76	**Minnesota**	**WHA**	57	26	38	64	4
	Indianapolis	WHA	12	3	7	10	2
1976-77	Minnesota	WHA	42	13	38	51	2
	New England	WHA	34	14	25	39	8
1977-78	New England	WHA	77	24	38	62	2
WHA TOTALS			**222**	**80**	**146**	**226**	**18**

WHA PLAYOFFS

YEAR	CLUB	GP	G	A	PTS	PIM
1976	Indianapolis	7	2	2	4	2
1977	New England	5	3	1	4	0
1978	New England	14	5	11	16	4
TOTALS		**26**	**10**	**14**	**24**	**6**

KIRK, GAVIN
KURK

CENTER
Height: 5'10"
Weight: 165 lbs.
Birthdate: December 6, 1951
Birthplace: London, England
Shoots: Left

REGULAR SEASON CAREER

SEASON	CLUB	LEAGUE	GP	G	A	PTS	PIM
1968-69	Markham	Jr. "B" OHA	27	24	22	46	62
1969-70	Toronto	Jr. "A" OHA	53	17	33	50	40
1970-71	Toronto	Jr. "A" OHA	62	38	69	107	101
1971-72	Phoenix	WHL	3	1	2	3	2
	Loyola	ECAC	29	24	41	65	48
1972-73	Ottawa	WHA	78	28	40	68	54
1973-74	Toronto	WHA	78	20	48	68	44
1974-75	Toronto	WHA	78	15	58	73	69
1975-76	Toronto	WHA	62	29	38	67	32
	Calgary	WHA	15	7	8	15	14
1976-77	Birmingham	WHA	29	9	18	27	34
	Edmonton	WHA	52	8	28	36	16
1977-78	Philadelphia	AHL	59	21	26	47	32
WHA TOTALS			392	116	238	354	263

WHA PLAYOFFS

YEAR	CLUB	GP	G	A	PTS	PIM
1973	Ottawa	5	2	3	5	4
1974	Toronto	12	2	4	6	4
1975	Toronto	6	5	6	11	2
1976	Calgary	10	4	6	10	19
1977	Edmonton	5	1	0	1	4
TOTALS		38	14	19	33	33

LACOMBE, FRANCOIS
lah - KOHM

DEFENSE
Height: 5'10"
Weight: 188 lbs.
Birthdate: February 22, 1948
Birthplace: Montreal, Quebec
Shoots: Left

REGULAR SEASON CAREER

SEASON	CLUB	LEAGUE	GP	G	A	PTS	PIM
1967-68	Montreal	Jr. "A" OHA	51	1	10	11	59
1968-69	Oakland	NHL	72	2	16	18	50
1969-70	Providence	AHL	70	9	16	25	64
	Oakland	NHL	2	0	0	0	0
1970-71	Salt Lake	WHL	70	11	39	50	89
	Buffalo	NHL	1	0	1	1	2
1971-72	Salt Lake	WHL	11	2	3	5	22
	Fort Worth	CHL	19	3	5	8	26
	Cincinnati	AHL	35	4	10	14	26
1972-73	**Quebec**	**WHA**	62	10	18	28	123
1973-74	**Quebec**	**WHA**	71	9	26	35	41
1974-75	Maine	NAHL	4	0	3	3	12
	Quebec	**WHA**	55	7	17	24	54
1975-76	**Calgary**	**WHA**	71	3	28	31	62
1976-77	**Quebec**	**WHA**	81	5	22	27	86
1977-78	**Quebec**	**WHA**	22	1	7	8	12
WHA TOTALS			**362**	**35**	**118**	**153**	**378**

WHA PLAYOFFS

YEAR	CLUB	GP	G	A	PTS	PIM
1975	Quebec	15	0	2	2	14
1976	Calgary	8	0	0	0	2
1977	Quebec	17	4	3	7	16
1978	Quebec	10	1	4	5	2
TOTALS		**50**	**5**	**9**	**14**	**34**

LACROIX, ANDRE
la - KWAH

CENTER
Height: 5'8"
Weight: 175 lbs.
Birthdate: June 5, 1945
Birthplace: Lauzon, Quebec
Shoots: Left

REGULAR SEASON CAREER

SEASON	CLUB	LEAGUE	GP	G	A	PTS	PIM
1964-65	Peterborough	Jr. "A" OHA	49	45	74	119	—
	Quebec	AHL	1	0	0	0	0
1965-66	Peterborough	Jr. "A" OHA	48	40	80	120	20
	Quebec	AHL	2	1	3	4	0
1966-67	Quebec	AHL	67	25	24	49	14
1967-68	Quebec	AHL	54	41	46	87	18
	Philadelphia	NHL	18	6	8	14	6
1968-69	Philadelphia	NHL	75	24	32	56	4
1969-70	Philadelphia	NHL	74	22	36	58	14
1970-71	Philadelphia	NHL	78	20	22	42	12
1971-72	Chicago	NHL	51	4	7	11	6
1972-73	**Philadelphia**	**WHA**	78	50	74	124	83
1973-74	**Jersey**	**WHA**	78	31	80	111	54
1974-75	**San Diego**	**WHA**	78	41	106	147	63
1975-76	**San Diego**	**WHA**	80	29	72	101	42
1976-77	**San Diego**	**WHA**	81	32	82	114	79
1977-78	**Houston**	**WHA**	78	36	77	113	57
WHA TOTALS			473	219	491	710	378

WHA PLAYOFFS

YEAR	CLUB	GP	G	A	PTS	PIM
1973	Philadelphia	4	0	2	2	18
1975	San Diego	10	3	9	12	2
1976	San Diego	11	4	6	10	4
1977	San Diego	7	1	6	7	6
1978	Houston	6	2	2	4	0
TOTALS		38	10	25	35	30

LAGACE, PIERRE
la - gah - SAY

CENTER
Height: 6'2"
Weight: 210 lbs.
Birthdate: October 27, 1957
Birthplace: Montreal, Quebec
Shoots: Left

REGULAR SEASON CAREER

SEASON	CLUB	LEAGUE	GP	G	A	PTS	PIM
1974-75	Trois-Rivieres	LJMQ	72	36	50	86	110
1975-76	Trois-Rivieres	LJMQ	71	13	29	42	146
1976-77	Quebec	QMJHL	71	22	30	52	168
1977-78	**Quebec**	**WHA**	17	2	4	6	2
WHA TOTALS			17	2	4	6	2

WHA PLAYOFFS

YEAR	CLUB	GP	G	A	PTS	PIM
1978	Quebec	1	0	0	0	0
TOTALS		1	0	0	0	0

95

LAHACHE, FLOYD
lah - HAHSH

DEFENSE
Height: 5'10"
Weight: 185 lbs.
Birthdate: September 17, 1957
Birthplace: Caughnawaga, Quebec
Shoots: Right

REGULAR SEASON CAREER

SEASON	CLUB	LEAGUE	GP	G	A	PTS	PIM
1973-74	Sherbrooke	QMJHL	70	2	13	15	155
1974-75	Sherbrooke	QMJHL	65	5	21	26	296
1975-76	Sherbrooke	QMJHL	71	11	49	60	159
1976-77	Sherbrooke	QMJHL	70	10	37	47	225
1977-78	Hampton	AHL	44	4	4	8	87
	Binghamton	AHL	12	0	1	1	11
	Cincinnati	**WHA**	**11**	**0**	**3**	**3**	**13**
WHA TOTALS			**11**	**0**	**3**	**3**	**13**

LANGEVIN, DAVE
LAHN - je - van

DEFENSE
Height: 6'2"
Weight: 200 lbs.
Birthdate: May 15, 1954
Birthplace: St. Paul, Minnesota
Shoots: Left

REGULAR SEASON CAREER

SEASON	CLUB	LEAGUE	GP	G	A	PTS	PIM
1973-74	U. of Minn.-Duluth	WCHA	37	2	11	13	56
1974-75	U. of Minn.-Duluth	WCHA	35	8	24	32	44
1975-76	U. of Minn.-Duluth	WCHA	34	19	26	45	82
1976-77	**Edmonton**	**WHA**	**77**	**7**	**16**	**23**	**94**
1977-78	**Edmonton**	**WHA**	**62**	**6**	**22**	**28**	**90**
WHA TOTALS			**139**	**13**	**38**	**51**	**184**

WHA PLAYOFFS

YEAR	CLUB	GP	G	A	PTS	PIM
1977	Edmonton	5	2	1	3	9
1978	Edmonton	5	0	2	2	10
TOTALS		**10**	**2**	**3**	**5**	**19**

LARIVIERE, GARRY
lah - RI - vee - EHR

DEFENSE
Height: 6'0"
Weight: 190 lbs.
Birthdate: December 6, 1954
Birthplace: St. Catharines, Ontario
Shoots: Right

REGULAR SEASON CAREER

SEASON	CLUB	LEAGUE	GP	G	A	PTS	PIM
1972-73	St. Catherines	OHA	55	5	32	37	140
1973-74	St. Catherines	Jr. "A" OHA	60	3	35	38	153
1974-75	Tulsa	CHL	76	15	38	53	168
	Phoenix	WHA	4	0	1	1	28
1975-76	Phoenix	WHA	79	7	17	24	100
1976-77	Phoenix	WHA	61	7	23	30	48
	Quebec	WHA	15	0	3	3	8
1977-78	Quebec	WHA	80	7	49	56	78
WHA TOTALS			239	21	93	114	262

WHA PLAYOFFS

YEAR	CLUB	GP	G	A	PTS	PIM
1975	Phoenix	1	0	0	0	0
1976	Phoenix	5	0	2	2	2
1977	Quebec	17	0	10	10	10
1978	Quebec	11	3	2	5	4
TOTALS		34	3	14	17	16

LAROSE, CLAUDE
lah - ROHZ

LEFT WING
Height: 5'10"
Weight: 170 lbs.
Birthdate: May 17, 1955
Birthplace: St. Jean, Quebec
Shoots: Left

REGULAR SEASON CAREER

SEASON	CLUB	LEAGUE	GP	G	A	PTS	PIM
1972-73	Drummondville	QMHL	61	63	50	113	12
1973-74	Drummondville	QMHL	61	56	77	133	16
1974-75	Sherbrooke	QHML	61	69	76	145	12
1975-76	Cincinnati	WHA	79	28	24	52	19
1976-77	Cincinnati	WHA	81	30	46	76	8
1977-78	Cincinnati	WHA	51	11	20	31	6
	Indianapolis	WHA	28	14	16	30	12
WHA TOTALS			239	83	106	189	45

WHA PLAYOFFS

YEAR	CLUB	GP	G	A	PTS	PIM
1977	Cincinnati	4	2	1	3	0
TOTALS		4	2	1	3	0

LARWAY, DON
LAHR - way

RIGHT WING
Height: 6'1"
Weight: 195 lbs.
Birthdate: February 12, 1954
Birthplace: Oak Lake, Manitoba
Shoots: Right

REGULAR SEASON CAREER

SEASON	CLUB	LEAGUE	GP	G	A	PTS	PIM
1973-74	Swift Current	WCHL	66	46	36	82	175
1974-75	Houston	WHA	76	21	13	34	59
1975-76	Houston	WHA	79	30	20	50	56
1976-77	Oklahoma City	CHL	2	1	0	1	17
	Houston	WHA	75	11	13	24	112
1977-78	Houston	WHA	69	24	35	59	52
WHA TOTALS			299	86	81	167	279

WHA PLAYOFFS

YEAR	CLUB	GP	G	A	PTS	PIM
1975	Houston	13	3	1	4	8
1976	Houston	16	7	5	12	21
1977	Houston	3	1	0	1	0
1978	Houston	6	1	2	3	4
TOTALS		38	12	8	20	33

LEDUC, RICHARD
le - DEWK

CENTER
Height: 5'11"
Weight: 170 lbs.
Birthdate: August 24, 1951
Birthplace: Ile Perrot, Quebec
Shoots: Left

REGULAR SEASON CAREER

SEASON	CLUB	LEAGUE	GP	G	A	PTS	PIM
1971-72	Cleveland	AHL	14	1	4	5	27
	Boston	AHL	61	26	27	53	92
1972-73	Boston	NHL	5	1	1	2	2
	Boston	AHL	65	31	42	73	75
1973-74	Boston	AHL	29	7	11	18	60
	Boston	NHL	28	3	3	6	12
1974-75	Cleveland	WHA	78	34	31	65	122
1975-76	Cleveland	WHA	79	36	22	58	76
1976-77	Cincinnati	WHA	81	52	55	107	75
1977-78	Cincinnati	WHA	54	27	31	58	44
	Indianapolis	WHA	28	10	15	25	38
WHA TOTALS			320	159	154	313	355

WHA PLAYOFFS

YEAR	CLUB	GP	G	A	PTS	PIM
1975	Cleveland	5	0	2	2	2
1976	Cleveland	3	2	1	3	2
1977	Cincinnati	4	1	3	4	16
TOTALS		**12**	**3**	**6**	**9**	**20**

LEGGE, BARRY
LEG

DEFENSE
Height: 6'0"
Weight: 186 lbs.
Birthdate: October 22, 1954
Birthplace: Winnipeg, Manitoba
Shoots: Left

REGULAR SEASON CAREER

SEASON	CLUB	LEAGUE	GP	G	A	PTS	PIM
1970-71	St. James	MJHL	47	7	22	29	98
1972-73	Winnipeg	WCHL	63	10	43	53	161
1973-74	Winnipeg	WCHL	66	13	34	47	198
1974-75	Greensboro	SHL	37	3	16	19	60
	Baltimore	WHA	36	3	18	21	20
1975-76	Ottawa	WHA	40	6	8	14	15
	Cleveland	WHA	35	0	7	7	22
1976-77	Minnesota	WHA	2	0	0	0	0
	Cincinnati	WHA	74	7	22	29	39
1977-78	Cincinnati	WHA	78	7	17	24	114
WHA TOTALS			**265**	**23**	**72**	**95**	**210**

WHA PLAYOFFS

YEAR	CLUB	GP	G	A	PTS	PIM
1976	Cleveland	3	0	1	1	12
1977	Cincinnati	4	0	0	0	0
TOTALS		**7**	**0**	**1**	**1**	**12**

LEROUX, GERRY
le - RHUE

LEFT WING
Height: 5'7"
Weight: 160 lbs.
Birthdate: June 9, 1958
Birthplace: St. Bernardin, Ontario
Shoots: Left

REGULAR SEASON CAREER

SEASON	CLUB	LEAGUE	GP	G	A	PTS	PIM
1977-78	Windsor	OHL	68	57	66	123	85

LESUK, BILL
LEZ - zook

LEFT WING
Height: 5'9"
Weight: 187 lbs.
Birthdate: November 1, 1946
Birthplace: Moose Jaw, Saskatchewan
Shoots: Left

REGULAR SEASON CAREER

SEASON	CLUB	LEAGUE	GP	G	A	PTS	PIM
1965-66	Weyburn	SJHL	55	25	33	58	73
1966-67	Weyburn	CMJHL	56	36	46	82	62
1967-68	Oklahoma City	CHL	67	14	10	24	53
1968-69	Oklahoma City	CHL	64	17	30	47	46
	Boston	NHL	5	0	1	1	0
1969-70	Hershey	AHL	70	20	20	40	82
	Boston	NHL	3	0	0	0	0
1970-71	Philadelphia	NHL	78	17	19	36	87
1971-72	Philadelphia	NHL	45	7	6	13	31
	Los Angeles	NHL	27	4	10	14	14
1972-73	Los Angeles	NHL	67	6	14	20	90
1973-74	Los Angeles	NHL	35	2	1	3	32
1974-75	Washington	NHL	79	8	11	19	77
1975-76	**Winnipeg**	**WHA**	**81**	**15**	**21**	**36**	**92**
1976-77	**Winnipeg**	**WHA**	**78**	**14**	**27**	**41**	**85**
1977-78	**Winnipeg**	**WHA**	**80**	**9**	**18**	**27**	**48**
WHA TOTALS			**239**	**38**	**66**	**104**	**225**

WHA PLAYOFFS

YEAR	CLUB	GP	G	A	PTS	PIM
1976	Winnipeg	13	2	2	4	8
1977	Winnipeg	18	2	1	3	22
1978	Winnipeg	9	2	5	7	12
TOTALS		**40**	**6**	**8**	**14**	**42**

LEVASSEUR, LOUIS
lev - ah - SUR

GOALTENDER
Height: 5'10"
Weight: 160 lbs.
Birthdate: June 16, 1949
Birthplace: Noranda, Quebec
Shoots: Right

REGULAR SEASON CAREER

SEASON	CLUB	LEAGUE	GP	GA	SO	GAA
1972-73	Orillia	Sr. "A" OHA	35	114	1	3.26
	Tulsa	CHL	4	13	1	4.62
1973-74	Orillia	Sr. "A" OHA	14	48	1	3.43
1974-75	Johnstown	NAHL	26	79	1	3.15
1975-76	Johnstown	NAHL	30	89	1	3.04
	Minnesota	**WHA**	4	10	0	3.11
1976-77	**Minnesota**	**WHA**	30	78	2	2.73
	Edmonton	**WHA**	21	88	0	4.35
1977-78	**New England**	**WHA**	27	91	3	3.30
WHA TOTALS			82	267	5	3.35

WHA PLAYOFFS

YEAR	CLUB	GP	GA	SO	GAA
1977	Edmonton	2	10	0	4.51
1978	New England	12	31	1	2.59
TOTALS		14	41	1	2.89

LEY, RICK
LEE

DEFENSE
Height: 5'9"
Weight: 185 lbs.
Birthdate: December 2, 1948
Birthplace: Orillia, Ontario
Shoots: Left

REGULAR SEASON CAREER

SEASON	CLUB	LEAGUE	GP	G	A	PTS	PIM
1968-69	Tulsa	CHL	19	0	5	5	23
	Toronto	NHL	38	1	11	12	39
1969-70	Toronto	NHL	48	2	13	15	102
1970-71	Toronto	NHL	76	4	16	20	151
1971-72	Toronto	NHL	67	1	14	15	124
1972-73	**New England**	**WHA**	76	3	27	30	108
1973-74	**New England**	**WHA**	72	6	35	41	148
1974-75	**New England**	**WHA**	62	6	36	42	50
1975-76	**New England**	**WHA**	67	8	30	38	78
1976-77	**New England**	**WHA**	55	2	21	23	102
1977-78	**New England**	**WHA**	73	3	41	44	95
WHA TOTALS			405	28	190	218	581

WHA PLAYOFFS

YEAR	CLUB	GP	G	A	PTS	PIM
1973	New England	15	3	7	10	24
1974	New England	7	1	5	6	18
1975	New England	6	1	1	2	32
1976	New England	17	1	4	5	49
1977	New England	5	0	4	4	4
1978	New England	14	1	8	9	4
TOTALS		64	7	29	36	131

LINDSTROM, WILLY
LIND - struhm

RIGHT WING
Height: 6'0"
Weight: 180 lbs.
Birthdate: May 5, 1951
Birthplace: Grums, Sweden
Shoots: Left

REGULAR SEASON CAREER

SEASON	CLUB	LEAGUE	GP	G	A	PTS	PIM
1975-76	Winnipeg	WHA	81	23	36	59	32
1976-77	Winnipeg	WHA	79	44	36	80	37
1977-78	Winnipeg	WHA	77	30	30	60	42
WHA TOTALS			237	97	102	199	111

WHA PLAYOFFS

YEAR	CLUB	GP	G	A	PTS	PIM
1976	Winnipeg	13	4	7	11	2
1977	Winnipeg	20	9	6	15	22
1978	Winnipeg	8	3	4	7	17
TOTALS		41	16	17	33	41

LIUT, MIKE
LEE - oot

GOALTENDER
Height: 6'2"
Weight: 180 lbs.
Birthdate: January 7, 1956
Birthplace: Weston, Ontario
Shoots: Right

REGULAR SEASON CAREER

SEASON	CLUB	LEAGUE	GP	GA	SO	GAA
1973-74	Bowling Green St. U.	CCHA	24	88	0	4.00
1974-75	Bowling Green St. U.	CCHA	20	78	0	3.99
1975-76	Bowling Green St. U.	CCHA	21	50	2	2.56
1976-77	Bowling Green St. U.	CCHA	24	61	2	2.75
1977-78	**Cincinnati**	**WHA**	27	86	0	4.25
WHA TOTALS			27	86	0	4.25

LONG, BARRY
LAWNG

DEFENSE
Height: 6'2"
Weight: 210 lbs.
Birthdate: January 31, 1949
Birthplace: Red Deer, Ontario
Shoots: Left

REGULAR SEASON CAREER

SEASON	CLUB	LEAGUE	GP	G	A	PTS	PIM
1968-69	Dallas	CHL	46	4	11	15	85
1969-70	Dallas	CHL	71	11	22	33	127
1970-71	Dallas	CHL	72	9	24	33	90
1971-72	Portland	WHL	66	14	22	47	52
1972-73	Los Angeles	NHL	70	2	13	15	48
1973-74	Los Angeles	NHL	60	3	19	22	118
1974-75	**Edmonton**	**WHA**	**78**	**20**	**40**	**60**	**116**
1975-76	**Edmonton**	**WHA**	**78**	**10**	**32**	**42**	**66**
1976-77	**Edmonton**	**WHA**	**2**	**0**	**1**	**1**	**2**
	Winnipeg	**WHA**	**71**	**9**	**38**	**47**	**54**
1977-78	**Winnipeg**	**WHA**	**78**	**7**	**24**	**31**	**42**
WHA TOTALS			**307**	**46**	**135**	**181**	**280**

WHA PLAYOFFS

YEAR	CLUB	GP	G	A	PTS	PIM
1976	Edmonton	4	0	0	0	4
1977	Winnipeg	20	1	5	6	10
1978	Winnipeg	9	0	5	5	6
TOTALS		**33**	**1**	**10**	**11**	**20**

LUKOWICH, MORRIS
LEWK - oh - wich

LEFT WING
Height: 5'9"
Weight: 170 lbs.
Birthdate: June 1, 1956
Birthplace: Saskatoon, Saskatchewan
Shoots: Left

REGULAR SEASON CAREER

SEASON	CLUB	LEAGUE	GP	G	A	PTS	PIM
1975-76	Medicine Hat	WCHL	72	65	77	142	195
1976-77	**Houston**	**WHA**	**62**	**27**	**18**	**45**	**67**
1977-78	**Houston**	**WHA**	**80**	**40**	**35**	**75**	**131**
WHA TOTALS			**142**	**67**	**53**	**120**	**198**

WHA PLAYOFFS

YEAR	CLUB	GP	G	A	PTS	PIM
1977	Houston	11	6	4	10	19
1978	Houston	6	1	2	3	17
TOTALS		**17**	**7**	**6**	**13**	**36**

103

LUKSA, CHUCK
LAHK - sah

DEFENSE
Height: 6'1"
Weight: 190 lbs.
Birthdate: February 19, 1954
Birthplace: Toronto, Ontario
Shoots: Left

REGULAR SEASON CAREER

SEASON	CLUB	LEAGUE	GP	G	A	PTS	PIM
1974-75	Nova Scotia	AHL	32	0	4	4	54
1975-76	Nova Scotia	AHL	73	5	13	18	75
1976-77	Nova Scotia	AHL	80	9	31	40	72
1977-78	Nova Scotia	AHL	66	3	23	26	89

LYLE, GEORGE
LYL

LEFT WING
Height: 6'2"
Weight: 210 lbs.
Birthdate: November 24, 1953
Birthplace: Vancouver, British Columbia
Shoots: Left

REGULAR SEASON CAREER

SEASON	CLUB	LEAGUE	GP	G	A	PTS	PIM
1973-74	Michigan Tech	WCHA	19	9	13	22	20
1974-75	Michigan Tech	WCHA	38	37	19	56	76
1975-76	Michigan Tech	WCHA	43	47	41	88	42
1976-77	**New England**	**WHA**	75	39	33	72	62
1977-78	**New England**	**WHA**	68	30	24	54	74
TOTALS			143	69	57	126	136

WHA PLAYOFFS

YEAR	CLUB	GP	G	A	PTS	PIM
1977	New England	5	1	0	1	4
1978	New England	12	2	1	3	13
TOTALS		17	3	1	4	17

MacDONALD, BLAIR
mak - DAH - nald

RIGHT WING
Height: 5'10"
Weight: 180 lbs.
Birthdate: November 17, 1953
Birthplace: Cornwall, Ontario
Shoots: Right

REGULAR SEASON CAREER

SEASON	CLUB	LEAGUE	GP	G	A	PTS	PIM
1972-73	Cornwall	QMJHL	64	63	39	102	44
1973-74	Edmonton	WHA	78	21	24	45	34
1974-75	Edmonton	WHA	72	22	24	46	14
1975-76	Edmonton	WHA	29	7	5	12	8
	Indianapolis	WHA	56	20	11	31	14
1976-77	Indianapolis	WHA	81	34	30	64	28
1977-78	Edmonton	WHA	80	34	34	68	11
WHA TOTALS			396	138	128	266	109

WHA PLAYOFFS

YEAR	CLUB	GP	G	A	PTS	PIM
1974	Edmonton	5	4	2	6	2
1976	Indianapolis	7	0	0	0	0
1977	Indianapolis	13	7	8	15	4
1978	Edmonton	5	1	1	2	0
TOTALS		30	12	11	23	6

MacKINNON, PAUL
mak - IN - on

DEFENSE
Height: 6'0"
Weight: 190 lbs.
Birthdate: November 6, 1958
Birthplace: Brantford, Ontario
Shoots: Right

REGULAR SEASON CAREER

SEASON	CLUB	LEAGUE	GP	G	A	PTS	PIM
1976-77	Peterborough	Jr. "A" OHA	65	2	38	40	96
1977-78	Peterborough	Jr. "A" OHA	60	1	25	26	77

MAGEE, DEAN
muh - GEE

LEFT WING
Height: 6'1"
Weight: 210 lbs.
Birthdate: April 29, 1955
Birthplace: Banff, Alberta

REGULAR SEASON CAREER

SEASON	CLUB	LEAGUE	GP	G	A	PTS	PIM
1974-75	Colorado	WCHA	36	15	13	28	130
1975-76	Colorado	WCHA	33	9	7	16	104
1976-77	Colorado	WCHA	39	23	18	41	144
1977-78	Colorado	WCHA	25	13	15	28	50

MARRIN, PETER
MEHR - rin

CENTER
Height: 5'10"
Weight: 185 lbs.
Birthdate: August 8, 1953
Birthplace: Toronto, Ontario
Shoots: Right

REGULAR SEASON CAREER

SEASON	CLUB	LEAGUE	GP	G	A	PTS	PIM
1972-73	Toronto	Jr. "A" OHA	59	42	64	106	26
1973-74	Mohawk Valley	NAHL	24	7	16	23	2
	Toronto	WHA	31	1	4	5	4
1974-75	Mohawk Valley	NAHL	54	33	45	78	36
	Toronto	WHA	4	3	1	4	0
1975-76	Toronto	WHA	64	22	16	38	16
1976-77	Birmingham	WHA	79	23	37	60	36
1977-78	Birmingham	WHA	80	28	43	71	53
WHA TOTALS			258	77	101	178	109

WHA PLAYOFFS

YEAR	CLUB	GP	G	A	PTS	PIM
1974	Toronto	3	0	1	1	0
1975	Toronto	6	0	4	4	2
1978	Birmingham	5	0	3	3	2
TOTALS		14	0	8	8	4

MARSH, PETER
MARSH

RIGHT WING
Height: 6'1"
Weight: 180 lbs.
Birthdate: December 21, 1956
Birthplace: Halifax, Nova Scotia
Shoots: Left

REGULAR SEASON CAREER

SEASON	CLUB	LEAGUE	GP	G	A	PTS	PIM
1973-74	Sherbrooke	Jr. "A" OHA	45	12	11	23	32
1974-75	Sherbrooke	Jr. "A" OHA	65	36	36	72	140
1975-76	Sherbrooke	Jr. "A" OHA	69	75	81	156	102
1976-77	Cincinnati	WHA	76	23	28	51	52
1977-78	Cincinnati	WHA	74	25	25	50	123
WHA TOTALS			150	48	53	101	175

WHA PLAYOFFS

YEAR	CLUB	GP	G	A	PTS	PIM
1977	Cincinnati	4	2	0	2	0

MATTSSON, MARKUS
MATT - sun

GOALTENDER
Height: 6'0"
Weight: 180 lbs.
Birthdate: July 30, 1957
Birthplace: Tampere, Finland
Shoots: Left

REGULAR SEASON CAREER

SEASON	CLUB	LEAGUE	GP	GA	SO	GAA
1977-78	Quebec	WHA	6	30	0	6.77
	Winnipeg	WHA	10	30	0	3.52
WHA TOTALS			16	60	0	4.63

MAYER, JIM
MAY - ur

RIGHT WING
Height: 6'0"
Weight: 190 lbs.
Birthdate: October 30, 1954
Birthplace: Capreol, Ontario
Shoots: Right

REGULAR SEASON CAREER

SEASON	CLUB	LEAGUE	GP	G	A	PTS	PIM
1976-77	Calgary	WHA	21	2	3	5	0
	Tidewater	SHL	23	11	12	23	8
	Erie	NAHL	14	5	4	9	15
1977-78	New England	WHA	51	11	9	20	21
WHA TOTALS			72	13	12	25	21

McKENZIE, JOHN
mak - KEN - zee

RIGHT WING
Height: 5'7"
Weight: 175 lbs.
Birthdate: December 12, 1937
Birthplace: High River, Alberta
Shoots: Right

REGULAR SEASON CAREER

SEASON	CLUB	LEAGUE	GP	G	A	PTS	PIM
1958-59	Chicago	NHL	32	3	4	7	22
1959-60	Detroit	NHL	59	8	12	20	50
1960-61	Detroit	NHL	16	3	1	4	13
1963-64	Chicago	NHL	45	9	9	18	50
1964-65	Chicago	NHL	51	8	10	18	46
1965-66	NY Rangers	NHL	35	6	5	11	36
1965-66	Boston	NHL	36	13	9	22	36
1966-67	Boston	NHL	69	17	19	36	98
1967-68	Boston	NHL	74	28	38	66	107
1968-69	Boston	NHL	60	29	27	56	99
1969-70	Boston	NHL	72	29	41	70	114
1970-71	Boston	NHL	65	31	46	77	120
1971-72	Boston	NHL	77	22	47	69	126
1972-73	**Philadelphia**	**WHA**	60	28	50	78	157
1973-74	**Vancouver**	**WHA**	45	14	38	52	71
1974-75	**Vancouver**	**WHA**	74	23	37	60	82
1975-76	**Minnesota**	**WHA**	57	21	26	47	48
	Cincinnati	**WHA**	12	3	10	13	6
1976-77	**Minnesota**	**WHA**	40	17	13	30	52
	New England	**WHA**	34	11	19	30	25
1977-78	**New England**	**WHA**	79	27	29	56	61
WHA TOTALS			401	144	222	366	502

WHA PLAYOFFS

YEAR	CLUB	GP	G	A	PTS	PIM
1973	Philadelphia	4	3	1	4	8
1977	New England	5	2	1	3	8
1978	New England	14	6	6	12	16
TOTALS		23	11	8	19	32

McLEOD, AL
mak - LOWD

DEFENSE
Height: 5'11"
Weight: 195 lbs.
Birthdate: June 17, 1949
Birthplace: Medicine Hat, Alberta
Shoots: Left

REGULAR SEASON CAREER

SEASON	CLUB	LEAGUE	GP	G	A	PTS	PIM
1968-69	Michigan Tech	WCHA	23	2	3	5	10
1969-70	Michigan Tech	WCHA	34	14	17	31	32
1970-71	Michigan Tech	WCHA	32	13	26	39	14
1971-72	Fort Worth	CHL	22	1	6	7	48
	Port Huron	IHL	35	1	12	13	15
1972-73	Virginia	AHL	76	4	15	19	105
1973-74	Virginia	AHL	54	1	13	14	52
	Detroit	NHL	26	2	2	4	24
1974-75	**Phoenix**	**WHA**	**77**	**3**	**16**	**19**	**98**
1975-76	**Phoenix**	**WHA**	**80**	**2**	**18**	**20**	**82**
1976-77	**Phoenix**	**WHA**	**29**	**1**	**5**	**6**	**35**
	Houston	**WHA**	**51**	**7**	**21**	**28**	**20**
1977-78	**Houston**	**WHA**	**80**	**2**	**22**	**24**	**54**
WHA TOTALS			**317**	**15**	**82**	**97**	**289**

WHA PLAYOFFS

YEAR	CLUB	GP	G	A	PTS	PIM
1975	Phoenix	5	0	4	4	4
1976	Phoenix	5	0	2	2	4
1977	Houston	10	1	3	4	9
1978	Houston	6	1	0	1	2
TOTALS		**26**	**2**	**9**	**11**	**19**

MELROSE, BARRY
MEL - rohz

DEFENSE
Height: 6'2"
Weight: 200 lbs.
Birthdate: July 15, 1956
Birthplace: Kelvington, Saskatchewan
Shoots: Right

REGULAR SEASON CAREER

SEASON	CLUB	LEAGUE	GP	G	A	PTS	PIM
1973-74	Weyburn	SJHL	50	2	19	21	162
1974-75	Kamloops	WCHL	70	6	18	24	95
1975-76	Kamloops	WCHL	72	12	49	61	112
1976-77	Springfield	AHL	23	0	3	3	17
	Cincinnati	**WHA**	**29**	**1**	**4**	**5**	**8**
1977-78	**Cincinnati**	**WHA**	**69**	**2**	**9**	**11**	**113**
WHA TOTALS			**98**	**3**	**13**	**16**	**121**

WHA PLAYOFFS

YEAR	TEAM	GP	G	A	PTS	PIM
1977	Cincinnati	2	0	0	0	0

MICHELETTI, JOE
MIK - ah - LET - tee

DEFENSE
Height: 6'0"
Weight: 185 lbs.
Birthdate: October 24, 1954
Birthplace: Hibbing, Minnesota
Shoots: Left

REGULAR SEASON CAREER

SEASON	CLUB	LEAGUE	GP	G	A	PTS	PIM
1973-74	U. of Minnesota	WCHA	21	2	5	7	10
1974-75	U. of Minnesota	WCHA	42	7	13	20	44
1975-76	U. of Minnesota	WCHA	33	7	24	31	46
1976-77	U. of Minnesota	WCHA	39	9	39	48	53
	Calgary	WHA	14	3	3	6	10
1977-78	Edmonton	WHA	56	14	34	48	56
WHA TOTALS			**70**	**17**	**37**	**54**	**66**

WHA PLAYOFFS

YEAR	CLUB	GP	G	A	PTS	PIM
1978	Edmonton	5	0	2	2	4
TOTALS		**5**	**0**	**2**	**2**	**4**

MILLER, WARREN
MIL - lur

RIGHT WING
Height: 5'11"
Weight: 180 lbs.
Birthdate: January 1, 1954
Birthplace: South St. Paul, Minnesota
Shoots: Right

REGULAR SEASON CAREER

SEASON	CLUB	LEAGUE	GP	G	A	PTS	PIM
1972-73	U. of Minnesota	WCHA	32	5	3	8	22
1973-74	U. of Minnesota	WCHA	40	11	16	27	34
1974-75	U. of Minnesota	WCHA	41	16	21	37	40
1975-76	U. of Minnesota	WCHA	44	26	31	57	52
	Calgary	WHA	3	0	0	0	0
1976-77	Calgary	WHA	80	23	32	55	51
1977-78	Edmonton	WHA	18	2	4	6	18
	Quebec	WHA	60	14	24	38	50
WHA TOTALS			**161**	**39**	**60**	**99**	**119**

WHA PLAYOFFS

YEAR	CLUB	GP	G	A	PTS	PIM
1976	Calgary	10	1	0	1	28
1977	Calgary	3	0	0	0	0
1978	Quebec	11	0	2	2	0
TOTALS		**24**	**1**	**2**	**3**	**28**

MIO, EDDIE
MEE - oh

GOALTENDER
Height: 5'10"
Weight: 180 lbs.
Birthdate: January 31, 1954
Birthplace: Windsor, Ontario
Shoots: Right

REGULAR SEASON CAREER

SEASON	CLUB	LEAGUE	GP	GA	SO	GAA
1972-73	Colorado College	WCHA	22	119	0	5.41
1973-74	Colorado College	WCHA	12	57	0	4.91
1974-75	Colorado College	WCHA	21	83	0	3.95
1975-76	Colorado College	WCHA	34	144	0	4.24
1976-77	Tidewater	SHL	19	66	1	3.53
	Erie	NAHL	17	42	0	3.27
1977-78	**Indianapolis**	**WHA**	17	64	0	4.27
	Hampton	AHL	19	53	2	3.35
WHA TOTALS			**17**	**64**	**0**	**4.27**

MOFFAT, LYLE
MAHF - fat

LEFT WING
Height: 5'10"
Weight: 185 lbs.
Birthdate: March 19, 1948
Birthplace: Calgary, Alberta
Shoots: Left

REGULAR SEASON CAREER

SEASON	CLUB	LEAGUE	GP	G	A	PTS	PIM
1968-69	Michigan Tech	WCHA	28	10	19	29	36
1969-70	Michigan Tech	WCHA	29	12	11	23	44
1971-72	Tulsa	CHL	70	15	16	31	82
1972-73	Tulsa	CHL	71	40	40	80	108
	Toronto	NHL	1	0	0	0	0
1973-74	Oklahoma	CHL	50	19	30	49	70
1974-75	Oklahoma	CHL	39	17	19	36	87
	Toronto	NHL	22	2	7	9	13
1975-76	**Cleveland**	**WHA**	33	4	7	11	33
	Winnipeg	**WHA**	42	13	9	22	44
1976-77	**Winnipeg**	**WHA**	74	13	11	24	90
1977-78	**Winnipeg**	**WHA**	57	9	16	25	39
WHA TOTALS			**206**	**39**	**43**	**82**	**206**

WHA PLAYOFFS

YEAR	CLUB	GP	G	A	PTS	PIM
1976	Winnipeg	13	3	3	6	9
1977	Winnipeg	17	2	0	2	6
1978	Winnipeg	9	5	7	12	9
TOTALS		**39**	**10**	**10**	**20**	**24**

MORETTO, ANGELO
more - ET - o

CENTER
Height: 6'3"
Weight: 212 lbs.
Birthdate: September 18, 1953
Birthplace: Toronto, Ontario
Shoots: Left

REGULAR SEASON CAREER

SEASON	CLUB	LEAGUE	GP	G	A	PTS	PIM
1972-73	Univ. of Michigan	WCHA	30	10	17	27	36
1973-74	Univ. of Michigan	WCHA	34	25	22	47	28
1974-75	Univ. of Michigan	WCHA	38	39	28	67	43
1975-76	Univ. of Michigan	WCHA	27	24	18	42	50
1976-77	Salt Lake City	CHL	71	19	13	32	19
	Cleveland	NHL	5	1	2	3	2
1977-78	Phoenix	CHL	14	1	6	7	22

MORRISON, KEVIN
MOR - ris - suhn

DEFENSE
Height: 5'11"
Weight: 205 lbs.
Birthdate: October 28, 1949
Birthplace: Sydney, Nova Scotia
Shoots: Left

REGULAR SEASON CAREER

SEASON	CLUB	LEAGUE	GP	G	A	PTS	PIM
1968-69	St. Jerome	QJHL	—	—	—	—	—
1969-70	New Haven	EHL	48	24	18	42	136
1970-71	New Haven	EHL	64	11	44	55	348
	Fort Worth	CHL	3	0	0	0	0
1971-72	Fort Worth	CHL	26	2	1	3	56
	Tidewater	AHL	11	0	2	2	18
	Rochester	AHL	29	2	0	2	49
1972-73	New Haven	AHL	74	7	28	35	154
1973-74	**Jersey**	**WHA**	**78**	**24**	**43**	**67**	**132**
1974-75	**San Diego**	**WHA**	**78**	**20**	**61**	**81**	**143**
1975-76	**San Diego**	**WHA**	**80**	**22**	**43**	**65**	**56**
1976-77	**San Diego**	**WHA**	**75**	**8**	**30**	**38**	**68**
1977-78	**Indianapolis**	**WHA**	**75**	**17**	**40**	**57**	**49**
WHA TOTALS			**386**	**91**	**217**	**308**	**448**

WHA PLAYOFFS

YEAR	CLUB	GP	G	A	PTS	PIM
1975	San Diego	10	0	7	7	2
1976	San Diego	11	1	5	6	12
1977	San Diego	7	1	3	4	8
TOTALS		**28**	**2**	**15**	**17**	**22**

112

NEILSON, JIM
NEEL - sun

DEFENSE
Height: 6'2"
Weight: 205 lbs.
Birthdate: November 28, 1941
Birthplace: Big River, Saskatchewan
Shoots: Left

REGULAR SEASON CAREER

SEASON	CLUB	LEAGUE	GP	G	A	PTS	PIM
1961-62	Kitch.-Waterloo	EPHL	70	9	33	42	78
1962-63	New York	NHL	69	5	11	16	38
1963-64	New York	NHL	69	5	24	29	93
1964-65	New York	NHL	62	0	13	13	58
1965-66	New York	NHL	65	4	19	23	84
1966-67	New York	NHL	61	4	11	15	65
1967-68	New York	NHL	67	6	29	35	60
1968-69	New York	NHL	76	10	34	44	95
1969-70	New York	NHL	62	3	20	23	75
1970-71	New York	NHL	77	8	24	32	69
1971-72	New York	NHL	78	7	30	37	56
1972-73	New York	NHL	52	4	16	20	35
1973-74	New York	NHL	72	4	7	11	38
1974-75	California	NHL	72	3	17	20	56
1975-76	California	NHL	26	1	6	7	20
1976-77	Cleveland	NHL	47	3	17	20	42
1977-78	Cleveland	NHL	68	2	21	23	20

NILSSON, KENT
NEEL - suhn

CENTER
Height: 6'1"
Weight: 185 lbs.
Birthdate: August 31, 1956
Birthplace: Nynashamn, Sweden
Shoots: Left

REGULAR SEASON CAREER

SEASON	CLUB	LEAGUE	GP	G	A	PTS	PIM
1976-77	AIK		36	30	19	49	18
1977-78	**Winnipeg**	**WHA**	**80**	**42**	**65**	**107**	**8**
WHA TOTALS			80	42	65	107	8

WHA PLAYOFFS

YEAR	CLUB	GP	G	A	PTS	PIM
1978	Winnipeg	9	2	8	10	10
TOTALS		9	2	8	10	10

113

NORWICH, CRAIG
NOR - wich

DEFENSE
Height: 5'11"
Weight: 175 lbs.
Birthdate: December 15, 1955
Birthplace: Edina, Minnesota
Shoots: Left

REGULAR SEASON CAREER

SEASON	CLUB	LEAGUE	GP	G	A	PTS	PIM
1974-75	U. of Wisconsin	WCHA	38	11	34	45	24
1975-76	U. of Wisconsin	WCHA	32	13	27	40	66
1976-77	U. of Wisconsin	WCHA	44	18	65	83	70
1977-78	**Cincinnati**	**WHA**	**65**	**7**	**23**	**30**	**48**
WHA TOTALS			**65**	**7**	**23**	**30**	**48**

NUGENT, KEVIN
NOO - gent

RIGHT WING
Height: 6'5"
Weight: 235 lbs.
Birthdate: June 7, 1955
Birthplace: Little Falls, Minnesota
Shoots: Right

REGULAR SEASON CAREER

SEASON	CLUB	LEAGUE	GP	G	A	PTS	PIM
1974-75	Notre Dame	WCHA	35	7	12	19	74
1975-76	Notre Dame	WCHA	29	17	18	35	59
1976-77	Notre Dame	WCHA	37	16	26	42	54
1977-78	Notre Dame	WCHA	23	13	15	28	85

O'NEIL, PAUL
oh - NEEL

CENTER
Height: 6'1"
Weight: 185 lbs.
Birthdate: August 24, 1953
Birthplace: Charlestown, Massachusetts
Shoots: Left

REGULAR SEASON CAREER

SEASON	CLUB	LEAGUE	GP	G	A	PTS	PIM
1971-72	Boston U.	NCAA	17	13	14	27	6
1972-73	Boston	ECAC	28	35	19	54	8
1973-74	Seattle	WHL	66	29	17	46	14
	Vancouver	NHL	5	0	0	0	0

1974-75	Seattle	CHL	49	16	19	35	7
1975-76	Rochester	AHL	49	35	16	51	17
	Boston	NHL	1	0	0	0	0
1976-77	Hampton	SHL	48	21	34	55	0
1977-78	Hampton	AHL	36	17	27	44	9
	San Diego	PHL	17	11	9	20	0

O'TOOLE, TOM
oh - TOOL

GOALTENDER
Height: 6'0"
Weight: 180 lbs.
Birthdate: August 12, 1955
Birthplace: Kingston, Ontario
Shoots: Right

REGULAR SEASON CAREER

SEASON	CLUB	LEAGUE	GP	GA	SO	GAA
1977-78	San Francisco	PHL	21	64	0	3.19

PARIZEAU, MICHEL
pehr - i - ZOH

CENTER
Height: 5'10"
Weight: 165 lbs.
Birthdate: April 9, 1948
Birthplace: Montreal, Quebec
Shoots: Left

REGULAR SEASON CAREER

SEASON	CLUB	LEAGUE	GP	G	A	PTS	PIM
1968-69	Omaha	CHL	71	22	39	61	20
1969-70	Omaha	CHL	71	13	16	29	30
1970-71	Omaha	CHL	72	35	49	84	43
1971-72	St. Louis	NHL	20	1	2	3	8
	Philadelphia	NHL	38	2	12	14	10
1972-73	**Quebec**	**WHA**	75	25	48	73	50
1973-74	**Quebec**	**WHA**	78	26	34	60	39
1974-75	**Quebec**	**WHA**	78	28	46	74	69
1975-76	**Quebec**	**WHA**	58	12	27	39	22
	Indianapolis	**WHA**	23	13	15	28	20
1976-77	**Indianapolis**	**WHA**	75	18	37	55	39
1977-78	**Indianapolis**	**WHA**	70	13	27	40	47
WHA TOTALS			457	135	234	369	286

WHA PLAYOFFS

YEAR	CLUB	GP	G	A	PTS	PIM
1975	Quebec	15	2	4	6	10
1976	Indianapolis	7	4	4	8	6
1977	Indianapolis	8	3	6	9	8
TOTALS		30	9	14	23	24

PARK, JIM
PAHRK

GOALTENDER
Height: 6'1"
Weight: 190 lbs.
Birthdate: June 22, 1952
Birthplace: Toronto, Ontario
Shoots: Right

REGULAR SEASON CAREER

SEASON	CLUB	LEAGUE	GP	GA	SO	GAA
1972-73	Jersey	EHL	31	120	0	3.87
	Richmond	AHL	4	8	0	2.82
	Des Moines	IHL	11	37	0	3.67
1973-74	Des Moines	IHL	32	89	1	3.77
1974-75	Mohawk Valley	NAHL	50	221	0	4.67
1975-76	Mohawk Valley	NAHL	37	168	0	4.48
	Indianapolis	**WHA**	**11**	**23**	**0**	**2.41**
1976-77	Mohawk Valley	NAHL	1	2	0	2.00
	Oklahoma City	CHL	3	11	0	3.69
	Indianapolis	**WHA**	**31**	**114**	**1**	**3.96**
1977-78	**Indianapolis**	**WHA**	**12**	**41**	**0**	**4.21**
WHA TOTALS			**54**	**178**	**1**	**3.70**

WHA PLAYOFFS

YEAR	CLUB	GP	GA	SO	GAA
1976	Indianapolis	6	12	2	2.45
TOTALS		**6**	**12**	**2**	**2.45**

PELOFFY, ANDRE
pel - UHF - fee

CENTER
Height: 5'8"
Weight: 160 lbs.
Birthdate: February 25, 1951
Birthplace: Sete, France
Shoots: Left

REGULAR SEASON CAREER

SEASON	CLUB	LEAGUE	GP	G	A	PTS	PIM
1969-70	Laval Saints	QJHL	0	37	43	80	69
1970-71	Rosemont Natl.	QJHL	60	49	69	118	67
1971-72	New Haven	EHL	42	32	44	76	31
	Providence	AHL	2	1	2	3	0
1972-73	Providence	AHL	62	16	23	39	24
1973-74	Providence	AHL	72	26	45	71	52
1974-75	Richmond	AHL	62	29	44	73	84
	Washington	NHL	9	0	0	0	0
1975-76	Richmond	AHL	67	29	30	59	78
1976-77	Springfield	AHL	79	42	57	99	106
1977-78	**New England**	**WHA**	**10**	**2**	**0**	**2**	**2**
	Springfield	AHL	67	33	55	88	73
WHA TOTALS			**10**	**2**	**0**	**2**	**2**

WHA PLAYOFFS

YEAR	CLUB	GP	G	A	PTS	PIM
1978	New England	2	0	0	0	0
TOTALS		**2**	**0**	**0**	**0**	**0**

PLUMB, RON
PLUHM

DEFENSE
Height: 5'10"
Weight: 175 lbs.
Birthdate: July 17, 1950
Birthplace: Kingston, Ontario
Shoots: Right

REGULAR SEASON CAREER

SEASON	CLUB	LEAGUE	GP	G	A	PTS	PIM
1967-68	Peterborough	Jr. "A" OHA	47	3	19	22	38
1968-69	Peterborough	Jr. "A" OHA	53	4	10	14	57
1969-70	Peterborough	Jr. "A" OHA	54	16	29	45	77
1970-71	Oklahoma City	CHL	72	3	19	22	73
1971-72	Oklahoma City	CHL	72	10	42	52	90
1972-73	**Philadelphia**	**WHA**	**78**	**10**	**41**	**51**	**66**
1973-74	**Vancouver**	**WHA**	**75**	**6**	**32**	**38**	**40**
1974-75	**San Diego**	**WHA**	**78**	**10**	**38**	**48**	**56**
1975-76	**Cincinnati**	**WHA**	**80**	**10**	**36**	**46**	**31**
1976-77	**Cincinnati**	**WHA**	**79**	**11**	**58**	**69**	**52**
1977-78	**Cincinnati**	**WHA**	**54**	**13**	**34**	**47**	**45**
	New England	**WHA**	**27**	**1**	**9**	**10**	**18**
WHA TOTALS			**471**	**61**	**248**	**309**	**308**

WHA PLAYOFFS

YEAR	CLUB	GP	G	A	PTS	PIM
1973	Philadelphia	4	0	2	2	13
1975	San Diego	10	2	3	5	19
1977	Cincinnati	4	1	2	3	0
1978	New England	14	1	5	6	16
TOTALS		**32**	**4**	**12**	**16**	**48**

PRESTON, RICH
PRES - tuhn

RIGHT WING
Height: 6'0"
Weight: 185 lbs.
Birthdate: May 22, 1952
Birthplace: Regina, Saskatchewan
Shoots: Right

REGULAR SEASON CAREER

SEASON	CLUB	LEAGUE	GP	G	A	PTS	PIM
1970-71	Denver University	WCHA	17	0	1	1	0
1971-72	Denver University	WCHA	33	3	11	14	18
1972-73	Denver University	WCHA	39	23	25	48	24
1973-74	Denver University	WCHA	38	20	25	45	36
1974-75	**Houston**	**WHA**	**78**	**20**	**21**	**41**	**10**
1975-76	**Houston**	**WHA**	**77**	**22**	**33**	**55**	**33**
1976-77	**Houston**	**WHA**	**80**	**38**	**41**	**79**	**54**
1977-78	**Houston**	**WHA**	**73**	**25**	**25**	**50**	**52**
WHA TOTALS			**308**	**105**	**120**	**225**	**149**

WHA PLAYOFFS

YEAR	CLUB	GP	G	A	PTS	PIM
1975	Houston	13	1	6	7	6
1976	Houston	17	4	6	10	8
1977	Houston	11	3	5	8	10
TOTALS		**41**	**8**	**17**	**25**	**24**

RAEDER, CAP
RAH - dur

GOALTENDER
Height: 6'0"
Weight: 175 lbs.
Birthdate: October 8, 1953
Birthplace: Portland, Maine
Shoots: Right

REGULAR SEASON CAREER

SEASON	CLUB	LEAGUE	GP	GA	SO	GAA
1972-73	U. New Hampshire	ECAC	20	67	1	3.35
1973-74	U. New Hampshire	ECAC	22	58	1	2.64
1974-75	U. New Hampshire	ECAC	27	94	0	3.62
1975-76	Cape Cod	NAHL	21	81	0	4.00
	Binghampton	NAHL	21	86	0	4.35
	New England	**WHA**	**2**	**8**	**0**	**4.80**
1976-77	**New England**	**WHA**	**26**	**69**	**2**	**3.12**
	Rhode Island	AHL	20	75	0	4.25
1977-78	Philadelphia	AHL	9	38	0	4.83
WHA TOTALS			**28**	**77**	**2**	**3.23**

RAMAGE, ROB
RAM - aj

DEFENSE
Height: 6'2"
Weight: 195 lbs.
Birthdate: January 11, 1959
Birthplace: Byron, Ontario
Shoots: Right

REGULAR SEASON CAREER

SEASON	CLUB	LEAGUE	GP	G	A	PTS	PIM
1975-76	London	OHA	65	12	31	43	113
1976-77	London	OHA	65	15	58	73	177
1977-78	London	Jr. "A" OHA	59	17	47	64	162

RIGGIN, PAT
RIG - in

GOALTENDER
Height: 5'9"
Weight: 163 lbs.
Birthdate: May 26, 1959
Birthplace: Kincardine, Ontario
Shoots: Right

REGULAR SEASON CAREER

SEASON	CLUB	LEAGUE	GP	GA	SO	GAA
1975-76	London	OHA	23	85	0	3.68
1976-77	London	OHA	48	140	2	2.95
1977-78	London	Jr. "A" OHA	37	140	0	3.65

ROBERTO, PHIL
ro - BURT - o

RIGHT WING
Height: 6'1"
Weight: 190 lbs.
Birthdate: January 1, 1949
Birthplace: Niagara Falls, Ontario
Shoots: Right

REGULAR SEASON CAREER

SEASON	CLUB	LEAGUE	GP	G	A	PTS	PIM
1965-66	Niagara Falls	Jr. "A" OHA	2	2	0	2	0
1966-67	Niagara Falls	OHA	14	1	0	1	6
1967-68	Niagara Falls	OHA	53	19	20	39	92
1968-69	Niagara Falls	OHA	52	29	65	94	152
1969-70	Montreal	AHL	54	20	19	39	160
	Montreal	NHL	8	0	1	1	8
1970-71	Montreal	AHL	32	19	22	41	127
	Montreal	NHL	39	14	7	21	76
1971-72	Montreal	NHL	27	3	2	5	22
	St. Louis	NHL	49	12	13	25	76
1972-73	St. Louis	NHL	77	20	22	42	99
1973-74	Denver	WHL	8	5	4	9	40
	St. Louis	NHL	15	1	1	2	10
1974-75	Denver	CHL	8	3	2	5	12
	St. Louis	NHL	7	0	2	2	2
	Detroit	NHL	46	13	27	40	30
1975-76	Detroit	NHL	37	1	7	8	68
	Kansas City	NHL	37	7	15	22	42
1976-77	Colorado	NHL	22	1	5	6	23
	Cleveland	NHL	21	3	4	7	8
1977-78	**Birmingham**	**WHA**	**53**	**8**	**20**	**28**	**91**

WHA PLAYOFFS

YEAR	CLUB	GP	G	A	PTS	PIM
1978	Birmingham	4	1	0	1	120
TOTALS		**4**	**1**	**0**	**1**	**20**

ROBERTS, GORDIE
RAH - burts

DEFENSE
Height: 6'1"
Weight: 190 lbs.
Birthdate: October 2, 1957
Birthplace: Detroit, Michigan
Shoots: Left

REGULAR SEASON CAREER

SEASON	CLUB	LEAGUE	GP	G	A	PTS	PIM
1974-75	Victoria	WCHL	53	19	45	64	145
1975-76	New England	WHA	77	3	19	22	102
1976-77	New England	WHA	77	13	33	46	169
1977-78	New England	WHA	78	15	46	61	118
WHA TOTALS			232	31	98	129	389

WHA PLAYOFFS

YEAR	CLUB	GP	G	A	PTS	PIM
1976	New England	17	2	9	11	36
1977	New England	5	2	2	4	6
1978	New England	14	0	5	5	29
TOTALS		36	4	16	20	71

ROGERS, MIKE

RAH - jurs

CENTER
Height: 5'9"
Weight: 170 lbs.
Birthdate: October 24, 1954
Birthplace: Calgary, Alberta
Shoots: Left

REGULAR SEASON CAREER

SEASON	CLUB	LEAGUE	GP	G	A	PTS	PIM
1973-74	Calgary	WCHL	66	67	73	140	32
1974-75	Edmonton	WHA	78	35	48	83	2
1975-76	Edmonton	WHA	44	12	15	27	10
	New England	WHA	36	18	14	32	10
1976-77	New England	WHA	78	25	57	82	10
1977-78	New England	WHA	80	28	43	71	46
WHA TOTALS			316	118	177	295	78

WHA PLAYOFFS

YEAR	CLUB	GP	G	A	PTS	PIM
1976	New England	17	5	8	13	2
1977	New England	5	1	1	2	2
1978	New England	14	5	6	11	8
TOTALS		36	11	15	26	12

ROLLINS, JERRY
RAWL - ins

DEFENSE
Height: 6'3"
Weight: 195 lbs.
Birthdate: March 22, 1955
Birthplace: New Westminster, British Columbia
Shoots: Right

REGULAR SEASON CAREER

SEASON	CLUB	LEAGUE	GP	G	A	PTS	PIM
1972-73	Flin Flon	WCHL	32	0	3	3	99
1973-74	Flin Flon	WCHL	64	4	12	16	338
1974-75	Flin Flon	WCHL	9	1	4	5	72
	Winnipeg	WCHL	53	6	17	23	401
1975-76	**Toronto**	**WHA**	**52**	**5**	**7**	**12**	**185**
1976-77	**Birmingham**	**WHA**	**8**	**0**	**0**	**0**	**17**
	Phoenix	**WHA**	**63**	**4**	**10**	**14**	**169**
1977-78	Kalamazoo	IHL	28	3	5	8	199
WHA TOTALS			**123**	**9**	**17**	**26**	**371**

RUSKOWSKI, TERRY
ruhs - KOW - skee

CENTER
Height: 5'9"
Weight: 170 lbs.
Birthdate: December 31, 1954
Birthplace: Prince Albert, Saskatchewan
Shoots: Left

REGULAR SEASON CAREER

SEASON	CLUB	LEAGUE	GP	G	A	PTS	PIM
1973-74	Swift Current	WCHL	68	40	93	133	243
1974-75	**Houston**	**WHA**	**71**	**10**	**36**	**46**	**134**
1975-76	**Houston**	**WHA**	**65**	**14**	**35**	**49**	**100**
1976-77	**Houston**	**WHA**	**80**	**24**	**60**	**84**	**146**
1977-78	**Houston**	**WHA**	**78**	**15**	**57**	**72**	**170**
WHA TOTALS			**294**	**63**	**188**	**251**	**550**

WHA PLAYOFFS

YEAR	CLUB	GP	G	A	PTS	PIM
1975	Houston	13	4	2	6	15
1976	Houston	16	6	10	16	64
1977	Houston	11	6	11	17	67
1978	Houston	4	1	1	2	5
TOTALS		**44**	**17**	**24**	**41**	**151**

ST. SAUVEUR, CLAUDE
SAN - soh - VUR

LEFT WING
Height: 6'0"
Weight: 170 lbs.
Birthdate: January 1, 1952
Birthplace: Sherbrooke, Quebec
Shoots: Left

REGULAR SEASON CAREER

SEASON	CLUB	LEAGUE	GP	G	A	PTS	PIM
1971-72	Sherbrooke	QMJHL	60	53	58	111	97
1972-73	Roanoke	EHL	62	55	52	107	99
	Philadelphia	**WHA**	**2**	**1**	**0**	**1**	**0**
1973-74	**Vancouver**	**WHA**	**70**	**38**	**30**	**68**	**55**
1974-75	**Vancouver**	**WHA**	**76**	**24**	**23**	**47**	**32**
1975-76	Atlanta	NHL	79	24	24	48	23
1976-77	**Calgary**	**WHA**	**17**	**0**	**3**	**3**	**2**
	Edmonton	**WHA**	**15**	**5**	**7**	**12**	**2**
1977-78	**Indianapolis**	**WHA**	**72**	**36**	**42**	**78**	**24**
WHA TOTALS			**252**	**104**	**105**	**209**	**115**

WHA PLAYOFFS

YEAR	CLUB	GP	G	A	PTS	PIM
1977	Edmonton	5	1	0	1	0
TOTALS		**5**	**1**	**0**	**1**	**0**

123

SANDBECK, CAL
SAND - bek

DEFENSE
Height: 6'1"
Weight: 218 lbs.
Birthdate: January 28, 1956
Birthplace: International Falls, Minnesota
Shoots: Right

REGULAR SEASON CAREER

SEASON	CLUB	LEAGUE	GP	G	A	PTS	PIM
1974-75	Denver University	WCHA	25	3	5	8	55
1975-76	Denver University	WCHA	29	2	12	14	58
1976-77	Denver University	WCHA	38	4	9	13	77
1977-78	Denver University	WCHA	39	8	24	32	60
	Edmonton	**WHA**	11	1	2	3	39
WHA TOTALS			11	1	2	3	39

WHA PLAYOFFS

YEAR	CLUB	GP	G	A	PTS	PIM
1978	Edmonton	5	0	0	0	10
TOTALS		5	0	0	0	10

SCHELLA, JOHN
SHEL - ah

DEFENSE
Height: 6'0"
Weight: 180 lbs.
Birthdate: May 9, 1947
Birthplace: Port Arthur, Ontario
Shoots: Right

REGULAR SEASON CAREER

SEASON	CLUB	LEAGUE	GP	G	A	PTS	PIM
1963-64	Fort William	TBJHL					
1964-65	Fort William	TBJHL	—	6	16	22	131
1965-66	Fort William	TBJHL	—	8	29	37	—
1966-67	Peterborough	Jr. "A" OHA	47	11	11	22	182
1967-68	Houston	CPHL	39	5	2	7	110
1968-69	Denver	WHL	69	4	22	26	152
1969-70	Denver	WHL	67	7	30	37	198
1970-71	Rochester	AHL	33	3	14	17	118
	Vancouver	NHL	38	0	5	5	58
1971-72	Vancouver	NHL	77	2	13	15	166
1972-73	**Houston**	**WHA**	77	2	24	26	239
1973-74	**Houston**	**WHA**	73	12	19	31	170
1974-75	**Houston**	**WHA**	78	10	42	52	176
1975-76	**Houston**	**WHA**	74	6	32	38	106
1976-77	**Houston**	**WHA**	20	0	6	6	28
1977-78	**Houston**	**WHA**	63	9	20	29	125
WHA TOTALS			385	39	143	182	844

WHA PLAYOFFS

YEAR	CLUB	GP	G	A	PTS	PIM
1973	Houston	10	0	2	2	12
1974	Houston	14	2	6	8	42
1975	Houston	13	0	8	8	12
1976	Houston	17	1	6	7	38
1977	Houston	6	1	2	3	6
1978	Houston	6	0	1	1	33
TOTALS		**66**	**4**	**25**	**29**	**143**

SELWOOD, BRAD
SEL - wood

DEFENSE
Height: 6'1"
Weight: 200 lbs.
Birthdate: March 18, 1948
Birthplace: Leamington, Ontario
Shoots: Left

REGULAR SEASON CAREER

SEASON	CLUB	LEAGUE	GP	G	A	PTS	PIM
1968-69	Tulsa	CHL	70	7	32	39	118
1969-70	Vancouver	WHL	72	9	24	33	93
1970-71	Tulsa	CHL	13	1	1	2	4
	Toronto	NHL	28	2	10	12	13
1971-72	Toronto	NHL	72	4	17	21	60
1972-73	New England	WHA	75	13	21	34	114
1973-74	New England	WHA	76	9	28	37	91
1974-75	New England	WHA	77	4	35	39	117
1975-76	New England	WHA	40	2	10	12	28
1976-77	New England	WHA	41	4	12	16	71
1977-78	New England	WHA	80	6	25	31	88
WHA TOTALS			**389**	**38**	**131**	**169**	**509**

WHA PLAYOFFS

YEAR	CLUB	GP	G	A	PTS	PIM
1973	New England	15	3	5	8	22
1974	New England	7	0	2	2	11
1975	New England	5	1	0	1	11
1976	New England	17	2	2	4	27
1977	New England	5	0	0	0	2
1978	New England	14	0	3	3	8
TOTALS		**63**	**6**	**12**	**18**	**81**

125

SEMENKO, DAVE
suh - MEN - koh

LEFT WING
Height: 6'3"
Weight: 210 lbs.
Birthdate: July 12, 1957
Birthplace: Winnipeg, Manitoba
Shoots: Left

REGULAR SEASON CAREER

SEASON	CLUB	LEAGUE	GP	G	A	PTS	PIM
1974-75	Brandon	MJHL	42	11	17	28	55
	Brandon	WCHL	12	2	1	3	12
1975-76	Brandon	WCHL	72	8	5	13	194
1976-77	Brandon	WCHL	61	27	33	60	265
1977-78	**Edmonton**	**WHA**	**65**	**6**	**6**	**12**	**140**
WHA TOTALS			**65**	**6**	**6**	**12**	**140**

WHA PLAYOFFS

YEAR	CLUB	GP	G	A	PTS	PIM
1978	Edmonton	5	0	0	0	8

SHEEHY, TIM
SHEE - hee

RIGHT WING
Height: 6'1"
Weight: 185 lbs.
Birthdate: September 3, 1948
Birthplace: Ft. Frances, Ontario
Shoots: Right

REGULAR SEASON CAREER

SEASON	CLUB	LEAGUE	GP	G	A	PTS	PIM
1967-68	Boston College	ECAC	30	27	30	57	—
1968-69	Boston College	ECAC	26	19	41	60	36
1969-70	Boston College	ECAC	24	28	40	68	20
1970-71	USA National Team						
1971-72	USA Olympic Team						
1972-73	New England	WHA	78	33	38	71	30
1973-74	New England	WHA	77	29	29	58	22
1974-75	New England	WHA	52	20	13	33	18
	Edmonton	WHA	29	8	20	28	4
1975-76	Edmonton	WHA	81	34	31	65	17
1976-77	Edmonton	WHA	28	15	8	23	4
	Birmingham	WHA	50	26	21	47	44
1977-78	Birmingham	WHA	13	4	2	6	5
	New England	WHA	25	8	11	19	12
WHA TOTALS			**433**	**177**	**173**	**350**	**156**

WHA PLAYOFFS

YEAR	CLUB	GP	G	A	PTS	PIM
1973	New England	15	9	14	23	13
1974	New England	7	4	2	6	4
1976	Edmonton	4	2	2	4	0
1978	New England	13	1	3	4	9
TOTALS		39	16	21	37	26

SHMYR, PAUL
SHMEER

DEFENSE
Height: 5'11"
Weight: 175 lbs.
Birthdate: January 28, 1946
Birthplace: Cudworth, Saskatchewan
Shoots: Left

REGULAR SEASON CAREER

SEASON	CLUB	LEAGUE	GP	G	A	PTS	PIM
1966-67	Fort Wayne	IHL	70	3	18	21	89
	Vancouver	WHL	1	0	0	0	0
1967-68	Dallas	CPHL	70	5	15	20	73
1968-69	Dallas	CHL	69	7	39	46	118
	Chicago	NHL	3	1	0	1	8
1969-70	Dallas	CHL	48	3	21	24	88
	Chicago	NHL	24	0	4	4	26
1970-71	Chicago	NHL	57	1	12	13	41
1971-72	California	NHL	69	6	21	27	156
1972-73	**Cleveland**	**WHA**	**73**	**5**	**43**	**48**	**169**
1973-74	**Cleveland**	**WHA**	**78**	**13**	**31**	**44**	**165**
1974-75	**Cleveland**	**WHA**	**49**	**7**	**14**	**21**	**103**
1975-76	**Cleveland**	**WHA**	**70**	**6**	**44**	**50**	**101**
1976-77	**San Diego**	**WHA**	**81**	**13**	**37**	**50**	**103**
1977-78	**Edmonton**	**WHA**	**80**	**9**	**40**	**49**	**100**
WHA TOTALS			**431**	**53**	**209**	**262**	**741**

WHA PLAYOFFS

YEAR	CLUB	GP	G	A	PTS	PIM
1973	Cleveland	8	1	3	4	19
1974	Cleveland	5	0	4	4	31
1975	Cleveland	5	2	1	3	15
1977	San Diego	7	0	2	2	8
1978	Edmonton	5	1	3	4	11
TOTALS		30	4	13	17	84

SHUTT, BYRON
SHUT

LEFT WING
Height: 6'1"
Weight: 195 lbs.
Birthdate: October 26, 1955
Birthplace: Toronto, Ontario
Shoots: Left

REGULAR SEASON CAREER

SEASON	CLUB	LEAGUE	GP	G	A	PTS	PIM
1974-75	Bowling Green	CCHA	27	10	15	25	61
1975-76	Bowling Green	CCHA	32	14	14	28	76
1976-77	Bowling Green	CCHA	38	14	27	41	123
1977-78	Bowling Green	CCHA	39	12	31	43	106

SJOBERG, LARS-ERIK
SHOO - burg

DEFENSE
Height: 5'8"
Weight: 179 lbs.
Birthdate: April 5, 1944
Birthplace: Falun, Sweden
Shoots: Left

REGULAR SEASON CAREER

SEASON	CLUB	LEAGUE	GP	G	A	PTS	PIM
1973-74	V. Frolunda	Sweden	41	4	35	39	21
1974-75	Winnipeg	WHA	75	7	53	60	30
1975-76	Winnipeg	WHA	81	5	36	41	12
1976-77	Winnipeg	WHA	52	2	38	40	31
1977-78	Winnipeg	WHA	78	11	39	50	72
WHA TOTALS			286	25	166	191	145

WHA PLAYOFFS

YEAR	CLUB	GP	G	A	PTS	PIM
1976	Winnipeg	13	0	5	5	12
1977	Winnipeg	20	0	6	6	22
1978	Winnipeg	9	0	9	9	4
TOTALS		42	0	20	20	38

SLEIGHER, LOUIS
SLAY - gur

RIGHT WING
Height: 5'11"
Weight: 195 lbs.
Birthdate: October 23, 1958
Birthplace: Nouvelle, Quebec
Shoots: Right

REGULAR SEASON CAREER

SEASON	CLUB	LEAGUE	GP	G	A	PTS	PIM
1976-77	Chicoutimi	QMJHL	70	53	48	101	49
1977-78	Chicoutimi	QMJHL	71	65	54	119	125

SMITH, AL
SMITH

GOALTENDER
Height: 6'1"
Weight: 200 lbs.
Birthdate: November 10, 1945
Birthplace: Toronto, Ontario
Shoots: Left

REGULAR SEASON CAREER

SEASON	CLUB	LEAGUE	GP	GA	SO	GAA
1965-66	Toronto	NHL	2	2	0	1.94
1966-67	Toronto	NHL	1	5	0	5.00
	Victoria	WHL	56	180	6	3.26
1967-68	Tulsa	CHL	40	126	0	3.32
1968-69	Toronto	NHL	7	16	0	2.87
	Tulsa	CHL	8	22	0	2.87
	Rochester	AHL	34	114	2	3.45
1969-70	Baltimore	AHL	3	8	0	2.67
	Pittsburgh	NHL	46	129	2	3.03
1970-71	Pittsburgh	NHL	46	128	2	3.10
1971-72	Detroit	NHL	43	135	4	3.24
1972-73	**New England**	**WHA**	51	162	3	3.17
1973-74	**New England**	**WHA**	55	164	2	3.08
1974-75	**New England**	**WHA**	59	202	2	3.47
1975-76	Buffalo	NHL	14	43	0	3.07
1976-77	Buffalo	NHL	7	19	0	4.30
1977-78	**New England**	**WHA**	55	174	2	3.22
WHA TOTALS			220	702	9	3.24

WHA PLAYOFFS

YEAR	CLUB	GP	GA	SO	GAA
1973	New England	15	49	0	3.23
1974	New England	7	21	1	3.16
1975	New England	6	28	0	4.59
1978	New England	3	14	0	7.00
TOTALS		31	112	1	3.75

SMITH, GARY
SMITH

GOALTENDER
Height: 6'4"
Weight: 215 lbs.
Birthdate: February 4, 1944
Birthplace: Ottawa, Ontario
Shoots: Left

REGULAR SEASON CAREER

SEASON	CLUB	LEAGUE	GP	GA	SO	GAA
1963-64	Toronto	Jr. "A" OHA	54½	186	3	3.41
1964-65	Rochester	AHL	⅓	0	0	0.00
	Tulsa	CPHL	1	5	0	5.00
	Victoria	WHL	7	30	0	4.29
1965-66	Toronto	NHL	3	7	0	3.50
	Rochester	AHL	38	97	2	2.86
1966-67	Toronto	NHL	2	7	0	3.63
	Victoria	WHL	16⅔	51	2	3.06
	Rochester	AHL	17	38	1	2.61
1967-68	Oakland	NHL	21	60	1	3.19
1968-69	Oakland	NHL	54	148	4	2.96
1969-70	Oakland	NHL	65	195	2	3.11
1970-71	California	NHL	71	256	2	3.86
1971-72	Chicago	NHL	28	62	5	2.41
1972-73	Chicago	NHL	23	79	0	3.54
1973-74	Vancouver	NHL	66	208	3	3.44
1974-75	Vancouver	NHL	72	197	6	3.09
1975-76	Vancouver	NHL	51	167	2	3.50
1976-77	Minnesota	NHL	36	139	1	3.99
1977-78	Washington	NHL	17	68	0	4.16
	Minnesota	NHL	3	9	0	3.00

SOBCHUK, DENNIS
SAWB - chuhk

CENTER
Height: 6'2"
Weight: 176 lbs.
Birthdate: January 12, 1954
Birthplace: Lang, Saskatchewan
Shoots: Left

REGULAR SEASON CAREER

SEASON	CLUB	LEAGUE	GP	G	A	PTS	PIM
1971-72	Regina	WCHL	68	56	67	123	115
1972-73	Regina	WCHL	66	67	80	147	128
1973-74	Regina	WCHL	66	68	78	146	78
1974-75	**Phoenix**	**WHA**	78	32	45	77	36
1975-76	**Cincinnati**	**WHA**	79	32	40	72	74
1976-77	**Cincinnati**	**WHA**	81	44	52	96	38
1977-78	**Cincinnati**	**WHA**	23	5	9	14	22
	Edmonton	WHA	13	6	3	9	4
WHA TOTALS			**274**	**119**	**149**	**268**	**174**

WHA PLAYOFFS

YEAR	CLUB	GP	G	A	PTS	PIM
1975	Phoenix	5	4	1	5	2
1977	Cincinnati	3	0	1	1	2
1978	Edmonton	5	1	0	1	4
TOTALS		**13**	**5**	**2**	**7**	**8**

STEPHENSON, BOB
STEEV - en - suhn

RIGHT WING
Height: 6'1"
Weight: 187 lbs.
Birthdate: February 1, 1954
Birthplace: Saskatoon, Saskatchewan
Shoots: Right

REGULAR SEASON CAREER

SEASON	CLUB	LEAGUE	GP	G	A	PTS	PIM
1976-77	St. Francis Xavier	MUAA	20	20	23	43	18
1977-78	**Birmingham**	**WHA**	39	7	6	13	33
	Hampton	AHL	1	0	0	0	0
	Flint	IHL	6	2	5	7	7
	Tulsa	CHL	9	1	1	2	7
WHA TOTALS			**39**	**7**	**6**	**13**	**33**

STEWART, JOHN C.
STOO - ahrt

CENTER
Height: 6'0"
Weight: 180 lbs.
Birthdate: January 2, 1954
Birthplace: Toronto, Ontario
Shoots: Left

REGULAR SEASON CAREER

SEASON	CLUB	LEAGUE	GP	G	A	PTS	PIM
1973-74	Bowling Green	CCHA	39	27	43	70	50
1974-75	Cape Cod	NAHL	13	5	11	16	14
	Cleveland	**WHA**	59	4	7	11	8
1975-76	Syracuse	NAHL	23	11	17	28	29
	Cleveland	**WHA**	42	2	9	11	15
1976-77	Syracuse	NAHL	18	18	36	54	4
	Birmingham	**WHA**	52	17	24	41	33
1977-78	Philadelphia	AHL	24	11	13	24	44
	Birmingham	**WHA**	48	13	26	39	52
WHA TOTALS			**201**	**36**	**66**	**102**	**108**

WHA PLAYOFFS

YEAR	CLUB	GP	G	A	PTS	PIM
1975	Cleveland	1	0	0	0	0
1978	Birmingham	5	1	1	2	6
TOTALS		**6**	**1**	**1**	**2**	**6**

STEWART, PAUL
STOO - ahrt

LEFT WING
Height: 6'1"
Weight: 205 lbs.
Birthdate: March 21, 1954
Birthplace: Boston, Massachusetts
Shoots: Left

REGULAR SEASON CAREER

SEASON	CLUB	LEAGUE	GP	G	A	PTS	PIM
1975-76	Binghamton	AHL	46	3	4	7	273
1976-77	**Edmonton**	**WHA**	2	0	0	0	2
	New Haven	AHL	1	0	0	0	6
	Binghamton	AHL	60	4	13	17	232
1977-78	Binghamton	AHL	21	5	2	7	69
	Cincinnati	**WHA**	40	1	5	6	241
WHA TOTALS			**42**	**1**	**5**	**6**	**243**

STOUGHTON, BLAINE
STOW - tuhn

RIGHT WING
Height: 5'10"
Weight: 185 lbs.
Birthdate: March 13, 1953
Birthplace: Gilbert Plains, Manitoba
Shoots: Right

REGULAR SEASON CAREER

SEASON	CLUB	LEAGUE	GP	G	A	PTS	PIM
1969-70	Flin Flon	WCHL	59	19	20	39	181
1970-71	Flin Flon	WCHL	35	26	24	50	96
1971-72	Flin Flon	WCHL	68	60	66	126	121
1972-73	Flin Flon	WCHL	66	58	60	118	86
1973-74	Hershey	AHL	47	23	17	40	35
	Pittsburgh	NHL	34	5	6	11	8
1974-75	Toronto	NHL	78	23	14	37	24
1975-76	Oklahoma City	CHL	30	14	22	36	24
	Toronto	NHL	43	6	11	17	8
1976-77	**Cincinnati**	**WHA**	81	52	52	104	39
1977-78	**Cincinnati**	**WHA**	30	6	13	19	36
	Indianapolis	WHA	47	13	13	26	28
WHA TOTALS			158	71	78	149	103

WHA PLAYOFFS

YEAR	CLUB	GP	G	A	PTS	PIM
1977	Cincinnati	4	0	3	3	2

SULLIVAN, PETER
SUHL - li - van

CENTER
Height: 5'9"
Weight: 170 lbs.
Birthdate: July 25, 1951
Birthplace: Toronto, Ontario
Shoots: Right

REGULAR SEASON CAREER

SEASON	CLUB	LEAGUE	GP	G	A	PTS	PIM
1968-69	Peterborough	Jr. "A" OHA	4	1	0	1	0
1969-70	Oshawa	Jr. "A" OHA	52	40	30	70	16
1970-71	Oshawa	Jr. "A" OHA	61	29	23	52	26
1971-72	Mount Royal	AJHL	26	14	19	33	4
	Muskegon	IHL	1	0	0	0	0
	St. Petersburg	EHL	5	2	1	3	0
1972-73	Nova Scotia	AHL	39	10	14	24	8
1973-74	Nova Scotia	AHL	74	30	40	70	22
1974-75	Nova Scotia	AHL	75	44	60	104	48
1975-76	**Winnipeg**	**WHA**	78	32	39	71	22
1976-77	**Winnipeg**	**WHA**	78	31	52	83	18
1977-78	**Winnipeg**	**WHA**	77	16	39	55	43
WHA TOTALS			233	79	130	209	83

WHA PLAYOFFS

YEAR	CLUB	GP	G	A	PTS	PIM
1976	Winnipeg	13	6	7	13	0
1977	Winnipeg	20	7	12	19	2
1978	Winnipeg	9	3	4	7	4
TOTALS		42	16	23	39	6

TARDIF, MARC
tahr - DEEF

LEFT WING
Height: 6'1"
Weight: 180 lbs.
Birthdate: September 23, 1947
Birthplace: Granby, Quebec
Shoots: Left

REGULAR SEASON CAREER

SEASON	CLUB	LEAGUE	GP	G	A	PTS	PIM
1968-69	Montreal	Jr. "A" OHA	51	31	41	72	121
1969-70	Montreal	Jr. "A" OHA	45	27	31	58	70
	Montreal	NHL	18	3	2	5	27
1970-71	Montreal	NHL	76	19	30	49	133
1971-72	Montreal	NHL	75	31	22	53	81
1972-73	Montreal	NHL	76	25	25	50	48
1973-74	Los Angeles	WHA	75	40	30	70	47
1974-75	Michigan	WHA	23	12	5	17	9
	Quebec	WHA	53	38	34	72	70
1975-76	Quebec	WHA	81	71	77	148	79
1976-77	Quebec	WHA	62	49	60	109	65
1977-78	Quebec	WHA	78	65	89	154	50
WHA TOTALS			372	275	295	570	320

WHA PLAYOFFS

YEAR	CLUB	GP	G	A	PTS	PIM
1975	Quebec	15	10	11	21	10
1976	Quebec	2	1	0	1	2
1977	Quebec	12	4	10	14	8
1978	Quebec	11	6	9	15	11
TOTALS		40	21	30	51	31

TEBBUTT, GREG
TEB - buht

DEFENSE
Height: 6'3"
Weight: 215 lbs.
Birthdate: May 11, 1957
Birthplace: Vancouver, British Columbia
Shoots: Left

REGULAR SEASON CAREER

SEASON	CLUB	LEAGUE	GP	G	A	PTS	PIM
1975-76	Victoria	WCHL	51	3	4	7	217
1976-77	Victoria	WCHL	29	7	12	19	98
	Regina	WCHL	40	8	17	25	138
1977-78	Flin Flon	WCHL	55	28	46	74	270

TERBENCHE, PAUL
tur - BENCH - e

DEFENSE
Height: 5'10"
Weight: 190 lbs.
Birthdate: September 16, 1945
Birthplace: Trail, British Columbia
Shoots: Left

REGULAR SEASON CAREER

SEASON	CLUB	LEAGUE	GP	G	A	PTS	PIM
1964-65	St. Catharines	Jr. "A" OHA	56	3	23	26	—
1965-66	St. Catharines	Jr. "A" OHA	48	5	31	36	26
	St. Louis	CHL	2	0	0	0	0
1966-67	St. Louis	CHL	63	4	14	18	39
1967-68	Chicago	NHL	68	3	7	10	8
1968-69	Dallas	CHL	26	0	4	4	2
1969-70	Portland	WHL	66	5	15	20	8
1970-71	Salt Lake	WHL	51	4	20	24	16
	Buffalo	NHL	3	0	0	0	2
1971-72	Salt Lake	WHL	64	1	31	32	10
	Buffalo	NHL	5	0	0	0	2
1972-73	Buffalo	NHL	42	0	7	7	8
1973-74	Buffalo	NHL	67	2	12	14	8
1974-75	**Vancouver**	**WHA**	**60**	**3**	**14**	**17**	**10**
1975-76	**Calgary**	**WHA**	**58**	**2**	**14**	**16**	**22**
1976-77	**Calgary**	**WHA**	**80**	**9**	**24**	**33**	**30**
1977-78	**Birmingham**	**WHA**	**11**	**1**	**0**	**1**	**0**
	Houston	WHA	—	—	—	—	—
WHA TOTALS			209	15	52	67	62

WHA PLAYOFFS

YEAR	CLUB	GP	G	A	PTS	PIM
1976	Calgary	10	0	6	6	6
1978	Houston	6	1	1	2	0
TOTALS		16	1	7	8	6

THOMAS, REG
TAH - mas

LEFT WING
Height: 5'10"
Weight: 185 lbs.
Birthdate: April 21, 1953
Birthplace: Lambeth, Ontario
Shoots: Left

REGULAR SEASON CAREER

SEASON	CLUB	LEAGUE	GP	G	A	PTS	PIM
1972-73	London	Jr. "A" OHA	61	52	83	135	41
1973-74	**Los Angeles**	**WHA**	**72**	**14**	**21**	**35**	**22**
1974-75	**Baltimore**	**WHA**	**50**	**8**	**13**	**21**	**42**

1975-76	Indianapolis	WHA	80	23	17	40	23
1976-77	Indianapolis	WHA	79	25	30	55	34
1977-78	Indianapolis	WHA	49	15	16	31	44
	Cincinnati	WHA	18	4	2	6	12
WHA TOTALS			348	89	99	188	177

WHA PLAYOFFS

YEAR	CLUB	GP	G	A	PTS	PIM
1976	Indianapolis	7	1	0	1	4
1977	Indianapolis	9	7	9	16	4
TOTALS		16	8	9	17	8

TREMBLAY, J.C.
trawm - BLAY

DEFENSE
Height: 5'11"
Weight: 190 lbs.
Birthdate: January 22, 1936
Birthplace: Bagotville, Quebec
Shoots: Left

REGULAR SEASON CAREER

SEASON	CLUB	LEAGUE	GP	G	A	PTS	PIM
1957-58	Hull-Ottawa	Sr. "A" OHA	39	5	17	22	16
1958-59	Hull-Ottawa	EOHL	44	4	13	17	22
	Rochester	AHL	3	0	0	0	0
1959-60	Montreal	NHL	11	0	1	1	0
	Hull-Ottawa	EPHL	55	25	31	56	55
1960-61	Hull-Ottawa	EPHL	37	7	33	40	28
	Montreal	NHL	29	1	3	4	18
1961-62	Montreal	NHL	70	3	17	20	18
1962-63	Montreal	NHL	69	1	17	18	10
1963-64	Montreal	NHL	70	5	16	21	24
1964-65	Montreal	NHL	68	3	17	20	22
1965-66	Montreal	NHL	59	6	29	35	8
1966-67	Montreal	NHL	60	8	26	34	14
1967-68	Montreal	NHL	73	4	26	30	18
1968-69	Montreal	NHL	75	7	32	39	18
1969-70	Montreal	NHL	58	2	19	21	7
1970-71	Montreal	NHL	76	11	52	63	23
1971-72	Montreal	NHL	76	6	51	57	24
1972-73	**Quebec**	**WHA**	75	14	75	89	32
1973-74	**Quebec**	**WHA**	68	9	44	53	10
1974-75	**Quebec**	**WHA**	68	16	56	72	18
1975-76	**Quebec**	**WHA**	80	12	77	89	16
1976-77	**Quebec**	**WHA**	53	4	31	35	16
1977-78	**Quebec**	**WHA**	54	5	37	42	26
WHA TOTALS			398	60	320	380	118

WHA PLAYOFFS

YEAR	CLUB	GP	G	A	PTS	PIM
1975	Quebec	11	0	10	10	2
1976	Quebec	5	0	3	3	0
1977	Quebec	17	2	9	11	2
1978	Quebec	1	0	1	1	0
TOTALS		34	2	23	25	4

TURKIEWICZ, JIM
TUR - ki - wits

DEFENSE
Height: 5'10"
Weight: 175 lbs.
Birthdate: April 13, 1955
Birthplace: Peterborough, Ontario
Shoots: Left

REGULAR SEASON CAREER

SEASON	CLUB	LEAGUE	GP	G	A	PTS	PIM
1973-74	Peterborough	Jr. "A" OHA	69	20	41	61	91
1974-75	Toronto	WHA	78	3	27	30	28
1975-76	Toronto	WHA	77	10	29	39	55
1976-77	Birmingham	WHA	80	6	25	31	54
1977-78	Birmingham	WHA	78	3	21	24	45
WHA TOTALS			313	22	102	124	182

WHA PLAYOFFS

YEAR	CLUB	GP	G	A	PTS	PIM
1975	Toronto	6	0	2	2	0
1978	Birmingham	5	1	1	2	0
TOTALS		11	1	3	4	0

VAIVE, RICK
VYV

RIGHT WING
Height: 6'0"
Weight: 180 lbs.
Birthdate: May 14, 1959
Birthplace: Ottawa, Ontario
Shoots: Right

REGULAR SEASON CAREER

SEASON	CLUB	LEAGUE	GP	G	A	PTS	PIM
1975-76	Charlottetown	PEI Jr.	34	42	37	79	95
1976-77	Sherbrooke	QMJHL	68	51	60	111	98
1977-78	Sherbrooke	QMJHL	68	76	79	155	199

WALSH, ED
WAWLSH

GOALTENDER
Height: 5'10"
Weight: 180 lbs.
Birthdate: August 18, 1951
Birthplace: Arlington, Massachusetts
Shoots: Right

REGULAR SEASON CAREER

SEASON	CLUB	LEAGUE	GP	GA	SO	GAA
1971-72	Boston University	ECAC	3	3	0	2.40
1972-73	Boston University	ECAC	27	79	2	2.94
1973-74	Boston University	ECAC	29	78	2	2.86
1974-75	Nova Scotia	AHL	46	128	2	2.77
1975-76	Nova Scotia	AHL	31	91	2	3.06
1976-77	Nova Scotia	AHL	40	115	3	2.86
1977-78	Binghamtom	AHL	18	76	0	4.98
	Springfield	AHL	13	64	0	5.16

WARNER, JIM
WORN - ur

RIGHT WING
Height: 5'11"
Weight: 180 lbs.
Birthdate: March 26, 1954
Birthplace: St. Paul, Minnesota
Shoots: Right

REGULAR SEASON CAREER

SEASON	CLUB	LEAGUE	GP	G	A	PTS	PIM
1974-75	Colorado Col.	WCHA	37	30	25	55	24
1975-76	Colorado Col.	WCHA	35	16	20	36	59
1976-77	Colorado Col.	WCHA	30	16	23	39	36
1977-78	Colorado Col.	WCHA	33	24	36	60	46

WEIR, STAN
WEER

CENTER
Height: 6'1"
Weight: 170 lbs.
Birthdate: March 17, 1952
Birthplace: Ponoka, Alberta
Shoots: Left

REGULAR SEASON CAREER

SEASON	CLUB	LEAGUE	GP	G	A	PTS	PIM
1969-70	Ponoka	AJHL	42	35	26	61	45
1970-71	Medicine Hat	WCHL	66	52	59	111	88
1971-72	Medicine Hat	WCHL	68	58	75	133	77
1972-73	California	NHL	78	15	24	39	16
1973-74	California	NHL	58	9	7	16	10
1974-75	California	NHL	80	18	27	45	12
1975-76	Toronto	NHL	64	19	32	51	22
1976-77	Toronto	NHL	65	11	19	30	14
1977-78	Toronto	NHL	30	12	5	17	4
	Tulsa	CHL	42	24	33	57	38

WEIR, WALLY
WEER

DEFENSE
Height: 6'2"
Weight: 195 lbs.
Birthdate: June 3, 1954
Birthplace: Verdun, Quebec
Shoots: Right

REGULAR SEASON CAREER

SEASON	CLUB	LEAGUE	GP	G	A	PTS	PIM
1975-76	Beauce	NAHL	56	6	20	26	180
1976-77	Quebec	WHA	69	3	17	20	197
1977-78	Quebec	WHA	13	0	0	0	47
WHA TOTALS			82	3	17	20	244

WHA PLAYOFFS

YEAR	CLUB	GP	G	A	PTS	PIM
1977	Quebec	17	1	5	6	13
1978	Quebec	11	1	2	3	50
TOTALS		28	2	7	9	63

WEST, STEVE
WEST

CENTER
Height: 5'8"
Weight: 150 lbs.
Birthdate: March 20, 1952
Birthplace: Peterborough, Ontario
Shoots: Left

REGULAR SEASON CAREER

SEASON	CLUB	LEAGUE	GP	G	A	PTS	PIM
1970-71	Oshawa	Jr. "A" OHA	2	2	0	2	0
1971-72	Oshawa	Jr. "A" OHA	63	30	43	73	40
1972-73	Jacksonville	AHL	76	27	42	69	51
1973-74	New Haven	AHL	76	50	60	110	41
1974-75	**Baltimore**	**WHA**	**50**	**15**	**18**	**33**	**4**
1975-76	Tucson	CHL	51	25	40	65	29
1976-77	Oklahoma City	CHL	76	33	63	96	42
	Houston	WHA	3	0	0	0	2
1977-78	**Houston**	**WHA**	**71**	**11**	**21**	**32**	**23**
WHA TOTALS			**124**	**26**	**39**	**65**	**29**

WHA PLAYOFFS

YEAR	CLUB	GP	G	A	PTS	PIM
1977	Houston	6	0	0	0	0
1978	Houston	6	1	0	1	0
TOTALS		**12**	**1**	**0**	**1**	**0**

WOOD, WAYNE
WOOD

GOALTENDER
Height: 6'1"
Weight: 195 lbs.
Birthdate: June 5, 1951
Birthplace: Toronto, Ontario
Shoots: Left

REGULAR SEASON CAREER

SEASON	CLUB	LEAGUE	GP	GA	SO	GAA
1970-71	Montreal	Jr. "A" OHA	48	177	1	3.66
1971-72	Omaha	CHL	17	55	1	3.38
	Providence	AHL	8	18	0	3.22
1972-73	Providence	AHL	58	171	4	3.02
1973-74	Albuquerque	CHL	14	41	2	2.80
	Providence	AHL	5	11	0	2.93
1974-75	Tulsa	CHL	8	23	0	2.88
	Vancouver	**WHA**	11	30	0	3.52
1975-76	**Calgary**	**WHA**	19	45	1	3.07
	Toronto	**WHA**	13	62	0	4.76
1976-77	**Birmingham**	**WHA**	23	78	0	4.13
1977-78	**Birmingham**	**WHA**	32	99	1	3.83
WHA TOTALS			98	314	2	3.88

WHA PLAYOFFS

YEAR	CLUB	GP	GA	SO	GAA
1978	Birmingham	1	3	0	6.15
TOTALS		1	3	0	6.15

YAKIWCHUK, DALE
YAHK - i - chuhk

CENTER
Height: 6'4"
Weight: 205 lbs.
Birthdate: October 17, 1958
Birthplace: Calgary, Alberta
Shoots: Left

REGULAR SEASON CAREER

SEASON	CLUB	LEAGUE	GP	G	A	PTS	PIM
1976-77	Portland	WCHL	59	24	53	77	151
1977-78	Portland	WCHL	64	32	52	84	312

142

REGULAR SEASON HISTORY

Cincinnati's Rick Dudley looks for another 40-goal season as the Stingers bid for post-season play under new Head Coach Floyd Smith. For career record of Dudley, see page 67.

ALL-TIME WHA PLAYER LISTING AND STATISTICS INCLUDING PLAYOFFS

			REGULAR SEASON					PLAYOFFS				
	POS		GP	G	A	TP	PIM	GP	G	A	TP	PIM
Abbey, Bruce	D	1975-76	17	1	0	1	12	—	—	—	—	—
Abgrall, Dennis	RW	1976-78	145	36	50	86	35	4	2	0	2	5
Abrahamsson, Thommy	D	1974-77	203	28	67	95	126	28	2	7	9	15
Adair, Jim	C	1973-74	70	12	17	29	10	—	—	—	—	—
Addouno, Ray	C	1973-78	221	45	152	197	67	28	12	18	30	38
Ahearn, Kevin	LW	1972-74	78	20	22	42	18	14	1	2	3	9
Ahrens, Chris	D	1977-78	4	0	0	0	15	—	—	—	—	—
Allan, Jeff	D	1977-78	2	0	0	0	0	—	—	—	—	—
Alley, Steve	LW	1977-78	27	8	12	20	11	5	1	0	1	5
Amodeo, Mike	D	1972-78	236	7	47	54	244	27	1	7	8	59
Anderson, Ron	D	1972-75	115	3	35	38	44	—	—	—	—	—
Anderson, Ron	RW	1972-74	91	19	17	36	47	1	0	0	0	0
Andrascik, Steve	RW	1974-76	97	9	13	22	79	—	—	—	—	—
Andrea, Paul	RW	1972-74	135	36	48	84	26	14	3	8	11	2
Angotti, Lou	C	1974-75	26	2	5	7	9	—	—	—	—	—
Antonovich, Mike	LW	1972-78	417	162	161	323	148	47	16	17	33	14
Arbour, John	D	1972-77	336	29	164	193	568	28	3	13	16	63
Archambault, Michel	LW	1972-73	57	12	25	37	36	—	—	—	—	—
Arndt, Danny	LW	1975-78	120	16	23	39	21	8	0	0	0	0
Ash, Bob	D	1972-75	200	6	46	52	88	17	1	4	5	6
Ashton, Ron	LW	1974-75	36	1	3	4	66	—	—	—	—	—
Asmundson, Duke	D	1972-76	258	16	54	70	211	29	4	5	9	21
Atkinson, Steve	C	1975-76	42	2	6	8	22	—	—	—	—	—
Backstrom, Ralph	C	1973-77	304	100	153	253	104	38	10	18	28	12
Baird, Ken	LW	1972-78	333	91	99	190	500	16	4	6	10	30
Ball, Blake	D	1972-73	—	—	—	—	—	2	0	0	0	2
Ball, Terry	D	1972-77	307	28	134	162	174	28	5	8	13	14
Balon, Dave	LW	1973-74	9	0	0	0	2	—	—	—	—	—
Baltimore, Bryon	D	1974-78	260	13	61	74	305	16	0	1	1	9
Barber, Butch	D	1972-74	78	4	19	23	41	—	—	—	—	—
Barlow, Bob	C	1974-75	51	6	20	26	8	—	—	—	—	—
Barrie, Doug	D	1972-77	351	37	122	159	620	12	1	1	2	31
Bateman, Jamie	RW	1974-76	31	1	3	4	100	5	0	0	0	16
Bathgate, Andy	RW	1974-75	11	1	6	7	2	—	—	—	—	—
Baxter, Paul	D	1974-78	194	15	53	68	722	26	6	9	15	87
Beaton, Frank	LW	1975-78	153	12	21	33	614	10	2	2	4	31
Beaudin, Norm	RW	1972-76	311	97	155	252	69	31	18	19	37	14
Beaudoin, Serge	D	1973-78	260	15	82	97	392	10	2	0	2	56
Beaule, Alain	D	1973-74	154	8	57	65	136	—	—	—	—	—
Bennett, John	LW	1972-73	34	4	6	10	18	—	—	—	—	—
Bennett, Wendell	D	1974-75	67	4	15	19	92	5	1	2	3	6
Benzelock, Jim	RW	1972-76	166	18	27	45	72	21	2	2	4	36
Bergeron, Yves	RW	1972-73	65	14	19	33	32	—	—	—	—	—
Bergman, Thommie	D	1974-78	234	22	97	119	261	13	3	10	13	8
Bernier, Jean	D	1974-78	260	17	84	101	50	32	4	7	11	4
Bernier, Serge	C	1973-78	352	194	290	484	415	49	28	46	74	39
Bignell, Larry	D	1975-76	41	5	5	10	43	—	—	—	—	—
Bilodeau, Gilles	LW	1975-78	107	4	9	13	429	3	0	0	0	27
Bilodeau, Yvon	D	1975-76	4	0	0	0	2	—	—	—	—	—
Black, Milt	RW	1972-75	186	28	31	59	55	18	2	4	6	10
Blackburn, Don	LW	1973-76	146	40	74	114	34	12	3	6	9	6
Blain, Jacques	D	1972-73	70	1	10	11	78	—	—	—	—	—
Blanchette, Bernie	RW	1972-73	47	7	7	14	10	—	—	—	—	—
Block, Ken	D	1972-78	433	14	184	198	182	16	0	6	6	8

144

	POS		REGULAR SEASON					PLAYOFFS				
			GP	G	A	TP	PIM	GP	G	A	TP	PIM
Boddy, Gregg	D	1976-77	64	2	19	21	60	4	1	2	3	14
Boland, Mike	RW	1972-73	41	1	15	16	44	1	0	0	0	12
Bolduc, Dan	RW	1975-78	88	15	13	28	51	30	3	10	13	8
Bond, Kerry	RW	1974-76	86	24	15	39	32	7	1	0	1	11
Bordeleau, Chris	C	1972-78	396	174	313	487	162	53	16	34	50	16
Bordeleau, Paulin	RW	1976-78	157	84	64	148	81	27	16	15	31	14
Borgeson, Don	RW	1974-76	145	59	52	111	66	8	1	2	3	2
Boucha, Henry	LW	1975-76	36	15	20	35	47	—	—	—	—	—
Boudreau, Bruce	C	1975-76	30	3	6	9	4	—	—	—	—	—
Boudreau, Michel	LW	1972-74	36	8	7	15	4	2	0	0	0	0
Boudrias, Andre	C	1976-78	140	22	48	70	34	28	3	14	17	10
Bowles, Brian	D	1975-76	3	0	0	0	0	—	—	—	—	—
Bowman, Kirk	LW	1973-74	10	0	2	2	0	—	—	—	—	—
Boyd, Bob	D	1973-75	54	1	14	15	35	7	0	0	0	4
Boyd, Jim	C	1974-77	169	49	80	129	68	10	4	3	7	4
Boyer, Wally	C	1972-73	69	6	28	34	27	14	4	2	6	4
Boylan, Dean	D	1973-75	64	1	5	6	122	—	—	—	—	—
Brackenbury, Curt	RW	1973-78	195	28	37	65	598	44	4	8	12	158
Bradley, Brian	LW	1972-75	190	41	61	102	38	6	0	1	1	2
Bray, Duane	D	1976-77	46	2	6	8	62	—	—	—	—	—
Bredin, Gary	RW	1974-76	144	26	31	57	49	—	—	—	—	—
Brewer, Carl	D	1973-74	77	2	23	25	42	12	0	4	4	11
Brindley, Doug	LW	1972-75	103	28	20	48	19	14	0	1	1	8
Brown, Arnie	D	1974-75	60	3	5	8	40	—	—	—	—	—
Brown, Bob	D	1972-74	80	7	17	24	46	—	—	—	—	—
Buetow, Brad	LW	1973-74	25	0	0	0	4	—	—	—	—	—
Buchanan, Ron	C	1972-76	205	83	102	185	48	14	7	3	10	2
Burgess, Don	LW	1972-78	443	106	121	228	87	22	4	9	13	4
Busniuk, Ron	D	1974-78	286	9	64	73	762	39	2	5	7	132
Butters, Bill	D	1974-78	217	4	51	55	530	34	1	4	5	87
Bye, Brian	LW	1975-76	1	0	0	0	0	—	—	—	—	—
Byers, Mike	RW	1972-76	263	83	74	157	40	25	10	11	21	20
Cadle, Brian	C	1972-73	56	4	4	8	39	3	0	0	0	0
Caffery, Terry	C	1972-76	164	59	111	170	30	8	3	7	10	0
Cahan, Larry	D	1972-74	78	1	10	11	46	—	—	—	—	—
Callighen, Brett	LW	1976-78	142	35	56	91	201	10	4	3	7	23
Campbell, Bryan	C	1972-78	433	123	253	376	219	8	3	2	5	6
Campbell, Colin	D	1973-74	78	3	20	23	191	—	—	—	—	—
Campbell, Scott	D	1977-78	75	8	29	37	116	6	1	1	2	8
Campeau, Rychard	D	1972-74	82	1	18	19	74	4	1	0	1	17
Cardiff, Jim	D	1972-75	200	4	47	51	398	4	0	0	0	11
Cardwell, Steve	LW	1973-75	152	32	36	68	227	15	0	1	1	34
Carleton, Wayne	C	1972-77	290	132	180	312	135	25	8	21	29	24
Carlin, Brian	LW	1972-74	70	13	22	35	6	—	—	—	—	—
Carlson, Jack	LW	1974-78	238	34	44	78	633	28	3	4	7	68
Carlson, Jeff	RW	1975-76	7	0	1	1	14	—	—	—	—	—
Carlson, Steve	C	1975-78	99	15	25	40	82	18	2	7	9	11
Carlyle, Steve	D	1972-75	221	13	59	72	109	5	0	1	1	4
Caron, Alain	RW	1972-75	193	82	50	132	30	—	—	—	—	—
Carroll, Greg	C	1976-78	151	30	66	96	116	4	1	2	3	0
Cartier, Jean-Yves	D	1972-73	15	0	3	3	8	—	—	—	—	—
Cassolato, Tony	RW	1976-78	120	31	37	68	85	7	0	0	0	8
Charlebois, Bob	LW	1972-76	188	32	50	82	34	16	2	1	3	8
Chartre, Claude	C	1972-75	18	2	3	5	0	—	—	—	—	—
Chernoff, Mike	LW	1973-75	39	11	10	21	4	—	—	—	—	—
Chipchase, Jack	D	1972-73	4	0	0	0	2	—	—	—	—	—
Chipperfield, Ron	C	1974-78	314	121	140	261	142	15	6	5	11	6
Christiansen, Keith	C	1972-74	138	23	55	78	60	15	1	1	2	2

	POS		REGULAR SEASON					PLAYOFFS				
			GP	G	A	TP	PIM	GP	G	A	TP	PIM
Clackson, Kim	D	1975-78	200	6	27	33	722	24	0	2	2	110
Clarke, Jim	D	1975-76	59	1	9	10	57	0	0	0	0	0
Clearwater, Ray	D	1972-77	214	27	77	104	141	18	2	3	5	10
Climie, Ron	LW	1972-77	248	98	106	204	68	15	4	0	4	2
Cloutier, Real	RW	1974-78	292	208	229	437	121	44	31	28	59	27
Coates, Brian	LW	1973-78	202	42	43	85	86	21	0	3	3	41
Colborne, Howie	LW	1973-74	2	0	0	0	0	—	—	—	—	—
Cole, Jim	LW	1976-77	2	0	1	1	0	—	—	—	—	—
Conacher, Brian	C	1972-73	69	8	19	27	32	5	1	3	4	4
Connelly, Gary	RW	1973-74	4	0	1	1	2	—	—	—	—	—
Connelly, Wayne	RW	1972-77	366	167	162	329	93	36	16	15	31	16
Connor, Cam	RW	1974-78	274	83	88	171	904	23	5	4	9	92
Conroy, Mike	C	1975-76	4	0	1	1	0	—	—	—	—	—
Constantin, Charles	LW	1974-78	190	28	35	63	229	20	0	2	2	19
Cormier, Michel	LW	1974-77	182	70	69	139	52	5	1	0	1	2
Cote, Alain	LW	1977-78	27	3	5	8	8	11	1	2	3	0
Cote, Roger	D	1972-75	153	3	14	17	104	2	0	0	0	0
Cournoyer, Norm	C	1973-77	32	4	7	11	14	—	—	—	—	—
Crashley, Bart	D	1972-74	148	22	53	75	26	6	0	2	2	2
Critch, Glen	D	1975-76	3	0	0	0	0	—	—	—	—	—
Cross, Jim	D	1977-78	2	0	0	0	0	—	—	—	—	—
Crowley, Paul	RW	1975-76	4	0	0	0	0	—	—	—	—	—
Cuddie, Steve	D	1972-75	222	17	47	64	235	26	1	9	10	32
Cunniff, John	LW	1972-76	65	10	10	20	35	18	2	2	4	2
Cunningham, Gary	D	1973-75	2	0	0	0	0	—	—	—	—	—
Cunningham, Rick	D	1972-77	323	23	91	114	458	21	1	6	7	33
Curtis, Paul	D	1974-75	76	4	15	19	32	—	—	—	—	—
D'Alvise, Bob	C	1975-76	59	5	8	13	10	—	—	—	—	—
Danby, John	C	1972-76	150	16	25	41	16	19	1	1	2	0
Davidson, Blair	D	1976-77	2	0	0	0	2	—	—	—	—	—
Davis, Bill	D	1977-78	12	0	0	0	2	—	—	—	—	—
Deadmarsh, Butch	LW	1974-78	255	63	66	129	570	8	0	1	1	14
Dean, Barry	LW	1975-76	71	9	25	34	110	—	—	—	—	—
Debol, Dave	C	1977-78	9	3	2	5	2	—	—	—	—	—
Delorenzi, Ray	RW	1974-76	42	8	12	20	4	—	—	—	—	—
Delorme, Ron	RW	1975-76	22	1	3	4	28	—	—	—	—	—
Demarco, Ab	D	1977-78	47	6	8	14	20	1	0	0	0	0
Derksen, Brian	D	1973-74	1	0	0	0	2	—	—	—	—	—
Deschamps, Andre	LW	1976-77	9	1	2	3	19	—	—	—	—	—
Descoteaux, Norm	D	1973-75	29	1	7	8	6	—	—	—	—	—
Desjardine, Ken	D	1972-76	154	4	24	28	148	—	—	—	—	—
Devine, Kevin	LW	1974-78	283	74	81	155	405	18	4	4	8	50
Dillabough, Bob	C	1972-73	72	8	8	16	8	9	1	0	1	0
Dillon, Wayne	C	1973-75	148	59	101	160	35	18	9	10	19	13
Dobek, Bob	C	1975-76	72	10	18	28	19	16	1	2	3	4
Donaldson, Gary	RW	1976-77	5	0	0	0	6	—	—	—	—	—
Donnelly, John	D	1972-73	15	1	1	2	44	—	—	—	—	—
Donnelly, Pat	C	1975-76	23	5	7	12	4	—	—	—	—	—
Dorey, Jim	D	1972-78	399	52	230	282	600	48	5	33	38	131
Dornseif, Dave	D	1977-78	3	0	1	1	0	—	—	—	—	—
Douglas, Kent	D	1972-73	60	3	15	18	74	—	—	—	—	—
Driscoll, Peter	LW	1974-78	249	70	77	147	445	10	2	5	7	41
Dube, Norm	LW	1976-78	112	31	49	80	25	24	5	14	19	17
Dubois, Michel	D	1975-77	59	2	5	7	117	2	0	1	1	0
Dudley, Rick	LW	1975-78	223	114	126	240	414	4	0	1	1	7
Dufour, Guy	RW	1972-74	84	30	25	55	32	—	—	—	—	—
Dunn, Dave	D	1976-78	106	9	31	40	208	29	5	6	11	23
Dupras, Richard	C	1973-74	2	0	0	0	0	—	—	—	—	—

146

	POS		REGULAR SEASON					PLAYOFFS				
			GP	G	A	TP	PIM	GP	G	A	TP	PIM
Durbano, Steve	D	1977-78	45	6	4	10	284	4	0	2	2	16
Earl, Tom	RW	1972-77	347	40	56	96	116	46	3	11	14	28
Edur, Tom	D	1973-76	217	17	79	96	116	13	3	5	8	0
Erickson, Grant	LW	1972-76	266	54	78	132	79	24	2	5	7	2
Evans, Chris	D	1975-78	204	11	51	62	136	10	5	5	10	4
Evo, Bill	RW	1974-76	97	14	18	32	64	—	—	—	—	—
Falkenberg, Bob	D	1972-78	376	14	74	88	183	28	1	5	6	24
Falkman, Craig	RW	1972-73	45	1	5	6	12	—	—	—	—	—
Farda, Richard	LW	1974-77	177	34	86	120	12	1	0	0	0	0
Featherstone, Tony	RW	1974-76	108	29	45	74	31	6	2	1	3	2
Fedorko, Mike	D	1976-77	4	0	0	0	0	—	—	—	—	—
Ferguson, Norm	RW	1972-78	436	181	184	365	45	26	10	9	19	9
Fisher, John	C	1972-73	40	0	5	5	0	—	—	—	—	—
Fitchner, Bob	C	1973-78	335	58	104	162	432	33	5	9	14	34
Fleming, Reg	LW	1972-74	120	25	57	82	142	12	0	4	4	12
Flett, Bill	RW	1976-78	121	75	48	124	54	5	0	2	2	2
Folco, Peter	D	1975-77	21	1	8	9	15	—	—	—	—	—
Foley, Rick	D	1975-76	11	1	2	3	6	—	—	—	—	—
Fontaine, Len	RW	1974-75	21	1	8	9	6	—	—	—	—	—
Fonteyne, Val	LW	1972-74	149	16	45	61	4	5	1	0	1	0
Ford, Mike	D	1974-78	233	33	99	132	172	34	5	25	30	20
Fortier, Dave	D	1977-78	54	1	15	16	86	—	—	—	—	—
Fortier, Florent	LW	1975-76	4	1	1	2	0	1	0	0	0	0
Fortunato, Joe	LW	1976-77	1	0	0	0	0	—	—	—	—	—
Fotiu, Nick	LW	1974-76	110	5	4	9	238	20	5	2	7	84
Fraser, Rick	D	1974-75	4	0	0	0	2	—	—	—	—	—
Fronoh, John	LW	1972-78	420	108	192	300	130	44	14	25	39	6
Ftorek, Robbie	C	1974-78	293	177	230	407	278	10	3	8	11	4
Gallant, Gord	LW	1973-77	273	31	59	90	849	14	2	2	4	98
Gambucci, Gary	LW	1974-76	112	29	24	53	33	12	4	0	4	6
Garneau, JC	LW	1974-75	17	0	5	5	27	—	—	—	—	—
Garwasiuk, Ron	LW	1973-74	51	6	13	19	100	—	—	—	—	—
Gateman, Marty	D	1975-76	12	0	1	1	6	—	—	—	—	—
Gaudette, Andre	C	1972-75	223	61	105	166	34	9	0	1	1	0
Gellard, Sam	LW	1972-74	28	7	4	11	15	3	0	0	0	0
Gendron, Jean-Guy	LW	1972-74	127	28	41	69	155	—	—	—	—	—
Gibbons, Brian	D	1972-76	217	15	88	103	251	22	3	7	10	26
Gibbons, Gerard	D	1973-76	31	2	4	6	30	1	0	0	0	0
Gibson, Jack	LW	1972-76	126	38	22	60	108	14	2	3	5	16
Gilbert, Jeannot	C	1973-75	131	24	60	84	32	11	3	6	9	2
Gilligan, Bill	C	1977-78	54	10	14	24	59	—	—	—	—	—
Gilmore, Tom	LW	1972-75	202	48	60	108	439	10	2	7	9	17
Gilmour, Dave	C	1975-76	1	0	0	0	0	—	—	—	—	—
Giroux, Rejean	RW	1972-74	71	15	18	33	55	—	—	—	—	—
Given, David	RW	1974-75	1	0	0	0	0	—	—	—	—	—
Glenwright, Brian	LW	1972-74	65	5	7	12	0	—	—	—	—	—
Globensky, Allan	D	1973-76	42	1	2	3	18	2	1	0	1	0
Goldsworthy, Bill	RW	1977-78	32	8	10	18	10	—	—	—	—	—
Goldthorpe, Bill	LW	1973-76	33	1	0	1	87	3	0	0	0	25
Golembrosky, Frank	RW	1972-73	60	8	12	20	53	—	—	—	—	—
Gordon, Don	RW	1973-75	94	18	14	32	43	18	4	8	12	4
Gorman, Dave	LW	1974-78	200	42	59	101	169	9	1	3	4	24
Gratton, Bill	LW	1975-76	6	0	1	1	2	—	—	—	—	—
Gratton, Jean-Guy	RW	1972-75	188	31	41	72	52	14	1	1	2	4
Gravel, John	D	1972-73	8	1	3	4	0	—	—	—	—	—
Gray, John	LW	1974-78	306	136	131	267	407	22	3	8	11	37
Green, Ted	D	1972-78	438	42	136	178	288	61	2	16	18	59
Greig, Bruce	LW	1976-78	39	4	2	6	67	—	—	—	—	—

	POS		REGULAR SEASON					PLAYOFFS				
			GP	G	A	TP	PIM	GP	G	A	TP	PIM
Grenier, Richard	LW	1976-77	34	11	9	20	4	—	—	—	—	—
Gresdal, Gary	D	1975-76	2	0	1	1	5	1	0	0	0	14
Grierson, Don	RW	1972-74	143	33	40	73	128	17	1	5	6	29
Gruen, Danny	LW	1974-77	181	56	61	117	185	3	0	1	1	0
Guindon, Bobby	LW	1972-78	392	104	127	231	135	57	22	18	40	33
Guite, Pierre	LW	1972-78	361	91	104	195	577	22	6	1	7	29
Gulka, Bud	RW	1974-75	5	1	0	1	10	—	—	—	—	—
Haas, Derek	C	1975-76	30	5	9	14	6	1	0	0	0	0
Hagman, Matti	C	1977-78	53	23	31	56	16	—	—	—	—	—
Hale, Larry	D	1972-78	413	12	95	107	214	65	4	15	19	22
Hall, Del	LW	1975-78	186	89	88	177	44	5	2	3	5	0
Hall, Murray	RW	1972-76	312	96	125	221	155	54	21	17	38	32
Hamilton, Al	D	1972-78	375	47	220	267	454	13	1	6	7	25
Hampson, Ted	LW	1972-76	305	60	143	203	51	33	8	14	22	18
Handrahan, Alf	RW	1977-78	14	1	3	4	42	—	—	—	—	—
Haney, Merv	D	1972-73	7	0	1	1	4	—	—	—	—	—
Hangsleben, Alan	D	1974-78	257	26	54	80	289	37	3	10	13	85
Hanmer, Craig	D	1974-75	27	1	0	1	15	—	—	—	—	—
Hanna, John	D	1972-73	66	6	20	26	68	—	—	—	—	—
Hansis, Ron	RW	1976-78	100	17	12	29	57	14	2	2	4	8
Hanson, Dave		1976-78	50	7	18	25	285	6	0	1	1	48
Harbaruk, Nick	RW	1974-77	181	45	44	89	78	13	3	1	4	10
Hardy, Joe	C	1972-75	210	46	94	140	201	27	4	10	14	13
Hargreaves, Jim	D	1973-76	175	12	20	32	151	15	1	0	1	8
Hargreaves, Ted	LW	1973-74	74	7	12	19	15	4	0	1	1	10
Harker, Derek	D	1972-73	29	0	5	5	46	—	—	—	—	—
Harris, Duke	RW	1972-75	193	53	47	100	52	28	7	7	14	6
Harris, Hugh	LW	1973-78	336	107	173	280	241	16	2	9	11	19
Harrison, Jim	C	1972-76	132	117	152	269	360	8	1	3	4	13
Hart, Richard	D	1976-77	4	0	0	0	0	—	—	—	—	—
Harvey, Michel	C	1972-73	40	6	13	19	14	—	—	—	—	—
Hatoum, Ed	RW	1972-74	52	4	13	17	10	—	—	—	—	—
Heatley, Murray	RW	1973-76	156	48	54	102	86	10	1	0	1	2
Heaver, Paul	D	1977-78	71	1	12	13	83	—	—	—	—	—
Hedberg, Anders	RW	1974-78	286	236	222	458	201	42	35	28	63	30
Heggedal, Howie	LW	1972-73	8	2	1	3	0	1	0	0	0	0
Heindl, Bill	LW	1973-74	67	4	14	18	4	5	0	1	1	2
Heiskala, Earl	LW	1972-74	94	14	23	37	195	5	1	1	2	4
Henderson, Paul	LW	1974-78	284	116	116	232	92	5	1	1	2	0
Henry, Pierre	LW	1972-73	19	2	3	5	13	—	—	—	—	—
Herriman, Don	LW	1972-75	155	36	71	107	143	4	1	0	1	14
Hicke, Bill	RW	1972-73	73	14	24	38	20	—	—	—	—	—
Hickey, Pat	LW	1973-75	152	60	63	123	102	17	3	4	7	16
Hillman, Larry	D	1973-76	192	6	49	55	182	17	1	5	6	40
Hillman, Wayne	D	1973-75	126	3	16	19	88	10	0	2	2	18
Hinse, Andre	LW	1973-77	256	102	151	253	69	42	15	16	31	28
Hislop, Jamie	RW	1976-78	126	31	62	93	23	4	0	1	1	4
Hobin, Mike	C	1975-77	77	18	19	37	16	—	—	—	—	—
Hodgson, Ted	RW	1972-74	107	18	34	52	121	9	1	3	4	13
Hoekstra, Ed	C	1972-74	97	13	28	41	12	9	1	2	3	0
Hoganson, Dale	D	1973-78	309	28	142	170	169	23	2	6	8	13
Holbrook, Terry	RW	1974-76	93	11	15	26	13	8	0	1	1	0
Holland, Jerry	LW	1977-78	22	2	1	3	14	—	—	—	—	—
Holmgren, Paul	C	1975-76	51	14	16	30	121	—	—	—	—	—
Hopiavouri, Ralph	D	1972-75	70	6	15	21	71	12	0	2	2	6
Hornung, Larry	D	1972-78	373	34	121	155	103	37	2	12	14	6
Horton, Billy	D	1972-75	193	4	35	39	131	9	0	1	1	10

	POS		REGULAR SEASON					PLAYOFFS				
			GP	G	A	TP	PIM	GP	G	A	TP	PIM
Houle, Rejean	RW	1973-76	204	118	139	257	115	20	12	6	18	10
Howe, Gordie	RW	1973-78	361	155	310	465	348	68	25	42	67	111
Howe, Mark	LW	1973-78	349	166	231	397	166	68	37	49	86	42
Howe, Marty	D	1973-78	383	58	102	160	429	66	9	13	22	77
Howell, Harry	D	1973-76	170	7	36	43	58	7	1	0	1	12
Huck, Fran	C	1973-78	228	67	127	194	133	16	3	15	18	14
Hughes, Brent	D	1975-78	220	20	76	96	159	22	2	9	11	18
Hughes, Frank	RW	1972-78	392	173	180	353	173	54	24	16	40	33
Hughes, John	D	1974-78	309	13	111	124	648	10	1	1	2	14
Hull, Bobby	LW	1972-78	407	301	332	633	183	60	43	37	80	38
Hull, Steve	RW	1975-77	60	11	17	28	6	—	—	—	—	—
Hurley, Paul	D	1972-77	311	10	76	86	181	25	0	8	8	18
Huston, Ron	C	1975-77	159	42	83	124	14	5	1	1	2	0
Hutchison, Dave	D	1972-74	97	0	15	15	185	3	0	0	0	2
Hyndman, Mike	RW	1972-74	86	12	22	34	32	6	0	3	3	17
Hynes, David	LW	1976-77	22	5	4	9	4	—	—	—	—	—
Inglis, Lee	LW	1973-75	10	0	2	2	0	—	—	—	—	—
Inkpen, Dave	D	1975-78	227	12	61	73	236	9	0	2	2	8
Irwin, Glen	D	1974-78	209	7	23	30	509	18	0	2	2	17
Israelson, Larry	LW	1974-77	105	22	31	53	36	3	0	0	0	0
Jacques, Jeff	RW	1974-77	199	50	68	118	231	6	0	4	4	2
Jacquith, Gary	D	1975-76	2	0	0	0	0	—	—	—	—	—
Jakubo, Mike	C	1972-73	7	0	0	0	0	—	—	—	—	—
Jarrett, Gary	LW	1972-76	298	104	119	223	239	22	9	8	17	34
Jarry, Pierre	LW	1977-78	18	4	10	14	4	5	1	0	1	4
Jodzio, Rick	RW	1974-77	137	15	16	31	357	2	0	0	0	14
Johnson, Danny	C	1972-75	232	53	58	111	62	18	5	1	6	5
Johnson, Jim	C	1972-75	157	32	71	103	54	16	3	5	8	6
Johnston, Larry	D	1974-75	49	0	9	9	93	—	—	—	—	—
Johnstone, Ed	RW	1974-75	23	4	4	8	43	—	—	—	—	—
Jones, Bobby	C	1972-76	161	30	48	78	60	—	—	—	—	—
Jones, Jim	D	1973-74	1	0	0	0	0	—	—	—	—	—
Jones, Jimmy	RW	1973-75	81	14	9	23	62	—	—	—	—	—
Jordan, Ric	D	1972-77	183	11	23	34	180	17	0	0	0	14
Joyal, Ed	C	1972-76	239	57	55	112	26	5	2	0	2	4
Justin, Dan	D	1975-77	23	0	2	2	6	—	—	—	—	—
Kannegeisser, Gord	D	1972-75	127	1	34	35	62	12	0	3	3	8
Karlander, Al	C	1973-77	269	63	109	172	107	21	3	7	10	6
Kassian, Dennis	LW	1972-73	50	6	7	13	14	—	—	—	—	—
Keeler, Mike	D	1973-74	1	0	0	0	0	1	0	0	0	0
Kennedy, Jamie	RW	1972-73	54	4	6	10	11	—	—	—	—	—
Kennett, Murray	D	1974-76	106	8	21	29	39	—	—	—	—	—
Keogan, Murray	C	1974-76	114	42	42	84	91	5	0	1	1	0
Keon, Dave	C	1975-78	212	80	146	226	18	26	10	14	24	6
Kerslake, Doug	RW	1974-76	23	5	1	6	14	—	—	—	—	—
Ketola, Veli-Pekka	C	1974-77	235	84	99	183	118	13	7	5	12	2
Ketter, Kerry	D	1975-76	48	1	9	10	20	—	—	—	—	—
King, Steve	RW	1972-74	136	32	56	88	54	17	0	4	4	18
Kirk, Gavin	C	1972-77	392	116	238	354	263	38	14	19	33	33
Klatt, Billy	RW	1972-74	143	50	28	78	34	16	4	5	9	23
Knibbs, Darrel	C	1972-73	41	3	8	11	0	—	—	—	—	—
Kokkola, Keith	D	1974-77	52	0	5	5	130	—	—	—	—	—
Konik, George	D	1972-73	54	4	12	16	34	—	—	—	—	—
Krake, Skip	RW	1972-76	207	52	77	129	318	19	2	4	6	66
Krezanski, Reg	D	1974-75	2	0	0	0	2	—	—	—	—	—
Krupicka, Jarda	C	1972-73	36	2	2	4	6	—	—	—	—	—
Kryskow, Dave	LW	1976-78	116	36	38	74	63	9	4	4	8	2
Kuzmicz, George	D	1974-76	35	0	12	12	22	—	—	—	—	—

	POS		REGULAR SEASON					PLAYOFFS				
			GP	G	A	TP	PIM	GP	G	A	TP	PIM
Labossiere, Gord	C	1972-76	301	102	162	264	144	50	16	28	44	46
Labraaten, Dan	LW	1976-78	111	42	43	85	51	24	8	18	26	23
Lacombe, Francois	D	1972-78	361	35	118	153	378	50	5	9	14	34
Lacroix, Andre	C	1972-78	473	219	491	710	378	38	10	25	35	30
Laframboise, Peter	C	1976-77	17	0	5	5	12	—	—	—	—	—
Lagace, Jean-Guy	D	1976-77	78	2	25	27	110	—	—	—	—	—
Lagace, Pierre	C	1977-78	17	2	4	6	2	1	0	0	0	0
Lahache, Floyd	D	1977-78	11	0	3	3	13	—	—	—	—	—
Laing, Bill	LW	1974-76	97	10	16	26	99	4	0	1	1	4
Lalonde, Rick	D	1975-76	2	0	0	0	0	—	—	—	—	—
Langevin, Dave	D	1976-78	139	13	38	51	184	10	2	3	5	19
Langway, Rod	D	1977-78	52	3	18	21	52	4	0	0	0	9
Lapierre, Camille	C	1972-74	33	5	12	17	2	4	0	2	2	0
Lariviere, Garry	D	1974-78	239	21	93	114	262	34	3	14	17	16
Larose, Claude	LW	1975-78	239	83	106	189	45	4	2	1	3	0
Larose, Paul	RW	1973-75	33	1	8	9	9	—	—	—	—	—
Larose, Ray	D	1972-74	86	1	11	12	45	8	0	0	0	2
Larway, Don	RW	1974-78	299	86	81	167	279	38	12	8	20	33
Laughton, Mike	C	1972-75	203	43	47	90	100	10	4	1	5	0
Lavender, Brian	LW	1975-76	37	2	0	2	7	—	—	—	—	—
Lawson, Danny	RW	1972-77	392	218	204	422	142	26	6	9	15	25
LeBlanc, JP	C	1972-76	248	56	134	190	232	6	0	5	5	2
Leclerc, Renald	RW	1972-78	403	129	170	299	443	30	10	11	21	52
Leduc, Bobby	LW	1972-75	168	47	66	113	109	17	4	8	12	46
Leduc, Rich	C	1974-78	320	159	154	313	355	12	3	6	9	20
Legge, Barry	D	1974-78	265	23	72	95	210	7	0	1	1	12
Legge, Randy	D	1974-77	192	3	31	34	166	10	0	0	0	18
Leiter, Bob	C	1975-76	51	17	17	34	8	3	2	0	2	0
Lemieux, Richard	C	1976-77	33	6	11	17	9	—	—	—	—	—
Lesuk, Bill	LW	1975-78	239	38	66	104	225	40	6	8	14	42
Ley, Rick	D	1972-78	405	28	190	218	581	64	7	29	36	131
Liddington, Bob	LW	1972-77	346	96	82	178	115	18	6	5	11	11
Lilyholm, Len	LW	1972-73	77	8	13	21	37	5	1	0	1	0
Lindh, Mats	C	1975-77	138	33	32	65	14	33	4	9	13	6
Lindskog, Doug	LW	1976-77	2	0	0	0	2	—	—	—	—	—
Lindstrom, Willy	RW	1975-78	237	97	102	199	111	41	16	17	33	41
Linseman, Ken	C	1977-78	71	38	38	76	126	5	2	2	4	15
Lloyd, Owen	D	1977-78	3	0	1	1	4	—	—	—	—	—
Locas, Jacques	C	1974-78	187	49	70	119	111	—	—	—	—	—
Lodboa, Dan	RW	1972-73	58	15	18	33	16	—	—	—	—	—
Lomenda, Mark	RW	1974-77	164	31	61	92	46	9	3	1	4	17
Long, Barry	D	1974-78	307	46	135	181	280	33	1	10	11	20
Long, Ted	D	1976-77	1	0	0	0	0	—	—	—	—	—
Lukowich, Bernie	RW	1975-77	21	5	3	8	18	10	3	4	7	8
Lukowich, Morris	LW	1976-78	142	67	53	120	198	17	7	6	13	36
Lund, Larry	C	1972-78	459	149	277	426	419	59	20	45	65	116
Lunde, Len	C	1973-74	72	26	22	48	8	5	0	1	1	0
Lyle, George	LW	1976-78	143	69	57	126	136	17	3	1	4	17
MacDonald, Blair	RW	1973-78	396	138	128	266	109	30	12	11	23	6
MacGregor, Bruce	RW	1974-76	135	37	38	75	23	4	0	1	1	0
MacGregor, Gary	C	1974-78	234	84	66	150	87	3	0	0	0	4
MacKenzie, Al	D	1973-74	2	0	0	0	0	—	—	—	—	—
MacMillan, Bob	C	1972-74	153	27	61	88	129	16	2	6	8	4
MacNeil, Bernie	LW	1972-76	119	19	19	38	131	3	0	0	0	4
MacSweyn, Ralph	D	1972-74	151	2	44	46	97	6	1	2	3	4
Maggs, Darryl	D	1973-78	375	47	163	210	518	34	5	9	14	95
Mahovlich, Frank	LW	1974-78	237	89	143	232	75	9	4	1	5	2
Mara, Peter	C	1974-76	97	20	28	48	24	—	—	—	—	—

150

	POS		REGULAR SEASON					PLAYOFFS				
			GP	G	A	TP	PIM	GP	G	A	TP	PIM
Marotte, Gilles	D	1977-78	73	3	20	23	76	—	—	—	—	—
Marrin, Peter	C	1973-78	258	77	101	178	109	14	0	8	8	4
Marsh, Jim	D	1976-77	1	0	0	0	0	—	—	—	—	—
Marsh, Peter	RW	1976-78	150	48	53	101	175	4	2	0	2	0
Martin, Tom	RW	1972-75	214	58	77	135	59	22	8	13	21	4
Mavety, Larry	D	1972-77	248	37	113	150	418	24	4	11	15	52
Maxwell, Bryan	D	1975-78	124	6	23	29	217	6	0	0	0	33
Mayer, Jim	RW	1976-78	72	13	12	25	21	0	0	0	0	0
Mazur, John	LW	1977-78	1	0	0	0	0	—	—	—	—	—
McAneeley, Bob	C	1972-76	163	29	34	63	133	7	2	0	2	0
McAneeley, Ted	D	1975-76	79	2	17	19	71	4	0	0	0	0
McCallum, Dunc	D	1972-75	100	9	30	39	136	10	2	3	5	6
McCaskill, Ted	C	1972-74	91	13	13	26	213	6	2	3	5	12
McCrimmon, Jim	D	1973-76	107	3	8	11	158	0	0	0	0	0
McCulloch, Don	D	1972-75	51	1	9	10	42	—	—	—	—	—
McDonald, Ab	LW	1972-74	148	29	41	70	24	18	2	6	8	4
McDonald, Brian	C	1972-77	304	89	101	190	268	26	6	5	11	61
McDonough, Al	RW	1974-77	200	66	73	139	52	8	3	1	4	2
McGlynn, Dick	D	1972-73	30	0	0	0	12	—	—	—	—	—
McKay, Ray	D	1974-78	212	14	44	58	134	7	0	1	1	8
McKenzie, Brian	LW	1973-75	87	19	20	39	72	5	0	1	1	0
McKenzie, John	RW	1972-78	401	144	222	366	502	23	11	8	19	32
McLeod, Al	D	1974-78	317	15	82	97	289	26	2	9	11	19
McMahon, Mike	D	1972-76	266	29	101	130	249	32	1	14	15	13
McManama, Bob	C	1975-76	37	3	10	13	28	12	4	3	7	4
McMasters, Jim	D	1972-74	83	1	7	8	41	9	0	1	1	6
McMullen, Dale	LW	1977-78	1	0	0	0	0	—	—	—	—	—
McNamara, Mike	D	1972-73	19	0	0	0	5	—	—	—	—	—
McNamee, Peter	RW	1973-77	175	16	31	47	189	18	1	2	3	32
Meloche, Denis	C	1972-74	45	7	14	21	18	—	—	—	—	—
Meloff, Chris	D	1972-73	28	1	6	7	40	—	—	—	—	—
Melrose, Barry	D	1976-78	98	3	13	16	121	2	0	0	0	2
Mercredi, Vic	C	1975-76	3	0	0	0	29	—	—	—	—	—
Merrell, Barry	C	1976-77	10	1	3	4	0	—	—	—	—	—
Methe, Gerry	D	1974-75	5	0	1	1	4	2	0	0	0	0
Micheletti, Joe	D	1976-78	70	17	37	54	66	5	0	2	2	4
Migneault, John	LW	1972-76	258	49	61	110	107	8	0	0	0	0
Milani, Tom	RW	1976-77	2	0	0	0	0	—	—	—	—	—
Miller, Perry	D	1974-77	201	31	60	91	309	20	4	6	10	27
Miller, Warren	RW	1975-78	161	39	60	99	119	24	1	2	3	28
Miszuk, John	D	1974-77	214	6	66	72	179	10	0	1	1	10
Moffat, Lyle	LW	1975-78	206	39	43	82	206	39	10	10	20	24
Mononen, Lauri	RW	1975-77	142	36	50	86	29	5	1	3	4	2
Morenz, Brian	RW	1972-76	223	53	57	110	165	21	2	4	6	19
Morgan, Ron	LW	1973-74	4	0	1	1	7	2	1	0	1	0
Morin, Wayne	D	1976-77	13	2	0	2	25	—	—	—	—	—
Morris, Billy	LW	1974-75	36	4	8	12	6	—	—	—	—	—
Morris, Peter	LW	1975-77	78	7	13	20	36	3	0	1	1	7
Morris, Rick	LW	1972-78	413	102	90	192	567	27	4	5	9	52
Morrison, George	LW	1972-77	361	123	142	265	110	38	14	17	31	14
Morrison, Kevin	D	1973-78	386	91	217	308	448	28	2	15	17	22
Mortson, Keke	C	1972-78	73	13	17	30	102	12	0	4	4	16
Mosdell, Wayne	D	1972-73	8	0	1	1	12	—	—	—	—	—
Mott, Darwin	LW	1972-73	1	0	0	0	0	—	—	—	—	—
Mott, Morris	RW	1976-77	2	0	1	1	5	—	—	—	—	—
Mowat, Bob	RW	1974-75	53	9	10	19	34	4	0	0	0	0
Muloin, Wayne	D	1972-76	257	10	43	53	178	20	2	4	6	18
Myers, Murray	RW	1972-76	148	37	36	73	44	2	0	0	0	0

151

			REGULAR SEASON					PLAYOFFS				
	POS		GP	G	A	TP	PIM	GP	G	A	TP	PIM
Napier, Mark	RW	1975-78	237	136	118	254	134	5	0	2	2	14
Neale, Robbie	C	1973-75	59	9	14	23	38	5	0	0	0	4
Nedomansky, Vaclav	C	1974-78	252	135	118	253	43	6	3	1	4	9
Neeld, Greg	D	1975-76	17	0	1	1	18	—	—	—	—	—
Nesterenko, Eric	RW	1973-74	29	2	5	7	8	—	—	—	—	—
Nevin, Bob	RW	1976-77	13	3	2	5	0	—	—	—	—	—
Newell, Rick	D	1974-75	25	0	4	4	39	5	0	1	1	2
Niekamp, Jim	D	1972-77	383	16	96	112	484	16	2	2	4	18
Nilsson, Kent	C	1977-78	80	42	65	107	8	9	2	8	10	10
Nilsson, Ulf	C	1974-78	300	140	344	484	341	42	14	53	67	51
Nistico, Lou	LW	1973-77	187	44	72	116	375	6	6	1	7	19
Noris, Joe	C	1975-78	198	72	116	188	60	18	4	5	9	12
Norwich, Craig	D	1977-78	65	7	23	30	48	—	—	—	—	—
O'Connell, Tim	RW	1976-77	16	0	3	3	4	—	—	—	—	—
O'Donnell, Fred	RW	1974-76	155	32	26	58	165	20	2	5	7	35
O'Donoghue, Don	RW	1972-76	147	25	37	62	63	4	0	1	1	0
Odrowski, Gerry	D	1972-76	182	16	114	130	230	11	1	4	5	6
Olds, Wally	D	1972-76	89	5	12	17	10	9	0	2	2	4
Orr, Billy	D	1973-74	44	3	9	12	16	12	1	0	1	6
O'Shea, Danny	C	1974-75	76	16	25	41	47	11	0	0	0	6
O'Shea, Kevin	RW	1974-75	68	10	10	20	42	1	0	0	0	0
Ouimet, Francois	D	1975-77	25	1	10	11	12	—	—	—	—	—
Paiement, Pierre	RW	1972-73	8	1	0	1	18	—	—	—	—	—
Paiement, Rosaire	RW	1972-78	455	146	221	367	602	44	13	22	35	72
Paradise, Dick	D	1972-74	144	5	22	27	260	12	0	1	1	8
Parizeau, Michel	C	1972-78	467	135	234	369	286	30	9	14	23	24
Patenaude, Rusty	RW	1972-78	431	159	131	290	368	10	1	6	7	22
Patrick, Craig	RW	1976-77	30	6	11	17	6	—	—	—	—	—
Patrick, Glenn	D	1976-77	23	0	4	4	62	2	0	0	0	0
Patry, Denis	RW	1974-75	3	1	2	3	2	—	—	—	—	—
Patterson, Dennis	D	1976-77	23	0	2	2	2	—	—	—	—	—
Payette, Jean	C	1972-74	107	19	40	59	52	—	—	—	—	—
Peacosh, Gene	LW	1972-77	367	165	165	330	134	30	12	9	21	27
Pearson, Mel	RW	1972-73	70	8	12	20	12	5	2	0	2	0
Peloffy, Andre	C	1977-78	10	2	0	2	2	2	0	0	0	0
Pelyk, Mike	D	1974-76	150	24	49	73	238	—	—	—	—	—
Pentland, Dwayne	D	1976-77	29	1	2	3	6	2	0	0	0	0
Perkins, Ross	C	1972-75	225	44	93	137	95	5	1	3	4	2
Perry, Brian	RW	1972-75	145	33	31	64	49	6	1	2	3	6
Pesut, George	D	1976-77	17	2	0	2	2	—	—	—	—	—
Peters, Garry	C	1972-74	57	4	12	16	42	—	—	—	—	—
Phaneuf, Jean-Luc	C	1975-77	78	10	15	25	6	—	—	—	—	—
Pinder, Gerry	RW	1972-78	356	93	141	234	436	18	5	10	15	40
Pizunski, Ed	RW	1975-76	1	0	0	0	0	—	—	—	—	—
Plante, Michel	C	1972-74	92	16	14	30	37	4	0	0	0	2
Pleau, Larry	C	1972-78	440	151	209	360	174	56	27	21	48	37
Plumb, Ron	D	1972-78	471	61	248	309	308	32	4	12	16	48
Polano, Nick	D	1972-73	17	0	3	3	24	—	—	—	—	—
Popiel, Jan	LW	1972-77	296	78	82	160	256	26	9	6	15	16
Popiel, Poul	D	1972-78	467	62	265	327	618	71	7	47	54	118
Powis, Lynn	C	1975-78	153	50	65	115	60	13	7	5	12	9
Pratt, Kelly	RW	1973-74	50	4	6	10	50	—	—	—	—	—
Prentice, Bill	D	1972-78	158	8	14	22	265	19	0	0	0	24
Preston, Rich	RW	1974-78	308	105	120	225	149	41	8	17	25	24
Price, Pat	D	1974-75	69	5	29	34	54	—	—	—	—	—
Primeau, Kevin	RW	1977-78	7	0	1	1	2	2	0	0	0	2
Pritchard, Jim	D	1974-75	2	0	0	0	0	—	—	—	—	—
Proceviat, Dick	D	1972-77	321	16	90	106	265	20	0	4	4	12

			REGULAR SEASON					PLAYOFFS			
	POS		GP	G	A	TP	PIM	GP	G	A	TP	PIM
Pumple, Rich	LW	1972-75	128	27	30	57	90	9	3	5	8	11
Rautakallio, Pekka	D	1975-77	151	15	70	85	16	5	0	2	2	0
Reed, Bill	D	1974-76	40	0	5	5	26	—	—	—	—	—
Reichmuth, Craig	LW	1972-75	189	25	25	50	322	—	—	—	—	—
Repo, Sepo	C	1976-77	80	29	31	60	10	—	—	—	—	—
Rhiness, Brad	C	1976-78	70	12	17	29	16	5	0	1	1	0
Richardson, Steve	LW	1974-76	72	9	22	31	74	—	—	—	—	—
Riihiranta, Heikki	D	1974-77	187	10	38	48	84	4	0	4	4	6
Riley, Ron	LW	1972-73	22	0	5	5	2	2	0	0	0	0
Rivers, Wayne	RW	1972-77	357	158	176	334	183	24	8	6	14	14
Rizzuto, Garth	LW	1972-74	102	13	14	27	40	14	0	1	1	14
Roberto, Phil	RW	1977-78	53	8	20	28	91	4	1	0	1	20
Roberts, Doug	D	1975-77	140	7	31	38	84	19	1	1	2	8
Roberts, Gordie	D	1975-78	232	31	98	129	389	36	4	16	20	71
Robertson, Joe	C	1974-75	29	5	8	13	27	—	—	—	—	—
Rochon, Francois	LW	1973-77	255	71	60	131	95	14	2	2	4	0
Rogers, John	RW	1975-76	44	9	8	17	34	—	—	—	—	—
Rogers, Mike	C	1974-78	316	118	177	295	78	36	11	15	26	12
Rollins, Jerry	D	1975-77	123	9	17	26	371	—	—	—	—	—
Rombough, Lorne	LW	1973-74	3	1	2	3	0	—	—	—	—	—
Roselle, Bob	LW	1975-76	1	0	0	0	0	—	—	—	—	—
Rota, Randy	LW	1976-78	93	17	28	45	20	10	4	3	7	4
Rouleau, Michel	C	1972-75	115	13	35	48	289	3	0	0	0	4
Rousseau, Dunc	LW	1972-74	135	26	25	51	114	18	3	2	5	2
Roy, Pierre	D	1972-77	315	22	84	106	862	23	1	12	13	76
Ruhnke, Kent	RW	1976-78	72	19	20	39	4	5	2	0	2	0
Rupp, Duane	D	1974-76	114	3	42	45	78	7	0	2	2	0
Ruskowski, Terry	C	1974-78	294	63	188	251	550	44	17	24	41	151
Russell, Bob	C	1975-77	115	20	24	44	60	5	1	0	1	0
Ryan, Terry	D	1972-73	76	13	6	19	13	5	0	2	2	0
Rycroft, Al	RW	1972-73	7	0	2	2	0	—	—	—	—	—
Rydman, Blaine	D	1972-74	39	0	1	1	90	1	0	0	0	0
St. Sauveur, Claude	C	1972-78	252	104	105	209	115	5	1	0	1	0
Sandbeck, Cal	D	1977-78	11	1	2	3	39	5	0	0	0	10
Sanders, Frank	D	1972-73	76	8	8	16	94	4	0	1	1	0
Sanderson, Derek	C	1972-73	8	3	3	6	69	—	—	—	—	—
Sarner, Craig	RW	1975-76	1	0	0	0	0	—	—	—	—	—
Sarrazin, Dick	RW	1972-73	68	7	15	22	2	—	—	—	—	—
Sather, Glen	LW	1976-77	81	19	34	53	77	5	1	1	2	2
Scharf, Ted	RW	1972-77	238	16	21	37	343	14	0	0	0	5
Schella, John	D	1972-78	385	39	143	182	844	66	4	25	29	143
Schneider, Buzz	LW	1976-77	4	0	0	0	2	—	—	—	—	—
Schraefel, Jim	C	1973-74	33	1	1	2	0	5	0	3	3	0
Selby, Brit	LW	1972-75	152	23	51	74	73	23	4	7	11	15
Selwood, Brad	D	1972-78	389	38	131	169	509	63	6	12	18	81
Semenko, Dave	LW	1977-78	65	6	6	12	140	5	0	0	0	8
Sentes, Rick	LW	1972-77	337	137	143	280	233	41	14	8	22	45
Serafini, Ron	D	1975-76	16	0	2	2	15	—	—	—	—	—
Serviss, Tom	C	1972-76	287	38	78	116	101	11	0	0	0	0
Sheehan, Bobby	C	1972-76	240	75	110	185	45	5	1	3	4	0
Sheehy, Tim	RW	1972-78	433	177	173	350	156	39	16	21	37	26
Sheridan, John	C	1974-76	69	18	13	31	20	—	—	—	—	—
Sherrit, Jim	C	1973-76	193	63	72	135	59	27	8	10	18	8
Shirton, Glen	D	1973-74	4	0	0	0	0	—	—	—	—	—
Shmyr, John	D	1972-75	89	2	8	10	58	3	0	1	1	2
Shmyr, Paul	D	1972-78	431	53	209	262	741	30	4	13	17	84
Sicinski, Bob	C	1972-77	353	76	184	260	56	34	6	11	17	6
Simpson, Tom	RW	1972-77	313	125	84	209	160	22	6	2	8	5

153

	POS		REGULAR SEASON				PLAYOFFS				
			GP	G	A	TP	PIM	GP	G	A	TP	PIM
Sittler, Gary	D	1974-75	5	1	1	2	14	—	—	—	—	—
Sjoberg, Lars-Erik	D	1974-78	286	25	166	191	143	42	0	20	20	38
Slater, Peter	RW	1972-74	92	13	13	26	89	6	0	0	0	2
Sleep, Mike	RW	1975-77	22	4	2	6	6	3	0	0	0	0
Smedsmo, Dale	LW	1975-78	110	10	22	32	291	2	0	1	1	0
Smith, Brian	LW	1972-73	48	7	6	13	19	10	0	2	2	0
Smith, Guy	LW	1972-74	39	4	8	12	31	11	2	0	2	4
Smith, Rick	D	1973-76	200	20	89	109	260	23	2	8	10	28
Smith, Ross	LW	1974-75	15	1	6	7	19	—	—	—	—	—
Snell, Ron	RW	1973-75	90	24	25	49	40	4	0	0	0	0
Sobchuk, Dennis	C	1974-78	274	119	149	268	174	13	5	2	7	8
Sobchuk, Gene	LW	1974-76	81	24	19	43	37	5	0	0	0	0
Speck, Fred	C	1972-75	123	22	42	64	96	6	3	2	5	2
Speer, Bill	D	1972-74	135	4	26	30	70	—	—	—	—	—
Spencer, Irv	D	1972-74	73	2	28	30	49	4	0	0	0	4
Spring, Danny	C	1973-76	200	39	51	90	38	6	1	2	3	0
Spring, Frank	RW	1977-78	13	2	4	6	2	—	—	—	—	—
Stanfield, Jack	LW	1972-74	113	9	15	24	10	16	1	0	1	2
Stapleton, Pat	D	1973-78	375	26	212	238	187	34	2	21	23	38
Steele, Billy	RW	1975-77	84	11	22	33	21	2	0	0	0	0
Stephanson, Ken	D	1972-74	106	3	23	26	117	8	1	3	4	18
Stephenson, Bob	RW	1977-78	39	7	6	13	33	—	—	—	—	—
Stevens, Mike	D	1974-76	76	2	16	18	71	5	0	1	1	0
Stewart, John A.	LW	1975-77	95	15	24	39	45	3	0	0	0	0
Stewart, JC	C	1974-78	201	36	66	102	105	6	1	1	2	6
Stewart, Paul	D	1976-77	42	1	5	6	243	—	—	—	—	—
Stoughton, Blaine	RW	1976-78	158	71	78	149	103	4	0	3	3	2
Sullivan, Peter	C	1975-78	233	79	130	209	83	42	16	23	39	6
Sutherland, Bill	RW	1972-74	60	10	21	31	40	18	5	9	14	13
Sutherland, Steve	LW	1972-78	379	97	76	173	805	52	9	6	15	112
Swain, Garry	C	1974-77	171	22	33	55	70	25	3	5	8	56
Swenson, Cal	C	1972-74	102	12	25	37	21	15	1	5	6	7
Syvret, Dave	D	1975-77	38	1	11	12	24	—	—	—	—	—
Szura, Joe	C	1972-74	115	21	39	60	29	12	0	0	0	0
Tamminen, Juhani	LW	1975-77	130	17	43	60	22	1	0	0	0	0
Tannahill, Don	C	1974-77	222	58	76	134	34	20	4	9	13	8
Tardif, Marc	LW	1973-78	372	275	295	570	320	40	21	30	51	31
Taylor, Ted	LW	1972-78	421	123	164	287	600	63	18	21	39	147
Terbenche, Paul	D	1974-78	209	15	52	67	62	16	1	7	8	6
Tetreault, Jean	LW	1974-76	9	1	1	2	0	—	—	—	—	—
Thomas, Reg	LW	1973-78	348	89	99	188	177	16	8	9	17	8
Tidey, Alex	RW	1975-78	74	16	11	27	46	11	3	6	9	10
Titcomb, Gord	LW	1974-75	2	0	1	1	0	—	—	—	—	—
Tonelli, John	C	1975-78	224	64	86	150	278	34	11	14	25	38
Topolnisky, Craig	D	1977-78	10	0	2	2	4	—	—	—	—	—
Tremblay, J.C.	D	1972-78	398	60	320	380	118	34	2	23	25	4
Trevelyn, Tom	C	1974-75	20	0	2	2	4	—	—	—	—	—
Trognitz, Willie	LW	1977-78	29	2	1	3	94	—	—	—	—	—
Trooien, Jerry	C	1972-73	2	0	0	0	0	—	—	—	—	—
Trottier, Guy	RW	1972-75	174	62	75	137	89	17	6	7	13	4
Troy, James	RW	1975-76	68	2	0	2	174	4	0	0	0	29
Turkiewicz, Jim	D	1974-78	313	22	102	124	182	11	1	3	4	0
Ullman, Norm	C	1975-77	144	47	83	130	40	9	1	6	7	2
Van Horlick, John	D	1975-76	2	0	0	0	12	—	—	—	—	—
Veneruzzo, Gary	LW	1972-77	348	151	123	274	212	18	5	0	5	11
Viau, Pierre	D	1972-73	4	0	0	0	0	—	—	—	—	—
Volmar, Doug	RW	1974-75	10	0	1	1	4	—	—	—	—	—
Walker, Russ	RW	1973-76	214	52	40	92	319	13	2	0	2	46

	POS		REGULAR SEASON					PLAYOFFS				
			GP	G	A	TP	PIM	GP	G	A	TP	PIM
Wall, Bob	D	1972-76	255	23	89	112	113	26	1	8	9	8
Walsh, Brian	C	1976-77	5	0	2	2	12	—	—	—	—	—
Walter, Dave	C	1973-76	26	2	3	5	8	—	—	—	—	—
Walters, Ron	RW	1972-75	166	44	41	85	74	—	—	—	—	—
Walton, Mike	RW	1973-76	211	136	145	281	148	23	20	15	35	26
Walton, Rob	C	1973-76	150	40	71	111	54	—	—	—	—	—
Ward, Ron	C	1972-77	359	170	210	380	103	13	3	4	7	4
Warr, Steve	D	1972-74	72	3	8	11	79	4	0	0	0	0
Watson, Jim	D	1972-76	231	8	33	41	228	22	2	4	6	20
Webster, Tom	RW	1972-78	352	220	205	425	241	43	28	26	54	19
Weir, Wally	D	1976-78	82	3	17	20	244	28	2	7	9	63
West, Steve	C	1974-78	124	26	39	65	29	12	1	0	1	0
Westrum, Pat	D	1974-78	237	7	45	52	356	9	0	2	2	21
White, Alton	RW	1972-75	145	38	46	84	45	6	1	0	1	0
Whitlock, Bobby	LW	1972-76	244	81	98	179	155	—	—	—	—	—
Widing, Juha	C	1977-78	71	18	24	42	8	5	0	1	1	0
Wilkins, Barry	D	1976-78	130	6	45	51	154	4	0	1	1	2
Williams, Butch	RW	1976-77	29	3	10	13	16	—	—	—	—	—
Williams, Tommy	C	1972-74	139	31	58	89	20	19	6	14	20	12
Williamson, Gary	LW	1973-74	9	2	6	8	0	12	0	0	0	0
Willis, Hal	D	1972-76	92	4	23	27	183	—	—	—	—	—
Winograd, Bob	D	1972-77	60	1	12	13	23	—	—	—	—	—
Wiste, Jim	C	1972-76	228	64	108	172	80	14	3	9	12	13
Woytowich, Bob	D	1972-76	242	9	51	60	140	18	1	1	2	4
Wyrozub, Randy	C	1975-76	55	11	14	25	8	—	—	—	—	—
Young, Bill	LW	1972-74	142	28	30	58	140	5	1	1	2	4
Young, Howie	RW	1974-77	98	17	25	42	109	—	—	—	—	—
Zaine, Rod	C	1972-75	214	11	33	44	58	18	2	1	3	2
Zanussi, Joe	D	1972-74	149	7	43	50	106	18	2	5	7	6
Zrymiak, Jerry	D	1972-77	156	7	40	47	112	2	1	0	1	2
Zuk, Wayne	RW	1973-74	2	0	0	0	0	—	—	—	—	—
Zuke, Mike	C	1976-78	86	26	38	64	49	5	2	3	5	0

ALL-TIME WHA GOALTENDING STATISTICS

GOALIE	YEARS	REGULAR SEASON							PLAYOFFS				
		GP	W- L- T	SO	AS'TS	PIM	GP	GAA	W- L	SO	AS'TS	PIM
Abrahamsson, Christer	74-77	102	3.58	41- 46- 7	3	2	18	3	3.33	0- 1	0	0	0
Archambault, Yves	72-74	11	5.05	2- 7- 0	0	1	0	3	4.31	0- 2	0	0	0
Aubry, Serge	72-77	142	3.75	63- 55- 5	5	4	88	3	3.33	0- 0	0	0	0
Berglund, Bill	73-75	5	3.61	2- 1- 0	0	0	0						
Binkley, Les	72-76	80	3.72	30- 36- 2	1	0	0	10	5.17	3- 6	0	0	0
Blanchet, Bob	72-74	4	3.13	2- 2- 0	0	0	0						
Blum, Frank	72-74	7	3.02	1- 0- 0	0	0	0						
Broderick, Ken	76-78	73	3.95	29- 31- 2	4	3	0	2	7.50	0- 2	0	0	9
Brodeur, Richard	72-78	263	3.73	140-101- 9	5	9	2	5	3.17	1- 3	0	0	0
Bromley, Gary	76-78	67	3.49	31- 21- 3	3	1	19	48	3.45	26-21	3	2	4
Brown, Andy	74-77	86	3.94	25- 50- 3	3	2	6	5	1.57	4- 0	3	0	2
Brown, Ken	72-75	52	3.55	21- 19- 0	3	1	75						
Burchell, Randy	76-77	5	3.53	1- 0- 0	0	1	4						
Caron, Jacques	75-77	26	2.91	14- 6- 3	3	1	0	1	12.86	0- 1	0	0	0
Cheevers, Gerry	72-76	191	3.12	99- 78- 9	14	2	134	19	3.28	7-12	0	0	10
Cooley, Gaye	75-76	0						1	0.00	0- 0	0	0	30
Corsi, Jim	77-78	23	4.52	10- 7- 0	0	1	2						
Cottringer, Tom	72-73	2	3.93	1- 1- 0	0	0	0						
Coutu, Rich	73-76	24	4.11	9- 13- 1	0	0	0						
Curran, Mike	72-77	130	3.44	63- 50- 8	7	1	58	7	3.64	2- 5	0	0	10
Daley, Joe	72-78	285	3.30	160-102-10	12	10	45	46	3.28	30-15	2	3	30
Deguise, Michel	73-76	50	3.62	18- 18- 3	1	0	0						
Desjardins, Gerry	74-75	41	4.26	9- 28- 1	1	2	13						
Dion, Michel	74-78	119	3.26	52- 52- 5	5	5	28	7	3.56	2- 4	0	0	0
Donnelly, Peter	72-76	100	3.71	44- 44- 2	5	1	11						
Doyle, Gary	73-74	1	4.00	1- 0- 0	0	0	0						
Dryden, Dave	74-78	179	3.72	71- 96- 8	5	6	6	5	4.55	0- 4	0	0	0
Dumas, Rich	74-75	1	0.00	0- 0- 0	0	0	0						
Dyck, Ed	74-75	32	4.36	3- 21- 3	0	0	6						
Gardner, George	73-78	79	3.89	23- 45- 5	1	1	2	3	5.67	1- 2	0	0	0
Garrett, John	73-78	282	3.51	128-134-11	12	7	69	24	4.03	11-12	1	1	16
Gill, Andre	72-74	46	3.92	8- 31- 2	0	0	6	11	3.71	6- 5	1	0	4
Gillow, Russ	72-76	109	3.50	37- 47- 6	4	1	12	9	2.95	1- 2	0	0	0
Grahame, Ron	73-77	143	2.99	102- 37- 3	12	2	28	36	3.23	22-14	4	2	0
Gratton, Gilles	72-75	161	3.69	81- 66- 7	4	9	46	13	3.35	5- 5	1	0	5
Grigg, Chris	75-76	2	9.75	0- 0- 0	0	0	0						
Hebenton, Clay	75-77	58	4.28	17- 30- 3	0	0	2						
Hoganson, Paul	73-78	143	4.11	44- 71- 4	5	0	18	5	2.93	3- 2	1	1	0
Holden, William	73-74	2	3.43	0- 1- 0	0	0	0						
Holmqvist, Leif	75-76	19	3.00	6- 9- 3	0	0	2						

Name	Season	GP	Avg	W-L-T			GP	Avg	W-L-T		
Hughes, Bill	72-73	3	3.88	0-1-1	0	0	—	—	—	—	—
Humphreys, Ed	75-77	30	3.60	14-13-1	1	0	1	0.00	0-0	0	0
Inness, Gary	77-78	52	4.21	14-30-1	0	0	—	—	—	—	—
Johnson, Bob	75-77	42	3.63	17-22-1	1	0	—	—	—	—	—
Junkin, Joe	75-77	69	3.68	27-32-4	2	42	2	4.00	0-2	0	0
Kiely, John	75-76	22	4.31	6-8-1	2	9	—	—	—	—	—
Kurt, Gary	72-77	176	4.17	72-86-7	3	9	4	3.48	1-2	0	0
Landon, Bruce	72-77	122	3.46	50-50-9	10	12	8	3.24	4-2	0-1	0
LaPointe, Norm	75-78	77	4.09	30-37-3	2	36	4	3.52	0-3	0-0	2
Larsson, Curt	74-77	68	4.16	30-30-2	1	8	3	3.23	2-0	0	0
Lemelin, Jacques	72-73	9	4.00	3-4-0	3	14	—	—	—	—	—
Levasseur, Louis	75-78	82	3.35	37-35-7	5	6	14	2.89	8-6	1	4
Liut, Mike	77-78	27	4.25	8-12-0	1	0	—	—	—	—	—
Lockett, Ken	76-77	45	3.70	18-19-1	0	15	5	4.38	1-3	0	0
Mattsson, Markus	77-78	16	4.63	5-8-0	1	2	—	—	—	—	—
McCartan, Jack	72-75	42	3.69	16-19-1	0	19	4	3.94	1-2	0	0
McDuffe, Peter	77-78	12	4.34	1-6-1	0	0	—	—	—	—	—
McLeod, Don	72-78	332	3.33	157-144-15	11	34	31	3.23	18-13	1	6
McLeod, Jim	72-75	97	3.76	32-51-3	2	4	—	—	—	—	—
Menard, Paul	72-73	1	6.67	0-1-0	43	0	—	—	—	—	—
Mio, Ed	77-78	17	4.27	6-8-0	1	0	—	—	—	—	—
Newton, Cam	73-76	102	3.46	48-51-3	0	0	11	4.39	2-6	0	0
Norris, Jack	72-76	191	3.16	86-82-12	2	0	10	4.24	2-7	0	2
Ouimet, Ted	74-75	1	9.00	0-0-0	9	10	—	—	—	—	—
Paille, Marcel	72-73	15	4.81	2-8-0	5	0	—	—	—	—	—
Parent, Bernie	72-73	63	3.61	33-28-0	0	36	1	11.46	0-1	0	0
Park, Jim	75-78	54	3.70	23-23-4	2	14	1	2.57	0-1	0	0
Perrault, Bob	72-73	1	2.00	1-0-0	1	0	6	2.45	3-2	2	0
Plante, Jacques	74-75	31	3.32	15-14-1	0	2	—	—	—	—	—
Raeder, Cap	75-77	29	3.24	12-11-1	1	2	—	—	—	—	—
Rutledge, Wayne	72-78	175	3.25	93-72-7	2	39	15	2.59	7-8	2	0
Sanza, Nick	75-76	1	15.00	0-1-0	6	0	16	2.88	9-6	1	2
Shaw, Jim	74-76	37	4.36	11-16-2	4	0	—	—	—	—	—
Smith, Al	72-78	220	3.24	106-81-10	0	94	5	4.12	2-2	0	0
Sullivan, Danny	72-74	2	5.00	1-1-0	9	7	31	3.75	17-13	1	14
Tataryn, Dave	75-76	23	4.76	7-12-1	0	0	—	—	—	—	—
Tumilson, Gordon	75-78	3	4.34	0-2-0	0	2	—	—	—	—	—
Turnbull, Frank	75-78	4	5.42	0-2-0	0	0	—	—	—	—	—
Vien, Mario	75-76	26	5.13	4-14-3	0	2	—	—	—	—	—
Wakely, Ernie	72-78	297	3.25	149-120-20	16	17	31	3.76	15-16	2	0
Wetzel, Carl	72-73	1	3.00	0-1-0	6	0	—	—	—	—	—
Whidden, Bob	72-76	98	3.43	34-51-9	7	11	2	—	—	—	2
Wilkie, Ian	72-74	33	4.01	15-13-1	1	0	1	5.85	0-1	0	0
Wood, Wayne	74-78	98	3.88	38-36-3	2	26	1	6.15	0-0	0	0
Worthy, Chris	73-76	82	3.97	27-39-4	4	22	4	4.37	1-2	0	0
Zimmerman, Lynn	75-78	28	4.15	12-15-1	1	4	4	5.28	1-2	0	6

WORLD HOCKEY ASSOCIATION RECORDS
(through 1977-78)
TEAM RECORDS

MOST POINTS, ONE SEASON:
106 — Winnipeg, 1975-76
— Houston, 1974-75, 1975-76, 1976-77

MOST POINTS WON ON HOME ICE, ONE SEASON:
70 — Houston, 1976-77

MOST POINTS WON ON THE ROAD, ONE SEASON:
50 — Houston, 1974-75

FEWEST POINTS, ONE SEASON:
39 — Indianapolis, 1974-75

FEWEST POINTS WON ON HOME ICE, ONE SEASON:
26 — Indianapolis, 1974-75

FEWEST POINTS WON ON THE ROAD, ONE SEASON:
13 — Indianapolis, 1974-75
— Michigan/Baltimore, 1974-75

MOST WINS, ONE SEASON:
53 — Houston, 1974-75, 1975-76

MOST WINS ON HOME ICE, ONE SEASON:
33 — Houston, 1975-76, 1976-77
— Quebec, 1975-76

MOST WINS ON THE ROAD, ONE SEASON:
25 — Houston, 1974-75

FEWEST WINS, ONE SEASON:
18 — Indianapolis, 1974-75

FEWEST WINS ON HOME ICE, ONE SEASON:
13 — Indianapolis, 1974-75

FEWEST WINS ON THE ROAD, ONE SEASON:
5 — Indianapolis, 1974-75
— Calgary, 1976-77

MOST LOSSES, ONE SEASON:
57 — Indianapolis, 1974-75

MOST LOSSES ON HOME ICE, ONE SEASON:
26 — Indianapolis, 1974-75

MOST LOSSES ON THE ROAD, ONE SEASON:
32 — Michigan/Baltimore, 1974-75
— Edmonton, 1975-76
— Toronto, 1975-76

FEWEST LOSSES, ONE SEASON:
24 — Houston, 1976-77

FEWEST LOSSES ON HOME ICE, ONE SEASON:
3 — Houston, 1976-77

FEWEST LOSSES ON THE ROAD, ONE SEASON:
14 — Houston, 1974-75

MOST TIES, ONE SEASON:
9 — Cleveland, 1973-74

MOST TIES ON HOME ICE:
6 — Phoenix, 1975-76

MOST TIES ON THE ROAD:
    5 — Los Angeles, 1972-73
       — Cleveland, 1973-74
       — New England, 1975-76
       — Indianapolis, 1976-77
       — Calgary, 1976-77

FEWEST TIES, ONE SEASON:
    0 — Philadelphia, 1972-73
       — Los Angeles, 1973-74
       — Quebec, 1974-75
       — Houston, 1974-75, 1975-76

FEWEST TIES ON HOME ICE, ONE SEASON:
    0 — 1972-73, Philadelphia and Chicago
       — 1973-74, Vancouver and Los Angeles
       — 1974-75, Quebec, Toronto, Indianapolis, Minnesota, Houston
       — 1975-76, Quebec, Houston, Winnipeg, Cincinnati
       — 1976-77, All teams had at least one tie
       — 1977-78, All teams had at least one tie

FEWEST TIES ON THE ROAD, ONE SEASON:
    0 — 1972-73, Philadelphia and Quebec
       — 1973-74, Los Angeles and Quebec
       — 1974-75, Houston, Chicago, Vancouver and Quebec
       — 1975-76, Houston and Phoenix
       — 1976-77, San Diego
       — 1977-78, Winnipeg

MOST CONSECUTIVE NON-TIE GAMES:
    187 — Houston, between Feb. 10, 1974 and Oct. 19, 1976
       — (current streak — 38 games since Winnipeg played a 4-4 game in Winnipeg vs. New England, Jan. 20, 1978)

MOST CONSECUTIVE NON-TIE GAMES ON HOME ICE:
    107 — Houston, Between Nov. 28, 1973 and Oct. 19, 1976
       — (current streak — 33 games since New England was tied at Home by Indianapolis, Nov. 23, 1977)

MOST CONSECUTIVE NON-TIE ROAD GAMES:
    139 — Quebec, Between Nov. 29, 1974 and Dec. 3, 1976
       — (current streak — 69 games since Winnipeg played a tie game on the road (at Houston), Nov. 26, 1976)

MOST PENALTY MINUTES CALLED ON ONE TEAM IN A SINGLE SEASON:
    2,177 — Birmingham, 1977-78

FEWEST PENALTY MINUTES CALLED ON ONE TEAM IN A SEASON:
    673 — Winnipeg, 1973-74

MOST CONSECUTIVE GAMES PLAYED WITHOUT A LOSS:
    15 — Winnipeg between Jan. 29, 1978 and Mar. 1, 1978 (all wins)

MOST CONSECUTIVE GAMES WON:
    15 — Winnipeg between Jan. 29 and Mar. 1, 1978

MOST CONSECUTIVE GAMES LOST:
    13 — Indianapolis between Nov. 13 and Dec. 5, 1974

MOST CONSECUTIVE GAMES WITHOUT A WIN:
    17 — Toronto between Jan. 22 and Feb. 29, 1976 (15 losses and two ties)

MOST CONSECUTIVE HOME GAMES WITHOUT A LOSS:
    22 — Houston between Mar. 19 and Dec. 3, 1975 (includes Playoffs

and two seasons)

21 — Houston between Dec. 21, 1976 and Mar. 25, 1977 (single season record)

MOST CONSECUTIVE GAMES WON ON HOME ICE:
22 — Houston between Mar. 19 and Dec. 3, 1975 (includes Playoffs and two seasons)

21 — Houston between Dec. 21, 1976 and Mar. 25, 1977 (single season record)

MOST CONSECUTIVE HOME GAMES LOST:
7 — Vancouver between Oct. 21 and Nov. 13, 1973
— Indianapolis between Nov. 19 and Dec. 5, 1974
— Baltimore between Feb. 2 and Feb. 18, 1975

MOST CONSECUTIVE HOME GAMES WITHOUT A WIN:
8 — Denver between the opening of the season and Nov. 15, 1975 (seven losses and one tie)

MOST CONSECUTIVE ROAD GAMES WITHOUT A LOSS:
9 — Houston between Oct. 29 and Dec. 4, 1974 (all wins)
— Indianapolis between Mar. 6, 1976 to end of season (seven wins, two ties — Racers lost first game of the following season)

MOST CONSECUTIVE ROAD GAMES WON:
9 — Houston between Oct. 29 and Dec. 4, 1974

MOST CONSECUTIVE ROAD GAMES WITHOUT A WIN:
25 — Michigan/Baltimore between Oct. 19, 1974 and Feb. 1, 1975 (24 losses, one tie)

MOST CONSECUTIVE ROAD GAMES LOST:
14 — Los Angeles between Jan. 29, 1974 and end of season. Team moved to Michigan the following season and won its first road game.

MOST CONSECUTIVE TIE-GAMES:
3 — Indianapolis between Mar. 18 and Mar. 23, 1976

MOST CONSECUTIVE OVERTIME GAMES:
4 — Alberta between Feb. 23 and Mar. 10, 1973 (won two, lost two)
— Chicago between Mar. 5 and Mar. 10, 1973 (won one, lost two, tied one)
— Indianapolis between Mar. 18 and Mar. 25, 1976 (won one, tied three)

MOST GOALS SCORED IN ONE SEASON BY A TEAM:
381 — Winnipeg, 1977-78 (4.76 goals per game)

MOST GOALS AGAINST A TEAM IN ONE SEASON:
398 — Toronto, 1975-76 (4.91 goals per game)

FEWEST GOALS SCORED BY A TEAM IN ONE SEASON:
205 — Michigan/Baltimore, 1974-75 (2.63 per game)

FEWEST GOALS ALLOWED BY A TEAM IN ONE SEASON:
219 — Houston, 1973-74 (2.81 per game)

MOST SCORING POINTS IN A SINGLE SEASON:
1,010 — Winnipeg, 1977-78, 381 goals — 629 assists (12.6 points per game)

FEWEST SCORING POINTS IN A SINGLE SEASON:
540 — Michigan/Baltimore, 1974-75, 205 goals — 335 assists (6.9 points per game)

MOST ASSISTS AWARDED A TEAM IN A SINGLE SEASON:
629 — Winnipeg, 1977-78 (1.65 assists per goal scored)
628 — Quebec, 1975-76 (1.69 assists per goal scored)

FEWEST ASSISTS AWARDED A TEAM IN A SINGLE SEASON:
335 — Michigan/Baltimore, 1974-75 (1.63 assists per goal)
MOST SHUTOUTS IN ONE SEASON:
7 — Houston, 1976-77
MOST SHUTOUTS ON HOME ICE, ONE SEASON:
5 — Minnesota, 1972-73
  — Houston, 1976-77
  — Cincinnati, 1976-77
MOST SHUTOUTS ON THE ROAD, ONE SEASON:
3 — Houston, 1974-75
FEWEST SHUTOUTS ONE SEASON:
0 — Quebec, 1974-75 and 1977-78
  — Ottawa, 1972-73
  — Phoenix, 1976-77
  — Indianapolis, 1977-78
FEWEST SHUTOUTS ON HOME ICE, ONE SEASON:
0 — Ottawa, 1972-73
  — Houston, 1972-73
  — Philadelphia, 1972-73
  — New York/New Jersey, 1973-74
  — Quebec, 1974-75, 1977-78
  — Phoenix, 1976-77
  — Indianapolis, 1977-78
FEWEST SHUTOUTS ON THE ROAD, ONE SEASON:
0 — Minnesota, 72/73
  — Quebec, 72/73, 74/75, 77/78
  — New York, 72/73
  — Chicago, 72/73, 73/74, 74/75 (never shutout an opponent on the road)
  — Ottawa, 72/73, Toronto, 75/76, Birmingham, 77/78
  — Alberta, 72/73, Edmonton, 75/76
  — Indianapolis, 74/75, 75/76, 76/77, 77/78 (never shutout an opponent on the road)
  — Vancouver, 74/75, Calgary, 75/76, 76/77
  — Cleveland, 75/76
  — Phoenix, 75/76, 76/77
  — Cincinnati, 77/78
MOST TIMES A TEAM HAS BEEN SHUTOUT IN ONE SEASON:
8 — Los Angeles, 73/74
  — Indianapolis, 74/75
MOST TIMES A TEAM HAS BEEN SHUTOUT ON HOME ICE, ONE SEASON:
5 — Los Angeles 73/74
  — Indianapolis 74/75
MOST TIMES A TEAM HAS BEEN SHUTOUT ON THE ROAD, ONE SEASON:
6 — Philadelphia, 72/73
FEWEST TIMES A TEAM HAS BEEN SHUTOUT, ONE SEASON:
0 — Toronto, 73/74, 74/75
  — Minnesota, 73/74, 74/75
  — Quebec, 74/75, 77/78
  — Houston, 74/75
  — San Diego, 75/76

— Winnipeg, 77/78

FEWEST TIMES A TEAM HAS BEEN SHUTOUT ON HOME ICE, ONE SEASON:
0 — Quebec, 72/73, 73/74, 74/75, 75/76, 76/77, 77/78
— Ottawa, 72/73, Toronto, 73/74, 74/75, 75/76, Birmingham, 76/77, 77/78
— Philadelphia, 72/73
— Winnipeg, 72/73, 74/75, 76/77, 77/78
— Minnesota, 72/73, 73/74, 74/75
— New England, 72/73, 74/75
— Edmonton, 73/74, 75/76, 77/78
— Cleveland, 73/74
— Houston, 74/75, 75/76
— San Diego, 74/75, 75/76
— Cincinnati, 75/76, 76/77
— Indianapolis, 77/78

FEWEST TIMES A TEAM HAS BEEN SHUTOUT ON THE ROAD, ONE SEASON:
0 — New York, 72/73, San Diego, 75/76
— Minnesota, 73/74, 74/75
— Houston, 73/74, 74/75
— Toronto, 73/74, 74/75
— Quebec, 74/75, 77/78
— Winnipeg, 75/76, 77/78

MOST CONSECUTIVE GAMES NOT SHUTOUT:
200 — Minnesota between Feb. 9, 1973 and Dec. 12, 1975 (Current streak — 95 games, Winnipeg was last shutout Mar. 15, 1977 by Edmonton at Winnipeg)

MOST CONSECUTIVE HOME GAMES NOT SHUTOUT:
238 — Birmingham (Ottawa/Toronto) has never been shutout on home ice (Total, including playoffs — 249 games)
— Quebec has never been shutout on home ice during regular season play
(They were shutout once in the playoffs — by Houston May 10, 1975)

MOST CONSECUTIVE ROAD GAMES NOT SHUTOUT:
106 — Ottawa/Toronto between Feb. 15, 1973 and Dec. 27, 1975 (Current streak — 54 games — Winnipeg was last shutout on the road Feb. 11, 1977 at Cincinnati, 4-0)

MOST POWERPLAY OPPORTUNITIES, ONE SEASON:
394 — Winnipeg, 75/76

MOST POWERPLAY GOALS, ONE SEASON:
90 — Winnipeg, 76/77

MOST GOALS ALLOWED WHILE ON POWERPLAY, ONE SEASON:
16 — Winnipeg, 74/75

MOST PROFICIENT POWERPLAY, ONE SEASON:
30.9% — Quebec, 75/76 (77 goals in 249 chances)

FEWEST POWERPLAY OPPORTUNITIES, ONE SEASON:
188 — Houston, 72/73

FEWEST POWERPLAY GOALS, ONE SEASON:
38 — Cleveland, 74/75
— New England, 74/75
— Calgary, 76/77

FEWEST GOALS ALLOWED WHILE ON POWERPLAY, ONE SEASON:
1 — Houston, 72/73

LEAST PROFICIENT POWERPLAY, ONE SEASON:
14.7% — Calgary, 76/77 (38 goals in 258 chances)
MOST SHORTHANDED SITUATIONS, ONE SEASON:
372 — Houston, 74/75
MOST GOALS SCORED WHILE SHORTHANDED, ONE SEASON:
20 — Minnesota, 73/74
MOST GOALS ALLOWED WHILE SHORTHANDED, ONE SEASON:
89 — Phoenix, 75/76
MOST EFFICIENT PENALTY-KILLING, ONE SEASON:
86.5% — New England, 74/75 (29 goals allowed in 215 situations)
FEWEST SHORTHANDED SITUATIONS, ONE SEASON:
194 — Quebec, 73/74
FEWEST GOALS SCORED WHILE SHORTHANDED, ONE SEASON:
1 — Quebec, 73/74
— Edmonton, 76/77
FEWEST GOALS ALLOWED WHILE SHORTHANDED, ONE SEASON:
29 — New England, 74/75
LEAST EFFICIENT PENALTY-KILLING, ONE SEASON:
70.3% — Cincinnati, 77/78 (76 goals allowed in 256 situations)
MOST 100-OR-MORE POINT SCORERS FROM ONE TEAM IN ONE SEASON:
5 — Quebec 75/76. Marc Tardif-148, Real Cloutier-114, Chris Bordeleau-109, Rejean Houle-103, Serge Bernier-102
MOST 60-OR-MORE GOAL SCORERS FROM ONE TEAM, ONE SEASON:
2 — Quebec, 75/76. Marc Tarduf-71, Real Cloutier-60
MOST 50-OR-MORE GOAL SCORERS FROM ONE TEAM, ONE SEASON:
3 — Quebec, 75/76. Marc Tardif-71, Real Cloutier-60, Rejean Houle-51
MOST 40-OR-MORE GOAL SCORERS FROM ONE TEAM, ONE SEASON:
4 — San Diego, 74/75. Andre Lacroix-41, Wayne Rivers-54, Rick Sentes-44, Gene Peacosh-43
— Cincinnati, 76/77. Rich Leduc-52, Blaine Stoughton-52, Dennis Sobchuk-44, Rick Dudley-41
— Quebec, 76/77. Real Cloutier-66, Marc Tardif-49, Serge Bernier-43, Paulin Bordeleau-42
MOST 30-OR-MORE GOAL SCORERS FROM ONE TEAM, ONE SEASON:
6 — Houston, 73/74. Frank Hughes-42, Mark Howe-38, Larry Lund-33, Gordie Howe-31, Jim Sherrit-30, Murray Hall-30
MOST 20-OR-MORE GOAL SCORERS FROM ONE TEAM, ONE SEASON:
10 — Houston, 74/75. Frank Hughes-48, Andre Hinse-39, Larry Lund-33, Gordie Howe-34, Mark Howe-36, Ted Taylor-26, Rich Preston-20, Don Larway-22, Jim Sherrit-22, Gord Labossiere-23
MOST TIMES PLAYERS HAVE HAD 4-OR-MORE GOAL NIGHTS FOR ONE TEAM, ONE SEASON:
4 — Philadelphia, 72/73. Andre Lacroix twice, Danny Lawson twice
— Toronto, 74/75. Tom Simpson three times, Jeff Jacques once
— Winnipeg, 76/77. Anders Hedberg three times, Perry Miller once
MOST TIMES 4-OR-MORE GOAL NIGHTS HAVE BEEN SCORED AGAINST ONE TEAM, ONE SEASON:
2 — Chicago, 72/73
— Quebec, 73/74
— Winnipeg, 73/74, 76/77

— Edmonton, 76/77
— San Diego, 76/77
— Indianapolis, 77/78

MOST TIMES PLAYERS HAVE HAD 3-OR-MORE GOAL NIGHTS FOR ONE TEAM, ONE SEASON:
14 — Quebec, 76/77

MOST TIMES 3-OR-MORE GOAL NIGHTS HAVE BEEN SCORED AGAINST A TEAM, ONE SEASON:
16 — Indianapolis, 77/78

LONGEST SHUTOUT SEQUENCE (AMOUNT OF TIME BETWEEN OPPONENT GOALS):
228 Minutes, 10 Seconds — Winnipeg between 8:25 of first period in game with Denver, Oct. 24, 1975 and 16:35 of third period in game with Quebec Nov. 2, 1975. Includes shutout games against Phoenix, Oct. 26 and Cincinnati, Oct. 30, 1975.

LONGEST TIME ONE TEAM HAS FAILED TO SCORE:
190 Minutes, 21 Seconds — Calgary. Between 13:05 of second period at New England, Mar. 18, 1977 and 3:26 of third period of Birmingham, Mar. 22, 1977. Included being shutout by Quebec, Mar. 19 and New England Mar. 20, 1977.

MOST GOALS SCORED BY BOTH TEAMS IN ONE GAME:
19 — Toronto 11 at Denver 8, Nov. 13, 1975
— Toronto 9 at Cleveland 10, Nov. 30, 1975

MOST GOALS SCORED BY ONE TEAM IN ONE GAME:
12 — Minnesota vs. Winnipeg, Jan. 27, 1974. Minn. 12, Wpg. 2
— Phoenix vs. Indianapolis, Mar. 1, 1975. Phx. 12, Indy. 2
— Quebec at Winnipeg, Dec. 26, 1976. Que. 12, Wpg. 3
— Birmingham vs. Cincinnati, Nov. 24, 1977. Bir. 12, Cin. 2

MOST GOALS SCORED BY A LOSING TEAM:
9 — Toronto lost to Cleveland 10-9, Nov. 30, 1975

MOST GOALS SCORED IN TWO CONSECUTIVE GAMES BY ONE TEAM:
21 — Winnipeg defeated Toronto 10-1, Nov. 1, 1974 and Michigan 11-3, Nov. 3, 1974

MOST GOALS SCORED IN THREE CONSECUTIVE GAMES BY ONE TEAM:
27 — Winnipeg defeated Phoenix 6-5, Oct. 30, 1974, Toronto 10-1, Nov. 1, 1974 and Michigan 11-3, Nov. 3, 1974
— Winnipeg defeated Toronto 10-1, Nov. 1, Michigan 11-3, Nov. 3, and Minnesota 6-4, Nov. 5, 1974

MOST GOALS ALLOWED IN TWO CONSECUTIVE GAMES BY ONE TEAM:
21 — Quebec lost to Cincinnati 11-7, Dec. 21 and 10-4 to San Diego, Dec. 23, 1975

MOST GOALS ALLOWED IN THREE CONSECUTIVE GAMES BY ONE TEAM:
28 — New York lost to Los Angeles 9-2, Jan. 28, to Alberta 11-3, Jan. 30 and 8-5, Feb. 1, 1973
— Quebec defeated Calgary 8-7, Dec. 20, lost to Cincinnati 11-7, Dec. 21 and lost to San Diego 10-4, Dec. 23, 1975

FEWEST GOALS BY BOTH TEAMS IN ONE GAME:
0 — Cleveland at Chicago, January 8, 1974
— New England at Minnesota, December 17, 1975

— Edmonton at Houston, December 3, 1976

FEWEST GOALS SCORED IN THREE CONSECUTIVE GAMES BY ONE TEAM:
- 1 — Indianapolis lost three games 5-0, 2-1 and 10-0 between Nov. 15 and Nov. 19, 1974
  - Chicago lost three games 4-0, 3-0 and 3-1 between Jan. 6 and Jan. 13, 1974
  - Winnipeg lost three games 7-1, 3-0 and 4-0 between Feb. 26 and Mar. 1, 1974
  - Birmingham lost three games 9-0, 7-0 and 4-1 between Feb. 8 and Feb. 14, 1978

MOST POINTS BY TWO TEAMS IN ONE GAME:
- 50 — Toronto defeated Denver 11-8 on Nov. 13, 1974 with Toronto collecting 19 assists, and Denver 12
  - Cleveland defeated Toronto 10-9 on Nov. 30, 1975 with Cleveland collecting 17 assists and Toronto 14

MOST POINTS BY ONE TEAM IN A GAME:
- 34 — Minnesota defeated Winnipeg 12-2, Jan. 27, 1974 collecting 22 assists

MOST PENALTIES CALLED ON BOTH TEAMS IN ONE GAME:
- 46 — Birmingham at Winnipeg, Mar. 12, 1978. Birmingham was called for 20 minors, 1 major and 7 misconducts. Winnipeg was called for 11 minors, 1 major and 6 misconducts. Winnipeg won game, 3-2.

MOST PENALTY MINUTES CALLED ON BOTH TEAMS IN ONE GAME:
- 228 — Cleveland at Indianapolis, Mar. 8, 1975. Cleveland won game 6-5 and was called for 11 minors, 5 majors and 7 misconducts or 117 minutes. Indianapolis was called for 111 minutes on 8 minors, 5 majors and 7 misconducts.

MOST PENALTIES CALLED ON ONE TEAM IN A GAME:
- 28 — Birmingham, at Winnipeg Nov. 26, 1977. 16 minors, 4 majors, 8 misconducts. Won game 4-3
  - Birmingham, at Winnipeg Mar. 12, 1978. 20 minors, 1 major, 7 misconducts. Lost game 3-2

MOST PENALTY MINUTES BY ONE TEAM IN ONE GAME:
- 137 — Phoenix, Feb. 7, 1975 vs. Minnesota in 4-1 win. 11 minors, 7 majors, 8 misconducts

MOST CONSECUTIVE GOALS BY A TEAM IN A SINGLE GAME:
- 11 — Winnipeg, Feb. 1, 1977 vs. Edmonton in 11-1 win

MOST CONSECUTIVE GOALS BY A TEAM:
- 17 — Cincinnati. Scored final three goals vs. Houston, Dec. 10 in 6-2 win, all eight in 8-0 win vs. Phoenix, Dec. 12, all five in 5-0 win vs. Minnesota, Dec. 15 and the first goal in 4-3 loss at Minnesota, Dec. 19, 1976.

MOST CONSECUTIVE GAMES WITH AN EMPTY NET GOAL:
- 3 — New England. Scored goals after opposition had pulled goalie for an extra forward in games vs. Edmonton, Nov. 10, vs. Indianapolis, Nov. 12 and at Indianapolis, Nov. 15, 1977

MOST PLAYERS WITH MULTIPLE GOAL NIGHTS BY ONE TEAM IN A SINGLE GAME:
- 6 — Phoenix, Mar. 1, 1975 vs. Indianapolis in 12-2 win. Two goals each were scored by Dennis Sobchuk, Robbie Ftorek, Jim Boyd, Michel

Cormier, John Gray and Bob Mowat

MOST POWERPLAY GOALS SCORED BY A TEAM IN ONE GAME:
- 6 — Indianapolis, Dec. 4, 1975 vs. Cincinnati in 7-1 win
- — Calgary, Mar. 9, 1976 vs. Quebec in 7-4 win
- — Winnipeg, Mar. 10, 1976 vs. Quebec in 10-3 win

MOST POWERPLAY GOALS SCORED IN TWO CONSECUTIVE GAMES BY ONE TEAM: (and) MOST GOALS ALLOWED WHILE SHORTHANDED BY ONE TEAM IN TWO CONSECUTIVE GAMES:
- 11 — Winnipeg scored 11 powerplay goals in back to back games with Quebec, Mar. 10 and Mar. 12, 1976

MOST POWERPLAY OPPORTUNITIES BY TWO TEAMS IN ONE GAME:
- 21 — Cincinnati at Indianapolis, Dec. 4, 1975. Indianapolis had 12 chances, Cincinnati, 9. Indy scored six powerplay goals, Cincinnati none and Indy won game 7-1.

NOTE: Soviet All Stars and Houston Aeros had a total of 26 powerplays in exhibition game played at Houston, Dec. 28, 1977. Soviets scored 4 goals in 24 chances to win game 7-3. Houston scored no goals in two chances.

MOST POWERPLAY OPPORTUNITIES BY ONE TEAM IN A GAME:
- 13 — Winnipeg, Oct. 21, 1975 vs. Cincinnati. Scored 3 pp goals to win game 7-0
- — Winnipeg, Mar. 10, 1976 vs. Quebec. Scored 6 powerplay goals to win 10-3
- — Winnipeg, Mar. 27, 1977 at Houston. Scored 4 powerplay goals to win 5-3

NOTE: Soviet All-Stars had 24 chances in exhibition game at Houston, Dec. 28, 1977. Eight of the 24 were two-man advantages. Soviet scored four powerplay goals in 7-3 win, three with the two man advantage. Soviets played 25 minutes, 42 seconds with a man advantage. Houston played 3 minutes nine seconds with man advantage.

MOST SHORTHANDED GOALS SCORED BY A TEAM IN ONE GAME:
- 3 — Minnesota, Mar. 6, 1974 in 8-6 win over New England
- — Winnipeg, Nov. 1, 1974 in 10-1 win over Toronto
- — Phoenix, Jan. 22, 1975 in 8-5 win over Chicago
- — Houston, Mar. 27, 1975 in 8-0 win over Winnipeg
- — Indianapolis, Nov. 27, 1976 in 8-2 win at Quebec
- — Quebec, Jan. 22, 1977 in 5-3 win over Calgary

MOST SHOTS ON GOAL BY BOTH TEAMS IN A GAME:
- 107 — Michigan at Winnipeg, Nov. 29, 1974. Michigan had 53 shots, Winnipeg 54. Wpg. won 7-6
- — San Diego at Toronto, Mar. 14, 1975. San Diego had 48 shots, Toronto 59. SD won 6-4

MOST SHOTS TAKEN BY ONE TEAM IN A GAME:
- 64 — San Diego, Dec. 23, 1975 vs. Quebec in 10-4 win

FEWEST SHOTS ON GOAL BY BOTH TEAMS IN A SINGLE GAME:
- 33 — Winnipeg at San Diego, Oct. 17, 1976. Winnipeg had 14 shots, San Diego, 19. SD won 3-1

FEWEST SHOTS TAKEN BY A TEAM IN A GAME:
- 11 — Indianapolis, Dec. 18, 1975 at Phoenix in 7-1 loss
- — Edmonton, Dec. 16, 1976 at San Diego in 3-0 loss

FEWEST SHOTS TAKEN BY A WINNING TEAM:
- 13 — New England at Los Angeles, Dec. 14, 1972 in 5-2 win

MOST SHOTS TAKEN BY A LOSING TEAM:
  59 — Toronto, Mar. 14, 1975 vs. San Diego in 6-4 loss
MOST GOALS SCORED BY BOTH TEAMS IN ONE PERIOD:
  9 — New England at Philadelphia, Dec. 16. 1972, third period. NE scored 5, Philly 4 in 10-6 Philadelphia win
  — Quebec at Ottawa, Jan. 9, 1973, first period. Quebec scored 4, Ottawa 5 in 7-5 Ottawa win
  — Los Angeles at New England, Jan. 13, 1974, first period. LA scored 4, New England 5 in 9-6 New England win
  — Houston at Winnipeg, Mar. 29, 1974, third period. Houston scored 3, Wpg. 6 in 7-5 Winnipeg win
  — San Diego at Cincinnati, Nov. 8, 1975, second period. SD scored 3, Cincy 6. Cincinnati won 7-4
  — Winnipeg at Indianapolis, Mar. 4, 1978, second period. Wpg. scored 5, Indy 4 in 8-6 Indianapolis win
MOST GOALS SCORED BY ONE TEAM IN A PERIOD:
  8 — Toronto, Dec. 9, 1973 in third period of 10-1 win vs. Minnesota
MOST PENALTIES BY BOTH TEAMS IN ONE PERIOD:
  37 — Birmingham at Winnipeg, Nov. 27, 1977. Birmingham has 12 minors, 4 majors and eight misconducts. Winnipeg had 7 minors, 4 majors, and 2 misconducts in third period of 4-3 Birmingham overtime win.
MOST PENALTY MINUTES BY BOTH TEAMS IN ONE PERIOD:
  192 — Cleveland at Indianapolis, Mar. 8, 1975. In the third period Cleveland received 94 minutes, Indianapolis 98. Cleveland won 6-5.
MOST PENALTIES ON ONE TEAM IN A SINGLE PERIOD: (and)
MOST PENALTY MINUTES BY ONE TEAM IN A SINGLE PERIOD:
  24 Penalties, 124 Minutes — Birmingham, Nov. 24, 1977 in third period at Winnipeg received 12 minors, 4 majors and 8 misconducts but won the game in overtime, 4-3.
MOST SHOTS ON GOAL BY BOTH TEAMS IN ONE PERIOD:
  41 — Indianapolis at Toronto, Feb 9 75. second period, Indy had 17 shots to 24 by Toronto. Toronto won game 7-5.
MOST SHOTS ON GOAL BY ONE TEAM IN A PERIOD:
  32 — San Diego, Dec 23 75, first period, San Diego defeated Quebec 10-4.
  Quebec, Jan 6 78, third period, Quebec lost at Cincinnati 5-3.
FEWEST SHOTS ON GOAL BY BOTH TEAMS:
  7 — Cleveland at Los Angeles, Nov 16 73, Los Angeles had 5 shots, Cleveland 2. Cleveland won game in overtime 4-3.
FEWEST SHOTS ON GOAL BY A TEAM IN ONE PERIOD:
  0 — New York, Nov 5 72 vs. Winnipeg, first period in game won by Winnipeg 3-1.
  Indianapolis, Mar 23 76 at San Diego, second period in game that ended in 8-8 tie.
FASTEST TWO GOALS BY TWO TEAMS:
  3 seconds — New England at Birmingham, Mar 10 78. Ken Linseman (B) scored at 3:00 and Gordie Howe (N) at 3:03 of first period in game won by New England in overtime 5-4.

FASTEST THREE GOALS BY TWO TEAMS:
27 seconds — New England at New York, Nov 29 72. John French (NE) scored at 12:53, Ron Ward (NY) at 13:11 and 13:20 of second period in game won by New York 7-6.

FASTEST FOUR GOALS BY TWO TEAMS:
54 seconds — Birmingham at Indianapolis, Apr 9 78. Claude St. Sauveur (I) scored at 18:43, Rod Langway (B) at 19:05, Ken Linseman (B) at 19:18 and Michel Parizeau (I) at 19:37 of third period of game won by Birmingham 9-7. The two Birmingham goals were scored into an empty net.

FASTEST FIVE GOALS BY TWO TEAMS:
2 minutes, 4 seconds — Winnipeg at Indianapolis, Mar 4 78. Rusty Patenaude (I) scored at 6:15, Dave Kryskow (W) at 6:41, Kent Nilsson (W) at 7:17, Ulf Nilsson (W) at 8:04 and Claude St. Sauveur (I) at 8:19 of second period in game won by Indianapolis 8-6.

FASTEST TWO GOALS BY ONE TEAM:
4 seconds — New England Dec 16 72 at Philadelphia. Terry Caffery scored at 2:49 and Brit Selby at 2:53 of third period in game won by New England 10-6.

FASTEST THREE GOALS BY ONE TEAM:
30 seconds — New England Mar 21 78 vs. Indianapolis. Gordie Howe scored at 14:25, Mike Antonovich at 14:36 and John McKenzie at 14:55 of second period of game won by New England 6-3.

FASTEST FOUR GOALS BY ONE TEAM:
1 minute, 45 seconds — Alberta vs. New York, Jan 30 73. Rusty Patenaude scored at 10:48, Doug Barrie at 11:48, Steve Carlyle at 12:00 and Jim Harrison at 12:33 of third period of game won by Alberta 11-3.

FASTEST FIVE GOALS BY ONE TEAM:
4 minutes, 48 seconds — Alberta Jan 30 73 vs. New York. Bernie Blanchette scored at 7:45, Rusty Patenaude at 10:48, Doug Barrie at 11:48, Steve Carlyle at 12:00 and Jim Harrison at 12:33 of third period in game won by Alberta 11-3.

FASTEST TWO POWERPLAY GOALS SCORED BY A TEAM:
11 seconds — Birmingham Nov 27 77 vs. Cincinnati. Tony Cassolato scored at 3:43 and Peter Marrin at 3:54 of third period in game won by Birmingham 12-2.

FASTEST THREE POWERPLAY GOALS BY ONE TEAM:
1 minute, 34 seconds — Cincinnati Feb 8 78 at Edmonton. Rich Leduc scored at 12:36, Claude Larose at 13:25 and Ron Plumb at 14:10 of third period in game that ended in 6-6 tie.

FASTEST TWO GOALS FROM THE START OF THE GAME BY TWO TEAMS:
43 seconds — Phoenix at New England, Mar 13 75. Robbie Ftorek (P) scored at 0:12 and Don Blackburn (N) at 0:43 in game that ended in 5-5 tie.

FASTEST THREE GOALS FROM THE START OF THE GAME BY TWO TEAMS:
2 minutes, 12 seconds — Vancouver at Toronto, Jan 27 74. Mike Chernoff (V) scored at 1:27, Wayne Dillon (T) at 1:58 and Tom

168

Simpson (T) at 2:12 in game won by Toronto 9-7.

FASTEST FOUR GOALS FROM THE START OF THE GAME BY TWO TEAMS:

3 minutes, 44 seconds — New England at Winnipeg, Oct 10 76. Ulf Nilsson (W) scored at 0:35, Rosaire Paiement (N) at 1:55, Nilsson again at 2:34 and Dan Bolduc (N) at 3:44 in game won by Winnipeg 5-2.

FASTEST FIVE GOALS FROM THE START OF THE GAME BY TWO TEAMS:

6 minutes, 1 second — Winnipeg at Denver, Oct 16 75. Willy Lindstrom (W) scored at 1:00, Veli Pekka Ketola (W) at 1:59 and 3:10, Bill Lesuk (W) at 5:27 and Francois Rochon at 6:01 in game won by Winnipeg at 7-3.

FASTEST SIX GOALS FROM THE START OF THE GAME BY TWO TEAMS:

6 minutes, 15 seconds — Winnipeg at Denver, Oct 16 75. Willy Lindstrom (W) scored at 1:00, Veli Pekka Ketola (W) at 1:59 and 3:10, Bill Lesuk (W) at 5:27, Francois Rochon (D) at 6:01 and Larry Bignell (D) at 6:15 of game won by Winnipeg 7-3.

FASTEST TWO GOALS SCORED BY TWO TEAMS FROM THE START OF THE SECOND PERIOD:

58 seconds — Houston at Los Angeles, Feb 15 74. Jim Sherrit (H) scored at 24 seconds and Gary Veneruzzo at 58 seconds in second period of game won by Houston 6-4.

FASTEST THREE GOALS SCORED BY TWO TEAMS FROM THE START OF THE SECOND PERIOD:

1 minute — Edmonton at Cincinnati, Oct 23 75. Rick Dudley (C) scored at 0:12 and 0:20, Rosaire Paiment (E) at 1:00 of second period of game won by Cincinnati 6-4.

FASTEST FOUR GOALS SCORED BY TWO TEAMS FROM THE START OF THE SECOND PERIOD:

1 minute, 18 seconds — Edmonton at Cincinnati, Oct 23 75. Rick Dudley (C) scored at 0:12 and 0:20, Rusty Patenaude (E) at 1:00 and Steve Andrascik (C) at 1:18 of second period in game won by Cincinnati at 6-4.

FASTEST FIVE GOALS SCORED BY TWO TEAMS FROM THE START OF THE SECOND PERIOD:

4 minutes, 19 seconds — Edmonton at Cincinnati, Oct 23 75. Rick Dudley (C) scored at 0:12 and 0:20, Rosaire Paiement (E) at 1:00, Steve Andrascik (C) at 1:18 and Skip Krake (E) at 4:19 of second period of game won by Cincinnati 6-4.

FASTEST TWO GOALS SCORED BY TWO TEAMS FROM THE START OF THE THIRD PERIOD:

45 seconds — Quebec at Cleveland, Dec 27 74. Rick Leduc (C) scored at 0:27 and Serge Bernier (Q) at 0:45 of third period of game won by Cleveland 4-3.

FASTEST THREE GOALS SCORED BY TWO TEAMS FROM THE START OF THE THIRD PERIOD:

1 minute, 55 seconds — Indianapolis at Phoenix, Mar 2 76. Robbie Ftorek (P) scored at 0:31, Dave Gorman (P) at 1:31 and Blair

MacDonald (I) at 1:55 of third period of game won by Phoenix 5-2.

FASTEST FOUR GOALS SCORED BY TWO TEAMS FROM THE START OF THE THIRD PERIOD:
3 minutes, 17 seconds — New England at Philadelphia, Dec 16 72. Larry Pleau (N) scored at 1:03, Terry Caffery (N) at 2:49, Brit Selby (N) at 2:53 and Danny Lawson at 3:17 of third period in game won by NE 10-6.

FASTEST FIVE GOALS SCORED BY TWO TEAMS FROM START OF THIRD PERIOD:
4 minutes, 13 seconds — New England at Houston, Feb 17 76. Larry Lund (H) scored at 1:38, Don Borgeson (N) at 2:29, Ted Taylor (H) at 3:21, Bob Charlesbois (N) at 3:57 and Rosaire Paiement (N) at 4:13 of third period in game won by Houston 4-3.

FASTEST GOAL FROM THE START OF A GAME BY A CLUB:
5 seconds — Cleveland, Feb 19 75 vs. Minnesota. Russ Walker scored at 0:05 in game won by Minnesota 5-3.

FASTEST TWO GOALS BY A TEAM, FROM THE START OF A GAME:
28 seconds — Minnesota, Feb 17 73 at Cleveland. Mike McMahon scored at 0:19 and George Morrison at 0:28 in game won by Minnesota 7-3.

FASTEST THREE GOALS BY A TEAM FROM THE START OF THE GAME:
2 minutes, 45 seconds — Edmonton Oct 14 73 vs. Houston. Jim Harrison scored at 0:13, Ron Climie at 0:35 and Ken Baird at 2:45 in game won by Edmonton 5-2.

FASTEST FOUR GOALS BY A TEAM FROM THE START OF A GAME:
5 minutes, 27 seconds — Winnipeg Oct 16 75 at Denver. Willy Lindstrom scored at 1:00, Veli Pekka Ketola at 1:59 and 3:10 and Bill Lesuk at 5:27 in game won by Winnipeg 7-3.

FASTEST FIVE GOALS SCORED BY A TEAM FROM THE START OF A GAME:
11 minutes, 4 seconds — Winnipeg Oct 29 76 vs. Edmonton. Ulf Nilsson scored at 3:11, Willy Lindstrom at 5:25, Barry Long at 6:41, Veli Pekka Ketola at 9:13 and Bill Lesuk at 11:04 in game won by Winnipeg 11-3.

FASTEST GOAL SCORED BY A TEAM FROM THE START OF SECOND PERIOD:
5 seconds — Cleveland Dec 7 74 vs. San Diego. Skip Krake scored at 0:05 of second period in game won by Cleveland 3-1.

FASTEST TWO GOALS BY A TEAM FROM THE START OF SECOND PERIOD:
20 seconds — Cincinnati Oct 23 75 vs. Edmonton. Rick Dudley scored at 0:12 and 0:20 of second period in game won by Cincinnati 6-4.

FASTEST THREE GOALS BY A TEAM FROM THE START OF SECOND PERIOD:
1 minute, 18 seconds — Cincinnati Oct 23 75 vs. Edmonton. Rick Dudley scored at 0:12 and 0:20 and Steve Andrascik at 1:18 of second period in game won by Cincinnati 6-4.

FASTEST FOUR GOALS BY A TEAM FROM THE START OF THE SECOND PERIOD:
    5 minutes, 54 seconds — Houston Mar 27 74 at Vancouver. Frank Hughes scored at 3:26, Jim Sherrit at 4:01, Don Grierson at 4:46 and Murray Hall at 5:54 of second period in game won by Houston 8-1.

FASTEST FIVE GOALS SCORED BY A TEAM FROM THE START OF THE SECOND PERIOD:
    8 minutes, 50 seconds — Minnesota Nov 15 75 vs. Indianapolis. John McKenzie scored at 0:13, Paul Holmgren at 1:33, Mike Walton at 1:51, Dave Keon at 7:37 and Holmgren again at 8:50 of second period in game won by Minnesota 9-7.

FASTEST GOAL BY A TEAM FROM THE START OF THE THIRD PERIOD:
    7 seconds — Minnesota Nov 30 72 at New York. Wayne Connelly scored at 0:07 of third period in game won by NY 5-2.

FASTEST TWO GOALS SCORED BY A TEAM FROM THE START OF THE THIRD PERIOD:
    47 seconds — Toronto Nov 9 74 at Minnesota. Paul Henderson scored at 0:23 and 0:47 of third period in game won by Toronto 7-4.

FASTEST THREE GOALS SCORED BY A TEAM FROM THE START OF THE THIRD PERIOD:
    2 minutes, 12 seconds — New England Nov 6 75 vs. Cincinnati. Rosaire Paiement scored at 0:25, Wayne Carleton at 1:35 and Thommy Abrahamsson at 2:12 of third period in game won by NE 8-3.

FASTEST FOUR GOALS BY A TEAM FROM THE START OF THE THIRD PERIOD:
    3 minutes, 51 seconds — Philadelphia Dec 13 72 vs. Winnipeg. Danny Lawson scored at 1:32, Michel Plante at 2:02 and 2:54 and Bryan Campbell at 3:51 of third period in game won by Philadelphia 7-4.

FASTEST FIVE GOALS SCORED BY A TEAM FROM THE START OF THE THIRD PERIOD:
    10 minutes, 12 seconds — Toronto Nov 13 75 at Denver. Gavin Kirk scored at 1:18, Bob D'Alvise at 3:36, Mike Amodeo at 4:34, Frank Mahovlich at 8:39 and Vaclav Nedomansky at 10:12 of third period in game won by Toronto 11-8.

INDIVIDUAL RECORDS

MOST GAMES PLAYED:
    473 — Andre Lacroix, with Philadelphia, New York/New Jersey, San Diego and Houston
    471 — Ron Plumb, with Philadelphia, Vancouver, San Diego, Cincinnati and New England
    467 — Michel Parizeau, with Quebec and Indianapolis
    467 — Poul Popiel, all with Houston

MOST WHA CAREER POINTS:
    710 — Andre Lacroix, in 472 games has 219 goals and 491 assists.
    633 — Bobby Hull, in 407 games has 301 goals and 332 assists.

MOST WHA CAREER GOALS:
- 301 — Bobby Hull, in 407 games
- 275 — Marc Tardif, in 372 games

MOST WHA CAREER ASSISTS:
- 491 — Andre Lacroix, in 473 games
- 344 — Ulf Nilsson, in 300 games

MOST WHA CAREER PENALTY MINUTES:
- 904 — Cam Connor, in 274 games
- 862 — Pierre Roy, in 315 games

MOST WHA CAREER 3-OR-MORE GOAL NIGHTS:
- 19 — Bobby Hull, in 407 games has 16 three-goal nights and three four-goal nights.
- 17 — Real Cloutier in 292 games has had 14 3-goal nights, two 4-goal and one 5-goal nights.

SINGLE SEASON RECORDS

MOST POINTS BY A PLAYER IN ONE SEASON:
- 154 — Mark Tardif, Quebec 1977-78, 65 goals, 89 assists in 78 games
- 148 — Marc Tardif, Quebec 1975-76, 71 goals, 77 assists in 81 games
- 147 — Andre Lacroix, San Diego 1974-75, 41 goals, 106 assists in 78 games

MOST GOALS BY A PLAYER IN A SEASON:
- 77 — Bobby Hull, Winnipeg 1974-75 in 78 games
- 71 — Marc Tardif, Quebec 1975-76 in 81 games
- 70 — Anders Hedberg, Winnipeg 1976-77 in 68 games

MOST ASSISTS BY A PLAYER IN A SEASON:
- 106 — Andre Lacroix, San Diego 1974-75 in 78 games
- 94 — Ulf Nilsson, Winnipeg 1974-75 in 78 games
- 89 — Ulf Nilsson, Winnipeg 1977-78 in 73 games
- — Marc Tardif, Quebec 1977-78 in 78 games

MOST PENALTY MINUTES BY A PLAYER IN ONE SEASON:
- 365 — Curt Brackenbury, Minnesota/Quebec 1975-76 in 74 games
- 351 — Kim Clackson, Indianapolis 1975-76 in 77 games (Rookie Season)
- 297 — Gord Gallant, Quebec 1975-76 in 63 games

MOST THREE-OR-MORE GOAL NIGHTS BY A PLAYER IN ONE SEASON:
- 8 — Real Cloutier, Quebec 1976-77 in 76 games had seven 3-goal nights and one 5-goal night.
- 6 — Danny Lawson, Philadelphia 1972-73 in 78 games had three 3-goal and three 4-goal nights.
- — Mike Walton, Minnesota 1973-74 in 78 games had four 3-goal and two 4-goal nights.
- — Bobby Hull, Winnipeg, 1974-75 in 78 games had five 3-goal and one 4-goal nights.

SINGLE SEASON RECORDS, BY POSITION

MOST POINTS IN A SEASON BY A RIGHT WING:
- 141 — Real Cloutier, Quebec 1976-77, in 76 games scored 66 goals and 75 assists.
- 131 — Anders Hedberg, Winnipeg 1976-77, in 68 games scored 70

goals and 61 assists.

129 — Real Cloutier, Quebec 1977-78, in 73 games scored 56 goals and 73 assists.

MOST GOALS IN A SEASON BY A RIGHT WING:

70 — Anders Hedberg, Winnipeg 1976-77 in 68 games

66 — Real Cloutier, Quebec 1976-77 in 76 games

63 — Anders Hedberg, Winnipeg 1977-78 in 77 games

MOST ASSISTS IN A SEASON BY A RIGHT WING:

75 — Real Cloutier, Quebec 1976-77 in 76 games

73 — Real Cloutier, Quebec 1977-78 in 73 games

69 — Gordie Howe, Houston 197e-74 in 78 games

MOST PENALTY MINUTES IN A SEASON BY A RIGHT WING:

365 — Curt Brackenbury, Minnesota/Quebec 1975-76 in 74 games

295 — Cam Connor, Houston 1975-76 in 72 games

224 — Cam Connor, Houston 1976-77 in 76 games

MOST THREE-OR-MORE GOAL NIGHTS IN A SEASON BY A RIGHT WING:

8 — Real Cloutier, 1976-77, seven 3-goal, one 5-goal night

MOST POINTS IN A SEASON BY A LEFT WING:

154 — Marc Tardif, Quebec 1977-78, in 78 games scored 65 goals and 89 assists.

148 — Marc Tardif, Quebec 1975-76, in 81 games scored 71 goals and 77 assists.

142 — Bobby Hull, Winnipeg 1974-75, in 78 games scored 77 goals and 65 assists.

MOST GOALS IN A SEASON BY A LEFT WING:

77 — Bobby Hull, Winnipeg 1974-75 in 78 games

71 — Marc Tardif, Quebec 1975-76 in 81 games

65 — Marc Tardif, Quebec 1977-78 in 78 games

MOST ASSISTS IN A SEASON BY A LEFT WING:

89 — Marc Tardif, Quebec 1977-78 in 78 games

77 — Marc Tardif, Quebec 1975-76 in 81 games

71 — Bobby Hull, Winnipeg 1977-78 in 77 games

70 — Bobby Hull, Winnipeg 1975-76 in 80 games

MOST PENALTY MINUTES IN A SEASON BY A LEFT WING:

297 — Gord Gallant, Quebec 1975-76 in 63 games

279 — Frank Beaton, Birmingham 1977-78 in 56 games

274 — Frank Beaton, Edmonton 1976-77 in 68 games

MOST THREE-OR-MORE GOAL NIGHTS IN A SEASON BY A LEFT WING:

6 — Bobby Hull, Winnipeg 1974-75 in 78 games, five 3-goal and one 4-goal nights

MOST POINTS IN A SEASON BY A CENTER:

147 — Andre Lacroix, San Diego 1974-75, in 78 games scored 41 goals and 106 assists.

126 — Ulf Nilsson, Winnipeg 1977-78, in 73 games scored 37 goals and 89 assists.

124 — Andre Lacroix, Philadelphia 1972-73, in 78 games scored 50 goals and 74 assists.

— Ulf Nilsson, Winnipeg 1976-77, in 71 games scored 38 goals and 85 assists.

MOST GOALS IN A SEASON BY A CENTER:
    59 — Robbie Ftorek, Cincinnati 1977-78 in 80 games
    56 — Vaclav Nedomansky, Toronto 1975-76 in 81 games
    54 — Serge Bernier, Quebec 1974-75 in 78 games

SINGLE SEASON RECORDS, BY POSITION

MOST ASSISTS IN A SEASON BY A CENTER:
    106 — Andre Lacroix, San Diego 1974-75 in 78 games
    94 — Ulf Nilsson, Winnipeg 1974-75 in 78 games
    89 — Ulf Nilsson, gwinnipeg 1977-78 in 73 games

MOST PENALTY MINUTES IN A SEASON BY A CENTER:
    170 — Terry Ruskowski, Houston 1977-78 in 78 games
    157 — Mike Rouleau, Philadelphia/Quebec 1972-73 in 58 games
    150 — Ted McCaskill, Los Angeles 1972-73 in 73 games

MOST THREE-OR-MORE GOAL NIGHTS IN A SEASON BY A CENTER:
    3 — Andre Lacroix, Philadelphia 1972-73, two 3-goal and one 4-goal nights
      — Claude St. Sauveur, Vancouver 1973-74, all 3-goal nights
      — Ron Ward, Los Angeles/Cleveland 1973-74, all 3-goal nights

MOST POINTS IN A SEASON BY A DEFENSEMAN:
    89 — J.C. Tremblay, Quebec 1972-73, in 78 games scored 14 goals and 75 assists.
      — J.C. Tremblay, Quebec 1975-76, in 80 games scored 12 goals and 77 assists.
    81 — Kevin Morrison, San Diego 1974-75, in 78 games scored 20 goals and 61 assists.

MOST GOALS IN A SEASON BY A DEFENSEMAN:
    24 — Kevin Morrison, NY/NJ 1973-74 in 78 games
    22 — Kevin Morrison, San Diego 1975-76 in 80 games
    20 — Kevin Morrison, San Diego 1974-75 in 78 games
      — Barry Long, Winnipeg 1974-75 in 78 games

MOST ASSISTS IN A SEASON BY A DEFENSEMAN:
    77 — J.C. Tremblay, Quebec 1975-76 in 81 games
    75 — J.C. Tremblay, Quebec 1972-73 in 78 games
    61 — Kevin Morrison, San Diego 1974-75 in 78 games

MOST PENALTY MINUTES IN A SEASON BY A DEFENSEMAN:
    351 — Kim Clackson, Indianapolis 1975-76 in 77 games
    284 — Steve Durbano, Birmingham 1977-78 in 45 games
    255 — Pierre Roy, Quebec 1975-76 in 78 games

MOST THREE-OR-MORE GOAL NIGHTS IN A SEASON BY A DEFENSEMAN:
    1 — Ken Baird, Edmonton, Nov 13 74 vs. Winnipeg
      — Kevin Morrison, NJ, Mar 18 74 vs. Toronto
      — Thommy Abrahamsson, NE, Nov 6 75 vs. Cincinnati
      — Perry Miller, Winnipeg, Feb 1 77 at Edmonton (scored 4th goal as a left wing)
      — Ab Demarco, Edmonton, Apr 5 78 vs. New England

MOST ASSISTS IN A SEASON BY A GOALTENDER:
    13 — Don McLeod, Calgary 1975-76 in 63 games
    10 — Don McLeod, Quebec/Edmonton 1977-78 in 40 games
    9 — Don McLeod, Calgary 1976-77 in 67 games

MOST PENALTY MINUTES IN A SEASON BY A GOALTENDER:
- 75 — Andy Brown, Indianapolis 1974-75 in 52 games
- 59 — Gerry Cheevers, Cleveland 1974-75 in 52 games
- 54 — Serge Aubry, Quebec 1972-73 in 52 games

SINGLE SEASON RECORDS
MOST POINTS IN A ROOKIE SEASON:
- 120 — Ulf Nilsson, Winnipeg 1974-75, in 78 games scored 26 goals and 94 assists.
- 107 — Kent Nilsson, Winnipeg 1977-78, in 80 games scored 42 goals and 65 assists.
- 100 — Terry Caffery, New England 1972-73, in 74 games scored 39 goals and 61 assists.
- — Anders Hedberg, Winnipeg 1974-75, in 65 games scored 53 goals and 47 assists.

MOST GOALS IN A SEASON BY A ROOKIE:
- 53 — Anders Hedberg, Winnipeg 1974-75 in 65 games
- 44 — Gary MacGregor, Chicago 1974-75 in 78 games
- 43 — Mark Napier, Toronto 1975-76 in 78 games
- 42 — Kent Nilsson, Winnipeg 1977-78 in 80 games

MOST ASSISTS IN A SEASON BY A ROOKIE:
- 94 — Ulf Nilsson, Winnipeg 1974-75 in 78 games
- 65 — Kent Nilsson, Winnipeg 1977-78 in 80 games
- 63 — Bob Sicinski, Chicago 1972-73 in 77 games

MOST PENALTY MINUTES IN A SEASON BY A ROOKIE:
- 351 — Kim Clackson, Indianapolis 1975-76 in 77 games
- 223 — Gord Gallant, Minnesota 1973-74 in 72 games
- 201 — John Hughes, Phoenix 1974-75 in 72 games
- — Paul Baxter, Cleveland 1975-76 in 67 games

MOST THREE-OR-MORE GOAL NIGHTS IN A ROOKIE SEASON:
- 3 — Anders Hedberg, Winnipeg 1974-75, in 65 games had two 3-goal and one 4-goal nights.

MOST POWER PLAY GOALS SCORED BY A PLAYER IN ONE SEASON:
- 27 — Bobby Hull, Winnipeg 1974-75
- 25 — Real Cloutier, Quebec 1976-77
- 22 — Anders Hedberg, Winnipeg 1976-77

MOST SHORTHANDED GOALS SCORED BY A PLAYER IN ONE SEASON:
- 9 — Mike Walton, Minnesota 1973-74
- 8 — Paulin Bordeleau, Quebec 1976-77
- 6 — Anders Hedberg, Winnipeg 1975-76 and 1977-78
- — Jim Harrison, Edmonton 1972-73
- — Bob Dillabough, Cleveland 1972-73
- — Terry Ryan, Minnesota 1972-73
- — Tom Earl, New England 1975-76
- — Mark Howe, Houston 1975-76
- — Rick Morris, Denver/Ottawa/Edmonton 1975-76
- — Joe Norris, San Diego 1976-77

FEWEST NUMBER OF GAMES NEEDED TO SCORE 20 GOALS:
- 18 — Bobby Hull, Winnipeg 1974-75
- — Real Cloutier, Quebec 1976-77

FEWEST NUMBER OF GAMES NEEDED TO SCORE 30 GOALS:
  29 — Bobby Hull, Winnipeg 1974-75
     — Marc Tardif, Quebec 1977-78
FEWEST NUMBER OF GAMES NEEDED TO SCORE 40 GOALS:
  41 — Bobby Hull, Winnipeg 1974-75
FEWEST NUMBER OF GAMES NEEDED TO SCORE 50 GOALS:
  47 — Anders Hedberg, Winnipeg 1976-77

SINGLE SEASON

FEWEST NUMBER OF GAMES NEEDED TO SCORE 60 GOALS:
  57 — Anders Hedberg, Winnipeg 1976-77
FEWEST NUMBER OF GAMES NEEDED TO SCORE 70 GOALS:
  68 — Anders Hedberg, Winnipeg 1976-77
MOST CONSECUTIVE GAMES PLAYED:
  439 — Rosaire Paiement, between Oct 12 72 and Jan 30 78, with Chicago, New England, and Indianapolis. Streak stopped by eye injury.
  429 — Andre Lacroix, between Oct 12 77 and Jan 6 78, with Philadelphia, New York, New Jersey, San Diego and Houston. Streak stopped by ankle injury.
CURRENT LONGEST CONSECUTIVE GAMES PLAYED STREAK:
  276 — Robbie Ftorek has played every game since Jan 18 75 with Phoenix and Cincinnati.
  226 — Ron Chipperfield has played every game since Nov 16 75 with Calgary and Edmonton.
  207 — Blair Macdonald has played every game since Jan 2 76 with Indianapolis and Edmonton.
  200 — Rich Leduc has played every game since Jan 21 76 with Cincinnati and Indianapolis.
MOST CONSECUTIVE GAMES WITH POINTS:
  32 — Andre Lacroix, San Diego. Collected 17 goals and 53 assists in 32 straight games between Jan 4 75 and Mar 19 75.
MOST CONSECUTIVE GAMES WITH GOALS:
  11 — Serge Bernier, Quebec. Collected 16 goals in 11 straight games between Dec 5 and Dec 22 74.
MOST CONSECUTIVE GAMES WITH ASSISTS:
  18 — Ulf Nilsson, Winnipeg. Between Oct 13 and Nov 27 77 collected 27 assists.
MOST CONSECUTIVE GAMES WITH PENALTIES:
  12 — Kim Clackson, Winnipeg. Collected 51 minutes in 12 straight games between Jan 18 and Feb 10 78.

INDIVIDUAL SINGLE GAME RECORDS

MOST POINTS BY A PLAYER IN A GAME:
  10 — Jim Harrison, Alberta, Jan 30 73 vs. New York. Scored three goals and seven assists in 11-3 Alberta win.
MOST GOALS BY A PLAYER IN A GAME:
  5 — Ron Ward, Jan 4 73 New York 9-4 win at Ottawa
    — Ron Ward, Nov 30 75 in Cleveland 10-9 win over Toronto
    — Ron Climie, Nov 6 73 in 9-0 Edmonton win vs. New York
    — Andre Hinse, Jan 15 75 in 9-2 Houston win at Edmonton
    — Vaclav Nedomansky, Nov 13 75, Toronto 10-9 win at Denver

176

— Wayne Connelly, Nov 27 75 in Minnesota 5-3 win vs. Cincinnati
— Real Cloutier, Oct 26 76 in Quebec 11-3 win vs. Phoenix

MOST ASSISTS BY A PLAYER IN ONE GAME:
7 — Jim Harrison, Alberta, Jan 30 73 in Oiler 11-3 win over New York
— Jim Harrison, Cleveland, Nov 30 75 in Crusader 10-9 win over Toronto

MOST PENALTY MINUTES CALLED ON A PLAYER IN A GAME:
46 — Dave Hanson, Birmingham Feb 5 78 at Indianapolis. Called for 3 minors, 2 majors and 3 misconduct penalties. Indy won game 6-1.

MOST PENALTIES CALLED ON A PLAYER IN A GAME:
8 — Kim Clackson, Indianapolis Nov 30 75, 4 minors, 3 majors, 1 misconduct, for 33 minutes in 4-2 loss to Denver
— Paul Baxter, Quebec Nov 2 76, 6 minors, 1 major and 1 misconduct for 27 minutes in 5-3 loss to Phoenix
— Wally Weir, Quebec Dec 12 76, 7 minors and a major for 19 minutes in 5-1 win vs. New England
— Dave Hanson, Birmingham Feb 5 78, 3 minors, 2 majors and 3 misconducts for 46 minutes in 6-1 loss at Indianapolis

PERIOD RECORDS

MOST POINTS IN A PERIOD:
5 — Jim Harrison, Alberta Jan 30 73, scored a goal and 4 assists in third period of 11-3 win over New York.
— Jim Harrison, Cleveland Jan 30 75, collected 5 assists in 10-9 win vs. Toronto, third period.
— Doug Barrie, Alberta Jan 30 73, scored a goal and 4 assists in third period of 11-3 win over New York.
— Real Cloutier, Quebec Dec 26 76, scored 2 goals and 3 assists in first period of 12-3 win at Winnipeg.

MOST GOALS BY A PLAYER IN A PERIOD:
4 — Ron Climie, Edmonton Nov 6 73, scored in third period of 8-0 win vs. New York.

MOST ASSISTS BY A PLAYER IN A PERIOD:
5 — Jim Harrison, Cleveland Jan 30 75, in third period of 10-9 win vs. Toronto

MOST PENALTIES BY A PLAYER IN A PERIOD: (and)
MOST PENALTY MINUTES BY A PLAYER IN A PERIOD:
6 penalties, 38 minutes — Curt Brackenbury, Minnesota Jan 17 76, had 2 minors, a major and 3 misconducts in 4-2 win at Phoenix, first period.

FASTEST TWO GOALS SCORED BY A PLAYER:
6 seconds — Dennis Sobchuk, Edmonton Dec 30 77, scored at 11:07 and 11:13 of first period in 8-5 win vs. Indianapolis. It was Sobchuk's first game as an Oiler.

FASTEST THREE GOALS BY A PLAYER:
43 seconds — George Morrison, Minnesota Apr 3 74, scored at 15:42, 15:56 and 16:25 of second period in 9-0 win vs. Vancouver.

FASTEST FOUR GOALS BY A PLAYER:
12 minutes, 11 seconds — Ron Climie, Edmonton Nov 6 73, scored at 3:28, 4:01, 7:10 and 15:39 of third period in 8-0 win vs. New York.

177

FASTEST FIVE GOALS SCORED BY A PLAYER:
  25 minutes, 53 seconds — Ron Ward, New York Jan 4 73, scored at 18:41, 19:16, 33:46, 39:01 and 44:34 in 9-4 win vs. Ottawa.

FASTEST OPENING GOAL BY A PLAYER FROM START OF THE GAME:
  5 seconds — Russ Walker, Cleveland Feb 19 75, in 5-3 loss vs. Minnesota

FASTEST ANSWERING GOAL BY A PLAYER, FOLLOWING A GOAL BY A PLAYER FROM OPPOSING TEAM:
  3 seconds — Gordie Howe, New England Mar 10 78, scored at 3:03 of first period in New England 5-4 overtime win at Birmingham. Ken Linseman had scored at 3:00.

FASTEST TWO GOALS FROM THE START OF THE GAME, BY A PLAYER:
  48 seconds — Anders Hedberg, Winnipeg Dec 26 77, scored at 0:16 and 0:48 in 9-4 win vs. Quebec.

FASTEST THREE GOALS BY A PLAYER FROM THE START OF THE GAME:
  5 minutes, 3 seconds — Jim Wiste, Cleveland Feb 16 74, scored at 0:20, 4:51 and 5:03 in 5-2 win vs. Quebec.

FASTEST FOUR GOALS BY A PLAYER FROM THE START OF THE GAME:
  27 minutes, 23 seconds — Danny Lawson, Philadelphia Feb 13 73, scored at 2:54, 15:00, 19:27 and 27:23 in 5-4 win vs. New England.

FASTEST FIVE GOALS FROM THE START OF THE GAME:
  42 minutes, 29 seconds — Andre Hinse, Houston Jan 15 75, scored at 8:28, 15:36, 33:23, 41:17 and 42:29 in 9-2 win vs. Edmonton.

FASTEST GOAL FROM THE START OF THE SECOND PERIOD:
  5 seconds — Skip Krake, Cleveland Dec 7 74, in 3-1 win vs. San Diego

FASTEST TWO GOALS FROM THE START OF THE SECOND PERIOD:
  20 seconds — Rick Dudley, Cincinnati Oct 23 75, scored at 0:12 and 0:20 in 6-4 win vs. Edmonton.

FASTEST THREE GOALS FROM THE START OF THE SECOND PERIOD:
  11 minutes, 25 seconds — Peter Marrin, Birmingham Nov 16 76, scored at 0:44, 7:37 and 11:25 in 5-4 loss to New England.

FASTEST FOUR GOALS FROM THE START OF THE SECOND PERIOD:
  29 minutes, 56 seconds — Brian McDonald, at Houston Dec 19 72, scored at 10:34, 16:14 of the second period and 9:46 and 9:56 of the third in 7-5 win vs. Los Angeles.

FASTEST FIVE GOALS BY A PLAYER FROM THE START OF THE SECOND PERIOD:
  No Player has ever scored five goals in the final 40 minutes of a game.

FASTEST GOAL FROM THE START OF THE THIRD PERIOD:
  7 seconds — Wayne Connelly, Minnesota Nov 30 72, in 5-2 loss at New York

FASTEST TWO GOALS FROM THE START OF THE THIRD PERIOD:
  47 seconds — Paul Henderson, Toronto Nov 9 74, scored at 0:23 and 0:47 in 7-4 win vs. Minnesota.

FASTEST THREE GOALS FROM THE START OF THE THIRD PERIOD:
  7 minutes, 10 seconds — Ron Climie, Edmonton Nov 6 73, scored at 3:28, 4:01 and 7:10 in 8-0 win vs. New York.

FASTEST FOUR GOALS FROM THE START OF THE THIRD PERIOD:
    15 minutes, 39 seconds — Ron Climie, Edmonton Nov 6 73, scored at 3:28, 4:01, 7:10 and 15:39 in 8-0 win vs. New York.
FASTEST FIVE GOALS FROM THE START OF THE THIRD PERIOD:
    No Player has ever scored five goals in the final 20 minutes of a game.
FASTEST GOAL FROM THE START OF AN OVERTIME PERIOD:
    4 seconds — John French, New England Nov 26 73, in 5-4 win at Quebec

GOALTENDER RECORDS

GOALIE CAREER
BEST CAREER GOALS AGAINST AVERAGE:
    2.99 — Ron Grahame, 4 seasons, 425 goals in 8,528 minutes
    3.12 — Gerry Cheevers, 4 seasons, 591 goals in 11,352 minutes
    3.16 — Jack Norris, 4 seasons, 582 goals in 11,030 minutes
MOST CAREER GAMES APPEARED IN:
    332 — Don McLeod, 6 seasons, with Houston/Vancouver/Calgary/Quebec and Edmonton
    297 — Ernie Wakely, 6 seasons with Winnipeg/San Diego/Cincinnati and Houston
    285 — Joe Daley, 6 seasons with Winnipeg
MOST MINUTES PLAYED IN WHA CAREER:
    18,926 — Don McLeod, 6 seasons with Houston/Vancouver/Calgary/Quebec and Edmonton
    17,272 — Ernie Wakely, 6 seasons with Winnipeg/San Diego/Cincinnati and Houston
    16,579 — Joe Daley, 6 seasons with Winnipeg
MOST CAREER WINS:
    160 — Joe Daley in six seasons with Winnipeg
    157 — Don McLeod in six seasons with Houston/Vancouver/Calgary/Quebec and Edmonton
    149 — Ernie Wakely in six seasons with Winnipeg/San Diego/Cincinnati and Houston
MOST CAREER LOSSES:
    144 — Don McLeod in six seasons with Houston/Vancouver/Calgary/Quebec and Edmonton
    134 — John Garrett in five seasons with Minnesota/Toronto and Birmingham
    120 — Ernie Wakely in six seasons with Winnipeg/San Diego/Cincinnati and Houston
MOST CAREER TIES:
    20 — Ernie Wakely in six seasons with Winnipeg/San Diego/Cincinnati and Houston
    15 — Don McLeod in six seasons with Houston/Vancouver/Calgary/Quebec and Edmonton
    12 — Jack Norris in four seasons with Edmonton and Phoenix
MOST SHOTS FACED IN WHA CAREER:
    9,293 — John Garrett in five seasons with Minnesota/Toronto and Birmingham
    9,196 — Don McLeod in six seasons with

Houston/Vancouver/Calgary/Quebec and Edmonton
8,875 — Ernie Wakely in six seasons with Winnipeg/San Diego/Cincinnati and Houston

HIGHEST SHOTS AGAINST AVERAGE PER GAME IN WHA CAREER:
36.6 — Gerry Desjardins faced 1,391 shots in 2,282 minutes.
35.3 — Mike Curran faced 4,344 shots in 7,377 minutes.
34.4 — Chris Worthy faced 2,506 shots in 4,368 minutes.

MOST GOALS ALLOWED IN WHA CAREER:
1,051 — Don McLeod in six seasons with Houston/Vancouver/Calgary/Quebec and Edmonton
961 — John Garrett in five seasons with Minnesota/Toronto and Birmingham
935 — Ernie Wakely in six seasons with Winnipeg/San Diego/Cincinnati and Houston

MOST SAVES MADE IN WHA CAREER:
8,332 — John Garrett in five seasons with Minnesota/Toronto and Birmingham
8,075 — Don McLeod in six seasons with Houston/Vancouver/Calgary/Quebec and Edmonton
7,940 — Ernie Wakely in six seasons with Winnipeg/San Diego/Cincinnati and Houston

HIGHEST SAVE PERCENTAGE IN WHA CAREER:
.905 — Gerry Cheevers in four seasons with Cleveland
.903 — Mike Curran in five seasons with Minnesota
.900 — Ron Grahame in four seasons with Houston

MOST CAREER SHUTOUTS:
16 — Ernie Wakely in six seasons with Winnipeg/San Diego and Houston
14 — Gerry Cheevers in four seasons with Cleveland
12 — Ron Grahame in four seasons with Houston
— John Garrett in five seasons with Minnesota/Toronto and Birmingham
— Joe Daley in six seasons with Winnipeg

GOALTENDER — SINGLE SEASONS (25 game minimum)
BEST SINGLE SEASON GOALS AGAINST AVERAGE:
2.56 — Don McLeod, Houston 1973-74, 127 goals in 2,971 minutes
2.74 — Ron Grahame, Houston 1976-77, 107 goals in 2,345 minutes
— Michel Dion, Indianapolis 1975-76, 85 goals in 1,860 minutes

MOST GAME APPEARANCES IN A SEASON:
72 — Don McLeod, Vancouver 1974-75
69 — Richard Brodeur, Quebec 1975-76
67 — Ernie Wakely, San Diego 1975-76
— Don McLeod, Calgary 1976-77

MOST MINUTES PLAYED IN A SEASON:
4,184 — Don McLeod, Vancouver 1974-75
3,967 — Richard Brodeur, Quebec 1975-76
3,824 — Ernie Wakely, San Diego 1975-76
3,818 — Joe Daley, Winnipeg 1976-77

MOST WINS IN A SEASON:
44 — Richard Brodeur, Quebec 1975-76

41 — Joe Daley, Winnipeg 1975-76
    39 — Joe Daley, Winnipeg 1976-77
       — Ron Grahame, Houston 1975-76

MOST LOSSES IN A SEASON:
    35 — Andy Brown, Indianapolis 1974-75
       — Don McLeod, Vancouver 1974-75
    34 — Don McLeod, Calgary 1976-77
       — Dave Dryden, Edmonton 1975-76
       — John Garrett, Birmingham 1976-77

MOST TIES IN A SEASON:
    6 — Gerry Cheevers, Cleveland 1973-74
    5 — Bruce Landon, New England 1975-76
      — Dave Dryden, Edmonton 1975-76
      — Don McLeod, Calgary 1976-77
      — Louis Levasseur, Minnesota/Edmonton 1976-77

MOST SHOTS FACED IN A SEASON:
    2,216 — Richard Brodeur, Quebec 1975-76
    2,212 — John Garrett, Birmingham 1976-77
    2,132 — Don McLeod, Vancouver 1974-75

HIGHEST SHOTS AGAINST AVERAGE FOR A SEASON:
    40.6 — Mario Vien, Toronto 1975-76, 830 shots in 1,228 minutes
    37.7 — Cam Newton, Chicago 1974-75, 1,196 shots in 1,905 minutes
    36.9 — Dave Dryden, Chicago 1974-75, 1,679 shots in 2,728 minutes

MOST GOALS ALLOWED IN A SEASON:
    244 — Richard Brodeur, Quebec 1975-76
    235 — Dave Dryden, Edmonton 1975-76
    233 — Don McLeod, Vancouver 1974-75

MOST SAVES IN A SEASON:
    1,988 — John Garrett, Birmingham 1976-77
    1,972 — Richard Brodeur, Quebec 1975-76
    1,899 — Don McLeod, Vancouver 1974-75

BEST SAVE PERCENTAGE FOR A SEASON:
    .912 — Gerry Cheevers, Cleveland 1972-73, 1546 saves on 1695 shots
    .911 — Don McLeod, Houston 1973-74, 1305 saves on 1432 shots
    .910 — Mike Curran, Minnesota 1973-74, 1314 saves on 1444 shots
       — Michel Dion, Indianapolis 1975-76, 857 saves on 942 shots

MOST SHUTOUTS IN A SEASON:
    5 — Gerry Cheevers, Cleveland 1972-73
      — Joe Daley, Winnipeg 1975-76
    4 — Gerry Cheevers, Cleveland 1973-74 and 1974-75
      — Ron Grahame, Houston 1974-75 and 1976-77
      — Mike Curran, Minnesota 1972-73
      — Ken Broderick, Edmonton 1976-77
      — John Garrett, Birmingham 1976-77
      — Michel Dion, Cincinnati 1977-78

MOST CONSECUTIVE GAME APPEARANCES:
    41 — Don McLeod, Vancouver, between Dec 26 74 and Mar 25 75

LONGEST UNDEFEATED STREAK: (and)
LONGEST WINNING STREAK:
    16 — Ron Grahame, Houston, between Jan 16 77 and the end of season

LONGEST UNDEFEATED STREAK ON HOME ICE:
   22 — Ron Grahame, Houston, between April 4 76 and the end of 1976-77 season, 21 wins, 1 tie

LONGEST UNDEFEATED STREAK ON THE ROAD: (and)
LONGEST WINNING STREAK ON THE ROAD
   7 — Ron Grahame, Houston, between Nov 19 and Dec 22 74

LONGEST WINNING STREAK ON HOME ICE:
   14 — Ron Grahame, Houston, between Dec 14 76 and end of season

MOST CONSECUTIVE GAMES WITHOUT A WIN:
   16 — George Gardner, Vancouver, between Nov 25 73 and end of season. These were the final 16 games of his WHA career. 15 losses, 1 tie
   — Ed Dyck, Indianapolis, between Nov 15 74 and Mar 13 75, 13 losses, 3 ties

MOST CONSECUTIVE HOME GAMES WITHOUT A WIN:
   8 — Andre Gill, Chicago, between Dec 14 72 and Mar 28 73, all losses
   — Ed Dyck, Indianapolis, between Nov 5 74 and Jan 19 75, all losses

MOST CONSECUTIVE ROAD GAMES WITHOUT A WIN:
   26 — Don McLeod, Calgary, between Oct 8 76 (first game of season) and March 25 77, 23 losses, 3 ties

MOST CONSECUTIVE GAMES LOST:
   12 — George Gardner, Vancouver, between Nov 25 73 and Mar 21 74

MOST CONSECUTIVE LOSSES ON HOME ICE:
   8 — Andre Gill, Chicago, between Dec 14 72 and Mar 28 73
   — Ed Dyck, Indianapolis, between Nov 5 74 and Jan 19 75

MOST CONSECUTIVE LOSSES ON THE ROAD:
   19 — Paul Hoganson, Los Angeles/Michigan/Baltimore, between Nov 11 73 and Mar 4 75. Streak lasted two seasons.

FEWEST SAVES BY A GOALTENDER IN A SHUTOUT:
   11 — Ernie Wakely, San Diego Dec 16 76 vs. Edmonton in 3-0 win

MOST SAVES NEEDED IN A SHUTOUT BY A GOALTENDER:
   48 — Louis Levasseur, Minnesota Nov 23 76 vs. Cincinnati in 4-0 win

MOST SAVES MADE BY A WINNING GOALTENDER:
   53 — John Garrett, Minnesota Dec 26 74 at Edmonton in 5-1 win
   52 — Serge Aubry, Quebec Feb 4 73 at Los Angeles in 5-3 win

LONGEST SHUTOUT SEQUENCE BY A GOALTENDER:
   228 minutes, 10 seconds — Joe Daley, Winnipeg, between 8:25 of first period vs. Denver Oct 24 and 16:35 of third period vs. Quebec Nov 2 75. Included shutouts over Phoenix and Cincinnati.

ALL-TIME WHA CLUB RECORDS

TEAM RECORDS	BIRMINGHAM		CINCINNATI		EDMONTON		INDIANAPOLIS		NEW ENGLAND		QUEBEC		WINNIPEG	
Most Points	88	1974-75	83	1976-77	79	1972-73 1973-74 1977-78	80	1976-77	94	1972-73	104	1975-76	106*	1975-76
Most Wins	43	1974-75	39	1976-77	38	1972-73 1973-74 1977-78	36	1976-77	46	1972-73	50	1975-76	52	1975-76
Most Ties	5	1975-76	5	1976-77	5	1975-76	8	1976-77	7	1975-76	5	1972-73	5	1973-74 1974-75
Most Losses	52	1975-76	44	1975-76	49	1975-76	57*	1974-75	40	1975-76 1976-77	40	1972-73	39	1973-74
Most Overtimes Played	14	1976-77	12	1976-77 1977-78	13	1977-78	17*	1976-77	15	1977-78	14	1977-78	15	1973-74
Most Overtimes Won	4	1973-74	6	1977-78	7*	1977-78	7*	1976-77	7*	1974-75	7*	1977-78	6	1975-76
Most Overtimes Lost	9*	1976-77	7	1976-77	5	1972-73	8	1974-75	6	1977-78	5	1977-78	7	1973-74
Most Goals Scored	349	1974-75	354	1976-77	309	1977-78	276	1976-77	335	1975-76	371	1975-76	381*	1977-78
Most Goals Against	398*	1975-76	340	1975-76	345	1975-76	353	1977-78	290	1975-76	347	1977-78	296	1973-74
Fewest Points	53	1975-76	71	1975-76	59	1975-76	39*	1974-75	73	1975-76	71	1972-73	73	1973-74
Fewest Wins	24	1975-76	35	1975-76 1977-78	27	1975-76	18*	1974-75	33	1975-76	33	1972-73	34	1973-74
Fewest Losses	33	1973-74 1974-75	37	1976-77	37	1972-73 1973-74	37	1976-77	30	1972-73 1974-75	27	1975-76	27	1975-76
Fewest Overtimes Played	5	1974-75	5	1975-76	8	1973-74	12	1974-75	7	1972-73	9	1976-77	6	1976-77
Fewest Overtimes Won	1	1975-76 1976-77	0*	1976-77	2	1973-74 1975-76	1	1974-75	2	1975-76 1976-77	2	1972-73	1	1977-78
Fewest Overtimes Lost	1	1974-75	2	1975-76	1	1976-77	2	1976-77	0*	1972-73 1974-75	2	1976-77	0*	1976-77
Fewest Goals Scored	279	1972-73	285	1975-76	243	1976-77	216	1974-75	255	1975-76	276	1972-73	264	1973-74
Fewest Goals Against	272	1973-74	303	1976-77	256	1972-73	247	1975-76	260	1973-74	280	1973-74	249	1975-76
Most Shutouts	5	1972-73	6	1976-77	5	1976-77	2	1974-75 1976-77	5	1977-78	4	1976-77	5	1975-76
Fewest Shutouts	1	1975-76	3	1975-76	2	1972-73 1975-76	0*	1977-78	2	1973-74 1975-76	0*	1974-75 1977-78	2	1977-78
Most Penalty Minutes	2177*	1977-78	1701	1977-78	1319	1976-77	1308	1975-76	1255	1977-78	1654	1975-76	991	1976-77
Fewest Penalty Minutes	871	1973-74	970	1976-77	843	1972-73	880	1976-77	858	1972-73	909	1973-74	673*	1973-74

*Indicates a League Record.

INDIVIDUAL RECORDS

	BIRMINGHAM		CINCINNATI		EDMONTON		INDIANAPOLIS		NEW ENGLAND		QUEBEC		WINNIPEG	
Most Goals Scored	60	Mark Napier 1976-77	59	Robbie Ftorek 1977-78	42	Rusty Patenaude 1975-76	37	Rich Leduc 1977-78	53	Tom Webster 1972-73	71	Marc Tardif 1975-76	77*	Bobby Hull 1974-75
Most Assists	66	Wayne Dillon 1976-77	58	Ron Plumb 1976-77	56	Norm Ullman 1975-76	55	Darryl Maggs 1976-77	62	Gordie Howe 1977-78	89	Marc Tardif 1977-78	94	Ulf Nilsson 1974-75
Most Total Points	98	Vaclav Nedomansky 1975-76	109	Robbie Ftorek 1977-78	87	Norm Ullman 1975-76	83	Rich Leduc 1977-78	103	Tom Webster 1972-73	154*	Marc Tardif 1977-78	142	Bobby Hull 1974-75
Most Penalty Minutes	284	Steve Durbano 1977-78	241	Paul Stewart 1977-78	274	Frank Beaton 1976-77	351	Kim Clackson 1975-76	192	Jack Carlson 1977-78	297	Gord Gallant 1975-76	203	Kim Clackson 1977-78
Most Shutouts	4	John Garrett 1977-78	4	Michel Dion 1977-78	4	Ken Broderick 1976-77	2	Andy Brown 1974-75	3	Al Smith 1972-73 Louis Levasseur 1977-78	2	Serge Aubry 1975-76 Richard Brodeur 1976-77	5*	Joe Daley 1975-76
Best Goals Against Average (at least 25 games played)	3.27	Les Binkley 1973-74	3.57	Michel Dion 1977-78	3.06	Jack Norris 1972-73	2.74	Michel Dion 1975-76	3.08	Al Smith 1973-74	3.29	Michel Deguise 1973-74	2.84	Joe Daley 1975-76

*Indicates a League Record.

REGULAR SEASON CAREER LEADERS

25 ALL-TIME GAMES PLAYED LEADERS
1. 473 Andre Lacroix
2. 471 Ron Plumb
3. 467 Poul Popiel
4. 459 Larry Lund
5. 457 Michel Parizeau
6. 455 Rosaire Paiement
7. 443 Don Burgess
8. 440 Larry Pleau
9. 438 Ted Green
10. 436 Norm Ferguson
11. 433 Ken Block
11. 433 Bryan Campbell
11. 433 Tim Sheehy
14. 431 Rusty Patenaude
14. 431 Paul Shmyr
16. 421 Ted Taylor
17. 420 John French
18. 417 Mike Antonovich
19. 413 Larry Hale
19. 413 Rick Morris
21. 407 Bobby Hull
22. 405 Rick Ley
23. 403 Ronald Leclerc
24. 401 John McKenzie
25. 399 Jim Dorey

25 ALL-TIME PENALTY LEADERS
1. 904 Cam Connor
2. 862 Pierre Roy
3. 849 Gord Gallant
4. 844 John Schella
5. 805 Steve Sutherland
6. 762 Ron Busniuk
7. 741 Paul Shmyr
8. 722 Paul Baxter
8. 722 Kim Clackson
10. 648 John Hughes
11. 633 Jack Carlson
12. 620 Doug Barrie
13. 618 Poul Popiel
14. 614 Frank Beaton
15. 602 Rosaire Paiement
16. 600 Jim Dorey
16. 600 Ted Taylor
18. 598 Curt Brackenbury
19. 581 Rick Ley
20. 577 Pierre Guite
21. 570 Butch Deadmarsh
22. 568 John Arbour
23. 567 Rick Morris
24. 550 Terry Ruskowski
25. 530 Bill Butters

25 ALL-TIME POINT LEADERS
1. 710 Andre Lacroix
2. 633 Bobby Hull
3. 570 Marc Tardif
4. 487 Chris Bordeleau
5. 484 Serge Bernier
5. 484 Ulf Nilsson
7. 465 Gordie Howe
8. 458 Anders Hedberg
9. 437 Real Cloutier
10. 426 Larry Lund
11. 425 Tom Webster
12. 422 Danny Lawson
13. 407 Robbie Ftorek
14. 397 Mark Howe
15. 380 Ron Ward
15. 380 J. C. Tremblay
17. 376 Bryan Campbell
18. 369 Michel Parizeau
19. 367 Rosaire Paiement
20. 366 John McKenzie
21. 365 Norm Ferguson
22. 360 Larry Pleau
23. 354 Gavin Kirk
24. 353 Frank Hughes
25. 350 Tim Sheehy

25 ALL-TIME GOAL SCORING LEADERS
1. 301 Bobby Hull
2. 275 Marc Tardif
3. 236 Anders Hedberg
4. 220 Tom Webster
5. 219 Andre Lacroix
6. 218 Danny Lawson
7. 208 Real Cloutier
8. 194 Serge Bernier
9. 181 Norm Ferguson
10. 177 Robbie Ftorek
10. 177 Tim Sheehy
12. 174 Chris Bordeleau
13. 173 Frank Hughes
14. 170 Ron Ward
15. 167 Wayne Connelly
16. 166 Mark Howe
17. 165 Gene Peacosh
18. 162 Mike Antonovich
19. 159 Rich Leduc
19. 159 Rusty Patenaude
21. 158 Wayne Rivers
22. 155 Gordie Howe
23. 151 Gary Veneruzzo
23. 151 Larry Pleau
25. 149 Larry Lund

25 ALL-TIME ASSIST LEADERS

1. 491 Andre Lacroix
2. 344 Ulf Nilsson
3. 332 Bobby Hull
4. 320 J. C. Tremblay
5. 313 Chris Bordeleau
6. 310 Gordie Howe
7. 295 Marc Tardif
8. 290 Serge Bernier
9. 277 Larry Lund
10. 265 Poul Popiel
11. 253 Bryan Campbell
12. 248 Ron Plumb
13. 238 Gavin Kirk
14. 234 Michel Parizeau
15. 231 Mark Howe
16. 230 Robbie Ftorek
16. 230 Jim Dorey
18. 229 Real Cloutier
19. 222 Anders Hedberg
20. 222 John McKenzie
21. 221 Rosaire Paiement
22. 220 Al Hamilton
23. 217 Kevin Morrison
24. 212 Pat Stapleton
25. 210 Ron Ward

WHA CAREER HAT TRICKS

PLAYER	HT	GOAL NIGHT 3	4	5	AT HOME	ON ROAD	FASTEST TIME 3-GLS	4-GLS	5-GLS
Abgrall, Dennis	1	1	-	-	1	0	40:06	—	—
Abrahamsson, Thommy	1	1	-	-	1	0	30:36	—	—
Alley, Steve	1	1	-	-	0	1	11:08	—	—
Antonovich, Mike	6	6	-	-	3	3	13:49	—	—
Backstrom, Ralph	2	2	-	-	2	0	21:15	—	—
Baird, Ken	2	2	-	-	2	0	21:40	—	—
Beaudin, Norm	1	1	-	-	1	0	15:59	—	—
Bernier, Serge	2	2	-	-	2	0	39:05	—	—
Blackburn, Don	1	1	-	-	1	0	49:20	—	—
Bordeleau, Chris	2	1	1	-	1	1	23:01	46:39	—
Bordeleau, Paulin	3	3	-	-	1	2	13:07	—	—
Borgeson, Don	3	3	-	-	1	2	31:21	—	—
Boyd, Jim	1	1	-	-	1	0	29:16	—	—
Buchanan, Ron	2	1	1	-	1	1	16:33	33:43	—
Byers, Mike	1	1	-	-	1	0	16:09	—	—
Caffery, Terry	2	2	-	-	2	0	48:43	—	—
Callighen, Brett	1	1	-	-	1	0	15:35	—	—
Campbell, Bryan	3	3	-	-	2	1	11:23	—	—
Cardwell, Steve	1	1	-	-	1	0	35:38	—	—
Carlson, Jack	2	2	-	-	2	0	31:26	—	—
Carleton, Wayne	2	2	-	-	1	1	18:48	—	—
Caron, Alain	2	2	-	-	2	0	28:36	—	—
Chipperfield, Ron	2	2	-	-	1	1	47:23	—	—
Climie, Ron	3	2	-	1	2	1	3:42	12:11	36:00
Cloutier, Real	17	14	2	1	9	8	11:17	25:06	50:03
Coates, Brian	1	1	-	-	1	0	32:59	—	—
Connelly, Wayne	4	3	-	1	2	2	14:51	26:25	40:28
Constantin, Charles	1	1	-	-	0	1	30:06	—	—
Cormier, Michel	3	3	-	-	1	2	29:39	—	—
Demarco, Ab	1	1	-	-	1	0	7:35	—	—
Devine, Kevin	1	1	-	-	0	1	52:33	—	—
Dillon, Wayne	1	-	1	-	1	0	13:29	31:18	—
Driscoll, Peter	1	1	-	-	1	0	32:35	—	—
Dudley, Rick	3	2	1	-	3	0	19:06	48:51	—
Ferguson, Norm	2	2	-	-	1	1	13:42	—	—
Fleming, Reg	1	1	-	-	0	1	29:39	—	—
Flett, Bill	3	2	1	-	2	1	14:23	23:08	—
French, John	1	-	1	-	1	0	36:10	51:18	—
Ftorek, Robbie	6	6	-	-	3	3	29:32	—	—

PLAYER	HT	GOAL NIGHT			AT HOME	ON ROAD	FASTEST TIME		
		3	4	5			3-GLS	4-GLS	5-GLS
Gaudette, Andre	1	1	—	—	1	0	55:00	—	—
Gilmore, Tom	2	1	1	—	1	1	27:10	60:08	—
Giroux, Rejean	1	1	—	—	1	0	50:32	—	—
Gorman, Dave	1	1	—	—	0	1	15:08	—	—
Gratton, Jean-Guy	1	1	—	—	1	0	27:12	—	—
Gray, John	3	3	—	—	1	2	18:14	—	—
Grierson, Don	1	1	—	—	1	0	32:09	—	—
Guindon, Bob	1	1	—	—	1	0	37:41	—	—
Guite, Pierre	2	2	—	—	1	1	24:06	—	—
Hagman, Matti	2	1	1	—	2	0	7:48	26:46	—
Hall, Del	3	3	—	—	3	0	20:41	—	—
Hall, Murray	2	2	—	—	2	0	9:44	—	—
Hardy, Joe	1	1	—	—	0	1	32:30	—	—
Harris, Hugh	1	1	—	—	0	1	57:39	—	—
Harrison, Jim	2	2	—	—	2	0	47:45	—	—
Hedberg, Anders	12	6	6	—	7	5	7:58	26.47	—
Henderson, Paul	5	5	—	—	4	1	2:16	—	—
Herriman, Don	2	2	—	—	1	1	15:17	—	—
Hickey, Pat	2	1	1	—	2	0	13:51	41:09	—
Hinse, Andre	2	1	—	1	1	1	9:06	26:53	34:01
Hodgson, Ted	1	1	—	—	0	1	46:14	—	—
Holmgren, Paul	1	1	—	—	1	0	15:41	—	—
Houle, Rejean	7	6	1	—	6	1	11:29	22:42	—
Howe, Gordie	3	1	2	—	1	2	7:45	30:35	—
Howe, Mark	7	7	—	—	4	3	7:30	—	—
Huck, Fran	2	2	—	—	2	0	13:56	—	—
Hughes, Frank	7	6	1	—	4	3	6:40	27:26	—
Hull, Bobby	19	16	3	—	13	6	9:00	40:52	—
Jacques, Jeff	1	—	1	—	0	1	8:43	35:08	—
Jarrett, Gary	1	1	—	—	0	1	52:55	—	—
Johnson, Danny	1	1	—	—	0	1	25:46	—	—
Karlander, Al	2	2	—	—	2	0	19:48	—	—
Keon, Dave	1	1	—	—	0	1	35:11	—	—
Ketola, Veli-Peka	2	2	—	—	1	1	39:16	—	—
Kirk, Gavin	1	1	—	—	1	0	32:16	—	—
Labossiere, Gord	3	3	—	—	3	0	27:09	—	—
Lacroix, Andre	5	4	1	—	3	2	22:35	31:05	—
Lawson, Danny	12	9	3	—	6	6	12:23	24:29	—
LeBlanc, J. P.	2	2	—	—	0	2	44:21	—	—
Leclerc, Rene	1	1	—	—	0	1	27:23	—	—
Leduc, Rich	5	4	1	—	4	1	17:30	45:05	—
Lindstrom, Willy	2	2	—	—	1	1	19:09	—	—
Linseman, Ken	1	1	—	—	0	1	31:38	—	—
Locas, Jacques	1	1	—	—	1	0	8:47	—	—
Lodboa, Dan	1	1	—	—	1	0	52:45	—	—
Lukowich, Morris	2	2	—	—	2	0	20:41	—	—
Lund, Larry	5	5	—	—	4	1	22:37	—	—
Lyle, George	1	1	—	—	1	0	15:17	—	—
MacDonald, Blair	4	3	1	—	2	2	29:17	46:49	—
MacGregor, Gary	2	2	—	—	0	2	23:54	—	—
Mahovlich, Frank	3	3	—	—	2	1	19:10	—	—
Mara, Peter	1	1	—	—	1	0	26:29	—	—
Marrin, Peter	1	1	—	—	1	0	10:41	—	—
Marsh, Peter	3	3	—	—	1	2	5:41	—	—
Martin, Tom	3	2	1	—	0	3	11:49	50:38	—
McDonald, Brian	3	2	1	—	3	0	13:42	19:22	—
McDonough, Al	1	1	—	—	0	1	25:41	—	—
McKenzie, John	5	5	—	—	4	1	9:57	—	—
Miller, Perry	1	—	1	—	0	1	8:36	25:31	—
Mononen, Lauri	2	2	—	—	2	0	12:30	—	—
Morris, Rick	1	1	—	—	1	0	27:02	—	—
Morrison, George	3	2	1	—	2	1	0:43	34:39	—

PLAYER	HT	GOAL NIGHT 3	4	5	AT HOME	ON ROAD	FASTEST TIME 3-GLS	4-GLS	5-GLS
Morrison, Kevin	1	1	-	-	1	0	34:07	—	—
Myers, Murray	3	3	-	-	2	1	14:34	—	—
Morenz, Brian	1	1	-	-	0	1	36:12	—	—
Napier, Mark	4	4	-	-	2	2	33:49	—	—
Nedomansky, Vaclav	4	3	-	1	1	3	13:33	25:40	40:28
Nilsson, Kent	2	2	-	-	0	2	29:58	—	—
Nilsson, Ulf	4	4	-	-	1	3	16:49	—	—
O'Donnell, Fred	1	1	-	-	1	0	16:46	—	—
Paiement, Rosaire	3	3	-	-	2	1	31:26	—	—
Parizeau, Michel	2	2	-	-	0	2	40:13	—	—
Patenaude, Rusty	3	3	-	-	3	0	49:10	—	—
Peacosh, Gene	6	6	-	-	2	4	6:01	—	—
Perkins, Ross	1	1	-	-	1	0	17:07	—	—
Pinder, Gerry	1	1	-	-	0	1	36:31	—	—
Pleau, Larry	5	5	-	-	4	1	13:52	—	—
Popiel, Jan	2	2	-	-	2	0	33:23	—	—
Powis, Lynn	1	1	-	-	1	0	46:39	—	—
Preston, Rich	1	1	-	-	1	0	42:17	—	—
Repo, Sepo	1	1	-	-	1	0	13:41	—	—
Richter, Pavel	1	1	-	-	0	1	30:26	—	—
Rivers, Wayne	4	4	-	-	3	1	29:23	—	—
Rochon, Francois	2	2	-	-	2	0	23:00	—	—
Rogers, Mike	2	2	-	-	1	1	21:15	—	—
Ruskowski, Terry	1	-	1	-	1	0	32:03	38:34	—
St. Sauveur, Claude	5	5	-	-	4	1	14:01	—	—
Selby, Brit	1	1	-	-	0	1	59:01	—	—
Sentes, Rick	4	3	1	-	3	1	12:17	33:44	—
Serviss, Tom	1	1	-	-	1	0	42:21	—	—
Sheehy, Tim	2	1	1	-	2	0	23:36	30:08	—
Sheehan, Bobby	2	2	-	-	2	0	19:55	—	—
Simpson, Tom	6	3	3	-	4	2	20:45	36:36	—
Sobchuk, Dennis	2	2	-	-	2	0	45:24	—	—
Stoughton, Blaine	2	1	1	-	0	2	12:51	35:24	—
Sullivan, Peter	2	2	-	-	0	2	10:17	—	—
Sutherland, Steve	1	1	-	-	0	1	26:13	—	—
Tardif, Marc	12	10	2	-	2	10	7:48	40:00	—
Taylor, Ted	2	2	-	-	1	1	26:36	—	—
Thomas, Reg	1	1	-	-	1	0	29:07	—	—
Tidey, Alex	1	1	-	-	1	0	7:15	—	—
Ullman, Norm	1	1	-	-	0	1	37:11	—	—
Veneruzzo, Gary	4	3	1	-	1	3	19:02	52:50	—
Walters, Ron	1	1	-	-	1	0	54:10	—	—
Walton, Mike	7	5	2	-	7	0	5:29	34:54	—
Ward, Ron	7	5	-	2	6	1	6:44	20:20	25:53
Webster, Tom	7	7	-	-	4	3	15:16	—	—
White, Alton	2	2	-	-	0	2	6:58	—	—
Whitlock, Bobby	1	1	-	-	0	1	20:19	—	—
Widing, Juha	1	1	-	-	1	0	24:28	—	—
Williams, Tommy	1	1	-	-	0	1	40:06	—	—
Wiste, Jim	1	1	-	-	1	0	4:43	—	—
Wyrozub, Randy	1	1	-	-	1	0	1:46	—	—
Young, Bill	1	1	-	-	0	1	40:04	—	—
Zuke, Mike	1	1	-	-	1	0	2:18	—	—
Totals	406	352	47	7	249	157	0:43	12:11	25:53

REGULAR SEASON PENALTY SHOTS

DATE	SHOOTER	DEFENDING GOALIE	PER	TIME	RESULT
1972-73 Season					
Oct 11 72	Billy Hicke	Les Binkley	1	16:37	SCORED
Nov 29 72	Ron Ward	Al Smith	1	5:24	failed
Jan 16 73	Renald Leclerc	Gilles Gratton	3	8:17	SCORED
Mar 25 73	Renald Leclerc	Jack Norris	3	6:15	SCORED
1973-74 Season					
Oct 11 73	Andre LaCroix	Cam Newton	3	18:28	failed
Oct 19 73	Denis Meloche	Jack Norris	3	15:19	failed
Oct 25 73	Andre LaCroix	Al Smith	2	8:57	failed
Nov 3 73	Ron Buchanan	Andre Gill	2	7:46	failed
Nov 22 73	Wayne Connelly	Al Smith	2	10:34	failed
Nov 23 73	Marc Tardif	Jack Norris	3	18:12	failed
Dec 22 73	Gary Veneruzzo	Don McLeod	3	15:08	failed
Dec 29 73	Andre LaCroix	Gerry Cheevers	1	19:09	failed
Mar 1 74	Brian Carlin	Don McLeod	3	19:50	SCORED
Mar 10 74	Ron Garwasiuk	Mike Curran	2	19:38	failed
Mar 14 74	Tom Martin	Cam Newton	2	3:39	failed
Mar 31 74	Brian Morenz	Gerry Cheevers	3	12:22	failed
Apr 1 74	Frank Hughes	Al Smith	2	7:10	failed
1974-75 Season					
Oct 24 74	Wayne Connelly	Andy Brown	1	11:44	failed
Nov 12 74	Gary MacGregor	Joe Junkin	1	10:19	failed
Dec 4 74	Eddie Joyal	Don McLeod	2	6:45	SCORED
Dec 26 74	Wayne Connelly	Jacques Plante	1	7:44	failed
Jan 4 75	Danny Lawson	Al Smith	3	19:42	SCORED
Jan 5 75	Bobby Leduc	Bob Whidden	1	9:49	failed
Jan 28 75	Norm Ferguson	Joe Daley	3	12:46	failed
Feb 11 75	Rejean Houle	Ernie Wakely	2	8:30	SCORED
Mar 1 75	Bob Mowat	Andy Brown	2	19:36	SCORED
Mar 12 75	Jim Harrison	Paul Hoganson	2	5:34	failed
1975-76 Season					
Oct 10 75	Kevin Devine	Gary Kurt	2	6:01	failed
Oct 28 75	Serge Bernier	Mario Vien	1	13:45	SCORED
Feb 6 76	Mark Napier	Joe Daley	3	13:43	SCORED
Feb 18 76	Al McDonough	Don McLeod	3	2:48	failed
Feb 18 76	Danny Gruen	Don McLeod	3	11:47	failed
Mar 2 76	Rick Morris	Don McLeod	1	18:33	SCORED
Mar 20 76	Chris Bordeleau	Don McLeod	1	8:46	failed
Mar 20 76	Rejean Houle	Don McLeod	1	10:21	failed
Mar 30 76	Florent Fortier	Chris Worthy	3	14:46	failed
1976-77 Season					
Oct 17 76	Danny Gruen	Wayne Wood	2	6:49	failed
Nov 11 76	Danny Lawson	Curt Larsson	2	14:30	failed
Dec 17 76	Robbie Ftorek	Ken Broderick	1	17:53	failed
Dec 26 76	Mark Napier	Wayne Rutledge	3	17:44	SCORED
Jan 20 77	Frank Hughes	Paul Hoganson	3	15:56	failed
Feb 18 77	Bruce Greig	Norm LaPointe	2	16:46	SCORED
1977-78 Season					

NO PENALTY SHOTS AWARDED DURING REGULAR SEASON

REGULAR SEASON
CAREER GOALTENDING LEADERS
(At Least 2100 Minutes Played)

TEN LOWEST G.A.A.'s
1. 2.99 Ron Grahame
2. 3.12 Gerry Cheevers
3. 3.16 Jack Norris
4. 3.24 Al Smith
5. 3.25 Ernie Wakely
6. 3.25 Wayne Rutledge
7. 3.26 Michel Dion
8. 3.30 Joe Daley
9. 3.33 Don McLeod
10. 3.35 Louis Levasseur

MOST LOSSES
1. 144 Don McLeod
2. 134 John Garrett
3. 120 Ernie Wakely
4. 102 Joe Daley
5. 101 Richard Brodeur
6. 96 Dave Dryden
7. 86 Gary Kurt
8. 82 Jack Norris
9. 81 Al Smith
10. 78 Gerry Cheevers

MOST GAME APPEARANCES
1. 332 Don McLeod
2. 297 Ernie Wakely
3. 285 Joe Daley
4. 282 John Garrett
5. 263 Richard Brodeur
6. 220 Al Smith
7. 191 Gerry Cheevers
7. 191 Jack Norris
9. 179 Dave Dryden
10. 176 Gary Kurt

MOST TIES
1. 20 Ernie Wakely
2. 15 Don McLeod
3. 12 Jack Norris
4. 11 John Garrett
5. 10 Al Smith
5. 10 Joe Daley
7. 9 Bob Whidden
7. 9 Bruce Landon
7. 9 Gerry Cheevers
7. 9 Richard Brodeur

MOST MINUTES PLAYED
1. 18,926 Don McLeod
2. 17,272 Ernie Wakely
3. 16,579 Joe Daley
4. 16,423 John Garrett
5. 14,668 Richard Brodeur
6. 12,993 Al Smith
7. 11,352 Gerry Cheevers
8. 11,030 Jack Norris
9. 10,372 Wayne Rutledge
10. 10,289 Dave Dryden

MOST SHOTS FACED
1. 9,293 John Garrett
2. 9,126 Don McLeod
3. 8,875 Ernie Wakely
4. 8,372 Joe Daley
5. 8,097 Richard Brodeur
6. 6,379 Al Smith
7. 6,203 Gerry Cheevers
8. 5,645 Jack Norris
9. 5,538 Dave Dryden
10. 5,282 Wayne Rutledge

MOST WINS
1. 160 Joe Daley
2. 157 Don McLeod
3. 149 Ernie Wakely
4. 140 Richard Brodeur
5. 128 John Garrett
6. 106 Al Smith
7. 102 Ron Grahame
8. 99 Gerry Cheevers
9. 93 Wayne Rutledge
10. 86 Jack Norris

HIGHEST SHOTS-AGAINST-AVERAGE
1. 36.6 Gerry Desjardins
2. 35.3 Mike Curran
3. 34.4 Chris Worthy
4. 34.1 Jim McLeod
5. 34.0 John Garrett
6. 33.8 Clay Hebenton
7. 33.4 Andre Gill
8. 33.3 Ken Brown
9. 33.1 Christer Abrahamsson
9. 33.1 Richard Brodeur

LOWEST SHOTS-AGAINST-AVERAGE
- 44. 28.9 Ken Broderick
- 44. 28.9 Don McLeod
- 43. 29.0 Russ Gillow
- 41. 29.5 Al Smith
- 41. 29.5 Gary Bromley
- 40. 30.0 Grahame
- 39. 30.3 Joe Daley
- 38. 30.6 Wayne Rutledge
- 36. 30.7 Jack Norris
- 36. 30.7 George Gardner

MOST GOALS ALLOWED
1. 1051 Don McLeod
2. 961 John Garrett
3. 935 Ernie Wakely
4. 912 Joe Daley
5. 911 Richard Brodeur
6. 702 Al Smith
7. 690 Gary Kurt
8. 638 Dave Dryden
9. 591 Gerry Cheevers
10. 582 Jack Norris

MOST SAVES MADE
1. 8,332 John Garrett
2. 8,075 Don McLeod
3. 7,940 Ernie Wakely
4. 7,460 Joe Daley
5. 7,186 Richard Brodeur
6. 5,677 Al Smith
7. 5,612 Gerry Cheevers
8. 5,063 Jack Norris
9. 4,900 Dave Dryden
10. 4,721 Wayne Rutledge

HIGHEST SAVE PERCENTAGE
1. .905 Gerry Cheevers
2. .903 Mike Curran
3. .900 Ron Grahame
4. .897 John Garrett
4. .897 Jack Norris
6. .896 Bob Whidden
7. .895 Ernie Wakely
8. .894 Wayne Rutledge
8. .894 Michel Dion
8. .894 Cam Newton

LOWEST SAVE PERCENTAGE
- 45. .863 Ken Broderick
- 44. .865 Gary Kurt
- 42. .870 Gary Inness
- 42. .870 Norm LaPointe
- 40. .871 Curt Larsson
- 40. .871 Paul Hoganson
- 38. .873 Clay Hebenton
- 38. .873 George Gardner
- 37. .873 Andy Brown
- 35. .880 Wayne Wood
- 35. .880 Russ Gillow

MOST SHUTOUTS
1. 16 Ernie Wakely
2. 14 Gerry Cheevers
3. 12 Ron Grahame
3. 12 John Garrett
3. 12 Joe Daley
6. 11 Don McLeod
7. 9 Al Smith
8. 8 Mike Curran
9. 6 Wayne Rutledge
10. 5 Eight Players

191

WHA CAREER SHUTOUTS

ABRAHAMSSON, Christer	3	JOHNSON, Bob	1
AUBRY, Serge	5	JUNKIN, Joe	2
BINKLEY, Les	1	KURT, Gary	3
BLANCHET, Bob	1	LANDON, Bruce	2
BRODERICK, Ken	4	LaPOINTE, Norm	2
BRODEUR, Richard	5	LARSSON, Curt	1
BROMLEY, Gary	1	LEVASSEUR, Louis	5
BROWN, Andy	3	LOCKETT, Ken	1
BROWN, Ken	3	McCARTEN, Jack	1
CARON, Jacques	3	McLEOD, Don	11
CHEEVERS, Gerry	14	McLEOD, Jim	2
CURRAN, Mike	7	NEWTON, Cam	2
DALEY, Joe	12	NORRIS, Jack	5
DEGUISE, Michel	1	PARENT, Bernie	2
DION, Michel	5	PARK, Jim	1
DONNELLY, Peter	5	PLANTE, Jacques	1
DRYDEN, Dave	5	RAEDER, Cap	2
GARDNER, George	1	RUTLEDGE, Wayne	6
GARRETT, John	12	SMITH, Al	9
GILLOW, Russ	4	WAKELY, Ernie	16
GRAHAME, Ron	12	WHIDDEN, Bobby	2
GRATTON, Gilles	4	WILKIE, Ian	1
HOGANSON, Paul	5	WOOD, Wayne	2
HUMPHREYS, Ed	1	WORTHY, Chris	3

PAST WINNERS OF THE HOWE TROPHY

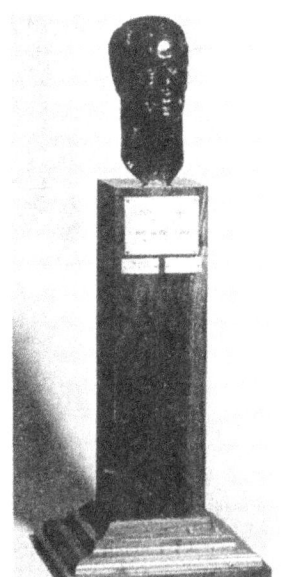

HOWE TROPHY
(Most Valuable Player)

Marc Tardif	1977-78
Robbie Ftorek	1976-77
Marc Tardif	1975-76
Bobby Hull	1974-75
Gordie Howe	1973-74
Bobby Hull	1972-73

The Howe Trophy

PAST WINNERS OF THE INDIVIDUAL TROPHY

HATSKIN TROPHY
(Best Goaltender)

Al Smith	1977-78
Ron Grahame	1976-77
Michel Dion	1975-76
Ron Grahame	1974-75
Don McLeod	1973-74
Gerry Cheevers	1972-73

HUNTER TROPHY
(Scoring Champion)

Marc Tardif	1977-78
Real Cloutier	1976-77
Marc Tardif	1975-76
Andre LaCroix	1974-75
Mike Walton	1973-74
Andre LaCroix	1972-73

The Individual Trophy

OUTSTANDING DEFENSEMAN

Lars-Eric Sjoberg	1977-78
Ron Plumb	1976-77
Paul Shmyr	1975-76
JC Tremblay	1974-75
Pat Stapleton	1973-74
JC Tremblay	1972-73

ROOKIE OF THE YEAR

Kent Nilsson	1977-78
George Lyle	1976-77
Mark Napier	1975-76
Anders Hedberg	1974-75
Mark Howe	1973-74
Terry Caffery	1972-73

MOST GENTLEMANLY PLAYER

Dave Keon	1977-78
Dave Keon	1976-77
Vaclav Nedomansky	1975-76
Mike Rogers	1974-75
Ralph Backstrom	1973-74
Ted Hampson	1972-73

SCHMERTZ TROPHY
(Coach of the Year)

Bill Dineen	1977-78
Bill Dineen	1976-77
Bobby Kromm	1975-76
Sandy Hucul	1974-75
Billy Harris	1973-74
Jack Kelley	1972-73

1972-78 OFFICIAL END OF SEASON ALL-STAR TEAMS

1977-78
FIRST TEAM	POS	SECOND TEAM
Al Smith	G	Ernie Wakely
Lars-Erik Sjoberg	D	Rick Ley
Al Hamilton	D	Barry Long
Ulf Nilsson	C	Robbie Ftorek
Anders Hedberg	RW	Real Cloutier
Marc Tardif	LW	Bobby Hull

1976-77
FIRST TEAM	POS	SECOND TEAM
John Garrett	G	Joe Daley
Darryl Maggs	D	Poul Popiel
Ron Plumb	D	Mark Howe
Robbie Ftorek	C	Ulf Nilsson
Anders Hedberg	RW	Real Cloutier
Marc Tardif	LW	Rick Dudley

1975-76
FIRST TEAM	POS	SECOND TEAM
Joe Daley	G	Ron Grahame
Paul Shmyr	D	Kevin Morrison
JC Tremblay	D	Pat Stapleton
Ulf Nilsson	C	Robbie Ftorek
Anders Hedberg	RW	Real Cloutier
Marc Tardif	LW	Bobby Hull

1974-75
FIRST TEAM	POS	SECOND TEAM
Ron Grahame	G	Gerry Cheevers
JC Tremblay	D	Poul Popiel
Kevin Morrison	D	Barry Long
Andre LaCroix	C	Serge Bernier
Gordie Howe	RW	Anders Hedberg
Bobby Hull	LW	Marc Tardif

1973-74
FIRST TEAM	POS	SECOND TEAM
Don McLeod	G	Gerry Cheevers
Pat Stapleton	D	JC Tremblay
Paul Shmyr	D	Al Hamilton
Andre LaCroix	C	Wayne Carleton
Gordie Howe	RW	Mike Walton
Bobby Hull	LW	Mark Howe

1972-73
FIRST TEAM	POS	SECOND TEAM
Gerry Cheevers	G	Bernie Parent
JC Tremblay	D	Jim Dorey
Paul Shmyr	D	Larry Hornung
Andre LaCroix	C	Ron Ward
Danny Lawson	RW	Tom Webster
Bobby Hull	LW	Gary Jarrett

AVCO WORLD TROPHY PLAYOFF HISTORY

Quebec's Serge Bernier was awarded the MVP trophy for the 1976-77 Avco playoffs. For career record of Bernier, see page 47.

AVCO WORLD TROPHY PLAYOFF CHAMPIONS

1978 — WINNIPEG JETS
General Manager Rudy Pilous,
Coach Larry Hillman,
Captain Lars-Erik Sjoberg,
Mike Amodeo, Ken Baird,
Gary Bromley, Kim Clackson,
Joe Daley, Bill Davis,
Dave Dunn, Mike Ford,
Ted Green, Bob Guindon,
Anders Hedberg, Bobby Hull,
Dave Kryskow, Dan Labraaten,
Bill Lesuk, Willy Lindstrom,
Barry Long, Markus Mattsson,
Lyle Moffat, Kent Nilsson,
Ulf Nilsson, Lynn Powis,
Kent Ruhnke, Peter Sullivan.

1977 — QUEBEC NORDIQUES
General Manager Maurice Filion,
Coach Marc Boileau,
Captain Marc Tardif, Serge Aubry,
Paul Baxter, Jean Bernier, Serge Bernier,
Chris Bordeleau, Paulin Bordeleau,
Andre Boudrias, Curt Brackenbury,
Richard Brodeur, Real Cloutier,
Charles Constantin, Jim Dorey,
Norm Dube, Bob Fitchner, Pierre Guite,
Ed Humphreys, Francois Lacombe,
Garry Lariviere, Steve Sutherland,
JC Tremblay, Wally Weir.

1976 — WINNIPEG JETS
General Manager Rudy Pilous,
Coach Bobby Kromm,
Captain Lars-Erik Sjoberg,
Duke Asmundson, Norm Beaudin,
Thommie Bergman, Joe Daley, Mike Ford,
Ted Green, Bobby Guindon,
Larry Hillman, Anders Hedberg,
Larry Hornung, Bobby Hull,
Veli Pekka Ketola, Curt Larsson,
Bill Lesuk, Mats Lindh,
Willy Lindstrom, Lyle Moffat, Ulf Nilsson,
Gerry Odrowski, Heikki Riihiranta,
Peter Sullivan.

1975 — HOUSTON AEROS
General Manager-Coach Bill Dineen,
Captain Ted Taylor, Ron Grahame,
Larry Hale, Murray Hall, Andre Hinse,
Gordie Howe, Mark Howe, Marty Howe,
Frank Hughes, Glen Irwin,
Gord Labossiere, Don Larway,
Larry Lund, Poul Popiel, Bill Prentice,
Rich Preston, Terry Ruskowski,
Wayne Rutledge, John Schella,
Jim Sherrit.

1974 — HOUSTON AEROS
General Manager-Coach Bill Dineen,
Captain Ted Taylor, Ron Grahame,
Don Grierson, Larry Hale, Murray Hall,
Andre Hinse, Gordie Howe, Mark Howe,
Marty Howe, Frank Hughes,
Gord Kannegeisser, Gord Labossiere,
Larry Lund, Dunc McCallum,
Don McLeod, Poul Popiel, Bill Prentice,
Wayne Rutledge, John Schella,
Jim Sherrit, Jack Stanfield, Joe Szura,
Gary Williamson.

1973 — NEW ENGLAND WHALERS
General Manager-Coach Jack Kelley,
Captain Ted Green, Kevin Ahearn,
Mike Byers, Terry Caffery, John Cuniff,
Jack Danby, Jim Dorey, Tom Earl,
John French, Paul Hurley,
Bruce Landon, Rick Ley, Larry Pleau,
Brit Selby, Brad Selwood, Tim Sheehy,
Al Smith, Guy Smith, Tom Webster,
Tommy Williams.

AVCO WORLD TROPHY STANDINGS
1973-1978

	YRS	SERIES	WON	LOST	GAMES	WON	LOST	GOALS FOR	GOALS AGAINST	TROPHIES
New England	6	12	7	5	64	36	28	233	211	1
Winnipeg	5	12	9	3	60	40	20	265	200	2
Quebec	4	9	6	3	48	26	22	196	168	1
Birmingham	4	5	1	4	28	11	17	101	127	—
Edmonton	4	4	0	4	19	3	16	50	87	—
Indianapolis	2	3	1	2	16	8	8	48	52	—
Cincinnati	1	1	0	1	4	0	4	9	19	—
Defunct Clubs		38	18	20	197	94	103	675	713	2
TOTALS	6	84	42	42	436	218	218	1577	1577	6

AVCO WORLD TROPHY
PLAYOFF RECORDS 1972-1978
TEAM RECORDS

MOST AVCO WORLD TROPHY CHAMPIONSHIPS:
    2 — Winnipeg Jets (1976/78)
    — Houston Aeros (1974/75)

MOST FINAL SERIES APPEARANCES:
    4 — Winnipeg Jets (1973/76/77/78)

MOST SEMI-FINAL SERIES APPEARANCES:
    5 — Houston Aeros (1973/74/75/76/77)
    4 — Winnipeg Jets (1973/76/77/78)

MOST PLAYOFF SERIES APPEARANCES:
    14 — Houston Aeros (won 10, lost 4)
    12 — Winnipeg Jets (won 9, lost 3)
    — New England Whalers (won 7, lost 5)

MOST YEARS IN PLAYOFFS:
    6 — New England Whalers (never missed playoffs)
    — Houston Aeros (never missed playoffs)
    5 — Winnipeg Jets

MOST PLAYOFF SERIES WON:
    10 — Houston Aeros
    9 — Winnipeg Jets
    7 — New England Whalers

MOST PLAYOFF SERIES LOST:
    5 — New England Whalers
    4 — Birmingham Bulls (includes series as Toronto and Ottawa)
    — Edmonton Oilers
    — Houston Aeros
    — Cleveland Crusaders

MOST GAMES PLAYED IN PLAYOFFS:
    71 — Houston Aeros (won 44, lost 27)
    64 — New England Whalers (won 36, lost 28)
    60 — Winnipeg Jets (won 40, lost 20)

MOST PLAYOFF GAMES WON:
  44 — Houston Aeros
  40 — Winnipeg Jets
  36 — New England Whalers

MOST PLAYOFF GAMES LOST:
  28 — New England Whalers
  27 — Houston Aeros
  22 — Quebec Nordiques

MOST GOALS SCORED IN PLAYOFFS:
  273 — Houston Aeros (71 games, 3.8 avg. per game)
  265 — Winnipeg Jets (60 games, 4.4 avg. per game)
  233 — New England Whalers (64 games, 3.6 per game)

MOST GOALS ALLOWED IN PLAYOFFS:
  224 — Houston Aeros (71 games, 3.2 avg. per game)
  211 — New England Whalers (64 games, 3.3 avg. per game)
  200 — Winnipeg Jets (60 games, 3.3 avg. per game)

FOUR GAME SERIES RECORDS

MOST FOUR-GAME SERIES INVOLVED IN:
  6 — Houston Aeros (won 4, lost 2)
  5 — Winnipeg Jets (won 4, lost 1)

MOST GOALS SCORED BY BOTH TEAMS IN A FOUR-GAME SERIES:
  35 — Winnipeg outscored Houston 24-11 in four-game sweep in 1976 finals.
  33 — Winnipeg outscored Edmonton 22-11 in four-game sweep in 1976 quarter-finals.
  32 — Houston outscored Winnipeg 23-9 in four-game sweep in 1974 quarter-finals.
     — Winnipeg outscored New England 24-8 in four-game sweep in 1978 finals.

FEWEST GOALS SCORED BY BOTH TEAMS IN FOUR-GAME SERIES:
  17 — Winnipeg outscored Houston 14-3 in four-game sweep in 1973 semi-finals.
  22 — Houston outscored San Diego 17-5 in four-game sweep in 1975 semi-finals.
  25 — Cleveland outscored Philadelphia in 1973 quarter-finals, 19-6.

MOST GOALS SCORED BY ONE TEAM IN A FOUR-GAME SERIES:
  24 — Winnipeg in 1976 final series vs. Houston
     — Winnipeg in 1978 final series vs. New England
  23 — Houston in 1974 quarter-final series vs. Winnipeg

FEWEST GOALS SCORED BY A TEAM IN A FOUR-GAME SERIES:
  3 — Houston in 1973 semi-final loss to Winnipeg
  5 — San Diego in 1975 semi-final loss to Houston
  6 — Philadelphia in 1973 quarter-final loss to Cleveland

MOST SHUTOUTS IN A FOUR-GAME SERIES:
  2 — Winnipeg shutout Houston twice in 1973 semi-final series won by Winnipeg 4-0.
    — Houston shutout San Diego twice in 1975 semi-final series won by Houston 4-0.

MOST PENALTIES BY BOTH TEAMS IN A FOUR-GAME SERIES:
  67 — Winnipeg had 27 penalties, Edmonton 40 in Winnipeg four-game

sweep in 1974 quarter-final series. Winnipeg had 74 penalty minutes, Edmonton 97.

66 — Cleveland had 35 penalties, Philadelphia 31 in Cleveland four-game sweep in 1973 quarter-final series. Cleveland had 82 penalty minutes, Philadelphia 95.

61 — Houston had 38 penalties, Winnipeg 23 in Houston four-game sweep in 1974 quarter-final series. Houston had 98 penalty minutes, Winnipeg 60.

MOST PENALTY MINUTES BY BOTH TEAMS IN A FOUR-GAME SERIES:

177 — Cleveland defeated Philadephia in four games in 1973 quarter-final series. Cleveland had 35 penalties for 82 minutes, Philadelphia 31 for 95 minutes.

171 — Winnipeg defeated Edmonton in 1976 quarter-finals. Winnipeg had 27 penalties for 74 minutes, Edmonton 40 for 97 minutes.

158 — Houston defeated Winnipeg in 1974 quarter-finals. Houston had 38 penalties for 98 minutes, Winnipeg had 23 for 60 minutes.

MOST PENALTIES BY ONE TEAM IN A FOUR-GAME SERIES:

40 — Edmonton in 1976 quarter-final loss to Winnipeg, 97 minutes

38 — Houston in 1974 quarter-final win over Winnipeg, 98 minutes

35 — Cleveland in 1973 quarter-final win over Philadelphia, 82 minutes

MOST PENALTY MINUTES BY ONE TEAM IN A FOUR-GAME SERIES:

98 — Houston in 1974 quarter-final win over Winnipeg

97 — Edmonton in 1976 quarter-final loss to Winnipeg

95 — Philadelphia in 1973 quarter-final loss to Cleveland

FEWEST PENALTIES BY BOTH TEAMS IN A FOUR-GAME SERIES:

31 — Houston/San Diego 1975 semi-finals. Houston had 18 penalties for 36 minutes, San Diego, 13 for 26 minutes. Houston won series.

40 — Winnipeg/Houston 1973 semi-finals. Winnipeg had 13 penalties for 29 minutes, Houston had 27 for 83 minutes. Winnipeg won series.

42 — Houston/Quebec 1975 finals. Houston had 23 penalties for 55 minutes, Quebec 19 for 47 minutes. Houston won series.

FEWEST PENALTY MINUTES BY BOTH TEAMS IN A FOUR-GAME SERIES:

62 — Houston/San Diego in 1975 semi-finals. Houston had 36 minutes, San Diego had 26. Houston won series.

102 — Houston/Quebec in 1975 finals. Houston had 55 minutes, Quebec 47. Houston won series.

104 — Winnipeg/New England 1978 finals. Winnipeg had 51 minutes, New England 53. Winnipeg won series.

FEWEST PENALTIES BY ONE TEAM IN A FOUR-GAME SERIES:

13 — Winnipeg 1973 semi-final win over Houston, 29 minutes
 — San Diego 1975 semi-final loss to Houston, 26 minutes

18 — Houston 1975 semi-final win over San Diego, 36 minutes

FEWEST PENALTY MINUTES BY ONE TEAM IN A FOUR-GAME SERIES:

26 — San Diego 1975 semi-final loss to Houston

29 — Winnipeg 193 semi-final win over Houston

36 — Houston 1975 semi-final win over San Diego

199

FIVE-GAME SERIES TEAM RECORDS
MOST GOALS BY BOTH TEAMS IN A FIVE-GAME SERIES:
- 48 — New England outscored Winnipeg 30-18 in 1973 finals won by New England, 4-1.
- 41 — New England outscored Ottawa 24-17 in 1973 quarter-finals won by New England, 4-1.
- — Winnipeg outscored Birmingham 29-12 in 1978 quarter-finals won by Winnipeg, 4-1.

FEWEST GOALS SCORED BY BOTH TEAMS IN A FIVE-GAME SERIES:
- 29 — Toronto outscored Cleveland 18-11 in 1974 quarter-finals won by Toronto, 4-1.
- 30 — New England outscored Cleveland 16-14 in 1973 semi-finals won by New England, 4-1.
- — San Diego outscored Phoenix 17-13 in 1976 preliminary round won by San Diego, 3-2.

MOST GOALS SCORED BY ONE TEAM IN A FIVE-GAME SERIES:
- 30 — New England outscored Winnipeg 30-18 in winning 1973 finals, 4-1.
- 29 — Winnipeg outscored Birmingham 29-12 in winning 1978 quarter-finals, 4-1.
- 25 — Quebec outscored Indianapolis 25-14 in winning 1977 semi-finals, 4-1.
- — New England outscored Quebec 25-14 in 1978 semi-finals, 4-1.

FEWEST GOALS SCORED BY ONE TEAM IN A FIVE-GAME SERIES:
- 9 — Edmonton was outscored by New England 23-9 in losing 1978 quarter-finals, 4-1.
- 11 — Cleveland was outscored by Toronto 18-11 in losing 1974 quarter-finals, 4-1.
- 12 — Phoenix was outscored by Quebec 23-12 in losing 1975 quarter-finals, 4-1.
- — Birmingham was outscored by Winnipeg 29-12 in losing 1978 quarter-finals, 4-1.

MOST SHUTOUTS BY BOTH TEAMS IN A FIVE-GAME SERIES:
- 1 — Quebec in 1975 quarter-finals vs. Phoenix won by Quebec, 4-1
- — Quebec in 1977 quarter-finals vs. New England won by Quebec, 4-1
- — Winnipeg in 1977 semi-finals vs. Calgary won by Winnipeg, 4-1
- — Indianapolis in 1977 semi-finals vs. Quebec won by Quebec, 4-1
- — Edmonton in 1978 quarter-finals vs. New England won by New England, 4-1

MOST PENALTIES BY BOTH TEAMS IN A FIVE-GAME SERIES:
- 106 — Winnipeg/Birmingham 1978 quarter-final series won by Winnipeg, 4-1. Winnipeg had 42 penalties for 172 minutes, Birmingham had 64 for 243 minutes.
- 94 — New England/Edmonton in 1978 quarter-finals won by New England, 4-1. New England had 45 penalties for 99 minutes, Edmonton had 49 for 115 minutes.
- 91 — Toronto/Cleveland in 1974 quarter-finals won by Toronto, 4-1. Toronto had 46 penalties for 124 minutes, Cleveland had 45 for 141 minutes.

MOST PENALTY MINUTES BY BOTH TEAMS IN A FIVE-GAME SERIES
- 415 — Winnipeg/Birmingham in 1978 quarter-final series won by Winnipeg, 4-1. Winnipeg had 172 minutes, Birmingham, 243.
- 311 — Calgary/Quebec in 1976 quarter-final series won by Calgary, 4-1. Calgary had 137 minutes, Quebec had 174.
- 265 — Toronto/Cleveland in 1974 quarter-finals won by Toronto, 4-1. Toronto had 124 minutes, Cleveland, 141.

MOST PENALTIES BY ONE TEAM IN A FIVE-GAME SERIES:
- 64 — Birmingham in 1978 quarter final loss to Winnipeg, 243 minutes
- 49 — Edmonton in 1978 quarter-final loss to New England, 115 minutes
- 46 — Cleveland in 1973 semi-final loss to New England, 112 minutes
  - Toronto in 1974 quarter-final win over Cleveland, 124 minutes
  - Quebec in 1976 quarter-final loss to Calgary, 174 minutes

MOST PENALTY MINUTES BY ONE TEAM IN A FIVE-GAME SERIES:
- 243 — Birmingham in 1978 quarter-final loss to Winnipeg
- 174 — Quebec in 1976 quarter-final loss to Calgary
- 172 — Winnipeg in 1978 quarter-final win over Quebec

FEWEST PENALTIES BY BOTH TEAMS IN A FIVE-GAME SERIES:
- 29 — Winnipeg/Minnesota in 1973 quarter-final series won by Winnipeg, 4-1. Winnipeg had 14 penalties for 39 minutes, Minnesota 15 for 33 minutes.
- 37 — Quebec/Phoenix in 1975 quarter-final series won by Quebec, 4-1. Quebec had 18 penalties for 47 minutes, Phoenix had 19 for 46 minutes.
- 38 — New England/Winnipeg in 1973 finals won by New England, 4-1. New England had 20 penalties for 40 minutes, Winnipeg 18 for 36 minutes.

FEWEST PENALTY MINUTES BY BOTH TEAMS IN A FIVE-GAME SERIES:
- 72 — Winnipeg/Minnesota in 1973 quarter-final series won by Winnipeg, 4-1. Winnipeg had 39 minutes, Minnesota had 33.
- 76 — New England/Winnipeg in 1973 finals won by New England, 4-1. New England had 40 minutes, Winnipeg had 36.
- 93 — Quebec/Phoenix in 1975 quarter-finals won by Quebec, 4-1. Quebec had 47 minutes, Phoenix had 46.

FEWEST PENALTIES BY ONE TEAM IN A FIVE-GAME SERIES
- 14 — Winnipeg in 1973 quarter-final win over Minnesota
- 15 — Minnesota in 1973 quarter-final loss to Winnipeg
- 18 — Winnipeg in 1973 finals loss to New England
  - Quebec in 1975 quarter-final win over Phoenix

FEWEST PENALTY MINUTES BY ONE TEAM IN A FIVE-GAME SERIES:
- 33 — Minnesota in 1973 quarter-final loss to Winnipeg
- 36 — Winnipeg in 1973 final series loss to New England
- 39 — Winnipeg in 1973 quarter-final win over Minnesota

SIX-GAME SERIES TEAM RECORDS
MOST GOALS BY BOTH TEAMS IN A SIX-TEAM SERIES:
- 56 — San Diego/Toronto in 1975 quarter-final series won by San Diego, 4-2. San Diego scored 29 goals, Toronto 27.
- 47 — Winnipeg/Houston in 1977 semi-finals won by Winnipeg, 4-2. Winnipeg scored 24 goals, Houston 23.

201

FEWEST GOALS SCORED BY BOTH TEAMS IN A SIX-GAME SERIES:
- 39 — Houston/Los Angeles in 1973 quarter-finals won by Houston, 4-2. Houston scored 23 goals, Los Angeles 16.
- 43 — Houston/Minnesota in 1974 semi-finals won by Houston, 4-2. Houston scored 26 goals, Minnesota 17.

MOST GOALS SCORED BY ONE TEAM IN A SIX-GAME SERIES
- 29 — Quebec outscored Minnesota 29-16 in winning 1975 semi-finals.
  - — San Diego outscored Toronto 29-27 in winning 1975 quarter-finals.
  - — Quebec outscored Houston 29-16 in winning 1978 quarter-finals.

FEWEST GOALS SCORED BY ONE TEAM IN A SIX-GAME SERIES:
- 16 — Los Angeles was outscored by Houston 23-16 in losing 1973 quarter-finals.
  - — Minnesota was outscored by Quebec 29-16 in losing 1975 semi-finals.
  - — Houston was outscored by Quebec 29-16 in 1978 quarter-finals.

MOST SHUTOUTS BY BOTH TEAMS IN A SIX-GAME SERIES:
- 1 — Minnesota in 1975 quarter-final win vs. New England
  - — Quebec in 1978 quarter-final win vs. Houston

MOST PENALTIES BY BOTH TEAMS IN A SIX-GAME SERIES:
- 125 — Quebec/Houston in 1978 quarter-finals won by Quebec, 4-2. Quebec had 67 penalties, Houston 58.
- 115 — Houston/Minnesota in 1974 semi-finals won by Houston, 4-2. Houston had 55 penalties, Minnesota 60.
- 103 — Minnesota/New England in 1975 quarter-finals won by Minnesota, 4-2. Minnesota had 53 penalties, New England 50.

MOST PENALTY MINUTES BY BOTH TEAMS IN A SIX-GAME SERIES:
- 383 — Houston/Minnesota in 1974 semi-finals won by Houston, 4-2. Houston had 170 minutes, Minnesota had 213.
- 379 — Minnesota/New England in 1975 quarter-finals won by Minnesota, 4-2. Minnesota had 182 minutes, New England 197.
- 314 — Quebec/Houston in 1978 quarter-finals won by Quebec, 4-2. Quebec had 189 minutes, Houston 152.

MOST PENALTIES BY ONE TEAM IN A SIX-GAME SERIES:
- 67 — Quebec in 1978 quarter-final win over Houston
- 60 — Minnesota in 1974 semi-final loss to Houston
  - — Houston in 1977 semi-final loss to Winnipeg

MOST PENALTY MINUTES BY ONE TEAM IN A SIX-GAME SERIES:
- 213 — Minnesota in 1974 semi-final loss to Houston
- 197 — New England in 1975 quarter-final loss to Minnesota
- 189 — Quebec in 1978 quarter-final win over Houston

FEWEST PENALTIES BY BOTH TEAMS IN A SIX-GAME SERIES:
- 64 — San Diego/Toronto in 1975 quarter-finals won by San Diego, 4-2. San Diego and Toronto both had 32 penalties.
- 71 — Quebec/Minnesota in 1975 semi-finals won by Quebec, 4-2. Quebec had 39 penalties, Minnesota 32.
- 75 — Houston/Los Angeles in 1973 quarter-finals won by Houston, 4-2. Houston had 39 penalties, Los Angeles 36.

FEWEST PENALTY MINUTES BY BOTH TEAMS IN A SIX-GAME SERIES:
- 164 — San Diego/Toronto in 1975 quarter-finals won by San Diego,

4-2. San Diego had 94 minutes, Toronto 70.
167 — Houston/Los Angeles in 1973 quarter-final series won by Houston, 4-2. Houston had 84 minutes, Los Angeles 83.
174 — Quebec/Minnesota in 1975 semi-finals won by Quebec, 4-2. Quebec had 95 minutes, Minnesota 79.

FEWEST PENALTIES BY ONE TEAM IN A SIX-GAME SERIES:
32 — San Diego in 1975 quarter-final win over Toronto
— Toronto in 1975 quarter-final loss to San Diego
— Minnesota in 1975 semi-final loss to Quebec

FEWEST PENALTY MINUTES BY ONE TEAM IN A SIX-GAME SERIES:
70 — Toronto in 1975 quarter-final loss to San Diego
79 — Minnesota in 1975 semi-final loss to Quebec
83 — Los Angeles in 1973 quarter-final loss to Houston

SEVEN-GAME SERIES RECORDS

MOST GOALS BY BOTH TEAMS IN A SEVEN-GAME SERIES:
61 — Chicago outscored Toronto 34-27 in winning 1974 semi-finals, 4-3.
59 — Quebec outscored Winnipeg 31-28 in winning 1977 finals, 4-3.

FEWEST GOALS SCORED BY BOTH TEAMS IN A SEVEN-GAME SERIES:
33 — New England outscored Indianpolis 18-15 in winning 1976 quarter-finals, 4-3.
40 — Houston was outscored by New England 19-21 in winning 1976 semi-finals, 4-3.

MOST GOALS SCORED BY ONE TEAM IN A SEVEN-GAME SERIES:
34 — Chicago outscored Toronto 34-27 in winning 1974 semi-finals, 4-3.
31 — Quebec outscored Winnipeg 31-28 in winning 1977 finals, 4-3.

FEWEST GOALS SCORED BY ONE TEAM IN A SEVEN-GAME SERIES:
15 — Indianapolis was outscored by New England 15-18 in losing 1976 quarter-finals, 3-4.
18 — New England outscored Indianpolis 18-15 in winning 1976 quarter-finals, 4-3.

MOST SHUTOUTS BY BOTH TEAMS IN A SEVEN-GAME SERIES:
4 — New England and Indianapolis shutout each other twice in route to New England's winning the 1976 quarter-finals, 4-3.

MOST PENALTIES BY BOTH TEAMS IN A SEVEN-GAME SERIES:
122 — Houston/New England in 1976 semi-finals won by Houston, 4-3. Houston had 55 penalties, New England 67.
94 — New England/Indianapolis in 1976 quarter-finals won by New England, 4-3. New England had 45 penalties, Indianapolis 49.

MOST PENALTY MINUTES BY BOTH TEAMS IN A SEVEN-GAME SERIES:
337 — Houston/New England in 1976 semi-finals won by Houston, 4-3. Houston had 142 minutes, New England 195.
278 — Chicago/New England in 1974 quarter-finals won by Chicago, 4-3. Chicago had 155 minutes, New England 123.

MOST PENALTIES BY ONE TEAM IN A SEVEN-GAME SERIES:
67 — New England in 1976 semi-final loss to Houston
55 — Houston in 1976 semi-final win over New England

MOST PENALTY MINUTES BY ONE TEAM IN A SEVEN-GAME SERIES:
- 195 — New England in 1976 semi-final loss to Houston
- 155 — Chicago in 1974 quarter-final win over New England

FEWEST PENALTIES BY BOTH TEAMS IN A SEVEN-GAME SERIES:
- 70 — Quebec/Winnipeg in 1977 finals won by Quebec, 4-3. Quebec had 42 penalties, Winnipeg had 28.
- 80 — Winnipeg/San Diego in 1977 quarter-finals won by Winnipeg, 4-3. Winnipeg had 42 penalties, San Diego 38.

FEWEST PENALTY MINUTES BY BOTH TEAMS IN A SEVEN-GAME SERIES:
- 160 — Quebec/Winnipeg in 1977 finals won by Quebec, 4-3. Quebec had 98 minutes, Winnipeg had 62.
- 222 — Winnipeg/San Diego in 1977 quarter-finals won by Winnipeg, 4-3. Winnipeg had 115 minutes, San Diego 107.

FEWEST PENALTIES BY ONE TEAM IN A SEVEN-GAME SERIES:
- 28 — Winnipeg in 1977 finals loss to Quebec
- 38 — Toronto in 1974 semi-final loss to Chicago
  — San Diego in 1977 quarter-final loss to Winnipeg

TEAM RECORDS — NO GAME RESTRICTION

MOST CONSECUTIVE PLAYOFF GAME VICTORIES:
- 13 — Houston between Apr 15/75 and Apr 27/76. Won final two games against Cleveland in quarter-finals, swept past San Diego and Quebec to win the AVCO World Trophy, and won the first three games with San Diego the following season in the quarter-final round.

MOST CONSECUTIVE PLAYOFF GAME LOSSES:
- 7 — Edmonton between Apr 14/74 and Apr 17/77. Lost final game with Minnesota in 1974 quarter-final round, was swept out by Winnipeg in 1976 quarter-finals, and lost first two games with Houston in 1977 quarter-finals.
  — Quebec Nordiques between May 3/75 and Apr 16/76. Lost four straight to Houston in 1975 finals and lost first three to Calgary in 1976 quarter-finals.

MOST WINS, ONE PLAYOFF SEASON:
- 12 — New England 1973
  — Houston 1974
  — Houston 1975
  — Winnipeg 1976
  — Quebec 1977

MOST WINS BY A TEAM THAT DID NOT WIN AVCO TROPHY:
- 11 — Winnipeg 1977
- 10 — New England 1976
- 9 — Winnipeg 1973

MOST LOSSES IN ONE PLAYOFF SEASON:
- 10 — Chicago 1974
- 9 — Houston 1976
  — Winnipeg 1977

FEWEST LOSSES BY A TEAM IN ONE PLAYOFF SEASON:
- 1 — Houston 1975
  — Winnipeg 1976

— Winnipeg 1978

MOST PLAYOFF GAMES PLAYED IN ONE PLAYOFF SEASON:
- 20 — Winnipeg 1977 (won 11, lost 9)
- 18 — Chicago 1974 (won 8, lost 10)
- 17 — Houston 1976 (won 8, lost 9)
- — Quebec 1977 (won 12, lost 5)

MOST POINTS SCORED BY A TEAM IN A PLAYOFF SEASON:
- 217 — Winnipeg 1977, in 20 games scored 80 goals, 137 assists for an average 10.9 per game.
- 204 — Quebec 1977, in 17 games scored 79 goals and 125 assists for an average 12 per game.
- 190 — New England 1973, in 15 games scored 70 and 120 assists for an average of 12.7 per game.

MOST GOALS SCORED BY A TEAM IN A PLAYOFF SEASON:
- 80 — Winnipeg 1977, in 20 games average of 4.0 per game
- 79 — Quebec 1977, in 17 games average of 4.7 per game
- 71 — Houston 1974, in 14 games average of 5.1 per game

MOST ASSISTS BY A TEAM IN ONE PLAYOFF SEASON:
- 137 — Winnipeg 1977, in 20 games, 6.9 per game, 1.7 per goal
- 125 — Quebec 1977, in 17 games, 7.4 per game, 1.6 per goal
- 120 — New England 1973, in 15 games, 8 per game, 1.7 per goal

MOST POINTS ALLOWED OPPONENTS IN ONE PLAYOFF SEASON:
- 196 — Chicago 1974, in 18 games allowed 72 goals, 124 assists, 10.9 per game
- 191 — Winnipeg 1977, in 20 games allowed 73 goals, 118 assists, 9.6 per game
- 173 — Houston 1976, in 17 games allowed 64 goals, 109 assists, 10.2 per game

MOST GOALS ALLOWED OPPOSITION IN ONE PLAYOFF SEASON:
- 73 — Winnipeg 1977, in 20 games, 3.7 per game
- 72 — Chicago 1974, in 18 games, 4.0 per game
- 64 — Houston 1976, in 17 games, 3.7 per game

MOST ASSISTS ALLOWED OPPOSITION IN ONE PLAYOFF SEASON:
- 124 — Chicago 1974, in 18 games, 6.9 per game, 1.7 per goal
- 118 — Winnipeg 1977, in 20 games, 5.9 per game, 1.6 per goal
- 109 — Houston 1976, i17 games, 6.4 per game, 1.7 per goal

MOST POWERPLAY OPPORTUNITIES BY A TEAM IN A PLAYOFF SEASON:
- 96 — Winnipeg 1977
- 87 — Winnipeg 1976
- 79 — Houston 1976

MOST POWERPLAY GOALS BY A TEAM IN A PLAYOFF SEASON:
- 19 — Winnipeg 1977
- 17 — Houston 1974
- 16 — Winnipeg 1978

MOST GOALS ALLOWED BY A TEAM WHILE ON THE POWERPLAY IN A PLAYOFF SEASON:
- 5 — Minnesota 1974
- 4 — Winnipeg 1977
- — Edmonton 1978

MOST PROFICIENT POWERPLAY BY A TEAM IN A PLAYOFF SEASON:
39.5% — Houston 1975. 15 powerplay goals in 39 opportunities
37.5% — Houston 1977. 12 powerplay goals in 32 opportunities
37.2% — Winnipeg 1978. 16 powerplay goals in 43 opportunities

LEAST PROFICIENT POWERPLAY BY A TEAM IN A PLAYOFF SEASON:
00.0% — Winnipeg 1974. Scored no powerplay goals in 25 opportunities
4.3% — Cleveland 1976. 1 powerplay goal in 15 opportunities
6.3% — Houston 1978. 2 powerplay goals in 32 opportunities

MOST SHORTHANDED SITUATIONS BY A TEAM IN A PLAYOFF SEASON:
  96 — New England 1976
  96 — Houston 1976
  81 — Chicago 1974

MOST GOALS SCORED WHILE SHORTHANDED BY A TEAM IN A PLAYOFF SEASON:
  7 — Houston 1974
  5 — New England 1978
  4 — Calgary 1976
    — Quebec 1977

MOST GOALS ALLOWED WHILE SHORTHANDED BY A TEAM IN A PLAYOFF SEASON:
  23 — Chicago 1974
  17 — Houston 1976
  15 — New England 1976
     — Quebec 1977

MOST EFFICIENT PENALTY KILLING BY A TEAM IN A PLAYOFF SEASON:
90.8% — Houston 1974. Skated off 69 of 76 situations
90.0% — Minnesota 1974. Skated off 45 of 50 situations
89.8% — Winnipeg 1976. Skated off 44 of 49 situations

LEAST EFFICIENT PENALTY KILLING BY A TEAM IN A PLAYOFF SEASON:
46.2% — Minnesota 1973. Skated off 6 of 13 situations
55.0% — Los Angeles 1973. Skated off 11 of 20 situations
60.0% — Edmonton 1977. Skated off 9 of 15 situations

MOST GOALS BY BOTH TEAMS IN A PLAYOFF GAME:
  15 — New England 9, Winnipeg 6 in final game of final series on May 6/73 at New England
     — Winnipeg 12, Quebec 3 in final series won by Quebec, May 24/77, at Winnipeg
  14 — New England 6, at Chicago 8 Apr 9/74 quarter-final series won by Chicago, 4-3
     — San Diego 6, at Houston 8 Apr 21/76 quarter-final series won by Houston, 4-3

MOST GOALS BY ONE TEAM IN A PLAYOFF GAME:
  12 — Winnipeg 12 May 24/77 vs. Quebec
  11 — Quebec 11 Apr 26/78 vs. Houston
  10 — Houston 10 Apr 13/74 vs. Winnipeg
     — Winnipeg 10 May 19/78 vs. New England 2

MOST GOALS SCORED BY A LOSING TEAM IN A PLAYOFF GAME:
  6 — Winnipeg lost at New England, 9-6, May 6/73.

- New England lost at Chicago, 8-6, Apr 9/74.
- Chicago lost to Toronto, 7-6, Apr 30/74.
- Toronto lost at San Diego, 7-6, Apr 12/75.
- San Diego lost at Houston, 8-6, Apr 21/76.

MOST GOALS SCORED BY A TEAM IN TWO CONSECUTIVE GAMES:
17 — Winnipeg defeated Birmingham 9-3 Apr 14 and 8-3 Apr 16/78.
15 — Houston defeated Winnipeg 10-9 Apr 13 and 5-4 Apr 14/74.
- Winnipeg defeated Houston 6-3 May 25 and 9-1 May 27/76.
- Winnipeg lost at Quebec 3-8 May 22, and defeated Quebec 12-3 May 24/77.
- Winnipeg defeated New England 5-2 May 14 and 10-2 May 19/78.
- Winnipeg defeated New England 10-2 May 19 and 5-3 May 22/78.

MOST GOALS SCORED BY A TEAM IN THREE CONSECUTIVE GAMES:
20 — Winnipeg defeated Houston 5-4 May 23, 9-3 May 25 and 9-1 May 27/76.
- Winnipeg defeated New England 5-2 May 14, 10-2 May 19 and 5-3 May 22/78.
19 — Houston defeated San Diego 8-6 Apr 21, 3-1 Apr 23 and 8-4 Apr 25/76.
- Quebec defeated Winnipeg 8-3 May 22, lost at Winnipeg 3-12 May 24, and won in Quebec 8-2 May 26/77.
- Winnipeg defeated Birmingham 9-3 Apr 14, 8-3 Apr 16 and lost at Birmingham 2-3 Apr 19/78.

MOST PENALTIES CALLED ON BOTH TEAMS IN ONE GAME:
41 — Minnesota at New England, Apr 11/75. Minnesota was called for 20 penalties, New England 21 in game won by New England, 3-2 in overtime.
39 — Calgary at Quebec, Apr 11/76. Calgary was called for 18 penalties, Quebec 21 in game won by Calgary, 8-4.
34 — Birmingham at Winnipeg, Apr 16/78. Birmingham was called for 22 penalties, Winnipeg 12 in game won by Winnipeg, 8-3.

MOST PENALTY MINUTES ASSESSED BOTH TEAMS IN A PLAYOFF GAME:
217 — Minnesota at New England, Apr 11/75. Minnesota was assessed 101 minutes, New England 116 in game won by New England, 3-2 in overtime.
207 — Calgary at Quebec, Apr 11/76. Calgary was assessed 91 minutes, Quebec 116 in game won by Calgary, 8-4.
176 — Birmingham at Winnipeg, Apr 16/78. Birmingham was assessed 106 minutes, Winnipeg 70 in game won by Winnipeg, 8-3.

MOST PENALTIES CALLED ON ONE TEAM IN A PLAYOFF GAME:
22 — Birmingham Apr 16/78 at Winnipeg in 8-3 loss
21 — New England Apr 11/75 vs. Minnesota in 3-2 overtime win
- Quebec Apr 11/76 vs. Calgary in 8-4 loss

MOST PENALTY MINUTES ASSESSED ONE TEAM IN A PLAYOFF GAME:
116 — New England, Apr 11/75 in 3-2 overtime win vs. Minnesota
- Quebec, Apr 11/76 in 8-4 loss to Calgary
106 — Birmingham, Apr 16/78 in 8-3 loss at Winnipeg

207

FEWEST PENALTIES CALLED ON BOTH TEAMS IN ONE GAME:
- 0 — San Diego at Phoenix, Apr 17/76. San Diego won game, 2-1.
- 3 — Minnesota at Winnipeg, Apr 15/73. Minnesota was called for 2 penalties, Winnipeg 1 in game won by Winnipeg, 8-5.
  - San Diego at Houston, May 1/75. San Diego was called for one penalty, Houston 2 in game won by Houston in overtime, 5-4.
  - Houston at Quebec, May 10/75. Houston was called for two penalties, Quebec 1 in game won by Houston, 2-0.

FEWEST PENALTY MINUTES ASSESSED BOTH TEAMS IN A PLAYOFF GAME:
- 0 — San Diego at Phoenix, Apr 17/76. San Diego won game, 2-1.
- 6 — Minnesota at Winnipeg, Apr 15/73. Minnesota was assessed four minutes, Winnipeg two in game won by Winnipeg, 8-5.
  - San Diego at Houston, May 1/75. San Diego was assessed two minutes, Houston four in game won by Houston, 5-4 in overtime.
  - Houston at Quebec, May 10/75. Houston was assessed four minutes, Quebec two in game won by Houston, 2-0.

FEWEST PENALTIES CALLED ON ONE TEAM IN A PLAYOFF GAME:
- 0 — San Diego, Apr 17/76 at Phoenix in 2-1 win
  - Phoenix, Apr 17/76 vs. San Diego in 2-1 loss
- 1 — Winnipeg, Apr 8/73 vs. Minnesota in 5-2 win
  - Winnipeg, Apr 15/73 vs. Minnesota in 8-5 win
  - San Diego, May 1/75 at Houston in 5-4 overtime loss
  - Quebec, May 10/75 vs. Houston in 2-0 loss
  - San Diego, Apr 30/76 vs. Houston in 3-2 loss
  - Edmonton, Apr 20/77 vs. Houston in 4-1 loss
  - Quebec, Apr 28/78 at New England in 5-1 loss

FEWEST PENALTY MINUTES ASSESSED ON ONE TEAM IN A PLAYOFF GAME:
- 0 — San Diego, Apr 17/76 at Phoenix in 2-1 win
  - Phoenix, Apr 17/76 vs. San Diego in 2-1 loss
- 2 — Winnipeg, Apr 8/73 vs. Minnesota in 5-2 win
  - Winnipeg, Apr 15/73 vs. Minnesota in 8-5 win
  - San Diego, May 1/75 at Houston in 5-4 overtime loss
  - Quebec, May 10/75 vs. Houston in 2-0 loss
  - San Diego, Apr 30/76 vs. Houston in 3-2 loss
  - Edmonton, Apr 20/77 vs. Houston in 4-1 loss
  - Quebec, Apr 28/78 at New England in 5-1 loss

MOST POWER PLAY OPPORTUNITIES BY BOTH TEAMS IN A PLAYOFF GAME:
- 20 — San Diego at Houston, Apr 21/76. San Diego had 13 chances, Houston 7 in game won by Houston, 8-6. Houston scored one PP goal and 2 SH goals, San Diego scored two PP goals.
- 17 — Quebec at Calgary, Apr 14/76. Quebec had 8 chances, Calgary 9. Quebec scored one powerplay goal, but lost the game to Calgary, 3-2.
  - Birmingham at Winnipeg, Apr 14/78. Birmingham had 3 chances, Winnipeg 14. The Jets scored 5 powerplay goals to win the game, 9-3.

MOST POWERPLAY OPPORTUNITIES BY ONE TEAM IN A PLAYOFF GAME:
- 14 — Winnipeg, Apr 14/78 vs. Birmingham in 9-3 win. Scored 5 PP goals.
- 13 — San Diego, Apr 21/76 at Houston in 8-6 loss. Scored 2 PP goals, Houston scored two shorthanded goals.
- 11 — Cleveland, Apr 10/76 vs. New England in 6-1 loss. Scored no PP goals.
  — Winnipeg, May 24/77 vs. Quebec in 12-3 win. Scored 4 PP goals.

MOST POWERPLAY GOALS BY BOTH TEAMS IN A PLAYOFF GAME:
- 6 — Chicago at Houston, May 19/74. Houston scored 5, Chicago 1 in 6-2 Houston win.
- 5 — Los Angeles at Houston, Apr 15/73. Houston scored 3, Los Angeles 2 in 6-3 Houston win.
  — Houston at Quebec, May 12/75. Houston scored 3, Quebec 2 in 7-2 Houston win.
  — Calgary at Quebec, Apr 11/76. Calgary scored 3, Quebec 2 in 8-4 Calgary win.
  — Quebec at Calgary, Apr 16/76. Calgary scored 3, Quebec 2 in 4-3 Quebec win.
  — Houston at New England, May 11/76. Houston scored 2, New England 3 in 4-3 Houston win.
  — Birmingham at Winnipeg, Apr 14/78. Winnipeg scored all 5 in 9-3 win.

MOST POWERPLAY GOALS BY ONE TEAM IN A PLAYOFF GAME:
- 5 — Houston, May 19/74 vs. Chicago in 6-2 win
  — Winnipeg, Apr 16/78 vs. Birmingham in 9-3 win
- 4 — Minnesota, Apr 13/75 vs. New England in 8-3 win
  — Winnipeg, May 24/77 vs. Quebec in 12-3 win
  — Winnipeg, Apr 16/78 vs. Birmingham in 8-3 win

MOST SHORTHANDED GOALS SCORED BY BOTH TEAMS IN A PLAYOFF GAME: (and) MOST SHORTHANDED GOALS SCORED BY ONE TEAM IN A PLAYOFF GAME:
- 2 — Houston, Apr 13/74 vs. Winnipeg in 10-1 win
  — Houston, Apr 29/74 vs. Minnesota in 9-4 win
  — New England, Apr 15/75 at Minnesota in 5-2 win
  — Houston, Apr 21/76 vs. San Diego in 8-6 win
  — New England, Apr 14/78 vs. Edmonton in 6-4 win
  — New England, Apr 16/78 vs. Edmonton in 4-1 win

MOST SHOTS ON GOAL BY BOTH TEAMS IN A PLAYOFF GAME:
- 111 — Indianapolis/Cincinnati, Apr 9/77. Indianapolis defeated Cincinnati, 4-3 in the third overtime period despite being outshot by the Stingers, 59-52.
- 92 — Toronto at San Diego, Apr 18/75. San Diego outshot Toronto, 55-37 and won the game, 4-3.
- 87 — San Diego at Houston, May 1/75. Houston outshot San Diego, 50-37 and won the game, 5-4 after 27 seconds of overtime.

MOST SHOTS ON GOAL BY ONE TEAM IN A PLAYOFF GAME:
- 62 — Winnipeg, Apr 11/76 in 5-4 win vs. Edmonton, after 54 seconds of overtime.
- 59 — Cincinnati, Apr 9/77 in 4-3 loss to Indianapolis after 48 minutes,

40 seconds of overtime.

  58 — New England, Apr 7/73 in 6-3 win vs. Ottawa.

  57 — New England, Apr 8/73 in 4-3 win vs. Ottawa after 3 minutes, 37 seconds of overtime.

LEAST NUMBER OF SHOTS ON GOAL BY BOTH TEAMS IN A PLAYOFF GAME:

  41 — New England at Quebec, Apr 9/77. Quebec outshot New England, 21-20 in 5-2 win.

  43 — Houston at Winnipeg, May 25/76. Winnipeg outshot Houston, 25-18 in 6-3 win.

    — Winnipeg at Houston, May 3/77. Houston outshot Winnipeg, 24-19 in 3-2 win.

FEWEST SHOTS ON GOAL BY ONE TEAM IN A PLAYOFF GAME:

  12 — Birmingham, Apr 14/78 at Winnipeg in 9-3 loss

  14 — Minnesota, Apr 20/74 in 5-2 loss at Houston

  15 — Winnipeg, Apr 22/77 in 3-1 loss at San Diego

MOST SHOTS ON GOAL TAKEN BY A LOSING TEAM IN A PLAYOFF GAME:

  59 — Cincinnati, Apr 9/77 in 4-3 loss at Indianapolis after 48 minutes, 40 seconds of overtime

  48 — San Diego, Apr 27/75 in 2-1 loss to Houston

  46 — Chicago, Apr 30/74 in 7-6 loss to Toronto

FEWEST NUMBER OF SHOTS ON GOAL TAKEN BY A WINNING TEAM:

  18 — Quebec, Apr 12/75 in 3-0 win at Phoenix

    — New England, May 5/76 in 4-2 win at Houston

  21 — Quebec, Apr 9/77 in 5-2 win over New England

    — Winnipeg, May 18/77 in 6-1 win over Quebec

    — Winnipeg, Apr 21/78 in 5-1 win at Birmingham

TEAM PERIOD RECORDS

MOST GOALS SCORED BY BOTH TEAMS IN ONE PERIOD:

  8 — San Diego at Houston, Apr 21/76. Houston outscored San Diego, 6-2 in 1st period of game won by Houston, 8-6.

  7 — Minnesota at Winnipeg, Apr 15/73. Winnipeg outscored Minnesota, 5-2 in the 2nd period of game won by Winnipeg, 8-5.

    — Winnipeg at New England, May 6/73. New England outscored Winnipeg, 5-2 in 1st period of game won by New England, 9-6.

    — Edmonton at Minnesota, Apr 7/74. Edmonton outscored Minnesota, 4-3 in the 3rd period of game won by Minnesota, 8-5.

    — New England at Chicago, Apr 9/74. New England outscored Chicago in 2nd period of game won by Chicago, 8-6.

    — Toronto at Chicago, Apr 30/74. Toronto outscored Chicago in 2nd period, 5-2, in game won by Toronto, 7-6.

    — Houston at Cleveland, Apr 15/75. Houston outscored Cleveland, 5-2 in 3rd period of game won by Houston, 7-2.

    — Quebec at Winnipeg, May 24/77. Winnipeg outscored Quebec, 4-3 in 1st period of game won by Winnipeg, 12-3.

    — Winnipeg at Quebec, May 26/77. Quebec outscored Winnipeg, 6-1 in 2nd period of game won by Quebec, 8-2.

MOST GOALS SCORED BY ONE TEAM IN ONE PERIOD:

  6 — Calgary, Apr 11/76 at Quebec in 3rd period of 8-4 win

    — Houston, Apr 21/76 vs. San Diego in 1st period of 8-6 win

— Quebec, May 26/77 vs. Winnipeg in 2nd period of 8-2 win
— Winnipeg, May 19/78 vs. New England in 1st period of 10-2 win

MOST PENALTIES CALLED ON BOTH TEAMS IN A SINGLE PERIOD: (and) MOST PENALTY MINUTES ASSESSED BOTH TEAMS IN A SINGLE PERIOD:

34 penalties, 189 minutes — Minnesota at New England, Apr 11/75, 2nd period. Minnesota received 16 penalties for 82 minutes, New England received 18 penalties for 107, in game won by New England after 6 minutes, 46 seconds of overtime.

32 penalties, 185 minutes — Calgary at Quebec, Apr 11/76, first period. Calgary was called for 15 penalties for 85 minutes, Quebec 17 penalties for 100 minutes in game won by Calgary, 8-4.

26 penalties, 146 minutes — Birmingham at Winnipeg, Apr 16/78, first period. Birmingham was called for 17 penalties and 85 minutes, Winnipeg 9 penalties and 61 minutes in game won by Winnipeg, 8-3.

MOST PENALTIES CALLED ON ONE CLUB IN A SINGLE PERIOD:

18 — New England, Apr 11/75, 2nd period in 3-2 overtime win vs. Minnesota

17 — Quebec, Apr 11/76, 1st period of 8-4 loss vs. Calgary
— Birmingham, Apr 16/78, 1st period of 8-3 loss at Winnipeg

MOST PENALTY MINUTES ASSESSED TO ONE CLUB IN A SINGLE PERIOD:

107 — New England, Apr 11/75, 2nd period of 3-2 overtime win vs. Minnesota

100 — Quebec, Apr 11/76, 1st period of 8-4 loss vs. Calgary

82 — Minnesota, Apr 11/75, 2nd period of 3-2 overtime loss at New England

MOST SHOTS ON GOAL BY BOTH TEAMS IN ONE PERIOD:

37 — Toronto at San Siego, Apr 18/75, 3rd period. San Diego outshot Toronto, 22-15 in game won by San Diego, 4-3.

36 — Ottawa at New England, Apr 7/73, 3rd period. New England outshot Ottawa, 20-16 in game won by New England, 6-3.

35 — Toronto at San Diego, Apr 12/75, 2nd period. San Diego outshot Toronto, 23-12 in game won by San Diego, 7-6.

MOST SHOTS ON GOAL BY ONE TEAM IN A SINGLE PERIOD:

25 — Houston, Apr 29/74, 1st period of 9-4 win vs. Minnesota

24 — Chicago, Apr 16/74, 3rd period of 3-2 win at New England
— Winnipeg, Apr 11/76, 1st period of 5-4 overtime win vs. Edmonton

FEWEST SHOTS ON GOAL BY BOTH TEAMS IN A SINGLE PERIOD:

9 — Houston at Winnipeg, Apr 10/74, 1st period. Winnipeg outshot Houston, 6-3 in game won by Houston, 3-2.
— Winnipeg at San Diego, Apr 17/77, 3rd period. Winnipeg outshot San Diego, 5-4 in game won by San Diego, 6-4. One of San Diego shots was an empty net goal.

10 — Edmonton at Houston, Apr 22/77, 3rd period. Houston outshot Edmonton, 7-3 in game won by Houston, 4-3.
— Quebec at Houston, Apr 23/78, 1st period. Houston outshot Quebec, 6-4 in game won by Houston, 5-2.

FEWEST SHOTS BY ONE TEAM IN A SINGLE PERIOD OF PLAYOFF HOCKEY:
  2 — Minnesota, Apr 30/74 in 3rd period of 5-2 loss at Houston
    — Edmonton, Apr 16/76 in 3rd period of 7-2 loss vs. Winnipeg
    — Winnipeg, Apr 22/77 in 1st period of 3-1 loss at San Diego
    — New England, May 14/78 in 1st period of 5-2 loss vs. Winnipeg

FASTEST TWO GOALS BY BOTH TEAMS IN A PLAYOFF GAME:
  8 seconds — Minnesota at Quebec, Apr 29/75. Mike Walton (M) 8:53; Marc Tardif (Q) 9:01 of 2nd period of 6-3 Quebec win
  10 seconds — Quebec at Indianapolis, Apr 28/77. Reg Thomas (I) 12:07; Paulin Bordeleau (Q) 12:17 of 1st period of 6-5 Quebec overtime win
  12 seconds — Minnesota at Houston, Apr 20/74. Wayne Connelly (M) 18:31; Murray Hall (H) 18:43 1st period of 5-2 Houston win
    — Houston at Winnipeg, May 1/77. Morris Lukowich (H) 16:21; Anders Hedberg (W) 16:33 of 2nd period in game won by Winnipeg, 6-4

FASTEST THREE GOALS BY BOTH TEAMS IN A PLAYOFF GAME:
  52 seconds — Winnipeg at Calgary, Apr 30/76. Danny Lawson (C) 3:12; Gavin Kirk (C) 3:52; Anders Hedberg (W) 4:04 of 1st period in 7-3 Calgary win
  56 seconds — Edmonton at Minnesota, Apr 7/74. Ted Hampson (M) 18:32; Blair MacDonald (E) 19:04; Mike Walton (M) empty net goal at 19:28 of 3rd period of 8-5 Minnesota win
  58 seconds — Quebec at Houston, May 6/75. Gord Labossiere (H) 2:06; Marc Tardif (Q) 2:23; Terry Ruskowski (H) 3:04 of 3rd period of 5-3 Houston win

FASTEST FOUR GOALS BY BOTH TEAMS IN A PLAYOFF GAME:
  2 minutes, 18 seconds — New England at Chicago, Apr 9/74. Jim Watson (C) 7:35; Don Blackburn (N) 8:48; John Cunnif (N) 9:23; John French (N) 9:53 of 2nd period of 6-5 Chicago win
  2 minutes, 50 seconds — San Diego at Houston, Apr 21/76. Andre Lacroix (S) 17:09; Gord Labossiere (H) on a penalty shot at 17:55; Terry Ruskowski (H) 19:29 and 19:59 of 1st period in game won by Houston, 8-6
  2 minutes, 53 seconds — New England at Chicago, Apr 9/74. Don Blackburn (N) 8:48; John Cunnif (N) 9:23; John French (N) 9:53; Bob Sicinski (C) 11:46 of 2nd period in game won by Chicago, 8-6

FASTEST TWO GOALS BY ONE TEAM:
  3 seconds — Calgary, Apr 28/76. Lynn Powis 4:08, Dan Tannahill 4:11 of 2nd period in 6-3 loss vs. Winnipeg
  9 seconds — Winnipeg, Apr 16/78. Kent Ruhnke 3:24 and Dave Kryskow 3:33 2nd period of 8-3 win vs. Birmingham. Both Goals were powerplays with Birmingham playing two-men short.
  12 seconds — Toronto, Apr 22/74. Bob Leduc scored at 8:55, Tom Martin at 9:07 of 2nd period in 4-3 loss vs. Chicago.
    — Winnipeg, May 22/78. Dave Kryskow scored at 3:26, Lyle Moffat at 3:38 of 2nd period in 5-3 Winnipeg win vs. New England.

212

FASTEST THREE GOALS BY ONE TEAM:
55 seconds — Cleveland, Apr 7/73. Jim Wiste 5:15, Gerry Pinder 5:51 and Gary Jarrett at 6:10 of 2nd period in 7-1 win vs. Philadelphia

INDIVIDUAL RECORDS

MOST PLAYOFF GAMES PLAYED:
- 71 — Poul Popiel, Houston 73/74/75/76/77/78
- 68 — Gordie Howe, Houston 74/75/76/77; New England 78
- — Mark Howe, Houston 74/75/76/77; New England 78

MOST POINTS IN PLAYOFF CAREER:
- 86 — Mark Howe, 37 gls-49 asts.
- 80 — Bobby Hull, 43 gls-37 asts.
- 74 — Serge Bernier, 28 gls-46 asts.

MOST GOALS SCORED IN PLAYOFF CAREER:
- 43 — Bobby Hull
- 37 — Mark Howe
- 35 — Anders Hedberg

MOST ASSISTS IN PLAYOFF CAREER:
- 53 — Ulf Nilsson
- 49 — Mark Howe
- 47 — Poul Popiel

MOST PENALTY MINUTES IN PLAYOFF CAREER:
- 159 — Curt Brackenbury
- 151 — Terry Ruskowski
- 147 — Ted Taylor

MOST POINTS IN ONE PLAYOFF YEAR:
- 39 — Serge Bernier, Quebec/77. 14 G/22 A.
- 29 — Anders Hedberg, Winnipeg/77. 13 G/16 A.
- 28 — Norm Beaudin, Winnipeg/73. 13 G/15 A.

MOST GOALS IN A SINGLE PLAYOFF SEASON:
- 14 — Serge Bernier, Quebec/77
  - — Real Cloutier, Quebec/77
- 13 — Norm Beaudin, Winnipeg/73
  - — Anders Hedberg, Winnipeg/76
  - — Anders Hedberg, Winnipeg/77
  - — Bobby Hull, Winnipeg/77

MOST ASSISTS IN A SINGLE PLAYOFF SEASON:
- 22 — Serge Bernier, Quebec/77
- 21 — Ulf Nilsson, Winnipeg/77
- 19 — Ulf Nilsson, Winnipeg/76

MOST PENALTY MINUTES IN A SINGLE PLAYOFF SEASON:
- 71 — Darryl Maggs, Chicago/74
- 67 — Gord Gallant, Minnesota/74
  - — Terry Ruskowski, Houston/77

MOST POINTS BY A PLAYER IN A FOUR-GAME SERIES:
- 9 — Gordie Howe, Houston/74. Collected 9 assists vs Chicago.
  - — Ulf Nilsson, Winnipeg/76. 3 goals, 6 assists vs Houston.
  - — Reggie Thomas, Indianapolis/77. 4 goals, 5 assists vs Cincinnati.

MOST GOALS IN A FOUR-GAME SERIES:
   6 — Anders Hedberg, Winnipeg/76 vs Houston
   5 — Andre Hinse, Houston/74 vs Chicago
     — Gordie Howe, Houston/75 vs Quebec
MOST ASSISTS IN A FOUR-GAME SERIES:
   9 — Gordie Howe, Houston/74
MOST POINTS BY A PLAYER IN A FIVE-GAME SERIES:
   15 — Norm Beaudin, Winnipeg/73, 5 g, 10 a.
MOST GOALS BY A PLAYER IN A FIVE-GAME SERIES:
   8 — Mark Howe, Houston/75
MOST ASSISTS BY A PLAYER IN A FIVE-GAME SERIES:
   10 — Norm Beaudin, Winnipeg/73
MOST POINTS BY A PLAYER IN A SIX-GAME SERIES:
   12 — Fran Huck, Minnesota/75
     — Ray Adduono, San Diego/75
     — Ulf Nilsson, Winnipeg/77
MOST GOALS BY A PLAYER IN A SIX-GAME SERIES:
   7 — Gene Peacosh, San Diego/75
     — Real Cloutier, Quebec/78
MOST ASSISTS BY A PLAYER IN A SIX-GAME SERIES:
   10 — Fran Huck, Minnesota/75
     — Ulf Nilsson, Winnipeg/77
MOST POINTS BY A PLAYER IN A SEVEN-GAME SERIES:
   13 — Serge Bernier, Quebec/77, 5 g, 8 a.
   12 — Real Cloutier, Quebec/77, 5 g, 7 a.
     — Dan Labraaten, Winnipeg/77, 5 g, 7 a.
MOST GOALS BY A PLAYER IN A SEVEN-GAME SERIES:
   7 — Rosaire Paiement, Chicago/74
     — Tom Webster, New England/76
     — Bobby Hull, Winnipeg/77
MOST ASSISTS BY A PLAYER IN A SEVEN-GAME SERIES:
   8 — Ralph Backstrom, Toronto/74
     — Serge Bernier, Quebec/77
MOST POINTS BY A PLAYER IN A QUARTER-FINAL SERIES:
   15 — Norm Beaudin, Winnipeg/73, 5 g, 10 a.
MOST GOALS BY A PLAYER IN A QUARTER-FINAL SERIES:
   8 — Mark Howe, Houston/75
   7 — Tom Webster, New England/73
     — Bobby Hull, Winnipeg/77
     — Real Cloutier, Quebec/78
MOST ASSISTS BY A PLAYER IN A QUARTER-FINAL SERIES:
   10 — Norm Beaudin, Winnipeg/73
     — Fran Huck, Minnesota/75
MOST POINTS BY A PLAYER IN A SEMI-FINAL SERIES:
   12 — Tim Sheehy, New England/73, 6 g, 6 a.
     — Serge Bernier, Quebec/77, 5 g, 7 a.
     — Ulf Nilsson, Winnipeg/77, 2 g, 10 a.
MOST GOALS BY A PLAYER IN A SEMI-FINAL SERIES:
   7 — Rosaire Paiement, Chicago/74
     — Tom Webster, New England/76

MOST ASSISTS BY A PLAYER IN A SEMI-FINAL SERIES:
   10 — Ulf Nilsson, Winnipeg/77
   8 — Ralph Backstrom, Chicago/74

MOST POINTS BY A PLAYER IN A FINAL SERIES:
   13 — Serge Bernier, Quebec/77

MOST GOALS BY A PLAYER IN A FINAL SERIES:
   6 — Anders Hedberg, Winnipeg/76

MOST ASSISTS BY A PLAYER IN A FINAL SERIES:
   9 — Tommy Williams, New England/73
      — Gordie Howe, Houston/74

MOST CONSECUTIVE PLAYOFF GAMES WITH POINTS:
   16 — Tim Sheehy, New England. Between Apr 12/73 and Apr 12/74 scored 13 goals and 16 assists.
   15 — Ulf Nilsson, Winnipeg. Between Apr 9/76 and Apr 12/77 scored 7 goals and 22 assists.

MOST CONSECUTIVE PLAYOFF GAMES WITH GOALS:
   9 — Anders Hedberg, Winnipeg. Between Apr 25/76 and Apr 12/77.
   8 — Bobby Hull, Winnipeg. Between Apr 14/74 and Apr 28/76.

MOST CONSECUTIVE PLAYOFF GAMES WITH ASSISTS:
   11 — Ulf Nilsson, Winnipeg. Between Apr 9/76 and May 25/76.

FASTEST GOAL FROM THE START OF THE GAME:
   15 Seconds — Jim Harrison, Cleveland Apr 10/75 in 8-5 loss at Houston
   21 Seconds — Tom Webster, New England May 6/73 in 9-6 win at New England

FASTEST TWO GOALS FROM THE START OF THE GAME:
   4 minutes, 28 seconds — Real Cloutier, Quebec May 24/77 in 12-3 loss at Winnipeg
   5 minutes, 31 seconds — Rich Preston, Houston Apr 21/76 in 8-6 win vs San Diego
   7 minutes, 31 seconds — Willy Lindstrom, Winnipeg May 19/78 in 10-2 win vs New England

FASTEST GOAL FROM THE START OF PERIOD (OTHER THAN FIRST):
   7 seconds — Mike Antonovich, Minnesota Apr 15/73 in 8-5 loss at Winnipeg, 2nd period.

FASTEST TWO GOALS FROM THE START OF A PERIOD (OTHER THAN FIRST):
   1 minute, 3 seconds — Bobby Hull, Winnipeg Apr 24/77 in 3rd period of 7-3 win vs San Diego.

FASTEST TWO GOALS BY A PLAYER:
   15 seconds — Mike Walton, Minnesota Apr 14/74 scored at 19:05 and 19:20 of 1st period in 5-4 win vs Edmonton.

FASTEST THREE GOALS BY A PLAYER:
   8 minutes, 42 seconds — Rick Sentes, Toronto Apr 12/74 scored at 10:41, 13:04 and 19:23 of 2nd period of 4-2 win at Cleveland.

MOST POINTS BY A PLAYER IN A SINGLE GAME:
   7 — Norm Beaudin, Winnipeg Apr 15/73 scored 3 goals and 4 assists in 8-5 win vs Minnesota

MOST GOALS IN A PLAYOFF GAME:
   4 — Larry Lund, Houston Apr 13/74 in 10-1 win at Winnipeg
      — Real Cloutier, Quebec Apr 26/78 in 11-2 win vs Houston

215

MOST ASSISTS BY A PLAYER IN A PLAYOFF GAME:
4 — Ulf Nilsson, Winnipeg May 1/77 in 6-4 win vs Houston
— Ulf Nilsson, Winnipeg May 24/77 in 12-3 win vs Quebec
— Jim Dorey, New England Apr 7/73 in 6-3 win vs Ottawa
— Bobby Hull, Winnipeg Apr 15/73 in 8-5 win vs Minnesota
— Bill Sutherland, Winnipeg Apr 15/73 in 8-5 win vs Minnesota
— Norm Beaudin, Winnipeg, Apr 15/73 in 8-5 win vs Minnesota
— Tommy Williams, New England May 6/73 in 9-6 win vs Winnipeg
— Poul Popiel, Houston May 19/74 in 6-2 win vs Chicago
— Gordie Howe, Houston May 19/74 in 6-2 win vs Chicago
— Marc Tardif, Quebec Apr 10/75 in 6-2 win vs Phoenix
— Larry Lund, Houston Apr 12/75 in 7-2 win at Quebec
— Ron Chipperfield, Calgary Apr 11/76 in 8-4 win at Quebec
— Mark Howe, Houston Apr 21/76 in 8-6 win vs San Diego
— Terry Ruskowski, Houston Apr 21/76 in 8-6 win vs San Diego
— Mike Ford, Winnipeg May 27/76 in 9-1 win vs Houston
— Serge Bernier, Quebec May 2/77 in 8-3 win vs Indianapolis
— Lars-Erik Sjoberg, Winnipeg Apr 14/78 in 9-3 win vs Birmingham

MOST PENALTIES BY A PLAYER IN A PLAYOFF GAME: (and)
MOST PENALTY MINUTES ON A PLAYER IN A PLAYOFF GAME:
7 penalties, 36 minutes — Ted Taylor, Houston Apr 28/74 in 4-1 win at Minnesota. Was called for 3 minors, 2 majors and 2 misconduct penalties.

MOST POINTS BY A PLAYER IN A SINGLE PERIOD:
4 — Norm Beaudin, Winnipeg Apr 15/73 in 2nd period of 8-5 win vs Minnesota. 2g/2a.
— Robbie Ftorek, Phoenix Apr 15/75 in 1st period of 6-5 Ovt. win vs Quebec. 1g/3a.
— Mike Walton, Minnesota Apr 24/75 in 2nd period of 5-3 win at Quebec. 2g/2a.

MOST GOALS BY A PLAYER IN A SINGLE PERIOD:
3 — Rick Sentes, Toronto Apr 12/74 in 4-2 win at Cleveland

MOST ASSISTS BY A PLAYER IN A SINGLE PERIOD:
3 — Wayne Dillon, Toronto Apr 30/74 in 2nd period of 7-6 win at Chicago
— Poul Popiel, Houston May 19/74 in 2nd period of 6-3 win vs Chicago
— Marc Tardif, Quebec Apr 10/75 in 2nd period of 6-2 win vs Phoenix
— Ray Adduono, San Diego Apr 12/75 in 2nd period of 7-6 win vs Toronto
— Robbie Ftorek, Phoenix Apr 15/75 in 1st period of 6-5 overtime win vs Quebec
— Al McLeod, Phoenix Apr 15/75 in 1st period of 6-5 overtime win vs Quebec
— Mark Howe, Houston Apr 21/76 in 1st period of 8-6 win vs San Diego
— Ken Block, Indianapolis Apr 27/76 in 2nd period of 5-3 win at New England
— Mike Ford, Winnipeg May 27/76 in 1st period of 9-1 win vs Houston

— Serge Bernier, Quebec Apr 26/78 in 3rd period of 11-2 win vs Houston

MOST PENALTIES BY A PLAYER IN A SINGLE PERIOD: (and)
MOST PENALTY MINUTES BY A PLAYER IN A SINGLE PERIOD:

7 penalties, 36 minutes — Ted Taylor, Houston Apr 28/74 in 1st period of 4-1 win at Minnesota. Received 3 minors, 2 majors and 2 misconduct penalties.

LOWEST PLAYOFF CAREER GOALS AGAINST AVERAGE, (at least 10 games):

2.59 — Cap Raeder, New England. 38 goals in 15 games.
2.88 — Wayne Rutledge, Houston. 42 goals in 16 games.
2.89 — Louis Levasseur, Edmonton/New England. 41 goals in 14 games.

MOST PLAYOFF GAME APPEARANCES BY A GOALTENDER:

48 — Richard Brodeur, Quebec
46 — Joe Daley, Winnipeg
36 — Ron Grahame, Houston

MOST MINUTES PLAYED IN PLAYOFF HOCKEY:

2,834 — Richard Brodeur, Quebec
2,669 — Joe Daley, Winnipeg
2,158 — Ron Grahame, Houston

MOST PLAYOFF VICTORIES FOR A GOALTENDER:

30 — Joe Daley, Winnipeg
26 — Richard Brodeur, Quebec
22 — Ron Grahame, Houston

MOST PLAYOFF GAMES LOST FOR A GOALTENDER:

21 — Richard Brodeur, Quebec
16 — Ernie Wakely, Winnipeg/San Diego
15 — Joe Daley, Winnipeg

MOST SHOTS FACED IN A PLAYOFF CAREER:

1,516 — Richard Brodeur, Quebec
1,190 — Joe Daley, Winnipeg
1,090 — Ron Grahame, Houston

HIGHEST SHOTS AGAINST AVERAGE FOR A PLAYOFF CAREER:

36.9 — Les Binkley, Ottawa/Toronto
35.7 — John Garrett, Minnesota/Birmingham
35.6 — Gilles Gratton, Ottawa/Toronto

MOST GOALS ALLOWED IN A PLAYOFF CAREER:

163 — Richard Brodeur, Quebec
146 — Joe Daley, Winnipeg
116 — Ron Grahame, Houston

MOST SAVES MADE IN A PLAYOFF CAREER:

1,355 — Richard Brodeur, Quebec
1,044 — Joe Daley, Winnipeg
974 — Ron Grahame, Houston

HIGHEST SAVE PERCENTAGE FOR A PLAYOFF CAREER:

.914 — Cap Raeder, New England
.909 — Wayne Rutledge, Houston
.906 — Gilles Gratton, Ottawa/Toronto

MOST SHUTOUTS IN A PLAYOFF CAREER:

4 — Ron Grahame, Houston

3 — Richard Brodeur, Quebec
2 — Jim Park, Indianapolis
— Cap Raeder, New England
— Ernie Wakely, Winnipeg
— Joe Daley, Winnipeg

MOST CONSECUTIVE WINS BY A GOALTENDER IN THE PLAYOFFS:
13 — Ron Grahame, Houston. Between Apr 15/75 and Apr 27/76.

MOST CONSECUTIVE WINS BY A GOALTENDER IN A SINGLE PLAYOFF SEASON:
10 — Ron Grahame, Houston. Won final 10 games in 1975 playoffs, also won first 3 in 76.

MOST SHUTOUTS BY A GOALTENDER IN A SINGLE PLAYOFF SEASON:
3 — Ron Grahame, Houston/75

MOST CONSECUTIVE SHUTOUTS IN THE PLAYOFFS: (and) LONGEST PERIOD OF TIME A GOALTENDER HAS GONE WITHOUT ALLOWING A GOAL:
2 games (145 minutes, 3 seconds) — Ernie Wakely, Winnipeg. Between 14:43 of 3rd period Apr 15 vs Minnesota and 19:46 of 1st period vs New England May 2. Includes back-to-back shutouts of Houston Apr 22 (8-0) and Apr 26/73 (3-0).

AVCO WORLD TROPHY PLAYOFF HISTORY CLUB vs. CLUB

BIRMINGHAM BULLS

BIRMINGHAM BULLS vs. New England Whalers

SERIES	WON	LOST	GAMES	WON	LOST	GOALS FOR	GOALS AGAINST
1	0	1	5	1	4	17	24

1973 Quarter Final — New England won best-of-seven series, 4-1. Outscoring Birmingham, 24-17.

BIRMINGHAM BULLS vs. Winnipeg Jets

SERIES	WON	LOST	GAMES	WON	LOST	GOALS FOR	GOALS AGAINST
1	0	1	5	1	4	12	29

1978 Quarter-Final — Winnipeg won best of seven series 4-1. Outscoring Birmingham, 29-12.

BIRMINGHAM (Ottawa/Toronto)

SERIES	WON	LOST	GAMES	WON	LOST	GOALS FOR	GOALS AGAINST
3	1	2	18	9	9	72	74

1974 Quarter-Final — Toronto defeated Cleveland in best-of-seven series 4-1. Outscoring the Crusaders, 18-11.
1974 Semi-Final — Chicago Cougars defeated Toronto in best-of-seven series 4-3. Outscoring the Toros, 34-27.
1975 Quarter-Final — San Diego defeated Toronto in best-of-seven series 4-2. Outscoring the Toros, 29-27.

SUMMARY OF BIRMINGHAM PLAYOFF SERIES
AVCO WORLD TROPHY CHAMPIONSHIPS — None
Final Series —0—
Semi-Final Series —1— Won 0; Lost 1.
Quarter-Final Series —4— Won 1; Lost 3.

CINCINNATI STINGERS

CINCINNATI STINGERS vs. Indianapolis Racers

SERIES	WON	LOST	GAMES	WON	LOST	GOALS FOR	GOALS AGAINST
1	0	1	4	0	4	9	19

1977 Quarter-Final — Indianapolis won best-of-seven series, 4-0. Outscoring Stingers, 19-9.

SUMMARY OF CINCINNATI PLAYOFF SERIES
AVCO WORLD TROPHY CHAMPIONSHIP — None
Final Series —0—
Semi-Final Series —0—
Quarter-Final Series —1— Won 0; Lost 1.

EDMONTON OILERS

EDMONTON OILERS vs. New England Whalers

SERIES	WON	LOST	GAMES	WON	LOST	GOALS FOR	GOALS AGAINST
1	0	1	5	1	4	9	23

1978 Quarter-Final — New England won best-of-seven series, 4-1. Outscoring Edmonton, 23-9.

EDMONTON OILERS vs. Winnipeg Jets

SERIES	WON	LOST	GAMES	WON	LOST	GOALS FOR	GOALS AGAINST
1	0	1	4	0	4	11	22

1976 Quarter-Final — Winnipeg won best-of-seven series, 4-0. Outscoring Edmonton, 22-11.

SUMMARY OF EDMONTON PLAYOFF SERIES
AVCO WORLD TROPHY CHAMPIONSHIPS — None
Final Series —0—
Semi-Final Series —0—
Quarter-Final Series —4— Won 0; Lost 4.

INDIANAPOLIS RACERS

INDIANAPOLIS RACERS vs. New England Whalers

SERIES	WON	LOST	GAMES	WON	LOST	GOALS FOR	GOALS AGAINST
1	0	1	7	3	4	15	18

1976 Quarter-Final — New England won best-of-seven series, 4-3. Outscoring the Racers, 18-15.

INDIANAPOLIS RACERS vs. Cincinnati Stingers

SERIES	WON	LOST	GAMES	WON	LOST	GOALS FOR	GOALS AGAINST
1	1	0	4	4	0	19	9

1977 Quarter-Final — Racers won best-of-seven series, 4-0. Outscoring Cincinnati, 19-9.

INDIANAPOLIS RACERS vs. Quebec Nordiques

SERIES	WON	LOST	GAMES	WON	LOST	GOALS FOR	GOALS AGAINST
1	0	1	1	0	1	14	25

1977 Semi-Final — Nordiques won best-of-seven series, 4-1. Outscoring Indianapolis, 25-14.

SUMMARY OF INDIANAPOLIS PLAYOFF SERIES
AVCO WORLD TROPHY CHAMPIONSHIPS — None
Final Series —0—
Semi-Final Series —1— Won 0; Lost 1.
Quarter-Final Series —2— Won 1; Lost 1.

NEW ENGLAND WHALERS

NEW ENGLAND WHALERS vs. Birmingham Bulls (Ottawa/Toronto)

SERIES	WON	LOST	GAMES	WON	LOST	GOALS FOR	GOALS AGAINST
1	1	0	5	4	1	24	17

1973 Quarter-Final — New England won best-of-seven series, 4-1. Outscoring Ottawa, 24-17.

NEW ENGLAND WHALERS vs. Edmonton Oilers

SERIES	WON	LOST	GAMES	WON	LOST	GOALS FOR	GOALS AGAINST
1	1	0	5	4	1	23	9

1978 Quarter-Final — New England won best-of-seven series, 4-1. Outscoring Oilers, 23-9.

NEW ENGLAND WHALERS vs. Indianapolis Racers

SERIES	WON	LOST	GAMES	WON	LOST	GOALS FOR	GOALS AGAINST
1	1	0	7	4	3	18	15

1976 Semi-Final — New England won best-of-seven series, 4-3. Outscoring Racers, 18-15.

NEW ENGLAND WHALERS vs. Quebec Nordiques

SERIES	WON	LOST	GAMES	WON	LOST	GOALS FOR	GOALS AGAINST
2	1	1	10	5	5	39	37

1977 Quarter-Final — Quebec won best-of-seven series, 4-1. Outscoring Whalers, 23-14.
1978 Semi-Final — New England won best-of-seven series, 4-1. Outscoring Nordiques, 25-14.

NEW ENGLAND WHALERS vs. Winnipeg Jets

SERIES	WON	LOST	GAMES	WON	LOST	GOALS FOR	GOALS AGAINST
2	1	1	9	4	5	38	42

1973 Final — New England won best-of-seven series, 4-3. Outscoring Jets, 30-18.
1978 Final — Winnipeg won best-of-seven series, 4-0. Outscoring Whalers, 24-8.

SUMMARY OF NEW ENGLAND PLAYOFF SERIES
AVCO WORLD TROPHY CHAMPIONSHIPS —1— Against Winnipeg.
Final Series —2— Won 1; Lost 1.
Semi-Final Series —3— Won 2; Lost 1.
Quarter-Final Series —6— Won 3; Lost 3.
Preliminary Series —1— Won 1.

QUEBEC NORDIQUES

QUEBEC NORDIQUES vs. Indianapolis Racers

SERIES	WON	LOST	GAMES	WON	LOST	GOALS FOR	GOALS AGAINST
1	1	0	5	4	1	25	14

1977 Semi-Final — Quebec won best-of-seven series, 4-1. Outscoring Racers, 25-14.

QUEBEC NORDIQUES vs. New England Whalers

SERIES	WON	LOST	GAMES	WON	LOST	GOALS FOR	GOALS AGAINST
2	1	1	10	5	5	37	39

1977 Quarter-Final — Quebec won best-of-seven series, 4-1. Outscoring Whalers, 23-14.
1978 Semi-Final — New England won best-of-seven series, 4-1. Outscoring Nordiques, 25-14.

QUEBEC NORDIQUES vs. Winnipeg Jets

SERIES	WON	LOST	GAMES	WON	LOST	GOALS FOR	GOALS AGAINST
1	0	1	7	3	4	31	28

1977 Final — Quebec won best-of-seven series, 4-3. Outscoring the Jets, 31-28.

SUMMARY OF QUEBEC PLAYOFF SERIES
AVCO WORLD TROPHY CHAMPIONSHIPS —1—
Final Series —2— Won 1; Lost 1.
Semi-Final Series —3— Won 2; Lost 1.
Quarter-Final Series —4— Won 3; Lost 1.

WINNIPEG JETS

WINNIPEG JETS vs. Birmingham Bulls

SERIES	WON	LOST	GAMES	WON	LOST	GOALS FOR	GOALS AGAINST
1	1	0	5	4	1	29	12

1978 Quarter-Final — Winnipeg won best-of-seven series, 4-1. Outscoring Bulls, 29-12.

WINNIPEG JETS vs. Edmonton Oilers

SERIES	WON	LOST	GAMES	WON	LOST	GOALS FOR	GOALS AGAINST
1	1	0	4	4	0	22	11

1976 Quarter-Final — Winnipeg won best-of-seven series, 4-0. Outscoring Oilers, 22-11.

WINNIPEG JETS vs. New England Whalers

SERIES	WON	LOST	GAMES	WON	LOST	GOALS FOR	GOALS AGAINST
2	1	1	9	5	4	42	38

1973 Final — New England won best-of-seven series, 4-1. Outscoring Jets, 30-18.
1978 Final — Winnipeg won best-of-seven series, 4-0. Outscoring the Whalers, 24-8.

WINNIPEG JETS vs. Quebec Nordiques

SERIES	WON	LOST	GAMES	WON	LOST	GOALS FOR	GOALS AGAINST
1	0	1	7	3	4	28	31

1977 Final — Quebec won best-of-seven series, 4-3. Outscoring Jets, 31-28.

SUMMARY OF WINNIPEG PLAYOFF SERIES
AVCO WORLD TROPHY CHAMPIONSHIPS —2—
Final Series —4— Won 2; Lost 2.
Semi-Final Series —3— Won 3; Lost 0.
Quarter-Final Series —5— Won 4; Lost 1.
Note: Jets, under '77-'78 playoff format, went to finals from quarter finals.

AVCO WORLD TROPHY PLAYOFF CAREER LEADERS

MOST PLAYOFF GAMES PLAYED

1. 71 Poul Popiel
2. 68 Gordie Howe
2. 68 Mark Howe
4. 66 Marty Howe
4. 66 John Schella
6. 65 Larry Hale
7. 64 Rick Ley
8. 63 Brad Selwood
8. 63 Ted Taylor
10. 61 Ted Green
11. 60 Bobby Hull
12. 59 Larry Lund
13. 57 Robert Guindon
14. 56 Joe Daley
14. 56 Larry Pleau
16. 54 Murray Hall
16. 54 Frank Hughes
18. 53 Chris Bordeleau
19. 52 Steve Sutherland
20. 50 Gordon Labossiere
20. 50 Francois Lacombe
22. 49 Serge Bernier
23. 48 Richard Brodeur
23. 48 Jim Dorey
25. 47 Mike Antonovich

PLAYOFF PENALTY LEADERS

1. 159 Curt Brackenbury
2. 151 Terry Ruskowski
3. 147 Ted Taylor
4. 143 John Schella
5. 132 Ron Busniuk
6. 131 Jim Dorey
6. 131 Rick Ley
8. 118 Poul Popiel
9. 116 Larry Lund
10. 112 Steve Sutherland
11. 111 Gordie Howe
12. 110 Kim Clackson
13. 98 Gord Gallant
14. 95 Darryl Maggs
15. 92 Cam Connor
16. 87 Paul Baxter
16. 87 Bill Butters
18. 85 Alan Hangsleben
19. 84 Nick Fotiu
19. 84 Paul Shmyr
21. 81 Brad Selwood
22. 77 Marty Howe
23. 76 Pierre Roy
24. 72 Rosaire Paiement
25. 71 Gordie Roberts

PLAYOFF POINT LEADERS

1. 86 Mark Howe
2. 80 Bobby Hull
3. 74 Serge Bernier
4. 67 Gordie Howe
4. 67 Ulf Nilsson
6. 65 Larry Lund
7. 63 Anders Hedberg
8. 59 Real Cloutier
9. 54 Tom Webster
9. 54 Poul Popiel
11. 51 Marc Tardif
12. 50 Chris Bordeleau
13. 48 Larry Pleau
14. 44 Gordon Labossiere
15. 41 Terry Ruskowski
16. 40 Frank Hughes
16. 40 Robert Guindon
18. 39 Ted Taylor
18. 39 Peter Sullivan
18. 39 John French
21. 38 Murray Hall
21. 38 Jim Dorey
23. 37 Norm Beaudin
23. 37 Tim Sheehy
25. 36 Rick Ley

PLAYOFF GOAL LEADERS

1. 43 Bobby Hull
2. 37 Mark Howe
3. 35 Anders Hedberg
4. 31 Real Cloutier
5. 28 Tom Webster
5. 28 Serge Bernier
7. 27 Larry Pleau
8. 25 Gordie Howe
9. 24 Frank Hughes
10. 22 Robert Guindon
11. 21 Mark Tardif
11. 21 Murray Hall
13. 20 Mike Walton
13. 20 Larry Lund
15. 18 Norm Beaudin
15. 18 Ted Taylor
17. 17 Terry Ruskowski
18. 16 Paulin Bordeleau
18. 16 Wayne Connelly
18. 16 Tim Sheehy
18. 16 Willy Lindstrom
18. 16 Peter Sullivan
18. 16 Mike Antonovich
18. 16 Gordon Labossiere
18. 16 Chris Bordeleau

PLAYOFF ASSIST LEADERS

1. 53 Ulf Nilsson
2. 49 Mark Howe
3. 47 Poul Popiel
4. 46 Serge Bernier
5. 45 Larry Lund
6. 42 Gordie Howe
7. 37 Bobby Hull
8. 34 Chris Bordeleau
9. 33 Jim Dorey
10. 30 Marc Tardif
11. 29 Rick Ley
12. 28 Anders Hedberg
12. 28 Real Cloutier
12. 28 Gordon Labossiere
15. 26 Tom Webster
16. 25 Mike Ford
16. 25 Andre Lacroix
16. 25 John French
16. 25 John Schella
20. 24 Terry Ruskowski
21. 23 J. C. Tremblay
21. 23 Peter Sullivan
23. 22 Rosaire Paiement
24. 21 Wayne Carleton
24. 21 Pat Stapleton
24. 21 Tim Sheehy
24. 21 Larry Pleau
24. 21 Ted Taylor

AVCO WORLD TROPHY PLAYOFF CAREER GOALTENDING LEADERS

TOP TEN PLAYOFF G.A.A.'s

1. 1.57 Gary Bromley
2. 2.45 Jim Park
3. 2.57 Bernie Parent
4. 2.59 Cap Raeder
5. 2.88 Wayne Rutledge
6. 2.89 Louis Levasseur
7. 2.93 Paul Hoganson
8. 2.95 Russ Gillow
9. 3.17 Ken Broderick
10. 3.23 Ron Grahame
10. 3.23 Don McLeod
10. 3.23 Curt Larsson

MOST PLAYOFF WINS

1. 30 Joe Daley
2. 26 Richard Brodeur
3. 22 Ron Grahame
4. 18 Don McLeod
5. 17 Al Smith
6. 15 Ernie Wakely
7. 11 John Garrett
8. 9 Wayne Rutledge
9. 7 Cap Raeder
9. 7 Gerry Cheevers

MOST PLAYOFF GAME APPEARANCES

1. 48 Richard Brodeur
2. 46 Joe Daley
3. 36 Ron Grahame
4. 31 Al Smith
4. 31 Don McLeod
4. 31 Ernie Wakely
7. 24 John Garrett
8. 19 Gerry Cheevers
9. 16 Wayne Rutledge
10. 15 Cap Raeder

MOST PLAYOFF LOSSES

1. 21 Richard Brodeur
2. 16 Ernie Wakely
3. 15 Joe Daley
4. 14 Ron Grahame
5. 13 Al Smith
5. 13 Don McLeod
7. 12 Gerry Cheevers
7. 12 John Garrett
9. 8 Cap Raeder
10. 7 Jack Norris

MOST PLAYOFF MINUTES PLAYED

1. 2,834 Richard Brodeur
2. 2,669 Joe Daley
3. 2,158 Ron Grahame
4. 1,794 Al Smith
5. 1,786 Don McLeod
6. 1,740 Ernie Wakely
7. 1,369 John Garrett
8. 1,151 Gerry Cheevers
9. 879 Cap Raeder
10. 874 Wayne Rutledge

HIGHEST DECISION PERCENTAGE

1. 1.000 Gary Bromley
1. 1.000 Curt Larsson
3. .667 Joe Daley
3. .667 Bruce Landon
5. .611 Ron Grahame
6. .600 Wayne Rutledge
6. .600 Paul Hoganson
6. .600 Jim Park
9. .581 Don McLeod
10. .571 Louis Levasseur

MOST SHOTS FACED
1. 1,516 Richard Brodeur
2. 1,190 Joe Daley
3. 1,090 Ron Grahame
4. 926 Ernie Wakely
5. 922 Al Smith
6. 876 Don McLeod
7. 814 John Garrett
8. 655 Gerry Cheevers
9. 460 Wayne Rutledge
10. 443 Cap Raeder

HIGHEST SHOTS-AGAINST-AVERAGE
1. 41.2 Dave Dryden
2. 39.4 Jim Shaw
3. 37.0 Frank Blum
4. 36.9 Les Binkley
5. 36.6 Jack McCartan
6. 36.0 Bernie Parent
7. 35.7 John Garrett
8. 35.6 Gilles Gratton
9. 35.1 Mike Curran
10. 34.5 Bob Johnson

LOWEST SHOTS-AGAINST-AVERAGE
39. 23.5 Gary Kurt
38. 24.8 Ken Broderick
37. 25.4 Curt Larsson
36. 25.8 Gary Bromley
35. 25.9 Yves Archambault
34. 26.8 Joe Daley
33. 27.3 Norm LaPointe
32. 28.6 Louis Levasseur
31. 29.4 Don McLeod
30. 29.5 George Gardner

MOST GOALS ALLOWED
1. 163 Richard Brodeur
2. 146 Joe Daley
3. 116 Ron Grahame
4. 112 Al Smith
5. 109 Ernie Wakely
6. 96 Don McLeod
7. 92 John Garrett
8. 63 Gerry Cheevers
9. 42 Wayne Rutledge
10. 41 Louis Levasseur

MOST SAVES MADE
1. 1,353 Richard Brodeur
2. 1,044 Joe Daley
3. 974 Ron Grahame
4. 817 Ernie Wakely
5. 810 Al Smith
6. 780 Don McLeod
7. 722 John Garrett
8. 592 Gerry Cheevers
9. 418 Wayne Rutledge
10. 405 Cap Raeder

HIGHEST SAVE PERCENTAGE
1. .939 Gary Bromley
2. .929 Bernie Parent
3. .923 Jim Park
4. .914 Cap Raeder
5. .911 Russ Gillow
6. .909 Wayne Rutledge
7. .906 Gilles Gratton
8. .905 Paul Hoganson
9. .904 Gerry Cheevers
10. .902 Christer Abrahamsson

LOWEST SAVE PERCENTAGE
39. .797 Frank Blum
38. .807 George Gardner
37. .824 Lynn Zimmerman
36. .833 Yves Archambault
35. .852 Gary Kurt
34. .858 Jack Norris
33. .860 Les Binkley
32. .862 Chris Worthy
31. .863 Cam Newton
30. .869 Ken Lockett

PLAYOFF SHUTOUTS
1. 4 Ron Grahame
2. 3 Richard Brodeur
3. 2 Jim Park
3. 2 Cap Raeder
3. 2 Ernie Wakely
3. 2 Joe Daley
7. 1 Paul Hoganson
7. 1 Gilles Gratton
7. 1 Louis Levasseur
7. 1 John Garrett
7. 1 Al Smith
7. 1 Don McLeod

PENALTY SHOTS IN AVCO WORLD TROPHY COMPETITION

DATE	PLAYER TAKING SHOT		GOALTENDER FACING SHOT	
Apr 19/74	Wayne Dillon, Toronto	vs.	Cam Newton, Chicago	SCORE
Apr 21/76	Gord Labossiere, Houston	vs.	Ernie Wakely, San Diego	SCORE
May 5/76	Tom Earl, New England	vs.	Ron Grahame, Houston	SAVE
Apr 14/78	Anders Hedberg, Winnipeg	vs.	John Garrett, Birmingham	SCORE

1978-79 REGULAR SEASON SCHEDULE

Edmonton's promising Joe Micheletti enters his third season of WHA regular season play. For career record of Micheletti, see page 110.

All regular season games are numbered 1-287.

All International exhibitions are numbered I-1 through I-11.

1	Fri	Oct 13	Winnipeg	.....	at Birmingham	.....
2			Cincinnati	.....	at Edmonton	.....
3	Sat	Oct 14	Winnipeg	.....	at Indianapolis	.....
4			New England	.....	at Quebec	.....
5	Sun	Oct 15	Birmingham	.....	at Indianapolis	.....
6			Cincinnati	.....	at Winnipeg	.....
7	Tue	Oct 17	New England	.....	at Edmonton	.....
8			Cincinnati	.....	at Quebec	.....
9	Wed	Oct 18	Indianapolis	.....	at Quebec	.....
10			New England	.....	at Winnipeg	.....
11	Fri	Oct 20	Birmingham	.....	at Cincinnati	.....
12			Edmonton	.....	at Indianapolis	.....
13	Sat	Oct 21	Edmonton	.....	at Cincinnati	.....
14			Quebec	.....	at New England	.....
15	Sun	Oct 22	New England	.....	at Indianapolis	.....
16			Birmingham	.....	at Quebec	.....
17			Edmonton	.....	at Winnipeg	.....
18	Tue	Oct 24	New England	.....	at Cincinnati	.....
19			Birmingham	.....	at Winnipeg	.....
20	Wed	Oct 25	Cincinnati	.....	at Quebec	.....
21			Birmingham	.....	at Winnipeg	.....
22	Thu	Oct 26	New England	.....	at Quebec	.....
23	Fri	Oct 27	Winnipeg	.....	at New England	.....
24			Indianapolis	.....	at Birmingham	.....
25	Sat	Oct 28	Quebec	.....	at Cincinnati	.....
26			Winnipeg	.....	at Indianapolis	.....
27	Sun	Oct 29	Quebec	.....	at Edmonton	.....
28			Cincinnati	.....	at New England	.....
29			Indianapolis	.....	at Winnipeg	.....
30	Tue	Oct 31	Quebec	.....	at Edmonton	.....
31	Wed	Nov 1	Birmingham	.....	at Cincinnati	.....
32	Fri	Nov 3	Winnipeg	.....	at Edmonton	.....
33			Quebec	.....	at Birmingham	.....
34			Indianapolis	.....	at New England	.....
35	Sat	Nov 4	Quebec	.....	at Birmingham	.....
36			New England	.....	at Indianapolis	.....
37	Sun	Nov 5	New England	.....	at Cincinnati	.....
38			Edmonton	.....	at Quebec	.....
39			Indianapolis	.....	at Winnipeg	.....
40	Tue	Nov 7	Winnipeg	.....	at Quebec	.....
41	Wed	Nov 8	Indianapolis	.....	at Cincinnati	.....
42			Edmonton	.....	at Quebec	.....
43	Thu	Nov 9	Winnipeg	.....	at Birmingham	.....
44			Edmonton	.....	at New England	.....
45	Fri	Nov 10	Winnipeg	.....	at Cincinnati	.....

46	Sat	Nov 11	Edmonton	.....	at Birmingham	.....
47			Cincinnati	.....	at New England	.....
48			Indianapolis	.....	at Quebec	.....
49	Sun	Nov 12	Edmonton	.....	at Cincinnati	.....
50			Quebec	.....	at Winnipeg	.....
51	Tue	Nov 14	New England	.....	at Birmingham	.....
52	Wed	Nov 15	New England	.....	at Cincinnati	.....
53			Winnipeg	.....	at Quebec	.....
54	Fri	Nov 17	New England	.....	at Birmingham	.....
55			Indianapolis	.....	at Edmonton	.....
56			Cincinnati	.....	at Winnipeg	.....
57	Sat	Nov 18	Birmingham	.....	at New England	.....
58	Sun	Nov 19	Cincinnati	.....	at Edmonton	.....
59			Indianapolis	.....	at Winnipeg	.....
60	Tue	Nov 21	Quebec	.....	at Edmonton	.....
61	Wed	Nov 22	Birmingham	.....	at Cincinnati	.....
62			Winnipeg	.....	at New England	.....
63	Thu	Nov 23	Cincinnati	.....	at Birmingham	.....
64			Winnipeg	.....	at Indianapolis	.....
65	Fri	Nov 24	Indianapolis	.....	at Cincinnati	.....
66			Quebec	.....	at Edmonton	.....
67	Sat	Nov 25	Cincinnati	.....	at Indianapolis	.....
68			Birmingham	.....	at New England	.....
69	Sun	Nov 26	Winnipeg	.....	at Quebec	.....
70			Birmingham	.....	at New England	.....
71	Tue	Nov 28	Indianapolis	.....	at Edmonton	.....
72			Birmingham	.....	at Quebec	.....
73	Wed	Nov 29	New England	.....	at Winnipeg	.....
74	Fri	Dec 1	Birmingham	.....	at Indianapolis	.....
75			New England	.....	at Edmonton	.....
76			Cincinnati	.....	at Winnipeg	.....
77	Sat	Dec 2	Indianapolis	.....	at Birmingham	.....
78			Cincinnati	.....	at Quebec	.....
79	Sun	Dec 3	New England	.....	at Edmonton	.....
80			Cincinnati	.....	at Indianapolis	.....
81			Winnipeg	.....	at Quebec	.....
82	Tue	Dec 5	New England	.....	at Cincinnati	.....
83	Wed	Dec 6	Edmonton	.....	at Quebec	.....
84	Thu	Dec 7	Cincinnati	.....	at Birmingham	.....
85			Winnipeg	.....	at Indianapolis	.....
86			Edmonton	.....	at New England	.....
87	Sat	Dec 9	Edmonton	.....	at Birmingham	.....
88			Sov. All-Stars	.....	at New England	.....
89			Cincinnati	.....	at Quebec	.....
90	Sun	Dec 10	Cincinnati	.....	at Birmingham	.....
91			Edmonton	.....	at Indianapolis	.....
92			Quebec	.....	at Winnipeg	.....
93	Tue	Dec 12	Edmonton	.....	at Cincinnati	.....
94			New England	.....	at Indianapolis	.....

95			Sov. All-Stars	..... at Quebec	.....
I-1	Thu	Dec 14	Sweden	..... at New England	.....
96			Birmingham	..... at Quebec	.....
97			Sov. All-Stars	..... at Winnipeg	.....
I-2	Fri	Dec 15	Sweden	..... at Winnipeg	.....
98			Sov. All-Stars	..... at Edmonton	.....
99	Sat	Dec 16	Birmingham	..... at Cincinnati	.....
100			Sov. All-Stars	..... at Indianapolis	.....
101			Quebec	..... at New England	.....
102	Sun	Dec 17	Indianapolis	..... at Birmingham	.....
I-3			Sweden	..... at Edmonton	.....
103			New England	..... at Quebec	.....
104			Cincinnati	..... at Winnipeg	.....
105	Tue	Dec 19	Edmonton	..... at Indianapolis	.....
I-4			Sweden	..... at Quebec	.....
106			Sov. All-Stars	..... at Birmingham	.....
107	Wed	Dec 20	Sov. All-Stars	..... at Cincinnati	.....
108	Thu	Dec 21	Quebec	..... at Indianapolis	.....
109	Fri	Dec 22	Quebec	..... at Birmingham	.....
110			Winnipeg	..... at Edmonton	.....
111	Sat	Dec 23	Quebec	..... at Cincinnati	.....
112			Indianapolis	..... at New England	.....
113	Tue	Dec 26	Indianapolis	..... at Birmingham	.....
I-5			Moscow Dynamo	..... at New England	.....
114			Edmonton	..... at Winnipeg	.....
115	Wed	Dec 27	Winnipeg	..... at Edmonton	.....
116			Czechoslovakia	..... at New England	.....
I-6			Moscow Dynamo	..... at Quebec	.....
117	Thu	Dec 28	Birmingham	..... at Cincinnati	.....
118			Czechoslovakia	..... at Quebec	.....
119	Fri	Dec 29	Cincinnati	..... at Indianapolis	.....
120	Fri	Dec 29	Birmingham	..... at New England	.....
I-7			Moscow Dynamo	..... at Edmonton	.....
121	Sat	Dec 30	Indianapolis	..... at Cincinnati	.....
122			Birmingham	..... at Quebec	.....
I-8			Moscow Dynamo	..... at Winnipeg	.....
123			Czechoslovakia	..... at Edmonton	.....
			— 1979 —		
124	Mon	Jan 1	Czechoslovakia	..... at Winnipeg	.....

WHA ALL-STAR SERIES
at EDMONTON COLISEUM

Tue Jan 2 Moscow Dynamo vs Team WHA
Thu Jan 4 Moscow Dynamo vs Team WHA
Fri Jan 5 Moscow Dynamo vs Team WHA

125	Sat	Jan 6	Czechoslovakia	.....	at Cincinnati	.....
126	Sun	Jan 7	Indianapolis	.....	at Edmonton	.....
127			Cincinnati	.....	at New England	.....
128			Quebec	.....	at Winnipeg	.....
129			Czechoslovakia	.....	at Birmingham	.....
130	Tue	Jan 9	Quebec	.....	at Cincinnati	.....
131			Indianapolis	.....	at Winnipeg	.....
132	Thu	Jan 11	Quebec	.....	at Indianapolis	.....
133			Winnipeg	.....	at New England	.....
134	Fri	Jan 12	Winnipeg	.....	at Birmingham	.....
135			Indianapolis	.....	at Cincinnati	.....
136	Sat	Jan 13	Winnipeg	.....	at Birmingham	.....
137			Quebec	.....	at Indianapolis	.....
138			Edmonton	.....	at New England	.....
139	Sun	Jan 14	Birmingham	.....	at Cincinnati	.....
140			Indianapolis	.....	at New England	.....
141			Edmonton	.....	at Quebec	.....
142	Tue	Jan 16	Birmingham	.....	at Edmonton	.....
143	Wed	Jan 17	New England	.....	at Cincinnati	.....
144			Indianapolis	.....	at Quebec	.....
145			Birmingham	.....	at Winnipeg	.....
146	Thu	Jan 18	Cincinnati	.....	at Indianapolis	.....
147			Quebec	.....	at New England	.....
148	Fri	Jan 19	Birmingham	.....	at Edmonton	.....
149			Indianapolis	.....	at Winnipeg	.....
150	Sat	Jan 20	Cincinnati	.....	at New England	.....
151			Winnipeg	.....	at Quebec	.....
152	Sun	Jan 21	Indianapolis	.....	at Edmonton	.....
153			Quebec	.....	at Winnipeg	.....
154	Tue	Jan 23	New England	.....	at Birmingham	.....
155			Quebec	.....	at Edmonton	.....
156	Wed	Jan 24	Winnipeg	.....	at Cincinnati	.....
157			New England	.....	at Indianapolis	.....
158	Fri	Jan 26	New England	.....	at Birmingham	.....
159			Cincinnati	.....	at Edmonton	.....
160	Sat	Jan 27	Birmingham	.....	at Indianapolis	.....
161			Winnipeg	.....	at Quebec	.....
162	Sun	Jan 28	Cincinnati	.....	at Edmonton	.....
163			Winnipeg	.....	at New England	.....
164	Tue	Jan 30	Quebec	.....	at Birmingham	.....
165			Winnipeg	.....	at New England	.....
166	Wed	Jan 31	Edmonton	.....	at Winnipeg	.....
167	Thu	Feb 1	Quebec	.....	at Birmingham	.....
168			Cincinnati	.....	at Indianapolis	.....
169	Fri	Feb 2	Edmonton	.....	at New England	.....
170			Indianapolis	.....	at Winnipeg	.....
171	Sat	Feb 3	New England	.....	at Birmingham	.....
172			Edmonton	.....	at Indianapolis	.....
173	Sun	Feb 4	New England	.....	at Indianapolis	.....

229

174			Cincinnati	.....	at Quebec	.....
175			Edmonton	.....	at Winnipeg	.....
176	Tue	Feb 6	Birmingham	.....	at Edmonton	.....
177			New England	.....	at Quebec	.....
178	Wed	Feb 7	Cincinnati	.....	at Edmonton	.....
179			Birmingham	.....	at Winnipeg	.....
180	Fri	Feb 9	Winnipeg	.....	at Cincinnati	.....
181			Birmingham	.....	at Edmonton	.....
182	Sat	Feb 10	Quebec	.....	at Indianapolis	.....
183	Sun	Feb 11	New England	.....	at Cincinnati	.....
184			Winnipeg	.....	at Edmonton	.....
185	Mon	Feb 12	Birmingham	.....	at Indianapolis	.....
186	Tue	Feb 13	Winnipeg	.....	at Edmonton	.....
187	Wed	Feb 14	Quebec	.....	at Cincinnati	.....
188			Indianapolis	.....	at New England	.....
189	Thu	Feb 15	Quebec	.....	at Indianapolis	.....
190	Fri	Feb 16	Winnipeg	.....	at Birmingham	.....
191			Edmonton	.....	at New England	.....
192	Sat	Feb 17	Winnipeg	.....	at Cincinnati	.....
193			Edmonton	.....	at Indianapolis	.....
194			Quebec	.....	at New England	.....
195	Sun	Feb 18	Edmonton	.....	at Birmingham	.....
196			Indianapolis	.....	at Cincinnati	.....
197			New England	.....	at Winnipeg	.....
198	Tue	Feb 20	Indianapolis	.....	at Birmingham	.....
199			Quebec	.....	at Cincinnati	.....
200			New England	.....	at Edmonton	.....
201	Wed	Feb 21	New England	.....	at Winnipeg	.....
202	Fri	Feb 23	Winnipeg	.....	at Birmingham	.....
203			Cincinnati	.....	at Edmonton	.....
204			Quebec	.....	at New England	.....
205	Sat	Feb 24	Indianapolis	.....	at Quebec	.....
206	Sun	Feb 25	Birmingham	.....	at Edmonton	.....
207			Winnipeg	.....	at New England	.....
208			Indianapolis	.....	at Quebec	.....
209	Tue	Feb 27	Cincinnati	.....	at Winnipeg	.....
210			New England	.....	at Edmonton	.....
211	Thu	Mar 1	Birmingham	.....	at Indianapolis	.....
212	Fri	Mar 2	Cincinnati	.....	at Edmonton	.....
213			New England	.....	at Winnipeg	.....
214	Sat	Mar 3	Edmonton	.....	at Cincinnati	.....
215			New England	.....	at Indianapolis	.....
216			Birmingham	.....	at Quebec	.....
217	Sun	Mar 4	Edmonton	.....	at Indianapolis	.....
218			Cincinnati	.....	at New England	.....
219			Birmingham	.....	at Quebec	.....
220	Tue	Mar 6	Winnipeg	.....	at Birmingham	.....
221	Wed	Mar 7	Winnipeg	.....	at Cincinnati	.....
222			Edmonton	.....	at Quebec	.....

223	Thu Mar 8	Winnipeg	.....	at Indianapolis	.....
224	Fri Mar 9	Edmonton	.....	at Birmingham	.....
225		Quebec	.....	at New England	.....
226	Sat Mar 10	Winnipeg	.....	at Cincinnati	.....
227		Quebec	.....	at Indianapolis	.....
228	Sun Mar 11	Edmonton	.....	at Birmingham	.....
229		Indianapolis	.....	at Cincinnati	.....
230		Quebec	.....	at Winnipeg	.....
231	Tue Mar 13	New England	.....	at Birmingham	.....
232		Edmonton	.....	at Cincinnati	.....
233	Wed Mar 14	Quebec	.....	at Winnipeg	.....
234	Thu Mar 15	Birmingham	.....	at New England	.....
235	Fri Mar 16	Cincinnati	.....	at Birmingham	.....
236		Quebec	.....	at Edmonton	.....
237		Indianapolis	.....	at Winnipeg	.....
238	Sat Mar 17	Cincinnati	.....	at New England	.....
239	Sun Mar 18	Indianapolis	.....	at Edmonton	.....
240		Birmingham	.....	at Winnipeg	.....
241	Tue Mar 20	Birmingham	.....	at Cincinnati	.....
242		Indianapolis	.....	at Edmonton	.....
I-9		Finland	.....	at Quebec	.....
243	Wed Mar 21	New England	.....	at Quebec	.....
244		Edmonton	.....	at Winnipeg	.....
245	Thu Mar 22	Birmingham	.....	at Indianapolis	.....
246	Fri Mar 23	Cincinnati	.....	at Birmingham	.....
I-10		Finland	.....	at Edmonton	.....
247		Quebec	.....	at New England	.....
248	Sat Mar 24	Quebec	.....	at Cincinnati	.....
249		Winnipeg	.....	at Edmonton	.....
250		Indianapolis	.....	at New England	.....
251	Sun Mar 25	Edmonton	.....	at Cincinnati	.....
252		Indianapolis	.....	at Quebec	.....
I-11		Finland	.....	at Winnipeg	.....
253	Tue Mar 27	New England	.....	at Birmingham	.....
254		Finland	.....	at Indianapolis	.....
255	Wed Mar 28	Edmonton	.....	at Quebec	.....
256		Cincinnati	.....	at Winnipeg	.....
257	Thu Mar 29	New England	.....	at Indianapolis	.....
258	Fri Mar 30	Quebec	.....	at Birmingham	.....
259		Edmonton	.....	at New England	.....
260		Cincinnati	.....	at Winnipeg	.....
261	Sat Mar 31	Quebec	.....	at Birmingham	.....
262		Cincinnati	.....	at Indianapolis	.....
263	Sun Apr 1	Edmonton	.....	at New England	.....
264		Winnipeg	.....	at Quebec	.....
265	Mon Apr 2	Edmonton	.....	at Indianapolis	.....
266	Tue Apr 3	Indianapolis	.....	at Birmingham	.....
267	Wed Apr 4	Indianapolis	.....	at Cincinnati	.....
268		Edmonton	.....	at Quebec	.....

269			New England	.....	at Winnipeg	.....
270	Thu	Apr 5	Birmingham	.....	at Indianapolis	.....
271	Fri	Apr 6	New England	.....	at Edmonton	.....
272			Birmingham	.....	at Winnipeg	.....
273	Sat	Apr 7	Quebec	.....	at Cincinnati	.....
274	Sun	Apr 8	Birmingham	.....	at Edmonton	.....
275			New England	.....	at Winnipeg	.....
276	Tue	Apr 10	Winnipeg	.....	at Edmonton	.....
277			New England	.....	at Quebec	.....
278	Wed	Apr 11	Birmingham	.....	at Winnipeg	.....
279			Cincinnati	.....	at Quebec	.....
280	Thu	Apr 12	Cincinnati	.....	at New England	.....
281	Fri	Apr 13	Edmonton	.....	at Birmingham	.....
282			Winnipeg	.....	at Indianapolis	.....
283	Sat	Apr 14	Cincinnati	.....	at Birmingham	.....
284			Indianapolis	.....	at New England	.....
285	Sun	Apr 15	Birmingham	.....	at New England	.....
286			Indianapolis	.....	at Quebec	.....
287			Edmonton	.....	at Winnipeg	.....

About The WHA Hall of Fame & Author

The World Hockey Association Hall of Fame is an independent organization of hockey historians, journalists and former WHA coaches, players and management who are dedicated to honoring the 1972-1979 major league.

Voting for the Honored Members of the WHA Hall of Fame was completed in 2010 and 2012. Induction ceremonies were completed throughout North America, featuring such WHA luminaries as Gordie, Mark and Marty Howe, Bobby Hull, Anders Hedberg and Ulf Nilsson, Pat Stapleton, Andre Lacroix, and many others.

The WHA HOF also conducts WHA reunions, film screenings, and seminars throughout the USA and Canada.

Visit the online archives of the WHA Hall of Fame at **www.WHAhof.com** and see our official display at the United States Hockey Hall of Fame Museum in Eveleth, Minnesota.

Author Timothy Gassen is president of the World Hockey Association Hall of Fame, and an acknowledged expert on the history of the WHA. He has written, produced, and directed the more than 12 hours of WHA video documentaries for the WHA Hall of Fame DVD and Blu-ray Disc series.

His other books on the World Hockey Association include "The WHA Hall of Fame: A Photographic History Of The Rebel League 1972-1979," published by St. Johann Press. It features many previously unpublished WHA photos and a complete league history. He is also author of "Positive Waves: a history of Indianapolis Racers hockey 1974-1979," published by the WHA HOF.

Gassen has won Arizona Press Club Awards for his hockey coverage, and he's served as a college hockey team media director, a college and pro hockey radio man and TV broadcaster. He has also been a longtime columnist for hockey magazines and the Arizona Daily Star newspaper. This is his fifth book.

Visit the author's company Web site at **www.purple-cactus.tv** and the WHA Hall of Fame at both **WHAhof.com** and **whaRACERS.com**

The author highly recommends two books by Scott Surgent to augment these media guides: "The Complete Historical and Statistical Reference to the World Hockey Association" and "The World Hockey Association Fact Book." Both are available at **www.surgent.net/wha/**

www.ingramcontent.com/pod-product-compliance
Lightning Source LLC
Chambersburg PA
CBHW071053230426
43666CB00009B/1709